ISBN 978-1-333-20874-5
PIBN 10473650

FB &c Ltd, Dalton House, 60 Windsor Avenue, London, SW19 2RR.
Company number 08720141. Registered in England and Wales.

DEPARTMENT OF COMMERCE AND LABOR

BUREAU OF THE CENSUS

E. DANA DURAND, DIRECTOR

SPECIAL REPORTS

RELIGIOUS BODIES: 1906

PART I

SUMMARY AND GENERAL TABLES

WASHINGTON
GOVERNMENT PRINTING OFFICE
1910

THIS REPORT IS PUBLISHED IN TWO PARTS, AS FOLLOWS:

PART I—SUMMARY AND GENERAL TABLES.

PART II—SEPARATE DENOMINATIONS:
HISTORY, DESCRIPTION, AND STATISTICS.

CONTENTS.

INTRODUCTION.

	Page.
Scope of the inquiry	9, 10
Methods pursued in collecting the statistics	10, 11
Sources of information	10
Plan of enumeration	10
Means of verification	11
Difficulties encountered	11
Special data, and how obtained	11, 13
History, doctrine, polity, and work of denominations	11
Undenominational Sunday schools	12
Independent churches	13
Plan of report	13
Classification of denominations at former census periods	13, 14
Names and classification of denominations in 1906	14, 16
Changes in the names of denominations	14
Changes in the names of denominational families	14
Disappearance of denominations and denominational families	15
New denominations and denominational families	15
List of denominations for 1906	16–18

SUMMARY

Summary of statistics for continental United States	21–41
Religious organizations	21
Communicants or members	24
Total number	24
Distribution by sex	28
Places of worship	32
Number of church edifices, halls, etc	32
Seating capacity of church edifices	33
Seating capacity of halls, etc	36
Value of church property	36
Debt on church property	39
Value of parsonages	40
Summary of statistics for states and territories	42 68
General summary for 1906	42
Average per organization	44
Distribution of communicants or members by principal families and denominations	45
Relation of church membership to population	58
Summary for counties	68
Distribution of communicants or members	68
Distribution of denominations	68
Summary of statistics for the principal cities	68–86
Sunday schools	86–91
Schools conducted by church organizations	86
Total number of schools, teachers, and scholars	86
Average number of scholars and teachers per school	87
Ratio of communicants to Sunday school scholars	88
All Sunday schools, including undenominational schools	88
Distribution by states and territories	89
Distribution by geographic divisions	90
Ministers	91–98
Total number	91
Ratio of organizations to ministers	92
Ratio of communicants or members to ministers	93
Average annual salaries paid to ministers	93

Page.
Date of establishment of religious organizations 99-105
Languages used in the conduct of church services 105-123
English only 106
Foreign languages 107
Languages by denominations 111
Alphabetical list 121
Geographic distribution 122
Work of denominations in domestic and foreign fields 123-136
Domestic work 124
Foreign work 130
Summary of contributions 134
Comparison of home and foreign work 135
Summary of statistics of colored organizations 136-146
General summary for 1906 136
Comparison of organizations, communicants or members, and value of church property, for 1906 and 1890 136
Statistics of denominations 138
Distribution of communicants or members by states and territories 145
Colored ministers 145

GENERAL TABLES.

Table 1.—Organizations, communicants or members, places of worship, value of church property, debt on church property, parsonages, and Sunday schools, by denominations (in detail), for continental United States: 1906 148
Table 2.—Organizations, communicants or members, places of worship, value of church property, debt on church property, parsonages, and Sunday schools, for all denominations, by states and territories: 1906 154
Table 3.—Organizations, communicants or members, places of worship, value of church property, debt on church property, parsonages, and Sunday schools, by denominations (in detail), for each state and territory: 1906 156

	Page.		Page.
Alabama	156	Nebraska	226
Arizona	158	Nevada	230
Arkansas	160	New Hampshire	232
California	162	New Jersey	234
Colorado	166	New Mexico	236
Connecticut	168	New York	238
Delaware	170	North Carolina	242
District of Columbia	172	North Dakota	244
Florida	176	Ohio	246
Georgia	178	Oklahoma	252
Idaho	180	Oregon	254
Illinois	182	Pennsylvania	258
Indiana	186	Rhode Island	262
Iowa	190	South Carolina	264
Kansas	194	South Dakota	266
Kentucky	198	Tennessee	270
Louisiana	202	Texas	272
Maine	204	Utah	276
Maryland	206	Vermont	276
Massachusetts	208	Virginia	278
Michigan	212	Washington	282
Minnesota	216	West Virginia	284
Mississippi	220	Wisconsin	288
Missouri	220	Wyoming	290
Montana	224		

Table 4.—Population in 1900 and communicants or members for selected denominations, for each state and territory, by counties: 1906 294

	Page.		Page
Alabama	294	Georgia	303
Arizona	296	Idaho	305
Arkansas	296	Illinois	305
California	298	Indiana	308
Colorado	300	Iowa	311
Connecticut	301	Kansas	314
Delaware	302	Kentucky	317
District of Columbia	302	Louisiana	321
Florida	302	Maine	322

	Page.
TABLE 4.—Population in 1900 and communicants or members for selected denominations, for each state and territory, by counties: 1906—(Continued)	294

	Page.		Page.
Maryland	322	Oklahoma	348
Massachusetts	323	Oregon	350
Michigan	324	Pennsylvania	350
Minnesota	327	Rhode Island	352
Mississippi	329	South Carolina	353
Missouri	331	South Dakota	353
Montana	334	Tennessee	354
Nebraska	335	Texas	357
Nevada	337	Utah	364
New Hampshire	338	Vermont	365
New Jersey	338	Virginia	365
New Mexico	338	Washington	368
New York	339	West Virginia	369
North Carolina	341	Wisconsin	371
North Dakota	344	Wyoming	373
Ohio	345		

Table 5.—Organizations, communicants or members, places of worship, value of church property, debt on church property, parsonages, and Sunday schools, for each city of 25,000 inhabitants or more in 1900, for all denominations: 1906	374
Table 6.—Population and communicants or members for each city of 25,000 inhabitants or more in 1900, by denominations (in detail): 1906	380
Table 7.—Organizations, communicants or members, places of worship, value of church property, debt on church property, parsonages, and Sunday schools, for each city of 25,000 inhabitants or more in 1900, by selected denominations: 1906	408
Table 8.—Comparison of organizations, communicants or members, ministers, church edifices, seating capacity of church edifices, number of halls, etc., and value of church property, by denominations (in detail), for continental United States: 1906 and 1890	514
Table 9.—Comparison of the total population, and organizations, communicants or members, church edifices, seating capacity of church edifices, number of halls, etc., and value of church property, for all denominations, by states and territories: 1906 and 1890	520
Table 10.—Comparison of communicants or members, by selected denominations, by states and territories: 1906 and 1890	522
Table 11.—Colored organizations, showing communicants or members, places of worship, value of church property, debt on church property, parsonages, and Sunday schools, by denominations (in detail), for continental United States: 1906	538
Table 12.—Colored organizations, showing communicants or members, places of worship, value of church property, debt on church property, parsonages, and Sunday schools, by states and territories: 1906	540
Table 13.—Colored organizations, showing communicants or members, places of worship, value of church property, debt on church property, parsonages, and Sunday schools, by denominations (in detail), for each state and territory: 1906	542

	Page.		Page.
Alabama	543	Montana	552
Arizona	543	Nebraska	554
Arkansas	543	New Hampshire	554
California	544	New Jersey	554
Colorado	544	New Mexico	554
Connecticut	544	New York	554
Delaware	544	North Carolina	556
District of Columbia	544	Ohio	556
Florida	546	Oklahoma	556
Georgia	546	Oregon	558
Illinois	546	Pennsylvania	558
Indiana	548	Rhode Island	558
Iowa	548	South Carolina	558
Kansas	548	South Dakota	560
Kentucky	548	Tennessee	560
Louisiana	550	Texas	560
Maine	550	Utah	560
Maryland	550	Virginia	562
Massachusetts	550	Washington	562
Michigan	550	West Virginia	562
Minnesota	552	Wisconsin	562
Mississippi	552	Wyoming	562
Missouri	552		

Table 14.—Comparison of colored organizations, showing communicants or members, church edifices, seating capacity of church edifices, number of halls, etc., and value of church property, by denominations (in detail), for continental United States: 1906 and 1890	564
Table 15.—Comparison of organizations or churches, accommodations, and property, by denominations, for continental United States: 1870, 1860, and 1850	565

DIAGRAMS.

Page.

Diagram 1.—Distribution of communicants or members, by principal families or denominations, for continental United States: 1890 and 1906 26

Diagram 2.—Distribution of communicants or members, by principal families or denominations, for each state and territory: 1906 .. 50-53

Diagram 3.—Proportion of the population reported as Protestant, Roman Catholic, and "all other" church members, and proportion not reported as church members, for continental United States: 1890 and 1906 59

Diagram 4.—Proportion of the population reported as Protestant, Roman Catholic, and "all other" church members, and proportion not reported as church members, for each state and territory: 1906 60

Diagram 5.—Number of communicants or members per 1,000 of the population, for 12 principal families or denominations, for each state and territory: 1906 .... 64, 65

Diagram 6.—Number of communicants or members per 1,000 of the population, arranged according to proportional strength, for 12 principal families or denominations, for each state and territory: 1906 .... 66, 67

Diagram 7.—Distribution of communicants or members in each principal family or denomination, for cities of 25,000 inhabitants or more in 1900 (arranged in four classes) and outside of cities: 1906 83

Diagram 8.—Distribution of communicants or members by principal families or denominations, for 24 principal cities: 1906 .... 84, 85

Diagram 9.—Proportion of the population reported as Protestant, Roman Catholic, and "all other" church members, and proportion not reported as church members, for 35 principal cities in detail: 1906 86

LETTER OF TRANSMITTAL.

DEPARTMENT OF COMMERCE AND LABOR,
BUREAU OF THE CENSUS,
Washington, D. C., February 23, 1910.

SIR:

I have the honor to transmit herewith Part I of a special report on religious bodies, in which are presented a summary of the results and general tables. Part II will present the statistics and general description of the separate denominations.

The statistics presented in this report have been compiled from material collected by the Bureau of the Census under the authority of section 7 of the permanent census act. Limited information of this character was first published in the census report for 1850, and similar information was included in the reports for 1860, 1870, and 1890, so that the present report, representing conditions, as near as may be, at the close of the year 1906, constitutes the fifth collection and publication of these statistics through the agency of the Census.

The essential results of the present inquiry have already been presented in a preliminary bulletin (Census Bulletin 103) in such form and detail as to meet, in most respects, the wants of the general public.

The complete report embraces not only all the material contained in the preliminary bulletin, but covers much additional information, including considerable data not comprehended by any of the former census reports on religious bodies, notably, the statistics of denominational and undenominational Sunday schools; a compilation of the average annual salaries paid to ministers; a statement of the languages used in the conduct of church services; and a sketch of the missionary, educational, and philanthropic work of the various denominations, both at home and abroad.

The statistics for this report were collected partly by correspondence and partly by the employment of special agents. The work was conducted under the supervision of Mr. William C. Hunt, chief statistician for population in this bureau.

Very respectfully,

E Dana Durand
Director of the Census.

Hon. CHARLES NAGEL,
Secretary of Commerce and Labor.

RELIGIOUS BODIES: 1906.

INTRODUCTION.

SCOPE OF THE INQUIRY.

The law of May 23, 1850, under which the censuses of 1850, 1860, and 1870 were taken, provided for the first time for the collection of social statistics, including among other subjects that of religious organizations. The inquiries to be made under each heading of the schedule were fixed by the census act, and under that of "religion" called for the return for each denomination of the number of churches, church accommodations, and value of church property. Information covering these items was collected at the censuses of 1850 and 1860, but the results of these inquiries showed that the term "Number of churches," as designated by the census law, was ambiguous, and that it was "impossible to feel any assurance, in any particular case, whether church organizations or church edifices had been returned."[1] To avoid the possibility of similar confusion at the census of 1870, therefore, this inquiry was divided in order to insure returns for both church organizations and church edifices.

The marshals and assistant marshals, who were charged with the duty of taking the census in 1850, were provided with detailed instructions concerning the manner in which the returns were to be made under each category of the schedule, and in the absence of any change in the law at the two succeeding censuses it is to be presumed that the same instructions, in effect, governed the work in 1860 and in 1870.[2]

[1] Census of 1870, Population and Social Statistics, page 502.

[2] The instructions of 1850 in this respect were as follows:

Columns 25, 26, 27, and 28. Under the heading entitled "Religion," insert a separate account of churches, and other places of worship, belonging to all religious denominations, in the town or county described, including halls and chapels, if statedly used as places of public worship. By number of sittings is meant the number of seats for individuals in such places of worship, or the number of persons they will accommodate.

Under "Value of church property," is to be inserted the present value of each of the churches or chapels, including the lands and estate, real and personal, owned by such religious societies. If a chapel or other place of worship is *rented*, its value is not to be here included; in such case you must include the name of denomination and the number of members, leaving blank the column numbered 28. As it is possible for a society to have property without a place of worship, the value of such property should be given in column 28. The facts relating to churches may generally be obtained with perfect accuracy from the pastor or clergyman having the same in charge; and, in case of his absence, application should be made to a warden, elder, or trustee.

An effort was made at the census of 1880 to secure, mainly by correspondence, very full and complete statistics concerning churches and Sunday schools, but the tabulations were not completed and no results are available for that census.

At the census of 1890 the inquiries concerning religious bodies were as follows: Organizations; church edifices and seating capacity; halls, schoolhouses, etc., and seating capacity; value of church property; and communicants or members. A statement was also requested of the number of ministers in each denomination as a whole, and care was taken to explain the meaning of the terms used, so as to insure results free from ambiguity.

The present inquiry, made in conformity to the provisions of section 7 of the permanent census act,[1] relates to the close of the year 1906. The inquiry covers information secured through the use of the following schedule:

1. Denomination.
2. Division (ecclesiastical).
3. Organization.
4. Location (city, town, or village; county; state).
5. Year in which established.
6. Number of church edifices.
7. Seating capacity.
8. Value of church property.
9. Amount of debt on church.
10. Value of parsonage, if any.
11. Language in which services are conducted.
12. Ministers (number of; salary).
13. Communicants or members (total number; males; females).
14. Sunday schools conducted by church organization (number of schools; number of officers and teachers; number of scholars).

The present inquiry covers, therefore, not only the same ground as that of 1890, but includes several additional items. The inquiries common to both censuses are those numbered 1, 2, 3, 4, 6, 7, and 8, and that part of 13 which relates to the return of the total number of communicants or members. The new inquiries—those numbered 5, 9, 10, 11, 12, 13 (in part), and 14—provide information for the first time in a United States census as to the date of establishment of the local church organization, amount of debt on church property, number and value of church parsonages, language in which services are conducted,

[1] Act of March 6, 1902, as amended by act of June 30, 1906.

salaries paid to ministers, sex of communicants or members, and the number and membership of Sunday schools conducted by church organizations.

The statistics of religious bodies, based upon these inquiries, refer to the close of the year 1906, as heretofore stated, and are limited to religious organizations in continental United States, no effort having been made to include any portion of the outlying territory.

Although one of these schedules was returned for each church organization represented in the statistics here given, yet in some instances the schedule was not filled in completely. In some cases, as is hereafter explained, the omissions are due simply to failure to answer the questions, and in others to the fact that the questions were not applicable to that particular organization. Because of these omissions a column has been inserted under each topic presented in the general tables for 1906 showing the number of organizations which made a report in regard to that topic. The difference between the number thus presented and the total number of organizations represents, in each case, the number of organizations for which no report was made.

METHODS PURSUED IN COLLECTING THE STATISTICS.

The general plan adopted for the collection of the statistics was by means of correspondence with the individual church organizations, together with such assistance from denominational officials as might be necessary, and as they were able and willing to render.

Sources of information.—In the carrying out of this plan it was necessary first to secure as complete a list as possible, by name and location, of the individual organizations in the several denominations, and for this the denominational officials were chiefly relied upon. The general officers of the various denominations were requested to furnish lists of the ecclesiastical divisions—associations, conferences, dioceses, presbyteries, etc.—composing them, with the names and addresses of their clerks or secretaries; and these divisional officers were in turn requested to furnish lists of organizations and ministers in their respective divisions.

For statistical purposes the natural divisions were found to be: For Baptist bodies the association; for Methodist bodies the district; for Presbyterian bodies the presbytery; for the Congregationalist churches the state conference (using the term recommended by the National Council); and in the Roman Catholic and Protestant Episcopal churches the diocese. Accordingly the clerk of the Baptist association, the presiding elder or district superintendent of the Methodist district, the stated clerk of the presbytery, the statistical secretary of the Congregational state conference, and the secretary of the Roman Catholic or Protestant Episcopal diocese, were applied to for the needed information.

This request for the assistance of the general and divisional officers of the various denominations met in most instances with a hearty response, and by this means a list of organizations, by ecclesiastical divisions, was obtained for each of the denominations having such divisions. In the case of those bodies which have no ecclesiastical divisions, lists of organizations were furnished by their general officers.

Plan of enumeration.—With these lists as a basis, a copy of the schedule already referred to, with the necessary instructions and a return franked envelope, was addressed to the pastor or clerk of each church organization. The original plan was to send these direct to the church organizations, and when filled out and properly signed have them sent to the divisional officer, to be in turn certified by him and forwarded to the Bureau of the Census. The purpose of this was to give the divisional officer an opportunity to see whether any of the churches under his jurisdiction had failed to report, and also whether the returns as made were substantially correct. It appeared, however, that according to the postal law the pastor or clerk of the church was not permitted to send the schedule under the frank of the Bureau to the divisional officer, since the latter was not an employee of the Government, and according to another law, could not be commissioned without compensation. Accordingly the plan was adopted of inclosing these addressed envelopes to the divisional officer, in the first instance, with the request that he make any needed correction in the addresses, see that the proper number of cards were inclosed in each envelope, namely, one for each church served by the pastor, and forward them to the church organizations. Also, in order to make sure that no churches were omitted, a number of blank envelopes, with schedules and instructions, were sent to him, to be forwarded to such organizations as might not have been included in the list. The schedules, when filled out and properly signed by the pastor or clerk, were then to be inclosed in the return franked envelope and sent direct to the Bureau of the Census.

In cases where the divisional officer declined to cooperate in this way, the schedules were sent to the individual organizations direct. The result was that the returns for about two-thirds of the entire number of organizations were secured through this method of direct correspondence with the individual organizations.

In the case of a considerable number of denominations, however, where for various reasons the work was attended with special difficulties, the statistics were collected in whole or in part through the general or statistical secretaries, or other prominent representatives, who were commissioned as special agents for the purpose, and who were willing for a nominal sum to cooperate with the Bureau of the Census in this way. Among the denominations for which the work was done, partly by direct correspondence and then placed in the hands of special agents for completion, are two branches of the Baptists—the Southern Baptist Convention and the National Baptist Convention (Colored)—the Primitive Baptists, and the Disciples of Christ. Among those for which the statistics were collected entirely under the supervision of their own representatives are the Roman Catholic Church, the Churches of Christ (Disciples), and the Jewish congregations. There were also a number of comparatively small bodies, many of them having but few organizations each, which could better be reached through their own representatives than through direct correspondence, because they either had no complete ecclesiastical system, or were not accustomed to furnishing statistics of their churches, or were opposed to doing so through conscientious scruples.

The returns for the National Baptist Convention (Colored) were finally completed by a personal canvass by agents sent out from the Bureau, as were also those for the three principal colored Methodist bodies, namely, the African Methodist Episcopal Church, the African Methodist Episcopal Zion Church, and the Colored Methodist Episcopal Church.

Means of verification.—All the items of information contained in the schedules for the various denominations were transferred to sheets, by individual organizations and ecclesiastical divisions, and by states, counties, and cities of 25,000 inhabitants or more, in this way bringing together, in the form most convenient for scrutiny and subsequent tabulation, all the information for each denomination.

For the purpose of verification, the returns for each individual church organization and for each ecclesiastical division and denomination were carefully compared with the yearbooks and minutes of the various bodies, and with all other available sources of information, and supplemental information was obtained by special correspondence, wherever this was found necessary.

In the case of some denominations it will be found that the number of organizations as given in this report is less than that shown by the yearbooks for 1906. In many instances this may be accounted for by the fact that the yearbooks include the names of churches which are either extinct or practically so, and for which no report could be obtained, and in other cases by the fact that the figures as given in the yearbooks include mere preaching places or unorganized missions, which, as will later appear, could not well be included in this report.

The employment of these different means of collecting and verifying the statistics, as circumstances required, has resulted in a very thorough and complete presentation.

Difficulties encountered.—The chief difficulty encountered in the prosecution of the work was that of securing prompt returns from the individual church organizations. A little more than one-half of the entire number sent in their reports with reasonable promptness, and had all done the same, the census might have been completed at a much earlier date, but many responded only after long delay and after repeated reminders had been sent to them. In many instances it was necessary to call upon the divisional officers for special assistance in securing returns for the delinquent churches, this assistance being rendered by them gratuitously.

Another difficulty was that of securing the complete and proper filling of the schedule by the pastor or clerk of the individual church organization. In many cases it could not be determined from the schedule to what ecclesiastical division or even to what denomination the church for which it was returned belonged, or in what county it was located. In other respects also the schedules as first returned were frequently imperfectly filled out. To supply the information lacking required a great amount of extra correspondence, and was the occasion of delaying greatly the completion of the work.

SPECIAL DATA, AND HOW OBTAINED.

Besides the statistics based on the returns from the individual church organizations, special provision was made for securing (1) an authoritative statement, for each denomination as a whole, as to its history, doctrine, polity, and work, the latter comprehending its activities in the home and foreign missionary fields and in educational, philanthropic, institutional, and other lines of work; (2) a statement covering the undenominational and union Sunday schools of the country, as a supplement to the statistics of Sunday schools connected with the local church organizations in the several denominations; and (3) substantially complete statistics of the independent, unassociated, or union churches scattered over the country, in which there has been a very considerable development in recent years.

History, doctrine, polity, and work of denominations.—The statements under this head follow in general the plan of similar statements in the report for 1890, except that they are more comprehensive and include under the title of work the missionary, educational, and philanthropic activities of the denominations both in the United States and in foreign lands.

For the preparation of them application was made to prominent men, usually officials, in the different bodies, and a general outline was furnished to each, covering the specific points which it was desired to set forth. This outline included different points under each head as follows: (1) History: The origin, development, and present status of the denomination. (2) Doctrine: General classification, whether Calvinistic, Arminian, Lutheran, Liberal, or other, together with the creeds or confessions recognized as furnishing the basis of church membership and of ordination to the ministry. (3) Polity: General classification, whether Congregational, Episcopal, Methodist, Presbyterian, etc., together with specific forms of organization, local and general. (4) Work: Home missionary, foreign missionary, educational, institutional, and general.

The statements received varied greatly. In some the history was given in full; in others the barest summary was furnished. The doctrinal statements were, with few exceptions, quite complete, while those on polity varied in their extent almost as much as those on history. The description of work done was in general quite full, though not infrequently detailed figures were not provided. In order to secure greater harmony and better proportion in all these parts, considerable correspondence was carried on both with those who furnished the original material and with others who were able to provide information on specific points. In every case also the yearbooks and histories of the denominations, as well as books of general reference, were consulted.

The original intention was to publish the statements either over the names of the writers or to give them credit. It appeared, however, that in many cases this was impracticable, and the editorial form was adopted for all. This naturally involved some changes in form of statement, and some rearrangement of material, in order to secure general uniformity of presentation. Whenever it seemed best for the sake of clearness or brevity to retain phrases which would be appropriate only from the specific standpoint of the denomination, quotation marks have been used. The final form has been submitted either to the author or, in a few instances where that was impracticable, to some one in the denomination competent to pass upon it.

In the historical sections the interrelations of the different bodies and the part they have had in the general life of the country have been kept in mind as well as their internal development. Wherever differing or opposing views had to be taken into consideration, the statement has been confined to the simple historical facts, and where interpretation was essential it has been made clear that it was from the standpoint of the interested body. It is indicative of the general character of the material furnished, that the instances of sharp divergence in this particular have been very few.

In the sections on doctrine and polity the specific points emphasized by each denomination are set forth as briefly as possible, reference being made in several cases to fuller statements in connection with other bodies. This is especially true of such families as the Methodist and Presbyterian, where the statement for the leading member of the family suffices in most respects for all. The various sections are generally set off by special headings, but in some of the smaller bodies the doctrine and polity are included under the head of history.

The section on work of the denominations includes both textual statement and a tabular presentation of certain items common to all, or the great number, of the denominations. In the preparation of this section certain difficulties, arising partly from diverse forms of organization, partly from the use of diverse methods and terms, but chiefly from incomplete or general rather than specific reports, prevented that completeness and accuracy which is essential to any thoroughly scientific census presentation.

In this connection it may be stated that a number of societies or associations directly connected with Christian work and similar to many of the denominational societies are not represented either in the textual statements or the tables. Among these are the Young Men's Christian Association, the Young Women's Christian Association, the Woman's Christian Temperance Union, and kindred organizations; the American Bible Society; and the American Tract Society. These are omitted not from any failure to recognize the character of their work, but because under the law governing this report it is limited to religious bodies, and those organizations not directly connected with some denomination are thus excluded.

It should be again emphasized that the presentation, whether in the statements or in the tables, does not include all the work done by the individual organizations of the various religious bodies. It includes only such as has been reported by the various general societies or organizations of the denominations. A vast amount of similar work is done on independent lines. Making, however, as stated in connection with the tables, due allowance for the conditions, the general presentation, it is believed, is reasonably accurate, and is a fairly clear survey of the subject.

Undenominational Sunday schools.—In addition to the Sunday schools conducted by individual church organizations in the various denominations, there are a large number of undenominational schools, which obviously could not be reached by means of the general schedule. As the statistics of these schools were necessary to an adequate presentation of the Sunday school work in the United States, provision was made for securing them through the International Sunday School Association, of which Marion Lawrance, of Chicago, Ill., is general secretary. The method employed by Mr. Lawrance was to obtain from the state secretary of the association in each state and territory a list of the county secretaries, and from these in turn to obtain a list, by name and location, of the undenominational Sunday schools in their respective counties, with the names and addresses of their superintendents, and the number of officers and teachers and the number of scholars in each school. In counties where the association had no secretaries the information was obtained from the county superintendents of public schools. Valuable assistance was also rendered to the association by lists of schools provided by the missionaries of the American Sunday School Union. The work was done in a thorough manner, and it is believed that the figures presented comprise substantially complete statistics of the undenominational Sunday schools of the country.

Independent churches.—With the request sent to the divisional officers of the various denominations for lists of their own churches, a form was inclosed on which they were requested to furnish also the name and location of any independent or unassociated churches known to them, within the bounds of their several jurisdictions. A similar form was inclosed with the schedules sent to the pastors of the denominational churches, and they were asked to give the name and location of any churches in their vicinity which were not identified with any denomination. In addition, a careful search was made in the directories of all the principal cities for the names of independent churches. A schedule was then sent to the pastor or clerk of each of the churches on the list so obtained, and he was requested, in filling out the schedule, to indicate whether the church was, as reported, an independent or unassociated church, and with what denomination, if any, it was affiliated. Returns for most of the organizations which have been classified under the general head of "Independent churches" were received in answer to these inquiries. Among them there are a considerable number which bear denominational names, but which appear to have no denominational connection. Most of these, after every effort had been made to classify them, were placed with the Independent churches. In some cases, however, it appeared that enough denominational affiliation existed to identify them practically with some ecclesiastical division, and in these cases they were added to the respective denominations.

PLAN OF REPORT.

The report on religious bodies comprises three general sections: The first section consists of a summary of the detailed statistics derived from the returns of the local church organizations, together with such explanations as are necessary to a proper understanding of the figures presented for the several denominations, and, in addition thereto, summary statements, by denominations only, covering the average annual salaries paid to ministers, the date of establishment of church organizations, and the languages used in the conduct of church services; the second section consists of a series of fifteen general tables giving the statistics for 1906 in detail for continental United States, for each state and territory, in part for counties and principal cities, and to a certain extent in comparison with similar statistics derived from previous census reports; these two sections form Part I of the report. The third section, forming Part II of the report, is devoted to a separate presentation for each denomination of the statistics for 1906, by states and territories and by ecclesiastical divisions, in conjunction with an authoritative statement of the history, doctrine, polity, and work of the denomination as a whole.

CLASSIFICATION OF DENOMINATIONS AT FORMER CENSUS PERIODS.

The first statistics of religious bodies, published in the report of the census of 1850, were presented for the principal or leading denominations, arranged simply in their alphabetical order. These were 18 in number and designated as follows: Baptist, Christian, Congregational, Dutch Reformed, Episcopal, Friends, German Reformed, Jews, Lutheran, Mennonite, Methodist, Moravian, Presbyterian, Roman Catholic, Swedenborgian, Tunker, Unitarian, and Universalist. The Congregational churches of Pennsylvania were grouped under the title "Orthodox Congregational," but could have been very properly included under the general denominational head. No attempt was made to distinguish between the various branches of the larger denominations—for example, the Baptists, Methodists, or Presbyterians—and all churches not easily included under one of the foregoing 18 titles were either grouped under the heads of "Free" or "Union" or combined under that of "Minor Sects." The last-named group, especially, included a number of churches in certain states which belonged to some of the 18 denominations specified, although in other states they were listed separately; subsequently, at the period of the census of 1870, they were transferred to their proper places and so presented in a summary given in the report for 1870. This summary was reprinted in the report for 1890 and is also included in the present report,[1] but the statistics for each denomination presented in the summary, while agreeing in total with those published in the original report for 1850 do not correspond in detail.

A classification by "family" groups first appeared in the report for 1860, but only two families were so registered—Baptists and Presbyterians; the former included Baptists and Freewill, Mennonite, Seventh-day, Tunker, and Winebrennerian Baptists, while the latter included Presbyterians and Cumberland, Reformed, and United Presbyterians. The Orthodox Congregationalists of Pennsylvania, separately listed in 1850, were grouped under their general denominational head, the Mennonites and Tunkers were included in the Baptist family, as above stated, and the Adventists, Shakers, and Spiritualists appeared as new denominations.

The classification in the report for 1870 was not as detailed as in that for 1860. All but the Regular Baptists were included under the head of "Other" Baptists, and a similar rule was followed with respect

[1] See Table 15, page 565.

to the Presbyterians. Three denominations—the Evangelical Association, Mormons, and United Brethren in Christ—appeared for the first time, but a large number of churches were classed under the heads of "Miscellaneous," "Unknown (local missions)," and "Unknown (union)."

The presentation of denominations in the report for 1890 was very complete, both as to families and as to separate denominations. The total number of denominations covered by the report was 145, including the three branches of Regular Baptists as separate and distinct denominations and counting the independent Lutheran congregations and the independent miscellaneous congregations as the equivalent of two denominations. Of the 145 denominations so listed in 1890, 120 were grouped in 18 families and 25 were listed separately.

NAMES AND CLASSIFICATION OF DENOMINATIONS IN 1906.

The statistics of religious bodies for 1906 embrace a total of 186 denominations in the United States, if the "Independent churches" be classed as one denomination. Of these 186 denominations, 154 are grouped in 27 families, and 32 are classed as unrelated or separate denominations. Since 1890 the number of denominations has increased by 41 and the number of denominational families by 9. The following summary indicates, in general, the movement in religious denominations between the two censuses:

Denominations reported in 1890		145
Denominations which have ceased to exist	12	
Denominations consolidated with other denominations	4	
Denominations which have disappeared through change in classification	4	
Total denominations which have disappeared		20
Denominations reported in both 1890 and 1906		125
Denominations added by division of denominations	13	
Other new denominations	48	
Total new denominations		61
Denominations reported in 1906		186

So far as the names and classification of the religious bodies in existence in 1890 are concerned, the present report agrees, in the main, with that of 1890. A few changes have been made in order to meet criticisms of the latter report. As the work of collecting the statistics for the several denominations progressed, it was found that there was some dissatisfaction with the terminology and classification previously used. It was evident, however, that no list of denominations, grouped as far as possible by denominational families, could be devised which would be entirely consistent and practical, and at the same time scientific, owing partly to the great diversity among religious bodies, partly to their predilections, and partly to the popular use of certain names which would render the adoption of the corporate names confusing or even misleading. As far as practicable, the predilections of each denomination have been consulted, and, the list of denominations finally adopted,[1] after a careful review of existing conditions and after extended conference with a number of persons actively identified with the religious work of the country, is deemed, on the whole, to meet the peculiar difficulties of the case. In addition to the changes made to meet the criticisms referred to, there are changes due to altered conditions. Separate denominations in the families are in general arranged in the order of the date of organization, though occasionally, for specific reasons, that has been modified.

The changes in the list of denominations from that given in the report for 1890 are indicated in detail under four heads: (1) Changes in the names of denominations; (2) changes in the names of denominational families; (3) disappearance of denominations and denominational families; and (4) new denominations and denominational families.

Changes in the names of denominations.—The report for 1890, in the case of some of the denominations, failed to use the corporate name, but substituted a short and more popular designation. The present report, with few exceptions, has adopted the corporate name. The only changes requiring notice are indicated in the following tabular statement giving the names by which the bodies in question have been known at the two periods:

1906	1890
Associate Synod of North America (Associate Presbyterian Church).	Associate Church of North America.
Christian Union	Churches of Christ in Christian Union, Independent.
Churches of God in North America, General Eldership of the.	Church of God (Winebrennerian).
Duck River and Kindred Associations of Baptists (Baptist Church of Christ).	Baptist Church of Christ.
Free Baptists	Freewill Baptists.
Freewill Baptists	Original Freewill Baptists.
National Baptist Convention (Colored)	Regular Baptists (Colored)
Northern Baptist Convention	Regular Baptists (North).
Presbyterian Church in the United States.	Presbyterian Church in the United States (Southern).
Presbyterian Church in the United States of America.	Presbyterian Church in the United States of America (Northern).
Reformed Zion Union Apostolic Church (Colored Methodist).	Zion Union Apostolic.
Southern Baptist Convention	Regular Baptists (South).
Temple Society in the United States (Friends of the Temple).	Friends of the Temple.
United Society of Believers (Shakers)	Society of Shakers.

Changes in the names of denominational families.—In the report for 1890, the denominational families were generally designated by the names usually given to the adherents of the constituent denominations, as Adventists, Baptists, etc. This procedure has been criticised, and the terms "bodies" and "churches," with the appropriate adjective prefixed, have been suggested. Since the term "churches" is also used in reference to local churches, the term "bodies" has been adopted. In a few cases where they seemed to be peculiarly appropriate, however, the terms "churches" and "societies" have been used, and in a

[1] For full list of denominations, as adopted for 1906, see page 18.

few cases, in order to avoid an awkward or undesirable phrase, the customary term has been retained.

Disappearance of denominations and denominational families.—The following 12 denominations, represented in the report for 1890, have been omitted from that for 1906, since no information indicating their denominational existence in 1906 has been found, and in the case of most of them a definite statement was received that they had been dissolved:

Adonai Shomo (Communistic).
Christian Missionary Association.
Church Triumphant or Koreshan Ecclesia (Communistic).
Church Triumphant (Schweinfurth).
Congregational Methodist (Colored).
Evangelist Missionary Church (Methodist).
Harmony Society (Communistic).
Independent Methodists.
New Icaria Society (Communistic).
Old Catholic Church.
Society of Altruists (Communistic).
Society of Separatists (Communistic).

In the report for 1890, 5 denominations were represented which have since been consolidated with other denominations. They are given in the following tabular statement, together with the denominations with which they have been respectively consolidated:

DENOMINATION CONSOLIDATED WITH ANOTHER DENOMINATION.	DENOMINATION WITH WHICH CONSOLIDATED.
Apostolic Mennonite Church	General Conference of Mennonites of North America.
Christian Church (South)	Christians (Christian Connection).
Danish Church Association (Lutheran)	United Danish Evangelical Lutheran Church in America.
German Augsburg Synod (Lutheran)	Evangelical Lutheran Synod of Michigan and Other States, and other Lutheran bodies.
Lutheran Independent congregations	Various Lutheran bodies and (in part) independent churches.

The Danish Church Association was combined with the Danish Evangelical Lutheran Church in North America, organized since the report for 1890, to form the United Danish Evangelical Lutheran Church in America, and on this account the consolidations given in the foregoing statement have reduced the number of denominations by only 4 as compared with 1890.

In addition, the number of denominations has been reduced by 4 through change in classification. In the report for 1890, the 3 Baptist bodies designated, respectively, Regular Baptists (North), Regular Baptists (South), and Regular Baptists (Colored) were classed as 3 separate denominations. This classification has occasioned considerable criticism, since it was maintained that they are not 3 denominations, but 1 as far as doctrine, polity, and usages are concerned, the distinction being purely for administrative purposes. In the present report they are classed as a single denomination, but the statistics are presented separately for each branch. The number of Jewish denominations has been reduced from 2 to 1, because the Jewish authorities who furnished the information for the present report did not accept the separation made in 1890 between Orthodox and Reformed Jews. The Greek Catholic Church (Uniat), classed as a separate denomination in 1890, is more properly a part of the Roman Catholic Church, and has been so classed in the present report.

Four denominational families which appeared in the report for 1890 do not appear in that for 1906. They are given in the following tabular statement, together with the reasons for their omission:

DENOMINATIONAL FAMILY.	REASON FOR OMISSION.
Catholic bodies Protestant Episcopal bodies	Predilection of some of the constituent denominations to be considered unrelated bodies.
Christians (Christian Connection)	Union of the constituent denominations.
Jewish congregations	Classification of the constituent denominations as one denomination.

New denominations and denominational families.—The following tabular statement gives the names of 17 denominations which have been added by division of denominations, as well as the names of the bodies from which they respectively branched off. The net gain in this manner, however, is only 13, since in 4 cases the denominations from which they respectively branched off were entirely reorganized into two or more new bodies.

DENOMINATION ADDED BY DIVISION OF A DENOMINATION.	DENOMINATION WITH WHICH FORMERLY INCLUDED.
American Salvation Army	Salvation Army.
Churches of Christ	Disciples of Christ.
Church of God (Adventist), Unattached Congregations.	Church of God (Seventh-day Adventist).
Colored Primitive Baptists in America	Primitive Baptists.
General Church of the New Jerusalem	Church of the New Jerusalem (Swedenborgian).
General Convention of the New Jerusalem in the United States of America.	Church of the New Jerusalem (Swedenborgian).
German Evangelical Lutheran Synod of Texas.	General Council of the Evangelical Lutheran Church in North America.
German Evangelical Protestant Ministers' Association.	German Evangelical Protestant Church.
German Evangelical Protestant Ministers' Conference.	German Evangelical Protestant Church.
Krimmer Brueder-Gemeinde	Bundes Conferenz der Mennoniten Brueder-Gemeinde.
Polish National Church of America	Roman Catholic Church.
Schellenberger Brueder-Gemeinde	Bundes Conferenz der Mennoniten Brueder-Gemeinde.
Theosophical Society, American Section.	Theosophical Society.
Theosophical Society in America	Theosophical Society.
Theosophical Society, New York	Theosophical Society.
Universal Brotherhood and Theosophical Society.	Theosophical Society.
United Evangelical Church	Evangelical Association.

These former denominations which have been completely reorganized are the Church of the New Jerusalem (Swedenborgian), German Evangelical Protestant Church, Bundes Conferenz der Mennoniten Brueder-Gemeinde, and the Theosophical Society.

In the following list 48 denominations are named which have been added otherwise than by division of denominations. Of these, 11 are the result of immigration; 29 are new denominations not the result of division of denominations existing in 1890; 7 are bodies in existence in 1890, but not included in the report for that year; and 1 is a denomination erroneously included with another body, in the report for 1890.

Denominations added through immigration:
- Eastern Orthodox Churches:
  - Servian Orthodox Church.
  - Syrian Orthodox Church.
- Evangelical Union of Bohemian and Moravian Brethren in North America.
- Hungarian Reformed Church in America.
- Japanese Temples.
- Lutheran bodies:
  - Church of the Lutheran Brethren of America (Norwegian).
  - Finnish Evangelical Lutheran National Church.
  - Slovak Evangelical Lutheran Synod of America.
- New Apostolic Church.
- Swedish Evangelical bodies:
  - Swedish Evangelical Free Mission.
  - Swedish Evangelical Mission Covenant of America.

New denominations not occasioned by ecclesiastical division:
- Bahais.
- Central Illinois Conference of Mennonites.
- Christian Catholic Church in Zion.
- Church of God and Saints of Christ (Colored).
- Churches of the Living God (Colored):
  - Church of Christ in God.
  - Church of the Living God (Apostolic Church).
  - Church of the Living God (Christian Workers for Friendship).
- Evangelistic associations:
  - Apostolic Christian Church.
  - Apostolic Faith Movement.
  - Christian Congregation.
  - Church of Daniel's Band.
  - Gospel Mission.
  - Heavenly Recruit Church.
  - Hephzibah Faith Missionary Association.
  - Lumber River Mission.
  - Metropolitan Church Association.
  - Missionary Church Association.
  - Peniel Missions.
  - Pentecost Bands of the World.
  - Pentecostal Union Church.
  - Voluntary Missionary Society in America (Colored).
- Free Christian Zion Church of Christ (Colored).
- International Apostolic Holiness Union.
- Nonsectarian Churches of Bible Faith.
- Norwegian Lutheran Free Church.
- Pentecostal Church of the Nazarene.
- United American Freewill Baptists (Colored).
- Vedanta Society.
- Volunteers of America.

Denominations in existence in 1890, but not included in the report for that year:
- Christian Israelite Church.
- Freewill Baptists (Bullockites).
- Lutheran bodies:
  - Apostolic Lutheran Church (Finnish).
  - Evangelical Lutheran Church in America, Eielsen's Synod.
  - Evangelical Lutheran Jehovah Conference.
- Nebraska and Minnesota Conference of Mennonites.
- Reformed Methodist Union Episcopal Church (Colored).

Denomination erroneously included, in 1890, in the General Council of the Evangelical Lutheran Church in America:
- Evangelical Lutheran Synod of Iowa and Other States.

Nine new denominational families appear in the report for 1906 through division of bodies existing in 1890 or through addition to them from abroad. They are given in the first of the following tables, together with the occasion of their formation.

Four new denominational families have originated otherwise than by division of bodies existing in 1890 or addition to them from abroad. They are given in the second of the following tables, together with the occasion of their formation:

DENOMINATIONAL FAMILY.	OCCASION OF FORMATION.
Buddhists	Addition of Japanese Buddhists, who have settled in the United States chiefly since 1890.
Catholic Apostolic Churches	Addition of the New Apostolic Church through immigration of its adherents from Germany.
Churches of the New Jerusalem	Division of the Church of the New Jerusalem (Swedenborgian) into two bodies.
Disciples or Christians	Division of the Disciples of Christ into two bodies.
Evangelical bodies	Division of the Evangelical Association into two bodies.
German Evangelical Protestant bodies.	Division of the German Evangelical Protestant Church into two bodies.
Moravian bodies	Organization, by immigrants from Europe, of a new denomination entitled Evangelical Union of Bohemian and Moravian Brethren of North America.
Salvationists	Withdrawal of the American Salvation Army from the Salvation Army.
Theosophical societies	Organization of four separate societies by members of the Theosophical Society.

Churches of the Living God (Colored).	Organization of a new denomination since 1890, and its subsequent division into three bodies.
Eastern Orthodox Churches	Formed of the Russian and the Greek Orthodox Churches, classed with Catholic bodies in the report for 1890, and of the Servian and the Syrian Orthodox Churches, organized in the United States since 1890.
Evangelistic associations	Formed of local churches, organized more or less closely for the purpose of carrying on evangelistic work.
Swedish Evangelical bodies	Formed of two bodies organized by Swedish immigrants since 1890.

LIST OF DENOMINATIONS FOR 1906.

The list of denominations as finally adopted for 1906 is as follows:

Adventist bodies:
- Evangelical Adventists.
- Advent Christian Church.
- Seventh-day Adventist Denomination.
- Church of God (Adventist).
- Churches of God (Adventist), Unattached Congregations.
- Life and Advent Union.
- Churches of God in Christ Jesus.

Armenian Church.

Bahais.

Baptist bodies:
- Baptists—
  - Northern Baptist Convention.
  - Southern Baptist Convention.
  - National Baptist Convention (Colored).
- General Six Principle Baptists.
- Seventh-day Baptists.
- Free Baptists.
- Freewill Baptists.
- General Baptists.
- Separate Baptists.
- United Baptists.
- Duck River and Kindred Associations of Baptists (Baptist Church of Christ).
- Primitive Baptists.
- Colored Primitive Baptists in America.
- Two-Seed-in-the-Spirit Predestinarian Baptists.
- Freewill Baptists (Bullockites).
- United American Freewill Baptists (Colored).

Brethren (Plymouth):
- Brethren (Plymouth)—I.
- Brethren (Plymouth)—II.
- Brethren (Plymouth)—III.
- Brethren (Plymouth)—IV.

Brethren (River):
- Brethren in Christ.
- Yorker, or Old Order, Brethren.
- United Zion's Children.

Buddhists:
- Chinese Temples.
- Japanese Temples.

Catholic Apostolic Churches:
- Catholic Apostolic Church.
- New Apostolic Church.

Christadelphians.
Christian Catholic Church in Zion.
Christian Israelite Church.
Christian Union.
Christians (Christian Connection).
Church of Christ, Scientist.
Church of God and Saints of Christ (Colored).
Churches of God in North America, General Eldership of the.
Churches of the Living God (Colored):
- Church of the Living God (Christian Workers for Friendship).
- Church of the Living God (Apostolic Church).
- Church of Christ in God.

Churches of the New Jerusalem:
- General Convention of the New Jerusalem in the United States of America.
- General Church of the New Jerusalem.

Communistic societies:
- United Society of Believers (Shakers).
- Amana Society.

Congregationalists.
Disciples or Christians:
- Disciples of Christ.
- Churches of Christ.

Dunkers or German Baptist Brethren:
- German Baptist Brethren Church (Conservative).
- Old Order German Baptist Brethren.
- The Brethren Church (Progressive Dunkers).
- German Seventh-day Baptists.

Eastern Orthodox Churches:
- Russian Orthodox Church.
- Servian Orthodox Church.
- Syrian Orthodox Church.
- Greek Orthodox Church.

Evangelical bodies:
- Evangelical Association.
- United Evangelical Church.

Evangelistic associations:
- Apostolic Faith Movement.
- Peniel Missions.
- Metropolitan Church Association.
- Hephzibah Faith Missionary Association.
- Missionary Church Association.
- Pentecost Bands of the World.
- Heavenly Recruit Church.
- Apostolic Christian Church.
- Christian Congregation.
- Gospel Mission.
- Church of Daniel's Band.
- Lumber River Mission.
- Pentecostal Union Church.
- Voluntary Missionary Society in America (Colored).

Free Christian Zion Church of Christ (Colored).
Friends:
- Society of Friends (Orthodox).
- Religious Society of Friends (Hicksite).
- Orthodox Conservative Friends (Wilburite).
- Friends (Primitive).

German Evangelical Protestant bodies:
- German Evangelical Protestant Ministers' Association.
- German Evangelical Protestant Ministers' Conference.

German Evangelical Synod of North America.
Independent churches.
International Apostolic Holiness Union.
Jewish congregations.
Latter-day Saints:
- Church of Jesus Christ of Latter-day Saints.
- Reorganized Church of Jesus Christ of Latter-day Saints.

Lutheran bodies:
- General Synod of the Evangelical Lutheran Church in the United States of America.
- United Synod of the Evangelical Lutheran Church in the South.
- General Council of the Evangelical Lutheran Church in North America.
- Evangelical Lutheran Synodical Conference of America.
- United Norwegian Lutheran Church in America.
- Evangelical Lutheran Joint Synod of Ohio and Other States.
- Lutheran Synod of Buffalo.
- Hauge's Norwegian Evangelical Lutheran Synod.
- Evangelical Lutheran Church in America, Eielsen's Synod.
- German Evangelical Lutheran Synod of Texas.
- Evangelical Lutheran Synod of Iowa and Other States.
- Synod for the Norwegian Evangelical Lutheran Church in America.
- Evangelical Lutheran Synod of Michigan and Other States.
- Danish Evangelical Lutheran Church in America.
- Icelandic Evangelical Lutheran Synod in North America.
- Immanuel Synod of the Evangelical Lutheran Church of North America.
- Finnish Evangelical Lutheran Church of America, or Suomi Synod.
- Norwegian Lutheran Free Church.
- United Danish Evangelical Lutheran Church in America.
- Slovak Evangelical Lutheran Synod of America.
- Finnish Evangelical Lutheran National Church.
- Apostolic Lutheran Church (Finnish).
- Church of the Lutheran Brethren of America (Norwegian).
- Evangelical Lutheran Jehovah Conference.

Mennonite bodies:
- Mennonite Church.
- Bruederhoef Mennonite Church.
- Amish Mennonite Church.
- Old Amish Mennonite Church.
- Reformed Mennonite Church.
- General Conference of Mennonites of North America.
- Church of God in Christ (Mennonite).
- Old (Wisler) Mennonite Church.
- Defenceless Mennonites.
- Mennonite Brethren in Christ.
- Bundes Conferenz der Mennoniten Brueder-Gemeinde—
  - Krimmer Brueder-Gemeinde.
  - Schellenberger Brueder-Gemeinde.
- Central Illinois Conference of Mennonites.
- Nebraska and Minnesota Conference of Mennonites.

Methodist bodies:
- Methodist Episcopal Church.
- Union American Methodist Episcopal Church (Colored).
- African Methodist Episcopal Church.
- African Union Methodist Protestant Church.
- African Methodist Episcopal Zion Church.
- Methodist Protestant Church.
- Wesleyan Methodist Connection of America.
- Methodist Episcopal Church, South.
- Congregational Methodist Church.
- New Congregational Methodist Church.
- Colored Methodist Episcopal Church.
- Reformed Zion Union Apostolic Church (Colored).
- Primitive Methodist Church in the United States of America.
- Free Methodist Church of North America.
- Reformed Methodist Union Episcopal Church (Colored).

Moravian bodies;
- Moravian Church (Unitas Fratrum).
- Evangelical Union of Bohemian and Moravian Brethren in North America.

Nonsectarian Churches of Bible Faith.
Pentecostal Church of the Nazarene.
Polish National Church of America.
Presbyterian bodies:
- Presbyterian Church in the United States of America.
- Cumberland Presbyterian Church.
- Colored Cumberland Presbyterian Church.
- Welsh Calvinistic Methodist Church.
- United Presbyterian Church of North America.
- Presbyterian Church in the United States.
- Associate Synod of North America (Associate Presbyterian Church).
- Associate Reformed Synod of the South.
- Synod of the Reformed Presbyterian Church of North America.
- Reformed Presbyterian Church in North America, General Synod.
- Reformed Presbyterian Church (Covenanted).
- Reformed Presbyterian Church in the United States and Canada.

Protestant Episcopal Church.
Reformed bodies:
- Reformed Church in America.
- Reformed Church in the United States.
- Christian Reformed Church.
- Hungarian Reformed Church in America.

Reformed Catholic Church.
Reformed Episcopal Church.
Roman Catholic Church.
Salvationists:
- Salvation Army.
- American Salvation Army.

Schwenkfelders.
Social Brethren.
Society for Ethical Culture.
Spiritualists.
Swedish Evangelical bodies:
- Swedish Evangelical Mission Covenant of America.
- Swedish Evangelical Free Mission.

Temple Society in the United States (Friends of the Temple).
Theosophical societies:
- Theosophical Society in America.
- Theosophical Society, New York.
- Theosophical Society, American Section.
- Universal Brotherhood and Theosophical Society.

Unitarians.
United Brethren bodies:
- Church of the United Brethren in Christ.
- Church of the United Brethren in Christ (Old Constitution).

Universalists.
Vedanta Society.
Volunteers of America.

SUMMARY

SUMMARY OF RESULTS.

SUMMARY OF STATISTICS FOR CONTINENTAL UNITED STATES.

The first broad division of this report relates to continental United States, and consists of a classification according to religious denominations of the material collected relative to each of the following topics: Organizations, communicants or members, places of worship, value of church property, debt on church property, and value of parsonages. These statistics, which are included in summarized form in the ensuing text, are given in detail in Tables 1 and 8 (pages 148 and 514).

For purposes of textual consideration the distinctively Protestant bodies—those which in history and general character are identified more or less closely with the Protestant Reformation or its subsequent development—are grouped under one head. Twenty-two bodies are not included in this group. They comprise those bodies which are distinctively non-Protestant, those which differ in some important characteristics from the Protestant bodies, and those into whose organization the question of Protestantism can scarcely be said to enter. These 22 bodies are grouped as follows:

(1) The Roman Catholic Church.

(2) The Jewish congregations.

(3) The Latter-day Saints, consisting of the Church of Jesus Christ of Latter-day Saints and the Reorganized Church of Jesus Christ of Latter-day Saints.

(4) The Eastern Orthodox Churches, consisting of the Russian Orthodox Church, the Servian Orthodox Church, the Syrian Orthodox Church, and the Greek Orthodox Church.

(5) All other bodies—consisting of the Armenian Church; the Bahais; the Buddhists, who comprise the worshipers in Chinese and Japanese Temples; the Communistic societies, which comprise the United Society of Believers (Shakers) and the Amana Society; the Polish National Church of America; the Society for Ethical Culture; the Spiritualists; the Theosophical societies, which comprise the Theosophical Society in America, the Theosophical Society, New York, the Theosophical Society, American Section, and the Universal Brotherhood and Theosophical Society; and the Vedanta Society.

RELIGIOUS ORGANIZATIONS.

The statistical unit in the presentation of religious bodies is the organization. The term is used in this report in the same sense as in that for 1890; it is a comprehensive designation for what is variously called a church, a congregation, a society, or a meeting, and embraces not only a church proper, but also each mission, station, or chapel, when separately organized. In the great majority of bodies the organization is distinctively a gathering for religious service. In one instance, the Chinese Temples, it represents the building, containing one or more shrines at which Chinese Buddhists worship, and in a number of instances, as in the case of the Bahais, the Society for Ethical Culture, and the Theosophical societies, it represents a gathering for conference on ethical, philosophical, or social subjects, as well as religious topics.

The total number of organizations covered by the present investigation is 212,230, as reported by 186 denominations. For purposes of presentation, as already explained, 154 of these bodies are arranged under 27 family heads, while 32 bodies are not so grouped but are listed separately in alphabetical order. The distribution of religious organizations by principal families and separate denominations in 1906 (those reporting 50,000 or more communicants or members), in comparison with similar figures for 1890, is given in the table on page 22.

Of the 212,230 organizations in 1906, shown by the following table, 195,618, or 92.2 per cent, are reported by the 164 Protestant bodies; 12,482, or 5.9 per cent, by the Roman Catholic Church; and 4,130, or about 2 per cent, by the remaining bodies, including Jewish congregations, Latter-day Saints, Eastern Orthodox Churches, and 14 minor bodies. The report for 1890 showed for continental United States a total of 165,151 organizations, of which 153,054, or 92.7 per cent, were reported by Protestant bodies; 10,239, or 6.2 per cent, by the Roman Catholic Church; and 1,858, or a little more than 1 per cent, by all the remaining bodies. According to these figures, between 1890 and 1906 the total number of religious organizations in the United States increased 47,079, or 28.5 per cent. For Protestant bodies the increase was 42,564, or 27.8 per cent; for the Roman Catholic Church 2,243, or 21.9 per cent; for Jewish congregations 1,236, or 231.9 per cent; and for Latter-day Saints, 328, or 38.3 per cent. The Eastern Orthodox Churches have practically come into existence since 1890, and this is also true with respect to several of the smaller denominations which are included under "All other bodies."

DENOMINATION.	Number of bodies: 1906.	RELIGIOUS ORGANIZATIONS. Number. 1906	Number. 1890	Per cent distribution. 1906	Per cent distribution. 1890	Increase from 1890 to 1906. Number.	Increase from 1890 to 1906. Per cent.
All denominations	186	212,230	[1]165,151	100.0	100.0	47,079	28.5
Protestant bodies	164	195,618	153,054	92.2	92.7	42,564	27.8
Adventist bodies	7	2,551	1,757	2	1	794	
Baptist bodies	14	54,880	42,909	9	0	11,971	
Christians (Christian Connection)	1	1,379	1,424	6	9	[2]45	
Church of Christ, Scientist	1	638	221	1.3	1.1	417	45.2
Congregationalists	1	5,713	4,868	28.7	28.9	845	[illegible]
Disciples or Christians	2	10,942	7,246	2	4	3,696	.
Dunkers or German Baptist Brethren	4	1,097	989	5	6	108	
Evangelical bodies	2	2,738	2,310	5.3	4.4	428	51.0
Friends	4	1,147	1,056	8.5	8.6	91	[illegible]
German Evangelical Synod of North America	1	1,205	870	6	5	335	38.5
Independent churches	1	1,079	155	5	1	924	596.1
Lutheran bodies	24	12,703	8,595	0.0	0.2	4,108	47.8
Mennonite bodies	14	604	550	6.3	6.3	54	9.8
Methodist bodies	15	64,701	51,489	5	.2	13,212	7
Presbyterian bodies	12	15,506	13,471	3	2	2,035	1
Protestant Episcopal Church	1	6,845	5,018	30.2	31.0	1,827	25.4
Reformed bodies	4	2,585	2,181	3.2	3.3	404	[illegible]
Unitarians	1	461	421	2	3	40	9.5
United Brethren bodies	2	4,304	4,526	0	7	[2]222	[2]4.9
Universalists		846	956	0.4	0.6	[2]110	[2]11.5
Other Protestant bodies	52	3,694	2,042	8.7	8.2	1,652	80.9
Roman Catholic Church	1	12,482	10,239	9	6.2	2,243	21.9
Jewish congregations	1	1,769	533	8	0.3	1,236	231.9
Latter-day Saints	2	1,184	856	6	0.5	328	38.3
Eastern Orthodox Churches	4	411	2	5.2	(3)	409	(4)
All other bodies	14	766	467	0.4	0.3	299	64.0

[1] Exclusive of 26 organizations in Alaska.
[2] Decrease.
[3] Less than one-tenth of 1 per cent.
[4] Per cent not shown where base is less than 100.

The general order or rank of the principal religious bodies in 1906 with respect to organizations is presented in the following summary:

DENOMINATION.	Number of organizations.	Rank in number of organizations.
Methodist bodies	64 701	1
Baptist bodies	54 880	2
Presbyterian bodies	15,506	3
Lutheran bodies	12 703	4
Roman Catholic Church	12,482	5
Disciples or Christians	10,942	6
Protestant Episcopal Church	6,845	7
Congregationalists	5,713	8
United Brethren bodies	4,304	9
Evangelical bodies	2,738	10
Reformed bodies	2,585	11
Adventist bodies	2,551	12
Jewish congregations	1,769	13
Christians (Christian Connection)	1,379	14
German Evangelical Synod of North America	1,205	15
Latter-day Saints	1,184	16
Friends	1,147	17
Dunkers or German Baptist Brethren	1,097	18

The Methodist bodies rank first in number of organizations, in 1906, reporting 64,701, or 30.5 per cent of the entire number in the United States. The Baptist bodies rank second, with 54,880 organizations, or 25.9 per cent of the whole number. As compared with 1890, the Methodist bodies show an increase in the number of organizations of 13,212,[1] or 25.7 per cent, and the Baptist bodies an increase of 11,971, or 27.9 per cent. These two families embrace considerably more than one-half (56.4 per cent) of the whole number of organizations, and also show more than one-half of the entire increase between 1890 and 1906, or 25,183 out of a total increase for all bodies of 47,079.

[1] Some of this increase is only apparent; see explanatory statement on page 23 concerning the returns for the African Methodist Episcopal Church.

Six other Protestant families, or denominations, comprise from 2 to more than 7 per cent of all the organizations in 1906, namely, Presbyterian bodies with 15,506 organizations, or 7.3 per cent of the total number; Lutheran bodies with 12,703, or 6 per cent; Disciples or Christians with 10,942, or 5.2 per cent; Protestant Episcopal Church with 6,845, or 3.2 per cent; Congregationalists with 5,713, or 2.7 per cent; and United Brethren bodies with 4,304, or 2 per cent. These 6, together with the Methodist and Baptist families, comprise 71 bodies, which represent substantially nine-tenths of the Protestant organizations, and 82.8 per cent of all the religious organizations in the United States.

The differences in the per cent distribution of organizations in 1906 as compared with 1890 are in general small and indicate that the relative importance of the several families and denominations has not changed essentially since the former report, so far as organizations are concerned.

Of the larger Protestant bodies only 3 show a decline in the number of organizations. These are the Christians (Christian Connection), which had 1,379 organizations in 1906 as against 1,424 in 1890, a loss of 45, or 3.2 per cent; United Brethren bodies, which had 4,304 organizations in 1906 as against 4,526 in 1890, a loss of 222, or 4.9 per cent; and the Universalists, which had 846 organizations in 1906 as against

956 in 1890, a loss of 110, or 11.5 per cent. It should be noted, however, that the loss in the United Brethren bodies (see Table 8, page 514) is confined entirely to one body, Church of the United Brethren in Christ (Old Constitution), the other body having substantially the same number of organizations in 1906 as in 1890.

The Jewish congregations, with 1,769 organizations in 1906 as compared with 533 in 1890, show a gain of 1,236 organizations, or 231.9 per cent. For the Latter-day Saints, comprising 2 bodies, the number of organizations has risen from 856 in 1890 to 1,184 in 1906, representing a gain of 328, or 38.3 per cent. The Eastern Orthodox Churches, which had only 2 organizations in 1890—Greek Orthodox and Russian Orthodox, 1 each—are now represented by 4 bodies comprising 411 organizations, of which 334 are Greek Orthodox churches.

The more detailed presentation in Table 8 (page 514) throws considerable light on the preceding statements for the principal families and denominations.

It shows, for example, that among the Adventist bodies the gain in organizations is contributed wholly by the Seventh-day branch, for which 1,889 organizations were reported in 1906 as against 995 in 1890. Each of the other 6 branches shows a slight loss in number of organizations.

The Baptist bodies show a gain between 1890 and 1906 of 11,971 organizations, but most of this gain is to be credited to 2 branches of the Baptist denomination, namely, the Southern Baptist Convention, with an increase of 4,866 organizations, and the National Baptist Convention (Colored), with an increase of 6,001. The 2 bodies of Primitive Baptists show an increase of 612 organizations; the Freewill Baptists, an increase of 441; and the Northern Baptist Convention, an increase of 370. Many of the remaining branches, however, show a loss, especially the Free Baptists, whose organizations decreased in number from 1,586 in 1890 to 1,346 in 1906, and the Two-Seed-in-the-Spirit Predestinarian Baptists, whose organizations decreased from 473 in 1890 to 55 in 1906. Evidently some readjustment of organizations has taken place, because certain churches reported in 1890 as affiliated with one body are now reported as connected with another.

The Church of Christ, Scientist, as indicated by the foregoing table, has experienced a rapid growth. The number of organizations increased from 221 in 1890 to 638 in 1906—a gain of 417, or 188.7 per cent.

The growth in the number of "Independent churches," has also been phenomenal. In 1890 the number of independent congregations reported was 155. The number given for 1906 is 1,079, indicating a gain of 924, or 596.1 per cent. There are included under this title in 1906 four classes of churches: (1) Churches which call themselves absolutely independent, owning no ecclesiastical association or affiliation; (2) churches using a denominational name but declining any ecclesiastical connection with a denominational body; (3) union churches, representing combinations of two or more denominations, but not ecclesiastically identified with any; (4) churches which, while generally agreeing in doctrine and frequently loosely associated so far as their ministers are concerned, yet have no general organization. A tendency is already manifest within them for more or less organization and consolidation, and whether their distinctive independency will continue is thus a matter of doubt.

The Lutheran bodies have increased in number of organizations from 8,595 to 12,703, a gain of 4,108, or 47.8 per cent. Each of the principal bodies shows a considerable gain in number of organizations. The largest numerical increase in any single body is that for the Evangelical Lutheran Synodical Conference of America, whose organizations rose in number from 1,934 in 1890 to 3,301 in 1906, a gain of 1,367, or 70.7 per cent.

Each of the Methodist bodies in existence in 1906 shows a gain in number of organizations since 1890. The principal gains, out of a total increase of 13,212 organizations for all Methodist bodies, were 4,082, or 15.8 per cent, for the Methodist Episcopal Church; and 2,814, or 18.7 per cent, for the Methodist Episcopal Church, South. The gain of 4,166, or 167.9 per cent, for the African Methodist Episcopal Church is largely apparent, because for that body circuits containing 2, 3, and 4 churches were counted as single organizations in 1890, whereas in 1906 each of these churches was counted separately.

The increase of 2,035 organizations among the Presbyterian bodies was mainly contributed by two denominations—the Presbyterian Church in the United States of America, which reported an increase of 1,223 organizations, and the Presbyterian Church in the United States, which reported an increase of 713. The Cumberland Presbyterian Church, taken, as near as may be, as it existed at the close of the ecclesiastical year in March, 1906, shows a gain since 1890 of only 59 organizations, or 2.1 per cent, while all but 3 of the 9 remaining Presbyterian bodies show a decrease.

At the censuses of 1850, 1860, and 1870 inquiry was made concerning churches, as already explained. The results of the inquiries for these three censuses, although the completeness of the returns is somewhat doubtful, are given by denominations in Table 15 (page 565), from which it appears that the number of "churches" reported was 38,061 in 1850 and 54,009 in 1860; and further, that at the census of 1870, under the division of the inquiries, the number of church organizations reported was 72,459 and the number of church edifices, 63,082. On the face of the returns, therefore, the number of churches increased 15,948, or 41.9 per cent, from 1850 to 1860. A comparison of the number of churches in 1860 with the number of church organizations in 1870 shows an increase of 18,450, or 34.2 per cent. These percentages may be regarded as indicating roughly the probable growth of religious bodies during the two decades in question. For the twenty years from 1870 to 1890, the basis of comparison is positive, and the figures show that the number of church organizations more than doubled, increasing from 72,459 in 1870 to 165,151 in 1890, a gain of 92,692, or 127.9 per cent, but part of this increase is due to the fact that the canvass was more thorough in 1890 than in 1870. As previously stated, the increase from 1890 to 1906 is 47,079, or 28.5 per cent.

COMMUNICANTS OR MEMBERS.

The term "communicants or members" includes, as in the report for 1890, all persons who are entitled or privileged to participate in the ordinance of communion, or the sacrament of the Lord's Supper, in denominations which observe it, and all members in other denominations.

Comparison between the different denominations in regard to their membership, to be valuable, must take into consideration the conditions of membership, particularly with respect to the age limits involved.

In all Protestant bodies, and in many of the other bodies, especially those on the society basis, membership implies definite action both by the applicant and by the official representatives of the denomination. It is therefore practically adult membership, although it may include those as young as 12 or 15 years.

In the Armenian, Eastern Orthodox, Polish National, and Roman Catholic churches all baptized persons, including infants, are regarded and returned as members. In the Armenian and Eastern Orthodox churches all are communicants, but the number of adult males without families is so large that the figures may be taken as fairly comparable with those of other bodies. In the Roman Catholic Church, as just stated, a report was made including as members all baptized persons, but, in accordance with the course pursued in 1890, 15 per cent of this number was deducted to cover those under 9 years of age, as this is the age at which the first communion is usually taken. The conditions in the Polish National Church are similar to those in the Roman Catholic Church, but no deduction has been made because of the small number involved.

In the Jewish congregations only heads of families, in some instances including females, are reported as members, but there is no basis for even an estimate as to the size of families or the proportion of children represented. In the Church of Jesus Christ of Latter-day Saints all, including children, are considered members, although in reporting membership an age limit of 8 years was adopted.

Total number.—The number of communicants or members is given for 1890 and 1906 by denominations in detail in Table 8 (page 514). The table on page 25 shows the situation in regard to membership in the principal denominational families and separate denominations, and gives, first, the number of organizations reporting membership in 1906 and the percentage which they form of the total number of organizations in the body; second, the total number of communicants or members reported by these organizations in 1906 as compared with the number reported in 1890; third, the per cent distribution of membership in 1890 and 1906; and, fourth, the actual and relative increase in membership during the sixteen years from 1890 to 1906.

Little difference exists between the various bodies with regard to the proportion of organizations making a report as to membership. Three bodies made a full report, while the majority made a report for from 99.2 to 99.9 per cent of the total number of organizations. The bodies which were most inadequately returned, and the percentage which the organizations reporting membership formed of the total number, are as follows: Universalists, 95.9; Unitarians, 94.4; "all other bodies," 91.6; and Jewish congregations, 65.1. The comparatively low percentage reported for "all other bodies" results from the fact that under this head are included the Chinese Temples and the Universal Brotherhood and Theosophical Society, for which no statistics of membership can be given.

Because of the small proportion of Jewish congregations for which a report of members was secured and because of the additional fact that the membership of these congregations, when reported, is limited to a statement of the number of heads of families, the returns of the Jewish membership for 1906 can not be compared with the corresponding returns for other bodies. The basis of reporting the members of Jewish congregations, moreover, was not the same in 1890 as it was in 1906, and hence no comparisons between the two periods are possible for the body itself.

The whole number of communicants or members reported by all the religious bodies in 1906 was 32,936,445, of which 20,287,742, or 61.6 per cent, were returned by the 164 Protestant bodies; 12,079,142, or 36.7 per cent, by the Roman Catholic Church; and 569,561, or 1.7 per cent, by 21 other bodies. Of the 20,597,954 communicants or members given in the report for 1890, the Protestant bodies contributed 14,007,187, or 68 per cent; the Roman Catholic Church 6,241,708, or 30.3 per cent; and all the remaining bodies 349,059, or 1.7 per cent.

In considering these figures showing the relative importance of the different bodies with respect to the number of communicants or members, it should be borne constantly in mind that among the Jewish congregations, the Roman Catholic Church, and the Protestant bodies, differences in the requirements for membership exist which prevent statistics based on membership from being an accurate index of the religious affiliations of the population of the United States. The Jewish congregations include as members only the heads of families. The Roman Catholic Church includes as members all persons baptized into the church, and it requires that all children of members shall be baptized as soon as possible, thereby themselves becoming members. The Protestant bodies, as a rule, admit as members only those who, after reaching fairly mature age, declare their desire to join the church. The difference in respect to age at membership between the Protestant bodies and the Roman Catholic Church has been in part eliminated, as explained on page 24, but this correction, even, does not make the figures an accurate index of the religious affiliations of the population. The membership of the Roman Catholic Church includes practically all persons who regard themselves as affiliated with that church. The rules of the Protestant bodies, on the other hand, are such that many persons who regard themselves as affiliated with these bodies are not included because they have not seen fit to fulfill the requirements of membership; and there is, furthermore, no reliable basis for determining the number of actual adherents of the various Protestant denominations. As an index of religious affiliation of the population, therefore, the statistics of membership here presented are misleading, for while giving practically the true number of Roman Catholics in the population at least 10 years of age, they largely understate the number of Hebrews, and, to a less degree, the number of Protestants. For this reason such figures should not be used, without reservation, to determine the religious affiliation of the population.

DENOMINATION.	ORGANIZATIONS REPORTING COMMUNICANTS OR MEMBERS: 1906.		COMMUNICANTS OR MEMBERS.					
			Number.		Per cent distribution.		Increase from 1890 to 1906.	
	Number.	Per cent of total.	1906	1890	1906	1890	Number.	Per cent.
All denominations	210,418	99.1	32,936,445	[1]20,597,954	100.0	100.0	[2]12,367,530	[2]60.4
Protestant bodies	194,497	99.4	20,287,742	14,007,187	61.6	68.0	6,280,555	44.8
Adventist bodies	2,537	99.5	92,735	60,491	0.3	0.3	32,244	53.3
Baptist bodies	54,707	99.7	5,662,234	3,712,468	17.2	18.0	1,949,766	52.5
Christians (Christian Connection)	1,354	98.2	110,117	103,722	0.3	0.5	6,395	6.2
Church of Christ, Scientist	635	99.5	85,717	8,724	0.3	(3)	76,993	882.5
Congregationalists	5,700	99.8	700,480	512,771	2.1	2.5	187,709	36.6
Disciples or Christians	10,909	99.7	1,142,359	641,051	3.5	3.1	501,308	78.2
Dunkers or German Baptist Brethren	1,090	99.4	97,144	73,795	0.3	0.4	23,349	31.6
Evangelical bodies	2,730	99.7	174,780	133,313	0.5	0.6	41,467	31.1
Friends	1,141	99.5	113,772	107,208	0.3	0.5	6,564	6.1
German Evangelical Synod of North America	1,198	99.4	293,137	187,432	0.9	0.9	105,705	56.4
Independent churches	1,065	98.7	73,673	13,360	0.2	0.1	60,313	451.4
Lutheran bodies	12,642	99.5	2,112,494	1,231,072	6.4	6.0	881,422	71.6
Mennonite bodies	604	100.0	54,798	41,541	0.2	0.2	13,257	31.9
Methodist bodies	64,255	99.3	5,749,838	4,589,284	17.5	22.3	1,160,554	25.3
Presbyterian bodies	15,471	99.8	1,830,555	1,277,851	5.6	6.2	552,704	43.3
Protestant Episcopal Church	6,725	98.2	886,942	532,048	2.7	2.6	354,894	66.7
Reformed bodies	2,583	99.9	449,514	309,458	1.4	1.5	140,056	45.3
Unitarians	435	94.4	70,542	67,749	0.2	0.3	2,793	4.1
United Brethren bodies	4,268	99.2	296,050	225,281	0.9	1.1	70,769	31.4
Universalists	811	95.9	64,158	49,194	0.2	0.2	14,964	30.4
Other Protestant bodies	3,637	98.5	226,703	129,374	0.7	0.6	97,329	75.2
Roman Catholic Church	12,472	99.9	12,079,142	6,241,708	36.7	30.3	5,837,434	93.5
Jewish congregations	1,152	65.1	[4]101,457	[4]130,496	0.3	0.6	(5)	(5)
Latter-day Saints	1,184	100.0	256,647	166,125	0.8	0.8	90,522	54.5
Eastern Orthodox Churches	411	100.0	129,606	600	0.4	(3)	129,006	21,501.0
All other bodies	702	91.6	81,851	51,838	0.2	0.3	30,013	57.9

[1] Exclusive of 14,852 communicants or members reported for 26 organizations in Alaska.
[2] Exclusive of Jewish congregations.
[3] Less than one-tenth of 1 per cent.
[4] In 1906, heads of families only. In 1890, members as well as heads of families included.
[5] As the figures for the two censuses are not comparable, the increase can not be shown.

Since the basis of determining membership in the Roman Catholic Church and in the Protestant bodies has not changed essentially between the two censuses, the figures for membership can be used to determine the relative growth of the two bodies. This is indicated by the figures given in the foregoing table, and is also presented graphically in Diagram 1. The membership of the Protestant bodies has increased 6,280,555, or 44.8 per cent, while the membership of the Roman Catholic Church has increased 5,837,434, or 93.5 per cent. In view of the great volume of immigration to this country since 1890,[1] the increase of 93.5 per cent for the Roman Catholic Church does not seem to be greater than would naturally be expected.

Among the Protestant bodies, the Methodist bodies rank first in number of members, with 5,749,838, or 17.5 per cent of the total number, and the Baptist bodies come next, with 5,662,234 members, or 17.2 per cent. These 2 families constitute somewhat more

[1] The number of immigrants from July 1, 1890, to December 31, 1906, was 9,162,772.

than one-third of the entire Protestant membership of the country. If to these be added the Lutheran bodies, with 2,112,494 members, the Presbyterian bodies, with 1,830,555 members, the Disciples or Christians, with 1,142,359 members—each comprising more than a million members—the 5 bodies combined include 16,497,480 members, or fully one-half (50.2 per cent) of the membership of all religious bodies in the United States and more than four-fifths (81.3 per cent) of all the members of Protestant bodies.

DIAGRAM 1.—*Distribution of communicants or members, by principal families or denominations, for continental United States: 1890 and 1906.*

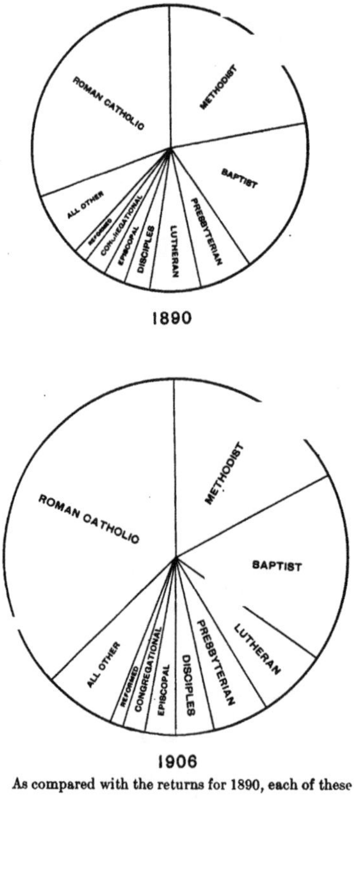

As compared with the returns for 1890, each of these increase in numbers the Baptist bodies lead with 1,949,766, and are followed by the Methodist bodies with 1,160,554, the Lutheran bodies with 881,422, the Presbyterian bodies with 552,704, and the Disciples or Christians with 501,308.

The rank of these 5 Protestant families in the percentage of increase shows, however, some notable variations from the rank as based on actual numbers. The Disciples or Christians lead with 78.2 per cent; then come the Lutheran bodies with 71.6 per cent, the Baptist bodies with 52.5 per cent, the Presbyterian bodies with 43.3 per cent, and the Methodist bodies with 25.3 per cent.

With respect to the membership reported for the Church of Christ, Scientist—85,717 in 1906—it should be noted that, in accordance with the policy and practice of this body, many are counted as members of the central organization in Boston, called the "Mother Church," who are also members of branch churches throughout the world. It is probable, as learned from an authoritative source, that the duplication of membership thus occasioned amounts to nearly, if not quite, one-half of the membership of the Mother Church (41,309). No deduction has been made on this account from the number of members reported for the body.

The summary on page 27 gives for the families, or denominations, having at least 50,000 members in 1906, the rank in number of members, in actual increase in membership, and in relative increase in membership.

Taking the figures given in this summary for the 5 leading denominational families, in conjunction with those for the membership as reported in detail for each denomination in Table 8 (page 514), it appears that of the 5,749,838 members reported for all Methodist bodies in 1906, fully four-fifths are contained in two denominations, namely, the Methodist Episcopal Church, with 2,986,154 members, and the Methodist Episcopal Church, South, with 1,638,480 members. In 1890 the Methodist Episcopal Church had 2,240,354 members, so that the figures for 1906 represent a gain for that church of 745,800, or 33.3 per cent. The Methodist Episcopal Church, South had 1,209,976 members in 1890, so that the gain for that church was 428,504, or 35.4 per cent. The membership of the African Methodist Episcopal Church, the next largest body, shows a gain of 42,052, or 9.3 per cent, having advanced from 452,725 in 1890 to 494,777 in 1906. Considerable gains are also noted for the Colored Methodist Episcopal Church (33.7 per cent) and for the Methodist Protestant Church (25.7 per cent).

The figures reported for the African Methodist Episcopal Zion Church, on the other hand, indicate a very decided loss in membership. According to the report for 1890, this denomination then had 349,788 members, but the number returned for 1906 is only 184,542, a loss of 165,246, or 47.2 per cent. The method of securing the statistics of this denomina-

ability of any great error with respect to either the number of communicants or any of the other items of inquiry. The statistics, in all cases, were obtained direct, from either the pastors or the presiding elders, and the greater part of them were secured by a personal canvass made by agents sent out from the Census Bureau. Furthermore, the figures have been subjected to a most careful scrutiny and verification from authoritative sources and are believed to be substantially correct; it is quite evident, therefore, that the number of communicants given in the report for 1890 was too high. This seems all the more probable, too, when it is considered that the statistics for 1906, as compared with those given in the report for 1890, show that, although the present number of communicants is not much more than one-half the former number, there have been substantial increases in the number of organizations (29.3 per cent) and in the number of church edifices (34.3 per cent) and a very material increase (78.1 per cent) in the value of church property.

The 3 conventions of the Baptist denomination have 5,323,183 members, out of a total of 5,662,234 for all Baptist bodies in 1906, and each shows a very considerable gain as compared with 1890. The Northern Baptist Convention, with 1,052,105 members in 1906, shows an increase since 1890 of 252,080, or 31.5 per cent; the Southern Baptist Convention, with 2,009,471 members in 1906, an increase of 729,405, or 57 per cent; and the National Baptist Convention (Colored), with 2,261,607 members in 1906, an increase of 912,618, or 67.7 per cent. It should be noted in this connection that churches belonging to colored Baptist associations in Northern states, which were included in the statistics for the Northern Baptist Convention in 1890, are now given in connection with the statistics for the National Baptist Convention, and that for this reason the figures for the 2 bodies for 1906 are not entirely comparable with those for 1890. It was the judgment of the Bureau of the Census, and it was concurred in by representatives of the 2 conventions, that Baptist associations composed exclusively of colored organizations, in whatever part of the country, should properly be included in the National Baptist Convention, since they appear to be claimed by that convention, and particularly in view of the fact, also, that such inclusion would not affect the totals for the Baptist denomination as a whole, including the 3 conventions. The 2 Primitive Baptist bodies show a gain since 1890 of 21,116, or 18.2 per cent, while of the smaller Baptist bodies, 4 show an increase, 5 a decrease, and 2 were not reported in 1890.

Of the 2,112,494 members reported for the 24 Lutheran bodies in 1906, fully nine-tenths are contained in 7 bodies, each comprising over 100,000 members, namely, Synodical Conference, 648,529 members; General Council, 462,177 members; General Synod, 270,221 members; United Norwegian Church, 185,027 members; Joint Synod of Ohio and Other States, 123,408 members; Synod of Iowa and Other States, 110,254 members; and Norwegian Synod, 107,712 members. As compared with 1890, each of these 7 bodies shows a very material increase in membership, the lowest being 54.2 per cent, for the United Norwegian Church, and the highest, 128 per cent, for the Synod of Iowa and Other States.

DENOMINATION.	COMMUNICANTS OR MEMBERS: 1906.					
	Number.	Increase over 1890.		Rank of denomination according to—		
		Number.	Per cent.	Number.	Increase over 1890.	
					Number.	Per cent.
Roman Catholic Church	12,079,142	5,837,434	5	1	1	4
Methodist bodies	5,749,838	1,160,554	3	2	3	20
Baptist bodies	5,662,234	1,949,766	5	3	2	11
Lutheran bodies	2,112,494	881,422	93.6	4	4	6
Presbyterian bodies	1,830,555	552,704	[illegible].3	5	5	13
Disciples or Christians	1,142,359	501,308	2	6	6	5
Protestant Episcopal Church	886,942	354,894	7	7	7	7
Congregationalists	700,480	187,709	.6	8	8	14
Reformed bodies	449,514	140,056	78.3	9	9	12
United Brethren bodies	296,050	70,769	[illegible].4	10	14	17
German Evangelical Synod of North America	293,137	105,705	4	11	11	8
Latter-day Saints	256,647	90,522	5	12	12	9
Evangelical bodies	174,780	41,467	.1	13	16	18
Eastern Orthodox Churches	129,606	129,006	21, 56.0	14	10	1
Friends	113,772	6,564	[illegible].1	15	21	22
Christians (Christian Connection)	110,117	6,395	2	16	22	21
Dunkers or German Baptist Brethren	97,144	23,349	.6	17	18	16
Adventist bodies	92,735	32,244	6.3	18	17	10
Church of Christ, Scientist	85,717	76,993	883.5	19	13	2
Independent churches	73,673	60,313	.4	20	15	3
Unitarians	70,542	2,793	1	21	23	23
Universalists	64,158	14,964	451 4	22	19	19
Mennonite bodies	54,798	13,257	38.9	23	20	15

Among the Presbyterian bodies the Presbyterian Church in the United States of America is much the largest body and, with 1,179,566 members in 1906, comprises very nearly two-thirds of the entire membership reported for these bodies as a whole; it had 787,743 members in 1890, showing a gain of 391,823, or 49.7 per cent. The Presbyterian Church in the United States, although a much smaller body, shows a substantially similar gain (48.2 per cent), having 266,345 members in 1906, as against 179,721 in 1890. The Cumberland Presbyterian Church, with 195,770 members, shows a gain since 1890 of 18.7 per cent, and the United Presbyterian Church of North America, with 130,342 members in 1906, a gain of 38.1 per cent. It should here be stated that, in view of the fact that the union between the Presbyterian Church in the United States of America and the Cumberland Presbyterian Church was not fully consummated at the close of the year 1906, but was in a state of transition, no attempt is made to give the statistics for the united body. On account, also, of this unsettled condition, the statistics here given separately for each of the 2 bodies represent as near as may be the condition at the close of the ecclesiastical year, March, 1906, before the union had taken place, instead of at the close of the calendar year, as in the case of the other denominations.

The Disciples or Christians, returned as a single body in 1890, show a large gain in membership, but the number of communicants or members reported for 1906 is very unevenly divided between the 2 bodies, the Disciples of Christ showing 982,701, or 86 per cent, and the Churches of Christ, 159,658, or 14 per cent.

In this general increase immigration has had a large share, especially in the Lutheran bodies, the German Evangelical Synod, the Roman Catholic Church, and the Eastern Orthodox Churches. That other influences have also been effective is apparent from the increase in several bodies not materially affected by immigration—for example, the Disciples or Christians, which show an increase of 78.2 per cent, and the Protestant Episcopal Church, which shows an increase of 66.7 per cent.

The figures thus far presented concerning communicants or members have dealt with the total number reported. The following table shows, for each of the principal families or denominations, the average number of communicants or members per organization in 1906.

The Roman Catholic Church reported the highest number of communicants or members per organization, 969. The Eastern Orthodox Churches, which ranked second in this respect, reported 315; while the German Evangelical Synod of North America, the Protestant body ranking highest as to membership per organization, reported 245. For the Protestant bodies as a whole the average number of members per organization was 104, less than one-ninth the average number for the Roman Catholic Church.

The average size of the organizations is, of course, the result of many factors. Denominations which are largely centered in urban communities naturally have much larger organizations than those which are scattered through rural districts. The concentration of the members of the Roman Catholic Church in the states of the North Atlantic division, which have a large proportion of urban population, doubtless accounts in part for the large average size of the organizations of that body. The form of government of the denominations also plays an important part. Those in which ecclesiastical authority is highly centralized can develop large organizations more readily than those in which each congregation is highly independent. Then, too, the general policy of the denominations enters into the question; and as a result of these factors it is not surprising to find a variation in the average number of members per organization from 37 in the case of the Adventist bodies to 969 in the case of the Roman Catholic Church.

DENOMINATION.	Organizations reporting communicants or members.	Communicants or members.	Average number of communicants or members per organization.
All denominations	210,418	32,936,445	157
Protestant bodies	194,497	20,287,742	104
Adventist bodies	2,537	92,735	37
Baptist bodies	54,707	5,662,234	104
Christians (Christian Connection)	1,354	110,117	81
Church of Christ, Scientist	635	85,717	135
Congregationalists	5,700	700,480	123
Disciples or Christians	10,909	1,142,359	105
Dunkers or German Baptist Brethren	1,090	97,144	89
Evangelical bodies	2,730	174,780	64
Friends	1,141	113,772	100
German Evangelical Synod of North America	1,198	293,137	245
Independent churches	1,065	73,673	69
Lutheran bodies	12,642	2,112,494	167
Mennonite bodies	604	54,798	91
Methodist bodies	64,255	5,749,838	89
Presbyterian bodies	15,471	1,830,555	118
Protestant Episcopal Church	6,725	886,942	132
Reformed bodies	2,583	449,514	174
Unitarians	435	70,542	162
United Brethren bodies	4,268	296,050	69
Universalists	811	64,158	79
Other Protestant bodies	3,637	226,703	62
Roman Catholic Church	12,472	12,079,142	969
Jewish congregations	1,152	[1] 101,457	[1] 88
Latter-day Saints	1,184	256,647	217
Eastern Orthodox Churches	411	129,606	315
All other bodies	702	81,851	117

[1] Heads of families only.

Distribution by sex.—An inquiry was made in 1890 and again in 1906 as to the total number of communicants or members, but at the latter investigation the inquiry was extended to include the number of males and females as well. Statistics are here presented for the first time, therefore, giving substantially the sex distribution of the members of all the religious bodies in the United States. The returns, although secured for the individual church organizations, had to be based in some cases upon estimates rather than upon an exact enumeration, but a comparison of these estimates with the returns in which the report of sex is complete shows such agreement that the figures presented may be considered to represent accurately the general situation in this regard.

The table on page 30 shows for each family or separate denomination comprising more than 25,000 members, first, the number and per cent of organizations reporting sex; second, the total number of communicants or members and the number and per cent for whom sex is reported; and third, the number and per cent of each sex so reported.

A full report in regard to the sex of communicants or members was made by a few bodies only, the Mennonites and some smaller bodies. For the Congregationalists, the report was substantially complete, as 99.2 per cent of the total number of organizations returned the sex of members. Other religious families and separate denominations furnishing approximately complete returns in regard to sex, with the percentage of organizations reporting in each case, are as follows: Spiritualists, 98.9; Swedish Evangelical bodies, 97.8; Friends, 97.7; Latter-day Saints, 97.3; and Dunkers, 96.6. In some families substantially complete returns were received for certain branches, but the percentage of organizations reporting for the family as a whole was reduced by the markedly incomplete returns for other branches. Thus, for example, the percentage for the Baptist bodies as a whole (92.9) is reduced somewhat by the small proportion of the organizations making a report among the Colored Primitive Baptists in America (40.8 per cent), the Primitive Baptists (73.2 per cent), the Free Baptists (83.9 per cent), and the 8 smaller Baptist bodies (61.7 per cent). Again, among the Lutheran bodies the percentage of organizations reporting for the body as a whole is made low by the small proportion reported for Hauge's Norwegian Evangelical Lutheran Synod (71.3 per cent) and the United Norwegian Lutheran Church in America (76.5 per cent).

The sex of communicants is reported for the Unitarians by only 73.1 per cent of its organizations; for the Universalists, by 77.1 per cent; for the Protestant Episcopal Church, by 84.3 per cent; and for the Roman Catholic Church, by 88.4 per cent. For the Eastern Orthodox Churches, also, there is a report of sex for only 25.1 per cent, but this is wholly due to the very incomplete report for the Greek Orthodox Church. In spite of the very low percentage of organizations in this church reporting sex (7.8), the number of members for whom the sex is reported constitutes, as shown in the fourth column of the table, more than one-half (54 per cent) of all the members reported for this body. No distribution by sex is given for the membership of the Jewish congregations, since their membership comprises largely male heads of families.

For some of the smaller bodies, or members of certain of the denominational families, as shown by Table 1 (page 148), a full report of sex has been made, the more notable being the Armenian Church, the Colored Cumberland Presbyterian Church, the Polish National Church, the Finnish Evangelical Lutheran Church of America, or Suomi Synod, and the Slovak Evangelical Lutheran Synod of America.

The percentages showing the proportion of members for whom sex is reported, also given in the table on page 30, are not essentially different from those for organizations, although as a rule they are somewhat larger. The more notable exceptions to this rule are found in the cases of "other Dunkers," the Christian Reformed Church, the German Evangelical Protestant bodies, the Protestant Episcopal Church, the German Evangelical Synod of North America, the Independent churches, and the Lutheran bodies.

The figures indicating the distribution by sex show that, of the total number of communicants or members for which these data were returned, 43.1 per cent are males and 56.9 per cent females. For the Protestant bodies as a whole the difference is greater, for in these bodies 39.3 per cent of the members are males and 60.7 per cent females. For the Roman Catholic Church the percentages are more nearly even, being 49.3 for males and 50.7 for females. For the Eastern Orthodox Churches and for "all other bodies," on the other hand, the percentages of males are very much larger than those for females.

The largest percentage of males shown for any single body is that for the Greek Orthodox Church (93.9) and the next largest is that for the Hungarian Reformed Church in America (68.7). The 3 other bodies of Eastern Orthodox Churches together show 74.3 per cent males, but the percentages for the individual bodies, based upon the figures given in Table 1 (page 148), differ widely. In the Servian Orthodox Church the males form 85.8 per cent of all communicants; in the Russian Orthodox Church, 67.6 per cent; and in the Syrian Orthodox Church, 60.5 per cent. Similarly, the percentage shown for "all other bodies" as a whole (63.7) is not indicative of the conditions existing in the numerous small bodies included thereunder, the percentages for the particular bodies ranging from 75.6 for the Armenian Church to as low as 21.3 for the United Society of Believers (Shakers).

In the Roman Catholic Church the communicants are, as already stated, about equally divided in respect to sex, and this is also true of a number of other bodies, especially among the Lutherans. The Church of Jesus Christ of Latter-day Saints, also, shows 48.6 per cent of males and the Christian Reformed Church, 47.9 per cent.

The Methodist and Baptist bodies, collectively, show the same percentages—38.5 per cent males and 61.5 per cent females. The proportion of organizations reporting sex is nearly the same in each, but it should be noted that in the Methodist Episcopal Church, South only 86.6 per cent of the organizations are included. The colored churches of both families are well represented, though in many cases the figures, as before stated, represent estimates rather than an exact enumeration.

DENOMINATION.	ORGANIZATIONS REPORTING SEX: 1906.		COMMUNICANTS OR MEMBERS: 1906.						
			Aggregate number.	Reported by sex.					
				Total.		Male.		Female.	
	Number.	Per cent of total.		Number.	Per cent of aggregate number.	Number.	Per cent of total.	Number.	Per cent of total.
All denominations	193,229	91.0	32,936,445	29,616,971	89.9	12,767,466	43.1	16,849,505	56.9
Protestant bodies	180,251	92.1	20,287,742	18,691,885	92.1	7,345,805	39.3	11,346,080	60.7
Adventist bodies	2,374	93.1	92,735	87,309	94.1	32,088	36.8	55,221	63.2
Advent Christian Church	497	90.4	26,799	24,987	93.2	10,187	40.8	14,800	2
Seventh-day Adventist Denomination	1,772	93.8	62,211	58,923	94.7	20,508	34.8	38,415	59.2
Other Adventists (5 bodies)	105	93.8	3,725	3,399	91.2	1,393	41.0	2,006	59.0
Baptist bodies	50,982	92.9	5,662,234	5,344,885	94.4	2,055,558	38.5	3,289,327	61.5
Baptists	45,838	7	5,323,183	5,079,794	95.4	1,953,538	5	3,126,256	.5
Northern Baptist Convention	7,652	5	1,052,105	979,132	93.1	357,749	5	621,383	5
Southern Baptist Convention	20,152	.5	2,009,471	1,899,113	94.5	773,627	7	1,125,486	3.
National Baptist Convention (Colored)	18,034	3	2,261,607	2,201,549	97.3	822,162	.3	1,379,387	.7
Free Baptists	1,129	9	81,359	69,825	85.8	26,051	.3	43,774	.7
Freewill Baptists	574	.4	40,280	38,185	94.8	15,702	.1	22,483	9
General Baptists	497	9	30,097	28,150	93.5	11,577	.1	16,573	9
Primitive Baptists	2,138	2	102,311	78,614	76.8	28,581	4	50,033	6.
Colored Primitive Baptists in America	325	95.8	35,076	17,779	50.7	6,341	38.7	11,438	61.3
Other Baptists (8 bodies)	481	[illegible].7	49,928	32,538	65.2	13,768	[illegible].3	18,770	[illegible].7
Christians (Christian Connection)	1,221	5	110,117	100,762	91.5	40,740	4	60,022	6
Church of Christ, Scientist	604	88.7	85,717	82,332	96.1	22,736	40.6	59,596	59.4
Congregationalists	5,666	98.2	700,480	694,583	99.2	236,968	[illegible].1	457,615	[illegible].9
Disciples or Christians	10,441	95.4	1,142,359	1,082,821	94.8	432,682	40.0	650,139	60.0
Disciples of Christ	7,799	94.0	982,701	923,698	94.0	366,681	39.7	557,017	60.3
Churches of Christ	2,642	99.7	159,658	159,123	99.7	66,001	41.5	93,122	58.5
Dunkers or German Baptist Brethren	1,060	96.6	97,144	93,604	96.4	39,928	42.7	53,676	57.3
German Baptist Brethren Church (Conservative)	802	97.6	76,547	75,417	98.5	32,232	42.7	43,185	57.3
Other Dunkers (3 bodies)	258	93.8	20,597	18,187	88.3	7,696	42.3	10,491	[illegible].7
Evangelical bodies	2,627	95.9	174,780	168,420	96.4	67,448	40.0	100,972	60.0
Evangelical Association	1,677	95.3	104,898	100,546	95.9	41,641	41.4	58,905	6.
United Evangelical Church	950	97.1	69,882	67,874	97.1	25,807	38.0	42,067	[illegible].0
Friends	1,121	97.7	113,772	111,952	98.4	51,708	46.2	60,244	53.8
Society of Friends (Orthodox)	855	97.9	91,161	89,778	98.5	41,468	46.2	48,310	53.8
Other Friends (3 bodies)	266	97.1	22,611	22,174	98.1	10,240	46.2	11,934	53.8
German Evangelical Protestant bodies	61	92.4	34,704	30,554	88.0	12,830	0	17,724	0
German Evangelical Synod of North America	1,072	89.0	293,137	250,115	85.3	111,681	42.7	138,434	58.3
Independent churches	986	91.4	73,673	64,907	88.1	26,895	41.4	38,012	58.6
Lutheran bodies	11,329	89.2	2,112,494	1,851,348	87.6	853,339	46.1	998,009	53.9
General Synod of the Evangelical Lutheran Church in the United States of America	1,615	93.1	270,221	252,443	93.4	102,544	40.6	149,899	59.4
United Synod of the Evangelical Lutheran Church in the South	407	90.6	47,747	41,669	87.3	18,555	44.5	23,114	55.5
General Council of the Evangelical Lutheran Church in North America	1,894	88.3	462,177	403,252	87.3	180,112	7	223,140	3
Evangelical Lutheran Synodical Conference of America	2,997	8	648,529	575,079	88.7	270,718	.1	304,361	.9
United Norwegian Lutheran Church in America	900	5	185,027	139,683	75.5	68,767	2	70,916	8
Evangelical Lutheran Joint Synod of Ohio and Other States	702	9	123,408	107,978	87.5	49,290	6	58,688	4
Hauge's Norwegian Evangelical Lutheran Synod	194	90.3	33,268	23,493	70.6	11,314	44.2	12,179	55.8
Evangelical Lutheran Synod of Iowa and Other States	797	[illegible].3	110,254	105,515	95.7	51,078	[illegible].4	54,437	[illegible].6
Synod for the Norwegian Evangelical Lutheran Church in America	813	87.7	107,712	93,119	.5	45,740	1	47,379	9
Norwegian Lutheran Free Church	296	92.5	26,928	22,971	.3	10,924	49.6	12,047	50.4
Other Lutherans (14 bodies)	714	91.9	97,223	86,146	88.6	44,297	[illegible].4	41,849	[illegible].6
Mennonite bodies	604	100.0	54,798	54,798	100.0	25,053	45.7	29,745	54.3
Methodist bodies	59,592	92.1	5,749,838	5,311,377	92.4	2,042,713	38.5	3,268,664	61.5
Methodist Episcopal Church	27,800	92.8	2,986,154	2,786,666	9 3	1,042,830	.4	1,743,836	6
Methodist Protestant Church	2,673	94.0	178,544	168,705	9 5	68,360	5	100,345	5
Methodist Episcopal Church, South	15,446	86.6	1,638,480	1,434,355	8 5	587,324	9	847,031	1
Free Methodist Church of North America	1,488	95.8	32,838	31,560	1	11,228	.6	20,332	4
African Methodists	11,188	97.4	869,710	848,722	9 6	316,591	.3	532,131	7
African Methodist Episcopal Church	6,486	97.6	494,777	481,997	9 4	177,837	37.9	304,160	1
African Methodist Episcopal Zion Church	2,156	97.8	184,542	180,501	.8	67,096	[illegible].2	113,405	8
Colored Methodist Episcopal Church	2,309	97.0	172,996	169,252	9 8	64,988	38.4	104,264	.6
Other African Methodists (4 bodies)	237	95.2	17,395	16,972	3.6	6,670	39.3	10,302	62.7
Other Methodists (4 bodies)	997	95.0	44,112	41,369	[illegible].8	16,380	39.6	24,989	[illegible].4
Presbyterian bodies	14,014	90.4	1,830,555	1,670,795	91.3	633,598	37.9	1,037,197	62.1
Presbyterian Church in the United States of America	7,340	92.5	1,179,566	1,075,774	.2	392,692	5	683,082	5
Cumberland Presbyterian Church	2,310	81.1	195,770	165,950	8	69,691	0	96,259	0
United Presbyterian Church of North America	940	97.1	130,342	127,261	.6	50,834	9	76,427	63.1
Presbyterian Church in the United States	2,789	89.9	266,345	245,099	91.0	95,474	39.0	149,625	[illegible].0
Other Presbyterians (8 bodies)	635	97.8	58,532	56,711	[illegible].9	24,907	[illegible].9	31,804	56.1

DENOMINATION.	ORGANIZATIONS REPORTING SEX: 1906.		COMMUNICANTS OR MEMBERS: 1906.						
			Aggregate number.	Reported by sex.					
				Total.		Male.		Female.	
	Number.	Per cent of total.		Number.	Per cent of aggregate number.	Number.	Per cent of total.	Number.	Per cent of total.
Protestant bodies—Continued.									
Protestant Episcopal Church	5,767	84.3	886,942	709,034	79.9	251,869	35.5	457,165	64.5
Reformed bodies	2,445	94.6	449,514	423,161	94.1	181,619	42.9	241,542	57.1
Reformed Church in America	632	95.9	124,938	117,059	93.7	44,673	38.2	72,386	61.8
Reformed Church in the United States	1,632	94.0	292,654	276,911	94.6	121,925	44.0	154,986	56.0
Christian Reformed Church	166	95.4	26,669	24,238	90.9	11,617	47.9	12,621	52.1
Hungarian Reformed Church in America	15	93.8	5,253	4,953	94.3	3,404	68.7	1,549	31.3
Swedish Evangelical bodies	399	97.8	27,712	26,798	96.7	11,977	44.7	14,821	55.3
Unitarians	337	73.1	70,542	55,683	78.9	21,817	39.2	33,866	60.8
United Brethren bodies	3,810	88.5	296,050	267,992	90.5	107,369	40.1	160,623	59.9
Church of the United Brethren in Christ	3,249	87.1	274,649	247,145	90.0	99,176	40.1	147,969	59.9
Church of the United Brethren in Christ (Old Constitution)	561	98.1	21,401	20,847	97.4	8,193	39.3	12,654	60.7
Universalists	652	77.1	64,158	51,625	80.5	18,279	35.4	33,346	64.6
Other Protestant bodies	3,087	95.9	164,287	157,030	95.6	66,910	42.6	90,120	57.4
Roman Catholic Church	11,028	88.4	12,079,142	10,510,100	87.0	5,184,922	49.3	5,325,178	50.7
Jewish congregations	......	......	[1] 101,457	......	......	......	......	......	......
Latter-day Saints	1,152	97.3	256,647	245,802	95.8	117,026	47.6	128,776	52.4
Church of Jesus Christ of Latter-day Saints	666	97.5	215,796	206,304	95.6	100,217	48.6	106,087	51.4
Reorganized Church of Jesus Christ of Latter-day Saints	486	97.0	40,851	39,498	96.7	16,809	42.6	22,689	57.4
Eastern Orthodox Churches	103	25.1	129,606	87,842	67.8	74,867	85.2	12,975	14.8
Greek Orthodox Church	26	7.8	90,751	48,987	54.0	46,005	93.9	2,982	6.1
Other Eastern Orthodox Churches (3 bodies)	77	100.0	38,855	38,855	100.0	28,862	74.3	9,993	25.7
Spiritualists	450	98.9	35,056	34,687	98.9	15,135	43.6	19,552	56.4
All other bodies	245	78.8	46,795	46,655	99.7	29,711	63.7	16,944	36.3

[1] Heads of families only.

Among the Presbyterian bodies the smallest percentage of males shown (36.5) is for the Presbyterian Church in the United States of America, and the highest percentage (42) for the Cumberland Presbyterian Church; for some of the 8 other Presbyterian bodies, however, as indicated by the figures in Table 1 (page 148), the percentages of males are considerably higher, as is the case in the Colored Cumberland Presbyterian Church, 46.5; in the Associate Reformed Synod of the South, 44.8; and in the Welsh Calvinistic Methodist Church, 44.4.

The smallest percentage of males shown (27.6) is that for the Church of Christ, Scientist, which is considerably less than that for the Congregationalists (34.1) or for the Seventh-day Adventist Denomination (34.8).

Probably the most important single factor in determining the proportion of the sexes in any denomination is the extent to which the membership of that denomination is composed of immigrants. At the census of 1900 males formed 54.4 per cent of the foreign born population, as contrasted with 50.5 per cent of the native population. The percentage formed by the males, moreover, has been far greater in recent immigration than it was in the foreign born population of 1900. The distribution, by sex, of the immigrants entering this country during the year ending June 30, 1907, is shown in the table on page 32, the figures for which were taken from the annual report of the Commissioner-General of Immigration.

Of the bodies not directly affected by immigration, those represented chiefly in the Southern states show a higher percentage of males than those in the Northern states. Thus the Methodist Episcopal Church, South, reports 40.9 per cent of males; the Southern Baptist Convention, 40.7 per cent; the Presbyterian Church in the United States, 39 per cent; and the Cumberland Presbyterian Church, 42 per cent; while the Methodist Episcopal Church reports 37.4 per cent of males; the Northern Baptist Convention, 36.5 per cent; and the Presbyterian Church in the United States of America, 36.5 per cent.

The Churches of Christ, mostly in the Southern states, show 41.5 per cent of male membership, while the Disciples of Christ, chiefly in the Northern states, report 39.7 per cent. The Adventist bodies, Congregationalists, Protestant Episcopal Church, Unitarians, and Universalists, which are strongest in the Northern and Western states, and are not affected to any extent by immigration, all rank below 40 per cent, while others, as the Evangelical and United Brethren bodies, chiefly in the Northern states, but also moderately affected by immigration, hold medium rank at about 40 per cent.

RACE OR PEOPLE.	IMMIGRANT ALIENS ADMITTED TO THE UNITED STATES DURING THE YEAR ENDING JUNE 30, 1907.				
	Total.	Male.		Female.	
		Number.	Per cent.	Number.	Per cent.
Total	1,285,349	929,976	72.4	355,373	27.6
African (black)	5,235	3,332	63.6	1,903	36.4
Armenian	2,644	1,874	70.9	770	29.1
Bohemian and Moravian	13,554	8,142	60.1	5,412	39.9
Bulgarian, Servian, and Montenegrin	27,174	26,423	97.2	751	2.8
Chinese	770	706	91.7	64	8.3
Croatian and Slovenian	47,826	40,538	84.8	7,288	15.2
Cuban	5,475	3,747	68.4	1,728	31.6
Dalmatian, Bosnian, and Herzegovinian	7,393	7,061	95.5	332	4.5
Dutch and Flemish	12,467	8,362	67.1	4,105	32.9
East Indian	1,072	1,056	98.5	16	1.5
English	51,126	33,100	64.7	18,026	35.3
Finnish	14,860	10,326	69.5	4,534	30.5
French	9,392	5,425	57.8	3,967	42.2
German	92,936	56,170	60.4	36,766	39.6
Greek	46,283	44,647	96.5	1,636	3.5
Hebrew	149,182	80,530	54.0	68,652	46.0
Irish	38,706	21,871	56.5	16,835	43.5
Italian (north)	51,564	40,949	79.4	10,615	20.6
Italian (south)	242,497	190,905	78.7	51,592	21.3
Japanese	30,824	27,845	90.3	2,979	9.7
Korean	39	36	(1)	3	(1)
Lithuanian	25,884	18,716	72.3	7,168	27.7
Magyar	60,071	44,804	74.6	15,267	25.4
Mexican	91	74	(1)	17	(1)
Pacific Islander	3	2	(1)	1	(1)
Polish	138,033	100,700	73.0	37,333	27.0
Portuguese	9,648	5,812	60.2	3,836	39.8
Roumanian	19,200	17,779	92.6	1,421	7.4
Russian	16,807	15,095	89.8	1,712	10.2
Ruthenian (Russniak)	24,081	18,451	76.6	5,630	23.4
Scandinavian	53,425	34,164	63.9	19,261	36.1
Scotch	20,516	13,666	66.6	6,850	33.4
Slovak	42,041	28,951	68.9	13,090	31.1
Spanish	9,495	7,268	76.5	2,227	23.5
Spanish-American	1,060	734	69.2	326	30.8
Syrian	5,880	4,276	72.7	1,604	27.3
Turkish	1,902	1,855	97.5	47	2.5
Welsh	2,754	1,852	67.2	902	32.8
West Indian (except Cuban)	1,381	778	56.3	603	43.7
All other peoples	2,058	1,954	94.9	104	5.1

[1] Per cent not shown where base is less than 100.

PLACES OF WORSHIP.

Under the head of "places of worship" are included church edifices, halls, schoolhouses, private houses, and other buildings in which religious services or meetings are held.

The term "church edifice" covers those buildings owned in whole or in part by the organizations using them. The building may be consecrated or unconsecrated, a principal building, a chapel, or a mission; if it is a separate building, used for services, and owned in whole or in part by the organization using it, it is classed as a church edifice. In some cases two or more organizations use the same building; if the ownership is divided, each organization is credited with an edifice; if the ownership is with one body and it is rented or used by another body, it is included, in the latter case, under the head of "halls, etc." In a number of cases an organization reports more than one church edifice.

Under the head of "halls, etc.," are included those buildings which are rented by the organizations using them, or which they are permitted by the owners to use for the purposes of their service. Such are church edifices owned by other denominations, college chapels, halls, schoolhouses, private houses, public edifices, etc.

Number of church edifices, halls, etc.—The following table, derived from Table 8 (page 514), shows for the principal families and separate denominations, first, the number of organizations reporting places of worship in 1906; second, the number and the per cent distribution of church edifices reported in 1890 and 1906, with the increase from 1890 to 1906; and third, the number and the per cent distribution of halls, etc., in 1890 and 1906.

DENOMINATION.	ORGANIZATIONS REPORTING PLACES OF WORSHIP: 1906.		CHURCH EDIFICES REPORTED.						HALLS, ETC., REPORTED.			
			Number.		Per cent distribution.		Increase from 1890 to 1906.		Number.		Per cent distribution.	
	Number.	Per cent of total.	1906	1890	1906	1890	Number.	Per cent.	1906	1890	1906	1890
All denominations	199,831	94.2	192,795	142,487	100.0	100.0	50,308	35.3	14,791	23,332	100.0	100.0
Protestant bodies	185,397	94.8	178,850	132,891	92.8	93.3	45,959	34.6	12,994	20,842	87.9	89.3
Adventist bodies	2,121	83.1	1,473	774	0.8	0.5	699	90.3	666	957	4.5	4.1
Baptist bodies	52,338	95.4	50,092	37,671	26.0	26.4	12,421	33.0	3,250	5,539	22.0	23.7
Christians (Christian Connection)	1,323	95.9	1,253	1,098	0.6	0.8	155	14.1	85	226	0.6	1.0
Church of Christ, Scientist	573	89.8	253	7	0.1	(1)	246	(2)	322	213	2.2	0.9
Congregationalists	5,507	96.4	5,792	4,736	3.0	3.3	1,056	22.3	164	456	1.1	2.0
Disciples or Christians	9,803	89.6	9,040	5,324	4.7	3.7	3,716	69.8	907	1,141	6.1	4.9
Dunkers or German Baptist Brethren	1,040	94.8	1,442	1,016	0.7	0.7	426	41.9	59	280	0.4	1.2
Evangelical bodies	2,661	97.2	2,537	1,899	1.3	1.3	638	33.6	152	425	1.0	1.8
Friends	1,134	98.9	1,097	995	0.6	0.7	102	10.3	39	99	0.3	0.4
German Evangelical Synod of North America	1,178	97.8	1,258	785	0.7	0.6	473	60.3	42	83	0.3	0.4
Independent churches	1,015	94.1	812	112	0.4	0.1	700	625.0	229	54	1.5	0.2
Lutheran bodies	11,892	93.6	11,194	6,701	5.8	4.7	4,493	67.0	1,197	1,314	8.1	5.6
Mennonite bodies	585	96.9	509	406	0.3	0.3	103	25.4	87	103	0.6	0.4
Methodist bodies	62,076	95.9	59,990	46,138	31.1	32.4	13,852	30.0	3,193	6,057	21.6	26.0
Presbyterian bodies	14,488	93.4	15,311	12,465	7.9	8.7	2,846	22.8	406	1,352	2.7	5.8
Protestant Episcopal Church	6,255	91.4	6,922	5,018	3.6	3.5	1,904	37.9	257	312	1.7	1.3
Reformed bodies	2,542	98.3	2,706	2,080	1.4	1.5	626	30.1	62	73	0.4	0.3
Unitarians	430	93.3	463	424	0.2	0.3	39	9.2	23	55	0.2	0.2
United Brethren bodies	4,109	95.5	3,900	3,415	2.0	2.4	485	14.2	255	989	1.7	4.2
Universalists	801	94.7	776	832	0.4	0.6	[3]56	[3]6.7	33	61	0.2	0.3
Other Protestant bodies	3,526	95.5	2,030	995	1.1	0.7	1,035	104.0	1,566	1,053	10.6	4.5
Roman Catholic Church	11,273	90.3	11,881	8,784	6.2	6.2	3,097	35.3	518	1,469	3.5	6.3
Jewish congregations	983	55.6	821	301	0.4	0.2	520	172.8	230	231	1.6	1.0
Latter-day Saints	1,059	89.4	933	388	0.5	0.3	545	140.5	214	432	1.4	1.9
Eastern Orthodox Churches	410	99.8	85	2	(1)	(1)	83	(2)	326	....	2.2	....
All other bodies	709	92.7	225	121	0.1	0.1	104	86.0	509	358	3.4	1.5

[1] Less than one-tenth of 1 per cent. [2] Per cent not shown where base is less than 100. [3] Decrease.

From this table it appears that, with two exceptions, a report as to places of worship has been made by all the denominational families and separate denominations for substantially 90 per cent or more of their organizations. The exceptions are the Jewish congregations, for which the report is very incomplete, covering only 55.6 per cent of the congregations, and the Adventist bodies, for which there is a report for 83.1 per cent of their organizations.

Out of a total of 212,230 organizations 199,831, or 94.2 per cent, made a report as to places of worship. In other words, 12,399 organizations furnished no specific information showing whether they owned a church edifice in whole or in part, or whether they held their services in a rented building, although of course every organization must have had some place of worship.

In number of church edifices the Methodist bodies lead with 59,990, and are followed by the Baptist bodies with 50,092; the Presbyterian bodies with 15,311; the Roman Catholic Church with 11,881; and the Lutheran bodies with 11,194. In regard to the number of halls, etc., the order is somewhat different. In this respect the Baptist bodies lead with 3,250; and are followed by the Methodist bodies with 3,193; the Lutheran bodies with 1,197; the Disciples or Christians with 907; the Adventist bodies with 666; the Roman Catholic Church with 518; and the Presbyterian bodies with 406.

The per cent distribution of church edifices shows that the Methodist bodies and Baptist bodies together own 57.1 per cent, or considerably more than one-half, of all the church edifices reported in 1906. Next to them in order come the Presbyterian bodies with 7.9 per cent; the Roman Catholic Church with 6.2 per cent; the Lutheran bodies with 5.8 per cent; the Disciples or Christians with 4.7 per cent; the Protestant Episcopal Church with 3.6 per cent; and the Congregationalists with 3 per cent.

The denominational families and separate denominations leading in the per cent distribution of halls, etc., are the Baptist bodies, 22 per cent; the Methodist bodies, 21.6 per cent; the Lutheran bodies, 8.1 per cent; the Disciples or Christians, 6.1 per cent; the Adventist bodies, 4.5 per cent; and the Roman Catholic Church, 3.5 per cent.

A comparison with the figures for 1890 shows an increase in the number of church edifices in the different bodies as follows: Methodist bodies, 13,852; Baptist bodies, 12,421; Lutheran bodies, 4,493; Disciples or Christians, 3,716; Roman Catholic Church, 3,097; Presbyterian bodies, 2,846; Protestant Episcopal Church, 1,904; and Congregationalists, 1,056.

In the percentage of increase in the number of church edifices the rank is naturally different. Aside from the Eastern Orthodox Churches and the Church of Christ, Scientist, which are virtually new bodies, and the Independent churches and Jewish congregations, where the conditions are such as scarcely to permit comparison, the order is as follows: Latter-day Saints, 140.5 per cent; Adventist bodies, 90.3 per cent; Disciples or Christians, 69.8 per cent; Lutheran bodies, 67 per cent; German Evangelical Synod of North America, 60.3 per cent; Dunkers, 41.9 per cent; Protestant Episcopal Church, 37.9 per cent; Roman Catholic Church, 35.3 per cent; Evangelical bodies, 33.6 per cent; Baptist bodies, 33 per cent; Reformed bodies, 30.1 per cent; and Methodist bodies, 30 per cent.

In the number of halls, etc., there has been a considerable decrease, accompanied by a general increase in the number of church edifices, showing that church edifices have taken the place of halls and the like. Thus in 1890 the Dunkers reported 1,016 church edifices and 280 halls, or a total of 1,296 places of worship. In 1906 they reported 1,442 church edifices and 59 halls, or a total of 1,501 places of worship, an increase of 205, or 15.8 per cent, in the places of worship, although in church edifices they showed an increase of 41.9 per cent. Similar conditions are found in other bodies. The Presbyterian bodies show an increase in church edifices of 2,846, a decrease in halls, etc., of 946, or a net increase in places of worship of 1,900. The United Brethren bodies show an increase of 485 in the number of church edifices and a decrease of 734 in halls, etc., or a net decrease of 249 in the total number of places of worship. This decrease is due largely to a decrease in the total number of organizations in 1906 as compared with 1890. The only bodies showing an increase in the number of halls, etc., used for worship are the Church of Christ, Scientist, Eastern Orthodox Churches, Independent churches, "other Protestant bodies," and "all other bodies." In regard to all of these the increase in this particular is due probably to comparatively recent organization, rapid growth and extension, and the formation of a considerable number of new organizations which are not strong enough to own church edifices.

Seating capacity of church edifices.—The term "seating capacity" signifies the total number of persons an edifice is arranged to seat. In this report, church edifices alone are taken into consideration, partly because they bear a closer and more significant relation to the church organization than do halls, schoolhouses, etc., and partly because returns for them are more complete. Two things are to be kept in mind: (1) That the figures are almost entirely estimates, since comparatively few church organizations are able to give exact reports; and (2) that in some instances, notably in the case of the Roman Catholic Church, the same edifice is used repeatedly, and by varying congregations.

The following table gives for the principal families and separate denominations, first, the total number of organizations making a report as to seating capacity and the percentage which that number bears to the total organizations reporting church edifices; and, second, the seating capacity of church edifices reported in 1890 and 1906, the per cent distribution at each period, and the increase from 1890 to 1906:

DENOMINATION.	ORGANIZATIONS REPORTING SEATING CAPACITY OF CHURCH EDIFICES: 1906.		SEATING CAPACITY OF CHURCH EDIFICES REPORTED.					
			Amount.		Per cent distribution.		Increase from 1890 to 1906.	
	Number.	Per cent of total reporting church edifices.	1906	1890	1906	1890	Amount.	Per cent.
All denominations	179,954	97.3	58,536,830	43,560,063	100.0	100.0	14,976,767	34.4
Protestant bodies	167,884	97.4	53,282,445	39,896,330	91.0	91.6	13,386,115	33.6
Adventist bodies	1,431	98.4	287,964	190,748	0.5	0.4	97,216	51.0
Baptist bodies	48,042	97.9	15,702,712	11,568,019	26.8	26.6	4,134,693	35.7
Christians (Christian Connection)	1,221	98.6	383,893	347,697	0.7	0.8	36,196	10.4
Church of Christ, Scientist	245	97.6	81,823	1,500	0.1	(1)	80,323	5,354.9
Congregationalists	5,244	98.1	1,794,997	1,553,080	3.1	3.6	241,917	15.6
Disciples or Christians	8,702	97.8	2,776,044	1,609,452	4.7	3.7	1,166,592	72.5
Dunkers or German Baptist Brethren	969	98.8	508,374	414,036	0.9	1.0	94,338	22.8
Evangelical bodies	2,461	98.1	659,391	479,335	1.1	1.1	180,056	37.6
Friends	1,088	99.4	304,204	302,218	0.5	0.7	1,986	0.7
German Evangelical Synod of North America	1,131	99.6	380,465	245,781	0.6	0.6	134,684	54.8
Independent churches	741	94.3	213,096	39,345	0.4	0.1	173,751	441.6
Lutheran bodies	10,493	98.1	3,344,654	2,205,635	5.7	5.1	1,139,019	51.6
Mennonite bodies	497	99.8	171,381	129,340	0.3	0.3	42,041	32.5
Methodist bodies	56,577	96.1	17,053,392	12,863,178	29.1	29.5	4,190,214	32.6
Presbyterian bodies	13,942	99.0	4,892,819	4,037,550	8.4	9.3	855,269	21.2
Protestant Episcopal Church	5,960	99.4	1,675,750	1,336,752	2.9	3.1	338,998	25.4
Reformed bodies	2,472	99.7	990,654	825,931	1.7	1.9	164,723	19.9
Unitarians	401	98.5	159,917	135,090	0.3	0.4	[2]5,173	[2]3.1
United Brethren bodies	3,637	94.4	1,060,560	991,138	1.8	2.3	69,422	7.0
Universalists	718	93.5	220,222	244,615	0.4	0.6	[2]24,393	[2]10.0
Other Protestant bodies	1,912	97.6	620,133	345,890	1.1	0.8	274,243	79.3
Roman Catholic Church	10,303	95.8	4,494,377	3,370,482	7.7	7.7	1,123,895	33.3
Jewish congregations	717	95.2	364,701	139,234	0.6	0.3	225,467	161.9
Latter-day Saints	837	99.1	280,747	122,892	0.5	0.3	157,855	128.5
Eastern Orthodox Churches	75	89.3	38,995	325	0.1	(1)	38,670	11,898.5
All other bodies	138	69.0	75,565	30,800	0.1	0.1	44,765	145.3

[1] Less than one-tenth of 1 per cent.

[2] Decrease.

The seating capacity of church edifices in 1906 is very fully reported, the only apparent exception being, as shown by the preceding table, that for "all other bodies." The low percentage there reported is due, in a measure, to the inclusion of the 62 Chinese Temples, for which no report of seating capacity, consistent with the facts, can be made.

The total seating capacity of church edifices in 1906, for all denominations, as reported by 179,954 organizations, was 58,536,830; for the Protestant bodies, as reported by 167,884 organizations, 53,282,445; for the Roman Catholic Church, as reported by 10,303 organizations, 4,494,377; and for the remaining bodies, as reported by 1,767 organizations, 760,008. Thus the average per organization for all denominations is 325; for the Protestant bodies, 317; for the Roman Catholic Church, 436; and for the remaining bodies, 430.

It should be stated that where two or more organizations use the same edifice the seating capacity is reported by each organization separately, and therefore some duplication may result where figures for different denominations are combined. The amount of duplication thus resulting in the grand total for all denominations has not been ascertained for 1906, but for 1890 it was said to be approximately 2,800,000 out of a total seating capacity for church edifices of 43,560,063.

A comparison between the figures for 1890 and those for 1906, if no allowance be made for duplications, indicates that the total seating capacity of church edifices increased in the sixteen years 14,976,767, or 34.4 per cent. The Protestant bodies furnished 89.4 per cent of this increase and the Roman Catholic Church 7.5 per cent. The rate of increase in seating capacity was practically the same in each case—33.6 for the Protestant bodies and 33.3 for the Roman Catholic Church.

Figures showing accommodations or sittings for the censuses of 1850, 1860, and 1870 are available and are presented in Table 15 (page 565). In round numbers, these figures show 14,000,000 seats in 1850, 19,000,000 in 1860, and 22,000,000 in 1870. It is rather interesting to note how this growth in the seating capacity of church edifices has kept pace with the growth of population, and therefore the following tabular statement has been prepared showing the ratio between population and seating capacity of church edifices at different censuses.

According to these figures, the seating capacity of church edifices, in proportion to population, was greater in 1906 than at any preceding census of religious bodies, although it was only slightly greater than in 1890. In 1906, as the summary indicates, the churches could have seated at one time 69.5 per cent of the population. This figure, however, exaggerates the seating capacity because it does not allow for the unknown amount of duplication resulting from the fact that the seating capacity of churches used by two or more organizations was counted for each organization. If it be assumed that this duplication was the same, in proportion to the total seating capacity, as it was said to be in 1890, then the net seating capacity in 1906 was about 54,790,473, and the churches of the country could in that year have seated 65 per cent of the population.

YEAR.	Population.	SEATING CAPACITY OF CHURCH EDIFICES.	
		Amount.	Per cent of population.
1906	[1]84,246,252	58,536	69.5
1890	[2]62,947,714	43,560,830	69.2
1880	50,155,783	(3),063	(3)
1870	38,558,371	[4]21,665,062	56.2
1860	31,443,321	[5]19,128,751	60.8
1850	23,191,876	[5]14,234,825	61.4

[1] Estimated.
[2] Includes the population of Indian Territory and Indian reservations.
[3] Not reported.
[4] Reported as "sittings."
[5] Reported as "accommodations."

Perhaps more significant is the relation between the church membership and the seating capacity of the church edifice. The figures for communicants or members given in this report were compiled from the returns of each organization without regard to the question whether the organization reported a church edifice, and if it reported one, whether it gave the seating capacity. As a result of this fact a direct comparison between seating capacity and membership would be somewhat misleading, as it would tend to overstate the number of members to be provided for in the church edifices. In the following table for 1906, therefore, the average membership per organization for all organizations reporting membership is compared with the average seating capacity per organization for all organizations reporting the seating capacity of church edifices.

With the single exception of the Roman Catholic Church, all the denominations show an average seating capacity considerably in excess of the average membership. For all the Protestant bodies combined, the average membership per organization reporting membership is 104, while the average seating capacity per organization reporting seating capacity is more than three times that number, or, to give the exact figure, 317. For the Roman Catholic Church the average membership, 969, is almost two and one-fourth times the average seating capacity.

DENOMINATION.	Organizations reporting communicants or members: 1906.	COMMUNICANTS OR MEMBERS: 1906.		Organizations reporting seating capacity of church edifices: 1906.	SEATING CAPACITY OF CHURCH EDIFICES: 1906.	
		Total number.	Average number per organization reporting.		Total amount.	Average amount per organization reporting.
All denominations	210,418	32,936,445	157	179,954	58,536,830	325
Protestant bodies	194,497	20,287,742	104	167,884	53,282,445	317
Adventist bodies	2,537	92,735	37	1,431	287,964	201
Baptist bodies	54,707	5,662,234	104	48,042	15,702,712	327
Christians (Christian Connection)	1,354	110,117	81	1,221	383,893	314
Church of Christ, Scientist	635	85,717	135	245	81,823	334
Congregationalists	5,700	700,480	123	5,244	1,794,997	342
Disciples or Christians	10,909	1,142,359	105	8,702	2,776,044	319
Dunkers or German Baptist Brethren	1,090	97,144	89	969	508,374	525
Evangelical bodies	2,730	174,780	64	2,461	659,391	268
Friends	1,141	113,772	100	1,088	304,204	280
German Evangelical Synod of North America	1,198	293,137	245	1,131	380,465	336
Independent churches	1,065	73,673	69	741	213,096	288
Lutheran bodies	12,642	2,112,494	167	10,493	3,344,654	319
Mennonite bodies	604	54,798	91	497	171,381	345
Methodist bodies	64,255	5,749,838	89	56,577	17,053,392	301
Presbyterian bodies	15,471	1,830,555	118	13,942	4,892,819	351
Protestant Episcopal Church	6,725	886,942	132	5,960	1,675,750	281
Reformed bodies	2,583	449,514	174	2,472	990,654	401
Unitarians	435	70,542	162	401	159,917	399
United Brethren bodies	4,268	296,050	69	3,637	1,060,560	292
Universalists	811	64,158	79	718	220,222	307
Other Protestant bodies	3,637	226,703	62	1,912	620,133	324
Roman Catholic Church	12,472	12,079,142	969	10,303	4,494,377	436
Jewish congregations	1,152	[1]101,457	[1]88	717	364,701	509
Latter-day Saints	1,184	256,647	217	837	280,747	335
Eastern Orthodox Churches	411	129,606	315	75	38,995	520
All other bodies	702	81,851	117	138	75,565	548

[1] Heads of families only.

Two factors probably combine to account in a large measure for this wide difference between the Protestant bodies and the Roman Catholic Church. Perhaps the more important is that the Roman Catholic Church conducts several services on Sunday morning, each attended by a largely distinct congregation. The Protestant bodies, on the other hand, usually have but one service each Sunday morning. Increasing membership can thus be met to some extent in the Roman Catholic Church by increasing the number of services, while in the Protestant bodies it is met either by increasing the seating capacity, when that in existence is exhausted, or by forming new organizations. The second factor is that the Protestant bodies have to provide for a relatively larger number of nonmembers than does the Roman Catholic Church. Practically all persons over 9 years of age who attend the Roman Catholic Church are included in these statistics as members of that church, but a large number of persons who attend the Protestant churches are not included in these statistics, as they have not become members of the churches.[1]

Another fact which must be borne in mind in using the averages given in the preceding table is, that for any denomination the average number of members per organization is not exactly equivalent to the average number of members per organization owning a church edifice. The average membership per organization owning a church is doubtless considerably larger than the average membership per organization, because the organizations which have not secured a church generally have few members. Thus their inclusion materially lowers the average, and tends to exaggerate the excess of seating capacity over membership, apparent for all bodies except the Roman Catholic Church.

Seating capacity of halls, etc.—Of the 14,791 organizations worshiping in "halls, etc.," in 1906, 9,817 organizations submitted a report on seating capacity, representing a total of 1,546,350, or an average per organization reporting of 158. These figures are not of much significance, however, because the buildings so included—for the most part halls and schoolhouses—were not specially built to meet the requirements of the church organizations using them, as is the case with respect to church edifices proper. The report for 1890 shows, exclusive of the returns for Alaska, a total seating capacity for halls, etc., of 2,450,518, as reported by 23,332 organizations, including, however, many private houses for which the seating capacity could not be given. For the reason stated, therefore, no figures indicating the seating capacity of halls, etc., are presented in the general tables.

VALUE OF CHURCH PROPERTY.

Under the head of "value of church property" is included the estimated value in 1906 of the buildings owned and used for worship by the organizations reporting, together with the value of their sites, and of their furniture, organs, bells, etc. It does not include the value of rented buildings or halls, nor of parsonages, parochial school buildings, theological seminaries, monasteries, convents, or the like. In some cases the church edifice was combined with a parish house, a parsonage, or a school, while the site sometimes included a cemetery. When these were identified with the church edifice, so that practically no distinction could be made between them, their value is necessarily included in the value of the church property reported. In the case of monasteries or convents, the value of chapels is not reported except where they were separate and distinct buildings. When an organization worshiped in a rented building but at the same time owned a lot on which it expected to build, the value of the lot is included. Wherever two or more organizations shared the ownership of a church edifice, each is credited with its proper proportion of the value—one-half, one-third, etc., as the case may be.

The value of church property is given for 1890 and 1906 by denominations in detail in Table 8 (page 514). The next table gives, for principal families and separate denominations, first, the number of organizations reporting the value of church property owned by them and the percentage which they represent of the total number reporting; second, the value of church property reported in 1890 and in 1906 together with the per cent distribution of this property in each year; and, third, the amount and per cent of increase in value of church property from 1890 to 1906.

According to that table, reports as to the value of church property owned were made by 186,132 organizations, or 87.7 per cent of the total number. The organizations for which no statistics as to property owned are presented consist largely of organizations which were worshiping in rented halls, in other rented buildings, or in private houses, and consequently owned no property which could be reported, although it is undoubtedly true that some organizations which owned property failed to make any report concerning it. In regard to the number of organizations reporting, the rank of the different denominations is much the same as in respect to places of worship, the largest number being shown for Methodist bodies.

[1] For a statement of the difference between the Roman Catholic Church and the Protestant bodies in respect to membership, see page 24.

DENOMINATION.	ORGANIZATIONS REPORTING VALUE OF CHURCH PROPERTY: 1906.		VALUE OF CHURCH PROPERTY REPORTED.					
	Number.	Per cent of total.	Amount.		Per cent distribution.		Increase from 1890 to 1906.	
			1906	1890	1906	1890	Amount.	Percent.
All denominations	186,132	87.7	$1,257,575,867	$679,426,489	100.0	100.0	$578,149,378	85.1
Protestant bodies	173,902	88.9	935,942,578	549,695,707	74.4	80.9	386,246,871	70.3
Adventist bodies	1,492	58.5	2,425,209	1,236,345	0.2	0.2	1,188,864	96.2
Baptist bodies	49,339	89.0	139,842,656	82,328,123	11.1	12.1	57,514,533	69.9
Christians (Christian Connection)	1,239	89.8	2,740,322	1,775,202	0.2	0.3	965,120	54.4
Church of Christ, Scientist	401	62.9	8,806,441	40,666	0.7	(1)	8,765,775	21,555.5
Congregationalists	5,366	93.9	63,240,305	43,335,437	5.0	6.4	19,904,868	45.9
Disciples or Christians	8,906	81.4	29,995,316	12,206,038	2.4	1.8	17,789,278	145.7
Dunkers or German Baptist Brethren	974	88.8	2,802,532	1,362,631	0.2	0.2	1,439,901	105.7
Evangelical bodies	2,515	91.9	8,999,979	4,785,680	0.7	0.7	4,214,299	88.1
Friends	1,097	95.6	3,857,451	4,541,334	0.3	0.7	[2] 683,883	[2] 15.1
German Evangelical Synod of North America	1,137	94.4	9,376,402	4,614,490	0.7	0.7	4,761,912	103.2
Independent churches	806	74.7	3,934,267	1,486,000	0.3	0.2	2,448,267	164.8
Lutheran bodies	10,779	84.9	74,826,389	35,060,354	6.0	5.2	39,766,035	113.4
Mennonite bodies	497	82.3	1,237,134	643,800	0.1	0.1	593,334	92.2
Methodist bodies	59,083	91.3	229,450,996	132,140,179	18.2	19.4	97,310,817	73.6
Presbyterian bodies	14,161	91.3	150,189,446	94,861,347	11.9	14.0	55,328,099	58.3
Protestant Episcopal Church	6,057	88.5	125,040,498	81,219,117	9.9	12.0	43,821,381	54.0
Reformed bodies	2,477	95.8	30,648,247	18,744,242	2.4	2.8	11,904,005	63.5
Unitarians	406	88.1	14,263,277	10,335,100	1.1	1.5	3,928,177	38.0
United Brethren bodies	3,839	89.2	9,073,791	4,937,583	0.7	0.7	4,136,208	83.8
Universalists	779	92.1	10,575,656	8,054,333	0.8	1.2	2,521,323	31.3
Other Protestant bodies	2,552	69.1	14,616,264	5,987,706	1.2	0.9	8,628,558	144.1
Roman Catholic Church	10,293	82.5	292,638,787	118,123,346	23.3	17.4	174,515,441	147.7
Jewish congregations	747	42.2	23,198,925	9,754,275	1.8	1.4	13,444,650	137.8
Latter-day Saints	909	76.8	3,168,548	1,051,791	0.3	0.2	2,116,757	201.3
Eastern Orthodox Churches	89	21.7	964,791	45,000	0.1	(1)	919,791	2,044.0
All other bodies	192	25.1	1,662,238	756,370	0.1	0.1	905,868	119.8

[1] Less than one-tenth of 1 per cent.

[2] Decrease.

The total value of church property reported in 1906, for all denominations, was $1,257,575,867, of which $935,942,578 was reported for Protestant bodies, $292,638,787 for the Roman Catholic Church, and $28,994,502 for all the remaining bodies. The following statement shows the principal families and separate denominations arranged in the order of the value of church property as reported by them, together with the average value per organization reporting:

DENOMINATION.	TOTAL VALUE OF CHURCH PROPERTY REPORTED: 1906.		AVERAGE VALUE OF CHURCH PROPERTY REPORTED PER ORGANIZATION REPORTING.	
	Amount.	Rank.	Amount.	Rank.
Roman Catholic Church	$292,638,787	1	$28,431	3
Methodist bodies	229,450,996	2	3,884	14
Presbyterian bodies	150,189,446	3	10,606	10
Baptist bodies	139,842,656	4	2,834	20
Protestant Episcopal Church	125,040,498	5	20,644	5
Lutheran bodies	74,826,389	6	6,942	12
Congregationalists	63,240,305	7	11,785	8
Reformed bodies	30,648,247	8	12,373	7
Disciples or Christians	29,995,316	9	3,368	18
Jewish congregations	23,198,925	10	31,056	2
Unitarians	14,263,277	11	35,131	1
Universalists	10,575,656	12	13,576	6
German Evangelical Synod of North America	9,376,402	13	8,247	11
United Brethren bodies	9,073,791	14	2,364	22
Evangelical bodies	8,999,979	15	3,579	15
Church of Christ, Scientist	8,806,441	16	21,961	4
Independent churches	3,934,267	17	4,881	13
Friends	3,857,451	18	3,516	16
Latter-day Saints	3,168,548	19	3,486	17
Dunkers or German Baptist Brethren	2,802,532	20	2,877	19
Christians (Christian Connection)	2,740,322	21	2,212	23
Adventist bodies	2,425,209	22	1,625	24
Mennonite bodies	1,237,134	23	2,489	21
Eastern Orthodox Churches	964,791	24	10,840	9

In the consideration of the foregoing statistics it must be kept in mind that some bodies are not very fully represented. For example, for the Jewish congregations only 747 organizations, or considerably less than one-half the entire number, reported the value of church property owned by them, and, similarly, for the Church of Christ, Scientist, only 401 organizations, or not much more than three-fifths of the entire number, made a report. For the Roman Catholic Church, only a little more than four-fifths of the total number of organizations made any report of property owned, while the Eastern Orthodox Churches as a whole show a report for only about one-fifth of all their organizations. In these, and in other cases, there has not been, therefore, a full report of the value of church property, and the total amounts shown, even though large in themselves, do not, in all probability, represent the whole amount of property owned and used for worship by the several denominations.

The figures given for 1890, like those for 1906, probably represent the value of church property so far as reported, and, similarly, do not stand for the entire value of church property owned and used for worship at that period.

It should also be noted that under the head of "other Protestant bodies" are included some denominations, as the Plymouth Brethren and Christadelphians, which are averse to the use of special buildings for worship; and others, as some of the Evangelistic associations and the Nonsectarian Churches of Bible Faith, which are principally evangelistic in character, or are widely scattered in small communities and worship to a considerable extent in tents, school buildings, or private houses.

The statement would seem to indicate that those religious bodies which are largely concentrated in cities, or which usually have large congregations to provide for, reported the highest average value of church property owned, while many bodies which show a large number of organizations and of communicants or members, but are principally located in rural districts, show a comparatively small average value. Thus the two families which together reported more than one-half of the total number of church edifices returned in 1906, the Methodists and Baptists, represent less than one-third of the total value of church property reported and have a low rank in average value per organization reporting, while the Unitarians, Jewish congregations, and Roman Catholic Church, which are largely concentrated in or near cities, stand at the head in respect to average value. The Unitarians, with church property valued at $14,263,277, as reported by 406 organizations, have a comparatively low rank in total value, but are first in point of average value, with an average of $35,131 for each organization reporting. The Jewish congregations, with property valued at $23,198,925, as reported by 747 organizations, rank just above the Unitarians in total value, but are second with respect to average value, with an average of $31,056. The Roman Catholic Church, which is first in point of total value of church property reported, $292,638,787, comes third in the average value per organization reporting, with $28,431, and is followed by the Church of Christ, Scientist, and the Protestant Episcopal Church, with average values per organization of $21,961 and $20,644, respectively.

The conditions in regard to single denominations in the denominational families are in many cases quite different, as indicated by the figures in Table 1 (page 148). The Northern Baptist Convention, with 17.6 per cent of the total number of organizations in the three Baptist conventions which reported value of church property, has 55.8 per cent of the total value of church property reported, and an average value per organization reporting of $9,573. On the other hand, the Southern Baptist Convention, with 42.1 per cent of the number of organizations reporting, has only 26 per cent of the total value of church property, and an average value per organization reporting of $1,860.

The situation is similar in the Methodist bodies. The Methodist Episcopal Church, with 47.2 per cent of the entire number of organizations in the family reporting value of church property, had 71.2 per cent of the total value of church property reported, and an average value per organization reporting of $5,858; while the Methodist Episcopal Church, South, with 26.8 per cent of the total number of organizations in the family reporting value of church property, shows 16.2 per cent of the total value of church property reported, and an average value per organization reporting of $2,351.

The Presbyterian Church in the United States of America, with 52.3 per cent of the entire number of Presbyterian organizations reporting, has 76.5 per cent of the total value of church property reported, and shows an average value per organization reporting of $15,514, as against an average value of $11,411 for the United Presbyterian Church, and of $5,665 for the Presbyterian Church in the United States.

It is also to be noted that those bodies which are numerically strongest in the Northern and Eastern states, as the Methodist Episcopal Church, the Presbyterian Church in the United States of America, and the Roman Catholic Church, show higher average values than those whose strength is chiefly in the Southern states, as the Methodist Episcopal Church, South, the Presbyterian Church in the United States, and the Southern Baptist Convention. The relatively high rank in average values held by those bodies most affected by immigration, as the Lutheran bodies and the German Evangelical Synod, may be considered as indicative in general of their prosperous character.

Of the total value of church property ($3,168,548) shown for the 2 bodies comprising the Latter-day Saints, $2,645,363 was reported for the Church of Jesus Christ of Latter-day Saints, more commonly known as the Utah branch. This sum represents the amount reported by the individual wards—equivalent to church organizations in other denominations—but is exclusive of the value of church property used for the purposes of the stakes and of the church in general, including the Temple, Tabernacle, and Assembly Hall at Salt Lake City, as well as other edifices, and representing an aggregate value of $7,766,750.

The increase from 1890 to 1906 in the value of church property reported was $578,149,378, of which $386,246,871 represents the increase in the value of the property reported by Protestant bodies, and $174,515,441 the increase in the value of the property reported by the Roman Catholic Church. The Methodist bodies reported the largest increase of any of the Protestant denominations, $97,310,817, and were followed by the Baptist bodies with an increase of $57,514,533, and the Presbyterian bodies with an increase of $55,328,099. The decrease shown for the Friends is explained partly by a general decrease in the value of the property reported by the Hicksite organizations, but more particularly by the fact that, probably as a result of a clerical error in the schedules for the Orthodox Friends for 1890, a church edifice, with a reported value in 1906 of $98,000, was given a value in 1890 of $1,000,000 instead of the more probable value, $100,000. If allowance is made for this, the 4 bodies of Friends would show a gain of over $216,000, instead of an apparent loss of $683,883, as shown in the table.

The percentage of increase shown for the different

families varies greatly. Leaving out of consideration the phenomenal increases shown for the Church of Christ, Scientist, and the Eastern Orthodox Churches, the property reported by the Latter-day Saints more than trebled in value, while the Independent churches, the Roman Catholic Church, the Disciples or Christians, the Jewish congregations, the Lutheran bodies, the Dunkers, and the German Evangelical Synod of North America, reported increases of more than 100 per cent. These large percentages of increase are explained partly by the change from the use of halls to the use of regular church edifices, and partly by the addition of new organizations as the result of immigration, notably in the Roman Catholic Church, the Lutheran bodies, the German Evangelical Synod of North America, and similar denominations.

The census reports for 1850, 1860, and 1870 also give the value of church property, the amounts being as shown in Table 15 (page 565). The following tabular statement shows the value of church property reported for each census at which such statistics were obtained, together with the percentage of increase between censuses:

YEAR.	VALUE OF CHURCH PROPERTY REPORTED.	
	Amount.	Per cent of increase over value at preceding census.
1906	$1,257,575,867	85.1
1890	679,426,489	91.7
1870	354,483,581	106.8
1860	171,397,932	96.3
1850	87,328,801	....

The figures shown for the earlier periods are undoubtedly subject to the same limitations as those already indicated in the case of the figures for 1906, but on their face show a very considerable advance from one census to another in the value of property held for purposes of worship. The per capita increase is shown in the following statement:

YEAR.	Population.	Per capita value of church property.
1906	[1] 84,246,252	$14.93
1890	[2] 62,947,714	10.79
1870	38,558,371	9.19
1860	31,443,321	5.45
1850	23,191,876	3.77

[1] Estimated.
[2] Includes the population of Indian Territory and Indian reservations.

The value of church property reported for 1870 is probably on a currency basis rather than a gold basis, but the report on religious statistics at that census does not afford definite information on this point.

DEBT ON CHURCH PROPERTY.

The amount of debt on church property owned and used for worship was ascertained for the first time in the present census investigation. A report was made on this point by 33,617 organizations out of a total of 186,132 organizations reporting value of church property—that is, less than one-fifth (18.1 per cent) of the organizations to which the inquiry was applicable report a debt. While there are probably some organizations which failed to make a report, it is to be presumed that the remaining 152,515 organizations for the most part held their church property free of debt. The total amount of debt reported, for all denominations, was $108,050,946, representing 8.6 per cent of the total value of all church property reported as owned and used for worship in 1906. The distribution of this amount of debt and its relation to the value of church property reported is given by principal families and separate denominations in the table on page 40.

Of the total number of organizations reporting debt, as shown by this table, 28,797 belonged to Protestant bodies, 4,104 to the Roman Catholic Church, and 716 to the remaining bodies. Of the Jewish congregations that reported the value of church property, 60.1 per cent also reported debt; while the corresponding percentage for the Roman Catholic Church is 39.9 per cent; for the German Evangelical Synod of North America, 35 per cent; for the Independent churches, 28.5 per cent; for the Lutheran bodies, 27.6 per cent; and for the Reformed bodies, 26.4 per cent. On the other hand, a debt on church property was reported by only 5.5 per cent of the organizations of Friends that reported the value of church property, 6.2 per cent of those connected with Mennonite bodies, and 7.8 per cent of those belonging to the Christians (Christian Connection).

Of the total amount of debt, $53,301,254 was reported by Protestant bodies, $49,488,055 by the Roman Catholic Church, $4,556,571 by the Jewish congregations, and $705,066 by all the remaining bodies. Among the Protestant bodies, the largest amount of debt reported is $12,272,463 for the Methodist bodies, while the Baptist bodies reported a debt of $8,323,862; the Lutheran bodies, a debt of $7,859,469; and the Presbyterian bodies, a debt of $6,545,025.

The amount of debt reported represents, for all denominations, as before stated, 8.6 per cent of the total value of church property reported. For the Protestant bodies as a whole the proportion is 5.7 per cent and for the Roman Catholic Church, 16.9 per cent. The highest proportion, 30.1 per cent, is shown for the Eastern Orthodox Churches, followed by the Jewish congregations with 19.6 per cent; the German Evangelical Synod of North America with 12.4 per cent; the Independent churches with 12.2 per cent; and the Lutheran bodies with 10.5 per cent. The smallest proportions shown are seven-tenths of 1 per cent for the Mennonite bodies, 1.1 per cent for the Friends, 2.3 per cent for the Unitarians, 3 per cent for the Dunkers, and 3.5 per cent for the Latter-day Saints.

DENOMINATION.	ORGANIZATIONS REPORTING DEBT ON CHURCH PROPERTY: 1906.		Value of church property reported: 1906.	DEBT REPORTED: 1906.		
	Number.	Per cent of organizations reporting value of church property.		Amount.	Per cent of value of church property.	Average per organization reporting.
All denominations	33,617	18.1	$1,257,575,867	$108,050,946	8.6	$3,214
Protestant bodies	28,797	16.6	935,942,578	53,301,254	5.7	1,851
Adventist bodies	183	12.3	2,425,209	167,812	6.9	917
Baptist bodies	6,199	12.6	139,842,656	8,323,862	6.0	1,343
Christians (Christian Connection)	97	7.8	2,740,322	101,561	3.7	1,047
Church of Christ, Scientist	88	21.9	8,806,441	391,338	4.4	4,447
Congregationalists	1,206	22.5	63,240,305	2,708,025	4.3	2,245
Disciples or Christians	1,234	13.9	29,995,316	1,868,821	6.2	1,514
Dunkers or German Baptist Brethren	115	11.8	2,802,532	83,199	3.0	723
Evangelical bodies	412	16.4	8,999,979	666,973	7.4	1,619
Friends	60	5.5	3,857,451	41,496	1.1	692
German Evangelical Synod of North America	398	35.0	9,376,402	1,161,776	12.4	2,919
Independent churches	230	28.5	3,934,267	478,425	12.2	2,080
Lutheran bodies	2,970	27.6	74,826,389	7,859,469	10.5	2,646
Mennonite bodies	31	6.2	1,237,134	9,082	0.7	293
Methodist bodies	10,430	17.7	229,450,996	12,272,463	5.3	1,177
Presbyterian bodies	2,102	14.8	150,189,446	6,545,025	4.4	3,114
Protestant Episcopal Church	1,011	16.7	125,040,498	4,930,914	3.9	4,877
Reformed bodies	654	26.4	30,648,247	2,377,014	7.8	3,635
Unitarians	85	20.9	14,263,277	332,330	2.3	3,910
United Brethren bodies	460	12.0	9,073,791	496,959	5.5	1,085
Universalists	132	16.9	10,575,656	464,755	4.4	3,521
Other Protestant bodies	700	27.4	14,616,264	2,017,955	13.8	2,883
Roman Catholic Church	4,104	39.9	292,638,787	49,488,055	16.9	12,058
Jewish congregations	449	60.1	23,198,925	4,556,571	19.6	10,148
Latter-day Saints	145	16.0	3,168,548	111,782	3.5	771
Eastern Orthodox Churches	58	(1)	964,791	290,674	30.1	5,012
All other bodies	64	33.3	1,662,238	302,610	18.2	4,728

1 Per cent not shown where base is less than 100.

In general a large number of organizations reporting debt, and a large amount of debt reported, indicate one of two conditions—rapid extension in the number of organizations to supply the demand of new communities, resulting largely from recent immigration, or enlargement in church accommodations to meet the congested conditions in cities. Certain of the smaller bodies (see Table 1, page 148), as the Plymouth Brethren, which as a rule do not own church edifices, report a small amount of property and very little debt. A few bodies make no report of debt, although in these cases it is not always clear whether they have failed to report, or whether they had no debt to report. The general presumption is, however, that they had no debt to report.

In some cases the smaller denominations report a greater debt than most of the larger bodies. Thus 9 out of the 11 organizations in the Hungarian Reformed Church reporting value of church property showed debts averaging $7,883, and representing 57.4 per cent of the total value of their church property. In the Metropolitan Church Association 4 organizations reported value of church property, and of these, 3 reported debts amounting to $74,000, or 62.6 per cent of the total value of church property reported, and averaging $24,667. The colored bodies, as a rule, show a higher percentage of organizations reporting debt, and the debts represent a higher percentage of the total value of church property reported, but the average debt per organization is lower than is the case in the white bodies. Thus in the African Methodist Episcopal Church 40.9 per cent of the organizations reporting value of church property showed debts amounting to 10.5 per cent of the total value given for the entire denomination, but averaging only $463 per organization, while in the Methodist Episcopal Church the debt as stated by 16.7 per cent of the organizations reporting value of church property amounted to only 5.3 per cent of the total value, while the average debt per organization reporting was $1,853. The situation in other colored churches is essentially the same as in the African Methodist Episcopal Church.

The average amount of debt per organization reporting varies from $12,058, for the Roman Catholic Church, to $293, for the Mennonite bodies. The highest averages after the Roman Catholic Church are: Jewish congregations, $10,148; Eastern Orthodox Churches, $5,012; Protestant Episcopal Church, $4,877; and Church of Christ, Scientist, $4,447. It thus appears that the heaviest debts are borne by those bodies largely represented in cities which aim to provide for large congregations and which erect elaborate edifices.

VALUE OF PARSONAGES.

In response to this inquiry, made for the first time in 1906, parsonages were reported by 54,214 organizations, constituting 25.5 per cent of all the organizations represented, as shown by the following table.

DENOMINATION.	ORGANIZATIONS REPORTING PARSONAGES: 1906.		VALUE OF PARSONAGES REPORTED: 1906.	
	Number.	Per cent of total.	Total.	Average per organization reporting.
All denominations	54,214	25.5	$143,495,853	$2,647
Protestant bodies	47,714	24.4	106,710,596	2,236
Adventist bodies	60	2.4	91,640	1,517
Baptist bodies	4,978	9.1	9,233,631	1,855
Christians (Christian Connection)	160	11.6	256,350	1,602
Church of Christ, Scientist	4	0.6	57,300	14,325
Congregationalists	2,693	47.1	6,761,148	2,511
Disciples or Christians	617	5.6	1,129,225	1,830
Dunkers or German Baptist Brethren	54	4.9	99,200	1,837
Evangelical bodies	1,026	37.5	1,907,917	1,860
Friends	145	12.6	181,874	1,254
German Evangelical Synod of North America	774	64.2	1,717,345	2,219
Independent churches	93	8.6	185,450	1,994
Lutheran bodies	4,994	39.3	11,521,988	2,307
Mennonite bodies	39	6.5	55,500	1,423
Methodist bodies	20,837	32.2	36,420,655	1,748
Presbyterian bodies	5,417	34.9	16,155,861	2,982
Protestant Episcopal Church	2,706	39.5	13,207,084	4,881
Reformed bodies	1,355	52.4	4,166,769	3,075
Unitarians	115	24.9	584,750	5,085
United Brethren bodies	1,106	25.7	1,507,932	1,363
Universalists	136	16.1	491,100	3,611
Other Protestant bodies	405	11.0	978,477	2,416
Roman Catholic Church	6,360	51.0	36,302,064	5,708
Jewish congregations	81	4.6	270,550	3,340
Latter-day Saints	8	0.7	7,800	975
Eastern Orthodox Churches	29	7.1	117,143	4,039
All other bodies	22	2.9	87,700	3,986

The largest proportion of organizations reporting parsonages shown in the table is for the German Evangelical Synod of North America, 64.2 per cent of all the organizations for this denomination reporting that parsonages were owned by them. Other denominations showing a relatively large number of organizations reporting parsonages are the Reformed bodies, for which the proportion is 52.4 per cent; the Roman Catholic Church, for which it is 51 per cent; and the Congregationalists, for which it is 47.1 per cent; while for the Protestant Episcopal Church, the Lutheran bodies, the Evangelical bodies, the Presbyterian bodies, and the Methodist bodies, it exceeded 30 per cent in each case. In many instances members of the same denominational family show wide variations. Thus, as indicated by the figures in Table 1 (page 148), 31.2 per cent of the organizations connected with the Northern Baptist Convention reported parsonages, as compared with 6 per cent for the Southern Baptist Convention and 3.8 per cent for the National Baptist Convention (Colored). Similarly, 40.8 per cent of the organizations reported for the Methodist Episcopal Church reported parsonages, against 22.4 per cent for the African Methodists as a whole.

Among the Reformed bodies the Christian Reformed Church and the Reformed Church in America lead, with percentages of 78.2 and 74.2, respectively, and these are the highest percentages reported by any denomination, exceeding considerably that already noted for the German Evangelical Synod (64.2). The Reformed Church in the United States, on the other hand, shows but 41.7 per cent. The Lutheran bodies, as a whole, show 39.3 per cent, but parsonages are reported by 54.9 per cent of the organizations in the Synodical Conference and 49 per cent of those in each of the Synods of Iowa and Ohio. It is noticeable that in general the highest percentages are reported by denominations of European origin, while those of British or distinctively American origin show much lower percentages.

The 54,214 parsonages thus reported are valued, in the aggregate, at $143,495,853, and are distributed as follows: Protestant bodies, 47,714 parsonages, valued at $106,710,596; Roman Catholic Church, 6,360 parsonages, valued at $36,302,064; and the remaining bodies, 140 parsonages, valued at $483,193. Among the Protestant denominations, the Methodist bodies lead with 20,837 parsonages, valued at $36,420,655, followed by the Presbyterian bodies, with 5,417 parsonages, valued at $16,155,861; the Protestant Episcopal Church, with 2,706 parsonages, valued at $13,207,084; and the Lutheran bodies, with 4,994 parsonages, valued at $11,521,988.

In average value of parsonages the Church of Christ, Scientist, leads with an average of $14,325, but this is based upon a report as to parsonages for less than 1 per cent of all the organizations in that denomination. The Roman Catholic Church is second, with an average of $5,708; and is followed by the Unitarians, with an average of $5,085; and by the Protestant Episcopal Church, with an average of $4,881. In a number of cases, especially in the Roman Catholic and Protestant Episcopal churches, parsonages are frequently combined with parish houses, which partially explains their high average values. In the Hungarian Reformed Church and the Eastern Orthodox Churches, only a few parsonages are reported, but the average value is high, $4,417 and $4,039, respectively.

The parsonages reported for Congregationalists, the Presbyterian, Baptist, and Methodist bodies, and to a certain extent also for the Lutheran bodies, are very largely in towns or country districts, and this accounts, in general, for the low averages.

SUMMARY OF STATISTICS FOR STATES AND TERRITORIES.

The statistics of religious bodies are presented in detail by states and territories in Tables 2, 3, and 9 of the general tables. Table 2 (page 154) gives a summary of the statistics for 1906 for all denominations; Table 3 (page 156) shows the distribution of the communicants or members reported for 1906 by denominations in detail; and Table 9 (page 520) presents a comparative statement of the population, number of church organizations, number of communicants or members, places of worship, and value of church property reported for 1890 and 1906, respectively.

GENERAL SUMMARY FOR 1906.

The following table shows for each state and territory the estimated population in 1906, the number of organizations and of communicants or members, the value of church property reported, and the amount of debt reported on church property, together with the proportion of the total for continental United States reported by each state and territory, and the rank of each. The states and territories are arranged under each head according to their rank.

It will be observed from the table that the several percentages for each particular state are approximately uniform and that with few exceptions no one state shows a marked variation. Thus Illinois has 6.4 per cent of the total population, 4.4 per cent of the number of organizations, 6.3 per cent of the number of communicants or members, 5.3 per cent of the value of church property, and 5.8 per cent of the

STATE OR TERRITORY.	1906						
	Population.[1]			Total organizations.			
	Number.	Per cent distribution.	Rank.	State or territory.	Number reported.	Per cent distribution.	Rank.
Continental United States	84,246,252	100.0	....	Continental United States	212,230	100.0	....
New York	8,226,990	9.8	1	Pennsylvania	12,834	6.0	1
Pennsylvania	6,928,515	8.2	2	Texas	12,354	5.8	2
Illinois	5,418,670	6.4	3	Georgia	10,097	4.8	3
Ohio	4,448,677	5.3	4	Ohio	9,890	4.7	4
Texas	3,536,618	4.2	5	New York	9,639	4.5	5
Missouri	3,363,153	4.0	6	Illinois	9,374	4.4	6
Massachusetts	3,043,346	3.6	7	Missouri	9,206	4.3	7
Indiana	2,710,898	3.2	8	Alabama	8,894	4.2	8
Michigan	2,584,533	3.1	9	North Carolina	8,592	4.0	9
Georgia	2,443,719	2.9	10	Tennessee	8,021	3.8	10
Kentucky	2,320,298	2.8	11	Mississippi	7,396	3.5	11
Wisconsin	2,260,930	2.7	12	Indiana	6,863	3.2	12
Iowa	2,205,690	2.6	13	Virginia	6,639	3.1	13
New Jersey	2,196,237	2.6	14	Kentucky	6,553	3.1	14
Tennessee	2,172,476	2.6	15	Iowa	6,293	3.0	15
North Carolina	2,059,326	2.4	16	Arkansas	6,208	2.9	16
Minnesota	2,025,615	2.4	17	Michigan	5,635	2.7	17
Alabama	2,017,877	2.4	18	South Carolina	5,385	2.5	18
Virginia	1,973,104	2.3	19	Kansas	4,994	2.4	19
Mississippi	1,708,272	2.0	20	Wisconsin	4,902	2.3	20
California	1,648,049	2.0	21	Minnesota	4,759	2.2	21
Kansas	1,612,471	1.9	22	Oklahoma[2]	4,497	2.1	22
Louisiana	1,539,449	1.8	23	West Virginia	4,042	1.9	23
South Carolina	1,453,818	1.7	24	Louisiana	3,855	1.8	24
Arkansas	1,421,574	1.7	25	Florida	3,370	1.6	25
Oklahoma[2]	[3]1,414,177	1.7	26	Nebraska	3,313	1.6	26
Maryland	1,275,434	1.5	27	Massachusetts	3,088	1.5	27
West Virginia	1,076,406	1.3	28	California	2,897	1.4	28
Nebraska	1,068,484	1.3	29	New Jersey	2,802	1.3	29
Connecticut	1,005,716	1.2	30	Maryland	2,773	1.3	30
Maine	714,494	0.8	31	North Dakota	1,993	0.9	31
Florida	629,341	0.7	32	South Dakota	1,801	0.8	32
Colorado	615,570	0.7	33	Washington	1,771	0.8	33
Washington	614,625	0.7	34	Maine	1,559	0.7	34
Rhode Island	490,387	0.6	35	Connecticut	1,384	0.7	35
Oregon	474,738	0.6	36	Oregon	1,304	0.6	36
South Dakota	465,908	0.6	37	Colorado	1,268	0.6	37
North Dakota	463,784	0.6	38	Vermont	909	0.4	38
New Hampshire	432,624	0.5	39	New Hampshire	856	0.4	39
Vermont	350,373	0.4	40	Idaho	676	0.3	40
Utah	316,331	0.4	41	New Mexico	625	0.3	41
District of Columbia	307,716	0.4	42	Montana	546	0.3	42
Montana	303,575	0.4	43	Utah	542	0.3	43
New Mexico	216,328	0.3	44	Rhode Island	521	0.2	44
Idaho	205,704	0.2	45	Delaware	468	0.2	45
Delaware	194,479	0.2	46	District of Columbia	289	0.1	46
Arizona	143,745	0.2	47	Arizona	237	0.1	47
Wyoming	103,673	0.1	48	Wyoming	228	0.1	48
Nevada	42,335	0.1	49	Nevada	88	([4])	49

[1] Estimated.
[2] Oklahoma and Indian Territory combined.
[3] Special census, 1907.
[4] Less than one-tenth of 1 per cent.

amount of debt on church property. Ohio reports 5.3 per cent of the population, 4.7 per cent of the number of organizations, 5.3 per cent of the number of communicants or members, 5.9 per cent of the value of church property, and 4.8 per cent of the amount of debt. Among the states of small population, Washington reports seven-tenths of 1 per cent of the population, eight-tenths of 1 per cent of the number of organizations, six-tenths of 1 per cent of the number of communicants or members, six-tenths of 1 per cent of the value of church property, and eight-tenths of 1 per cent of the amount of debt. Greater variations, however, may be noted in respect to the value of church property and the amount of debt on church property. Although New York has only 9.8 per cent of the total population and Pennsylvania only 8.2 per cent, New York reports 20.3 per cent of the entire amount of church property in the country and Pennsylvania 13.8 per cent; while in respect to debt, New York reports 26.3 per cent of the entire amount and Pennsylvania 14.4 per cent.

With regard to the relative rank of the states under the several heads, however, there is considerable variation. Thus New York ranks first in population, in number of communicants or members, in value of church property, and in amount of debt on church property, but fifth in number of organizations. Pennsylvania ranks first in number of organizations and second in every other particular. Ohio ranks fourth in every particular except in debt on church prop-

1906—Continued.

Communicants or members.				Value of church property.				Debt on church property.			
State or territory.	Number reported.	Per cent distribution.	Rank.	State or territory.	Amount reported.	Per cent distribution.	Rank.	State or territory.	Amount reported.	Per cent distribution.	Rank.
Continental United States.	32,936,445	100.0	......	Continental United States.	$1,257,575,867	100.0	......	Continental United States.	$108,050,946	100.0	......
New York	3,591,974	10.9	1	New York	255,166,284	20.3	1	New York	28,382,866	26.3	1
Pennsylvania	2,977,022	9.0	2	Pennsylvania	173,605,141	13.8	2	Pennsylvania	15,562,196	14.4	2
Illinois	2,077,197	6.3	3	Massachusetts	84,729,445	6.7	3	Massachusetts	8,203,412	7.6	3
Ohio	1,742,873	5.3	4	Ohio	74,670,765	5.9	4	New Jersey	6,786,368	6.3	4
Massachusetts	1,562,621	4.7	5	Illinois	66,222,514	5.3	5	Illinois	6,317,919	5.8	5
Texas	1,226,906	3.7	6	New Jersey	50,907,123	4.0	6	Ohio	5,202,205	4.8	6
Missouri	1,199,239	3.6	7	Missouri	38,059,233	3.0	7	Missouri	3,257,740	3.0	7
Georgia	1,029,037	3.1	8	Indiana	31,081,500	2.5	8	Wisconsin	2,885,247	2.7	8
Wisconsin	1,000,908	3.0	9	Iowa	30,464,860	2.4	9	Connecticut	2,776,588	2.6	9
Michigan	962,479	3.0	10	Connecticut	29,196,128	2.3	10	California	2,541,148	2.4	10
Indiana	938,405	2.8	11	California	28,065,261	2.2	11	Maryland	2,095,293	1.9	11
Kentucky	858,324	2.6	12	Wisconsin	27,277,837	2.2	12	Minnesota	2,066,006	1.9	12
New Jersey	857,548	2.6	13	Michigan	27,144,250	2.2	13	Michigan	1,729,978	1.6	13
Minnesota	834,442	2.5	14	Minnesota	26,063,159	2.1	14	Indiana	1,723,109	1.6	14
North Carolina	824,385	2.5	15	Maryland	23,765,172	1.9	15	District of Columbia	1,570,609	1.5	15
Alabama	824,209	2.5	16	Texas	22,949,976	1.8	16	Iowa	1,517,992	1.4	16
Virginia	793,546	2.4	17	Virginia	19,699,014	1.6	17	Rhode Island	1,064,432	1.0	17
Iowa	788,667	2.4	18	Kentucky	18,044,389	1.4	18	Virginia	996,367	0.9	18
Louisiana	778,901	2.4	19	Georgia	17,929,183	1.4	19	Texas	944,057	0.9	19
Tennessee	697,570	2.1	20	Tennessee	14,469,012	1.2	20	Kentucky	862,993	0.8	20
South Carolina	665,933	2.0	21	North Carolina	14,053,505	1.1	21	Georgia	848,770	0.8	21
Mississippi	657,381	2.0	22	Kansas	14,053,454	1.1	22	Washington	833,258	0.8	22
California	611,464	1.9	23	Alabama	13,314,993	1.1	23	Louisiana	689,072	0.6	23
Connecticut	502,560	1.5	24	Nebraska	12,114,817	1.0	24	New Hampshire	625,807	0.6	24
Maryland	473,257	1.4	25	Louisiana	10,456,146	0.8	25	Colorado	619,367	0.6	25
Kansas	458,190	1.4	26	South Carolina	10,209,043	0.8	26	Maine	614,198	0.6	
Arkansas	426,179	1.3	27	District of Columbia	10,025,122	0.8	27	Kansas	567,254	0.5	26
Nebraska	345,803	1.0	28	Maine	9,955,363	0.8	28	Nebraska	531,042	0.5	28
West Virginia	301,565	0.9	29	West Virginia	9,733,585	0.8	29	Alabama	527,479	0.5	29
Rhode Island	264,712	0.8	30	Rhode Island	9,533,543	0.8	30	West Virginia	512,412	0.5	30
Oklahoma [1]	257,100	0.8	31	Mississippi	9,482,229	0.8	31	North Carolina	498,043	0.5	31
Florida	221,318	0.7	32	Washington	8,082,986	0.6	32	Vermont	470,095	0.4	32
Maine	212,988	0.6	33	New Hampshire	7,864,991	0.6	33	North Dakota	463,890	0.4	33
Colorado	205,666	0.6	34	Colorado	7,723,200	0.6	34	Tennessee	445,709	0.4	34
Washington	191,976	0.6	35	Arkansas	6,733,375	0.5	35	Oklahoma [1]	435,569	0.4	35
New Hampshire	190,298	0.6	36	Vermont	5,939,492	0.5	36	Florida	430,351	0.4	36
Utah	172,814	0.5	37	Florida	5,795,859	0.5	37	Arkansas	361,011	0.3	37
South Dakota	161,961	0.5	38	Oklahoma [1]	4,933,843	0.4	38	South Carolina	350,527	0.3	38
North Dakota	159,053	0.5	39	Oregon	4,620,793	0.4	39	Mississippi	345,304	0.3	39
Vermont	147,223	0.4	40	North Dakota	4,576,157	0.4	40	Oregon	257,815	0.2	40
New Mexico	137,009	0.4	41	South Dakota	4,538,013	0.4	41	Delaware	248,720	0.2	
District of Columbia	136,759	0.4	42	Utah	3,612,422	0.3	42	South Dakota	232,123	0.2	
Oregon	120,229	0.4	43	Delaware	3,250,105	0.3	43	Montana	195,122	0.2	
Montana	98,984	0.3	44	Montana	2,809,779	0.2	44	Utah	152,131	0.1	41
Idaho	74,578	0.2	45	Idaho	1,726,734	0.1	45	Idaho	119,677	0.1	48
Delaware	71,251	0.2	46	New Mexico	956,605	0.1		Arizona	71,441	0.1	
Arizona	45,067	0.1	47	Arizona	798,975	0.1	46	New Mexico	53,535	(2)	46
Wyoming	23,945	0.1	48	Wyoming	778,142	0.1	48	Wyoming	45,394	(2)	48
Nevada	14,944	(2)	49	Nevada	402,350	(2)	49	Nevada	19,305	(2)	49

[1] Oklahoma and Indian Territory combined.

[2] Less than one-tenth of 1 per cent.

erty, in which respect it occupies the sixth place. Texas ranks fifth in population, second in number of organizations, sixth in number of communicants or members, sixteenth in value of church property, and nineteenth in amount of debt on church property. Rhode Island ranks thirty-fifth in population, forty-fourth in number of organizations, thirtieth in number of communicants or members and in value of church property, but seventeenth in amount of debt on church property. The only 2 states which hold the same rank in every particular are the lowest on the list—Wyoming and Nevada.

The 10 leading states in respect to population include 50.7 per cent, more than one-half, of the entire population of the country, but only 41.9 per cent of the total number of organizations reported. On the other hand, they contain 52.4 per cent of the total communicants or members, 62.9 per cent of the value of church property reported, and 66.8 per cent of the total amount of debt reported on church property. Of the 10 states ranking highest in population, Massachusetts, Indiana, and Michigan are superseded, though not in the same order, by Alabama, North Carolina, and Tennessee, when the 10 ranking highest in respect to number of organizations are considered; similarly Texas, Michigan, and Georgia are superseded, in value of church property, by New Jersey, Iowa, and Connecticut; and Texas, Indiana, Michigan, and Georgia, in amount of debt on church property, by New Jersey, Wisconsin, Connecticut, and California.

In regard to the number of communicants or members, Wisconsin, which ranks ninth in respect to church membership, stands twelfth in population; while Indiana, which ranks eighth in population, is eleventh in respect to church membership. The relative rank of the states depends largely on the relative number of Roman Catholic inhabitants. Where there is a large representation of members of this church the state ranks relatively high in communicants, value of church property, and debt on church property. This explains why Wisconsin, with a Roman Catholic membership constituting 50.5 per cent of the total church membership of the state, stands three places higher in respect to church membership than in respect to population; and why Indiana, with a Roman Catholic membership constituting only 18.6 per cent of the total, stands three places lower in respect to church membership than in respect to population.

Average per organization.—A comparison of the number of communicants or members, the value of church property, and the amount of debt on church property, with the number of organizations reported for the different states, shows a considerable difference in the average per organization under these heads, as is set forth in the following table, in which the states and territories are arranged in the order of the number of communicants or members:

STATE OR TERRITORY.	1906		
	Communicants or members, average per organization reporting.	Value of church property, average per organization reporting.	Debt, average per organization reporting.
Continental United States	157	$6,756	$3,214
New York	389	30,581	12,400
Pennsylvania	234	14,564	4,936
Illinois	223	8,135	4,237
Ohio	178	8,102	3,764
Massachusetts	516	30,500	8,608
Texas	100	2,413	716
Missouri	131	4,778	3,132
Georgia	103	1,901	549
Wisconsin	205	6,225	2,753
Michigan	175	5,773	1,663
Indiana	137	4,843	1,793
Kentucky	132	3,138	1,385
New Jersey	312	19,686	6,313
Minnesota	177	6,347	2,042
North Carolina	96	1,742	559
Alabama	93	1,660	483
Virginia	120	3,209	1,226
Iowa	126	5,307	1,767
Louisiana	204	2,946	939
Tennessee	88	1,998	649
South Carolina	124	1,966	487
Mississippi	89	1,377	826
California	215	11,427	4,322
Connecticut	368	22,845	7,029
Maryland	172	9,112	3,180
Kansas	92	3,450	960
Arkansas	69	1,309	519
Nebraska	105	4,333	1,224
West Virginia	75	2,919	1,352
Rhode Island	522	20,502	7,144
Oklahoma[1]	58	1,830	628
Florida	66	1,918	1,013
Maine	139	7,081	2,659
Colorado	163	8,079	2,017
Washington	109	5,712	2,187
New Hampshire	229	10,006	4,376
Utah	322	7,342	1,769
South Dakota	90	3,167	1,006
North Dakota	81	3,485	1,189
Vermont	163	7,012	3,535
New Mexico	220	2,053	991
District of Columbia	475	41,256	10,983
Oregon	93	4,392	1,276
Montana	183	7,186	2,243
Idaho	111	3,399	942
Delaware	153	7,206	1,777
Arizona	191	4,592	1,931
Wyoming	106	4,894	1,565
Nevada	174	5,748	1,207

[1] Oklahoma and Indian Territory combined.

From this table it appears that the highest average church membership per organization is reported by Rhode Island, 522. It is followed by Massachusetts with 516, the District of Columbia with 475, and New York with 389. The smallest averages reported are by Oklahoma, 58; Florida, 66; Arkansas, 69; and West Virginia, 75. An average membership of less than 100 is reported by 12 states; of 100 or over but less than 200, by 23 states; of 200 or over but less than 300, by 7 states; and of 300 or over, by 7 states.

In respect to the value of church property, an average per organization of $10,000 or over is reported by 9 states; of over $5,000 but less than $10,000, by 15 states; of over $2,000 but less than $5,000, by 16 states; and of less than $2,000, by 9 states. The highest average reported is for the District of Columbia, $41,256; the second highest, for New York, $30,581; and the third, for Massachusetts, $30,500. The lowest averages are those reported by Arkansas, $1,309, and Mississippi, $1,377. In regard to the amount of debt, an average per organization of $10,000 or over is reported by 2 states; of over $5,000 but less than $10,000, by 4 states; of $1,000 or over but less than $5,000, by 30 states; and of less than $1,000, by 13 states. The highest average is reported by New York, $12,400, and the lowest by Mississippi, $325.

The high averages under each head are reported in most instances by states in which a large proportion of the church membership belongs to the Roman Catholic Church, which, as has been shown previously (see pages 28 and 40), reported the largest average membership, and the largest average amount of debt, per organization, of any of the more important religious bodies. The relative proportions of urban and rural population in the different states also have an influence upon the figures. Thus the average size of the organization will naturally be much smaller in states where the population is distributed to a large extent through small rural communities than where it is concentrated in cities or large towns, and similarly the average value of property, and the average amount of debt, will be relatively high in states which are largely urban in character, and low in states where the population is mainly rural.

DISTRIBUTION OF COMMUNICANTS OR MEMBERS BY PRINCIPAL FAMILIES AND DENOMINATIONS.

The next two tables give the number and per cent distribution, by principal families and separate denominations, of the total church membership reported for the several states and territories in 1890 and 1906. The distribution of communicants or members, by principal families or denominations, as set forth in these tables, is also illustrated in Diagram 2.

From the table showing the communicants or members for 1906 it appears that a majority of the communicants or members reported in 29 states belonged to Protestant bodies; in 16 states, to the Roman Catholic Church; and in 1 state, to the Latter-day Saints.

In 1890 a majority of the communicants or members in 34 states belonged to Protestant bodies; in 12 states, to the Roman Catholic Church; and in 2 states, to the Latter-day Saints; while in 1 state the Roman Catholic Church had a plurality. The changes from 1890 to 1906 are as follows: 6 states—Maine, New Hampshire, Vermont, New Jersey, Michigan, and Wisconsin—formerly showing a majority for Protestant bodies, are now in the Roman Catholic column; 1 state—Minnesota—formerly Roman Catholic, is now Protestant; 2 states—Colorado and Wyoming—which showed a Roman Catholic majority in 1890, now show Roman Catholic pluralities; 1 state—Connecticut—has changed its Roman Catholic plurality to a majority; and 1 state—Idaho—which in 1890 showed a majority for the Latter-day Saints, now shows a plurality for that body. In the three changes from majorities to pluralities the principal gain was reported for the Protestant bodies in Colorado and Idaho, and for the Latter-day Saints in Wyoming.

In addition to the foregoing, there have been other notable changes in many states, although not sufficient to call for a different classification. Thus in Pennsylvania the percentage of communicants or members in Protestant bodies in 1890 was 66.8, and in 1906 it was only 57.7, nearly all the difference going to the Roman Catholic Church. Iowa, on the other hand, shows an increase in the percentage of Protestant membership, from 68.6 per cent in 1890 to 72.2 per cent in 1906.

A comparison of the percentages for continental United States shows that the Protestant bodies have fallen off from 68 per cent of the total membership in 1890 to 61.6 per cent in 1906; that the Roman Catholic Church has increased from 30.3 per cent in 1890 to 36.7 per cent in 1906; while the Latter-day Saints maintain the same proportion, eight-tenths of 1 per cent.

Comparing the geographic divisions it appears that the greatest change has been in the North Atlantic division, where the proportion represented by the Protestant bodies decreased from 50.9 per cent to 41.7 per cent, and the Roman Catholic Church advanced from 47.6 per cent to 56.6 per cent. The South Atlantic division shows virtually the same percentages for both 1890 and 1906. The North Central and South Central divisions show practically the same changes as are shown for the country as a whole; the Protestant bodies losing in the one case 4.7 per cent and in the other 6.6 per cent, while the Roman Catholic Church shows a corresponding gain. In the Western division, on the other hand, the percentage for the Protestant bodies advanced from 30.2 in 1890 to 36.6 in 1906; the percentage for the Roman Catholic Church fell from 50.7 in 1890 to 49.2 in 1906; and the percentage for the Latter-day Saints fell from 17.5 in 1890 to 12.1 in 1906.

STATE OR TERRITORY.	COMMUNICANTS OR MEMBERS: 1906.																
	Total.	Protestant bodies.															
		Total.		Baptist bodies.		Congregationalists.		Disciples or Christians.		German Evangelical Synod of North America.		Lutheran bodies.		Methodist bodies.		Presbyterian bodies.	
		Number.	Per cent of total.	Number.	Per cent of total.	Number.	Per cent of total.	Number.	Per cent of total.	Number.	Per cent of total.	Number.	Per cent of total.	Number.	Per cent of total.	Number.	Per cent of total.
Continental United States	32,936,445	20,287,742	61.6	5,662,234	17.2	700,480	2.1	1,142,359	3.5	293,137	0.9	2,112,494	6.4	5,749,838	17.5	1,830,555	5.6
North Atlantic division	10,306,946	4,296,706	41.7	571,346	5.5	337,502	3.3	39,771	0.4	35,359	0.3	522,606	5.1	958,008	9.3	617,944	6.0
Maine	212,988	96,341	45.2	32,854	15.4	21,093	9.9	397	0.2	......	......	1,045	0.5	20,112	9.4	364	0.2
New Hampshire	190,298	64,264	33.8	15,974	8.4	19,070	10.0	4	[1]	......	......	1,070	0.6	12,529	6.6	842	0.4
Vermont	147,223	63,895	43.4	9,951	6.8	22,109	15.0	316	0.2	......	......	408	0.3	17,671	12.0	1,636	1.1
Massachusetts	1,562,621	449,358	28.8	80,894	5.2	119,196	7.6	1,527	0.1	......	......	13,063	0.8	65,498	4.2	8,559	0.5
Rhode Island	264,712	64,141	24.2	19,878	7.5	9,858	3.7	79	[1]	......	......	2,873	1.1	7,892	3.0	1,741	0.7
Connecticut	502,560	196,248	39.0	27,872	5.5	65,554	13.0	866	0.2	......	......	19,713	3.9	34,663	6.9	2,425	0.5
New York	3,591,974	1,237,992	34.5	176,981	4.9	57,351	1.6	9,168	0.3	26,183	0.7	124,644	3.5	313,689	8.7	199,923	5.6
New Jersey	857,548	407,430	47.5	65,248	7.6	8,460	1.0	227	[1]	2,305	0.3	24,147	2.8	122,511	14.3	79,912	9.3
Pennsylvania	2,977,022	1,717,037	57.7	141,694	4.8	14,811	0.5	27,187	0.9	6,871	0.2	335,643	11.3	363,443	12.2	322,542	10.8
South Atlantic division	4,517,051	4,142,451	91.7	1,984,710	43.9	15,685	0.3	77,820	1.7	9,582	0.2	91,951	2.0	1,464,023	32.4	213,488	4.7
Delaware	71,251	46,779	65.7	2,921	4.1	......	......	75	0.1	......	......	731	1.0	32,402	45.5	5,200	7.3
Maryland	473,257	302,393	63.9	30,928	6.5	812	0.2	3,343	0.7	8,384	1.8	32,246	6.8	137,156	29.0	17,895	3.8
District of Columbia	136,759	91,474	66.9	37,024	27.1	2,984	2.2	2,170	1.6	350	0.3	3,104	2.3	20,077	14.7	8,636	6.3
Virginia	793,546	761,996	96.0	415,987	52.4	238	[1]	26,248	3.3	564	0.1	15,010	1.9	200,771	25.3	39,628	5.0
West Virginia	301,565	259,804	86.2	67,044	22.2	228	0.1	13,323	4.4	95	[1]	6,506	2.2	115,825	38.4	19,668	6.5
North Carolina	824,385	819,099	99.4	401,043	48.6	2,699	0.3	13,637	1.7	......	......	17,740	2.2	277,282	33.6	55,837	6.8
South Carolina	665,933	653,843	98.2	341,456	51.3	456	0.1	2,021	0.3	......	......	12,652	1.9	249,169	37.4	35,533	5.3
Georgia	1,029,037	1,007,205	97.9	596,319	57.9	5,581	0.5	13,749	1.3	189	[1]	3,233	0.3	349,079	33.9	24,040	2.3
Florida	221,318	199,858	90.3	91,988	41.6	2,687	1.2	3,254	1.5	......	......	729	0.3	82,262	37.2	7,051	3.2
North Central division	10,689,212	6,632,820	62.1	771,329	7.2	278,687	2.6	616,578	5.8	220,090	2.1	1,405,788	13.2	1,676,275	15.7	609,739	5.7
Ohio	1,742,873	1,171,084	67.2	92,112	5.3	43,555	2.5	88,787	5.1	35,138	2.0	132,439	7.6	355,444	20.4	138,768	8.0
Indiana	938,405	757,843	80.8	92,705	9.9	5,405	0.6	118,447	[illegible]	21,624	2.3	55,768	5.9	233,443	24.9	58,633	[illegible]
Illinois	2,077,197	1,109,764	53.4	152,870	7.4	54,875	2.6	105,068	.1	59,973	2.9	202,566	9.8	263,344	12.7	115,602	
Michigan	982,479	481,996	49.1	50,136	5.1	32,553	3.3	10,629	.1	20,436	2.1	105,803	10.8	128,675	13.1	37,900	
Wisconsin	1,000,903	490,871	49.0	21,716	2.2	26,163	2.6	1,715	.2	19,861	2.0	284,286	28.4	57,473	5.7	21,243	
Minnesota	834,442	450,434	54.0	24,309	2.9	22,264	2.7	3,560	.4	9,183	1.1	267,322	32.0	47,637	5.7	27,569	
Iowa	788,667	569,734	72.2	44,096	5.6	37,061	4.7	57,425	.3	11,681	1.5	117,668	14.9	164,329	20.8	60,081	
Missouri	1,199,239	802,116	66.9	218,353	18.2	11,046	0.9	166,137	1 .9	32,715	2.7	46,868	3.9	214,004	17.8	71,599	
North Dakota	159,053	97,361	61.2	4,596	2.9	5,290	3.3	147	.1	1,655	1.0	59,923	37.7	10,223	6.4	6,727	
South Dakota	161,961	100,625	62.1	6,198	3.8	8,599	5.3	1,478	.9	325	0.2	45,018	27.8	16,143	10.0	6,990	
Nebraska	345,803	240,516	69.6	17,939	5.2	16,629	4.8	19,613	.7	3,882	1.1	59,485	17.2	64,352	18.6	23,862	
Kansas	458,190	360,476	78.7	46,299	10.1	15,247	3.3	43,572	.5	3,617	0.8	28,642	6.3	121,208	26.5	40,765	
South Central division	5,726,570	4,595,464	80.2	2,262,933	39.5	16,062	0.3	349,944	6.1	25,877	0.5	49,586	0.9	1,479,745	25.8	287,949	5.0
Kentucky	858,324	689,326	80.3	311,583	36.3	996	0.1	136,110	15.9	12,189	1.4	4,940	0.6	156,007	18.2	47,822	5.6
Tennessee	697,570	677,947	97.2	277,170	39.7	2,426	0.3	56,315	8.1	......	......	3,225	0.5	241,396	34.6	79,337	11.4
Alabama	824,209	777,125	94.3	452,559	54.9	5,395	0.7	17,970	2.2	710	0.1	1,111	0.1	254,373	30.9	30,722	3.7
Mississippi	657,381	626,845	95.4	371,518	56.5	595	0.1	9,864	1.5	......	......	970	0.1	212,105	32.3	22,471	3.4
Louisiana	778,901	298,946	38.4	185,554	23.8	1,773	0.2	2,548	0.3	4,353	0.6	5,793	0.7	79,464	10.2	8,350	1.1
Arkansas	426,179	392,571	92.1	193,244	45.3	344	0.1	21,275	5.0	250	0.1	2,060	0.5	142,569	33.5	21,156	5.0
Oklahoma[2]	257,100	218,787	85.1	69,585	27.1	2,677	1.0	32,306	12.6	630	0.2	4,030	1.6	76,336	29.7	16,001	6.2
Texas	1,226,906	913,917	74.5	401,720	32.7	1,856	0.2	73,556	6.0	7,745	0.6	27,437	2.2	317,495	25.9	62,090	5.1
Western division	1,696,666	620,301	36.6	71,916	4.2	52,544	3.1	58,246	3.4	2,229	0.1	42,563	2.5	171,787	10.1	101,435	6.0
Montana	96,984	24,156	24.4	2,029	2.0	954	1.0	2,006	2.0	......	......	3,059	3.1	7,022	7.1	4,096	4.1
Idaho	74,578	22,796	30.6	2,374	3.2	1,487	2.0	3,252	4.	......	......	1,968	2.6	5,884	7.9	3,770	5.1
Wyoming	23,945	7,502	31.3	838	3.5	833	3.5	292	1.	125	0.5	908	3.8	1,657	6.9	984	4.1
Colorado	205,666	96,878	48.1	13,011	6.3	8,951	4.4	8,635	4.	833	0.4	5,053	2.5	27,867	13.5	18,957	9.2
New Mexico	137,009	14,593	10.7	2,403	1.8	270	0.	1,092	0.	......	......	100	0.1	6,560	4.8	2,935	2.1
Arizona	45,057	9,052	20.1	1,034	2.3	405	0.	536	1.	......	......	......	......	2,667	5.9	2,884	6.4
Utah	172,814	8,193	4.7	987	0.6	1,174	0.	250	0.	50	[1]	453	0.3	1,567	0.9	1,902	1.1
Nevada	14,944	3,199	21.4	316	2.1	180	1.	100	0.	......	......	148	1.0	618	4.1	520	3.5
Washington	191,976	114,070	59.4	12,807	6.7	10,025	5.	10,628	5.	......	......	13,464	7.0	31,700	16.5	16,758	8.7
Oregon	120,229	81,855	68.1	11,316	9.4	4,575	3.	10,420	8.	......	......	6,039	5.0	21,717	18.1	10,947	9.1
California	611,464	236,007	38.6	24,801	4.1	23,690	3.	21,033	3.	1,221	0.2	11,371	1.9	64,528	10.6	37,682	6.2

[1] Less than one-tenth of 1 per cent.

[2] Oklahoma and Indian Territory combined.

STATE OR TERRITORY.	COMMUNICANTS OR MEMBERS: 1906—continued.													
	Protestant bodies—Continued.								Roman Catholic Church.		Latter-day Saints.		All other bodies.	
	Protestant Episcopal Church.		Reformed bodies.		United Brethren bodies.		Other Protestant bodies.							
	Number.	Per cent of total.	Number.	Per cent of total.	Number.	Per cent of total.	Number.	Per cent of total.	Number.	Per cent of total.	Number.	Per cent of total.	Number.	Per cent of total.
Continental United States	886,942	2.7	449,514	1.4	296,050	0.9	1,164,139	3.5	12,079,142	36.7	256,647	0.8	312,914	1.0
North Atlantic division	467,067	4.5	290,131	2.8	57,081	0.6	399,891	3.9	5,833,658	56.6	2,911	(1)	173,671	1.7
Maine	5,520	2.6					14,956	7.0	113,419	53.3	507	0.2	2,721	1.3
New Hampshire	4,892	2.6					9,883	5.2	119,863	63.0			6,171	3.2
Vermont	5,278	3.6					6,526	4.4	82,272	55.9			1,056	0.7
Massachusetts	51,636	3.3	393	(1)			108,592	6.9	1,080,706	69.2	679	(1)	31,878	2.0
Rhode Island	15,443	5.8					6,377	2.4	195,951	74.0	306	0.1	4,314	1.6
Connecticut	37,466	7.5	1,262	0.3			6,427	1.3	299,513	59.6	44	(1)	6,755	1.3
New York	193,890	5.4	69,828	1.9	1,507	(1)	64,828	1.8	2,285,768	63.6	388	(1)	67,826	1.9
New Jersey	53,921	6.3	37,298	4.3			13,401	1.6	441,432	51.5			8,686	1.0
Pennsylvania	99,021	3.3	181,350	6.1	55,574	1.9	168,901	5.7	1,214,734	40.8	987	(1)	44,264	1.5
South Atlantic division	126,982	2.8	22,273	0.5	34,377	0.8	101,560	2.2	354,736	7.9	6,686	0.1	13,178	0.3
Delaware	3,796	5.3					1,654	2.3	24,228	34.0			244	0.3
Maryland	34,965	7.4	13,461	2.8	6,541	1.4	16,662	3.5	166,941	35.3	115	(1)	3,808	0.8
District of Columbia	13,692	10.0	580	0.4	260	0.2	2,597	1.9	43,778	32.0			1,507	1.1
Virginia	28,487	3.6	2,488	0.3	7,021	0.9	25,554	3.2	28,700	3.6	1,021	0.1	1,829	0.2
West Virginia	5,230	1.7	886	0.3	19,993	6.6	11,006	3.6	40,011	13.3	1,385	0.5	365	0.1
North Carolina	13,890	1.7	4,718	0.6			32,253	3.9	3,981	0.5	976	0.1	329	(1)
South Carolina	8,557	1.3	140	(1)			3,859	0.6	10,317	1.5	1,101	0.2	672	0.1
Georgia	9,790	1.0			521	0.1	4,704	0.5	19,273	1.9	386	(1)	2,173	0.2
Florida	8,575	3.9			41	(1)	3,271	1.5	17,507	7.9	1,702	0.8	2,251	1.0
North Central division	183,107	1.7	132,643	1.2	191,777	1.8	546,807	5.1	3,946,752	36.9	31,947	0.3	77,693	0.7
Ohio	32,399	1.9	51,328	2.9	71,338	4.1	129,776	7.4	557,650	32.0	1,507	0.1	12,632	0.7
Indiana	7,653	0.8	9,216	1.0	52,700	5.6	102,249	10.	174,849	18.6	1,090	0.	4,623	0.5
Illinois	36,364	1.8	9,946	0.5	19,701	0.9	89,455	4.	932,084	44.9	2,960	0.	32,389	1.6
Michigan	26,439	2.7	28,345	2.9	7,383	0.8	33,697	3.	492,135	50.1	4,335	0.	4,013	0.4
Wisconsin	16,527	1.7	11,459	1.1	2,180	0.2	28,248	2.	505,264	50.5	1,184	0.	3,584	0.4
Minnesota	18,763	2.2	2,255	0.3	1,282	0.2	26,290	3.	378,288	45.3	522	0.	5,198	0.6
Iowa	8,990	1.1	11,517	1.5	11,236	1.4	45,650	5.	207,607	26.3	8,328	1.	2,998	0.4
Missouri	13,328	1.1	1,284	0.1	3,616	0.3	23,166	1.	382,642	31.9	8,042	0.	6,439	0.5
North Dakota	2,227	1.4	1,059	0.7			5,514	3.	61,261	38.5	242	0.	189	0.1
South Dakota	7,065	4.4	2,711	1.7	257	0.2	5,851	3.	61,014	37.7	85	0.	237	0.1
Nebraska	6,903	2.0	,108	0.6	6,086	1.8	19,657	5.	100,763	29.1	1,568	0.	2,956	0.9
Kansas	6,459	1.4	1,415	0.3	15,998	3.5	37,254	8.	93,195	20.3	7,084	0.	2,435	0.5
South Central division	60,285	1.1	3,142	0.1	7,233	0.1	52,708	0.9	1,109,096	19.4	9,547	0.2	12,463	0.2
Kentucky	8,091	0.9	2,101	0.2	993	0.1	8,434	1.0	165,908	19.3	1,407	0.2	1,663	0.2
Tennessee	7,874	1.1	234	(1)	2,875	0.4	7,095	1.0	17,252	2.5	1,013	0.1	1,358	0.2
Alabama	8,961	1.1			30	(1)	5,294	0.6	42,285	5.1	2,124	0.3	2,675	0.3
Mississippi	5,704	0.9					3,618	0.6	28,576	4.3	1,214	0.2	746	0.1
Louisiana	9,070	1.2			361	(1)	1,680	0.2	477,774	61.3	455	0.1	1,726	0.2
Arkansas	4,315	1.0	60	(1)			7,278	1.7	32,397	7.6	538	0.1	673	0.2
Oklahoma [2]	2,024	0.8	747	0.3	2,974	1.2	11,477	4.5	36,548	14.2	1,296	0.5	469	0.2
Texas	14,246	1.2					7,772	0.6	308,356	25.1	1,500	0.1	3,133	0.3
Western division	49,501	2.9	1,325	0.1	5,582	0.3	63,173	3.7	834,900	49.2	205,556	12.1	35,909	2.1
Montana	3,290	3.3	135	0.1			1,563	1.6	72,359	73.1	510	0.5	1,959	2.0
Idaho	1,846	2.5			310	0.4	1,905	2.6	18,057	24.2	32,425	43.5	1,300	1.7
Wyoming	1,741	7.3					124	0.	10,264	42.9	5,211	21.	968	4.0
Colorado	6,832	3.3	111	0.1	720	0.4	7,908	3.	99,820	48.5	2,755	1.	4,213	2.0
New Mexico	869	0.6	70	0.1			294	0.	121,558	88.7	738	0.	120	0.1
Arizona	1,059	2.4					467	1.	29,810	66.2	6,175	13.	20	(1)
Utah	977	0.6					833	0.	8,356	4.8	151,525	87.	4,740	2.7
Nevada	1,210	8.1					107	0.	9,970	66.7	1,105	7.	670	4.5
Washington	6,780	3.5	379	0.2	1,079	0.6	10,450	5.	74,981	39.1	461	0.	2,464	1.3
Oregon	3,580	3.0	512	0.4	2,129	1.8	10,620	8.	35,317	29.4	1,817	1.	1,240	1.0
California	21,317	3.5	118	(1)	1,344	0.2	28,902	4.	354,408	58.0	2,834	0.	18,215	3.0

[1] Less than one-tenth of 1 per cent.

[2] Oklahoma and Indian Territory combined.

STATE OR TERRITORY.	COMMUNICANTS OR MEMBERS: 1890.																	
	Total.	Protestant bodies.																
		Total.		Baptist bodies.		Congregationalists.		Disciples or Christians.		German Evangelical Synod of North America.		Lutheran bodies.		Methodist bodies.		Presbyterian bodies.	
		Number.	Per cent of total.	Number.	Per cent of total.	Number.	Per cent of total.	Number.	Per cent of total.	Number.	Per cent of total.	Number.	Per cent of total.	Number.	Per cent of total.	Number.	Per cent of total.
Continental United States	20,597,954	14,007,187	68.0	3,712,468	18.0	512,771	2.5	641,051	3.1	187,432	0.9	1,231,072	6.0	4,589,284	22.3	1,277,851	6.2
North Atlantic division	6,176,015	3,142,031	50.9	435,043	7.0	290,352	4.7	18,132	0.3	24,502	0.4	333,736	5.4	774,544	12.5	454,530	7.4
Maine	159,846	99,194	62.1	35,038	21.9	21,523	13.5	293	0.2	......	......	904	0.6	23,041	14.4	224	0.1
New Hampshire	102,941	62,099	60.3	16,772	16.3	19,712	19.1	......	......	......	......	520	0.5	12,354	12.0	956	0.9
Vermont	106,315	61,495	57.8	11,258	10.6	20,465	19.2	262	0.2	......	......	174	0.2	17,527	16.5	1,267	1.2
Massachusetts	942,751	317,405	33.7	62,966	6.7	101,890	10.8	777	0.1	......	......	4,137	0.4	61,138	6.5	5,105	0.5
Rhode Island	148,008	49,590	33.5	17,293	11.7	7,192	4.9	35	(1)	......	......	590	0.4	7,353	5.0	828	0.6
Connecticut	309,341	152,300	49.2	22,600	7.3	59,154	19.1	337	0.1	......	......	5,762	1.9	30,815	10.0	1,864	0.6
New York	2,171,822	965,034	44.4	142,736	6.6	45,686	2.1	4,316	0.2	17,409	0.8	89,046	4.1	265,551	12.2	168,564	7.8
New Jersey	508,351	280,680	55.2	39,760	7.8	4,912	1.0	105	(1)	1,890	0.4	12,878	2.5	96,377	19.0	59,464	11.7
Pennsylvania	1,726,640	1,154,234	66.8	86,620	5.0	9,818	0.6	12,007	0.7	5,293	0.3	219,725	12.7	260,388	15.1	216,248	12.5
South Atlantic division	3,295,916	3,028,646	91.9	1,297,371	39.4	8,469	0.3	43,775	1.3	5,219	0.2	67,721	2.1	1,279,623	38.8	142,263	4.3
Delaware	48,679	36,903	75.8	2,006	4.1	......	......	95	0.2	......	......	296	0.6	25,786	53.0	4,622	9.5
Maryland	379,418	233,688	61.6	16,238	4.3	336	0.1	1,774	0.5	4,405	1.2	24,648	6.5	123,618	32.6	12,483	3.3
District of Columbia	94,203	55,150	58.5	19,372	20.6	1,399	1.5	700	0.7	......	......	2,997	3.2	16,309	17.4	5,128	5.4
Virginia	569,235	555,509	97.6	303,134	53.3	156	(1)	14,100	2.5	700	0.1	12,220	2.1	154,693	27.2	27,746	4.9
West Virginia	189,917	173,443	91.3	42,854	22.6	136	0.1	5,807	3.1	114	0.1	4,176	2.2	85,102	44.8	10,952	5.8
North Carolina	685,194	682,060	99.5	310,920	45.4	1,002	0.1	12,437	1.8	......	......	12,326	1.8	276,336	40.3	36,102	5.3
South Carolina	508,485	502,102	98.7	203,959	40.1	376	0.1	2,880	0.6	......	......	8,757	1.7	251,477	49.5	26,118	5.1
Georgia	679,051	665,393	98.0	357,241	52.6	3,880	0.6	4,676	0.7	......	......	1,932	0.3	275,784	40.6	14,538	2.1
Florida	141,734	124,398	87.8	41,647	29.4	1,184	0.8	1,306	0.9	......	......	369	0.3	70,458	49.7	4,574	3.2
North Central division	6,738,989	4,499,795	66.8	568,662	8.4	185,359	2.8	365,442	5.4	149,145	2.2	793,897	11.8	1,260,402	18.7	427,629	6.3
Ohio	1,215,409	867,099	71.3	68,033	5.6	32,281	2.7	54,425	4.5	31,617	2.6	89,569	7.4	272,737	22.4	103,607	8.5
Indiana	693,860	570,043	82.2	70,380	10.	3,081	0.	78,942	11.4	15,274	2.2	41,832	6.0	179,613	25.9	43,351	6.2
Illinois	1,202,588	713,467	59.3	109,640	9.	35,830	3.	60,867	5.1	37,138	3.1	116,807	9.7	189,358	15.7	77,218	6.4
Michigan	569,504	339,437	59.6	39,580	6.	24,582	4.	5,788	1.0	10,926	1.9	62,897	11.0	101,951	17.9	25,931	4.6
Wisconsin	556,355	304,591	54.7	16,913	3.	15,841	2.	1,317	0.2	11,410	2.1	160,919	28.9	43,696	7.9	14,154	2.5
Minnesota	532,590	258,663	48.6	16,441	3.	13,624	2.	1,917	0.4	5,567	1.0	145,907	27.4	32,199	6.0	15,055	2.8
Iowa	556,817	382,173	68.6	33,962	6.	23,733	4.	30,988	5.6	6,902	1.2	63,725	11.4	122,607	22.0	40,528	7.3
Missouri	735,839	564,295	76.7	159,371	21.	7,617	1.	97,773	13.3	25,676	3.5	27,099	3.7	162,514	22.1	53,510	7.3
North Dakota	59,496	33,039	55.5	2,298	3.	1,616	2.	20	(1)	440	0.7	18,269	30.7	4,889	8.2	3,044	5.1
South Dakota	85,490	59,682	69.8	4,052	4.	5,164	6.	490	0.6	......	......	23,314	27.3	12,116	14.2	4,778	5.6
Nebraska	194,466	140,512	72.3	13,481	6.	10,045	5.	7,715	4.0	2,142	1.1	27,297	14.0	42,941	22.1	15,065	7.7
Kansas	336,575	266,794	79.3	34,511	10.	11,945	3.	25,200	7.5	2,053	0.6	16,262	4.8	95,781	28.5	31,393	9.3
South Central division	3,555,324	3,085,283	86.8	1,382,992	38.9	6,640	0.2	192,390	5.4	8,026	0.2	25,567	0.7	1,193,379	33.6	213,113	6.0
Kentucky	606,397	512,018	4	229,524	37.9	449	0.1	77,	12.8	4,912	0.8	2,394	0.4	141,521	23.3	40,880	6.7
Tennessee	551,673	530,690	2	185,189	33.6	1,429	0.3	41,447	7.5	......	......	2,975	0.5	223,116	40.4	66,573	12.1
Alabama	559,171	542,181	.0	258,405	46.2	1,683	0.3	9,285	1.6	......	......	791	0.1	242,624	43.4	21,502	3.8
Mississippi	430,557	417,642	0	224,612	52.2	210	(1)	5,729	1.3	......	......	533	0.1	164,589	38.2	18,250	4.2
Louisiana	399,991	184,624	2	98,552	24.6	1,057	0.3	202	0.1	1,250	0.3	2,952	0.7	65,693	16.4	5,864	1.5
Arkansas	296,208	291,534	4	128,724	43.5	669	0.2	14,385	4.9	......	......	1,386	0.5	123,316	41.6	18,022	6.1
Oklahoma[2]	34,176	31,594	84.4	9,463	27.7	297	0.9	2,242	6.6	......	......	......	......	13,630	39.9	4,211	12.3
Texas	677,151	575,000	[illegible].9	248,523	36.7	846	0.1	41,859	6.2	1,864	0.3	14,556	2.1	218,890	32.3	37,811	5.6
Western division	831,710	251,432	30.2	28,400	3.4	21,951	2.6	21,312	2.6	450	0.1	10,131	1.2	81,336	9.8	40,326	4.8
Montana	32,478	7,047	21.7	683	2.1	345	1.1	785	2.4	......	......	394	1.2	2,425	7.5	1,232	3.8
Idaho	24,036	4,255	17.7	745	3.	105	0.4	350	1.5	......	......	401	1.7	1,162	4.8	815	3.4
Wyoming	11,705	3,134	26.8	262	2.	339	2.9	48	0.4	......	......	721	6.2	912	7.8	364	3.1
Colorado	86,837	36,627	42.2	4,944	5.	3,217	3.7	2,400	2.8	135	0.2	1,208	1.4	10,850	12.5	6,968	8.0
New Mexico	105,749	4,667	4.4	355	0.	175	0.2	65	0.1	......	......	64	0.1	2,360	2.2	1,275	1.2
Arizona	26,972	1,472	5.5	197	0.	162	0.6	78	0.3	......	......	......	......	656	2.4	188	0.7
Utah	128,115	3,776	2.9	327	0.	460	0.4	270	0.2	......	......	84	0.1	1,055	0.8	688	0.5
Nevada	5,877	1,397	23.8	63	1.	50	0.9	......	......	......	......	......	......	418	7.1	275	4.7
Washington	58,798	37,192	63.3	3,941	6.	3,154	5.4	5,816	9	......	......	1,912	3.3	12,097	21.6	4,343	7.4
Oregon	70,524	38,267	54.3	[illegible],500	7.	2,037	2.9	4,067	9.8	......	......	1,080	1.5	11,927	16.9	5,244	7.4
California	280,619	113,598	40.5	1,383	4.	1,907	4.2	7,433	2.6	315	0.1	4,267	1.5	36,874	13.1	18,934	6.7

[1] Less than one-tenth of 1 per cent.

[2] Oklahoma and Indian Territory combined.

STATE OR TERRITORY.	COMMUNICANTS OR MEMBERS: 1890—continued.													
	Protestant bodies—Continued.								Roman Catholic Church.		Latter-day Saints.		All other bodies.	
	Protestant Episcopal Church.		Reformed bodies.		United Brethren bodies.		Other Protestant bodies.							
	Number.	Per cent of total.	Number.	Per cent of total.	Number.	Per cent of total.	Number.	Per cent of total.	Number.	Per cent of total.	Number.	Per cent of total.	Number.	Per cent of total.
Continental United States	532,048	2.6	309,458	1.5	225,281	1.1	788,471	3.8	6,241,708	30.3	166,125	0.8	182,934	0.9
North Atlantic division	285,543	4.6	207,095	3.4	34,904	0.6	283,570	4.6	2,939,986	47.6	1,736	[1]	92,262	1.5
Maine	3,291	2.1					14,880	9.3	57,548	36.0	442	0.3	2,662	1.7
New Hampshire	2,911	2.8					8,874	8.6	39,920	38.8			922	0.9
Vermont	4,335	4.1					6,207	5.8	42,810	40.3			2,010	1.9
Massachusetts	26,855	2.8	62	[1]			54,475	5.8	614,627	65.2	457	[1]	10,262	1.1
Rhode Island	9,458	6.4					6,841	4.6	96,755	65.4	233	0.2	1,430	1.0
Connecticut	26,652	8.6	150	[1]			4,966	1.6	152,945	49.4	8	[1]	4,088	1.3
New York	127,218	5.9	55,973	2.6	953	[1]	47,582	2.2	1,153,130	53.1	158	[1]	53,500	2.5
New Jersey	30,103	5.9	26,210	5.2			8,981	1.8	223,274	43.9	21	[1]	4,376	0.9
Pennsylvania	54,720	3.2	124,700	7.2	33,951	2.0	130,764	7.6	558,977	32.4	417	[1]	13,012	0.8
South Atlantic division	81,078	2.5	16,627	0.5	22,284	0.7	64,216	1.9	254,883	7.7	1,395	[1]	10.992	0.3
Delaware	2,719	5.6	69	0.1			1,310	2.7	11,776	24.2				
Maryland	23,938	6.3	10,741	2.8	4,736	1.2	10,771	2.8	141,410	37.3	75	[1]	4,245	1.1
District of Columbia	7,476	7.9	301	0.3			1,408	1.5	37,593	39.9			1,400	1.5
Virginia	20,371	3.6	1,819	0.3	5,306	0.9	15,264	2.7	12,356	2.2	171	[1]	1,199	0.2
West Virginia	2,906	1.5	794	0.4	12,242	6.4	8,360	4.4	15,653	8.2	406	0.2	415	0.2
North Carolina	8,186	1.2	2,903	0.4			21,848	3.2	2,640	0.4	108	[1]	386	0.1
South Carolina	5,742	1.1					2,793	0.5	5,360	1.1	203	[1]	820	0.2
Georgia	5,515	0.8					1,827	0.3	11,228	1.7	175	[1]	2,255	0.3
Florida	4,225	3.0					635	0.4	16,867	11.9	257	0.2	212	0.1
North Central division	107,850	1.6	83,582	1.2	162,196	2.4	395,629	5.9	2,172,330	32.2	15,816	0.2	51,048	0.8
Ohio	17,454	1.4	36,255	3.0	53,500	4.4	107,621	8.9	336,114	27.7	678	0.1	11,518	0.9
Indiana	5,185	0.7	6,761	1.	42,697	6.2	82,927	12.0	119,100	17.2	380	0.1	4,337	0.6
Illinois	19,099	1.6	5,385	0.	16,622	1.4	45,508	3.8	475,324	39.5	1,909	0.2	11,888	1.0
Michigan	18,034	3.2	15,404	2.	10,803	1.9	23,541	4.1	222,261	39.0	1,540	0.3	6,266	1.1
Wisconsin	10,457	1.9	7,765	1.	1,750	0.3	20,369	3.7	249,164	44.8	341	0.1	2,259	0.4
Minnesota	11,142	2.1	968	0.	803	0.2	15,040	2.8	271,769	51.0	224	[1]	1,934	0.4
Iowa	6,481	1.2	5,741	1.	10,673	1.9	36,833	6.6	164,522	29.5	5,303	1.0	4,819	0.9
Missouri	8,828	1.2	586	0.	4,361	0.6	16,960	2.3	162,864	22.1	3,189	0.4	5,491	0.7
North Dakota	892	1.5	287	0.			1,284	2.2	26,427	44.4			30	0.1
South Dakota	2,649	3.1	1,883	2.	602	0.7	4,634	5.4	25,720	30.1	88	0.1		
Nebraska	4,036	2.1	1,408	0.	6,031	3.1	10,351	5.3	51,503	26.5	1,058	0.5	1,393	0.7
Kansas	3,593	1.1	1,139	0.	14,356	4.3	30,561	9.1	67,562	20.1	1,106	0.3	1,113	0.3
South Central division	37,222	1.0	1,586	[1]	1,708	[1]	22,640	0.6	452,841	12.7	1,779	0.1	15,421	0.4
Kentucky	7,161	1.2	1,350	0.2	567	0.1	5,613	0.9	92,504	15.3	249	[1]	1,626	0.3
Tennessee	5,671	1.0	236	[1]	1,141	0.2	3,235	0.6	17,950	3.3	198	[1]	2,835	0.5
Alabama	6,085	1.1					1,890	0.3	13,230	2.4	592	0.1	3,168	0.6
Mississippi	3,560	0.8					159	[1]	11,348	2.6	197	[1]	1,370	0.3
Louisiana	5,162	1.3					3,802	1.0	211,763	52.9			3,604	0.9
Arkansas	2,381	0.8					2,651	0.9	3,845	1.3	60	[1]	769	0.3
Oklahoma [2]	105	0.3					1,646	4.8	2,510	7.3	46	0.1	26	0.1
Texas	7,097	1.0					3,554	0.5	99,691	14.7	437	0.1	2,023	0.3
Western division	20,355	2.4	568	0.1	4,187	0.5	22,416	2.7	421,668	50.7	145,399	17.5	13,211	1.6
Montana	1,104	3.4					79	0.2	25,149	77.4	122	0.4	160	0.5
Idaho	364	1.5			100	0.4	213	0.9	4,809	20.0	14,972	62.6		
Wyoming	467	4.0					21	0.2	7,185	61.4	1,336	11.	50	0.4
Colorado	3,814	4.4	35	[1]	585	0.7	2,471	2.8	47,111	54.3	1,762	2.	1,337	1.5
New Mexico	373	0.4							100,576	95.1	456	0.	50	[1]
Arizona	179	0.7					12	[1]	19,000	70.4	6,500	24.		
Utah	751	0.6					141	0.1	5,958	4.7	118,201	92.	180	0.1
Nevada	535	9.1					56	1.0	3,955	67.3	525	8.		
Washington	1,696	2.9	167	0.3	1,100	1.9	2,364	4.0	20,848	35.5	34	0.	724	1.2
Oregon	1,849	2.6	298	0.4	1,696	2.4	4,569	6.5	30,231	42.9	95	0.	1,931	2.7
California	9,221	3.3	68	[1]	706	0.3	12,490	4.5	156,846	55.9	1,396	0.	8,779	3.1

[1] Less than one-tenth of 1 per cent.

[2] Oklahoma and Indian Territory combined.

DIAGRAM 2.—DISTRIBUTION OF COMMUNICANTS OR MEMBERS, BY PRINCIPAL FAMILIES OR DENOMINATIONS, FOR EACH STATE AND TERRITORY: 1906.

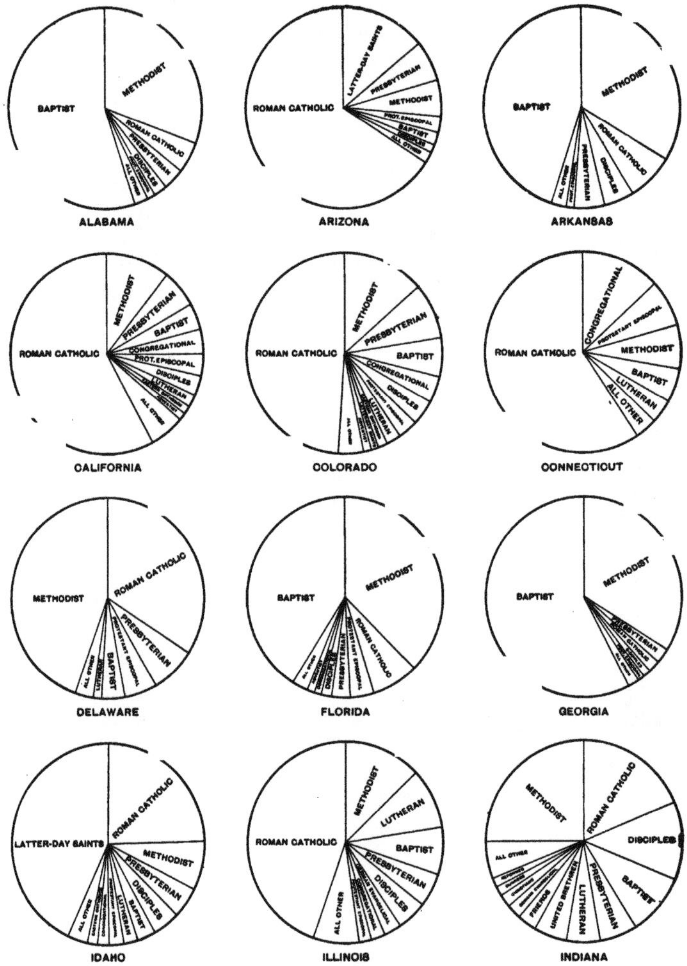

DIAGRAM 2.—DISTRIBUTION OF COMMUNICANTS OR MEMBERS, BY PRINCIPAL FAMILIES OR DENOMINATIONS, FOR EACH STATE AND TERRITORY: 1906—Continued.

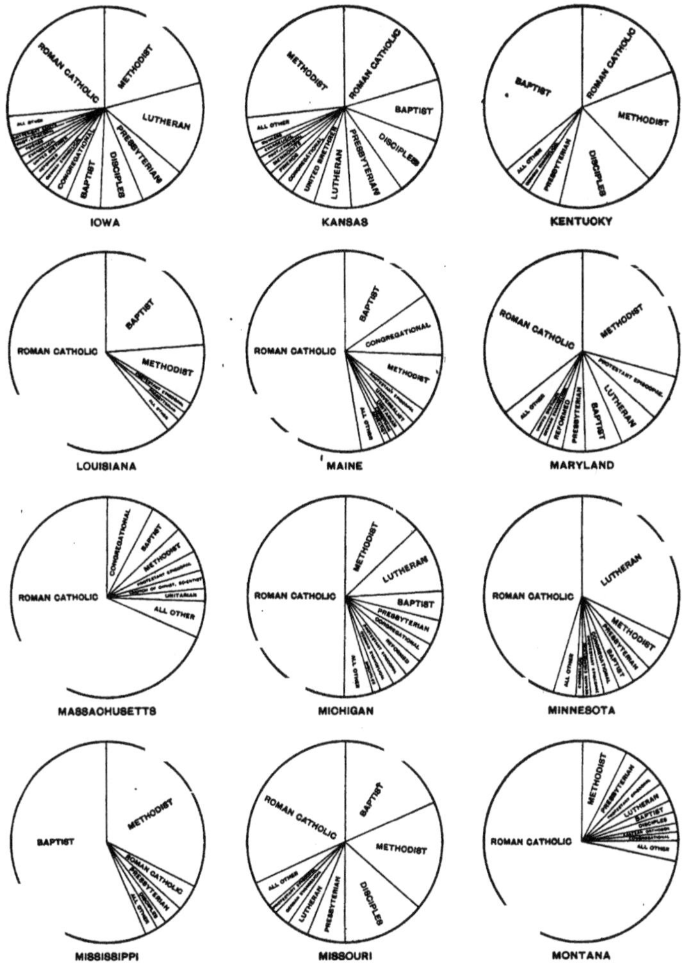

DIAGRAM 2.—DISTRIBUTION OF COMMUNICANTS OR MEMBERS, BY PRINCIPAL FAMILIES OR DENOMINATIONS, FOR EACH STATE AND TERRITORY: 1906—Continued.

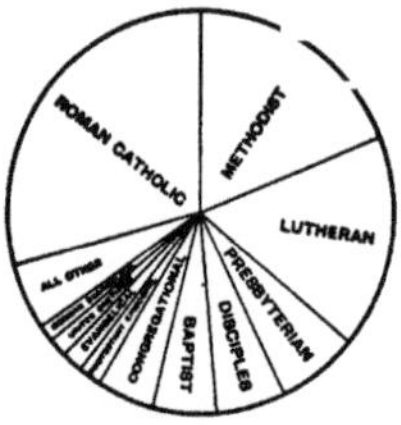

NEBRASKA

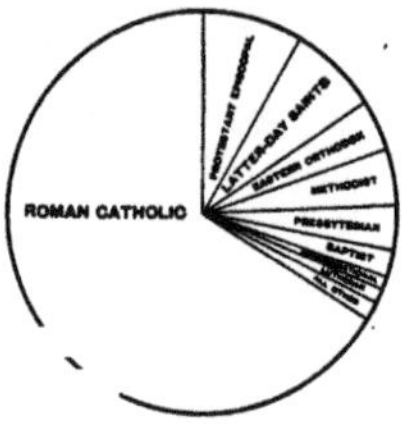

NEVADA

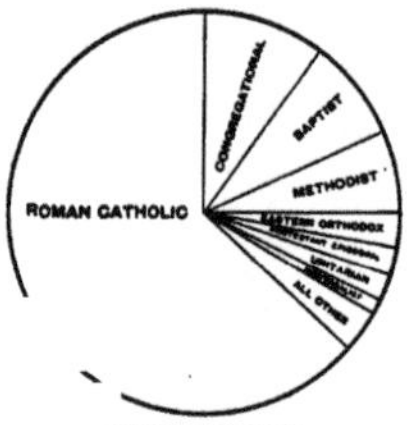

NEW HAMPSHIRE

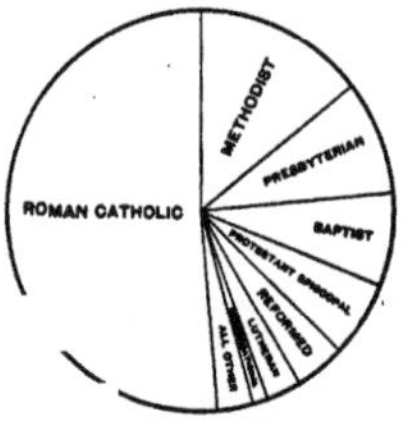

NEW JERSEY

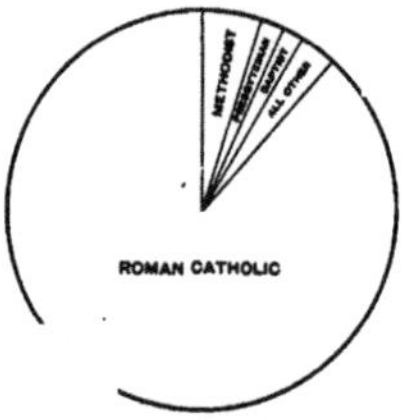

NEW MEXICO

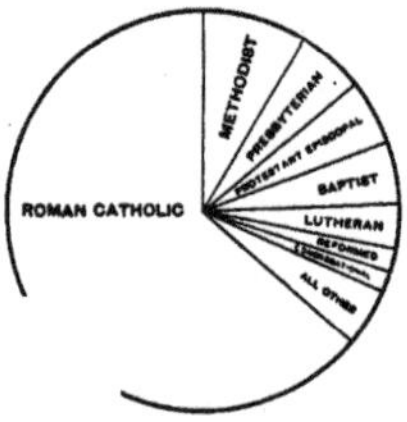

NEW YORK

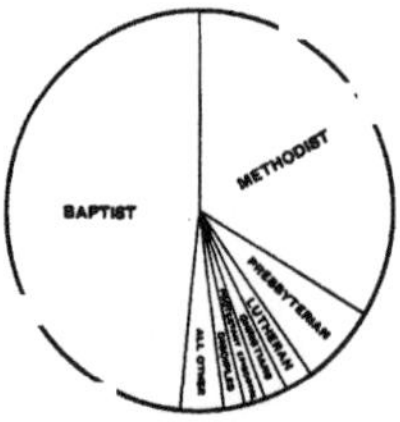

NORTH CAROLINA

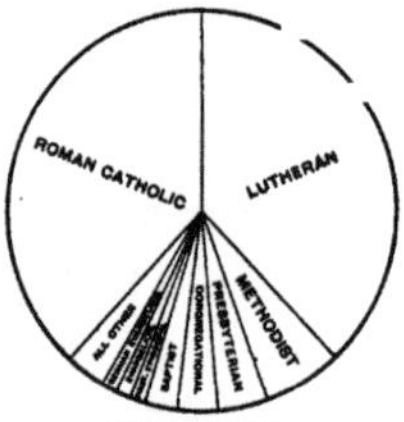

NORTH DAKOTA

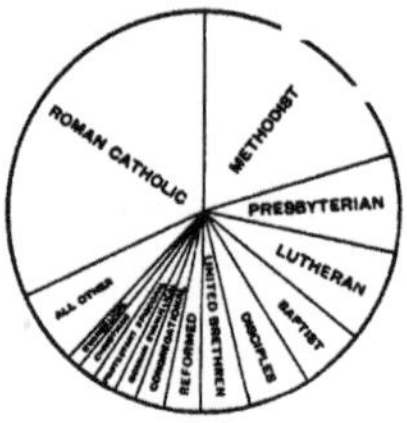

OHIO

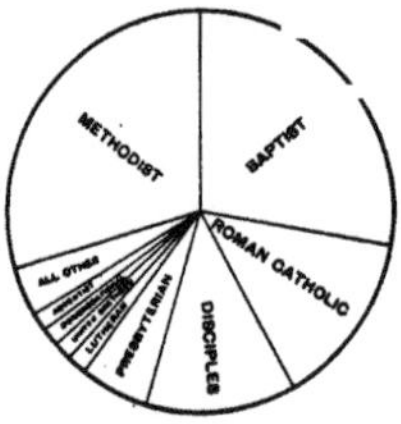

OKLAHOMA

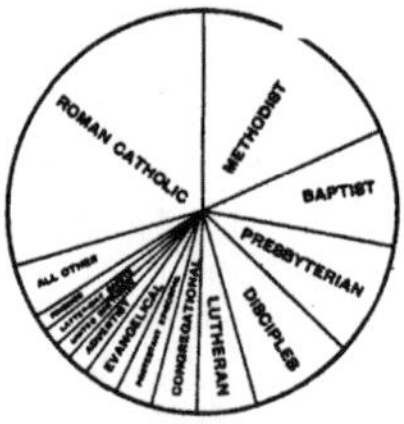

OREGON

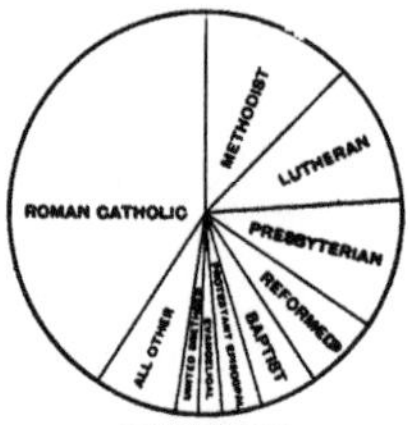

PENNSYLVANIA

DIAGRAM 2.—DISTRIBUTION OF COMMUNICANTS OR MEMBERS, BY PRINCIPAL FAMILIES OR DENOMINATIONS, FOR EACH STATE AND TERRITORY: 1906—Continued.

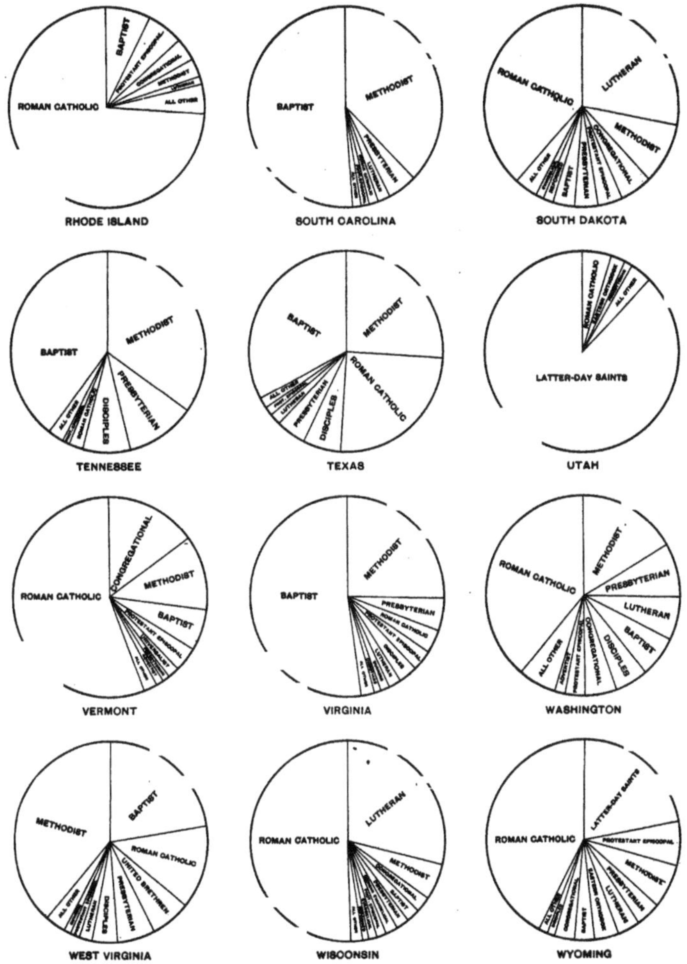

In the North Atlantic division the 41.7 per cent of the communicants or members shown for the Protestant bodies is made up as follows: Methodist bodies, 9.3 per cent; Presbyterian bodies, 6 per cent; Baptist bodies, 5.5 per cent; Lutheran bodies, 5.1 per cent; Protestant Episcopal Church, 4.5 per cent; and Congregationalists, 3.3 per cent. As compared with the figures for 1890, all share in the general falling off, although this is most marked in the Methodist bodies, which report only 9.3 per cent of all communicants in 1906, as compared with 12.5 per cent in 1890.

In the South Atlantic and South Central divisions the Baptist bodies lead, and their percentage of the total church membership shows an increase over 1890 of 4.5 in the South Atlantic states and of six-tenths of 1 in the South Central. The percentage for the Methodist bodies shows a decrease in each division—6.4 in the South Atlantic states and 7.8 in the South Central.

In the North Central division the 62.1 per cent of the total members shown for the Protestant bodies is made up as follows: Methodist bodies, 15.7 per cent; Lutheran bodies, 13.2 per cent; Baptist bodies, 7.2 per cent; Disciples or Christians, 5.8 per cent; Presbyterian bodies, 5.7 per cent; and Congregationalists, 2.6 per cent. As compared with 1890, the percentage for the Lutheran bodies shows an increase of 1.4, and that for the Disciples or Christians an increase of four-tenths of 1; while the percentages for the other bodies show a decrease.

In the Western division the general increase in Protestant membership from 30.2 per cent in 1890 to 36.6 per cent in 1906 is shared by most of the bodies. For 1906 the Methodist bodies report 10.1 per cent; Presbyterian bodies, 6 per cent; Baptist bodies, 4.2 per cent; Disciples or Christians, 3.4 per cent; Congregationalists, 3.1 per cent; and the Protestant Episcopal Church, 2.9 per cent.

The Roman Catholic Church reports 56.6 per cent of all the members in the North Atlantic division; 49.2 per cent in the Western; 36.9 per cent in the North Central; 19.4 per cent in the South Central; and 7.9 per cent in the South Atlantic. As compared with the report for 1890, the percentage that the Roman Catholic membership represents of the total membership shows an increase of 9 in the North Atlantic division; 4.7 in the North Central; 6.7 in the South Central; two-tenths of 1 in the South Atlantic; and a loss of 1.5 in the Western.

The Latter-day Saints, while showing a considerable increase in members over 1890 (90,522), retain the same percentage of the entire membership, but in the Western division, where they are strongest, they have fallen from 17.5 per cent to 12.1 per cent of the total membership.

These general statements support what has already been said under the head of communicants or members (see page 28), that the change in the relative strength of the religious bodies is due primarily to the influence of immigration. Where immigration has been inconsiderable, as in the South Atlantic division, there have been no material changes in the relative strength of the different bodies.

The following tabular statement for 1906 shows for each state and territory the 5 leading families or separate denominations arranged in the order of their rank, together with the proportion which their membership bears to the total church membership reported in each case:

STATE OR TERRITORY.	PRINCIPAL FAMILY OR SEPARATE DENOMINATION RANKING IN 1906— First. Name.	First. Per cent of total membership for state or territory.	Second. Name.	Second. Per cent of total membership for state or territory.	Third. Name.	Third. Per cent of total membership for state or territory.
Continental United States:						
North Atlantic division—						
Maine	Roman Catholic Church	53.3	Baptist bodies	15.4	Congregationalists	9.9
New Hampshire	Roman Catholic Church	63.0	Congregationalists	10.0	Baptist bodies	8.4
Vermont	Roman Catholic Church	55.9	Congregationalists	15.0	Methodist bodies	12.0
Massachusetts	Roman Catholic Church	69.2	Congregationalists	7.6	Baptist bodies	5.2
Rhode Island	Roman Catholic Church	74.0	Baptist bodies	7.5	Protestant Episcopal Church	5.8
Connecticut	Roman Catholic Church	59.6	Congregationalists	13.0	Protestant Episcopal Church	7.5
New York	Roman Catholic Church	63.6	Methodist bodies	8.7	Presbyterian bodies	5.6
New Jersey	Roman Catholic Church	51.5	Methodist bodies	14.3	Presbyterian bodies	9.3
Pennsylvania	Roman Catholic Church	40.8	Methodist bodies	12.2	Lutheran bodies	11.3
South Atlantic division—						
Delaware	Methodist bodies	45.5	Roman Catholic Church	34.0	Presbyterian bodies	7.3
Maryland	Roman Catholic Church	35.3	Methodist bodies	29.0	Protestant Episcopal Church	7.4
District of Columbia	Roman Catholic Church	32.0	Baptist bodies	27.1	Methodist bodies	14.7
Virginia	Baptist bodies	52.4	Methodist bodies	25.3	Presbyterian bodies	5.0
West Virginia	Methodist bodies	38.4	Baptist bodies	22.2	Roman Catholic Church	13.3
North Carolina	Baptist bodies	48.6	Methodist bodies	33.6	Presbyterian bodies	6.8
South Carolina	Baptist bodies	51.3	Methodist bodies	37.4	Presbyterian bodies	5.3
Georgia	Baptist bodies	57.9	Methodist bodies	33.9	Presbyterian bodies	2.3
Florida	Baptist bodies	41.6	Methodist bodies	37.2	Roman Catholic Church	7.9
North Central division—						
Ohio	Roman Catholic Church	32.0	Methodist bodies	20.4	Presbyterian bodies	8.0
Indiana	Methodist bodies	24.9	Roman Catholic Church	18.6	Disciples or Christians	12.6
Illinois	Roman Catholic Church	44.9	Methodist bodies	12.7	Lutheran bodies	9.8
Michigan	Roman Catholic Church	50.1	Methodist bodies	13.1	Lutheran bodies	10.8
Wisconsin	Roman Catholic Church	50.5	Lutheran bodies	28.4	Methodist bodies	5.7
Minnesota	Roman Catholic Church	45.3	Lutheran bodies	32.0	Methodist bodies	5.7
Iowa	Roman Catholic Church	26.3	Methodist bodies	20.8	Lutheran bodies	14.9
Missouri	Roman Catholic Church	31.9	Baptist bodies	18.2	Methodist bodies	17.8
North Dakota	Roman Catholic Church	38.5	Lutheran bodies	37.7	Methodist bodies	6.4
South Dakota	Roman Catholic Church	37.7	Lutheran bodies	27.8	Methodist bodies	10.0
Nebraska	Roman Catholic Church	29.1	Methodist bodies	18.6	Lutheran bodies	17.2
Kansas	Methodist bodies	26.5	Roman Catholic Church	20.3	Baptist bodies	10.1
South Central division—						
Kentucky	Baptist bodies	36.3	Roman Catholic Church	19.3	Methodist bodies	18.2
Tennessee	Baptist bodies	39.7	Methodist bodies	34.6	Presbyterian bodies	11.4
Alabama	Baptist bodies	54.9	Methodist bodies	30.9	Roman Catholic Church	5.1
Mississippi	Baptist bodies	56.5	Methodist bodies	32.3	Roman Catholic Church	4.3
Louisiana	Roman Catholic Church	61.3	Baptist bodies	28.8	Methodist bodies	10.2
Arkansas	Baptist bodies	45.3	Methodist bodies	33.5	Roman Catholic Church	7.6
Oklahoma[1]	Methodist bodies	29.7	Baptist bodies	27.1	Roman Catholic Church	14.2
Texas	Baptist bodies	32.7	Methodist bodies	25.9	Roman Catholic Church	25.1
Western division—						
Montana	Roman Catholic Church	73.1	Methodist bodies	7.1	Presbyterian bodies	4.1
Idaho	Latter-day Saints	43.5	Roman Catholic Church	24.2	Methodist bodies	7.9
Wyoming	Roman Catholic Church	42.9	Latter-day Saints	21.8	Protestant Episcopal Church	7.3
Colorado	Roman Catholic Church	48.5	Methodist bodies	13.5	Presbyterian bodies	9.2
New Mexico	Roman Catholic Church	88.7	Methodist bodies	4.8	Presbyterian bodies	2.1
Arizona	Roman Catholic Church	66.2	Latter-day Saints	13.7	Presbyterian bodies	6.4
Utah	Latter-day Saints	87.7	Roman Catholic Church	4.8	Presbyterian bodies	1.1
Nevada	Roman Catholic Church	66.7	Protestant Episcopal Church	8.1	Latter-day Saints	7.4
Washington	Roman Catholic Church	39.1	Methodist bodies	16.5	Presbyterian bodies	8.7
Oregon	Roman Catholic Church	29.4	Methodist bodies	18.1	Baptist bodies	9.4
California	Roman Catholic Church	58.0	Methodist bodies	10.6	Presbyterian bodies	6.2

[1] Oklahoma and Indian Territory combined.

STATE OR TERRITORY.	PRINCIPAL FAMILY OR SEPARATE DENOMINATION RANKING IN 1906—continued.			
	Fourth.		Fifth.	
	Name.	Per cent of total membership for state or territory.	Name.	Per cent of total membership for state or territory.
Continental United States:				
North Atlantic division—				
Maine	Methodist bodies	9.4	Protestant Episcopal Church	2.
New Hampshire	Methodist bodies	6.6	Protestant Episcopal Church	2.
Vermont	Baptist bodies	6.8	Protestant Episcopal Church	3.
Massachusetts	Methodist bodies	4.2	Protestant Episcopal Church	3.
Rhode Island	Congregationalists	3.7	Methodist bodies	3.6
Connecticut	Methodist bodies	6.9	Baptist bodies	5.8
New York	Protestant Episcopal Church	5.4	Baptist bodies	4.9
New Jersey	Baptist bodies	7.6	Protestant Episcopal Church	6.2
Pennsylvania	Presbyterian bodies	10.8	Reformed bodies	6.7
South Atlantic division				
Delaware	Protestant Episcopal Church	5.3	Baptist bodies	4.1
Maryland	Lutheran bodies	6.8	Baptist bodies	6.5
District of Columbia	Protestant Episcopal Church	10.0	Presbyterian bodies	6.3
Virginia	Roman Catholic Church	3.6	Protestant Episcopal Church	3.6
West Virginia	United Brethren bodies	6.6	Presbyterian bodies	6.5
North Carolina	Lutheran bodies	2.2	Protestant Episcopal Church	1.7
South Carolina	Lutheran bodies	1.9	Roman Catholic Church	1.5
Georgia	Roman Catholic Church	1.9	Disciples or Christians	1.3
Florida	Protestant Episcopal Church	3.9	Presbyterian bodies	3.2
North Central division—				
Ohio	Lutheran bodies	7.6	Baptist bodies	5.3
Indiana	Baptist bodies	9.9	Presbyterian bodies	6.2
Illinois	Baptist bodies	7.4	Presbyterian bodies	5.6
Michigan	Baptist bodies	5.1	Presbyterian bodies	3.9
Wisconsin	Congregationalists	2.6	Baptist bodies	2.2
Minnesota	Presbyterian bodies	3.3	Baptist bodies	2.9
Iowa	Presbyterian bodies	7.6	Disciples or Christians	7.3
Missouri	Disciples or Christians	13.9	Presbyterian bodies	6.0
North Dakota	Presbyterian bodies	4.2	Congregationalists	3.3
South Dakota	Congregationalists	5.3	Protestant Episcopal Church	4.4
Nebraska	Presbyterian bodies	6.9	Disciples or Christians	5.7
Kansas	Disciples or Christians	9.5	Presbyterian bodies	8.9
South Central division—				
Kentucky	Disciples or Christians	15.9	Presbyterian bodies	5.6
Tennessee	Disciples or Christians	8.1	Roman Catholic Church	2.5
Alabama	Presbyterian bodies	3.7	Disciples or Christians	2.2
Mississippi	Presbyterian bodies	3.4	Disciples or Christians	1.5
Louisiana	Protestant Episcopal Church	1.2	Presbyterian bodies	1.1
Arkansas	Disciples or Christians	5.0	Presbyterian bodies	5.0
Oklahoma[1]	Disciples or Christians	12.6	Presbyterian bodies	6.2
Texas	Disciples or Christians	6.0	Presbyterian bodies	5.1
Western division—				
Montana	Protestant Episcopal Church	3.3	Lutheran bodies	3.1
Idaho	Presbyterian bodies	5.1	Disciples or Christians	4.4
Wyoming	Methodist bodies	6.9	Presbyterian bodies	4.1
Colorado	Baptist bodies	6.3	Congregationalists	4.4
New Mexico	Baptist bodies	1.8	Disciples or Christians	0.8
Arizona	Methodist bodies	5.9	Protestant Episcopal Church	2.4
Utah	Methodist bodies	0.9	Congregationalists	0.7
Nevada	Methodist bodies	4.1	Presbyterian bodies	3.5
Washington	Lutheran bodies	7.0	Baptist bodies	6.7
Oregon	Presbyterian bodies	9.1	Disciples or Christians	8.7
California	Baptist bodies	4.1	Congregationalists	3.9

[1] Oklahoma and Indian Territory combined.

It is to be observed from the foregoing statement that in most cases the 5 leading families or separate denominations listed contain at least three-fourths of the total church membership in 1906 and that in a few instances the proportion thus represented falls but little short of the entire membership reported, as, for example, in New Mexico and Mississippi, due in the first case to the predominance of members of the Roman Catholic Church and in the latter case to the large proportion represented by members of the Baptist and Methodist bodies.

The 5 states containing the largest proportions of the members reported for each principal family or separate denomination in 1906 are given in the order of their rank in the following tabular statement:

DENOMINATION.	STATE OR TERRITORY RANKING IN 1906— First.		Second.		Third.		Fourth.		Fifth.	
	Name.	Per cent of total membership for denomination.	Name.	Per cent of total membership for denomination.	Name.	Per cent of total membership for denomination.	Name.	Per cent of total membership for denomination.	Name.	Per cent of total membership for denomination.
All denominations	New York	10.9	Pennsylvania	9.0	Illinois	6.3	Ohio	5.3	Massachusetts	4.7
Protestant bodies	Pennsylvania	8.5	New York	6.1	Ohio	5.8	Illinois	5.5	Georgia	5.0
Baptist bodies	Georgia	10.5	Alabama	8.0	Virginia	7.3	Texas	7.1	North Carolina	7.1
Congregationalists	Massachusetts	17.0	Connecticut	9.4	New York	8.2	Illinois	7.8	Ohio	6.2
Disciples or Christians	Missouri	14.5	Kentucky	11.9	Indiana	10.4	Illinois	9.2	Ohio	7.8
German Evangelical Synod of North America.	Illinois	20.5	Ohio	12.0	Missouri	11.2	New York	8.9	Indiana	7.4
Lutheran bodies	Pennsylvania	15.9	Wisconsin	13.5	Minnesota	12.7	Illinois	9.6	Ohio	6.8
Methodist bodies	Pennsylvania	6.3	Ohio	6.2	Georgia	6.1	Texas	5.5	New York	5.5
Presbyterian bodies	Pennsylvania	17.6	New York	10.9	Ohio	7.6	Illinois	6.3	New Jersey	4.4
Protestant Episcopal Church	New York	21.9	Pennsylvania	11.2	New Jersey	6.1	Massachusetts	5.8	Connecticut	4.2
Reformed bodies	Pennsylvania	40.3	New York	15.5	Ohio	11.4	New Jersey	8.3	Michigan	6.3
United Brethren bodies	Ohio	24.1	Pennsylvania	18.8	Indiana	17.8	West Virginia	6.8	Illinois	6.7
Other Protestant bodies	Pennsylvania	14.5	Ohio	11.1	Massachusetts	9.3	Indiana	8.8	Illinois	7.7
Roman Catholic Church	New York	18.9	Pennsylvania	10.1	Massachusetts	8.9	Illinois	7.7	Ohio	4.6
Latter-day Saints	Utah	59.0	Idaho	12.6	Iowa	3.2	Missouri	3.1	Arizona	2.4
All other bodies	New York	21.7	Pennsylvania	14.1	Illinois	10.4	Massachusetts	10.2	California	5.8

As indicated by the foregoing statement, the 5 leading states shown for the Protestant bodies, taken as a whole, contained only a little more than three-tenths (30.9 per cent) of all the members so included for 1906, whereas the 5 states shown for the Roman Catholic Church contained fully one-half (50.2 per cent) of all the members reported for that denomination, and those shown for the Latter-day Saints four-fifths (80.3 per cent) of all their reported membership.

In the case of all but 2 of the Protestant families and denominations represented, the 5 leading states contained either very nearly or more than one-half of their reported membership, the percentages ranging from 46.8 for the Presbyterian bodies to as high as 81.8 for the Reformed bodies. The 5 states listed for the Baptist bodies contained, on the other hand, only two-fifths (40 per cent) of the membership reported by the constituent denominations, and, similarly, the 5 states listed for the Methodist bodies contained less than three-tenths (29.6 per cent) of their reported membership. For each of these 2 families more than 5,000,000 members were reported in 1906, but this membership was very widely scattered over the country. As shown by the table on page 46, there were in 1906 over 100,000 members of Baptist bodies in each of 15 states, and, similarly, of Methodist bodies in each of 22 states.

The membership of Baptist bodies is especially large in the Southern states, and the 5 leading states in point of membership, as before stated, are all Southern states. For 1 of them (Georgia) there were reported 4 states, between 400,000 and 500,000 members; for each of 3 other states, also, there were reported between 300,000 and 400,000 members; for each of 2 other states, between 200,000 and 300,000 members; and for 5 states, between 100,000 and 200,000 members.

Of the 5 leading states shown for the Methodist bodies, however, the first, second, and fifth were Northern states and the third and fourth Southern states. For each of the first 2 states (Pennsylvania and Ohio) there were reported somewhat more than 350,000 members, and for each of the remaining 3 states, between 300,000 and 350,000 members; but besides these states there were 9 other states for each of which between 200,000 and 300,000 members were reported, and 8 other states for each of which between 100,000 and 200,000 members were reported.

The membership of the Roman Catholic Church, on the other hand, although also widely distributed among the states and territories, is more nearly concentrated in the larger and more thickly settled states of the North and East. There are 23 states for each of which there were reported in 1906 over 100,000 members of the Roman Catholic Church, but the 5 leading states, as before stated, contained fully one-half of its entire reported membership. Considerably more than 2,000,000 members were shown for New York, more than 1,000,000 members each for Pennsylvania and Massachusetts, very nearly 1,000,000 members for Illinois, and more than 500,000 members for Ohio;

500,000 members were reported for 1 other state (Wisconsin); between 400,000 and 500,000 members for each of 3 states; between 300,000 and 400,000 members for each of 4 states; between 200,000 and 300,000 members for each of 2 states; and between 100,000 and 200,000 members for each of 8 states.

RELATION OF CHURCH MEMBERSHIP TO POPULATION.

Statistics showing the relation between the church membership of the different states and territories and the total population possess a certain amount of interest, although too much importance should not be attached to them, owing to the fact that the percentage of the population which is presumably barred from membership by reason of childhood or youth, varies considerably in the different states, as does also the number of those, already referred to, affiliated with churches but not registered as members. The following table shows, for each state and territory, in 1890 and 1906, respectively, the proportion of the total population reported as church members, classified according to membership in Protestant bodies, the Roman Catholic Church, or other bodies. The distribution of the population of continental United States according to church membership is also given for 1890 and 1906, respectively, in Diagram 3, and a similar distribution of the population of each state or territory, for 1906 only, in Diagram 4.

STATE OR TERRITORY.	POPULATION.											
	Total.		Percentage—									
			Reported as church members.								Not reported as church members.	
			Total.		Protestant.		Roman Catholic.		All other.			
	1906[1]	1890	1906	1890	1906	1890	1906	1890	1906	1890	1906	1890
Continental United States	84,246,252	[2]62,947,714	39.1	32.7	24.1	22.3	14.3	9.9	0.7	0.6	60.9	67.3
North Atlantic division	23,388,682	17,406,969	44.1	35.5	18.4	18.1	24.9	16.9	0.8	0.5	55.9	64.5
Maine	714,494	661,086	29.8	24.2	13.5	15.0	15.9	8.7	0.5	0.5	70.2	75.8
New Hampshire	432,624	376,530	44.0	27.3	14.9	16.5	27.7	10.6	1.4	0.2	56.0	72.7
Vermont	350,373	332,422	42.0	32.0	18.2	18.5	23.5	12.9	0.3	0.6	58.0	68.0
Massachusetts	3,043,346	2,238,947	51.3	42.1	14.8	14.2	35.5	27.5	1.1	0.5	48.7	57.9
Rhode Island	490,387	345,506	54.0	42.8	13.1	14.4	40.0	28.0	0.9	0.5	46.0	57.2
Connecticut	1,005,716	746,258	50.0	41.5	19.5	20.4	29.8	20.5	0.7	0.5	50.0	58.5
New York	8,226,990	6,003,174	43.7	36.2	15.0	16.1	27.8	19.2	0.8	0.9	56.3	63.8
New Jersey	2,196,237	1,444,933	39.0	35.2	18.6	19.4	20.1	15.5	0.4	0.3	61.0	64.8
Pennsylvania	6,928,515	5,258,113	43.0	32.8	24.8	22.0	17.5	10.6	0.7	0.3	57.0	67.2
South Atlantic division	11,413,343	8,857,922	39.6	37.2	36.3	34.2	3.1	2.9	0.2	0.1	60.4	62.8
Delaware	194,479	168,493	36.6	28.9	24.1	21.9	12.5	7.0	0.1	....	63.4	71.1
Maryland	1,275,434	1,042,390	37.1	36.4	23.7	22.4	13.1	13.6	0.3	0.4	62.9	63.6
District of Columbia	307,716	230,392	44.4	40.9	29.7	23.9	14.2	16.3	0.5	0.6	55.6	59.1
Virginia	1,973,104	1,655,980	40.2	34.4	38.6	33.5	1.5	0.7	0.1	0.1	59.8	65.6
West Virginia	1,076,406	762,794	28.0	24.9	24.1	22.7	3.7	2.1	0.2	0.1	72.0	75.1
North Carolina	2,059,326	1,617,949	40.0	42.3	39.8	42.2	0.2	0.2	0.1	(3)	60.0	57.7
South Carolina	1,453,818	1,151,149	45.8	44.2	45.0	43.6	0.7	0.5	0.1	0.1	54.2	55.8
Georgia	2,443,719	1,837,353	42.1	37.0	41.2	36.2	0.8	0.6	0.1	0.1	57.9	63.0
Florida	629,341	391,422	35.2	36.2	31.8	31.8	2.8	4.3	0.6	0.1	64.8	63.8
North Central division	28,628,813	22,410,417	37.3	30.1	23.2	20.1	13.8	9.7	0.4	0.3	62.7	69.9
Ohio	4,448,677	3,672,329	39.2	33.1	26.3	23.6	12.5	9.2	0.3	0.3	60.8	66.9
Indiana	2,710,898	2,192,404	34.6	31.6	28.0	26.0	6.4	5.4	0.2	0.2	65.4	68.4
Illinois	5,418,670	3,826,352	38.3	31.4	20.5	18.6	17.2	12.4	0.7	0.4	61.7	68.6
Michigan	2,584,533	2,093,890	38.0	27.2	18.6	16.2	19.0	10.6	0.3	0.4	62.0	72.8
Wisconsin	2,260,930	1,693,330	44.3	32.9	21.7	18.0	22.3	14.7	0.2	0.2	55.7	67.1
Minnesota	2,025,615	1,310,283	41.2	40.6	22.2	19.7	18.7	20.7	0.3	0.2	58.8	59.4
Iowa	2,205,690	1,912,297	35.8	29.1	25.8	20.0	9.4	8.6	0.5	0.5	64.2	70.9
Missouri	3,363,153	2,679,185	35.7	27.5	23.9	21.1	11.4	6.1	0.4	0.3	64.3	72.5
North Dakota	463,784	190,983	34.3	31.2	21.0	17.3	13.2	13.8	0.1	(3)	65.7	68.8
South Dakota	465,908	348,600	34.8	24.5	21.6	17.1	13.1	7.4	0.1	(3)	65.2	75.5
Nebraska	1,068,484	1,062,656	32.4	18.3	22.5	13.2	9.4	4.8	0.4	0.2	67.6	81.7
Kansas	1,612,471	1,428,108	28.4	23.6	22.4	18.7	5.8	4.7	0.3	0.2	71.6	76.4
South Central division	16,130,741	11,170,137	35.5	31.8	28.5	27.6	6.9	4.1	0.1	0.2	64.5	68.2
Kentucky	2,320,298	1,858,635	37.0	32.6	29.7	27.5	7.2	0	1	0.1	63.0	67.4
Tennessee	2,172,476	1,767,518	32.1	31.2	31.2	30.0	0.8	0	1	0.2	67.9	68.8
Alabama	2,017,877	1,513,401	40.8	36.9	38.5	35.8	2.1	9	2	0.2	59.2	63.1
Mississippi	1,708,272	1,289,600	38.5	33.4	36.7	32.4	1.7	5.9	1	0.1	61.5	66.6
Louisiana	1,539,449	1,118,588	50.6	35.8	19.4	16.5	31.0	18.9	1	0.3	49.4	64.2
Arkansas	1,421,574	1,128,211	30.0	26.3	27.6	25.8	2.3	0.3	1	0.1	70.0	73.7
Oklahoma[4]	[5]1,414,177	258,657	18.2	13.2	15.5	12.2	2.6	1.0	0.1	(3)	81.8	86.8
Texas	3,536,618	2,235,527	34.7	30.3	25.8	25.7	8.7	4.5	0.1	0.1	65.3	69.7
Western division	4,684,673	3,102,269	36.2	26.8	13.2	8.1	17.8	13.6	5.2	5.1	63.8	73.2
Montana	303,575	142,924	32.6	22.7	8.0	4.9	23.8	17.6	8	0.2	67.4	77.3
Idaho	205,704	88,548	36.3	27.1	11.1	4.8	8.8	5.4	4	16.9	63.7	72.9
Wyoming	103,673	62,555	23.1	18.7	7.2	5.0	9.9	11.5	0	2.2	76.9	81.3
Colorado	615,570	413,249	33.4	21.0	16.1	8.9	16.2	11.4	1	0.7	66.6	79.0
New Mexico	216,328	160,282	63.3	66.0	6.7	2.9	56.2	62.7	4	0.3	36.7	34.0
Arizona	143,745	88,243	31.3	30.6	6.3	1.7	20.7	21.5	3	7.4	68.7	69.4
Utah	316,331	210,779	54.6	60.8	2.6	1.8	2.6	2.8	4	56.2	45.4	39.2
Nevada	42,335	47,355	35.3	12.4	7.6	3.0	23.6	8.4	2	1.1	64.7	87.6
Washington	614,625	357,232	31.2	16.5	18.6	10.4	12.2	5.8	5	0.2	68.8	83.5
Oregon	474,738	317,704	25.3	22.2	17.2	12.0	7.4	9.5	0.6	0.6	74.7	77.8
California	1,648,049	1,213,398	37.1	23.1	14.3	9.4	21.5	12.9	[illegible].3	0.8	62.9	76.9

[1] Estimated.
[2] Includes the population of Indian Territory and Indian reservations.
[3] Less than one-tenth of 1 per cent.
[4] Oklahoma and Indian Territory combined.
[5] Special census, 1907.

Diagram 3.—*Proportion of the population reported as Protestant, Roman Catholic, and "all other" church members, and proportion not reported as church members, for continental United States: 1890 and 1906.*

[*Note.*—The designation "not church members" represents the difference between the number reported as communicants or members and the total population; it embraces, therefore, children too young to become church members, as well as that portion of the population which is eligible to church membership, although not affiliated with any religious denomination.]

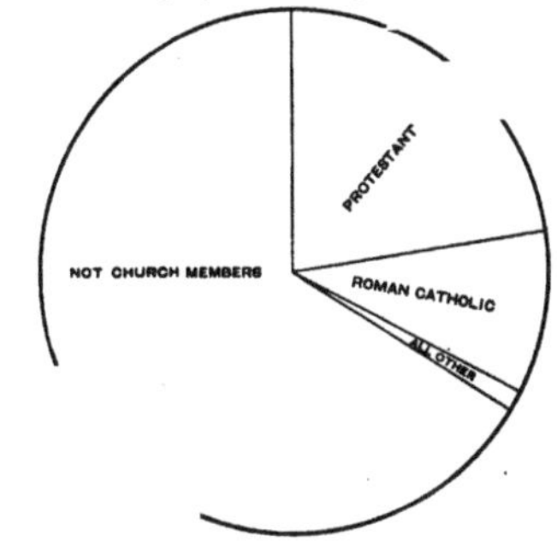

1890

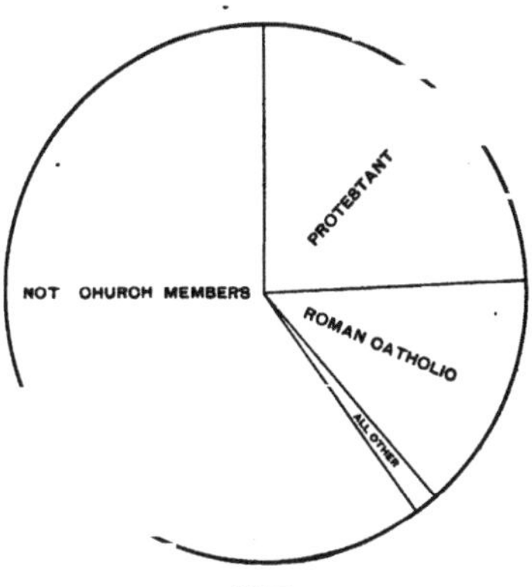

1906

Of the total estimated population of continental United States in 1906, 39.1 per cent, or not quite two-fifths, were reported as church members. The corresponding percentage for 1890 was 32.7, or somewhat less than one-third, so that the proportion of the population included within the churches was larger by 6.4 per cent in 1906 than at the time of the earlier census. Compared with 1890, as represented by the difference (6.4) between the percentages shown for the two years, is divided among the three classes of members as follows: Protestant bodies, 1.8; Roman Catholic Church, 4.4; "all other bodies," one-tenth of 1 per cent.

The percentage of total population reported as church members varied considerably in the different states, ranging for 1906 from 18.2 in Oklahoma to 63.3 in New Mexico. The low percentage in Oklahoma is probably partly due to the fact that this state is of comparatively recent settlement, while the high percentage for New Mexico results from the fact that the majority of the population is affiliated with the Roman Catholic Church, which reports as communicants a larger proportion of those affiliated with it than do most Protestant bodies.

There were, in 1906, 6 states and territories in which at least 50 per cent of the population were church members, and 12 others in which between 40 and 50 per cent of the population were church members. The following statement shows these states and territories arranged according to the percentage which church members represent of the total population, together with the percentage of the total population reported for each of the three main denominational groupings:

STATE OR TERRITORY.	PERCENTAGE OF TOTAL POPULATION REPRESENTED IN 1906 BY MEMBERS OF—			
	All religious bodies.	Protestant bodies.	Roman Catholic Church.	All other bodies.
New Mexico	63.3	6.7	56.2	0.4
Utah	54.6	2.6	2.6	49.4
Rhode Island	54.0	13.1	40.0	9
Massachusetts	51.3	14.8	35.5	1
Louisiana	50.6	19.4	31.0	1
Connecticut	50.0	19.5	29.8	7
South Carolina	45.8	45.0	0.7	1
District of Columbia	44.4	29.7	14.2	5
Wisconsin	44.3	21.7	22.3	3
New Hampshire	44.0	14.9	27.7	4
New York	43.7	15.0	27.8	8
Pennsylvania	43.0	24.8	17.5	7
Georgia	42.1	41.2	0.8	1
Vermont	42.0	18.2	23.5	3
Minnesota	41.2	22.2	18.7	3
Alabama	40.8	38.5	2.1	0.2
Virginia	40.2	38.6	1.5	0.1
North Carolina	40.0	39.8	0.2	0.1

It will be observed that in 12 out of the 18 states shown in the statement at least 10 per cent of the total population were communicants of the Roman Catholic Church, the proportion rising to over 56 per cent in New Mexico and exceeding 25 per cent in 6 other states. In general, the table shows that states having a relatively large Roman Catholic population will as a rule show a higher percentage of church members than states in which this church has a relatively small representation. This of course merely reflects the fact, already alluded to, that in the case of the Roman Catholic Church the communicants reported represent a much larger proportion of the total population affiliated with the church in question than is the case with respect to Protestant bodies, so that where those of Catholic affiliation represent a large proportion of the total population, the proportion reported as church

DIAGRAM 4.—PROPORTION OF THE POPULATION REPORTED AS PROTESTANT, ROMAN CATHOLIC, AND "ALL OTHER" CHURCH MEMBERS, AND PROPORTION NOT REPORTED AS CHURCH MEMBERS, FOR EACH STATE AND TERRITORY: 1906.

[*Note.*—The designation "not church members" represents the difference between the number reported as communicants or members and the total population; it embraces, therefore, children too young to become church members, as well as that portion of the population which is eligible to church membership, although not affiliated with any religious denomination.]

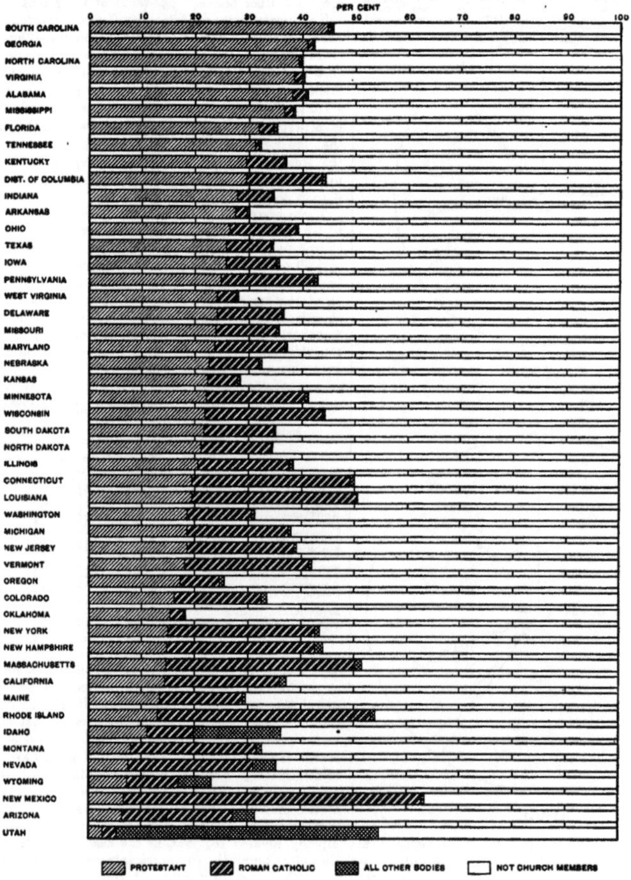

Referring to the table on page 58 it will be seen that the proportion of the total population represented in the membership of Protestant churches varies much less widely for the different states than does the corresponding proportion for communicants of the Roman Catholic Church. The membership of Protestant bodies is least important relatively in Utah, where it represents only 2.6 per cent of the total population, and most important in South Carolina, where it represents 45 per cent of the total population. The corresponding percentages for the Roman Catholic Church, on the other hand, vary from two-tenths of 1 per cent in North Carolina to 56.2 per cent in New Mexico, showing a much wider range of variation than was shown for Protestant bodies, and indicating a much more uneven distribution of the members of this communion.

It appears, in general, as already indicated, that communicants of the Roman Catholic Church are most numerous relatively in the states into which there is a large influx resulting from immigration, and in the states and territories of the Southwest adjoining the Catholic country of Mexico, and least numerous in the Southern states, into which immigration has so far been relatively slight.

The large percentage of the population of Utah shown in the table under the heading "all other" results from the preponderance of the Latter-day Saints in that state.

It also should be stated here that the percentages given in the last two columns of the table represent, for each state and territory in 1890 and 1906, respectively, simply the difference between the number of communicants or members reported and the total population, and that they cover, therefore, children and infants too young to become church members as well as that portion of the population which is eligible to church membership, although not affiliated with any religious denomination.

The table on page 58 also shows that in 13 states the proportion of the total population reported as being communicants or members of religious organizations was greater by at least 10 per cent in 1906 than in 1890. The following statement shows for each of these states the relative gain (or loss) in the percentage for 1906 over that for 1890 of the total population represented by members of all religious organizations, and by members of Protestant bodies, the Roman Catholic Church, and all other religious bodies, respectively:

STATE.	RELATIVE GAIN IN THE PERCENTAGE FOR 1906 OVER THAT FOR 1890 OF THE TOTAL POPULATION REPORTED AS MEMBERS OF—			
	All religious bodies.	Protestant bodies.	Roman Catholic Church.	All other bodies.
Nevada	22.9	4.6	15.2	3.1
New Hampshire	16.7	[1]1.6	17.1	1.2
Louisiana	14.8	2.9	12.1	[1]0.2
Washington	14.7	8.2	6.4	0.3
Nebraska	4.1	9.3	4.6	0.2
California	4.0	4.9	8.6	0.5
Colorado	2.4	7.2	4.8	0.4
Wisconsin	1.4	3.7	7.6	(²)
Rhode Island	1.2	[1]1.3	12.0	0.4
Michigan	0.8	2.4	8.4	[1]0.1
South Dakota	0.3	4.5	5.7	0.1
Pennsylvania	0.2	2.8	6.9	0.4
Vermont	10.0	[1]0.3	10.6	[1]0.3

[1] Decrease. [2] Less than one-tenth of 1 per cent.

Of the following tabular statements, one presents the 10 states showing the largest relative gains in the percentage for 1906 over that for 1890 of the total population represented by communicants of Protestant bodies and of the Roman Catholic Church, respectively, while the other makes a corresponding presentation for the states showing relative losses:

STATES AND TERRITORIES SHOWING RELATIVE GAINS IN THE PERCENTAGE FOR 1906 OVER THAT FOR 1890 OF THE TOTAL POPULATION REPORTED AS MEMBERS OF—

Protestant bodies.		Roman Catholic Church.	
Name.	Relative gain.	Name.	Relative gain.
Nebraska	9.3	New Hampshire	17.1
Washington	8.2	Nevada	15.2
Colorado	7.2	Louisiana	12.1
Idaho	6.3	Rhode Island	12.0
District of Columbia	5.8	Vermont	10.6
Iowa	5.8	Connecticut	9.3
Oregon	5.2	New York	8.6
Virginia	5.1	California	8.6
Georgia	5.0	Michigan	8.4
California	4.9	Massachusetts	8.0

STATES AND TERRITORIES SHOWING RELATIVE LOSS IN THE PERCENTAGE FOR 1906 OVER THAT FOR 1890 OF THE TOTAL POPULATION REPORTED AS MEMBERS OF—

Protestant bodies.		Roman Catholic Church.	
Name.	Relative loss.	Name.	Relative loss.
North Carolina	2.4	New Mexico	6.5
New Hampshire	1.6	District of Columbia	2.1
Maine	1.5	Oregon	2.1
Rhode Island	1.3	Minnesota	2.0
New York	1.1	Wyoming	1.6
Connecticut	0.9	Florida	1.5
New Jersey	0.8	Arizona	0.8
Vermont	0.3	North Dakota	0.6
		Maryland	0.5
		Utah	0.2
		Tennessee	0.2

From a study of the preceding figures it appears that the largest gains in the proportion of the total population represented by church members have been for the most part in those states which are most affected by immigration, and that they are more or less generally coincident with the growth of the Roman Catholic Church. It is to be noted, however, that in New Mexico, where communicants of the Roman Catholic Church represented more than one-half the total population in 1906, there has been a relative loss in the percentage of the total population reported as members of that denomination, from 62.7 in 1890 to 56.2 in 1906. This is probably to some extent due to the fact that there has been a large influx of new settlers into this territory since 1890, which has reduced not only the proportion of the total population having Catholic affiliation, as just stated, but also the proportion reported as having any church connection, in the latter case from 66 in 1890 to 63.3 in 1906. A similar instance is shown for Utah, where the percentage representing "all others" (comprising Latter-day Saints largely) has decreased from 56.2 in 1890 to 49.4 in 1906 and, as a result, that representing all church members, from 60.8 in 1890 to 54.6 in 1906.

The following table and Diagram 5 show, by states and territories, the number of communicants per 1,000 population in 1906 for each of the 12 principal families and separate denominations—those for which 250,000 members or more were reported, and Diagram 6 shows their proportional strength:

STATE OR TERRITORY.	Estimated population: 1906.	NUMBER OF COMMUNICANTS OR MEMBERS PER 1,000 POPULATION: 1906.														
		All Protestant bodies.	Baptist bodies.	Congregationalists.	Disciples or Christians.	German Evangelical Synod of North America.	Lutheran bodies.	Methodist bodies.	Presbyterian bodies.	Protestant Episcopal Church.	Reformed bodies.	United Brethren bodies.	Other Protestant bodies.	Roman Catholic Church.	Latter-day Saints.	All other bodies.
Continental United States	84,246,252	241	67	8	14	3	25	68	22	11	5	4	14	143	3	4
North Atlantic division	23,388,682	184	24	14	2	2	22	41	26	20	12	2	17	249	(1)	7
Maine	714,494	185	46	30	1	......	1	28	1	8	......	......	21	159	1	4
New Hampshire	432,624	149	37	44	(1)	......	2	29	2	11	......	......	23	277	......	14
Vermont	350,373	182	28	63	1	......	1	50	5	15	......	......	19	235	......	3
Massachusetts	3,043,346	148	27	39	1	......	4	22	3	17	(1)	......	36	355	(1)	10
Rhode Island	490,387	131	41	20	(1)	......	6	16	4	31	......	......	13	400	1	9
Connecticut	1,005,716	195	28	65	1	......	20	34	2	37	1	......	6	298	(1)	7
New York	8,226,990	150	22	7	1	3	15	38	24	24	8	(1)	8	278	(1)	8
New Jersey	2,196,237	186	30	4	(1)	1	11	56	36	25	17	......	6	201	......	4
Pennsylvania	6,928,515	248	20	2	4	1	48	52	47	14	26	8	24	175	(1)	6
South Atlantic division	11,413,343	363	174	1	7	1	8	128	19	11	2	3	9	31	1	1
Delaware	194,479	241	15	......	(1)	......	4	167	27	20	......	......	9	125	......	1
Maryland	1,275,434	237	24	1	3	7	25	108	14	27	11	5	13	131	(1)	3
District of Columbia	307,716	297	120	10	7	1	10	65	28	44	2	1	8	142	......	5
Virginia	1,973,104	386	211	(1)	13	(1)	8	102	20	14	1	4	13	15	1	1
West Virginia	1,076,406	241	62	(1)	12	(1)	6	108	18	5	1	19	10	37	1	(1)
North Carolina	2,059,326	398	195	1	7	......	9	135	27	7	2	......	16	2	(1)	(1)
South Carolina	1,453,818	450	235	(1)	1	......	9	171	24	6	(1)	......	3	7	1	(1)
Georgia	2,443,719	412	244	2	6	(1)	1	148	10	4	......	(1)	2	8	(1)	1
Florida	629,341	318	146	4	5	......	1	131	11	14	......	(1)	5	28	3	4
North Central division	28,628,813	232	27	10	22	8	49	59	21	6	5	7	19	138	1	3
Ohio	4,448,677	263	21	10	20	8	30	80	31	7	12	16	29	125	(1)	3
Indiana	2,710,898	280	34	2	44	8	21	86	22	3	3	19	38	64	(1)	2
Illinois	5,418,670	205	28	10	19	11	37	49	21	7	2	4	17	172	1	6
Michigan	2,584,533	186	19	13	4	8	41	50	15	10	11	3	13	190	2	2
Wisconsin	2,260,930	217	10	12	1	9	126	25	9	7	5	1	12	223	1	2
Minnesota	2,025,615	222	12	11	2	5	182	24	14	9	1	1	13	187	(1)	3
Iowa	2,205,690	258	20	17	26	5	53	75	27	4	5	5	21	94	4	1
Missouri	3,363,153	239	65	3	49	10	14	64	21	4	(1)	1	7	114	2	2
North Dakota	463,784	210	10	11	(1)	4	129	22	15	5	2	......	12	132	1	(1)
South Dakota	465,908	216	13	18	3	1	97	35	15	15	6	1	13	131	(1)	1
Nebraska	1,068,484	225	17	16	18	4	56	60	22	6	2	6	18	94	1	3
Kansas	1,612,471	224	29	9	27	2	18	75	25	4	1	10	23	58	1	2
South Central division	16,130,741	285	140	1	22	2	3	92	18	4	(1)	(1)	3	69	1	1
Kentucky	2,320,298	297	134	(1)	59	5	2	67	21	3	1	(1)	4	72	1	1
Tennessee	2,172,476	312	128	1	26	......	1	111	37	4	(1)	1	3	8	(1)	1
Alabama	2,017,877	385	224	3	9	(1)	1	126	15	4	......	(1)	3	21	1	1
Mississippi	1,708,272	367	217	(1)	6	......	1	124	13	3	......	......	2	17	1	(1)
Louisiana	1,539,449	194	121	1	2	3	4	52	5	6	......	(1)	1	310	(1)	1
Arkansas	1,421,574	276	136	(1)	15	(1)	1	100	15	3	(1)	......	5	23	(1)	(1)
Oklahoma[2]	[3]1,414,177	155	49	2	23	(1)	3	54	11	1	1	2	8	26	1	(1)
Texas	3,536,618	258	114	1	21	2	8	90	18	4	......	......	2	87	(1)	1
Western division	4,684,673	132	15	11	12	(1)	9	37	22	11	(1)	1	13	178	44	8
Montana	303,575	80	7	3	7	......	10	23	13	11	(1)	......	5	238	2	6
Idaho	205,704	111	12	7	16	......	10	29	18	9	......	2	9	88	158	6
Wyoming	103,673	72	8	8	3	1	9	16	9	17	......	......	1	99	50	9
Colorado	615,570	161	21	15	14	1	8	45	31	11	(1)	1	13	162	4	7
New Mexico	216,328	67	11	1	5	......	(1)	30	14	4	(1)	......	1	562	3	1
Arizona	143,745	63	7	3	4	......	......	19	20	7	......	......	3	207	43	(1)
Utah	316,331	26	3	4	1	(1)	1	5	6	3	......	......	3	26	479	15
Nevada	42,335	76	7	4	2	......	3	15	12	29	......	......	3	236	26	16
Washington	614,625	186	21	16	17	......	22	52	27	11	1	2	17	122	1	4
Oregon	474,738	172	24	10	22	......	13	46	23	8	1	4	22	74	4	3
California	1,648,049	143	15	14	13	1	7	39	23	13	(1)	1	18	215	2	11

[1] Less than 1 per 1,000 of population.
[2] Oklahoma and Indian Territory combined
[3] Special census, 1907.

According to the foregoing table, the Roman Catholic Church had in 1906 at least 100 communicants per 1,000 population in 28 states, the Baptist bodies in 13 states, the Methodist bodies in 12 states, the Lutheran bodies in 3 states, and the Latter-day Saints in 2 states.

Considering the states having at least 100 communicants per 1,000 population, it appears that, for the Roman Catholic Church, the range is from 562 for New Mexico to 114 for Missouri. For Rhode Island, the proportion, although not so high as for New Mexico, is very large, or 400 per 1,000 population, and for 2 other states—Massachusetts and Louisiana—it is between 300 and 400.

For the Baptist bodies the range in the 13 states under consideration is very much narrower—from 244 for Georgia to 114 for Texas, 5 states showing a proportion of over 200 members, and 8 states between 100 and 200 members in every 1,000 population.

For the Methodist bodies there is no state for which the proportion of members per 1,000 population is in excess of 200, the highest shown for any of the 12 states considered being 171 for South Carolina, and the lowest 100 for Arkansas.

The Lutheran bodies have 132 members per 1,000 population in Minnesota, 129 in North Dakota, and 126 in Wisconsin; and, similarly, the Latter-day Saints have 479 in Utah and 158 in Idaho.

DIAGRAM 5.—NUMBER OF COMMUNICANTS OR MEMBERS PER 1,000 OF THE POPULATION, FOR 12 PRINCIPAL FAMILIES OR DENOMINATIONS, FOR EACH STATE AND TERRITORY: 1906.

ROMAN CATHOLIC CHURCH.

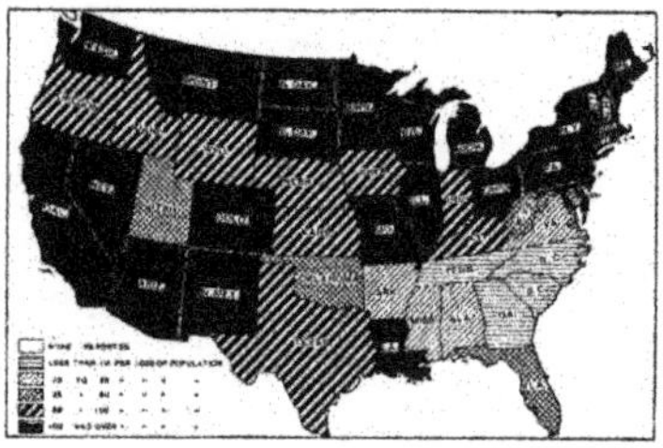

METHODIST BODIES.

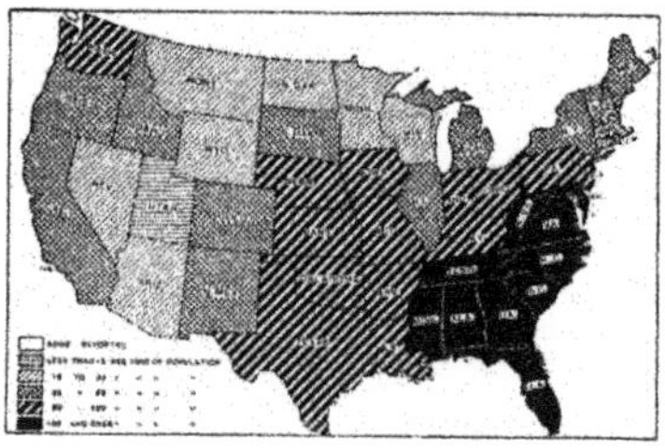

BAPTIST BODIES.

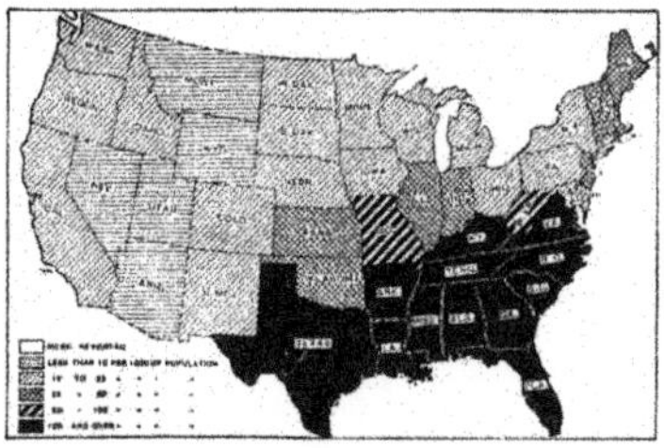

LUTHERAN BODIES.

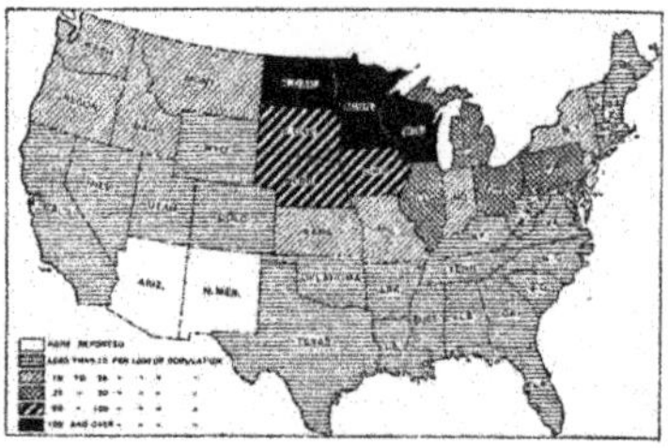

PRESBYTERIAN BODIES.

DISCIPLES OR CHRISTIANS.

DIAGRAM 5.—NUMBER OF COMMUNICANTS OR MEMBERS PER 1,000 OF THE POPULATION, FOR 12 PRINCIPAL FAMILIES OR DENOMINATIONS, FOR EACH STATE AND TERRITORY: 1906—Continued.

PROTESTANT EPISCOPAL CHURCH.

CONGREGATIONALISTS.

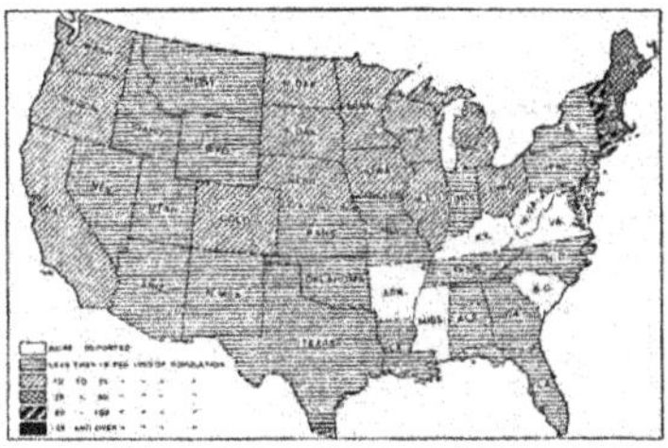

REFORMED BODIES.

UNITED BRETHREN BODIES.

GERMAN EVANGELICAL SYNOD OF NORTH AMERICA.

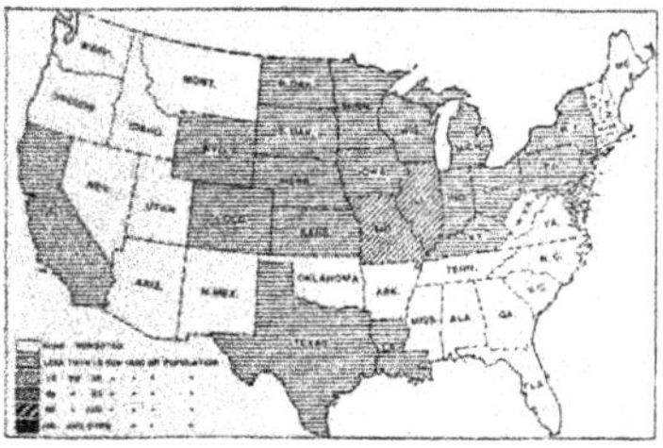

LATTER-DAY SAINTS.

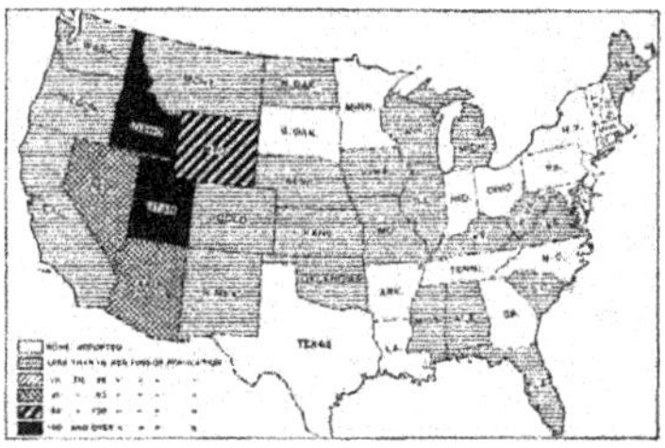

DIAGRAM 6.—NUMBER OF COMMUNICANTS OR MEMBERS PER 1,000 OF THE POPULATION, ARRANGED ACCORDING TO PROPORTIONAL STRENGTH, FOR 12 PRINCIPAL FAMILIES OR DENOMINATIONS, FOR EACH STATE AND TERRITORY: 1906.

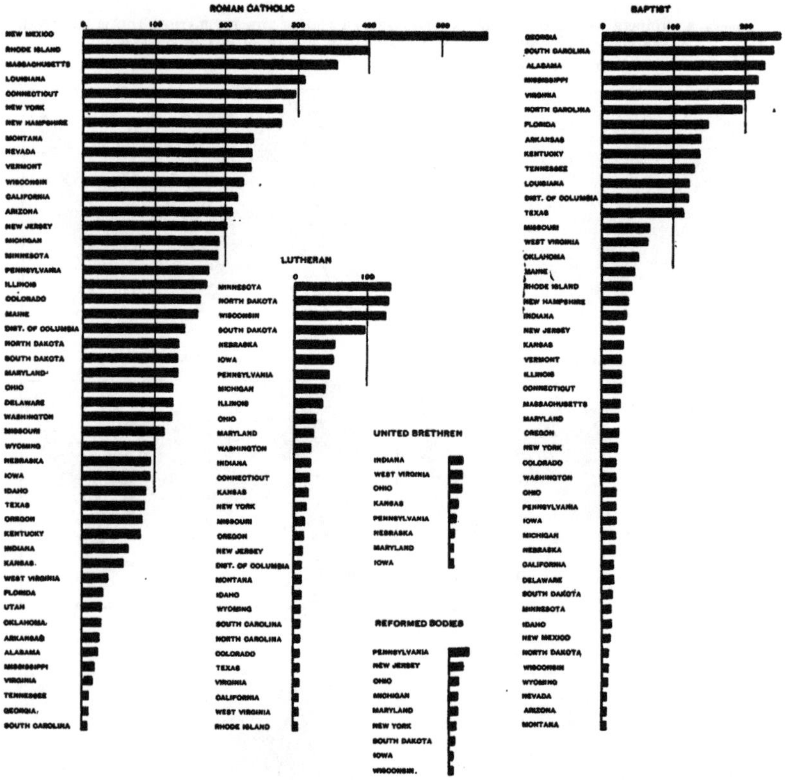

DIAGRAM 6.—NUMBER OF COMMUNICANTS OR MEMBERS PER 1,000 OF THE POPULATION, ARRANGED ACCORDING TO PROPORTIONAL STRENGTH, FOR 12 PRINCIPAL FAMILIES OR DENOMINATIONS, FOR EACH STATE AND TERRITORY: 1906—Continued.

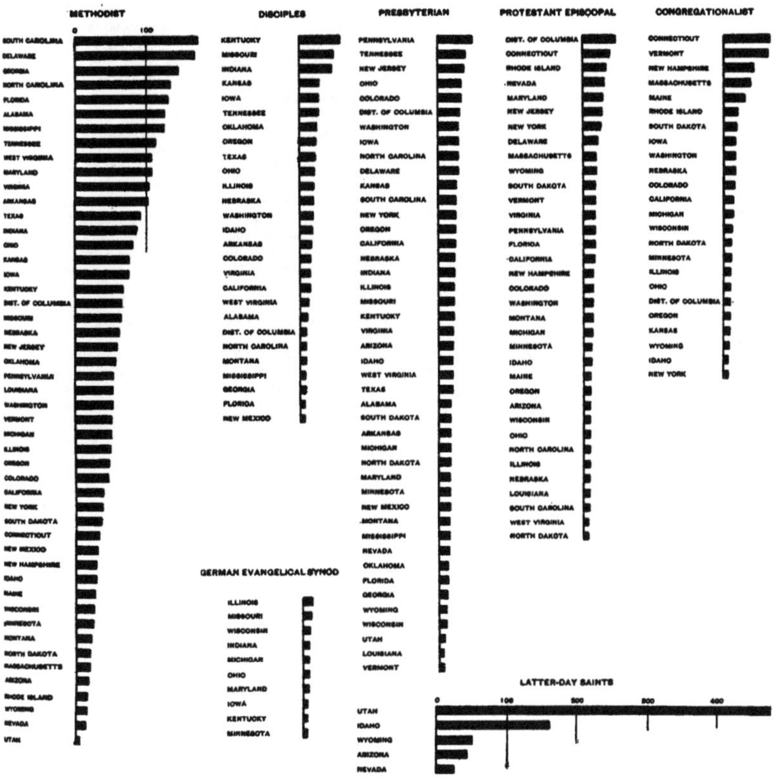

SUMMARY FOR COUNTIES.

The statistics of communicants or members for each state and territory by counties are given in Table 4 of the general tables, together with the total population according to the census of 1900, the total membership for Protestant bodies, and the membership for a selected list of Protestant denominations, for the Roman Catholic Church, Jewish congregations, etc. The list varies with the states, the design being to present in each case those bodies which according to the reports sent in by the individual organizations are most strongly represented in the particular state. In the few cases where denominations have been consolidated, it is indicated either in the boxhead or in footnotes.

Distribution of communicants or members.—A study of Table 4 of the general tables shows that out of over 2,900 counties in continental United States, only 9 make no report of communicants or members. Of these, 1 is in California, in the heart of the Sierras; and the other 8 in western Texas, where there are few facilities for intercommunication. Seven of these counties had, in 1900, a population, respectively, of from 4 to 87, and the eighth, on the Mexican border, with a population of 4,760, is probably, like the adjoining counties, peopled by Spanish-speaking Roman Catholics, although no returns were received from the priests.

The distribution of communicants within the states naturally corresponds very closely to the distribution of population, the same general proportion being usually found in the respective counties as in the states at large. In general, those counties which report a smaller number of communicants or members in proportion to the population are isolated and have poor facilities for intercourse. Thus the membership in Forest and Pike counties in Pennsylvania, which are practically without railroad communication, represents but 16 per cent of their total population, although the general percentage for the state is 47.2. In North Carolina, while the general percentage for the state is 43.5, Clay and Graham counties in the mountain section of the western part of the state, with no facilities for intercommunication, show percentages of 33.7 and 26.2. In Illinois only 2 counties report less than 2,000 members—Hardin and Putnam; the former has little railroad communication, the latter is very small; and the proportion of membership to the population is 25.4 and 26.3, against 43.1 for the state as a whole.

Distribution of denominations.—The Methodist bodies are the most widely distributed. In 29 states communicants of either the Methodist Episcopal Church or the Methodist Episcopal Church South, are to be found in every county, and in over 2,900 counties in continental United States, there are less than 100 in which at least one of these bodies is not represented. Next in order come the Baptist bodies, members of one or more of the three Baptist conventions being found in every county in 20 states, and in the great majority of the counties of continental United States. The Presbyterians are likewise very widely represented, while the Roman Catholics are represented in every county in 12 states.

Certain denominations especially prominent in particular states are also, as a rule, well distributed over those states. Thus the Disciples of Christ who are strong in Indiana, reporting 108,188 members, are found in every county in the state, and are well distributed, only 5 counties reporting over 3,000, while 53 out of the 92 counties in the state have less than 1,000 members each. Similar conditions exist among the United Brethren, the Congregationalists, the Protestant Episcopal Church, and others. Among the Lutherans there is more of a tendency to concentrate in particular counties, except in the case of the Synodical Conference, whose membership is distributed quite evenly over the sections of the states where it is strong.

So far as concerns the number of denominations represented in particular counties, the largest numbers are naturally found in those counties containing large cities. There are comparatively few counties in which every denomination represented in the state has members, and those are generally in the more densely populated states.

SUMMARY OF STATISTICS FOR THE PRINCIPAL CITIES.

The statistics of the religious bodies for 1906 for the cities having a population of 25,000 and over in 1900 are presented in detail in Tables 5, 6, and 7 of the general tables. Table 5 (page 374) gives, for each city, a summary of the statistics for all denominations together; Table 6 (page 380) gives the estimated population of the cities for 1906, and the number of communicants or members by denominations in detail; and Table 7 (page 408) presents, for each city, a summary of the statistics by selected denominations.

In these general tables and in the following textual discussion the 160 principal cities—those having 25,000 inhabitants or more in 1900—are divided into four classes according to population, as follows: 11 cities of the first class—those having over 300,000 inhabitants; 27 cities of the second class—those having from 100,000 to 300,000 inhabitants; 40 cities of the third class—those having from 50,000 to 100,000 inhabitants; and 82 cities of the fourth class—those having from 25,000 to 50,000 inhabitants.

It should be noted that the estimated population for 1906 as given in the various tables and diagrams does not include Los Angeles and San Francisco, California.[1]

It should also be noted that the figures given in the various tables for Rochester, N. Y., do not include the statistics of the Roman Catholic Church, since these were not furnished separately by cities for the diocese of Rochester. For the same reason the figures for the cities of Auburn and Elmira, N. Y., which belong to this diocese, are similarly affected. For the diocese of Cleveland, Ohio, a part only of the statistics of the Roman Catholic Church were furnished separately by cities, and hence in the figures given for the city of Cleveland and for the cities of Canton, Toledo, and Youngstown, which belong to this diocese, only a part of the statistics of this body are included. No statistics for this body are given for Jackson, Mich., as only a part of the statistics for the diocese of Detroit, to which Jackson belongs, were furnished separately by cities. These facts affect somewhat not only the figures for the cities named, but also the general totals for cities, and the totals for the various classes of cities to which those in question belong.

The proportion of organizations reporting on the various items of inquiry as compared with the reports for the whole country is shown by classes of cities in the following table:

CLASS OF CITY.	1906								
	Total organizations.	Communicants or members.		Sex of communicants or members.		Places of worship.			
						Organizations reporting.			Per cent of total.
		Organizations reporting.	Per cent of total.	Organizations reporting.	Per cent of total.	Total.	Church edifices.	Halls, etc.	
Continental United States	212.230	210,418	99.1	193,229	91.0	199,831	185,040	14,791	94.2
Principal cities in 1900	17,906	17,290	96.6	14,965	83.6	16,787	14,875	1,912	93.8
Cities of 300,000 and over	6,455	6,017	93.2	4,942	76.6	5,818	5,113	705	90.1
Cities of 100,000 to 300,000	4,127	4,067	98.5	3,567	86.4	3,959	3,536	423	95.9
Cities of 50,000 to 100,000	3,264	3,218	98.6	2,907	89.1	3,140	2,807	333	96.2
Cities of 25,000 to 50,000	4,060	3,988	98.2	3,549	87.4	3,870	3,419	451	95.3
Outside of principal cities	194,324	193,128	99.4	178,264	91.7	183,044	170,165	12,879	94.2

CLASS OF CITY.	1906									
	Seating capacity of church edifices.		Value of church property.		Debt on church property.		Value of parsonages.		Sunday schools.	
	Organizations reporting.	Per cent of organizations reporting church edifices.	Organizations reporting.	Per cent of total.	Organizations reporting.	Per cent of total reporting value.	Organizations reporting.	Per cent of total.	Organizations reporting.	Per cent of total.
Continental United States	179,954	97.3	186.132	87.7	33,617	18.1	54.214	25.5	167,574	79.0
Principal cities in 1900	14,514	97.6	15,093	84.3	7,509	49.8	6,193	34.6	15.269	85.3
Cities of 300,000 and over	5.021	98.2	5.174	80.2	2,778	53.7	2.131	33.0	5.149	79.8
Cities of 100,000 to 300,000	3,400	96.2	3.541	85.8	1,769	50.0	1,326	32.1	3,624	87.8
Cities of 50,000 to 100,000	2.766	98.5	2,868	87.9	1,335	46.5	1,120	34.3	2,892	88.6
Cities of 25,000 to 50,000	3,327	97.3	3,510	86.5	1,627	46.4	1.016	39.8	3,604	88.8
Outside of principal cities	165,440	97.2	171.039	88.0	26,108	15.3	48,021	24.7	152,305	78.4

From this table it appears that the reports from the principal cities were in general not as complete as from the country as a whole. The percentages of organizations which furnished figures for communicants or members, sex of members, and value of church property, were noticeably smaller, but in regard to other items the reports from the cities were more complete than those from the country as a whole. Among the different classes of cities those of the first class in general furnished the smallest percentages of organizations reporting. The percentage of organizations reporting debt on church property was considerably larger for the cities, especially for those of the first class, but this does not indicate fuller reports, inasmuch as organizations having no debt evidently made no mention of the fact, but simply that a larger proportion of city than country organizations had such debts.

The following table shows, for the different classes of cities, the number and per cent distribution of population, organizations, and communicants or members in 1890 and 1906:

[1] No estimates were made for Los Angeles in compliance with the request of the city officials, and none for San Francisco on account of the great loss occasioned by the earthquake of April 18, 1906.

CLASS OF CITY.	NUMBER OF CITIES.		POPULATION.				ORGANIZATIONS.				COMMUNICANTS OR MEMBERS.			
			1906		1890		1906		1890		1906		1890	
	1906	1890	Number.	Per cent distribution.	Number.	Per cent distribution.	Number.	Per cent distribution.	Number.	Per cent distribution.	Number.	Per cent distribution.	Number.	Per cent distribution.
Continental United States	......	......	[1] 84,246,252	100.0	[2] 62,947,714	100.0	212,230	100.0	165,151	100.0	32,936,445	100.0	20,597,954	100.0
Principal cities in 1900	160	124	[3] 22,425,548	26.6	13,989,568	22.2	17,906	8.4	10,241	6.2	10,511,178	31.9	5,302,018	25.7
Cities of 300,000 and over	11	7	[4] 10,971,688	13.0	5,803,144	9.2	6,455	3.0	3,117	1.9	4,985,085	15.1	2,141.127	10.4
Cities of 100,000 to 300,000	27	21	[5] 4,992,494	5.9	3,894,816	6.2	4,127	1.9	2,840	1.7	2,358,318	7.2	1,483,835	7.2
Cities of 50,000 to 100,000	40	30	3,127,827	3.7	2,022,822	3.2	3,264	1.5	1,859	1.1	1,555,030	4.7	790,304	3.8
Cities of 25,000 to 50,000	82	66	3,333,539	4.0	2,268,786	3.6	4,060	1.9	2,425	1.5	1,612,745	4.9	886,752	4.3
Outside of principal cities	......	......	61,820,704	73.4	48,958,146	77.8	194,324	91.6	154,910	93.8	22,425,267	68.1	15,295,936	74.3

[1] Estimated.
[2] Includes the population of Indian Territory and Indian reservations.
[3] Exclusive of Los Angeles and San Francisco.
[4] Exclusive of San Francisco.
[5] Exclusive of Los Angeles.

In 1906 the estimated population of the 160 principal cities (exclusive of Los Angeles and San Francisco) was 22,425,548, or 26.6 per cent of the total estimated population of continental United States; while they reported 17,906 religious organizations, or 8.4 per cent of the total number, and 10,511,178 communicants or members, or 31.9 per cent of the total number. There was thus, in 1906, in the principal cities, 1 organization to every 1,252 of the population, and in cities of the first class, 1 to every 1,700 of the population; while for the country as a whole the proportion was 1 to every 397 of the population. Of the 22,425,548 population in the principal cities, 10,511,178, or 46.9 per cent, were reported as communicants or members, while the percentage for the country as a whole is only 39.1. Of the different classes of cities, the third shows the highest ratio of communicants to population, 49.7 per cent, and is followed by the fourth with 48.4 per cent.

As compared with 1890, it appears that for the principal cities the rate of increase in the number of organizations and in number of communicants or members is much greater than the rate of increase in population, but for the area outside these cities, the rate of increase in the number of organizations is approximately the same as the rate of increase in population, and in number of communicants or members it is considerably greater. Among the different classes of cities the first class shows the most notable increase, more than doubling the number of organizations and of communicants; the third and fourth classes follow closely; while the second has a much lower rate, and outside of the principal cities the rate of increase was even less.

The following table shows, for the different classes of cities, the number of communicants or members in comparison with the total population in 1890 and 1906:

CLASS OF CITY.	1906			1890		
	Population.	Communicants or members.	Number of communicants per 1,000 population.	Population.	Communicants or members.	Number of communicants per 1,000 population.
Continental United States	[1] 84,246,252	32,936,445	391	[2] 62,947,714	20,597,954	327
Principal cities in 1900	[3] 22,425,548	10,511,178	469	13,989,568	5,302,C18	379
Cities of 300,000 and over	[4] 10,971,688	4,985,085	454	5,803,144	2,141,127	369
Cities of 100,000 to 300,000	[5] 4,992,494	2,358,318	472	3,894,816	1,483,835	381
Cities of 50,000 to 100,000	3,127,827	1,555,030	497	2,022,822	790,304	391
Cities of 25,000 to 50,000	3,333,539	1,612,745	484	2,268,786	886,752	391
Outside of principal cities	61,820,704	22,425,267	363	48,958,146	15,295,936	312

[1] Estimated.
[2] Includes the population of Indian Territory and Indian reservations.
[3] Exclusive of Los Angeles and San Francisco.
[4] Exclusive of San Francisco.
[5] Exclusive of Los Angeles.

The number of communicants or members in each 1,000 of population for 1906 is, for the principal cities, 469; for the whole country, 391; and for the sections outside of the principal cities, 363. The ratio of communicants to population is thus considerably greater for the principal cities than for the country as a whole. Comparing the different classes of cities it appears that the ratios for cities of the first and second classes are considerably smaller than for the other two classes, due probably in part to the omission of the statistics of the Roman Catholic Church in certain cities, as already indicated.

As compared with the report for 1890, the table shows a gain of 90 communicants in each 1,000 of population for the principal cities, and of 51 outside of the principal cities, the gain in the proportion of communicants to population thus being far greater in the principal cities than outside of these cities, or than in the country as a whole. Among the different classes of cities, the largest gain—106 communicants per 1,000 population—is found in cities of the third class, while the smallest gain appears in those of the first class, and the next smallest in those of the second class, these smaller gains being due, in part, as already stated, to incomplete statistics for the Roman Catholic Church.

The high ratios of communicants or members to population shown for the principal cities, as compared with the area outside these cities, are due chiefly to the greater strength of the Roman Catholic Church in the cities; and the greater proportionate increase in communicants or members between 1890 and 1906 shown for these cities is also largely due to the same cause. The fact that in 1906 the number of principal cities was larger by 36 than in 1890, and that in addition, during the interval between 1890 and 1906, a considerable territory had been annexed to various cities, augments to a noticeable extent the rates of increase for the principal cities and diminishes the rates of increase for the area outside these cities. Of course this last fact does not materially affect the changes between 1890 and 1906 in the ratios of communicants or members to population.

The following table shows, for the different classes of cities, the sex distribution of communicants or members in 1906:

CLASS OF CITY.	COMMUNICANTS OR MEMBERS: 1906.						
	Aggregate number.	Reported by sex.					
		Total.		Male.		Female.	
		Number.	Per cent of aggregate number.	Number.	Per cent of total.	Number.	Per cent of total.
Continental United States	32,936,445	29,616,971	89.9	12,767,466	43.1	16,849,505	56.9
Principal cities in 1900	10,511,178	9,125,366	86.8	4,082,420	44.7	5,042,946	55.3
Cities of 300,000 and over	4,985,065	4,274,107	85.7	1,960,466	45.9	2,313,641	54.1
Cities of 100,000 to 300,000	2,358,318	1,985,731	84.2	867,360	43.7	1,118,371	56.3
Cities of 50,000 to 100,000	1,555,080	1,435,188	92.3	635,716	44.3	799,472	55.7
Cities of 25,000 to 50,000	1,612,745	1,430,340	88.7	618,878	43.3	811,462	56.7
Outside of principal cities	22,425,267	20,491,605	91.4	8,685,046	42.4	11,806,559	57.6

There were in continental United States 4,082,039, or 32 per cent, more female than male members, while in the principal cities the excess of female members was proportionately less, being 960,526, or 23.5 per cent. Comparing the different classes of cities, it appears that in those of the first class the excess of female members over male members was only 18 per cent; in the second class, 28.9 per cent; in the third class, 25.8 per cent; in the fourth class, 31.1 per cent; and outside of these cities, 35.9 per cent. The greater proportion of males in the principal cities is largely due to the greater proportionate strength of the Roman Catholic Church in these cities.

The following table shows, for the different classes of cities, the distribution of church edifices in 1890 and 1906, and a similar distribution for 1906 only, of halls, etc., and the seating capacity of church edifices:

CLASS OF CITY.	CHURCH EDIFICES REPORTED.				HALLS, ETC., REPORTED.		SEATING CAPACITY OF CHURCH EDIFICES REPORTED.	
	1906		1890		1906		1906	
	Number.	Per cent distribution.	Number.	Per cent distribution.	Number.	Per cent distribution.	Amount.	Per cent distribution.
Continental United States	192,795	100.0	142,487	100.0	14,791	100.0	58,536,830	100.0
Principal cities in 1900	16,517	8.6	9,722	6.8	1,912	12.9	8,251,853	14.1
Cities of 300,000 and over	5,770	3.0	2,950	2.1	705	4.8	3,169,748	5.4
Cities of 100,000 to 300,000	3,903	2.0	2,693	1.9	423	2.9	1,865,562	3.2
Cities of 50,000 to 100,000	3,075	1.6	1,805	1.3	333	2.3	1,514,977	2.6
Cities of 25,000 to 50,000	3,769	2.0	2,274	1.6	451	3.0	1,701,566	2.9
Outside of principal cities	176,278	91.4	132,765	93.2	12,879	87.1	50,284,977	85.9

Comparing the preceding table with the tables on page 70 it appears that, exclusive of Los Angeles and San Francisco, there was, in 1906, in the principal cities, 1 church edifice to every 1,358 of the population, while for the whole country the proportion was 1 to every 437. Comparing the different classes, the cities of the first class show 1 for every 1,902 of the population; of the second class 1 for every 1,279; of the third class 1 for every 1,017; and of the fourth class 1 for every 884. Thus it appears that the smaller cities provide more church edifices in proportion to their population than do the larger cities.

It appears also that the seating capacity reported for the principal cities for 1906 represented 36.8 per cent of their population, while for the whole country it represented 69.5 per cent. Among the different classes of cities, the smallest percentage under this head, 28.9, was for cities of the first class, and the largest, 51 per cent, for those of the fourth class. The increase between 1890 and 1906 in the number of church edifices in the principal cities was 69.9 per cent, as compared with 74.8 per cent in the number of organizations and 98.2 per cent in communicants or members.

In this connection it should be remembered, as already noted (page 71), that the relation of the seating capacity of church edifices to church membership and to the population, especially in large cities, is materially affected by the high average membership in the Roman Catholic Church, and the fact that in the cities are congregated the great majority of those who are not identified in any way with religious organizations. These two facts account in great measure for the low percentages presented in the table.

The following table shows, for the different classes of cities, the value of church property in 1890 and 1906, and the debt on church property and value of parsonages, in 1906 only:

CLASS OF CITY.	VALUE OF CHURCH PROPERTY REPORTED.				DEBT ON CHURCH PROPERTY REPORTED.		VALUE OF PARSONAGES REPORTED.	
	1906		1890		1906		1906	
	Amount.	Per cent distribution.	Amount.	Per cent distribution.	Amount.	Per cent distribution.	Amount.	Per cent distribution.
Continental United States	$1,257,575,867	100.0	$679,426,489	100.0	$108,050,946	100.0	$143,495,853	100.0
Principal cities in 1900	612,833,315	48.7	313,537,247	46.1	70,262,228	65.0	43,098,769	30.0
Cities of 300,000 and over	340,430,592	27.1	146,916,242	21.6	40,063,622	37.1	20,497,480	14.3
Cities of 100,000 to 300,000	110,357,931	8.8	79,422,746	11.7	14,052,537	13.0	8,000,528	5.6
Cities of 50,000 to 100,000	82,271,671	6.5	42,693,776	6.3	8,076,972	7.5	6,583,350	4.6
Cities of 25,000 to 50,000	79,773,121	6.3	44,504,483	6.6	8,069,097	7.5	8,017,411	5.6
Outside of principal cities	644,742,552	51.3	365,889,242	53.9	37,788,718	35.0	100,397,084	70.0

It appears that although they had less than 9 per cent of the organizations and less than 32 per cent of the communicants, the principal cities reported nearly one-half the entire amount of church property, considerably more than one-half the debt on church property, and about one-third the value of parsonages. Moreover, under each head the cities of the first class reported much the largest percentages. The explanation as to the value of church property and the debt on church property is found, undoubtedly, in the higher value of land in the cities, especially those of the first class, and in the more elaborate church edifices, while the small proportion of the value of parsonages is explained probably by the greater need of such provision outside of the cities. As compared with 1890, the increase of church property in the principal cities was 95.5 per cent, as compared with 85.1 per cent for the country as a whole. In the different classes of cities the increase ranges from 131.7 per cent for cities of the first class to 79.2 per cent for those of the fourth class, with the exception of those of the second class, for which it was only 39 per cent. The rate of increase in the value of church property outside of the principal cities was 76.2 per cent.

The first table on page 73 shows, for the different classes of cities, the Sunday schools conducted by church organizations in 1906.

From this table it appears that while the proportion of Sunday schools in these cities is small, a much larger proportion of officers and teachers and a still larger proportion of scholars are found in them. Comparing these figures with the population, it appears that in the principal cities there was 1 Sunday school to every 1,276 of the population, as compared with 1 to every 473 for the whole country. In the cities of the first class, there was 1 school for every 1,811 of the population, while for the area outside of the principal cities there was 1 for every 385. The Sunday school scholars represented 16.1 per cent of the population in the principal cities, as compared with 17.4 per cent for the country as a whole. Of the different classes of cities, the smallest proportion is shown for the first class, 13.8 per cent, while outside of the principal cities it is 17.9 per cent. Comparing the number of schools with the number of communicants or members, it appears that in the principal cities there was 1 school to every 598 communicants, and in the cities of the first class, 1 to every 823 communicants, while for the country as a whole the ratio is 1 to every 185 communicants.

CLASS OF CITY.	SUNDAY SCHOOLS CONDUCTED BY CHURCH ORGANIZATIONS: 1906.								
	Sunday schools reported.		Officers and teachers.		Scholars.		Average teachers per school.	Average scholars per school.	Average scholars per teacher.
	Number.	Per cent distribution.	Number.	Per cent distribution.	Number.	Per cent distribution.			
Continental United States	178,214	100.0	1,648,664	100.0	14,685,997	100.0	9.3	82	8.9
Principal cities in 1900	17,568	9.9	309,618	18.8	3,603,872	24.5	17.6	205	11.6
Cities of 300,000 and over	6,058	3.4	120,368	7.3	1,511,809	10.3	19.9	250	12.6
Cities of 100,000 to 300,000	4,149	2.3	70,873	4.3	802,078	5.5	17.1	193	11.3
Cities of 50,000 to 100,000	3,316	1.9	56,937	3.5	610,933	4.2	17.2	184	10.7
Cities of 25,000 to 50,000	4,045	2.3	61,440	3.7	679,052	4.6	15.2	168	11.1
Outside of principal cities	160,646	90.1	1,339,046	81.2	11,082,125	75.5	8.3	69	8.3

The following table shows for continental United States the principal cities, and the area outside of these cities, the average per organization reporting for the following items: Communicants or members, seating capacity of church edifices, value of church property, debt on church property, and value of parsonages.

CLASS OF CITY.	1906					
	Communicants or members.			Seating capacity of church edifices.		
	Organizations reporting.	Total number.	Average number per organization reporting.	Organizations reporting.	Seating capacity reported.	Average seating capacity per organization reporting.
Continental United States	210,418	32,936,445	157	179,954	58,536,830	325
Principal cities in 1900	17,290	10,511,178	608	14,514	8,251,853	569
Cities of 300,000 and over	6,017	4,965,085	829	5,021	3,169,748	631
Cities of 100,000 to 300,000	4,067	2,358,318	580	3,400	1,865,562	549
Cities of 50,000 tc 100,000	3,218	1,555,030	483	2,766	1,514,977	548
Cities of 25,000 to 50,000	3,988	1,612,745	404	3,327	1,701,566	511
Outside of principal cities	193,128	22,425,267	116	165,440	50,284,977	304

CLASS OF CITY.	1906—continued.								
	Value of church property.			Debt on church property.			Value of parsonages.		
	Organizations reporting.	Total value reported.	Average value per organization reporting.	Organizations reporting.	Total debt reported.	Average debt per organization reporting.	Organizations reporting.	Total value reported.	Average value per organization reporting.
Continental United States	186,132	$1,257,575,867	$6,756	33,617	$108,050,946	$3,214	54,214	$143,495,853	$2,647
Principal cities in 1900	15,093	612,833,315	40,604	7,509	70,2[illegible]2,228	9,357	6,193	43,098,769	6,959
Cities of 300,000 and over	5,174	340,430,592	65,796	2,778	40,063,622	14,422	2,131	20,497,490	9,619
Cities of 100,000 to 300,000	3,541	110,357,931	31,166	1,769	14,052,587	7,944	1,326	8,000,528	6,034
Cities of 50,000 to 100,000	2,868	82,271,671	28,686	1,335	8,076,972	6,050	1,120	6,583,350	5,878
Cities of 25,000 to 50,000	3,510	79,773,121	22,727	1,627	8,069,097	4,959	1,616	8,017,411	4,961
Outside of principal cities	171,039	644,742,552	3,770	26,108	37,788,718	1,447	48,021	100,397,084	2,091

The average number of communicants or members reported by the organizations throughout the country was 157, while the average number reported by the organizations in the principal cities was 608. Of the different classes of cities, the first class shows an average of 829, and the others follow with steadily decreasing numbers. For the country as a whole the average seating capacity per organization reporting was 325, and for the principal cities, 569. The cities of the first class led with 631, while the figures for the second and third classes were very nearly alike, 549 and 548. Outside the principal cities the average was 304.

The average value of church property per organization reporting was $6,756 for the country as a whole, and for the principal cities, $40,604. The cities of the first class reported an average of $65,796, and the other classes show steadily diminishing figures as in the case of average membership per organization. In respect to debt on church property, the situation is similar. The average debt per organization reporting is, for the entire country, $3,214; for the principal cities, $9,357; and for the cities of the first class, $14,422, with the other classes of cities following in order.

The following table and the table on page 76 give for the principal families and separate denominations the total communicants or members, value of church property, and debt on church property, as reported for the different classes of cities and for the area outside of the principal cities, with the averages under each head for the organizations reporting.

DENOMINATION.	COMMUNICANTS OR MEMBERS: 1906.									AVERAGE NUMBER OF COMMUNICANTS OR MEMBERS PER ORGANIZATION REPORTING: 1906.							
	Aggregate number reported.	In cities of 300,000 and over.		In cities of 100,000 to 300,000.		In cities of 25,000 to 100,000.		Outside of principal cities.		In cities of 300,000 and over.		In cities of 100,000 to 300,000.		In cities of 25,000 to 100,000.		Outside of principal cities.	
		Total number reported.	Per cent of aggregate number.	Total number reported.	Per cent of aggregate number.	Total number reported.	Per cent of aggregate number.	Total number reported.	Per cent of aggregate number.	Organizations reporting.	Average number.	Organizations reporting.	Average number.	Organizations reporting.	Average number.	Organizations reporting.	Average number.
All denominations	32,936,445	4,985,085	15.1	2,358,318	7.2	3,167,775	9.6	22,425,267	68.1	6,017	829	4,067	580	7,206	440	193,128	116
Protestant bodies	20,287,742	1,478,145	7.3	954,485	4.7	1,502,711	7.4	16,352,401	80.6	4,453	332	3,277	291	5,968	252	180,799	90
Adventist bodies	92,735	3,840	4.1	4,893	5.3	9,394	10.1	74,608	80.5	49	78	61	80	146	64	2,281	33
Baptist bodies	5,662,234	198,569	3.5	176,527	3.1	311,688	5.5	4,975,450	87.9	562	353	591	299	1,053	296	52,501	95
Christians (Christian Connection)	110,117	242	0.2	1,163	1.1	2,212	2.0	106,500	96.7	3	81	9	129	15	147	1,327	80
Church of Christ, Scientist	85,717	52,339	61.1	9,457	11.0	8,976	10.5	14,945	17.4	31	1,688	39	242	113	79	452	33
Congregationalists	700,480	68,553	9.8	58,763	8.4	90,191	12.9	482,973	68.9	240	286	197	298	328	275	4,935	98
Disciples or Christians	1,142,359	27,602	2.4	41,441	3.6	61,712	5.4	1,011,604	88.6	104	265	118	351	216	286	10,471	97
Dunkers or German Baptist Brethren	97,144	1,459	1.5	769	0.8	3,683	3.8	91,233	93.9	12	122	10	77	28	132	1,040	88
Evangelical bodies	174,780	8,984	5.1	5,612	3.2	18,953	10.8	141,231	80.8	71	127	45	125	124	153	2,490	57
Friends	113,772	7,743	6.8	2,211	1.9	3,175	2.8	100,643	88.5	33	235	15	147	38	84	1,055	95
German Evangelical Synod of North America	293,137	61,080	20.8	40,793	13.9	20,181	6.9	171,083	58.4	106	576	57	716	43	469	992	172
Independent churches	73,673	16,805	22.8	4,793	6.5	8,855	12.0	43,220	58.7	92	183	39	123	88	101	846	51
Lutheran bodies	2,112,494	210,093	9.9	141,597	6.7	169,804	8.0	1,591,000	75.3	495	424	347	408	522	325	11,278	141
Mennonite bodies	54,798	562	1.0	....	......	614	1.1	53,622	97.9	4	141	....	......	11	56	589	91
Methodist bodies	5,749,838	255,371	4.4	192,928	3.4	363,800	6.3	4,937,739	85.9	918	278	726	266	1,439	253	61,172	81
Presbyterian bodies	1,830,555	208,752	11.4	122,447	6.7	172,576	9.4	1,326,780	72.5	567	368	375	327	602	287	13,927	95
Protestant Episcopal Church	886,942	221,274	24.9	99,244	11.2	133,448	15.0	432,976	48.8	539	411	305	325	453	295	5,428	80
Reformed bodies	449,514	58,767	13.1	20,673	4.6	58,497	13.0	311,577	69.3	187	314	70	295	160	366	2,166	144
Unitarians	70,542	13,776	19.5	6,553	9.3	12,511	17.7	37,702	53.4	46	299	27	243	63	199	299	126
United Brethren bodies	296,050	3,179	1.1	2,840	1.0	18,475	6.2	271,556	91.7	21	151	19	149	83	223	4,145	66
Universalists	64,158	6,321	9.9	5,381	8.4	10,006	15.6	42,450	66.2	28	226	22	245	60	167	701	61
Other Protestant bodies	226,703	52,834	23.3	16,400	7.2	23,960	10.6	133,509	58.9	345	153	205	80	383	63	2,704	49
Roman Catholic Church	12,079,142	[1]3,375,453	27.9	[2]1,361,132	11.3	[3]1,570,944	13.0	5,771,613	47.8	[1]917	3,681	[2]494	2,755	[3]716	2,194	10,345	558
Jewish congregations	[4]101,457	58,324	57.5	15,412	15.2	16,211	16.0	11,510	11.3	496	118	142	109	216	75	298	39
Latter-day Saints	256,647	2,315	0.9	3,514	1.4	27,743	10.8	223,075	86.9	18	129	23	153	73	380	1,070	208
Eastern Orthodox Churches	129,606	44,257	34.1	13,115	10.1	34,304	26.5	37,930	29.3	25	1,770	32	410	94	365	260	146
All other bodies	81,851	26,591	32.5	10,660	13.0	15,862	19.4	28,738	35.1	108	246	99	108	139	114	356	81

[1] Exclusive of statistics for Roman Catholic Church not reported separately by cities for part of Cleveland diocese.
[2] Exclusive of statistics for Roman Catholic Church not reported separately by cities for Rochester diocese and part of Cleveland diocese.
[3] Exclusive of statistics for Roman Catholic Church not reported separately by cities for Rochester diocese and parts of Cleveland and Detroit dioceses.
[4] Heads of families only.

Of the aggregate number of communicants reported for Protestant bodies, 20,287,742, the preceding table shows that 1,478,145, or 7.3 per cent, were in cities of the first class; 4.7 per cent in cities of the second class; and 7.4 per cent in cities of the third and fourth classes combined, while 80.6 per cent were outside of the principal cities. The proportion is considerably less for each class of cities than that for all denominations taken together, while for the area outside of the principal cities it is much greater.

Of the aggregate number of communicants reported by the Roman Catholic Church, 3,375,453, or 27.9 per cent, were in cities of the first class; 1,361,132, or 11.3 per cent, in cities of the second class; 1,570,944, or 13 per cent, in cities of the third and fourth classes combined; and 5,771,613, or 47.8 per cent, outside of the principal cities. It thus appears that the number of members of the Roman Catholic Church reported in cities of the first class was considerably more than double the number reported by all the Protestant bodies, while outside of the principal cities the number reported by the Roman Catholic Church was only a little over one-third the number reported by all the Protestant bodies. In this connection it should be remembered that, as stated on page 25, the numerical strength of the Protestant bodies, as compared with the Roman Catholic Church, is greatly understated.

Of the Protestant bodies shown in the table, only two report a majority of their membership in the principal cities, namely, the Church of Christ, Scientist, 82.6 per cent, and the Protestant Episcopal Church, 51.2 per cent; while of the membership of the Jewish congregations, 88.7 per cent are in the principal cities, and of the Eastern Orthodox Churches, 70.7 per cent. The religious bodies showing the largest percentages of members outside of the principal cities are: The Mennonite bodies, 97.9 per cent; the Christians (Christian Connection), 96.7 per cent; the Dunkers or German Baptist Brethren, 93.9 per cent; the United Brethren bodies, 91.7 per cent; the Disciples or Christians, 88.6 per cent; the Friends, 88.5 per cent; the Baptist bodies, 87.9 per cent; the Latter-day Saints, 86.9 per cent; and the Methodist bodies, 85.9 per cent.

Of the total number of communicants or members reported for the principal cities by all denominations, 6,307,529, or 60 per cent, belonged to the Roman Catholic Church, and 3,935,341, or 37.4 per cent, to Protestant bodies. Of the total number reported by Protestant bodies for these cities, 2,524,152, or 64.1 per cent, were returned by four denominational families, the Methodist, Baptist, Lutheran, and Presbyterian, in the order named.

The average number of communicants or members per organization reporting ranged, for Protestant bodies, from 332 for cities of the first class to 90 for the area outside of the principal cities; for the Roman Catholic Church, from 3,681 for cities of the first class to 558 for the area outside of the principal cities; and for the Eastern Orthodox Churches, from 1,770 for cities of the first class to 146 for the area outside of the principal cities. For the Church of Christ, Scientist, the number ranged from 1,688 for cities of the first class to 33 for the area outside of the principal cities. Of the Protestant bodies, the Church of Christ, Scientist, shows the largest average membership per organization for cities of the first class, and is followed by the German Evangelical Synod of North America. The latter body shows the largest average membership among Protestant bodies in the cities of the second class and in the cities of the third and fourth classes combined. The bodies showing the largest averages outside of the principal cities are the Roman Catholic Church, 558; Latter-day Saints, 208; German Evangelical Synod of North America, 172; Eastern Orthodox Churches, 146; Reformed bodies, 144; and Lutheran bodies, 141. In a number of religious bodies, notably the Christians (Christian Connection), Disciples or Christians, German Evangelical Synod, United Brethren bodies, and Latter-day Saints, larger averages are shown for either the second class, or the third and fourth classes combined, than for the first class. With the exception of four bodies—Dunkers or German Baptist Brethren, Friends, Mennonite bodies, and Latter-day Saints—the average number of communicants or members per organization is lower outside of the principal cities than in any of the different classes of cities.

The number of communicants or members given in the report for 1890 for cities of 25,000 inhabitants and over was 5,302,018; of these the Protestant bodies were credited with 2,137,748, or 40.3 per cent, and the Roman Catholic Church, with 3,010,646, or 56.8 per cent. Of the total number reported by Protestant bodies at that time, the four leading families—the Methodist, Baptist, Presbyterian, and Lutheran, in the order named—were credited with 1,403,699, or 65.7 per cent. In 1906 the same families led, but the Lutheran and Presbyterian bodies had changed places.

Comparison with the report for 1890 shows that in general there has been an increase in the proportion of communicants or members in the principal cities as compared with those outside of these cities. In 1906 the percentage of the total number of communicants in these cities, for all denominations, was 31.9, as compared with 25.7 in 1890. The percentages for the two periods, as shown by some of the principal families and separate denominations, are as follows: Adventist bodies, 19.5 per cent in 1906 as compared with 14 in 1890; Baptist bodies, 12.1 per cent as compared with 9.4; Congregationalists, 31.5 per cent as compared with 25.6; Lutheran bodies, 24.7 per cent as compared with 21.6; Methodist bodies, 14.1 per cent as compared with 10.8; Presbyterian bodies, 27.5 per cent as compared with 22.9; Reformed bodies, 30.7 per cent as compared with 22.7; the Protestant Episcopal Church, 51.2 per cent as compared with 48; and the Roman Catholic Church, 52.2 per cent as compared with 48.2.

DENOMINATION.	VALUE OF CHURCH PROPERTY: 1906.								
	Aggregate value reported.	In cities of 300,000 and over.		In cities of 100,000 to 300,000.		In cities of 25,000 to 100,000.		Outside of principal cities.	
		Total value reported.	Per cent of aggregate value.	Total value reported.	Per cent of aggregate value.	Total value reported.	Per cent of aggregate value.	Total value reported.	Per cent of aggregate value.
All denominations	$1,257,575,867	$340,430,592	27.1	$110,257,931	8.8	$162,044,792	12.9	$644,742,552	51.3
Protestant bodies	935,942,578	217,074,122	23.2	81,911,860	8.8	116,183,079	12.4	520,773,517	55.6
Adventist bodies	2,425,209	188,464	7.8	146,045	6.0	367,036	15.1	1,723,664	71.1
Baptist bodies	139,842,656	23,624,875	16.9	12,035,995	8.6	17,274,403	12.4	86,907,383	62.1
Christians (Christian Connection)	2,740,322	95,000	3.5	99,500	3.6	213,100	8.6	2,332,722	85.1
Church of Christ, Scientist	8,806,441	5,379,111	61.1	1,261,845	14.3	932,299	1	1,233,186	14.0
Congregationalists	63,240,305	12,457,890	19.7	7,104,533	11.2	10,506,235	1	33,171,647	52.5
Disciples or Christians	29,995,316	1,887,175	6.3	2,396,050	8.0	2,907,358	9.7	22,804,733	76.0
Dunkers or German Baptist Brethren	2,802,532	203,100	7.2	44,700	1.6	162,100	5.8	2,392,632	85.4
Evangelical bodies	8,999,979	1,091,853	12.1	504,375	5.6	1,280,350	14.2	6,123,401	68.0
Friends	3,857,451	887,500	23.0	201,700	5.2	317,550	8.2	2,450,701	63.5
German Evangelical Synod of North America	9,376,402	2,478,900	26.4	1,511,192	16.1	937,100	10.0	4,449,210	47.5
Independent churches	3,934,267	2,117,375	53.8	157,965	4.0	386,123	9.8	1,272,804	32.4
Lutheran bodies	74,826,389	15,596,002	20.8	6,665,225	8.9	9,750,873	13.0	42,815,289	57.2
Mennonite bodies	1,237,134	36,000	2.9	....	....	30,430	2	1,170,704	94.6
Methodist bodies	229,450,996	33,540,265	14.6	17,028,247	7.4	24,325,894	10.6	154,556,590	67.4
Presbyterian bodies	150,189,446	41,631,502	27.7	14,570,375	9.7	18,630,098	12.4	75,357,471	50.2
Protestant Episcopal Church	125,040,498	49,997,383	40.0	12,170,818	9.7	17,348,628	13.9	45,523,669	36.4
Reformed bodies	30,648,247	10,228,777	33.4	1,894,800	6.2	4,308,560	14.1	14,216,110	46.4
Unitarians	14,263,277	5,970,900	41.9	1,197,300	8.4	2,313,300	16.2	4,781,777	33.5
United Brethren bodies	9,073,791	213,700	2.4	207,000	2.3	942,828	10.4	7,710,263	85.0
Universalists	10,575,656	2,343,792	22.2	1,242,300	11.7	1,821,850	17.2	5,167,714	48.9
Other Protestant bodies	14,616,264	7,105,558	48.6	1,471,895	10.1	1,426,964	9.8	4,611,847	31.6
Roman Catholic Church	293,638,787	[1]106,891,559	36.5	[2]25,045,137	8.6	[3]41,824,824	14.3	118,877,767	40.6
Jewish congregations	23,198,925	15,186,350	65.5	3,059,000	13.2	3,132,700	13.5	1,820,875	7.8
Latter-day Saints	3,168,548	64,721	2.0	51,389	1.6	492,929	15.6	2,559,509	80.8
Eastern Orthodox Churches	964,791	446,820	46.3	98,100	10.2	283,910	29.4	135,961	14.1
All other bodies	1,662,238	767,020	46.1	192,445	11.6	127,850	7.7	574,923	34.6

DENOMINATION.	AVERAGE VALUE OF CHURCH PROPERTY PER ORGANIZATION REPORTING: 1906.							
	In cities of 300,000 and over.		In cities of 100,000 to 300,000.		In cities of 25,000 to 100,000.		Outside of principal cities.	
	Organizations reporting.	Average value.	Organizations reporting.	Average value.	Organizations reporting.	Average value.	Organizations reporting	Average value.
All denominations	5,174	$65,796	3,541	$31,166	6,378	$25,407	171,039	$3,770
Protestant bodies	4,049	53,612	3,007	27,240	5,471	21,236	161,375	3,227
Adventist bodies	22	8,567	33	4,426	90	4,078	1,347	1,280
Baptist bodies	504	46,875	549	21,923	1,003	17,223	47,283	1,838
Christians (Christian Connection)	2	47,500	6	16,583	15	14,207	1,216	1,918
Church of Christ, Scientist	24	224,130	30	42,062	69	13,512	278	4,436
Congregationalists	230	54,165	193	36,811	314	33,459	4,629	7,166
Disciples or Christians	89	21,204	113	21,204	197	14,758	8,507	2,681
Dunkers or German Baptist Brethren	12	16,925	10	4,470	27	6,004	925	2,587
Evangelical bodies	71	15,378	45	11,208	122	10,495	2,277	2,689
Friends	28	31,696	14	14,407	35	9,073	1,020	2,403
German Evangelical Synod of North America	104	23,836	57	26,512	43	21,793	933	4,769
Independent churches	62	34,151	24	6,582	63	6,129	657	1,937
Lutheran bodies	453	34,426	331	20,137	486	20,064	9,509	4,503
Mennonite bodies	4	9,000	....	....	10	3,043	483	2,424
Methodist bodies	877	38,244	697	24,431	1,380	17,627	56,129	2,754
Presbyterian bodies	549	75,832	366	39,810	588	31,684	12,658	5,953
Protestant Episcopal Church	503	99,398	295	41,257	440	39,429	4,819	9,447
Reformed bodies	177	57,790	65	29,151	156	27,619	2,079	6,838
Unitarians	47	127,040	26	46,050	57	40,584	276	17,326
United Brethren bodies	21	10,176	16	12,938	80	11,785	3,722	2,072
Universalists	28	83,707	20	62,115	59	30,879	672	690
Other Protestant bodies	242	29,362	117	12,580	237	6,021	1,956	358
Roman Catholic Church	[1]807	132,455	[2]385	65,052	[3]637	65,658	8,464	14,045
Jewish congregations	271	56,038	102	29,990	163	19,219	211	8,630
Latter-day Saints	8	8,090	16	3,212	59	8,355	826	3,099
Eastern Orthodox Churches	16	27,926	11	8,918	25	11,356	37	3,675
All other bodies	23	33,349	20	9,622	23	5,559	126	4,563

[1] Exclusive of statistics for Roman Catholic Church not reported separately by cities for part of Cleveland diocese.
[2] Exclusive of statistics for Roman Catholic Church not reported separately by cities for Rochester diocese and part of Cleveland diocese.
[3] Exclusive of statistics for Roman Catholic Church not reported separately by cities for Rochester diocese and parts of Cleveland and Detroit dioceses.

Of the total value of church property in the principal cities, $415,169,061, or 67.7 per cent, was reported by Protestant bodies, and $173,761,020, or 28.4 per cent, by the Roman Catholic Church. Of the total reported by Protestant bodies for these cities, $282,178,483, or 68 per cent, was reported by four of the bodies listed—the Protestant Episcopal Church and the Methodist, Presbyterian, and Baptist bodies—in the order named. The Protestant bodies, as a whole, reported 23.2 per cent of the total value of their church property in cities of the first class, 8.8 per cent in cities of the second class, 12.4 per cent in cities of the third and fourth classes combined, and 55.6 per cent outside of the principal cities. Among Protestant bodies reporting the largest percentage of their property in the principal cities are: The Church of Christ, Scientist, 86 per cent, 61.1 per cent being in cities of the first class; Independent churches, 67.6 per cent, 53.8 per cent being in cities of the first class; the Unitarians, 66.5 per cent, 41.9 per cent being in cities of the first class; and the Protestant Episcopal Church, 63.6 per cent, 40 per cent being in cities of the first class.

The Roman Catholic Church reported 59.4 per cent of the value of its church property as being in the principal cities, 36.5 per cent being in cities of the first class; the Jewish congregations, 92.2 per cent, 65.5 per cent being in cities of the first class; and the Eastern Orthodox Churches, 85.9 per cent, 46.3 per cent being in cities of the first class.

Among the religious bodies having an exceptionally large percentage of their church property outside of the principal cities were the Mennonite bodies, 94.6 per cent; the Dunkers or German Baptist Brethren, 85.4 per cent; the Christians (Christian Connection), 85.1 per cent; the United Brethren bodies, 85 per cent; and the Latter-day Saints 80.8 per cent.

The average value of church property per organization reporting corresponds in general with the grades of the cities, ranging, for all denominations, from $65,796 for cities of the first class to $25,407 for cities of the third and fourth classes combined. The average outside of the principal cities was $3,770. For Protestant bodies the average ranges from $53,612 for cities of the first class to $21,236 for cities of the third and fourth classes combined, and $3,227 outside of the principal cities, the average being considerably less in each instance than that for all denominations taken together. For the Roman Catholic Church the averages are $132,455 for cities of the first class, $65,052 for cities of the second class, $65,658 for cities of the third and fourth classes, and $14,045 for the area outside of the principal cities, each of these averages being more than twice the corresponding average for all denominations combined. The denomination showing the highest average value of church property per organization for cities of the first class is the Church of Christ, Scientist, while those next in order are the Roman Catholic Church and the Unitarians. The Roman Catholic Church leads in cities of the second class and in those of the third and fourth classes combined, and is followed by the Universalists in cities of the second class, and by the Unitarians in cities of the third and fourth classes. The Unitarians and the Roman Catholic Church report the highest average values outside of the principal cities. Among the bodies showing exceptionally low average values outside of the principal cities are the Adventist bodies, $1,280; the Baptist bodies, $1,838; the Christians (Christian Connection), $1,918; and the Independent churches, $1,937.

The total value of church property given in the report for 1890 for cities of over 25,000 inhabitants was $313,537,247; of this, $238,813,328, or 76.2 per cent, was returned by Protestant bodies, and $65,045,650, or 20.7 per cent, by the Roman Catholic Church. Of the total value returned by Protestant bodies, $170,072,381, or 71.2 per cent, was reported by the same four subclasses of Protestants which led in 1906, although in a somewhat different order: Protestant Episcopal Church, and the Presbyterian, Methodist, and Baptist bodies.

In general there has been an increase in the proportion of the value of church property in the principal cities as compared with that outside of these cities. In 1906 the percentage, for the principal cities, of the total value for all denominations was 48.7 per cent, as compared with 46.1 per cent in 1890. The percentages in these cities at the two periods, shown by some of the principal families and denominations, are as follows: Adventist bodies, 28.9 per cent in 1906, as compared with 24.7 in 1890; Baptist bodies, 37.9 per cent, as compared with 36.5; Congregationalists, 47.5 per cent, as compared with 41.6; Lutheran bodies, 42.8 per cent, as compared with 41.7; Methodist bodies, 32.6 per cent, as compared with 31.9; Presbyterian bodies, 49.8 per cent, as compared with 49.8; the Protestant Episcopal Church, 63.6 per cent, as compared with 62.3; and the Roman Catholic Church, 59.4 per cent, as compared with 55.1 in 1890.

DENOMINATION.	Aggregate debt reported.	AMOUNT OF DEBT ON CHURCH PROPERTY: 1906. In cities of 300,000 and over. Total debt reported.	Per cent of aggregate debt.	In cities of 100,000 to 300,000. Total debt reported.	Per cent of aggregate debt.	In cities of 25,000 to 100,000. Total debt reported.	Per cent of aggregate debt.	Outside of principal cities. Total debt reported.	Per cent of aggregate debt.
All denominations	$108,050,946	$40,063,622	37.1	$14,052,537	13.0	$16,146,069	14.9	$37,788,718	35.0
Protestant bodies	53,301,254	16,188,708	30.4	7,578,307	14.2	8,310,747	15.6	21,223,492	39.8
Adventist bodies	167,812	48,629	29.0	14,215	8.5	51,100	30.5	53,868	32.1
Baptist bodies	8,323,862	2,647,519	31.8	948,249	11.4	1,294,402	15.6	3,433,692	41.3
Christians (Christian Connection)	101,561	12,500	12.3	11,550	11.4	10,700	10.5	66,811	65.8
Church of Christ, Scientist	391,338	12,100	3.1	173,581	44.4	94,350	24.1	111,307	28.4
Congregationalists	2,708,025	671,633	24.8	429,580	15.9	515,906	19.1	1,090,906	40.3
Disciples or Christians	1,868,821	268,565	14.4	208,463	11.2	201,444	10.8	1,190,349	63.7
Dunkers or German Baptist Brethren	83,199	26,800	32.2	3,000	3.6	14,150	17.0	39,249	47.2
Evangelical bodies	666,973	176,340	26.4	54,555	8.2	142,251	21.3	293,827	44.1
Friends	41,496	3,800	9.2	6,701	16.1	2,500	6.0	28,495	68.7
German Evangelical Synod of North America	1,161,776	468,344	40.3	288,162	24.8	120,928	10.4	284,342	24.5
Independent churches	478,425	256,635	53.6	46,220	9.7	77,830	16.3	97,740	20.4
Lutheran bodies	7,859,469	2,749,814	35.0	1,180,161	15.0	1,240,560	15.8	2,688,934	34.2
Mennonite bodies	9,082	400	4.4	....	....	1,000	11.0	7,682	84.6
Methodist bodies	12,272,463	2,785,782	22.7	1,527,180	12.4	1,864,064	15.2	6,095,437	49.7
Presbyterian bodies	6,545,025	2,034,988	31.1	1,183,143	18.1	920,291	14.1	2,406,603	36.8
Protestant Episcopal Church	4,930,914	2,047,045	41.5	905,605	18.4	602,444	12.2	1,375,820	27.9
Reformed bodies	2,377,014	732,150	30.8	239,460	10.1	600,183	25.2	805,221	33.9
Unitarians	332,330	149,200	44.9	18,350	5.5	83,870	25.2	80,910	24.3
United Brethren bodies	498,959	14,560	2.9	35,737	7.2	113,908	22.8	334,754	67.1
Universalists	464,755	96,500	20.8	57,800	12.4	121,950	26.2	188,505	40.6
Other Protestant bodies	2,017,955	985,404	48.8	246,595	12.2	236,916	11.7	549,040	27.2
Roman Catholic Church	49,488,055	[1]20,554,725	41.5	[2]5,768,680	11.7	[3]7,098,142	14.3	16,066,508	32.5
Jewish congregations	4,556,571	3,068,760	67.3	641,200	14.1	574,250	12.6	272,361	6.0
Latter-day Saints	111,782	10,700	9.6	875	0.8	18,170	16.3	82,037	73.4
Eastern Orthodox Churches	290,674	112,029	38.5	32,675	11.2	98,600	33.9	47,370	16.3
All other bodies	302,610	128,700	42.5	30,800	10.2	46,160	15.3	96,950	32.0

DENOMINATION.	AVERAGE AMOUNT OF DEBT PER ORGANIZATION REPORTING: 1906. In cities of 300,000 and over. Organizations reporting.	Average debt.	In cities of 100,000 to 300,000. Organizations reporting.	Average debt.	In cities of 25,000 to 100,000. Organizations reporting.	Average debt.	Outside of principal cities. Organizations reporting.	Average debt.
All denominations	2,778	$14,422	1,769	$7,944	2,962	$5,451	26,108	$1,447
Protestant bodies	2,004	8,078	1,439	5,266	2,417	3,438	22,937	925
Adventist bodies	12	4,052	12	1,185	34	1,503	125	431
Baptist bodies	285	9,290	262	3,619	453	2,857	5,199	660
Christians (Christian Connection)	2	6,250	3	3,850	5	2,140	87	768
Church of Christ, Scientist	2	6,050	10	17,358	21	4,493	55	2,024
Congregationalists	92	7,300	79	5,438	129	3,999	906	1,204
Disciples or Christians		5,595	52	4,009	83	2,427	1,051	1,133
Dunkers or German Baptist Brethren		3,829	2	1,500	13	1,088	93	422
Evangelical bodies	48	4,766	20	2,728	57	2,496	298	986
Friends	37	950	4	1,675	4	625	48	594
German Evangelical Synod of North America	80	5,854	44	6,549	29	4,170	245	1,161
Independent churches	29	8,849	13	3,555	36	2,162	152	643
Lutheran bodies	327	8,409	227	5,199	308	4,028	2,108	1,276
Mennonite bodies	1	400	....	....	1	1,000	29	265
Methodist bodies		6,617	341	4,479	627	2,973	9,041	674
Presbyterian bodies		9,126	147	8,049	204	4,511	1,528	1,575
Protestant Episcopal Church	421	10,606	113	8,014	132	4,564	573	2,401
Reformed bodies	223	7,707	40	5,987	97	6,187	422	1,908
Unitarians		10,657	5	3,670	22	3,812	44	1,839
United Brethren bodies	14	2,427	8	4,467	42	2,712	404	829
Universalists	16	8,773	10	5,780	26	4,690	85	2,218
Other Protestant bodies	115	8,569	47	5,247	94	2,520	444	1,237
Roman Catholic Church	[1]577	35,623	[2]237	24,340	[3]395	17,970	2,895	5,550
Jewish congregations	175	17,536	75	8,549	108	5,317	91	2,993
Latter-day Saints	3	3,567	2	438	13	1,398	127	646
Eastern Orthodox Churches	11	10,184	7	4,668	17	5,800	23	2,060
All other bodies	8	16,088	9	3,422	12	3,847	35	2,770

[1] Exclusive of statistics for Roman Catholic Church not reported separately by cities for part of Cleveland diocese.
[2] Exclusive of statistics for Roman Catholic Church not reported separately by cities for Rochester diocese and part of Cleveland diocese.
[3] Exclusive of statistics for Roman Catholic Church not reported separately by cities for Rochester diocese and parts of Cleveland and Detroit dioceses.

It is noteworthy that of the total debt for cities of the first class more than one-half was reported by the Roman Catholic Church. Other families or separate denominations reporting exceptionally large amounts of debt for this class of cities are the Jewish congregations, $3,068,760, or 67.3 per cent of their total debt; the Methodist bodies, $2,785,782, or 22.7 per cent of their total debt; the Lutheran bodies, $2,749,814, or 35 per cent of their total debt; and the Baptist bodies, $2,647,519, or 31.8 per cent of their total debt. The highest figures reported for the area outside of the principal cities are: $16,066,508, by the Roman Catholic Church; $6,095,437, by Methodist bodies; $3,433,692, by Baptist bodies; $2,688,934, by Lutheran bodies; and $2,406,603, by Presbyterian bodies.

The average debt per organization reporting corresponds in general, as in the case of the value of church property, with the grade of the cities, ranging, for all denominations together, from $14,422 for cities of the first class to $5,451 for cities of the third and fourth classes combined, while for the area outside of the principal cities, it was only $1,447. For Protestant bodies, the averages range from $8,078 for cities of the first class to $3,438 for cities of the third and fourth classes combined, and $925 for the area outside of the principal cities, the average in each instance being much less than that for all denominations.

For the Roman Catholic Church the averages are $35,623 for cities of the first class, $24,340 for those of the second class, and $17,970 for those of the third and fourth classes combined, while the average for the area outside of the principal cities is $5,550. In four cases only the averages reported for cities of the second class are larger than those for the first class, namely, the Church of Christ, Scientist, $17,358 as compared with $6,050; the German Evangelical Synod of North America, $6,549 as compared with $5,854; the United Brethren bodies, $4,467 as compared with $2,427; and the Friends, $1,675 as compared with $950. The United Brethren bodies report a still higher average for cities of the third and fourth classes combined than for those of the first class, namely $2,712 as compared with $2,427. In no case is the average for the area outside of the principal cities larger than the average for any one of the several classes of cities.

The next table gives, for 1906, the number of communicants or members of the principal denominational families and separate denominations in the 38 cities having in 1900 a population of over 100,000, together with the percentage that the membership in each case constitutes of the total membership in the city.

As already shown, the total number of communicants or members in the principal cities in 1906 was 10,511,178. Of this number, 7,343,403, or 69.9 per cent, were reported by the 38 cities of over 100,000 population, and of these, 2,432,630, or 33.1 per cent, belonged to Protestant bodies, and 4,736,585, or 64.5 per cent, to the Roman Catholic Church, this denomination having in these 38 cities about three-fourths—75.1 per cent—of its entire membership in cities of over 25,000 inhabitants. As already stated, the statistics of the Roman Catholic Church for Rochester are not included. Of the total membership reported for cities of over 100,000 inhabitants, the Methodist bodies are credited with 6.1 per cent; the Baptist bodies, with 5.1 per cent; the Lutheran bodies, with 4.8 per cent; and the Presbyterian bodies, with 4.5 per cent, while other Protestant bodies showing low percentages are the United Brethren bodies, one-tenth of 1 per cent; the Disciples or Christians, nine-tenths of 1 per cent; the Reformed bodies, 1.1 per cent; the German Evangelical Synod of North America, 1.4 per cent; and the Congregationalists, 1.7 per cent. The Latter-day Saints had in these cities only 5,829 communicants, or one-tenth of 1 per cent of the total number reported for the cities in question, and "all other bodies" 168,359, or 2.3 per cent.

In 13 of the cities (including Rochester), as shown by the table, more than one-half of the communicants or members reported belonged to Protestant bodies, while in 23 the majority belonged to the Roman Catholic Church. Aside from Rochester, the cities showing the largest proportions of Protestant communicants are Memphis, 84.4 per cent; Toledo, 70 per cent; Washington, 66.9 per cent; Kansas City, Mo., 66.2 per cent; and Indianapolis, 62.1 per cent; while the cities showing the largest percentages of Roman Catholic communicants are Fall River, 86.5 per cent; San Francisco, 81.1 per cent; New Orleans, 79.7 per cent; New York, 76.9 per cent; and Providence, 76.5 per cent.

Naturally the city reporting the largest number of communicants or members is New York, with 1,838,482, or considerably more than twice the number reported by any other city; and of these 20.3 per cent were Protestants and 76.9 per cent Roman Catholics. The Protestant denominations having the largest number of members in this city are the Protestant Episcopal Church, 92,534, or 5 per cent of the total communicants or members in the city; the Methodist bodies, 57,021, or 3.1 per cent; the Presbyterian bodies, 51,547, or 2.8 per cent; and the Lutheran bodies, 51,285, or 2.8 per cent. The city which stands second in respect to the number of communicants or members reported is Chicago, with 833,441, and of these 28.5 per cent are Protestants and 68.2 per cent Roman Catholics. The leading Protestant bodies in Chicago are the Lutheran bodies, with 64,897 communicants, or 7.8 per cent of the total for the city; the Methodist bodies, with 34,034, or 4.1 per cent; the Presbyterian bodies, with 24,427, or 2.9 per cent; and the Baptist bodies, with 23,931, also 2.9 per cent.

CITY.	COMMUNICANTS OR MEMBERS: 1906.														
	Total.	Protestant bodies.													
		Total.		Baptist bodies.		Congregationalists.		Disciples or Christians.		German Evangelical Synod of North America.		Lutheran bodies.		Methodist bodies.	
		Number.	Per cent of total.	Number.	Per cent of total.	Number.	Per cent of total.	Number.	Per cent of total.	Number.	Per cent of total.	Number.	Per cent of total.	Number.	Per cent of total.
Cities of 25,000 and over	10,511,178	3,935,341	37.4	686,784	6.5	217,507	2.1	130,756	1.2	122,064	1.2	521,494	5.0	812,099	7.7
Cities of 100,000 and over	7,343,403	2,432,630	33.1	375,096	5.1	127,316	1.7	69,043	0.9	101,873	1.4	351,690	4.8	448,209	6.1
Allegheny, Pa.	61,456	29,000	47.2	1,328	2.2	147	0.2	1,[illegible]	3.2	1,467	2.4	6,790	11.0	5,528	9.0
Baltimore, Md.	224,968	120,985	53.8	24,703	11.0	676	0.3	1,[illegible]	0.7	7,105	3.2	12,914	5.7	3[illegible], 18	15.9
Boston, Mass.	376,728	111,563	[illegible]	17,349	4.6	12,127	3.2		.1	......	......	3,683	1.0	,283	2.2
Buffalo, N. Y.	195,302	64,114		6,022	3.1	1,036	0.5	1,	6	13,256	6.8	12,189	6.2	,727	4.0
Chicago, Ill.	833,441	237,220	.	23,931	2.9	15,621	1.9	6,	8	17,063	2.0	64,897	7.8	34,034	4.1
Cincinnati, Ohio	159,663	51,520	32.3	7,767	4.9	1,248	0.8	2,951	1.8	3,275	2.1	1,431	0.9	10,386	6.5
Cleveland, Ohio	146,338	76,174	52,[illegible]	7,365	5.0	7,692	5.3	3,[illegible]	[illegible],3	[illegible],981	4.1	12,744	8.7	11,100	7.6
Columbus, Ohio	63,261	33,645		3,249	5.1	2,444	3.9	1,	.8	,800	4.4	3,346	5.3	11,184	17.7
Denver, Colo.	58,699	30,646		3,989	6.8	3,223	5.5	2,	.6	681	1.2	1,574	2.7	7,824	13.3
Detroit, Mich.	194,160	64,039		5,570	2.9	2,636	1.4	1,202	6	7,214	3.7	18,694	9.6	9,308	4.8
Fall River, Mass.	71,877	8,611	12.0	1,900	2.6	1,072	1.5	......	......	......	......	......	......	2,237	3.1
Indianapolis, Ind.	84,815	52,655	[illegible]	9,586	11.3	1,187	1.4	8,102	9.6	2,008	2.4	3,423	4.0	14,744	17.4
Jersey City, N. J.	104,637	26,578		2,781	2.7	1,379	1.3	......	......	......	......	5,776	5.5	4,653	4.4
Kansas City, Mo.	61,503	40,732		9,163	14.9	2,022	3.3	7,437	12.1	428	0.[illegible]	1,542	2.5	9,960	16.2
Los Angeles, Cal.	81,771	41,691	5	4,489	5.5	3,402	4.2	3,408	4.2	130	0.	1,522	1.9	11,542	14.1
Louisville, Ky.	147,330	60,680	41.2	20,464	13.9	133	0.1	5,129	3.5	9,260	6.3	2,965	2.0	10,759	7.3
Memphis, Tenn.	37,477	31,623	84.[illegible]	11,562	30.9	401	1.1	1,347	3.6	......	......	250	0.7	11,375	30.4
Milwaukee, Wis.	155,206	52,606	33	2,355	1.5	1,778	1.1	330	2	3,635	2.[illegible]	32,186	20.7	3,898	2.5
Minneapolis, Minn.	96,819	48,814	50.	5,947	6.1	5,934	6.1	593	.6	350	0.	11,918	12.3	7,066	7.3
Newark, N. J.	115,307	41,196	35	6,361	5.5	784	0.7	......	......	1,360	1.	2,035	1.8	8,368	7.3
New Haven, Conn.	67,650	21,675	32.0	3,061	4.5	6,895	10.2	......	......	......	......	1,915	2.8	4,124	6.1
New Orleans, La.	18[illegible],497	36,875	19.[illegible]	10,580	5.7	363	0.2	185	0.1	4,353	2.[illegible]	5,015	2.7	7,028	3.8
New York, N. Y.	1,838,482	372,090	20	45,078	2.5	21,096	1.1	1,819	.1	940	0.	51,285	2.8	57,021	3.1
Omaha, [illegible]ebr.	33,900	16,612	49	1,923	5.7	1,184	3.5	1,184	.5	128	0.	2,235	6.6	3,230	9.5
Paterson, N. J.	45,967	17,329	37	2,525	5.5	155	0.3	......	......	......	......	803	1.7	3,665	8.0
Philadelphia, Pa.	558,866	254,812	45.6	44,430	8.0	2,357	0.4	1,160	0.2	......	......	21,733	3.9	52,068	9.3
Pittsburg, Pa.	205,847	78,170	38.[illegible]	9,625	4.7	858	0.4	2,[illegible]	[illegible].3	......	......	9,846	4.8	16,268	7.9
Providence, R. I.	131,214	27,656	21.	8,009	6.1	4,603	3.5		.1	......	......	884	0.7	3,500	2.7
Rochester, N. Y.	41,951	40,768	97	6,199	14.8	297	0.7		.7	3,400	8.[illegible]	7,512	17.9	6,184	14.7
San Francisco, Cal.	142,919	21,776	15	1,356	0.9	2,400	1.7		.5	542	0.	2,863	2.0	3,556	2.5
St. Joseph, Mo.	25,280	14,255	56.4	2,476	9.8	324	1.3	2,123	8.4	862	3.4	638	2.5	4,083	16.2
St. Louis, Mo.	302,531	89,121	[illegible]	10,943	3.6	3,442	1.1	[illegible]	[illegible].6	12,928	4.[illegible]	16,508	5.5	19,210	6.3
St. Paul, Minn.	103,639	29,465	.	2,776	2.7	2,267	2.2		3	855	0.	9,685	9.3	4,076	3.9
Scranton, Pa.	70,776	21,901		3,887	5.5	1,610	2.3		4	962	1.	2,471	3.5	4,999	7.1
Syracuse, N. Y.	66,697	23,162	34.7	3,184	4.8	1,936	2.9	320	0.5	550	0.8	3,193	4.8	5,274	7.9
Toledo, Ohio	44,082	30,870	[illegible]	2,648	6.0	2,914	6.6	1,[illegible]	2.4	......	......	10,455	23.7	4,811	10.9
Washington, D. C.	136,759	91,474		37,024	27.1	2,984	2.2	2,	1.6	350	0.3	3,104	2.3	20,077	14.7
Worcester, Mass.	69,588	19,927		3,491	5.0	6,699	9.6	64	0.9	......	......	1,646	2.4	3,431	4.9

CITY.	COMMUNICANTS OR MEMBERS: 1906—continued. Protestant bodies—Continued. Presbyterian bodies. Number.	Presbyterian bodies. Per cent of total.	Protestant Episcopal Church. Number.	Protestant Episcopal Church. Per cent of total.	Reformed bodies. Number.	Reformed bodies. Per cent of total.	United Brethren bodies. Number.	United Brethren bodies. Per cent of total.	Other Protestant bodies. Number.	Other Protestant bodies. Per cent of total.	Roman Catholic Church. Number.	Roman Catholic Church. Per cent of total.	Latter-day Saints. Number.	Latter-day Saints. Per cent of total.	All other bodies. Number.	All other bodies. Per cent of total.
Cities of 25,000 and over	508,775	4.8	453,966	4.3	137,937	1.3	24,494	0.2	324,476	3.1	6,307,529	60.0	33,572	0.3	234,736	2.2
Cities of 100,000 and over	331,199	4.5	320,518	4.4	79,440	1.1	6,019	0.1	222,137	3.0	4,736,585	64.5	5,829	0.1	168,359	2.3
Allegheny, Pa	8,264	13.4	920	1.5	200	0.3	......	......	2,367	3.9	30,313	49.3	168	0.3	1,975	3.2
Baltimore, Md	9,484	4.2	16,812	7.5	4,496	2.0	1,485	0.7	6,123	2.7	100,397	44.6	39	(1)	3,547	1.6
Boston, Mass	3,066	0.8	13,352	3.5	118	(1)	......	......	53,235	14.1	258,936	68.7	109	(1)	6,120	1.6
Buffalo, N. Y	6,724	3.4	8,483	4.3	3,714	1.9	218	0.1	3,496	1.8	126,396	64.7	......	......	4,793	2.5
Chicago, Ill	24,427	2.9	19,275	2.3	5,240	0.6	219	(1)	26,604	3.1	568,764	68.2	400	(1)	27,067	3.2
Cincinnati, Ohio	8,068	5.1	4,308	2.7	1,717	1.1	388	0.2	9,981	6.3	106,211	66.5	......	......	1,932	1.2
Cleveland, Ohio	8,391	5.7	5,880	4.0	4,831	3.3	654	0.4	8,163	5.6	[2]66,432	45.4	98	0.1	3,634	2.5
Columbus, Ohio	4,575	7.2	1,332	2.1	390	0.6	506	0.8	2,649	4.2	28,398	44.9	84	0.1	1,134	1.8
Denver, Colo	5,307	9.0	2,712	4.6	90	0.2	98	0.2	3,087	5.2	25,993	44.3	262	0.4	1,796	3.1
Detroit, Mich	8,620	4.4	8,041	4.1	602	0.3	......	......	2,162	1.1	128,477	66.2	247	0.1	1,397	0.7
Fall River, Mass	370	0.5	2,053	2.9	......	......	......	......	979	1.4	62,195	86.5	164	0.2	907	1.3
Indianapolis, Ind	5,307	6.3	1,916	2.3	1,179	1.4	433	0.5	4,770	5.6	31,351	37.0	14	(1)	795	0.9
Jersey City, N. J	2,973	2.8	4,810	4.6	3,497	3.3	......	......	709	0.7	77,279	73.9	......	......	780	0.7
Kansas City, Mo	4,870	7.9	2,217	3.6	78	0.1	13	(1)	3,002	4.9	19,077	31.0	476	0.8	1,218	2.0
Los Angeles, Cal	6,820	8.3	3,657	4.5	......	......	211	0.3	6,510	8.0	36,695	44.9	562	0.7	2,833	3.5
Louisville, Ky	6,117	4.2	3,632	2.5	1,129	0.8	32	(1)	1,040	0.7	85,170	57.8	66	(1)	1,414	1.0
Memphis, Tenn	3,938	10.5	2,269	6.0	......	......	......	......	491	1.3	5,270	14.1	......	......	584	1.6
Milwaukee, Wis	2,412	1.6	2,798	1.8	575	0.4	......	......	2,639	1.7	101,453	65.4	90	0.1	1,057	0.7
Minneapolis, Minn	6,238	6.4	4,785	4.9	......	......	70	0.1	5,913	6.1	45,642	47.1	67	0.1	2,296	2.4
Newark, N. J	10,629	9.2	5,195	4.5	4,214	3.7	......	......	2,250	2.0	71,845	62.3	......	......	2,266	2.0
New Haven, Conn	300	0.4	4,896	7.2	......	......	......	......	484	0.7	45,383	67.1	......	......	592	0.9
New Orleans, La	3,667	2.0	5,178	2.8	......	......	......	......	506	0.3	148,579	79.7	......	......	1,043	0.6
New York, N. Y	51,547	2.8	92,534	5.0	25,848	1.4	......	......	25,522	1.4	1,413,775	76.9	270	(1)	51,747	2.8
Omaha, Nebr	3,205	9.5	2,094	6.2	36	0.1	......	......	1,393	4.1	15,053	44.4	320	0.9	1,915	5.6
Paterson, N. J	2,734	5.9	2,521	5.5	4,351	9.5	......	......	575	1.3	27,961	60.8	......	......	677	1.5
Philadelphia, Pa	57,874	10.4	46,644	8.3	11,218	2.0	215	(1)	17,113	3.1	289,615	51.8	270	(1)	14,169	2.5
Pittsburg, Pa	25,582	12.4	5,550	2.7	1,173	0.6	......	......	6,679	3.2	120,232	58.4	151	0.1	7,294	3.5
Providence, R. I	1,006	0.8	6,350	4.8	......	......	......	......	3,225	2.5	100,324	76.5	268	0.2	2,976	2.3
Rochester, N. Y	9,170	21.9	4,434	10.6	1,404	3.3	......	......	1,888	4.5	(3)	......	......	......	1,183	2.8
San Francisco, Cal	3,558	2.5	2,846	2.0	......	......	......	......	3,903	2.7	115,921	81.1	491	0.3	4,731	3.3
St. Joseph, Mo	2,028	8.0	765	3.0	85	0.3	......	......	871	3.4	9,980	39.5		2.5	418	1.7
St. Louis, Mo	10,081	3.3	5,590	1.8	412	0.1	......	......	5,087	1.7	208,775	69.0		0.2	4,148	1.4
St. Paul, Minn	4,039	3.9	3,418	3.3	180	0.2	......	......	1,849	1.8	72,899	70.3	627	(1)	1,249	1.2
Scranton, Pa	5,096	7.2	1,764	2.5	99	0.1	......	......	758	1.1	46,738	66.0	[illegible]	0.1	2,089	3.0
Syracuse, N. Y	3,642	5.5	3,146	4.7	565	0.8	......	......	1,362	2.0	42,649	63.9	......	......	886	1.3
Toledo, Ohio	2,285	5.2	2,852	6.5	1,429	3.2	1,217	2.8	1,199	2.7	[4]12,072	27.4	43	0.1	1,097	2.5
Washington, D. C	8,636	6.3	13,692	10.0	580	0.4	260	0.2	2,597	1.9	43,778	32.0	......	......	1,507	1.1
Worcester, Mass	199	0.3	1,807	2.6	......	......	......	......	2,007	2.9	46,560	66.9	......	......	3,101	4.5

[1] Less than one-tenth of 1 per cent.
[2] Exclusive of statistics for Roman Catholic Church not reported separately by cities for part of Cleveland diocese.
[3] Statistics not reported separately by cities for Rochester diocese.
[4] Exclusive of statistics for Roman Catholic Church not reported separately by cities for Rochester diocese and parts of Cleveland and Detroit dioceses.

The third city in respect to the number of communicants or members reported is Philadelphia, with 558,866, and of these 45.6 per cent are Protestants and 51.8 per cent Roman Catholics. The leading Protestant bodies in Philadelphia are the Presbyterian bodies, with 57,874 communicants, or 10.4 per cent of the total for the city; the Methodist bodies, with 52,068, or 9.3 per cent; the Protestant Episcopal Church, with 46,644, or 8.3 per cent; and the Baptist bodies, with 44,430, or 8 per cent. The fourth city is Boston, with 376,728 communicants or members, and of this number 29.6 per cent are Protestants and 68.7 per cent Roman Catholics. The leading Protestant bodies are the Baptist bodies, with 17,349 communicants, or 4.6 per cent of the total; the Protestant Episcopal Church, 13,352, or 3.5 per cent; and the Congregationalists, 12,127, or 3.2 per cent. The city fifth in order is St. Louis, with 302,531 communicants or members, 29.5 per cent being Protestants and 69 per cent Roman Catholics. The Methodist bodies report 19,210 communicants, or 6.3 per cent of the total; the Lutheran bodies, 16,508, or 5.5 per cent; and the German Evangelical Synod of North America, 12,928, or 4.3 per cent.

In the percentage of communicants reported by Protestant bodies (not including "other Protestant bodies") in the 38 cities shown in the table, the Methodist bodies lead in 11 cities, namely, Baltimore, Cincinnati, Columbus, Denver, Fall River, Indianapolis, Kansas City, Mo., Los Angeles, St. Joseph, St. Louis, and Syracuse; the Lutheran bodies in 8, namely, Chicago, Cleveland, Detroit, Jersey City, Milwaukee, Minneapolis, St. Paul, and Toledo; the Baptist bodies in 6, namely, Boston, Louisville, Memphis, New Orleans, Providence, and Washington; the Presbyterian bodies in 6, namely, Allegheny, Newark, Philadelphia, Pittsburg, Rochester, and Scranton; the Congregationalists in 2, namely, New Haven and Worcester; the German Evangelical Synod of North America in 1, Buffalo; the Protestant Episcopal Church in 1, New York; and the Reformed bodies in 1, Paterson, N. J. In both Omaha and San Francisco the Methodist and Presbyterian bodies show the same percentage of communicants, which is in each case higher than that for any other Protestant body.

In regard to the absolute numerical strength of the leading Protestant bodies in the cities mentioned in the table, it appears that the Baptist bodies have their greatest strength in New York, Philadelphia, and Washington; the Congregationalists, in New York, Chicago, and Boston; the Disciples or Christians, in Indianapolis, Kansas City, Mo., and Chicago; the German Evangelical Synod of North America, in Chicago, Buffalo, and St. Louis; the Lutheran bodies, in Chicago, New York, and Milwaukee; the Methodist bodies, in New York, Philadelphia, Baltimore, and Chicago; the Presbyterian bodies, in Philadelphia, New York, and Pittsburg; the Protestant Episcopal Church, in New York, Philadelphia, and Chicago; the Reformed bodies, in New York and Philadelphia; and the United Brethren bodies, in Baltimore.

In the 5 leading cities the proportion of communicants to population is as follows: New York, 44.7 per cent; Chicago, 40.7 per cent; Philadelphia, 38.8 per cent; Boston, 62.6 per cent; and St. Louis, 46.6 per cent. In general, cities which have a relatively large Roman Catholic population show a higher percentage of church members than cities in which this body has a comparatively small representation. In Fall River, as shown by the table, 86.5 per cent of the total number of communicants reported are Roman Catholics, the church membership represents 67.8 per cent of the population, while in Memphis, where 84.4 per cent of the communicants reported belong to Protestant bodies, the church membership is only 30 per cent of the population.

The following diagrams illustrate the relative strength in membership of the principal families and separate denominations. Diagram 7 shows that strength in the different classes of cities; diagram 8 shows it in a selected list of cities; and diagram 9 shows the relative strength of Protestant, Roman Catholic, and all other bodies, and of those not reported in connection with any religious organization.

Diagram 7.—DISTRIBUTION OF COMMUNICANTS OR MEMBERS IN EACH PRINCIPAL FAMILY OR DENOMINATION, FOR CITIES OF 25,000 INHABITANTS OR MORE IN 1900 (ARRANGED IN FOUR CLASSES) AND OUTSIDE OF CITIES: 1906.

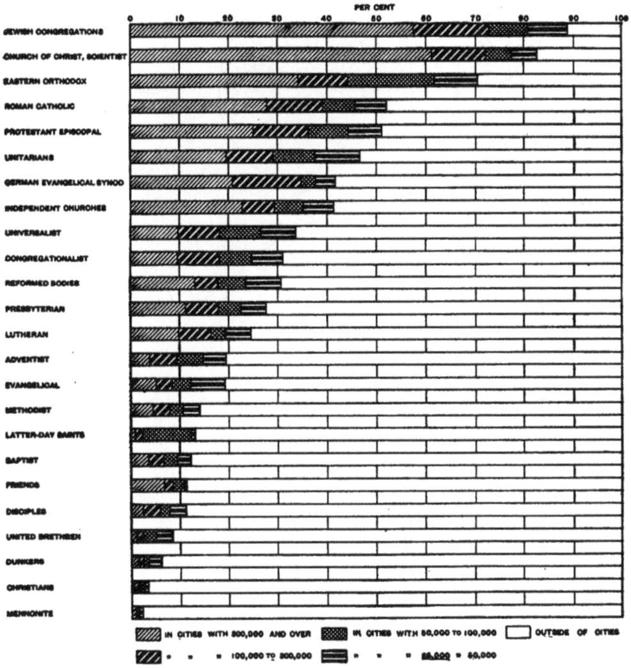

Diagram 8.—DISTRIBUTION OF COMMUNICANTS OR MEMBERS BY PRINCIPAL FAMILIES OR DENOMINATIONS, FOR 24 PRINCIPAL CITIES: 1906.

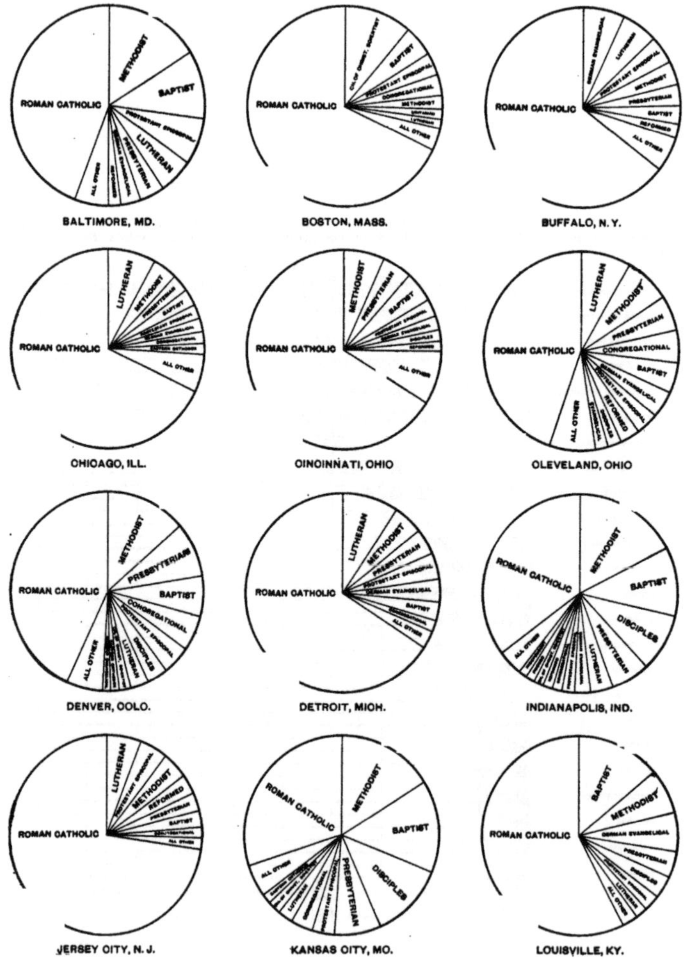

Diagram 8.—DISTRIBUTION OF COMMUNICANTS OR MEMBERS BY PRINCIPAL FAMILIES OR DENOMINATIONS, FOR 24 PRINCIPAL CITIES: 1906—Continued.

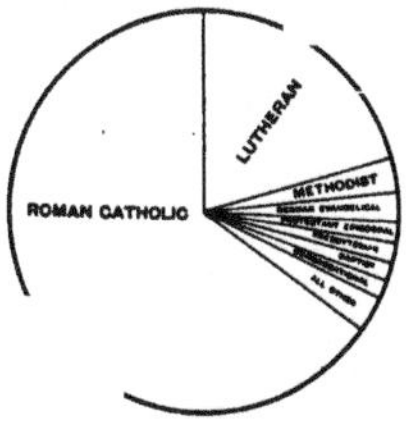

MILWAUKEE, WIS.

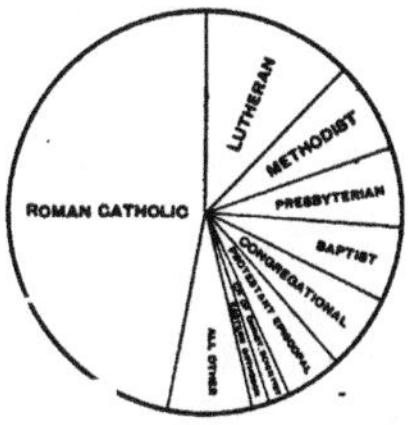

MINNEAPOLIS, MINN.

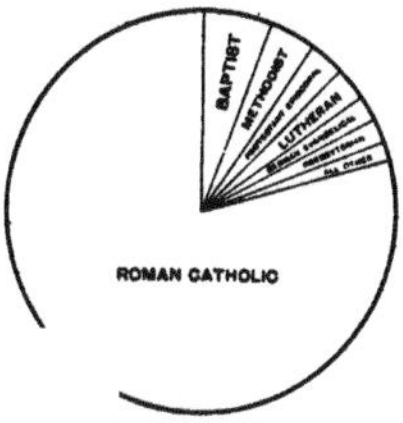

NEW ORLEANS, LA.

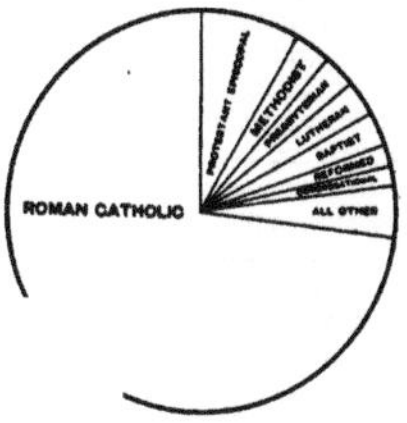

NEW YORK, N. Y.

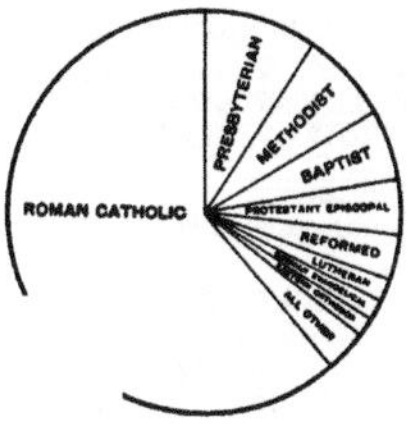

NEWARK, N. J.

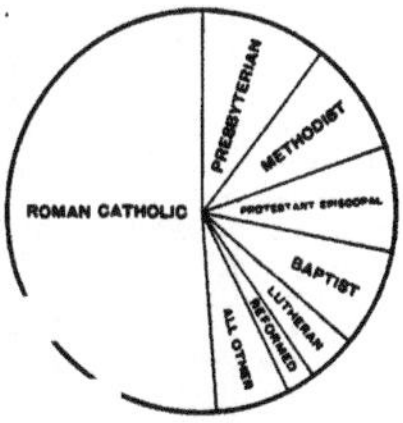

PHILADELPHIA, PA.

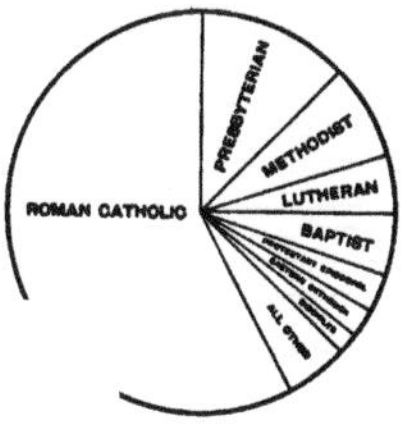

PITTSBURG, PA.

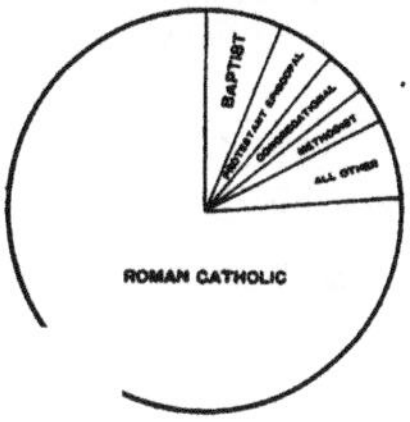

PROVIDENCE, R. I.

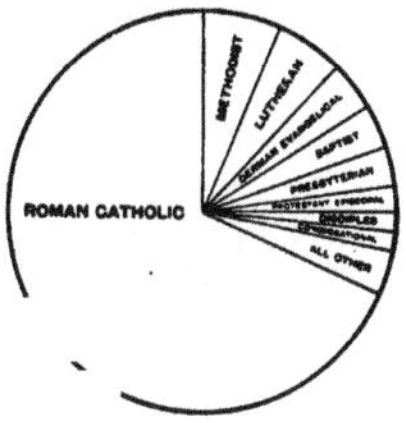

ST. LOUIS, MO.

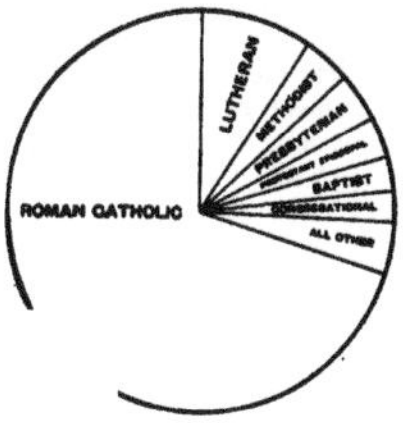

ST. PAUL, MINN.

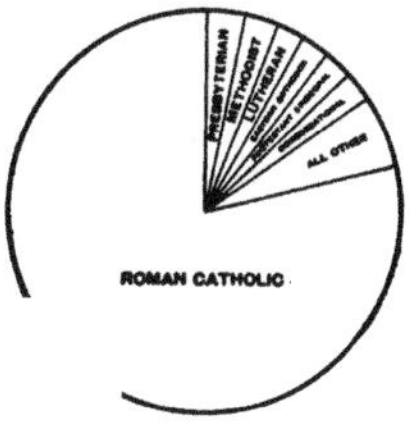

SAN FRANCISCO, CAL.

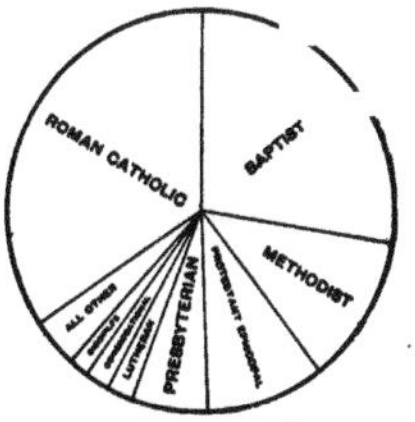

WASHINGTON, D. C.

DIAGRAM 9.—PROPORTION OF THE POPULATION REPORTED AS PROTESTANT, ROMAN CATHOLIC, AND "ALL OTHER" CHURCH MEMBERS, AND PROPORTION NOT REPORTED AS CHURCH MEMBERS, FOR 35 PRINCIPAL CITIES IN DETAIL: 1906.

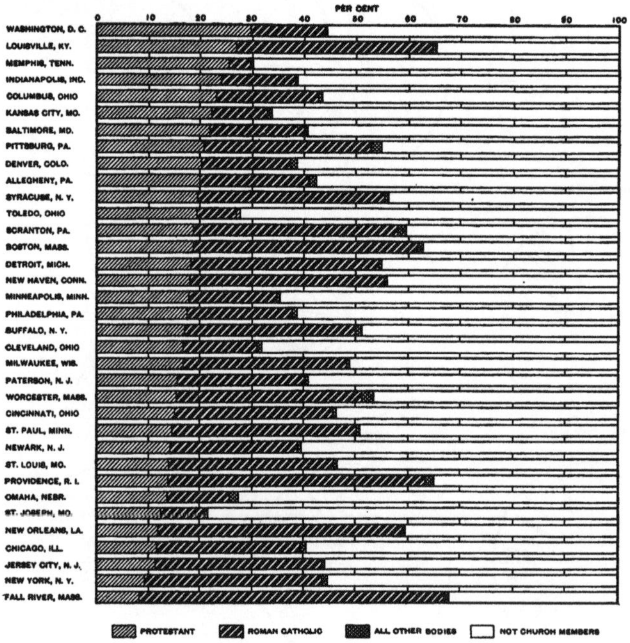

SUNDAY SCHOOLS.

SCHOOLS CONDUCTED BY CHURCH ORGANIZATIONS.

The statistics of Sunday schools, which are limited to 1906, are given in detail by denominations in Table 1 (page 148), and include only those Sunday schools which are conducted by church organizations. They are derived, as in other cases, from the returns for the individual organizations in the several denominations.

Total number of schools, teachers, and scholars.—The following table shows, for 1906, by principal families and separate denominations, the number and per cent of organizations reporting Sunday schools and the number and per cent distribution of Sunday schools, officers and teachers, and scholars.

DENOMINATION.	1906							
	Organizations reporting Sunday schools.		Sunday schools reported.		Sunday school officers and teachers.		Sunday school scholars.	
	Number.	Per cent of total.	Number.	Per cent distribution.	Number.	Per cent distribution.	Number.	Per cent distribution.
All denominations	167,574	79.0	178,214	100.0	1,648,664	100.0	14,685,997	100.0
Protestant bodies	156,437	80.0	165,128	92.7	1,564,821	94.9	13,018,434	88.6
Adventist bodies	2,078	81.5	2,242	1.3	14,286	0.9	69,110	0.5
Baptist bodies	41,165	75.0	43,178	24.2	323,473	19.6	2,898,914	19.7
Christians (Christian Connection)	1,136	82.4	1,149	0.6	10,510	0.6	72,963	0.5
Church of Christ, Scientist	550	86.2	551	0.3	3,155	0.2	16,116	0.1
Congregationalists	5,327	93.2	5,741	3.2	75,801	4.6	638,089	4.3
Disciples or Christians	7,901	72.2	8,078	4.5	70,476	4.3	634,504	4.3
Dunkers or German Baptist Brethren	866	78.9	1,223	0.7	10,789	0.7	78,575	0.5
Evangelical bodies	2,454	89.6	2,549	1.4	32,113	1.9	214,998	1.5
Friends	846	73.8	887	0.5	7,735	0.5	53,761	0.4
German Evangelical Synod of North America	1,086	90.1	1,111	0.6	12,079	0.7	116,106	0.8
Independent churches	826	76.6	922	0.5	6,732	0.4	57,680	0.4
Lutheran bodies	8,682	68.3	9,450	5.3	83,891	5.1	782,786	5.3
Mennonite bodies	411	66.0	439	0.2	5,041	0.3	44,922	0.3
Methodist bodies	55,227	85.4	57,464	32.2	569,296	34.5	4,472,930	30.5
Presbyterian bodies	13,048	84.1	14,452	8.1	176,647	10.7	1,511,175	10.3
Protestant Episcopal Church	5,211	76.1	5,601	3.1	51,048	3.1	464,351	3.2
Reformed bodies	2,345	90.7	2,588	1.5	38,710	2.3	361,548	2.5
Unitarians	358	77.7	364	0.2	3,592	0.2	24,006	0.2
United Brethren bodies	3,777	87.8	3,870	2.2	42,169	2.6	301,320	2.1
Universalists	596	70.4	600	0.3	6,585	0.4	42,201	0.3
Other Protestant bodies	2,547	68.9	2,669	1.5	20,698	1.3	162,380	1.1
Roman Catholic Church	9,406	75.4	11,172	6.3	62,470	3.8	1,481,535	10.1
Jewish congregations	561	31.7	600	0.3	2,239	0.1	49,514	0.3
Latter-day Saints	1,036	87.5	1,169	0.7	18,507	1.1	130,085	0.9
Eastern Orthodox Churches	7	1.7	7	(1)	10	(1)	509	(1)
All other bodies	127	16.6	138	0.1	617	(1)	5,920	(1)

1 Less than one-tenth of 1 per cent.

From this table it appears that only 79 per cent of the total number of organizations reported Sunday schools, although in several denominations the percentage was much higher. The reason for the low average is chiefly found in the fact that certain bodies, as shown in Table 1 (page 148), report no Sunday schools. The percentage for the Baptist bodies as a whole is considerably lowered by the small percentage reported for the Southern Baptist Convention, as well as by the fact that the Primitive Baptists report no Sunday schools. For the Lutheran bodies, it should be noted that the parochial schools, in which religious as well as secular instruction is given, to a considerable extent take the place of Sunday schools. This fact affects the percentage of organizations reporting Sunday schools, especially in the Evangelical Lutheran Synodical Conference of America and the Synod for the Norwegian Evangelical Lutheran Church in America.

Among the Eastern Orthodox Churches there are but few Sunday schools, more attention being given to parish schools in which both secular and religious instruction is given. A comparatively small percentage also of the Jewish congregations report Sunday schools, the religious instruction of their children being provided for by other schools and by private teaching. Similarly, the small percentage reported for "all other bodies" is due to the fact that four of these bodies—Chinese Temples, Theosophical Society in America, Amana Society, and Vedanta Society—maintain no Sunday schools, and with nearly all of the remainder Sunday schools are the exception.

Among the Protestant bodies, the Methodist and Baptist bodies together report 56.4 per cent of the entire number of denominational Sunday schools. Next in order come the Presbyterian and Lutheran bodies and the Disciples or Christians, the five families combined reporting 132,622 Sunday schools, or nearly three-fourths (74.4 per cent) of the entire number, and more than four-fifths (80.3 per cent) of all those reported by Protestant bodies.

From Table 1 (page 148) it appears that in the different families there is frequently a concentration in 2 or 3 bodies. Thus the Methodist Episcopal Church and the Methodist Episcopal Church, South, the 3 branches of Baptists, the Presbyterian Church in the United States of America, and the Lutherans—General Council, General Synod, and Synodical Conference—report by far the greater part of the Sunday schools in their respective families. The situation is essentially the same in regard to the officers and teachers, and scholars.

Average number of scholars and teachers per school.—The average number of scholars and of teachers per Sunday school, and the average number of scholars per teacher are given for each of the principal families and separate denominations in the following table.

DENOMINATION.	1906		
	Scholars, average per school.	Teachers, average per school.	Scholars, average per teacher.
All denominations	82	9.3	8.9
Protestant bodies	79	9.5	8.3
Adventist bodies	31	6.4	4.8
Baptist bodies	67	7.5	9.0
Christians (Christian Connection)	64	9.1	6.9
Church of Christ, Scientist	29	5.7	5.1
Congregationalists	111	13.2	8.4
Disciples or Christians	79	8.7	9.0
Dunkers or German Baptist Brethren	64	8.8	7.3
Evangelical bodies	84	12.6	6.7
Friends	61	8.7	7.0
German Evangelical Synod of North America	105	10.9	9.6
Independent churches	63	7.3	8.6
Lutheran bodies	83	8.9	9.3
Mennonite bodies	102	11.5	8.9
Methodist bodies	78	9.9	7.9
Presbyterian bodies	105	12.2	8.6
Protestant Episcopal Church	83	9.1	9.1
Reformed bodies	140	15.0	9.3
Unitarians	66	9.9	6.7
United Brethren bodies	78	10.9	7.1
Universalists	70	11.0	6.4
Other Protestant bodies	61	7.8	7.8
Roman Catholic Church	133	5.6	23.7
Jewish congregations	83	3.7	22.1
Latter-day Saints	111	15.8	7.0
Eastern Orthodox Churches	73	1.4	50.9
All other bodies	43	4.5	9.6

The average number of scholars per school for all denominations, as shown by the above table, is 82, the largest average shown being 140, for the Reformed bodies, and the lowest, 29, for the Church of Christ, Scientist. But this table should be examined in connection with Table 1 (page 148) on account of the divergencies in the families. Thus the average membership for the Reformed bodies, 140, includes averages varying from 159, for the Reformed Church in America, to 45, for the Hungarian Reformed Church in America; the average for the Presbyterian bodies, 105, covers a range from 132, as reported for the single school of the Reformed Presbyterian Church in the United States and Canada, to as low as 32 for the Associate Synod of North America (Associate Presbyterian Church). The situation is essentially the same in regard to the average number of teachers (including officers) per school, and the average number of scholars per teacher. In some cases, as in the Roman Catholic Church, the Eastern Orthodox Churches, and the Jewish congregations, the small average number of teachers is probably due to different methods adopted or to the small number of Sunday schools reported, while the large average of scholars per teacher corresponds to the small average of teachers.

Ratio of communicants to Sunday school scholars.—In order to show the ratio of communicants or members to Sunday school scholars the following table is presented, giving by principal families and separate denominations the average number of communicants per individual church organization, the average number of scholars per school for schools conducted by church organizations, and the ratio of communicants to Sunday school scholars:

DENOMINATION.	1906		
	Communicants or members, average per organization.	Scholars, average per school.	Communicants or members to 1 scholar.
All denominations	157	82	1.9
Protestant bodies	104	79	1.3
Adventist bodies	37	31	1.2
Baptist bodies	104	67	1.6
Christians (Christian Connection)	81	64	1.3
Church of Christ, Scientist	136	29	4.7
Congregationalists	123	111	1.1
Disciples or Christians	105	79	1.3
Dunkers or German Baptist Brethren	89	64	1.4
Evangelical bodies	64	84	0.8
Friends	100	61	1.6
German Evangelical Synod of North America	245	105	2.3
Independent churches	69	63	1.1
Lutheran bodies	167	83	2.0
Mennonite bodies	91	102	0.9
Methodist bodies	89	78	1.1
Presbyterian bodies	118	105	1.1
Protestant Episcopal Church	132	83	1.6
Reformed bodies	174	140	1.2
Unitarians	162	66	2.5
United Brethren bodies	69	78	0.9
Universalists	79	70	1.1
Other Protestant bodies	62	61	1.0
Roman Catholic Church	969	133	7.3
Jewish congregations	[1] 88	83	1.1
Latter-day Saints	217	111	2.0
Eastern Orthodox Churches	315	73	4.3
All other bodies	117	43	2.7

[1] Heads of families only.

As shown by this table, the number of communicants to each scholar, for all denominations, is 1.9. There are 3 bodies which show a greater average number of scholars per Sunday school than of communicants per organization, namely, the Mennonite bodies and the United Brethren bodies, each with a ratio of 0.9 communicants to each scholar, and the Evangelical bodies, with 0.8. Of the remaining bodies, those which show a marked variation from the general average for all denominations, are the Roman Catholic Church, with 7.3 communicants per scholar, the Church of Christ, Scientist, with 4.7, and the Eastern Orthodox Churches, with 4.3.

ALL SUNDAY SCHOOLS, INCLUDING UNDENOMINATIONAL SCHOOLS.

In addition to the Sunday schools conducted by church organizations, there are a large number of undenominational and union Sunday schools, and, as the statistics of these are essential to an adequate presentation of the Sunday school work in the United States, they were secured through the agency of the International Sunday School Association. Including these, the total number of Sunday schools reported for 1906 was 192,722, with 1,746,074 officers and teachers, and 15,337,811 scholars, as shown by the following summary:

KIND OF SUNDAY SCHOOL.	1906		
	Number of Sunday schools reported.	Number of officers and teachers.	Number of scholars.
All Sunday schools	192,722	1,746,074	15,337,811
Denominational	178,214	1,648,664	14,685,997
Undenominational and union	14,508	97,410	651,814

These figures do not include the mission Sunday schools which are maintained by some bodies, notably the Congregationalists and the Presbyterian Church in the United States of America, but which are not connected with local organizations. With these exceptions, however, it is believed that the figures given in the summary represent a substantially full report of the Sunday schools of the country.

Distribution by states and territories.—The general statistics of denominational and undenominational Sunday schools at the close of the year 1906 are given by states and territories, in the table which follows:

STATE OR TERRITORY.	1906								
	All Sunday schools.			Denominational Sunday schools.			Undenominational and union Sunday schools.		
	Sunday schools.	Officers and teachers.	Scholars.	Sunday schools.	Officers and teachers.	Scholars.	Sunday schools.	Officers and teachers.	Scholars.
Continental United States	192,722	1,746,074	15,337,811	178,214	1,648,664	14,685,997	14,508	97,410	651,814
North Atlantic division	34,082	469,310	4,418,106	31,768	447,634	4,282,562	2,314	21,676	135,544
Maine	1,657	14,811	113,596	1,450	13,420	107,440	207	1,391	6,156
New Hampshire	835	8,097	66,741	763	7,815	64,865	72	282	1,876
Vermont	902	8,429	62,624	872	8,200	61,277	30	229	1,347
Massachusetts	3,111	52,834	497,782	2,999	51,882	491,697	112	952	6,085
Rhode Island	506	8,330	81,791	491	8,187	80,901	15	143	890
Connecticut	1,396	19,803	182,502	1,340	19,320	179,673	56	483	2,829
New York	9,189	126,839	1,273,300	8,795	123,319	1,247,051	394	3,520	26,249
New Jersey	3,004	44,502	416,021	2,785	42,613	404,095	219	1,889	11,926
Pennsylvania	13,482	185,665	1,723,749	12,273	172,878	1,645,563	1,209	12,787	78,186
South Atlantic division	37,414	283,604	2,481,930	35,763	273,704	2,412,617	1,651	9,900	69,313
Delaware	448	5,655	50,313	441	5,604	49,926	7	51	387
Maryland	2,672	32,038	266,471	2,606	31,174	261,440	66	864	5,031
District of Columbia	302	5,392	57,550	297	5,338	56,771	5	54	779
Virginia	6,521	53,207	451,667	5,965	50,229	430,452	556	2,978	21,215
West Virginia	3,699	29,037	223,777	3,486	27,577	212,577	213	1,460	11,200
North Carolina	7,511	54,245	495,403	7,293	53,132	487,261	218	1,113	8,142
South Carolina	5,099	35,669	334,072	5,020	35,054	328,829	79	615	5,243
Georgia	8,456	52,478	474,780	8,052	50,246	460,769	404	2,232	14,011
Florida	2,706	15,883	127,897	2,603	15,350	124,592	103	533	3,305
North Central division	64,905	611,991	5,080,905	58,705	570,384	4,805,135	6,200	41,607	275,770
Ohio	9,683	114,752	967,534	9,226	111,122	939,469	457	3,630	28,065
Indiana	6,222	65,741	532,074	5,879	63,042	516,809	343	2,699	15,265
Illinois	8,713	97,318	856,526	8,173	92,913	825,323	540	4,405	31,203
Michigan	5,537	55,319	452,244	4,830	49,847	414,421	707	5,472	37,823
Wisconsin	4,381	30,406	289,187	4,036	28,770	278,691	345	1,636	10,496
Minnesota	4,498	32,301	291,399	3,975	29,521	273,223	523	2,780	18,176
Iowa	6,105	57,279	434,551	5,57	54,016	413,548	530	3,263	21,003
Missouri	7,599	64,158	537,622	6,91	59,678	504,770	682	4,480	32,852
North Dakota	1,616	7,977	64,864	1,51[illegible]	7,407	61,199	105	570	3,665
South Dakota	1,765	10,128	80,763	1,463	8,587	71,554	302	1,541	9,209
Nebraska	3,376	27,712	210,927	2,845	24,242	192,443	531	3,470	18,484
Kansas	5,410	48,900	363,214	4,275	41,239	313,685	1,135	7,661	49,529
South Central division	46,142	289,672	2,562,972	42,951	272,087	2,433,161	3,191	17,585	129,811
Kentucky	5,275	37,241	343,991	4,723	33,833	314,667	552	3,408	29,324
Tennessee	6,494	42,767	369,217	6,101	40,875	355,550	393	1,892	13,667
Alabama	6,917	40,904	365,868	6,808	40,238	361,279	109	666	4,589
Mississippi	6,053	33,177	290,525	5,911	32,422	286,257	142	755	4,268
Louisiana	3,493	18,681	184,410	3,320	17,963	177,739	173	718	6,671
Arkansas	4,842	30,337	248,531	4,398	27,979	230,238	444	2,358	18,293
Oklahoma [1]	3,684	24,499	201,947	3,012	20,684	173,896	672	3,815	28,051
Texas	9,384	62,066	558,483	8,678	58,093	533,535	706	3,973	24,948
Western division	10,179	91,497	793,898	9,027	84,855	752,522	1,152	6,642	41,376
Montana	508	3,454	35,226	477	3,298	33,891	31	156	1,335
Idaho	663	6,390	47,828	599	6,043	45,437	64	347	2,391
Wyoming	290	1,969	15,920	202	1,556	13,472	88	413	2,448
Colorado	1,407	12,351	108,736	1,099	10,446	96,919	308	1,905	11,817
New Mexico	409	1,924	21,257	364	1,716	20,050	45	208	1,207
Arizona	237	1,841	15,682	217	1,703	14,967	20	138	715
Utah	599	10,783	90,608	575	10,681	89,887	24	102	721
Nevada	91	589	5,085	84	550	4,641	7	39	444
Washington	1,810	15,064	121,778	1,631	13,870	114,467	179	1,194	7,311
Oregon	1,277	10,653	81,466	1,090	9,545	75,119	187	1,108	6,347
California	2,888	26,479	250,312	2,689	25,447	243,672	199	1,032	6,640

[1] Oklahoma and Indian Territory combined.

From this table it appears that Pennsylvania has the largest number of Sunday schools, followed closely by Ohio, Texas, and New York. Pennsylvania also leads in the number of denominational Sunday schools, with Ohio second, followed in order by New York and Texas.

Distribution by geographic divisions.—The following table gives the distribution of denominational and undenominational Sunday schools according to geographic divisions, and, in addition, shows for continental United States and for each geographic division separately the per cent which each class bears to all Sunday schools:

GEOGRAPHIC DIVISION.	1906							
	All Sunday schools.		Denominational Sunday schools.		Undenominational Sunday schools.		Per cent of all Sunday schools.	
	Number.	Per cent distribution.	Number.	Per cent distribution.	Number.	Per cent distribution.	Denominational.	Undenominational.
Continental United States.	192,722	100.0	178,214	100.0	14,508	100 0	92.5	7.5
North Atlantic	34,082	17.7	31,768	17.8	2,314	15.9	93.2	6.8
South Atlantic	37,414	19.4	35,763	20.1	1,651	11.4	95.6	4.4
North Central	64,905	33.7	58,705	32.9	6,200	42.7	90.4	9.6
South Central	46,142	23.9	42,951	24.1	3,191	22.0	93.1	6.9
Western	10,179	5.3	9,027	5.1	1,152	7.9	88.7	11.3

From this table it appears that the percentages for all Sunday schools and for denominational Sunday schools in the various geographic divisions correspond very closely. For the undenominational Sunday schools, however, as already intimated, there is considerable variation. The highest percentage for these schools, 42.7 per cent, shown for the North Central division, is considerably above the percentages for denominational Sunday schools and all Sunday schools for the same division, and the percentage for the Western division is likewise relatively high; while that for the South Atlantic division, 11.4 per cent, is much below the percentages for denominational Sunday schools and all Sunday schools for that division. In the North Atlantic and South Central divisions the percentages for the three classes are approximately the same.

With regard to the relation of denominational and undenominational Sunday schools to the total number of Sunday schools, it is notable that the denominational Sunday schools represent 92.5 per cent of the total and the undenominational 7.5 per cent. If the geographic divisions be considered, the highest percentage of denominational Sunday schools, 95.6, is shown for the South Atlantic division, and the lowest, 88.7, for the Western division, and, conversely, for undenominational Sunday schools, the highest percentage, 11.3, is shown for the Western division; and the lowest, 4.4, for the South Atlantic division. From the last two tables it appears that, in general, the largest representation of the undenominational and union Sunday schools is in those divisions and in those states that are more distinctively rural in character, or which have been settled most recently.

The following table gives for continental United States and for the geographic divisions the average number of scholars per school, the average number of teachers per school, and the average number of scholars per teacher, for all Sunday schools and for the denominational and undenominational Sunday schools separately:

GEOGRAPHIC DIVISION.	1906								
	All Sunday schools.			Denominational Sunday schools.			Undenominational Sunday schools.		
	Scholars, average per school.	Teachers, average per school.	Scholars, average per teacher.	Scholars, average per school.	Teachers, average per school.	Scholars, average per teacher.	Scholars, average per school.	Teachers, average per school.	Scholars, average per teacher.
Continental United States	80	9.1	8.8	82	9.3	8.9	45	6.7	6.7
North Atlantic	130	13.8	9.4	135	14.1	9.6	59	9.4	6.3
South Atlantic	66	7.6	8.8	67	7.7	8.8	42	6.0	7.0
North Central	78	9.4	8.3	82	9.7	8.4	44	6.7	6.6
South Central	56	6.3	8.8	57	6.3	8.9	41	5.5	7.4
Western	78	9.0	8.7	83	9.4	8.9	36	5.8	6.2

For continental United States, as shown by the above table, the average number of scholars per school, for the denominational and undenominational schools taken together, is 80; for the denominational schools, 82; and for the undenominational, 45. The geographic division showing the largest average number of scholars per school, both for denominational and undenominational schools, is the North Atlantic, while the division showing the smallest average number for denominational schools is the South Central, and for undenominational, the Western.

The average number of teachers per school, for continental United States, for all Sunday schools, is 9.1; for the denominational schools, 9.3; and for the undenominational schools, 6.7. The geographic division showing the largest average number of teachers per school, for both the denominational and undenominational schools, is the North Atlantic, and the division showing the smallest average number for each is the South Central.

The average number of scholars per teacher for continental United States, for both classes of schools, is 8.8; for the denominational schools, 8.9; and for the undenominational, 6.7. The geographic division showing the largest average number for denominational schools is the North Atlantic, and for undenominational, the South Central, while the division showing the smallest average number for denominational schools is the North Central, and for undenominational, the Western.

MINISTERS.

The statistics for ministers are given by denominations only. They have been obtained from various authoritative sources, either from the published reports of the several denominations or through correspondence with representatives. They include, in nearly every instance, only those who are duly authorized to administer the sacraments and to perform all the usual functions of the ministry, whether or not in active service as pastors in charge of churches. Licentiates and other similar classes who are sometimes regarded as ministers are not included. The number of ministers is estimated for the following 6 denominations which furnished no returns or only partial returns, namely: United Baptists, Two-Seed-in-the-Spirit Predestinarian Baptists, United American Freewill Baptists (Colored), Church of God and Saints of Christ (Colored), Churches of Christ (Disciples), and African Methodist Episcopal Church. For 2 bodies—the Apostolic Faith Movement and the Independent churches—ministers are not reported, since the number could not be reasonably estimated from the information received. The first of these bodies is small, having but 6 organizations. The Independent churches number 1,079, but since they have no central organization from which a report on the number of ministers could be obtained, and since many of them appear to be supplied by ministers connected with some of the various denominations, no attempt was made to arrive at an estimate of the number of ministers. Two bodies, having 1 organization each—the Reformed Presbyterian Church (Covenanted) and the Reformed Presbyterian Church in the United States and Canada—report no ministers, as the former is supplied by a theological student, and the latter by ministers from other Presbyterian bodies. There are 15 denominations which report no regular ministry, namely, the Bahais, Christadelphians, Christian Israelite Church, Plymouth Brethren (4 bodies), United Society of Believers (Shakers), Amana Society, Society for Ethical Culture, the 4 Theosophical societies, and the Vedanta Society.

TOTAL NUMBER.

The number of ministers, as reported for 1890 and 1906, is given in detail by denominations in Table 8 (page 514). The following table shows, by principal families and separate denominations, the number of ministers as reported for 1890 and 1906, together with the actual and relative increase since 1890:

DENOMINATION.	NUMBER OF MINISTERS.		INCREASE FROM 1890 TO 1906.	
	1906	1890	Number.	Per cent.
All denominations	164,830	[1]111,036	53,794	48.4
Protestant bodies	146,451	99,605	46,846	47.0
Adventist bodies	1,152	1,364	[2]212	[2]15.5
Baptist bodies	43,790	25,646	18,144	70.7
Christians (Christian Connection)	1,011	1,435	[2]424	[2]29.5
Church of Christ, Scientist	1,276	26	1,250	(3)
Congregationalists	5,802	5,058	744	14.7
Disciples or Christians	8,741	3,773	4,968	131.7
Dunkers or German Baptist Brethren	2,255	2,088	167	8.0
Evangelical bodies	1,495	1,235	260	21.1
Friends	1,479	1,277	202	15.8
German Evangelical Synod of North America	972	680	292	42.9
Independent churches	(4)	[1]54	[2]54	(3)
Lutheran bodies	7,841	4,591	3,250	70.8
Mennonite bodies	1,006	905	101	11.2
Methodist bodies	39,737	30,000	9,737	32.5
Presbyterian bodies	12,456	[1]10,448	2,008	19.2
Protestant Episcopal Church	5,368	[1]4,146	1,222	29.5
Reformed bodies	2,039	1,506	533	35.4
Unitarians	541	515	26	5.0
United Brethren bodies	2,435	2,798	[2]363	[2]13.0
Universalists	724	708	16	2.3
Other Protestant bodies	6,331	1,352	4,979	368.3
Roman Catholic Church	15,177	[1]9,166	6,011	65.6
Jewish congregations	1,084	200	884	442.0
Latter-day Saints	1,774	2,043	[2]269	[2]13.2
Eastern Orthodox Churches	108	[1]14	94	(3)
All other bodies	236	8	228	(3)

[1] Includes figures for Alaska, not returned separately.
[2] Decrease.
[3] Per cent not shown where base is less than 100.
[4] Not reported.

The family reporting the greatest number of ministers for 1906 is the Baptist, with 43,790, or 26.6 per cent of the total, while the Methodist bodies come next in order, with 39,737, or 24.1 per cent of the total. These 2 families show a little more than one-half the entire number of ministers. The Presbyterian bodies report 12,456 ministers, the Disciples or Christians, 8,741, and the Lutheran bodies, 7,841.

According to the figures given in the table, the total increase in the number of ministers since 1890 is 53,794, or 48.4 per cent. The Protestant bodies show an increase of 46,846, or 47 per cent, and the Roman Catholic Church an increase of 6,011, or 65.6 per cent. Among the Protestant bodies, those showing the greatest absolute increase are the Baptist bodies, with a gain of 18,144, or 70.7 per cent; the Methodist bodies, with a gain of 9,737, or 32.5 per cent; the Disciples or Christians, with a gain of 4,968, or 131.7 per cent; the Lutheran bodies, with a gain of 3,250, or 70.8 per cent; and the Presbyterian bodies, with a gain of 2,008, or 19.2 per cent.

Of the Baptist bodies, as indicated by the figures in Table 8 (page 514), the National Baptist Convention (Colored) leads, with an increase of 11,649 ministers, or 213 per cent; and is followed by the Southern Baptist Convention, with an increase of 4,359, or 48.7 per cent. The Freewill Baptists show a gain of 482, or 408.5 per cent. Among the Methodist bodies, the African Methodist Episcopal Church leads, with an increase of 2,879 ministers, or 86.7 per cent; and is followed by the Methodist Episcopal Church, with an increase of 2,056, or 13.3 per cent; and the African Methodist Episcopal Zion Church, with an increase of 1,517, or 96.9 per cent. Among the Lutheran bodies, the Synodical Conference comes first, with an increase of 1,103 ministers, or 86 per cent; and is followed by the General Synod, with an increase of 345, or 35.7 per cent; and the United Norwegian Lutheran Church, with an increase of 344, or 315.6 per cent. Among the Presbyterian bodies, the Presbyterian Church in the United States of America ranks first, with an increase of 1,669 ministers, or 28.1 per cent, and the Presbyterian Church in the United States comes next, with an increase of 477, or 42.2 per cent.

The great increase shown for the Church of Christ, Scientist, is apparently due in large part to a difference in the organization of the church, the returns for 1906 showing 2 ministers, or "readers," to each organization, whereas the report for 1890 showed only 26 ministers to 221 organizations. In the case of the Jewish congregations also, the large increase is probably due chiefly to a difference in the basis of reporting. Moreover, it is possible that the report concerning ministers of this denomination for 1890 was incomplete on account of the special difficulty, in this case, of obtaining complete statistics.

The decrease in the number of ministers, as shown in the table, for the Adventist bodies appears mainly in connection with the Advent Christian Church, while in the case of the Latter-day Saints, it appears wholly in the Reorganized Church of Jesus Christ of Latter-day Saints. The decrease shown for these bodies, as well as for the Christians (Christian Connection) and the United Brethren bodies, may in some instances be due to an actual decrease in the number of ministers, but is probably due in most instances either to incomplete returns, or to a difference in the basis of reporting the ministers at the two periods. The Latter-day Saints, especially, have numerous orders in the ministry, and the question might have arisen as to how many of them should be included, as properly corresponding with the regular ordained ministry of other denominations.

The figures given for "other Protestant bodies" and for "all other bodies" for 1906 are not comparable with those for 1890, since the bodies composing these two classes are not entirely the same for the two periods, some being included in each class for 1906 which were not in existence, or not reported, in 1890.

Ratio of organizations to ministers.—The ratio of organizations to ministers for 1906 and 1890, respectively, is shown for the principal families and separate denominations in the following table:

DENOMINATION.	NUMBER OF ORGANIZATIONS PER MINISTER.	
	1906	1890
All denominations	1.3	1.5
Protestant bodies	1.3	1.5
Adventist bodies	2.2	1.3
Baptist bodies	1.3	1.7
Christians (Christian Connection)	1.4	1.0
Church of Christ, Scientist	0.5	8.5
Congregationalists	1.0	1.0
Disciples or Christians	1.3	1.9
Dunkers or German Baptist Brethren	0.5	0.5
Evangelical bodies	1.8	1.9
Friends	0.8	0.8
German Evangelical Synod of North America	1.2	1.3
Independent churches	(1)	2.9
Lutheran bodies	1.6	1.9
Mennonite bodies	0.6	0.6
Methodist bodies	1.6	1.7
Presbyterian bodies	1.2	1.3
Protestant Episcopal Church	1.3	1.2
Reformed bodies	1.3	1.4
Unitarians	0.9	0.8
United Brethren bodies	1.8	1.6
Universalists	1.2	1.4
Other Protestant bodies	0.6	1.5
Roman Catholic Church	0.8	1.1
Jewish congregations	1.6	2.7
Latter-day Saints	0.7	0.4
Eastern Orthodox Churches	3.8	0.1
All other bodies	3.2	58.4

[1] Ministers not reported.

From this table it appears that for all denominations the average number of organizations to each minister for 1906 was 1.3, as compared with 1.5 for 1890. The Protestant bodies showing the most marked changes are the Adventist bodies and the Church of Christ, Scientist. The increase shown for the Adventist bodies—from 1.3 organizations per minister in 1890 to 2.2 in 1906—is due mainly to a decrease in the number of ministers reported for 1906, by the Advent Christian Church. The figures for the Church of Christ, Scientist, on the other hand, show 0.5 organization per minister for 1906 as against 8.5 for 1890, this great disproportion being due apparently, as already explained, to a difference in the organization of the church at the two periods. The Roman Catholic Church had 0.8 organization to each minister in 1906, as against 1.1 in 1890, a difference due apparently to an actual relative increase in the number of ministers. The Jewish congregations had 1.6 organizations per minister in 1906, as against 2.7 in 1890, while the Latter-day Saints had 0.7 in 1906, as against 0.4 in 1890, the difference in both cases being probably in large part due, as already indicated, to a difference in the basis of reporting for the two periods. The large increase in the number of organizations per minister shown by the Eastern Orthodox Churches—from 0.1 in 1890 to 3.8 in 1906—is due mainly to the large increase of organizations belonging to the Greek Orthodox Church, as compared with the increase in the number of ministers. Owing to the impossibility of obtaining the number of ministers connected with the Independent churches for 1906, the figures for these churches are not presented in the table.

Ratio of communicants or members to ministers.—The following table shows for each of the principal families and separate denominations the average number of communicants or members to each minister reported for 1906 and 1890, respectively:

DENOMINATION.	NUMBER OF COMMUNICANTS OR MEMBERS PER MINISTER.	
	1906	1890
All denominations	200	186
Protestant bodies	139	141
Adventist bodies	80	44
Baptist bodies	129	145
Christians (Christian Connection)	109	72
Church of Christ, Scientist	67	336
Congregationalists	121	101
Disciples or Christians	131	170
Dunkers or German Baptist Brethren	43	35
Evangelical bodies	117	106
Friends	77	84
German Evangelical Synod of North America	302	276
Independent churches	(1)	247
Lutheran bodies	269	268
Mennonite bodies	54	46
Methodist bodies	145	153
Presbyterian bodies	147	122
Protestant Episcopal Church	165	128
Reformed bodies	220	205
Unitarians	130	132
United Brethren bodies	122	81
Universalists	89	69
Other Protestant bodies	36	96
Roman Catholic Church	796	681
Jewish congregations[2]	.....	.....
Latter-day Saints	145	81
Eastern Orthodox Churches	1,200	43
All other bodies	347	6,480

[1] Ministers not reported. [2] Membership not comparable.

For all denominations, as shown by the above table, the average number of members to a minister for 1906 was 200, as compared with 186 for 1890. For Protestant bodies the average for 1906 was 139 members to each minister, as compared with 141 for 1890; and for the Roman Catholic Church, 796 for 1906, as compared with 681 for 1890. The increase in the figures shown in the table for the Adventist bodies is due mainly, as already stated, to a decrease in the number of ministers reported in 1906 for the Advent Christian Church, while the marked decrease shown for the Church of Christ, Scientist—from 336 members per minister in 1890 to 67 in 1906—is apparently due, as already explained, to a difference in the organization of the church at the two periods. Owing to the impossibility of obtaining the number of ministers connected with the Independent churches for 1906, no figures are presented in the above table for these churches, and on account of the difference in the basis of reporting the membership of the Jewish congregations at the two periods, as already explained, the figures for this body, also, are omitted from the table. The difference between 1906 and 1890 in the average number of communicants per minister shown for the Latter-day Saints is mainly due to a difference in the basis of reporting the ministers, already referred to, while the large difference shown for the Eastern Orthodox Churches is due mainly to the large increase in the number of communicants, as compared with ministers in the Greek Orthodox Church.

AVERAGE ANNUAL SALARIES PAID TO MINISTERS.

In connection with this report an attempt has been made for the first time to secure official statistics concerning the salaries paid to ministers in the respective denominations. They were collected by means of the general schedule, by which it was sought to obtain a report of the amount of annual salary received by each minister serving one or more churches. The results are not entirely satisfactory, on account of the failure of some to report the salary and of others to report with sufficient clearness. In some instances it could not be determined whether the amount reported was the yearly or monthly salary, and in other instances whether it was that paid to a single minister or to two or more serving jointly or in succession during the same year. In cases where a minister served more than one church it was not always clear whether he had reported his entire salary on each schedule returned by him or only that part of it which was paid by the particular church for which the schedule was filled. In addition to this, 15 of the 186 denominations, as already stated, have no regular ministry, and 69 others either pay no stated salaries to their ministers or made returns which were not sufficiently complete to warrant tabulation. Of the 201,351 organizations composing the 102 remaining denominations, 164,229, or 81.6 per cent, made returns to this inquiry which there is reason to believe are substantially complete and accurate, and it is thought that they embrace a sufficient number of organizations of the respective denominations to be fairly representative of conditions as to the average salaries paid to ministers. These returns are presented in the following table, which gives for each denomination represented the total number of organizations, the number of organizations reporting salaries, the number of ministers whose salaries are reported, the total amount of salary reported, and the average salary per minister. These figures are given for continental United States, for each of the four principal classes of cities, and for the area outside of the principal cities. It should be remembered that the table is not designed to show the total amount of money paid for salaries by these bodies, since, as already stated, all of the organizations and ministers connected with them are not represented, but simply shows the average annual salary paid, as indicated by the returns for the organizations which are represented in the table.

DENOMINATION.	Total number of organizations: 1906.	SALARIES OF MINISTERS: 1906. In continental United States.				In cities of 300,000 and over in 1900.				In cities of 100,000 to 300,000 in 1900.			
		Number of organizations reporting.	Number whose salaries are reported.	Total amount of salary reported.	Average salary per minister reporting.	Number of organizations reporting.	Number whose salaries are reported.	Total amount of salary reported.	Average salary per minister reporting.	Number of organizations reporting.	Number whose salaries are reported.	Total amount of salary reported.	Average salary per minister reporting.
Total for denominations represented	201,351	164,229	105,133	$69,667,587	$663	4,848	6,661	$8,145,001	$1,223	3,307	3,968	$4,405,083	$1,110
Protestant bodies:													
Adventist bodies—													
Advent Christian Church	550	294	241	99,768	414	6	6	4,720	787	7	7	5,554	793
Life and Advent Union	12	5	5	2,999	600	1	1	1,200	1,200	1	1	400	400
Churches of God in Christ Jesus	62	20	9	3,354	373	1	1	624	624	....	....	....	....
Baptist bodies—													
Baptists—													
Northern Baptist Convention	8,272	6,027	5,119	4,264,171	833	319	355	561,056	1,580	232	256	363,493	1,420
Southern Baptist Convention	21,104	14,819	8,950	3,284,289	367	32	35	62,770	1,793	56	63	93,862	1,490
National Baptist Convention (Colored)	18,534	16,482	11,241	2,774,850	247	124	123	74,415	605	221	215	116,140	540
Seventh-day Baptists	77	58	51	27,339	536	2	2	2,200	1,100	....	....	....	....
Free Baptists	1,346	760	568	262,449	462	9	9	9,450	1,050	7	7	7,444	1,063
General Baptists	518	313	170	20,586	121	....	....	....	....	....	....	....	....
Separate Baptists	76	29	16	1,823	114	....	....	....	....	....	....	....	....
Colored Primitive Baptists in America	797	156	105	24,786	236	....	....	....	....	....	....	....	....
United American Freewill Baptists (Colored)	251	167	86	10,695	124	....	....	....	....	....	....	....	....
Christian Catholic Church in Zion	17	15	39	40,440	1,037	5	9	11,440	1,271	4	4	2,770	693
Christian Union	217	150	63	19,219	305	....	....	....	....	....	....	....	....
Christians (Christian Connection)	1,379	884	492	218,763	445	2	2	2,000	1,000	6	6	6,950	1,158
Church of Christ, Scientist	638	426	845	198,095	234	24	48	45,968	958	29	58	32,740	564
Churches of God in North America, General Eldership of the	518	413	207	77,080	372	2	2	2,150	1,075	....	....	....	....
Churches of the New Jerusalem—													
General Convention of the New Jerusalem in the United States of America	119	64	59	72,745	1,233	20	21	34,690	1,652	10	9	9,600	1,067
General Church of the New Jerusalem	14	8	7	6,394	913	5	4	4,150	1,038	....	....	....	....
Congregationalists	5,713	474	3,967	4,154,786	1,042	208	233	451,621	1,938	181	197	335,010	1,701
Disciples or Christians—													
Disciples of Christ	8,293	945	4,353	2,554,476	587	76	79	104,741	1,326	100	105	137,908	1,313
Churches of Christ	2,649	326	288	76,711	266	....	....	....	....	5	6	6,200	1,033
Dunkers or German Baptist Brethren—													
The Brethren Church (Progressive Dunkers)	202	135	93	49,538	533	4	4	3,980	995	2	2	1,850	925
Evangelical bodies—													
Evangelical Association	1,760	1,736	883	531,823	602	54	52	42,205	812	38	38	29,413	774
United Evangelical Church	978	962	472	277,477	588	18	18	15,275	849	5	5	3,600	720
Evangelistic associations—													
Lumber River Mission	5	5	5	300	60	....	....	....	....	....	....	....	....
Friends—													
Society of Friends (Orthodox)	873	423	360	134,766	374	2	2	1,420	710	4	4	3,420	855
German Evangelical Protestant bodies—													
German Evangelical Protestant Ministers' Association	44	42	39	34,525	885	17	16	17,670	1,104	2	2	2,200	1,100
German Evangelical Protestant Ministers' Conference	22	18	17	15,340	902	7	7	9,100	1,300	1	1	1,000	1,000
German Evangelical Synod of North America	1,205	141	854	560,912	657	106	106	95,572	902	56	56	52,860	944
Independent churches	1,079	316	292	178,851	613	45	52	71,002	1,365	13	15	11,966	798
Lutheran bodies—													
General Synod of the Evangelical Lutheran Church in the United States of America	1,734	,570	1,020	869,020	852	71	71	99,780	1,405	52	51	59,400	1,165
United Synod of the Evangelical Lutheran Church in the South	449	391	173	111,743	646	....	....	....	....	....	....	....	....
General Council of the Evangelical Lutheran Church in North America	2,146	1,866	1,306	1,109,899	850	159	160	192,540	1,203	85	84	88,795	1,057
Evangelical Lutheran Synodical Conference of America	3,301	3,051	2,060	1,150,839	559	150	157	128,218	817	100	101	74,120	734
United Norwegian Lutheran Church in America	1,177	1,073	390	281,603	722	15	15	14,310	954	5	5	4,300	860
Evangelical Lutheran Joint Synod of Ohio and Other States	772	746	475	283,201	596	16	17	12,480	734	32	32	26,982	843
Lutheran Synod of Buffalo	33	33	23	11,615	505	1	1	1,000	1,000	2	2	1,100	550
Hauge's Norwegian Evangelical Lutheran Synod	272	232	88	55,340	629	6	5	5,340	1,068	2	2	1,400	700
German Evangelical Lutheran Synod of Texas	25	25	13	5,140	395	....	....	....	....	....	....	....	....
Evangelical Lutheran Synod of Iowa and Other States	828	807	434	238,007	548	2	2	1,550	775	10	10	7,685	769
Synod for the Norwegian Evangelical Lutheran Church in America	927	821	285	178,052	625	15	13	9,010	693	11	11	7,010	637
Evangelical Lutheran Synod of Michigan and Other States	55	53	36	18,503	514	....	....	....	....	3	3	2,550	850
Danish Evangelical Lutheran Church in America	92	73	48	29,186	608	7	6	5,455	909	4	3	1,764	588
Icelandic Evangelical Lutheran Synod in North America	14	11	3	2,525	842	....	....	....	....	....	....	....	....
Immanuel Synod of the Evangelical Lutheran Church of North America	11	11	11	8,125	739	....	....	....	....	1	1	1,800	1,800
Finnish Evangelical Lutheran Church of America, or Suomi Synod	105	84	24	21,434	893	2		,060	1,060	1	1	720	720
Norwegian Lutheran Free Church	320	285	107	49,557	463	....	....	....	....	5	5	3,105	621
United Danish Evangelical Lutheran Church in America	198	141	89	48,081	540	8	8	5,080	635	3	3	1,700	567
Slovak Evangelical Lutheran Synod of America	59	24	23	14,220	618	5	5	3,270	654		3	1,800	600
Finnish Evangelical Lutheran National Church	66	52	14	9,654	690	....	....	....	....	....	....	....	....
Church of the Lutheran Brethren of America (Norwegian)	16	3	2	650	325	....	....	....	....	....	....	....	....
Evangelical Lutheran Jehovah Conference	9	5	5	1,997	399			600	600	2	2	,140	570

SALARIES OF MINISTERS: 1906—continued.

DENOMINATION.	In cities of 50,000 to 100,000 in 1900.				In cities of 25,000 to 50,000 in 1900.				Outside of principal cities.			
	Number of organizations reporting.	Number whose salaries are reported.	Total amount of salary reported.	Average salary per minister reporting.	Number of organizations reporting.	Number whose salaries are reported.	Total amount of salary reported.	Average salary per minister reporting.	Number of organizations reporting.	Number whose salaries are reported.	Total amount of salary reported.	Average salary per minister reporting.
Total for denominations represented	2,573	3,034	$3,223,695	$1,063	3,228	3,677	$3,574,747	$972	150,278	87,793	$50,319,061	$573
Protestant bodies:												
Adventist bodies—												
Advent Christian Church	13	14	11,068	790	11	11	8,262	751	257	203	70,164	346
Life and Advent Union	1	1	425	425	1	1	350	350	1	1	624	624
Churches of God in Christ Jesus					1	1	400	400	18	7	2,330	333
Baptist bodies—												
Baptists—												
Northern Baptist Convention	200	216	298,283	1,381	186	197	245,914	1,248	5,090	4,095	2,795,425	683
Southern Baptist Convention	62	66	99,325	1,505	81	89	120,895	1,358	14,586	8,697	2,907,437	334
National Baptist Convention (Colored)	128	126	76,080	604	231	228	114,825	504	15,778	10,549	2,393,390	227
Seventh-day Baptists									56	49	25,139	513
Free Baptists	12	10	11,080	1,108	13	13	8,983	691	719	529	225,492	426
General Baptists	1	1	612	612					312	169	19,974	118
Separate Baptists									29	16	1,823	114
Colored Primitive Baptists in America					4	4	1,550	388	152	101	23,236	230
United American Freewill Baptists (Colored)									167	86	10,695	124
Christian Catholic Church in Zion	2	2	2,040	1,020					4	24[1]	24,190[1]	1,008
Christian Union									150	63	19,219	305
Christians (Christian Connection)	8	7	7,800	1,114	4	4	4,040	1,010	864	473	197,973	419
Church of Christ, Scientist	34	68	24,508	360	56	112	23,727	212	283	559	71,157	127
Churches of God in North America, General Eldership of the	5	5	2,930	586	6	6	3,370	562	400	194	68,630	354
Churches of the New Jerusalem—												
General Convention of the New Jerusalem in the United States of America	5	5	5,600	1,120	3	3	5,120	1,707	26	21	17,735	845
General Church of the New Jerusalem	1	1	200	200					2	2	2,044	1,022
Congregationalists	147	154	271,633	1,764	148	162	244,979	1,512	3,790	3,241	2,851,543	880
Disciples or Christians—												
Disciples of Christ	50	54	69,291	1,283	102	107	133,790	1,250	4,617	4,008	2,108,746	526
Churches of Christ	3	4	2,600	650	3	3	3,000	1,000	315	275	64,911	236
Dunkers or German Baptist Brethren—												
The Brethren Church (Progressive Dunkers)	1	1	800	800	6	8	4,870	609	122	78	38,038	488
Evangelical bodies—												
Evangelical Association	32	31	22,874	738	46	44	29,375	668	566	718	407,956	568
United Evangelical Church	11	11	10,090	917	34	33	26,368	799	894	405	222,144	549
Evangelistic associations—												
Lumber River Mission									5	5	300	60
Friends—												
Society of Friends (Orthodox)	8	6	5,660	943					409	348	124,266	357
German Evangelical Protestant bodies—												
German Evangelical Protestant Ministers' Association					4	4	4,300	1,075	19	17	10,355	609
German Evangelical Protestant Ministers' Conference					1	1	900	900	9	8	4,340	543
German Evangelical Synod of North America	17	18	17,530	974	24	23	18,930	823	938	651	376,020	578
Independent churches	5	5	5,820	1,164	11	11	10,060	915	242	209	80,003	383
Lutheran bodies—												
General Synod of the Evangelical Lutheran Church in the United States of America	39	38	43,720	1,151	60	60	71,310	1,189	848	800	594,810	744
United Synod of the Evangelical Lutheran Church in the South	8	8	11,400	1,425	5	5	4,760	952	378	160	95,583	597
General Council of the Evangelical Lutheran Church in North America	73	72	73,038	1,014	85	80	77,242	966	1,464	910	678,284	745
Evangelical Lutheran Synodical Conference of America	29	29	20,434	705	68	68	45,055	663	2,704	1,705	883,012	518
United Norwegian Lutheran Church in America	8	8	7,750	969	7	6	6,710	1,118	1,038	356	248,533	698
Evangelical Lutheran Joint Synod of Ohio and Other States	11	10	7,200	720	18	18	13,850	769	609	398	222,689	560
Lutheran Synod of Buffalo									30	20	9,515	476
Hauge's Norwegian Evangelical Lutheran Synod	1	1	575	575	2	2	1,600	800	221	78	46,425	595
German Evangelical Lutheran Synod of Texas									26	13	5,140	396
Evangelical Lutheran Synod of Iowa and Other States	6	6	3,945	658	9	9	5,510	612	780	407	219,317	539
Synod for the Norwegian Evangelical Lutheran Church in America	8	9	4,970	552	4	4	2,300	575	783	248	154,762	624
Evangelical Lutheran Synod of Michigan and Other States					3	3	1,450	483	47	30	14,503	483
Danish Evangelical Lutheran Church in America	4	4	2,160	540	1	1	800	800	57	34	19,007	559
Icelandic Evangelical Lutheran Synod in North America									11	3	2,525	842
Immanuel Synod of the Evangelical Lutheran Church of North America									10	10	6,325	633
Finnish Evangelical Lutheran Church of America, or Suomi Synod									81	22	19,654	893
Norwegian Lutheran Free Church	3	3	1,900	633	3	3	1,700	567	274	96	42,852	446
United Danish Evangelical Lutheran Church in America	3	3	2,400	800	6	6	3,980	663	121	69	34,921	506
Slovak Evangelical Lutheran Synod of America	1	1	720	720	2	2	1,060	540	13	12	7,350	613
Finnish Evangelical Lutheran National Church									52	14	9,654	690
Church of the Lutheran Brethren of America (Norwegian)									3	2	650	325
Evangelical Lutheran Jehovah Conference									2	2	257	129

[1] Includes 21 ministers reported at Zion City, Ill. (headquarters) with salaries as follows: 4 at $1,500, and 17 at $950.

DENOMINATION.	Total number of organizations: 1906.	SALARIES OF MINISTERS: 1906. In continental United States. Number of organizations reporting.	Number whose salaries are reported.	Total amount of salary reported.	Average salary per minister reporting.	In cities of 300,000 and over in 1900. Number of organizations reporting.	Number whose salaries are reported.	Total amount of salary reported.	Average salary per minister reporting.	In cities of 100,000 to 300,000 in 1900. Number of organizations reporting.	Number whose salaries are reported.	Total amount of salary reported.	Average salary per minister reporting.
Protestant bodies—Continued.													
Methodist bodies—													
Methodist Episcopal Church	29,943	28,958	15,219	$12,356,051	$812	694	707	$1,005,493	$1,422	472	471	$600,700	$1,275
Union American Methodist Episcopal Church (Colored)	77	63	61	16,934	278	10	10	3,600	360	2	2	713	357
African Methodist Episcopal Church	6,647	6,171	3,846	1,335,186	347	66	65	54,303	835	69	65	49,739	765
African Union Methodist Protestant Church	69	63	56	21,856	390	4	4	2,250	563	1	1	500	500
African Methodist Episcopal Zion Church	2,204	2,045	1,203	421,429	350	31	31	21,630	698	33	32	22,990	718
Methodist Protestant Church	2,843	2,606	1,033	448,557	434	26	26	26,010	1,000	15	14	15,380	1,099
Wesleyan Methodist Connection of America	594	521	288	89,647	311					2	4	1,250	313
Methodist Episcopal Church, South	17,831	17,695	5,463	3,900,853	714	24	24	39,415	1,642	66	67	83,585	1,248
Congregational Methodist Church	325	176	94	10.415	111	1	1	500	500				
Colored Methodist Episcopal Church	2,381	2,261	1,254	408,151	325	8	8	2,796	350	19	17	10.200	600
Reformed Zion Union Apostolic Church (Colored)	45	43	23	3,322	144								
Primitive Methodist Church in the United States of America	96	91	68	48,479	713	7	7	5,850	836	5	5	4,850	970
Free Methodist Church of North America	1,553	1,193	724	267,793	370	13	13	8,700	669	18	17	9,945	585
Moravian bodies—													
Moravian Church (Unitas Fratrum)	117	109	87	58,215	669	12	12	11,650	971	1	1	1,000	1,000
Evangelical Union of Bohemian and Moravian Brethren in North America	15	13	3	1,560	520								
Pentecostal Church of the Nazarene	100	66	63	41,263	655	7	7	6,680	954	7	8	6,750	844
Presbyterian bodies—													
Presbyterian Church in the United States of America	7,935	6,418	5,378	6,331,851	1,177	416	486	1,054,052	2,169	282	275	521,486	1,896
Cumberland Presbyterian Church	2,850	1,757	951	515.834	542	10	10	13,463	1,346	11	11	13,478	1,225
Colored Cumberland Presbyterian Church	196	170	113	18,984	168	1	1	720	720				
Welsh Calvinistic Methodist Church	147	95	64	54,055	845	6	6	8,100	1,350	7	6	6,200	1,033
United Presbyterian Church of North America	968	819	745	816,799	1,096	76	80	126,990	1,587	42	42	69,600	1,657
Presbyterian Church in the United States	3,104	2,259	1,308	1,249,950	956	8	8	19,600	2,450	38	39	68,482	1,756
Associate Synod of North America (Associate Presbyterian Church)	22	10	8	4,170	521								
Associate Reformed Synod of the South	141	128	89	58,072	652					2	2	1,700	850
Synod of the Reformed Presbyterian Church of North America	114	91	86	86,650	1,008	15	15	24,300	1,620	5	5	7,600	1,520
Reformed Presbyterian Church in North America, General Synod	27	16	15	13,650	910	4	4	5,700	1,425	1	1	600	600
Protestant Episcopal Church	6,845	5,063	3,934	4,887,092	1,242	477	672	1,258,468	1,873	272	313	479,820	1,533
Reformed bodies—													
Reformed Church in America	659	549	531	621,026	1,170	83	87	168,600	1,938	30	32	56,425	1,763
Reformed Church in the United States	1,736	1,578	904	729,544	807	82	82	95,670	1,167	25	23	23,750	1,033
Christian Reformed Church	174	118	117	90,750	776	8	8	7,600	950	5	5	5,000	1,000
Hungarian Reformed Church in America	16	15	15	12,850	857	2	2	1,800	900				
Reformed Catholic Church	5	5	6	4,000	667	4	5	3,500	700	1	1	500	500
Reformed Episcopal Church	81	72	54	53,203	985	26	27	39,844	1,476	1	1	1,600	1,600
Salvationists—													
Salvation Army	694	682	1,532	349,094	228	101	272	57,092	210	49	122	31,012	254
Swedish Evangelical bodies—													
Swedish Evangelical Mission Covenant of America	281	199	188	116,837	621	18	18	16,965	943	9	9	10,220	1,136
Swedish Evangelical Free Mission	127	73	70	38,635	552	4	4	3,480	870	4	4	3,500	875
Temple Society in the United States (Friends of the Temple)	3	3	3	1,680	560	1	1	480	480				
Unitarians	461	377	379	626,485	1,653	49	53	155,800	2,940	25	25	61,800	2,472
United Brethren bodies—													
Church of the United Brethren in Christ	3,732	3,557	1,415	817,477	578	20	20	18,752	938	17	17	15,800	929
Church of the United Brethren in Christ (Old Constitution)	572	523	209	59,302	284								
Universalists	846	500	373	461,915	1,238	24	25	59,050	2,362	19	22	43,050	1,957
Volunteers of America	71	70	186	50,690	273	14	37	11,827	320	16	54	12,962	240
Roman Catholic Church	12,482	9,427	9,646	6,779,130	703	766	1,895	1,296,930	684	368	744	497,356	668
Jewish congregations	1,769	496	656	801,436	1,222	154	242	360,820	1,491	78	118	141,760	1,201
Eastern Orthodox Churches:													
Russian Orthodox Church	59	42	38	33,360	878	7	11	11,569	1,052	3	3	2,769	923
Servian Orthodox Church	10	8	8	7,740	968	2	2	2,220	1,110				
Syrian Orthodox Church	8	8	8	5,340	668	2	2	2,520	1,260	2	2	1,140	570
Greek Orthodox Church	334	27	28	27,222	972	10	11	11,060	1,005	6	6	5,580	930
Armenian Church	73	7	8	4,950	619	2	2	1,600	800	2	2	1,200	600
Buddhists:													
Japanese Temples	12	10	12	11,800	983	1	2	3,000	1,500	1	1	1,000	1,000
Polish National Church of America	24	24	26	18,562	714	5	7	5,440	777	3	3	2,340	780

DENOMINATION.	SALARIES OF MINISTERS: 1906—continued.											
	In cities of 50,000 to 100,000 in 1900.				In cities of 25,000 to 50,000 in 1900.				Outside of principal cities.			
	Number of organizations reporting.	Number whose salaries are reported.	Total amount of salary reported.	Average salary per minister reporting.	Number of organizations reporting.	Number whose salaries are reported.	Total amount of salary reported.	Average salary per minister reporting.	Number of organizations reporting.	Number whose salaries are reported.	Total amount of salary reported.	Average salary per minister reporting.
Protestant bodies—Continued.												
Methodist bodies—												
Methodist Episcopal Church	336	329	$397,120	$1,207	433	421	$499,773	$1,187	27,023	13,291	$9,852,965	$741
Union American Methodist Episcopal Church (Colored)	4	4	1,720	430	4	4	1,500	375	43	41	9,401	229
African Methodist Episcopal Church	95	87	54,879	631	114	113	67,622	598	5,827	3,516	1,108,643	315
African Union Methodist Protestant Church	9	9	4,650	517	6	6	2,600	433	43	36	11,856	329
African Methodist Episcopal Zion Church	20	20	12,990	650	54	51	29,485	578	1,907	1,069	334,334	313
Methodist Protestant Church	8	8	5,534	692	8	9	9,190	1,021	2,549	976	392,443	402
Wesleyan Methodist Connection of America	4	3	1,450	483	7	8	2,434	304	508	273	84,513	310
Methodist Episcopal Church, South	71	67	94,865	1,416	104	103	142,878	1,387	17,480	5,202	3,540,110	681
Congregational Methodist Church	1	1	200	200					174	92	9,715	106
Colored Methodist Episcopal Church	12	12	5,900	492	26	24	11,821	493	2,196	1,193	377,434	316
Reformed Zion Union Apostolic Church (Colored)					1	1	200	200	42	22	3,122	142
Primitive Methodist Church in the United States of America	6	6	5,450	908	2	2	1,600	800	71	48	30,729	640
Free Methodist Church of North America	16	15	8,800	587	24	24	12,154	506	1,122	655	228,194	348
Moravian bodies—												
Moravian Church (Unitas Fratrum)	2	2	1,450	725	4	4	3,400	850	90	68	40,715	599
Evangelical Union of Bohemian and Moravian Brethren in North America									13	3	1,560	520
Pentecostal Church of the Nazarene	4	4	4,192	1,048	4	4	2,980	745	44	40	20,661	517
Presbyterian bodies—												
Presbyterian Church in the United States of America	168	174	297,741	1,711	201	212	328,135	1,524	5,381	4,231	4,135,437	977
Cumberland Presbyterian Church	17	16	18,649	1,166	13	13	20,200	1,554	1,706	901	450,044	499
Colored Cumberland Presbyterian Church					2	2	580	290	167	110	17,684	161
Welsh Calvinistic Methodist Church	3	3	4,010	1,337	3	3	3,400	1,133	76	46	32,345	703
United Presbyterian Church of North America	21	21	26,700	1,271	33	33	44,000	1,333	647	569	549,509	966
Presbyterian Church in the United States	41	41	72,060	1,758	53	54	90,010	1,667	2,119	1,166	999,798	857
Associate Synod of North America (Associate Presbyterian Church)									10	8	4,170	521
Associate Reformed Synod of the South	1	1	1,200	1,200	1	1	850	850	124	85	54,322	639
Synod of the Reformed Presbyterian Church of North America	3	3	3,500	1,167	3	3	3,300	1,100	65	60	47,950	799
Reformed Presbyterian Church in North America, General Synod									11	10	7,350	735
Protestant Episcopal Church	192	207	322,413	1,558	201	192	291,254	1,517	3,911	2,550	2,535,137	994
Reformed bodies—												
Reformed Church in America	17	17	21,050	1,238	13	13	22,290	1,715	406	382	352,661	923
Reformed Church in the United States	35	33	35,400	1,073	60	59	64,302	1,090	1,376	707	510,422	722
Christian Reformed Church	10	11	10,380	944	2	2	1,850	925	93	91	65,920	724
Hungarian Reformed Church in America	2	2	1,800	900	2	2	1,450	725	9	9	7,800	867
Reformed Catholic Church												
Reformed Episcopal Church	7	5	3,735	747	1	1	900	900	37	20	7,124	356
Salvationists—												
Salvation Army	52	124	32,097	259	70	165	41,349	251	410	849	187,544	221
Swedish Evangelical bodies—												
Swedish Evangelical Mission Covenant of America	9	9	8,280	920	10	10	8,480	848	153	142	72,892	513
Swedish Evangelical Free Mission	3	3	1,800	600	5	5	3,260	652	57	54	26,595	498
Temple Society in the United States (Friends of the Temple)					1	1	800	800	1	1	400	400
Unitarians	27	27	55,300	2,048	30	29	54,400	1,876	246	245	299,185	1,221
United Brethren bodies—												
Church of the United Brethren in Christ	34	32	30,875	965	43	44	39,591	900	3,443	1,302	712,459	547
Church of the United Brethren in Christ (Old Constitution)	2	2	725	363					521	207	58,577	283
Universalists	30	29	54,175	1,868	25	26	38,150	1,467	402	271	267,490	987
Volunteers of America	9	21	6,782	323	15	38	9,429	248	16	36	9,690	269
Roman Catholic Church	280	594	384,550	647	322	575	373,904	650	7,691	5,838	4,226,390	724
Jewish congregations	60	72	85,724	1,191	66	75	87,870	1,172	137	149	125,262	841
Eastern Orthodox Churches:												
Russian Orthodox Church	4	4	3,569	892	5	5	4,481	896	23	15	10,972	731
Servian Orthodox Church	1	1	600	600	2	2	2,220	1,110	3	3	2,700	900
Syrian Orthodox Church	1	1	300	300	1	1	600	600	2	2	780	390
Greek Orthodox Church	8	8	8,482	1,060	2	2	1,380	690	1	1	720	720
Armenian Church	1	1	500	500					2	3	1,650	550
Buddhists:												
Japanese Temples	3	3	2,600	867	1	1	1,000	1,000	4	5	4,200	840
Polish National Church of America	4	4	3,042	761	2	2	1,320	660	10	10	6,420	642

As shown by this table, the average annual salary per minister for all denominations represented, for continental United States as a whole, is $663. The denomination showing the highest average is the Unitarian, with $1,653, while the denominations next in order are the Protestant Episcopal Church, $1,242; the Universalists, $1,238; the General Convention of the New Jerusalem in the United States of America, $1,233; the Jewish congregations, $1,222; the Presbyterian Church in the United States of America, $1,177; the Reformed Church in America, $1,170; the United Presbyterian Church of North America, $1,096; the Congregationalists, $1,042; the Christian Catholic Church in Zion, $1,037; and the Synod of the Reformed Presbyterian Church of North America, $1,008. Among the denominations showing an average salary considerably lower than the general average for the United States are the Advent Christian Church; all the Baptist bodies except the Northern Baptist Convention; the Christian Union; the Christians (Christian Connection); the Church of Christ, Scientist; the General Eldership of the Churches of God in North America; the Society of Friends (Orthodox); the colored Methodist bodies; the Methodist Protestant, Wesleyan Methodist, and Free Methodist churches; the Salvation Army; and the Volunteers of America. In the case of most of these last-named bodies, as shown by the table, many of the organizations reporting are outside of the principal cities, and many of them are doubtless in rural regions, and this fact accounts largely for the comparatively low average salary. The low average shown for the Church of Christ, Scientist, is due to the fact that most of those who serve as ministers, or readers, are persons having other vocations and not dependent on the salaries paid by the churches. In the case of the Salvation Army and the Volunteers of America, the allowance made for the officers serving at the various posts is usually based upon their probable expenses, and is practically limited to these expenses.

The average salary shown for the large cities is considerably higher as a rule than the general average for the denomination, while for the area outside of the principal cities it is usually somewhat less. Moreover, the average salary generally corresponds to the grade of the cities. For all denominations together it ranges from $1,223 for cities of the first class to $1,110 for those of the second class; $1,063 for those of the third class; $972 for those of the fourth class; and $573 for the area outside of the principal cities. In individual denominations the conditions vary. In the Northern Baptist Convention the average for cities of the first class is $1,580; of the second class, $1,420; of the third class, $1,381; of the fourth class, $1,248; and for the area outside of the principal cities, $683. The figures for the Disciples of Christ show a regular gradation from $1,326 per minister for cities of the first class to $1,250 for those of the fourth class; for the Methodist Episcopal Church, from $1,422 for cities of the first class to $1,187 for those of the fourth class; and for the Presbyterian Church in the United States of America, from $2,169 for those of the first class to $1,524 for those of the fourth class.

In the Southern Baptist Convention, the average salary ranges from $1,793 for cities of the first class to $1,358 for those of the fourth class, and among the Congregationalists from $1,938 for cities of the first class to $1,512 for those of the fourth class, but in the case of both these denominations the average for cities of the third class is a little larger than for those of the second class. Among the Lutheran bodies there is considerable difference; some, as the General Council, showing a regular gradation; others, as the United Norwegian, showing larger averages for cities of the third and fourth classes.

The lower average salary shown by some denominations for a higher class of cities than for a lower is in most cases due to the existence in the higher class of cities of an unusually large number of weak or mission churches. For example, in the case of the Southern Baptist Convention, which shows an average salary per minister of $1,505 for cities of the third class and only $1,490 for cities of the second class, the churches in the third class have an average membership of 472, and in the second class of only 362, indicating that the churches in the third class are also financially stronger on the average than those in the second class.

In the Protestant Episcopal Church the average is from $1,873 in cities of the first class to $1,517 in those of the fourth, there being but little difference in the figures for the second, third, and fourth classes of cities. In the case of the Roman Catholic Church, the figures show but little difference between the general average and that for the various classes of cities or for the area outside of the principal cities, the reason being that in this denomination the salaries are fixed for the diocese, being in general the same for the rural districts as for the large cities. Of the 24 ministers reported by the 4 organizations of the Christian Catholic Church in Zion, for the area outside the principal cities, 21 are reported at Zion City, and are probably connected with the headquarters of the denomination at that place.

Among the denominations included in this report with those not paying regular salaries to their ministers, and hence not represented in this table, there are several, as for example, the Freewill Baptists and the German Baptist Brethren Church (Conservative), in which a considerable number of the organizations pay stated salaries, although it is not a general custom. Some of these denominations, among which are the ones just mentioned, appear to be in the transitional state from the unsalaried to the salaried ministry basis.

DATE OF ESTABLISHMENT OF RELIGIOUS ORGANIZATIONS.

An inquiry was made in 1906 as to the date of establishment, meaning the year in which the local church was organized. From the nature of the reports made, however, it is evident that to a certain extent the inquiry was misunderstood, and that in some cases the date given refers either to the founding of the denomination to which the church belongs or to matters of general ecclesiastical history, such as the origin of the Christian Church, or the date of the Reformation, rather than to the date of establishment of the local church.

With a view to presenting the origin and growth of the various denominations, the years reported have been arranged by periods, and the following have been selected as on the whole the most significant: Prior to 1800; from 1800 to 1849; from 1850 to 1899, by decades; and from 1900 to 1906. The years 1800 to 1849 have been included in one period chiefly because this was a period of preparation, the forward movement in denominational life beginning practically about the middle of the century.

The following table shows by denominations in detail the total number of organizations, the number of organizations reporting date of establishment and the percentage which they form of the total number of organizations in the body, and the number of organizations established during each of the different periods mentioned:

DENOMINATION.	Total number of organizations: 1906.	ORGANIZATIONS REPORTING DATE OF ESTABLISHMENT.		ORGANIZATIONS ESTABLISHED—							
		Number.	Per cent of total.	Prior to 1800.	1800 to 1849.	1850 to 1859.	1860 to 1869.	1870 to 1879.	1880 to 1889.	1890 to 1899.	1900 to 1906.
All denominations	212,230	179,331	84.5	3,637	21,929	12,816	16,114	25,851	32,771	34,827	31,386
Adventist bodies	2,551	2,345	91.9		15	36	124	254	424	650	842
Evangelical Adventists	18	17	(1)		2	3	5	5		2	
Advent Christian Church	550	503	91.5		9	18	33	84	94	143	122
Seventh-day Adventist Denomination	1,889	1,740	92.1		3	6	73	155	314	481	708
Church of God (Adventist)	10	10	(1)				1	2	3	1	3
Churches of God (Adventist), Unattached Congregations	10	10	(1)					1	4	3	2
Life and Advent Union	12	12	(1)			2	2		3	4	1
Churches of God in Christ Jesus	62	53	(1)		1	7	10	7	6	16	6
Armenian Church	73	73	(1)						5	15	53
Bahais	24	24	(1)							10	14
Baptist bodies	54,880	49,110	89.5	779	5,902	2,608	4,240	7,689	9,761	9,852	8,279
Baptists	47,910	44,060	92.0	663	4,668	2,280	3,920	7,046	9,008	8,994	7,481
Northern Baptist Convention	8,272	7,937	96.0	306	1,956	789	679	874	1,248	1,255	830
Southern Baptist Convention	21,104	18,513	87.7	356	2,613	1,410	1,186	2,163	3,316	3,576	3,893
National Baptist Convention (Colored)	18,534	17,610	95.0	1	99	81	2,055	4,009	4,444	4,163	2,758
General Six Principle Baptists	16	16	(1)	5	4	5		2			
Seventh-day Baptists	77	74	(1)	7	31	5	4	9	10	4	4
Free Baptists	1,346	1,003	74.5	21	234	92	103	150	139	162	102
Freewill Baptists	608	578	95.1	3	35	18	20	91	92	173	146
General Baptists	518	491	94.8		11	12	23	51	93	130	171
Separate Baptists	76	60	(1)		17	2	9	6	14	3	9
United Baptists	196	73	37.2		7	5	4	12	12	13	20
Duck River and Kindred Associations of Baptists (Baptist Church of Christ)	93	89	(1)		30	8	6	11	14	12	8
Primitive Baptists	2,922	2,132	73.0	78	818	177	122	216	279	236	206
Colored Primitive Baptists in America	797	330	41.4		12	1	25	65	80	76	71
Two-Seed-in-the-Spirit Predestinarian Baptists	55	39	(1)		28			11			
Freewill Baptists (Bullockites)	15	13	(1)	2	6	3	1	1			
United American Freewill Baptists (Colored)	251	152	60.6		1		3	18	20	49	61
Brethren (Plymouth)	403	398	98.8		1	5	14	50	93	144	91
Brethren (Plymouth)—I	134	134	100.0		1	1	8	23	30	41	30
Brethren (Plymouth)—II	128	126	98.4					7	35	52	32
Brethren (Plymouth)—III	81	78	(1)			4	6	11	20	26	11
Brethren (Plymouth)—IV	60	60	(1)					9	8	25	18
Brethren (River)	111	110	99.1	3	2	4	12	19	37	20	13
Brethren in Christ	74	73	(1)			1	6	13	29	17	7
Yorker, or Old Order, Brethren	9	9	(1)	3	2		2		2		
United Zion's Children	28	28	(1)			3	4	6	6	3	6
Buddhists	74	74	(1)						21	33	20
Chinese Temples	62	62	(1)						21	32	9
Japanese Temples	12	12	(1)							1	11
Catholic Apostolic Churches	24	24	(1)		1	1	2	3	3	2	12
Catholic Apostolic Church	11	11	(1)		1	1	2	3	3	1	
New Apostolic Church	13	13	(1)							1	12
Christadelphians	70	70	(1)		1	4	15	6	15	18	11
Christian Catholic Church in Zion	17	17	(1)					1		12	4
Christian Israelite Church	5	5	(1)		1					4	
Christian Union	217	205	94.5		1	3	60	23	35	40	48
Christians (Christian Connection)	1,379	1,172	85.0		246	125	118	157	202	174	150
Church of Christ, Scientist	638	626	98.1					1	15	312	298
Church of God and Saints of Christ (Colored)	48	48	(1)						1	3	44
Churches of God in North America, General Eldership of the	518	454	87.6		46	44	44	90	81	75	74

1 Per cent not shown where base is less than 100.

DENOMINATION.	Total number of organizations: 1906.	ORGANIZATIONS REPORTING DATE OF ESTABLISHMENT.		ORGANIZATIONS ESTABLISHED—							
		Number.	Per cent of total.	Prior to 1800.	1800 to 1849.	1850 to 1859.	1860 to 1869.	1870 to 1879.	1880 to 1889.	1890 to 1899.	1900 to 1906.
Churches of the Living God (Colored)	68	67	(1)						3	32	32
Church of the Living God (Christian Workers for Friendship)	44	44	(1)						3	15	26
Church of the Living God (Apostolic Church)	15	14	(1)							14	
Church of Christ in God	9	9	(1)							3	6
Churches of the New Jerusalem	133	121	91.0		23	15	11	17	15	19	21
General Convention of the New Jerusalem in the United States of America	119	107	89.9		23	15	10	14	12	16	17
General Church of the New Jerusalem	14	14	(1)				1	3	3	3	4
Communistic societies	22	22	(1)	10	4	4	3			1	
United Society of Believers (Shakers)	15	15	(1)	10	4					1	
Amana Society	7	7	(1)			4	3				
Congregationalists	5,713	5,642	98.8	686	964	416	363	536	963	1,074	640
Disciples or Christians	10,942	8,108	74.1		574	426	541	954	1,538	1,953	2,122
Disciples of Christ	8,293	5,678	68.5		473	330	422	711	1,130	1,408	1,204
Churches of Christ	2,649	2,430	91.7		101	96	119	243	408	545	918
Dunkers or German Baptist Brethren	1,097	966	88.1	14	87	91	70	108	207	212	177
German Baptist Brethren Church (Conservative)	822	763	92.8	11	87	89	69	104	113	156	134
Old Order German Baptist Brethren	68		(1)								
The Brethren Church (Progressive Dunkers)	202	198	98.0			1		4	94	56	43
German Seventh-day Baptists	5	5	(1)	3		1	1				
Eastern Orthodox Churches	411	104	25.3				1		2	31	70
Russian Orthodox Church	59	59	(1)				1		2	27	29
Servian Orthodox Church	10	10	(1)							1	
Syrian Orthodox Church	8	8	(1)							1	9
Greek Orthodox Church	334	27	8.1							2	25
Evangelical bodies	2,738	2,419	88.3		172	229	295	380	369	635	339
Evangelical Association	1,760	1,556	88.4		124	192	234	291	296	218	201
United Evangelical Church	978	863	88.2		48	37	61	89	73	417	138
Evangelistic associations	182	174	95.6		1	5	10	12	11	46	89
Apostolic Faith Movement	6	6	(1)								6
Peniel Missions	11	11	(1)						3	5	3
Metropolitan Church Association	6	6	(1)							1	5
Hephzibah Faith Missionary Association	10	10	(1)						1	3	6
Missionary Church Association	32	29	(1)						1	8	20
Pentecost Bands of the World	16	15	(1)							6	9
Heavenly Recruit Church	27	26	(1)							16	10
Apostolic Christian Church	42	41	(1)		1	5	10	12	6	2	5
Christian Congregation	9	9	(1)								9
Gospel Mission	8	6	(1)							2	4
Church of Daniel's Band	4	4	(1)							3	1
Lumber River Mission	5	5	(1)								5
Pentecostal Union Church	3	3	(1)								3
Voluntary Missionary Society in America (Colored)	3	3	(1)								3
Free Christian Zion Church of Christ (Colored)	15	13	(1)								13
Friends	1,147	812	70.8	30	203	39	41	70	113	136	80
Society of Friends (Orthodox)	873	664	76.1	80	145	35	29	60	106	133	76
Religious Society of Friends (Hicksite)	218	99	45.4	48	41	2	3	2	1	1	1
Orthodox Conservative Friends (Wilburite)	48	41	(1)	2	17	1	5	5	6	2	3
Friends (Primitive)	8	8	(1)			1	4	3			
German Evangelical Protestant bodies	66	64	(1)		18	11	10	10	7	5	3
German Evangelical Protestant Ministers' Association	44	44	(1)		15	8	5	5	5	4	2
German Evangelical Protestant Ministers' Conference	22	20	(1)		3	3	5	5	2	1	1
German Evangelical Synod of North America	1,205	1,186	98.4		116	128	156	170	231	212	173
Independent churches	1,079	963	89.2	3	26	21	24	37	118	276	458
International Apostolic Holiness Union	74	72	(1)							3	69
Jewish congregations	1,769	1,112	62.9	4	31	50	63	92	212	321	339
Latter-day Saints	1,184	1,112	93.9		38	44	118	160	212	284	256
Church of Jesus Christ of Latter-day Saints	683	627	91.8		23	40	65	91	127	139	142
Reorganized Church of Jesus Christ of Latter-day Saints	501	485	96.8		15	4	53	69	85	145	114
Lutheran bodies	12,703	11,930	93.9	258	907	828	991	1,628	2,306	2,626	2,386
General Synod of the Evangelical Lutheran Church in the United States of America	1,734	1,567	90.4	105	345	194	145	167	188	218	205
United Synod of the Evangelical Lutheran Church in the South	449	392	87.3	40	97	45	21	45	43	63	38
General Council of the Evangelical Lutheran Church in North America	2,146	2,104	98.0	111	235	131	162	319	384	472	290
Evangelical Lutheran Synodical Conference of America	3,301	3,109	94.2	2	108	196	340	429	678	687	669
United Norwegian Lutheran Church in America	1,177	1,106	94.0		14	59	61	180	308	271	213
Evangelical Lutheran Joint Synod of Ohio and Other States	772	717	92.9		76	82	68	54	127	171	139
Lutheran Synod of Buffalo	33	32	(1)		7	3	3	6	1	10	2
Hauge's Norwegian Evangelical Lutheran Synod	272	241	88.6		1	10	10	41	62	61	56
Evangelical Lutheran Church in America, Eielsen's Synod	26	26	(1)			1	4	2	4	9	6
German Evangelical Lutheran Synod of Texas	25	24	(1)			1	4	2	4	6	7
Evangelical Lutheran Synod of Iowa and Other States	828	804	97.1		8	48	73	106	204	188	177
Synod for the Norwegian Evangelical Lutheran Church in America	927	896	96.7		12	48	75	166	138	184	273

[1] Per cent not shown where base is less than 100.

DENOMINATION.	Total number of organizations: 1906.	ORGANIZATIONS REPORTING DATE OF ESTABLISHMENT.		ORGANIZATIONS ESTABLISHED—							
		Number.	Per cent of total.	Prior to 1800.	1800 to 1849.	1850 to 1859.	1860 to 1869.	1870 to 1879.	1880 to 1889.	1890 to 1899.	1900 to 1906.
Lutheran bodies—Continued.											
Evangelical Lutheran Synod of Michigan and Other States	55		(1)		2	7	9	10	11	7	8
Danish Evangelical Lutheran Church in America	92	[illegible]	(1)				1	26	25	23	15
Icelandic Evangelical Lutheran Synod in North America	14	[illegible]	(1)					1	12	1	
Immanuel Synod of the Evangelical Lutheran Church of North America	11	11	(1)		2	1	2	2	1	1	2
Finnish Evangelical Lutheran Church of America, or Suomi Synod	105	102	97.1					2	8	44	48
Norwegian Lutheran Free Church	320	306	95.6			1	11	33	60	94	107
United Danish Evangelical Lutheran Church in America	198	148	74.7			1	2	34	28	51	32
Slovak Evangelical Lutheran Synod of America	59	57	(1)						6	19	32
Finnish Evangelical Lutheran National Church	66	66	(1)						3	17	46
Apostolic Lutheran Church (Finnish)	68	40	(1)					3	8	19	10
Church of the Lutheran Brethren of America (Norwegian)	16	15	(1)						1	6	8
Evangelical Lutheran Jehovah Conference	9	9	(1)						2	4	3
Mennonite bodies	604	497	82.3	39	78	31	34	56	68	92	99
Mennonite Church	220	190	86.4	27	48	6	17	16	23	25	28
Bruederhoef Mennonite Church	8	8	(1)					1	2	1	4
Amish Mennonite Church	57	56	(1)	1	13	8	7	4	4	8	11
Old Amish Mennonite Church	46	43	(1)	5	7	7	3	5	5	3	8
Reformed Mennonite Church	34		(1)								
General Conference of Mennonites of North America	90	86	(1)	6	7	4	3	14	11	17	24
Church of God in Christ (Mennonite)	18		(1)								
Old (Wisler) Mennonite Church	9	8	(1)		3	2		2		1	
Defenceless Mennonites	14	14	(1)				2		5	6	1
Mennonite Brethren in Christ	68	63	(1)			2	1	5	13	22	20
Bundes Conferenz der Mennoniten Brueder-Gemeinde:											
Krimmer Brueder-Gemeinde	6	6	(1)					3	1	2	
Schellenberger Brueder-Gemeinde	13	3	(1)					3			
Central Illinois Conference of Mennonites	13	13	(1)			2	1	1	1	7	1
Nebraska and Minnesota Conference of Mennonites	8	7	(1)					2	3		2
Methodist bodies	64,701	49,534	76.6	267	6,755	4,125	5,254	8,152	9,052	8,282	7,647
Methodist Episcopal Church	29,943	23,155	77.3	202	4,110	2,489	2,672	3,614	4,000	3,489	2,579
Union American Methodist Episcopal Church (Colored)	77	74	(1)		12	7	6	1	7	14	27
African Methodist Episcopal Church	6,647	5,637	84.8		192	69	706	1,183	1,268	1,129	1,091
African Union Methodist Protestant Church	69	48	(1)		3	5	8	10	10	3	9
African Methodist Episcopal Zion Church	2,204	2,043	92.7		57	27	337	475	396	354	398
Methodist Protestant Church	2,843	2,375	83.5		351	229	256	333	382	421	403
Wesleyan Methodist Connection of America	594	513	86.4		50	45	40	62	74	103	139
Methodist Episcopal Church, South	17,831	11,837	66.4	65	1,962	1,234	1,007	1,567	2,088	1,886	2,028
Congregational Methodist Church	325	275	84.6			10	5	16	23	56	165
New Congregational Methodist Church	35	35	(1)						15	10	10
Colored Methodist Episcopal Church	2,381	2,021	84.9		8	4	104	722	441	356	386
Reformed Zion Union Apostolic Church (Colored)	45	43	(1)				11	11	9	8	4
Primitive Methodist Church in the United States of America	96	86	(1)		6	5	6	24	26	11	8
Free Methodist Church of North America	1,553	1,334	85.9		4	1	90	130	289	428	392
Reformed Methodist Union Episcopal Church (Colored)	58	58	(1)				7	4	25	14	8
Moravian bodies	132	122	92.4	17	7	17	16	17	16	16	16
Moravian Church (Unitas Fratrum)	117	107	91.5	17	7	17	15	15	16	10	10
Evangelical Union of Bohemian and Moravian Brethren in North America	15	15	(1)				1	2		6	6
Nonsectarian Churches of Bible Faith	204	199	97.5			1		14	57	63	64
Pentecostal Church of the Nazarene	100	96	96.0						3	23	70
Polish National Church of America	24	24	(1)							11	13
Presbyterian bodies	15,506	14,060	90.7	594	2,879	1,330	1,103	1,847	2,318	2,278	1,711
Presbyterian Church in the United States of America	7,935	7,487	94.4	353	1,555	663	629	975	1,248	1,140	924
Cumberland Presbyterian Church	2,850	2,259	79.3	1	374	247	198	351	436	403	249
Colored Cumberland Presbyterian Church	196	193	98.5			1	12	50	62	41	27
Welsh Calvinistic Methodist Church	147	143	97.3		42	32	20	21	19	6	3
United Presbyterian Church of North America	968	936	96.7	39	246	132	71	97	96	127	128
Presbyterian Church in the United States	3,104	2,761	88.9	171	583	227	156	310	425	527	362
Associate Synod of North America (Associate Presbyterian Church)	22	19	(1)		11		3		3	1	1
Associate Reformed Synod of the South	141	130	92.2	24	24	11	5	15	17	22	12
Synod of the Reformed Presbyterian Church of North America	114	107	93.9	3	37	11	9	24	10	8	5
Reformed Presbyterian Church in North America, General Synod	27	23	(1)	3	7	6		3	1	3	
Reformed Presbyterian Church (Covenanted)	1	1	(1)					1			
Reformed Presbyterian Church in the United States and Canada	1	1	(1)						1		
Protestant Episcopal Church	6,845	6,070	88.7	315	943	538	543	757	961	1,111	902
Reformed bodies	2,585	2,411	93.3	288	516	266	253	218	293	340	237
Reformed Church in America	659	650	98.6	111	145	79	43	52	65	99	56
Reformed Church in the United States	1,736	1,573	90.6	176	364	182	194	151	188	184	134
Christian Reformed Church	174	172	98.9	1	7	5	16	15	40	52	36
Hungarian Reformed Church in America	16	16	(1)							5	11
Reformed Catholic Church	5	5	(1)					1	1	1	2
Reformed Episcopal Church	81	80	(1)					39	19	16	6
Roman Catholic Church	12,482	10,473	83.9	107	828	1,001	1,097	1,565	1,958	1,800	2,117
Salvationists	714	712	99.7					2	128	291	291
Salvation Army	694	692	99.7					2	128	288	274
American Salvation Army	20	20	(1)							3	17
Schwenkfelders	8	4	(1)	2						1	1
Social Brethren	17	17	(1)				2	4	1	7	3
Society for Ethical Culture	5	5	(1)					1	3		1
Spiritualists	455	454	99.8			6	11	16	25	118	278

[1] Per cent not shown where base is less than 100.

DENOMINATION.	Total number of organizations: 1906.	ORGANIZATIONS REPORTING DATE OF ESTABLISHMENT.		ORGANIZATIONS ESTABLISHED—							
		Number.	Per cent of total.	Prior to 1800.	1800 to 1849.	1850 to 1859.	1860 to 1869.	1870 to 1879.	1880 to 1889.	1890 to 1899.	1900 to 1906.
Swedish Evangelical bodies	408	389	95.3				3	41	120	151	74
Swedish Evangelical Mission Covenant of America	281	264	94.0				3	39	85	89	48
Swedish Evangelical Free Mission	127	125	98.4					2	35	62	26
Temple Society in the United States (Friends of the Temple)	3	3	(1)			1	1		1		
Theosophical societies	85	84	(1)					4	6	47	27
Theosophical Society in America	14	14	(1)					1	2	7	4
Theosophical Society, New York	1	1	(1)							1	
Theosophical Society, American Section	69	68	(1)					2	4	39	23
Universal Brotherhood and Theosophical Society	1	1	(1)					1			
Unitarians	461	456	98.9	108	78	21	41	26	72	61	49
United Brethren bodies	4,304	3,199	74.3	4	250	265	351	532	595	746	456
Church of the United Brethren in Christ	3,732	2,655	71.1	4	216	227	294	450	517	554	393
Church of the United Brethren in Christ (Old Constitution)	572	544	95.1		34	38	57	82	78	192	63
Universalists	846	720	85.1	9	215	77	79	92	74	104	70
Vedanta Society	4	4	(1)							1	3
Volunteers of America	71	71	(1)							37	34

[1] Per cent not shown where base is less than 100.

From this table it appears that 179,331 organizations, or 84.5 per cent of the total number, made a report as to the date of establishment. For most of the smaller denominations—those having less than 100 organizations in 1906—there was either a full report as to date of establishment or a report from all but a few organizations. Three of these smaller bodies, however—Old Order German Baptist Brethren, Reformed Mennonite Church, and Church of God in Christ (Mennonites)—made no report whatever, while for the Apostolic Lutheran Church (Finnish), the African Union Methodist Protestant Church, the Separate Baptists, and one or two other bodies, the returns were very incomplete. Among the denominations having 100 or more organizations in 1906, the following stand highest in respect to the percentage of organizations reporting date of establishment: The Brethren (Plymouth)—I, 100 per cent; Spiritualists, 99.8 per cent; Salvation Army, 99.7 per cent; Christian Reformed Church, 98.9 per cent; Unitarians, 98.9 per cent; Congregationalists, 98.8 per cent; Reformed Church in America, 98.6 per cent; and Colored Cumberland Presbyterian Church, 98.5 per cent.

Among the denominations for which comparatively low percentages are shown are the Disciples of Christ, 68.5 per cent; Methodist Episcopal Church, South, 66.4 per cent; Jewish congregations, 62.9 per cent; United American Freewill Baptists (Colored), 60.6 per cent; Friends (Hicksite), 45.4 per cent; Colored Primitive Baptists in America, 41.4 per cent; United Baptists, 37.2 per cent; and Greek Orthodox Church, 8.1 per cent.

There were 44 denominations reporting organizations established prior to 1800. It does not follow, however, that all of them had a denominational existence at that time. In some cases churches organized prior to that date subsequently joined denominations of more recent formation.

Fifty denominations report their earliest organization in the period from 1800 to 1849, but among these, also, there are cases in which churches now connected with a certain denomination were at that time identified with some other body.

For purposes of further comparison the following table is presented, which shows, for all denominations and for each family or separate denomination for which a report as to date of establishment was made by more than 100 organizations, the percentage of organizations established during each of the different periods specified:

DENOMINATION.	PER CENT OF ORGANIZATIONS ESTABLISHED—							
	Prior to 1800.	1800 to 1849.	1850 to 1859.	1860 to 1869.	1870 to 1879.	1880 to 1889.	1890 to 1899.	1900 to 1906.
All denominations	2.0	12.2	7.1	9.0	14.4	18.3	19.4	17.5
Adventist bodies	....	0.6	1.5	5.3	10.8	18.1	27.7	35.9
Advent Christian Church	....	1.8	3.6	6.6	16.7	18.7	28.4	24.3
Seventh-day Adventist Denomination	....	0.2	0.3	4.2	8.9	18.0	27.6	40.7
Baptist bodies	1.6	12.0	5.3	8.6	15.7	19.9	20.1	16.9
Baptists	1.5	10.6	5.2	8.9	16.0	20.4	20.4	17.0
Northern Baptist Convention	3.9	24.6	9.9	8.6	11.0	15.7	15.8	10.5
Southern Baptist Convention	1.9	14.1	7.6	6.4	11.7	17.9	19.3	21.0
National Baptist Convention (Colored)	(1)	0.6	0.5	11.7	22.8	2	23.6	15.7
Free Baptists	2.1	23.3	9.2	10.3	5.0	9	16.2	10.2
Freewill Baptists	0.5	6.1	3.1	3.5	5.7	9	29.9	25.3
General Baptists	....	2.2	2.4	4.7	0.4	9	26.5	34.8
Primitive Baptists	3.7	38.4	8.3	5.7	0.1	1	11.1	9.7
Colored Primitive Baptists in America	....	3.6	0.3	7.6	9.7	25.2	23.0	21.5
United American Freewill Baptists (Colored)	....	0.7	....	2.0	11.8	28.2	32.2	40.1
Brethren (Plymouth)	....	0.3	1.3	3.5	12.6	23.4	36.2	22.9
Brethren (Plymouth)—I	....	0.7	0.7	6.0	17.2	22.4	30.6	22.4
Brethren (Plymouth)—II	....	....	....	....	5.6	27.8	41.3	25.4
Brethren (River)	2.7	1.8	3.6	10.9	17.3	33.6	18.2	11.8
Christian Union	....	0.5	1.5	29.3	11.2	17.1	19.5	21.0
Christians (Christian Connection)	....	21.0	10.7	10.1	13.4	17.2	14.8	12.8
Church of Christ, Scientist	....	....	....	....	0.2	2.4	49.8	47.6
Churches of God in North America, General Eldership of the	....	10.1	9.7	9.7	19.8	17.8	16.5	16.3
Churches of the New Jerusalem	....	19.0	12.4	9.1	14.0	12.4	15.7	17.4
General Convention of the New Jerusalem in the United States of America	....	21.5	14.0	9.3	13.1	11.2	15.0	15.9
Congregationalists	12.2	17.1	7.4	6.4	9.5	17.1	19.0	11.3
Disciples or Christians	....	7.1	5.3	6.7	11.8	19.0	24.1	26.2
Disciples of Christ	....	8.3	5.8	7.4	12.5	19.9	24.8	21.2
Churches of Christ	....	4.2	4.0	4.9	10.0	16.8	22.4	37.8
Dunkers or German Baptist Brethren	1.4	9.0	9.4	7.2	11.2	21.4	21.9	18.3
German Baptist Brethren Church (Conservative)	1.4	11.4	11.7	9.0	13.6	14.8	20.4	17.6
The Brethren Church (Progressive Dunkers)	....	....	0.5	....	2.0	47.5	28.3	21.7
Eastern Orthodox Churches	....	....	....	1.0	....	1.9	29.8	67.3
Evangelical bodies	....	7.1	9.5	12.2	15.7	15.3	26.3	14.0
Evangelical Association	....	8.0	12.3	15.0	18.7	19.0	14.0	12.9
United Evangelical Church	....	5.6	4.3	7.1	10.3	8.5	48.3	16.0
Evangelistic associations	....	0.6	2.9	5.7	6.9	6.3	26.4	51.1
Friends	16.0	25.0	4.8	5.0	8.6	13.9	16.7	9.9
Society of Friends (Orthodox)	12.0	21.8	5.3	4.4	9.0	16.0	20.0	11.4
German Evangelical Synod of North America	....	9.8	10.8	13.2	14.3	19.5	9	14.6
Independent churches	0.3	2.7	2.2	2.5	3.8	12.3	17.7	47.6
Jewish congregations	0.4	2.8	4.5	5.7	8.3	19.1	28.9	30.5
Latter-day Saints	....	3.4	4.0	10.6	14.4	19.1	25.5	23.0
Church of Jesus Christ of Latter-day Saints	....	3.7	6.4	10.4	14.5	20.3	22.2	22.6
Reorganized Church of Jesus Christ of Latter-day Saints	....	3.1	0.8	10.9	14.2	17.5	29.9	23.5
Lutheran bodies	2.2	7.6	6.9	8.3	13.6	19.3	22.0	20.0
General Synod of the Evangelical Lutheran Church in the United States of America	6.7	22.0	12.4	9.3	10.7	12.0	13.9	13.1
United Synod of the Evangelical Lutheran Church in the South	10.2	24.7	11.5	5.4	11.5	11.0	16.1	9.7
General Council of the Evangelical Lutheran Church in North America	5.3	11.2	6.2	7.7	15.2	18.3	22.4	13.8
Evangelical Lutheran Synodical Conference of America	0.1	3.5	6.3	10.9	13.8	21.8	22.1	21.5
United Norwegian Lutheran Church in America	....	1.3	5.3	5.5	16.3	27.8	24.5	19.3
Evangelical Lutheran Joint Synod of Ohio and Other States	....	10.6	11.4	9.5	7.5	17.7	23.8	19.4
Hauge's Norwegian Evangelical Lutheran Synod	....	0.4	4.1	4.1	17.0	25.7	25.3	23.2
Evangelical Lutheran Synod of Iowa and Other States	....	1.0	6.0	9.1	13.2	25.4	23.4	22.0
Synod for the Norwegian Evangelical Lutheran Church in America	....	1.3	5.4	8.4	18.5	15.4	20.5	30.5
Finnish Evangelical Lutheran Church of America, or Suomi Synod	....	....	....	....	2.0	7.8	43.1	47.1
Norwegian Lutheran Free Church	....	....	0.3	3.6	10.8	19.6	30.7	35.0
United Danish Evangelical Lutheran Church in America	....	....	0.7	1.4	23.0	18.9	34.5	21.6
Mennonite bodies	7.8	15.7	6.2	6.8	11.3	13.7	18.5	19.
Mennonite Church	14.2	25.3	3.2	8.9	8.4	12.1	13.2	14.9
Methodist bodies	0.5	13.6	8.3	10.6	16.5	18.3	16.7	15.4
Methodist Episcopal Church	0.9	17.7	10.7	11.5	15.6	17.3	15.1	11.1
African Methodist Episcopal Church	....	3.4	1.2	12.5	21.0	22.5	20.0	19.4
African Methodist Episcopal Zion Church	....	2.8	1.3	16.5	23.3	19.3	17.3	19.5
Methodist Protestant Church	....	14.8	9.6	10.8	14.0	16.1	17.7	17.0
Wesleyan Methodist Connection of America	....	9.7	8.8	7.8	12.1	14.4	20.1	27.1
Methodist Episcopal Church, South	0.5	16.6	10.4	8.5	13.2	17.6	15.9	17.1
Congregational Methodist Church	....	....	3.6	1.8	5.8	8.4	20.4	60.0
Colored Methodist Episcopal Church	....	0.4	0.2	5.1	35.7	21.8	17.6	19.1
Free Methodist Church of North America	....	0.3	0.1	6.7	9.7	21.7	32.1	29.4
Moravian bodies	13.9	5.7	13.9	13.1	13.9	13.1	13.1	13.1
Moravian Church (Unitas Fratrum)	15.9	6.5	15.9	14.0	14.0	15.0	9.3	9.3
Nonsectarian Churches of Bible Faith	....	....	0.5	....	7.0	28.6	31.7	32.2

[1] Less than one-tenth of 1 per cent.

DENOMINATION.	PER CENT OF ORGANIZATIONS ESTABLISHED—							
	Prior to 1800.	1800 to 1849.	1850 to 1859.	1860 to 1869.	1870 to 1879.	1880 to 1889.	1890 to 1899.	1900 to 1906.
Presbyterian bodies	4.2	20.5	9.5	7.8	13.1	16.5	16.2	12.2
Presbyterian Church in the United States of America	4.7	20.8	8.9	8.4	13.0	16.7	15.2	12.3
Cumberland Presbyterian Church	(1)	16.6	10.9	8.8	15.5	19.3	17.8	11.0
Colored Cumberland Presbyterian Church			0.5	6.2	25.9	32.1	21.2	14.0
Welsh Calvinistic Methodist Church		29.4	22.4	14.0	14.7	13.3	4.2	3.1
United Presbyterian Church of North America	4.2	26.3	14.1	7.6	10.4	10.3	13.6	13.7
Presbyterian Church in the United States	6.2	21.1	8.2	5.7	11.2	15.4	19.1	13.1
Associate Reformed Synod of the South	18.5	18.5	8.5	3.8	11.5	13.1	16.9	9.2
Synod of the Reformed Presbyterian Church of North America	2.8	34.6	10.3	8.4	22.4	9.3	7.5	4.7
Protestant Episcopal Church	5.2	15.5	8.9	8.9	12.5	15.8	18.3	14.9
Reformed bodies	11.9	21.4	11.0	10.5	9.0	12.2	14.1	9.8
Reformed Church in America	17.1	22.3	12.2	6.6	8.0	10.0	15.2	8.6
Reformed Church in the United States	11.2	23.1	11.6	12.3	9.6	12.0	11.7	8.5
Christian Reformed Church	0.6	4.1	2.9	9.3	8.7	23.3	30.2	20.9
Roman Catholic Church	1.0	7.9	9.6	10.5	14.9	18.7	17.2	20.2
Salvationists					0.3	18.0	40.9	40.9
Salvation Army					0.3	18.5	41.6	39.6
Spiritualists			1.3	2.4	3.5	5.5	26.0	61.2
Swedish Evangelical bodies				0.8	10.5	30.8	38.8	19.0
Swedish Evangelical Mission Covenant of America				1.1	14.8	32.2	33.7	18.2
Swedish Evangelical Free Mission					1.6	28.0	40.6	20.8
Unitarians	23.7	17.1	4.6	9.0	5.7	15.8	13.4	10.7
United Brethren bodies	0.1	7.8	8.3	11.0	16.6	18.6	23.3	14.3
Church of the United Brethren in Christ	0.2	8.1	8.5	11.1	16.9	19.5	20.9	14.8
Church of the United Brethren in Christ (Old Constitution)		6.3	7.0	10.5	15.1	14.3	35.3	11.6
Universalists	1.3	29.9	10.7	11.0	12.8	10.3	14.4	9.7

[1] Less than one-tenth of 1 per cent.

The 179,331 organizations which were in existence at the close of 1906 and for which the date of establishment was reported, are subdivided as follows, according to the different periods of organization shown by the two tables preceding:

PERIOD.	Number.	Per cent of total.
Total	179,331	100.0
Prior to 1800	3,637	2.0
1800 to 1849	21,929	12.2
1850 to 1859	12,816	7.1
1860 to 1869	16,114	9.0
1870 to 1879	25,851	14.4
1880 to 1889	32,771	18.3
1890 to 1899	34,827	19.4
1900 to 1906	31,386	17.5

Considering the figures for all denominations together, it is noticeable that beginning with the middle of the last century, they are much larger for each successive period, making allowance for the fact that the latest period includes only seven years. If organizations are established at a corresponding rate during the remaining three years of the present decade, the number for the entire decade will be 44,837, and the percentage 23.3. Part of this steady advance in the number of organizations established in the successive decades is of course only apparent. Some organizations disappear within a longer or shorter time after their establishment, and the more remote the decade, the smaller is the proportion of all organizations established in that decade that still survive, and the greater the understatement in the table of the total number of organizations established in that decade. But the chief cause of the steady advance is the fact that the population of the country is constantly increasing.

The denominations showing the largest percentages of organizations established before 1800 are as follows:

Unitarians	23.7
Associate Reformed Synod of the South (Presbyterian)	18.5
Reformed Church in America	17.1
Moravian Church (Unitas Fratrum)	15.9
Mennonite Church	14.2
Congregationalists	12.2
Friends (Orthodox)	12.0
Reformed Church in the United States	11.2
United Synod in the South (Lutheran)	10.2

Of the 9 denominations listed, the Unitarian is the only one for which the percentage for the period prior to 1800 is equaled by that of no period later. In the case of the Associate Reformed Synod of the South (Presbyterian), the Moravian Church (Unitas Fratrum), and the Reformed Church in America, the percentage for the period prior to 1800 is equaled once; in the case of the Mennonite Church, twice; in the case of the Congregationalists and the Friends (Orthodox), three times; and in the case of the Reformed Church in the United States and the United Synod in the South (Lutheran), five times.

The percentages for the decade 1860 to 1869 are only a little larger than for the decade 1850 to 1859, but for the decade 1870 to 1879, the figures are much larger than for the preceding decade. The number of organizations established in the decade 1860 to 1869 was undoubtedly reduced on account of the Civil War and the reduction would have been greater had it not been for the remarkable extension of the colored denominations through the South immediately after that war. Thus 11.7 per cent of the organizations of the Colored Baptists were established in the decade 1860 to 1869, 12.5 per cent of the organizations of the African Methodist Episcopal Church, and 16.5 per cent of the African Methodist Episcopal Zion Church, as compared with five-tenths of 1 per cent, 1.2 per cent, and 1.3 per cent, respectively, for the preceding decade.

The decade 1870 to 1879 was one of general prosperity, which marked the beginning of a large amount of immigration, and shows a corresponding advance in the percentages. The impulse received in that decade, however, was not continued to the same extent through the succeeding decade, 1880 to 1889, and the influence of the period of general financial depression which occurred in the decade 1890 to 1899 is manifest in the slight increase in per cent of organizations formed during that period. In general, the record of these tables accords very closely with the history of the times and of the denominations.

The seven years 1900 to 1906 show a notable increase, their percentage of the total, as already indicated, being at the rate of 23.3 for the whole decade. A high percentage for the latest period is shown even for some of the older denominations. The Freewill Baptists, with a percentage of 29.9 for 1890 to 1899, showed a percentage of 25.3 for 1900 to 1906, and the General Baptists, Congregational Methodists, and Seventh-day Adventists seem likewise to have entered on a new period of expansion.

Among the bodies showing a decline in the number of new organizations formed during this period are the Northern Baptist Convention, the National Baptist Convention (Colored), the Congregationalists, the United Evangelical Church, the Society of Friends (Orthodox), the Reformed Church in America, the Swedish Evangelical Mission Covenant, the Swedish Evangelical Free Mission, the United Brethren (Old Constitution), and the Universalists. The United Evangelical Church was organized as a denomination in the decade 1890 to 1899, and reported 48.3 per cent of its organizations as established in that decade. The Swedish Evangelical Mission Covenant and the Swedish Evangelical Free Mission both reported high figures in the two preceding decades, 1880 to 1889 and 1890 to 1899, as the result of immigration. It was of course not to be expected that the same rate of increase would be maintained for these denominations in the period 1900 to 1906. In the case of the other denominations mentioned the retrogression is slight.

For the bodies most affected by immigration, especially the Lutheran bodies, the percentages for the later decades are naturally comparatively high. The percentage for the Lutheran bodies as a whole for the decade 1880 to 1889 was 19.3 per cent; for that of 1890 to 1899, 22 per cent; and for the seven years 1900 to 1906, 20 per cent. It is noteworthy that the percentage for the Roman Catholic Church for the decade 1890 to 1899 (17.2) was somewhat less than for the preceding decade (18.7), but for the seven years 1900 to 1906 the percentage was 20.2, which represents a much higher decennial rate.

The denominations showing the largest percentages of organizations formed during the seven years from 1900 to 1906 are:

Eastern Orthodox Churches	67.3
Spiritualists	61.2
Congregational Methodist Church	60.0
Evangelistic associations	51.1
Church of Christ, Scientist	47.6
Independent churches	47.6
Finnish Evangelical Lutheran Church (Suomi Synod)	47.1
Seventh-day Adventist Denomination	40.7
United American Freewill Baptist Church (Colored)	40.1
Salvation Army	39.6
Churches of Christ (Disciples or Christians)	37.8
Norwegian Lutheran Free Church	35.0
General Baptists	34.8

A high percentage for a denomination in any particular decade indicates either its organization as a denomination or some special influence, such as immigration, though, as already indicated, the formal organization of a denomination does not preclude the report of individual organizations showing an earlier date. Thus the Primitive Baptists became a distinct denomination in the period 1800 to 1849, as indicated by the percentage reported, 38.4. Among those churches, however, there were some, 3.7 per cent of the total, which were organized prior to 1800.

LANGUAGES USED IN THE CONDUCT OF CHURCH SERVICES.

In the census of 1906, for the first time, an attempt was made to secure complete reports from the various denominations as to the languages used in the conduct of religious services. This was considered in the report for 1890 an important element in the statement of the work of the churches, especially among the foreign population, but there was no general enumeration or classification, although summaries, recognized as approximate, were given of the languages used in the Lutheran bodies and the Methodist Episcopal Church, and mention was made of those used in other bodies.

In the schedules sent out in 1906 each organization was asked to state the language used in church services. Of the 186 denominations, 91 made a full report as to the language used in the church services; 83 furnished reports from at least 90 per cent of their organizations; and only 12 from less than 90 per cent. The total number of organizations reporting was 204,268, or 96.2 per cent of the total. A considerable number of organizations which made no report apparently took it for granted, as will be seen later, that it would be understood that English was used. It follows therefore that the record of the languages used in church services is reasonably complete.

The organizations reporting are classified under three heads: (1) Those using English only; (2) those using English and one or more foreign languages; and (3) those using one or more foreign languages. The American Indian languages are classed as foreign.

English only.—The following table shows the denominations which report the use of English only; the total number of organizations and of communicants or members reported by them; the number of organizations reporting services conducted in English only; and the per cent which these constitute of the total organizations of the respective denominations:

DENOMINATION.	Total organizations.	Total communicants or members.	ORGANIZATIONS REPORTING SERVICES CONDUCTED IN ENGLISH ONLY.	
			Number.	Per cent of total organizations.
All denominations represented	15,844	1,023,672	14,125	89.2
Adventist bodies:				
Evangelical Adventists	18	481	18	100.0
Church of God (Adventist)	10	354	9	90.0
Churches of God (Adventist), Unattached Congregations	10	257	10	100.0
Life and Advent Union	12	509	12	100.0
Churches of God in Christ Jesus	62	2,124	59	95.2
Bahais	24	1,280	24	100.0
Baptist bodies:				
General Six Principle Baptists	16	685	16	100.0
Seventh-day Baptists	77	8,381	76	98.7
Free Baptists	1,346	81,359	1,167	86.7
Freewill Baptists	608	40,280	590	97.0
General Baptists	518	30,097	511	98.6
Separate Baptists	76	5,180	64	84.2
United Baptists	196	13,698	128	65.3
Duck River and Kindred Associations of Baptists (Baptist Church of Christ)	93	6,416	89	95.7
Primitive Baptists	2,922	102,311	2,246	76.9
Colored Primitive Baptists in America	797	35,076	340	42.7
Two-Seed-in-the-Spirit Predestinarian Baptists	55	781	39	70.9
Freewill Baptists (Bullockites)	15	298	15	100.0
United American Freewill Baptists (Colored)	251	14,489	153	61.0
Brethren (Plymouth):				
Brethren (Plymouth)—I	134	2,933	134	100.0
Brethren (Plymouth)—II	128	4,752	125	97.7
Christadelphians	70	1,412	70	100.0
Christian Israelite Church	5	78	5	100.0
Christian Union	217	13,905	214	98.6
Church of Christ, Scientist	638	85,717	617	96.7
Church of God and Saints of Christ (Colored)	48	1,823	48	100.0
Churches of the Living God (Colored):				
Church of the Living God (Christian Workers for Friendship)	44	2,676	44	100.0
Church of the Living God (Apostolic Church)	15	752	15	100.0
Church of Christ in God	9	848	9	100.0
Churches of the New Jerusalem:				
General Church of the New Jerusalem	14	635	14	100.0
Communistic societies:				
United Society of Believers (Shakers)	15	516	15	100.0
Dunkers or German Baptist Brethren:				
Old Order German Baptist Brethren	68	3,388	61	89.7
The Brethren Church (Progressive Dunkers)	202	17,042	200	99.0
Evangelistic associations:				
Apostolic Faith Movement	6	538	6	100.0
Peniel Missions	11	703	11	100.0
Metropolitan Church Association	6	466	6	100.0
Pentecost Bands of the World	16	487	16	100.0
Heavenly Recruit Church	27	938	27	100.0
Christian Congregation	9	395	9	100.0
Gospel Mission	8	196	8	100.0
Church of Daniel's Band	4	92	4	100.0
Lumber River Mission	5	265	5	100.0
Pentecostal Union Church	3	230	3	100.0
Voluntary Missionary Society in America (Colored)	3	425	3	100.0
Free Christian Zion Church of Christ (Colored)	15	1,835	15	100.0
Friends:				
Religious Society of Friends (Hicksite)	218	18,560	216	99.1
Friends (Primitive)	8	171	8	100.0
International Apostolic Holiness Union	74	2,774	73	98.6
Methodist bodies:				
Union American Methodist Episcopal Church (Colored)	77	4,347	76	98.7
African Union Methodist Protestant Church	69	5,592	68	98.6
African Methodist Episcopal Zion Church	2,204	184,542	2,178	98.8
Congregational Methodist Church	325	14,729	323	99.4
New Congregational Methodist Church	35	1,782	35	100.0
Colored Methodist Episcopal Church	2,381	172,996	2,352	98.8
Reformed Zion Union Apostolic Church (Colored)	45	3,059	43	95.6
Primitive Methodist Church in the United States of America	96	7,558	96	100.0
Reformed Methodist Union Episcopal Church (Colored)	58	4,397	56	96.6
Presbyterian bodies:				
Colored Cumberland Presbyterian Church	196	18,066	195	99.5
Associate Synod of North America (Associate Presbyterian Church)	22	786	22	100.0
Associate Reformed Synod of the South	141	13,201	141	100.0
Reformed Presbyterian Church in North America, General Synod	27	3,620	26	96.3
Reformed Presbyterian Church (Covenanted)	1	17	1	100.0
Reformed Presbyterian Church in the United States and Canada	1	440	1	100.0
Reformed Episcopal Church	81	9,682	81	100.0
Social Brethren	17	1,262	17	100.0
Society for Ethical Culture	5	2,040	4	80.0
Theosophical societies:				
Theosophical Society in America	14	166	14	100.0
Theosophical Society, New York	1	90	1	100.0
Universal Brotherhood and Theosophical Society	1	[1]	1	100.0
Universalists	846	64,158	772	91.3
Vedanta Society	4	340	4	100.0
Volunteers of America	71	2,194	71	100.0

[1] No statistics are available.

From this table it appears that the number of denominations reporting the use of English only is 72, the total number of organizations reported by them, 15,844, and the total number of communicants or members, 1,023,672. While the aggregate is large, many of the denominations of which it is composed are small, and, as a whole, they represent only 7.5 per cent of the total number of church organizations in continental United States and 3.1 per cent of the communicants or members. Only 6 have over 50,000 members each, and of these 2 are colored. More than 60 per cent of the communicants or members belong to bodies located chiefly in the Southern states where the foreign element is small; while the larger bodies included in the list which are located chiefly in the Northern states, such as the Free Baptists; Church of Christ, Scientist; Religious Society of Friends

(Hicksite); Universalists, etc., are, as appears in the statements descriptive of the respective denominations, not identified with work among the foreign population. It is noteworthy that among them are included some bodies, as the Brethren Church (Progressive Dunkers), which, while chiefly of non-English speaking origin, emphasize the use of English in the church services.

In regard to the organizations belonging to the denominations listed in this table which make no report as to language, it is to be noted that they constitute only 10.8 per cent of the total number of organizations, and that in nearly every case they belong to denominations so thoroughly identified with the use of English that it might naturally seem superfluous to mention the language. Such are the Separate, United, and Primitive Baptists, the Freewill Colored Baptists, the colored Methodist bodies, etc. It may thus be safely assumed that the comparatively few organizations not reporting may be properly classed as using English only, so that the figures given, 15,844 organizations, with 1,023,672 communicants or members, may be considered to represent those denominations which use the English language exclusively in church services.

Foreign languages.—The following table shows the denominations which report a part or all of their organizations as using a foreign language; the total number of organizations and of communicants or members reported by the denominations in question; the number of organizations with membership, (1) reporting services conducted in English only; (2) reporting a foreign language alone or in addition to English; and (3) not reporting language.

DENOMINATION.	Total organizations.	Total communicants or members.	ORGANIZATIONS REPORTING SERVICES CONDUCTED IN— English only.		ORGANIZATIONS REPORTING SERVICES CONDUCTED IN— Foreign languages alone or in addition to English.		ORGANIZATIONS NOT REPORTING AS TO LANGUAGE.	
			Organizations.	Membership.	Organizations.	Membership.	Organizations.	Membership.
All denominations represented	196,386	31,912,773	165,549	22,624,595	24,594	8,394,229	6,243	893,949
Adventist bodies	2,439	89,010	2,155	81,343	189	6,154	95	1,513
Advent Christian Church	550	26,799	535	26,375	2	65	13	359
Seventh-day Adventist Denomination	1,889	62,211	1,620	54,968	187	6,089	82	1,154
Armenian Church	73	19,889	....	....	71	19,554	2	335
Baptist bodies	47,910	5,323,183	46,648	5,211,632	744	71,035	518	40,516
Baptists	47,910	5,323,183	46,648	5,211,632	744	71,035	518	40,516
Northern Baptist Convention	8,272	1,052,105	7,516	979,662	662	66,692	94	5,751
Southern Baptist Convention	21,104	2,009,471	20,905	1,995,331	80	4,304	119	9,836
National Baptist Convention (Colored)	18,534	2,261,607	18,227	2,236,639	2	39	305	24,929
Brethren (Plymouth)	141	2,881	119	2,469	22	412	....	....
Brethren (Plymouth)—III	81	1,724	67	1,429	14	295	....	....
Brethren (Plymouth)—IV	60	1,157	52	1,040	8	117	....	....
Brethren (River)	111	4,569	57	1,882	53	2,675	1	12
Brethren in Christ	74	3,397	53	1,814	21	1,583	....	....
Yorker, or Old Order, Brethren	9	423	3	33	6	390	....	....
United Zion's Children	28	749	1	35	26	702	1	12
Buddhists	74	3,165	....	....	74	3,165	....	....
Chinese Temples	62	(1)	....	....	62	(1)	....	....
Japanese Temples	12	3,165	....	....	12	3,165	....	....
Catholic Apostolic Churches	24	4,927	8	1,301	16	3,626	....	....
Catholic Apostolic Church	11	2,907	8	1,301	3	1,606	....	....
New Apostolic Church	13	2,020	....	....	13	2,020	....	....
Christian Catholic Church in Zion	17	5,865	13	1,570	4	4,295	....	....
Christians (Christian Connection)	1,379	110,117	1,342	109,375	1	32	36	710
Churches of God in North America, General Eldership of the	518	24,356	505	23,780	8	401	5	175
Churches of the New Jerusalem	119	6,612	101	5,920	12	613	6	79
General Convention of the New Jerusalem in the United States of America	119	6,612	101	5,920	12	613	6	79
Communistic societies	7	1,756	....	....	7	1,756	....	....
Amana Society	7	1,756	....	....	7	1,756	....	....
Congregationalists	5,713	700,480	5,200	658,517	466	38,184	47	3,779
Disciples or Christians	10,942	1,142,359	10,786	1,132,937	6	190	150	9,232
Disciples of Christ	8,293	982,701	8,150	973,647	5	169	138	8,885
Churches of Christ	2,649	159,658	2,636	159,290	1	21	12	347
Dunkers or German Baptist Brethren	827	76,714	794	71,224	28	5,328	5	162
German Baptist Brethren Church (Conservative)	822	76,547	791	71,164	27	5,301	4	82
German Seventh-day Baptists	5	167	3	60	1	27	1	80

1 Not reported.

DENOMINATION.	Total organizations.	Total communicants or members.	ORGANIZATIONS REPORTING SERVICES CONDUCTED IN— English only. Organizations.	English only. Membership.	Foreign languages alone or in addition to English. Organizations.	Foreign languages alone or in addition to English. Membership.	ORGANIZATIONS NOT REPORTING AS TO LANGUAGE. Organizations.	ORGANIZATIONS NOT REPORTING AS TO LANGUAGE. Membership.
Eastern Orthodox Churches	411	129,606			411	129,606		
Russian Orthodox Church	59	19,111			59	19,111		
Serviap Orthodox Church	10	15,742			10	15,742		
Syrian Orthodox Church	8	4,002			8	4,002		
Greek Orthodox Church	334	90,751			334	90,751		
Evangelical bodies	2,738	174,780	1,606	100,428	1,075	72,005	57	2,347
Evangelical Association	1,760	104,898	792	43,212	917	59,527	51	2,159
United Evangelical Church	978	69,882	814	57,216	158	12,478	6	188
Evangelistic associations	84	6,107	20	634	60	5,085	4	388
Hephzibah Faith Missionary Association	10	293	8	238	2	55		
Missionary Church Association	32	1,256	12	396	20	860		
Apostolic Christian Church	42	4,558			38	4,170	4	388
Friends	921	95,041	902	93,800	7	416	12	825
Society of Friends (Orthodox)	873	91,161	858	90,279	4	148	11	734
Orthodox Conservative Friends (Wilburite)	48	3,880	44	3,521	3	268	1	91
German Evangelical Protestant bodies	66	34,704	1	50	62	32,954	3	1,700
German Evangelical Protestant Ministers' Association	44	23,518			44	23,518		
German Evangelical Protestant Ministers' Conference	22	11,186	1	50	18	9,436	3	1,700
German Evangelical Synod of North America	1,205	293,137	14	2,264	1,188	288,693	3	2,180
Independent churches	1,079	73,673	923	55,170	137	17,594	19	909
Jewish congregations	1,769	[1] 101,457	111	8,203	951	82,844	707	10,410
Latter-day Saints	1,184	256,647	1,138	240,530	19	7,818	27	8,299
Church of Jesus Christ of Latter-day Saints	683	215,796	644	200,113	14	7,439	25	8,244
Reorganized Church of Jesus Christ of Latter-day Saints	501	40,851	494	40,417	5	379	2	55
Lutheran bodies	12,703	2,112,494	2,735	344,157	9,808	1,754,355	160	13,982
General Synod of the Evangelical Lutheran Church in the United States of America	1,734	270,221	1,448	222,091	262	46,385	24	1,745
United Synod of the Evangelical Lutheran Church in the South	449	47,747	440	45,685	5	1,733	4	329
General Council of the Evangelical Lutheran Church in North America	2,146	462,177	534	38,699	1,586	421,568	26	1,910
Evangelical Lutheran Synodical Conference of America	3,301	648,529	126	17,843	3,147	628,239	28	2,447
United Norwegian Lutheran Church in America	1,177	185,027	6	842	1,136	180,669	35	3,516
Evangelical Lutheran Joint Synod of Ohio and Other States	772	123,408	159	16,574	606	104,723	7	2,111
Lutheran Synod of Buffalo	33	5,270			33	5,270		
Hauge's Norwegian Evangelical Lutheran Synod	272	33,268	3	539	256	32,277	13	452
Evangelical Lutheran Church in America, Eielsen's Synod	26	1,013			26	1,013		
German Evangelical Lutheran Synod of Texas	25	2,440			25	2,440		
Evangelical Lutheran Synod of Iowa and Other States	828	110,254	4	697	819	108,892	5	665
Synod for the Norwegian Evangelical Lutheran Church in America	927	107,712	12	1,042	902	106,393	13	277
Evangelical Lutheran Synod of Michigan and Other States	55	9,697			55	9,697		
Danish Evangelical Lutheran Church in America	92	12,541			90	12,315	2	226
Icelandic Evangelical Lutheran Synod in North America	14	2,101			14	2,101		
Immanuel Synod of the Evangelical Lutheran Church of North America	11	3,275			10	3,125	1	150
Finnish Evangelical Lutheran Church of America, or Suomi Synod	105	12,907			105	12,907		
Norwegian Lutheran Free Church	320	26,928			319	26,864	1	64
United Danish Evangelical Lutheran Church in America	198	16,340	3	145	195	16,195		
Slovak Evangelical Lutheran Synod of America	59	12,141			59	12,141		
Finnish Evangelical Lutheran National Church	66	10,111			66	10,111		
Apostolic Lutheran Church (Finnish)	68	8,170			67	8,080	1	90
Church of the Lutheran Brethren of America (Norwegian)	16	482			16	482		
Evangelical Lutheran Jehovah Conference	9	735			9	735		
Mennonite bodies	604	54,798	225	13,449	378	41,306	1	43
Mennonite Church	220	18,674	146	8,771	74	9,903		
Bruederhoef Mennonite Church	8	275			8	275		
Amish Mennonite Church	57	7,640	9	939	48	6,701		
Old Amish Mennonite Church	46	5,043			46	5,043		
Reformed Mennonite Church	34	2,079			34	2,079		
General Conference of Mennonites of North America	90	11,661	7	916	82	10,702	1	43
Church of God in Christ (Mennonite)	18	562			18	562		
Old (Wisler) Mennonite Church	9	655			9	655		
Defenceless Mennonites	14	967			14	967		
Mennonite Brethren in Christ	68	2,801	57	2,084	11	717		
Bundes Conferenz der Mennoniten Brueder-Gemeinde:								
Krimmer Brueder-Gemeinde	6	708			6	708		
Schellenberger Brueder-Gemeinde	13	1,825			13	1,825		
Central Illinois Conference of Mennonites	13	1,363	6	739	7	624		
Nebraska and Minnesota Conference of Mennonites	8	545			8	545		
Methodist bodies	59,411	5,350,836	55,238	5,073,516	1,552	105,745	2,621	171,575
Methodist Episcopal Church	29,943	2,986,154	27,558	2,824,161	1,400	99,404	985	62,589
African Methodist Episcopal Church	6,647	494,777	6,508	486,340	1	33	138	8,404
Methodist Protestant Church	2,843	178,544	2,752	174,972	3	150	88	3,422
Wesleyan Methodist Connection of America	594	20,043	584	19,758	2	72	8	213
Methodist Episcopal Church, South	17,831	1,638,480	16,311	1,535,723	142	5,978	1,378	96,779
Free Methodist Church of North America	1,553	32,838	1,525	32,562	4	108	24	168
Moravian bodies	132	17,926	70	9,813	61	8,029	1	84
Moravian Church (Unitas Fratrum)	117	17,155	70	9,813	46	7,258	1	84
Evangelical Union of Bohemian and Moravian Brethren in North America	15	771			15	771		
Nonsectarian Churches of Bible Faith	204	6,396	184	5,914	13	364	7	118
Pentecostal Church of the Nazarene	100	6,657	98	6,562	2	95		
Polish National Church of America	24	15,473			24	15,473		

[1] Heads of families only.

DENOMINATION.	Total organizations.	Total communicants or members.	ORGANIZATIONS REPORTING SERVICES CONDUCTED IN— English only. Organizations.	English only. Membership.	Foreign languages alone or in addition to English. Organizations.	Foreign languages alone or in addition to English. Membership.	ORGANIZATIONS NOT REPORTING AS TO LANGUAGE. Organizations.	ORGANIZATIONS NOT REPORTING AS TO LANGUAGE. Membership.
Presbyterian bodies	15,118	1,794,425	14,040	1,715,329	574	57,990	504	21,106
Presbyterian Church in the United States of America	7,935	1,179,566	7,401	1,128,535	376	41,906	158	9,125
Cumberland Presbyterian Church	2,850	195,770	2,611	187,866	17	284	222	7,620
Welsh Calvinistic Methodist Church	147	13,280	6	183	141	13,097	....	....
United Presbyterian Church of North America	968	130,342	961	129,363	6	619	1	360
Presbyterian Church in the United States	3,104	266,345	2,951	260,396	31	1,976	122	3,973
Synod of the Reformed Presbyterian Church of North America	114	9,122	110	8,986	3	108	1	28
Protestant Episcopal Church	6,845	886,942	6,439	853,738	177	25,105	229	8,099
Reformed bodies	2,585	449.514	1,477	236,917	1,085	209,947	23	2,650
Reformed Church in America	659	124,938	436	92,531	222	32,364	1	43
Reformed Church in the United States	1,736	292,654	1,021	142,872	694	147,195	21	2,587
Christian Reformed Church	174	26,669	20	1,514	153	25,135	1	20
Hungarian Reformed Church in America	16	5,253	....	....	16	5,253	....	....
Reformed Catholic Church	5	1,250	4	1,100	1	150	....	....
Roman Catholic Church	12,482	12,079,142	7,080	6,159,822	4,711	5,342,023	691	577,297
Salvationists	714	23,344	630	20,630	79	2,693	5	21
Salvation Army	694	22,908	613	20,280	77	2,613	4	15
American Salvation Army	20	436	17	350	2	80	1	6
Schwenkfelders	8	725	2	120	6	605	....	....
Spiritualists	455	35,056	427	33,555	23	938	5	563
Swedish Evangelical bodies	408	27,712	....	....	406	27,687	2	25
Swedish Evangelical Mission Covenant of America	281	20,760	....	....	279	20,735	2	25
Swedish Evangelical Free Mission	127	6,952	....	....	127	6,952	....	....
Temple Society in the United States (Friends of the Temple)	3	376	....	....	3	376	....	....
Theosophical societies	69	2,080	66	1,957	1	27	2	96
Theosophical Society, American Section	69	2,080	66	1,957	1	27	2	96
Unitarians	461	70,542	450	69,870	6	653	5	19
United Brethren bodies	4,304	296,050	3,941	275,117	73	6,233	290	14,700
Church of the United Brethren in Christ	3,732	274,649	3,397	254,504	67	6,028	268	14,117
Church of the United Brethren in Christ (Old Constitution)	572	21,401	544	20,613	6	205	22	583

From this table it appears that the number of denominations which report a part or all of their organizations as using a foreign language is 114, with 196,386 organizations, or 92.5 per cent of the total number in continental United States, and 31,912,773 communicants or members, or 96.9 per cent of the total in the United States. Of these organizations, 165,549, with 22,624,595 members, report services conducted in English only; 24,594, with 8,394,229 members, report the use of a foreign language alone or in addition to English; and 6,243, with 893,949 members, make no report of the language used in their church services.

It shows that in those denominations which report the use, in whole or in part, of one or more foreign languages, 84.3 per cent of their organizations, with 70.9 per cent of the members, report English only in their church services; while 12.5 per cent of their organizations, with 26.3 per cent of their membership, report foreign languages alone or in addition to English. If the organizations presented in the table on page 108, which shows the denominations reporting the use of English only, be combined with the organizations in this table reporting English only the result is 181,393, the total number of organizations reporting the use of English only, or 85.5 per cent of all the organizations in continental United States, with a membership of 23,648,267, or 71.8 per cent of the total membership.

It is probable also that of the 6,243 organizations in this table, with 893,949 members, which make no report of language, a large number, as already suggested in regard to those in the preceding table which make no report, failed to do so because they took it for granted that it would be understood that English was used. This will be evident from an inspection of the denominations in question. In the National Baptist Convention (Colored) only 2 organizations out of 18,534 report any language other than English, and as will be seen from a succeeding table, they use an American Indian language; it is therefore extremely probable that the great majority, at least, of the 305 organizations of this body which make no report, use English and English only. The same may be said in regard to the Christians (Christian Connection); the Disciples or Christians; the Methodist Episcopal Church, South; the African Methodist Episcopal Church; the Cumberland Presbyterian Church, and others. With regard to certain bodies, however, as the Evangelical Association, the Lutheran bodies, the Methodist Episcopal Church, the Presbyterian Church in the United States of America, the Protestant Episcopal Church, and other bodies which report a considerable number of organizations using some language other than English, and especially with regard to the Jewish congregations and the Roman Catholic Church, the same can not be said. No line, therefore, can be drawn, and the nonreporting organizations must be left out of account, although it is necessary to remember that they undoubtedly include a considerable proportion of English speaking congregations. It is also to be remembered that, as appears in a succeeding table, a considerable proportion of the organizations which report some other language than English use English also. The number of organizations reporting the use of English in connection with some other language is given as 7,906, and their membership as 3,371,628, while 16,688 organizations, with a membership of 5,022,601, are reported as using foreign languages only. It thus appears that only 7.9 per cent of the total number of organizations and 15.2 per cent of the membership, or 6 per cent of the estimated population of the United States in 1906, are reported as using foreign languages only in church services. As approximately 2,000,000 immigrants, using foreign languages, entered the country during the years 1905 and 1906, it is evident that the adoption of English by these immigrant communities has progressed rapidly. In this connection it should be noted that by no means all of these immigrants are identified with church life.

The significance of the figures depends somewhat upon the denominations reporting them. The denominations reporting a part or all of their organizations as using a foreign language may be divided into four classes: (1) Those in which the use of English is predominant, and in which the organizations reporting the use of a foreign language may be considered the result of evangelistic or mission work; (2) those which are also predominantly English speaking, but in which organizations using foreign languages are provided to meet the needs of immigrant communities naturally affiliated with the particular denomination; (3) those which are solely or very largely made up of the immigrant element, to which the use of English, whether in church services or in ordinary life, is as yet unfamiliar, and in which there are comparatively few English speaking organizations; and (4) those which report no organizations using English only.

In the first class the percentage of organizations using a foreign language is naturally small; in the second class it is more nearly equal to that of organizations using English only; and in the third it is of course exceedingly large. It is noticeable also that in the first class the average membership of the organizations using foreign languages is generally smaller than in those reporting English only; in the second class it is about the same as for those reporting English only; in the third class it is somewhat larger; while the largest averages of membership in congregations using foreign languages are in most cases found in the fourth class.

Among the denominations of the first class interested particularly in evangelistic work in immigrant communities are the Baptists, Congregationalists, Methodist Episcopal Church, Presbyterian Church in the United States of America, and the Protestant Episcopal Church. Of the Baptist organizations, 1.6 per cent report the use of a foreign language, and they have an average membership of 95, as compared with 112 for those reporting English only. Of the Congregational organizations, 8.2 per cent use a foreign language, and their average membership is 82, as compared with 127 for those reporting English only. In the Methodist Episcopal Church the percentage of organizations reporting a foreign language is 4.7, and their average membership, 71, as compared with 102 for those reporting English only; and for the Presbyterian Church in the United States of America the percentage is also 4.7, and the average membership, 111, as compared with 152 for those reporting English only. In the Protestant Episcopal Church the percentage is 2.6, but the average membership is 142, as compared with 133 for those using English only; an exception explained by the fact shown in the following table that an unusually large average is reported by the Indian mission churches in the West.

Among the denominations in the second class, in which special provision is made for affiliated non-English speaking immigrants, are the Evangelical, Moravian, and Reformed bodies, and the Roman Catholic Church. In the Evangelical bodies the percentage of organizations reporting other languages than English is 39.3, and the average membership, 67, as compared with 63 for those reporting English only; in the Moravian bodies, the percentage is 46.2, and the average membership, 132, as compared with 140; and in the Reformed bodies, the percentage is 42, and the average membership, 193, as compared with 160. In the last case the situation is affected by the Reformed Hungarian (Magyar) Church which uses Magyar only. In the Roman Catholic Church 37.7 per cent of the organizations report the use of some foreign language, and an average membership of 1,134, as compared with 870 for those reporting English only.

The leading bodies in the third class, largely made up of non-English speaking organizations, are the Jewish congregations, the German Evangelical Synod, and the Lutheran bodies. Of the Jewish congregations, those reporting a foreign language represent 53.8 per cent of the total, and an average membership of 87, as compared with 74 for those using English only. It should be remembered in this connection that 40 per cent of the Jewish congregations made no report as to language, and only heads of families are returned as members. Among the Lutheran bodies conditions vary greatly. Of the 24 bodies, 14 report no organizations using English only, but they are the smaller bodies. Of the larger bodies, the General Synod and the United Synod, South, are predominantly English, and the remainder predominantly foreign, in regard to the language used in church services. Taking the Lutheran bodies as a whole, 77.2 per cent of the organizations report the use of a foreign language, while the average membership in these organizations is 179, as compared with 126 for those reporting English only.

In the fourth class, denominations reporting no organizations using English only, are included the Armenian Church, the Buddhists, the Eastern Orthodox Churches, and the Swedish Evangelical bodies. In most cases one or more organizations are reported which use English in addition to the foreign language. In regard to these bodies, the average size of organizations is noteworthy. In the Armenian Church the average membership is 272; in the Japanese Temples, 264; and in the Eastern Orthodox Churches, 315.

The comparative importance of these four classes, as indicated by their relative size, is as follows:

	Organizations.	Membership.
Total	196,386	31,912,773
First class	155,954	16,020,909
Second class	23,068	13,094,126
Third class	16,371	2,601,517
Fourth class	993	196,221

Languages by denominations.—The following table shows the denominations reporting organizations using a foreign language, with the languages given in alphabetical order; the aggregate number of organizations, with membership, making such report; the number of organizations, with membership, using the specified foreign languages only; and the number of organizations, with membership, using the specified foreign languages and English:

DENOMINATION AND LANGUAGE.	ORGANIZATIONS REPORTING SERVICES CONDUCTED IN—					
	Specified languages.		Specified languages only.		Specified languages and English.	
	Organizations.	Membership.	Organizations.	Membership.	Organizations.	Membership.
All denominations represented	24,594	8,394,229	16,688	5,022,601	7,906	3,371,628
Adventist bodies:						
Advent Christian Church	2	65	1	40	1	25
German	2	65	1	40	1	25
Seventh-day Adventist Denomination	187	6,089	118	3,672	69	2,417
Dutch or Flemish	1	18			1	18
French	4	125	1	26	3	99
French and Swedish	1	8	1	8		
German	83	3,185	58	2,035	25	1,150
German and Spanish	1	59			1	59
German and Swedish	1	34			1	34
German, Italian, and Scandinavian	1	100			1	100
Indian (American)	1	32			1	32
Italian	1	30	1	30		
Russian	1	50	1	50		
Scandinavian—						
Danish	27	700	10	247	17	453
Danish and Norwegian	2	170	2	170		
Norwegian	11	149	8	103	3	46
Norwegian and Swedish	1	55	1	55		
Swedish	28	625	20	413	8	212
Not specified	14	564	8	380	6	184
Spanish	9	185	7	155	2	30
Armenian Church	71	19,554	71	19,554		
Armenian	71	19,554	71	19,554		
Baptist bodies:						
Baptists—						
Northern Baptist Convention	662	66,692	548	46,669	114	20,023
Bohemian	3	231	2	226	1	5
Chinese	3	114	3	114		
Chinese, Greek, Magyar, Polish, and Slovak	1	323			1	323
Croatian and Magyar	1	52	1	52		
Dutch or Flemish	1	60	1	60		
Finnish	3	128	2	46	1	82
Finnish and Swedish	3	231	2	128	1	103
French	12	3,683	2	128	10	3,555
French and Spanish	1	667			1	667
German	190	21,656	177	20,952	13	704
German and Roumanian	1	1,010			1	1,010
Indian (American)	5	387	5	387		
Italian	11	3,265	4	199	7	3,066
Italian and Swedish	2	958			2	958
Japanese	1	69	1	69		
Lettish	2	262	2	262		
Magyar	2	184	1	48	1	136
Polish	5	320	5	320		
Portuguese	2	349			2	349
Ruthenian	1	490			1	490

DENOMINATION AND LANGUAGE.	ORGANIZATIONS REPORTING SERVICES CONDUCTED IN—					
	Specified languages.		Specified languages only.		Specified languages and English.	
	Organizations.	Membership.	Organizations.	Membership.	Organizations.	Membership.
Baptist bodies—Continued.						
Baptists—Continued.						
Northern Baptist Convention—Continued.						
Scandinavian—						
Danish	48	3,407	34	2,319	14	1,088
Danish and Norwegian	2	174	2	174	.....	.....
Norwegian	38	1,704	33	1,319	5	385
Norwegian and Swedish	1	11	.....	.....	1	11
Swedish	280	22,452	256	19,274	24	3,178
Not specified	5	200	3	129	2	71
Slovak	1	58	1	58	.....	.....
Spanish	6	178	5	167	1	11
Welsh	31	4,069	6	238	25	3,831
Southern Baptist Convention	80	4,304	71	3,543	9	761
German	22	1,696	21	1,552	1	144
Indian (American)	38	1,872	30	1,255	8	617
Lettish	1	43	1	43	.....	.....
Scandinavian—						
Swedish	4	276	4	276	.....	.....
Spanish	15	417	15	417	.....	.....
National Baptist Convention (Colored)	2	39	.....	.....	2	39
Indian (American)	2	39	.....	.....	2	39
Brethren (Plymouth):						
Brethren (Plymouth)—III	14	295	8	111	6	184
French	4	70	2	52	2	18
German	9	215	5	49	4	166
Polish	1	10	1	10	.....	.....
Brethren (Plymouth)—IV	8	117	4	49	4	68
French	2	37	1	5	1	32
German	1	3	.....	.....	1	3
Italian	1	7	.....	.....	1	7
Scandinavian—						
Norwegian	1	26	.....	.....	1	26
Swedish	3	44	3	44	.....	.....
Brethren (River):						
Brethren in Christ	21	1,583	.....	.....	21	1,583
German	21	1,583	.....	.....	21	1,583
Yorker, or Old Order, Brethren	6	390	.....	.....	6	390
German	6	390	.....	.....	6	390
United Zion's Children	26	702	.....	.....	26	702
German	26	702	.....	.....	26	702
Buddhists:						
Chinese Temples	62	(1)	62	(1)	.....	.....
Chinese	62	(1)	62	(1)	.....	.....
Japanese Temples	12	3,165	11	2,823	1	342
Japanese	12	3,165	11	2,823	1	342
Catholic Apostolic Churches:						
Catholic Apostolic Church	3	1,606	1	450	2	1,156
German	3	1,606	1	450	2	1,156
New Apostolic Church	13	2,020	12	1,520	1	500
German	13	2,020	12	1,520		500
Christian Catholic Church in Zion	4	4,295	1	250		4,045
German	4	4,295	1	250	3	4,045
Christians (Christian Connection)	1	32	.....	.....	1	32
Chinese	1	32	.....	.....	1	32
Churches of God in North America, General Eldership of the	8	401	3	174	5	227
German	6	261	1	34	5	227
Slavic	2	140	2	140	.....	.....
Churches of the New Jerusalem:						
General Convention of the New Jerusalem in the United States of America	12	613	6	324	6	289
German	11	570	6	324	5	246
Scandinavian—						
Swedish	1	43	.....	.....	1	43
Communistic societies:						
Amana Society	7	1,756	7	1,756	.....	.....
German	7	1,756	7	1,756	.....	.....

1 Not reported.

DENOMINATION AND LANGUAGE.	ORGANIZATIONS REPORTING SERVICES CONDUCTED IN—					
	Specified languages.		Specified languages only.		Specified languages and English.	
	Organizations.	Membership.	Organizations.	Membership.	Organizations.	Membership.
Congregationalists	466	38,184	341	23,345	125	14,839
Arabic and Armenian	1	357			1	357
Armenian	5	631	4	320	1	311
Armenian, Italian, and Syriac	1	1,108			1	1,108
Bohemian	10	551	5	298	5	253
Bohemian and Polish	1	227			1	227
Chinese	2	150	1	111	1	39
Finnish	6	694	5	248	1	446
French	11	789	10	732	1	57
German	158	9,539	130	7,550	28	1,989
Indian (American)	19	1,401	10	487	9	914
Italian	11	1,517	6	354	5	1,163
Japanese	1	21	1	21		
Scandinavian:						
Danish	3	129	3	129		
Danish and Norwegian	2	109	2	109		
Norwegian	7	681	5	323	2	358
Swedish	114	9,970	109	9,695	5	275
Not specified	6	201	4	146	2	55
Slavic	1	21	1	21		
Slovak	4	176	3	146	1	30
Spanish	4	621	3	91	1	530
Welsh	99	9,291	39	2,564	60	6,727
Disciples or Christians:						
Disciples of Christ	5	169	2	54	3	115
Chinese	1	23	1	23		
French	1	31	1	31		
German	2	57			2	57
Scandinavian— Norwegian	1	58			1	58
Churches of Christ	1	21	1	21		
German	1	21	1	21		
Dunkers or German Baptist Brethren:						
German Baptist Brethren Church (Conservative)	27	5,301	2	129	25	5,172
German	27	5,301	2	129	25	5,172
German Seventh-day Baptists	1	27			1	27
German	1	27			1	27
Eastern Orthodox Churches:						
Russian Orthodox Church	59	19,111	51	14,013	8	5,098
Greek	1	61			1	61
Greek and Slavic	7	2,987	3	800	4	2,187
Greek, Roumanian, and Slavic	1	300			1	300
Slavic	50	15,763	48	13,213	2	2,550
Servian Orthodox Church	10	15,742	10	15,742		
Servian and Slavic	1	1,190	1	1,190		
Slavic	9	14,552	9	14,552		
Syrian Orthodox Church	8	4,002	8	4,002		
Syro-Arabic	8	4,002	8	4,002		
Greek Orthodox Church	334	90,751	334	90,751		
Greek	334	90,751	334	90,751		
Evangelical bodies:						
Evangelical Association	917	59,527	554	33,797	363	25,730
German	917	59,527	554	33,797	363	25,730
United Evangelical Church	158	12,478	36	1,598	122	10,880
German	158	12,478	36	1,598	122	10,880
Evangelistic associations:						
Hephzibah Faith Missionary Association	2	55	2	55		
German	2	55	2	55		
Missionary Church Association	20	860	5	151	15	709
German	19	840	5	151	14	689
Scandinavian— Swedish	1	20			1	20
Apostolic Christian Church	38	4,170	34	3,938	4	232
German	38	4,170	34	3,938	4	232

DENOMINATION AND LANGUAGE.	ORGANIZATIONS REPORTING SERVICES CONDUCTED IN—					
	Specified languages.		Specified languages only.		Specified languages and English.	
	Organizations.	Membership.	Organizations.	Membership.	Organizations.	Membership.
Friends:						
Society of Friends (Orthodox)	4	148			4	148
Indian (American)	2	18			2	18
Scandinavian—						
Norwegian	2	130			2	130
Orthodox Conservative Friends (Wilburite)	3	268			3	268
Scandinavian—						
Danish	1	152			1	152
Norwegian	2	116			2	116
German Evangelical Protestant bodies:						
German Evangelical Protestant Ministers' Association	44	23,518	27	12,898	17	10,620
German	44	23,518	27	12,898	17	10,620
German Evangelical Protestant Ministers' Conference	18	9,436	7	2,175	11	7,261
German	18	9,436	7	2,175	11	7,261
German Evangelical Synod of North America	1,188	288,693	952	201,137	236	87,556
German	1,188	288,693	952	201,137	236	87,556
Independent churches	137	17,594	93	10,713	44	6,881
Bohemian	5	851	5	851		
Dutch or Flemish	12	1,641	12	1,641		
French	2	117	1	85	1	32
German	66	10,672	37	6,149	29	4,523
German and Hebrew	1	398			1	398
German and Scandinavian	1	300			1	300
German, Lithuanian, Polish, Slavic, and Yiddish	1	35			1	35
Indian (American)	1	10	1	10		
Italian	1	1,275			1	1,275
Lithuanian	1	34	1	34		
Scandinavian:						
Danish	2	53	2	53		
Danish and Swedish	1	14			1	14
Norwegian	14	981	12	866	2	115
Norwegian and Swedish	2	91	2	91		
Swedish	13	517	12	442	1	75
Not specified	8	205	4	107	4	98
Slavic	1	20	1	20		
Spanish	2	33	1	17	1	16
Welsh	2	347	2	347		
Yiddish	1	(1)			1	(1)
Jewish congregations	951	[2] 82,844	752	[2] 58,988	199	[2] 23,856
German	7	1,125	1	5	6	1,120
German and Hebrew	13	1,866	5	424	8	1,442
Hebrew	931	79,853	746	58,559	185	21,294
Latter-day Saints:						
Church of Jesus Christ of Latter-day Saints	14	7,439			14	7,439
German	7	2,885			7	2,885
Indian (American)	1	104			1	104
Scandinavian—						
Danish	3	2,529			3	2,529
Swedish	1	622			1	622
Not specified	2	1,299			2	1,299
Reorganized Church of Jesus Christ of Latter-day Saints	5	379			5	379
German	1	80			1	80
Portuguese	1	26			1	26
Scandinavian—						
Swedish	1	166			1	166
Not specified	1	36			1	36
Welsh	1	71			1	71
Lutheran bodies:						
General Synod of the Evangelical Lutheran Church in the United States of America	262	46,385	145	17,506	117	28,879
German	261	46,273	144	17,394	117	28,879
Scandinavian—						
Swedish	1	112	1	112		
United Synod of the Evangelical Lutheran Church in the South	5	1,733			5	1,733
German	5	1,733			5	1,733
General Council of the Evangelical Lutheran Church in North America	1,586	421,568	984	186,401	602	235,167
German	598	244,827	179	57,303	419	187,524
Scandinavian—						
Swedish	984	175,741	801	128,098	183	47,643
Slovak	4	1,000	4	1,000		

[1] Not reported.

[2] Heads of families only.

DENOMINATION AND LANGUAGE.	ORGANIZATIONS REPORTING SERVICES CONDUCTED IN— Specified languages.		Specified languages only.		Specified languages and English.	
	Organizations.	Membership.	Organizations.	Membership.	Organizations.	Membership.
Lutheran bodies—Continued.						
Evangelical Lutheran Synodical Conference of America	3,147	628,239	2,433	456,734	714	171,505
Esthonian	2	36	2	36		
Finnish and German	2	211			2	211
Finnish, German, and Swedish	1	66			1	66
German	3,110	623,452	2,403	453,296	707	170,156
German and Norwegian	1	80			1	80
German and Polish	6	2,269	5	1,283	1	986
German and Wendish	1	656	1	656		
Indian (American)	2	6			2	6
Lettish	7	378	7	378		
Lithuanian	7	490	7	490		
Polish	5	201	5	201		
Scandinavian—						
Danish	2	247	2	247		
Swedish	1	147	1	147		
United Norwegian Lutheran Church in America	1,136	180,669	807	119,802	329	60,867
Scandinavian—						
Danish	3	103	3	103		
Danish and Norwegian	1	270	1	270		
Norwegian	1,130	180,089	801	119,222	329	60,867
Not specified	2	207	2	207		
Evangelical Lutheran Joint Synod of Ohio and Other States	606	104,723	351	50,040	255	54,683
German	606	104,723	351	50,040	255	54,683
Lutheran Synod of Buffalo	33	5,270	31	4,899	2	371
German	33	5,270	31	4,899	2	371
Hauge's Norwegian Evangelical Lutheran Synod	256	32,277	189	23,297	67	8,980
Scandinavian—						
Norwegian	256	32,277	189	23,297	67	8,980
Evangelical Lutheran Church in America, Eielsen's Synod	26	1,013	25	1,003	1	10
Scandinavian—						
Danish	1	30	1	30		
Norwegian	25	983	24	973	1	10
German Evangelical Lutheran Synod of Texas	25	2,440	25	2,440		
German	25	2,440	25	2,440		
Evangelical Lutheran Synod of Iowa and Other States	819	108,892	722	92,113	97	16,779
German	819	108,892	722	92,113	97	16,779
Synod for the Norwegian Evangelical Lutheran Church in America	902	106,393	601	64,751	301	41,642
German	1	250			1	250
German and Norwegian	1	196			1	196
Lappish and Norwegian	1	10	1	10		
Scandinavian—						
Danish	26	1,587	19	780	7	807
Danish and Norwegian	8	514	4	156	4	358
Norwegian	865	103,836	577	63,805	288	40,031
Evangelical Lutheran Synod of Michigan and Other States	55	9,697	37	6,018	18	3,679
German	55	9,697	37	6,018	18	3,679
Danish Evangelical Lutheran Church in America	90	12,315	90	12,315		
Scandinavian—						
Danish	90	12,315	90	12,315		
Icelandic Evangelical Lutheran Synod in North America	14	2,101	14	2,101		
Scandinavian—						
Icelandic	14	2,101	14	2,101		
Immanuel Synod of the Evangelical Lutheran Church of North America	10	3,125	9	2,875	1	250
German	10	3,125	9	2,875	1	250
Finnish Evangelical Lutheran Church of America, or Suomi Synod	105	12,907	105	12,907		
Finnish	105	12,907	105	12,907		
Norwegian Lutheran Free Church	319	26,864	275	21,815	44	5,049
Scandinavian—						
Norwegian	319	26,864	275	21,815	44	5,049
United Danish Evangelical Lutheran Church in America	195	16,195	182	14,415	13	1,780
Scandinavian—						
Danish	195	16,195	182	14,415	13	1,780
Slovak Evangelical Lutheran Synod of America	59	12,141	59	12,141		
Slovak	59	12,141	59	12,141		
Finnish Evangelical Lutheran National Church	66	10,111	66	10,111		
Finnish	66	10,111	66	10,111		

DENOMINATION AND LANGUAGE.	ORGANIZATIONS REPORTING SERVICES CONDUCTED IN—					
	Specified languages.		Specified languages only.		Specified languages and English.	
	Organizations.	Membership.	Organizations.	Membership.	Organizations.	Membership.
Lutheran bodies—Continued.						
Apostolic Lutheran Church (Finnish)	67	8,080	67	8,080	....	....
Finnish	66	8,061	66	8,061	....	....
Finnish and Swedish	1	19	1	19	....	....
Church of the Lutheran Brethren of America (Norwegian)	16	482	16	482	....	....
Scandinavian—						
Norwegian	16	482	16	482	....	....
Evangelical Lutheran Jehovah Conference	9	735	9	735	....	....
German	9	735	9	735	....	....
Mennonite bodies:						
Mennonite Church	74	9,903	18	3,387	56	6,516
German	74	9,903	18	3,387	56	6,516
Bruederhoef Mennonite Church	8	275	8	275	....	....
German	8	275	8	275	....	....
Amish Mennonite Church	48	6,701	14	1,142	34	5,559
German	48	6,701	14	1,142	34	5,559
Old Amish Mennonite Church	46	5,043	45	5,004	1	39
German	46	5,043	45	5,004	1	39
Reformed Mennonite Church	34	2,079	....	....	34	2,079
German	34	2,079	....	....	34	2,079
General Conference of Mennonites of North America	82	10,702	51	6,361	31	4,341
German	77	10,543	50	6,297	27	4,246
Indian (American)	5	159	1	64	4	95
Church of God in Christ (Mennonite)	18	562	18	562	....	....
German	18	562	18	562	....	....
Old (Wisler) Mennonite Church	9	655	6	487	3	168
German	9	655	6	487	3	168
Defenceless Mennonites	14	967	12	701	2	266
German	14	967	12	701	2	266
Mennonite Brethren in Christ	11	717	1	62	10	655
German	11	717	1	62	10	655
Bundes Conferenz der Mennoniten Brueder-Gemeinde:						
Krimmer Brueder-Gemeinde	6	708	6	708	....	....
German	6	708	6	708	....	....
Schellenberger Brueder-Gemeinde	13	1,825	13	1,825	....	....
German	13	1,825	13	1,825	....	....
Central Illinois Conference of Mennonites	7	624	....	....	7	624
German	7	624	....	....	7	624
Nebraska and Minnesota Conference of Mennonites	8	545	8	545	....	....
German	8	545		545	....	....
Methodist bodies:						
Methodist Episcopal Church	1,400	99,404	1,228	84,530	172	14,874
Armenian, Chinese, Hebrew, and Italian	1	120	....	....	1	120
Bohemian	9	804	6	344	3	460
Chinese	9	339	8	264	1	75
Finnish	6	101	5	69	1	32
French	8	356	1	42	7	314
German	864	64,574	768	56,078	96	8,496
Indian (American)	21	1,456	4	162	17	1,294
Italian	26	2,686	18	1,400	8	1,286
Japanese	14	851	13	683	1	168
Portuguese	3	111	2	64	1	47
Scandinavian—						
Danish	9	442	9	442	....	....
Danish and Norwegian	31	2,092	28	1,988	3	104
Norwegian	93	4,910	85	4,036	8	874
Norwegian and Swedish	1	30	....	....	1	30
Swedish	242	17,883	224	16,426	18	1,457
Not specified	5	74	1	35	4	39
Slovak	1	17	1	17	....	....
Spanish	55	2,393	53	2,315	2	78
Welsh	2	165	2	165	....	....
African Methodist Episcopal Church	1	33	....	....	1	33
Indian (American)	1	33	....	....	1	33

DENOMINATION AND LANGUAGE.	ORGANIZATIONS REPORTING SERVICES CONDUCTED IN—					
	Specified languages.		Specified languages only.		Specified languages and English.	
	Organizations.	Membership.	Organizations.	Membership.	Organizations.	Membership.
Methodist bodies—Continued.						
Methodist Protestant Church	3	150	....	....	3	
German	1	120	....	....	1	150
Indian (American)	2	30	....	....	2	120
Wesleyan Methodist Connection of America	2	72	2	72	....	....
Indian (American)	2	72	2	72	....	....
Methodist Episcopal Church, South	142	5,978	120	4,941	22	1,037
French	2	130	2	130	....	....
German	35	1,700	19	931	16	769
Indian (American)	73	2,426	69	2,270	4	156
Italian	1	75	1	75	....	....
Spanish	31	1,647	29	1,535	2	112
Free Methodist Church of North America	4	108	....	....	4	108
German	3	95	....	....	3	95
Indian (American)	1	13	....	....	1	13
Moravian bodies:						
Moravian Church (Unitas Fratrum)	46	7,258	17	1,125	29	6,133
German	41	6,886	15	1,015	26	5,871
Indian (American)	2	49	....	....	2	49
Scandinavian—						
Danish	2	110	2	110	....	....
Not specified	1	213	....	....	1	213
Evangelical Union of Bohemian and Moravian Brethren in North America	15	771	15	771	....	....
Bohemian	15	771	15	771	....	....
Nonsectarian Churches of Bible Faith	13	364	1	15	12	349
German	13	364	1	15	12	349
Pentecostal Church of the Nazarene	2	95	1	70	1	25
Indian (American)	1	25	....	....	1	25
Spanish	1	70	1	70	....	....
Polish National Church of America	24	15,473	24	15,473	....	....
Polish	24	15,473	24	15,473	....	....
Presbyterian bodies:						
Presbyterian Church in the United States of America	376	41,906	269	20,635	107	21,271
Arabic	1	30	1	30	....	....
Armenian	4	552	2	97	2	455
Bohemian	27	2,487	25	1,829	2	658
Bohemian and Slavic	1	35	1	35	....	....
Chinese	3	337	2	286	1	51
Dutch or Flemish	10	1,096	4	374	6	722
French	9	1,040	6	606	3	434
Gaelic	2	69	....	....	2	69
German	143	17,448	106	10,348	37	7,100
German and Swedish	1	316	....	....	1	316
Greek, Italian, and Yiddish	1	384	....	....	1	384
Indian (American)	77	5,000	53	2,726	24	2,274
Italian	17	7,193	7	506	10	6,687
Japanese	6	721	3	75	3	646
Magyar	12	2,243	11	1,693	1	550
Portuguese	1	64	....	....	1	64
Scandinavian—						
Danish	1	200	....	....	1	200
Norwegian	1	25	....	....	1	25
Norwegian and Swedish	1	11	....	....	1	11
Swedish	2	68	1	18	1	50
Slavic	1	68	1	68	....	....
Slovak	1	105	1	105	....	....
Spanish	45	1,817	42	1,670	3	147
Welsh	9	597	3	169	6	428
Cumberland Presbyterian Church	17	284	17	284	....	....
Chinese	1	42	1	42	....	....
Indian (American)	16	242	16	242	....	....
Welsh Calvinistic Methodist Church	141	13,097	80	7,104	61	5,993
Welsh	141	13,097	80	7,104	61	5,993
United Presbyterian Church of North America	6	619	2	140	4	479
French	1	112	1	112	....	....
Indian (American)	2	85	....	....	2	85
Italian	3	422	1	28	2	394
Presbyterian Church in the United States	31	1,976	23	1,085	8	891
French	3	176	....	....	3	176
German	2	469	....	....	2	469
Indian (American)	9	369	6	123	3	246
Italian	1	72	1	72	....	....
Spanish	16	890	16	890	....	....
Synod of the Reformed Presbyterian Church of North America	3	108	1	(1)	2	108
Chinese	1	10	....	....	1	10
Indian (American)	1	98	....	....	1	98
Yiddish	1	(1)	1	(1)	....	....

[1] Not reported.

DENOMINATION AND LANGUAGE.	ORGANIZATIONS REPORTING SERVICES CONDUCTED IN—					
	Specified languages.		Specified languages only.		Specified languages and English.	
	Organizations.	Membership.	Organizations.	Membership.	Organizations.	Membership.
Protestant Episcopal Church	177	25,105	89	6,337	88	18,768
Armenian, Chinese, German, and Swedish	2	2,952			2	2,952
Armenian, French, and Italian	1	1,000			1	1,000
Chinese	1	412			1	412
Danish and Welsh	1	1,311			1	1,311
French	4	346	3	249	1	97
German	15	4,379			15	4,379
Greek	1	174			1	174
Indian (American)	118	6,592	69	3,475	49	3,117
Italian	6	3,116	3	645	3	2,471
Japanese	1	19	1	19		
Modern Syriac (Nestorian)	1	1,250			1	1,250
Scandinavian:						
Swedish	26	3,554	13	1,949	13	1,605
Reformed bodies:						
Reformed Church in America	222	32,364	115	13,841	107	18,523
Dutch or Flemish	151	23,830	69	8,947	82	14,883
German	68	8,161	44	4,750	24	3,411
Indian (American)	3	373	2	144	1	229
Reformed Church in the United States	694	147,195	260	41,574	434	105,621
Bohemian	2	114	2	114		
German	674	143,023	241	37,408	433	105,615
Indian (American)	1	6			1	6
Magyar	17	4,052	17	4,052		
Christian Reformed Church	153	25,135	146	24,058	7	1,077
Dutch or Flemish	138	24,085	133	23,139	5	946
Dutch or Flemish, and German	4	366	3	311	1	55
German	11	684	10	608	1	76
Hungarian Reformed Church in America	16	5,253	16	5,253		
Magyar	15	5,153	15	5,153		
Magyar and Slavic	1	100	1	100		
Reformed Catholic Church	1	150			1	150
Polish	1	150			1	150
Roman Catholic Church	4,711	5,342,023	2,176	3,064,436	2,535	2,277,587
Arabic	1	255	1	255		
Arabic and Greek	1	213	1	213		
Austrian (German)	3	908	1	425	2	483
Austrian (German), Croatian, French, German, and Slovak	1	1,629			1	1,629
Austrian (German), French, and German	1	94			1	94
Austrian (German), French, German, and Indian (American)	1	1,484			1	1,484
Austrian (German) and Montenegrin	1	176			1	176
Belgian[1]	1	4,250	1	4,250		
Belgian[1] and German	1	744			1	744
Bohemian	143	154,073	99	111,509	44	42,564
Bohemian and German	40	32,107	16	18,160	24	13,947
Bohemian and Polish	2	951	2	951		
Bohemian, Croatian, German, Magyar, and Slovak	1	777	1	777		
Bohemian, Dutch or Flemish, French, and German	1	1,445			1	1,445
Bohemian, French, and German	1	441			1	441
Bohemian, French, German, and Polish	1	245			1	245
Bohemian, German, and Polish	5	3,903			5	3,903
Bohemian, Polish, Slavic, and Spanish	1	1,751			1	1,751
Croatian	16	24,630	9	15,545	7	9,085
Croatian and German	1	1,275			1	1,275
Croatian and Italian	2	379	2	379		
Croatian and Slavic	1	298	1	298		
Croatian and Slovak	2	3,145	1	170	1	2,975
Croatian and Slovenian	3	6,545	3	6,545		
Croatian, German, and Italian	1	536			1	536
Dutch or Flemish	14	12,799	3	1,689	11	11,110
Dutch or Flemish, and French	4	3,841			4	3,841
Dutch or Flemish, and German	4	2,168			4	2,168
Dutch or Flemish, French, and German	2	2,822			2	2,822
Dutch or Flemish, French, and Polish	1	2,678			1	2,678
French	723	1,031,530	254	566,689	469	464,841
French and German	42	38,973	1	637	41	38,336
French and Indian (American)	5	1,054			5	1,054
French and Italian	11	23,186	1	212	10	22,974
French and Polish	15	19,793			15	19,793
French and Portuguese	1	1,292			1	1,292
French and Spanish	2	1,063			2	1,063
French, German, and Italian	4	8,481			4	8,481
French, German, and Slavic	2	3,015			2	3,015
French, German, Italian, and Polish	2	8,200			2	8,200
French, Italian, and Polish	1	317			1	317
German	1,881	1,519,978	584	625,972	1,297	894,006
German and Greek	1	17			1	17
German and Indian (American)	1	77			1	77
German and Italian	9	3,693	1	162	8	3,531
German and Lithuanian	1	3,769			1	3,769
German and Magyar	1	763	1	763		
German and Polish	24	23,180	7	6,536	17	16,644
German and Slavic	2	756			2	756
German and Slovak	3	1,672	2	1,462	1	210
German and Slovenian	1	468	1	468		
German and Spanish	4	2,940	1	1,334	3	1,606
German, Indian (American), and Italian	1	1,275			1	1,275
German, Italian, and Polish	2	2,839			2	2,839
German, Italian, Magyar, and Polish	1	1,339			1	1,339
German, Italian, Polish, and Spanish	1	118			1	118
German, Lithuanian, and Polish	1	1,275			1	1,275
German, Magyar, and Slavic	1	434	1	434		
German, Magyar, and Slovak	1	298			1	298

[1] Whether Flemish or French not specified.

DENOMINATION AND LANGUAGE.	ORGANIZATIONS REPORTING SERVICES CONDUCTED IN—					
	Specified languages.		Specified languages only.		Specified languages and English.	
	Organizations.	Membership.	Organizations.	Membership.	Organizations.	Membership.
Roman Catholic Church—Continued.						
German, Polish, and Slavic	1	680			1	680
Greek	12	15,964	3	14,535	9	1,429
Greek and Russian	1	1,275	1	1,275		
Greek and Slavic	1	340	1	340		
Greek, Magyar, Roumanian, and Russian	1	1,706	1	1,706		
Indian (American)	108	32,647	23	4,705	85	27,942
Indian (American) and Spanish	2	144	2	144		
Italian	291	826,023	165	451,816	126	374,207
Italian and Polish	6	10,897	1	577	5	10,320
Italian and Portuguese	3	10,030	1	8,075	2	1,955
Italian and Slavic	2	1,494	1	49	1	1,445
Italian and Slovak	1	680			1	680
Italian and Slovenian	1	52	1	52		
Italian and Spanish	21	8,544	2	2,198	19	6,346
Italian, Lithuanian, and Polish	2	2,930			2	2,930
Italian, Lithuanian, and Slavic	1	680			1	680
Italian, Polish, and Slavic	6	3,578			6	3,578
Italian, Slovak, and Slovenian	1	383			1	383
Lithuanian	50	82,530	47	81,462	3	1,068
Lithuanian and Polish	7	13,158	5	7,007	2	6,151
Little Russian	2	2,063	2	2,063		
Magyar	20	26,472	17	16,082	3	10,390
Magyar and Ruthenian	2	1,275	2	1,275		
Magyar and Slavic	3	2,314	1	1,326	2	988
Magyar and Slovak	1	2,125	1	2,125		
Magyar, Polish, and Slovak	1	425	1	425		
Polish	437	736,150	371	687,871	66	48,279
Polish and Slavic	5	9,726	1	3,307	4	6,419
Polish and Slovak	3	4,408	2	2,491	1	1,917
Portuguese	40	48,227	15	32,189	25	16,038
Russian	3	1,501	3	1,501		
Russian and Slavic	1	1,360	1	1,360		
Ruthenian	13	16,551	13	16,551		
Ruthenian and Slavic	6	4,257	6	4,257		
Slavic	54	47,491	34	34,551	20	12,940
Slavic and Slovak	1	467	1	467		
Slovak	60	78,353	54	69,826	6	8,527
Slovenian	10	15,558	10	15,558		
Spanish	514	356,329	378	226,769	136	129,560
Syriac	16	4,879	14	4,666	2	213
Salvationists:						
Salvation Army	77	2,613	72	2,455	5	158
Finnish	4	73	4	73		
German	11	190	9	133	2	57
Italian	1	12	1	12		
Scandinavian—						
Danish	1	16	1	16		
Norwegian	4	120	4	120		
Swedish	55	2,115	53	2,101	2	14
Spanish	1	87			1	87
American Salvation Army	2	80			2	80
German	2	80			2	80
Schwenkfelders	6	605			6	605
German	6	605			6	605
Spiritualists	23	938	8	474	15	464
Bohemian	1	27	1	27		
French	2	150	2	150		
German	19	741	4	277	15	464
Scandinavian—						
Swedish	1	20	1	20		
Swedish Evangelical bodies:						
Swedish Evangelical Mission Covenant of America	279	20,735	274	20,351	5	384
Scandinavian—						
Danish and Swedish	1	12	1	12		
Norwegian and Swedish	1	10	1	10		
Swedish	277	20,713	272	20,329	5	384
Swedish Evangelical Free Mission	127	6,952	125	6,917	2	35
Scandinavian—						
Danish and Swedish	1	18	1	18		
Norwegian	2	32	1	23	1	9
Norwegian and Swedish	1	100	1	100		
Swedish	118	6,543	118	6,543		
Not specified	5	259	4	233	1	26
Temple Society in the United States (Friends of the Temple)	3	376	2	190	1	186
German	3	376	2	190	1	186
Theosophical societies:						
Theosophical Society, American Section		27			1	27
Scandinavian—						
Norwegian	1	27			1	27
Unitarians	6	653	4	321	2	332
Dutch or Flemish	1	165	1	165		
Scandinavian:						
Norwegian	4	452	2	120	2	332
Swedish	1	36	1	36		
United Brethren bodies:						
Church of the United Brethren in Christ	67	6,028	24	1,667	43	4,361
German	67	6,028	24	1,667	43	4,361
Church of the United Brethren in Christ (Old Constitution)	6	205			6	205
German	6	205			6	205

From this table it appears that of the 24,594 organizations with 8,394,229 members which reported the use of a foreign language, 16,688 organizations with 5,022,601 members use the specified foreign language or languages only; while 7,906 organizations with 3,371,628 members use English also. The religious bodies reporting a membership of over 25,000 belonging to organizations which use the specified foreign languages only are: The Lutheran bodies, 7,242 organizations with 1,122,981 members; the Roman Catholic Church, 2,176 organizations with 3,064,436 members; the Methodist Episcopal Church, 1,228 organizations with 84,530 members; the German Evangelical Synod of North America, 952 organizations with 201,137 members; the Jewish congregations, 752 organizations with 58,988 members; the Evangelical Association, 554 organizations with 33,797 members; the Northern Baptist Convention, 548 organizations with 46,669 members; the Greek Orthodox Church, 334 organizations with 90,751 members; and the Reformed Church in the United States, 260 organizations with 41,574 members. Of the Lutheran bodies the Synodical Conference reports 2,433 organizations with 456,734 members; the General Council, 984 organizations with 186,401 members; the United Norwegian Lutheran Church, 807 organizations with 119,802 members; and the Synod of Iowa, 722 organizations with 92,113 members.

Of organizations which use the specified foreign language or languages and English, the Lutheran bodies report 2,566 with 631,374 members; and the Roman Catholic Church, 2,535 with 2,277,587 members. The only other denominations which report a membership of over 25,000 belonging to such organizations are: The Reformed Church in the United States, 434 organizations with 105,621 members; the Evangelical Association, 363 organizations with 25,730 members; and the the German Evangelical Synod of North America, 236 organizations with 87,556 members.

In the case of nearly all the religious bodies, the number of organizations using the specified foreign languages and English is considerably smaller than the number using the specified foreign languages only. The principal denominations in which the number of organizations using English also is larger than the number using the specified foreign languages only are the Roman Catholic Church and the Reformed Church in the United States. Among the Lutheran bodies, the United Synod in the South reports no organizations using a foreign language only, and only 5 using a foreign language and English. Three of the larger Lutheran bodies, the General Synod, the General Council, and the Synod of Ohio, while reporting a greater number of organizations using the specified foreign languages only, at the same time report a greater number of members belonging to organizations using English also.

The average membership of the organizations which use the specified foreign languages and English is, as a rule, larger, and in many instances much larger, than that of the organizations which use the specified foreign languages only. A notable exception is the Roman Catholic Church, where the average membership of the organizations using the specified foreign languages only is 1,408, while the average membership of those that use the specified foreign languages and English is only 898. A partial explanation of this is found in the fact that a considerable number of Roman Catholic organizations using foreign languages only report a very large membership. Thus, a French parish in California reports 6,800 members, and an Italian and Portuguese parish, 8,075 members; while in Illinois 32 Polish parishes aggregate 122,341 members, an average of 3,823; and 9 Bohemian parishes, 34,955 members, an average of 3,884. Similar conditions exist elsewhere and indicate large non-English speaking communities provided in each case with a single church which, with its numerous services, meets the needs of the community.

It proved difficult in some instances to know the languages reported. Sometimes the nationality rather than the language appears to have been given, and sometimes the language of the liturgy rather than that of the sermon or address, while in still other cases both were reported. The following instances call for special mention. Several organizations reported the use of the Austrian language. As there is no distinctively Austrian language, the presumption is that German is intended, inasmuch as great care is taken to specify the other languages—Bohemian, Croatian, Magyar, etc.—used in that polyglot empire. Accordingly whenever Austrian is used the term (German) follows. Similarly a number of organizations reported Belgian, but in these cases there was nothing to indicate whether French or Flemish was intended, and a note to that effect is appended. Considerable difficulty was experienced in regard to the various forms of Slavic. The terms reported included Slav, Slavonic, Slavonish, Slavish, Ancient Slavonic, Old Slavish, Old Slavonian, Old Slavonic, and Vetero Slavish. From the type of organizations reporting it is probable that in the great majority of cases the language referred to was what may be called the Old Church Slavic, the language of the liturgy, which is the basis for all the Slavic languages. Accordingly all of these have been included under the term Slavic. It is noticeable that the term Russian was not reported by the organizations of the Russian Orthodox Church, although that is uniformly the language of the sermon or address, but Slavic, or its equivalent, Old Russian, was reported. On the other hand the Roman Catholic churches did not report Latin, the language of the liturgy of all except the Uniat churches, but did report the spoken language. Hebrew, as reported by the Jewish congregations, is evidently the language of the service, but as reported by the Protestant denominations, at least in a considerable number of cases, it is undoubtedly equivalent to Yiddish, the two terms being used interchangeably by many. The term Syro-Arabic is used to indicate the form of Arabic used in Syria, which differs somewhat, though not materially, from the forms used in Egypt, Arabia, etc.

Scarcely less significant than the variety of languages used is the combination of languages in use in the same local organization. Some combinations seem natural, as when one language is evidently that of the liturgy and the other that of the address, as Slavic and Servian, or when two cognate languages are used, as Norwegian and Swedish, but such combinations as "German, Italian, Scandinavian, and English;" or "Chinese, Greek, Magyar, Polish, Slovak, and English;" or "Armenian, Chinese, Hebrew, Italian, and English," illustrate very vividly the cosmopolitan character of the congregations. This is particularly noticeable in the Roman Catholic Church and in those Protestant bodies which are more closely identified with evangelistic work among the foreign population.

Alphabetical list.—In no other way, perhaps, is the cosmopolitan character of the United States brought out more clearly than by the number and diversity of the languages used in the conduct of church services. Undoubtedly many others are spoken by individuals, but the fact that these have a definite place in the religious service of so many communities is of the greatest significance. In the following table the languages reported are arranged alphabetically, and the number of denominations and of organizations, with membership, reporting them, whether alone or in conjunction with some other language, is given. Since many organizations report the use of two or more languages it is evident that there is much duplication in the figures.

LANGUAGE.	Number of denominations reporting.	ORGANIZATIONS REPORTING SERVICES CONDUCTED IN—					
		Specified language.		Specified language only.		Specified language and one or more other languages (including English).	
		Organizations.	Membership.	Organizations.	Membership.	Organizations.	Membership.
Arabic	4	12	4,857	2	285	10	4,572
Armenian	5	86	26,274	77	19,971	9	6,303
Austrian (German)	1	7	4,291	1	425	6	3,866
Belgian [1]	1	2	4,994	1	4,250	1	744
Bohemian	9	269	201,791	160	115,969	109	85,822
Chinese [2]	10	88	4,854	78	840	10	4,014
Croatian	3	30	42,241	9	15,545	21	26,696
Danish	19	464	42,899	358	31,206	106	11,693
Dutch or Flemish	8	344	77,014	223	36,015	121	40,999
Esthonian	1	2	36	2	36	...	...
Finnish	8	263	32,602	253	31,515	10	1,087
French	15	889	1,160,420	287	569,037	602	591,383
Gaelic	1	2	69	...	...	2	69
German	77	13,034	3,601,943	8,014	1,746,065	5,020	1,855,878
Greek	6	363	114,495	337	105,286	26	9,209
Hebrew	3	946	82,237	746	58,559	200	23,678
Icelandic	1	14	2,101	14	2,101	...	...
Indian (American)	25	524	57,578	291	16,122	233	41,456
Italian	13	457	938,994	208	455,137	249	483,857
Japanese	6	35	4,846	30	3,690	5	1,156
Lappish	1	1	10	...	...	1	10
Lettish	2	10	683	10	683	...	...
Lithuanian	3	71	104,901	55	81,986	16	22,915
Little Russian	1	2	2,063	2	2,063	...	...
Magyar	5	82	50,035	61	27,028	21	23,007
Modern Syriac (Nestorian)	1	1	1,250	...	...	1	1,250
Montenegrin	1	1	176	...	...	1	176
Norwegian	22	2,849	357,865	2,032	236,504	817	121,361
Polish	8	570	867,549	406	703,875	164	163,674
Portuguese	5	51	60,099	17	32,253	34	27,846
Roumanian	3	3	3,016	...	...	3	3,016
Russian	2	7	5,892	4	1,551	3	4,341
Ruthenian	2	22	22,573	13	16,551	9	6,022
Scandinavian (not specified)	10	51	3,658	26	1,237	25	2,421
Servian	1	1	1,190	...	...	1	1,190
Slavic	8	164	113,852	96	62,565	68	51,287
Slovak	7	147	108,182	123	83,293	24	24,889
Slovenian	2	16	23,006	10	15,558	6	7,448
Spanish	11	732	379,953	550	234,096	182	145,857
Swedish	21	2,177	266,603	1,890	205,923	287	60,680
Syriac	3	25	9,989	14	4,666	11	5,323
Welsh	8	286	28,948	132	10,587	154	18,361
Wendish	1	1	656	...	...	1	656
Yiddish	3	[3] 4	419	1	([4])	[5] 3	419

[1] Whether Flemish or French not specified.
[2] Not including the Chinese Temples which made no specific report.
[3] Includes 2 organizations for which no membership is reported.
[4] Not reported.
[5] Includes 1 organization for which no membership is reported.

From the table it appears that German (aside from Austrian) is reported by 77 denominations; the American Indian languages, by 25; Norwegian, by 22; Swedish, by 21; Danish, by 19; French, by 15; and Italian, by 13. In respect to the number of organizations, German is reported by 13,034; Norwegian, by 2,849; Swedish, by 2,177; Hebrew, by 946; French, by 889; Spanish, by 732; Polish, by 570; and Indian (American), by 524. In respect to the membership of organizations using the various languages, German continues to lead with 3,601,943, but the second place is held by French, with 1,160,420, the third place by Italian, with 938,994, and the fourth place by Polish, with 867,549. Other leading languages, with membership of the organizations using them, are Spanish, with 379,953, Norwegian, with 357,865, Swedish, with 266,603, Bohemian, with 201,791, Greek, with 114,495, and Slavic, with 113,852. The large figures shown for French are chiefly attributed to the large number of French Canadians in the country. In the case of the figures for all languages, it should be remembered that a greater or less proportion represents members who in their worship use English or a foreign language other than that specified.

Geographic distribution.—The 24,594 organizations which report the use of a foreign language, either alone or in connection with English, are distributed among the geographic divisions as follows:

North Atlantic division	5,177
South Atlantic division	340
North Central division	15,685
South Central division	1,445
Western division	1,947

The states reporting more than 100 organizations using a foreign language are as follows:

Minnesota	2,793	Indiana	555
Wisconsin	2,592	California	452
Pennsylvania	2,318	Massachusetts	444
Illinois	1,738	New Mexico	419
New York	1,409	New Jersey	382
Iowa	1,401	Oklahoma	375
Michigan	1,150	Washington	355
North Dakota	1,132	Connecticut	266
Ohio	1,097	Colorado	245
South Dakota	960	Louisiana	170
Nebraska	950	Oregon	158
Missouri	709	Maryland	144
Texas	640	Maine	104
Kansas	608		

Of the 41 individual languages tabulated on page 121, New York naturally reports the largest number, 29. Pennsylvania reports 28; Illinois, 26; and Ohio, 24; while 5 states, Massachusetts, Michigan, Wisconsin, Minnesota, and Washington, report 21 each. Three states—South Carolina, Georgia, and Kentucky—report only 3 languages, and 17 others less than 10 languages. Of these 17, only 2—Louisiana and New Mexico—are included among the states reporting more than one hundred organizations using a foreign language, and in each of these states some one language greatly preponderates—in Louisiana, French; and in New Mexico, Spanish.

Any comparison between the membership of church organizations reporting the use of foreign languages, and the foreign-born element of the population, however interesting, is impracticable on account of the widely different dates for which the information in the two cases is available, the figures for church membership being for 1906 and those for the foreign-born population for 1900. Such comparison is also rendered difficult by the facts that a portion of the foreign-born population is not identified with church life, and that in some sections, especially in the West, it is so scattered that organizations have not been formed, and consequently there is no report of membership.

The distribution throughout the country of organizations using a foreign language is shown in the next table.

STATE OR TERRITORY.	Number of languages reported.	ORGANIZATIONS REPORTING A FOREIGN LANGUAGE.	
		Number.	Membership.
Continental United States	....	24,594	8,394,229
North Atlantic division	....	5,177	3,149,250
Maine	11	104	75,631
New Hampshire	9	94	94,797
Vermont	7	74	41,312
Massachusetts	21	444	426,377
Rhode Island	11	86	94,782
Connecticut	18	266	184,486
New York	29	1,409	1,016,087
New Jersey	19	382	197,082
Pennsylvania	28	2,318	1,018,696
South Atlantic division	....	340	109,902
Delaware	5	11	10,512
Maryland	11	144	63,301
District of Columbia	4	11	2,736
Virginia	10	43	6,302
West Virginia	11	48	18,686
North Carolina	6	17	1,108
South Carolina	3	13	1,574
Georgia	3	25	2,623
Florida	6	28	3,050
North Central division	....	15,685	3,900,579
Ohio	24	1,097	412,015
Indiana	14	555	157,396
Illinois	26	1,738	772,888
Michigan	21	1,150	383,526
Wisconsin	21	2,592	720,823
Minnesota	21	2,793	542,056
Iowa	12	1,401	234,735
Missouri	19	709	256,953
North Dakota	16	1,132	110,298
South Dakota	13	960	89,157
Nebraska	17	950	133,989
Kansas	13	608	86,743
South Central division	....	1,445	762,457
Kentucky	3	78	54,926
Tennessee	7	26	4,524
Alabama	7	58	12,296
Mississippi	6	30	2,272
Louisiana	7	170	373,152
Arkansas	7	68	18,718
Oklahoma [1]	10	375	22,068
Texas	14	640	274,501
Western division	....	1,947	472,041
Montana	15	88	30,236
Idaho	8	82	8,891
Wyoming	6	23	3,043
Colorado	18	245	57,995
New Mexico	5	419	122,192
Arizona	5	74	29,579
Utah	8	44	10,919
Nevada	4	7	820
Washington	21	355	35,777
Oregon	15	158	20,411
California	20	452	152,169

[1] Oklahoma and Indian Territory combined.

The statement in the report for 1890 of the languages used in church services is so meager that comparison is scarcely possible. A tabular statement for the Lutheran bodies in that report shows that 8,364 organizations, with 1,189,119 members, reported services in English, German, German-English, Swedish, Norwegian, Danish, Icelandic, and Finnish, while the report for 1906 shows that in addition to these, the following languages were used: Esthonian, Indian (American), Lappish, Lettish, Lithuanian, Polish, Slovak, and Wendish. With the exception of the 1,178 organizations which in 1890 reported German-English, there is nothing to indicate to what extent English was used with the other languages. According to the returns for 1906, out of 12,703 organizations, with 2,112,494 members, 2,735 organizations, with 344,157 members, reported services in English only, while 9,808 organizations, with 1,754,355 members, reported the use of one or more foreign languages, and 160 organizations, with 13,982 members, made no report at all. If the 1,816 organizations which in 1890 reported English used English only, the percentage of those reporting English only has not materially changed, being 21.7 per cent of the total Lutheran organizations reporting as to language in 1890, and 21.8 per cent in 1906. In view of the very large immigration since 1890, this is not surprising, but the impossibility of knowing the number using English with the other languages in 1890 makes the comparison of little value.

In the case of the Methodist Episcopal Church, the report for 1890 shows services conducted in German, Spanish, Swedish, Norwegian, and Danish. The 1906 report shows in addition to these Armenian, Bohemian, Chinese, Finnish, French, Hebrew, Indian (American), Italian, Japanese, Portuguese, Slovak, and Welsh. In 1890 the number of organizations reporting a foreign language was 1,261, with a membership of 76,400, while in 1906 the number of organizations was 1,400, with a membership of 99,404. In the case of all other denominations, the statements as to languages used are too fragmentary to be useful.

A general survey of the situation in regard to the use of foreign languages in church services, as illustrated by the preceding tables, shows that, as already indicated, in local organizations originally made up of the non-English speaking immigrant element, the trend is toward the use, first of English in connection with the foreign language, and then to the exclusive use of English. The same thing appears in the statements of the history and work of the various bodies. In the early life of the Methodist Episcopal Church the feeling that English alone should be used was so strong that a distinct denomination, the Evangelical Association, grew out of the necessity of providing for those who knew no English. In the Roman Catholic Church one of the causes of disturbance in its early history was the effort to place English speaking priests in charge of the spiritual interests of non-English speaking communities. In the Lutheran bodies there has been a more general comprehension of the need for the immigrants on their arrival of the use of the mother tongue, but an equally clear recognition of the temporary character of such services.

WORK OF DENOMINATIONS IN DOMESTIC AND FOREIGN FIELDS.

The descriptive statements which accompany the statistics of denominations (pages 11 to 662, Part II) include, in addition to a review of the history, doctrine, and polity of each body, a sketch of its missionary, educational, and philanthropic work, both at home and abroad. The specific items called for under each head were as follows:

1. Home missionary work, including general evangelism and church erection: Agencies or societies employed; sections occupied; special features emphasized; total contributions for all departments during the calendar year 1906 and for such years prior thereto as information is available.

2. Foreign missionary work: Agencies or societies employed; countries occupied and languages used; number of mission stations, of churches and communicants, of missionaries and native helpers; value of mission property; amount of contributions during 1906 and for such previous years as information is available.

3. Educational work: Number and kind of schools, including parochial schools, supported in whole or in part by the denomination; number of teachers and pupils; value of property devoted to educational work; amount of contributions during the year 1906 and for such years prior thereto as information is available.

4. Institutional and general work: Hospitals, orphanages, homes for the aged, asylums, and the like (number, value of property, cost of maintenance, persons accommodated, etc.); Epworth leagues, Christian Endeavor societies, and the like (number of persons enrolled, amount contributed, for what purpose, etc.); brotherhoods and similar organizations (nature and extent of work); any other kind of work.

As indicated in the introduction, certain general difficulties were encountered, preventing that completeness and accuracy essential to a thoroughly scientific census presentation. Among these are the different forms of organization, the diverse methods of financial statements, and particularly the incomplete returns.

In most of the larger and more thoroughly organized bodies, as the Congregationalists, and the Methodist and Presbyterian bodies, and in some of the smaller denominations, the different phases of work are under the care of distinct societies. Thus, there is one society for home missions, emphasizing general evangelism; another for the erection of church buildings or parsonages; another for special evangelistic and educational work among negroes, Indians, and the foreign born population; another for Sunday school organization and the supplying of religious literature; another for the assistance of educational institutions or of students; another for foreign missionary work; besides a considerable number of minor societies for special objects. With the exception of the society for foreign work these cover largely the same territory and often have similar general aims, but are independent of each other. In some instances, as in the Protestant Episcopal Church, a single general society nominally covers the whole field, but practically a considerable amount of the work in each department is done by diocesan organizations. In the Roman Catholic Church there is no general organization for any one of these various departments, but the religious orders, and sometimes the dioceses, carry on the work on mutually independent lines under general ecclesiastical supervision. In the smaller bodies there is a smaller number of societies, and in a few there is no organization at all for the carrying on of general religious, benevolent, or foreign work, all initiative in these directions being taken by individual churches or by the regular ecclesiastical divisions.

As to methods of work and terms used there is almost as much diversity as in the forms of society organization. A mission in one of the Protestant bodies is an entirely different thing from a mission in the Roman Catholic Church, and in the Protestant bodies there is considerable variety as to the status of mission workers. It was also frequently difficult to determine the grade or character of the educational institutions.

Another serious difficulty arose from the very diverse methods of financial statement. The general purpose was to show the amount contributed by the churches of the United States for the various departments of missionary and benevolent work during the year under review. The reports that came in included in many cases not merely the contributions of the churches, but income from invested funds, fees for tuition, or for treatment in hospitals or asylums, etc. In other instances the figures sent in covered not the exact income during the year, but amounts expended or even appropriated for the respective departments of work. So far as possible these sources have been specially noted, but in many cases this was impracticable.

The greatest difficulty of all, however, arose from incomplete returns. In very few cases were all the questions answered, and frequently such figures as were given were incomplete. Schools were mentioned but no hint given as to their grade, no pupils were reported, and no value of property given; again the value of property was in some instances given, but with no indication of what the item covered. An effort was made to learn the number and membership of the young people's societies, but the returns were varied and incomplete. Sometimes correspondence elicited the necessary information, but in a number of instances it was evident that the authorities of the denominations themselves had no complete or accurate information as to the points in review.

With a view to a comprehensive presentation of the principal facts, tables have been prepared, the first relating to the domestic work, missionary, educational, and philanthropic; the second relating to the foreign mission work; and the third giving a summary of the contributions for these different departments.

In the preparation of these tables it was found necessary to limit the items presented to those which were common to many of the denominations, if not to all, and which admitted of classification; therefore some interesting and valuable information has been omitted from them. The conditions are set forth more fully in the general descriptive text which follows these tables, but it may be said here that the general presentation in the tables is reasonably accurate, and gives a fairly complete review of the work of the different bodies. It should be remembered also that the figures represent less rather than more than the entire amount of work done.

Of the 186 denominations, 75 made no report such as could be presented in tabular form. Of the remaining 111 denominations, 75 are represented in both the domestic and foreign work tables, 29 in the domestic work table, but not in the foreign, and 7 in the foreign work table, but not in the domestic. The domestic table, therefore, gives a survey of 104 denominations and the foreign table, of 82 denominations. The general summary of contributions includes reports for only 92 denominations, as several bodies reporting other items gave no figures of this nature.

Domestic work.—The table for domestic work which follows gives, for the 104 denominations listed, the amount contributed during the year 1906 for home missions, education, and philanthropic work; the number of persons employed in home missionary work and the number of churches aided; the number of colleges, academies, etc., with the number of their students; and the number of philanthropic institutions, including hospitals, asylums, orphanages, homes for the aged, etc., with the number of inmates and patients treated; the value of property and endowments for educational and philanthropic purposes.

Under home missions are combined all the evangelistic departments in the various denominations. The number of missionaries includes ministers, whether pastors supported by the home mission societies or general evangelists, and teachers in mission schools. Under churches aided are given those organizations supplied by home missionaries, or which have received aid in the conduct of their church work, or in the erection of church buildings. Under educational work are included only institutions of higher grade—colleges, academies, etc. In some denominations the amounts reported as contributed for education include those for the support of parochial schools, and in others the amounts reported as contributed for home missions include those for the support of mission schools. Wherever practicable, a note to this effect is appended. So far as possible the number of persons treated in the various hospitals, as well as those resident in the asylums and homes, have been given. An attempt was made to distinguish between value of property and amount of endowments, but there were so many instances in which this was difficult that these two items have been combined.

The denominations are arranged by families and separate denominations, the Protestant bodies being classed together.

DENOMINATION.	DOMESTIC WORK: 1906.					
	Amount contributed.				Home missions.	
	Total.	Home missions.	Education.	Hospitals, asylums, etc.	Number of missionaries.	Number of churches aided.
All denominations represented	$38,675,919	$12,762,271	$17,665,445	$8,248,203	20,044	22,591
Protestant bodies	33,781,752	12,616,210	17,337,265	3,828,277	19,118	22,555
Adventist bodies	275,937	163,033	28,404	84,500	1,206	89
Advent Christian Church	9,838	1,434	8,404		6	11
Seventh-day Adventist Denomination	265,599	161,099	20,000	84,500	1,197	78
Church of God (Adventist)					2	
Life and Advent Union	500	500				
Baptist bodies	13,125,325	2,145,401	10,738,969	240,955	2,900	5,759
Baptists	13,049,363	2,081,411	10,726,997	240,955	2,856	5,701
Northern Baptist Convention	11,732,896	1,811,799	9,921,097	(1)	1,925	2,573
Southern Baptist Convention	1,218,839	251,984	726,900	240,955	865	3,128
National Baptist Convention (Colored)	97,628	17,628	80,000	(1)	66	
General Six Principle Baptists					1	
Seventh-day Baptists	13,202	8,000	5,202		31	38
Free Baptists	62,760	55,990	6,770		12	20
General Baptists			(1)			
Brethren (Plymouth)					40	
Brethren (Plymouth)—I		(1)			40	
Brethren (River)	4,504	977		3,527	15	7
Brethren in Christ	4,504	977	(1)	3,527	15	7
Christian Catholic Church in Zion			(1)			
Christian Union	2,000	2,000			(1)	(1)
Christians (Christian Connection)	15,000	10,000	5,000	(1)	25	30
Churches of God in North America, General Eldership of the	21,550	7,000	14,550			6
Churches of the New Jerusalem	18,995	17,462	475	1,058	7	16
General Convention of the New Jerusalem in the United States of America	14,000	14,000	(1)		7	16
General Church of the New Jerusalem	4,995	3,462	475	1,058		
Congregationalists	1,034,154	969,789	64,365		2,494	2,249
Disciples or Christians	1,735,456	641,456	1,044,000	50,000	1,206	384
Disciples of Christ	1,735,456	641,456	1,044,000	50,000	1,206	384
Churches of Christ			(1)			
Dunkers or German Baptist Brethren	127,106	23,500	79,606	24,000	50	103
German Baptist Brethren Church (Conservative)	118,106	20,000	74,106	24,000	40	96
The Brethren Church (Progressive Dunkers)	9,000	3,500	5,500		10	7
German Seventh-day Baptists				(1)		
Evangelical bodies	413,965	317,842	61,366	34,757	907	1,185
Evangelical Association	275,508	199,880	40,871	34,757	622	900
United Evangelical Church	138,457	117,962	20,495		285	285
Evangelistic associations					75	
Metropolitan Church Association				(1)		
Hephzibah Faith Missionary Association			(1)	(1)		
Pentecost Bands of the World		(1)	(1)	(1)	75	
Friends	75,000	14,000	1,000	60,000	20	10
Society of Friends (Orthodox)	14,000	14,000	(1)		20	10
Religious Society of Friends (Hicksite)	60,000		(1)	60,000		
Orthodox Conservative Friends (Wilburite)	1,000		1,000			
German Evangelical Synod of North America	173,327	27,000	44,457	101,870	83	108
International Apostolic Holiness Union	11,100		7,500	3,600		
Lutheran bodies	2,112,120	630,055	826,672	655,393	1,397	2,840
General Synod of the Evangelical Lutheran Church in the United States of America	319,546	168,380	51,666	99,500	262	212
United Synod of the Evangelical Lutheran Church in the South	132,855	21,380	93,475	18,000	29	50
General Council of the Evangelical Lutheran Church in North America	328,255	147,647	171,650	8,958	359	728
Evangelical Lutheran Synodical Conference of America	635,726	137,726	[2] 158,000	340,000	301	924
United Norwegian Lutheran Church in America	308,625	43,166	149,300	116,159	97	365
Evangelical Lutheran Joint Synod of Ohio and Other States	57,000	25,000	22,000	10,000	76	
Lutheran Synod of Buffalo	2,580	580	2,000			4
Hauge's Norwegian Evangelical Lutheran Synod	45,584	8,584	32,000	5,000	50	60
Evangelical Lutheran Church in America, Eielsen's Synod	3,827	827		3,000	1	
German Evangelical Lutheran Synod of Texas	365	179	61	125	3	3
Evangelical Lutheran Synod of Iowa and Other States	54,108	15,082	21,481	17,545	65	160
Synod for the Norwegian Evangelical Lutheran Church in America	122,695	43,551	59,144	20,000	80	140
Evangelical Lutheran Synod of Michigan and Other States	5,487	678	4,809		5	8
Danish Evangelical Lutheran Church in America	10,500	1,500	6,600	2,400	10	10
Icelandic Evangelical Lutheran Synod in North America	2,200	1,000	1,200		7	20
Immanuel Synod of the Evangelical Lutheran Church of North America	850	850			4	2
Finnish Evangelical Lutheran Church of America, or Suomi Synod	15,800	800	15,000		1	
Norwegian Lutheran Free Church	46,196	6,759	27,331	12,106	30	90
United Danish Evangelical Lutheran Church in America	11,829	3,558	[2] 5,671	2,600	11	14
Slovak Evangelical Lutheran Synod of America						
Finnish Evangelical Lutheran National Church	5,000	2,500	2,500		4	40
Church of the Lutheran Brethren of America (Norwegian)	3,092	308	[2] 2,784		2	10

[1] Not reported.

[2] Parochial schools included.

DOMESTIC WORK: 1906—continued.

DENOMINATION.	Colleges, academies, etc.		Hospitals, asylums, etc.		Value of property and endowments.		
	Number.	Students.	Number.	Inmates and patients.	Total.	For educational purposes.	For philanthropic purposes.
All denominations represented	2,532	401,018	1,857	454,280	$297,510,918	$239,690,727	$57,820,191
Protestant bodies	1,472	272,352	848	142,117	291,928,527	234,584,986	57,343,541
Adventist bodies	44	3,590	46	9,434	2,614,427	938,233	1,676,194
Advent Christian Church	3	216			8,800	8,800	
Seventh-day Adventist Denomination	41	3,374	46	9,434	2,605,627	929,433	1,676,194
Church of God (Adventist)							
Life and Advent Union							
Baptist bodies	207	49,156	78	2,851	61,858,888	58,088,888	3,770,000
Baptists	193	46,734	78	2,851	59,271,888	55,501,888	3,770,000
Northern Baptist Convention	65	19,983	41	(1)	47,680,799	45,193,799	2,487,000
Southern Baptist Convention	102	21,551	23	[2]1,851	10,891,089	9,708,089	1,183,000
National Baptist Convention (Colored)	26	5,200	14	1,000	700,000	600,000	100,000
General Six Principle Baptists							
Seventh-day Baptists	3	572			752,000	752,000	
Free Baptists	10	1,700			1,765,000	1,765,000	
General Baptists	1	150			70,000	70,000	
Brethren (Plymouth)							
Brethren (Plymouth)—I							
Brethren (River)	1	26	1	29	17,881	7,881	10,000
Brethren in Christ	1	26	1	29	17,881	7,881	10,000
Christian Catholic Church in Zion	1	2,136			(1)	(1)	
Christian Union							
Christians (Christian Connection)	9	1,000	2	(1)	1,205,000	1,175,000	30,000
Churches of God in North America, General Eldership of the	2	479			237,500	237,500	
Churches of the New Jerusalem	4	177			943,001	943,001	
General Convention of the New Jerusalem in the United States of America	3	120			443,820	443,820	
General Church of the New Jerusalem	1	57	(1)	(1)	499,181	499,181	(1)
Congregationalists	87	13,258			(1)	(1)	
Disciples or Christians	61	10,198	12	780	6,311,000	6,036,000	275,000
Disciples of Christ	50	8,684	12	780	6,005,500	5,730,500	275,000
Churches of Christ	11	1,514			305,500	305,500	
Dunkers or German Baptist Brethren	12	2,073	14	229	1,357,000	1,048,000	309,000
German Baptist Brethren Church (Conservative)	11	1,921	12	225	1,194,000	890,000	304,000
The Brethren Church (Progressive Dunkers)	1	152			163,000	158,000	[3]5,000
German Seventh-day Baptists			2	4	(1)		(1)
Evangelical bodies	6	1,041	3	549	1,109,000	874,000	235,000
Evangelical Association	3	591	3	549	834,000	599,000	235,000
United Evangelical Church	3	450			275,000	275,000	
Evangelistic associations	2	145	6	318	106,500	1,000	105,500
Metropolitan Church Association			1	45	(1)		(1)
Hephzibah Faith Missionary Association	1	70	1	23	(1)	(1)	(1)
Pentecost Bands of the World	1	75	4	250	106,500	1,000	105,500
Friends	72	8,063	12	264	9,804,600	9,364,600	440,000
Society of Friends (Orthodox)	36	5,163			7,614,600	7,614,600	
Religious Society of Friends (Hicksite)	32	2,750	12	264	2,190,000	1,750,000	440,000
Orthodox Conservative Friends (Wilburite)	4	150			(1)	(1)	
German Evangelical Synod of North America	2	188	8	2,086	940,350	409,850	530,500
International Apostolic Holiness Union	1	75	4	(1)	[3]11,000	(1)	[3]11,000
Lutheran bodies	106	14,511	128	26,924	25,615,774	17,869,661	7,746,113
General Synod of the Evangelical Lutheran Church in the United States of America	11	1,508	8	289	2,685,000	2,295,000	390,000
United Synod of the Evangelical Lutheran Church in the South	9	1,226	1	55	894,845	819,845	75,000
General Council of the Evangelical Lutheran Church in North America	18	3,633	40	[2]11,920	15,151,715	10,321,715	4,830,000
Evangelical Lutheran Synodical Conference of America	21	[2]2,696	40	9,000	3,059,000	1,559,000	1,500,000
United Norwegian Lutheran Church in America	10	1,879	17	2,206	1,250,818	940,992	309,826
Evangelical Lutheran Joint Synod of Ohio and Other States	4	408	2	108	440,400	365,400	75,000
Lutheran Synod of Buffalo	1	12			35,000	35,000	
Hauge's Norwegian Evangelical Lutheran Synod	2	254	1	50	191,000	156,000	35,000
Evangelical Lutheran Church in America, Eielsen's Synod			1	6	3,500		3,500
German Evangelical Lutheran Synod of Texas		[4]1					
Evangelical Lutheran Synod of Iowa and Other States	4	228	3	218	316,360	163,860	152,500
Synod for the Norwegian Evangelical Lutheran Church in America	15	1,956	7	1,853	1,047,636	809,849	237,787
Evangelical Lutheran Synod of Michigan and Other States	1	(1)			18,000	18,000	
Danish Evangelical Lutheran Church in America	3	200	1	35	108,000	91,000	17,000
Icelandic Evangelical Lutheran Synod in North America	(1)	(1)				(1)	
Immanuel Synod of the Evangelical Lutheran Church of North America		[4]3					
Finnish Evangelical Lutheran Church of America, or Suomi Synod	1	87			53,000	53,000	
Norwegian Lutheran Free Church	3	247	5	1,149	293,500	183,000	110,500
United Danish Evangelical Lutheran Church in America	1	130	2	38	40,000	30,000	10,000
Slovak Evangelical Lutheran Synod of America		[4]26					
Finnish Evangelical Lutheran National Church	1	27			3,000	3,000	
Church of the Lutheran Brethren of America (Norwegian)	1	60			25,000	25,000	

[1] Not reported.
[2] Partial report. See denominational text.
[3] Endowment fund only. See denominational text.
[4] Special or correspondence students.

DENOMINATION.	DOMESTIC WORK: 1906—continued.					
	Amount contributed.				Home missions.	
	Total.	Home missions.	Education.	Hospitals, asylums, etc.	Number of missionaries.	Number of churches aided.
Protestant bodies—Continued.						
Mennonite bodies	$86,290	$41,807	$22,000	$22,483	100	61
Mennonite Church	58,190	35,707	(1)	22,483	....	11
Amish Mennonite Church						
General Conference of Mennonites of North America	23,100	1,100	22,000	(1)	....	....
Mennonite Brethren in Christ	5,000	5,000	....	....	100	50
Methodist bodies	6,186,433	2,963,903	2,019,428	1,203,102	2,147	2,378
Methodist Episcopal Church	4,277,723	2,413,286	1,008,066	856,371	(1)	365
Methodist Protestant Church	62,974	15,600	45,874	1,500	28	35
Wesleyan Methodist Connection of America	28,942	4,127	24,815	....	12	....
Methodist Episcopal Church, South	1,447,689	432,454	690,235	325,000	1,983	1,758
Congregational Methodist Church	....	....	(1)	....	....	....
Primitive Methodist Church in the United States of America	5,916	4,416	1,500	....	14	17
Free Methodist Church of North America	63,669	15,000	28,438	20,231	15	96
African Methodists	299,520	79,020	220,500	....	95	107
Union American Methodist Episcopal Church (Colored)	900	400	500	....	....	....
African Methodist Episcopal Church	162,280	37,280	125,000	....	....	....
African Methodist Episcopal Zion Church	23,000	23,000	(1)	....	....	....
Colored Methodist Episcopal Church	113,340	18,340	95,000	....	95	107
Moravian bodies	32,528	22,550	3,378	6,600	57	75
Moravian Church (Unitas Fratrum)	32,495	22,517	3,378	6,600	54	73
Evangelical Union of Bohemian and Moravian Brethren in North America	33	33	....	....	3	2
Pentecostal Church of the Nazarene	8,879	7,590	1,289	....	(1)	....
Presbyterian bodies	4,631,391	2,913,460	1,558,957	158,974	3,866	4,259
Presbyterian Church in the United States of America	3,062,771	2,215,188	847,583	....	3,217	3,369
Cumberland Presbyterian Church	101,962	82,597	15,000	3 355	75	98
Colored Cumberland Presbyterian Church	2,950	450	2,500	....	17	8
Welsh Calvinistic Methodist Church	3,478	3,478	....	....	30	40
United Presbyterian Church of North America	443,866	325,060	51,476	67 330	350	307
Presbyterian Church in the United States	948,120	232,757	632,000	83 363	146	378
Associate Synod of North America (Associate Presbyterian Church)	605	605	....	....	4	9
Associate Reformed Synod of the South	13,913	13,913	(1)	(1)	(1)	(1)
Synod of the Reformed Presbyterian Church of North America	53,211	37,896	10,398	4 917	28	50
Reformed Presbyterian Church in North America, General Synod	....	....	(1)	....	....	....
Reformed Presbyterian Church in the United States and Canada	526	526	....	....	1	....
Protestant Episcopal Church	2,665,133	1,068,155	442,142	1,154 836	1,983	2,077
Reformed bodies	502,584	249,085	252,499	1,000	383	509
Reformed Church in America	169,824	115,085	54,739	....	177	239
Reformed Church in the United States	203,099	110,000	93,099	(1)	192	238
Christian Reformed Church	129,661	24,000	104,661	1,000	14	32
Reformed Episcopal Church	18,861	16,766	2,095	(1)	(1)	....
Salvationists	11,622	....	....	11,622	....	....
Salvation Army	....	....	....	(1)	....	....
American Salvation Army	11,622	....	....	11,622	....	....
Schwenkfelders	3,500	3,500	(1)	....	(1)	(1)
Unitarians	185,000	185,000	....	....	....	....
United Brethren bodies	238,671	109,558	119,113	10,000	131	362
Church of the United Brethren in Christ	177,671	64,558	103,113	10,000	44	52
Church of the United Brethren in Christ (Old Constitution)	61,000	45,000	16,000	....	87	310
Universalists	65,321	65,321	(1)	(1)	75	53
Roman Catholic Church	....	....	(1)	(1)	....	....
Jewish congregations	4,419,563	....	115,391	4,304,172	....	....
Latter-day Saints	393,789	137,000	174,789	82,000	926	36
Church of Jesus Christ of Latter-day Saints	246,709	(1)	171,709	75,000	926	36
Reorganized Church of Jesus Christ of Latter-day Saints	147,080	137,000	3,080	7,000	(1)	(1)
Eastern Orthodox Churches	2,000	....	....	2,000	....	....
Russian Orthodox Church	2,000	....	(1)	2,000	....	....
All other bodies	78,815	9,061	38,000	31,754	....	....
Buddhists	3,861	3,861	....	....	....	....
Japanese Temples	3,861	3,861	(1)	....	(1)	(1)
Society for Ethical Culture	70,454	700	38,000	31,754	(1)	(1)
Spiritualists	4,500	4,500	(1)	....	(1)	(1)

[1] Not reported.

DENOMINATION.	DOMESTIC WORK: 1906—continued.						
	Colleges, academies, etc.		Hospitals, asylums, etc.		Value of property and endowments.		
	Number.	Students.	Number.	Inmates and patients.	Total.	For educational purposes.	For philanthropic purposes.
Protestant bodies—Continued.							
Mennonite bodies	7	825	7	188	$297,800	$171,000	$126,800
Mennonite Church	1	225	4	188	187,800	61,000	126,800
Amish Mennonite Church							
General Conference of Mennonites of North America	6	600	3	(1)	110,000	110,000	(1)
Mennonite Brethren in Christ							
Methodist bodies	372	99,048	144	38,536	72,946,069	61,743,180	11,202,889
Methodist Episcopal Church	124	[2] 52,507	126	35,127	50,499,160	41,678,756	8,820,404
Methodist Protestant Church	7	1,034	1	25	1,169,836	1,169,836	(1)
Wesleyan Methodist Connection of America	3	209			128,000	128,000	
Methodist Episcopal Church, South	193	34,683	14	[3] 3,237	19,242,588	16,931,853	2,310,735
Congregational Methodist Church	1	55			(1)	(1)	
Primitive Methodist Church in the United States of America		[4] 50					
Free Methodist Church of North America	8	1,300	3	147	384,435	312,685	71,750
African Methodists	36	9,210			1,522,050	1,522,050	
Union American Methodist Episcopal Church (Colored)	1	60			3,500	3,500	
African Methodist Episcopal Church	20	5,700			975,000	975,000	
African Methodist Episcopal Zion Church	11	2,000			150,000	150,000	
Colored Methodist Episcopal Church	4	1,450			393,550	393,550	
Moravian bodies	6	1,069	6		907,000	822,000	85,000
Moravian Church (Unitas Fratrum)	6	1,069	6	(1)	907,000	822,000	[3] 85,000
Evangelical Union of Bohemian and Moravian Brethren in North America							
Pentecostal Church of the Nazarene	2	(1)			47,000	47,000	
Presbyterian bodies	308	47,592	24	2,714	49,012,148	47,678,207	1,333,941
Presbyterian Church in the United States of America	110	22,005			35,937,078	35,937,078	
Cumberland Presbyterian Church	14	3,025	2	40	1,960,000	1,905,000	55,000
Colored Cumberland Presbyterian Church	3	350			6,750	6,750	
Welsh Calvinistic Methodist Church							
United Presbyterian Church of North America	12	4,279	3	1,141	2,398,137	1,973,137	425,000
Presbyterian Church in the United States	162	17,170	13	1,444	8,004,226	7,200,285	803,941
Associate Synod of North America (Associate Presbyterian Church)							
Associate Reformed Synod of the South	3	337	1	9	258,000	253,000	5,000
Synod of the Reformed Presbyterian Church of North America	2	281	5	80	298,211	253,211	45,000
Reformed Presbyterian Church in North America, General Synod	2	145			149,746	149,746	
Reformed Presbyterian Church in the United States and Canada							
Protestant Episcopal Church	106	8,098	136	47,236	46,359,726	17,057,622	29,302,104
Reformed bodies	26	3,211	7	402	3,783,000	3,743,000	40,000
Reformed Church in America	9	650			743,000	743,000	
Reformed Church in the United States	16	2,400	4	322	2,726,000	2,726,000	(1)
Christian Reformed Church	1	161	3	80	314,000	274,000	40,000
Reformed Episcopal Church	1	16	1	(1)	225,000	217,000	8,000
Salvationists			203	9,587	6,500		6,500
Salvation Army			190	9,242	(1)		(1)
American Salvation Army			13	345	6,500		6,500
Schwenkfelders	1	300			50,000	50,000	
Unitarians							
United Brethren bodies	16	3,730	2	40	1,811,629	1,711,629	100,000
Church of the United Brethren in Christ	13	3,500	2	40	1,761,629	1,661,629	100,000
Church of the United Brethren in Christ (Old Constitution)	3	230			50,000	50,000	
Universalists	10	2,362	4	(1)	4,350,734	4,350,734	(1)
Roman Catholic Church	1,011	121,343	878	271,180	(1)	(1)	(1)
Jewish congregations	14	(1)	121	[3] 38,116	[5] 3,288,000	[5] 3,288,000	(1)
Latter-day Saints	17	5,980	7	1,998	1,450,391	1,031,741	418,650
Church of Jesus Christ of Latter-day Saints	16	5,780	4	1,998	1,361,741	991,741	370,000
Reorganized Church of Jesus Christ of Latter-day Saints	1	200	3	(1)	88,650	40,000	48,650
Eastern Orthodox Churches	2	25	1	12	65,000	55,000	10,000
Russian Orthodox Church	2	[4] 25	1	12	65,000	55,000	10,000
All other bodies	16	1,318	2	857	779,000	731,000	48,000
Buddhists	14	748			6,000	6,000	
Japanese Temples	14	748			6,000	6,000	
Society for Ethical Culture	1	550	2	857	748,000	700,000	48,000
Spiritualists	1	20			25,000	25,000	

[1] Not reported.
[2] Includes teachers.
[3] Partial report. See denominational text.
[4] Special or correspondence students.
[5] Endowment fund only. See denominational text.

It appears from this table that the total amount reported as contributed by the religious bodies in continental United States during the year 1906 for missionary, educational, and philanthropic work within this country was $38,675,919. Of this sum, $33,781,752, or 87.3 per cent, was given by the Protestant bodies; $4,419,563, or 11.4 per cent, by the Jewish congregations; and the balance, $474,604, or 1.2 per cent, largely by the Latter-day Saints. The figures for contributions reported by the Roman Catholic Church are so incomplete (only one organization reporting) that they are omitted. Several other bodies also made no report of contributions.

Among the Protestant bodies the Baptists reported contributions amounting to $13,125,325; the Methodist bodies, $6,186,433; the Presbyterian bodies, $4,631,391; the Protestant Episcopal Church, $2,665,133; the Lutheran bodies, $2,112,120; the Disciples or Christians, $1,735,456; and the Congregationalists, $1,034,154. The Northern Baptist Convention alone reported $11,732,896; the Methodist Episcopal Church, $4,277,723; and the Presbyterian Church in the United States of America, $3,062,771.

The total amount contributed for home missions, or general evangelism, was $12,762,271, of which the Methodist bodies reported $2,963,903; the Presbyterian bodies, $2,913,460; the Baptist bodies, $2,145,401; the Protestant Episcopal Church, $1,068,155; the Congregationalists, $969,789; and the Disciples or Christians, $641,456. For education the total amount reported is $17,665,445, apportioned in part as follows: Baptist bodies, $10,738,969; Methodist bodies, $2,019,428; Presbyterian bodies, $1,558,957; Disciples or Christians, $1,044,000; and Lutheran bodies, $826,672. In this connection it should be noted that the contributions for education by the Baptist bodies appear to include something over $6,000,000 for the University of Chicago. For philanthropic work the total amount contributed was $8,248,203, of which the Jewish congregations reported $4,304,172; the Methodist bodies, $1,203,102; the Protestant Episcopal Church, $1,154,836; and the Lutheran bodies, $655,393.

In the distinctively home mission department the total number of persons employed as missionaries or teachers was 20,044. The Presbyterian bodies lead with 3,868, and are followed by the Baptist bodies with 2,900; the Congregationalists, with 2,494; the Methodist bodies, with 2,147; the Protestant Episcopal Church, with 1,933; the Lutheran bodies, with 1,397; and the Disciples or Christians, with 1,206. The total number of churches aided was 22,591, of which the Baptist bodies reported 5,759; the Presbyterian bodies, 4,259; the Lutheran bodies, 2,840; the Methodist bodies, 2,378; the Congregationalists, 2,249; and the Protestant Episcopal Church, 2,077.

Under the head of education, 2,532 colleges, academies, etc., are reported, with 401,018 students. The Roman Catholic Church reported 1,011 institutions, with 121,343 students; the Methodist bodies, 372 institutions, with 99,048 students; the Presbyterian bodies, 308 institutions, with 47,592 students; and the Baptist bodies, 207 institutions, with 49,156 students.

Under the head of philanthropic institutions, 1,857 hospitals and asylums are reported, with 454,280 patients or inmates. The Roman Catholic Church reports 878 institutions, with 271,180 patients or inmates; the Salvationists, 203 institutions, with 9,587 inmates; the Methodist bodies, 144 institutions, with 38,536 inmates; the Protestant Episcopal Church, 136 institutions, with 47,236 inmates; the Lutheran bodies, 128 institutions, with 26,924 inmates; and the Jewish congregations, 121 institutions, with 38,116 inmates.

The total value of property and endowment reported was $297,510,918, of which $239,690,727 was for educational purposes, and $57,820,191 for philanthropic purposes. Of the total for educational purposes, the Methodist bodies reported $61,743,180; the Baptist bodies, $58,088,888; the Presbyterian bodies, $47,678,207; the Lutheran bodies, $17,869,661; and the Protestant Episcopal Church, $17,057,622. Of the total value of property and endowment for philanthropic purposes, the Protestant Episcopal Church reported $29,302,104; the Methodist bodies, $11,202,889; and the Lutheran bodies, $7,746,113.

It will be noticed that in a considerable number of cases no report was made, and in others only a partial report. The large amount reported for educational purposes by the Jewish congregations includes the Baron de Hirsch fund, which is not entirely educational in its purpose, but this seemed, on the whole, the best disposition that could be made of it.

Foreign work.—The table for foreign mission work presents for each denomination listed the amount contributed by the churches in the United States for the conduct of this work in its various departments; the total value of property; the number of countries and central stations occupied; the number of American missionaries and native helpers employed; the number of organized churches with their membership; the number of schools, together with the number of pupils; and the number of philanthropic institutions, together with the number of inmates. In view of the fact that the same country and sometimes the same city or town are often occupied by several denominations, no totals are given for the number of countries occupied or for the number of stations. The term "American missionaries," in accordance with the general usage in the United States and Great Britain, includes all those of either sex commissioned by the missionary societies. Of late the term has been held to include also the wives of missionaries. The term "native helpers" includes all those native to the country, whether preachers, teachers, colporters, or other workers of either sex, in the employ of a missionary society, but not the pastors of self-supporting native churches. The terms "churches" and "members" are used in the same sense as in the report on religious conditions in the United States. The schools are, in the main, schools of higher grade—colleges, academies, normal schools, etc.—the primary schools connected with the missionary boards being to a considerable degree supported by the native churches themselves, and not included in the reports presented. The philanthropic institutions include hospitals, dispensaries, asylums, and orphanages. Under the head of inmates it is intended to include all patients who were treated during the year, as well as regular inmates; in some instances, however, the capacity is given rather than the total number of inmates. The property includes all buildings, whether for educational or philanthropic purposes, or for use as residences for missionaries. Sometimes it includes church buildings, but these commonly are not owned by the missionary society.

DENOMINATION.	FOREIGN MISSION WORK: 1906.											
	Amount contributed.	Countries.		Missionaries.		Churches.		Schools.		Philanthropic institutions.		Value of property.
		Number.	Stations.	American.	Native helpers.	Number.	Members.	Number.	Pupils.	Number.	Inmates and patients.	
All denominations represented	$8,744,627	...	...	7,731	35,388	8,323	922,567	8,708	321,452	549	1,492,647	$26,496,672
Protestant bodies	8,655,981	...	...	6,131	31,303	8,100	860,516	8,699	319,968	549	1,492,647	26,196,084
Adventist bodies	299,638	...	...	305	1,168	677	27,853	47	2,472	21	5,124	995,359
Advent Christian Church	32,982	3	12	21	60	11	654	30	1,723	2	120	41,500
Seventh-day Adventist Denomination	266,656	45	126	284	1,108	666	27,199	17	749	19	5,004	953,859
Baptist bodies	1,306,156	...	...	824	7,204	2,656	275,687	2,188	66,537	68	83,809	1,689,650
Baptists	1,238,174	...	...	789	6,885	2,631	274,122	2,059	62,282	58	80,750	1,579,650
Northern Baptist Convention	815,636	17	113	578	6,456	2,365	252,611	1,919	53,892	50	62,750	1,250,000
Southern Baptist Convention	403,811	7	46	203	297	233	13,437	108	2,609	8	18,000	300,000
National Baptist Convention (Colored)	18,727	5	72	8	132	33	8,074	32	5,781	...	...	29,650
Seventh-day Baptists	5,400	4	7	9	19	6	235	7	150	3	2,892	25,000
Free Baptists	62,582	1	9	26	300	19	1,330	122	4,105	7	[1]167	85,000
Brethren (Plymouth)	...		...	605	...	...	...	...	...	...	...	...
Brethren (Plymouth)—I	([2])	...	...	5	...	...	...	...	...	...	...	...
Brethren (Plymouth)—II	([2])	...	...	600	...	...	...	...	...	...	...	...
Brethren (River)	1,324	...	...	14	6	...	...	5	125	...	...	...
Brethren in Christ	1,324	2	5	14	6	...	...	5	125	...	...	([2])
Christians (Christian Connection)	13,879	2	6	14	21	15	688	2	12	...	...	14,960
Churches of God in North America, General Eldership of the	5,000	1	2	4	10	2	73	...	...	1	([2])	560
Churches of the New Jerusalem	1,000	...	...	...	4	...	300	...	...	...	...	...
General Convention of the New Jerusalem in the United States of America	1,000	6	11	...	4	([2])	300	...	...	...	...	([2])
Congregationalists	891,979	13	105	569	4,135	580	68,952	1,468	65,152	123	373,500	1,500,000
Disciples or Christians	446,353	...	...	231	575	152	14,860	153	9,499	64	66,661	736,000
Disciples of Christ	446,353	19	87	231	575	152	14,860	153	9,499	64	66,661	736,000
Dunkers or German Baptist Brethren	70,051	...	...	29	16	9	1,270	2	600	2	200	2,000
German Baptist Brethren Church (Conservative)	[3]66,961	1	14	23	15	8	1,200	2	600		[1]200	([2])
The Brethren Church (Progressive Dunkers)	3,090	3	3	6	1	1	70	...	...	...	...	2,000
Evangelical bodies	70,250	...	...	30	620	460	27,997	6	133	15	11,416	1,151,588
Evangelical Association	44,600	5	2	16	617	456	27,897	3	53	15	11,416	1,132,000
United Evangelical Church	25,650	1	3	14	3	4	100	3	80	...	...	19,588
Evangelistic associations	12,040	...	...	56	15	3	250	2	250	2	200	35,000
Apostolic Faith Movement	([2])	7	...	([2])	...	...	...	...	...	...	...	...
Metropolitan Church Association	2,340	3	...	15	...	...	...	...	...	...	...	...
Hephzibah Faith Missionary Association	5,200	4	7	24	...	...	...	...	...	...	...	...
Pentecost Bands of the World	4,500	3	10	17	15	3	250	2	250	2	200	35,000
Friends	97,500	...	...	115	250	29	4,190	55	3,000	5	...	...
Society of Friends (Orthodox)	97,500	12	41	115	250	29	4,190	55	3,000	5	([2])	([2])
German Evangelical Synod of North America	29,067	1	4	12	154	4	1,814	39	1,601	11	12,759	50,000
International Apostolic Holiness Union	12,400	4	10	25	...	...	...	3	([2])	...	...	27,000

[1] Partial report. See denominational text.
[2] Not reported.
[3] For work in 6 countries; figures for all other details are for India only.

DENOMINATION.	FOREIGN MISSION WORK: 1906.											
	Amount contributed.	Countries.		Missionaries.		Churches.		Schools.		Philanthropic institutions.		Value of property.
		Number.	Stations.	American.	Native helpers.	Number.	Members.	Number.	Pupils.	Number.	Inmates and patients.	
Protestant bodies—Continued.												
Lutheran bodies	$257,216			158	1,209	826	23,357	684	19,660	24	24,207	$352,100
General Synod of the Evangelical Lutheran Church in the United States of America	73,172	2	8	38	610	502	12,725	301	8,829	5	8,507	175,000
United Synod of the Evangelical Lutheran Church in the South	7,150	1	1	3	7	9	200					6,000
General Council of the Evangelical Lutheran Church in North America	39,245	1	5	21	300	241	6,135	196	5,736	2	4,000	100,000
Evangelical Lutheran Synodical Conference of America	14,021	1	4	7	9	4	60	14	687			10,000
United Norwegian Lutheran Church in America	57,430	2	8	39	81	47	1,183	11	529	8	2,125	38,000
Evangelical Lutheran Joint Synod of Ohio and Other States	[1] 6,600	2										
Lutheran Synod of Buffalo	[1] 650	1										
Hauge's Norwegian Evangelical Lutheran Synod	27,000	1	4	16	65	15	284	30	854	4	1,030	13,000
German Evangelical Lutheran Synod of Texas	[1] 104											
Evangelical Lutheran Synod of Iowa and Other States	[1] 9,721											
Synod for the Norwegian Evangelical Lutheran Church in America	4,003	1		16	32		1,811	9	462	3	57	(2)
Danish Evangelical Lutheran Church in America	[1] 196											
Finnish Evangelical Lutheran Church of America, or Suomi Synod	[1] 529											
Norwegian Lutheran Free Church	13,993	1	3	7	100	3	929	60	2,493	2	488	7,900
United Danish Evangelical Lutheran Church in America	2,022	1	1	4	3	1	30	1	30			(2)
Finnish Evangelical Lutheran National Church	[1] 50											
Church of the Lutheran Brethren of America (Norwegian)	1,330	1	1	7	2			2	40			2,200
Mennonite bodies	67,188			70	25	4	1,177	5	285	5	900	148,300
Mennonite Church; Amish Mennonite Church	31,688	1	3	13	13	4	782	3	285	2	550	62,000
General Conference of Mennonites of North America	[3] 21,500	1	2			(2)	60	2	(2)	2	(2)	[3] 72,000
Defenceless Mennonites	(2)	1	1	2								
Mennonite Brethren in Christ	14,000	5		38						1	[4] 350	(2)
Bundes Conferens der Mennoniten Brueder-Gemeinde—												
Krimmer Brueder-Gemeinde; Schellenberger Brueder-Gemeinde	(2)	2	4	12	12	(2)	335					14,300
Central Illinois Conference of Mennonites	(2)	1		5								
Methodist bodies	2,177,827			1,193	10,370	1,801	293,894	2,151	80,944	28	123,022	11,491,664
Methodist Episcopal Church	1,302,698	28	172	827	9,463	1,455	259,782	2,016	70,588	22	[5] 59,522	9,513,801
Methodist Protestant Church	28,606	1	5	13	15	12	1,000	5	900			63,500
Wesleyan Methodist Connection of America	10,061	1	1	5	5	1	50	2	30			5,000
Methodist Episcopal Church, South	766,627	6	50	281	795	318	20,990	100	8,691	6	63,500	1,800,963
Primitive Methodist Church in the United States of America	800	1	1		1	1	75	1	150			(2)
Free Methodist Church of North America	56,285	6	18	52	91	11	1,047	24	685			90,400
African Methodists	12,750			15		3	10,950	3				18,000
Union American Methodist Episcopal Church (Colored)	(2)	1				3	150					5,000
African Methodist Episcopal Church	9,750	8				(2)	[5] 10,800					
African Methodist Episcopal Zion Church	3,000	4		15				3	(2)			13,000
Moravian bodies	24,507			40								
Moravian Church (Unitas Fratrum)	24,474			40								
Evangelical Union of Bohemian and Moravian Brethren in North America	[1] 33											
Pentecostal Church of the Nazarene	4,000	2		8	6	3	100	2	(2)	2	(2)	6,000
Presbyterian bodies	1,941,704			1,361	3,918	621	96,771	1,448	51,360	148	587,585	5,921,571
Presbyterian Church in the United States of America	1,182,516	15	136	890	2,611	443	63,480	995	32,430	118	442,756	4,000,000
Cumberland Presbyterian Church	72,121	3	11	35		11	1,299	4	500	1	8,000	55,000
Welsh Calvinistic Methodist Church	3,450	1	1	3		1	18					(2)
United Presbyterian Church of North America	366,164	3	93	176	86	90	19,798	365	13,750	10	116,418	1,437,250
Presbyterian Church in the United States	266,318	7	49	206	888	55	10,824	61	3,471	4	15,000	250,000
Associate Synod of North America (Associate Presbyterian Church)	740	1	1	2	7	1	57	3	189	2	2,897	(2)
Associate Reformed Synod of the South	19,650	2		13	12	11	342	6	300	2	[4] 14	48,450
Synod of the Reformed Presbyterian Church of North America	20,965	3	5	36	44	2	403	14	720	3	2,500	126,871
Reformed Presbyterian Church in North America, General Synod	9,455	1			26	7	550			3	(2)	4,000
Reformed Presbyterian Church in the United States and Canada	325	1			1							
Protestant Episcopal Church	549,070	7	387	221	761	96	9,890	180	6,950	18	95,323	[5] 1,271,548

[1] In aid of work carried on by foreign societies.
[2] Not reported.
[3] Includes work for Indians in the United States.
[4] Capacity, not patients.
[5] Partial report. See denominational text.

DENOMINATION.	FOREIGN MISSION WORK: 1906.												
	Amount contributed.	Countries.		Missionaries.		Churches.		Schools.		Philanthropic institutions.		Value of property.
		Number.	Stations.	American.	Native helpers.	Number.	Members.	Number.	Pupils.	Number.	Inmates and patients.	
Protestant bodies—Continued.												
Reformed bodies	$275,967	......	......	154	671	88	8,662	223	10,023	11	86,511	$566,063
Reformed Church in America	179,867	4	23	100	551	35	5,062	217	9,398	8	84,361	301,063
Reformed Church in the United States	96,100	2	3	54	120	53	3,600	6	625	3	2,150	265,000
Reformed Episcopal Church	8,159	1	5	[1] 12	......	......	......	......	......	3	([2])	100,000
Schwenkfelders	[3] 500	......	......	......	......	......	......	......	......	......	......	......
Swedish Evangelical bodies	......	......	......	15	20	12	446	......	......	......	......	......
Swedish Evangelical Mission Covenant of America	([2])	1	3	15	20	12	446	......	......	......	......	([2])
United Brethren bodies	84,706	......	......	61	139	57	2,078	36	1,365	3	21,370	116,771
Church of the United Brethren in Christ	82,206	5	......	56	133	51	2,028	34	1,285	3	21,370	111,771
Church of the United Brethren in Christ (Old Constitution)	2,500	1	3	5	6	6	50	2	80	......	......	5,000
Universalists	8,500	1	11		6	5	207	......	......	......	......	20,000
Latter-day Saints	88,646	......	......	1,600	4,085	223	62,051	9	1,484	......	......	300,588
Church of Jesus Christ of Latter-day Saints	75,646	14	15	1,600	4,085	85	53,996	9	1,484	......	......	285,588
Reorganized Church of Jesus Christ of Latter-day Saints	13,000	11	......	([2])	......	138	8,055	......	......	......	......	15,000

[1] Includes native helpers. [2] Not reported. [3] In aid of work carried on by foreign societies.

According to this table the total amount contributed in continental United States for the work of foreign missions in the year 1906 was $8,744,627. Of this amount, $8,655,981, or 99 per cent, was contributed by Protestant bodies, and the balance, $88,646, by the Latter-day Saints. The Roman Catholic Church in the United States (see page 607, Part II) does not contribute directly to foreign missions, although gifts are sent to the Society for the Propagation of the Faith and are then distributed in different foreign fields, but of this there is no definite record. In eight cases denominations which report missionaries and other items make no report of contributions, and in nine cases denominations contribute to foreign work through the societies of other bodies either in this country or in Europe.

The religious bodies which reported the largest contributions are as follows: Methodist bodies, $2,177,827; Presbyterian bodies, $1,941,704; Baptist bodies, $1,306,156; Congregationalists, $891,979; and the Protestant Episcopal Church, $549,070.

The total number of missionaries reported is 7,731, of whom 6,131 are reported by the Protestant bodies and 1,600 by the Latter-day Saints. The Presbyterian bodies reported 1,361; the Methodist bodies, 1,193; the Baptist bodies, 824; and the Congregationalists, 569. The number of native helpers employed is 35,388, of whom 31,303 are under the care of the Protestant bodies and 4,085 under the care of the Latter-day Saints. The Methodist bodies reported 10,370; Baptist bodies, 7,204; Congregationalists, 4,135; Presbyterian bodies, 3,918; and Lutheran bodies, 1,209. The Northern Baptist Convention and the Methodist bodies (see pages 51 and 436, Part II) have in Europe a large force, classed as native helpers, of a somewhat different type from those reported by other bodies.

The total number of churches reported is 8,323, with a membership of 922,567; and of these, 8,100 churches, with 860,516 members, belong to the Protestant bodies, and 223 churches, with 62,051 members, to the Latter-day Saints. The Baptist bodies reported 2,656 churches, with 275,687 members; the Methodist bodies, 1,801 churches, with 293,894 members; the Lutheran bodies, 826 churches, with 23,357 members; the Presbyterian bodies, 621 churches, with 96,771 members; and the Congregationalists, 580 churches, with 68,952 members.

The number of schools of various grades, but chiefly of the higher grades, reported by the different bodies is 8,708, and the number of pupils, 321,452. Of these, 8,699 schools with 319,968 pupils belong to the Protestant bodies, and 9 schools with 1,484 pupils to the Latter-day Saints. The Baptist bodies lead with 2,188 schools and 66,537 pupils. The Methodist bodies reported 2,151 schools, with 80,944 pupils; the Congregationalists, 1,468 schools, with 65,152 pupils; the Presbyterian bodies, 1,448 schools, with 51,360 pupils; and the Lutheran bodies, 684 schools, with 19,660 pupils.

The 549 philanthropic institutions reported, with their 1,492,647 inmates, including patients treated in hospitals and dispensaries, belong exclusively to the Protestant bodies. The Presbyterian bodies reported 143 institutions, with 587,585 inmates; the Congregationalists, 123 institutions, with 373,500 inmates; the Baptist bodies, 68 institutions, with 83,809 inmates; and the Methodist bodies, 28 institutions, with 123,022 inmates.

The value of property reported is $26,496,672, of which $26,196,084 belongs to the Protestant bodies and $300,588 to the Latter-day Saints. The Methodist bodies reported $11,491,664; the Presbyterian bodies, $5,921,571; the Baptist bodies, $1,689,650; the Congregationalists, $1,500,000; and the Protestant Episcopal Church, $1,271,548.

Summary of contributions.—The following summary of contributions as presented in the two preceding tables shows first, the total membership of the denominations reporting contributions; second, the total contributed for both domestic and foreign work, together with the amount under each head, and the per cent of the total; third, the total contributed specifically for home missions and foreign missions, with the amount under each head, and the per cent of the total; and fourth, the average amount contributed per member of the denominations reporting contributions.

DENOMINATION	Communicants or members.	CONTRIBUTIONS: 1906. Domestic work and foreign mission work. Total amount contributed.	Domestic work. Amount.	Domestic work. Per cent.	Foreign mission work. Amount.	Foreign mission work. Per cent.	Average per member for denominations reporting.	Home and foreign missions. Total amount contributed.	Home missions. Amount.	Home missions. Per cent.	Foreign missions. Amount.	Foreign missions. Per cent.	Average per member for denominations reporting.
All denominations reporting	19,918,048	$47,420,546	$38,675,919	81.6	$8,744,627	18.4	$2.38	$21,506,898	$12,762,271	59.3	$8,744,627	40.7	$1.08
Protestant bodies	19,500,572	42,437,733	33,781,752	79.6	8,655,981	20.4	2.18	21,272,191	12,616,210	59.3	8,655,981	40.7	1.09
Adventist bodies	89,519	575,575	275,937	47.9	299,638	52.1	6.43	462,671	163,033	35.2	299,638	64.8	5.17
Seventh-day Adventist Denomination	62,211	532,255	265,599	49.9	266,656	50.1	8.56	427,755	161,099	37.7	266,656	62.3	6.88
Other Adventist bodies (2 bodies)	27,308	43,320	10,338	23.9	32,982	76.1	1.59	34,916	1,934	5.5	32,982	94.5	1.28
Baptist bodies	5,412,923	14,431,481	13,125,325	90.9	1,306,156	9.1	2.67	3,451,557	2,145,401	62.2	1,306,156	37.8	0.64
Baptists:													
Northern Baptist Convention	1,052,105	12,548,532	11,732,896	93.5	815,636	6.5	11.93	2,627,435	1,811,799	69.0	815,636	31.0	2.50
Southern Baptist Convention	2,009,471	1,622,650	1,218,839	75.1	403,811	24.9	0.81	655,795	251,984	38.4	403,811	61.6	0.33
Other Baptist bodies (3 bodies)	2,351,347	260,299	173,590	66.7	86,709	33.3	0.11	168,327	81,618	48.5	86,709	51.5	0.07
Congregationalists	700,480	1,926,133	1,034,154	53.7	891,979	46.3	2.75	1,861,768	969,789	52.1	891,979	47.9	2.66
Disciples or Christians	982,701	2,181,809	1,735,456	79.5	446,353	20.5	2.22	1,087,809	641,456	59.0	446,353	41.0	1.11
Disciples of Christ	982,701	2,181,809	1,735,456	79.5	446,353	20.5	2.22	1,087,809	641,456	59.0	446,353	41.0	1.11
Evangelical bodies (2 bodies)	174,780	484,215	413,965	85.5	70,250	14.5	2.77	388,092	317,842	81.9	70,250	18.1	2.22
German Evangelical Synod of North America	293,137	202,394	173,327	85.6	29,067	14.4	0.69	56,067	27,000	48.2	29,067	51.8	0.19
Lutheran bodies	2,091,448	2,369,336	2,112,120	89.1	257,216	10.9	1.18	887,271	630,055	71.0	257,216	29.0	0.42
General Synod of the Evangelical Lutheran Church in the United States of America	270,221	392,718	319,546	81.4	73,172	18.6	1.45	241,552	168,380	69.7	73,172	30.3	0.89
General Council of the Evangelical Lutheran Church in North America	462,177	367,500	328,255	89.3	39,245	10.7	0.80	186,892	147,647	79.0	39,245	21.0	0.40
Evangelical Lutheran Synodical Conference of America	648,529	649,747	635,726	97.8	14,021	2.2	1.00	151,747	137,726	90.8	14,021	9.2	0.23
United Norwegian Lutheran Church in America	185,027	366,055	308,625	84.3	57,430	15.7	1.98	100,596	43,166	42.9	57,430	57.1	0.54
Other Lutheran bodies (17 bodies)	525,494	593,316	519,968	87.6	73,348	12.4	1.13	206,484	133,136	64.5	73,348	35.5	0.39
Methodist bodies	5,720,279	8,364,260	6,186,433	74.0	2,177,827	26.0	1.46	5,141,730	2,963,903	57.6	2,177,827	42.4	0.90
Methodist Episcopal Church	2,986,154	5,580,421	4,277,723	76.7	1,302,698	23.3	1.87	3,715,984	2,413,286	64.9	1,302,698	35.1	1.24
Methodist Episcopal Church, South	1,638,480	2,214,316	1,447,689	65.4	766,627	34.6	1.35	1,199,081	432,454	36.1	766,627	63.9	0.73
Other Methodist bodies (8 bodies)	1,095,645	569,523	461,021	80.9	108,502	19.1	0.52	226,665	118,163	52.1	108,502	47.9	0.21
Presbyterian bodies	1,826,918	6,573,095	4,631,391	70.5	1,941,704	29.5	3.60	4,855,164	2,913,460	60.0	1,941,704	40.0	2.66
Presbyterian Church in the United States of America	1,179,566	4,245,287	3,062,771	72.1	1,182,516	27.9	3.60	3,397,704	2,215,188	65.2	1,182,516	34.8	2.88
United Presbyterian Church of North America	130,342	810,029	443,865	54.8	366,164	45.2	6.21	691,214	325,050	47.0	366,164	53.0	5.30
Presbyterian Church in the United States	266,345	1,214,438	948,120	78.1	266,318	21.9	4.56	499,075	232,757	46.6	266,318	53.4	1.87
Other Presbyterian bodies (7 bodies)	250,665	303,341	176,635	58.2	126,706	41.8	1.21	267,171	140,465	52.6	126,706	47.4	1.07
Protestant Episcopal Church	886,942	3,214,203	2,665,133	82.9	549,070	17.1	3.62	1,617,225	1,068,155	66.0	549,070	34.0	1.82
Reformed bodies (3 bodies)	444,261	778,551	502,584	64.6	275,967	35.4	1.75	525,052	249,085	47.4	275,967	52.6	1.18
United Brethren bodies (2 bodies)	296,050	323,377	238,671	73.8	84,706	26.2	1.09	194,264	109,558	56.4	84,706	43.6	0.66
Other Protestant bodies (27 bodies)	581,124	1,013,304	687,256	67.8	326,048	32.2	1.74	743,521	417,473	56.1	326,048	43.9	1.28
Jewish congregations	[1] 101,457	4,419,563	4,419,563	100.0	....	.....	[2] 43.56	....	....	.....	....	.....	.....
Latter-day Saints (2 bodies)	256,647	482,435	393,789	81.6	88,646	18.4	1.88	225,646	137,000	60.7	88,646	39.3	0.88
Other bodies (4 bodies)	59,372	80,815	80,815	100.0	....	.....	1.36	9,061	9,061	100.0	....	.....	0.15

[1] Heads of families only.

[2] Average per head of family.

From this table it appears that of the 111 denominations represented in the preceding tables as conducting evangelistic, educational, or philanthropic work at home or abroad, only 92 made a specific report of contributions. Many of the bodies making no report are small, with no general organization, and have only a few missionaries or schools, probably supported in a private way rather than by denominational collections. The Plymouth Brethren make no collections for their missionary work, and the domestic work of the Evangelistic associations and of some other bodies is on a similar basis. The only large body not reporting is the Roman Catholic Church, and in this case the failure to report is due, as already stated, to the peculiar organization for the conduct of benevolent work.

Comparing evangelistic work with educational and philanthropic work, it appears that $21,506,898, or 45.4 per cent of the total amount contributed, went to evangelistic work at home and abroad, and $25,913,648, or 54.6 per cent, to educational and philanthropic work in this country.

While home and foreign mission work includes educational and philanthropic work, it is in general of a different type from that reported under the head of education and of hospitals, asylums, etc. The latter is more of the nature of establishing permanent institutions, including both property and endowments, so that the contributions are to a considerable degree, though by no means entirely, of the nature of permanent investments. Illustrations are found in the large amount given to Chicago University and credited to the Northern Baptist Convention, and the Baron de Hirsch fund credited to the Jewish congregations. A considerable portion of the amounts credited to other bodies are evidently of the same general nature. On the other hand, the contributions for work of this type in both home and foreign missions are chiefly for running expenses.

If the amounts contributed for domestic work be compared with the total amounts reported by the different denominations, it appears that with the exception of the Jewish congregations, which reported no foreign work, and the Northern Baptist Convention, whose high percentage for domestic work, 93.5, was apparently due to exceptional conditions, the highest percentages are for bodies whose members are chiefly of German or Scandinavian extraction. The general percentage for all Lutheran bodies is 89.1, while for the Synodical Conference it is 97.8; the General Council, 89.3; the United Norwegian Church, 84.3; and the General Synod, 81.4. With these may also be classed the German Evangelical Synod of North America, 85.6 per cent, and the Evangelical bodies, 85.5 per cent. Aside from these, the highest percentages are those for the Protestant Episcopal Church, 82.9; the Latter-day Saints, 81.6; the Disciples of Christ, 79.5; the Presbyterian Church in the United States, 78.1; and the Methodist Episcopal Church, 76.7.

Comparison of home and foreign work.—Comparing the home mission work with the foreign mission work, like conditions appear. Thus the percentage for the Lutheran bodies in general is 71 per cent for the home work and 29 per cent for the foreign work. The Synodical Conference reported 90.8 per cent for the home work, the General Council 79 per cent, and the General Synod 69.7 per cent. For similar reasons the two Evangelical bodies directly interested in work among the foreign born population in this country show for the home work 81.9 per cent. High percentages reported by other bodies are: The Northern Baptist Convention, 69; the Protestant Episcopal Church, 66; and the Presbyterian Church in the United States of America, 65.2. For the foreign work, the highest percentage for any single body shown in the table is for the Methodist Episcopal Church, South, 63.9 per cent. High percentages are also shown for the Seventh-day Adventists, 62.3; the Southern Baptist Convention, 61.6; the United Norwegian Lutheran Church in America, 57.1; the Presbyterian Church in the United States, 53.4; and the United Presbyterian Church of North America, 53.

The highest average of total contributions per member reported by any one denomination is $11.93 for the Northern Baptist Convention. Other high averages are $8.56 for the Seventh-day Adventists, $6.21 for the United Presbyterian Church, $4.56 for the Presbyterian Church in the United States, $3.62 for the Protestant Episcopal Church, and $3.60 for the Presbyterian Church in the United States of America.

The highest averages for distinctively mission work, both home and foreign, are $6.88 for the Seventh-day Adventists, $5.30 for the United Presbyterian Church of North America, $2.88 for the Presbyterian Church in the United States of America, $2.66 for the Congregationalists, $2.50 for the Northern Baptist Convention, and $2.22 for the Evangelical bodies.

It is noticeable that most of the bodies which show a higher percentage of contributions for foreign missions than for home missions are such as, for one reason or another, chiefly because of the section in which they are located, are not affected by the immigrant element in this country; among them are the Adventists, the Southern Baptist Convention, the Methodist Episcopal Church, South, the United Presbyterian Church of North America, the Presbyterian Church in the United States, etc. The single prominent exception is the United Norwegian Lutheran Church in America, and this is probably explained by the intimate relations this body holds to the very successful foreign mission enterprise of the mother church in Norway.

As previously stated, these tables are far from complete. Only such sums are included as have been reported by the benevolent societies or ecclesiastical authorities in the various denominations, and the sums expended in the conduct of local work, often of a distinctively missionary character, do not appear. No attempt has been made to present the total benefactions, whether of the local churches or of individual members. Incomplete, however, as they are, they furnish a valuable and interesting exhibit. Perhaps the most important result of a study of these tables would be that the various religious bodies should come to realize the desirability of keeping a complete record of their benevolences so that a clear statement of them in every particular may be available. There is an increasing demand for definite financial statements in every department of activity, including the benevolences of the people, and particularly of the churches. That those in charge of these benevolences were not only willing but glad to make such statements is abundantly evident from the correspondence in connection with these tables. Not less evident, however, is the fact that there is as yet not enough uniformity or even harmony of presentation to enable one not personally acquainted with denominational methods to gain an accurate conception of the work the religious bodies are doing.

SUMMARY OF STATISTICS OF COLORED ORGANIZATIONS.

This summary includes statistics for all colored organizations reported, whether these organizations were connected with denominations consisting entirely of such organizations, or with denominations in which colored organizations represented only a part of the membership. The term "colored organization," as used in this connection, signifies an organization whose membership is composed wholly of negroes or those of negro descent. Including the National Baptist Convention (a branch of the regular Baptists), 17 bodies are reported which are wholly made up of colored organizations, as against 10 given in the report for 1890. Of those given in the report for 1890, two—the Congregational Methodist Church and the Evangelist Missionary Church—have disappeared, while the following 9 appear for the first time in the report for 1906: Colored Primitive Baptists in America; United American Freewill Baptists; Church of God and Saints of Christ; Churches of the Living God (3 bodies); Voluntary Missionary Society in America; Free Christian Zion Church of Christ; and Reformed Methodist Union Episcopal Church. The denominations composed in part of colored organizations are 26 in number, as against 18 in 1890. For these denominations the general and divisional officers were requested to indicate either the divisions (associations, conferences, etc.) that were made up wholly of colored organizations, or the scattered organizations that were composed wholly of colored members, and this method was supplemented, in the case of several denominations, by special correspondence, through which additional lists of colored organizations were secured. In this way an attempt was made to secure a substantially full report of colored organizations, although it is probable that some distinctively colored churches have been omitted. This effort was restricted, however, to churches comprising colored members only, and no attempt was made to ascertain the number of colored communicants belonging to local white churches.

GENERAL SUMMARY FOR 1906.

The general statistics for all the colored organizations at the close of the year 1906 are given in Tables 11, 12, and 14 (pages 538, 540, and 564). The total number of organizations reported for 1906, as shown by these tables, is 36,770. The total number of communicants or members, as reported by 36,563 organizations, is 3,685,097; of these, as shown by the returns for 34,648 organizations, 37.5 per cent are males and 62.5 per cent females.

According to the statistics, these organizations have 35,160 church edifices; a seating capacity for church edifices of 10,481,738, as reported by 33,091 organizations; church property valued at $56,636,159, against which there appears an indebtedness of $5,005,905; halls, etc., used for worship by 1,261 organizations; and parsonages valued at $3,727,884. The number of Sunday schools, as reported by 33,538 organizations, is 34,681, with 210,148 officers and teachers and 1,740,099 scholars.

Compared with the report for 1890, these figures show increases of 13,308 in the number of colored organizations, 1,011,120 in the number of communicants or members, 11,390 in the number of church edifices, and $30,009,711 in the value of church property.

COMPARISON OF ORGANIZATIONS, COMMUNICANTS OR MEMBERS, AND VALUE OF CHURCH PROPERTY, FOR 1906 AND 1890.

The next table shows for 1890 and 1906, by denominations in detail, the number of colored organizations, the number of communicants or members, and the value of church property.

Of the total number of organizations reported for 1906, as shown by this table, 31,393, with 3,207,307 communicants and church property valued at $44,673,049, belonged to the denominations made up wholly of colored organizations, while 5,377, with 477,790 communicants and church property valued at $11,963,110, were connected with denominations made up only in part of colored organizations.

Including denominations made up either wholly or in part of colored organizations in 1906, 6 Baptist bodies reported 19,891 organizations, with 2,354,789 communicants, and church property valued at $26,562,845; and 10 Methodist bodies reported 15,317 organizations, with 1,182,131 communicants and church property valued at $25,771,262. These 2 denominational families reported 35,208 organizations, or 95.8 per cent of the total number of colored organizations reported; 3,536,920 communicants, or 96 per cent of the total number of colored communicants reported; and church property valued at $52,334,107, or 92.4 per cent of the total value of church property reported by colored organizations.

DENOMINATION.	NUMBER OF COLORED[1] ORGANIZATIONS.		NUMBER OF COMMUNICANTS OR MEMBERS REPORTED.		VALUE OF CHURCH PROPERTY REPORTED.	
	1906	1890	1906	1890	1906	1890
All denominations consisting in whole or in part of colored[1] organizations	36,770	23,462	3,685,097	2,673,977	$56,636,159	$26,626,448
Denominations consisting wholly of colored organizations	31,393	19,158	3,207,307	2,321,313	44,673,049	20,525,141
Baptist bodies:						
Baptists—National Convention	18,534	12,533	2,261,607	1,348,989	24,437,272	9,038,549
Colored Primitive Baptists in America[2]	797	323	35,076	18,162	296,539	135,427
United American Freewill Baptists	251	....	14,489	....	79,278	....
Church of God and Saints of Christ	48	....	1,823	....	6,000	....
Churches of the Living God:						
Church of the Living God (Christian Workers for Friendship)	44	....	2,676	....	23,175	....
Church of the Living God (Apostolic Church)	15	....	752	....	25,700	....
Church of Christ in God	9	....	848	....	9,700	....
Evangelistic associations:						
Voluntary Missionary Society in America	3	....	425	....	2,400	....
Free Christian Zion Church of Christ	15	....	1,835	....	5,975	....
Methodist bodies:						
Union American Methodist Episcopal Church	77	42	4,347	2,279	170,150	187,600
African Methodist Episcopal Church	6,647	2,481	494,777	452,725	11,303,489	6,468,280
African Union Methodist Protestant Church	69	40	5,592	3,415	183,697	54,440
African Methodist Episcopal Zion Church	2,204	1,704	184,542	349,788	4,833,207	2,714,128
Congregational Methodist Church	....	9	....	319	....	525
Colored Methodist Episcopal Church	2,381	1,759	172,996	129,383	3,017,849	1,713,366
Reformed Zion Union Apostolic Church	45	32	3,059	2,346	37,875	15,000
Reformed Methodist Union Episcopal Church	58	....	4,397	....	36,965	....
Evangelist Missionary Church	....	11	....	951	....	2,000
Presbyterian bodies:						
Colored Cumberland Presbyterian Church	196	224	18,066	12,956	203,778	195,826
Denominations consisting in part of colored[1] organizations	5,377	4,304	477,790	352,664	11,963,110	6,101,307
Adventist bodies:						
Advent Christian Church	2	....	72	....	3,800	....
Seventh-day Adventist Denomination	29	....	562	....	6,474	....
Baptist bodies:						
Baptists—Northern Convention	108	406	32,639	35,221	1,561,326	1,087,518
Baptists—Southern Convention	....	7	....	651	....	3,875
Free Baptists	197	5	10,876	271	186,130	13,300
Primitive Baptists[3]	4	....	102	....	2,300	....
Two-Seed-in-the-Spirit Predestinarian Baptists	....	15	....	265	....	930
Christians (Christian Connection)	92	63	7,545	4,989	69,506	23,500
Churches of God in North America, General Eldership of the	15	....	329	....	5,500	....
Congregationalists	156	85	11,960	6,908	459,497	246,125
Disciples or Christians:						
Disciples of Christ	129	277	9,705	18,578	170,265	176,795
Churches of Christ	41		1,528		14,950	
Independent churches	12	....	490	....	2,750	....
Lutheran bodies:						
United Synod of the Evangelical Lutheran Church in the South	....	5	....	94	....	1,750
General Council of the Evangelical Lutheran Church in North America	1	....	15	....	5,000	....
Evangelical Lutheran Synodical Conference of America	6	5	224	211	10,000	13,400
Methodist bodies:						
Methodist Episcopal Church	3,750	2,984	308,551	246,249	6,104,379	3,630,093
Methodist Protestant Church	64	54	2,612	3,183	62,651	35,445
Wesleyan Methodist Connection of America	22	....	1,258	....	21,000	....
Independent Methodists	....	2	....	222	....	4,675
Moravian bodies:						
Moravian Church (Unitas Fratrum)		....	351	....	8,000	....
Presbyterian bodies:						
Presbyterian Church in the United States of America	417	233	27,799	14,961	752,387	391,650
Cumberland Presbyterian Church	1	....	50	....	1,000	....
Presbyterian Church in the United States	44	45	1,183	1,568	32,850	22,200
Associate Reformed Synod of the South	1	....	18	....	200	....
Synod of the Reformed Presbyterian Church of North America	....	1	....	76	....	1,500
Protestant Episcopal Church	198	49	19,098	2,977	1,773,279	192,750
Reformed bodies:						
Reformed Church in America	2	....	59	....	....	....
Reformed Episcopal Church	38	37	2,252	1,723	28,287	18,401
Roman Catholic Church	36	31	38,235	14,517	678,480	237,400
United Brethren bodies:						
Church of the United Brethren in Christ	10	....	277	....	3,100	....

[1] Negroes or persons of negro descent.
[2] The organizations shown for this denomination in 1890 were returned at that census as belonging to the Primitive Baptists.
[3] The colored organizations returned for this denomination in 1890 are included in the present report as belonging to the Colored Primitive Baptists in America.

Of the total increase in the number of organizations, 12,235, or 91.9 per cent, were in denominations consisting wholly of colored organizations; of the total increase in the number of communicants, 885,994, or 87.6 per cent; and of the total increase in the value of church property, $24,147,908, or 80.5 per cent. Including the denominations made up either wholly or in part of colored organizations, the Baptist bodies show an increase over 1890 of 6,602 organizations, or 49.7 per cent, and the Methodist bodies of 6,199, or 68 per cent, these 2 families reporting an increase of 12,801 organizations, or 96.2 per cent of the total. The increase in the number of communicants reported by the Baptist bodies is 951,230, or 67.8 per cent, which is 94.1 per cent of the total increase. For the Methodist bodies the figures show a slight decrease in the number of communicants, owing to the decrease in the number reported for the African Methodist Episcopal Zion Church, due, as already explained (see page 26), to the fact that the number given in the report for 1890 was too high. The increase in the value of church property shown by the Baptist bodies is $16,283,246, or 158.4 per cent, and by the Methodist bodies, $10,945,710, or 73.8 per cent, these 2 families showing an increase in the value of church property of $27,228,956, or 90.7 per cent of the total increase.

It is to be noted that the figures for the Baptists—Northern Convention, include only those colored organizations and members connected with white associations, while those organizations and members connected with exclusively colored associations have been transferred to the Baptists—National Convention (Colored). As a result, in the comparison with 1890 there appears a decrease in the figures for the Baptists—Northern Convention, though the total for the two conventions is not affected. It should be stated, also, that the decrease shown for the Disciples or Christians in the number of organizations and of communicants is probably due in part to incomplete returns for 1906.

STATISTICS OF DENOMINATIONS.

The following tables furnish detailed statistics for those denominations, for each of which at least 10,000 members of colored organizations were reported in 1906, the remaining 26 denominations being combined under one head as "all other bodies." Those denominations composed in part only of colored organizations are indicated by the word "part" connected with the title. The selected denominations are given in each table in the order of their rank according to the membership reported for 1906.

DENOMINATION.	COLORED[1] ORGANIZATIONS.							
	Number.		Per cent distribution.		Increase from 1890 to 1906.		Rank in number.	
	1906	1890	1906	1890	Number.	Per cent.	1906	1890
Total	36,770	23,462	100.0	100.0	13,308	56.7	....	....
Baptists—National Convention (Colored)	18,534	12,533	50.4	53.4	6,001	47.9	1	1
African Methodist Episcopal Church	6,647	2,481	18.1	10.6	4,166	167.9	2	3
Methodist Episcopal Church (part)	3,750	2,984	10.2	12.7	766	25.7	3	2
African Methodist Episcopal Zion Church	2,204	1,704	6.0	7.3	500	29.3	5	5
Colored Methodist Episcopal Church	2,381	1,759	6.5	7.5	622	35.4	4	4
Roman Catholic Church (part)	36	31	0.1	0.1	5	(2)	15	13
Colored Primitive Baptists in America[3]	801	323	2.2	1.4	478	148.0	6	7
Baptists—Northern Convention (part)	108	406	0.3	1.7	[4]298	[4]73.4	14	6
Presbyterian Church in the United States of America (part)	417	233	1.1	1.0	184	79.0	7	9
Protestant Episcopal Church (part)	198	49	0.5	0.2	149	(2)	9	12
Colored Cumberland Presbyterian Church	196	224	0.5	1.0	[4]28	[4]12.5	11	10
United American Freewill Baptists (Colored)	251	....	0.7	....	251	....	8	....
Congregationalists (part)	156	85	0.4	0.4	71	(2)	13	11
Disciples or Christians (part)[5]	170	277	0.5	1.2	[4]107	[4]38.6	12	8
Free Baptists (part)	197	5	0.5	(6)	192	(2)	10	14
All other bodies (26)	724	368	2.0	1.6	356	96.7	....	....

[1] Negroes or persons of negro descent.
[2] Percentage not shown where base is less than 100.
[3] For 1906 includes 4 organizations reported by the Primitive Baptists.
[4] Decrease.
[5] Includes Disciples of Christ and Churches of Christ.
[6] Less than one-tenth of 1 per cent.

The body reporting the greatest number of organizations for 1906 is the Baptists—National Convention (Colored), with 18,534, or 50.4 per cent of the total number of colored organizations in the country, while the African Methodist Episcopal Church is next in order with 6,647, or 18.1 per cent of the entire number. The 3 leading colored Methodist bodies taken together, with the addition of the colored organizations belonging to the Methodist Episcopal Church, report an aggregate of 14,982 colored Methodist organizations, or 40.7 per cent of the entire number of colored organizations. These 5 bodies, therefore, contain 33,516 colored organizations, or 91.2 per cent of the entire number reported.

The denomination showing the greatest absolute increase in the number of organizations from 1890 to 1906 is the Baptists—National Convention (Colored), with 6,001, the African Methodist Episcopal Church coming next, with 4,166. In the per cent of increase, however, the African Methodist Episcopal Church leads, with 167.9 per cent, while that of the Baptists—National Convention (Colored)—is 47.9 per cent. The decrease shown in the table in the number of colored organizations connected with the Baptists—Northern Convention—and with the Disciples or Christians is due to the reasons already stated. It will be seen from the table that while the rank of the different denominations in 1906 differs considerably from that in 1890, the relative position of the 5 principal bodies is the same for the two years, except that the Methodist Episcopal Church (part), which was second in 1890 in the number of colored organizations, changed places in 1906 with the African Methodist Episcopal Church, which was third in 1890.

COLORED[1] ORGANIZATIONS—COMMUNICANTS OR MEMBERS.

DENOMINATION.	Organizations reporting communicants or members: 1906.		Number of communicants or members reported.		Per cent distribution.		Increase from 1890 to 1906.		Rank in 1906.			Average per organization reporting.
	Number.	Per cent.	1906	1890	1906	1890	Number.	Per cent.	Number.	Increase. Number.	Increase. Per cent.	
Total	36,563	99.4	3,685,097	2,673,977	100.0	100.0	1,011,120	37.8	......	......	......	
Baptists—National Convention (Colored)	18,492	99.8	2,261,607	1,348,989	61.4	50.4	912,618	67.7	1	1	7	[illegible]
African Methodist Episcopal Church	6,608	99.4	494,777	452,725	13.4	16.9	42,052	9.3	2	4	11	[illegible]
Methodist Episcopal Church (part)	3,682	98.2	308,551	246,249	8.4	9.2	62,302	25.3	3	2	10	84
African Methodist Episcopal Zion Church	2,197	99.7	184,542	349,788	5.0	13.1	[2] 165,246	[2] 47.2	4	15	14	84
Colored Methodist Episcopal Church	2,365	99.3	172,996	129,383	4.7	4.8	43,613	33.7	5	3	9	73
Roman Catholic Church (part)	36	100.0	38,235	14,517	1.0	0.5	23,718	163.4	6	5	3	1,062
Colored Primitive Baptists in America[3]	791	98.8	35,178	18,162	1.0	0.7	17,016	93.7	7	6	4	44
Baptists—Northern Convention (part)	108	100.0	32,639	35,221	0.9	1.3	[2] 2,582	[2] 7.3	8	13	12	302
Presbyterian Church in the United States of America (part)	417	100.0	27,799	14,961	0.8	0.6	12,838	85.8	9	9	5	
Protestant Episcopal Church (part)	193	97.5	19,098	2,977	0.5	0.1	16,121	541.5	10	7	2	
Colored Cumberland Presbyterian Church	196	100.0	18,066	12,956	0.5	0.5	5,110	39.4	11	11	8	67
United American Freewill Baptists (Colored)	247	98.4	14,489	......	0.4	......	14,489	......	12	8	......	[illegible]
Congregationalists (part)	156	100.0	11,960	6,908	0.3	0.3	5,052	73.1	13	12	6	
Disciples or Christians (part)[4]	170	100.0	11,233	18,578	0.3	0.7	[2] 7,345	[2] 39.5	14	14	13	
Free Baptists (part)	195	99.0	10,876	271	0.3	(5)	10,605	3,913.3	15	10	1	77
All other bodies (26)	710	98.1	43,061	22,292	1.2	0.8	20,759	93.1	......	......	......	[illegible]

[1] Negroes or persons of negro descent.
[2] Decrease.
[3] For 1906 includes 4 organizations, having 102 members, reported by the Primitive Baptists.
[4] Includes Disciples of Christ and Churches of Christ.
[5] Less than one-tenth of 1 per cent.

The body reporting the greatest number of communicants or members for 1906 is the Baptists—National Convention (Colored), with 2,261,607, or 61.4 per cent of the entire membership of colored organizations, while the denominations next in order are the African Methodist Episcopal Church, 494,777, or 13.4 per cent of the total; Methodist Episcopal Church (part), 308,551, or 8.4 per cent; African Methodist Episcopal Zion Church, 184,542, or 5 per cent; and the Colored Methodist Episcopal Church, 172,996, or 4.7 per cent. The 3 leading colored Methodist bodies, with the addition of the colored organizations belonging to the Methodist Episcopal Church, report a total of 1,160,866 members, or 31.5 per cent of the entire membership of colored organizations; and with the further addition of the Baptists—National Convention (Colored), a total of 3,422,473 members, or 92.9 per cent of the entire membership of colored organizations.

The denomination showing the greatest absolute increase in the number of communicants from 1890 to 1906 is the Baptists—National Convention (Colored), with 912,618; followed by the Methodist Episcopal Church (part), with 62,302, and the African Methodist Episcopal Church with 42,052. In the per cent of increase, however, the Free Baptists (part) lead with 3,913.3 per cent, the report for this body with respect to communicants in colored organizations in 1890 having apparently been incomplete. Next in order are the Protestant Episcopal Church (part), with 541.5 per cent, and the Roman Catholic Church (part), with 163.4 per cent.

In respect to the average number of members per organization, as shown by the table, the Roman Catholic Church (part), leads with 1,062, this being in keeping with the usual large average shown by this body. It is followed by the Baptists—Northern Convention (part), with 302; and the Baptists—National Convention (Colored), with 122.

DENOMINATION.	COLORED[1] ORGANIZATIONS—COMMUNICANTS OR MEMBERS: 1906.								
	Organizations reporting sex.		Communicants or members.						
			Total number.	Reported by sex.					
				Total.		Male.		Female.	
	Number.	Per cent of total.		Number.	Per cent.	Number.	Per cent.	Number.	Per cent.
Total	34,648	94.2	3,685,097	3,527,660	95.7	1,324,123	37.5	2,203,537	62.5
Baptists—National Convention (Colored)	18,034	97.3	2,261,607	2,201,549	97.3	822,162	37.3	1,379,387	62.7
African Methodist Episcopal Church	6,486	97.6	494,777	481,997	97.4	177,837	36.9	304,160	63.1
Methodist Episcopal Church (part)	3,183	84.9	308,551	271,821	88.1	102,740	37.8	169,081	62.2
African Methodist Episcopal Zion Church	2,156	97.8	184,542	180,501	97.8	67,095	37.2	113,406	62.8
Colored Methodist Episcopal Church	2,309	97.0	172,996	169,252	97.8	64,988	38.4	104,264	61.6
Roman Catholic Church (part)	33	(2)	38,235	35,430	92.7	16,838	47.5	18,592	52.5
Colored Primitive Baptists in America [3]	329	41.1	35,178	17,881	50.8	6,386	35.7	11,495	64.3
Baptists—Northern Convention (part)	98	90.7	32,639	29,802	91.3	10,694	35.9	19,108	64.1
Presbyterian Church in the United States of America (part)	356	85.4	27,790	23,898	86.0	8,935	37.4	14,963	62.6
Protestant Episcopal Church (part)	151	76.3	19,098	15,487	81.1	5,446	35.2	10,041	64.8
Colored Cumberland Presbyterian Church	196	100.0	18,066	18,066	100.0	8,405	46.5	9,661	53.5
United American Freewill Baptists (Colored)	135	53.8	14,489	7,835	54.1	3,438	43.9	4,397	56.1
Congregationalists (part)	155	99.4	11,960	11,952	99.9	4,613	38.6	7,339	61.4
Disciples or Christians (part) [4]	168	98.8	11,233	11,179	99.5	4,414	39.5	6,765	60.5
Free Baptists (part)	175	88.8	10,876	8,951	82.3	3,397	38.0	5,554	62.0
All other bodies (26)	684	94.5	43,051	42,059	97.7	16,734	39.8	25,325	60.2

[1] Negroes or persons of negro descent.
[2] Percentage not shown where base is less than 100.
[3] Includes 4 organizations having 102 members—45 males and 57 females—reported by the Primitive Baptists.
[4] Includes Disciples of Christ and Churches of Christ.

From the foregoing table it appears that 34,648 organizations, or 94.2 per cent of the total number, made report as to the sex of communicants; that the number of communicants thus reported was 3,527,660, or 95.7 per cent of the total, and that of this number, 1,324,123, or 37.5 per cent, were males and 2,203,537, or 62.5 per cent, were females. The denominations showing the largest proportion of males are the Roman Catholic Church (part), 47.5 per cent; the Colored Cumberland Presbyterian Church, 46.5 per cent; and the United American Freewill Baptists (Colored), 43.9 per cent. The denominations showing the smallest proportion of males are the Protestant Episcopal Church (part), 35.2 per cent; the Colored Primitive Baptists in America, 35.7 per cent; and the Baptists—Northern Convention (part), 35.9 per cent.

Comparing the colored bodies with the corresponding white bodies, it appears that in almost every instance the colored bodies show a slightly lower percentage of males. Thus the per cent of males for the Methodist bodies as a whole is 38.5; of the African Methodist bodies, 37.3; of the Methodist Episcopal Church, 37.4; of the colored organizations in that body, 37.8; of the Baptists—Northern Convention, 36.5; of the colored organizations, 35.9; of the Protestant Episcopal Church, 35.5; of the colored organizations, 35.2; of the Roman Catholic Church, 49.3; of the colored organizations, 47.5. In 2 bodies reporting both white and colored organizations, the Congregationalists and Presbyterian Church in the United States of America, the reverse is true, the percentage of males for the Congregationalists being 34.1, for the colored organizations, 38.6; of the Presbyterian Church in the United States of America, 36.5; of the colored organizations, 37.4.

As shown by the next table, places of worship, either church edifices or halls, etc., were reported by all but 2.7 per cent of the total number of colored organizations. Of the 35,160 church edifices reported for 1906, the Baptists—National Convention (Colored) are credited with 17,913, or 50.9 per cent; the African Methodist Episcopal Church, with 18.6 per cent; the Methodist Episcopal Church (part), with 10.4 per cent; the Colored Methodist Episcopal Church, with 6.6 per cent; and the African Methodist Episcopal Zion Church, with 6.1 per cent, the per cent distribution for the various bodies corresponding very closely to that for 1890. As compared with 1890, the table shows an increase in the number of church edifices of 11,390, or 47.9 per cent. The denominations showing the greatest absolute increase are the Baptists—National Convention (Colored), with 5,926, and the African Methodist Episcopal Church, with 2,414. Of the denominations reporting more than 100 church edifices in 1890, the Presbyterian Church in the United States of America shows the highest per cent of increase in the number of church edifices for colored organizations, 91.5 per cent. The total number of halls, etc., reported for 1906 was 1,261 as against 1,358 for 1890. Of these the Baptists—National Convention (Colored), are credited with 40.3 per cent, as compared with 48.8 per cent in 1890, and the African Methodist Episcopal Church, with 21.3 per cent, as compared with 2.3 per cent in 1890.

COLORED[1] ORGANIZATIONS—PLACES OF WORSHIP.

DENOMINATION.	Organizations reporting places of worship: 1906.		Organizations reporting church edifices: 1906.	Church edifices reported.						Organizations reporting halls, etc.: 1906.			
				Number.		Per cent distribution.		Increase from 1890 to 1906.		Number.		Per cent distribution.	
	Number.	Per cent of total.		1906	1890	1906	1890	Number.	Per cent.	1906	1890	1906	1890
Total	35,767	97.3	34,506	35,160	23,770	100.0	100.0	11,390	47.9	1,261	1,358	100.0	100.0
Baptists—National Convention (Colored)	18,340	99.0	17,832	17,913	11,987	50.9	50.4	5,926	49.4	508	663	40.3	48.8
African Methodist Episcopal Church	6,560	98.7	6,292	6,538	4,124	18.6	17.3	2,414	58.5	268	31	21.3	2.3
Methodist Episcopal Church (part)	3,631	96.8	3,556	3,672	2,800	10.4	11.8	872	31.1	75	165	5.9	12.2
African Methodist Episcopal Zion Church	2,157	97.9	2,079	2,131	1,587	6.1	6.7	544	34.3	78	114	6.2	8.4
Colored Methodist Episcopal Church	2,330	97.9	2,252	2,327	1,653	6.6	7.0	674	40.8	78	64	6.2	4.7
Roman Catholic Church (part)	36	100.0	34	36	27	0.1	0.1	9	(2)	2	3	0.2	0.2
Colored Primitive Baptists in America[3]	545	68.0	501	505	291	1.4	1.2	214	73.5	44	33	3.5	2.4
Baptists—Northern Convention (part)	105	97.2	99	106	324	0.3	1.4	[4]218	[4]67.3	6	72	0.5	5.3
Presbyterian Church in the United States of America (part)	380	91.1	363	383	200	1.1	0.8	183	91.5	17	21	1.3	1.5
Protestant Episcopal Church (part)	161	81.3	150	171	53	0.5	0.2	118	(2)	11	2	0.9	0.1
Colored Cumberland Presbyterian Church	196	100.0	195	195	183	0.6	0.8	12	6.6	1	34	0.1	2.5
United American Freewill Baptists (Colored)	157	62.5	149	152	......	0.4	......	152	......	8	......	0.6	......
Congregationalists (part)	147	94.2	133	137	69	0.4	0.3	68	(2)	14	11	1.1	0.8
Disciples or Christians (part)[5]	161	94.7	137	140	183	0.4	0.8	[4]43	[4]23.5	24	75	1.9	5.5
Free Baptists (part)	178	90.4	173	173	3	0.5	(6)	170	(2)	5	2	0.4	0.1
All other bodies (26)	683	94.3	561	581	286	1.7	1.2	295	103.1	122	68	9.7	5.0

[1] Negroes or persons of negro descent.
[2] Percentage not shown where base is less than 100.
[3] For 1906 includes 4 organizations, having 4 church edifices, reported by the Primitive Baptists.
[4] Decrease.
[5] Includes Disciples of Christ and Churches of Christ.
[6] Less than one-tenth of 1 per cent.

The next table shows that 33,091 colored organizations, or 95.9 per cent of the total number reporting church edifices, reported a seating capacity of 10,481,738. Of this number the Baptists—National Convention (Colored) reported 53.5 per cent; the African Methodist Episcopal Church, 17.5 per cent; the Methodist Episcopal Church (part), 8.6 per cent; the Colored Methodist Episcopal Church, 7.2 per cent; and the African Methodist Episcopal Zion Church, 6.6 per cent—these 5 bodies showing 93.4 per cent of the entire seating capacity reported by colored organizations.

COLORED[1] ORGANIZATIONS—SEATING CAPACITY OF CHURCH EDIFICES.

DENOMINATION.	Organizations reporting seating capacity of church edifices: 1906.		Seating capacity of church edifices reported.						Average per organization reporting.
			Amount.		Per cent distribution.		Increase from 1890 to 1906.		
	Number.	Per cent of total reporting church edifices.	1906	1890	1906	1890	Amount.	Per cent.	
Total	33,091	95.9	10,481,738	6,800,035	100.0	100.0	3,681,703	54.1	317
Baptists—National Convention (Colored)	17,316	97.1	5,610,301	3,440,970	53.5	50.6	2,169,331	63.0	324
African Methodist Episcopal Church	6,178	98.2	1,832,600	1,160,838	17.5	17.1	671,762	57.9	297
Methodist Episcopal Church (part)	3,094	87.0	901,812	635,252	8.6	9.3	266,560	42.0	291
African Methodist Episcopal Zion Church	2,048	98.5	690,951	565,577	6.6	8.3	125,374	22.2	337
Colored Methodist Episcopal Church	2,214	98.3	758,328	541,464	7.2	8.0	216,864	40.1	343
Roman Catholic Church (part)	32	(2)	12,640	8,370	0.1	0.1	4,270	51.0	395
Colored Primitive Baptists in America[3]	322	64.3	95,423	96,699	0.9	1.4	[4]1,276	[4]1.3	296
Baptists—Northern Convention (part)	94	(2)	41,860	92,660	0.4	1.4	[4]50,800	[4]54.8	445
Presbyterian Church in the United States of America (part)	360	99.2	113,701	56,280	1.1	0.8	57,421	102.0	316
Protestant Episcopal Church (part)	148	98.7	42,700	11,885	0.4	0.2	30,815	259.3	289
Colored Cumberland Presbyterian Church	191	97.9	71,165	52,139	0.7	0.8	19,026	36.5	373
United American Freewill Baptists (Colored)	137	91.9	39,825	....	0.4	....	39,825	....	291
Congregationalists (part)	130	97.7	39,500	19,360	0.4	0.3	20,140	104.0	304
Disciples or Christians (part)[5]	133	97.1	34,320	41,590	0.3	0.6	[4]7,270	[4]17.5	258
Free Baptists (part)	165	95.4	43,850	800	0.4	(6)	43,050	5,381.3	266
All other bodies (26)	529	94.3	152,762	76,151	1.5	1.1	76,611	100.6	289

[1] Negroes or persons of negro descent.
[2] Percentage not shown where base is less than 100.
[3] For 1906 includes 4 organizations having 4 church edifices with seating capacity of 1,200, reported by the Primitive Baptists.
[4] Decrease.
[5] Includes Disciples of Christ and Churches of Christ.
[6] Less than one-tenth of 1 per cent.

The per cent distribution for the several denominations, as shown by the table, does not vary much from that for 1890. The increase in seating capacity from 1890 to 1906, according to the table, was 3,681,703, or 54.1 per cent. The denominations showing the greatest absolute increase are the Baptists—National Convention (Colored), 2,169,331, and the African Methodist Episcopal Church, 671,762. In per cent of increase, however, the Free Baptists (part), lead with 5,381.3 per cent, this large increase being due apparently, as previously stated, to incomplete returns in 1890. Next comes the Protestant Episcopal Church (part), with 259.3 per cent.

The average seating capacity per organization reporting, as shown by the table, is 317, ranging from 445 for the Baptists—Northern Convention (part), to 258 for the Disciples or Christians (part).

COLORED[1] ORGANIZATIONS—VALUE OF CHURCH PROPERTY.

DENOMINATION.	Organizations reporting value of church property: 1906.		Value of church property reported.							Average per organization reporting.	
			Amount.		Per cent distribution.		Increase from 1890 to 1906.		Rank in 1906.		
	Number.	Per cent of total.	1906	1890	1906	1890	Amount.	Per cent.		Amount.	Rank.
Total	34,660	94.3	$56,636,159	$26,626,448	100.0	100.0	$30,009,711	112.7	....	$1,634	....
Baptists—National Convention (Colored)	17,890	96.5	24,437,272	9,038,549	43.1	33.9	15,398,723	170.4	1	1,366	9
African Methodist Episcopal Church	6,299	94.8	11,303,489	6,468,280	20.0	24.3	4,835,209	74.8	2	1,794	7
Methodist Episcopal Church (part)	3,585	95.6	6,104,379	3,630,093	10.8	13.6	2,474,286	68.2	3	1,703	8
African Methodist Episcopal Zion Church	2,104	95.5	4,833,207	2,714,128	8.5	10.2	2,119,079	78.1	4	2,297	5
Colored Methodist Episcopal Church	2,264	95.1	3,017,849	1,713,366	5.3	6.4	1,304,483	76.1	5	1,333	10
Roman Catholic Church (part)	32	(2)	678,480	237,400	1.2	0.9	441,080	185.8	9	21,203	1
Colored Primitive Baptists in America[3]	512	63.9	298,839	135,427	0.5	0.5	163,412	120.7	11	584	14
Baptists—Northern Convention (part)	97	89.8	1,561,326	1,087,518	2.8	4.1	473,808	43.6	7	16,096	2
Presbyterian Church in the United States of America (part)	365	87.5	752,387	391,650	1.3	1.5	360,737	92.1	8	2,061	6
Protestant Episcopal Church (part)	159	80.3	1,773,279	192,750	3.1	0.7	1,580,529	820.0	6	11,153	3
Colored Cumberland Presbyterian Church	192	98.0	203,778	195,826	0.4	0.7	7,952	4.1	12	1,061	13
United American Freewill Baptists (Colored)	151	60.2	79,278	....	0.1	....	79,278	....	15	525	15
Congregationalists (part)	137	87.8	459,497	246,125	0.8	0.9	213,372	86.7	10	3,354	4
Disciples or Christians (part)[4]	141	82.9	185,215	176,795	0.3	0.7	8,420	4.8	14	1,314	11
Free Baptists (part)	173	87.8	186,130	13,300	0.3	(5)	172,830	1,299.5	13	1,076	12
All other bodies (26)	559	77.2	761,754	385,241	1.3	1.4	376,513	97.7	....	1,363	....

[1] Negroes or persons of negro descent.
[2] Percentage not shown where base is less than 100.
[3] For 1906 includes 4 organizations having church property valued at $2,300, reported by the Primitive Baptists.
[4] Includes Disciples of Christ and Churches of Christ.
[5] Less than one-tenth of 1 per cent.

Of the total number of colored organizations, 34,660, or 94.3 per cent, reported value of church property in 1906. Of the total value reported, $56,636,159, the Baptists—National Convention (Colored) reported 43.1 per cent; the African Methodist Episcopal Church, 20 per cent; the Methodist Episcopal Church (part), 10.8 per cent; the African Methodist Episcopal Zion Church, 8.5 per cent; and the Colored Methodist Episcopal Church, 5.3 per cent, these 5 principal bodies holding 87.7 per cent of the entire value of church property reported in 1906 by colored organizations, as compared with 88.4 per cent in 1890. If the Baptists—Northern Convention (part), and the Protestant Episcopal Church (part), are added to these 5 bodies, the 7 bodies represent 93.6 per cent of the value of church property reported in 1906 as compared with 93.2 per cent for the same bodies in 1890. The increase in value from 1890 to 1906, as shown by the table, is $30,009,711, or 112.7 per cent. In absolute increase, the Baptists—National Convention (Colored) rank first; the African Methodist Episcopal Church, second; the Methodist Episcopal Church (part), third; the African Methodist Episcopal Zion Church, fourth; the Protestant Episcopal Church (part), fifth; and the Colored Methodist Episcopal Church, sixth. In per cent of increase, however, the Free Baptists (part) come first, with the Protestant Episcopal Church (part), second. In the average value of church property per organization reporting, as shown by the table, the Roman Catholic Church ranks first, with $21,203; and is followed by the Baptists—Northern Convention (part), with $16,096; and the Protestant Episcopal Church (part), with $11,153. The denomination showing the lowest average value is the United American Freewill Baptists (Colored), with $525, and the one showing the next lowest average, the Colored Primitive Baptists in America, with $584.

DENOMINATION.	COLORED[1] ORGANIZATIONS—DEBT ON CHURCH PROPERTY: 1906.				
	Organizations reporting debt on church property.		Debt reported.		
	Number.	Per cent of organizations reporting value of church property.	Amount.	Per cent of value of church property.	Average per organization reporting.
Total	9,003	26 0	$5,005,905	8.8	$556
Baptists—National Convention (Colored)	3,100	17.3	1,757,190	7.2	567
African Methodist Episcopal Church	2,574	40 9	1,191,921	10.5	463
Methodist Episcopal Church (part)	1,372	38.3	611,166	10.0	445
African Methodist Episcopal Zion Church	724	34.4	474,209	9.8	655
Colored Methodist Episcopal Church	692	30.6	215,111	7.1	311
Roman Catholic Church (part)	8	(2)	75,650	11.1	9,456
Colored Primitive Baptists in America[3]	34	6.6	6,968	2.3	205
Baptists—Northern Convention (part)	55	(2)	356,993	22.9	6,491
Presbyterian Church in the United States of America (part)	59	16.2	39,208	5.2	665
Protestant Episcopal Church (part)	28	17.6	113,246	6.4	4,045
Colored Cumberland Presbyterian Church	18	9.4	10,407	5.1	578
United American Freewill Baptists (Colored)	22	14.6	3,485	4.4	158
Congregationalists (part)	32	23.4	32,106	7.0	1,003
Disciples or Christians (part)[4]	36	25.5	18,029	9.7	501
Free Baptists (part)	43	24.9	16,227	8.7	377
All other bodies (26)	206	36.9	83,929	11.0	407

[1] Negroes or persons of negro descent.
[2] Percentage not shown where base is less than 100.
[3] Includes 4 organizations, having no debt on church property, reported by the Primitive Baptists.
[4] Includes Disciples of Christ and Churches of Christ.

Of the 34,660 colored organizations reporting value of church property, 9,003, or 26 per cent, reported debt on church property. In the case of the African Methodist Episcopal Church, 40.9 per cent of the organizations reporting property also report debt; and of the Methodist Episcopal Church (part), 38.3 per cent. In the case of the Baptists—Northern Convention (part), for which, however, only 97 organizations reported the value of church property, practically 4 out of 7 report debt. The denomination showing the lowest percentage is the Colored Primitive Baptists in America, only 6.6 per cent of the organizations which reported value of church property also reporting debt.

The total amount of debt reported, as shown by the table, is $5,005,905, or 8.8 per cent of the value of church property reported. The denominations showing the highest percentage of debt as compared with the value of property are the Baptists—Northern Convention (part), 22.9, and the Roman Catholic Church, 11.1; while the denomination showing the lowest percentage is the Colored Primitive Baptists in America, 2.3 per cent. The average for each organization reporting debt is $556. The denominations showing the highest average per organization are the Roman Catholic Church, $9,456; the Baptists—Northern Convention (part), $6,491; and the Protestant Episcopal Church (part), $4,045. The denominations showing the lowest are the United American Freewill Baptists (Colored), $158, and the Colored Primitive Baptists in America, $205. By comparison with the previous table it will be seen that the 5 bodies named rank the same in respect to average debt as in respect to average value of church property reported.

DENOMINATION.	COLORED[1] ORGANIZATIONS—PARSONAGES: 1906.			
	Organizations reporting parsonages.		Value of parsonages reported.	
	Number.	Per cent of total.	Total.	Average per organization reporting.
Total	4,779	13.0	$3,727,884	$780
Baptists—National Convention (Colored)	709	3.8	617,241	871
African Methodist Episcopal Church	1,783	26.8	1,255,246	704
Methodist Episcopal Church (part)	1,206	32.2	777,715	645
African Methodist Episcopal Zion Church	348	15.8	350,690	1,008
Colored Methodist Episcopal Church	421	17.7	237,547	564
Roman Catholic Church (part)	22	(2)	109,400	4,973
Colored Primitive Baptists in America[3]	21	2.6	10,095	481
Baptists—Northern Convention (part)	17	15.7	35,500	2,088
Presbyterian Church in the United States of America (part)	75	18.0	66,430	886
Protestant Episcopal Church (part)	58	29.3	164,950	2,844
Colored Cumberland Presbyterian Church	8	4.1	5,825	728
United American Freewill Baptists (Colored)	6	2.4	1,475	246
Congregationalists (part)	36	23.1	46,125	1,281
Disciples or Christians (part)[4]	4	2.4	1,950	488
Free Baptists (part)	13	6.6	13,100	1,008
All other bodies (26)	52	7.2	34,595	665

[1] Negroes or persons of negro descent.
[2] Percentage not shown where base is less than 100.
[3] Includes 4 organizations having no parsonages, reported by the Primitive Baptists.
[4] Includes Disciples of Christ and Churches of Christ.

The table shows that of the 36,770 colored organizations, 4,779, or 13 per cent, reported parsonages. The denomination showing the highest proportion of parsonages as compared with church organizations is the Roman Catholic Church (part). Of the 36 colored organizations reported by this body, 22, or nearly two-thirds, owned parsonages. Of the total number of colored organizations reported by the Methodist Episcopal Church (part), 1,206, or 32.2 per cent, reported parsonages. For the Protestant Episcopal Church (part), the percentage is 29.3; for the African Methodist Episcopal Church, 26.8; and for the Congregationalists (part), 23.1. The denominations showing the lowest percentages are the United American Freewill Baptists (Colored), and the Disciples or Christians, with 2.4 each. The total value of parsonages reported, as shown by the table, is $3,727,884. Of this amount, the African Methodist Episcopal Church reported $1,255,246, or a little more than one-third, while the next in order are the Methodist Episcopal Church (part); Baptists—National Convention (Colored); African Methodist Episcopal Zion Church; and Colored Methodist Episcopal Church, these 5 bodies together reporting $3,238,430, or 86.9 per cent of the total value of parsonages reported. The average value for each organization reporting is $780. The denominations showing the highest average per organization reporting are the Roman Catholic Church (part), $4,973; the Protestant Episcopal Church (part), $2,844; Baptists—Northern Convention (part), $2,088; and Congregationalists (part), $1,281. The denominations showing the lowest are the United American Freewill Baptists (Colored), $246; the Colored Primitive Baptists in America, $481; and the Disciples or Christians (part), $488.

DENOMINATION.	COLORED[1] ORGANIZATIONS—SUNDAY SCHOOLS CONDUCTED BY CHURCH ORGANIZATIONS: 1906.							
	Organizations reporting Sunday schools.		Sunday schools reported.		Sunday school officers and teachers.		Sunday school scholars.	
	Number.	Per cent of total.	Number.	Per cent distribution.	Number.	Per cent distribution.	Number.	Per cent distribution.
Total	33,538	91.2	34,681	100.0	210,148	100.0	1,740,099	100.0
Baptists—National Convention (Colored)	17,478	94.3	17,910	51.6	100,069	47.6	924,665	53.1
African Methodist Episcopal Church	6,056	91.1	6,285	18.1	41,941	20.0	292,689	16.8
Methodist Episcopal Church (part)	3,522	93.9	3,745	10.8	26,044	12.4	204,810	11.8
African Methodist Episcopal Zion Church	2,060	98.5	2,092	6.0	16,245	7.7	107,692	6.2
Colored Methodist Episcopal Church	2,207	92.7	2,328	6.7	12,375	5.9	92,457	5.3
Roman Catholic Church (part)	30	(2)	33	0.1	220	0.1	3,151	0.2
Colored Primitive Baptists in America[3]	166	20.7	166	0.5	911	0.4	6,224	0.4
Baptists—Northern Convention (part)	102	94.4	106	0.3	1,382	0.7	12,827	0.7
Presbyterian Church in the United States of America (part)	405	97.1	433	1.2	2,791	1.3	24,904	1.4
Protestant Episcopal Church (part)	180	90.9	188	0.5	1,189	0.6	13,779	0.8
Colored Cumberland Presbyterian Church	192	98.0	192	0.6	933	0.4	6,962	0.4
United American Freewill Baptists (Colored)	100	39.8	100	0.3	382	0.2	3,307	0.2
Congregationalists (part)	150	96.2	174	0.5	1,056	0.5	10,339	0.6
Disciples or Christians (part)[4]	134	78.8	141	0.4	712	0.3	4,916	0.3
Free Baptists (part)	168	85.3	177	0.5	868	0.4	5,732	0.3
All other bodies (26)	588	81.2	611	1.8	3,030	1.4	25,655	1.5

[1] Negroes or persons of negro descent.
[2] Percentage not shown where base is less than 100.
[3] Includes 4 organizations making no returns for Sunday schools, reported by the Primitive Baptists.
[4] Includes Disciples of Christ and Churches of Christ.

The table shows that of the total colored organizations, 33,538, or 91.2 per cent, reported Sunday schools. The denominations showing the highest percentages of Sunday schools, as compared with the total number of organizations, are the Colored Cumberland Presbyterian Church, with 98 per cent, and the Presbyterian Church in the United States of America, with 97.1 per cent. The denominations showing the lowest percentages, as compared with the total number of organizations, are the Colored Primitive Baptists in America, with 20.7 per cent, and the United American Freewill Baptists (Colored), with 39.8 per cent, the low percentage shown for these 2 bodies probably being due in part to incomplete returns.

The total number of Sunday schools reported is 34,681. Of these, the Baptists—National Convention (Colored) reported 51.6 per cent, a little more than one-half; the African Methodist Episcopal Church, 18.1 per cent; the Methodist Episcopal Church (part), 10.8 per cent; the Colored Methodist Episcopal Church, 6.7 per cent; and the African Methodist Episcopal Zion Church, 6 per cent, these 5 bodies reporting 32,360 Sunday schools, or 93.3 per cent of the total number reported by colored organizations.

The total number of Sunday school officers and teachers reported was 210,148. Of these the Baptists—National Convention (Colored) reported nearly one-half; the African Methodist Episcopal Church, 20 per cent; the Methodist Episcopal Church (part), 12.4 per cent; the African Methodist Episcopal Zion Church, 7.7 per cent; and the Colored Methodist Episcopal Church, 5.9 per cent, these 5 bodies reporting 196,674 Sunday school officers and teachers, or 93.6 per cent of the entire number reported by colored organizations.

The total number of Sunday school scholars reported by colored organizations is 1,740,099. Of these, the

Baptists—National Convention (Colored) reported 924,665, or a little more than one-half; the African Methodist Episcopal Church, 16.8 per cent; the Methodist Episcopal Church (part), 11.8 per cent; the African Methodist Episcopal Zion Church, 6.2 per cent; and the Colored Methodist Episcopal Church, 5.3 per cent, these 5 bodies reporting 1,622,313 Sunday school scholars, or 93.2 per cent of the entire number reported by colored organizations.

DISTRIBUTION OF COMMUNICANTS OR MEMBERS BY STATES AND TERRITORIES.

The statistics of colored organizations for 1906, for all denominations, are given by states and territories in Table 12 (page 540). The following table shows this distribution for communicants or members alone for 1890 and 1906, and the relative position of each state at the two periods:

STATE OR TERRITORY.	COLORED[1] ORGANIZATIONS—COMMUNICANTS OR MEMBERS.			
	1906		1890	
	Number.	Rank.	Number.	Rank.
Total[2]	3,685,097	....	2,673,977	....
Georgia	507,005	1	341,433	1
Alabama	397,178	2	297,161	3
South Carolina	394,149	3	317,020	2
Mississippi	358,708	4	224,404	6
Virginia	307,374	5	238,617	5
North Carolina	283,707	6	290,755	4
Texas	227,032	7	186,038	7
Louisiana	185,918	8	108,872	9
Tennessee	172,867	9	131,015	8
Arkansas	146,319	10	106,445	10
Kentucky	116,918	11	92,768	11
Florida	105,678	12	64,337	12
Maryland	71,797	13	58,566	13
Pennsylvania	60,161	14	26,753	15
Missouri	50,074	15	42,452	14
District of Columbia	46,249	16	22,965	16
Ohio	33,667	17	19,827	17
Illinois	32,058	18	15,635	19
New York	30,482	19	17,216	18
Oklahoma[3]	29,115	20	880	33
New Jersey	28,015	21	12,720	21
Indiana	23,133	22	13,404	20
Kansas	17,273	23	9,750	22
West Virginia	14,949	24	7,160	23
Delaware	10,583	25	6,595	24
Massachusetts	9,402	26	3,638	27
California	4,564	27	3,720	26
Connecticut	4,492	28	1,624	30
Iowa	4,108	29	2,643	28
Michigan	3,235	30	3,957	25
Colorado	2,507	31	1,171	31
Rhode Island	2,114	32	1,999	29
Minnesota	1,453	33	958	32
Nebraska	1,007	34	399	34
Washington	614	35	66	39
Wisconsin	310	36	268	36
New Mexico	221	37	62	40
Arizona	208	38	155	37
Oregon	160	39	291	35
Montana	135	40	32	42
Wyoming	45	41	154	38
South Dakota	38	42	....	....
Utah	30	43	7	43
Maine	25	44	45	41
New Hampshire	20	45	....	....

[1] Negroes or persons of negro descent.
[2] Idaho, Nevada, North Dakota, and Vermont had no colored organizations in 1906 or 1890.
[3] Oklahoma and Indian Territory combined.

From the number of communicants given in this table, it appears that 1 state reports a membership of over 500,000; 4 report a membership of from 300,000 to 400,000; and 7, a membership of from 100,000 to 300,000. These 12 states report a total colored membership in 1906 of 3,202,853, or 86.9 per cent of the entire membership of colored organizations. The same states reported a membership in 1890 of 2,398,865, or 89.7 per cent of the entire membership of colored organizations at that time. The relative position of the different states varied somewhat at the two censuses. Georgia was the leading state at each census, while 5 others of the 12 states—Arkansas, Florida, Kentucky, Texas, and Virginia—held the same relative position in 1906 as in 1890. On the other hand, South Carolina, which was second in 1890, changed places in 1906 with Alabama, which was third in 1890, while North Carolina changed places with Mississippi, and Louisiana with Tennessee.

In addition to the 12 states already named, Delaware, Maryland, West Virginia, and the District of Columbia, in the South Atlantic division, and Oklahoma, in the South Central division, reported a comparatively large colored membership. These 2 geographic divisions, the South Atlantic and South Central (see Table 12), reported in 1906 a total membership for colored organizations of 3,375,546, and in 1890 the same states reported a corresponding membership of 2,495,031, or somewhat more than nine-tenths—91.6 and 93.3 per cent, respectively—of the total colored membership reported for continental United States at each census.

Outside of the South Atlantic and South Central divisions, the states reporting in 1906 the largest membership for colored organizations are, Pennsylvania, 60,161; Missouri, 50,074; Ohio, 33,667; Illinois, 32,058; and New York, 30,482. Ohio held the same relative position in 1906 as in 1890, while Pennsylvania changed places with Missouri, and Illinois with New York. Of all the states and territories, Oklahoma shows the highest percentage of increase in members of colored organizations, namely, 3,208.5 per cent. Five states—North Carolina, Michigan, Oregon, Wyoming, and Maine—report a smaller number of members in 1906 than in 1890. The decrease shown for North Carolina is due largely to the decrease in the number of members reported for the African Methodist Episcopal Zion Church, which is especially strong in North Carolina. The states reporting no members of colored organizations either in 1890 or 1906 are Idaho, Nevada, North Dakota, and Vermont.

COLORED MINISTERS.

The number of ordained colored ministers connected with denominations made up wholly of colored organizations, as reported for 1890 and 1906, is given in detail by denominations in Table 8 (page 514). The table following shows for each of these denominations the number of ministers and the number of organizations reported in 1906.

DENOMINATION.	Colored[1] organizations in 1906.	Colored ministers in 1906.
Total number	31,393	31,624
Baptists—National Convention (Colored)	18,534	17,117
African Methodist Episcopal Church	6,647	6,200
African Methodist Episcopal Zion Church	2,204	3,082
Colored Methodist Episcopal Church	2,381	2,671
Colored Primitive Baptists in America	797	1,480
Colored Cumberland Presbyterian Church	196	375
United American Freewill Baptists (Colored)	251	136
Other bodies:		
Church of God and Saints of Christ (Colored)	48	75
Churches of the Living God (Colored)—3 bodies	68	101
Voluntary Missionary Society in America (Colored)	3	11
Free Christian Zion Church of Christ (Colored)	15	20
Union American Methodist Episcopal Church (Colored)	77	64
African Union Methodist Protestant Church	69	187
Reformed Zion Union Apostolic Church (Colored)	45	33
Reformed Methodist Union Episcopal Church (Colored)	58	72

[1] Negroes or persons of negro descent.

The table shows that for the denominations made up wholly of colored organizations, the total number of ministers reported for 1906 was 31,624, and the total number of organizations 31,393. Of the total number of ministers, 17,117, or 54.1 per cent, were connected with the Baptists—National Convention (Colored); 6,200, or 19.6 per cent, with the African Methodist Episcopal Church; 3,082, or 9.7 per cent, with the African Methodist Episcopal Zion Church; 2,671, or 8.4 per cent, with the Colored Methodist Episcopal Church; and 1,480, or 4.7 per cent, with the Colored Primitive Baptists in America, these 5 bodies having 30,550 ministers, or 96.6 per cent of the entire number of ordained ministers reported for denominations composed wholly of colored organizations. For 3 of these bodies, namely, United American Freewill Baptists (Colored), the Church of God and Saints of Christ (Colored), and the African Methodist Episcopal Church, the number of ministers is estimated because complete information was not obtainable. The number of colored ministers connected with denominations partly made up of colored organizations is not known. Estimating it on the basis of the number of ministers per organization for each of these denominations as a whole, the number is approximately 3,600. If this number be added to the number connected with denominations composed wholly of colored organizations, an estimated total is obtained of 35,224 ministers of colored organizations in continental United States, as compared with 36,770 colored organizations belonging to the denominations in question.

GENERAL TABLES

TABLE 1.—ORGANIZATIONS, COMMUNICANTS OR MEMBERS, PLACES OF WORSHIP, VALUE OF CHURCH PROPERTY, CONTINENTAL

	DENOMINATION.	Total number of organizations.	COMMUNICANTS OR MEMBERS.				
			Number of organizations reporting.	Total number reported.	Sex.		
					Number of organizations reporting.	Male.	Female.
1	All denominations	212,230	210,418	32,936,445	193,229	12,767,466	16,849,505
2	Adventist bodies	2,551	2,537	92,735	2,374	32,088	55,221
3	Evangelical Adventists	18	18	481	17	183	270
4	Advent Christian Church	550	541	26,799	497	10,187	14,800
5	Seventh-day Adventist Denomination	1,889	1,884	62,211	1,772	20,508	38,415
6	Church of God (Adventist)	10	10	354	10	167	187
7	Churches of God (Adventist), Unattached Congregations	10	10	257	9	72	95
8	Life and Advent Union	12	12	509	12	229	280
9	Churches of God in Christ Jesus	62	62	2,124	57	742	1,174
10	Armenian Church	73	73	19,889	73	15,037	4,852
11	Bahais	24	24	1,280	24	438	842
12	Baptist bodies	54,880	54,707	5,662,234	50,962	2,065,558	3,289,327
13	Baptists	47,910	47,814	5,323,183	45,838	1,953,538	3,126,256
14	Northern Baptist Convention	8,272	8,247	1,052,105	7,652	357,749	621,383
15	Southern Baptist Convention	21,104	21,075	2,009,471	20,152	773,627	1,125,486
16	National Baptist Convention (Colored)	18,534	18,492	2,261,607	18,034	822,162	1,379,387
17	General Six Principle Baptists	16	16	685	14	251	398
18	Seventh-day Baptists	77	76	8,381	70	3,312	4,708
19	Free Baptists	1,346	1,338	81,359	1,129	26,051	43,774
20	Freewill Baptists	608	608	40,280	574	15,702	22,483
21	General Baptists	518	518	30,097	497	11,577	16,573
22	Separate Baptists	76	73	5,180	55	1,918	2,518
23	United Baptists	196	190	13,698	84	2,152	2,875
24	Duck River and Kindred Associations of Baptists (Baptist Church of Christ)	93	92	6,416	85	2,432	3,519
25	Primitive Baptists	2,922	2,878	102,311	2,138	28,581	50,033
26	Colored Primitive Baptists in America	797	787	35,076	325	6,341	11,438
27	Two-Seed-in-the-Spirit Predestinarian Baptists	55	55	781	24	173	204
28	Freewill Baptists (Bullockites)	15	15	298	14	92	151
29	United American Freewill Baptists (Colored)	251	247	14,489	135	3,438	4,397
30	Brethren (Plymouth)	403	403	10,566	402	4,390	6,161
31	Brethren (Plymouth)—I	134	134	2,933	134	1,240	1,693
32	Brethren (Plymouth)—II	128	128	4,752	128	1,981	2,771
33	Brethren (Plymouth)—III	81	81	1,724	80	692	1,017
34	Brethren (Plymouth)—IV	60	60	1,157	60	477	680
35	Brethren (River)	111	110	4,569	110	1,823	2,746
36	Brethren in Christ	74	73	3,397	73	1,341	2,056
37	Yorker, or Old Order, Brethren	9	9	423	9	154	269
38	United Zion's Children	28	28	749	28	328	421
39	Buddhists	74	12	3,165	12	2,387	778
40	Chinese Temples	62					
41	Japanese Temples	12	12	3,165	12	2,387	778
42	Catholic Apostolic Churches	24	24	4,927	24	1,914	3,013
43	Catholic Apostolic Church	11	11	2,907	11	1,117	1,790
44	New Apostolic Church	13	13	2,020	13	797	1,223
45	Christadelphians	70	70	1,412	70	626	786
46	Christian Catholic Church in Zion	17	17	5,865	17	2,330	3,535
47	Christian Israelite Church	5	5	78	5	45	33
48	Christian Union	217	216	13,905	196	5,626	7,406
49	Christians (Christian Connection)	1,379	1,354	110,117	1,221	40,740	60,022
50	Church of Christ, Scientist	638	635	85,717	604	22,736	59,596
51	Church of God and Saints of Christ (Colored)	48	48	1,823	48	550	1,273
52	Churches of God in North America, General Eldership of the	518	511	24,356	487	9,198	14,012
53	Churches of the Living God (Colored)	68	67	4,276	67	1,686	2,590
54	Church of the Living God (Christian Workers for Friendship)	44	44	2,676	44	984	1,692
55	Church of the Living God (Apostolic Church)	15	14	752	14	291	461
56	Church of Christ in God	9	9	848	9	411	437
57	Churches of the New Jerusalem	133	133	7,247	127	2,579	4,489
58	General Convention of the New Jerusalem in the United States of America	119	119	6,612	113	2,335	4,098
59	General Church of the New Jerusalem	14	14	635	14	244	391
60	Communistic societies	22	22	2,272	22	966	1,306
61	United Society of Believers (Shakers)	15	15	516	15	110	406
62	Amana Society	7	7	1,756	7	856	900
63	Congregationalists	5,713	5,700	700,480	5,666	236,968	457,615
64	Disciples or Christians	10,942	10,909	1,142,359	10,441	432,682	650,139
65	Disciples of Christ	8,293	8,260	982,701	7,799	366,681	557,017
66	Churches of Christ	2,649	2,649	159,658	2,642	66,001	93,122
67	Dunkers or German Baptist Brethren	1,097	1,090	97,144	1,060	39,928	53,676
68	German Baptist Brethren Church (Conservative)	822	815	76,547	802	32,282	43,185
69	Old Order German Baptist Brethren	68	68	3,388	68	1,900	1,488
70	The Brethren Church (Progressive Dunkers)	202	202	17,042	185	5,729	8,903
71	German Seventh-day Baptists	5	5	167	5	67	100

DEBT ON CHURCH PROPERTY, PARSONAGES, AND SUNDAY SCHOOLS, BY DENOMINATIONS (IN DETAIL), FOR UNITED STATES: 1906.

PLACES OF WORSHIP.					VALUE OF CHURCH PROPERTY.		DEBT ON CHURCH PROPERTY.		PARSONAGES.		SUNDAY SCHOOLS CONDUCTED BY CHURCH ORGANIZATIONS.				
Number of organizations reporting—		Number of church edifices reported.	Seating capacity of church edifices.		Number of organizations reporting.	Value reported.	Number of organizations reporting.	Amount of debt reported.	Number of organizations reporting.	Value of parsonages reported.	Number of organizations reporting.	Number of Sunday schools reported.	Number of officers and teachers.	Number of scholars.	
Church edifices.	Halls, etc.		Number of organizations reporting.	Seating capacity reported.											
185,040	14,791	192,795	179,954	58,536,830	186,132	$1,257,575,867	33,617	$108,050,946	54,214	$143,495,853	167,574	178,214	1,648,664	14,685,997	1
1,455	666	1,473	1,431	287,964	1,492	2,425,209	183	167,812	60	91,040	2,078	2,242	14,286	69,110	2
16	2	16	16	4,050	15	27,050			1	1,200	9	9	57	264	3
424	90	428	420	104,339	428	854,323	57	78,828	44	72,675	362	367	2,876	16,941	4
968	539	981	950	169,740	998	1,454,067	121	77,984	14	14,165	1,656	1,813	11,033	50,225	5
3	6	3	3	1,200	3	4,000	1	700			9	11	52	326	6
2	8	2	2	350	3	2,300					5	5	30	200	7
6	5	6	6	1,150	9	29,799	4	10,300			7	7	45	259	8
36	16	37	34	7,135	36	53,650			1	8,000	30	30	193	895	9
3	60	3	3	1,300	3	38,000	1	4,000	1	2,500	4	4	9	340	10
	23										1	1	7	32	11
49,088	3,250	50,092	48,042	15,702,712	49,339	139,842,656	6,199	8,323,862	4,978	9,233,631	41,165	43,178	323,473	2,898,914	12
44,098	2,759	45,035	43,353	14,239,735	44,357	133,781,179	5,872	8,145,890	4,561	8,645,944	39,195	41,165	308,592	2,790,624	13
7,729	254	8,244	7,625	2,584,801	7,795	74,620,025	1,557	5,149,678	2,581	5,535,612	7,346	8,220	102,506	851,269	14
18,537	1,997	18,878	18,412	6,044,633	18,672	34,723,882	1,215	1,239,022	1,271	2,493,091	14,371	15,035	106,017	1,014,690	15
17,832	506	17,913	17,316	5,610,301	17,890	24,437,272	3,100	1,757,190	709	617,241	17,478	17,910	100,069	924,665	16
13	1	14	13	2,870	13	19,450			1	1,500	9	9	94	414	17
69	7	71	69	19,400	68	292,250	7	1,942	39	69,440	67	68	843	5,117	18
1,090	61	1,111	1,072	275,601	1,092	2,974,130	122	138,233	318	454,226	1,059	1,089	9,170	65,101	19
554	45	556	534	158,540	554	296,585	37	3,536	8	3,400	263	263	1,440	12,720	20
376	119	380	372	117,095	382	252,019	28	6,999	6	8,900	230	240	1,520	11,658	21
60	4	60	60	19,070	59	66,980	4	380			45	45	312	1,962	22
76	22	77	64	16,745	75	36,715	2	115	1	200	21	23	168	1,360	23
86	2	86	85	27,508	87	44,221	3	107	1	156	9	9	37	402	24
1,974	176	2,003	1,925	679,190	1,953	1,674,810	68	16,207	16	38,295					25
497	44	501	318	94,223	508	296,539	34	6,968	21	10,095	166	166	911	6,224	26
38		38	32	11,350	32	21,500									27
8	2	8	8	1,560	8	6,900					1	1	4	25	28
149	8	152	137	39,825	151	79,278	22	3,485	6	1,475	100	100	382	3,307	29
4	398	4	3	600	9	18,200	2	2,400			199	210	892	8,911	30
	134										78	80	306	2,716	31
3	124	3	3	600	6	17,500	2	2,400			93	102	514	5,475	32
1	80	1			3	700					28	28	72	720	33
	60														34
92	19	93	92	33,060	92	165,850	3	1,475	4	8,000	41	42	473	2,812	35
72	2	73	72	25,860	72	143,000	2	475	4	8,000	39	40	455	2,695	36
	9														37
20	8	20	20	7,200	20	22,850	1	1,000			2	2	18	117	38
69	5	69	7	2,110	8	88,000	1	2,000			12	19	48	913	
62		62			1	30,000									39
7	5	7	7	2,110	7	58,000	1	2,000			12	19	48	913	40
9	15	9	8	1,970	9	161,500	4	16,000			6	9	20	420	42
7	4	7	6	1,270	7	153,000	2	10,000			3	6	10	170	43
2	11	2	2	700	2	8,500	2	6,000			3	3	10	250	44
4	31	4	4	850	23	3,245					22	22	78	480	
	17														45
1	4	1	1	120	2	30,150					1	1	2	12	46
188	16	188	187	61,566	185	299,250	13	5,288	3	2,200	168	169	1,514	9,234	48
1,238	85	1,253	1,221	383,893	1,239	2,740,322	97	101,561	160	256,350	1,136	1,149	10,510	72,963	49
251	322	253	245	81,823	401	8,806,441	88	391,338	4	57,300	550	551	3,155	16,116	
1	47	1	1	400	1	6,000					1	1	6	150	
410	54	417	409	124,213	419	1,050,706	26	44,350	79	130,051	398	411	4,253	29,487	50
45	23	45	43	10,635	46	58,575	10	3,410	2	1,500	61	62	210	1,760	53
27	17	27	27	5,985	28	23,175	7	1,710			43	43	122	886	
12	3	12	11	3,100	12	25,700	2	1,600	2	1,500	13	13	67	585	55
6	3	6	5	1,550	6	9,700	1	100			5	6	21	289	56
89	31	94	86	19,498	95	1,791,041	20	56,875	18	67,400	84	85	530	3,544	57
84	22	89	81	18,978	87	1,760,691	17	49,625	17	64,400	77	78	510	3,434	
5	9	5	5	520	8	30,350	3	7,250	1	3,000	7	7	20	110	
10	12	24	10	4,300	22	31,190	1	80	3	7,500	5	6	17	103	59
3	12	3	3	800	15	17,100	1	80	3	7,500	5	6	17	103	
7		21	7	3,500	7	14,090									
5,343	164	5,792	5,244	1,794,997	5,366	63,240,305	1,206	2,708,025	2,693	6,761,148	5,327	5,741	75,801	638,089	61
8,896	907	9,040	8,702	2,776,044	8,906	29,995,316	1,234	1,868,821	617	1,129,225	7,901	8,078	70,476	634,504	64
6,969	214	7,066	6,777	2,176,597	6,944	27,439,944	1,041	1,792,613	596	1,106,325	6,676	6,818	65,364	578,418	65
1,927	693	1,974	1,925	599,447	1,962	2,555,372	193	76,208	21	22,900	1,225	1,260	5,112	56,086	66
981	59	1,442	969	508,374	974	2,802,532	115	83,199	54	99,200	866	1,223	10,789	78,575	67
744	47	1,186	736	432,854	741	2,198,957	84	38,109	33	56,600	708	1,057	9,212	66,595	68
58		66	57	19,250	57	89,800									69
175	11	184	172	54,220	172	472,975	29	41,490	20	41,700	156	164	1,564	11,850	70
4	1	6	4	2,050	4	40,800	2	3,600	1	900	2	2	13	130	71

TABLE 1.—ORGANIZATIONS, COMMUNICANTS OR MEMBERS, PLACES OF WORSHIP, VALUE OF CHURCH PROPERTY, CONTINENTAL UNITED

	DENOMINATION.	Total number of organizations.	COMMUNICANTS OR MEMBERS.				
			Number of organizations reporting.	Total number reported.	Sex.		
					Number of organizations reporting.	Male.	Female.
72	Eastern Orthodox Churches	411	411	129,606	103	74,867	12,975
73	Russian Orthodox Church	59	59	19,111	59	12,925	6,186
74	Servian Orthodox Church	10	10	15,742	10	13,514	2,228
75	Syrian Orthodox Church	8	8	4,002	8	2,423	1,579
76	Greek Orthodox Church	334	334	90,751	26	46,005	2,982
77	Evangelical bodies	2,738	2,730	174,780	2,627	67,448	100,972
78	Evangelical Association	1,760	1,755	104,898	1,677	41,641	58,905
79	United Evangelical Church	978	975	69,882	950	25,807	42,067
80	Evangelistic associations	182	179	10,842	172	4,397	5,790
81	Apostolic Faith Movement	6	6	538	6	221	317
82	Peniel Missions	11	11	703	10	480	173
83	Metropolitan Church Association	6	6	466	6	183	283
84	Hephzibah Faith Missionary Association	10	10	293	10	141	152
85	Missionary Church Association	32	30	1,256	27	415	596
86	Pentecost Bands of the World	16	16	487	16	191	296
87	Heavenly Recruit Church	27	27	938	27	407	531
88	Apostolic Christian Church	42	41	4,558	38	1,729	2,469
89	Christian Congregation	9	9	395	9	172	223
90	Gospel Mission	8	8	196	8	80	116
91	Church of Daniel's Band	4	4	92	4	38	54
92	Lumber River Mission	5	5	265	5	97	168
93	Pentecostal Union Church	3	3	230	3	93	137
94	Voluntary Missionary Society in America (Colored)	3	3	425	3	150	275
95	Free Christian Zion Church of Christ (Colored)	15	14	1,835	14	740	1,095
96	Friends	1,147	1,141	113,772	1,121	51,708	60,244
97	Society of Friends (Orthodox)	873	867	91,161	855	41,468	48,310
98	Religious Society of Friends (Hicksite)	218	218	18,560	210	8,345	9,778
99	Orthodox Conservative Friends (Wilburite)	48	48	3,880	48	1,826	2,054
100	Friends (Primitive)	8	8	171	8	69	102
101	German Evangelical Protestant bodies	66	65	34,704	61	12,830	17,724
102	German Evangelical Protestant Ministers' Association	44	44	23,518	43	9,284	12,934
103	German Evangelical Protestant Ministers' Conference	22	21	11,186	18	3,546	4,790
104	German Evangelical Synod of North America	1,205	1,198	293,137	1,072	111,681	138,434
105	Independent churches	1,079	1,065	73,673	986	26,895	38,012
106	International Apostolic Holiness Union	74	74	2,774	73	1,082	1,665
107	Jewish congregations	1,769	1,152	[1] 101,457	.....	.....	.....
108	Latter-day Saints	1,184	1,184	256,647	1,152	117,026	128,776
109	Church of Jesus Christ of Latter-day Saints	683	683	215,796	666	100,217	106,087
110	Reorganized Church of Jesus Christ of Latter-day Saints	501	501	40,851	486	16,809	22,689
111	Lutheran bodies	12,703	12,642	2,112,494	11,329	853,339	998,009
112	General Synod of the Evangelical Lutheran Church in the United States of America	1,734	1,734	270,221	1,615	102,544	149,
113	United Synod of the Evangelical Lutheran Church in the South	449	449	47,747	407	18,555	23,899
114	General Council of the Evangelical Lutheran Church in North America	2,146	2,133	462,177	1,894	180,112	223,1[illegible]
115	Evangelical Lutheran Synodical Conference of America	3,301	3,284	648,529	2,997	270,718	304,361
116	United Norwegian Lutheran Church in America	1,177	1,167	185,027	900	68,767	70,916
117	Evangelical Lutheran Joint Synod of Ohio and Other States	772	772	123,408	702	49,290	58,
118	Lutheran Synod of Buffalo	33	33	5,270	29	2,276	2,
119	Hauge's Norwegian Evangelical Lutheran Synod	272	265	33,268	194	11,314	12,
120	Evangelical Lutheran Church in America, Eielsen's Synod	26	26	1,013	26	478	
121	German Evangelical Lutheran Synod of Texas	25	24	2,440	23	885	1,
122	Evangelical Lutheran Synod of Iowa and Other States	828	828	110,254	797	51,078	54,
123	Synod for the Norwegian Evangelical Lutheran Church in America	927	917	107,712	813	45,740	47,
124	Evangelical Lutheran Synod of Michigan and Other States	55	55	9,697	48	3,992	4,
125	Danish Evangelical Lutheran Church in America	92	92	12,541	68	4,027	4,
126	Icelandic Evangelical Lutheran Synod in North America	14	14	2,101	7	349	
127	Immanuel Synod of the Evangelical Lutheran Church of North America	11	11	3,275	11	1,295	1,
128	Finnish Evangelical Lutheran Church of America, or Suomi Synod	105	105	12,907	105	6,834	6,
129	Norwegian Lutheran Free Church	320	317	26,928	296	10,924	12,
130	United Danish Evangelical Lutheran Church in America	198	198	16,340	182	6,827	7,
131	Slovak Evangelical Lutheran Synod of America	59	59	12,141	59	7,629	4,
132	Finnish Evangelical Lutheran National Church	66	66	10,111	66	5,315	4,688
133	Apostolic Lutheran Church (Finnish)	68	68	8,170	66	3,782	3,[illegible]
134	Church of the Lutheran Brethren of America (Norwegian)	16	16	482	16	263	219
135	Evangelical Lutheran Jehovah Conference	9	9	735	8	345	370
136	Mennonite bodies	604	604	54,798	604	25,053	29,745
137	Mennonite Church	220	220	18,674	220	8,404	10,270
138	Bruederhoef Mennonite Church	8	8	275	8	129	146
139	Amish Mennonite Church	57	57	7,640	57	3,629	4,011
140	Old Amish Mennonite Church	46	46	5,043	46	2,370	2,673
141	Reformed Mennonite Church	34	34	2,079	34	877	1,202
142	General Conference of Mennonites of North America	90	90	11,661	90	5,534	6,127
143	Church of God in Christ (Mennonite)	18	18	562	18	261	301
144	Old (Wisler) Mennonite Church	9	9	655	9	307	348
145	Defenceless Mennonites	14	14	967	14	435	532
146	Mennonite Brethren in Christ	68	68	2,801	68	1,070	1,731
	Bundes Conferenz der Mennoniten Brueder-Gemeinde:						
147	Krimmer Brueder-Gemeinde	6	6	708	6	307	401
148	Schellenberger Brueder-Gemeinde	13	13	1,825	13	830	995
149	Central Illinois Conference of Mennonites	13	13	1,363	13	650	713
150	Nebraska and Minnesota Conference of Mennonites	8	8	545	8	250	295

[1] Heads of families only.

DEBT ON CHURCH PROPERTY, PARSONAGES, AND SUNDAY SCHOOLS, BY DENOMINATIONS (IN DETAIL), I
STATES: 1906—Continued.

PLACES OF WORSHIP.					VALUE OF CHURCH PROPERTY.		DEBT ON CHURCH PROPERTY.		PARSONAGES.		SUNDAY SCHOOLS CONDUCTED BY CHURCH ORGANIZATIONS.			
Number of organizations reporting—		Number of church edifices reported.	Seating capacity of church edifices.		Number of organizations reporting.	Value reported.	Number of organizations reporting.	Amount of debt reported.	Number of organizations reporting.	Value of parsonages reported.	Number of organizations reporting.	Number of Sunday schools reported.	Number of officers and teachers.	Number of scholars.
Church edifices.	Halls, etc.		Number of organizations reporting.	Seating capacity reported.										
84	326	85	75	38,995	89	$964,791	58	$290,674	29	$117,143	7	7	10	509
45	13	46	45	20,345	53	484,371	36	131,774	25	112,243	1	1	2	75
8	2	8	8	2,800	9	62,460	7	19,000	2	2,100	1	1	1	13
2	6	2	2	700	8	32,160	...	...	...	...	1	1	1	50
29	305	29	20	15,150	19	385,800	15	139,900	2	2,800	4	4	6	371
2,509	152	2,537	2,461	659,391	2,515	8,999,979	412	666,973	1,026	1,907,917	2,454	2,549	32,113	214,998
1,598	100	1,617	1,554	390,199	1,609	5,819,620	204	374,969	680	1,297,666	1,571	1,631	19,977	121,822
911	52	920	907	269,192	906	3,180,359	208	292,004	346	610,251	883	918	12,136	93,176
120	52	124	112	34,590	122	532,185	31	102,700	9	34,000	136	147	947	7,615
1	5	1	1	200	2	450	...	...	...	...	5	6	30	245
1	10	1	1	500	3	40,250	...	...	...	...	7	7	40	308
4	2	4	4	2,025	4	118,300	3	74,000	1	13,000	4	4	29	360
9	1	9	9	1,450	9	11,300	1	175	...	...	9	9	75	402
19	12	19	18	4,735	22	33,135	4	1,500	1	1,000	28	34	271	1,916
15	1	16	14	3,780	15	69,550	7	6,625	6	19,500	13	14	83	477
8	15	8	7	2,800	7	8,950	3	700	1	500	14	14	116	527
41	1	44	37	11,475	38	141,550	6	6,500	...	...	31	32	130	1,932
5	1	5	5	1,550	5	7,200	2	600	...	...	7	7	73	332
4	3	4	4	750	5	3,100	1	500	...	...	7	9	34	245
2	1	2	2	500	2	2,400	1	100	...	...	1	1	3	50
5	...	5	5	2,600	5	3,000	...	...	...	...	5	5	28	256
3	...	3	2	900	3	90,600	2	11,000	...	...	2	2	14	175
3	...	3	3	1,325	2	2,400	1	1,000	...	...	3	3	21	390
14	1	14	14	5,201	13	5,975	7	1,150	2	450	7	7	63	340
1,095	39	1,097	1,088	304,204	1,097	3,857,451	60	41,496	145	181,874	846	887	7,735	53,761
830	32	832	823	224,898	833	2,719,551	60	41,496	145	181,874	723	762	6,931	47,612
214	2	214	214	66,290	213	1,037,650	...	...	...	...	116	118	771	5,944
47	1	47	47	12,216	47	93,500	...	...	...	...	7	7	33	205
4	4	4	4	800	4	6,750	...	...	...	...	...	...	...	...
66	...	71	63	37,409	66	2,556,550	38	161,650	47	186,150	60	61	1,225	11,362
44	...	49	43	25,179	44	939,950	29	91,250	36	138,750	41	42	834	8,211
22	...	22	20	12,230	22	1,616,600	9	70,400	11	47,400	19	19	391	3,151
1,136	42	1,258	1,131	380,465	1,137	9,376,402	398	1,161,776	774	1,717,345	1,086	1,111	12,079	116,106
786	229	812	741	213,096	806	3,934,267	230	478,425	93	185,450	826	922	6,732	57,680
41	31	44	41	15,115	44	80,150	23	13,246	10	7,125	66	68	503	3,276
753	230	821	717	364,701	747	23,198,925	449	4,556,571	81	270,550	561	600	2,239	49,514
845	214	933	837	280,747	909	3,168,548	145	111,782	8	7,800	1,036	1,169	18,507	130,085
544	93	624	543	214,409	594	2,645,363	104	75,793	3	1,700	660	766	14,765	113,139
301	121	309	294	66,338	315	523,185	41	35,989	5	6,100	376	403	3,742	16,946
10,695	1,197	11,194	10,493	3,344,654	10.779	74,826,389	2,970	7,859,469	4,994	11,521,988	8,682	9,450	83,891	782,786
1,667	41	1,720	1,629	582,008	1,680	16,875,429	412	1,593,778	688	1,815,250	1,628	1,696	26,288	225,94
429	13	442	426	153,520	429	1,509,760	41	49,692	149	339,550	380	385	3,901	30,039
1,983	75	2,106	1,947	734,068	2,008	22 394,618	732	2,944,683	797	2,607,237	1,914	2,110	28,845	254,88
2,707	351	2,868	2,688	826,993	2,731	18,916,407	865	2,178,741	1,813	3,587,760	1,434	1,546	6,168	94,00
980	102	1,018	939	284,711	956	3 668,588	167	166,203	246	651,370	842	995	5,109	43,71
693	53	712	675	199,797	694	3 606,285	192	333,580	378	746,204	601	624	4,395	47,60
33	...	34	33	8,759	32	130,000	10	10,314	20	36,400	13	14	58	62
218	22	226	205	57,426	222	682,135	54	55,205	51	103,149	194	218	1,101	8,99
6	20	6	6	1,200	6	15,900	1	50	1	1,500	6	6	13	11
18	5	18	17	2,834	18	30,050	3	1,000	14	10,850	17	18	57	80
671	109	705	658	162,847	676	2,327,093	140	116,505	406	627,853	614	640	2,449	27,64
630	138	649	621	168,889	648	2,469,713	145	165,053	203	566,805	370	443	1,945	18,71
49	4	53	49	13,795	49	184,700	17	12,775	35	51,050	38	39	239	2,46
63	20	70	62	14,250	66	248,700	26	37,514	42	72,200	58	64	231	2,98
14	...	14	13	3,355	14	32,350	4	998	2	2,300	12	13	49	49
11	...	11	11	5,300	11	89,300	3	6,250	7	34,300	11	11	124	1,12
44	60	50	44	11,643	44	151,345	19	19,550	16	28,750	77	108	571	4,51
218	68	219	216	54,605	230	660,310	55	38,628	46	91,000	211	233	1,127	7,47
136	57	140	135	27,294	138	418,450	45	43,425	60	103,900	142	153	775	6,11
29	30	31	28	9,775	31	219,300	19	60,700	10	33,100	12	12	13	58
43	23	43	43	10,095	43	95,150	9	12,500	2	2,000	62	69	272	2,14
35	3	37	31	7,725	35	62,856	3	1,200	1	2,000	22	27	78	1,03
10	3	10	10	2,315	10	16,400	4	3,575	1	1,100	15	16	62	39
8	...	12	7	1,450	8	21,550	4	7,550	6	6,300	9	10	21	35
498	87	509	497	171,381	497	1,237,134	31	9,082	39	55,500	411	439	5,041	44,92
202	13	207	202	77,451	202	500,112	6	1,215	5	6,700	156	170	1,967	15,79
8	...	8	8	650	8	9,100	...	...	...	...	...	...	...	...
52	5	52	52	17,487	52	122,275	7	1,321	...	...	54	57	798	6,36
4	41	4	4	1,025	4	6,700	...	...	...	...	6	6	66	49
29	5	29	29	7,465	29	52,650	...	...	...	...	...	...	...	...
84	5	89	84	33,800	84	303,400	9	5,690	9	19,050	84	89	1,148	12,47
2	5	2	2	350	2	1,600	...	...	...	...	...	...	...	...
9	...	10	9	2,440	9	17,950	...	...	...	...	...	...	...	...
13	1	13	13	3,095	13	16,800	...	...	1	500	13	13	142	1,10
58	9	58	57	16,248	57	140,747	8	756	23	28,850	59	60	578	3,72
6	...	6	6	3,175	6	17,900	1	100	1	400	6	7	61	68
13	...	13	13	3,550	13	13,000	...	...	...	...	13	15	120	2,55
12	1	12	12	3,075	12	25,900	...	...	...	...	12	12	116	95
6	2	6	6	1,570	6	9,000	...	...	...	...	8	10	45	73

TABLE 1.—ORGANIZATIONS, COMMUNICANTS OR MEMBERS, PLACES OF WORSHIP, VALUE OF CHURCH PROPERTY, CONTINENTAL UNITED

	DENOMINATION.	Total number of organizations.	COMMUNICANTS OR MEMBERS.				
			Number of organizations reporting.	Total number reported.	Sex.		
					Number of organizations reporting.	Male.	Female.
151	**Methodist bodies**	64,701	64,255	5,749,838	59,592	2,042,713	3,268,664
152	Methodist Episcopal Church	29,948	29,742	2,986,154	27,800	1,042,830	1,743,836
153	Union American Methodist Episcopal Church (Colored)	77	77	4,347	77	1,785	2,562
154	African Methodist Episcopal Church	6,647	6,608	494,777	6,486	177,837	304,160
155	African Union Methodist Protestant Church	69	69	5,592	67	1,972	3,493
156	African Methodist Episcopal Zion Church	2,204	2,197	184,542	2,156	67,096	113,405
157	Methodist Protestant Church	2,843	2,825	178,544	2,673	68,360	100,345
158	Wesleyan Methodist Connection of America	594	591	20,043	572	7,440	11,803
159	Methodist Episcopal Church, South	17,831	17,683	1,638,480	15,446	587,324	847,031
160	Congregational Methodist Church	325	324	14,729	296	5,672	7,341
161	New Congregational Methodist Church	35	35	1,782	35	655	1,127
162	Colored Methodist Episcopal Church	2,381	2,365	172,996	2,309	64,968	104,264
163	Reformed Zion Union Apostolic Church (Colored)	45	45	3,059	36	1,139	1,624
164	Primitive Methodist Church in the United States of America	96	96	7,558	94	2,613	4,718
165	Free Methodist Church of North America	1,553	1,541	32,838	1,488	11,228	20,332
166	Reformed Methodist Union Episcopal Church (Colored)	58	57	4,397	57	1,774	2,623
167	**Moravian bodies**	132	132	17,926	119	6,532	9,189
168	Moravian Church (Unitas Fratrum)	117	117	17,155	104	6,173	8,777
169	Evangelical Union of Bohemian and Moravian Brethren in North America	15	15	771	15	359	412
170	Nonsectarian Churches of Bible Faith	204	203	6,396	203	3,368	3,028
171	Pentecostal Church of the Nazarene	100	100	6,657	99	1,968	3,289
172	Polish National Church of America	24	24	15,473	24	8,627	6,846
173	**Presbyterian bodies**	15,506	15,471	1,830,555	14,014	633,598	1,037,197
174	Presbyterian Church in the United States of America	7,935	7,927	1,179,566	7,340	392,092	683,082
175	Cumberland Presbyterian Church	2,850	2,846	195,770	2,310	69,691	96,259
176	Colored Cumberland Presbyterian Church	196	196	18,066	196	8,405	9,661
177	Welsh Calvinistic Methodist Church	147	147	13,280	143	5,683	7,106
178	United Presbyterian Church of North America	968	964	130,342	940	50,834	76,427
179	Presbyterian Church in the United States	3,104	3,086	266,345	2,789	95,474	149,625
180	Associate Synod of North America (Associate Presbyterian Church)	22	22	786	22	300	486
181	Associate Reformed Synod of the South	141	141	13,201	134	5,629	6,942
182	Synod of the Reformed Presbyterian Church of North America	114	113	9,122	113	3,470	5,652
183	Reformed Presbyterian Church in North America, General Synod	27	27	3,620	25	1,220	1,700
184	Reformed Presbyterian Church (Covenanted)	1	1	17	1	7	10
185	Reformed Presbyterian Church in the United States and Canada	1	1	440	1	193	247
186	Protestant Episcopal Church	6,845	6,725	886,942	5,767	251,869	457,165
187	**Reformed bodies**	2,585	2,583	449,514	2,445	181,619	241,542
188	Reformed Church in America	659	657	124,938	632	44,673	72,386
189	Reformed Church in the United States	1,736	1,736	292,654	1,632	121,925	154,986
190	Christian Reformed Church	174	174	26,669	166	11,617	12,621
191	Hungarian Reformed Church in America	16	16	5,253	15	3,404	1,549
192	Reformed Catholic Church	5	5	1,250	5	730	520
193	Reformed Episcopal Church	81	79	9,682	76	3,296	5,686
194	Roman Catholic Church	12,482	12,472	12,079,142	11,028	5,184,922	5,325,178
195	**Salvationists**	714	682	23,344	680	11,977	11,360
196	Salvation Army	694	662	22,908	661	11,744	11,163
197	American Salvation Army	20	20	436	19	233	197
198	Schwenkfelders	8	8	725	8	318	407
199	Social Brethren	17	17	1,262	17	487	775
200	Society for Ethical Culture	5	5	2,040	5	1,303	737
201	Spiritualists	455	454	35,056	450	15,135	19,552
202	**Swedish Evangelical bodies**	408	407	27,712	399	11,977	14,821
203	Swedish Evangelical Mission Covenant of America	281	281	20,760	279	9,059	11,593
204	Swedish Evangelical Free Mission	127	126	6,952	120	2,918	3,228
205	Temple Society in the United States (Friends of the Temple)	3	3	376	3	158	218
206	**Theosophical societies**	85	84	2,336	84	853	1,483
207	Theosophical Society in America	14	14	166	14	79	87
208	Theosophical Society, New York	1	1	90	1	37	53
209	Theosophical Society, American Section	69	69	2,080	69	737	1,343
210	Universal Brotherhood and Theosophical Society [1]	1	....	....	....	....	....
211	Unitarians	461	435	70,542	337	21,817	33,866
212	**United Brethren bodies**	4,304	4,268	296,050	3,810	107,369	160,623
213	Church of the United Brethren in Christ	3,732	3,699	274,649	3,249	99,176	147,969
214	Church of the United Brethren in Christ (Old Constitution)	572	569	21,401	561	8,193	12,654
215	Universalists	846	811	64,158	652	18,279	33,346
216	Vedanta Society	4	4	340	1	100	100
217	Volunteers of America	71	65	2,194	65	1,140	1,054

[1] No statistics are available.

DEBT ON CHURCH PROPERTY, PARSONAGES, AND SUNDAY SCHOOLS, BY DENOMINATIONS (IN DETAIL), FOR STATES: 1906—Continued.

PLACES OF WORSHIP.					VALUE OF CHURCH PROPERTY.		DEBT ON CHURCH PROPERTY.		PARSONAGES.		SUNDAY SCHOOLS CONDUCTED BY CHURCH ORGANIZATIONS.				
Number of organizations reporting— Church edifices.	Number of organizations reporting— Halls, etc.	Number of church edifices reported.	Seating capacity of church edifices. Number of organizations reporting.	Seating capacity of church edifices. Seating capacity reported.	Number of organizations reporting.	Value reported.	Number of organizations reporting.	Amount of debt reported.	Number of organizations reporting.	Value of parsonages reported.	Number of organizations reporting.	Number of Sunday schools reported.	Number of officers and teachers.	Number of scholars.	
58,883	3,193	59,990	56,577	17,053,392	59,083	$229,450,996	10,430	$12,272,463	20,837	$36,420,655	55,227	57,464	569,296	4,472,930	151
27,810	1,211	28,345	26,866	7,983,742	27,888	163,357,805	4,662	8,640,273	12,215	25,508,417	26,869	28,102	351,312	2,700,742	152
60	16	60	59	16,046	59	170,150	39	40,796	4	6,400	76	78	481	3,372	153
6,292	268	6,538	6,178	1,832,600	6,299	11,303,489	2,574	1,191,921	1,783	1,255,246	6,056	6,285	41,941	292,689	154
68	1	71	67	21,955	68	183,697	41	20,917	7	7,500	66	66	441	5,266	155
2,079	78	2,131	2,048	690,951	2,104	4,833,207	724	474,269	348	350,690	2,060	2,092	16,245	107,692	156
2,435	230	2,457	2,370	721,464	2,442	6,053,048	244	247,524	661	910,645	2,118	2,181	18,970	141,086	157
477	64	489	473	123,571	480	637,117	49	18,914	176	189,175	475	505	3,442	21,463	158
15,798	970	15,933	14,704	4,484,290	15,859	37,278,424	1,195	1,256,093	4,566	7,265,610	13,846	14,306	113,328	1,040,160	159
256	33	262	251	82,355	250	194,275	19	9,477	1	1,500	181	182	1,146	8,785	160
34	1	34	34	11,000	33	27,650	...	...	...	...	27	27	143	1,298	161
2,252	78	2,327	2,214	758,328	2,264	3,017,849	692	215,111	421	237,547	2,207	2,328	12,375	92,457	162
41	1	43	38	15,700	41	37,875	7	825	...	...	35	36	212	1,508	163
93	3	101	93	30,390	93	630,700	45	90,965	49	103,600	91	98	1,563	13,177	164
1,130	239	1,140	1,124	262,265	1,145	1,688,745	112	61,124	598	612,050	1,066	1,124	7,493	41,443	165
58	...	59	58	18,735	58	36,965	27	4,254	8	2,275	54	54	204	1,792	166
121	11	137	120	44,625	123	936,650	12	31,635	79	207,325	109	121	1,419	12,998	167
113	4	129	112	41,525	113	922,900	12	31,635	77	206,625	107	119	1,413	12,901	168
8	7	8	8	3,100	10	13,750	...	...	2	700	2	2	6	97	169
40	156	41	33	5,700	33	25,910	2	3,300	...	...	33	33	158	1,976	170
69	26	69	68	19,770	71	393,990	40	97,224	7	22,500	80	82	824	5,039	171
23	1	27	23	12,130	24	494,700	23	216,960	14	74,000	20	22	26	1,289	172
14,082	406	15,311	13,942	4,892,819	14,161	150,189,446	2,102	6,545,025	5,417	16,155,861	13,048	14,452	176,647	1,511,175	173
7,395	208	8,185	7,362	2,692,561	7,405	114,882,781	1,484	5,116,899	3,465	11,503,460	7,393	8,300	118,602	1,045,056	174
2,398	108	2,474	2,325	767,348	2,451	5,803,960	157	208,876	436	658,400	1,817	1,846	15,596	120,311	175
195	1	195	191	71,165	192	203,778	18	10,407	8	5,825	192	192	933	6,952	176
144	2	156	143	40,282	145	761,350	17	27,425	34	66,916	136	138	1,681	11,347	177
936	19	984	935	322,950	943	10,760,208	151	546,557	450	1,155,750	948	991	12,841	115,963	178
2,722	60	3,012	2,698	898,087	2,734	15,488,489	239	539,111	942	2,598,485	2,301	2,699	24,327	189,767	179
19	1	19	19	4,575	20	28,825	...	...	...	...	9	9	13	289	180
136	3	142	132	50,075	134	436,550	17	16,680	51	96,975	126	131	1,109	9,732	181
110	3	116	110	34,110	110	1,258,105	12	48,650	23	52,800	103	122	1,270	9,613	182
26	...	27	26	11,016	26	365,400	6	25,420	8	17,250	22	23	255	2,013	183
...	1	...	...	...	...	...	...	...	...	...	...	...	...	...	184
1	...	1	1	650	1	200,000	1	5,000	...	...	1	1	20	132	185
5,998	257	6,922	5,960	1,675,750	6,067	125,040,498	1,011	4,930,914	2,706	13,207,084	5,211	5,601	51,048	464,351	186
2,480	62	2,706	2,472	990,654	2,477	30,648,247	654	2,377,014	1,355	4,166,769	2,345	2,588	38,710	361,548	187
640	15	773	638	283,447	639	15,553,250	198	729,225	489	2,022,450	639	757	12,089	120,705	188
1,670	30	1,740	1,666	640,745	1,667	14,067,897	349	1,360,552	724	1,827,569	1,569	1,677	25,191	222,324	189
159	13	181	157	62,334	160	903,600	98	216,287	136	290,250	133	150	1,424	18,340	190
11	4	12	11	4,128	11	123,500	9	70,950	6	26,500	4	4	6	179	191
1	4	1	1	200	1	60,000	1	15,000	...	...	...	...	...	...	192
76	5	87	76	25,053	76	1,469,787	23	67,143	14	48,950	76	89	959	9,864	193
10,755	518	11,881	10,303	4,494,377	10,293	292,638,787	4,104	49,488,055	6,360	36,302,064	9,406	11,172	62,470	1,481,535	194
161	541	161	147	53,273	686	3,184,854	313	1,157,801	8	23,300	576	581	2,455	17,521	195
159	523	159	145	52,223	681	3,175,154	311	1,154,901	7	21,500	574	579	2,437	17,346	196
2	18	2	2	1,050	5	9,700	2	2,900	1	1,800	2	2	18	175	197
8	...	8	8	2,950	8	38,700	1	1,700	...	...	5	5	101	991	198
15	2	15	15	9,200	15	13,800	...	...	...	...	6	6	23	180	199
...	5	...	...	...	...	...	...	...	...	...	5	5	64	466	200
93	322	100	93	55,125	132	958,048	38	79,570	4	3,700	75	76	436	2,699	201
375	18	389	370	111,480	379	1,638,675	125	194,987	122	238,526	373	418	3,794	32,504	202
258	9	268	254	82,368	261	1,225,220	83	121,694	91	184,500	258	291	2,862	24,888	203
117	9	121	116	29,112	118	413,455	42	73,293	31	54,026	115	127	932	7,616	204
3	...	3	3	830	3	11,000	...	...	1	1,000	3	3	21	168	205
...	79	...	...	...	1	300	...	...		...	5	5	10	78	206
...	9	...	...	...	...	...	...	...	...	...	...	...	...	...	207
...	1	...	...	...	...	...	...	...	...	...	1	1	5	45	208
...	69	...	...	...	1	300	...	...	...	...	4	4	5	33	209
...	...	...	...	...	...	...	...	...	...	...	...	...	...	...	210
407	23	463	401	159,917	406	14,263,277	85	332,330	115	584,750	358	364	3,592	24,005	211
3,854	255	3,900	3,637	1,060,560	3,839	9,073,791	460	498,959	1,106	1,507,932	3,777	3,870	42,169	301,320	212
3,369	191	3,410	3,157	937,055	3,356	8,401,539	417	489,035	1,004	1,423,282	3,325	3,409	37,993	278,764	213
485	64	490	480	123,505	483	672,252	43	9,924	102	84,650	452	461	4,176	22,556	214
768	33	776	718	220,222	779	10,575,656	132	464,755	136	491,100	596	600	6,585	42,201	215
2	2	2	2	600	2	52,000	...	...	...	...	...	...	...	...	216
7	64	10	7	1,825	31	83,521	6	40,621	...	...	36	36	223	1,736	217

TABLE 2.—ORGANIZATIONS, COMMUNICANTS OR MEMBERS, PLACES OF WORSHIP, VALUE OF CHURCH BY STATES AND

	STATE OR TERRITORY.	Total number of organizations.	COMMUNICANTS OR MEMBERS.				
			Number of organizations reporting.	Total number reported.	Sex.		
					Number of organizations reporting.	Male.	Female.
1	Continental United States	212,230	210,418	32,936,445	193,229	12,767,466	16,849,505
2	North Atlantic division	33,592	32,893	10,306,946	29,977	4,212,717	5,220,736
3	Maine	1,559	1,532	212,988	1,441	84,755	119,971
4	New Hampshire	856	832	190,298	773	79,376	100,340
5	Vermont	909	902	147,223	866	62,284	82,472
6	Massachusetts	3,088	3,031	1,562,621	2,795	639,844	813,961
7	Rhode Island	521	507	264,712	460	111,609	131,202
8	Connecticut	1,384	1,364	502,560	1,283	221,144	264,356
9	New York	9,639	9,227	3,591,974	8,067	1,456,047	1,794,081
10	New Jersey	2,802	2,750	857,548	2,497	302,345	408,929
11	Pennsylvania	12,834	12,748	2,977,022	11,795	1,255,313	1,505,424
12	South Atlantic division	41,655	41,434	4,517,051	37,958	1,658,517	2,483,965
13	Delaware	468	467	71,251	431	27,828	38,151
14	Maryland	2,773	2,756	473,257	2,464	157,412	229,087
15	District of Columbia	289	288	136,759	259	41,634	72,723
16	Virginia	6,639	6,605	793,546	5,937	296,766	436,929
17	West Virginia	4,042	4,019	301,565	3,665	118,553	159,538
18	North Carolina	8,592	8,554	824,385	7,915	311,655	463,395
19	South Carolina	5,385	5,373	665,933	4,969	243,348	375,754
20	Georgia	10,097	10,026	1,029,037	9,217	379,781	583,173
21	Florida	3,370	3,346	221,318	3,101	81,540	125,215
22	North Central division	69,023	68,615	10,689,212	63,265	3,998,569	5,196,707
23	Ohio	9,890	9,807	1,742,873	9,002	640,472	875,713
24	Indiana	6,863	6,829	938,405	6,329	369,516	514,938
25	Illinois	9,374	9,308	2,077,197	8,273	645,767	842,686
26	Michigan	5,635	5,605	982,479	5,138	291,315	387,461
27	Wisconsin	4,902	4,880	1,000,903	4,531	436,411	503,178
28	Minnesota	4,759	4,721	834,442	4,247	353,828	414,771
29	Iowa	6,293	6,259	788,667	5,900	316,088	428,603
30	Missouri	9,206	9,172	1,199,239	8,560	474,791	636,091
31	North Dakota	1,993	1,961	159,053	1,783	71,326	76,480
32	South Dakota	1,801	1,798	161,961	1,662	68,612	78,242
33	Nebraska	3,313	3,300	345,803	3,133	142,682	184,718
34	Kansas	4,994	4,975	458,190	4,707	182,761	253,826
35	South Central division	57,778	57,402	5,726,570	52,625	2,174,410	3,084,978
36	Kentucky	6,553	6,512	858,324	5,725	316,610	432,232
37	Tennessee	8,021	7,963	697,570	7,205	249,870	373,888
38	Alabama	8,894	8,858	824,209	8,096	307,978	455,838
39	Mississippi	7,396	7,361	657,381	6,761	232,451	370,870
40	Louisiana	3,855	3,813	778,901	3,491	327,111	419,082
41	Arkansas	6,208	6,144	426,179	5,762	164,535	239,099
42	Oklahoma[1]	4,497	4,466	257,100	4,183	100,312	139,515
43	Texas	12,354	12,285	1,226,906	11,402	475,543	654,454
44	Western division	10,182	10,074	1,696,666	9,404	728,253	863,119
45	Montana	546	542	98,984	522	48,255	49,285
46	Idaho	676	673	74,578	625	31,228	36,827
47	Wyoming	228	226	23,945	202	9,416	10,598
48	Colorado	1,268	1,261	205,666	1,179	87,077	105,861
49	New Mexico	625	624	137,009	536	57,012	59,746
50	Arizona	237	236	45,057	209	17,490	18,802
51	Utah	542	537	172,814	523	82,872	86,664
52	Nevada	88	86	14,944	73	6,595	6,474
53	Washington	1,771	1,759	191,976	1,672	78,115	99,422
54	Oregon	1,304	1,290	120,229	1,214	47,094	66,459
55	California	2,897	2,840	611,464	2,649	263,099	322,981

[1] Oklahoma and Indian Territory combined.

PROPERTY, DEBT ON CHURCH PROPERTY, PARSONAGES, AND SUNDAY SCHOOLS, FOR ALL DENOMINATIONS, TERRITORIES: 1906.

PLACES OF WORSHIP.					VALUE OF CHURCH PROPERTY.		DEBT ON CHURCH PROPERTY.		PARSONAGES.		SUNDAY SCHOOLS CONDUCTED BY CHURCH ORGANIZATIONS.				
Number of organizations reporting— Church edifices.	Number of organizations reporting— Halls, etc.	Number of church edifices reported.	Seating capacity of church edifices. Number of organizations reporting.	Seating capacity of church edifices. Seating capacity reported.	Number of organizations reporting.	Value reported.	Number of organizations reporting.	Amount of debt reported.	Number of organizations reporting.	Value of parsonages reported.	Number of organizations reporting.	Number of Sunday schools reported.	Number of officers and teachers.	Number of scholars.	
185,040	14,791	192,795	179,954	58,536,830	186,132	$1,257,575,867	33,617	$108,050,946	54,214	$143,495,853	167,574	178,214	1,648,664	14,685,997	1
30,269	2,137	32,991	29,744	11,788,803	30,410	626,897,510	8,521	64,485,962	14,286	63,282,199	28,956	31,768	447,634	4,282,562	2
1,381	104	1,511	1,366	412,833	1,406	9,955,363	231	614,198	583	1,435,201	1,304	1,450	13,420	107,440	3
772	61	851	765	254,017	786	7,864,991	143	625,807	481	1,313,525	723	763	7,815	64,865	4
836	46	891	822	235,661	847	5,939,492	133	470,095	511	1,207,900	812	872	8,200	61,277	5
2,706	288	2,983	2,678	1,313,564	2,778	84,729,445	953	8,203,412	1,377	7,772,560	2,774	2,999	51,882	491,697	6
452	50	493	446	195,688	465	9,533,543	149	1,064,432	181	960,980	453	491	8,187	80,901	7
1,255	87	1,414	1,245	522,941	1,278	29,196,128	395	2,776,588	818	3,995,148	1,251	1,340	19,320	179,673	8
8,444	623	9,193	8,190	3,191,267	8,344	255,166,284	2,289	28,382,866	4,638	22,283,225	7,968	8,795	123,319	1,247,051	9
2,558	174	2,875	2,524	1,015,903	2,586	50,907,123	1,075	6,786,368	1,289	6,376,490	2,495	2,785	42,613	404,095	10
11,865	704	12,780	11,708	4,646,929	11,920	173,605,141	3,153	15,562,196	4,408	17,937,170	11,176	12,273	172,878	1,645,563	11
38,368	1,628	39,627	37,159	12,250,279	38,492	114,460,588	5,797	7,551,092	6,511	13,557,541	33,838	35,763	273,704	2,412,617	12
450	13	478	431	130,267	451	3,250,105	140	248,720	168	470,605	425	441	5,604	49,926	13
2,615	81	2,814	2,548	810,701	2,608	23,765,172	659	2,095,293	951	2,758,674	2,437	2,606	31,174	261,440	14
235	43	264	232	142,311	243	10,025,122	143	1,570,609	74	612,741	263	297	5,338	56,771	15
6,135	242	6,480	5,983	1,974,332	6,139	19,699,014	813	996,367	1,141	2,471,251	5,441	5,965	50,229	430,452	16
3,317	463	3,428	3,217	949,812	3,335	9,733,585	379	512,412	659	1,622,566	3,212	3,486	27,577	212,577	17
8,004	229	8,188	7,832	2,715,567	8,068	14,053,505	891	498,043	1,028	1,681,622	6,969	7,293	53,132	487,261	18
5,176	99	5,290	5,004	1,774,437	5,194	10,209,043	802	350,527	824	1,352,263	4,829	5,020	35,054	328,829	19
9,427	275	9,624	9,070	3,063,866	9,432	17,929,183	1,545	848,770	1,089	1,696,113	7,752	8,052	50,246	460,769	20
3,009	183	3,061	2,842	688,986	3,022	5,795,859	425	430,351	577	891,706	2,510	2,603	15,350	124,592	21
59,999	4,806	62,256	58,739	17,844,755	60,286	356,256,559	10,479	26,494,505	22,524	48,781,303	55,374	58,705	570,384	4,805,135	22
9,163	379	9,519	8,991	3,102,819	9,216	74,670,765	1,382	5,202,205	2,961	7,916,108	8,733	9,226	111,122	939,469	23
6,390	250	6,580	6,288	2,132,181	6,418	31,081,500	961	1,723,109	1,705	3,623,538	5,690	5,879	63,042	516,809	24
8,262	423	8,626	7,964	2,685,352	8,140	66,222,514	1,491	6,317,919	3,284	8,640,258	7,736	8,173	92,913	825,323	25
4,661	523	4,882	4,561	1,353,180	4,702	27,144,250	1,040	1,729,978	2,155	3,946,747	4,563	4,830	49,847	414,421	26
4,352	327	4,562	4,273	1,206,385	4,382	27,277,837	1,048	2,885,247	2,072	4,837,471	3,698	4,036	28,770	278,691	27
4,086	356	4,280	3,973	1,104,317	4,105	26,053,159	1,012	2,066,006	1,709	4,044,430	3,544	3,975	29,521	273,223	28
5,699	368	5,921	5,606	1,617,467	5,741	30,464,860	859	1,517,992	2,686	5,481,894	5,291	5,575	54,016	413,548	29
7,924	646	8,146	7,786	2,391,498	7,966	38,059,233	1,040	3,257,740	1,744	3,448,045	6,670	6,917	59,678	504,770	30
1,274	355	1,325	1,243	262,251	1,313	4,576,157	390	463,890	500	957,814	1,332	1,511	7,407	61,199	31
1,412	240	1,461	1,381	285,197	1,433	4,538,013	231	232,123	639	1,111,745	1,337	1,463	8,587	71,554	32
2,756	337	2,847	2,716	649,132	2,796	12,114,817	434	531,042	1,432	2,304,069	2,701	2,845	24,242	192,443	33
4,020	602	4,107	3,957	1,054,976	4,074	14,053,454	591	567,254	1,667	2,469,184	4,079	4,275	41,239	313,685	34
48,514	4,957	49,594	46,572	14,478,100	48,805	100,383,963	6,906	4,611,194		11,305,354	41,282	42,951	272,087	2,433,161	35
5,757	285	5,894	5,617	1,775,123	5,751	18,044,389	623	862,993		1,637,943	4,543	4,723	33,833	314,667	36
7,232	489	7,400	6,972	2,323,285	7,243	14,469,012	687	445,709	7,848	1,346,711	5,919	6,101	40,875	355,550	37
8,026	379	8,183	7,667	2,423,175	8,023	13,314,993	1,091	527,479	886	1,443,022	6,584	6,808	40,238	361,279	38
6,879	222	6,997	6,581	2,041,665	6,888	9,482,229	1,063	345,304	870	1,237,829	5,714	5,911	32,422	286,257	39
3,537	127	3,630	3,324	1,046,850	3,549	10,456,146	734	689,072	726	1,314,247	3,096	3,320	17,963	177,739	40
5,097	685	5,192	4,921	1,446,892	5,145	6,733,375	695	361,011	768	778,190	4,248	4,398	27,979	230,238	41
2,642	1,051	2,709	2,434	598,650	2,696	4,933,843	694	435,569	674	682,806	2,870	3,012	20,684	173,896	42
9,344	1,719	9,589	9,056	2,822,460	9,510	22,949,976	1,319	944,057	2,090	2,864,606	8,308	8,678	58,093	533,535	43
7,890	1,263	8,327	7,740	2,174,893	8,139	59,577,247	1,914	4,908,193	3,045	6,569,456	8,124	9,027	84,855	752,522	44
367	82	407	383	100,665	391	2,809,779	87	196,122	193	450,110	423	477	3,298	33,891	45
477	107	495	468	121,775	508	1,726,734	127	119,677	137	217,375	538	509	6,043	45,437	46
156	37	160	155	35,250	159	778,142	29	45,394	66	144,650	175	202	1,556	13,472	47
917	190	956	908	255,469	956	7,723,200	307	619,367	419	863,920	987	1,099	10,446	96,919	48
470		522	451	129,745	466	956,605	54	53,535	124	186,770	323	364	1,716	20,050	49
166		181	165	40,954	174	798,975	37	71,441	65	121,525	189	217	1,703	14,967	50
459	56	516	459	169,369	492	3,612,422	86	152,131	45	107,690	505	575	10,681	89,887	51
62	[illegible]	67	58	15,015	70	402,350	16	19,305	34	68,700	71	84	550	4,641	52
1,370	217	1,416	1,349	341,812	1,415	8,082,986	381	833,258	540	902,801	1,	1,631	13,870	114,467	53
1,055	138	1,086	1,038	270,329	1,052	4,620,793	202	257,815	425	623,290	1 464	1,090	9,545	75,119	54
2,392	331	2,521	2,331	694,510	2,456	28,065,261	588	2,541,148	997	2,882,625	2,[illegible]	2,689	25,447	243,672	55

TABLE 3.—ORGANIZATIONS, COMMUNICANTS OR MEMBERS, PLACES OF WORSHIP, VALUE OF CHURCH PROPERTY, EACH STATE AND

ALABAMA.

	DENOMINATION.	Total number of organizations.	COMMUNICANTS OR MEMBERS.				
			Number of organizations reporting.	Total number reported.	Sex.		
					Number of organizations reporting.	Male.	Female.
1	All denominations	8,894	8,858	824,209	8,096	307,978	455,838
2	Adventist bodies	25	25	728	24	306	410
3	Advent Christian Church	10	10	413	9	172	229
4	Seventh-day Adventist Denomination	15	15	315	15	134	181
5	Bahais	1	1	29	1	14	15
6	Baptist bodies	4,477	4,470	452,559	4,147	169,425	259,068
7	Baptists	3,884	3,881	422,270	3,775	161,919	247,178
8	Southern Baptist Convention	1,907	1,907	162,445	1,840	63,659	90,876
9	National Baptist Convention (Colored)	1,977	1,974	259,825	1,935	98,260	156,302
10	Seventh-day Baptists	1	1	24	1	9	15
11	Free Baptists	21	21	1,200	13	121	209
12	Freewill Baptists	42	42	2,213	41	957	1,190
13	Duck River and Kindred Associations of Baptists (Baptist Church of Christ)	28	28	1,947	25	741	1,065
14	Primitive Baptists	306	303	9,772	224	2,901	4,706
15	Colored Primitive Baptists in America	187	186	14,829	63	2,714	4,547
16	Two-Seed-in-the-Spirit Predestinarian Baptists	2	2	32	2	16	16
17	United American Freewill Baptists (Colored)	6	6	272	3	47	142
18	Christians (Christian Connection)	25	25	1,890	20	658	901
19	Church of Christ, Scientist	3	3	94	3	25	69
20	Churches of the Living God (Colored)	2	2	37	2	18	19
21	Church of the Living God (Christian Workers for Friendship)	1	1	25	1	10	15
22	Church of Christ in God	1	1	12	1	8	4
23	Churches of the New Jerusalem	1	1	10	1	5	5
24	General Convention of the New Jerusalem in the United States of America	1	1	10	1	5	5
25	Congregationalists	114	113	5,395	113	2,247	3,148
26	Disciples or Christians	311	309	17,970	309	7,383	10,587
27	Disciples of Christ	154	152	8,756	152	3,496	5,260
28	Churches of Christ	157	157	9,214	157	3,887	5,327
29	Dunkers or German Baptist Brethren	1	1	52	1	26	26
30	German Baptist Brethren Church (Conservative)	1	1	52	1	26	26
31	Eastern Orthodox Churches	10	10	1,505	1	266	36
32	Greek Orthodox Church	10	10	1,505	1	266	36
33	Evangelistic associations	3	3	425	3	150	275
34	Voluntary Missionary Society in America (Colored)	3	3	425	3	150	275
35	Friends	1	1	37	1	15	22
36	Society of Friends (Orthodox)	1	1	37	1	15	22
37	German Evangelical Synod of North America	2	2	710	2	310	400
38	Independent churches	26	26	1,116	25	430	646
39	Jewish congregations	14	13	[1] 1,141	.....	.....	.....
40	Latter-day Saints	9	9	2,124	8	485	587
41	Church of Jesus Christ of Latter-day Saints	1	1	1,052	.....	.....	.....
42	Reorganized Church of Jesus Christ of Latter-day Saints	8	8	1,072	8	485	587
43	Lutheran bodies	21	21	1,111	21	495	616
44	United Synod of the Evangelical Lutheran Church in the South	1	1	50	1	20	30
45	General Council of the Evangelical Lutheran Church in North America	4	4	130	4	75	55
46	Evangelical Lutheran Synodical Conference of America	15	15	895	15	385	510
47	Evangelical Lutheran Joint Synod of Ohio and Other States	1	1	36	1	15	21
48	Methodist bodies	3,174	3,151	254,373	2,825	91,333	136,830
49	Methodist Episcopal Church	377	368	20,450	336	7,279	11,100
50	African Methodist Episcopal Church	557	555	39,617	527	14,324	23,852
51	African Methodist Episcopal Zion Church	389	385	36,705	382	13,076	23,410
52	Methodist Protestant Church	95	95	5,403	71	1,825	2,350
53	Methodist Episcopal Church, South	1,401	1,395	125,702	1,160	44,249	60,351
54	Congregational Methodist Church	59	59	3,355	58	1,422	1,837
55	Colored Methodist Episcopal Church	292	290	23,112	287	9,146	13,913
56	Free Methodist Church of North America	4	4	29	4	12	17
57	Nonsectarian Churches of Bible Faith	10	10	293	10	168	125

[1] Heads of families only.

DEBT ON CHURCH PROPERTY, PARSONAGES, AND SUNDAY SCHOOLS, BY DENOMINATIONS (IN DETAIL), FOR TERRITORY: 1906.

ALABAMA.

PLACES OF WORSHIP.					VALUE OF CHURCH PROPERTY.		DEBT ON CHURCH PROPERTY.		PARSONAGES.		SUNDAY SCHOOLS CONDUCTED BY CHURCH ORGANIZATIONS.				
Number of organizations reporting—		Number of church edifices reported.	Seating capacity of church edifices.		Number of organizations reporting.	Value reported.	Number of organizations reporting.	Amount of debt reported.	Number of organizations reporting.	Value of parsonages reported.	Number of organizations reporting.	Number of Sunday schools reported.	Number of officers and teachers.	Number of scholars.	
Church edifices.	Halls, etc.		Number of organizations reporting.	Seating capacity reported.											
8,026	379	8,183	7,667	2,423,175	8,023	$13,314,993	1,091	$527,479	934	$1,443,022	6,584	6,808	40,238	361,279	1
16	8	16	16	3,535	17	7,260	2	450	......	......	16	21	97	395	2
9	......	9	9	2,600	8	2,225	1	50	......	......	2	2	14	65	3
7	8	7	7	935	9	5,035	1	400	......	......	14	19	83	330	4
......	1	......	......	......	......	......	......	......	......	......	......	......	......	......	5
4,147	111	4,194	4,043	1,306,051	4,147	4,469,311	463	153,039	144	248,705	3,209	3,297	18,511	176,910	6
3,756	101	3,802	3,690	1,185,790	3,762	4,260,263	436	151,019	141	247,705	3,131	3,219	18,181	174,236	7
1,832	62	1,862	1,827	545,075	1,839	2,370,615	112	83,650	88	202,350	1,249	1,281	8,125	74,460	8
1,924	39	1,940	1,863	640,715	1,923	1,889,648	324	67,369	53	45,355	1,882	1,938	10,056	99,776	9
1	......	1	1	200	1	1,000	......	......	......	......	......	......	......	......	10
13	......	13	8	1,005	13	4,750	3	300	......	......	12	12	39	273	11
40	1	40	40	10,800	40	15,150	3	215	......	......	11	11	53	502	12
24	1	24	24	8,845	24	11,525	1	40	......	......	1	1	3	50	13
221	5	221	213	77,031	213	123,123	10	911	2	550	......	......	......	......	14
86	1	87	64	21,855	86	51,950	8	548	1	450	51	51	221	1,722	15
2	......	2	2	450	2	450	......	......	......	......	......	......	......	......	16
4	2	4	1	75	6	1,100	2	6	......	......	3	3	14	127	17
22	......	22	22	7,725	20	11,800	......	......	......	......	16	16	97	736	18
1	2	1	1	200	2	6,396	1	3,000	......	......	3	3	11	59	19
1	1	1	1	100	1	500	......	......	......	......	1	1	3	15	20
......	1	......	......	......	......	......	......	......	......	......	1	1	3	15	21
1	......	1	1	100	1	500	......	......	......	......	......	......	......	......	22
......	1	......	......	......	......	......	......	......	......	......	......	......	......	......	23
......	1	......	......	......	......	......	......	......	......	......	......	......	......	......	24
93	7	93	92	24,115	99	126,095	6	3,849	9	9,100	79	85	454	3,854	25
204	41	214	204	55,550	208	320,515	19	21,731	3	5,825	171	175	789	7,128	26
91	2	95	91	22,672	92	204,750	9	20,293	2	5,800	67	68	421	3,110	27
113	39	119	113	32,878	116	115,765	10	1,438	1	25	104	107	368	4,018	28
1	......	1	1	200	1	1,000	1	150	......	......	1	1	6	60	29
1	......	1	1	200		1,000	1	150	......	......	1	1	6	60	30
1	9	1	1	200	1	10,000	1	4,500	......	......	......	......	......	......	31
1	9	1	1	200	1	10,000	1	4,500	......	......	......	......	......	......	32
3	......	3	3	1,325		2,400	1	1,000	......	......		3	21	390	33
3	......	3	3	1,325	2	2,400	1	1,000	......	......	3	3	21	390	34
	......	1	1	150	1	500	......	......	......	......	1	1	10	40	35
1	......	1	1	150	1	500	......	......	......	......	1	1	10	40	36
2	......	2	2	900	2	16,000	1	2,000	1	1,100	2	2	18	265	37
23	......	23	19	4,977	21	19,525	9	3,138	1	150	22	25	92	781	38
12	1	14	11	5,250	12	198,800	3	47,000	2	700	9	12	48	746	39
8	1	8	7	1,475	8	23,175	......	......	......	......	6	6	48	203	40
1	......	1	1	100	1	375	......	......	......	......	......	......	......	......	41
7	1	7	6	1,375	7	22,800	......	......	......	......	6	6	48	203	42
11	6	13	9	2,610	10	36,250	2	4,900	5	8,350	13	13	34	307	43
1	......	1	1	800	1	200	......	......	......	......	1	1	3	28	44
1	1	1	1	250	2	1,850	......	......	......	......	2	2	7	50	45
9	4	11	7	1,560	7	34,200	2	4,900	5	8,350	9	9	23	217	46
......	1	......	......	......	......	......	......	......	......	......	1	1	1	12	47
2,937	142	2,994	2,710	846,673	2,925	4,496,235	536	201,173	628	696,067	2,571	2,664	16,870	142,265	48
333	23	346	303	93,628	333	353,316	65	13,152	71	29,161	287	302	1,916	14,167	49
505	42	517	474	153,650	501	599,907	179	46,375	120	61,403	480	502	3,012	21,616	50
375	7	387	364	121,785	377	701,841	112	22,046	57	48,103	355	358	2,456	17,202	51
87	1	87	77	26,195	86	89,726	8	25	11	9,600	63	66	308	2,497	52
1,300	55	1,306	1,159	338,709	1,290	2,426,669	81	97,575	308	516,395	1,074	1,105	7,481	74,825	53
52	6	54	52	19,300	53	31,600	4	1,309	1	1,500	35	35	249	1,917	54
284	8	296	280	93,306	284	292,676	87	20,691	60	29,905	275	294	1,440	9,996	55
1	......	1	1	100	1	500	......	......	......	......	2	2	8	45	56
3	6	3	3	550	3	2,100	......	......	......	......	1	1	6	100	57

TABLE 3.—ORGANIZATIONS, COMMUNICANTS OR MEMBERS, PLACES OF WORSHIP, VALUE OF CHURCH PROPERTY, EACH STATE AND

ALABAMA—Continued.

	DENOMINATION.	Total number of organizations.	COMMUNICANTS OR MEMBERS. Number of organizations reporting.	Total number reported.	Sex. Number of organizations reporting.	Male.	Female.
58	Presbyterian bodies	444	444	30,722	373	11,163	15,663
59	Presbyterian Church in the United States of America	7	7	303	5	87	188
60	Cumberland Presbyterian Church	162	162	8,588	122	2,759	3,790
61	Colored Cumberland Presbyterian Church	55	55	5,805	55	2,586	3,219
62	United Presbyterian Church of North America	6	6	249	6	108	141
63	Presbyterian Church in the United States	208	208	15,368	179	5,477	8,002
64	Associate Reformed Synod of the South	5	5	320	5	124	196
65	Synod of the Reformed Presbyterian Church of North America	1	1	89	1	22	67
66	Protestant Episcopal Church	102	101	8,961	96	2,432	4,467
67	Roman Catholic Church	98	98	42,285	97	20,414	21,727
68	Salvationists	8	7	79	7	33	46
69	Salvation Army	8	7	79	7	33	46
70	United Brethren bodies	1	a	30	....	....	....
71	Church of the United Brethren in Christ	1	1	30	....	....	....
72	Universalists	11	11	533		177	210

ARIZONA.

	DENOMINATION.	Total number of organizations.	COMMUNICANTS OR MEMBERS. Number of organizations reporting.	Total number reported.	Sex. Number of organizations reporting.	Male.	Female.
1	All denominations	237	236	45,057	209	17,490	18,802
2	Adventist bodies	10	9	214	9	82	132
3	Seventh-day Adventist Denomination	10	9	214	9	82	132
4	Baptist bodies	15	15	1,034	15	366	668
5	Baptists: Northern Baptist Convention	15	15	1,034	15	366	668
6	Brethren (River)	1	1	17	1	6	11
7	Brethren in Christ	1	1	17	1	6	11
8	Christadelphians	1	1	2	1	1	1
9	Church of Christ, Scientist	3	3	78	3	22	56
10	Congregationalists	7	7	405	7	120	285
11	Disciples or Christians	8	8	536	8	199	337
12	Disciples of Christ	4	4	484	4	182	302
13	Churches of Christ	4	4	52	4	17	35
14	Dunkers or German Baptist Brethren	1	1	36	1	15	21
15	German Baptist Brethren Church (Conservative)	1	1	36	1	15	21
16	Evangelistic associations	1	1	50	....	....	....
17	Missionary Church Association	a	a	50	....	....	....
18	Independent churches	4	4	25	4	13	12
19	Jewish congregations	1	1	[1] 20	....	....	....
20	Latter-day Saints	34	34	6,175	34	3,085	3,090
21	Church of Jesus Christ of Latter-day Saints	34	34	6,175	34	3,085	3,090
22	Mennonite bodies	1	1		1	1	2
23	General Conference of Mennonites of North America	1	1	3	1	1	2
24	Methodist bodies	51	51	2,667	49	1,049	1,449
25	Methodist Episcopal Church	34		1,734	32	725	840
26	African Methodist Episcopal Church	2		82	2	24	58
27	Methodist Episcopal Church, South	10		682	10	247	435
28	Colored Methodist Episcopal Church	3		126	3	42	84
29	Free Methodist Church of North America	2	34 1[illegible]	43	2	11	32
30	Presbyterian bodies	25	25	2,884	24	999	1,385
31	Presbyterian Church in the United States of America	25	25	2,884	24	999	1,385
32	Protestant Episcopal Church	13	13	1,059	10	211	456
33	Roman Catholic Church	58	58	29,810	39	11,296	10,880
34	Salvationists	3	3	42	3	25	17
35	Salvation Army	3	3	42	3	25	17

[1] Heads of families only.

DEBT ON CHURCH PROPERTY, PARSONAGES, AND SUNDAY SCHOOLS, BY DENOMINATIONS (IN DETAIL), FOR TERRITORY: 1906—Continued.

ALABAMA—Continued.

PLACES OF WORSHIP.					VALUE OF CHURCH PROPERTY.		DEBT ON CHURCH PROPERTY.		PARSONAGES.		SUNDAY SCHOOLS CONDUCTED BY CHURCH ORGANIZATIONS.				
Number of organizations reporting—		Number of church edifices reported.	Seating capacity of church edifices.		Number of organizations reporting.	Value reported.	Number of organizations reporting.	Amount of debt reported.	Number of organizations reporting.	Value of parsonages reported.	Number of organizations reporting.	Number of Sunday schools reported.	Number of officers and teachers.	Number of scholars.	
Church edifices.	Halls, etc.		Number of organizations reporting.	Seating capacity reported.											
393	11	415	379	125,137	390	$1,334,696	27	$50,859	78	$207,475	307	321	2,364	18,710	58
5	......	6	5	2,000	5	12,900	1	800	1	1,500	7	8	40	370	59
151	4	164	139	40,600	150	231,585	4	9,525	16	45,850	89	89	587	4,480	60
55	......	55	53	21,125	53	42,331	3	85	5	1,625	55	55	291	1,997	61
1	5	1	1	400	1	2,000	......	......	1	750	6	6	44	922	62
175	2	183	175	58,062	175	1,029,575	18	40,049	52	152,450	146	158	1,372	10,567	63
5	......	5	5	2,500	5	13,300	1	400	2	3,500	3	3	18	174	64
1	......	1	1	450	1	3,005	......	......	1	1,800	1	2	12	200	65
76	4	82	76	19,703	75	1,006,600	5	3,275	31	120,250	73	75	436	3,550	66
61	20	72	61	15,499	60	1,210,110	13	27,365	31	142,800	67	73	271	4,362	67
1	7	1	......	......	8	4,565	1	50	......	......	7	7	23	195	68
1	7	1	......	......	8	4,565	1	50	......	......	7	7	23	195	69
......	......	......	......	......	......	......	......	......	......	......	......	......	......	......	70
......	......	......	......	......	......	......	......	......	......	......	......	......	......	......	71
9	......	9	5	1,250	10	11,160	......	......		2,500	6	6	29	208	72

ARIZONA.

Church edifices.	Halls, etc.	Number of church edifices reported.	Number of organizations reporting (seating).	Seating capacity reported.	Number of organizations reporting (value).	Value reported.	Number of organizations reporting (debt).	Amount of debt reported.	Number of organizations reporting (parsonages).	Value of parsonages reported.	Number of organizations reporting (Sunday schools).	Number of Sunday schools reported.	Number of officers and teachers.	Number of scholars.	
166	37	181	165	40,954	174	$798,975	37	$71,441	65	$121,525	189	217	1,708	14,967	1
5	3	5	5	730	5	8,050	......	......	1	60	10	11	50	218	2
5	3	5	5	730	5	8,050	......	......	1	60	10	11	50	218	3
13	......	13	13	3,169	14	65,800	6	6,015	4	6,150	15	15	127	1,038	4
13	......	13	13	3,169	14	65,800	6	6,015	4	6,150	15	15	127	1,038	5
1	......	1	1	300	1	750	......	......	......	......	......	......	......	......	6
1	......	1	1	300	1	750	......	......	......	......	......	......	......	......	7
......	......	......	......	......	......	......	......	......	......	......	......	......	......	......	8
......	3	......	......	......	3	1,563	......	......	......	......	3	3	14	46	9
7	......	7	7	1,400	7	37,900	3	5,750	4	6,800	7	12	100	607	10
5	3	5	5	1,225	5	35,000	2	1,800	1	800	7	7	47	385	11
4	......	4	4	1,150	4	34,500	2	1,800	1	800	4	4	41	345	12
1	3	1	1	75	1	500	......	......	......	......	3	3	6	40	13
1	......	1	1	400	1	2,000	......	......	......	......	1	1	7	100	14
1	......	1	1	400	1	2,000	......	......	......	......	1	1	7	100	15
......	1	......	......	......	......	......	......	......	......	......	1	1	10	100	16
......	1	......	......	......	......	......	......	......	......	......	1	1	10	100	17
......	4	......	......	......	......	......	......	......	......	......	......	......	......	......	18
......	......	......	......	......	......	......	......	......	......	......	......	......	......	......	19
24	8	29	24	8,665	27	92,037	5	3,650	......	......	34	40	648	4,176	20
24	8	29	24	8,665	27	92,037	5	3,650	......	......	34	40	648	4,176	21
1	......	1	1	200	1	2,000	......	......	1	4,000	1	1	2	65	22
1	......	1	1	200	1	2,000	......	......	1	4,000	1	1	2	65	23
39	2	39	38	8,505	40	179,600	4	6,630	23	35,750	46	50	378	3,065	24
26	1	26	25	5,610	26	132,400	2	3,000	16	26,900	29	32	271	2,178	25
1	1	1	1	120	1	5,000	1	130	......	......	2	2	9	36	26
9	......	9	9	2,075	10	35,600	1	3,500	5	8,250	10	11	66	721	27
1	......	1	1	300	1	2,500	......	......	......	......	3	3	15	85	28
2	......	2	2	400	2	4,100	......	......	2	600	2	2	17	65	29
21	3	24	21	5,245	22	103,800	4	2,550	9	13,715	21	23	184	2,128	30
21	3	24	21	5,245	22	103,800	4	2,550	9	13,715	21	23	184	2,128	31
9	2	10	9	1,945	9	75,000	1	870	4	7,000	9	10	61	569	32
38	7	44	38	8,845	36	186,775	10	41,607	18	47,250	33	42	72	2,430	33
2	1	2	2	325	3	8,700	2	2,569	......	......	1	1	3	20	34
2	1	2	2	325	3	8,700	2	2,569	......	......	1	1	3	20	35

TABLE 3.—ORGANIZATIONS, COMMUNICANTS OR MEMBERS, PLACES OF WORSHIP, VALUE OF CHURCH PROPERTY, EACH STATE AND

ARKANSAS.

	DENOMINATION.	Total number of organizations.	COMMUNICANTS OR MEMBERS.				
			Number of organizations reporting.	Total number reported.	Sex.		
					Number of organizations reporting.	Male.	Female.
1	All denominations	6,208	6,144	426,179	5,762	164,535	239,099
2	Adventist bodies	25	25	664	17	201	299
3	Advent Christian Church	3	3	120	3	51	69
	Seventh-day Adventist Denomination	22	22	544	14	150	230
5	Baptist bodies	2,784	2,774	193,244	2,656	75,664	111,747
6	Baptists	2,534	2,528	184,995	2,486	73,367	108,546
7	Southern Baptist Convention	1,419	1,415	91,631	1,387	36,078	53,387
8	National Baptist Convention (Colored)	1,115	1,113	93,364	1,099	37,289	55,159
9	Seventh-day Baptists	4	4	254	4	128	126
10	Free Baptists	8	8	337	6	80	115
11	Freewill Baptists	10	10	371	10	153	218
12	General Baptists	54	54	2,035	53	827	1,148
13	United Baptists	35	33	1,646	21	401	468
14	Primitive Baptists	109	108	2,591	66	625	984
15	Colored Primitive Baptists in America	20	19	840	10	83	142
16	Two-Seed-in-the-Spirit Predestinarian Baptists	10	10	175	.....	.....	.....
17	Christadelphians	3	3	74	3	35	39
18	Christians (Christian Connection)	5	5	157	4	68	77
19	Church of Christ, Scientist	3	3	82	3	17	65
20	Churches of God in North America, General Eldership of the	23	23	737	21	324	353
21	Churches of the Living God (Colored)	20	20	1,118	20	413	705
22	Church of the Living God (Christian Workers for Friendship)	11	11	765	11	287	478
23	Church of the Living God (Apostolic Church)	8	8	338	8	118	220
24	Church of Christ in God	1	1	15	1	8	7
25	Churches of the New Jerusalem	2	2	54	2	28	26
26	General Convention of the New Jerusalem in the United States of America	2	2	54	2	28	26
27	Congregationalists	4	4	344	4	124	220
28	Disciples or Christians	346	344	21,275	329	8,298	11,679
29	Disciples of Christ	156	154	10,269	140	3,647	5,344
30	Churches of Christ	190	190	11,006	189	4,651	6,335
31	Dunkers or German Baptist Brethren	10	10	199	9	85	90
32	German Baptist Brethren Church (Conservative)	9	9	172	8	67	81
33	The Brethren Church (Progressive Dunkers)	1	1	27	1	18	9
34	Free Christian Zion Church of Christ (Colored)	14	13	1,635	13	665	970
35	German Evangelical Synod of North America	3	3	250	3	115	135
36	Independent churches	38	37	1,629	34	578	940
37	Jewish congregations	11	11	[1]673	.....	.....	.....
38	Latter-day Saints	5	5	538	5	218	320
39	Church of Jesus Christ of Latter-day Saints	1	1	248	1	91	157
40	Reorganized Church of Jesus Christ of Latter-day Saints	4	4	290	4	127	163
41	Lutheran bodies	26	26	2,080	24	934	1,036
42	Evangelical Lutheran Synodical Conference of America	22	22	1,886	20	851	925
43	Evangelical Lutheran Synod of Iowa and Other States	4	4	194	4	83	111
44	Mennonite bodies	1	1	45	1	23	22
45	Amish Mennonite Church	1	1	45	1	23	22
46	Methodist bodies	2,323	2,274	142,569	2,111	51,468	79,628
47	Methodist Episcopal Church	252	246	12,569	225	4,108	7,068
48	African Methodist Episcopal Church	485	482	26,903	481	10,247	16,636
49	African Methodist Episcopal Zion Church	65	65	2,404	65	932	1,472
50	Methodist Protestant Church	166	166	6,658	150	2,663	3,468
51	Methodist Episcopal Church, South	1,110	1,075	81,699	955	28,786	43,596
52	Congregational Methodist Church	26	26	684	26	284	400
53	Colored Methodist Episcopal Church	211	206	11,506	202	4,382	6,894
54	Free Methodist Church of North America	8	8	146	7	66	74
55	Nonsectarian Churches of Bible Faith	21	21	640	21	335	305
56	Presbyterian bodies	388	388	21,156	338	7,815	11,579
57	Presbyterian Church in the United States of America	23	23	809	17	236	388
58	Cumberland Presbyterian Church	260	260	11,990	222	4,476	6,345
59	United Presbyterian Church of North America	3	3	146	3	64	82
60	Presbyterian Church in the United States	89	89	7,357	83	2,680	4,269
61	Associate Reformed Synod of the South	13	13	854	13	359	495

[1] Heads of families only.

DEBT ON CHURCH PROPERTY, PARSONAGES, AND SUNDAY SCHOOLS, BY DENOMINATIONS (IN DETAIL), FOR TERRITORY: 1906—Continued.

ARKANSAS.

PLACES OF WORSHIP.					VALUE OF CHURCH PROPERTY.		DEBT ON CHURCH PROPERTY.		PARSONAGES.		SUNDAY SCHOOLS CONDUCTED BY CHURCH ORGANIZATIONS.				
Number of organizations reporting—		Number of church edifices reported.	Seating capacity of church edifices.		Number of organizations reporting.	Value reported.	Number of organizations reporting.	Amount of debt reported.	Number of organizations reporting.	Value of parsonages reported.	Number of organizations reporting.	Number of Sunday schools reported.	Number of officers and teachers.	Number of scholars.	
Church edifices.	Halls, etc.		Number of organizations reporting.	Seating capacity reported.											
5,097	685	5,192	4,921	1,446,892	5,145	$6,733,375	695	$361,011	768	$778,190	4,248	4,398	27,979	230,238	1
13	7	13	13	1,910	12	4,950	3	306	...	...	23	24	119	578	2
1	2	1	1	300	1	250	...	...	...	...	3	3	9	85	3
12	5	12	12	1,610	11	4,700	3	306	...	...	20	21	110	493	4
2,318	337	2,323	2,246	652,924	2,321	2,105,911	245	108,554	99	96,385	1,823	1,861	10,862	93,213	5
2,189	280	2,192	2,143	625,231	2,199	2,062,379	239	107,967	98	96,185	1,797	1,831	10,723	92,013	6
1,103	264	1,105	1,094	321,660	1,109	1,224,715	72	78,811	46	64,450	748	765	4,860	44,797	7
1,086	16	1,087	1,049	303,571	1,090	837,664	167	29,156	52	31,735	1,049	1,066	5,863	47,216	8
2	2	2	2	500	2	1,600	1	200	...	...	3	3	29	152	9
4	...	4	4	850	5	2,450	1	25	...	...	4	6	6	85	10
9	...	9	8	2,025	8	2,250	...	...	...	...	3	3	23	95	11
25	26	25	25	6,750	25	8,750	2	237	...	...	15	17	79	748	12
14	8	14	3	1,100	13	3,180	...	...	1	200	1	1	2	120	13
56	18	58	54	15,293	56	21,942	1	10	...	...	...	...	...	...	14
13	3	13	7	1,175	13	3,360	1	115	...	...	...	...	...	...	15
6	...	6	...	...	...	...	...	...	...	...	...	...	...	...	16
...	2	...	...	...	...	...	...	...	...	...	1	1	3	30	17
1	4	1	1	200	1	200	...	...	...	...	4	4	19	114	18
1	2	1	1	300	2	8,600	...	...	...	...	3	3	5	24	19
7	6	9	7	2,105	9	3,375	1	10	...	...	8	9	38	310	20
18	2	18	18	4,110	18	18,100	3	550	1	1,000	19	19	75	439	21
9	2	9	9	1,610	9	9,400	1	50	...	...	11	11	33	244	22
8	...	8	8	2,000	8	7,200	1	400	1	1,000	7	7	37	175	23
1	...	1	1	500	1	1,500	1	100	...	...	1	1	5	20	24
1	1	1	1	150	1	600	...	...	...	...	2	2	5	59	25
1	1			150	1	600	...	...	...	...	2	2	5	59	26
3	1	3	3	1,100	3	6,000	1	300	1	1,000	4	4	39	315	27
258	62	271	258	80,495	265	312,405	37	25,434	10	12,650	169	171	1,119	8,627	28
119	14	122	119	36,295	122	222,665	21	22,615	10	12,650	99	99	804	5,803	29
139	48	149	139	44,200	143	89,740	16	2,819	...	...	70	72	315	2,824	30
5	2	5	5	1,350	5	3,000	1	100	1	100	2	2	9	60	31
5	2	5	5	1,350	5	3,000	1	100	1	100	2	2	9	60	32
...	...	...	...	...	...	...	...	...	...	...	...	...	...	...	33
13	1	13	13	4,401	12	4,975	7	1,150	2	450	7	7	63	340	34
3	...	4	3	775	3	8,650	2	1,440	2	3,500	2	2	16	90	35
23	12	23	23	6,750	23	21,858	3	646	3	2,600	28	34	181	1,479	36
9	1	10	8	2,900	8	125,200	3	20,000	1	2,000	8	8	28	351	37
2	2	2	2	300	4	1,550	...	...	...	...	4	8	39	173	38
...	...	...	...	...	...	...	...	...	...	...	1	5	18	81	39
2	2	2	2	300	4	1,550	...	...	...	...	3	3	21	92	40
22	2	25	21	4,670	21	107,575	5	4,825	12	15,200	14	16	49	472	41
20	...	23	20	4,470	20	105,575	5	4,825	11	14,200	12	13	37	387	42
2	2	2	1	200	1	2,000	...	...	1	1,000	2	3	12	85	43
1	...	1	1	150	1	500	...	...	...	...	1	1	8	50	44
1	...	1	1	150	1	500	...	...	...	...	1	1	8	50	45
1,968	185	2,015	1,869	559,661	1,987	2,259,067	323	88,688	516	392,980	1,773	1,846	12,836	102,894	46
194	32	196	188	53,055	201	269,270	45	11,647	82	47,525	190	203	1,444	9,749	47
466	14	492	466	131,992	466	375,762	128	20,947	92	34,289	445	465	3,077	17,005	48
57	3	66	57	17,651	59	57,279	22	4,827	11	5,600	52	53	326	1,775	49
116	26	117	105	37,700	113	62,945	4	238	19	8,800	79	81	461	3,585	50
936	93	939	856	262,107	946	1,322,138	72	40,133	267	281,585	808	822	6,295	62,515	51
11	7	11	11	3,025	10	4,200	...	...	...	...	16	16	90	722	52
185	9	191	183	53,131	189	165,273	51	10,878	45	15,181	179	202	1,119	6,852	53
3	1	3	3	1,000	3	2,200	1	18	...	...	4	4	24	191	54
4	17	4	4	600	3	900	...	...	...	...	2	2	7	85	55
306	25	316	303	94,245	314	756,134	27	39,100	65	114,725	252	280	2,060	15,896	56
14	2	14	14	3,075	16	22,100	1	300	4	3,850	21	21	93	773	57
194	21	197	192	62,610	202	285,634	14	12,740	24	29,175	141	144	1,079	8,162	58
2	1	2	2	450	2	6,000	1	400	1	700	3	4	21	165	59
83	1	89	82	24,235	82	426,850	9	24,510	32	77,000	75	79	768	5,871	60
13	...	14	13	3,875	12	15,550	2	1,150	4	4,000	12	12	99	925	61

TABLE 3.—ORGANIZATIONS, COMMUNICANTS OR MEMBERS, PLACES OF WORSHIP, VALUE OF CHURCH PROPERTY, EACH STATE AND

ARKANSAS—Continued.

	DENOMINATION.	Total number of organizations.	COMMUNICANTS OR MEMBERS.				
			Number of organizations reporting.	Total number reported.	Sex.		
					Number of organizations reporting.	Male.	Female.
62	Protestant Episcopal Church	67	66	4,315	66	1,589	2,726
63	Reformed bodies	1	1	60	....	....	....
64	Reformed Church in the United States	1	1	60	....	....	....
65	Roman Catholic Church	77	77	32,397	70	15,427	16,005
66	Salvationists	5	5	159	5	77	82
67	Salvation Army	5	5	159	5	77	82
68	Universalists	3	3	85	3	34	51

CALIFORNIA.

	DENOMINATION.	Total number of organizations.	Number of organizations reporting.	Total number reported.	Number of organizations reporting.	Male.	Female.
1	All denominations	2,897	2,840	611,464	2,649	263,099	322,981
2	Adventist bodies	109	109	7,071	108	2,529	4,493
3	Advent Christian Church	15	15	675	15	267	408
4	Seventh-day Adventist Denomination	94	94	6,396	93	2,262	4,085
5	Armenian Church	4	4	2,134	4	1,386	748
6	Bahais	2	2	110	2	31	79
7	Baptist bodies	217	217	24,801	203	8,507	14,270
8	Baptists	215	215	24,683	201	8,462	14,197
9	Northern Baptist Convention	190	190	22,600	182	8,127	13,611
10	National Baptist Convention (Colored)	25	25	2,083	19	335	586
11	Free Baptists	2	2	118	2	45	73
12	Brethren (Plymouth)	25	25	613	25	263	350
13	Brethren (Plymouth)—I	10	10	155	10	58	97
14	Brethren (Plymouth)—II	7	7	210	7	95	115
15	Brethren (Plymouth)—III	5	5	175	5	81	94
16	Brethren (Plymouth)—IV	3	3	73	3	29	44
17	Brethren (River)	1	1	51	1	24	27
18	Brethren in Christ	1	1	51	1	24	27
19	Buddhists	41	9	2,629	9	1,975	654
20	Chinese Temples	32	....	....	....	....	....
21	Japanese Temples	9	9	2,629	9	1,975	654
22	Catholic Apostolic Churches	1	1	369	1	137	232
23	Catholic Apostolic Church	1	1	369	1	137	232
24	Christadelphians	4	4	51	4	19	32
25	Christian Catholic Church in Zion	2	2	220	2	90	130
26	Church of Christ, Scientist	35	35	2,753	32	682	1,855
27	Churches of the New Jerusalem	5	5	294	5	126	168
28	General Convention of the New Jerusalem in the United States of America	5	5	294	5	126	168
29	Congregationalists	214	214	23,690	213	8,145	15,425
30	Disciples or Christians	163	163	21,033	153	7,680	12,711
31	Disciples of Christ	140	140	20,272	130	7,343	12,287
32	Churches of Christ	23	23	761	23	337	424
33	Dunkers or German Baptist Brethren	26	25	1,518	24	652	839
34	German Baptist Brethren Church (Conservative)	17	16	1,070	15	480	563
35	Old Order German Baptist Brethren	2	2	69	2	38	31
36	The Brethren Church (Progressive Dunkers)	7	7	379	7	134	245
37	Eastern Orthodox Churches	30	30	9,110	3	5,175	475
38	Russian Orthodox Church	1	1	650	1	525	125
39	Servian Orthodox Church	1	1	2,800	1	2,500	300
40	Greek Orthodox Church	28	28	5,660	1	2,150	50
41	Evangelical bodies	16	16	918	13	341	477
42	Evangelical Association	15	15	872	12	326	446
43	United Evangelical Church	1	1	46	1	15	31
44	Evangelistic associations	11	11	583	11	429	154
45	Peniel Missions	8	8	528	8	405	123
46	Missionary Church Association	2	2	44	2	20	24
47	Pentecostal Union Church	1	1	11	1	4	7

DEBT ON CHURCH PROPERTY, PARSONAGES, AND SUNDAY SCHOOLS, BY DENOMINATIONS (IN DETAIL), FOR TERRITORY: 1906—Continued.

ARKANSAS—Continued.

PLACES OF WORSHIP.					VALUE OF CHURCH PROPERTY.		DEBT ON CHURCH PROPERTY.		PARSONAGES.		SUNDAY SCHOOLS CONDUCTED BY CHURCH ORGANIZATIONS.				
Number of organizations reporting—		Number of church edifices reported.	Seating capacity of church edifices.		Number of organizations reporting.	Value reported.	Number of organizations reporting.	Amount of debt reported.	Number of organizations reporting.	Value of parsonages reported.	Number of organizations reporting.	Number of Sunday schools reported.	Number of officers and teachers.	Number of scholars.	
Church edifices.	Halls, etc.		Number of organizations reporting.	Seating capacity reported.											
48	7	51	48	11,710	54	$323,525	11	$10,840	21	$55,200	43	44	255	2,012	62
...	...	...	...	...	...	...	...	...	...	...	1	1	5	41	63
...	...	...	...	...	...	...	...	...	...	...	1	1	5	41	64
70	2	80	70	15,386	70	653,250	20	57,920	34	80,400	49	63	110	2,907	65
...	5	...	...	...	5	1,350	2	148	...	...	4	4	18	133	66
...	5	...	...	...	5	1,350	2	148	...	...	4	4	18	133	67
3	...	3	3	700	3	5,700	1	1,000	...	...	2	2	11	46	68

CALIFORNIA.

Church edifices.	Halls, etc.	Number of church edifices reported.	Number of organizations reporting.	Seating capacity reported.	Number of organizations reporting.	Value reported.	Number of organizations reporting.	Amount of debt reported.	Number of organizations reporting.	Value of parsonages reported.	Number of organizations reporting.	Number of Sunday schools reported.	Number of officers and teachers.	Number of scholars.	
2,392	331	2,521	2,331	694,510	2,456	$28,065,261	588	$2,541,148	997	$2,882,625	2,439	2,689	25,447	243,672	1
78	17	80	77	15,650	78	251,365	12	8,250	5	5,600	100	103	1,005	5,492	2
12	1	12	12	2,350	12	45,700	1	2,750	3	3,500	12	12	106	575	3
66	16	68	65	13,300	66	205,665	11	5,500	2	2,100	88	91	899	4,917	4
1	2	1	1	400	1	9,000	...	...	...	...	1	1	2	100	5
...	2	...	...	...	...	...	...	...	...	...	...	...	...	...	6
200	11	209	197	60,515	205	1,860,126	48	139,170	64	109,550	212	246	2,462	22,112	7
198	11	207	195	60,115	203	1,851,126	48	139,170	64	109,550	210	244	2,447	22,011	8
177	8	186	174	54,670	181	1,689,776	40	116,247	57	102,550	187	220	2,297	20,832	9
21	3	21	21	5,445	22	161,350	8	22,923	7	7,000	23	24	150	1,179	10
2	...	2	2	400	2	9,000	...	...	...	...	2	2	15	101	11
...	25	...	...	...	...	...	...	...	...	...	14	15	35	373	12
...	10	...	...	...	...	...	...	...	...	...	5	5	10	110	13
...	7	...	...	...	...	...	...	...	...	...	6	7	18	168	14
...	5	...	...	...	...	...	...	...	...	...	3	3	7	95	15
...	3	...	...	...	...	...	...	...	...	...	...	...	...	...	16
1	...	1	1	350	1	2,700	...	...	...	...		1	13	105	17
1	...	1		350	1	2,700	...	...	...	...	1	1	13	105	18
38	3	38		1,960	6	56,000	1	2,000	...	...	9	15	39	725	19
32	...	32	...	...	...	...	...	...	...	...	...	...	...	...	20
6	3	6	6	1,960	6	56,000	1	2,000	...	...	9	15	39	725	21
1	...	1	1	250	1	6,000	...	...	...	...	...	...	...	...	22
1	...	1	1	250	1	6,000	...	...	...	...	...	...	...	...	23
...	1	...	...	...	1	50	...	...	...	...	1	1	3	15	24
...	2	...	...	...	...	...	...	...	...	...	...	...	...	...	25
20	13	20	19	6,542	27	458,020	6	12,050	...	...	31	31	195	1,336	26
5	...	5	5	1,150	5	87,000	1	1,700	...	...	5	5	26	154	27
5	...	5	5	1,150	5	87,000	1	1,700	...	...	5	5	26	154	28
190	4	200	189	52,055	194	2,271,688	41	78,235	68	162,050	197	214	2,514	21,662	29
141	19	143	140	45,070	144	1,157,900	37	123,579	21	30,400	142	150	1,686	15,899	30
132	5	134	132	43,410	134	1,147,500	33	121,639	21	30,400	133	141	1,654	15,534	31
9	14	9	8	1,660	10	10,400	4	1,940	...	...	9	9	32	365	32
20	1	20	20	5,965	20	50,417	2	650	1	2,000	20	20	206	1,574	33
14	1	14	14	4,265	14	38,750	1	150	...	...	16	16	173	1,369	34
1	...	1	1	250	1	1,400	...	...	...	...	...	...	...	...	35
5	...	5	5	1,450	5	10,267	1	500	1	2,000	4	4	33	205	36
3	27	3	2	2,300	3	27,000	1	3,000	1	700	...	...	...	...	37
...	1	...	...	...	1	3,000	...	...	...	...	...	...	...	...	38
1	...	1	1	300	1	4,000	...	...	1	700	...	...	...	...	39
2	26	2	1	2,000	1	20,000	1	3,000	...	...	...	...	...	...	40
14	...	15	14	2,800	14	123,950	4	6,550	9	27,550	16	16	172	1,000	41
13	...	13	13	2,600	13	111,950	3	5,550	8	25,350	15	15	151	873	42
1	...	2	1	200	1	12,000	1	1,000	1	2,200	1	1	21	127	43
2	8	2	1	500	4	45,850	1	3,000	...	...	6	6	37	283	44
1	7	1	1	500	3	40,250	...	...	...	...	6	6	37	283	45
...	1	...	...	...	...	...	...	...	...	...	...	...	...	...	46
1	...	1	...	...	1	5,600	1	3,000	...	...	...	...	...	...	47

TABLE 3.—ORGANIZATIONS, COMMUNICANTS OR MEMBERS, PLACES OF WORSHIP, VALUE OF CHURCH PROPERTY, EACH STATE AND

CALIFORNIA—Continued.

	DENOMINATION.	Total number of organizations.	COMMUNICANTS OR MEMBERS. Number of organizations reporting.	Total number reported.	Sex. Number of organizations reporting.	Male.	Female.
48	Friends	15	15	2,664	15	1,165	1,499
49	Society of Friends (Orthodox)	14	14	2,535	14	1,113	1,422
50	Orthodox Conservative Friends (Wilburite)	1	1	129	1	52	77
51	German Evangelical Protestant bodies	1	1	635	1	225	410
52	German Evangelical Protestant Ministers' Conference	1	1	635	1	225	410
53	German Evangelical Synod of North America	14	14	1,221	14	539	682
54	Independent churches	42	41	2,749	38	903	1,295
55	Jewish congregations	28		[1] 2,028			
56	Latter-day Saints	23	24 23	2,834	23	1,112	1,722
57	Church of Jesus Christ of Latter-day Saints	4	4	613	4	246	367
58	Reorganised Church of Jesus Christ of Latter-day Saints	19	19	2,221	19	866	1,355
59	Lutheran bodies	110	110	11,371	98	4,499	5,817
	General Synod of the Evangelical Lutheran Church in the United States of America	21	21	2,190	20	893	1,267
	General Council of the Evangelical Lutheran Church in North America	14	14	1,575	14	755	820
	Evangelical Lutheran Synodical Conference of America	46	46	5,247	38	1,874	2,703
	United Norwegian Lutheran Church in America	2	2	105			
	Hauge's Norwegian Evangelical Lutheran Synod	1	1	54	1	22	32
	Synod for the Norwegian Evangelical Lutheran Church in America	18	18	1,696	17	708	738
60	United Danish Evangelical Lutheran Church in America	6	6	428	6	216	212
[illegible]	Apostolic Lutheran Church (Finnish)	2	2	76	2	31	45
68	Mennonite bodies	2	2	100	2	49	51
69	General Conference of Mennonites of North America	2	2	100	2	49	51
70	Methodist bodies	697	687	64,528	662	24,263	38,135
71	Methodist Episcopal Church		495	50,985	484	19,563	30,060
72	African Methodist Episcopal Church	505	22	1,533	19	443	803
73	African Methodist Episcopal Zion Church	28	14	902	14	350	552
74	Methodist Episcopal Church, South	127	127	10,222	118	3,606	6,152
75	Free Methodist Church of North America	29	29	886	27	301	568
76	Moravian bodies	3	3	101	3	51	50
77	Moravian Church (Unitas Fratrum)	3	3	101	3	51	50
78	Pentecostal Church of the Nazarene	23	23	2,433	22	409	624
79	Presbyterian bodies	325	323	37,682	306	13,150	23,468
	Presbyterian Church in the United States of America	261	259	32,449	249	11,343	20,683
	Cumberland Presbyterian Church	36	36	2,908	29	901	1,366
	United Presbyterian Church of North America	23	23	2,213	23	855	1,358
80	Synod of the Reformed Presbyterian Church of North America	3	3	92	3	44	48
[illegible]	Reformed Presbyterian Church in North America, General Synod	2	2	20	2	7	13
85	Protestant Episcopal Church	223	219	21,317	187	5,479	11,404
86	Reformed bodies	1	1	118	1	53	65
87	Reformed Church in the United States	1	1	118	1	53	65
88	Reformed Catholic Church	1	1	150	1	75	75
89	Roman Catholic Church	346	346	354,408	340	169,656	180,257
	Salvationists	33	31	1,272	31	749	523
90 91	Salvation Army	33	31	1,272	31	749	523
	Spiritualists	25	25	1,808	25	814	994
	Swedish Evangelical bodies	11	11	436	11	220	216
	Swedish Evangelical Mission Covenant of America	6	6	339	6	169	170
	Swedish Evangelical Free Mission	5	5	97	5	51	46
	Theosophical societies	15	14	306	14	122	184
	Theosophical Society in America	3	3	35	3	20	15
92	Theosophical Society, American Section	11	11	271	11	102	169
[illegible]	Universal Brotherhood and Theosophical Society [2]	1					
100	Unitarians	19	19	3,204	14	692	1,239
101	United Brethren bodies	24	24	1,344	20	427	691
102	Church of the United Brethren in Christ	18	18	1,195	14	379	590
103	Church of the United Brethren in Christ (Old Constitution)	6	6	149	6	48	101
104	Universalists	4	4	605	4	211	394
105	Vedanta Society	2	2	90			
106	Volunteers of America	4	4	112		45	67

DEBT ON CHURCH PROPERTY, PARSONAGES, AND SUNDAY SCHOOLS, BY DENOMINATIONS (IN DETAIL), FOR TERRITORY: 1906—Continued.

CALIFORNIA—Continued.

PLACES OF WORSHIP.					VALUE OF CHURCH PROPERTY.		DEBT ON CHURCH PROPERTY.		PARSONAGES.		SUNDAY SCHOOLS CONDUCTED BY CHURCH ORGANIZATIONS.				
Number of organizations reporting—		Number of church edifices reported.	Seating capacity of church edifices.		Number of organizations reporting.	Value reported.	Number of organizations reporting.	Amount of debt reported.	Number of organizations reporting.	Value of parsonages reported.	Number of organizations reporting.	Number of Sunday schools reported.	Number of officers and teachers.	Number of scholars.	
Church edifices.	Halls, etc.		Number of organizations reporting.	Seating capacity reported.											
15	...	15	15	3,610	15	$104,150	2	$1,150	5	$9,000	12	12	191	1,422	48
14	...	14	14	3,460	14	97,150	2	1,150	5	9,000	12	12	191	1,422	49
1	...	1	1	150	1	7,000	...	...	...	...	...	...	...	...	50
1	...	1	1	1,000	1	95,000	1	3,200	...	...	1	1	25	255	51
1	...	1	1	1,000	1	95,000	1	3,200	...	...	1	1	25	255	52
10	2	10	10	2,500	12	84,300	6	18,000	4	13,300	12	12	76	771	53
32	8	32	29	5,145	33	158,250	2	10,000	13	13,150	33	38	241	2,006	54
11	3	15	11	6,100	12	598,750	4	104,300	...	...	15	15	45	1,371	55
7	9	7	7	1,170	14	22,795	...	...	...	...	17	21	186	866	56
...	2	...	...	...	4	1,490	...	...	...	...	4	8	53	324	57
7	7	7	7	1,170	10	21,305	...	...	...	...	13	13	133	542	58
70	24	73	70	19,840	79	895,390	40	126,168	19	90,600	90	97	664	5,186	59
15	3	15	15	5,460	17	304,900	12	47,888	1	2,500	21	21	261	1,731	60
11	1	11	11	3,350	13	124,700	7	10,000	5	23,000	12	12	91	731	61
27	12	28	27	7,095	32	330,190	14	52,450	9	56,100	34	38	217	1,759	62
1	1	1	1	300	1	17,000	...	...	...	...	2	2	10	76	63
1	...	1	1	300	1	3,000	...	...	...	...	1	1	4	30	64
8	6	9	8	1,875	8	73,000	5	8,430	2	4,000	13	15	44	605	65
5	1	6	5	1,300	5	41,800	2	7,400	2	5,000	5	6	34	214	66
2	...	2	2	160	2	800	...	...	...	...	2	2	3	40	67
2	...	2	2	320	2	6,500	...	...	...	...	2	2	17	145	68
2	...	2	2	320	2	6,500	...	...	...	...	2	2	17	145	69
630	37	643	622	183,043	642	5,194,087	122	232,518	410	782,200	622	679	7,737	68,222	70
464	26	473	460	136,408	472	4,135,100	91	193,359	291	567,900	459	501	6,275	55,932	71
21	...	23	21	6,425	22	125,150	9	5,750	11	13,050	21	21	154	934	72
13	1	13	12	4,955	14	129,587	6	15,173	7	3,550	12	12	93	484	73
113	5	114	110	31,515	115	747,950	12	17,722	88	170,650	109	121	1,030	9,664	74
19	5	20	19	3,740	19	56,300	4	514	13	27,050	21	24	185	1,208	75
3	...	3	3	350	3	1,200	...	...	3	1,400	3	3	6	209	76
3	...	3	3	350	3	1,200	...	...		1,400	3	3	6	209	77
18	5	18	18	5,650	18	149,815	9	25,305	...	...	17	17	179	1,405	78
299	15	322	296	91,805	304	3,967,460	59	148,500	106	268,500	302	339	3,960	35,150	79
242	11	262	239	75,575	247	3,472,160	49	139,430	77	195,050	243	275	3,362	29,377	80
34	1	35	34	9,045	33	124,600	4	3,150	18	23,850	33	37	307	2,932	81
21	1	23	21	6,785	22	350,700	5	4,800	10	47,300	23	24	270	2,675	82
1	2	1	1	300	1	15,000	...	...	1	2,300	2	2	14	82	83
1	...	1	1	100	1	5,000	1	1,120	...	...	1	1	7	84	84
189	14	213	186	38,867	201	2,201,815	48	186,289	75	270,365	160	172	1,197	10,000	85
1	...	1	1	175	1	1,300	...	...	...	...	1	1	6	65	86
1	...	1	1	175	1	1,300	...	...	...	...	1	1	6	65	87
...	1	...	...	...	...	...	...	...	...	...	...	...	...	...	88
325	17	360	325	114,244	323	7,191,735	112	1,279,186	171	1,067,350	312	369	1,904	41,523	89
7	25	7	5	1,500	32	151,665	13	11,725	...	...	23	23	84	604	90
7	25	7		1,500	32	151,665	13	11,725	...	...	23	23	84	604	91
7	14	7	7	6,950	9	48,250	3	4,200	...	...	6	6	53	215	92
11	...	11	10	2,675	10	32,200	6	5,075	3	5,300	11	13	99	632	93
6	...	6	6	1,925	6	23,000	3	3,400	2	3,500	6	8	63	443	94
5	...	5	4	750	4	9,200	3	1,675	1	1,800	5	5	36	189	95
...	12	...	...	...	...	...	...	...	...	...	1	1	2	3	96
...	1	...	...	...	...	...	...	...	...	...	...	...	...	...	97
...	11	...	...	...	...	...	...	...	...	...	1	1	2	3	98
...	...	...	...	...	...	...	...	...	...	...	...	...	...	...	99
15	2	18	15	6,024	15	519,500	...	...	1	5,000	16	16	115	884	100
20	3	20	20	5,685	20	101,551	5	4,150	17	15,610	22	22	218	1,428	101
16	1	16	16	4,760	16	98,500	4	4,125	12	13,860	17	17	188	1,305	102
4	2	4	4	925	4	3,051	1	25	5	2,050	5	5	30	123	103
3	1	3	3	1,550	3	103,000	1	350	1	3,000	4	4	37	285	104
1	1	1	1	300	1	12,000	...	...	...	...	...	...	...	...	105
1	3	1	1	500	2	17,482	1	2,848	...	...	2	2	10	195	106

[1] No statistics are available.

TABLE 3.—ORGANIZATIONS, COMMUNICANTS OR MEMBERS, PLACES OF WORSHIP, VALUE OF CHURCH PROPERTY, EACH STATE AND

COLORADO.

	DENOMINATION.	Total number of organizations.	COMMUNICANTS OR MEMBERS. Number of organizations reporting.	Total number reported.	Sex. Number of organizations reporting.	Male.	Female.
1	All denominations	1,268	1,261	205,666	1,179	87,077	105,861
2	Adventist bodies	50	50	2,344	49	854	1,463
3	Advent Christian Church	1	1	33	1	14	19
4	Seventh-day Adventist Denomination	49	49	2,311	48	840	1,444
5	Baptist bodies	90	90	13,011	85	4,141	7,775
	Baptists:						
6	Northern Baptist Convention	87	87	12,917	82	4,109	7,713
7	Seventh-day Baptists	1	1	63	1	21	42
8	Primitive Baptists	2	2	31	2	11	20
9	Brethren (Plymouth)	5	5	99	5	35	64
10	Brethren (Plymouth)—I	1	1	7	1	3	4
11	Brethren (Plymouth)—II	2	2	64	2	23	41
12	Brethren (Plymouth)—III	2	2	28	2	9	19
13	Christadelphians	1	1	25	1	9	16
14	Christian Union	5	5	190	2	19	26
15	Church of Christ, Scientist	20	20	1,489	20	407	1,082
16	Churches of the New Jerusalem	2	2	46	2	15	31
17	General Convention of the New Jerusalem in the United States of America	1	1	36	1	11	25
18	General Church of the New Jerusalem	1	1	10	1	4	6
19	Congregationalists	88	88	8,951	87	3,138	5,613
20	Disciples or Christians	51	51	8,635	39	2,146	3,699
21	Disciples of Christ	47	47	8,521	35	2,099	3,632
22	Churches of Christ	4	4	114	4	47	67
23	Dunkers or German Baptist Brethren	7	7	357	7	180	177
24	German Baptist Brethren Church (Conservative)	6	6	339	6	170	169
25	Old Order German Baptist Brethren	1	1	18	1	10	8
26	Eastern Orthodox Churches	16	16	2,905	4	1,317	208
27	Russian Orthodox Church	3	3	725	3	525	200
28	Greek Orthodox Church	13	13	2,180	1	792	8
29	Evangelical bodies	9	9	345	9	176	169
30	Evangelical Association	9	9	345	9	176	169
31	Evangelistic associations	2	2	187	2	71	116
32	Hephzibah Faith Missionary Association	1	1	24	1	8	16
33	Pentecostal Union Church	1	1	163	1	63	100
34	Friends	2	2	94	2	36	58
35	Society of Friends (Orthodox)	2	2	94	2	36	58
36	German Evangelical Synod of North America	6	6	833	6	318	515
37	Independent churches	7	7	346	7	147	199
38	Jewish congregations	18	13	[1]853	.....	.....	.....
39	Latter-day Saints	19	19	2,755	15	1,168	1,252
40	Church of Jesus Christ of Latter-day Saints	9	9	2,194	5	921	938
41	Reorganized Church of Jesus Christ of Latter-day Saints	10	10	561	10	247	314
42	Lutheran bodies	66	66	5,053	63	2,204	2,559
43	General Synod of the Evangelical Lutheran Church in the United States of America	7	7	820	7	327	493
44	General Council of the Evangelical Lutheran Church in North America	14	14	1,235	14	549	686
45	Evangelical Lutheran Synodical Conference of America	26	26	1,651	24	686	740
46	Evangelical Lutheran Joint Synod of Ohio and Other States	6	6	425	6	223	202
47	Evangelical Lutheran Synod of Iowa and Other States	6	6	670	6	338	332
48	Synod for the Norwegian Evangelical Lutheran Church in America	5	5	82	5	40	42
49	United Danish Evangelical Lutheran Church in America	2	2	170	1	41	64
50	Mennonite bodies	3	3	169	3	85	84
51	Mennonite Church	3	3	169	3	85	84
52	Methodist bodies	270	270	27,867	258	9,137	15,611
53	Methodist Episcopal Church	220	220	24,830	212	8,334	14,001
54	African Methodist Episcopal Church	15	15	1,139	14	325	679
55	Methodist Episcopal Church, South	15	15	1,465	13	331	670
56	Free Methodist Church of North America	20	20	433	19	147	261

[1] Heads of families only.

DEBT ON CHURCH PROPERTY, PARSONAGES, AND SUNDAY SCHOOLS, BY DENOMINATIONS (IN DETAIL), FOR TERRITORY: 1906—Continued.

COLORADO.

PLACES OF WORSHIP.					VALUE OF CHURCH PROPERTY.		DEBT ON CHURCH PROPERTY.		PARSONAGES.		SUNDAY SCHOOLS CONDUCTED BY CHURCH ORGANIZATIONS.				
Number of organizations reporting—		Number of church edifices reported.	Seating capacity of church edifices.		Number of organizations reporting.	Value reported.	Number of organizations reporting.	Amount of debt reported.	Number of organizations reporting.	Value of parsonages reported.	Number of organizations reporting.	Number of Sunday schools reported.	Number of officers and teachers.	Number of scholars.	
Church edifices.	Halls, etc.		Number of organizations reporting.	Seating capacity reported.											
917	190	956	908	255,469	956	$7,723,200	307	$619,367	419	$863,920	967	1,099	10,446	96,919	1
28	6	28	28	5,425	28	52,885	5	1,910	2	330	44	46	291	1,308	2
	1														3
28	5	28	28	5,425	28	52,885	5	1,910	2	330	44	46	291	1,308	4
76	7	79	76	22,955	82	628,325	32	52,736	31	64,900	83	100	1,170	10,187	5
75	6	78	75	22,755	81	624,825	32	52,736	31	64,900	82	99	1,159	10,138	6
1		1	1	200	1	3,500					1	1	11	49	7
	1														8
	5										1			20	9
	1														10
	2										1	1	3	20	11
	2														12
	1														13
3		3	3	950	3	5,200					4	4	30	180	14
5	11	5	4	1,987	9	188,675	1	7,000	1	300	20	20	166	917	15
2		2	2	130	2	7,000	1	750			1	1	10	41	16
1		1	1	100	1	4,500					1	1	10	41	17
1		1	1	30	1	2,500	1	750							18
72	7	78	71	23,820	72	599,950	28	41,706	33	58,650	85	108	1,082	9,725	19
47	3	47	47	14,185	48	382,550	15	18,450	9	15,550	45	46	565	5,724	20
43	3	43	43	13,560	44	376,900	15	18,450	9	15,550	43	44	554	5,654	21
4		4	4	625	4	5,650					2	2	11	70	22
5	1	5	5	1,440	5	8,700	2	550			6	7	55	411	23
5	1	5	5	1,440	5	8,700	2	550			6	7	55	411	24
															25
3	13	3	3	1,700	4	21,500	4	4,085	2	3,000					26
2	1	2	2	800	3	12,300	3	3,185	1	1,200					27
1	12	1	1	900	1	9,200	1	900	1	1,800					28
6	3	6	6	1,100	6	14,200	2	850	4	6,400	9	9	86	418	29
6	3	6	6	1,100	6	14,200	2	850	4	6,400	9	9	86	418	30
2		2	2	875	2	80,150	1	8,000			2	2	19	155	31
1		1	1	75	1	150					1	1	11	30	32
1		1	1	800	1	80,000	1	8,000			1	1	8	125	33
	2										2	2	18	107	34
	2										2	2	18	107	35
4		5	4	1,000	5	18,700	3	4,400	3	3,600	6	6	38	387	36
3	4	3	3	775	3	4,850					4	4	22	190	37
11	1	11	11	5,550	10	149,300	7	17,300	1	3,000	6	8	34	605	38
10	4	10	10	2,325	11	16,550	1	117			17	24	253	1,600	39
7	1	7	7	2,050	7	14,500					9	15	173	1,360	40
3	3	3	3	275	4	2,050	1	117			8	9	80	240	41
42	11	43	42	8,960	43	203,625	23	29,772	17	27,065	43	44	249	2,385	42
7		7	7	1,945	7	54,000	6	13,245	3	5,700	6	6	74	841	43
12	1	13	12	3,285	13	89,400	3	2,480	4	8,300	13	14	92	659	44
10	9	10	10	1,790	10	33,600	4	7,500	6	8,800	12	12	34	348	45
5	1	5	5	600	5	11,350	5	1,597	1	1,500	4	4	17	190	46
5		5	5	960	5	4,775	3	1,150	3	2,765	5	5	16	257	47
1		1	1	120	1	4,000	1	3,000			1	1	3	10	48
2		2	2	260	2	6,500	1	800			2	2	13	80	49
3		4	3	1,020	3	10,050	[illegible]	825			3	5	59	345	50
3		4	3	1,020	3	10,050	3	825			3	5	59	345	51
220	15	224	213	61,785	225	1,769,180	67	132,754	152	258,925	246	266	3,237	28,196	52
181	9	184	175	53,106	184	1,486,900	54	125,032	115	211,575	206	226	2,944	25,802	53
14	1	14	14	3,435	15	159,455	11	6,572	12	17,400	14	14	92	607	54
15		15	14	3,515	15	107,200			14	23,800	15	15	125	1,247	55
10	5	11	10	1,730	11	15,625	2	1,150	11	6,150	11	11	76	540	56

TABLE 3.—ORGANIZATIONS, COMMUNICANTS OR MEMBERS, PLACES OF WORSHIP, VALUE OF CHURCH PROPERTY, EACH STATE AND

COLORADO—Continued.

	DENOMINATION.	Total number of organizations.	COMMUNICANTS OR MEMBERS. Number of organizations reporting.	Total number reported.	Sex. Number of organizations reporting.	Male.	Female.
57	Nonsectarian Churches of Bible Faith	1	1	15	1	7	8
58	Pentecostal Church of the Nazarene	1	1	50	1	22	28
59	Presbyterian bodies	146	146	18,957	140	6,760	10,834
60	Presbyterian Church in the United States of America	128	126	16,055	122	5,543	9,149
61	Cumberland Presbyterian Church	4	4	718	4	319	399
62	Welsh Calvinistic Methodist Church	1	1	131	1	50	81
63	United Presbyterian Church of North America	9	9	1,798	9	739	1,059
64	Synod of the Reformed Presbyterian Church of North America	4	4	255	4	109	146
65	Protestant Episcopal Church	104	102	6,832	97	2,354	4,168
66	Reformed bodies	2	2	111	2	42	69
67	Reformed Church in the United States	1	1	90	1	31	59
68	Christian Reformed Church	1	1	21	1	11	10
69	Roman Catholic Church	224	224	99,820	222	51,064	48,411
70	Salvationists	13	13	454	13	230	224
71	Salvation Army	13	13	454	13	230	224
72	Spiritualists	5	5	406	5	173	233
73	Swedish Evangelical bodies	11	11	726	11	295	431
74	Swedish Evangelical Mission Covenant of America	4	4	208	4	88	120
75	Swedish Evangelical Free Mission	7	7	518	7	207	311
76	Theosophical societies	3	3	49	3	12	37
77	Theosophical Society in America	1	1	7	1	....	7
78	Theosophical Society, American Section	2	2	42	2	12	30
79	Unitarians	6	6	723	4	128	183
80	United Brethren bodies	12	12	720	11	267	389
81	Church of the United Brethren in Christ	12	12	720	11	267	389
82	Universalists	2	2	229	2	106	121
83	Volunteers of America	1	1	20	1	12	8

CONNECTICUT.

	DENOMINATION.	Total number of organizations.	COMMUNICANTS OR MEMBERS. Number of organizations reporting.	Total number reported.	Sex. Number of organizations reporting.	Male.	Female.
1	All denominations	1,384	1,364	502,560	1,283	221,144	264,356
2	Adventist bodies	38	38	2,042	38	764	1,278
3	Advent Christian Church	22	22	1,645	22	618	1,027
4	Seventh-day Adventist Denomination	12	12	269	12	80	189
5	Life and Advent Union	4	4	128	4	66	62
6	Armenian Church	3	3	579	3	471	108
7	Baptist bodies	158	157	27,872	157	10,572	17,300
8	Baptists	154	153	27,535	153	10,419	17,116
9	Northern Baptist Convention	141	140	25,317	140	9,651	15,666
10	National Baptist Convention (Colored)	13	13	2,218	13	768	1,450
11	Seventh-day Baptists	1	1	38	1	12	26
12	Free Baptists	3	3	299	3	141	158
13	Brethren (Plymouth)	5	5	49	5	23	26
14	Brethren (Plymouth)—II	2	2	24	2	12	12
15	Brethren (Plymouth)—IV	3	3	25	3	11	14
16	Buddhists	1	....	....	....	....	....
17	Chinese Temples	1	....	....	....	....	....
18	Catholic Apostolic Churches	3	3	163	3	52	111
19	Catholic Apostolic Church	3	3	163	3	52	111
20	Christians (Christian Connection)	2	2	103	1	36	37
21	Church of Christ, Scientist	10	10	521	10	149	372
22	Church of God and Saints of Christ (Colored)	4	4	42	4	9	33
23	Churches of the New Jerusalem	1	1	46	1	17	29
24	General Convention of the New Jerusalem in the United States of America	1	1	46	1	17	29

DEBT ON CHURCH PROPERTY, PARSONAGES, AND SUNDAY SCHOOLS, BY DENOMINATIONS (IN DETAIL), FOR TERRITORY: 1906—Continued.

COLORADO—Continued.

PLACES OF WORSHIP.					VALUE OF CHURCH PROPERTY.		DEBT ON CHURCH PROPERTY.		PARSONAGES.		SUNDAY SCHOOLS CONDUCTED BY CHURCH ORGANIZATIONS.				
Number of organizations reporting—Church edifices.	Number of organizations reporting—Halls, etc.	Number of church edifices reported.	Seating capacity of church edifices. Number of organizations reporting.	Seating capacity of church edifices. Seating capacity reported.	Number of organizations reporting.	Value reported.	Number of organizations reporting.	Amount of debt reported.	Number of organizations reporting.	Value of parsonages reported.	Number of organizations reporting.	Number of Sunday schools reported.	Number of officers and teachers.	Number of scholars.	
....	1	....	....	....	....	....	....	....	....	....	....	....	....	....	57
1	....	1	1	300	1	$800	....	....	....	....	1	1	6	48	58
119	11	125	119	38,779	120	1,224,050	33	$93,530	59	$153,050	138	159	1,930	18,644	59
102	10	108	102	33,079	103	1,018,550	29	80,589	51	133,550	120	141	1,642	15,886	60
4	....	4	4	1,450	4	35,000	....	....	3	4,000	4	4	50	664	61
1	....	1	1	175	1	5,000	....	....	....	....	1	1	15	75	62
9	....	9	9	3,500	9	152,500	4	12,950	5	15,500	9	9	177	1,664	63
3	1	3	3	575	3	13,000	....	....	....	....	4	4	46	355	64
72	14	74	72	14,509	73	771,035	18	36,552	38	89,000	63	65	469	4,119	65
1	1	1	1	250	1	12,500	1	6,500	1	2,000	2	2	20	195	66
1	....	1	1	250	1	12,500	1	5,500	1	2,000	1	1	19	175	67
....	1	....	....	....	....	....	....	....	....	....	1	1	1	20	68
155	45	168	155	37,534	159	1,239,395	44	139,012	52	154,600	115	123	296	8,523	69
....	13	....	....	....	13	3,000	5	209	....	....	12	12	41	334	70
....	13	....	....	....	13	3,000	5	209	....	....	12	12	41	334	71
....	5	....	....	....	....	....	....	....	....	....	....	....	....	....	72
10	1	12	10	3,225	11	57,330		7,950	2	1,800	10	13	107	780	73
3	1	4	3	900	4	21,080	3	4,200	1	1,000	3	4	23	180	74
7	....	8	7	2,325	7	36,250	2	3,750	1	800	7	9	84	600	75
....	3	....	....	....	....	....	....	....	....	....	....	....	....	....	76
....	1	....	....	....	....	....	....	....	....	....	....	....	....	....	77
....			....	....	....	....	....	....	....	....	....	....	....	....	78
5	....	5	5	1,750	5	163,200	2	6,400	1	3,000	5	5	36	265	79
11	....	11	11	2,940	11	59,500	3	4,500	11	18,750	12	14	134	970	80
11	....	11	11	2,940	11	59,500	3	4,500	11	18,750	12	14	134	970	81
1	1	1	1	200	1	31,000	1	3,500	....	....	1	1	12	90	82
....	1	....	....	....	....	....	....	....	....	....	1	1	8	50	83

CONNECTICUT.

1,255	87	1,414	1,245	522,941	1,278	$29,196,128	395	$2,776,588	818	$3,995,148	1,251	1,340	19,320	179,673	1
23	13	23	23	4,915	26	90,704	6	8,125	2	9,500	32	33	278	1,529	2
19	3	19	19	4,425	19	80,300	3	5,250	2	9,500	18	18	203	1,180	3
2	8	2	2	290	3	4,530	1	275	....	....	11	12	59	284	4
2	2	2	2	200	4	5,874	2	2,600	....	....	3	3	16	65	5
....	3	....	....	....	....	....	....	....	....	....	....	....	....	....	6
155	3	164	154	53,054	157	2,254,550	41	161,870	82	221,875	148	162	2,346	18,925	7
151	3	160	150	52,354	153	2,247,300	41	161,870	82	221,875	145	159	2,318	18,746	8
138	3	147	137	48,233	140	2,140,800	34	147,220	80	220,575	132	146	2,191	17,584	9
13	....	13	13	4,121	13	106,500	7	14,650	2	1,300	13	13	127	1,162	10
	....	1	1	200	1	2,000	....	....	....	....	1	1	9	54	11
3	....	3	3	500	3	5,250	....	....	....	....	2	2	19	125	12
....	5	....	....	....	....	....	....	....	....	....	2	2	5	24	13
....	2	....	....	....	....	....	....	....	....	....	2	2	5	24	14
....	3	....	....	....	....	....	....	....	....		....	....	....	....	15
	..		....	....	....	....	....	....	....	....	....	....	....	..	16
1	....		....	....	....	....	....	....	....	....	....	....	....	....	17
	1	2	2	320	2	20,000	....	....	....	....	....	....	....	....	18
	1	2	2	320	2	20,000	....	....	....	....	....	....	....	....	19
2	....	2	2	300	2	3,500	....	....	[illegible]	1,500	2	2	13	94	20
[illegible]	6	4	2	750	7	92,783	1	8,750	....	....	7	7	51	175	21
....	4	....	....	....	....	....	....	....	....	....	....	....	....	....	22
....	....	....	....	....	....	....	....	....	....	....	....	....	....	....	23
....	....	....	....	....	....	....	....	....	....	....	....	....	....	....	24

TABLE 3.—ORGANIZATIONS, COMMUNICANTS OR MEMBERS, PLACES OF WORSHIP, VALUE OF CHURCH PROPERTY, EACH STATE AND

CONNECTICUT—Continued.

	DENOMINATION.	Total number of organizations.	COMMUNICANTS OR MEMBERS.				
			Number of organizations reporting.	Total number reported.	Sex.		
					Number of organizations reporting.	Male.	Female.
25	Communistic societies	1	1	40	1	10	30
26	United Society of Believers (Shakers)	1	1	40	1	10	30
27	Congregationalists	333	333	65,554	333	22,536	43,018
28	Disciples or Christians	4	4	866	4	351	515
29	Disciples of Christ	4	4	866	4	351	515
30	Eastern Orthodox Churches	12	12	3,127	4	951	601
31	Russian Orthodox Church	4	4	1,552	4	951	601
32	Greek Orthodox Church	8	8	1,575	...	...	...
33	Evangelical bodies	1	1	76	1	25	51
34	Evangelical Association	1	1	76	1	25	51
35	Evangelistic associations	1	1	200	...	...	...
36	Apostolic Christian Church	1	1	200	...	...	...
37	Independent churches	9	9	639	9	246	393
38	Jewish congregations	31	18	[1]1,733	...	...	...
39	Latter-day Saints	1	1	44	1	16	28
40	Reorganized Church of Jesus Christ of Latter-day Saints	1	1	44	1	16	28
41	Lutheran bodies	75	75	19,713	70	8,351	9,857
42	General Synod of the Evangelical Lutheran Church in the United States of America	2	2	231	2	105	126
43	General Council of the Evangelical Lutheran Church in North America	48	48	13,951	45	5,905	7,006
44	Evangelical Lutheran Synodical Conference of America	19	19	4,156	17	1,662	2,029
45	Danish Evangelical Lutheran Church in America	4	4	550	4	279	271
46	Slovak Evangelical Lutheran Synod of America	2	2	825	2	400	425
47	Methodist bodies	233	232	34,663	213	11,319	20,128
48	Methodist Episcopal Church	206	206	32,878	188	10,711	19,104
49	Union American Methodist Episcopal Church (Colored)	1	1	60	1	20	40
50	African Methodist Episcopal Church	5	5	335	4	62	120
51	African Methodist Episcopal Zion Church	17	16	1,229	16	457	772
52	Methodist Protestant Church	4	4	161	4	69	92
53	Nonsectarian Churches of Bible Faith	1	1	25	1	15	10
54	Pentecostal Church of the Nazarene	3	3	81	3	26	55
55	Polish National Church of America	1	1	300	1	140	160
56	Presbyterian bodies	9	9	2,425	6	441	917
57	Presbyterian Church in the United States of America	8	8	2,252	6	441	917
58	United Presbyterian Church of North America	1	1	173	...	...	...
59	Protestant Episcopal Church	189	186	37,466	164	10,812	19,249
60	Reformed bodies	4	4	1,262	4	652	610
61	Reformed Church in the United States	3	3	1,012	3	507	505
62	Hungarian Reformed Church in America	1	1	250	1	145	105
63	Roman Catholic Church	211	211	299,513	211	151,913	147,600
64	Salvationists	15	15	476	15	224	252
65	Salvation Army	15	15	476	15	224	252
66	Spiritualists	7	6	976	6	418	558
67	Unitarians	5	5	446	3	150	156
68	Universalists	12	12	1.478	10	434	855
69	Volunteers of America	1	1	40	1	21	19

DELAWARE.

	DENOMINATION.	Total number of organizations.	Number of organizations reporting.	Total number reported.	Number of organizations reporting.	Male.	Female.
1	All denominations	468	467	71,251	431	27,828	38,151
	Adventist bodies	3	3	155	3	52	103
3	Seventh-day Adventist Denomination	3	3	155	3	52	103
4	Baptist bodies	23	23	2,921	19	688	1,457
	Baptists:						
5	Northern Baptist Convention	16	16	2,694	14	632	1,331
6	Primitive Baptists	7	7	227	5	56	126

[1] Heads of families only.

DEBT ON CHURCH PROPERTY, PARSONAGES, AND SUNDAY SCHOOLS, BY DENOMINATIONS (IN DETAIL), FOR TERRITORY: 1906—Continued.

CONNECTICUT—Continued.

PLACES OF WORSHIP: Number of organizations reporting—Church edifices.	PLACES OF WORSHIP: Number of organizations reporting—Halls, etc.	PLACES OF WORSHIP: Number of church edifices reported.	PLACES OF WORSHIP: Seating capacity of church edifices: Number of organizations reporting.	PLACES OF WORSHIP: Seating capacity of church edifices: Seating capacity reported.	VALUE OF CHURCH PROPERTY: Number of organizations reporting.	VALUE OF CHURCH PROPERTY: Value reported.	DEBT ON CHURCH PROPERTY: Number of organizations reporting.	DEBT ON CHURCH PROPERTY: Amount of debt reported.	PARSONAGES: Number of organizations reporting.	PARSONAGES: Value of parsonages reported.	SUNDAY SCHOOLS CONDUCTED BY CHURCH ORGANIZATIONS: Number of organizations reporting.	SUNDAY SCHOOLS CONDUCTED BY CHURCH ORGANIZATIONS: Number of Sunday schools reported.	SUNDAY SCHOOLS CONDUCTED BY CHURCH ORGANIZATIONS: Number of officers and teachers.	SUNDAY SCHOOLS CONDUCTED BY CHURCH ORGANIZATIONS: Number of scholars.	
....	1	....	....	....	1	$1,800	....	....	....	....	....	....	....	....	25
....	1	....	....	....	1	1,800	....	....	....	....	....	....	....	....	26
323		412	323	145,626	325	6,710,825	66	$193,216	250	$1,022,318	326	357	6,532	50,932	27
2		2	2	925	4	38,700	....	....	....	....	2	2	33	340	28
2	1	2	2	925	4	38,700	....	....	....	....	2	2	33	340	29
4	8	4	4	2,300	4	33,500	3	12,100	3	12,000	....	....	....	....	30
4	....	4	4	2,300	4	33,500	3	12,100	3	12,000	....	....	....	....	31
....	8	....	....	....	....	....	....	....	....	....	....	....	....	....	32
1	....	1	1	300	1	4,800	1	1,650	....	....	1	1	16	150	33
1	....	1	1	300	1	4,800	1	1,650	....	....	1	1	16	150	34
1	....	1	1	200	1	6,000	1	2,500	....	....	1	1	3	100	35
1	....	1	1	200	1	6,000	1	2,500	....	....	1	1	3	100	36
9	....	9	9	1,725	9	24,400		5,000	2	4,500	8	8	69	576	37
16	1	17	16	7,975	17	367,000	13	97,700	1	300	8	8	40	620	38
1	....	1	1	200	1	1,500	....	....	....	....	1	1	7	14	39
1	....	1	1	200	1	1,500	....	....	....	....	1	1	7	14	40
59	9	60	59	21,535	62	754,101	47	199,079	31	116,200	66	69	861	6,949	41
2	....	2	2	475	2	21,000	2	10,800	....	....	2	2	23	180	42
40	3	40	40	15,010	42	525,801	30	140,594	21	82,700	46	49	690	5,271	43
13	5	14	13	5,105	13	183,800	11	40,185	9	30,000	15	15	131	1,323	44
3	....	3	3	645	3	15,700	3	4,500	1	3,500	2	2	16	135	45
1	1	1	1	300	2	7,800	1	3,000	....	....	1	1	1	40	46
229	4	241	223	74,972	229	3,185,815	56	196,269	175	637,000	224	232	4,105	27,540	47
205	1	217	199	67,969	204	2,946,810	42	166,114	163	607,000	197	205	3,814	26,109	48
1	....	1	1	300	1	7,000	....	....	....	....	1	1	11	40	49
5	....	5	5	1,175	5	14,600	3	3,939	2	4,500	5	5	39	270	50
14	3	14	14	4,728	15	204,505	9	23,107	8	23,500	17	17	208	946	51
4	....	4	4	800	4	12,900	2	3,109	2	2,000	4	4	33	175	52
....		....	....	....	....	....	....	....	....	....	....	....	....	....	53
1	2	1	1	350	1	3,000	1	900	....	....	2	2	14	50	54
1	....	1	1	300	1	15,000	1	9,000	1	15,000	1	1	1	30	55
9	....	12	9	5,050	9	559,000	3	21,000	3	38,000	9	9	185	1,802	56
8	....	11	8	4,650	8	539,000	3	21,000	3	38,000	8	8	165	1,681	57
1	....	1	1	400	1	20,000	....	....	....	....	1	1	20	121	58
181	4	209	181	65,356	177	4,951,725	12	58,793	117	690,675	172	185	2,146	17,558	59
4	....	7	4	2,650	4	65,000	4	28,150	4	10,500	4	5	55	605	60
3	....	5	3	2,300	3	53,500	3	18,150	3	7,500	3	4	53	545	61
1	....	2	1	350	1	11,500	1	10,000	1	3,000	1	1	2	60	62
202	7	215	202	124,614	205	9,332,950	124	1,709,310	140	1,180,180	209	224	2,333	49,955	63
7	8	7	7	2,650	15	75,575	9	44,679	....	....	12	15	48	370	64
		7	7	2,650	15	75,575	9	44,679	....	....	12	15	48	370	65
3	1	3	3	1,050	3	17,500	....	....	....	....	1	1	9	40	66
3	1	3	3	1,224	3	44,300	1	3,150	....	....	4	4	25	189	67
12	....	12	12	4,600	12	542,100	2	15,347	6	35,600	9	9	145	1,106	68
....	1	....	....	....	....	....	....	....	....	....	....	....	....	....	69

DELAWARE.

450	13	478	431	130,267	451	$3,250,105	140	$248,720	168	$470,605	425	441	5,604	49,926	1
2	....	2	1	200	2	1,200	1	40	....	....	2	3	10	85	2
2	....	2	1	200	2	1,200	1	40	....	....	2	3	10	85	
21	....	23	20	7,750	21	241,800	4	6,650	4	16,500	15	15	358	2,437	4
16	....	17	15	6,000	16	223,300	3	5,650	3	9,500	15	15	358	2,437	5
5	....	6	5	1,750	5	18,500	1	1,000	1	7,000	....	....	....	....	

TABLE 3.—ORGANIZATIONS, COMMUNICANTS OR MEMBERS, PLACES OF WORSHIP, VALUE OF CHURCH PROPERTY, EACH STATE AND

DELAWARE—Continued.

	DENOMINATION.	Total number of organizations.	COMMUNICANTS OR MEMBERS.				
			Number of organizations reporting.	Total number reported.	Sex.		
					Number of organizations reporting.	Male.	Female.
7	Brethren (Plymouth)	3	3	42	3	21	21
8	Brethren (Plymouth)—I	2	2	32	2	16	16
9	Brethren (Plymouth)—IV	1	1	10	1	5	5
10	Church of Christ, Scientist	1	1	74	1	25	49
11	Church of God and Saints of Christ (Colored)	2	2	54	2	25	29
12	Churches of the New Jerusalem	1	1	59	1	21	38
13	General Convention of the New Jerusalem in the United States of America	1	1	59	1	21	38
14	Disciples or Christians	1	1	75	1	25	50
15	Disciples of Christ	1	1	75	1	25	50
16	Friends	6	6	621	6	296	325
17	Society of Friends (Orthodox)	1	1	109	1	48	61
18	Religious Society of Friends (Hicksite)	5	5	512	5	248	264
19	Independent churches	3	3	66	2	21	30
20	International Apostolic Holiness Union	1	1	168	1	67	101
21	Jewish congregations	2	2	[1]207	.....	.....	.....
22	Lutheran bodies	4	4	731	4	382	349
23	General Synod of the Evangelical Lutheran Church in the United States of America	1	1	38	1	16	22
24	General Council of the Evangelical Lutheran Church in North America	2	2	665	2	351	314
25	Evangelical Lutheran Joint Synod of Ohio and Other States	1	1	28	1	15	13
26	Methodist bodies	314	314	32,402	293	11,450	18,429
27	Methodist Episcopal Church	207	207	24,269	190	8,732	13,805
28	Union American Methodist Episcopal Church (Colored)	12	12	686	12	270	416
29	African Methodist Episcopal Church	39	39	2,553	38	689	1,281
30	African Union Methodist Protestant Church	13	13	1,264	11	412	725
31	African Methodist Episcopal Zion Church	4	4	167	3	44	42
32	Methodist Protestant Church	39	39	3,463	39	1,303	2,160
33	Presbyterian bodies	38	38	5,200	36	1,596	3,228
34	Presbyterian Church in the United States of America	37	37	5,086	35	1,556	3,154
35	United Presbyterian Church of North America	1	1	114	1	40	74
36	Protestant Episcopal Church	39	38	3,796	32	806	1,615
37	Reformed Episcopal Church	1	1	100	1	36	64
38	Roman Catholic Church	23	23	24,228	23	12,167	12,061
39	Salvationists	1	1	65	1	34	31
40	Salvation Army	1	1	65	1	34	31
41	Spiritualists	1	1	37	1	16	21
42	Unitarians	1	1	250	1	100	150

DISTRICT OF COLUMBIA.

	DENOMINATION.	Total number of organizations.	Number of organizations reporting.	Total number reported.	Number of organizations reporting.	Male.	Female.
1	All denominations	289	288	136,759	259	41,634	72,723
2	Adventist bodies	3	3	382	3	161	221
3	Seventh-day Adventist Denomination	3	3	382	3	161	221
4	Armenian Church	1	1	75	1	62	13
5	Bahais	1	1	74	1	13	61
6	Baptist bodies	82	82	37,024	78	10,180	23,986
7	Baptists	80	80	36,980	76	10,164	23,958
8	Northern Baptist Convention	20	20	10,777	18	3,635	7,009
9	National Baptist Convention (Colored)	60	60	26,203	58	6,529	16,949
10	Primitive Baptists	2	2	44	2	16	28
11	Brethren (Plymouth)	3	3	38	3	13	25
12	Brethren (Plymouth)—I	1	1	14	1	3	11
13	Brethren (Plymouth)—III	1	1	17	1	5	12
14	Brethren (Plymouth)—IV	1	1	7	1	5	2
15	Christadelphians	1	1	28	1	14	14
16	Church of Christ, Scientist	1	1	347	1	91	256
17	Church of God and Saints of Christ (Colored)	1	1	70	1	20	50

[1] Heads of families only.

DEBT ON CHURCH PROPERTY, PARSONAGES, AND SUNDAY SCHOOLS, BY DENOMINATIONS (IN DETAIL), FOR TERRITORY: 1906—Continued.

DELAWARE—Continued.

PLACES OF WORSHIP.					VALUE OF CHURCH PROPERTY.		DEBT ON CHURCH PROPERTY.		PARSONAGES.		SUNDAY SCHOOLS CONDUCTED BY CHURCH ORGANIZATIONS.				
Number of organizations reporting—		Number of church edifices reported.	Seating capacity of church edifices.		Number of organizations reporting.	Value reported.	Number of organizations reporting.	Amount of debt reported.	Number of organizations reporting.	Value of parsonages reported.	Number of organizations reporting.	Number of Sunday schools reported.	Number of officers and teachers.	Number of scholars.	
Church edifices.	Halls, etc.		Number of organizations reporting.	Seating capacity reported.											
	3														7
	2														8
	1														9
1		1	1	150	1	$8,000					1	1	8	40	10
	2														11
1		1	1	175	1	30,000			1	$8,000	1	1	6	25	12
1		1	1	175	1	30,000			1	8,000	1	1	6	25	13
1		1	1	300	1	1,600					1	1	5	30	14
1		1	1	300	1	1,600					1	1	5	30	15
6		6	6	1,500	6	43,000					4	4	28	164	16
1		1	1	250	1	16,000									17
5		5	5	1,250	5	27,000					4	4	28	164	18
2	1	2	2	500	3	2,248	3	$197			3	3	19	82	19
1		1	1	300	1	1,600			1	1,200	1	1	14	150	20
1	1	1	1	324	1	10,000	1	2,000			1	1	5	65	21
4		4	4	1,350	4	49,600	2	4,450			4	4	64	737	22
1		1	1	150	1	6,000					1	1	12	135	23
2		2	2	1,050	2	42,000	1	3,000			2	2	44	575	24
1		1	1	150	1	1,600	1	1,450			1	1	8	27	25
314		328	298	83,310	314	1,467,832	116	94,533	109	210,005	307	315	4,018	33,570	26
207		218	191	55,271	207	1,191,350	56	57,572	84	174,200	206	211	3,062	25,473	27
12		12	12	3,041	12	25,400	9	5,421	1	1,500	12	14	109	657	28
39		39	39	8,955	39	89,710	26	12,600	8	7,650	35	35	260	2,034	29
13		15	13	4,825	13	38,347	11	4,375	4	5,400	13	13	109	1,463	30
4		4	4	1,083	4	11,925	4	3,043			3	3	20	100	31
39		40	39	10,135	39	111,100	10	11,522	12	21,255	39	39	458	3,843	32
36		42	36	12,755	36	416,500	2	10,400	17	63,600	34	38	563	5,454	33
35		41	35	12,455	35	400,500	1	6,900	17	63,600	33	37	550	5,319	34
1		1	1	300	1	16,000	1	3,500			1	1	13	135	35
39		45	39	11,253	39	430,475	4	4,700	20	92,500	30	31	272	2,482	36
1		1	1	200	1	10,000					1	1	11	89	37
19	4	19	18	9,800	18	516,000	7	125,750	16	78,800	18	20	201	4,396	38
	1				1	250					1	1	12	70	39
	1				1	250					1	1	12	70	40
	1														41
1		1	1	400	1	20,000					1	1	10	50	42

DISTRICT OF COLUMBIA.

235	43	264	232	142,311	243	$10,025,122	143	$1,570,609	74	$612,741	263	297	5,338	56,771	1
2	1	2	2	700	2	20,000	1	2,400			3	3	42	304	
		2	2	700	2	20,000	1	2,400			3	3	42	304	[illegible]
															4
	1														5
61	21	65	60	39,382	61	1,851,400	40	215,986	4	8,800	77	83	1,219	13,913	6
61	19	65	60	39,382	61	1,851,400	40	215,986	4	8,800	77	83	1,219	13,913	7
18	2	21	17	12,045	18	888,500	7	35,600	2	7,500	20	25	737	8,314	8
43	17	44	43	27,337	43	962,900	33	180,386	2	1,300	57	58	482	5,599	9
	2														10
	3										1	1	3	21	11
	1										1	1	3	21	12
	1														13
	1														14
	1				1	50					1	1	6	20	15
1		1	1	600	1	32,000	1	12,000			1	1	14	90	16
1		1	1	400	1	6,000									17

TABLE 3.—ORGANIZATIONS, COMMUNICANTS OR MEMBERS, PLACES OF WORSHIP, VALUE OF CHURCH PROPERTY, EACH STATE AND

DISTRICT OF COLUMBIA—Continued.

	DENOMINATION.	Total number of organizations.	COMMUNICANTS OR MEMBERS.				
			Number of organizations reporting.	Total number reported.	Sex.		
					Number of organizations reporting.	Male.	Female.
18	Churches of the New Jerusalem	1	1	132	1	47	85
19	General Convention of the New Jerusalem in the United States of America	1		132	1	47	85
20	Congregationalists	6	[illegible]	2,984	6	1,137	1,847
21	Disciples or Christians	5	5	2,170	5	959	1,211
22	Disciples of Christ	5	5	2,170	5	959	1,211
23	Dunkers or German Baptist Brethren	2	2	256	2	99	157
24	German Baptist Brethren Church (Conservative)	1	1	110	1	43	67
25	The Brethren Church (Progressive Dunkers)	1	1	146	1	56	90
26	Eastern Orthodox Churches	1	[illegible]	450	1	400	50
27	Greek Orthodox Church	1	1	450	1	400	50
28	Friends	2	2	156	2	68	88
29	Society of Friends (Orthodox)	1	1	61	1	28	33
30	Religious Society of Friends (Hicksite)	1	1	95	1	40	55
31	German Evangelical Synod of North America	1	1	350	1	125	225
32	Independent churches	1	1	150	1	90	60
33	Jewish congregations	4	3	[1]698	....	....	....
34	Lutheran bodies	14	14	3,104	13	1,114	1,790
35	General Synod of the Evangelical Lutheran Church in the United States of America	9	9	2,129	8	711	1,218
36	General Council of the Evangelical Lutheran Church in North America	1	1	75	1	32	43
37	Evangelical Lutheran Synodical Conference of America	2	2	432	2	177	255
38	Evangelical Lutheran Joint Synod of Ohio and Other States	2	2	468	2	194	274
39	Methodist bodies	70	70	20,077	64	6,859	11,911
40	Methodist Episcopal Church	37	37	11,019	33	3,664	6,550
41	African Methodist Episcopal Church	7	7	1,928	7	724	1,204
42	African Union Methodist Protestant Church	1	1	45	1	20	25
43	African Methodist Episcopal Zion Church	6	6	2,615	6	988	1,627
44	Methodist Protestant Church	5	5	1,415	4	479	659
45	Methodist Episcopal Church, South	7	7	1,922	6	627	1,070
46	Colored Methodist Episcopal Church	5	5	1,110	5	348	762
47	Free Methodist Church of North America	2	2	23	2	9	14
48	Pentecostal Church of the Nazarene	1	1	166	1	60	106
49	Presbyterian bodies	19	19	8,636	18	2,486	4,988
50	Presbyterian Church in the United States of America	17	17	8,182	16	2,339	4,681
51	Presbyterian Church in the United States	2	2	454	2	147	307
52	Protestant Episcopal Church	38	38	13,692	33	3,747	7,877
53	Reformed bodies	2	2	580	1	109	161
54	Reformed Church in the United States	2	2	580	1	109	161
55	Roman Catholic Church	21	21	43,778	13	13,245	16,734
56	Salvationists	1	1	18	1	8	10
57	Salvation Army	1	1	18		8	10
58	Spiritualists	2	2	143	[illegible]	64	79
59	Theosophical societies	2	2	67	2	26	41
60	Theosophical Society in America	1	1	16	1	8	8
61	Theosophical Society, American Section	1	1	51	1	18	33
62	Unitarians	1	1	700	1	300	400
63	United Brethren bodies	1	1	260	1	95	165
64	Church of the United Brethren in Christ	1	1	260	1	95	165
65	Universalists	1	1	154	1	42	112

[1] Heads of families only.

DEBT ON CHURCH PROPERTY, PARSONAGES, AND SUNDAY SCHOOLS, BY DENOMINATIONS (IN DETAIL), FOR TERRITORY: 1906—Continued.

DISTRICT OF COLUMBIA—Continued.

PLACES OF WORSHIP.					VALUE OF CHURCH PROPERTY.		DEBT ON CHURCH PROPERTY.		PARSONAGES.		SUNDAY SCHOOLS CONDUCTED BY CHURCH ORGANIZATIONS.				
Number of organizations reporting—		Number of church edifices reported.	Seating capacity of church edifices.												
Church edifices.	Halls, etc.		Number of organizations reporting.	Seating capacity reported.	Number of organizations reporting.	Value reported.	Number of organizations reporting.	Amount of debt reported.	Number of organizations reporting.	Value of parsonages reported.	Number of organizations reporting.	Number of Sunday schools reported.	Number of officers and teachers.	Number of scholars.	
1	....	1	1	600	1	$100,000	....	....	....	....	1	1	7	70	18
1	....	1	1	600	1	100,000	....	....	....	....	1	1	7	70	19
5	....	6	5	4,050	6	329,000	3	$53,500	1	$4,000	6	8	168	2,311	20
5	....	6	5	2,600	5	141,000	4	25,013	....	....	5	5	123	1,495	21
5	....	6	5	2,600	5	141,000	4	25,013	....	....	5	5	123	1,495	22
2	....	2	2	900	2	24,000	1	2,500	....	....	2	2	27	305	23
1	....	1	1	600	1	18,000	....	....	....	....	1	1	15	190	24
1	....	1	1	300	1	6,000	1	2,500	....	....	1	1	12	115	25
1	....	1	1	250	1	3,500	....	....	....	....	....	....	....	....	26
1	....	1	1	250	1	3,500	....	....	....	....	....	....	....	....	27
2	....	2	2	575	2	54,000	....	....	....	....	2	2	12	76	28
1	....	1	1	300	1	25,000	....	....	....	....	1	1	9	60	29
1	....	1	1	275	1	29,000	....	....	....	....	1	1	3	16	30
1	....	1	1	650	1	53,000	1	1,000	1	5,500	1	1	20	160	31
....	1	....	....	....	....	....	....	....	....	....	....	....	....	....	32
3	....	3	3	3,100	3	210,000	3	115,000	....	....	3	3	12	325	33
14	....	15	14	5,435	14	581,700	11	85,300	4	41,500	14	15	274	2,273	34
9	....	9	9	3,910	9	476,700	6	59,300	3	36,500	9	9	220	1,794	35
1	....	1	1	350	1	22,000	1	10,000	....	....	1	1	10	98	36
2	....	3	2	600	2	40,000	2	1,300	1	5,000	2	3	20	154	37
2	....	2	2	575	2	48,000	2	14,700	....	....	2	2	24	227	38
66	4	67	64	36,162	67	1,968,272	44	214,923	30	170,560	68	78	1,443	15,111	39
36	1	36	34	17,439	36	1,178,705	24	84,098	20	138,260	37	41	934	9,569	40
7	....	7	7	4,150	7	127,987	6	29,350	4	8,800	7	7	98	1,116	41
....	1	....	....	....	....	....	....	....	....	....	1	1	4	40	42
6	....	6	6	3,230	6	207,000	5	38,900	2	9,000	6	7	102	1,037	43
5	....	5	5	3,843	5	169,500	3	24,500	2	10,000	5	5	126	1,466	44
7	....	8	7	3,100	7	141,000	3	18,075	1	3,500	7	7	130	1,378	45
5	....	5	5	4,400	5	139,000	3	20,000	1	1,000	5	5	49	505	46
....	2	....	....	....	1	80	....	....	....	....	....	....	....	....	47
....	1	....	....	....	....	....	....	....	....	....	1	1	9	50	48
19	....	27	1	13,120	19	1,238,500	8	107,450	6	57,000	19	25	636	6,994	49
17	....	25	17	12,560	17	1,198,500	7	101,450	6	57,000	17	23	606	6,809	50
2	....	2	2	560	2	40,000	1	6,000	....	....	2	2	30	185	51
33	5	43	33	18,267	37	1,864,850	17	208,318	13	117,500	38	46	677	6,606	52
2	....	2	2	1,200	2	90,000	....	....	2	12,000	2	2	38	421	53
2	....	2	2	1,200	2	90,000	....	....	2	12,000	2	2	38	421	54
13	....	15	13	11,670	13	1,259,550	8	514,919	13	195,881	13	19	526	5,620	55
....	1	....	....	....	1	300	....	....	....	....	1	1	6	55	56
....	1	....	....	....	1	300	....	....	....	....	1	1	6	55	57
....	2	....	....	....	....	....	....	....	....	....	1	1	3	25	58
....	1	....	....	....	....	....	....	....	....	....	....	....	....	....	59
....	....	....	....	....	....	....	....	....	....	....	....	....	....	....	60
....	1	....	....	....	....	....	....	....	....	....	....	....	....	....	61
1	....	1	1	700	1	100,000	....	....	....	....	1	1	20	150	62
1	....	2	1	950	1	53,000	1	12,300	....	....	1	1	33	266	63
1	....	2	1	950	1	53,000	1	12,300	....	....	1	1	33	266	64
1	....	1	1	1,000	1	50,000	....	....	....	....	1	1	20	110	65

TABLE 3.—ORGANIZATIONS, COMMUNICANTS OR MEMBERS, PLACES OF WORSHIP, VALUE OF CHURCH PROPERTY, EACH STATE AND

FLORIDA.

	DENOMINATION.	Total number of organizations.	COMMUNICANTS OR MEMBERS. Number of organizations reporting.	Total number reported.	Sex. Number of organizations reporting.	Male.	Female.
1	All denominations	3,370	3,346	221,318	3,101	81,540	125,215
2	Adventist bodies	46	46	2,212	38	761	1,068
3	Advent Christian Church	29	29	1,801	21	631	807
4	Seventh-day Adventist Denomination	17	17	411	17	130	281
5	Baptist bodies	1,447	1,441	91,988	1,361	34,179	54,839
6	Baptists	1,211	1,206	83,017	1,173	31,077	49,896
7	Southern Baptist Convention	551	548	34,646	520	13,008	19,956
8	National Baptist Convention (Colored)	660	658	48,371	653	18,069	29,940
9	Freewill Baptists	26	26	1,424	26	610	814
10	Primitive Baptists	61	60	1,781	48	541	954
11	Colored Primitive Baptists in America	128	128	5,350	98	1,767	3,007
12	Two-Seed-in-the-Spirit Predestinarian Baptists	3	3	28	....	....	....
13	United American Freewill Baptists (Colored)	18	18	388	16	184	166
14	Brethren (Plymouth)	9	9	96	9	50	46
15	Brethren (Plymouth)—I	4	4	54	4	30	24
16	Brethren (Plymouth)—III	5	5	42	5	20	22
17	Christadelphians	2	2	11	2	3	8
18	Church of Christ, Scientist	6	6	171	4	19	50
19	Churches of the New Jerusalem	1	1	13	1	3	10
20	General Convention of the New Jerusalem in the United States of America	1	1	13	1	3	10
21	Communistic societies	1	1	6	1	3	3
22	United Society of Believers (Shakers)	1	1	6	1	3	3
23	Congregationalists	57	57	2,687	57	1,035	1,652
24	Disciples or Christians	61	61	3,254	61	1,328	1,926
25	Disciples of Christ	33	33	2,194	33	876	1,318
26	Churches of Christ	28	28	1,060	28	452	608
27	Eastern Orthodox Churches	5	5	1,500	....	....	....
28	Greek Orthodox Church	5	5	1,500	....	....	....
29	Independent churches	19	19	553	13	168	228
30	Jewish congregations	7	5	[1]323	....	....	....
31	Latter-day Saints	7	7	1,702	6	136	182
32	Church of Jesus Christ of Latter-day Saints	1	1	1,384	....	....	....
33	Reorganized Church of Jesus Christ of Latter-day Saints	6	6	318	6	136	182
34	Lutheran bodies	12	12	729	12	308	421
35	United Synod of the Evangelical Lutheran Church in the South	2	2	268	2	116	152
36	General Council of the Evangelical Lutheran Church in North America	3	3	89	3	42	47
37	Evangelical Lutheran Synodical Conference of America	7	7	372	7	150	222
38	Methodist bodies	1,357	1,347	82,262	1,240	29,613	46,437
39	Methodist Episcopal Church	153	152	8,287	121	2,437	4,379
40	African Methodist Episcopal Church	583	582	35,713	580	13,824	21,793
41	African Methodist Episcopal Zion Church	64	64	3,223	64	1,153	2,070
42	Methodist Protestant Church	8	8	168	8	65	103
43	Wesleyan Methodist Connection of America	8	8	195	8	73	122
44	Methodist Episcopal Church, South	482	474	32,330	401	11,219	16,536
45	Congregational Methodist Church	4	4	156	4	74	82
46	New Congregational Methodist Church	7	7	332	7	86	246
47	Colored Methodist Episcopal Church	48	48	1,858	47	682	1,106
48	Presbyterian bodies	118	117	7,051	109	2,566	4,089
49	Presbyterian Church in the United States of America	32	31	1,307	29	453	828
50	Cumberland Presbyterian Church	4	4	126	3	42	69
51	Presbyterian Church in the United States	81	81	5,534	76	2,040	3,139
52	Associate Reformed Synod of the South	1	1	84	1	31	53
53	Protestant Episcopal Church	141	138	8,575	115	2,689	4,730
54	Roman Catholic Church	59	59	17,507	59	8,392	9,115
55	Salvationists	3	2	28	2	14	14
56	Salvation Army	3	2	28	2	14	14
57	Spiritualists	4	4	422	4	177	245
58	Unitarians	2	2	105	2	50	55
59	United Brethren bodies	2	1	41		19	22
60	Church of the United Brethren in Christ	2	1	41	1	19	22
61	Universalists	4	4	82	4	27	55

[1] Heads of families only.

DEBT ON CHURCH PROPERTY, PARSONAGES, AND SUNDAY SCHOOLS, BY DENOMINATIONS (IN DETAIL), FOR TERRITORY: 1906—Continued.

FLORIDA.

PLACES OF WORSHIP.					VALUE OF CHURCH PROPERTY.		DEBT ON CHURCH PROPERTY.		PARSONAGES.		SUNDAY SCHOOLS CONDUCTED BY CHURCH ORGANIZATIONS.				
Number of organizations reporting—		Number of church edifices reported.	Seating capacity of church edifices.												
Church edifices.	Halls, etc.		Number of organizations reporting.	Seating capacity reported.	Number of organizations reporting.	Value reported.	Number of organizations reporting.	Amount of debt reported.	Number of organizations reporting.	Value of parsonages reported.	Number of organizations reporting.	Number of Sunday schools reported.	Number of officers and teachers.	Number of scholars.	
3,009	183	3,061	2,842	688,986	3,022	$5,795,859	425	$430,351	577	$891,706	2,510	2,603	15,350	124,592	1
35	4	35	35	8,380	36	60,250	9	16,606	2	3,500	27	28	149	892	2
23	3	23	23	6,150	23	48,050	4	15,610	2	3,500	11	11	67	474	3
12	1	12	12	2,230	13	12,200	5	996	...	...	16	17	82	418	4
1,336	73	1,342	1,270	299,320	1,341	1,386,847	120	72,010	92	109,375	1,040	1,061	5,432	48,239	5
1,128	64	1,133	1,089	251,310	1,133	1,271,072	111	68,977	79	101,575	934	955	4,981	45,029	6
486	51	490	479	120,800	492	678,934	28	24,472	28	67,500	320	334	1,881	18,122	7
642	13	643	610	130,510	641	592,138	83	44,505	51	34,075	614	621	3,100	26,907	8
24	2	24	24	5,175	24	5,625	...	...	...	...	11	11	46	455	9
46	1	46	44	11,450	46	13,375	...	...	...	...	...	...	...	...	10
122	5	122	98	28,060	122	92,805	6	2,275	12	7,450	79	79	353	2,445	11
...	...	...	...	...	...	...	...	...	...	...	...	...	...	...	12
16	1	17	15	3,325	16	3,970	3	758	1	350	16	16	52	310	13
...	9	...	...	...	...	...	...	...	...	...	2	2	8	87	14
...	4	...	...	...	...	...	...	...	...	...	1	1	7	75	15
...	5	...	...	...	...	...	...	...	...	...	1	1	1	12	16
...	...	...	...	...	...	...	...	...	...	...	...	...	...	...	17
2	...		2	500	3	25,500	1	4,000	...	...	2	2	7	50	18
...	1	...	...	...	1	100	...	...	...	...	...	...	...	...	19
...	1	...	...	...	1	100	...	...	...	...	...	...	...	...	20
...	1	...	...	...	1	200	...	...	...	...	...	...	...	...	21
...	1	...	...	...	1	200	...	...	...	...	...	...	...	...	22
44	3	46	44	10,143	48	165,475	7	4,900	10	26,550	41	42	288	2,206	23
50	9	52	50	13,180	51	131,075	13	21,432	1	1,500	33	37	217	2,236	24
27	4	29	27	7,450	28	106,450	7	19,390	1	1,500	20	24	175	1,823	25
23	5	23	23	5,730	23	24,625	6	2,042	...	...	13	13	42	413	26
...	5	...	...	...	...	...	...	...	...	...	...	...	...	...	27
...	5	...	...	...	...	...	...	...	...	...	...	...	...	...	28
17	...	17	4	520	17	6,505	2	130	...	...	17	22	56	656	29
5	...	6	5	1,900	5	64,000	1	5,000	...	...	6	6	17	203	30
4	...	6	4	1,900	4	3,625	...	...	...	...	2	2	12	58	31
1	...	3	1	1,200	1	2,725	...	...	...	...	...	...	...	...	32
3	...	3	3	700	3	900	...	...	...	...	2	2	12	58	33
9	2	9	8	1,435	9	47,000	2	3,800	4	12,300	8	8	41	304	34
2	...	2	2	750	2	20,900	1	2,000	2	5,300	2	2	18	110	35
2	1	2	2	175	2	3,300	...	...	1	2,000	2	2	6	24	36
5	1	5	4	510	5	22,800	1	1,800	1	5,000	4	4	17	170	37
1,222	65	1,249	1,144	286,528	1,219	1,927,600	231	97,573	357	414,431	1,117	1,169	7,669	56,945	38
145	1	147	117	29,074	144	370,050	40	28,949	50	84,325	130	137	913	6,599	39
537	38	557	528	139,179	529	580,305	126	31,258	146	81,865	516	543	3,566	24,496	40
61	2	61	60	18,598	63	101,840	23	6,142	16	15,100	59	60	339	2,791	41
6	1	6	6	1,000	6	3,825	1	20	...	...	6	6	18	132	42
5	...	5	5	1,250	5	2,800	1	140	...	...	5	5	26	230	43
415	20	420	379	84,637	420	827,805	26	24,686	135	231,080	349	364	2,571	21,001	44
4	...	4	4	1,200	3	1,300	...	...	...	...	2	2	11	86	45
7	...	7	7	1,950	6	3,600	...	...	...	...	6	6	28	225	46
42	3	42	38	9,640	43	36,075	14	6,378	10	2,061	44	46	197	1,383	47
107	2	109	107	28,345	102	624,267	15	9,975	37	123,400	90	92	732	5,180	48
31	...	31	31	7,065	31	319,500	9	4,375	12	51,000	28	28	202	1,325	49
2	...	2	2	405	2	4,000	...	...	...	...	2	2	14	84	50
73	2	75	73	20,525	68	296,267	6	5,600	25	72,400	59	61	507	3,698	51
1	...	1	1	350	1	4,500	...	...	...	...	1	1	9	73	52
124	...	130	115	22,994	128	736,065	18	73,625	53	137,050	79	79	455	4,390	53
47	2	50	47	11,921	47	601,975	5	120,600	20	62,000	38	45	231	2,943	54
...	3	...	...	...	3	475	...	...	...	...	3	3	8	60	55
...	3	...	...	...	3	475	...	...	...	...	3	3	8	60	56
1	1	2	1	1,000	1	3,500	1	700	1	1,600	1	1	7	35	57
1	...	1	1	150	1	900	...	...	...	...	1	1	5	15	58
1	...	1	1	200	1	1,000	...	...	...	...	1	1	8	29	59
1	...	1	1	200	1	1,000	...	...	...	...	1	1	8	29	60
4	...	4	4	570	4	9,500	...	...	...	...	2	2	8	62	61

TABLE 3.—ORGANIZATIONS, COMMUNICANTS OR MEMBERS, PLACES OF WORSHIP, VALUE OF CHURCH PROPERTY, EACH STATE AND

GEORGIA.

	DENOMINATION.	Total number of organizations.	COMMUNICANTS OR MEMBERS.				
			Number of organizations reporting.	Total number reported.	Sex.		
					Number of organizations reporting.	Male.	Female.
1	All denominations	10,097	10,026	1,029,087	9,217	379,781	583,173
2	Adventist bodies	22	22	1,122	19	383	595
3	Advent Christian Church	14	14	917	11	301	472
4	Seventh-day Adventist Denomination	8	8	205	8	82	123
5	Baptist bodies	5,445	5,426	596,319	5,042	218,618	350,703
6	Baptists	4,663	4,652	566,631	4,492	210,175	337,012
7	Southern Baptist Convention	2,159	2,157	232,688	2,045	87,574	129,188
8	National Baptist Convention (Colored)	2,504	2,495	333,943	2,447	122,601	207,824
9	Free Baptists	14	14	776	11	221	302
10	Freewill Baptists	77	77	4,500	77	1,884	2,616
11	Primitive Baptists	443	439	16,157	329	4,491	7,508
12	Colored Primitive Baptists in America	150	146	4,531	63	771	1,850
13	Two-Seed-in-the-Spirit Predestinarian Baptists	5	5	44	....	....	....
14	United American Freewill Baptists (Colored)	93	93	3,680	70	1,076	1,415
15	Brethren (Plymouth)	5	5	33	5	17	16
16	Brethren (Plymouth)—I	2	2	6	2	3	3
17	Brethren (Plymouth)—II	1	1	6	1	4	2
18	Brethren (Plymouth)—III	2	2	21	2	10	11
19	Christians (Christian Connection)	9	9	657	9	263	394
20	Church of Christ, Scientist	7	7	397	6	98	279
21	Church of God and Saints of Christ (Colored)	2	2	32	2	11	21
22	Churches of the New Jerusalem	3	3	38	3	18	20
23	General Convention of the New Jerusalem in the United States of America	2	2	23	2	8	15
24	General Church of the New Jerusalem	1	1	15	1	10	5
25	Congregationalists	85	84	5,581	84	2,353	3,228
26	Disciples or Christians	151	150	13,749	148	5,536	7,998
27	Disciples of Christ	129	128	12,703	126	5,099	7,389
28	Churches of Christ	22	22	1,046	22	437	609
29	Eastern Orthodox Churches	10	10	1,270	2	950	50
30	Greek Orthodox Church	10	10	1,270	2	950	50
31	German Evangelical Synod of North America	1	1	189	1	91	98
32	Independent churches	13	13	738	8	200	363
33	Jewish congregations	17	13	[1]897	....	....	....
34	Latter-day Saints	1	1	386	....	....	....
35	Church of Jesus Christ of Latter-day Saints	1	1	386	....	....	....
36	Lutheran bodies	22	22	3,233	19	1,311	1,619
37	United Synod of the Evangelical Lutheran Church in the South	22	22	3,233	19	1,311	1,619
38	Methodist bodies	3,794	3,764	349,079	3,447	128,782	189,817
39	Methodist Episcopal Church	357	348	28,579	300	9,599	14,115
40	African Methodist Episcopal Church	1,226	1,212	93,626	1,201	35,011	57,350
41	African Methodist Episcopal Zion Church	68	68	3,630	66	1,298	2,232
42	Methodist Protestant Church	77	77	4,970	75	2,145	2,708
43	Wesleyan Methodist Connection of America	37	37	1,096	37	444	652
44	Methodist Episcopal Church, South	1,546	1,544	178,307	1,304	65,717	89,246
45	Congregational Methodist Church	47	47	2,656	46	1,050	1,446
46	New Congregational Methodist Church	28	28	1,450	28	569	881
47	Colored Methodist Episcopal Church	402	397	34,501	385	12,852	21,026
48	Free Methodist Church of North America	4	4	102	3	42	54
49	Reformed Methodist Union Episcopal Church (Colored)	2	2	162	2	55	107
50	Nonsectarian Churches of Bible Faith	1	1	800	1	500	300
51	Presbyterian bodies	278	277	24,040	253	8,583	13,670
52	Presbyterian Church in the United States of America	29	29	2,243	25	738	1,351
53	Cumberland Presbyterian Church	10	10	599	10	259	340
54	Presbyterian Church in the United States	227	226	20,258	206	7,155	11,470
55	Associate Reformed Synod of the South	12	12	940	12	431	509
56	Protestant Episcopal Church	121	108	9,790	63	1,967	3,517
57	Roman Catholic Church	77	77	19,273	77	9,500	9,773
58	Salvationists	4	4	61	4	39	22
59	Salvation Army	3	3	57	3	37	20
60	American Salvation Army	1	1	4	1	2	2
61	Spiritualists	1	1	6	1	5	1
62	Unitarians	2	2	170	2	62	108
63	United Brethren bodies	6	6	521	6	241	280
64	Church of the United Brethren in Christ	6	6	521	6	241	280
65	Universalists	20	20	656	15	253	301

DEBT ON CHURCH PROPERTY, PARSONAGES, AND SUNDAY SCHOOLS, BY DENOMINATIONS (IN DETAIL), FOR TERRITORY: 1906—Continued.

GEORGIA.

PLACES OF WORSHIP.					VALUE OF CHURCH PROPERTY.		DEBT ON CHURCH PROPERTY.		PARSONAGES.		SUNDAY SCHOOLS CONDUCTED BY CHURCH ORGANIZATIONS.				
Number of organizations reporting— Church edifices.	Number of organizations reporting— Halls, etc.	Number of church edifices reported.	Seating capacity of church edifices. Number of organizations reporting.	Seating capacity of church edifices. Seating capacity reported.	Number of organizations reporting.	Value reported.	Number of organizations reporting.	Amount of debt reported.	Number of organizations reporting.	Value of parsonages reported.	Number of organizations reporting.	Number of Sunday schools reported.	Number of officers and teachers.	Number of scholars.	
9,427	275	9,624	9,070	3,063,866	9,432	$17,929,183	1,545	$848,770	1,069	$1,696,113	7,752	8,052	50,246	460,769	1
16	4	16	16	4,050	17	23,940	1	1,200			13	13	77	472	2
11	1	11	11	3,100	12	15,140	1	1,200			6	6	38	252	3
5	3	5	5	950	5	8,800					7	7	39	220	4
5,111	125	5,165	4,969	1,762,003	5,112	6,984,298	495	210,497	134	262,885	3,943	4,052	22,020	228,060	5
4,511	109	4,552	4,435	1,572,413	4,517	6,595,033	460	206,562	126	260,460	3,852	3,961	21,648	225,071	6
2,083	53	2,116	2,071	711,965	2,086	3,979,289	126	110,911	92	228,625	1,501	1,573	10,590	103,109	7
2,428	56	2,436	2,364	860,448	2,431	2,615,744	334	95,651	34	31,835	2,351	2,388	11,058	121,962	8
12		12	12	1,940	13	2,750					6	6	25	204	9
70	7	71	70	20,200	70	36,950	1	75			18	18	97	864	10
326	4	334	318	122,640	322	252,450	7	558	1	300					11
109		112	59	18,810	107	46,557	10	581	2	1,000	3	3	15	168	12
															13
83	5	84	75	26,000	83	50,558	17	2,721	5	1,125	64	64	235	1,753	14
	5										1	1	1	15	15
	2										1	1	1	15	16
	1														17
	2														18
9		9	9	2,775	9	12,050	1	50	1	1,000	7	7	42	420	19
3	4	3	3	750	4	17,850					7	7	21	104	20
	2														21
1	2	1	1	200	1	5,000									22
1	1	1	1	200	1	5,000									23
	1														24
74	3	74	74	23,825	77	205,750	22	24,436	11	12,550	61	67	441	3,954	25
130	2	130	128	41,680	130	413,020	15	8,630	6	15,250	89	91	586	4,937	26
110		110	108	36,805	110	399,620	14	8,130	6	15,250	77	79	540	4,470	27
20	2	20	20	4,875	20	13,400	1	500			12	12	46	467	28
2	8	2	2	1,100	2	19,000	2	4,000			1	1	1	100	29
2	8	2	2	1,100	2	19,000	2	4,000			1	1	1	100	30
1		1	1	400	1	8,000	1	300	1	3,000	1	1	8	70	31
9	4	9	9	3,725	12	7,606	7	177			12	13	52	531	32
13	1	16	13	5,720	14	296,400	10	37,850	2	7,000	11	13	57	1,006	33
															34
															35
19	2	19	19	7,800	20	192,975	4	13,650	10	20,400	16	17	224	1,782	36
19	2	19	19	7,800	20	192,975	4	13,650	10	20,400	16	17	224	1,782	37
3,618	89	3,725	3,410	1,078,672	3,615	5,908,305	938	314,487	807	942,253	3,241	3,383	23,513	192,529	38
333	3	350	288	90,148	336	403,607	99	19,319	99	51,378	320	338	2,521	19,016	39
1,175	39	1,230	1,144	337,455	1,174	1,205,432	552	93,679	244	140,055	1,100	1,142	7,318	50,833	40
64	2	64	64	20,105	66	66,915	21	3,187	7	2,750	63	63	370	2,454	41
73	3	74	70	22,900	72	97,740	11	1,393	9	6,345	57	57	331	2,489	42
28	4	30	27	9,225	27	18,400	4	283	3	1,550	25	27	187	1,125	43
1,482	29	1,495	1,360	414,469	1,481	3,505,336	111	141,177	376	685,150	1,253	1,317	10,326	94,967	44
43	3	43	43	14,425	41	39,275	5	3,675			23	23	143	1,074	45
27	1	27	27	9,050	27	24,050					21	21	115	1,073	46
389	5	408	383	159,895	388	544,850	132	51,210	69	55,025	375	391	2,231	19,418	47
2		2	2	400	1	500	1	50			2	2	13	45	48
2		2	2	600	2	2,200	2	514			2	2	8	35	49
	1										1	1	25	500	50
251	4	266	251	85,667	250	1,774,975	25	89,358	79	247,475	223	248	2,289	17,876	51
25	2	27	25	9,275	26	59,025			5	2,450	28	28	193	2,325	52
10		10	10	3,700	10	31,550	1	7,000	1	3,000	6	6	39	295	53
204	2	216	204	68,927	202	1,649,300	22	77,258	65	232,800	180	203	1,962	14,510	54
12		13	12	3,765	12	35,100	2	5,100	8	9,225	9	11	95	746	55
112	6	128	111	24,299	113	1,101,989	13	53,510	24	91,000	67	73	541	4,786	56
32	9	32	32	10,375	27	862,900	7	62,600	13	91,800	43	46	258	2,971	57
1	3	1	1	125	3	30,275	1	25,000			3	3	9	72	58
1	2	1	1	125	3	30,275	1	25,000			3	3	9	72	59
	1														60
	1														61
2		2	2	350	2	10,850					1	1	8	60	62
6		8	6	6,950	6	16,500	2	2,925	1	1,500	4	7	36	311	63
6		8	6	6,950	6	16,500	2	2,925	1	1,500	4	7	36	311	64
17		17	13	3,400	17	37,500	1	100			7	7	37	213	65

TABLE 3.—ORGANIZATIONS, COMMUNICANTS OR MEMBERS, PLACES OF WORSHIP, VALUE OF CHURCH PROPERTY, EACH STATE AND

IDAHO.

	Denomination.	Total number of organizations.	Communicants or members: Number of organizations reporting.	Total number reported.	Sex: Number of organizations reporting.	Male.	Female.
1	All denominations	676	673	74,578	625	31,228	36,827
2	Adventist bodies	14	14	518	14	197	321
3	Advent Christian Church	2	2	88	2	48	40
4	Seventh-day Adventist Denomination	12	12	430	12	149	281
5	Baptist bodies	47	47	2,374	44	798	1,422
	Baptists:						
6	Northern Baptist Convention	45	45	2,331	42	781	1,396
7	Primitive Baptists	2	2	43	2	17	26
8	Brethren (Plymouth)	1	1	19	1	7	12
9	Brethren (Plymouth)—II	a	a	19	1	7	12
10	Buddhists	2	....	....	....	....	....
11	Chinese Temples	2	....	....	....	....	....
12	Church of Christ, Scientist	3	3	119	3	40	79
13	Congregationalists	25	25	1,487	25	471	1,016
14	Disciples or Christians	56	56	3,252	55	1,301	1,901
15	Disciples of Christ	54	54	3,206	53	1,279	1,877
16	Churches of Christ	2	2	46	2	22	24
17	Dunkers or German Baptist Brethren	7	7	476	7	229	247
18	German Baptist Brethren Church (Conservative)	7		476	7	229	247
19	Eastern Orthodox Churches	o	o	1,200	....	....	....
20	Greek Orthodox Church	8	8	1,200	....	....	....
21	Friends		4	273	4	135	138
22	Society of Friends (Orthodox)	a	a	273	4	135	138
23	Independent churches	1	1	66	1	33	33
24	Jewish congregations	1	....	....	....	....	....
25	Latter-day Saints	153	153	32,425	152	15,873	16,481
26	Church of Jesus Christ of Latter-day Saints	144	144	32,159	144	15,774	16,385
27	Reorganized Church of Jesus Christ of Latter-day Saints	9	9	266	8	99	96
28	Lutheran bodies	42	42	1,968	38	913	872
29	General Council of the Evangelical Lutheran Church in North America	9	9	821	9	420	401
30	Evangelical Lutheran Synodical Conference of America	12	12	206	12	99	107
31	United Norwegian Lutheran Church in America	9	9	424	5	126	115
32	Evangelical Lutheran Joint Synod of Ohio and Other States	4	4	292	4	148	144
33	Hauge's Norwegian Evangelical Lutheran Synod	1	1	64	1	35	29
34	Synod for the Norwegian Evangelical Lutheran Church in America	7	7	161	7	85	76
35	Mennonite bodies	1	1	56	1	25	31
36	Mennonite Church	1	1	56	1	25	31
37	Methodist bodies	99	99	5,884	93	2,312	3,438
38	Methodist Episcopal Church	81	81	5,313	76	2,078	3,121
39	Methodist Episcopal Church, South	12	12	503	12	213	290
40	Free Methodist Church of North America	6	6	68	5	21	27
41	Pentecostal Church of the Nazarene	1	1	30	1	11	19
42	Presbyterian bodies	62	62	3,770	53	1,113	2,041
43	Presbyterian Church in the United States of America	59	59	3,698	50	1,076	2,006
44	United Presbyterian Church of North America	3	3	72	3	37	35
45	Protestant Episcopal Church	48	43	1,846	37	441	1,167
46	Roman Catholic Church	80	80	18,067	75	6,992	7,188
47	Salvationists	5	5	186	5	84	102
48	Salvation Army	5	5	186	5	84	102
49	Spiritualists	1	1	100	1	40	60
50	Swedish Evangelical bodies	3	3	108	3	61	47
51	Swedish Evangelical Mission Covenant of America	3	3	108	3	61	47
52	Unitarians	1	1	54	1	26	28
53	United Brethren bodies	11	11	310	11	126	184
54	Church of the United Brethren in Christ	4	4	113	4	46	67
55	Church of the United Brethren in Christ (Old Constitution)	7	7	197	7	80	117

DEBT ON CHURCH PROPERTY, PARSONAGES, AND SUNDAY SCHOOLS, BY DENOMINATIONS (IN DETAIL), FOR TERRITORY: 1906—Continued.

IDAHO.

PLACES OF WORSHIP.					VALUE OF CHURCH PROPERTY.		DEBT ON CHURCH PROPERTY.		PARSONAGES.		SUNDAY SCHOOLS CONDUCTED BY CHURCH ORGANIZATIONS.				
Number of organizations reporting— Church edifices.	Number of organizations reporting— Halls, etc.	Number of church edifices reported.	Seating capacity of church edifices. Number of organizations reporting.	Seating capacity of church edifices. Seating capacity reported.	Number of organizations reporting.	Value reported.	Number of organizations reporting.	Amount of debt reported.	Number of organizations reporting.	Value of parsonages reported.	Number of organizations reporting	Number of Sunday schools reported.	Number of officers and teachers.	Number of scholars.	
477	107	495	468	121,775	508	$1,726,734	127	$119,677	137	$217,375	538	599	6,043	45,437	1
7	3	7	7	1,080	8	10,500	1	100			13	18	98	518	2
1		1	1	300	1	1,200	1	100			2	2	9	118	3
6	3	6	6	780	7	9,300					11	16	89	400	4
36	5	38	34	7,595	39	107,225	13	6,128	13	11,325	39	41	357	2,765	5
36	3	38	34	7,595	39	107,225	13	6,128	13	11,325	39	41	357	2,765	6
	2														7
	1										1		5	55	8
	1										1	1	5	55	9
2		2													10
2		2													11
2	1	2	2	255	3	10,450	1	1,500			3	3	18	87	12
20	4	20	20	5,175	22	83,210	6	5,950	9	9,950	24	27	205	1,954	13
28	3	29	28	7,195	28	54,200	8	4,183	2	3,500	28	30	243	1,772	14
27	2	28	27	7,120	27	54,100	8	4,183	2	3,500	27	29	240	1,742	15
1	1	1	1	75	1	100					1	1	3	30	16
7		7	6	1,850	7	15,400	1	500			7	8	82	571	17
7		7	6	1,850	7	15,400	1	500			7		82	571	18
															19
	8														20
3		3	2	550	3	3,900	1	400	1	800	3	3	25	155	21
3		3	2	550	3	3,900	1	400	1	800	3	3	25	155	22
	1										1	1	11	150	23
															24
115	23	121	115	42,300	132	434,199	37	25,411	1	1,000	151	173	3,108	20,276	25
114	18	120	114	42,050	131	433,699	37	25,411	1	1,000	144	166	3,060	20,079	26
1	5	1	1	250	1	500					7	7	48	197	27
26	12	27	25	4,295	28	37,100	12	4,085	8	10,750	25	25	92	702	28
9		9	8	1,220	9	19,000	5	2,270	2	5,500	8	8	47	325	29
2	8	2	2	175	3	1,250	1	280	1	300					30
7	2	7	7	1,700	7	6,700	2	700	1	1,500	9	9	28	234	31
4		5	4	700	4	6,250	2	450	3	1,650	3	3	5	71	32
1		1	1	200	1	1,000	1	200			1	1	3	20	33
3	2	3	3	300	4	2,900	1	185	1	1,800	4	4	9	52	34
1		1	1	300	1	2,000					1	2	15	132	35
1		1	1	300	1	2,000					1	2	15	132	36
81	14	82	81	19,145	81	296,700	20	32,488	45	54,400	86	97	898	7,251	37
68	10	69	68	16,570	68	282,600	19	32,428	40	50,350	70	80	780	6,374	38
11	1	11	11	2,275	11	12,800	1	60	3	3,000	11	12	91	756	39
2	3	2	2	300	2	1,300			2	1,050	5	5	27	121	40
1		1	1	250	1	1,250	1	450			1	1	11	60	41
48	7	49	48	11,070	49	173,900	9	6,612	21	38,300	57	61	485	4,511	42
47	7	48	47	10,970	47	172,100	9	6,612	21	38,300	54	58	468	4,369	43
1		1	1	100	2	1,800					3	3	17	142	44
34	3	35	34	5,850	36	195,800	8	14,810	18	43,850	36	40	193	1,916	45
53	15	57	52	10,190	54	249,850	6	3,485	16	41,400	46	52	107	1,979	46
2	3	2	2	500	5	28,550	1	12,000			4	4	12	87	47
2	3	2	2	500	5	28,550	1	12,000			4	4	12	87	48
	1														49
3		3	3	625	3	9,200	2	1,575	1	1,000	3	3	15	132	50
3		3	3	625	3	9,200	2	1,575	1	1,000	3	3	15	132	51
1		1			1	5,000					1	1	6	34	52
7	3	8	7	3,550	7	8,300			2	1,100	8	8	57	330	53
4		4	4	1,450	4	3,700			1	500	3	3	21	120	54
3	3	4	3	2,100	3	4,600			1	600	5	5	36	210	55

TABLE 3.—ORGANIZATIONS, COMMUNICANTS OR MEMBERS, PLACES OF WORSHIP, VALUE OF CHURCH PROPERTY, EACH STATE AND

ILLINOIS.

	DENOMINATION.	Total number of organizations.	COMMUNICANTS OR MEMBERS.				
			Number of organizations reporting.	Total number reported.	Sex.		
					Number of organizations reporting.	Male.	Female.
	All denominations	9,374	9,308	2,077,197	8,273	645,767	842,686
2	Adventist bodies	84	84	3,258	82	1,069	2,141
3	Advent Christian Church	17	17	1,054	17	402	652
4	Seventh-day Adventist Denomination	56	56	1,906	54	555	1,303
5	Churches of God (Adventist), Unattached Congregations	1	1	24	1	10	14
6	Churches of God in Christ Jesus	10	10	274	10	102	172
7	Armenian Church	5	5	1,446	5	1,211	235
8	Bahais	1	1	492	1	158	334
9	Baptist bodies	1,412	1,404	152,870	1,278	52,864	86,158
10	Baptists	1,103	1,098	134,965	1,009	46,577	76,314
11	Northern Baptist Convention	945	940	118,884	854	40,729	66,156
12	National Baptist Convention (Colored)	158	158	16,081	155	5,848	10,158
13	Seventh-day Baptists	3	3	290	3	125	165
14	Free Baptists	123	122	7,755	117	2,993	4,549
15	General Baptists	48	48	3,621	43	1,227	1,980
16	Separate Baptists	15	15	1,076	14	442	586
17	Primitive Baptists	120	118	5,163	92	1,500	2,564
18	Brethren (Plymouth)	23	23	967	22	399	553
19	Brethren (Plymouth)—I	6	6	159	6	72	87
20	Brethren (Plymouth)—II	8	8	539	8	231	308
21	Brethren (Plymouth)—III	7	7	182	6	64	103
22	Brethren (Plymouth)—IV	2	2	87	2	32	55
23	Brethren (River)	3	3	93	3	35	58
24	Brethren in Christ	3	3	93	3	35	58
25	Buddhists	1	....	....	....	....	....
26	Chinese Temples	1	....	....	....	....	....
27	Catholic Apostolic Churches	2	2	1,446	2	581	865
28	Catholic Apostolic Church	1	1	1,046	1	431	615
29	New Apostolic Church	1	1	400	1	150	250
30	Christadelphians	7	7	180	7	77	103
31	Christian Catholic Church in Zion	4	4	4,880	4	977	2,903
32	Christian Israelite Church	1	1	5	1	5	....
33	Christian Union	4	4	123	1	8	22
34	Christians (Christian Connection)	112	112	8,654	105	3,352	5,018
35	Church of Christ, Scientist	54	54	5,675	49	1,403	3,424
36	Churches of God in North America, General Eldership of the	32	32	1,555	30	544	929
37	Churches of the Living God (Colored)	2	2	55	2	22	33
38	Church of the Living God (Christian Workers for Friendship)	2	2	55	2	22	33
39	Churches of the New Jerusalem	17	17	712	15	230	357
40	General Convention of the New Jerusalem in the United States of America	15	15	613	13	190	298
41	General Church of the New Jerusalem	2	2	99	2	40	59
42	Congregationalists	339	339	54,875	331	18,778	35,135
43	Disciples or Christians	827	826	105,068	804	39,234	62,682
44	Disciples of Christ	769	768	101,516	746	37,851	60,513
45	Churches of Christ	58	58	3,552	58	1,383	2,169
46	Dunkers or German Baptist Brethren	60	59	4,666	58	2,012	2,634
47	German Baptist Brethren Church (Conservative)	49	48	3,848	48	1,693	2,155
48	Old Order German Baptist Brethren	4	4	102	4	58	44
49	The Brethren Church (Progressive Dunkers)	7	7	716	6	261	435
50	Eastern Orthodox Churches	27	27	17,536	7	12,944	1,282
51	Russian Orthodox Church	4	4	1,226	4	783	443
52	Servian Orthodox Church	2	2	3,000	2	2,661	339
53	Greek Orthodox Church	21	21	13,310	1	9,500	500
54	Evangelical bodies	213	212	15,107	208	6,015	8,866
55	Evangelical Association	127	126	8,660	123	3,532	4,952
56	United Evangelical Church	86	86	6,447	85	2,483	3,914
57	Evangelistic associations	21	20	2,780	19	1,105	1,550
58	Metropolitan Church Association	2	2	110	2	42	68
59	Missionary Church Association	2	2	85	2	26	59
60	Pentecost Bands of the World	1	1	26	1	16	10
61	Heavenly Recruit Church	1	1	44	1	18	26
62	Apostolic Christian Church	15	14	2,515	13	1,008	1,387

DEBT ON CHURCH PROPERTY, PARSONAGES, AND SUNDAY SCHOOLS, BY DENOMINATIONS (IN DETAIL), FOR TERRITORY: 1906—Continued.

ILLINOIS.

PLACES OF WORSHIP.					VALUE OF CHURCH PROPERTY.		DEBT ON CHURCH PROPERTY.		PARSONAGES.		SUNDAY SCHOOLS CONDUCTED BY CHURCH ORGANIZATIONS.				
Number of organizations reporting— Church edifices.	Number of organizations reporting— Halls, etc.	Number of church edifices reported.	Seating capacity of church edifices. Number of organizations reporting.	Seating capacity of church edifices. Seating capacity reported.	Number of organizations reporting.	Value reported.	Number of organizations reporting.	Amount of debt reported.	Number of organizations reporting.	Value of parsonages reported.	Number of organizations reporting.	Number of Sunday schools reported.	Number of officers and teachers.	Number of scholars.	
8,262	423	8,626	7,964	2,685,352	8,140	$66,222,514	1,491	$6,317,919	3,254	$8,640,258	7,736	8,173	92,913	825,323	1
47	25	48	47	9,960	50	109,654	12	16,859	3	4,000	73	81	511	2,570	2
16	1	16	16	3,820	16	42,150	3	1,050	3	4,000	14	14	127	767	3
25	19	26	25	4,965	28	57,354	9	15,209	....	....	51	59	343	1,608	4
....	1	....	....	....	....	....	....	....	....	....	....	....	....	....	5
6	4	6	6	1,175	6	10,150	....	....	....	....	8	8	41	195	6
....	5	....	....	....	....	....	....	....	....	....	....	....	....	....	7
....	1	....	....	....	....	....	....	....	....	....	....	....	....	....	8
1,322	39	1,360	1,310	431,547	1,330	5,702,544	184	456,472	215	434,960	1,097	1,186	11,937	100,448	9
1,054	27	1,090	1,043	350,122	1,062	5,378,719	163	440,243	202	420,310	950	1,031	10,819	92,901	10
909	17	945	900	309,767	914	4,956,921	114	386,029	183	401,860	798	875	9,764	85,607	11
145	10	145	143	40,355	148	421,798	49	54,214	19	18,450	152	156	1,055	7,294	12
2	1	2	2	600	2	8,000	....	....	2	2,000	3	3	39	206	13
118	2	118	118	33,410	118	153,365	18	15,761	10	10,650	103	109	745	5,307	14
43	4	45	43	14,075	43	29,350	....	....	1	2,000	28	30	225	1,460	15
14	....	14	14	4,120	14	15,000	....	....	....	....	13	13	109	574	16
91	5	91	90	29,220	91	118,110	3	468	....	....	....	....	....	....	17
....	22	....	....	....	....	....	....	....	....	....	13	13	80	804	18
....	6	....	....	....	....	....	....	....	....	....	3	3	14	95	
....	7	....	....	....	....	....	....	....	....	....	7	7	58	634	
....	7	....	....	....	....	....	....	....	....	....	3	3	8	75	19
....	2	....	....	....	....	....	....	....	....	....	....	....	....	....	
3	....	3	3	1,050	3	5,000		75	....	....	2	2	23	190	2
3	....	3	3	1,050	3	5,000	1	75	....	....	2	2	23	190	24
1	....	1	....	....	....	....	....	....	....	....	....	....	....	....	25
1	....	1	....	....	....	....	....	....	....	....	....	....	....	....	26
1	1	1	1	400	1	35,000	1	8,000	....	....	1	1	3	65	27
1	....	1	1	400	1	35,000	1	8,000	....	....	....	....	....	....	28
....	1	....	....	....	....	....	....	....	....	....	1	1	3	65	29
1	4	1	1	200	2	550	....	....	....	....	2	2	6	50	30
....	4	....	....	....	....	....	....	....	....	....	....	....	....	....	31
....	1	....	....	....	....	....	....	....	....	....	....	....	....	....	32
1	....	1	1	300	1	1,000	....	....	....	....	1	1	4	50	33
108	3	109	101	32,732	109	147,125	4	760	9	8,950	94	97	974	5,661	34
17	29	17	17	9,276	24	820,395	4	10,700	....	....	44	44	376	2,044	35
32	....	32	32	8,910	32	57,381	....	....	16	21,000	28	28	262	1,384	36
1	1	1	1	150	1	900		250	....	....	2	2	4	11	37
1	1	1	1	150	1	900	1	250	....	....	2	2	4	11	38
10	3	11	9	1,595	12	119,095	1	2,000	2	5,500	9	9	43	281	39
9	2	10	8	1,495	10	111,095	....	....	1	2,500	8	8	40	269	40
1	1	1	1	100	2	8,000	1	2,000	1	3,000	1	1	3	12	41
336	3	359	309	111,398	337	4,257,740	84	241,245	174	451,250	335	366	5,552	52,661	42
521	22	529	508	175,951	512	2,336,432	80	130,129	76	134,950	704	715	7,526	65,729	43
470	15	477	457	160,266	460	2,273,090	72	129,001	74	132,350	688	699	7,433	64,802	
51	7	52	51	15,685	52	63,342	8	1,128	2	2,600	16	16	93	927	
58	1	75	56	27,470	56	151,600	6	8,830	5	10,700	51	60	624	4,476	
49	....	66	48	25,130	48	127,700	3	4,700	3	4,200	45	63	555	3,990	
3	....	3	3	650	3	3,000	....	....	....	....	....	....	....	....	
6	1	6	5	1,690	5	20,900	3	4,130	2	6,500	6	6	69	486	
5	22	5	5	2,700	6	86,800	5	22,200	2	17,500	....	....	....	....	
3	1	3	3	1,400	4	32,800	4	17,200	2	17,500	....	....	....	....	
1	1	1	1	100	1	9,000	1	5,000	....	....	....	....	....	....	
1	20	1	1	1,200	1	45,000	....	....	....	....	....	....	....	....	
207	5	208	206	55,040	207	889,850	16	39,472	111	222,800	203	212	3,001	19,028	
123	3	123	123	32,020	123	577,850	7	26,212	62	132,250	119	123	1,797	10,434	
84	2	85	83	23,020	84	312,000	9	13,260	49	90,550	84	89	1,204	8,594	
19	2	20	17	7,175	17	87,700	3	14,600	1	13,000	16	16	87	1,035	
1	1	1	1	825	1	15,000	1	12,000	1	13,000	1	1	4	50	58
2	....	2	2	400	2	4,200	1	1,000	....	....	2	2	16	105	59
1	....	1	1	250	1	2,000	....	....	....	....	1	1	6	30	60
....	1	....	....	....	....	....	....	....	....	....	1	1	8	35	61
15	....	16	13	5,700	13	66,500		1,600	....	....	11	11	53	815	62

Table 3.—ORGANIZATIONS, COMMUNICANTS OR MEMBERS, PLACES OF WORSHIP, VALUE OF CHURCH PROPERTY, EACH STATE AND

ILLINOIS—Continued.

	DENOMINATION.	Total number of organizations.	COMMUNICANTS OR MEMBERS.				
			Number of organizations reporting.	Total number reported.	Sex.		
					Number of organizations reporting.	Male.	Female.
63	Friends	26	26	2,343	26	1,078	1,265
64	Society of Friends (Orthodox)	21	21	1,902	21	862	1,040
65	Religious Society of Friends (Hicksite)	5	5	441	5	216	225
66	German Evangelical Protestant bodies	5	4	2,630	3	569	861
67	German Evangelical Protestant Ministers' Association	3	3	1,430	3	569	861
68	German Evangelical Protestant Ministers' Conference	2	1	1,200			
69	German Evangelical Synod of North America	219	219	59,973	191	23,609	30,041
70	Independent churches	49	47	9,431	45	4,079	5,263
71	Jewish congregations	81	56	5,286[1]			
72	Latter-day Saints	35	35	2,960	35	1,203	1,757
73	Church of Jesus Christ of Latter-day Saints	5	5	518	5	197	321
74	Reorganized Church of Jesus Christ of Latter-day Saints	30	30	2,442	30	1,006	1,436
75	Lutheran bodies	782	778	202,566	708	81,358	94,363
76	General Synod of the Evangelical Lutheran Church in the United States of America	112	112	14,768	110	6,123	8,575
77	General Council of the Evangelical Lutheran Church in North America	128	127	36,366	116	14,253	17,769
78	Evangelical Lutheran Synodical Conference of America	340	339	113,527	314	47,130	53,148
79	United Norwegian Lutheran Church in America	34	34	7,374	20	1,989	2,501
80	Evangelical Lutheran Joint Synod of Ohio and Other States	22	22	5,651	20	2,153	2,348
81	Lutheran Synod of Buffalo	2	2	194	2	93	101
82	Hauge's Norwegian Evangelical Lutheran Synod	13	12	2,547	9	585	780
83	Evangelical Lutheran Synod of Iowa and Other States	88	88	14,005	86	6,350	6,909
84	Synod for the Norwegian Evangelical Lutheran Church in America	14	14	2,692	9	848	1,011
85	Danish Evangelical Lutheran Church in America	9	9	2,580	3	84	109
86	Finnish Evangelical Lutheran Church of America, or Suomi Synod	3	3	563	3	393	170
87	Norwegian Lutheran Free Church	2	1	42	1	20	22
88	United Danish Evangelical Lutheran Church in America	9	9	470	9	215	255
89	Slovak Evangelical Lutheran Synod of America	5	5	1,777	5	1,116	661
90	Church of the Lutheran Brethren of America (Norwegian)	1	1	10	1	6	4
91	Mennonite bodies	35	35	3,755	35	1,759	1,996
92	Mennonite Church	8	8	772	8	347	425
93	Amish Mennonite Church	7	7	993	7	493	500
94	Old Amish Mennonite Church	4	4	267	4	121	146
95	Reformed Mennonite Church	1	1	72	1	30	42
96	General Conference of Mennonites of North America	1	1	146	1	73	73
97	Church of God in Christ (Mennonite)	1	1	7	1	3	4
98	Defenceless Mennonites	2	2	290	2	122	168
99	Central Illinois Conference of Mennonites	11	11	1,208	11	570	638
100	Methodist bodies	2,538	2,528	263,344	2,372	91,093	155,483
101	Methodist Episcopal Church	2,028	2,021	235,092	1,899	81,763	138,805
102	African Methodist Episcopal Church	116	115	9,833	113	3,154	6,359
103	African Methodist Episcopal Zion Church	9	9	870	9	247	623
104	Methodist Protestant Church	106	104	5,512	92	1,937	3,031
105	Wesleyan Methodist Connection of America	5	5	308	5	107	201
106	Methodist Episcopal Church, South	114	114	7,198	98	2,381	3,697
107	Colored Methodist Episcopal Church	11	11	603	11	233	370
108	Primitive Methodist Church in the United States of America	3	3	331	2	36	87
109	Free Methodist Church of North America	146	146	3,597	143	1,235	2,310
110	Moravian bodies	2	2	266	2	108	158
111	Moravian Church (Unitas Fratrum)	2	2	266	2	108	158
112	Nonsectarian Churches of Bible Faith	6	6	52	6	26	26
113	Pentecostal Church of the Nazarene	11	11	797	11	295	502
114	Polish National Church of America	3	3	2,545	3	1,515	1,030
115	Presbyterian bodies	761	759	115,602	694	40,074	67,567
116	Presbyterian Church in the United States of America	473	471	86,251	453	29,634	52,143
117	Cumberland Presbyterian Church	193	193	17,208	148	5,723	8,338
118	Colored Cumberland Presbyterian Church	9	9	913	9	418	495
119	Welsh Calvinistic Methodist Church	2	2	502	2	238	264
120	United Presbyterian Church of North America	72	72	9,555	70	3,594	5,621
121	Associate Synod of North America (Associate Presbyterian Church)	1	1	5	1	2	3
122	Synod of the Reformed Presbyterian Church of North America	6	6	512	6	183	329
123	Reformed Presbyterian Church in North America, General Synod	5	5	656	5	282	374
124	Protestant Episcopal Church	210	209	36,364	194	11,187	20,004
125	Reformed bodies	71	71	9,946	71	4,379	5,567
126	Reformed Church in America	31	31	4,962	31	2,134	2,828
127	Reformed Church in the United States	31	31	2,652	31	1,177	1,475
128	Christian Reformed Church	9	9	2,332	9	1,068	1,264
129	Reformed Catholic Church	1	1	150	1	80	70
130	Reformed Episcopal Church	8	8	1,663	6	534	889
131	Roman Catholic Church	720	720	932,084	373	223,911	219,335

[1] Heads of families only.

DEBT ON CHURCH PROPERTY, PARSONAGES, AND SUNDAY SCHOOLS, BY DENOMINATIONS (IN DETAIL), FOR TERRITORY: 1906—Continued.

ILLINOIS—Continued.

PLACES OF WORSHIP.					VALUE OF CHURCH PROPERTY.		DEBT ON CHURCH PROPERTY.		PARSONAGES.		SUNDAY SCHOOLS CONDUCTED BY CHURCH ORGANIZATIONS.				
Number of organizations reporting—		Number of church edifices reported.	Seating capacity of church edifices.												
Church edifices.	Halls, etc.		Number of organizations reporting.	Seating capacity reported.	Number of organizations reporting.	Value reported.	Number of organizations reporting.	Amount of debt reported.	Number of organizations reporting.	Value of parsonages reported.	Number of organizations reporting.	Number of Sunday schools reported.	Number of officers and teachers.	Number of scholars.	
24	2	24	23	5,500	25	$53,100	1	$1,800	5	$7,000	20	20	167	1,082	63
20	1	20	19	4,800	21	50,400	1	1,800		7,000	17	17	155	983	64
4	1	4	4	700	4	2,700	....	....	....	....	3	3	12	99	65
5	....	6	3	1,500	5	35,500	3	4,800	3	6,000	3	3	40	414	66
3	....	4	3	1,500	3	14,500	3	4,800	3	6,000	3	3	40	414	67
2	....	2	....	....	2	21,000	....	....	....	....	....	....	....	....	68
212	2	246	210	70,777	211	1,656,055	57	150,981	165	370,650	204	207	2,669	24,046	69
36	10	39	34	13,480	37	423,950	9	13,425	6	19,000	40	42	634	5,750	70
43	4	45	39	23,835	43	1,066,100	32	210,850	4	41,000	34	36	137	3,499	71
20	13	22	20	5,470	25	48,910	2	1,200	....	....	31	34	343	1,363	72
2	3	2	2	750	3	18,875	....	....	....	....	5	5	43	232	73
18	10	20	18	4,720	22	30,035	2	1,200	....	....	26	29	300	1,131	74
712	40	747	706	258,468	717	6,156,298	254	885,593	463	1,103,725	539	584	5,392	60,462	75
108	2	108	105	34,532	109	841,700	30	89,150	61	131,900	103	104	1,367	12,050	76
114	6	122	114	48,863	118	1,387,661	61	206,149	68	237,200	122	131	2,146	20,886	77
317	12	333	316	124,993	318	2,929,215	113	444,109	240	520,525	157	180	628	13,875	78
32	1	34	32	8,770	32	156,500	8	22,750	9	31,500	32	38	359	3,502	79
21	1	22	21	7,750	21	128,200	6	19,800	16	24,950	16	17	92	1,473	80
2	....	2	2	475	2	4,900	....	....	1	1,500	....	....	....	....	81
13	....	14	13	4,075	13	103,050	6	20,300	4	17,500	12	12	166	2,055	82
76	9	81	74	19,659	74	329,267	12	20,180	52	97,450	69	70	362	3,787	83
11	2	11	11	3,790	12	136,700	8	23,974	4	19,500	10	12	161	1,700	84
5	2	6	5	1,700	5	46,500	3	11,681	4	8,000	5	7	47	585	85
2	1	2	2	688	2	11,000	1	1,500	1	3,000	2	2	9	80	86
2	....	2	2	215	2	5,000	1	300	....	....	1	1	7	45	87
6	2	6	6	1,358	6	28,100	4	7,700	1	1,700	7	7	43	304	88
3	2	4	3	1,600	3	48,500	1	18,000	2	9,000	2	2	2	95	89
....	....	....	....	....	....	....	....	....	....	....	1	1	3	25	90
29	5	29	29	8,052	29	95,500	....	....	2	3,000	28	31	406	3,139	91
8	....	8	8	2,220	8	24,300	....	....	....	....	8	11	129	935	92
7	....	7	7	2,132	7	40,500	....	....	....	....	7	7	120	971	93
....	4	....	....	....	....	....	....	....	....	....	....	....	....	....	94
1	....	1	1	400	1	2,500	....	....	....	....	....	....	....	....	95
1	....	1	1	300	1	2,500	....	....	1	2,500	1	1	14	70	96
....	....	....	....	....	....	....	....	....	....	....	....	....	....	....	97
2	....	2	2	575	2	4,300	....	....	1	500	2	2	48	310	98
10	1	10	10	2,425	10	21,400	....	....	....	....	10	10	95	853	99
2,479	40	2,528	2,421	723,296	2,474	13,615,437	261	564,987	1,111	2,251,019	2,327	2,394	31,361	239,672	100
1,997	21	2,039	1,945	594,093	1,989	12,533,612	178	471,290	901	2,031,749	1,899	1,961	27,881	216,614	101
107	8	111	105	28,518	110	423,925	63	77,986	45	46,850	107	110	833	5,316	102
8	1	8	8	2,300	8	46,300	6	7,027	4	1,220	9	9	65	550	103
102	3	102	102	30,550	103	192,050	2	2,400	50	48,450	78	78	748	5,280	104
5	....	6	5	1,395	5	13,000	....	....	4	7,100	5	5	59	424	105
112	1	113	110	29,360	111	130,000	1	562	40	31,700	96	96	797	5,462	106
10	1	10	10	2,800	10	25,600	7	2,068	4	2,600	10	10	65	318	107
3	....	3	3	800	3	27,500	1	700	3	6,500	3	3	49	429	108
135	5	136	133	33,480	135	223,450	3	2,954	60	74,850	120	122	864	5,279	109
2	....	2	2	850	2	9,500	....	....	2	3,200	2	2	26	251	110
2	....	2	2	850	2	9,500	....	....	2	3,200	2	2	26	251	111
1	5	1	....	....	....	....	....	....	....	....	....	....	....	....	112
7	3	7	7	1,525	8	26,825	2	1,500	2	7,500	7	7	86	490	113
3	....	3	3	1,600	3	57,000	8	11,000	2	4,000	3	3	5	292	114
737	5	790	735	276,037	748	7,869,025	116	358,355	369	944,600	712	772	11,092	105,498	115
461	5	504	460	185,973	463	6,645,425	91	299,573	256	711,925	454	507	8,069	79,979	116
182	....	185	182	58,295	190	599,450	8	16,960	57	88,425	165	169	1,756	14,053	117
9	....	9	9	3,450	9	23,950	6	8,732	1	3,500	9	9	60	672	118
2	....	2	2	1,070	2	42,300	....	....	....	....	2	2	32	238	119
71	....	78	70	23,324	72	503,100	11	33,100	52	132,750	72	75	1,066	9,608	120
1	....	1	1	400	1	800	....	....	....	....	....	....	....	....	121
6	....	6	6	1,725	6	38,500	....	....	1	4,000	5	5	56	522	122
5	....	5	5	1,800	5	15,500	....	....	2	4,000	5	5	53	426	123
192	5	222	191	60,463	201	4,039,500	60	305,825	82	425,550	174	180	1,634	14,203	124
69	2	71	69	24,492	69	467,750	18	53,600	54	134,900	70	75	971	9,133	125
31	....	33	31	12,367	31	270,700	8	15,100	28	80,200	31	34	539	5,600	126
29	2	29	29	7,475	29	136,200	4	17,000	19	31,700	31	33	329	2,118	127
9	....	9	9	4,650	9	60,850	6	21,500	7	23,000	8	8	103	1,415	128
....	1	....	....	....	....	....	....	....	....	....	....	....	....	....	129
7	1	8	7	3,310	7	176,800	1	5,000	1	25,000	8	10	160	1,911	130
537	4	590	440	201,722	341	13,201,065	178	2,548,340	248	1,759,317	411	477	1,856	63,648	131

TABLE 3.—ORGANIZATIONS, COMMUNICANTS OR MEMBERS, PLACES OF WORSHIP, VALUE OF CHURCH PROPERTY, EACH STATE AND

ILLINOIS—Continued.

	DENOMINATION.	Total number of organizations.	COMMUNICANTS OR MEMBERS.				
			Number of organizations reporting.	Total number reported.	Sex.		
					Number of organizations reporting.	Male.	Female.
132	Salvationists	51	50	1,928	50	993	935
133	Salvation Army	51	50	1,928	50	993	935
134	Social Brethren	17	17	1,262	17	487	775
135	Society for Ethical Culture	1	1	217	1	108	109
136	Spiritualists	32	32	4,547	32	2,069	2,478
137	Swedish Evangelical bodies	58	58	7,304	57	3,054	4,150
138	Swedish Evangelical Mission Covenant of America	41	41	5,762	40	2,335	3,327
139	Swedish Evangelical Free Mission	17	17	1,542	17	719	823
140	Theosophical societies	4	4	320	4	108	212
141	Theosophical Society, American Section	4	4	320	4	108	212
142	Unitarians	22	19	2,339	13	586	878
143	United Brethren bodies	313	310	19,701	237	6,223	9,279
144	Church of the United Brethren in Christ	287	284	18,705	211	5,843	8,663
145	Church of the United Brethren in Christ (Old Constitution)	26	26	996	26	380	616
146	Universalists	54	54	5,165	45	1,221	2,285
147	Volunteers of America	8	7	214	7	88	126

INDIANA.

	DENOMINATION.	Total number of organizations.	Number of organizations reporting.	Total number reported.	Number of organizations reporting (Sex).	Male.	Female.
1	All denominations	6,863	6,829	938,405	6,329	369,516	514,938
2	Adventist bodies	95	95	3,394	90	942	2,043
3	Advent Christian Church	10	10	669	9	180	288
4	Seventh-day Adventist Denomination	72	72	2,029	71	577	1,432
5	Churches of God in Christ Jesus	13	13	696	10	185	323
6	Baptist bodies	857	856	92,705	792	33,930	53,560
7	Baptists	577	577	73,729	535	27,166	42,888
8	Northern Baptist Convention	489	489	60,203	448	22,259	34,569
9	National Baptist Convention (Colored)	88	88	13,526	87	4,907	8,319
10	Free Baptists	31	31	1,931	31	743	1,188
11	General Baptists	73	73	6,671	71	2,679	3,865
12	Separate Baptists	25	24	2,201	21	854	1,145
13	Primitive Baptists	147	147	8,132	131	2,472	4,454
14	Two-Seed-in-the-Spirit Predestinarian Baptists	4	4	41	3	16	20
15	Brethren (Plymouth)	7	7	135	7	44	91
16	Brethren (Plymouth)—I	1	1	15	1	9	6
17	Brethren (Plymouth)—II	4	4	53	4	15	38
18	Brethren (Plymouth)—IV	2	2	67	2	20	47
19	Brethren (River)	4	4	143	4	53	90
20	Brethren in Christ	3	3	138	3	50	88
21	Yorker, or Old Order, Brethren	1	1	5	1	3	2
22	Catholic Apostolic Churches	2	2	85	2	30	55
23	New Apostolic Church	2	2	85	2	30	55
24	Christian Catholic Church in Zion	1	1	70	1	20	50
25	Christian Israelite Church	1	1	6	1	5	1
26	Christian Union	15	15	1,488	15	665	823
27	Christians (Christian Connection)	228	224	21,397	199	8,002	11,281
28	Church of Christ, Scientist	25	25	1,931	24	652	1,263
29	Churches of God in North America, General Eldership of the	35	35	1,999	30	645	1,019
30	Churches of the Living God (Colored)	2	2	120	2	44	76
31	Church of the Living God (Christian Workers for Friendship)	1	1	85	1	35	50
32	Church of Christ in God	1	1	35	1	9	26
33	Churches of the New Jerusalem	3	3	131	3	46	85
34	General Convention of the New Jerusalem in the United States of America	3	3	131	3	46	85
35	Congregationalists	58	58	5,405	57	1,745	3,396
36	Disciples or Christians	782	773	118,447	717	42,996	65,631
37	Disciples of Christ	670	661	108,188	605	38,703	59,665
38	Churches of Christ	112	112	10,259	112	4,293	5,966

DEBT ON CHURCH PROPERTY, PARSONAGES, AND SUNDAY SCHOOLS, BY DENOMINATIONS (IN DETAIL), FOR TERRITORY: 1906—Continued.

ILLINOIS—Continued.

PLACES OF WORSHIP.					VALUE OF CHURCH PROPERTY.		DEBT ON CHURCH PROPERTY.		PARSONAGES.		SUNDAY SCHOOLS CONDUCTED BY CHURCH ORGANIZATIONS.				
Number of organizations reporting—		Number of church edifices reported.	Seating capacity of church edifices.		Number of organizations reporting.	Value reported.	Number of organizations reporting.	Amount of debt reported.	Number of organizations reporting.	Value of parsonages reported.	Number of organizations reporting.	Number of Sunday schools reported.	Number of officers and teachers.	Number of scholars.	
Church edifices.	Halls, etc.		Number of organizations reporting.	Seating capacity reported.											
11	39	11	11	3,833	50	$151,245	22	$78,546	1	$300	42	42	194	1,397	132
11	39	11	11	3,833	50	151,245	22	78,546	1	300	42	42	194	1,397	133
15	2	15	15	9,200	15	13,800					6	6	23	180	134
	1										1	1	6	50	135
7	23	7	7	1,200	7	11,650					8	8	38	221	136
55	3	55	55	24,207	55	496,549	31	93,231	10	40,925	54	56	1,075	10,249	137
40	1	40	40	18,312	40	373,228	20	55,595	9	38,000	39	41	832	8,275	138
15	2	15	15	5,895	15	123,321	11	37,636	1	2,925	15	15	243	1,974	139
	4														140
	4														141
20	1	21	20	6,720	20	427,900	6	16,400	5	12,900	16	16	110	724	142
300	3	305	245	66,841	297	526,840	25	14,694	93	103,762	278	280	3,045	17,999	143
276	1	281	222	61,516	273	488,340	22	13,889	85	95,112	259	261	2,866	17,025	144
24	2	24	23	5,325	24	38,500	3	805	8	8,650	19	19	179	974	145
49	4	51	48	17,120	49	787,350	8	46,200	12	52,300	39	39	396	2,973	146
	8				2	104					4	4	34	190	147

INDIANA.

6,390	250	6,580	6,288	2,132,181	6,418	$31,081,500	961	$1,723,109	1,705	$3,623,538	5,690	5,879	63,042	516,809	1
69	5	69	67	12,675	70	73,165	3	1,016	2	1,625	68	68	318	1,984	
7	3	7	7	2,075	8	10,610	1	216	2	1,625	6	6	51	360	3
52	1	52	52	8,375	52	48,675	2	800			56	56	218	1,374	4
10	1	10	8	2,225	10	13,880					6	6	49	250	5
819	16	838	812	281,196	818	2,790,368	113	108,759	79	150,650	615	642	6,365	49,123	6
560	10	576	557	193,041	560	2,394,138	86	97,919	67	128,550	517	544	5,527	43,366	7
477	5	492	475	166,516	479	2,147,363	48	61,416	56	110,950	431	455	4,869	38,564	8
83	5	84	82	26,525	81	246,775	38	36,503	11	17,600	86	89	658	4,802	9
29	1	29	27	7,014	29	79,100	10	5,305	6	13,400	29	29	276	1,694	10
70	2	71	70	26,565	70	93,100	8	3,875	4	6,100	50	50	419	3,217	11
24	1	24	24	7,425	25	41,530	4	380			19	19	143	846	12
133	2	135	131	45,700	131	176,500	5	1,280	2	2,600					13
3		3	3	1,450	3	6,000									14
	7										3	3	15	140	15
	1										1	1	6	30	16
	4										2	2	9	110	17
	2														18
3	1	3	3	900	3	4,400					3	3	28	190	19
3		3	3	900	3	4,400					3	3	28	190	20
	1														21
	2														22
	2														23
	1														24
	1														25
15		15	15	5,215	15	86,500					11	11	113	500	26
223	1	229	221	73,775	223	481,030	17	9,856	10	16,900	205	205	2,065	13,685	27
4	13	4	4	1,153	11	68,138	2	10,900			19	19	82	407	28
35		35	33	11,180	35	67,600	1	1,800	3	4,800	31	31	317	1,913	29
	2										1	1	3	25	30
	1										1	1	3	25	31
	1														32
2	1	2	2	210	2	8,000			1	5,000	3	3	15	82	33
2	1	2	2	210	2	8,000			1	5,000	3	3	15	82	34
57		57	57	21,370	57	466,600	22	29,563	15	28,000	54	54	550	4,663	35
745	17	752	725	259,360	747	2,883,511	111	177,104	43	103,025	580	586	6,420	59,891	36
639	11	646	619	222,425	641	2,739,186	99	173,964	42	101,525	560	566	6,316	58,753	37
106	6	106	106	36,935	106	144,325	12	3,140	1	1,500	20	20	104	1,138	38

TABLE 3.—ORGANIZATIONS, COMMUNICANTS OR MEMBERS, PLACES OF WORSHIP, VALUE OF CHURCH PROPERTY, EACH STATE AND

INDIANA—Continued.

	DENOMINATION.	Total number of organizations.	COMMUNICANTS OR MEMBERS.				
			Number of organizations reporting.	Total number reported.	Sex.		
					Number of organizations reporting.	Male.	Female.
39	Dunkers or German Baptist Brethren	145	143	14,539	137	5,867	7,572
40	German Baptist Brethren Church (Conservative)	103	101	9,949	96	4,069	5,360
41	Old Order German Baptist Brethren	13	13	790	13	447	343
42	The Brethren Church (Progressive Dunkers)	29	29	3,800	28	1,351	2,169
43	Eastern Orthodox Churches	13	13	1,155	1	290	10
44	Greek Orthodox Church	13	13	1,155	1	290	10
45	Evangelical bodies	114	113	8,872	112	3,316	5,344
46	Evangelical Association	112	111	8,787	110	3,300	5,275
47	United Evangelical Church	2	2	85	2	16	69
48	Evangelistic associations	56	56	2,432	56	1,023	1,409
49	Missionary Church Association	5	5	362	5	149	213
50	Pentecost Bands of the World	12	12	427	12	158	269
51	Heavenly Recruit Church	26	26	894	26	389	505
52	Apostolic Christian Church	6	6	380	6	167	213
53	Christian Congregation	7	7	369	7	160	209
54	Friends	208	207	30,621	203	14,068	16,008
55	Society of Friends (Orthodox)	192	191	29,255	187	13,466	15,264
56	Religious Society of Friends (Hicksite)	9	9	1,013	9	469	544
57	Orthodox Conservative Friends (Wilburite)	7	7	353	7	153	200
58	German Evangelical Protestant bodies	10	10	2,633	10	1,172	1,461
59	German Evangelical Protestant Ministers' Association	7	7	2,256	7	1,038	1,218
60	German Evangelical Protestant Ministers' Conference	3	3	377	3	134	243
61	German Evangelical Synod of North America	91	90	21,624	81	8,892	10,436
62	Independent churches	35	35	3,020	34	1,076	1,894
63	International Apostolic Holiness Union	11	11	370	11	130	240
64	Jewish congregations	36	29	[1]1,383	....	....	....
65	Latter-day Saints	16	16	1,090	14	455	536
66	Church of Jesus Christ of Latter-day Saints	3	3	411	3	215	196
67	Reorganized Church of Jesus Christ of Latter-day Saints	13	13	679	11	240	340
68	Lutheran bodies	309	309	55,768	295	24,026	28,440
69	General Synod of the Evangelical Lutheran Church in the United States of America	89	89	7,753	85	3,080	4,469
70	General Council of the Evangelical Lutheran Church in North America	47	47	5,445	42	2,370	2,663
71	Evangelical Lutheran Synodical Conference of America	123	123	34,028	120	15,465	17,654
72	Evangelical Lutheran Joint Synod of Ohio and Other States	46	46	8,310	44	2,977	3,556
73	Synod for the Norwegian Evangelical Lutheran Church in America	2	2	125	2	64	61
74	Finnish Evangelical Lutheran Church of America, or Suomi Synod	1	1	30	1	15	15
75	Slovak Evangelical Lutheran Synod of America	1	1	77	1	55	22
76	Mennonite bodies	49	49	4,808	49	2,165	2,643
77	Mennonite Church	14	14	1,138	14	504	634
78	Amish Mennonite Church	8	8	1,078	8	506	572
79	Old Amish Mennonite Church	6	6	627	6	289	338
80	Reformed Mennonite Church	2	2	37	2	16	21
81	General Conference of Mennonites of North America	2	2	920	2	437	483
82	Church of God in Christ (Mennonite)	1	1	4	1	2	2
83	Old (Wisler) Mennonite Church	2	2	241	2	117	124
84	Defenceless Mennonites	4	4	250	4	115	135
85	Mennonite Brethren in Christ	9	9	448	9	149	299
86	Central Illinois Conference of Mennonites	1	1	65	1	30	35
87	Methodist bodies	2,073	2,067	233,443	1,959	83,981	137,223
88	Methodist Episcopal Church	1,726	1,724	210,593	1,626	75,682	123,299
89	African Methodist Episcopal Church	66	64	5,769	63	1,882	3,772
90	African Methodist Episcopal Zion Church	8	8	1,281	8	439	842
91	Methodist Protestant Church	130	128	10,408	124	4,039	6,018
92	Wesleyan Methodist Connection of America	88	88	3,459	83	1,241	2,057
93	Methodist Episcopal Church, South	8	8	818	8	330	488
94	Colored Methodist Episcopal Church	1	1	40	1	15	25
95	Free Methodist Church of North America	46	46	1,075	46	353	722
96	Moravian bodies	3	3	368	3	130	238
97	Moravian Church (Unitas Fratrum)	3	3	368	3	130	238
98	Nonsectarian Churches of Bible Faith	6	6	131	6	67	64
99	Pentecostal Church of the Nazarene	2	2	141	2	55	86
100	Polish National Church of America	1	1	450	1	250	200

[1] Heads of families only.

DEBT ON CHURCH PROPERTY, PARSONAGES, AND SUNDAY SCHOOLS, BY DENOMINATIONS (IN DETAIL), FOR TERRITORY: 1906—Continued.

INDIANA—Continued.

PLACES OF WORSHIP.					VALUE OF CHURCH PROPERTY.		DEBT ON CHURCH PROPERTY.		PARSONAGES.		SUNDAY SCHOOLS CONDUCTED BY CHURCH ORGANIZATIONS.				
Number of organizations reporting— Church edifices.	Number of organizations reporting— Halls, etc.	Number of church edifices reported.	Seating capacity of church edifices. Number of organizations reporting.	Seating capacity of church edifices. Seating capacity reported.	Number of organizations reporting.	Value reported.	Number of organizations reporting.	Amount of debt reported.	Number of organizations reporting.	Value of parsonages reported.	Number of organizations reporting.	Number of Sunday schools reported.	Number of officers and teachers.	Number of scholars.	
140	1	183	140	73,839	139	$399,132	13	$6,305	5	$6,300	123	150	1,468	10,556	39
100	1	142	100	60,034	100	316,417	9	2,105	5	6,300	94	119	1,134	7,992	40
12	....	13	12	4,250	12	19,100	....	....	....	....	....	....	....	....	41
28	....	28	28	9,555	27	63,615	4	4,200	....	....	29	31	334	2,564	42
1	12	1	1	300	1	800	....	....	....	....	1	1	1	100	43
1	12	1	1	300	1	800	....	....	....	....	1	1	1	100	44
110	3	110	110	31,225	111	402,100	9	13,100	38	70,950	106	106	1,585	10,880	45
109	3	109	109	30,925	109	396,100	9	13,100	37	69,450	104	104	1,561	10,730	46
1	....	1	1	300	2	6,000	....	....	1	1,500	2	2	24	150	47
32	19	33	30	9,840	32	106,450	12	8,325	6	19,000	39	41	333	1,936	48
3	2	3	3	1,210	4	8,100	....	....	....	....	5	6	70	545	49
11	1	12	10	2,855	11	64,400	6	6,025	5	18,500	10	11	63	382	50
8	14	8	7	2,800	7	8,950	3	700	1	500	13	13	108	492	51
5	1	5	5	1,425	5	17,800	1	1,000	....	....	4	4	19	185	52
5	1	5	5	1,550	5	7,200	2	600	....	....	7	7	73	332	53
207	....	207	207	60,790	208	549,700	12	11,785	25	37,674	191	194	1,944	14,105	54
192	....	192	192	56,620		502,000	12	11,785	25	37,674	186	189	1,904	13,831	55
8	....	8	8	2,270	192	36,900	....	....	....	....	5	5	40	274	56
7	....	7	7	1,900	9	10,800	....	....	....	....	....	....	....	....	57
10	....	11	10	5,209	10	80,250	4	5,950	5	7,700	8	9	64	574	58
7	....	8	7	3,909	7	63,750	3	5,550	5	7,700	5	6	52	477	59
3	....	3	3	1,300	3	16,500	1	400	....	....	3	3	12	97	60
90	....	99	89	31,996	90	681,678	26	34,732	68	123,050	84	84	940	8,728	61
24	10	24	23	7,125	28	44,777	6	6,350	5	3,200	26	37	234	1,777	62
4	7	4	4	1,200	5	6,650	3	3,092	....	....	10	10	69	457	63
18	4	20	18	5,460	15	175,000	5	23,140	....	....	17	17	43	612	64
8	4	9	8	2,500	7	4,720	....	....	....	....	9	9	52	310	65
1	2	1	1	250	1	720	....	....	....	....	3	3	21	86	66
7	2	8	7	2,250	6	4,000	....	....	....	....	6	6	31	224	67
292	9	298	291	98,345	293	2,123,350	62	154,010	164	354,614	212	216	1,950	16,379	68
89	....	90	89	26,631	88	429,550	13	22,575	30	54,900	83	83	1,111	7,294	69
45	1	46	45	14,775	45	269,200	12	9,695	18	41,500	42	43	434	2,992	70
112	5	115	111	42,694	112	1,181,000	29	88,590	84	188,300	43	46	122	2,853	71
45	....	46	45	14,045	46	250,800	8	33,150	31	68,414	41	41	276	3,187	72
1	1	1	1	200	1	2,000	....	....	1	1,500	2	2	5	43	73
....	1	....	....	....	....	....	....	....	....	....	1	1	2	10	74
....	1	....	....	....	1	800	....	....	....	....	....	....	....	....	75
36	12	36	36	13,125	35	78,000	3	480	3	5,000	31	31	461	4,149	76
13	1	13	13	4,700	13	24,300	....	....	1	1,500	11	11	136	1,446	77
6	2	6	6	2,675	6	14,650	2	480	....	....	6	6	109	970	78
....	6	....	....	....	....	....	....	....	....	....	....	....	....	....	79
1	1	1	1	100	1	700	....	....	....	....	....	....	....	....	80
2	....	2	2	1,500	2	12,500	....	....	....	....	2	2	98	900	81
....	....	....	....	....	....	....	....	....	....	....	....	....	....	....	82
2	....	2	2	650	2	6,250	....	....	....	....	....	....	....	....	83
4	....	4	4	1,000	4	4,600	....	....	....	....	4	4	41	309	84
7	2	7	7	2,250	6	13,500	1	50	2	3,500	7	7	67	449	85
1	....	1	1	250	1	1,500	....	....	....	....	1	1	10	75	86
2,016	29	2,026	1,987	642,247	2,013	8,264,038	266	323,688	720	1,215,975	1,885	1,904	23,716	184,409	87
1,692	15	1,701	1,665	549,672	1,691	7,602,538	191	288,263	601	1,094,400	1,562	1,572	20,875	166,371	88
65	1	66	65	19,250	65	223,500	40	18,091	41	35,750	59	60	458	2,728	89
8	....	8	8	2,875	8	33,800	6	5,243	2	2,400	8	8	63	527	90
127	3	127	126	36,260	127	250,275	6	4,050	37	49,825	125	125	1,286	8,647	91
76	7	76	76	21,675	75	87,425	14	4,378	19	14,850	82	89	663	3,938	92
8	....	8	8	2,300	7	13,600	....	....	1	1,800	8	8	87	735	93
1	....	1	....	....	1	800	1	600	....	....	1	2	3	16	94
39	3	39	39	10,215	39	52,100	8	3,063	19	16,950	40	40	281	1,447	95
3	....	3	3	1,435	3	18,100	1	1,280	1	2,000	2	2	40	344	96
3	....	3	3	1,435	3	18,100	1	1,280	1	2,000	2	2	40	344	97
2	4	2	2	300	2	1,000	....	....	....	....	1	1	5	47	98
1	1	1	1	400	2	6,250	1	4,000	....	....	2	2	20	133	99
1	....	1	1	300	1	11,000	1	4,000	1	3,000	1	1	1	50	100

TABLE 3.—ORGANIZATIONS, COMMUNICANTS OR MEMBERS, PLACES OF WORSHIP, VALUE OF CHURCH PROPERTY, EACH STATE AND

INDIANA—Continued.

	DENOMINATION.	Total number of organizations.	COMMUNICANTS OR MEMBERS. Number of organizations reporting.	Total number reported.	Sex. Number of organizations reporting.	Male.	Female.
101	Presbyterian bodies	420	420	58,633	384	20,100	33,850
102	Presbyterian Church in the United States of America	328	328	49,041	297	16,455	28,160
103	Cumberland Presbyterian Church	57	57	6,376	52	2,374	3,745
104	Welsh Calvinistic Methodist Church	1	1	9	1	4	5
105	United Presbyterian Church of North America	27	27	2,802	27	1,099	1,703
106	Associate Synod of North America (Associate Presbyterian Church)	3	3	57	3	24	33
107	Synod of the Reformed Presbyterian Church of North America	3	3	305	3	127	178
108	Reformed Presbyterian Church in North America, General Synod	1	1	43	1	17	26
109	Protestant Episcopal Church	71	71	7,653	67	2,342	4,681
110	Reformed bodies	65	65	9,216	50	3,651	4,441
111	Reformed Church in America	4	4	268	4	118	150
112	Reformed Church in the United States	58	58	8,289	43	3,223	3,942
113	Christian Reformed Church	3	3	659	3	310	349
114	Roman Catholic Church	256	256	174,849	252	85,553	87,988
115	Salvationists	15	15	353	15	191	162
116	Salvation Army	14	14	344	14	186	158
117	American Salvation Army	1	1	9	1	5	4
118	Spiritualists	29	29	1,608	29	765	843
119	Swedish Evangelical bodies	5	5	179	5	75	104
120	Swedish Evangelical Mission Covenant of America	5	5	179	5	75	104
121	Theosophical societies	2	2	27	2	16	11
122	Theosophical Society in America	2	2	27	2	16	11
123	Unitarians	4	4	253	1	71	99
124	United Brethren bodies	656	654	52,700	569	18,954	27,873
125	Church of the United Brethren in Christ	558	556	48,059	474	17,266	25,199
126	Church of the United Brethren in Christ (Old Constitution)	98	98	4,641	95	1,688	2,674
127	Universalists	44	44	2,506	34	932	1,258
128	Volunteers of America	3	3	124	3	64	60

IOWA.

	DENOMINATION.	Total number of organizations.	Number of organizations reporting.	Total number reported.	Number of organizations reporting.	Male.	Female.
1	All denominations	6,293	6,259	788,667	5,900	316,088	428,603
2	Adventist bodies	143	143	3,910	131	1,230	2,433
3	Advent Christian Church	14	14	608	13	211	387
4	Seventh-day Adventist Denomination	121	121	3,097	110	933	1,927
5	Church of God (Adventist)	2	2	60	2	26	34
6	Churches of God in Christ Jesus	6	6	145	6	60	85
7	Baptist bodies	477	472	44,096	427	14,762	25,308
8	Baptists	423	418	41,745	379	13,960	24,060
9	Northern Baptist Convention	390	385	39,393	346	13,081	22,587
10	National Baptist Convention (Colored)	33	33	2,352	33	879	1,473
11	Seventh-day Baptists	2	2	131	1	20	25
12	Free Baptists	27	27	1,563	26	595	948
13	Primitive Baptists	25	25	657	21	187	275
14	Brethren (Plymouth)	22	22	434	22	178	256
15	Brethren (Plymouth)—I	7	7	122	7	57	65
16	Brethren (Plymouth)—II	6	6	114	6	52	62
17	Brethren (Plymouth)—III	5	5	150	5	53	97
18	Brethren (Plymouth)—IV	4	4	48	4	16	32
19	Brethren (River)	4	4	70	4	32	38
20	Brethren in Christ	3	3	47	3	22	25
21	Yorker, or Old Order, Brethren	1	1	23	1	10	13
22	Christadelphians	2	2	29	2	10	19
23	Christian Union	15	15	655	13	205	315
24	Christians (Christian Connection)	41	40	3,568	35	1,337	2,012
25	Church of Christ, Scientist	35	34	1,485	33	404	1,010
26	Churches of God in North America, General Eldership of the	24	24	913	24	391	522
27	Churches of the New Jerusalem	2	2	75	2	36	39
28	General Convention of the New Jerusalem in the United States of America	2	2	75	2	36	39

DEBT ON CHURCH PROPERTY, PARSONAGES, AND SUNDAY SCHOOLS, BY DENOMINATIONS (IN DETAIL), FOR TERRITORY: 1906—Continued.

INDIANA—Continued.

PLACES OF WORSHIP.					VALUE OF CHURCH PROPERTY.		DEBT ON CHURCH PROPERTY.		PARSONAGES.		SUNDAY SCHOOLS CONDUCTED BY CHURCH ORGANIZATIONS.				
Number of organizations reporting— Church edifices.	Number of organizations reporting— Halls, etc.	Number of church edifices reported.	Seating capacity of church edifices. Number of organizations reporting.	Seating capacity of church edifices. Seating capacity reported.	Number of organizations reporting.	Value reported.	Number of organizations reporting.	Amount of debt reported.	Number of organizations reporting.	Value of parsonages reported.	Number of organizations reporting.	Number of Sunday schools reported.	Number of officers and teachers.	Number of scholars.	
408	7	453	406	146,858	410	$3,931,200	63	$155,703	150	$418,750	387	418	5,287	46,265	101
319	6	348	319	117,057	321	3,306,750	57	150,143	115	355,350	302	325	4,295	38,126	102
54	1	69	52	19,275	54	263,250	4	2,560	20	29,700	53	55	657	5,323	103
1	...	1	1	350	1	2,800	1	1,000	...	...	1	1	5	25	104
27	...	28	27	8,525	27	345,700	1	2,000	14	31,700	26	28	275	2,364	105
3	...	3	3	620	3	1,700	...	...	...	...	2	2	2	57	106
3	...	3	3	775	3	10,000	...	...	1	2,000	3	7	53	370	107
1	...	1	1	256	1	1,000	...	...	...	...	...	...	...	...	108
65	2	77	65	17,289	67	1,019,800	20	65,685	27	129,600	52	54	396	3,188	109
60	...	62	60	20,110	60	419,950	15	32,995	39	78,200	58	59	801	6,486	110
4	...	5	4	800	4	19,400	2	1,170	4	5,700	4	4	33	219	111
53	...	54	53	18,340	53	390,950	11	30,325	33	69,500	52	53	787	5,819	112
3	...	3	3	970	3	9,600	2	1,500	2	3,000	2	2	31	448	113
205	3	225	205	88,835	203	4,293,065	95	449,283	158	637,250	213	262	477	27,694	114
2	13	2	2	675	14	13,640	5	3,073	...	...	14	14	62	385	115
2	12	2	2	675	14	13,640		3,073	...	...	13	13	60	360	116
...	1	...	...	...	...	...	...	...	...	...	1	1	2	25	117
5	21	5	5	4,750	7	17,675	1	2,500	...	...	3	3	15	137	118
5	...	5	5	850	5	9,300	3	1,280	...	...	4	4	30	226	119
5	...	5	5	850	5	9,300	3	1,280	...	...	4	4	30	226	120
...	1	...	...	...	...	...	...	...	...	...	...	...	...	...	121
...	1	...	...	...	...	...	...	...	...	...	...	...	...	...	122
3	...	3	3	650	3	18,500	1	2,000	...	...	2	2	10	88	123
633	16	639	605	191,275	630	1,320,338	65	71,355	133	185,575	594	600	6,561	43,211	124
544	7	550	517	167,195	542	1,198,838	61	70,125	122	174,475	514	517	5,791	38,817	125
89	9	89	88	24,080	88	121,500	4	1,230	11	11,100	80	83	770	4,394	126
37	2	37	32	8,220	40	145,550	...	...	4	15,700	19	19	165	856	127
...	3	...	...	...	3	175	...	...	...	...	3	3	21	124	128

IOWA.

5,699	368	5,921	5,606	1,617,467	5,741	$30,464,860	859	$1,517,992	2,686	$5,481,894	5,291	5,575	54,016	413,548	1
80	38	80	79	14,963	81	90,377	6	1,493	2	2,700	121	129	746	2,992	2
12	2	12	12	2,760	11	15,000	1	330	2	2,700	13	13	95	384	3
64	32	64	63	11,403	66	71,177	5	1,163	...	...	102	110	615	2,438	4
1	1	1	1	200	1	1,200	...	...	...	...	2	2	10	55	5
3	3	3	3	600	3	3,000	...	...	...	...	4	4	26	115	6
436	12	450	425	122,912	433	1,934,920	81	111,571	165	272,160	402	433	4,521	32,404	7
396	9	410	385	113,142	393	1,866,170	81	111,571	150	251,160	379	410	4,281	30,841	8
369	3	383	359	107,172	366	1,812,195	71	105,540	144	247,260	350	381	4,104	29,608	9
27	6	27	26	5,970	27	53,975	10	6,031	6	3,900	29	29	177	1,233	10
2	...	2	2	400	2	5,500	...	...	2	2,600	2	2	22	115	11
23	1	23	23	5,210	23	51,500	...	...	12	16,400	21	21	218	1,448	12
15	2	15	15	4,160	15	11,750	...	...	1	2,000	...	...	...	...	13
1	21	1	...	...	1	500	...	...	...	...	9	9	27	218	14
...	7	...	...	...	...	...	...	...	...	...	2	2	4	26	15
...	6	...	...	...	...	...	...	...	...	...	4	4	11	80	16
1	4	1	...	...	1	500	...	...	...	...	3	3	12	112	17
...	4	...	...	...	...	...	...	...	...	...	...	...	...	...	18
3	1	3	3	775	3	11,800	...	...	1	2,000	2	2	15	70	19
3	...	3	3	775	3	11,800	...	...	1	2,000	2	2	15	70	20
...	1	...	...	...	...	...	...	...	...	...	...	...	...	...	21
...	1	...	...	...	1	25	...	...	...	...	1	1	4	25	22
14	...	14	13	3,800	14	13,200	...	...	...	...	11	11	83	562	23
38	2	38	38	10,930	39	74,107	3	4,520	4	3,700	33	33	294	1,838	24
18	16	18	18	4,085	28	142,825	6	11,370	1	2,000	29	29	131	506	25
21	1	21	21	5,360	21	44,100	...	...	4	3,900	20	20	188	933	26
1	...	1	1	175	1	1,000	...	...	...	...	1	1	6	31	27
1	...	1		175	1	1,000	...	...	...	...	1	1	6	31	28

TABLE 3.—ORGANIZATIONS, COMMUNICANTS OR MEMBERS, PLACES OF WORSHIP, VALUE OF CHURCH PROPERTY, EACH STATE AND

IOWA—Continued.

	DENOMINATION.	Total number of organizations.	COMMUNICANTS OR MEMBERS.				
			Number of organizations reporting.	Total number reported.	Sex.		
					Number of organizations reporting.	Male.	Female.
29	Communistic societies	7	7	1,756	7	856	900
30	Amana Society	7	7	1,756	7	856	900
31	Congregationalists	297	296	37,061	293	12,813	23,831
32	Disciples or Christians	463	460	57,425	452	21,982	34,526
33	Disciples of Christ	440	437	55,948	429	21,392	33,639
34	Churches of Christ	23	23	1,477	23	590	887
35	Dunkers or German Baptist Brethren	57	55	3,378	54	1,338	1,880
36	German Baptist Brethren Church (Conservative)	43	41	2,504	40	993	1,351
37	Old Order German Baptist Brethren	1	1	22	1	10	12
38	The Brethren Church (Progressive Dunkers)	13	13	852	13	335	517
39	Eastern Orthodox Churches	2	2	325	....	....	....
40	Greek Orthodox Church	2	2	325	....	....	....
41	Evangelical bodies	194	194	10,446	186	4,211	5,886
42	Evangelical Association	110	110	5,429	104	2,272	2,928
43	United Evangelical Church	84	84	5,017	82	1,939	2,958
44	Evangelistic associations	6	6	327	6	154	173
45	Hephzibah Faith Missionary Association	2	2	135	2	70	65
46	Pentecost Bands of the World	1	1	8	1	5	3
47	Apostolic Christian Church	3	3	184	3	79	105
48	Friends	99	99	10,088	99	4,668	5,420
49	Society of Friends (Orthodox)	85	85	8,762	85	4,016	4,746
50	Religious Society of Friends (Hicksite)	3	3	239	3	129	110
51	Orthodox Conservative Friends (Wilburite)	11	11	1,087	11	523	564
52	German Evangelical Protestant bodies	2	2	80	2	34	46
53	German Evangelical Protestant Ministers' Association	2	2	80	2	34	46
54	German Evangelical Synod of North America	81	81	11,681	78	5,246	5,965
55	Independent churches	29	29	2,706	29	1,369	1,337
56	International Apostolic Holiness Union	3	3	55	3	26	29
57	Jewish congregations	19	12	[1] 412	....	....	....
58	Latter-day Saints	76	76	8,328	75	3,449	4,765
59	Church of Jesus Christ of Latter-day Saints	1	1	189	1	84	105
60	Reorganized Church of Jesus Christ of Latter-day Saints	75	75	8,139	74	3,365	4,660
61	Lutheran bodies	742	742	117,668	665	49,488	53,362
62	General Synod of the Evangelical Lutheran Church in the United States of America	33	33	5,207	31	1,601	2,634
63	General Council of the Evangelical Lutheran Church in North America	72	72	13,771	61	5,515	6,365
64	Evangelical Lutheran Synodical Conference of America	163	163	25,528	149	10,902	11,388
65	United Norwegian Lutheran Church in America	119	119	23,287	101	9,776	9,912
66	Evangelical Lutheran Joint Synod of Ohio and Other States	22	22	2,643	21	1,131	1,112
67	Hauge's Norwegian Evangelical Lutheran Synod	30	30	5,523	20	1,886	2,157
68	Evangelical Lutheran Church in America, Eielsen's Synod	6	6	335	6	163	172
69	Evangelical Lutheran Synod of Iowa and Other States	171	171	23,082	159	10,160	10,825
70	Synod for the Norwegian Evangelical Lutheran Church in America	58	58	11,027	55	5,223	5,534
71	Danish Evangelical Lutheran Church in America	17	17	2,836	13	999	1,069
72	Immanuel Synod of the Evangelical Lutheran Church of North America	1	1	150	1	100	50
73	Norwegian Lutheran Free Church	4	4	158	3	55	50
74	United Danish Evangelical Lutheran Church in America	46	46	4,121	45	1,977	2,074
75	Mennonite bodies	13	13	1,669	13	756	913
76	Mennonite Church	1	1	25	1	12	13
77	Amish Mennonite Church	6	6	666	6	310	356
78	Old Amish Mennonite Church	2	2	211	2	92	119
79	General Conference of Mennonites of North America	4	4	767	4	342	425
80	Methodist bodies	1,811	1,801	164,329	1,748	59,431	99,796
81	Methodist Episcopal Church	1,586	1,576	156,576	1,528	56,537	94,993
82	African Methodist Episcopal Church	35	35	1,617	35	554	1,063
83	Methodist Protestant Church	57	57	2,994	57	1,230	1,764
84	Wesleyan Methodist Connection of America	25	25	712	24	263	420
85	Methodist Episcopal Church, South	7	7	562	7	208	354
86	Primitive Methodist Church in the United States of America	2	2	30	2	10	20
87	Free Methodist Church of North America	99	99	1,838	95	629	1,181
88	Moravian bodies	2	2	59	2	23	36
89	Moravian Church (Unitas Fratrum)	2	2	59	2	23	36

[1] Heads of families only.

DEBT ON CHURCH PROPERTY, PARSONAGES, AND SUNDAY SCHOOLS, BY DENOMINATIONS (IN DETAIL), FOR TERRITORY: 1906—Continued.

IOWA—Continued.

PLACES OF WORSHIP.					VALUE OF CHURCH PROPERTY.		DEBT ON CHURCH PROPERTY.		PARSONAGES.		SUNDAY SCHOOLS CONDUCTED BY CHURCH ORGANIZATIONS.				
Number of organizations reporting— Church edifices.	Number of organizations reporting— Halls, etc.	Number of church edifices reported.	Seating capacity of church edifices. Number of organizations reporting.	Seating capacity of church edifices. Seating capacity reported.	Number of organizations reporting.	Value reported.	Number of organizations reporting.	Amount of debt reported.	Number of organizations reporting.	Value of parsonages reported.	Number of organizations reporting.	Number of Sunday schools reported.	Number of officers and teachers.	Number of scholars.	
7	....	21	7	3,500	7	$14,090	....	....	....	....	....	....	....	....	29
7	....	21	7	3,500	7	14,090	....	....	....	....	....	....	....	....	30
291	3	296	284	90,115	292	2,049,400	57	$82,810	171	$315,000	277	288	3,528	28,632	31
443	7	456	440	138,114	446	1,823,607	59	59,293	56	100,100	407	418	4,400	36,256	
423	6	436	420	133,134	427	1,790,765	57	57,968	55	98,900	398	409	4,355	35,855	32
20	1	20	20	4,980	19	32,842	2	1,325	1	1,200	9	9	45	401	33
51	3	63	51	18,050	50	111,388	1	500	2	2,900	45	51	440	2,972	35
38	2	50	38	14,650	38	86,950	1	500	....	....	36	42	363	2,501	36
1	....	1	1	300	1	1,200	....	....	....	....	....	....	....	....	37
12	1	12	12	3,100	11	23,238	....	....	2	2,900	9	9	77	471	38
....	2	....	....	....	....	....	....	....	....	....	....	....	....	....	39
....	2	....	....	....	....	....	....	....	....	....	....	....	....	....	
176	12	178	173	39,090	175	420,777	7	9,575	101	153,025	179	186	2,020	10,903	
97	7	98	95	20,755	96	227,850	....	....	53	93,925	99	101	1,121	5,526	
79	5	80	78	18,335	79	192,927	7	9,575	48	59,100	80	85	899	5,377	
6	....	6	6	1,500	6	14,300	2	800	1	1,000	5	5	29	255	
2	....	2	2	550	2	6,800	....	....	....	....	2	2	20	170	
1	....	1	1	300	1	2,000	1	600	1	1,000	1	1	5	25	
3	....	3	3	650	3	5,500	1	200	....	....	2	2	4	60	
94	5	94	93	24,082	95	172,600	8	2,630	31	37,550	76	79	744	4,552	40
80	5	80	79	20,682	81	155,400	8	2,630	31	37,550	73	76	730	4,510	49
3	....	3	3	650	3	2,500	....	....	....	....	3	3	14	42	50
11	....	11	11	2,750	11	14,700	....	....	....	....	....	....	....	....	51
2	....	2	2	280	2	4,700	1	800	1	650	2	2	10	37	52
2	....	2	2	280	2	4,700	1	800	1	650	2	2	10	37	53
76	5	81	76	20,700	76	331,980	26	19,440	60	101,350	75	75	579	4,235	54
21	5	22	20	4,780	23	58,350	3	115	5	7,100	26	32	212	1,677	55
1	2	1	1	200	1	1,200	....	....	....	....	3	3	17	133	56
8	....	9	8	2,770	7	50,000	5	6,500	1	1,000	9	9	19	215	57
54	14	54	54	11,762	55	89,150	6	1,769	1	400	70	77	796	3,516	58
....	....	....	....	....	....	....	....	....	....	....	1	1	9	23	59
54	14	54	54	11,762	55	89,150	6	1,769	1	400	69	76	787	3,493	60
644	78	681	637	185,035	647	2,779,598	141	117,552	369	729,244	508	548	3,226	26,536	61
31	1	32	31	11,625	31	299,925	10	30,000	16	31,300	33	33	437	3,266	62
68	2	75	67	21,521	68	457,605	18	19,797	45	105,900	67	69	648	4,318	63
143	17	149	143	39,339	145	514,100	30	18,100	107	171,500	67	67	161	2,416	64
118	....	122	118	37,680	118	450,500	16	8,700	35	105,300	90	112	761	5,257	65
18	2	18	18	4,221	18	57,000	8	3,150	14	20,300	21	22	79	782	66
26	3	27	22	7,525	26	73,200	2	2,000	6	6,400	27	29	184	1,265	67
2	4	2	2	350	2	6,000	1	50	....	....	2	2	7	55	68
142	23	152	141	,403	143	532,535	29	18,947	97	166,344	130	138	609	5,847	69
53	4	58	53	35,560	53	262,583	7	3,240	23	76,400	22	22	123	1,285	70
11	4	12	11	12,870	12	39,400	9	7,068	9	15,200	10	11	34	521	71
1	....	1	1	300	1	1,800	....	....	....	....	1	1	6	50	72
2	1	2	2	550	2	4,000	2	450	....	....	4	4	12	80	73
29	17	31	28	6,091	28	80,950	9	6,050	17	30,600	34	38	165	1,394	74
11	2	11	11	2,990	11	21,300	....	....	....	....	13	13	198	1,530	75
1	....	1	1	200	1	1,200	....	....	....	....	1	1	9	40	
4	2	4	4	1,240	4	6,800	....	....	....	....	6	6	81	630	
2	....	2	2	500	2	4,600	....	....	....	....	2	2	40	230	76
4	....	4	4	1,050	4	8,700	....	....	....	....	4	4	68	630	77
1,719	72	1,738	1,702	462,509	1,727	6,815,988	124	159,088	828	1,417,725	1,613	1,656	19,920	142,061	80
1,521	52	1,	1,505	415,469	1,526	488	98	149,502	722	1,319,075	1,440	1,469	18,634	135,217	
30	4		29	7,335	30	850	17	7,180	16	12,900	32	32	213	968	81
55	2		55	13,460	55	400	1	400	22	25,750	48	54	424	2,459	82
21	2		21	4,535	21	400	....	....	13	12,300	19	20	125	684	84
7	....		7	1,750	7	900	....	....	3	3,150	6	6	53	232	
2	....	538	2	500	2	6,486,000	2	300	1	600	2	2	20	120	85
83	12	[illegible]	83	19,460	86	[illegible],950	6	1,706	51	43,950	66	73	451	2,371	86
2	....	2	2	292	2		....	....	2	1,400	2	2	9	59	88
2	....	2	2	292	2	2,300	....	....	2	1,400	2	2	9	59	89
						2,300									

TABLE 3.—ORGANIZATIONS, COMMUNICANTS OR MEMBERS, PLACES OF WORSHIP, VALUE OF CHURCH PROPERTY, EACH STATE AND

IOWA—Continued.

	DENOMINATION.	Total number of organizations.	COMMUNICANTS OR MEMBERS.				
			Number of organizations reporting.	Total number reported.	Sex.		
					Number of organizations reporting.	Male.	Female.
90	Nonsectarian Churches of Bible Faith	3	3	76	3	49	27
91	Pentecostal Church of the Nazarene	1	1	23	1	8	15
92	Presbyterian bodies	553	552	60,081	518	21,118	35,080
93	Presbyterian Church in the United States of America	426	426	48,326	395	16,499	28,335
94	Cumberland Presbyterian Church	19	19	1,190	17	425	651
95	Welsh Calvinistic Methodist Church	8	8	539	8	237	302
96	United Presbyterian Church of North America	87	86	8,890	85	3,491	5,122
97	Associate Synod of North America (Associate Presbyterian Church)	5	5	237	5	82	155
98	Synod of the Reformed Presbyterian Church of North America	8	8	899	8	384	515
99	Protestant Episcopal Church	91	91	8,990	87	2,881	5,735
100	Reformed bodies	122	122	11,517	118	5,154	6,082
101	Reformed Church in America	47	47	4,835	46	2,166	2,578
102	Reformed Church in the United States	44	44	3,692	41	1,541	1,961
103	Christian Reformed Church	31	31	2,990	31	1,447	1,543
104	Roman Catholic Church	552	552	207,607	520	96,380	102,079
105	Salvationists	17	16	472	16	255	217
106	Salvation Army	17	16	472	16	255	217
107	Spiritualists	11	11	505	11	219	286
108	Swedish Evangelical bodies	42	42	2,248	41	981	1,250
109	Swedish Evangelical Mission Covenant of America	25	25	1,492	25	621	871
110	Swedish Evangelical Free Mission	17	17	756	16	360	379
111	Unitarians	13	13	1,482	10	584	611
112	United Brethren bodies	196	195	11,236	154	3,615	5,840
113	Church of the United Brethren in Christ	187	186	11,082	145	3,554	5,747
114	Church of the United Brethren in Christ (Old Constitution)	9	9	154	9	61	93
115	Universalists	21	21	1,389	14	406	600
116	Volunteers of America	3	2	14	2	9	5

KANSAS.

	DENOMINATION.	Total number of organizations.	Number of organizations reporting.	Total number reported.	Number of organizations reporting.	Male.	Female.
1	All denominations	4,994	4,975	458,190	4,707	182,761	253,826
2	Adventist bodies	90	90	2,689	85	933	1,648
3	Advent Christian Church	4	4	247	4	87	160
4	Seventh-day Adventist Denomination	83	83	2,394	78	826	1,460
5	Churches of God in Christ Jesus	3	3	48	3	20	28
6	Baptist bodies	611	608	46,299	564	16,412	26,773
7	Baptists	583	583	45,003	543	15,924	26,019
8	Northern Baptist Convention	445	445	34,975	406	12,254	19,941
9	Southern Baptist Convention	1	1	17	1	6	11
10	National Baptist Convention (Colored)	137	137	10,011	136	3,664	6,067
11	Seventh-day Baptists	1	1	263	1	104	159
12	Free Baptists	13	12	826	12	321	505
13	Primitive Baptists	14	12	207	8	63	90
14	Brethren (Plymouth)	18	18	308	18	137	171
15	Brethren (Plymouth)—I	3	3	57	3	30	27
16	Brethren (Plymouth)—II	11	11	215	11	93	122
17	Brethren (Plymouth)—III	3	3	33	3	13	20
18	Brethren (Plymouth)—IV	1	1	3	1	1	2
19	Brethren (River)	10	10	450	10	204	246
20	Brethren in Christ	10	10	450	10	204	246
21	Christadelphians	3	3	58	3	44	14
22	Christian Union	4	4	99	4	43	56
23	Christians (Christian Connection)	26	26	1,034	24	401	633
24	Church of Christ, Scientist	31	31	1,131	30	305	733
25	Church of God and Saints of Christ (Colored)	3	3	78	3	28	50
26	Churches of God in North America, General Eldership of the	12	12	613	12	238	375
27	Churches of the Living God (Colored)	3	3	135	3	51	84
28	Church of the Living God (Christian Workers for Friendship)	3	3	135	3	51	84
29	Churches of the New Jerusalem		3	144	3	73	71
30	General Convention of the New Jerusalem in the United States of America	3	3	144	3	73	71

DEBT ON CHURCH PROPERTY, PARSONAGES, AND SUNDAY SCHOOLS, BY DENOMINATIONS (IN DETAIL), FOR TERRITORY: 1906—Continued.

IOWA—Continued.

PLACES OF WORSHIP.					VALUE OF CHURCH PROPERTY.		DEBT ON CHURCH PROPERTY.		PARSONAGES.		SUNDAY SCHOOLS CONDUCTED BY CHURCH ORGANIZATIONS.				
Number of organizations reporting— Church edifices.	Number of organizations reporting— Halls, etc.	Number of church edifices reported.	Seating capacity of church edifices. Number of organizations reporting.	Seating capacity of church edifices. Seating capacity reported.	Number of organizations reporting.	Value reported.	Number of organizations reporting.	Amount of debt reported.	Number of organizations reporting.	Value of parsonages reported.	Number of organizations reporting.	Number of Sunday schools reported.	Number of officers and teachers.	Number of scholars.	
....	3	....	....	....	....	....	....	....	....	....	....	....	....	....	90
....	1	....	....	....	....	....	....	....	....	....	1	1	8	35	91
520	13	548	516	155,759	522	$3,231,445	88	$110,762	306	$651,200	510	548	6,985	52,523	92
395	12	422	392	120,063	397	2,669,995	80	98,2°2	230	506,950	388	425	5,653	41,956	93
18	....	18	17	4,575	18	46,100	1	1,600	6	7,100	16	16	161	961	94
8	....	9	8	2,170	8	18,700	....	....	2	2,200	8	8	71	438	95
86	1	86	86	25,381	86	449,950	6	10,350	67	132,950	87	87	991	8,167	96
5	....	5	5	1,230	5	11,200	....	....	....	....	3	3	3	94	97
8	....	8	8	2,340	8	35,500	1	600	1	2,000	8	9	106	907	98
79	....	92	78	20,543	79	1,084,705	13	41,000	34	146,650	59	59	484	3,589	99
114	8	126	113	32,534	114	465,350	35	46,115	86	154,550	106	117	1,098	10,178	100
44	3	51	44	13,744	44	210,640	14	14,165	39	77,600	44	48	553	5,404	101
43	1	43	43	10,900	43	169,160	4	11,000	23	38,000	41	44	424	3,061	102
27	4	32	26	7,890	27	85,550	17	20,950	24	38,950	21	25	121	1,713	103
514	6	567	513	180,750	513	7,760,210	142	700,825	350	1,215,690	433	485	1,092	29,979	104
4	13	4	3	575	17	31,515	5	5,709	....	....	14	14	40	275	105
4	13	4	3	575	17	31,515	5	5,709	....	....	14	14	40	275	106
2	9	3	2	2,250	2	26,500	1	500	....	....	4	4	18	135	107
39	3	41	38	9,765	40	115,157	12	10,935	20	42,500	38	42	334	2,588	108
25	....	26	24	6,640	25	77,107	7	6,465	14	27,350	23	26	223	1,787	109
14	3	15	14	3,125	15	38,050	5	4,470	6	15,150	15	16	111	801	110
10	1	10	9	2,695	10	167,900	2	1,140	4	9,200	11	11	105	885	111
180	6	180	153	40,132	179	389,964	25	11,180	75	96,700	164	170	1,606	9,691	112
172	5	172	145	38,232	171	382,864	25	11,180	74	96,400	158	164	1,567	9,474	113
8	1	8	8	1,900	8	7,100	....	....	1	300	6	6	39	217	114
19	....	19	16	3,696	19	118,000	....	....	5	10,500	12	12	89	532	115
....	3	....	....	....	2	532	....	....	....	....	....	....	....	....	116

KANSAS.

4,020	602	4,107	3,957	1,054,976	4,074	$14,053,454	591	$567,254	1,667	$2,469,184	4,079	4,275	41,239	313,685	1
51	26	52	50	9,422	52	84,768	2	600	1	1,500	84	86	535	2,310	2
3	1	4	3	650	3	4,500	....	....	1	1,500	4	4	35	175	3
46	25	46	45	8,447	47	78,768	2	600	....	....	79	81	494	2,115	4
2	....	2	2	325	2	1,500	....	....	....	....	1	1	6	20	5
510	53	520	501	134,204	526	1,434,512	89	50,803	121	167,334	507	539	4,873	34,045	6
496	51	505	488	130,704	512	1,406,687	88	50,303	115	161,234	497	529	4,765	33,344	7
362	47	372	357	97,183	379	1,138,845	40	37,373	94	145,000	365	397	3,878	28,233	8
1	....	1	1	150	1	300	....	....	....	....	....	....	....	....	9
132	4	132	130	33,371	132	267,542	48	12,930	21	16,234	132	132	887	5,111	10
1	....	1	1	350	1	12,000	....	....	1	3,000	1	1	21	174	11
11	....	11	11	2,850	11	13,225	1	500	5	3,100	9	9	87	527	12
3	2	3	1	300	2	2,600	....	....	....	....	....	....	....	....	13
....	18	....	....	....	....	....	....	....	....	....	6	6	15	147	14
....	3	....	....	....	....	....	....	....	....	....	1	1	3	37	15
....	11	....	....	....	....	....	....	....	....	....	4	4	11	101	16
....	3	....	....	....	....	....	....	....	....	....	1	1	1	9	17
....	1	....	....	....	....	....	....	....	....	....	....	....	....	....	18
9				3,025		23,700	....	....	....	....		9	115	585	19
9	-	-	-	3,025		23,700	....	....	....	....	-	-	115	585	20
....	....	....	....	....	....	....	....	....	....	....	....	....	....	....	21
1	3	1	1	50	1	150	1	18	....	....	3	3	21	120	22
13	9	13	13	3,525	13	17,055	....	....	....	....	20	20	166	1,007	23
18	7	18	17	2,355	24	50,500	6	4,135	....	....	22	22	97	452	24
....	3	....	....	....	....	....	....	....	....	....	....	....	....	....	25
8	3	8	8	2,600	9	11,750	....	....	....	....	8	8	80	568	26
1	2	1	1	125	2	1,800	2	100	....	....	3		7	56	27
1	2	1	1	125	2	1,800	2	100	....	....	3	3	7	56	28
2	1	2	2	390	2	4,400	....	....	1	1,000	2	2	10	83	29
2	1	2	2	390	2	4,400	....	....	1	1,000	2	2	10	83	30

TABLE 3.—ORGANIZATIONS, COMMUNICANTS OR MEMBERS, PLACES OF WORSHIP, VALUE OF CHURCH PROPERTY, EACH STATE AND

KANSAS—Continued.

	DENOMINATION.	Total number of organizations.	COMMUNICANTS OR MEMBERS.				
			Number of organizations reporting.	Total number reported.	Sex.		
					Number of organizations reporting.	Male.	Female.
31	Congregationalists	168	167	15,247	167	5,402	9,845
32	Disciples or Christians	409	405	43,572	370	14,907	24,074
33	Disciples of Christ	343	339	40,356	304	13,600	22,165
34	Churches of Christ	66	66	3,216	66	1,307	1,909
35	Dunkers or German Baptist Brethren	81	81	4,821	79	2,079	2,673
36	German Baptist Brethren Church (Conservative)	62	62	3,905	60	1,698	2,138
37	Old Order German Baptist Brethren	3	3	106	3	62	44
38	The Brethren Church (Progressive Dunkers)	16	16	810	16	319	491
39	Eastern Orthodox Churches	2	2	750	1	550	50
40	Servian Orthodox Church	1	1	600	1	550	50
41	Greek Orthodox Church	1	1	150			
42	Evangelical bodies	102	102	5,388	101	2,309	2,914
43	Evangelical Association	88	88	4,841	87	2,065	2,611
44	United Evangelical Church	14	14	547	14	244	303
45	Evangelistic associations	11	10	649	9	249	365
46	Apostolic Faith Movement	3	3	140	3	50	90
47	Hephzibah Faith Missionary Association	1	1	29	1	14	15
48	Missionary Church Association	3	2	63	2	28	35
49	Apostolic Christian Church	4	4	417	3	157	225
50	Friends	76	76	7,925	75	3,804	4,061
51	Society of Friends (Orthodox)	72	72	7,304	71	3,473	3,791
52	Orthodox Conservative Friends (Wilburite)	4	4	621	4	331	290
53	German Evangelical Synod of North America	35	35	3,617	34	1,645	1,798
54	Independent churches	28	27	685	27	270	415
55	International Apostolic Holiness Union	2	2	51	2	18	33
56	Jewish congregations	7	5	[1]175			
57	Latter-day Saints	28	28	2,084	28	955	1,129
58	Church of Jesus Christ of Latter-day Saints	2	2	356	2	155	201
59	Reorganized Church of Jesus Christ of Latter-day Saints	26	26	1,728	26	800	928
60	Lutheran bodies	280	279	28,642	266	13,398	14,216
61	General Synod of the Evangelical Lutheran Church in the United States of America	55	55	4,583	53	1,886	2,520
62	General Council of the Evangelical Lutheran Church in North America	43	43	7,782	42	3,670	3,852
63	Evangelical Lutheran Synodical Conference of America	118	117	12,036	112	5,846	5,909
64	United Norwegian Lutheran Church in America	8	8	482	6	149	148
65	Evangelical Lutheran Joint Synod of Ohio and Other States	16	16	721	16	376	345
66	Hauge's Norwegian Evangelical Lutheran Synod	3	3	99	3	46	53
67	Evangelical Lutheran Synod of Iowa and Other States	32	32	2,529	32	1,281	1,248
68	Synod for the Norwegian Evangelical Lutheran Church in America	2	2	65			
69	Danish Evangelical Lutheran Church in America	1	1	60			
70	Norwegian Lutheran Free Church	1	1	255	1	134	121
71	United Danish Evangelical Lutheran Church in America	1	1	30	1	10	20
72	Mennonite bodies	61	61	7,445	61	3,491	3,954
73	Mennonite Church	9	9	537	9	253	284
74	Amish Mennonite Church	3	3	101	3	51	50
75	Old Amish Mennonite Church	5	5	467	5	219	248
76	General Conference of Mennonites of North America	21	21	3,581	21	1,726	1,855
77	Church of God in Christ (Mennonite)	5	5	314	5	144	170
78	Defenceless Mennonites	1	1	83	1	41	42
	Bundes Conferenz der Mennoniten Brueder-Gemeinde:						
79	Krimmer Brueder-Gemeinde	3	3	509	3	216	293
80	Schellenberger Brueder-Gemeinde	13	13	1,825	13	830	995
81	Nebraska and Minnesota Conference of Mennonites	1	1	28	1	11	17
82	Methodist bodies	1,629	1,625	121,208	1,563	43,591	72,280
83	Methodist Episcopal Church	1,299	1,295	108,097	1,244	38,995	64,236
84	African Methodist Episcopal Church	92	92	4,934	90	1,633	3,142
85	African Methodist Episcopal Zion Church	1	1	6	1	3	3
86	Methodist Protestant Church	41	41	2,050	38	745	1,193
87	Wesleyan Methodist Connection of America	36	36	1,077	33	420	585
88	Methodist Episcopal Church, South	43	43	2,332	41	837	1,388
89	Colored Methodist Episcopal Church	19	19	917	19	304	613
90	Free Methodist Church of North America	98	98	1,795	97	654	1,120
91	Nonsectarian Churches of Bible Faith	15	15	331	15	159	172
92	Pentecostal Church of the Nazarene	2	2	119	2	45	74

[1] Heads of families only.

DEBT ON CHURCH PROPERTY, PARSONAGES, AND SUNDAY SCHOOLS, BY DENOMINATIONS (IN DETAIL), FOR TERRITORY: 1906—Continued.

KANSAS—Continued.

PLACES OF WORSHIP. Number of organizations reporting— Church edifices.	PLACES OF WORSHIP. Number of organizations reporting— Halls, etc.	PLACES OF WORSHIP. Number of church edifices reported.	PLACES OF WORSHIP. Seating capacity of church edifices. Number of organizations reporting.	PLACES OF WORSHIP. Seating capacity of church edifices. Seating capacity reported.	VALUE OF CHURCH PROPERTY. Number of organizations reporting.	VALUE OF CHURCH PROPERTY. Value reported.	DEBT ON CHURCH PROPERTY. Number of organizations reporting.	DEBT ON CHURCH PROPERTY. Amount of debt reported.	PARSONAGES. Number of organizations reporting.	PARSONAGES. Value of parsonages reported.	SUNDAY SCHOOLS CONDUCTED BY CHURCH ORGANIZATIONS. Number of organizations reporting.	SUNDAY SCHOOLS CONDUCTED BY CHURCH ORGANIZATIONS. Number of Sunday schools reported.	SUNDAY SCHOOLS CONDUCTED BY CHURCH ORGANIZATIONS. Number of officers and teachers.	SUNDAY SCHOOLS CONDUCTED BY CHURCH ORGANIZATIONS. Number of scholars.	
155	3	156	150	37,433	156	$705,775	36	$26,615	78	$114,450	147	153	1,761	14,069	31
352	29	354	343	99,527	348	986,660	61	47,705	33	43,250	321	328	3,353	28,923	32
307	11	309	298	89,392	301	927,250	53	44,305	33	43,250	300	307	3,271	27,887	33
45	18	45	45	10,135	47	59,410	8	3,400			21	21	82	1,036	34
68	6	77	67	22,910	68	123,650	11	4,150	2	1,000	68	81	641	4,657	35
55	4	62	54	19,210	55	101,550	10	3,900	1	500	57	68	543	4,054	36
2		2	2	550	2	2,600									37
11	2	13	11	3,150	11	19,500	1	250	1	500	11	13	98	603	38
1	1	1	1	300	1	3,000	1	1,500	1	1,400					39
1		1	1	300	1	3,000	1	1,500	1	1,400					40
	1														41
80	15	80	80	18,230	80	169,650	5	1,117	41	42,650	93	94	1,125	6,754	42
73	10	73	73	16.830	73	154,100	3	455	37	37,850	80	81	1,014	6,036	43
7	5	7	7	1,400	7	15,550	2	662	4	4,800	13	13	111	718	44
7	4	8	4	1,025	6	13,950					8	8	50	417	45
	3										2	2	16	100	46
1		1	1	75	1	150					1	1	8	25	47
2	1	2	1	200	2	2,800					3	3	21	165	48
4		5	2	750	3	11,000					2	2	5	127	49
60	11	60	59	14,805	59	89,650	4	1,440	13	8,200	60	63	533	3,464	50
56	11	56	55	13,895	55	74,650	4	1,440	13	8,200	59	62	527	3,424	51
4		4	4	910	4	15,000					1	1	6	40	52
30	3	30	30	7,590	30	84,350	7	4,168	25	35,900	31	31	164	1,272	53
14	6	14	14	3,900	16	12,850	2	900			16	16	97	570	54
2		2	2	450	2	2,800	1	875			2	2	14	75	55
3		3	3	1,000	3	26,200	1	1,300	1	1,000	1	1	4	40	56
14	8	14	14	2,761	14	16,000	1	608			20	22	208	943	57
1		1	1	300	1	1,000					2	2	17	77	58
13	8	13	13	2,461	13	15,000	1	608			18	20	191	866	59
216	43	227	214	52,330	219	768,938	35	23,031	136	216,625	167	174	1,094	9,207	60
52	3	52	52	12,590	52	226,050	12	10,650	24	40,950	48	48	497	3,516	61
42	1	45	40	11,212	42	199,300	4	2,729	24	67,850	41	45	364	3,005	62
84	17	90	84	21,278	85	270,425	10	5,150	64	84,400	40	43	77	1,240	63
5	2	5	5	840	5	6,758			3	3,525	7	7	33	150	64
9	6	10	9	1,680	9	19,200			6	6,400	10	10	61	566	65
1	2	1	1	200	1	800			1	900					66
20	11	21	20	3,980	22	41,305	9	4,502	13	11,800	19	19	47	700	67
1		1	1	100	1	300									68
1		1	1	200	1	2,300			1	800	1	1	5	80	69
1		1	1	250	1	2,500					1	1	10	50	70
	1														71
51	9	53	51	20,220	51	129,500	1	1,500	1	400	48	56	565	7,441	72
8		8	8	1,925	8	10,900					7	7	83	595	73
3		3	3	800	3	2,900					3	3	18	135	74
	5														75
21		23	21	10,745	21	86,500	1	1,500			20	25	292	3,519	76
1	4	1	1	200	1	1,400									77
1		1	1	250	1	1,000					1	1	9	112	78
3		3	3	2,550	3	13,000			1	400	3	4	39	490	79
13		13	13	3,550	13	13,000					13	15	120	2,550	80
1		1	1	200	1	800					1	1	4	40	81
1,304	209	1,313	1,296	346,494	1,315	3,849,728	157	108,457	694	847,925	1,393	1,456	16,913	119,234	82
1,058	153	1,067	1,054	287,307	1,065	3,400,532	90	84,303	544	739,910	1,128	1,181	14,934	108,034	83
85	4	85	85	22,530	87	170,841	40	12,863	44	24,665	85	87	596	3,128	84
1		1	1	30	1	150					1	1	2	11	85
31	10	31	29	6,514	33	76,200	6	2,440	18	15,900	34	36	313	2,120	86
25	6	25	24	5,200	25	31,500	4	3,200	15	12,750	28	29	200	1,138	87
39	1	39	38	8,641	39	93,100	3	429	17	19,050	34	35	300	1,865	88
18	1	18	18	5,970	18	27,625	11	5,076	9	3,700	18	18	107	502	89
47	34	47	47	10,302	47	49,780	3	146	47	31,950	65	69	461	2,436	90
	15										5	5	27	283	91
2		2	2	500	2	700	1	150			2	2	16	63	92

TABLE 3.—ORGANIZATIONS, COMMUNICANTS OR MEMBERS, PLACES OF WORSHIP, VALUE OF CHURCH PROPERTY, EACH STATE AND

KANSAS—Continued.

	DENOMINATION.	Total number of organizations.	COMMUNICANTS OR MEMBERS. Number of organizations reporting.	Total number reported.	Sex. Number of organizations reporting.	Male.	Female.
93	Presbyterian bodies	407	406	40,765	379	14,879	23,944
94	Presbyterian Church in the United States of America	304	304	33,465	289	11,957	20,064
95	Cumberland Presbyterian Church	34	34	1,937	23	629	834
96	Colored Cumberland Presbyterian Church	1	1	85	1	45	40
97	Welsh Calvinistic Methodist Church	2	2	90	2	39	51
98	United Presbyterian Church of North America	51	50	4,061	49	1,729	2,308
99	Associate Synod of North America (Associate Presbyterian Church)	4	4	144	4	68	76
100	Synod of the Reformed Presbyterian Church of North America	10	10	907	10	379	528
101	Reformed Presbyterian Church in North America, General Synod	1	1	76	1	33	43
102	Protestant Episcopal Church	90	90	6,459	70	1,829	3,830
103	Reformed bodies	16	16	1,415	16	585	830
104	Reformed Church in America	2	2	213	2	93	120
105	Reformed Church in the United States	12	12	967	12	378	589
106	Christian Reformed Church	2	2	235	2	114	121
107	Roman Catholic Church	340	340	93,195	332	46,026	45,736
108	Salvationists	16	16	555	16	266	289
109	Salvation Army	16	16	555	16	266	289
110	Spiritualists	14	14	1,496	14	653	843
111	Swedish Evangelical bodies	21	21	1,114	21	512	602
112	Swedish Evangelical Mission Covenant of America	18	18	1,073	18	489	584
113	Swedish Evangelical Free Mission	3	3	41	3	23	18
114	Temple Society in the United States (Friends of the Temple)	1	1	150	1	70	80
115	Theosophical societies	1	1	14	1	2	12
116	Theosophical Society, American Section	1	1	14	1	2	12
117	Unitarians	4	4	345	3	94	128
118	United Brethren bodies	322	321	15,998	285	5,776	8,158
119	Church of the United Brethren in Christ	293	293	15,159	257	5,434	7,661
120	Church of the United Brethren in Christ (Old Constitution)	29	28	839	28	342	497
121	Universalists	12	12	937	10	328	547

KENTUCKY.

	DENOMINATION.	Total number of organizations.	Number of organizations reporting.	Total number reported.	Sex. Number of organizations reporting.	Male.	Female.
1	All denominations	6,553	6,512	858,324	5,725	316,610	432,232
2	Adventist bodies	19	19	343	17	102	221
3	Seventh-day Adventist Denomination	19	19	343	17	102	221
4	Baptist bodies	2,660	2,647	311,563	2,314	115,409	167,042
5	Baptists	2,234	2,230	287,791	2,087	109,8[illegible]2	159,304
6	Southern Baptist Convention	1,703	1,701	211,552	1,581	80,026	114,623
7	National Baptist Convention (Colored)	531	529	76,239	506	29,796	44,681
8	Free Baptists	39	39	2,165	28	627	896
9	General Baptists	98	98	6,881	90	2,598	3,385
10	Separate Baptists	30	28	1,765	16	582	719
11	United Baptists	82	79	7,167	14	604	858
12	Primitive Baptists	163	159	5,442	74	1,093	1,762
13	Colored Primitive Baptists in America	5	5	228	2	55	74
14	Two-Seed-in-the-Spirit Predestinarian Baptists	9	9	144	3	28	44
15	Brethren (Plymouth)	1	1	18	1	5	13
16	Brethren (Plymouth)—III	1	1	18	1	5	13
17	Christadelphians	2	2	129	2	57	72
18	Christian Union	5	5	139	5	60	79
19	Christians (Christian Connection)	49	46	2,310	21	449	580
20	Church of Christ, Scientist	4	4	137	4	28	109
21	Churches of the Living God (Colored)	5	5	174	5	67	107
22	Church of the Living God (Christian Workers for Friendship)	3	3	94	3	39	55
23	Church of Christ in God	2	2	80	2	28	52
24	Churches of the New Jerusalem	1	1	14	1	7	7
25	General Convention of the New Jerusalem in the United States of America	1	1	14	1	7	7

DEBT ON CHURCH PROPERTY, PARSONAGES, AND SUNDAY SCHOOLS, BY DENOMINATIONS (IN DETAIL), FOR TERRITORY: 1906—Continued.

KANSAS—Continued.

PLACES OF WORSHIP.					VALUE OF CHURCH PROPERTY.		DEBT ON CHURCH PROPERTY.		PARSONAGES.		SUNDAY SCHOOLS CONDUCTED BY CHURCH ORGANIZATIONS.				
Number of organizations reporting—		Number of church edifices reported.	Seating capacity of church edifices.												
Church edifices.	Halls, etc.		Number of organizations reporting.	Seating capacity reported.	Number of organizations reporting.	Value reported.	Number of organizations reporting.	Amount of debt reported.	Number of organizations reporting.	Value of parsonages reported.	Number of organizations reporting.	Number of Sunday schools reported.	Number of officers and teachers.	Number of scholars.	
380	11	392	373	105,185	379	$1,872,675	62	$66,235	184	$353,950	378	400	4,733	38,566	93
281	11	292	281	81,350	281	1,583,150	50	58,175	143	290,200	282	302	3,717	31,218	94
33		34	26	7,045	32	60,225	4	2,850	4	3,800	30	31	318	1,975	95
1		1	1	300	1	1,500			1	400	1	1	5	35	96
2		2	2	350	2	2,300					2	2	14	75	97
49		49	49	12,720	49	181,000	8	5,210	34	55,950	50	50	546	4,289	98
3		3	3	650	3	4,200					2	2	2	78	99
10		10	10	2,650	10	39,800			1	2,000	16	11	123	836	100
1		1	1	120	1	500			1	1,600	1	1	8	60	101
78	3	80	78	14,330	83	416,200	6	5,050	29	75,400	66	67	355	2,701	102
16		17	16	4,110	16	56,900	4	4,600	13	16,000	16	17	185	1,417	103
2		2	2	425	2	3,800	1	800	2	1,100	2	2	26	192	104
12		12	12	3,085	12	49,400	2	3,200	9	12,400	12	12	143	998	105
2		3	2	600	2	3,700	1	600	2	2,500	2	3	16	227	106
311	16	334	308	86,215	311	2,583,243	67	188,425	175	416,600	246	264	435	13,644	107
3	13	3	3	1,025	16	34,970	9	9,899			16	16	85	553	108
3	13	3		1,025	16	34,970	9	9,899			16	16	85	553	109
	13										2	2	12	42	110
21		22	21	5,350	21	49,800	3	2,200	12	19,000	18	19	165	1,245	111
18		19	18	4,850	18	46,200	2	1,700	12	19,000	18	19	165	1,245	112
3		3	3	500	3	3,600	1	500							113
1		1	1	200	1	2,000			1	1,000	1	1	8	75	114
	1														115
															116
3	1	3	3	900	3	33,000	1	2,000			3	3	17	106	117
230	56	232	218	51,390	229	375,230	13	8,573	103	101,600	280	289	2,705	18,108	118
212	46	213	200	46,960	211	346,105	10	7,623	98	95,950	256	264	2,520	17,013	119
18	10	19	18	4,430	18	29,125	3	950	5	5,650	24	25	185	1,095	120
5		5	4	1,100	7	17,400	2	1,100	2	3,000	7	7	55	343	121

KENTUCKY.

5,757	285	5,894	5,617	1,775,123	5,751	$18,044,389	623	$862,993	856	$1,637,943	4,543	4,723	33,833	314,667	1
6	5	6	5	1,005	6	8,000	3	1,525			16	16	67	325	2
6	5	6	5	1,005	6	8,000	3	1,525			16	16	67	325	3
2,324	134	2,347	2,298	738,488	2,330	4,423,671	183	148,310	109	211,450	1,673	1,745	11,781	108,553	4
2,084	113	2,106	2,062	664,483	2,089	4,271,239	166	113,580	106	207,950	1,585	1,653	11,295	104,491	5
1,579	95	1,600	1,568	516,442	1,579	3,310,037	74	71,926	77	185,400	1,090	1,155	8,060	79,276	6
505	18	506	499	148,041	510	961,202	92	41,654	29	22,550	495	498	3,235	25,215	7
29		29	29	6,605	29	21,400	5	2,975	1	1,000	31	33	162	1,075	8
88		89	86	29,430	89	51,272	7	1,140			39	41	218	2,055	9
19	8	19	19	6,950	19	10,050					13	13	60	542	10
18		18	18	3,645	17	4,560					5	5	46	390	11
76	10	76	74	23,775	77	59,300	5	615	2	2,500					12
1	1	1	1	500	1	2,000									13
9		9	9	3,100	9	3,850									14
											1	1	2	20	15
											1	1	2	20	16
1		1	1	300	1	750									17
3	1	3	3	950	3	2,300									18
22	23	23	22	6,705	21	8,900	1	60			14	14	84	496	19
	4				2	325					4	4	12	42	20
1	4	1			1	200					4	4	11	85	21
	3										3	3	9	45	22
1	1	1			1	200					1	1	2	40	23
	1														24
	1														25

TABLE 3.—ORGANIZATIONS, COMMUNICANTS OR MEMBERS, PLACES OF WORSHIP, VALUE OF CHURCH PROPERTY, EACH STATE AND

KENTUCKY—Continued.

	DENOMINATION.	Total number of organizations.	COMMUNICANTS OR MEMBERS.		Sex.		
			Number of organizations reporting.	Total number reported.	Number of organizations reporting.	Male.	Female.
26	Communistic societies	2	2	37	2	13	24
27	United Society of Believers (Shakers)	2	2	37	2	13	24
28	Congregationalists	18	18	996	18	470	526
29	Disciples or Christians	992	992	136,110	976	57,911	75,793
30	Disciples of Christ	841	841	123,659	827	52,942	68,561
31	Churches of Christ	151	151	12,451	149	4,969	7,232
32	Dunkers or German Baptist Brethren	1	1	14	1	4	10
33	German Baptist Brethren Church (Conservative)	1	1	14	1	4	10
34	Eastern Orthodox Churches	1	1	80	....	....	....
35	Greek Orthodox Church	1	1	80	....	....	....
36	Evangelical bodies	2	2	270	1	35	55
37	Evangelical Association	2	2	270	1	35	55
38	German Evangelical Protestant bodies	6	6	2,813	6	1,250	1,563
39	German Evangelical Protestant Ministers' Association	3	3	1,245	3	540	705
40	German Evangelical Protestant Ministers' Conference	3	3	1,568	3	710	858
41	German Evangelical Synod of North America	19	19	12,189	17	2,607	3,582
42	Independent churches	26	26	815	25	236	469
43	International Apostolic Holiness Union	5	5	142	5	49	93
44	Jewish congregations	11	10	1,147[1]	....	....	....
45	Latter-day Saints	5	5	1,407	4	110	147
46	Church of Jesus Christ of Latter-day Saints	1	1	1,150	....	....	....
47	Reorganized Church of Jesus Christ of Latter-day Saints	4	4	257	4	110	147
48	Lutheran bodies	28	28	4,940	28	2,079	2,861
49	General Synod of the Evangelical Lutheran Church in the United States of America	17	17	3,190	17	1,263	1,927
50	General Council of the Evangelical Lutheran Church in North America	1	1	100	1	55	45
51	Evangelical Lutheran Synodical Conference of America	6	6	1,511	6	693	818
52	Evangelical Lutheran Joint Synod of Ohio and Other States	4	4	139	4	68	71
53	Methodist bodies	1,815	1,804	156,007	1,605	55,063	83,836
54	Methodist Episcopal Church	425	423	30,158	375	10,286	15,910
55	African Methodist Episcopal Church	130	130	10,047	129	3,482	6,482
56	African Methodist Episcopal Zion Church	59	59	5,773	58	2,008	3,650
57	Methodist Protestant Church	43	43	2,341	39	989	1,214
58	Methodist Episcopal Church, South	1,047	1,038	99,355	894	35,133	51,447
59	Colored Methodist Episcopal Church	98	98	8,137	97	3,121	5,001
60	Free Methodist Church of North America	13	13	196	13	64	132
61	Nonsectarian Churches of Bible Faith	2	2	93	2	48	45
62	Presbyterian bodies	503	498	47,822	445	16,745	25,294
63	Presbyterian Church in the United States of America	83	82	8,543	72	2,604	4,235
64	Cumberland Presbyterian Church	205	205	16,916	169	5,966	8,021
65	Colored Cumberland Presbyterian Church	26	26	2,042	26	899	1,143
66	Presbyterian Church in the United States	184	180	20,143	173	7,204	11,789
67	Associate Reformed Synod of the South	5	5	178	5	72	106
68	Protestant Episcopal Church	86	83	8,091	81	2,373	4,832
69	Reformed bodies	12	12	2,101	2	165	250
70	Reformed Church in the United States	12	12	2,101	2	165	250
71	Roman Catholic Church	232	232	165,908	104	60,381	63,367
72	Salvationists	4	4	123	4	53	70
73	Salvation Army	4	4	123	4	53	70
74	Spiritualists	6	6	419	6	168	251
75	Unitarians	1	1	440	1	190	250
76	United Brethren bodies	22	16	993	13	240	380
77	Church of the United Brethren in Christ	22	16	993	13	240	280
78	Universalists	9	9	520	9	216	304

[1] Heads of families only.

DEBT ON CHURCH PROPERTY, PARSONAGES, AND SUNDAY SCHOOLS, BY DENOMINATIONS (IN DETAIL), FOR TERRITORY: 1906—Continued.

KENTUCKY—Continued.

PLACES OF WORSHIP.					VALUE OF CHURCH PROPERTY.		DEBT ON CHURCH PROPERTY.		PARSONAGES.		SUNDAY SCHOOLS CONDUCTED BY CHURCH ORGANIZATIONS.				
Number of organizations reporting—		Number of church edifices reported.	Seating capacity of church edifices.												
Church edifices.	Halls, etc.		Number of organizations reporting.	Seating capacity reported.	Number of organizations reporting.	Value reported.	Number of organizations reporting.	Amount of debt reported.	Number of organizations reporting.	Value of parsonages reported.	Number of organizations reporting.	Number of Sunday schools reported.	Number of officers and teachers.	Number of scholars.	
	2				2	$800									26
	2				2	800									27
15		15	15	3,695	15	36,350	3	$7,203	4	$8,600	12	12	107	936	28
924	24	929	921	266,518	929	2,599,855	57	99,413	30	69,900	786	794	5,541	55,837	29
784	13	787	781	222,651	788	2,434,155	47	93,456	30	69,900	708	715	5,174	51,760	30
140	11	142	140	43,867	141	165,700	10	5,957			78	79	367	4,077	31
1		1	1	125	1	500					1	1	6	60	32
1		1	1	125	1	500					1	1	6	60	33
	1														34
	1														35
2		2	2	500	2	12,400			2	2,800	2	2	47	348	36
2		2	2	500	2	12,400			2	2,800	2	2	47	348	37
6		6	6	2,720	6	75,600	3	4,000	4	13,900	6	6	102	938	38
3		3	3	1,900	3	49,000	1	1,400	3	10,300	3	3	46	569	39
3		3	3	820	3	26,600	2	2,600	1	3,600	3	3	56	369	40
16	2	18	16	9,200	16	402,000	9	78,100	12	66,000	17	17	364	3,957	41
19	6	19	17	2,900	18	6,650	8	809			15	15	106	855	42
1	4	2	1	100	1	500					2	2	14	70	43
9		15	9	5,950	9	271,000	6	58,000	3	8,200	7	7	31	517	44
4	1	5	4	1,300	5	1,965					2	2	15	47	45
1		2	1	500	1	340									46
3	1	3	3	800	4	1,625					2	2	15	47	47
25		27	25	8,226	25	267,460	9	48,905	7	11,900	22	22	318	3,045	48
17		17	17	6,226	17	237,760	6	43,005	2	2,200	15	15	287	2,670	49
1		1	1	150	1	1,000			1	500	1	1	3	40	50
5		7	5	1,500	5	25,700	3	5,900	3	8,200	5	5	20	300	51
2		2	2	350	2	3,000			1	1,000	1	1	8	35	52
1,715	52	1,746	1,658	511,855	1,718	4,128,758	252	166,273	509	630,518	1,411	1,450	10,878	88,395	53
403	9	419	389	118,177	402	896,688	53	15,618	124	138,570	317	323	2,690	20,041	54
129	1	132	129	33,475	130	265,930	68	23,441	62	37,403	116	123	690	4,461	55
56	3	57	56	16,005	57	111,350	17	6,993	16	8,950	54	58	408	3,229	56
29	8	32	29	9,650	33	16,970	2	540	4	1,120	26	32	173	1,239	57
993	28	998	953	304,733	991	2,635,895	70	103,320	265	423,450	801	815	6,337	55,034	58
96	1	99	93	27,140	96	196,725	42	16,361	38	21,025	91	93	548	4,184	59
9	2	9	9	2,675	9	5,200					6	6	32	207	60
1	1	1	1	200	1	600									61
478	6	521	468	160,070	479	2,447,730	42	40,427	99	275,925	371	417	3,466	27,821	62
78	1	89	77	25,140	79	762,750	7	3,710	21	58,325	66	84	707	6,684	63
194	3	199	185	67,895	193	351,895	13	14,035	16	31,150	129	133	968	7,671	64
25	1	25	25	7,855	25	29,410	3	475			24	24	120	935	65
177		204	177	57,905	178	1,284,825	19	22,207	61	183,950	148	171	1,642	12,360	66
4	1	4	4	1,275	4	18,850			1	2,500	4	5	29	171	67
53	2	60	53	20,136	56	1,074,380	14	37,550	26	96,350	53	60	479	4,401	68
2		2	2	630	2	13,500	2	900	1	2,500	11	11	134	1,553	69
2		2	2	630	2	13,500	2	900	1	2,500	11	11	134	1,553	70
102	3	106	69	26,050	70	2,193,275	25	197,782	48	237,600	97	104	171	15,590	71
	4				4	675	3	361			4	4	11	54	72
	4				[illegible]	675	3	361			4	4	11	54	73
3	3	3	3	1,400	4	10,770	2	3,300							74
1		2	1	800	1	24,000					1	2	13	120	75
15	1	16	8	3,100	15	19,775	1	75	1	300	9	9	61	527	76
15	1	16	8	3,100	15	19,775	1	75	1	300	9	9	61	527	77
8		8	8	2,200	8	11,700			1	2,000	2	2	12	75	78

TABLE 3.—ORGANIZATIONS, COMMUNICANTS OR MEMBERS, PLACES OF WORSHIP, VALUE OF CHURCH PROPERTY, EACH STATE AND

LOUISIANA.

	Denomination.	Total number of organizations.	Communicants or members.				
			Number of organizations reporting.	Total number reported.	Sex.		
					Number of organizations reporting.	Male.	Female.
1	All denominations	3,856	3,813	778,901	3,491	327,111	419,082
2	Adventist bodies	21	21	536	20	180	336
3	Advent Christian Church	2	2	34	1	6	8
4	Seventh-day Adventist Denomination	19	19	502	19	174	328
5	Baptist bodies	2,096	2,093	185,554	1,990	65,420	111,940
6	Baptists	2,021	2,019	183,130	1,972	65,131	111,552
7	Southern Baptist Convention	610	609	49,620	587	19,310	27,803
8	National Baptist Convention (Colored)	1,411	1,410	133,510	1,385	45,821	83,749
9	Seventh-day Baptists	1	1	60	1	21	39
10	Free Baptists	31	31	1,382	3	40	52
11	Primitive Baptists	38	38	781	13	178	222
12	Colored Primitive Baptists in America	4	4	201	1	50	75
13	Church of Christ, Scientist	1	1	63	1	13	50
14	Churches of the New Jerusalem	2	2	24	2	10	14
15	General Convention of the New Jerusalem in the United States of America	1	1	14	1	6	8
16	General Church of the New Jerusalem	1	1	10	1	4	6
17	Congregationalists	28	28	1,773	28	634	1,139
18	Disciples or Christians	35	35	2,548	35	1,106	1,442
19	Disciples of Christ	25	25	2,127	25	910	1,217
20	Churches of Christ	10	10	421	10	196	225
21	Dunkers or German Baptist Brethren	3	3	98	3	37	61
22	German Baptist Brethren Church (Conservative)	3	3	98	3	37	61
23	German Evangelical Synod of North America	4	4	4,353	2	1,125	1,308
24	Independent churches	12	12	592	12	235	357
25	Jewish congregations	24	20	[1]1,618			
26	Latter-day Saints	1	1	455	1	165	290
27	Church of Jesus Christ of Latter-day Saints	1	1	455	1	165	290
28	Lutheran bodies	25	24	5,793	23	2,098	3,635
29	Evangelical Lutheran Synodical Conference of America	23	22	5,253	21	1,865	3,328
30	Evangelical Lutheran Joint Synod of Ohio and Other States	2	2	540	2	233	307
31	Methodist bodies	1,172	1,143	79,464	994	25,436	43,113
32	Methodist Episcopal Church	279	264	19,763	180	4,447	9,243
33	African Methodist Episcopal Church	178	177	9,462	174	3,263	6,145
34	African Methodist Episcopal Zion Church	44	44	2,539	41	656	1,242
35	Methodist Protestant Church	91	91	3,513	80	1,341	1,666
36	Methodist Episcopal Church, South	381	370	31,639	322	10,794	17,204
37	Congregational Methodist Church	18	18	711	18	264	447
38	Colored Methodist Episcopal Church	171	169	11,728	169	4,633	7,095
39	Free Methodist Church of North America	10	10	109	10	38	71
40	Nonsectarian Churches of Bible Faith	4	4	45	4	26	19
41	Presbyterian bodies	115	114	8,350	103	2,805	5,291
42	Cumberland Presbyterian Church	27	27	1,152	25	467	576
43	Presbyterian Church in the United States	88	87	7,196	78	2,338	4,715
44	Protestant Episcopal Church	80	75	9,070	51	1,813	4,176
45	Roman Catholic Church	214	214	477,774	203	225,685	245,443
46	Salvationists	4	4	72	4	28	44
47	Salvation Army	4	4	72	4	28	44
48	Spiritualists	2	2	85	2	28	57
49	Theosophical societies	1		23	1	9	14
50	Theosophical Society, American Section	1	1	23		9	14
51	Unitarians	1	1	250	1	100	150
52	United Brethren bodies	11	11	361	11	158	203
53	Church of the United Brethren in Christ	11	11	361	11	158	203

[1] Heads of families only.

DEBT ON CHURCH PROPERTY, PARSONAGES, AND SUNDAY SCHOOLS, BY DENOMINATIONS (IN DETAIL), FOR TERRITORY: 1906—Continued.

LOUISIANA.

PLACES OF WORSHIP. Number of organizations reporting—Church edifices.	PLACES OF WORSHIP. Number of organizations reporting—Halls, etc.	PLACES OF WORSHIP. Number of church edifices reported.	PLACES OF WORSHIP. Seating capacity of church edifices. Number of organizations reporting.	PLACES OF WORSHIP. Seating capacity of church edifices. Seating capacity reported.	VALUE OF CHURCH PROPERTY. Number of organizations reporting.	VALUE OF CHURCH PROPERTY. Value reported.	DEBT ON CHURCH PROPERTY. Number of organizations reporting.	DEBT ON CHURCH PROPERTY. Amount of debt reported.	PARSONAGES. Number of organizations reporting.	PARSONAGES. Value of parsonages reported.	SUNDAY SCHOOLS CONDUCTED BY CHURCH ORGANIZATIONS. Number of organizations reporting.	SUNDAY SCHOOLS CONDUCTED BY CHURCH ORGANIZATIONS. Number of Sunday schools reported.	SUNDAY SCHOOLS CONDUCTED BY CHURCH ORGANIZATIONS. Number of officers and teachers.	SUNDAY SCHOOLS CONDUCTED BY CHURCH ORGANIZATIONS. Number of scholars.	
3,537	127	3,620	3,324	1,046,850	3,549	$10,456,146	734	$689,072	726	$1,314,247	3,096	3,320	17,963	177,730	1
9	1	9	9	2,100	9	7,400	...	...	...	...	18	18	110	416	2
2	...	2	2	600	2	1,000	...	...	...	...	1	1	5	30	3
7	1	7	7	1,500	7	6,400	...	...	...	...	17	17	105	386	4
1,961	58	1,968	1,890	571,775	1,975	2,352,457	304	91,749	129	121,102	1,741	1,799	9,117	84,769	5
1,937	58	1,944	1,872	566,750	1,951	2,340,332	304	91,749	126	119,852	1,716	1,774	8,985	83,992	6
562	33	563	559	164,789	566	688,725	37	10,688	32	62,300	396	421	2,179	21 164	7
1,375	25	1,381	1,313	401,961	1,385	1,651,607	267	81,061	94	57,552	1,320	1,353	6,806	62,828	8
1	...	1	1	400	1	2,000	...	...	1	1,000	1	1	9	45	9
7	...	7	6	2,150	7	3,275	...	...	1	100	24	24	123	732	10
12	...	12	10	2,275	12	5,500	...	...	...	...	...	...	...	...	11
4	...	4	1	200	4	1,350	...	...	1	150	...	...	...	...	12
1	...	2	1	300	1	5,000		4,000	...	...	1	1	14	20	13
...	1	...	...	...	...	...	...	...	...	...	...	...	...	...	14
...	...	...	...	...	...	...	...	...	...	...	...	...	...	...	15
...		...	...	...	...	...	...	...	...	...	...	...	...	...	16
23		23	22	6,500	23	65,550	8	2,040	12	16,900	28	37	208	1,816	17
28	2	29	28	9,650	29	97,400	8	14,040	2	4,000	23	23	156	1,292	18
20	...	21	20	7,650	21	89,400	8	14,040	2	4,000	19	19	144	1,189	19
8	2	8	8	2,000	8	8,000	...	...	...	...	4	4	12	103	20
2		2	2	500	2	2,300	...	...	...	...	2	2	11	95	21
2	1	2	2	500	2	2,300	...	...	...	...	2	2	11	95	22
4	...	5	4	2,700	4	150,500	2	22,500	4	19,000	4	6	174	2,161	23
9	2	10	9	2,500	10	6,330	3	693	...	...	12	14	71	520	24
16		17	16	6,060	17	412,550	3	19,400	3	14,000	17	18	64	761	25
...	...	...	...	...	...	...	...	...	...	...	1	4	16	72	26
...	...	...	...	...	...	...	...	...	...	...	1	4	16	72	27
22		22	22	5,565	21	153,250	7	7,086	11	27,325	20	20	155	2,382	28
20	2	20	20	5,115	19	140,250	7	7,086	10	24,325	18	18	122	2,037	29
2	...	2	2	450	2	13,000	...	...	1	3,000	2	2	33	345	30
1,075	43	1,093	944	284,445	1,080	2,080,989	331	144,069	365	355,210	954	1,004	5,874	50,876	31
266	3	267	173	51,220	264	513,475	151	40,991	143	104,900	252	274	1,572	15,095	32
171	6	175	171	52,220	174	261,305	77	19,829	71	39,335	168	175	958	7,600	33
39	1	39	37	9,695	41	31,925	19	1,291	6	4,500	32	32	199	1,183	34
71	11	71	70	22,000	73	43,675	9	1,816	10	6,350	46	46	195	1,732	35
338	17	345	306	85,365	337	966,384	33	65,450	104	175,800	285	294	2,077	18,770	36
17	...	17	17	5,900	17	11,200	...	...	...	...	11	11	52	370	37
163	5	168	160	55,095	164	249,125	42	14,692	30	23,925	154	166	791	5,974	38
10	...	11	10	2,950	10	3,900	...	...	1	400	6	6	30	152	39
2	2	2	1	150	2	440	...	...	...	...	...	...	...	...	40
102	1	106	100	33,175	103	721,960	13	44,095	28	89,750	78	90	788	6,195	41
27	...	27	26	8,925	25	13,900	1	100	3	2,100	14	14	81	483	42
75	1	79	74	24,250	78	708,050	12	43,995	25	87,650	64	76	707	5,712	43
69	2	75	69	18,128	57	816,975	13	88,700	27	116,850	58	58	462	3,927	44
205	1	258	198	101,517	203	3,557,330	39	252,614	143	547,110	131	217	690	22,072	45
...	4	...	...	...	4	600	1	36	...	...	2	2	4	20	46
...		...	...	...	4	600	1	36	...	...	2	2	4	20	47
...		...	...	...	...	...	...	...	...	...	...	...	...	...	48
...	1	...	...	...	...	...	...	...	...	...	...	...	...	...	49
...	1	...	...	...	...	...	...	...	...	...	...	...	...	...	50
1	...	1	1	160	.	15,000	...	...	...	...	1	1	9	50	51
8	1	8	8	1,625	8	10,125	1	50	2	3,000	5	6	40	295	52
8	1	8	8	1,625	8	10,125	1	50	2	3,000	5	6	40	295	53

TABLE 8.—ORGANIZATIONS, COMMUNICANTS OR MEMBERS, PLACES OF WORSHIP, VALUE OF CHURCH PROPERTY, EACH STATE AND

MAINE.

	DENOMINATION.	Total number of organizations.	COMMUNICANTS OR MEMBERS.				
			Number of organizations reporting.	Total number reported.	Sex.		
					Number of organizations reporting.	Male.	Female.
1	All denominations	1,559	1,532	212,988	1,441	84,755	119,971
2	Adventist bodies	61	61	2,159	61	820	1,339
3	Advent Christian Church	37	37	1,610	37	646	964
4	Seventh-day Adventist Denomination	22	22	527	22	164	363
5	Life and Advent Union	2	2	22	2	10	12
6	Armenian Church	4	4	318	4	249	69
7	Baptist bodies	451	451	32,854	420	10,484	20,426
	Baptists:						
8	Northern Baptist Convention	237	237	20,813	225	6,500	13,124
9	Free Baptists	199	199	11,698	181	3,871	7,127
10	Primitive Baptists	2	2	68	2	28	40
11	Freewill Baptists (Bullockites)	13	13	275	12	85	135
12	Christadelphians	1	1	2	1	1	1
13	Christians (Christian Connection)	34	33	2,210	32	918	1,276
14	Church of Christ, Scientist	14	14	384	14	96	288
15	Churches of the New Jerusalem	3	3	135	3	35	100
16	General Convention of the New Jerusalem in the United States of America	3	3	135	3	35	100
17	Communistic societies	2	2	75	2	13	62
18	United Society of Believers (Shakers)	2	2	75	2	13	62
19	Congregationalists	257	254	21,098	254	5,952	15,141
20	Disciples or Christians	14	14	397	13	123	254
21	Disciples of Christ	7	7	260	6	76	164
22	Churches of Christ	7	7	137	7	47	90
23	Eastern Orthodox Churches	5	5	780	....	....	....
24	Greek Orthodox Church	5	5	780	....	....	....
25	Evangelical bodies	2	2	64	2	24	40
26	Evangelical Association	2	2	64	2	24	40
27	Friends	26	26	1,713	26	768	945
28	Society of Friends (Orthodox)	26	26	1,713	26	768	945
29	Independent churches	12	12	346	9	104	117
30	Jewish congregations	7	4	[1]205	....	....	....
31	Latter-day Saints	9	9	507	8	150	257
32	Reorganized Church of Jesus Christ of Latter-day Saints	9	9	507	8	150	257
33	Lutheran bodies	8	8	1,045	6	358	387
34	General Council of the Evangelical Lutheran Church in North America	3	3	220	3	120	100
35	United Norwegian Lutheran Church in America	1	1	340	1	150	190
36	Danish Evangelical Lutheran Church in America	2	2	300	....	....	....
37	United Danish Evangelical Lutheran Church in America	2	2	185	2	88	97
38	Methodist bodies	317	312	20,112	295	6,202	12,905
39	Methodist Episcopal Church	316	311	20,087	294	6,192	12,890
40	African Methodist Episcopal Zion Church	1	1	25	1	10	15
41	Pentecostal Church of the Nazarene	3	3	94	3	28	66
42	Presbyterian bodies	2	2	364	2	110	254
43	Presbyterian Church in the United States of America	2	2	364	2	110	254
44	Protestant Episcopal Church	49	49	5,520	48	1,694	3,596
45	Roman Catholic Church	140	139	113,419	132	53,699	57,217
46	Salvationists	12	12	384	12	223	161
47	Salvation Army	12	12	384	12	223	161
48	Spiritualists	13	13	1,343	13	562	781
49	Unitarians	26	23	2,762	18	985	1,577
50	Universalists	86	75	4,686	62	1,142	2,710
51	Volunteers of America	1	1	17	1	15	2

[1] Heads of families only.

DEBT ON CHURCH PROPERTY, PARSONAGES, AND SUNDAY SCHOOLS, BY DENOMINATIONS (IN DETAIL), FOR TERRITORY: 1906—Continued.

MAINE.

PLACES OF WORSHIP.					VALUE OF CHURCH PROPERTY.		DEBT ON CHURCH PROPERTY.		PARSONAGES.		SUNDAY SCHOOLS CONDUCTED BY CHURCH ORGANIZATIONS.				
Number of organizations reporting—		Number of church edifices reported.	Seating capacity of church edifices.		Number of organizations reporting.	Value reported.	Number of organizations reporting.	Amount of debt reported.	Number of organizations reporting.	Value of parsonages reported.	Number of organizations reporting.	Number of Sunday schools reported.	Number of officers and teachers.	Number of scholars.	
Church edifices.	Halls, etc.		Number of organizations reporting.	Seating capacity reported.											
1,381	104	1,511	1,366	412,833	1,406	$9,955,363	231	$614,198	583	$1,435,201	1,304	1,450	13,420	107,440	1
38	16	39	38	7,668	39	63,568	5	1,663	2	2,500	51	53	363	2,058	2
28	8	29	28	5,893	30	53,968	5	1,663	2	2,500	32	33	268	1,640	3
9	8	9	9	1,575	8	8,800	...	...	...	...	19	20	95	418	4
1	...	1	1	200	1	800	...	...	...	...	...	...	...	...	5
...	3	...	...	...	...	...	...	...	...	...	...	...	...	...	6
414	9	452	412	114,287	415	1,716,777	35	41,839	167	281,251	368	409	4,001	30,728	7
226	3	255	225	66,531	226	1,132,377	23	21,360	104	189,800	209	246	2,468	19,055	8
179	4	188	178	45,646	181	576,500	12	20,479	62	89,651	158	162	1,529	11,648	9
2	...	2	2	700	1	1,500	...	...	1	1,800	...	...	...	...	10
7	2	7	7	1,410	7	6,400	...	...	...	...	1	1	4	25	11
...	...	...	...	...	...	...	...	...	...	...	...	...	...	...	12
32	1	34	32	7,805	31	107,950	4	3,275	10	16,600	26	28	252	1,491	13
1	12	1	1	312	8	16,600	...	...	...	...	10	10	20	93	14
3	...	3	2	505	3	20,000	...	...	...	...	3	3	21	104	15
3	...	3	2	505	3	20,000	...	...	...	...	3	3	21	104	16
...	2	...	...	...	2	1,900	...	...	...	...	2	3	10	35	17
...	2	...	...	...	2	1,900	...	...	...	...	2	3	10	35	18
250	6	288	247	81,056	250	1,869,200	34	69,253	117	257,900	234	255	2,702	20,027	19
7	6	8	7	1,575	7	16,100	...	...	...	...	7	7	61	358	20
4	2	4	4	900	4	11,100	...	...	...	...	5	5	54	303	21
3	4	4	3	675	3	5,000	...	...	...	...	2	2	7	55	22
...	5	...	...	...	...	...	...	...	...	...	...	...	...	...	23
...	5	...	...	...	...	...	...	...	...	...	...	...	...	...	24
2	...	2	2	250	2	2,000	...	...	1	1,200	2	3	20	94	25
2	...	2	2	250	2	2,000	...	...	1	1,200	2	3	20	94	26
24	2	24	24	6,485	24	78,600	1	250	1	1,000	24	26	199	1,174	27
24	2	24	24	6,485	24	78,600	1	250	1	1,000	24	26	199	1,174	28
9	2	10	9	1,800	9	10,810	...	...	...	...	7	8	35	290	29
2	...	2	1	200	2	12,000	1	2,500	1	600	1	1	2	40	30
7	2	9	7	1,800	7	9,500	2	310	...	...	7	9	61	280	31
7	2	9	7	1,800	7	9,500	2	310	...	...	7	9	61	280	32
7	...	8	7	1,875	7	46,500	6	7,765	3	4,850	8	8	58	377	33
3	...	3	3	900	3	21,500	2	3,700	1	650	3	3	17	92	34
1	...	1	1	275	1	15,000	1	150	...	...	1	1	18	120	35
1	...	2	1	350	1	5,000	1	3,015	1	2,500	2	2	7	60	36
2	...	2	2	350	2	5,000	2	900	1	1,700	2	2	16	105	37
308	7	330	308	83,249	308	1,475,725	49	49,142	176	298,650	292	345	3,452	24,790	38
307	7	329	307	83,049	307	1,472,725	48	47,542	176	298,650	291	344	3,444	24,760	39
1	...	1	1	200	1	3,000	1	1,600	...	...	1	1	8	30	40
2	1	2	2	450	2	10,750	1	4,300	1	2,500	3	3	20	67	41
2	...	3	2	1,200	2	23,300	1	2,900	1	3,000	2	4	28	316	42
2	...	3	2	1,200	2	23,300	1	2,900	1	3,000	2	4	28	316	43
48	...	58	48	12,587	48	638,000	4	3,920	23	111,800	46	47	317	2,630	44
113	7	120	113	53,787	115	2,497,000	54	371,066	64	403,650	116	133	886	16,549	45
...	12	...	...	...	12	2,460	8	296	...	...	8	8	17	128	46
...	12	...	...	...	12	2,460	8	296	...	...	8	8	17	128	47
3	9	3	3	3,300	7	20,103	1	3,000	...	...	4	4	24	160	48
26	...	28	26	9,250	25	392,500	6	8,050	7	23,100	16	16	139	969	49
83	1	87	75	23,392	80	924,000	19	44,669	9	26,600	66	66	730	4,667	50
...	1	...	...	...	1	20	...	...	...	...	1	1	2	15	51

TABLE 3.—ORGANIZATIONS COMMUNICANTS OR MEMBERS, PLACES OF WORSHIP, VALUE OF CHURCH PROPERTY, EACH STATE AND

MARYLAND.

	DENOMINATION.	Total number of organizations.	COMMUNICANTS OR MEMBERS.				
			Number of organizations reporting.	Total number reported.	Sex.		
					Number of organizations reporting.	Male.	Female.
1	All denominations	2,773	2,756	473,257	2,464	157,412	229,087
2	Adventist bodies	11	11	401	11	124	277
3	Seventh-day Adventist Denomination	11	11	401	11	124	277
4	Bahais	1	1	28	1	13	15
5	Baptist bodies	164	162	30,928	140	8,531	15,944
6	Baptists	140	140	29,435	127	8,439	15,687
7	Northern Baptist Convention	4	4	252	4	119	133
8	Southern Baptist Convention	71	71	11,232	70	3,840	7,172
9	National Baptist Convention (Colored)	65	65	17,951	53	4,480	8,382
10	Free Baptists	12	10	1,242	4	49	133
11	Primitive Baptists	12	12	251	9	43	124
12	Brethren (Plymouth)	5	5	129	5	49	80
13	Brethren (Plymouth)—I	2	2	45	2	17	28
14	Brethren (Plymouth)—III	2	2	44	2	17	27
15	Brethren (Plymouth)—IV	1	1	40	1	15	25
16	Brethren (River)	1	1	26	1	8	18
17	Brethren in Christ	1	1	26	1	8	18
18	Christadelphians	2	2	62	2	21	41
19	Christians (Christian Connection)	1	1	51	1	27	24
20	Church of Christ, Scientist	2	2	223	2	61	162
21	Church of God and Saints of Christ (Colored)	2	2	44	2	9	35
22	Churches of God in North America, General Eldership of the	25	25	1,204	25	435	769
23	Churches of the New Jerusalem	6	6	237	6	103	134
24	General Convention of the New Jerusalem in the United States of America	5	5	219	5	95	124
25	General Church of the New Jerusalem	1	1	18	1	8	10
26	Congregationalists	7	7	812	7	293	519
27	Disciples or Christians	26	26	3,343	23	1,188	1,855
28	Disciples of Christ	26	26	3,343	23	1,188	1,855
29	Dunkers or German Baptist Brethren	30	30	4,450	30	1,731	2,719
30	German Baptist Brethren Church (Conservative)	23	23	3,667	23	1,425	2,242
31	Old Order German Baptist Brethren	2	2	167	2	90	77
32	The Brethren Church (Progressive Dunkers)	5	5	616	5	216	400
33	Eastern Orthodox Churches	6	6	400	1	210	40
34	Greek Orthodox Church	6	6	400	1	210	40
35	Evangelical bodies	23	23	2,309	23	785	1,524
36	Evangelical Association	8	8	540	8	189	351
37	United Evangelical Church	15	15	1,769	15	596	1,173
38	Friends	24	24	2,079	24	982	1,097
39	Society of Friends (Orthodox)	6	6	508	6	239	269
40	Religious Society of Friends (Hicksite)	18	18	1,571	18	743	828
41	German Evangelical Protestant bodies	1	1	970	1	401	569
42	German Evangelical Protestant Ministers' Association	1	1	970	1	401	569
43	German Evangelical Synod of North America	17	17	8,384	12	2,402	3,522
44	Independent churches	19	18	1,738	16	609	1,062
45	International Apostolic Holiness Union	10	10	406	10	166	240
46	Jewish congregations	34	31	2,153			
47	Latter-day Saints	3	3	115	3	53	62
48	Church of Jesus Christ of Latter-day Saints	2	2	58	2	28	30
49	Reorganized Church of Jesus Christ of Latter-day Saints	1	1	57	1	25	32
50	Lutheran bodies	160	159	32,246	147	12.002	17,235
51	General Synod of the Evangelical Lutheran Church in the United States of America	115	115	24,824	109	9,275	13,657
52	General Council of the Evangelical Lutheran Church in North America	1	1	56			
53	Evangelical Lutheran Synodical Conference of America	21	20	4,062	17	1,389	1,762
54	Evangelical Lutheran Joint Synod of Ohio and Other States	22	22	3,254	20	1,318	1,786
55	Evangelical Lutheran Jehovah Conference	1	1	50	1	20	30
56	Mennonite bodies	22	22	953	22	419	534
57	Mennonite Church	16	16	689	16	293	396
58	Amish Mennonite Church	1	1	24	1	12	12
59	Old Amish Mennonite Church	3	3	165	3	79	86
60	Reformed Mennonite Church	2	2	75	2	35	40

[1] Heads of families onl .

DEBT ON CHURCH PROPERTY, PARSONAGES, AND SUNDAY SCHOOLS, BY DENOMINATIONS (IN DETAIL), FOR TERRITORY: 1906—Continued.

MARYLAND.

PLACES OF WORSHIP. Number of organizations reporting— Church edifices.	PLACES OF WORSHIP. Number of organizations reporting— Halls, etc.	PLACES OF WORSHIP. Number of church edifices reported.	PLACES OF WORSHIP. Seating capacity of church edifices. Number of organizations reporting.	PLACES OF WORSHIP. Seating capacity of church edifices. Seating capacity reported.	VALUE OF CHURCH PROPERTY. Number of organizations reporting.	VALUE OF CHURCH PROPERTY. Value reported.	DEBT ON CHURCH PROPERTY. Number of organizations reporting.	DEBT ON CHURCH PROPERTY. Amount of debt reported.	PARSONAGES. Number of organizations reporting.	PARSONAGES. Value of parsonages reported.	SUNDAY SCHOOLS CONDUCTED BY CHURCH ORGANIZATIONS. Number of organizations reporting.	SUNDAY SCHOOLS CONDUCTED BY CHURCH ORGANIZATIONS. Number of Sunday schools reported.	SUNDAY SCHOOLS CONDUCTED BY CHURCH ORGANIZATIONS. Number of officers and teachers.	SUNDAY SCHOOLS CONDUCTED BY CHURCH ORGANIZATIONS. Number of scholars.	
2,615	81	2,514	2,548	810,701	2,608	$23,765,172	659	$2,095,293	961	$2,758,674	2,437	2,606	31,174	261,440	1
4	6	5	4	700	4	2,250	1	250	......	......	11	14	88	386	2
4	6	5	4	700	4	2,250	1	250	......	......	11	14	88	386	3
......	1	......	......	......	......	......	......	......	......	......	......	......	......	......	4
141	7	146	132	46,860	143	1,310,783	55	142,157	22	45,700	135	154	1,729	17,110	5
128	7	133	120	44,110	130	1,280,233	51	140,777	21	45,300	127	146	1,657	16,697	6
3	......	3	3	810	4	12,800	1	150	1	1,800	4	4	43	271	7
67	3	72	67	24,565	68	953,450	20	93,985	14	35,100	64	80	1,064	10,219	8
58	4	58	50	18,735	58	313,983	30	46,642	6	8,400	59	62	550	6,207	9
4	......	4	4	900	4	8,050	4	1,380	1	400	8	8	72	413	10
9	......	9	8	1,850	9	22,500	......	......	......	......	......	......	......	......	11
......	5	......	......	......	......	......	......	......	......	......	3	3	14	115	12
......	2	......	......	......	......	......	......	......	......	......	2	2	12	105	13
......	2	......	......	......	......	......	......	......	......	......	1	1	2	10	14
......	1	......	......	......	......	......	......	......	......	......	......	......	......	......	15
1	......	1	1	500	1	4,000	......	......	......	......	......	......	......	......	16
1	......	1	1	500	1	4,000	......	......	......	......	......	......	......	......	17
......	1	......	......	......	1	150	......	......	......	......	......	......	......	......	18
1	......	1	1	600	1	1,200	1	500	......	......	1	1	9	50	19
1	1	1	1	400	2	64,000	......	......	......	......	2	2	19	124	20
......	2	......	......	......	......	......	......	......	......	......	......	......	......	......	21
25	......	25	25	6,175	25	34,900	2	393	3	2,501	18	18	220	1,710	22
5	1	5	5	1,000	6	58,900	2	2,000	1	3,000	5	5	41	161	23
5	......	5	5	1,000	5	58,750	2	2,000	1	3,000	4	4	38	147	24
......	1	......	......	......	1	150	......	......	......	......	1	1	3	14	25
7	......	7	7	2,460	7	151,000	4	15,945	1	1,000	7	7	91	890	26
26	......	26	26	8,000	26	231,700	6	45,300	1	2,500	25	26	320	2,949	27
26	......	26	26	8,000	26	231,700	6	45,300	1	2,500	25	26	320	2,949	28
30	......	58	29	18,800	30	107,800	2	699	3	2,350	27	54	511	4,508	29
23	......	50	23	16,900	23	84,100	2	699	2	850	23	49	460	4,138	30
2	......	2	2	600	2	3,700	......	......	......	......	......	......	......	......	31
5	......	6	4	1,300	5	20,000	......	......	1	1,500	4	5	51	370	32
1	5	1	1	250	......	......	......	......	......	......	......	......	......	......	33
1	5	1	1	250	......	......	......	......	......	......	......	......	......	......	34
22	1	22	22	6,425	22	148,303	7	39,425	10	17,300	22	24	363	2,846	35
8	......	8	8	2,075	8	71,450	3	16,400	2	1,400	7	7	89	512	36
14		14	14	4,350	14	76,853	4	23,025	8	15,900	15	17	274	2,334	37
24	...	24	24	7,310	24	175,700	......	......	......	......	15	18	110	987	38
6	......	6	6	1,910	6	69,000	......	......	......	......	5	8	66	572	39
18	......	18	18	5,400	18	106,700	......	......	......	......	10	10	44	415	40
	......	1	1	780	1	20,000	1	5,000	......	......	1	1	22	316	41
1	......	1	1	780	1	20,000	1	5,000	......	......	1	1	22	316	42
16	......	19	16	7,700	16	353,600	8	27,850	13	69,400	17	18	334	3,669	43
16	2	18	16	5,285	15	162,850	8	39,672	3	3,400	16	16	175	1,615	44
9	1	9	9	2,425	9	18,800	6	1,931	2	1,100	10	10	76	485	45
25	3	26	21	13,222	21	760,900	17	181,350	2	6,200	13	13	42	975	46
1	2	1	1	100	1	500	......	......	......	......	3	3	20	109	47
......	2	......	......	......	......	......	......	......	......	......	2	2	13	77	48
1	......	1	1	100	1	500	......	......	......	......	1	1	7	32	49
156	......	165	155	60,650	157	1,756,080	44	176,529	73	205,033	148	157	3,098	25,619	50
114	......	122	113	48,015	114	1,391,950	25	104,854	52	156,083	109	115	2,622	20,832	51
1	......	1	1	150	1	2,500	1	375	......	......	1	1	1	25	52
18	......	19	18	6,560	19	222,700	8	37,650	12	31,000	17	20	222	2,075	53
22	......	22	22	5,775	22	137,130	10	33,650	9	17,960	20	20	250	2,647	54
1	......	1	1	150	1	1,800	......	......	......	......	1	1	3	40	55
18	3	18	18	6,255	18	27,500	......	......	......	......	13	13	122	841	56
13	2	13	13	5,200	13	22,800	......	......	......	......	9	9	94	591	57
1	......	1	1	130	1	800	......	......	......	......	1	1	8	51	58
2	1	2	2	525	2	2,100	......	......	......	......	3	3	20	199	59
2	......	2	2	400	2	1,800	......	......	......	......	......	......	......	......	60

TABLE 3.—ORGANIZATIONS, COMMUNICANTS OR MEMBERS, PLACES OF WORSHIP, VALUE OF CHURCH PROPERTY, EACH STATE AND

MARYLAND—Continued.

	DENOMINATION.	Total number of organizations.	COMMUNICANTS OR MEMBERS. Number of organizations reporting.	Total number reported.	Sex. Number of organizations reporting.	Male.	Female.
61	Methodist bodies	1,471	1,466	137,156	1,371	48,499	79,055
62	Methodist Episcopal Church	966	963	95,207	889	34,096	54,237
63	Union American Methodist Episcopal Church (Colored)	12	12	936	12	372	564
64	African Methodist Episcopal Church	107	107	9,613	97	2,693	4,953
65	African Union Methodist Protestant Church	26	26	1,059	26	376	683
66	African Methodist Episcopal Zion Church	14	14	923	14	362	561
67	Methodist Protestant Church	181	181	16,373	178	6,079	10 069
68	Methodist Episcopal Church, South	153	152	12,642	144	4,353	7 753
69	Colored Methodist Episcopal Church	5	5	240	5	104	136
70	Free Methodist Church of North America	7	6	163	6	64	99
71	Moravian bodies	2	2	122	2	47	75
72	Moravian Church (Unitas Fratrum)	2	2	122	2	47	75
73	Pentecostal Church of the Nazarene	3	3	82	3	42	40
74	Polish National Church of America	1	1	1,132	1	523	609
75	Presbyterian bodies	111	111	17,895	102	5,966	10,915
76	Presbyterian Church in the United States of America	95	95	15,927	87	5,331	9,720
77	United Presbyterian Church of North America	2	2	340	2	140	200
78	Presbyterian Church in the United States	14	14	1,628	13	495	995
79	Protestant Episcopal Church	262	257	34,965	223	9,805	17,404
80	Reformed bodies	79	79	13,461	76	5,141	7,667
81	Reformed Church in America	1	1	19	1	9	10
82	Reformed Church in the United States	78	78	13,442	75	5,132	7,657
83	Reformed Episcopal Church	3	3	332	3	96	236
84	Roman Catholic Church	165	165	166,941	105	54,061	60,755
85	Salvationists	5	5	94	4	46	47
86	Salvation Army	5	5	94	4	46	47
87	Spiritualists	2	2	92	2	30	62
88	Theosophical societies	1	1	3	1	1	2
89	Theosophical Society in America	1	1	3	1	1	2
90	Unitarians	1	1	500	1	250	250
91	United Brethren bodies	64	64	6,541	55	2,283	3,493
92	Church of the United Brethren in Christ	63	63	6,445	54	2,249	3,431
93	Church of the United Brethren in Christ (Old Constitution)	1	1	96	1	34	62
94	Universalists	1	1	250	....	....	....

MASSACHUSETTS.

	DENOMINATION.	Total number of organizations.	Number of organizations reporting.	Total number reported.	Sex. Number of organizations reporting.	Male.	Female.
1	All denominations	3,088	3,031	1,562,621	2,795	639,844	813,961
2	Adventist bodies	70	69	4,061	68	1,455	2,433
3	Evangelical Adventists	1	1	36	1	14	22
4	Advent Christian Church	42	41	3,053	40	1,116	1,764
5	Seventh-day Adventist Denomination	26	26	926	26	303	623
6	Life and Advent Union	1	1	46	1	22	24
7	Armenian Church	29	29	6,960	29	5,199	1,761
8	Bahais	1	1	70	1	20	50
9	Baptist bodies	379	379	80,894	367	25,047	51,699
10	Baptists	358	358	78,165	348	24,206	50,018
11	Northern Baptist Convention	332	332	72,891	322	22,352	46,598
12	National Baptist Convention (Colored)	26	26	5,274	26	1,854	3,420
13	Free Baptists	20	20	2,720	18	839	1,674
14	Primitive Baptists	1	1	9	1	2	7
15	Brethren (Plymouth)	15	15	621	15	219	402
16	Brethren (Plymouth)—I	4	4	105	4	43	62
17	Brethren (Plymouth)—II	8	8	415	8	143	272
18	Brethren (Plymouth)—III	2	2	36	2	14	22
19	Brethren (Plymouth)—IV	1	1	65	1	19	46
20	Buddhists	1	....	....	....	....	....
21	Chinese Temples	1	....	....	....	....	....

DEBT ON CHURCH PROPERTY, PARSONAGES, AND SUNDAY SCHOOLS, BY DENOMINATIONS (IN DETAIL), FOR TERRITORY: 1906—Continued.

MARYLAND—Continued.

PLACES OF WORSHIP.					VALUE OF CHURCH PROPERTY.		DEBT ON CHURCH PROPERTY.		PARSONAGES.		SUNDAY SCHOOLS CONDUCTED BY CHURCH ORGANIZATIONS.				
Number of organizations reporting— Church edifices.	Number of organizations reporting— Halls, etc.	Number of church edifices reported.	Seating capacity of church edifices. Number of organizations reporting.	Seating capacity of church edifices. Seating capacity reported.	Number of organizations reporting.	Value reported.	Number of organizations reporting.	Amount of debt reported.	Number of organizations reporting.	Value of parsonages reported.	Number of organizations reporting.	Number of Sunday schools reported.	Number of officers and teachers.	Number of scholars.	
1,441	23	1,477	1,399	386,062	1,440	$6,857,575	352	$448,682	487	$1,001,075	1,404	1,448	16,665	129,962	61
951	13	980	909	254,242	949	4,916,475	242	300,245	335	700,400	934	973	12,085	92,292	
9	3	9	9	2,700	9	14,850	3	4,800	1	500	12	12	62	709	
104		106	104	28,230	102	337,850	57	69,951	39	38,000	97	98	709	7,120	
26		27	25	7,150	26	45,050	6	1,876	1	300	23	23	89	649	
14		15	14	4,535	13	44,100	10	19,025	1	4,000	13	13	86	871	
180	1	182	181	49,135	181	873,700	24	33,395	66	160,475	176	178	2,195	17,127	
149	3	150	149	38,570	150	616,700	8	19,100	44	97,400	138	140	1,359	10,650	
4	1	4	4	825	4	2,750	2	290			5	5	29	134	62
4	2	4	4	675	6	6,100					6	6	51	410	[illegible]
[illegible]		2	2	500	2	2,500					2	2	19	77	71
2			2	500	2	2,500					2	2	19	77	72
3		3	3	500	3	1,800	1	100			2	2	12	29	73
1		1	1	480	1	37,000	1	29,000	1	15,000	1	1	1	48	74
108	1	127	108	45,859	108	2,414,200	24	67,924	63	303,950	105	118	1,923	15,460	75
92		109	92	40,254	92	2,152,400	20	52,924	52	236,500	91	101	1,703	13,882	76
2		2		780	2	47,000	1	700	1	10,000	2	2	45	390	77
14		16	14	4,825	14	214,800	3	14,300	10	57,450	12	15	175	1,188	78
256	2	317	256	75,321	251	3,429,341	39	140,302	129	501,425	206	236	1,997	17,800	79
76	1	81	76	29,784	77	760,750	16	46,050	32	94,200	69	69	1,315	9,702	80
															81
76		81	76	29,784	77	760,750	16	46,050	32	94,200	69	69	1,315	9,702	82
3		3	3	990	3	65,000			1	2,000	3	3	39	333	83
132	2	157	123	55,348	124	3,991,315	51	671,834	85	438,200	86	100	877	14,680	84
	5				5	1,125	4	200			5	5	12	92	85
	5				5	1,125	4	200			5	5	12	92	86
1	1		1	500	2	14,400					2	2	10	71	87
	1														88
															89
1		2	1	600	1	500,000					1	1	16	100	90
60	4	63	60	18,860	60	267,250	7	12,200	19	43,340	58	61	856	7,481	91
59	4	62	59	18,660	59	264,250	7	12,200	18	41,540	57	60	838	7,396	92
1		1	1	200	1	3,000			1	1,800	1	1	18	85	93
1		1			1	32,000					1	1	28	140	94

MASSACHUSETTS.

2,706	288	2,983	2,678	1,313,564	2,778	$84,729,445	953	$8,203,412	1,377	$7,772,560	2,774	2,999	51,882	491,697	1
39	25	39	38	9,087	44	181,510	14	21,081	2	3,000	57	59	509	2,895	2
1		1	1	300	1	9,000									3
35	7	35	34	7,987	37	159,900	13	21,021	2	3,000	35	35	371	2,324	4
3	17	3	3	800	6	12,610	1	60			21	23	131	536	5
	1										1	1	7	35	6
1	21	1	1	500		17,000			1	2,500	2	2	4	190	7
	1														8
366	7	399	364	164,701	370	8,950,875	124	940,767	145	427,990	368	415	8,214	70,580	9
345	7	378	343	157,656	349	8,657,875	115	903,217	143	423,990	349	396	7,850	67,791	10
324	5	357	322	148,081	326	8,373,825	96	808,723	142	420,990	323	370	7,567	65,271	11
21	2	21	21	9,575	23	284,050	19	94,494	1	3,000	26	26	283	2,520	12
20		20	20	6,845	20	285,000	9	37,550	2	4,000	19	19	364	2,789	13
1		1	1	200	1	8,000									14
2	13	2	2	300	2	4,500	2	2,400			12	12	69	541	15
	4										3	3	11	66	16
2	6	2	2	300	2	4,500	2	2,400			8	8	56	455	17
	2										1	1	2	20	18
	1														19
1		1													20
1		1													21

TABLE 3.—ORGANIZATIONS, COMMUNICANTS OR MEMBERS, PLACES OF WORSHIP, VALUE OF CHURCH PROPERTY, EACH STATE AND

MASSACHUSETTS—Continued.

	DENOMINATION.	Total number of organizations.	COMMUNICANTS OR MEMBERS.				
			Number of organizations reporting.	Total number reported.	Sex.		
					Number of organizations reporting.	Male.	Female.
22	Catholic Apostolic Churches	1	1	101	1	30	71
23	Catholic Apostolic Church	1	1	101	1	30	71
24	Christadelphians	7	7	147	7	70	77
25	Christian Catholic Church in Zion	1	1	40	1	20	20
26	Christians (Christian Connection)	27	27	2,114	25	619	1,233
27	Church of Christ, Scientist	34	33	43,547	32	11,564	31,960
28	Church of God and Saints of Christ (Colored)	2	2	202	2	76	126
29	Churches of the New Jerusalem	17	17	1,535	15	446	1,059
30	General Convention of the New Jerusalem in the United States of America	17	17	1,535	15	446	1,059
31	Communistic societies	3	3	53	3	9	44
32	United Society of Believers (Shakers)	3	3	53	3	9	44
33	Congregationalists	615	615	119,196	611	37,692	79,972
34	Disciples or Christians	9	9	1,527	8	479	913
35	Disciples of Christ	9	9	1,527	8	479	913
36	Eastern Orthodox Churches	24	24	14,145	[illegible]	9,045	1,635
37	Russian Orthodox Church	1	1	470	1	400	70
38	Syrian Orthodox Church	3	3	1,200	3	710	490
39	Greek Orthodox Church	20	20	12,475	5	7,935	1,075
40	Evangelical bodies	10	10	590	10	180	410
41	Evangelical Association	10	10	590	10	180	410
42	Evangelistic associations	1	1	45	1	15	30
43	Metropolitan Church Association	1	1	45	1	15	30
44	Friends	30	30	1,798	30	756	1,042
45	Society of Friends (Orthodox)	28	28	1,734	28	722	1,012
46	Orthodox Conservative Friends (Wilburite)	1	1	55	1	28	27
47	Friends (Primitive)	1	1	9	1	6	3
48	Independent churches	35	35	2,013	34	699	1,251
49	International Apostolic Holiness Union	1	1	40	1	17	23
50	Jewish congregations	77	48	[1]14,388			
51	Latter-day Saints	9	9	679	9	261	418
52	Church of Jesus Christ of Latter-day Saints	1	1	109	1	46	63
53	Reorganized Church of Jesus Christ of Latter-day Saints	8	8	570	8	215	355
54	Lutheran bodies	74	73	13,063	68	5,049	6,364
55	General Council of the Evangelical Lutheran Church in North America	34	34	6,645	31	2,594	3,313
56	Evangelical Lutheran Synodical Conference of America	20	19	3,966	17	1,300	1,754
57	Synod for the Norwegian Evangelical Lutheran Church in America	1	1	200	1	75	125
58	Danish Evangelical Lutheran Church in America	2	2	140	2	65	75
59	Immanuel Synod of the Evangelical Lutheran Church of North America	1	1	200	1	75	125
60	Finnish Evangelical Lutheran Church of America, or Suomi Synod	6	6	1,055	6	565	490
61	United Danish Evangelical Lutheran Church in America	2	2	117	2	47	70
62	Finnish Evangelical Lutheran National Church	3	3	622	3	275	347
63	Apostolic Lutheran Church (Finnish)	5	5	118	5	53	65
64	Methodist bodies	445	444	65,498	419	19,818	38,840
65	Methodist Episcopal Church	413	412	61,626	390	18,761	36,900
66	African Methodist Episcopal Church	14	14	1,364	11	127	362
67	African Methodist Episcopal Zion Church	7	7	1,215	7	479	736
68	Primitive Methodist Church in the United States of America	9	9	1,264	9	434	830
69	Free Methodist Church of North America	2	2	29	2	17	12
70	Nonsectarian Churches of Bible Faith	2	2	40	2	25	15
71	Pentecostal Church of the Nazarene	11	11	926	11	313	613
72	Polish National Church of America	5	5	2,141	5	1,288	853
73	Presbyterian bodies	38	38	8,559	37	2,766	5,468
74	Presbyterian Church in the United States of America	23	23	5,678	23	1,780	3,898
75	United Presbyterian Church of North America	12	12	2,540	11	863	1,352
76	Synod of the Reformed Presbyterian Church of North America	3	3	341	3	123	218
77	Protestant Episcopal Church	229	228	51,636	183	14,166	24,638
78	Reformed bodies	3	3	393	2	113	145
79	Reformed Church in the United States	2	2	253	1	48	70
80	Christian Reformed Church	1	1	140	1	65	75

[1] Heads of families only.

DEBT ON CHURCH PROPERTY, PARSONAGES, AND SUNDAY SCHOOLS, BY DENOMINATIONS (IN DETAIL), FOR TERRITORY: 1906—Continued.

MASSACHUSETTS—Continued.

PLACES OF WORSHIP.					VALUE OF CHURCH PROPERTY.		DEBT ON CHURCH PROPERTY.		PARSONAGES.		SUNDAY SCHOOLS CONDUCTED BY CHURCH ORGANIZATIONS.				
Number of organizations reporting—		Number of church edifices reported.	Seating capacity of church edifices.		Number of organizations reporting.	Value reported.	Number of organizations reporting.	Amount of debt reported.	Number of organizations reporting.	Value of parsonages reported.	Number of organizations reporting.	Number of Sunday schools reported.	Number of officers and teachers.	Number of scholars.	
Church edifices.	Halls, etc.		Number of organizations reporting.	Seating capacity reported.											
...	1	...	...	...	...	...	...	...	...	...	...	...	...	...	22
...	1	...	...	...	...	...	...	...	...	...	...	...	...	...	23
...	7	...	...	...	5	$355	...	...	...	...	6	6	19	140	24
...	1	...	...	...	...	...	...	...	...	...	...	...	...	...	25
27	...	27	26	8,550	25	285,600	2	$16,050	10	$23,900	26	27	415	2,429	26
7	25	7	7	6,135	21	2,321,031	5	22,000	...	...	32	33	190	1,023	27
...	2	...	...	...	...	...	...	...	...	...	...	...	...	...	28
15	...	18	15	4,568	15	374,146	3	11,600	5	23,500	14	14	119	931	29
15	...	18	15	4,568	15	374,146	3	11,600	5	23,500	14	14	119	931	30
3	...	3	3	800	3	2,900	...	...	3	7,500	1	1	2	9	31
3	...	3	3	800	3	2,900	...	...	3	7,500	1	1	2	9	32
597	14	691	594	286,899	598	15,880,624	120	534,929	343	1,342,980	609	657	12,664	114,663	33
9	...	9	9	2,450	9	89,340	5	12,230	2	7,200	8	8	118	1,149	34
9	...	9	9	2,450	9	89,340	5	12,230	2	7,200	8	8	118	1,149	35
5	19	5	4	3,350	8	120,910	4	51,500	...	...	1	1	3	21	36
1	...	1	1	250	1	3,500	...	...	...	...	...	...	...	...	37
...	3	...	...	...	3	410	...	...	...	...	...	...	...	...	38
4	16	4	3	3,100	4	117,000	4	51,500	...	...	1	1	3	21	39
9	...	9	9	1,850	9	54,175	8	28,990	1	2,000	10	11	115	641	40
9	...	9	9	1,850	9	54,175	8	28,990	1	2,000	10	11	115	641	41
...	1	...	...	...	...	...	...	...	...	...	1	1	4	50	42
...	1	...	...	...	...	...	...	...	...	...	1	1	4	50	43
29	1	29	29	5,950	29	163,100	3	2,200	1	2,000	22	23	234	1,347	44
28	...	28	28	5,825	28	161,100	3	2,200	1	2,000	22	23	234	1,347	45
1	...	1	1	125	1	2,000	...	...	...	...	...	...	...	...	46
...	1	...	...	...	...	...	...	...	...	...	...	...	...	...	47
25	10	25	25	5,360	25	164,700	9	17,276	3	9,000	30	31	314	2,431	48
...	1	...	...	...	1	200	...	...	...	...	1	1	4	35	49
32	6	40	30	19,011	30	869,750	24	239,450	9	29,600	20	20	58	1,521	50
6	3	6	6	1,075	6	17,850	4	5,775	...	...	9	10	125	484	51
...	1	...	...	...	...	...	...	...	...	...	1	1	13	49	52
6	2	6	6	1,075	6	17,850	4	5,775	...	...	8	9	112	435	53
49	14	55	47	16,335	55	604,987	40	152,389	11	48,000	62	69	800	5,488	54
28	3	30	28	9,190	30	304,537	26	87,439	5	18,000	33	36	467	3,116	55
12	2	15	12	4,745	14	215,150	8	50,300	4	21,000	15	15	244	1,656	56
1	...	1	1	400	1	35,000	1	3,000	...	...	1	2	9	80	57
...	2	...	...	...	...	...	...	...	1	6,000	1	1	2	24	58
1	...	1	1	500	1	4,000	...	...	1	3,000	1	1	12	75	59
3	3	4	3	1,000	3	24,000	3	6,500	...	...	6	9	42	382	60
...	2	...	...	...	2	6,000	...	...	...	...	2	2	8	45	61
2	1	2	2	500	2	16,000	2	5,150	...	...	3	3	16	110	62
2	1	2	...	...	2	300	...	...	...	...	...	...	...	...	63
429	9	486	429	172,699	429	7,205,475	135	594,897	278	957,320	434	448	8,996	66,251	64
401	5	408	401	161,164	401	6,756,600	115	512,583	268	922,870	405	419	8,564	62,391	65
13	1	13	13	4,750	12	154,350	8	17,500	4	12,950	11	11	101	756	66
6	1	6	6	2,785	7	104,025	5	39,614	1	2,500	7	7	109	893	67
9	...	9	9	4,000	9	190,500	7	25,200	5	19,000	9	9	212	2,155	68
...	2	...	...	...	...	...	...	...	...	...	2	2	10	56	69
1	1	1	1	100	1	6,000	1	3,000	...	...	...	...	...	...	70
8	3	8	8	2,960	8	79,2[illegible]2	8	31,600	3	8,500	11	11	136	879	71
4	1	5	4	1,900	5	58,700	4	28,000	3	9,000	4	4	5	206	72
37	...	41	37	19,955	37	862,600	18	140,950	5	23,700	38	42	712	6,008	73
22	...	25	22	11,930	22	559,100	11	67,000	4	20,700	23	25	468	4,177	74
12	...	13	12	6,475	12	208,500	5	45,850	1	3,000	12	14	212	1,621	75
3	...	3	3	1,550	3	95,000	2	28,100	...	...	3	3	32	210	76
217	10	264	216	75,888	222	9,633,276	44	183,945	108	649,050	219	234	3,059	26,605	
3	...	3	3	1,000	3	56,000	2	7,265	1	4,000	3	3	31	284	
2	...	2	2	700	2	46,000	1	4,365	...	...	2	2	27	224	[illegible]
1	...	1	1	300	1	10,000	1	2,900	1	4,000	1	1	4	60	[illegible]

TABLE 3.—ORGANIZATIONS, COMMUNICANTS OR MEMBERS, PLACES OF WORSHIP, VALUE OF CHURCH PROPERTY, EACH STATE AND

MASSACHUSETTS—Continued.

	DENOMINATION.	Total number of organizations.	COMMUNICANTS OR MEMBERS. Number of organizations reporting.	Total number reported.	Sex. Number of organizations reporting.	Male.	Female.
81	Reformed Catholic Church	1	1	600	1	400	200
82	Roman Catholic Church	473	473	1,080,706	451	485,036	531,386
83	Salvationists	51	48	1,597	48	746	851
84	Salvation Army	51	48	1,597	48	746	851
85	Spiritualists	42	42	3,885	42	1,624	2,261
86	Swedish Evangelical bodies	1	1	86	1	22	64
87	Swedish Evangelical Free Mission	1	1	86	1	22	64
88	Theosophical societies	7	7	236	7	63	173
89	Theosophical Society, American Section	7	7	236	7	63	173
90	Unitarians	189	180	35,440	144	10,876	17,837
91	Universalists	114	106	12,983	92	3,586	7,593
92	Volunteers of America	5	3	66	3	35	31

MICHIGAN.

	DENOMINATION.	Total number of organizations.	Number of organizations reporting.	Total number reported.	Sex. Number of organizations reporting.	Male.	Female.
1	All denominations	5,635	5,605	982,479	5,138	291,315	387,461
2	Adventist bodies	204	203	7,974	193	2,659	5,028
3	Advent Christian Church	14	14	451	14	164	287
4	Seventh-day Adventist Denomination	175	174	7,042	165	2,348	4,497
5	Churches of God (Adventist), Unattached Congregations	6	6	153	5	23	40
6	Churches of God in Christ Jesus	9	9	328	9	124	204
7	Armenian Church	2	2	168	2	136	32
8	Bahais	2	2	28	2	6	22
9	Baptist bodies	528	528	50,136	504	16,699	31,156
10	Baptists	434	434	45,120	414	15,074	27,961
11	Northern Baptist Convention	420	420	44,373	400	14,781	27,507
12	National Baptist Convention (Colored)	14	14	747	14	293	454
13	Seventh-day Baptists	1	1	18	1	9	9
14	Free Baptists	92	92	4,977	89	1,616	3,186
15	Primitive Baptists	1	1	21	....	....	....
16	Brethren (Plymouth)	20	20	556	20	220	336
17	Brethren (Plymouth)—I	5	5	186	5	68	118
18	Brethren (Plymouth)—II	9	9	286	9	117	169
19	Brethren (Plymouth)—III	3	3	70	3	28	42
20	Brethren (Plymouth)—IV	3	3	14	3	7	7
21	Brethren (River)	3	3	61	3	27	34
22	Brethren in Christ	3	3	61	o	27	34
23	Catholic Apostolic Churches	2	2	135	2	55	80
24	New Apostolic Church	2	2	135	2	55	80
25	Christian Catholic Church in Zion	1	1	20	1	8	12
26	Christian Israelite Church	1	1	18	1	7	11
27	Christians (Christian Connection)	18	16	1,018	12	323	606
28	Church of Christ, Scientist	33	33	1,580	32	400	1,110
29	Churches of God in North America, General Eldership of the	12	12	320	10	101	164
30	Churches of the New Jerusalem	3	3	161	3	52	109
31	General Convention of the New Jerusalem in the United States of America	3	3	161	3	52	109
32	Congregationalists	323	321	32,553	321	10,551	22,002
33	Disciples or Christians	124	124	10,629	118	3,406	5,832
34	Disciples of Christ	116	116	9,791	110	3,100	5,300
35	Churches of Christ	8	8	838	8	306	532
36	Dunkers or German Baptist Brethren	26	26	1,213	25	519	674
37	German Baptist Brethren Church (Conservative)	18	18	914	18	405	509
38	Old Order German Baptist Brethren	3	3	98	3	53	45
39	The Brethren Church (Progressive Dunkers)	5	5	201	4	61	120
40	Eastern Orthodox Churches	2	2	500	....	....	....
41	Greek Orthodox Church	2	2	500	....	....	....

DEBT ON CHURCH PROPERTY, PARSONAGES, AND SUNDAY SCHOOLS, BY DENOMINATIONS (IN DETAIL), FOR TERRITORY: 1906—Continued.

MASSACHUSETTS—Continued.

PLACES OF WORSHIP.					VALUE OF CHURCH PROPERTY.		DEBT ON CHURCH PROPERTY.		PARSONAGES.		SUNDAY SCHOOLS CONDUCTED BY CHURCH ORGANIZATIONS.				
Number of organizations reporting— Church edifices.	Number of organizations reporting— Halls, etc.	Number of church edifices reported.	Seating capacity of church edifices. Number of organizations reporting.	Seating capacity of church edifices. Seating capacity reported.	Number of organizations reporting.	Value reported.	Number of organizations reporting.	Amount of debt reported.	Number of organizations reporting.	Value of parsonages reported.	Number of organizations reporting.	Number of Sunday schools reported.	Number of officers and teachers.	Number of scholars.	
....	1	....	....	....	....	....	....	....	....	....	....	....	....	....	81
465	9	504	454	364,772	454	$25,723,238	270	$1,616,620	355	$3,744,470	453	533	10,998	157,992	82
11	37	11	11	4,890	48	444,395	23	192,483	1	10,000	41	41	172	1,248	83
11	37	11	11	4,890	48	444,395	23	192,483	1	10,000	41	41	172	1,248	84
13	27	15	13	9,325	18	402,350	5	10,350	....	....	9	9	85	415	85
1	....	1	1	250	1	8,000	1	1,700	....	....	1	1	8	46	86
1	....	1	1	250	1	8,000	1	1,700	....	....			8	46	87
....	7	....	....	....	....	....	....	....	....	....			1	3	88
....	7	....	....	....	....	....	....	....	....	....	1	1	1	3	89
182	6	215	182	79,972	180	7,541,677	31	142,870	63	346,350	166	168	1,926	12,822	90
113	....	113	110	42,932	113	2,604,664	44	191,095	24	91,000	101	101	1,771	12,347	91
....	5	....	....	....	3	245	....	....	....	....	2	2	7	23	92
MICHIGAN.															
4,661	523	4,882	4,561	1,353,180	4,702	$27,144,250	1,040	$1,729,978	2,155	$3,946,747	4,563	4,830	49,847	414,421	1
129	56	132	128	27,230	133	226,615	15	6,617	3	4,300	176	188	1,237	5,336	2
9	4	9	9	2,550	9	13,350	....	....	1	1,000	4	4	40	135	3
114	45	117	113	23,430	117	206,265	15	6,617	2	3,300	168	180	1,170	5,035	4
2	4	2	2	350	3	2,300	....	....	....	....	4	4	27	166	5
4	3	4	4	900	4	4,700	....	....	....	....	....	....	....	....	6
....	2	....	....	....	....	....	....	....	....	....	....	....	....	....	7
....	1	....	....	....	....	....	....	....	....	....	....	....	....	....	8
499	12	522	486	141,588	507	2,690,920	96	113,911	213	293,250	478	521	6,081	46,598	9
416	7	439	404	120,772	422	2,497,420	84	109,436	181	261,700	394	437	5,204	41,112	10
403	7	426	391	117,312	408	2,465,470	79	107,811	177	258,000	381	424	5,105	40,614	11
13	....	13	13	3,460	14	31,950	5	1,625	4	3,700	13	13	99	498	12
....	....	....	....	....	....	....	....	....	....	....	1	1	5	25	13
83	5	83	82	20,816	85	193,500	12	4,475	32	31,550	83	83	872	5,461	14
....	....	....	....	....	....	....	....	....	....	....	....	....	....	....	15
1	19	1	1	300	2	8,100	....	....	....	....	7	9	48	523	16
....	5	....	....	....	....	....	....	....	....	....	3	5	29	260	17
1	8	1	1	300	1	8,000	....	....	....	....	3	3	17	248	18
....	3	....	....	....	1	100	....	....	....	....	1	1	2	15	19
....	3	....	....	....	....	....	....	....	....	....	....	....	....	....	20
3	....	3	3	500	3	2,950	....	....	....	....	1	1	8	40	21
3	....	3	3	500	3	2,950	....	....	....	....	1	1	8	40	22
1	1	1	1	200	1	2,500	1	2,000	....	....	....	....	....	....	23
1	1	1	1	200	1	2,500	1	2,000	....	....	....	....	....	....	24
....	1	....	....	....	....	....	....	....	....	....	....	....	....	....	25
....	1	....	....	....	....	....	....	....	....	....	....	....	....	....	26
16	....	16	16	3,900	16	36,050	....	....	4	6,000	11	11	122	774	27
15	13	16	15	4,244	23	149,450	6	12,545	....	....	29	29	125	548	28
10	1	10	10	3,100	10	9,350	....	....	....	....	9	9	60	345	29
3	....	3	3	400	3	33,200	1	3,000	1	1,400	1	1	9	55	30
3	....	3	3	400	3	33,200	1	3,000	1	1,400	1	1	9	55	31
310	9	316	309	101,961	310	2,131,633	87	95,063	152	260,800	298	308	3,891	31,780	32
101	11	103	101	28,685	103	417,200	22	30,860	18	18,500	112	115	1,102	8,525	33
94	10	96	94	27,055	96	391,400	22	30,860	18	18,500	107	110	1,052	7,963	34
7	1	7	7	1,630	7	25,800	....	....	....	....	5	5	50	562	35
23	1	28	23	7,010	23	45,800	2	465	....	....	20	25	190	1,075	36
16	1	21	16	5,060	16	37,600	2	465	....	....	16	21	158	925	37
2	....	2	2	450	2	1,800	....	....	....	....	....	....	....	....	38
5	....	5	5	1,500	5	6,400	....	....	....	....	4	4	32	150	39
....	2	....	....	....	....	....	....	....	....	....	....	....	....	....	40
....	2	....	....	....	....	....	....	....	....	....	....	....	....	....	41

TABLE 3.—ORGANIZATIONS, COMMUNICANTS OR MEMBERS, PLACES OF WORSHIP, VALUE OF CHURCH PROPERTY, EACH STATE AND

MICHIGAN—Continued.

	DENOMINATION.	Total number of organizations.	COMMUNICANTS OR MEMBERS.				
			Number of organizations reporting.	Total number reported.	Sex.		
					Number of organizations reporting.	Male.	Female.
42	Evangelical bodies	140	140	7,700	138	3,099	4,471
43	Evangelical Association	139	139	7,575	137	3,049	4,396
44	United Evangelical Church	1	1	125	1	50	75
45	Evangelistic associations	10	9	226	9	98	128
46	Missionary Church Association	5	4	100	4	46	54
47	Apostolic Christian Church	1	1	34	1	14	20
48	Church of Daniel's Band	4	4	92	4	38	54
49	Friends	20	20	1,351	20	578	773
50	Society of Friends (Orthodox)	19	19	1,348	19	576	772
51	Religious Society of Friends (Hicksite)	1	1	3	1	2	1
52	German Evangelical Protestant bodies	1	1	21	1	9	12
53	German Evangelical Protestant Ministers' Association	1	1	21	1	9	12
54	German Evangelical Synod of North America	68	68	20,436	65	8,175	10,271
55	Independent churches	32	31	2,035	30	954	1,067
56	International Apostolic Holiness Union	16	16	518	16	163	355
57	Jewish congregations	32	21	[1] 1,530	......	......	......
58	Latter-day Saints	75	75	4,335	72	1,698	2,448
59	Church of Jesus Christ of Latter-day Saints	1	1	108	1	26	82
60	Reorganized Church of Jesus Christ of Latter-day Saints	74	74	4,227	71	1,672	2,366
61	Lutheran bodies	555	555	105,803	504	44,660	48,292
62	General Synod of the Evangelical Lutheran Church in the United States of America	13	13	1,944	13	736	1,208
63	General Council of the Evangelical Lutheran Church in North America	68	68	9,693	66	4,457	5,042
64	Evangelical Lutheran Synodical Conference of America	207	207	50,031	184	20,045	22,256
65	United Norwegian Lutheran Church in America	17	17	2,760	13	793	853
66	Evangelical Lutheran Joint Synod of Ohio and Other States	30	30	9,702	26	4,060	4,908
67	Lutheran Synod of Buffalo	5	5	700	2	135	141
68	Hauge's Norwegian Evangelical Lutheran Synod	2	2	225	1	93	87
69	Evangelical Lutheran Synod of Iowa and Other States	38	38	6,817	37	3,268	3,389
70	Synod for the Norwegian Evangelical Lutheran Church in America	17	17	820	17	394	426
71	Evangelical Lutheran Synod of Michigan and Other States	50	50	7,801	43	3,110	3,044
72	Danish Evangelical Lutheran Church in America	11	11	[illegible],071	7	358	430
73	Finnish Evangelical Lutheran Church of America, or Suomi Synod	40	40	,121	40	3,240	2,881
74	Norwegian Lutheran Free Church	4	4	584	4	315	269
75	United Danish Evangelical Lutheran Church in America	7	7	688	7	392	296
76	Finnish Evangelical Lutheran National Church	15	15	3,539	15	1,909	1,630
77	Apostolic Lutheran Church (Finnish)	23	23	2,622	22	1,030	1,092
78	Evangelical Lutheran Jehovah Conference	8	8	685	7	325	340
79	Mennonite bodies	42	42	1,560	42	703	857
80	Mennonite Church	6	6	313	6	144	169
81	Amish Mennonite Church	2	2	178	2	93	85
82	Old Amish Mennonite Church	2	2	194	2	98	96
83	Reformed Mennonite Church	3	3	63	3	28	35
84	Church of God in Christ (Mennonite)	3	3	61	3	30	31
85	Old (Wisler) Mennonite Church	1	1	61	1	28	33
86	Mennonite Brethren in Christ	25	25	690	25	282	408
87	Methodist bodies	1,831	1,826	128,675	1,757	44,555	78,762
88	Methodist Episcopal Church	1,312	1,308	114,326	1,252	39,347	69,994
89	African Methodist Episcopal Church	22	22	1,737	22	651	1,086
90	African Methodist Episcopal Zion Church	2	2	60	2	19	41
91	Methodist Protestant Church	155	154	5,077	154	1,935	3,142
92	Wesleyan Methodist Connection of America	92	92	2,354	91	858	1,466
93	Free Methodist Church of North America	248	248	5,121	236	1,745	3,033
94	Moravian bodies	1	1	197	1	100	97
95	Moravian Church (Unitas Fratrum)	1	1	197	1	100	97
96	Nonsectarian Churches of Bible Faith	5	5	94	5	47	47
97	Presbyterian bodies	284	284	37,900	268	11,396	23,054
98	Presbyterian Church in the United States of America	269	269	36,710	253	10,956	22,304
99	United Presbyterian Church of North America	12	12	1,017	12	369	648
100	Synod of the Reformed Presbyterian Church of North America	3	3	173	3	71	102
101	Protestant Episcopal Church	201	196	26,439	179	7,088	14,617
102	Reformed bodies	148	148	28,345	141	11,936	13,954
103	Reformed Church in America	63	63	11,260	62	4,691	6,419
104	Reformed Church in the United States	18	18	1,666	17	708	935
105	Christian Reformed Church	66	66	14,719	61	6,037	6,400
106	Hungarian Reformed Church in America	1	1	700	1	500	200

[1] Heads of families only.

DEBT ON CHURCH PROPERTY, PARSONAGES, AND SUNDAY SCHOOLS, BY DENOMINATIONS (IN DETAIL), FOR TERRITORY: 1906—Continued.

MICHIGAN—Continued.

PLACES OF WORSHIP.					VALUE OF CHURCH PROPERTY.		DEBT ON CHURCH PROPERTY.		PARSONAGES.		SUNDAY SCHOOLS CONDUCTED BY CHURCH ORGANIZATIONS.				
Number of organizations reporting—		Number of church edifices reported.	Seating capacity of church edifices.		Number of organizations reporting.	Value reported.	Number of organizations reporting.	Amount of debt reported.	Number of organizations reporting.	Value of parsonages reported.	Number of organizations reporting.	Number of Sunday schools reported.	Number of officers and teachers.	Number of scholars.	
Church edifices.	Halls, etc.		Number of organizations reporting.	Seating capacity reported.											
132	4	133	129	32,894	134	$343,695	27	$26,346	54	$69,925	133	139	1,803	10,535	42
131	4	132	128	32,394	133	335,695	27	26,346	53	67,425	132	138	1,790	10,425	43
1		1	1	500	1	8,000			1	2,500	1	1	13	110	44
4	5	4	4	850	5	6,450	2	300			5	7	39	269	45
1	4	1	1	200	2	1,050					4	6	36	219	46
1		1	1	150	1	3,000	1	200							47
2	1	2	2	500	2	2,400	1	100			1		3	50	48
19	1	19	19	4,810	19	33,500	1	650	6	6,100	14	14	136	831	49
18	1	18	18	4,710	18	33,000	1	650	6	6,100	14	14	136	831	50
1		1	1	100	1	500									51
1		1	1	75	1	900									52
1		1	1	75	1	900									53
65	2	76	65	26,869	65	649,400	30	100,200	44	83,900	62	62	685	6,917	54
23	6	23	22	6,775	24	81,600	10	19,770	7	16,400	19	20	135	1,024	55
5	10	5	5	990	5	10,900	4	2,573	5	2,925	13	13	84	453	56
14	2	15	14	7,875	12	297,850	8	58,500	4	11,000	13	13	42	818	57
39	21	41	38	7,775	41	49,225	5	1,005	1	700	49	55	464	1,846	58
	1										1	3	13	51	59
39	20	41	38	7,775	41	49,225	5	1,005	1	700	48	52	451	1,795	60
465	52	505	458	141,256	463	2,193,860	178	310,766	288	493,512	345	387	2,300	23,331	61
13		14	13	5,030	13	146,000	7	43,250	6		12	13	200	1,936	62
64	1	67	64	17,255	64	289,255	19	27,688	26		60	66	720	4,698	63
185	13	200	183	62,206	184	1,003,650	80	148,465	139		79	83	264	4,668	64
17		20	16	4,600	15	50,300	3	1,400	7		15	16	105	800	65
30		32	28	11,425	30	202,625	15	46,125	24	16,900	28	28	190	3,029	66
5		5	5	1,775	5	21,000	4	4,700	3	[illegible]	3	4	14	133	67
2		2	2	450	2	5,500	2	1,030			2	2	16	92	68
33	3	36	33	9,475	33	117,950	10	6,900	22	30,800	27	27	106	1,319	69
8	2	8	8	1,385	9	18,175	1	100	4	5,800	9	9	29	253	70
44	4	47	44	11,720	44	146,300	15	9,775	31	41,450	33	34	140	1,694	71
11		11	11	1,735	11	24,700	4	2,350	6	9,500	10	10	36	370	72
21	19	26	21	6,085	21	63,655	7	3,150	8	11,850	31	54	326	2,563	73
4		4	4	1,000	4	19,000	2	1,283	2	5,500	3	3	39	290	74
6	1	6	6	950	6	7,700	1	300	2	3,200	4	4	9	120	75
7	8	7	7	2,100	7	26,000	3	6,000	1	1,500	15	19	62	709	76
8	1	9	7	2,765	8	32,300	1	700	1	2,000	6	6	26	347	77
7		11	6	1,300	7	19,750	4	7,550	6	6,300	8	9	18	310	78
28	11	29	28	6,073	28	60,517	3	291	11	7,450	29	29	246	1,498	79
3	2	3	3	950	3	2,800					5	5	49	321	80
2		2	2	450	2	1,800	2	190			2	2	29	200	81
	2														82
	3														83
1		1	1	150	1	200									84
1		2	1	250	1	650									85
21	4	21	21	4,273	21	55,067	1	101	11	7,450	22	22	168	977	86
1,618	155	1,644	1,591	414,211	1,623	6,419,775	266	310,348	797	1,127,980	1,617	1,701	19,577	139,822	87
1,191	89	1,212	1,168	317,934	1,193	5,733,325	217	282,912	577	947,445	1,208	1,261	16,210	122,304	88
22		23	21	6,710	22	97,400	12	13,609	18	16,860	22	22	210	1,052	89
2		2	2	750	2	4,700	1	1,400			2	2	7	27	90
132	20	132	129	29,342	132	278,700	18	5,447	57	52,325	137	146	1,277	7,016	91
68	17	71	68	13,730	70	92,550			41	34,875	76	83	569	3,225	92
203	29	204	203	45,745	204	213,100	18	6,980	104	76,475	172	187	1,304	6,198	93
1		1	1	325	1	3,000			1	3,000	1	1	8	108	94
1		1	1	325	1	3,000			1	3,000	1	1	8	108	95
	5														96
277	2	293	274	91,738	273	2,972,305	64	88,455	122	291,855	266	277	4,434	35,461	97
262	2	277	259	87,448	258	2,910,905	63	88,105	116	279,955	251	261	4,257	34,082	98
12		13	12	3,740	12	55,700	1	350	6	11,900	12	12	151	1,192	99
3		3	3	550	3	5,700					3	4	26	187	100
170	7	204	169	49,770	174	2,328,025	36	138,647	72	318,300	144	156	1,468	12,104	101
141	5	159	141	60,221	142	925,200	72	133,937	116	261,600	134	139	1,907	22,036	102
61	1	68	61	23,290	62	455,700	27	36,825	49	125,900	63	63	1,009	10,652	103
16	1	17	16	4,247	16	80,700	4	6,350	9	14,400	17	18	189	1,388	104
63	3	73	63	32,184	63	374,800	40	81,562	58	121,300	54	58	709	9,996	105
1		1	1	500	1	14,000	1	9,200							106

TABLE 3.—ORGANIZATIONS, COMMUNICANTS OR MEMBERS, PLACES OF WORSHIP, VALUE OF CHURCH PROPERTY, EACH STATE AND

MICHIGAN—Continued.

	DENOMINATION.	Total number of organizations.	COMMUNICANTS OR MEMBERS.				
			Number of organizations reporting.	Total number reported.	Sex.		
					Number of organizations reporting.	Male.	Female.
107	Reformed Episcopal Church	1	1	66	1	33	33
108	Roman Catholic Church	527	527	492,135	317	114,759	112,142
109	Salvationists	39	38	1,371	38	678	693
110	Salvation Army	38	37	1,368	37	677	691
111	American Salvation Army	1	1	3	1	1	2
112	Spiritualists	35	35	1,667	34	695	942
113	Swedish Evangelical bodies	36	36	2,124	36	936	1,188
114	Swedish Evangelical Mission Covenant of America	33	33	1,974	33	872	1,102
115	Swedish Evangelical Free Mission	3	3	150	3	64	86
116	Theosophical societies	7	7	120	7	52	68
117	Theosophical Society, American Section	7	7	120	7	52	68
118	Unitarians	13	13	1,452	10	440	635
119	United Brethren bodies	183	182	7,383	174	2,696	4,372
120	Church of the United Brethren in Christ	66	66	3,446	62	1,291	2,033
121	Church of the United Brethren in Christ (Old Constitution)	117	116	3,937	112	1,405	2,339
122	Universalists	26	26	1,866	21	571	942
123	Volunteers of America	3	3	60	3	27	33

MINNESOTA.

	DENOMINATION.	Total number of organizations.	Number of organizations reporting.	Total number reported.	Number of organizations reporting.	Male.	Female.
1	All denominations	4,759	4,721	834,442	4,247	353,828	414,771
2	Adventist bodies	82	82	2,452	76	804	1,488
3	Advent Christian Church	5	5	349	5	142	207
	Seventh-day Adventist Denomination	77	77	2,103	71	662	1,281
	Baptist bodies	270	270	24,309	253	8,867	14,294
	Baptists:						
6	Northern Baptist Convention	248	248	22,786	232	8,283	13,369
7	Seventh-day Baptists	2	2	207	2	83	124
8	Free Baptists	20	20	1,316	19	501	801
9	Brethren (Plymouth)	26	26	531	26	201	330
10	Brethren (Plymouth)—I	15	15	311	15	125	186
11	Brethren (Plymouth)—II	5	5	158	5	50	108
12	Brethren (Plymouth)—III	3	3	21	3	9	12
13	Brethren (Plymouth)—IV	3	3	41	3	17	24
14	Christadelphians	1	1	4	1	2	2
15	Christian Catholic Church in Zion	1	1	40	1	15	25
16	Church of Christ, Scientist	20	20	2,387	19	699	1,647
17	Churches of God in North America, General Eldership of the	1	1	21	1	10	11
18	Churches of the New Jerusalem	2	2	67	1	18	31
19	General Convention of the New Jerusalem in the United States of America	2	2	67	1	18	31
20	Congregationalists	210	210	22,264	205	7,681	14,066
21	Disciples or Christians	43	43	3,560	39	1,207	1,982
22	Disciples of Christ	43	43	3,560	39	1,207	1,982
23	Dunkers or German Baptist Brethren	8	8	365	8	171	194
24	German Baptist Brethren Church (Conservative)	8	8	365	8	171	194
25	Eastern Orthodox Churches	6	6	1,614	4	770	444
26	Russian Orthodox Church	3	3	964	3	548	416
27	Greek Orthodox Church	3	3	650	1	222	28
28	Evangelical bodies	139	139	7,942	139	3,497	4,445
29	Evangelical Association	126	126	7,450	126	3,262	4,188
30	United Evangelical Church	13	13	492	13	235	257
31	Evangelistic associations	1	1	20	1	10	10
32	Missionary Church Association	1	1	20	1	10	10
33	Friends	3	3	274	3	130	144
34	Society of Friends (Orthodox)	3	3	274	3	130	144

DEBT ON CHURCH PROPERTY, PARSONAGES, AND SUNDAY SCHOOLS, BY DENOMINATIONS (IN DETAIL), FOR TERRITORY: 1906—Continued.

MICHIGAN—Continued.

PLACES OF WORSHIP.					VALUE OF CHURCH PROPERTY.		DEBT ON CHURCH PROPERTY.		PARSONAGES.		SUNDAY SCHOOLS CONDUCTED BY CHURCH ORGANIZATIONS.				
Number of organizations reporting—		Number of church edifices reported.	Seating capacity of church edifices.		Number of organizations reporting.	Value reported.	Number of organizations reporting.	Amount of debt reported.	Number of organizations reporting.	Value of parsonages reported.	Number of organizations reporting.	Number of Sunday schools reported.	Number of officers and teachers.	Number of scholars.	
Church edifices.	Halls, etc.		Number of organizations reporting.	Seating capacity reported.											
1	....	1	1	200	1	$4,500	1	$2,300	....	....	1	1	15	138	107
303	26	327	267	115,255	275	3,899,445	44	179,017	152	$571,200	319	333	1,203	46,834	108
11	28	11	10	4,125	38	131,825	18	58,637	2	6,000	30	30	165	1,347	109
11	27	11	10	4,125	38	131,825	18	58,637	2	6,000	30	30	165	1,347	110
....	1	....	....	....	....	....	....	....	....	....	....	....	....	....	111
	23	7	7	4,900	11	24,060	4	3,550	1	400	3	3	18	97	112
33	1	35	31	7,837	33	91,100	11	6,955	13	15,500	33	39	332	2,722	113
30	1	32	28	7,312	30	85,900	9	6,105	12	14,800	30	33	312	2,592	114
3	....	3	3	525	3	5,200	2	850	1	700	3	6	20	130	115
....	7	....	....	....	....	....	....	....	....	....	....	....	....	....	116
....	7	....	....	....	....	....	....	....	....	....	....	....	....	....	117
12	1	13	12	4,100	12	274,500	4	3,295	2	9,000	8	8	68	536	118
159	15	163	156	39,133	162	279,600	18	7,275	62	50,450	162	165	1,684	9,011	119
58	3	60	56	15,418	61	118,050	13	5,975	23	19,500	61	61	694	3,830	120
101	12	103	100	23,715	101	161,550	5	1,300	39	30,950	101	104	990	5,181	121
22	1	22	22	6,005	26	309,250	4	12,700	4	15,300	20	20	147	1,067	122
....	3	....	....	....	....	....	....	....	....	....	1	1	5	17	123

MINNESOTA.

4,086	356	4,280	3,973	1,104,317	4,105	$26,053,159	1,012	$2,066,006	1,709	$4,044,430	3,544	3,975	29,521	273,223	1
48	21	48	46	7,066	48	56,400	1	250	3	5,100	68	77	494	2,167	2
4	....	4	4	816	4	8,450	....	....	1	3,000	5	5	44	277	3
44	21	44	42	6,250	44	47,950	1	250	2	2,100	63	72	450	1,890	4
236	13	255	232	62,443	238	1,509,983	48	48,243	77	118,050	230	283	2,687	21,150	5
216	11	233	212	57,568	217	1,413,158	46	47,643	65	102,850	210	263	2,482	19,862	6
2	....	2	2	600	2	2,800	....	....	1	2,000	2	2	29	141	7
18	2	20	18	4,275	19	94,025	2	600	11	13,200	18	18	176	1,147	8
....	26	....	....	....	1	1,000	....	....	....	....	15	17	50	599	9
....	15	....	....	....	....	....	....	....	....	....	11	11	35	364	10
....	5	....	....	....	1	1,000	....	....	....	....	4	6	15	235	11
....	3	....	....	....	....	....	....	....	....	....	....	....	....	....	12
....	3	....	....	....	....	....	....	....	....	....	....	....	....	....	13
....		....	....	....	....	....	....	....	....	....	....	....	....	....	14
....	1	....	....	....	....	....	....	....	....	....	....	....	....	....	15
11		11	11	4,370	12	195,850	2	3,700	....	....	17	17	146	696	16
....	....	....	....	....	....	....	....	....	....	....	1	1	6	40	17
2	....	2	1	150	1	15,000	....	....	....	....	1	1	4	35	18
2	....	2	1	150	1	15,000	....	....	....	....	1	1	4	35	19
203	4	214	203	55,059	199	1,619,585	61	69,505	87	168,675	200	220	2,453	22,283	20
37	4	37	36	8,885	38	192,850	12	15,595	5	5,000	39	40	338	2,471	21
37	4	37	36	8,885	38	192,850	12	15,595	5	5,000	39	40	338	2,471	22
8	....	9	8	2,225	8	13,900	....	....	1	1,500	8	10	92	568	23
8	....	9	8	2,225	8	13,900	....	....	1	1,500	8	10	92	568	24
3	3	3	3	1,300	3	48,000	2	16,375	1	2,000	1	1	2	75	25
2	1	2	2	1,100	2	31,000	1	13,375	1	2,000	1	1	2	75	26
1	2	1	1	200	1	17,000	1	3,000	....	....	....	....	....	....	27
126	9	129	126	26,825	128	351,925	3	8,425	59	107,250	130	134	1,677	7,303	28
116	6	119	116	24,650	118	322,725	2	8,300	54	98,850	118	121	1,542	6,769	29
10	3	10	10	2,175	10	29,200	1	125	5	8,400	12	13	135	534	30
1	....	1	1	100	1	650	1	300	....	....	1	1	4	15	31
1	....	1	1	100	1	650	1	300	....	....	1	1	4	15	32
3	....	3	3	500	3	9,200	....	....	2	700	3	3	18	89	33
3	....	3	3	500	3	9,200	....	....	2	700	3	3	18	89	34

TABLE 8.—ORGANIZATIONS, COMMUNICANTS OR MEMBERS, PLACES OF WORSHIP, VALUE OF CHURCH PROPERTY, EACH STATE AND

MINNESOTA—Continued.

	DENOMINATION.	Total number of organizations.	COMMUNICANTS OR MEMBERS.				
			Number of organizations reporting.	Total number reported.	Sex.		
					Number of organizations reporting.	Male.	Female.
35	German Evangelical Synod of North America	69	67	9,183	64	4,062	4,664
36	Independent churches	27	27	1,300	24	536	634
37	Jewish congregations	26	22	[1]11,725			
38	Latter-day Saints	8	8	522	7	182	259
39	Church of Jesus Christ of Latter-day Saints	2	2	143	2	53	90
40	Reorganized Church of Jesus Christ of Latter-day Saints	6	6	379	5	129	169
41	Lutheran bodies	1,798	1,784	267,322	1,474	106,445	112,946
42	General Council of the Evangelical Lutheran Church in North America	290	286	49,830	235	21,063	22,865
43	Evangelical Lutheran Synodical Conference of America	370	309	61,092	325	26,100	27,995
44	United Norwegian Lutheran Church in America	354	347	59,204	227	19,414	20,433
45	Evangelical Lutheran Joint Synod of Ohio and Other States	67	67	9,656	61	4,282	4,507
46	Lutheran Synod of Buffalo	3	3	368	3	193	175
47	Hauge's Norwegian Evangelical Lutheran Synod	89	89	12,857	63	4,436	4,631
48	Evangelical Lutheran Church in America, Eielsen's Synod	10	10	285	10	125	160
49	Evangelical Lutheran Synod of Iowa and Other States	57	57	8,460	54	4,048	4,257
50	Synod for the Norwegian Evangelical Lutheran Church in America	302	300	38,903	258	15,312	16,037
51	Danish Evangelical Lutheran Church in America	9	9	1,061	9	548	533
52	Icelandic Evangelical Lutheran Synod in North America	4	4	551	4	265	286
53	Finnish Evangelical Lutheran Church of America, or Suomi Synod	20	20	1,548	20	797	751
54	Norwegian Lutheran Free Church	141	141	13,546	131	5,266	5,972
55	United Danish Evangelical Lutheran Church in America	20	20	2,376	13	650	735
56	Slovak Evangelical Lutheran Synod of America	2	2	538	2	356	182
57	Finnish Evangelical Lutheran National Church	27	27	2,589	27	1,368	1,221
58	Apostolic Lutheran Church (Finnish)	26	26	4,299	25	2,156	2,133
59	Church of the Lutheran Brethren of America (Norwegian)	7	7	139	7	66	73
60	Mennonite bodies	5	5	659	5	313	346
61	Mennonite Church	1	1	24	1	13	11
62	General Conference of Mennonites of North America	1	1	262	1	122	140
63	Nebraska and Minnesota Conference of Mennonites	3	3	373	3	178	195
64	Methodist bodies	678	669	47,637	640	17,176	27,710
65	Methodist Episcopal Church	643	634	46,351	606	16,811	27,069
66	African Methodist Episcopal Church	5	5	755	4	172	283
67	Wesleyan Methodist Connection of America	2	2	80	2	30	50
68	Free Methodist Church of North America	28	28	451	28	163	288
69	Moravian bodies	11	11	830	11	404	426
70	Moravian Church (Unitas Fratrum)	11	11	830	11	404	426
71	Polish National Church of America	1	1	1,000	1	650	350
72	Presbyterian bodies	310	310	27,569	291	9,698	16,419
73	Presbyterian Church in the United States of America	296	296	26,412	277	9,168	15,792
74	Welsh Calvinistic Methodist Church	13	13	1,063	13	496	567
75	Synod of the Reformed Presbyterian Church of North America	1	1	94	1	34	60
76	Protestant Episcopal Church	223	221	18,763	206	6,447	11,193
77	Reformed bodies	28	28	2,255	26	1,022	1,074
78	Reformed Church in America	11	11	852	11	423	429
79	Reformed Church in the United States	7	7	788	6	286	367
80	Christian Reformed Church	10	10	615	9	313	278
81	Roman Catholic Church	575	575	378,288	556	178,513	194,382
82	Salvationists	16	15	581	15	294	287
83	Salvation Army	16	15	581	15	294	287
84	Spiritualists	13	13	715	13	307	408
85	Swedish Evangelical bodies	100	99	6,237	97	2,682	3,208
86	Swedish Evangelical Mission Covenant of America	80	80	5,017	79	2,241	2,768
87	Swedish Evangelical Free Mission	20	19	1,220	18	441	440
88	Theosophical societies	5	5	144	5	58	86
89	Theosophical Society, American Section	5	5	144	5	58	86
90	Unitarians	11	10	1,160	6	289	384
91	United Brethren bodies	32	28	1,282	24	439	604
92	Church of the United Brethren in Christ	32	28	1,282	24	439	604
93	Universalists	8	8	1,220	3	117	200
94	Volunteers of America	2	2	200	2	112	88

[1] Heads of families only.

DEBT ON CHURCH PROPERTY, PARSONAGES, AND SUNDAY SCHOOLS, BY DENOMINATIONS (IN DETAIL), FOR TERRITORY: 1906—Continued.

MINNESOTA—Continued.

PLACES OF WORSHIP.					VALUE OF CHURCH PROPERTY.		DEBT ON CHURCH PROPERTY.		PARSONAGES.		SUNDAY SCHOOLS CONDUCTED BY CHURCH ORGANIZATIONS.				
Number of organizations reporting— Church edifices.	Number of organizations reporting— Halls, etc.	Number of church edifices reported.	Seating capacity of church edifices. Number of organizations reporting.	Seating capacity of church edifices. Seating capacity reported.	Number of organizations reporting.	Value reported.	Number of organizations reporting.	Amount of debt reported.	Number of organizations reporting.	Value of parsonages reported.	Number of organizations reporting.	Number of Sunday schools reported.	Number of officers and teachers.	Number of scholars.	
61	5	62	61	15,030	61	$193,230	14	$9,300	33	$54,200	52	52	252	2,319	35
23	4	23	23	4,135	24	38,050	8	3,325	5	4,150	23	24	103	958	36
12	2	14	11	5,404	11	212,000	10	31,650	1	1,000	7	8	29	687	37
3	3	3	3	320	3	2,900	....	....	....	....	2	4	28	99	38
....	2	....	....	....	....	....	....	....	....	....	1	3	15	54	39
3	1	3	3	320	3	2,900	....	....	....	....	1	1	13	45	40
1,490	164	1,560	1,447	419,138	1,484	5,822,097	348	330,507	556	1,228,220	1,051	1,211	6,307	55,552	41
265	9	285	257	80,525	269	1,425,829	76	84,541	102	265,160	239	280	2,343	17,961	42
309	30	329	309	84,408	309	1,415,177	78	96,742	208	366,060	143	152	423	6,843	43
308	19	321	279	94,927	287	1,113,275	55	40,790	68	197,300	225	265	1,366	11,502	44
63	1	64	63	14,110	64	174,790	18	15,820	40	67,200	39	42	157	1,783	45
3	....	3	3	700	3	9,800	....	....	2	2,500	1	1	1	8	46
73	3	76	68	19,436	75	216,000	19	16,525	16	38,950	70	78	370	3,012	47
2	8	2	2	400	2	2,900	....	....	....	....	2	2	3	35	48
50	5	51	50	12,082	50	148,250	12	8,795	26	42,600	36	37	139	1,521	49
237	37	245	236	68,135	241	819,260	44	36,444	58	183,250	123	158	667	6,561	50
6	2	8	6	2,025	6	21,300	1	650	5	6,600	4	7	15	267	51
4	....	4	4	1,450	4	12,600	1	400	1	1,500	3	3	15	142	52
4	15	4	4	800	4	10,500	2	1,400	1	1,900	11	11	51	418	53
109	22	110	109	27,130	113	337,710	29	22,790	23	42,300	101	114	561	3,634	54
18	2	18	18	3,470	18	53,000	6	1,660	5	11,800	16	17	71	617	55
2	....	2	2	350	2	5,500	....	....	....	....	1	1	1	40	56
18	9	18	18	4,055	18	27,050	4	1,350	....	....	23	24	66	642	57
14	....	15	14	3,960	14	20,856	2	500	....	....	8	13	38	446	58
5	2	5	5	1,175	5	8,300	1	2,100	1	1,100	6	6	20	120	59
5	....	5	5	1,975	5	13,500	....	....	....	....	5	5	57	868	60
1	....	1	1	100	1	1,000	....	....	....	....	1	1	8	40	61
1	....	1	1	875	1	7,000	....	....	....	....	1	1	27	350	62
3	....	3	3	1,000	3	5,500	....	....	....	....	3	3	22	478	63
622	29	635	616	141,626	628	2,966,920	135	122,165	287	523,600	591	630	6,458	47,755	64
600	21	613	594	136,951	606	2,923,920	131	117,703	274	510,975	573	61	6,325	46,900	65
5	....	5	5	1,375	5	28,500	4	4,462	2	5,200	3		30	155	66
1	....	1	1	150	1	1,800	....	....	1	1,300	2		28	185	67
16	8	16	16	3,150	16	12,700	....	....	10	6,125	13	12	75	515	68
11	....	11	11	1,715	11	26,850	....	....	9	12,550	11	11	70	481	69
11	....	11	11	1,715	11	26,850	....	....	9	12,550	11	11	70	481	70
1	....	1	1	300	1	10,000	1	8,000	....	....	1	1	1	100	71
283	9	296	282	73,327	281	2,187,431	60	64,940	101	220,900	281	307	4,196	31,865	72
269	9	282	268	69,927	267	2,147,831	60	64,940	98	215,400	267	293	4,047	30,767	73
13	....	13	13	3,150	13	37,600	....	....	2	4,000	13	13	137	1,013	74
1	....	1	1	250	1	2,000	....	....	1	1,500	1	1	12	85	75
188	9	197	188	37,170	195	1,523,875	24	67,725	75	195,400	158	167	1,123	9,986	76
23	5	23	23	4,460	24	52,150	10	6,305	19	29,100	23	23	187	1,469	77
10	1	10	10	1,905	10	17,800	4	1,605	7	13,600	10	10	116	784	78
7	....	7	7	1,285	7	18,700	1	350	6	8,100	6	6	40	314	79
6	4	6	6	1,270	7	15,650	5	4,350	6	7,400	7	7	31	371	80
542	6	583	494	190,780	542	8,063,138	229	1,196,326	355	1,317,350	480	568	1,547	54,243	81
6	10	6	6	2,025	16	66,800	11	17,594	....	....	14	14	42	293	82
6	10	6	6	2,025	16	66,800	11	17,594	....	....	14	14	42	293	83
3	10	3	3	750	3	3,600	2	420	....	....	2	2	9	64	84
89	3	95	89	26,314	90	344,875	18	25,987	18	31,900	91	105	784	6,758	85
70	3	74	70	21,119	71	270,525	14	14,938	16	28,200	72		651	5,687	86
19	....	21	19	5,195	19	74,350	4	11,049	2	3,700	19	[illegible]	133	1,071	87
....	5	....	....	....	....	....	....	....	....	....	....	....	....	....	88
....	5	....	....	....	....	....	....	....	....	....	....	....	....	....	89
11	....	12	10	3,015	11	153,500	4	11,275	2	3,800	8	8	53	375	90
26	2	27	22	4,460	26	46,100	6	2,594	11	9,285	21	21	207	1,273	91
26	2	27	22	4,460	26	46,100	6	2,594	11	9,285	21	21	207	1,273	
8	....	8	7	3,150	8	304,800	2	5,500	2	4,700	8	8	93	623	92
1	1	3	1	300	1	7,000	....	....	....	....	1	1	4	14	93

TABLE 3.—ORGANIZATIONS, COMMUNICANTS OR MEMBERS, PLACES OF WORSHIP, VALUE OF CHURCH PROPERTY, EACH STATE AND

MISSISSIPPI.

	DENOMINATION.	Total number of organizations.	COMMUNICANTS OR MEMBERS.				
			Number of organizations reporting.	Total number reported.	Sex.		
					Number of organizations reporting.	Male.	Female.
	All denominations	7,396	7,361	657,381	6,761	232,451	370,870
2	Adventist bodies	28	25	569	23	192	315
3	Advent Christian Church	7	5	189	4	70	84
4	Seventh-day Adventist Denomination	21	20	380	19	122	231
5	Baptist bodies	3,785	3,776	371,518	3,560	131,284	221,967
6	Baptists	3,586	3,578	364,339	3,414	129,124	218,615
7	Southern Baptist Convention	1,350	1,346	123,357	1,259	47,833	65,580
8	National Baptist Convention (Colored)	2,236	2,232	240,982	2,155	81,291	153,035
9	Free Baptists	47	47	2,804	43	843	1,466
10	Freewill Baptists	1	1	35	1	10	25
11	Duck River and Kindred Associations of Baptists (Baptist Church of Christ)	8	8	370	8	166	204
12	Primitive Baptists	116	115	3,416	84	1,070	1,568
13	Colored Primitive Baptists in America	27	27	554	10	71	89
14	Church of Christ, Scientist	2	2	92	2	32	60
15	Churches of the Living God (Colored)	5	5	253		104	149
16	Church of the Living God (Christian Workers for Friendship)	5	5	253		104	149
17	Congregationalists	7	7	595	6	246	341
18	Disciples or Christians	152	152	9,864	150	4,257	5,557
19	Disciples of Christ	105	105	6,709	103	2,857	3,802
20	Churches of Christ	47	47	3,155	47	1,400	1,755
21	Independent churches	19	19	2,274	16	491	828
22	Jewish congregations	19	17	[1] 746	......	......	......
23	Latter-day Saints	4	4	1,214	3	108	88
24	Church of Jesus Christ of Latter-day Saints	1	1	1,018	......	......	......
25	Reorganized Church of Jesus Christ of Latter-day Saints	3	3	196	3	108	88
26	Lutheran bodies	24	24	970	22	387	465
27	United Synod of the Evangelical Lutheran Church in the South	15	15	722	15	318	404
28	Evangelical Lutheran Synodical Conference of America	8	8	198	6	44	36
29	Finnish Evangelical Lutheran Church of America, or Suomi Synod	1	1	50	1	25	25
30	Methodist bodies	2,773	2,757	212,105	2,455	73,955	113,297
31	Methodist Episcopal Church	564	559	50,695	479	16,877	27,863
32	Union American Methodist Episcopal Church (Colored)	6	6	122	6	49	73
33	African Methodist Episcopal Church	460	460	28,797	455	9,983	18,352
34	African Methodist Episcopal Zion Church	144	144	5,602	144	2,131	3,471
35	Methodist Protestant Church	94	93	4,517	88	1,828	2,454
36	Methodist Episcopal Church, South	1,113	1,105	94,845	912	32,719	45,464
37	Congregational Methodist Church	38	38	1,640	37	767	862
38	Colored Methodist Episcopal Church	348	346	25,814	328	9,573	14,713
39	Free Methodist Church of North America	6	6	73	6	28	45
40	Nonsectarian Churches of Bible Faith	4	4	130	4	82	48
41	Presbyterian bodies	394	390	22,471	345	8,247	11,927
42	Presbyterian Church in the United States of America	6	6	192	6	63	129
43	Cumberland Presbyterian Church	119	119	5,991	99	2,362	3,011
44	United Presbyterian Church of North America	1	1	70	1	25	45
45	Presbyterian Church in the United States	262	258	15,641	234	5,588	8,495
46	Associate Reformed Synod of the South	6	6	577	5	209	247
47	Protestant Episcopal Church	81	81	5,704	76	1,961	3,496
48	Roman Catholic Church	90	90	28,576	86	10,951	12,186
49	Salvationists	4	3	15	3	4	11
50	Salvation Army	4	3	15	3	4	11
51	Universalists	[illegible]	5	285	5	150	135

MISSOURI.

	DENOMINATION.	Total number of organizations.	Number of organizations reporting.	Total number reported.	Number of organizations reporting.	Male.	Female.
1	All denominations	9,206	9,172	1,199,239	8,560	474,791	636,091
2	Adventist bodies	73	72	2,378	57	752	1,139
3	Advent Christian Church	9	9	323	7	134	157
4	Seventh-day Adventist Denomination	56	55	1,805	43	495	859
5	Church of God (Adventist)	4	4	159	4	82	77
6	Churches of God (Adventist), Unattached Congregations	2	2	44	2	20	24
7	Churches of God in Christ Jesus	2	2	47	1	21	22

[1] Heads of families only.

DEBT ON CHURCH PROPERTY, PARSONAGES, AND SUNDAY SCHOOLS, BY DENOMINATIONS (IN DETAIL), FOR TERRITORY: 1906—Continued.

MISSISSIPPI.

PLACES OF WORSHIP. Number of organizations reporting— Church edifices.	PLACES OF WORSHIP. Number of organizations reporting— Halls, etc.	PLACES OF WORSHIP. Number of church edifices reported.	PLACES OF WORSHIP. Seating capacity of church edifices. Number of organizations reporting.	PLACES OF WORSHIP. Seating capacity of church edifices. Seating capacity reported.	VALUE OF CHURCH PROPERTY. Number of organizations reporting.	VALUE OF CHURCH PROPERTY. Value reported.	DEBT ON CHURCH PROPERTY. Number of organizations reporting.	DEBT ON CHURCH PROPERTY. Amount of debt reported.	PARSONAGES. Number of organizations reporting.	PARSONAGES. Value of parsonages reported.	SUNDAY SCHOOLS CONDUCTED BY CHURCH ORGANIZATIONS. Number of organizations reporting.	SUNDAY SCHOOLS CONDUCTED BY CHURCH ORGANIZATIONS. Number of Sunday schools reported.	SUNDAY SCHOOLS CONDUCTED BY CHURCH ORGANIZATIONS. Number of officers and teachers.	SUNDAY SCHOOLS CONDUCTED BY CHURCH ORGANIZATIONS. Number of scholars.	
6,879	222	6,997	6,581	2,041,665	6,888	$9,482,229	1,063	$345,304	870	$1,237,829	5,714	5,911	32,422	286,257	1
13	7	14	10	2,143	12	12,250	2	1,300	1	2,000	19	20	90	465	2
4	3	4	4	1,100	4	1,250	......	......	......	......	2	2	8	64	3
9	4	10	6	1,043	8	11,000	2	1,300	1	2,000	17	18	82	401	4
3,631	82	3,667	3,543	1,107,931	3,623	3,750,941	371	121,699	149	228,175	2,947	3,019	15,591	153,363	5
3,483	73	3,516	3,409	1,062,116	3,484	3,678,140	360	120,843	147	228,005	2,903	2,972	15,425	152,025	6
1,296	36	1,325	1,285	435,682	1,298	1,707,903	62	61,741	92	186,675	803	830	4,626	47,200	7
2,188	37	2,191	2,124	626,434	2,186	1,970,237	298	59,102	55	41,330	2,100	2,142	10,799	104,825	8
43	1	43	41	15,440	41	24,080	8	579	1	150	38	41	144	1,111	9
1	......	1	1	400	1	600	......	......	......	......	......	......	......	......	10
8	......	8	7	3,950	8	8,600	1	17	......	......	6	6	22	227	11
83	2	86	79	24,875	77	34,621	2	260	1	20	......	......	......	......	12
13	6	13	6	1,150	12	4,900	......	......	......	......	......	......	......	......	13
1	1	1	1	250	1	4,000	......	......	......	......	2	2	7	26	14
5	......	5	5	850	5	3,200	1	360	......	......	5	5	14	87	15
5	......	5	5	850	5	3,200		360	......	......	5	5	14	87	16
6	1	6	6	2,300	7	19,331	2	120	1	200	6	10	40	741	17
121	14	121	118	37,075	123	166,885	14	7,035	7	11,400	86	89	389	3,552	18
83	5	83	80	23,025	85	136,235	10	6,210	6	10,400	61	62	315	2,687	19
38	9	38	38	14,050	38	30,650	4	825	1	1,000	25	27	74	865	20
16	......	17	13	7,175	17	33,625	5	7,265	1	1,000	13	18	86	927	21
13	2	13	12	3,950	14	202,900	5	29,700	2	8,000	9	9	40	360	22
3	......	5	3	1,020	3	2,035	......	......	......	......	3	3	23	88	23
1	......	3	1	700	1	1,435	......	......	......	......	......	......	......	......	24
2	......	2	2	320	2	600	......	......	......	......	3	3	23	88	25
14	8	15	14	3,300	13	9,975	1	200	4	2,900	13	14	58	462	26
10	3	11	10	2,600	9	5,175	1	200	2	1,500	8	8	39	325	27
4	4	4	4	700	4	4,800	......	......	2	1,400	4	4	13	97	28
......	1	......	......	......	......	......	......	......	......	......	1	2	6	40	29
2,591	77	2,656	2,400	749,293	2,595	3,212,218	621	119,532	553	578,646	2,290	2,386	13,898	109,028	30
551	2	567	488	151,696	549	519,360	201	29,520	142	74,186	540	573	3,744	28,333	31
2	4	2	1	75	1	200	1	100	......	......	6	6	30	182	32
442	11	471	438	131,337	440	436,267	173	28,482	91	51,840	421	434	2,418	16,437	33
135	6	137	129	40,880	136	117,605	71	8,537	17	6,585	127	129	742	3,952	34
87	3	87	84	27,025	85	44,708	9	1,494	3	1,150	65	67	263	2,697	35
1,000	46	1,012	886	265,245	1,005	1,776,603	73	43,409	274	434,835	787	813	5,033	44,902	36
33	......	33	33	11,125	33	24,025	......	......	......	......	21	21	102	931	37
336	5	342	336	120,458	341	291,050	93	7,990	26	10,050	320	340	1,548	11,482	38
5	......	5	5	1,450	5	2,400	......	......	......	......	3	3	18	112	39
......	4	......	......	......	......	......	......	......	......	......	1	1	1	35	40
318	14	322	310	90,453	325	872,450	17	17,497	90	189,000	217	224	1,697	11,727	41
4	1	4	4	1,200	5	5,800	2	1,015	......	......	6	7	39	378	42
96	4	97	94	29,783	102	138,475	3	2,250	17	19,350	48	48	414	1,915	43
1	......	1	1	250	1	5,000	......	......	1	2,000	1	1	9	50	44
212	9	215	207	57,720	213	714,175	11	13,732	70	165,650	158	164	1,191	8,970	45
5	......	5	4	1,500	4	9,000	1	500	2	2,000	4	4	44	414	46
72	......	76	72	16,220	71	583,094	12	24,250	31	119,058	55	56	810	2,254	47
70	9	74	69	17,105	71	604,000	11	16,331	31	97,450	42	49	144	2,742	48
......	3	......	......	......	3	325	1	15	......	......	2	2	2	20	49
......	3	......	......	......	3	325	1	15	......	......	2	2	2	20	50
5	......	5	5	2,600	κ	5,000	......	......	......	......	4	4	32	380	51

MISSOURI.

7,924	646	8,146	7,786	2,391,498	7,966	$38,059,233	1,040	$3,257,740	1,744	$3,448,045	6,670	6,917	59,678	504,770	1
42	13	42	42	8,600	43	54,455	4	2,940	1	400	63	65	396	1,971	2
6	2	6	6	1,425	6	5,630	......	......	1	400	7	7	51	285	3
33	8	33	33	5,975	34	45,355	3	2,240	......	......	51	53	322	1,543	4
2	1	2	2	1,000	2	2,800	1	700	......	......	3	3	18	84	5
......	2	......	......	......	......	......	......	......	......	......	1	1	3	34	6
1	......	1	1	200	1	700	......	......	......	......	1	1	2	25	7

TABLE 3.—ORGANIZATIONS, COMMUNICANTS OR MEMBERS, PLACES OF WORSHIP, VALUE OF CHURCH PROPERTY, EACH STATE AND

MISSOURI—Continued.

	DENOMINATION.	Total number of organizations.	COMMUNICANTS OR MEMBERS.				
			Number of organizations reporting.	Total number reported.	Sex.		
					Number of organizations reporting.	Male.	Female.
8	Armenian Church	1	1	230	1	210	20
9	Baptist bodies	2,636	2,632	218,353	2,480	79,691	124,438
10	Baptists	2,184	2,184	198,459	2,080	72,537	113,666
11	Northern Baptist Convention	2	2	115	2	40	75
12	Southern Baptist Convention	1,894	1,894	176,208	1,800	65,403	100,356
13	National Baptist Convention (Colored)	288	288	22,136	278	7,094	13,235
14	Free Baptists	121	119	5,825	110	2,133	3,141
15	General Baptists	186	186	9,048	181	3,490	5,110
16	United Baptists	28	28	1,267	22	374	594
17	Primitive Baptists	116	114	4,040	87	1,157	1,927
18	Two-Seed-in-the-Spirit Predestinarian Baptists	1	1	14			
19	Brethren (Plymouth)	12	12	502	12	200	302
20	Brethren (Plymouth)—I	3	3	86	3	34	52
21	Brethren (Plymouth)—II	5	5	309	5	124	185
22	Brethren (Plymouth)—III	3	3	101	3	40	61
23	Brethren (Plymouth)—IV	1	1	6	1	2	4
24	Buddhists	1					
25	Chinese Temples	1					
26	Christadelphians	3	3	36	3	14	22
27	Christian Union	33	33	2,433	30	981	1,315
28	Christians (Christian Connection)	27	27	1,177	24	393	645
29	Church of Christ, Scientist	20	20	2,644	19	733	1,751
30	Church of God and Saints of Christ (Colored)	1	1	34	1	11	23
31	Churches of God in North America, General Eldership of the	37	37	1,053	36	457	566
32	Churches of the Living God (Colored)	3	3	695	3	353	342
33	Church of the Living God (Christian Workers for Friendship)	1	1	75	1	25	50
34	Church of Christ in God	2	2	620	2	328	292
35	Churches of the New Jerusalem	5	5	375	5	155	220
36	General Convention of the New Jerusalem in the United States of America	5	5	375	5	155	220
37	Congregationalists	76	76	11,046	76	3,991	7,055
38	Disciples or Christians	1,545	1,543	166,137	1,482	62,878	96,561
39	Disciples of Christ	1,424	1,422	159,050	1,363	60,104	92,293
40	Churches of Christ	121	121	7,087	119	2,774	4,268
41	Dunkers or German Baptist Brethren	45	45	1,984	44	798	1,096
42	German Baptist Brethren Church (Conservative)	41	41	1,881	40	751	1,040
43	Old Order German Baptist Brethren	2	2	59	2	33	26
44	The Brethren Church (Progressive Dunkers)	2	2	44	2	14	30
45	Eastern Orthodox Churches	6	6	2,455	1	1,450	25
46	Greek Orthodox Church	6	6	2,455	1	1,450	25
47	Evangelical bodies	22	22	1,081	22	467	614
48	Evangelical Association	22	22	1,081	22	467	614
49	Evangelistic associations	2	2	46	2	23	23
50	Hephzibah Faith Missionary Association	2	2	46	2	23	23
51	Friends	6	6	603	6	281	322
52	Society of Friends (Orthodox)	6	6	603	6	281	322
53	German Evangelical Protestant bodies	2	2	1,510	2	660	850
54	German Evangelical Protestant Ministers' Conference	2	2	1,510	2	660	850
55	German Evangelical Synod of North America	162	162	32,715	150	13,773	16,957
56	Independent churches	64	64	2,725	60	1,086	1,489
57	Jewish congregations	20	18	[1] 2,392			
58	Latter-day Saints	64	64	8,042	62	3,465	4,414
59	Church of Jesus Christ of Latter-day Saints	1	1	162	1	66	96
60	Reorganized Church of Jesus Christ of Latter-day Saints	63	63	7,880	61	3,399	4,318
61	Lutheran bodies	225	225	46,868	202	17,558	20,484
62	General Synod of the Evangelical Lutheran Church in the United States of America	20	20	2,104	20	791	1,313
63	General Council of the Evangelical Lutheran Church in North America	6	6	846	6	380	466
64	Evangelical Lutheran Synodical Conference of America	175	175	41,185	152	14,978	17,381
65	Evangelical Lutheran Joint Synod of Ohio and Other States	2	2	195	2	80	115
66	Evangelical Lutheran Synod of Iowa and Other States	17	17	2,137	17	1,074	1,063
67	United Danish Evangelical Lutheran Church in America	2	2	83	2	35	48
68	Slovak Evangelical Lutheran Synod of America	3	3	318	3	220	98

[1] Heads of families only.

DEBT ON CHURCH PROPERTY, PARSONAGES, AND SUNDAY SCHOOLS, BY DENOMINATIONS (IN DETAIL), FOR TERRITORY: 1906—Continued.

MISSOURI—Continued.

PLACES OF WORSHIP.					VALUE OF CHURCH PROPERTY.		DEBT ON CHURCH PROPERTY.		PARSONAGES.		SUNDAY SCHOOLS CONDUCTED BY CHURCH ORGANIZATIONS.				
Number of organizations reporting—		Number of church edifices reported.	Seating capacity of church edifices.		Number of organizations reporting.	Value reported.	Number of organizations reporting.	Amount of debt reported.	Number of organizations reporting.	Value of parsonages reported.	Number of organizations reporting.	Number of Sunday schools reported.	Number of officers and teachers.	Number of scholars.	
Church edifices.	Halls, etc.		Number of organizations reporting.	Seating capacity reported.											
	1														8
2,248	277	2,272	2,224	676,970	2,273	$5,042,415	182	$201,450	99	$179,425	1,814	1,873	14,077	117,656	9
1,945	178	1,969	1,926	593,936	1,964	4,830,347	165	194,881	95	177,525	1,673	1,730	13,224	111,900	10
2		2	2	600	2	1,800					2	2	13	75	11
1,681	160	1,703	1,666	523,155	1,699	4,116,097	92	99,347	74	146,675	1,402	1,459	11,619	102,116	12
262	18	264	258	70,181	263	712,450	73	95,534	21	30,850	269	269	1,592	9,709	13
83	23	83	81	17,914	85	57,042	5	2,937	3	1,100	59	59	354	2,512	14
121	55	121	119	32,295	122	58,401	8	1,562	1	800	75	77	444	2,954	15
26	2	26	25	7,250	27	16,325					7	7	55	290	16
73	19	73	73	25,575	75	80,300	4	2,070							17
															18
	12				1	100					7	7	38	497	19
	3										2	2	12	185	20
	5										4	4	19	232	21
	3					100					1	1	7	80	22
	1														23
1		1													24
1		1													25
	1														26
31	2	31	31	11,400	30	40,100	4	600			27	27	203	1,449	27
16	8	16	16	4,525	16	17,850	1	1,300			16	16	112	763	28
8	12	8	8	5,986	13	701,980	4	132,400			17	17	160	792	29
	1														30
14	4	14	14	4,725	14	25,250					19	19	141	811	31
2	1	2	2	550	2	6,500					3	4	13	220	32
	1										1	1	4	30	33
2		2	2	550	2	6,500					2	3	9	190	34
4	1	4	4	860	4	35,200	2	2,500	1	3,000	4	4	21	181	35
4	1	4	4	860	4	35,200	2	2,500	1	3,000	4	4	21	181	36
76		78	76	26,379	76	1,102,300	34	75,320	24	45,800	70	78	1,082	10,230	37
1,229	49	1,236	1,221	409,105	1,224	3,320,454	92	115,143	40	80,000	1,113	1,124	9,790	85,793	38
1,139	21	1,146	1,132	383,430	1,135	3,228,754	86	114,063	39	79,750	1,069	1,076	9,572	83,362	39
90	28	90	89	25,675	89	91,700	6	1,080	1	250	44	48	218	2,431	40
36	4	39	35	11,875	36	41,700	3	450	1	800	30	39	274	1,700	41
35	4	38	34	11,625	35	40,700	3	450	1	800	30	39	274	1,700	42
1		1	1	250	1	1,000									43
															44
	6								1	1,000					45
	6								1	1,000					46
20		20	20	5,025	21	63,900	5	3,450	9	13,200	18	18	217	1,328	47
20	2	20	20	5,025	21	63,900	5	3,450	9	13,200	18	18	217	1,328	48
2		2	2	325	2	1,400					1	1	4	50	49
2		2	2	325	2	1,400					1	1	4	50	50
6		6	6	1,155	6	10,325					6	8	75	349	51
6		6	6	1,155	6	10,325					6	8	75	349	52
2		2	2	2,050	2	95,000			2	11,000	2	2	49	544	53
2		2	2	2,050	2	95,000			2	11,000	2	2	49	544	54
155	4	177	155	45,295	156	1,122,675	62	195,757	112	236,100	144	150	1,347	13,007	55
50	12	58	50	14,025	50	117,200	10	4,696	1	2,500	46	52	332	2,933	56
15	1	16	15	11,300	14	773,500	12	219,000			10	11	50	1,482	57
51	8	52	50	13,540	50	136,070	8	9,075	1	500	52	55	616	3,576	58
											1	2	18	79	59
51	8	52	50	13,540	50	136,070	8	9,075	1	500	51	53	598	3,497	60
204	16	214	201	64,864	201	1,598,297	52	162,465	148	265,950	86	88	566	6,865	61
18	2	18	18	5,340	18	208,862	6	34,075	4	6,050	16	16	185	1,440	62
6		6	6	2,250	6	83,500	1	9,600	3	10,300	3	3	41	372	63
162	10	170	159	52,705	159	1,243,935	42	115,540	126	228,300	59	61	307	4,740	64
2		2	2	500	2	19,000	1	2,500	2	4,500	1	1	7	72	65
15		17	15	3,769	15	38,500	2	750	12	14,300	6	6	16	176	66
1	1	1	1	300	1	4,500			1	2,500	1	1	10	65	67
	3														68

TABLE 3.—ORGANIZATIONS, COMMUNICANTS OR MEMBERS, PLACES OF WORSHIP, VALUE OF CHURCH PROPERTY, EACH STATE AND

MISSOURI—Continued.

	DENOMINATION.	Total number of organizations.	COMMUNICANTS OR MEMBERS.				
			Number of organizations reporting.	Total number reported.	Sex.		
					Number of organizations reporting.	Male.	Female.
69	Mennonite bodies	17	17	1,032	17	477	555
70	Mennonite Church	7	7	317	7	145	172
71	Amish Mennonite Church	3	3	392	3	182	210
72	Old Amish Mennonite Church	2	2	88	2	40	48
73	General Conference of Mennonites of North America	1	1	130	1	60	70
74	Church of God in Christ (Mennonite)	2	2	58	2	28	30
75	Defenceless Mennonites	2	2	47	2	22	25
76	Methodist bodies	2,533	2,517	214,004	2,347	73,446	121,647
77	Methodist Episcopal Church	1,009	1,001	80,334	953	27,105	45,312
78	African Methodist Episcopal Church	154	154	11,318	150	3,603	7,422
79	African Methodist Episcopal Zion Church	11	11	1,765	11	396	1,369
80	Methodist Protestant Church	97	97	4,712	91	1,712	2,603
81	Methodist Episcopal Church, South	1,178	1,170	112,058	1,063	39,193	62,687
82	Congregational Methodist Church	27	27	1,118	22	446	546
83	Colored Methodist Episcopal Church	24	24	1,980	24	696	1,284
84	Free Methodist Church of North America	33	33	719	33	295	424
85	Moravian bodies	5	5	78	5	34	44
86	Moravian Church (Unitas Fratrum)	5	5	78	5	34	44
87	Nonsectarian Churches of Bible Faith	9	9	224	9	108	116
88	Presbyterian bodies	788	787	71,599	676	25,001	39,179
89	Presbyterian Church in the United States of America	225	225	25,991	204	8,963	15,045
90	Cumberland Presbyterian Church	380	379	28,637	301	9,944	13,890
91	Colored Cumberland Presbyterian Church	3	3	410	3	170	240
92	Welsh Calvinistic Methodist Church	2	2	73	2	36	37
93	United Presbyterian Church of North America	15	15	1,589	15	636	953
94	Presbyterian Church in the United States	160	160	14,713	148	5,	8,883
95	Associate Reformed Synod of the South	1	1	75	1	197	46
96	Synod of the Reformed Presbyterian Church of North America	2	2	111	2	26	85
97	Protestant Episcopal Church	125	125	13,328	121	4,329	8,192
98	Reformed bodies	10	10	1,284	7	405	484
99	Reformed Church in the United States	10	10	1,284	7	405	484
100	Reformed Catholic Church	1	1	150	1	75	75
101	Roman Catholic Church	457	456	382,642	436	177,380	181,065
102	Salvationists	19	18	980	18	496	484
103	Salvation Army	18	17	970	17	490	480
104	American Salvation Army	1	1	10	1	6	4
105	Society for Ethical Culture	1	1	360	1	231	129
106	Spiritualists	16	16	874	16	386	488
107	Swedish Evangelical bodies	2	2	108	2	43	65
108	Swedish Evangelical Mission Covenant of America	2	2	108	2	43	65
109	Theosophical societies	5	5	128	5	42	86
110	Theosophical Society, American Section	5	5	128	5	42	86
111	Unitarians	4	3	482	3	184	298
112	United Brethren bodies		93	3,616	90	1,370	2,079
113	Church of the United Brethren in Christ	97	83	3,321	80	1,280	1,874
114	Church of the United Brethren in Christ (Old Constitution)	[illegible]	10	295	10	90	205
115	Universalists	24	24	786	24	379	407
116	Volunteers of America	2	2	50	2	25	25

MONTANA.

1	All denominations	546	542	98,984	522	48,255	49,285
2	Adventist bodies	25	24	565	23	174	359
3	Seventh-day Adventist Denomination	25	24	565	23	174	359
4	Baptist bodies	26	26	2,029	26	663	1,366
5	Baptists: Northern Baptist Convention	26	26	2,029	26	663	1,366
6	Christians (Christian Connection)	1	1	18	1	11	7
7	Church of Christ, Scientist	6	6	213	5	49	124
8	Congregationalists	15	15	954	15	292	662

DEBT ON CHURCH PROPERTY, PARSONAGES, AND SUNDAY SCHOOLS, BY DENOMINATIONS (IN DETAIL), FOR TERRITORY: 1906—Continued.

MISSOURI—Continued.

PLACES OF WORSHIP.					VALUE OF CHURCH PROPERTY.		DEBT ON CHURCH PROPERTY.		PARSONAGES.		SUNDAY SCHOOLS CONDUCTED BY CHURCH ORGANIZATIONS.				
Number of organizations reporting— Church edifices.	Number of organizations reporting— Halls, etc.	Number of church edifices reported.	Seating capacity of church edifices. Number of organizations reporting.	Seating capacity of church edifices. Seating capacity reported.	Number of organizations reporting.	Value reported.	Number of organizations reporting.	Amount of debt reported.	Number of organizations reporting.	Value of parsonages reported.	Number of organizations reporting.	Number of Sunday schools reported.	Number of officers and teachers.	Number of scholars.	
12	2	12	12	3,295	12	$12,150	1	$190			13	15	142	1,106	69
6	1	6	6	1,800	6	5,900	1	190			7	9	71	496	70
3		3	3	925	3	3,800					2	2	30	280	71
	1										1	1	6	64	72
1		1	1	300	1	1,000					1	1	25	200	73
															74
2		2	2	270	2	1,450					2	2	10	64	75
2,319	120	2,358	2,238	629,902	2,318	7,708,279	266	368,082	834	$1,101,120	1,960	2,007	19,714	148,043	76
931	53	949	905	248,526	935	3,497,707	114	220,180	353	477,405	798	821	9,267	64,370	77
140	11	142	140	38,060	141	462,105	62	50,291	81	53,415	132	134	903	5,467	78
10	1	10	10	3,450	10	70,400	7	21,250	2	2,250	11	11	63	700	79
81	11	83	81	23,780	81	105,167	6	502	19	22,500	57	58	467	2,711	80
1,100	31	1,116	1,047	300,097	1,096	3,500,750	66	70,938	359	535,475	910	930	8,667	72,538	81
14	4	14	13	5,000	13	7,350	2	80			14	14	101	590	82
24		25	24	6,064	24	46,550	8	4,332	8	4,525	22	22	150	1,073	83
19	9	19	18	4,925	19	18,250	1	500	12	5,550	16	17	96	594	84
5		5	5	675	5	5,350			1	1,800	3	3	12	112	85
5			5	675	5	5,350			1	1,800	3	3	12	112	86
5	4		2	400	2	1,500					4	4	17	191	87
737	14	757	719	219,432	737	3,826,211	79	177,825	163	307,650	615	661	7,487	59,559	88
212	2	231	212	68,354	211	1,924,400	42	84,836	69	136,400	197	228	3,141	27,389	89
353	5	362	346	102,192	360	837,500	16	24,655	44	54,400	273	275	2,683	19,472	90
3		3	3	1,050	3	21,250	1	100			3	3	12	125	91
1	1	1	1	160	1	350			1	250	2	2	11	75	92
15		15	15	4,300	15	163,361	5	10,700	5	17,000	14	15	206	1,874	93
140	6	142	139	42,526	144	853,350	14	56,034	43	98,000	123	135	1,408	10,457	94
1		1	1	350	1	2,000			1	1,600	1	1	8	42	95
2		2	2	500	2	24,000	1	1,500			2	2	18	125	96
109	5	120	109	25,727	113	1,553,030	23	108,547	26	110,900	93	96	724	6,420	97
10		10	10	3,025	10	71,200	4	25,000	4	6,150	10	10	106	943	98
10		10	10	3,025	10	71,200	4	25,000	4	6,150	10	10	106	943	99
	1														100
420	14	489	415	161,693	418	10,326,114	170	1,428,304	259	1,067,650	319	358	1,061	30,999	101
3	15	3	2	475	17	26,420	9	5,631			16	16	83	578	102
3	14	3		475	17	26,420	9	5,631			16	16	83	578	103
	1														104
	1										1	1	20	100	105
5	9	5	[illegible]	1,550	6	27,570	2	9,500			4	4	17	132	106
2		2	2	500	2	8,500	1	1,800			2	[illegible]	12	98	107
2		2	2	500	2	8,500	1	1,800			2	2	12	98	108
	5														109
	5														110
3		3	3	755	3	58,000	1	3,000			4	4	36	200	111
80	7	80	78	22,780	77	92,610	6	1,915	17	13,100	66	66	877	3,496	112
74	4	74	72	21,475	71	87,710	4	1,700	16	12,300	59	59	521	3,251	113
6	3	6	6	1,305	6	4,900	2	215	1	800	7	7	56	245	114
12	12	12	12	2,735	11	35,600	3	1,400			10	10	76	486	115
	2				1	28					2	2	11	110	116

MONTANA.

367	82	407	363	100,665	391	$2,809,779	87	$195,122	193	$450,110	423	477	3,298	33,891	1
8	6	8	8	1,070	9	18,050	1	400			22	24	130	547	[illegible]
8	6	8	8	1,070	9	18,050		400			22	24	130	547	
20	1	23	19	4,895	20	141,574	9	18,100	10	23,950	22	26	231	2,309	
20	1	23	19	4,895	20	141,574	9	18,100	10	23,950	22	26	231	2,309	5
	1										1	1	5	23	6
1	5	1	1	150	4	13,035	1	850			6	6	13	85	7
13	1	14	13	2,525	13	67,000	3	2,150	7	14,000	14	15	114	954	8

TABLE 3.—ORGANIZATIONS, COMMUNICANTS OR MEMBERS, PLACES OF WORSHIP, VALUE OF CHURCH PROPERTY, EACH STATE AND

MONTANA—Continued.

	DENOMINATION.	Total number of organizations.	COMMUNICANTS OR MEMBERS. Number of organizations reporting.	Total number reported.	Sex. Number of organizations reporting.	Male.	Female.
9	Disciples or Christians	22	22	2,008	20	632	1,226
10	Disciples of Christ	22	22	2,008	20	632	1,226
11	Dunkers or German Baptist Brethren	1	1	16	1	4	12
12	German Baptist Brethren Church (Conservative)	1	1	16	1	4	12
13	Eastern Orthodox Churches	1	1	1,500	1	1,400	100
14	Servian Orthodox Church	1	1	1,500	1	1,400	100
15	Jewish congregations	3	3	[1]152	....	....	....
16	Latter-day Saints	6	6	510	5	158	247
17	Church of Jesus Christ of Latter-day Saints	2	2	242	2	90	152
18	Reorganized Church of Jesus Christ of Latter-day Saints	4	4	268	3	68	95
19	Lutheran bodies	47	46	3,059	44	1,476	1,418
20	General Council of the Evangelical Lutheran Church in North America	6	6	473	5	166	187
21	Evangelical Lutheran Synodical Conference of America	7	7	690	7	290	400
22	United Norwegian Lutheran Church in America	9	8	575	7	334	196
23	Synod for the Norwegian Evangelical Lutheran Church in America	24	24	1,290	24	670	620
24	Finnish Evangelical Lutheran Church of America, or Suomi Synod	1	1	31	1	16	15
25	Mennonite bodies	2	2	26	2	12	14
26	Old Amish Mennonite Church	1	1	21	1	10	11
27	General Conference of Mennonites of North America	1	1	5	1	2	3
28	Methodist bodies	156	155	7,022	151	2,368	4,409
29	Methodist Episcopal Church	127	126	5,819	124	1,984	3,620
30	African Methodist Episcopal Church	6	6	135	6	35	100
31	Methodist Episcopal Church, South	23	23	1,068	21	349	689
32	Presbyterian bodies	62	62	4,096	61	1,462	2,619
33	Presbyterian Church in the United States of America	62	62	4,006	61	1,402	2,619
34	Protestant Episcopal Church	57	57	3,290	53	849	2,207
35	Reformed bodies	2	2	135	2	78	57
36	Christian Reformed Church	2	2	135	2	78	57
37	Roman Catholic Church	91	90	72,359	89	38,155	33,898
38	Salvationists	8	8	172	8	97	75
39	Salvation Army	8	8	172	8	97	75
40	Spiritualists	3	3	237	3	100	137
41	Swedish Evangelical bodies	4	4	116	4	49	67
42	Swedish Evangelical Mission Covenant of America	4	4	116	4	49	67
43	Theosophical societies	5	5	70	5	29	41
44	Theosophical Society, American Section	5	5	70	5	29	41
45	Unitarians	3	3	437	3	197	240

NEBRASKA.

1	All denominations	3,313	3,300	345,803	3,133	142,682	184,718
2	Adventist bodies	76	76	2,872	70	724	1,341
3	Advent Christian Church	6	6	305	5	102	158
4	Seventh-day Adventist Denomination	64	64	2,415	59	573	1,080
5	Church of God (Adventist)	2	2	56	2	22	34
6	Churches of God in Christ Jesus	4	4	96	4	27	69
7	Baptist bodies	243	243	17,939	222	6,413	10,587
	Baptists:						
8	Northern Baptist Convention	210	210	16,895	195	6,016	10,057
9	Seventh-day Baptists	2	2	221	2	149	172
10	Free Baptists	19	19	491	14	173	240
11	General Baptists	6	6	103	6	40	63
12	United Baptists	1	1	11	1	5	6
13	Primitive Baptists	5	5	118	4	30	49

[1] Heads of families only.

DEBT ON CHURCH PROPERTY, PARSONAGES, AND SUNDAY SCHOOLS, BY DENOMINATIONS (IN DETAIL), FOR TERRITORY: 1906—Continued.

MONTANA—Continued.

PLACES OF WORSHIP.					VALUE OF CHURCH PROPERTY.		DEBT ON CHURCH PROPERTY.		PARSONAGES.		SUNDAY SCHOOLS CONDUCTED BY CHURCH ORGANIZATIONS.				
Number of organizations reporting— Church edifices.	Number of organizations reporting— Halls, etc.	Number of church edifices reported.	Seating capacity of church edifices. Number of organizations reporting.	Seating capacity of church edifices. Seating capacity reported.	Number of organizations reporting.	Value reported.	Number of organizations reporting.	Amount of debt reported.	Number of organizations reporting.	Value of parsonages reported.	Number of organizations reporting.	Number of Sunday schools reported.	Number of officers and teachers.	Number of scholars.	
18		18	18	5,150	19	$92,600	6	$7,585	5	$10,300	20	21	190	1,291	9
18		18	18	5,150	19	92,600	6	7,585	5	10,300	20	21	190	1,291	10
															11
															12
1		1	1	300	1	20,000	1	8,000							13
1		1	1	300	1	20,000	1	8,000							14
3		3	3	1,200	3	53,000					[illegible]	[illegible]	5	75	15
2	3	2	2	300	2	1,700					4	5	50	207	16
	2										2	2	24	121	17
2	1	2	2	300	2	1,700					2	3	26	86	18
17	14	18	17	3,170	20	92,800	9	15,305	7	14,300	28	30	113	945	19
5	1	5	5	1,015	5	26,800	2	2,400			6	6	39	295	20
5	1	6	5	915	5	42,500	3	10,800	4	8,800	5	5	17	224	21
3	5	3	3	500	3	5,200	1	100	2	3,500	5	6	27	168	22
4	6	4	4	740	7	18,100	3	2,005	1	2,000	11	12	27	248	23
	1										1	1	3	10	24
1	1	1	1	100	1	1,000			1	1,200					25
															26
1		1	1	100	1	1,000			1	1,200					27
129	12	133	129	26,625	131	476,390	23	19,748	89	119,925	124	140	1,110	8,870	28
102	12	106	102	21,250	104	380,640	18	19,226	70	93,175	103	115	962	7,743	29
6		6	6	1,175	6	11,650	4	432	4	3,600	5	5	30	134	30
21		21	21	4,200	21	84,100	1	90	15	23,150	16	20	118	993	31
51	3	55	50	9,655	52	252,500	10	14,250	24	51,300	59	64	642	5,134	32
51	3	55	50	9,655	52	252,500	10	14,250	24	51,300	59	64	642	5,134	33
38	5	38	38	5,740	42	259,375	2	5,250	20	63,585	36	37	230	2,198	34
1		1	1	250	1	5,000	1	1,650	1	2,000	2	2	6	110	35
1		1	1	250	1	5,000	1	1,650	1	2,000	2	2	6	110	36
58	14	85	57	37,985	61	1,248,300	14	86,760	27	143,050	70	90	402	10,619	37
1	7	1	1	200	7	21,305	4	8,174	1	4,000	6	6	22	277	38
1	7	1	1	200	7	21,305	4	8,174	1	4,000	6	6	22	277	39
											[illegible]	1	4	40	40
3		3	3	950		17,500	2	3,400	1	2,500	3	4	17	125	41
3		3	3	950	3	17,500	2	3,400	1	2,500	3	4	17	125	42
	5										1	1	1	12	43
	5										1	1	1	12	44
2	1	2	1	400	2	29,150	1	3,500			2	[illegible]	13	70	45

NEBRASKA.

2,756	337	2,847	2,716	649,132	2,796	$12,114,817	434	$531,042	1,432	$2,304,069	2,701	2,845	24,242	192,443	1
42	26	42	41	7,150	42	45,100	1	1,200	2	2,000	70	72	585	2,420	2
5	1	5	5	1,000	5	5,150	1	1,200	2	2,000	5	5	30	209	3
36	22	36	35	6,050	36	39,550					60	62	533	2,081	4
	2										2	2	8	69	5
1	1	1	1	100	1	400					3	3	14	61	6
215	10	222	209	47,960	215	710,770	30	11,174	82	116,690	206	222	2,041	15,441	7
197	5	203	191	44,715	197	680,760	30	11,174	75	111,040	190	206	1,915	14,534	8
1	1	1	1	350	1	6,000			2	2,700	2	2	34	297	9
15		16	15	2,445	15	21,510			5	2,950	12	12	81	430	10
	3										2	2	11	180	11
															12
2	1	2	2	450	2	2,500									13

TABLE 3.—ORGANIZATIONS, COMMUNICANTS OR MEMBERS, PLACES OF WORSHIP, VALUE OF CHURCH PROPERTY, EACH STATE AND

NEBRASKA—Continued.

	DENOMINATION.	Total number of organizations.	COMMUNICANTS OR MEMBERS.				
			Number of organizations reporting.	Total number reported.	Sex.		
					Number of organizations reporting.	Male.	Female.
14	Brethren (Plymouth)	12	12	178	12	78	100
15	Brethren (Plymouth)—II	2	2	25	2	10	15
16	Brethren (Plymouth)—III	1	1	6	1	3	3
17	Brethren (Plymouth)—IV	9	9	147	9	65	82
18	Catholic Apostolic Churches	1	1	30	1	12	18
19	New Apostolic Church	1	1	30	1	12	18
20	Christians (Christian Connection)	2	2	169	2	68	101
21	Church of Christ, Scientist	18	18	994	18	270	724
22	Churches of God in North America, General Eldership of the	12	12	329	9	113	96
23	Congregationalists	195	195	16,629	195	6,225	10,404
24	Disciples or Christians	189	187	19,613	179	6,720	10,680
25	Disciples of Christ	178	176	19,121	168	6,535	10,373
26	Churches of Christ	11	11	492	11	185	307
27	Dunkers or German Baptist Brethren	29	29	1,594	29	687	907
28	German Baptist Brethren Church (Conservative)	24	24	1,096	24	500	593
29	Old Order German Baptist Brethren	1	1	27	1	16	11
30	The Brethren Church (Progressive Dunkers)	4	4	471	4	171	300
31	Eastern Orthodox Churches	5	5	2,105	1	70	50
32	Syrian Orthodox Church	1	1	120	1	70	50
33	Greek Orthodox Church	4	4	1,985	....	....	....
34	Evangelical bodies	128	126	6,192	124	2,538	3,578
35	Evangelical Association	66	66	3,200	66	1,385	1,815
36	United Evangelical Church	62	60	2,992	58	1,153	1,763
37	Evangelistic associations	5	5	87	5	36	51
38	Hephzibah Faith Missionary Association	2	2	24	2	12	12
39	Missionary Church Association	2	2	57	2	22	35
40	Pentecost Bands of the World	1	1	6	1	2	4
41	Friends	25	25	1,358	25	592	766
42	Society of Friends (Orthodox)	23	23	1,243	23	539	704
43	Religious Society of Friends (Hicksite)	2	2	115	2	53	62
44	German Evangelical Synod of North America	28	28	3,882	25	1,761	1,782
45	Independent churches	15	15	764	15	330	434
46	Jewish congregations	11	8	[1]435	....	....	....
47	Latter-day Saints	19	19	1,578	16	486	697
48	Church of Jesus Christ of Latter-day Saints	2	2	75	....	....	....
49	Reorganized Church of Jesus Christ of Latter-day Saints	17	17	1,503	16	485	697
50	Lutheran bodies	530	529	59,485	497	27,146	28,204
51	General Synod of the Evangelical Lutheran Church in the United States of America	124	124	12,807	118	5,505	6,552
52	General Council of the Evangelical Lutheran Church in North America	47	47	7,303	41	3,195	3,384
53	Evangelical Lutheran Synodical Conference of America	207	206	25,730	197	12,042	12,169
54	United Norwegian Lutheran Church in America	8	8	338	8	173	165
55	Evangelical Lutheran Joint Synod of Ohio and Other States	10	10	1,259	10	645	614
56	Hauge's Norwegian Evangelical Lutheran Synod	4	4	532	4	262	270
57	Evangelical Lutheran Synod of Iowa and Other States	60	60	6,859	56	3,030	2,934
58	Synod for the Norwegian Evangelical Lutheran Church in America	16	16	1,212	10	538	527
59	Danish Evangelical Lutheran Church in America	14	14	1,325	14	686	639
60	United Danish Evangelical Lutheran Church in America	40	40	2,120	39	1,070	950
61	Mennonite bodies	19	19	1,468	19	708	760
62	Mennonite Church	1	1	89	1	40	49
63	Amish Mennonite Church	5	5	370	5	186	184
64	General Conference of Mennonites of North America	5	5	679	5	331	348
65	Church of God in Christ (Mennonite)	2	2	24	2	10	14
66	Defenceless Mennonites	1	1	36	1	17	19
	Bundes Conferenz der Mennoniten Brueder-Gemeinde:						
67	Krimmer Brueder-Gemeinde	1	1	50	1	21	29
68	Central Illinois Conference of Mennonites	1	1	90	1	50	40
69	Nebraska and Minnesota Conference of Mennonites	3	3	130	3	53	77
70	Methodist bodies	821	819	64,352	784	23,036	37,739
71	Methodist Episcopal Church	746	744	62,586	711	22,437	36,729
72	African Methodist Episcopal Church	6	6	509	5	175	322
73	Wesleyan Methodist Connection of America	5	5	67	5	24	43
74	Methodist Episcopal Church, South	3	3	181	3	67	114
75	Free Methodist Church of North America	61	61	1,009	60	333	531

[1] Heads of families only.

DEBT ON CHURCH PROPERTY, PARSONAGES, AND SUNDAY SCHOOLS, BY DENOMINATIONS (IN DETAIL), FOR TERRITORY: 1906—Continued.

NEBRASKA—Continued.

PLACES OF WORSHIP.					VALUE OF CHURCH PROPERTY.		DEBT ON CHURCH PROPERTY.		PARSONAGES.		SUNDAY SCHOOLS CONDUCTED BY CHURCH ORGANIZATIONS.				
Number of organizations reporting— Church edifices.	Number of organizations reporting— Halls, etc.	Number of church edifices reported.	Seating capacity of church edifices. Number of organizations reporting.	Seating capacity of church edifices. Seating capacity reported.	Number of organizations reporting.	Value reported.	Number of organizations reporting.	Amount of debt reported.	Number of organizations reporting.	Value of parsonages reported.	Number of organizations reporting.	Number of Sunday schools reported.	Number of officers and teachers.	Number of scholars.	
	12										3	3	8	70	14
	2										2	2	5	40	15
	1										1	1	3	30	16
	9														17
	1														18
	1														19
1	1	1	1	350	1	$1,500			1	$1,000	1	1	16	141	20
7	8	7	7	2,150	13	31,510					16	16	69	339	21
3	3	3	3	700	5	5,000					7	9	47	314	22
169	11	171	157	37,565	169	728,559	37	$20,842	99	154,350	185	192	1,912	15,438	23
163	10	164	163	42,687	166	527,270	22	29,120	33	33,950	159	162	1,613	12,716	24
156	6	157	156	41,612	159	516,870	21	29,010	33	36,950	155	158	1,596	12,574	25
7	4	7	7	1,075	7	10,400	1	110			4	4	17	142	26
20	6	26	20	6,850	20	51,800	5	1,400	3	7,000	21	25	199	1,209	27
15	6	19	15	5,150	15	35,300	4	1,150	1	1,500	18	22	169	968	28
1		1	1	250	1	1,000									29
4		6	4	1,450	4	15,500	1	250	2	5,500	3	3	30	241	30
2	2	2	1	100	1	1,200									31
1		1	1	100	1	1,200									32
1	3	1													33
114	6	115	114	23,015	114	247,101	19	9,944	68	112,491	121	130	1,318	7,525	34
62	2	63	62	11,680	62	128,950	8	6,658	36	71,266	62	69	713	3,888	35
52	4	52	52	11,335	52	118,151	11	3,286	32	41,225	59	61	605	3,637	36
3	2	3	3	500	3	3,050					4	6	35	195	37
1	1	1	1	150	1	1,000					2	2	18	60	38
1	1	1	1	175	1	1,400					2	4	17	135	39
1		1	1	175	1	650									40
20	4	20	20	3,580	22	18,510	3	515	7	4,700	17	17	132	626	41
19	4	19	19	3,380	21	17,310	3	515	7	4,700	16	16	131	616	42
1		1	1	200	1	1,200					1	1	1	10	43
26	2	26	26	5,935	26	90,350	8	5,295	22	34,500	23	23	154	1,389	44
10	3	10	10	2,350	9	9,000			2	4,200	13	13	86	631	45
6		6	6	1,650	6	91,000	3	27,500	1	350	4	4	12	195	46
10	5	10	9	1,695	9	10,500					18	21	150	620	47
											2	3	8	36	48
10	5	10	9	1,695	9	10,500					16	18	142	584	49
446	49	465	440	105,921	452	1,707,187	74	60,056	292	431,345	319	330	1,590	14,488	50
108	8	111	105	25,246	112	521,317	26	27,562	64	89,600	109	111	758	6,457	51
46		51	46	13,168	46	303,295	6	12,150	30	78,700	44	45	375	2,676	52
176	15	184	175	42,212	178	519,875	29	14,464	132	179,875	63	68	103	1,693	53
5	2	5	5	1,000	5	7,000			2	1,800	5	5	23	112	54
10		10	10	2,475	10	32,800	1	100	5	5,500	9	9	37	401	55
4		4	4	850	4	9,300			2	2,800	2	2	15	107	56
51	7	54	50	12,865	51	157,500	8	2,855	35	41,370	48	50	123	1,768	57
9		9	9	2,030	9	24,900	1	725	5	11,200	3	3	19	165	58
11	3	11	10	1,780	11	32,600			7	8,800	9	9	12	242	59
26	14	26	26	4,295	26	48,000	3	2,200	10	11,700	27	28	125	867	60
15	3	15	15	4,350	15	31,225	2	513			17	17	153	1,669	61
1		1	1	400	1	2,400					1	1	15	130	62
5		5	5	980	5	7,675	2	513			5	5	53	394	63
4	1	4	4	1,825	4	11,700							48	808	64
	1														65
1		1	1	150	1	750					1	1	6	40	66
1		1	1	225	1	3,000					1	1	5	45	67
1		1	1	400	1	3,000					1	1	11	30	68
2	1	2	2	370	2	2,700					3	3	15	222	69
696	91	707	668	169,885	699	2,364,050	62	69,439	419	555,273	703	745	8,633	60,970	70
655	67	665	647	162,110	656	2,296,600	58	68,389	393	535,723	659	698	8,330	59,304	71
5	1	5	5	1,775	5	29,300	2	650	2	2,200	6	6	59	371	72
1	4	1	1	100	2	1,000									73
3		3	3	550	3	4,200			1	1,800	3	3	24	175	74
32	19	33	32	5,350	33	32,950	2	400	23	15,550	35	38	220	1,120	75

TABLE 3.—ORGANIZATIONS, COMMUNICANTS OR MEMBERS, PLACES OF WORSHIP, VALUE OF CHURCH PROPERTY, EACH STATE AND

NEBRASKA—Continued.

	DENOMINATION.	Total number of organizations.	COMMUNICANTS OR MEMBERS. Number of organizations reporting.	COMMUNICANTS OR MEMBERS. Total number reported.	Sex. Number of organizations reporting.	Sex. Male.	Sex. Female.
76	Nonsectarian Churches of Bible Faith	3	3	121	3	53	68
77	Presbyterian bodies	258	258	23,862	240	8,751	13,888
78	Presbyterian Church in the United States of America		223	20,684	209	7,449	12,105
79	Cumberland Presbyterian Church		6	307	3	107	160
80	Welsh Calvinistic Methodist Church		3	242	3	116	126
81	United Presbyterian Church of North America	223	23	2,459	22	1,005	1,401
82	Synod of the Reformed Presbyterian Church of North America	28	3	170	3	74	96
83	Protestant Episcopal Church	126	125	6,903	113	1,937	3,648
84	Reformed bodies	21	21	2,108	21	1,029	1,079
85	Reformed Church in America	2	2	432	2	215	217
86	Reformed Church in the United States	18	18	1,616	18	789	827
87	Christian Reformed Church	1	1	60	1	25	35
88	Roman Catholic Church	328	328	100,763	328	49,030	51,733
89	Salvationists	7	6	154	6	78	76
90	Salvation Army	7	6	154		78	76
91	Spiritualists	2	2	387	1	32	48
92	Swedish Evangelical bodies	45	45	2,864		1,219	1,395
93	Swedish Evangelical Mission Covenant of America	20	20	1,625		711	914
94	Swedish Evangelical Free Mission	25	25	1,239		508	481
95	Theosophical societies	2	2	29		7	22
96	Theosophical Society, American Section	2	2	29		7	22
97	Unitarians	4	4	403	[illegible]	136	217
98	United Brethren bodies	130	129	6,086	121	2,355	3,487
99	Church of the United Brethren in Christ	126	125	6,045	117	2,340	3,461
100	Church of the United Brethren in Christ (Old Constitution)	4	4	41	4	15	26
101	Universalists	1	1	10	1	4	6
102	Volunteers of America	3	3	70	3	38	32

NEVADA.

	DENOMINATION.	Total number of organizations.	COMMUNICANTS OR MEMBERS. Number of organizations reporting.	COMMUNICANTS OR MEMBERS. Total number reported.	Sex. Number of organizations reporting.	Sex. Male.	Sex. Female.
1	All denominations	88	86	14,944	73	6,595	6,474
	Adventist bodies	2	2	76	2	28	48
	Seventh-day Adventist Denomination	2	2	76	2	28	48
	Baptist bodies	4	4	316	3	108	189
6	Baptists: Northern Baptist Convention	4	4	316	3	108	189
	Buddhists	1	....	....	....	....	....
	Chinese Temples	1	....	....	....	....	....
8	Congregationalists	1	1	180	1	50	
9	Disciples or Christians	1	1	100	1	33	
10	Disciples of Christ	1	1	100	1	33	130 67
11	Eastern Orthodox Churches	3	[illegible]	670	....	....	....
12	Greek Orthodox Church	3	3	670	....	....	....
13	Jewish congregations			....	....	....	....
14	Latter-day Saints	6	6	1,105	6	552	553
15	Church of Jesus Christ of Latter-day Saints	[illegible]	[illegible]	1,105	6	552	553
16	Lutheran bodies	2		148	1	2	10
17	Evangelical Lutheran Synodical Conference of America	2	2	148	1	2	10
18	Methodist bodies	18	18	618	15	171	389
19	Methodist Episcopal Church	18	18	618	15	171	389
20	Presbyterian bodies	14	14		13	167	346
21	Presbyterian Church in the United States of America	14	14	520 520	13	167	346

DEBT ON CHURCH PROPERTY, PARSONAGES, AND SUNDAY SCHOOLS, BY DENOMINATIONS (IN DETAIL), FOR TERRITORY: 1906—Continued.

NEBRASKA—Continued.

PLACES OF WORSHIP.					VALUE OF CHURCH PROPERTY.		DEBT ON CHURCH PROPERTY.		PARSONAGES.		SUNDAY SCHOOLS CONDUCTED BY CHURCH ORGANIZATIONS.				
Number of organizations reporting—		Number of church edifices reported.	Seating capacity of church edifices.												
Church edifices.	Halls, etc.		Number of organizations reporting.	Seating capacity reported.	Number of organizations reporting.	Value reported.	Number of organizations reporting.	Amount of debt reported.	Number of organizations reporting.	Value of parsonages reported.	Number of organizations reporting.	Number of Sunday schools reported.	Number of officers and teachers.	Number of scholars.	
1	2	1	1	200	1	$1,200	...	...	...	...	1	1	8	150	76
242	7	249	242	59,744	244	1,128,850	50	$49,309	122	$212,650	243	260	2,842	24,315	77
208	7	215	208	50,623	210	971,700	46	41,748	103	182,000	208	224	2,416	20,712	78
5	...	5	5	1,150	5	11,000	1	125	1	1,000	6	6	52	390	79
3	...	3	3	540	3	3,700	...	...	2	2,800	3	3	37	303	80
23	...	23	23	6,651	23	135,450	3	7,436	15	25,650	23	24	312	2,731	81
3	...	3	3	780	3	7,000	...	...	1	1,200	3	3	25	179	82
87	16	94	86	15,390	92	712,370	12	30,134	41	92,960	69	73	443	3,627	83
19	2	22	19	4,985	19	64,950	4	15,750	9	13,510	21	22	128	1,520	84
2	...	3	2	950	2	11,200	...	...	1	3,000	2	2	19	382	85
16	2	18	16	3,735	16	51,250	3	15,200	7	9,010	18	19	102	1,088	86
1	...	1	1	300	1	2,500	1	550	1	1,500	1	1	7	50	87
296	13	323	295	71,405	303	3,139,900	77	172,851	156	423,600	301	318	567	16,822	88
2	5	2	1	400	7	26,975	4	6,130	...	...	4	4	9	95	89
2		2	1	400	7	26,975	4	6,130	...	...	4			95	90
...	2	...	...	...	...	...	...	...	...	...	1	1	2	7	91
39	5	39	38	11,010	40	154,685	10	5,210	25	50,200	43	45	347	3,063	92
18	1	18	17	6,300	18	99,050	4	2,850	12	29,800	20	22	194	1,598	93
21	4	21	21	4,710	22	55,635	6	2,360	13	20,400	23	23	153	1,465	94
...	2	...	...	...	...	...		...	...	...	...	...	...	...	95
...	2	...	...	...	...	...	...	...	...	...	...	...	...	...	96
4	...	4	4	925	4	51,000		11,450	...	...	3	3	19	158	97
97	24	97	96	20,530	97	158,200		3,210	48	50,300	105	107	1,107	6,207	98
96	21	96	95	20,430	96	158,100	7	3,210	48	50,300	105	107	1,107	6,207	99
1	3	1	1	100	1	100	...	...	...	...	...	...	...	...	100
1	...	1	1	150	1	2,000	...	...	...	...	...	...	...	...	101
...	3	...	...	...	1	5	...	...	...	...	3	3	17	83	102
NEVADA.															
62	10	67	58	15,015	70	$402,350	16	$19,305	34	$68,700	71	84	550	4,641	1
1	...	1	1	150	1	2,000	...	...	...	...	2	[illegible]	11	55	2
1	...	1	1	150	1	2,000	...	...	...	...	2		11	55	3
3	...	4		975	4	25,350	2	1,000		1,000	4		39	400	4
3	...	4	3	975	4	25,350	2	1,000	1	1,000	4	5	39	400	5
1	...	1	...	...	...	...	...	...	...	...	...	...	...	...	6
1	...	1	...	...	...	...	...	...	...	...	...	...	...	...	7
1	...	1	1	500	1	17,000	...	...	1	4,000	1	1	15	175	8
...	...	...	...	...	...	...	...	...	...	...	1	1	10	40	9
...	...	...	...	...	...	...	...	...	...	...	1	1	10	40	10
...	3	...	...	...	...	...	...	...	...	...	...	...	...	...	11
...	3	...	...	...	...	...	...	...	...	...	...	...	...	...	12
...	...	...	...	...	...	...	...	...	...	...	...	...	...	...	13
5	1	5	5	1,275	6	9,875	1	175	...	...	6	7	100	635	14
5	1	5	5	1,275	6	9,875	1	175	...	...	6	7	100	635	15
1	...	1	1	125	1	4,000	...	...	1	1,800	2	2	5	88	16
1	...	1	1	125	1	4,000	...	...	1	1,800	2	2	5	88	17
16	1	16	13	3,310	17	52,900	4	460	11	16,100	18	25	154	1,273	18
16	1	16	13	3,310	17	52,900	4	460	11	16,100	18	25	154	1,273	19
9	1	10	9	2,170	9	53,400	1	200	6	9,850	11	15	112	812	20
9	1	10	9	2,170	9	53,400	1	200	6	9,850	11	15	112	812	21

TABLE 3.—ORGANIZATIONS, COMMUNICANTS OR MEMBERS, PLACES OF WORSHIP, VALUE OF CHURCH PROPERTY, EACH STATE AND

NEVADA—Continued.

	DENOMINATION.	Total number of organizations.	COMMUNICANTS OR MEMBERS.				
			Number of organizations reporting.	Total number reported.	Sex.		
					Number of organizations reporting.	Male.	Female.
22	Protestant Episcopal Church	21	21	1,210	18	510	565
23	Roman Catholic Church	10	10	9,970	9	4,954	4,166
24	Salvationists	3	3	25	3	17	8
25	Salvation Army	3		25	3	17	8
26	Volunteers of America	1		6	1	3	3

NEW HAMPSHIRE.

	DENOMINATION.	Total number of organizations.	Number of organizations reporting.	Total number reported.	Number of organizations reporting.	Male.	Female.
1	All denominations	856	832	190,298	773	79,376	100,340
2	Adventist bodies	47	46	1,723	44	679	994
3	Advent Christian Church	41	40	1,608	38	631	927
4	Seventh-day Adventist Denomination	6	6	115	6	48	67
5	Armenian Church	4	4	465	4	386	79
6	Baptist bodies	173	173	15,974	160	5,230	9,838
7	Baptists	87	87	9,741	83	3,112	6,106
8	Northern Baptist Convention	86	86	9,721	82	3,104	6,094
9	National Baptist Convention (Colored)	1	1	20	1	8	12
10	Free Baptists	84	84	6,210	75	2,111	3,716
11	Freewill Baptists (Bullockites)	2	2	23	2	7	16
12	Brethren (Plymouth)	1	1	15	1	7	8
13	Brethren (Plymouth)—I	1	1	15	1	7	8
14	Christians (Christian Connection)	19	19	1,303	19	454	849
15	Church of Christ, Scientist	7	7	431	7	137	294
16	Churches of the New Jerusalem	2	2	60	2	24	36
17	General Convention of the New Jerusalem in the United States of America	2	2	60	2	24	36
18	Communistic societies	2	2	133	2	15	118
19	United Society of Believers (Shakers)	2	2	133	2	15	118
20	Congregationalists	185	184	19,070	184	5,786	13,284
21	Disciples or Christians	1	1	4	1	1	3
22	Disciples of Christ	1	1	4	1	1	3
23	Eastern Orthodox Churches	8	8	5,210	1	2,800	200
24	Greek Orthodox Church	8	8	5,210	1	2,800	200
25	Friends	12	12	357	12	144	2:3
26	Society of Friends (Orthodox)	12	12	357	12	144	213
27	Independent churches	1	1	10	1	2	8
28	Jewish congregations	5	2	[1] 80	.....	.....	.....
29	Lutheran bodies	4	4	1,070	4	492	578
30	General Council of the Evangelical Lutheran Church in North America	2	2	550	2	254	296
31	Evangelical Lutheran Synodical Conference of America	1	1	260	1	98	162
32	United Norwegian Lutheran Church in America	1	1	260	1	140	120
33	Methodist bodies	142	142	12,579	133	3,839	7,322
34	Methodist Episcopal Church	142	142	12,529	133	3,839	7,322
35	Pentecostal Church of the Nazarene	2	2	53	2	21	32
36	Presbyterian bodies	8	8	842	8	278	564
37	Presbyterian Church in the United States of America	8	8	842	8	278	564
38	Protestant Episcopal Church	61	50	4,892	44	1,241	2,396
39	Roman Catholic Church	104	103	119,863	93	56,253	60,744
40	Salvationists	6	6	144	6	65	79
41	Salvation Army	6	6	144	6	65	79
42	Spiritualists	3	3	283	3	112	171
43	Swedish Evangelical bodies	1	1	165	1	67	98
44	Swedish Evangelical Mission Covenant of America	1	1	165	1	67	98
45	Unitarians	28	25	3,629	20	893	1,506
46	Universalists	30	26	1,993	21	450	926

[1] Heads of families only.

DEBT ON CHURCH PROPERTY, PARSONAGES, AND SUNDAY SCHOOLS, BY DENOMINATIONS (IN DETAIL), FOR TERRITORY: 1906—Continued.

NEVADA—Continued.

PLACES OF WORSHIP.					VALUE OF CHURCH PROPERTY.		DEBT ON CHURCH PROPERTY.		PARSONAGES.		SUNDAY SCHOOLS CONDUCTED BY CHURCH ORGANIZATIONS.				
Number of organizations reporting—		Number of church edifices reported.	Seating capacity of church edifices.		Number of organizations reporting.	Value reported.	Number of organizations reporting.	Amount of debt reported.	Number of organizations reporting.	Value of parsonages reported.	Number of organizations reporting.	Number of Sunday schools reported.	Number of officers and teachers.	Number of scholars.	
Church edifices.	Halls, etc.		Number of organizations reporting.	Seating capacity reported.											
13	2	15	13	3,300	17	$135,400	3	$9,500	7	$16,500	15	15	79	805	22
10	...	11	10	2,985	10	91,400	2	4,300	7	19,450	8	8	21	326	23
1	2	1	1	100	3	1,025	2	170	...	...	2	2	2	20	24
1	2	1	1	100	3	1,025	2	170	...	...	2	2	2	20	25
1	...	1	1	125	1	10,000	1	3,500	...	...	1	1	2	12	26

NEW HAMPSHIRE.

772	61	851	765	254,017	786	$7,864,991	143	$625,807	481	$1,313,525	723	763	7,815	64,865	1
34	10	34	33	7,513	34	79,700	3	7,800	6	11,200	37	37	261	1,243	2
33	6	33	32	7,333	33	79,200	3	7,800	6	11,200	32	32	243	1,180	3
1	4	1	1	180	1	500	...	...	...	...	5	5	18	63	4
...	4	...	...	...	...	...	...	...	...	...	...	...	...	...	5
168	1	189	167	49,055	165	1,137,700	14	19,598	108	208,325	154	161	1,785	13,630	6
85	1	101	84	27,580	85	790,700	11	16,253	61	115,400	83	88	1,096	8,189	7
85	1	101	84	27,580	85	790,700	11	16,253	61	115,400	82	87	1,093	8,165	8
...	...	...	...	...	...	...	...	...	...	...	1	1	3	24	9
82	...	87	82	21,325	79	346,500	3	3,345	47	92,925	71	73	689	5,441	10
1	...	1	1	150	1	500	...	...	...	...	...	...	...	...	11
...	1	...	...	...	...	...	...	...	...	...	...	...	...	...	12
...	1	...	...	...	...	...	...	...	...	...	...	...	...	...	13
19	...	19	19	4,700	19	88,000	2	8,000	10	16,700	19	19	205	1,150	14
3	3	3	3	1,325	7	216,950	1	800	...	...	7	7	17	70	15
2	...	2	2	350	2	7,500	1	1,000	...	...	1	1	16	70	16
2	...	2	2	350	2	7,500	.	1,000	...	...	1	1	16	70	17
...	2	...	...	...	2	2,200	1	80	...	...	9	2	5	59	18
...	2	...	...	...	2	2,200	1	80	...	...	2	2	5	59	19
184	1	214	184	67,379	184	1,782,150	16	10,400	146	329,700	174	185	2,278	17,200	20
...		...	...	...	...	...	...	...	...	...	...	...	...	...	21
...	1	...	...	...	...	...	...	...	...	...	...	...	...	...	22
2		2	...	...	1	20,000	1	7,000	...	...	...	...	...	...	23
2		2	...	...	1	20,000	1	7,000	...	...	...	...	...	...	24
11		11	11	1,643	11	13,000	...	...	...	...	8	8	48	242	25
11		11	11	1,643	11	13,000	...	...	...	...	8	8	48	242	26
...	1	...	...	...	...	...	...	...	...	...	...	...	...	...	27
2	...	2	2	130	1	3,000	1	900	2	400	1	1	1	18	28
4	...	4	4	1,770	4	40,600	4	6,300	2	8,800	4	5	67	414	29
2	...	2	2	750	2	24,400	2	3,000	1	5,000	2	3	45	203	30
1	...	1	1	320	1	5,200	1	1,800	...	...	1	1	3	68	31
1	...	1	1	700	1	11,000	1	1,500	1	3,800	1	1	19	143	32
139	2	143	130	41,413	139	774,600	19	22,730	97	177,100	135	145	1,675	12,016	33
139	2	143	139	41,413	139	774,600	19	22,730	97	177,100	135	145	1,675	12,016	34
1	...	1	1	300	1	5,000	1	2,400	...	...	1	1	8	40	35
8	...	9	8	2,700	8	68,500	1	570	4	6,700	8	8	88	761	36
8	...	9	8	2,700	8	68,500	1	570	4	6,700	8	8	88	761	37
54	6	65	54	13,529	59	713,881	9	19,175	20	76,400	40	42	283	2,222	38
90	9	95	90	45,524	91	2,281,560	64	506,504	64	400,100	85	92	628	13,326	39
...	6	...	...	...	6	1,200	...	...	...	...	5	5	7	85	40
...	6	...	...	...	6	1,200	...	...	...	...	5	5	7	85	41
1	2	1	1	500	2	5,150	...	...	...	...	2	2	8	50	42
1	...	1	1	500	1	14,000	1	1,500	1	3,000	1	1	18	75	43
1	...	1	1	500	1	14,000	1	1,500	1	3,000	1	1	18	75	44
23	3	30	22	8,631	24	316,700	1	1,200	13	51,700	18	20	145	856	45
26	2	26	24	7,055	25	[illegible]	3	9,850	8	23,400	21	21	272	1,338	46

TABLE 3.—ORGANIZATIONS, COMMUNICANTS OR MEMBERS, PLACES OF WORSHIP, VALUE OF CHURCH PROPERTY, EACH STATE AND

NEW JERSEY.

	DENOMINATION.	Total number of organizations.	COMMUNICANTS OR MEMBERS. Number of organizations reporting.	Total number reported.	Sex. Number of organizations reporting.	Male.	Female.
1	All denominations	2,802	2,750	857,548	2,497	302,345	408,929
2	Adventist bodies	22	22	599	22	157	442
3	Evangelical Adventists	1	1	36	1	13	23
4	Seventh-day Adventist Denomination	18	18	451	18	88	363
5	Life and Advent Union	2	2	82	2	38	44
6	Churches of God in Christ Jesus	1	1	30	1	18	12
7	Armenian Church	1	1	550	1	430	120
8	Bahais	2	2	58	2	24	34
9	Baptist bodies	365	364	65,248	345	21,640	40,131
10	Baptists	356	355	64,238	338	21,295	39,558
11	Northern Baptist Convention	286	286	54,354	269	18,396	32,573
12	National Baptist Convention (Colored)	70	69	9,884	69	2,899	6,985
13	Seventh-day Baptists	4	4	735	4	299	436
14	Free Baptists	1	1	50	....	....	....
15	Primitive Baptists	4	4	225	3	46	137
16	Brethren (Plymouth)	29	29	988	29	412	576
17	Brethren (Plymouth)—I	10	10	322	10	139	183
18	Brethren (Plymouth)—II	10	10	440	10	185	255
19	Brethren (Plymouth)—III	5	5	148	5	64	84
20	Brethren (Plymouth)—IV	4	4	78	4	24	54
21	Buddhists	1	....	....	....	....	....
22	Chinese Temples	1	....	....	....	....	....
23	Catholic Apostolic Churches	2	2	80	2	30	50
24	New Apostolic Church	2	2	80	2	30	50
25	Christadelphians	3	3	58	3	28	30
26	Christian Israelite Church	1	1	25	1	16	9
27	Christians (Christian Connection)	13	13	1,406	12	389	757
28	Church of Christ, Scientist	12	12	540	12	162	378
29	Church of God and Saints of Christ (Colored)	5	5	253	5	62	191
30	Churches of the New Jerusalem	3	3	133	3	51	82
31	General Convention of the New Jerusalem in the United States of America	3	3	133	3	51	82
32	Congregationalists	44	44	8,460	43	2,999	5,397
33	Disciples or Christians	3	3	227	2	18	24
34	Disciples of Christ	2	2	213	1	12	16
35	Churches of Christ	1	1	14	1	6	8
36	Dunkers or German Baptist Brethren	4	4	143	4	51	92
37	German Baptist Brethren Church (Conservative)	2	2	43	2	13	30
38	The Brethren Church (Progressive Dunkers)	2	2	100	2	38	62
39	Eastern Orthodox Churches	10	10	2,466	4	1,144	362
40	Russian Orthodox Church	3	3	606	3	344	262
41	Greek Orthodox Church	7	7	1,860	1	800	100
42	Evangelical bodies	9	9	762	8	276	416
43	Evangelical Association	9	9	762	8	276	416
44	Evangelistic associations	2	2	106	2	46	60
45	Apostolic Christian Church	1	1	50	1	20	30
46	Pentecostal Union Church	1	1	56	1	26	30
47	Friends	48	48	3,324	45	1,441	1,789
48	Society of Friends (Orthodox)	20	20	1,043	20	445	598
49	Religious Society of Friends (Hicksite)	28	28	2,281	25	996	1,191
50	German Evangelical Synod of North America	7	7	2,305	7	898	1,407
51	Independent churches	22	22	1,584	21	658	851
52	International Apostolic Holiness Union	1	1	20	1	8	12
53	Jewish congregations	87	56	[1]4,603	....	....	....
54	Lutheran bodies	120	120	24,147	108	9,228	13,643
55	General Synod of the Evangelical Lutheran Church in the United States of America	27	27	4,997	26	1,828	3,041
56	General Council of the Evangelical Lutheran Church in North America	63	63	15,323	55	5,787	8,598
57	Evangelical Lutheran Synodical Conference of America	16	16	2,240	15	885	1,330
58	United Norwegian Lutheran Church in America	1	1	25	1	15	10
59	Synod for the Norwegian Evangelical Lutheran Church in America	3	3	546	3	266	280
60	Danish Evangelical Lutheran Church in America	4	4	271	2	39	47
61	Immanuel Synod of the Evangelical Lutheran Church of North America	1	1	75	1	35	40
62	United Danish Evangelical Lutheran Church in America	1	1	15	1	7	8
63	Slovak Evangelical Lutheran Synod of America	4	4	655	4	366	289

DEBT ON CHURCH PROPERTY, PARSONAGES, AND SUNDAY SCHOOLS, BY DENOMINATIONS (IN DETAIL), FOR TERRITORY: 1906—Continued.

NEW JERSEY.

PLACES OF WORSHIP.					VALUE OF CHURCH PROPERTY.		DEBT ON CHURCH PROPERTY.		PARSONAGES.		SUNDAY SCHOOLS CONDUCTED BY CHURCH ORGANIZATIONS.				
Number of organizations reporting—		Number of church edifices reported.	Seating capacity of church edifices.		Number of organizations reporting.	Value reported.	Number of organizations reporting.	Amount of debt reported.	Number of organizations reporting.	Value of parsonages reported.	Number of organizations reporting.	Number of Sunday schools reported.	Number of officers and teachers.	Number of scholars.	
Church edifices.	Halls, etc.		Number of organizations reporting.	Seating capacity reported.											
2,558	174	2,875	2,524	1,015,903	2,586	$50,907,123	1,075	$6,786,368	1,289	$6,376,490	2,495	2,785	42,613	404,095	1
3	19	3	3	550	4	6,170	1	1,200			20	20	109	492	2
	1										1	1	8	20	3
1	17	1	1	200	2	1,650					18	18	94	437	4
1	1	1	1	250	1	4,500	1	1,200			1	1	7	35	5
1		1	1	100	1	20									6
		1	1	400	1	12,000	1	4,000			1	1	3	50	7
	2														8
352	8	396	350	149,474	356	5,385,580	172	563,472	141	418,790	349	392	6,444	52,214	9
344	8	387	342	145,974	348	5,310,580	171	562,922	136	403,290	345	388	6,366	51,812	10
281	3	324	279	125,559	281	4,984,745	122	493,397	129	392,390	277	320	5,855	47,631	11
63	5	63	63	20,415	67	325,835	49	69,525	7	10,900	68	68	511	4,181	12
4		5	4	1,550	4	60,500	1	550	4	10,500	4	4	78	402	13
															14
4		4	4	1,950	4	14,500				5,000					15
	29										21	23	115	1,132	16
	10										10	10	31	259	17
	10										9	11	78	824	18
	5										2	2	6	49	19
	4														20
1		1													21
1		1													22
	2														23
	2														24
	2				2	200					2	2	5	30	25
	1				1	150					1	1	2	12	26
13		13	13	3,700	13	76,900	2	2,700	8	16,000	10	10	163	1,056	27
2	10	2	2	475	4	48,023	1	2,313			12	12	54	221	28
	5										1	1	6	150	29
			2	400	3	19,500	1	1,600			1	1	6	25	30
2		2	2	400	3	19,500	1	1,600			1	1	6	25	31
41	1	48	41	17,400	42	1,261,800	20	80,060	11	66,700	41	45	706	6,307	32
2	1	2	2	1,260	2	44,000	2	16,955			2	2	24	335	33
2		2	2	1,260	2	44,000	2	16,955			2	2	24	335	34
	1														35
4		4	4	1,100	4	6,400	1	800	2	2,800	4	4	26	120	36
2		2	2	700	2	2,700			1	1,800	2	2	14	55	37
2		2	2	400	2	3,700	1	800	1	1,000	2	2	12	65	38
3	6	3	3	800	4	16,050	3	7,630			1	1	1	150	39
2		2	2	550	3	14,000	2	6,630							40
1	6	1	1	250	1	2,050	1	1,000			1	1	1	150	41
9		11	9	2,850	9	78,250	6	20,300	6	21,800	9	11	153	1,185	42
9		11	9	2,850	9	78,250	6	20,300	6	21,800	9	11	153	1,185	43
2		2	2	300	2	9,000	1	1,000			2	2	8	100	44
1		1	1	200	1	4,000	1	1,000			1	1	2	50	45
1		1	1	100	1	5,000					1	1	6	50	46
48		49	48	14,225	48	281,215					19	19	150	1,076	47
20		21	20	5,525	20	141,715									48
28		28	28	8,700	28	139,500					19	19	150	1,076	49
7		7	7	2,700	7	108,674	4	25,220	3	12,500	7	7	128	1,556	50
18	4	18	18	3,746	18	73,780	9	18,450	2	5,000	19	22	215	1,917	51
1		1	1	250	1	1,500	1	600			1	1	10	50	52
49	3	55	42	16,615	47	730,075	35	190,100	3	4,000	31	34	92	2,500	53
102	12	105	100	33,341	105	1,463,952	74	352,472	45	170,750	109	119	1,833	18,560	54
24	3	24	24	9,000	25	328,350	14	93,475	14	47,300	27	27	481	4,534	55
54	5	55	52	18,441	56	982,202	41	208,652	23	97,250	59	65	1,109	11,323	56
14	1	15	14	3,325	14	89,300	12	35,745	6	19,700	14	18	151	1,718	57
1		1	1	125	1	5,000					1	1	10	60	58
3		3	3	800	3	28,500	3	8,200	2	6,500	3	3	59	405	59
2	1	2	2	550	2	14,600	2	4,850			2	2	15	310	60
1		1	1	150	1	2,500	1	1,250			1	1	5	75	61
	1														62
3	1	4	3	950	3	13,500		300			2	2	3	135	63

TABLE 3.—ORGANIZATIONS, COMMUNICANTS OR MEMBERS, PLACES OF WORSHIP, VALUE OF CHURCH PROPERTY, EACH STATE AND

NEW JERSEY—Continued.

	DENOMINATION.	Total number of organizations.	COMMUNICANTS OR MEMBERS.				
			Number of organizations reporting.	Total number reported.	Sex.		
					Number of organizations reporting.	Male.	Female.
64	Methodist bodies	826	824	122,511	797	42,809	74,296
65	Methodist Episcopal Church	634	633	106,505	609	37,445	64,339
66	Union American Methodist Episcopal Church (Colored)	15	15	538	15	220	318
67	African Methodist Episcopal Church	69	69	5,971	69	1,891	4,080
68	African Union Methodist Protestant Church	12	12	1,575	12	583	992
69	African Methodist Episcopal Zion Church	35	34	2,180	34	702	1,478
70	Methodist Protestant Church	50	50	5,248	49	1,859	2,939
71	Congregational Methodist Church	5	5	403	4	98	120
72	Free Methodist Church of North America	6	6	91	5	11	30
73	Moravian bodies	4	4	375	4	151	224
74	Moravian Church (Unitas Fratrum)	4	4	375	4	151	224
75	Nonsectarian Churches of Bible Faith	2	2	16	2	8	8
76	Pentecostal Church of the Nazarene	1	1	20	1	11	9
77	Polish National Church of America	3	3	800	3	460	340
78	Presbyterian bodies	355	355	79,912	334	26,218	46,845
79	Presbyterian Church in the United States of America	346	346	78,490	325	25,624	46,017
80	Cumberland Presbyterian Church	2	2	79	2	33	46
81	United Presbyterian Church of North America	7	7	1,343	7	561	782
82	Protestant Episcopal Church	271	257	53,921	217	15,279	26,774
83	Reformed bodies	162	162	37,298	153	13,878	21,309
84	Reformed Church in America	133	133	32,290	126	11,336	19,008
85	Reformed Church in the United States	6	6	1,094	5	486	548
86	Christian Reformed Church	17	17	2,392	16	1,018	1,269
87	Hungarian Reformed Church in America	6	6	1,522	6	1,038	484
88	Reformed Episcopal Church	3	2	212	2	60	152
89	Roman Catholic Church	316	316	441,432	262	162,098	170,393
90	Salvationists	21	20	640	20	312	328
91	Salvation Army	20	19	620	19	302	318
92	American Salvation Army	1	1	20	1	10	10
93	Spiritualists	5	5	209	5	53	156
94	Unitarians	9	9	934	8	323	576
95	Universalists	5	4	910	4	368	542
96	Volunteers of America	3	3	273	3	149	124

NEW MEXICO.

1	All denominations	625	624	137,009	536	57,012	59,746
2	Adventist bodies	6	6	218	6	82	136
3	Seventh-day Adventist Denomination	6	6	218	6	82	136
4	Baptist bodies	62	62	2,403	54	802	1,134
5	Baptists	62	62	2,403	54	802	1,134
6	Northern Baptist Convention	57	57	2,331	49	776	1,088
7	Southern Baptist Convention	4	4	61	4	22	39
8	National Baptist Convention (Colored)	1	1	11	1	4	7
9	Brethren (Plymouth)	1	1	6	1	2	4
10	Brethren (Plymouth)—I	1	1	6	1	2	4
11	Christadelphians	1	1	10	1	4	6
12	Congregationalists	5	5	270	5	101	169
13	Disciples or Christians	16	16	1,092	16	427	665
14	Disciples of Christ	11	11	963	11	377	586
15	Churches of Christ	5	5	129	5	50	79
16	Independent churches	1	1	30	1	10	20
17	Jewish congregations	3	3	[1]120	....	....	....
18	Latter-day Saints	6	6	738	6	345	393
19	Church of Jesus Christ of Latter-day Saints	5	5	684	5	328	356
20	Reorganized Church of Jesus Christ of Latter-day Saints	1	1	54	1	17	37
21	Lutheran bodies	3	3	100	3	32	68
22	General Synod of the Evangelical Lutheran Church in the United States of America	2	2	59	2	15	44
23	Evangelical Lutheran Joint Synod of Ohio and Other States	1	1	41	1	17	24

[1] Heads of families only.

DEBT ON CHURCH PROPERTY, PARSONAGES, AND SUNDAY SCHOOLS, BY DENOMINATIONS (IN DETAIL), FOR TERRITORY: 1906—Continued.

NEW JERSEY—Continued.

PLACES OF WORSHIP.					VALUE OF CHURCH PROPERTY.		DEBT ON CHURCH PROPERTY.		PARSONAGES.		SUNDAY SCHOOLS CONDUCTED BY CHURCH ORGANIZATIONS.				
Number of organizations reporting—		Number of church edifices reported.	Seating capacity of church edifices.		Number of organizations reporting.	Value reported.	Number of organizations reporting.	Amount of debt reported.	Number of organizations reporting.	Value of parsonages reported.	Number of organizations reporting.	Number of Sunday schools reported.	Number of officers and teachers.	Number of scholars.	
Church edifices.	Halls, etc.		Number of organizations reporting.	Seating capacity reported.											
798	21	820	785	273,549	800	$9,126,570	301	$907,614	430	$1,495,550	798	851	14,768	117,432	64
620	11	641	608	221,592	622	8,191,195	202	739,630	365	1,371,100	617	669	12,835	101,573	65
10	5	10	10	2,100	10	13,800	7	2,850			14	14	64	276	66
68	1	68	68	20,042	68	371,300	31	62,214	34	52,450	66	66	610	4,601	67
12		12	12	3,750	12	28,800	12	5,270	1	800	12	12	121	1,628	68
29	4	29	28	8,775	30	136,000	19	27,023	5	9,800	33	33	252	1,903	69
50		50	50	15,490	49	355,275	23	67,127	24	59,900	49	50	821	6,979	70
5		6	5	950	5	15,200	4	3,000			5	5	48	362	71
4		4	4	850	4	15,000	3	500	1	1,500	2	2	17	110	72
4		4	4	1,150	4	27,500	1	850	4	7,300	4	4	55	421	73
4		4	4	1,150	4	27,500	1	850	4	7,300	4	4	55	421	74
	2														75
1		1	1	200	1	1,000	1	250			1	1	9	60	76
3		3	3	1,000	3	27,000	3	11,460			1	1	1	30	77
353	1	452	353	168,471	352	10,104,506	99	578,392	228	1,221,750	353	425	8,235	73,243	78
344	1	443	344	164,796	343	9,986,506	95	566,542	227	1,219,950	344	414	8,037	71,139	79
2		2	2	325	2	3,500	1	350	1	1,800	2	2	13	55	80
7		7	7	3,350	7	114,500	3	11,500			7	9	185	2,049	81
257	9	312	256	78,036	257	6,272,314	59	280,275	112	842,300	239	263	3,244	30,759	82
160	2	202	159	82,178	160	3,406,750	61	272,300	121	586,300	151	192	3,663	34,001	83
133		173	132	71,205	133	3,094,750	47	200,050	101	518,100	130	171	3,339	30,964	84
6		8	6	1,950	6	46,000	3	3,500	5	10,200	5	5	70	451	85
16	1	16	16	7,055	16	219,500	7	47,500	14	53,000	15	15	253	2,548	86
5	1	5	5	1,968	5	46,500	4	21,250	1	5,000	1	1	1	38	87
3		3	3	1,125	3	52,000			1	4,000	3	3	23	233	88
301	10	336	295	155,458	298	11,925,589	203	3,396,771	171	1,497,950	250	283	2,137	57,130	89
3	18	3	3	1,030	20	42,175	7	17,261			18	18	92	553	90
3	17	3	3	1,030	20	42,175	,	17,261			18	18	92	553	91
	1														92
	4										1	1	3	35	93
9		10	8	2,020	9	102,000	3	2,250			7	7	75	379	94
5		5	5	1,800	5	174,000	2	8,600	1	3,000	4	4	42	463	95
1	2	1	1	300	1	22,500	1	21,473				2	13	118	96

NEW MEXICO.

470	56	522	451	129,745	466	$956,605	54	$53,535	124	$186,770	323	364	1,716	20,050	1
2	3	2	2	500	4	2,500					6	8	38	223	2
2	3	2	2	500	4	2,500					6	8	38	223	3
28	20	29	27	6,175	31	67,350	13	6,939	9	9,350	37	40	248	2,145	4
28	20	29	27	6,175	31	67,350	13	6,939	9	9,350	37	40	248	2,145	5
27	16	28	26	6,075	30	66,550	13	6,939	9	9,350	36	39	246	2,136	6
	4														7
1		1	1	100	1	800					1	1	2	9	8
	1										1	1	4	35	9
	1										1	1	4	35	10
															11
4	1	4	4	940	5	20,150	1	1,000			4	6	29	235	12
5	5	5	5	1,725	8	42,900	2	2,500	2	1,200	9	9	65	654	13
5	1	5	5	1,725	8	42,900	2	2,500	2	1,200	8	8	63	624	14
	4										1	1	2	30	15
1		1	1	150	1	4,000									16
1		1	1	155	1	5,000					2	2	4	45	17
4		6	4	1,210	4	7,665	1	1,150			6	7	116	467	18
4		6	4	1,210	4	7,665	1	1,150			5	6	113	450	19
											1	1	3	17	20
2		2	2	350	2	4,600	1	1,900	1	1,500	3	3	16	129	21
2		2	2	350	2	4,600	1	1,900	1	1,500	2	2	13	99	22
											1	1	3	30	23

TABLE 3.—ORGANIZATIONS, COMMUNICANTS OR MEMBERS, PLACES OF WORSHIP, VALUE OF CHURCH PROPERTY, EACH STATE AND

NEW MEXICO—Continued.

	DENOMINATION.	Total number of organizations.	COMMUNICANTS OR MEMBERS.				
			Number of organizations reporting.	Total number reported.	Sex.		
					Number of organizations reporting.	Male.	Female.
24	Methodist bodies	115	114	6,560	105	2,353	3,305
25	Methodist Episcopal Church	62	61	3,513	54	1,288	1,597
26	African Methodist Episcopal Church	2	2	83	2	20	63
27	Methodist Episcopal Church, South	48	48	2,882	46	1,024	1,584
28	Colored Methodist Episcopal Church	3	3	82	3	21	61
29	Presbyterian bodies	54	54	2,935	53	1,057	1,628
30	Presbyterian Church in the United States of America	53	53	2,864	52	1,033	1,581
31	Presbyterian Church in the United States	1	1	71	1	24	47
32	Protestant Episcopal Church	18	18	869	15	237	495
33	Reformed bodies	2	2	70	2	34	36
34	Christian Reformed Church	2	2	70	2	34	36
35	Roman Catholic Church	330	330	121,558	266	51,507	51,676
36	Salvationists	2	2	30	2	19	11
37	Salvation Army	2	2	30	2	19	11
	NEW YORK.						
1	All denominations	9,639	9,227	3,591,974	8,067	1,456,047	1,794,061
2	Adventist bodies	126	126	4,022	118	1,234	2,526
3	Advent Christian Church	24	24	1,145	24	433	712
4	Seventh-day Adventist Denomination	99	99	2,614	91	692	1,660
5	Life and Advent Union	2	2	200	2	81	119
6	Churches of God in Christ Jesus	1	1	63	1	28	35
7	Armenian Church	10	10	3,295	10	2,311	984
8	Bahais	2	2	23	2	5	18
9	Baptist bodies	1,093	1,087	176,981	1,003	59,029	107,260
10	Baptists	937	934	165,710	874	55,550	101,382
11	Northern Baptist Convention	924	921	163,947	862	54,935	100,268
12	National Baptist Convention (Colored)	13	13	1,763	12	615	1,114
13	Seventh-day Baptists	27	26	2,926	22	1,055	1,609
14	Free Baptists	109	107	7,910	89	2,322	3,948
15	Primitive Baptists	20	20	435	18	102	321
16	Brethren (Plymouth)	42	42	1,572	42	692	880
17	Brethren (Plymouth)—I	14	14	421	14	180	241
18	Brethren (Plymouth)—II	15	15	728	15	333	395
19	Brethren (Plymouth)—III	7	7	184	7	63	121
20	Brethren (Plymouth)—IV	6	6	239	6	116	123
21	Brethren (River)	2	2	58	2	19	39
22	Brethren in Christ	2	2	58	2	19	39
23	Buddhists	15					
24	Chinese Temples	15					
25	Catholic Apostolic Churches	7	7	2,246	7	901	1,345
26	Catholic Apostolic Church	4	4	1,096	4	426	670
27	New Apostolic Church	3	3	1,150	3	475	675
28	Christadelphians	7	7	132	7	56	76
29	Christian Israelite Church	1	1	24	1	12	12
30	Christians (Christian Connection)	86	86	5,492	75	1,855	3,216
31	Church of Christ, Scientist	51	51	5,671	48	1,406	3,566
32	Church of God and Saints of Christ (Colored)	7	7	102	7	30	72
33	Churches of the New Jerusalem	8	8	578	8	212	366
34	General Convention of the New Jerusalem in the United States of America	7	7	558	7	205	353
35	General Church of the New Jerusalem	1	1	20	1	7	13
36	Communistic societies	2	2	126	2	29	97
37	United Society of Believers (Shakers)	2	2	126	2	29	97
38	Congregationalists	302	302	57,351	298	19,298	36,513

DEBT ON CHURCH PROPERTY, PARSONAGES, AND SUNDAY SCHOOLS, BY DENOMINATIONS (IN DETAIL), FOR TERRITORY: 1906—Continued.

NEW MEXICO—Continued.

PLACES OF WORSHIP.					VALUE OF CHURCH PROPERTY.		DEBT ON CHURCH PROPERTY.		PARSONAGES.		SUNDAY SCHOOLS CONDUCTED BY CHURCH ORGANIZATIONS.				
Number of organizations reporting— Church edifices.	Number of organizations reporting— Halls, etc.	Number of church edifices reported.	Seating capacity of church edifices. Number of organizations reporting.	Seating capacity of church edifices. Seating capacity reported.	Number of organizations reporting.	Value reported.	Number of organizations reporting.	Amount of debt reported.	Number of organizations reporting.	Value of parsonages reported.	Number of organizations reporting.	Number of Sunday schools reported.	Number of officers and teachers.	Number of scholars.	
80	9	81	73	15,866	84	$205,425	15	$8,685	46	$53,365	87	92	624	5,234	24
50	3	51	45	10,434	50	125,785	6	5,725	26	29,050	51	55	348	2,759	25
2	...	2	2	450	2	5,000	1	300	2	1,500	2	2	12	59	26
25	6	25	23	4,720	29	70,890	6	2,520	17	22,515	31	41	247	2,362	27
3	...	3	3	262	3	3,750	2	140	1	300	3	4	17	54	28
44	...	45	44	8,500	45	112,525	5	5,600	15	23,700	50	54	294	2,789	29
43	...	44	43	8,350	44	109,025	5	5,600	14	21,200	49	53	286	2,719	30
1	...	1	1	150	1	3,500	...	...	1	2,500	1	1	8	70	31
13	...	14	13	2,175	16	66,750	1	240	8	19,800	15	15	73	532	32
1	...	1	1	150	1	600	1	100	1	400	1	3	6	250	33
1	...	1	1	150	1	600	1	100	1	400	1	3	6	250	34
284	16	330	273	91,399	262	406,990	12	21,912	42	77,455	100	122	191	7,262	35
1	1	1		450	2	10,150	2	3,509	...	...	2	2	8	50	36
1	1	1	1	450	2	10,150	2	3,509	...	...	2	2	8	50	37

NEW YORK.

8,444	623	9,193	8,190	3,191,267	8,344	$255,166,284	2,289	$28,382,866	4,638	$22,283,225	7,968	8,795	123,319	1,247,051	1
60	43	62	59	9,935	64	130,131	12	29,050	6	12,900	100	106	582	2,750	2
23	1	23	22	4,230	23	57,330	3	13,650	5	10,900	19	20	151	846	3
35	41	37	35	5,205	39	54,301	8	8,900	1	2,000	79	84	418	1,783	4
2	...	2	2	500	2	18,500	1	6,500	...	...	1	1	10	100	5
...	1	...	...	...	...	...	...	...	...	...	1	1	3	21	6
...	9	...	...	...	...	...	...	...	...	...	...	...	...	...	7
...	2	...	...	...	...	...	...	...	...	...	...	...	...	...	8
1,046	19	1,097	1,038	372,883	1,043	19,219,831	231	1,382,206	543	1,237,800	981	1,039	16,174	136,979	9
916	14	964	909	339,033	917	18,729,206	219	1,373,589	484	1,139,800	861	914	14,935	128,425	10
905	12	953	900	335,423	907	18,649,331	215	1,347,601	484	1,139,800	850	903	14,845	127,806	11
11	2	11	9	3,610	10	79,875	4	25,988	...	...	11	11	90	619	12
25	2	26	25	6,850	25	78,050	3	1,067	14	22,400	21	21	304	1,725	13
90	3	92	90	22,000	88	367,675	9	7,550	44	63,600	99	104	935	6,829	14
15	...	15	14	5,000	13	44,900	...	...	1	12,000	...	...	...	...	15
...	42	...	...	...	...	...	...	...	...	...	18	19	87	1,133	16
...	14	...	...	...	...	...	...	...	...	...	9	9	34	278	17
...	15	...	...	...	...	...	...	...	...	...	9	10	53	855	18
...	7	...		...	...	...	...	...	...	...	...	...	...	...	19
...	6	...	...	...	...	...	...	...	...	...	...	...	...	...	20
2	...	2	2	500		3,500	...	...	1	1,000	2	2	20	145	21
2	...	2	2	500		3,500	...	...	1	1,000	2	2	20	145	22
15	...	15	...	...		30,000	...	...	...	...	...	...	...	...	23
15	...	15	...	...		30,000	...	...	...	...	...	...	...	...	24
4		4	3	800	4	98,000	2	6,000	...	...	4	5	14	290	25
3	1	3	2	300	3	92,000	1	2,000	...	...	2	3	7	105	26
1	2	1	1	500	1	6,000	1	4,000	...	...	2	2	7	185	27
...	2	...	...	...	3	175	...	...	...	...	3	3	13	70	28
1	...	1	1	120	1	30,000	...	...	...	...	...	...	...	...	29
82	1	83	82	19,597	81	224,100	3	2,700	44	59,500	71	72	676	4,329	30
24	25	24	24	8,442	33	2,138,775	10	33,281	2	55,000	48	48	305	1,504	31
...	7	...	...	...	...	...	...	...	...	...	...	...	...	...	32
5	3	5	5	1,535		364,500	2	14,900	1	2,500	7	8	41	277	33
5	2	5	5	1,535	5	364,500	2	14,900	1	2,500	7	8	41	277	34
...	1	...	...	...	...	...	...	...	...	...	...	...	...	...	35
...	2	...	...	...		5,300	...	...	...	...	...	...	...	...	36
...	2	...	...	...	2	5,300	...	...	...	...	...	...	...	...	37
296	4	338	293	123,461	295	6,879,503	70	387,191	169	473,550	291	313	6,247	47,882	38

TABLE 3.—ORGANIZATIONS, COMMUNICANTS OR MEMBERS, PLACES OF WORSHIP, VALUE OF CHURCH PROPERTY, EACH STATE AND

NEW YORK—Continued.

	DENOMINATION.	Total number of organizations.	COMMUNICANTS OR MEMBERS. Number of organizations reporting.	Total number reported.	Sex. Number of organizations reporting.	Male.	Female.
39	Disciples or Christians	55	55	9,168	45	2,938	4,847
40	Disciples of Christ	53	53	9,124	43	2,914	4,827
41	Churches of Christ	2	2	44	2	24	20
42	Dunkers or German Baptist Brethren	1	1	100	1	45	55
43	German Baptist Brethren Church (Conservative)	1	1	100	1	45	55
44	Eastern Orthodox Churches	36	36	19,302	8	14,463	2,039
45	Russian Orthodox Church	4	4	1,767	4	1,181	586
46	Syrian Orthodox Church	2	2	2,435	2	1,507	928
47	Greek Orthodox Church	30	30	15,100	2	11,775	525
48	Evangelical bodies	71	70	5,755	68	2,205	3,375
49	Evangelical Association	65	64	5,597	62	2,152	3,270
50	United Evangelical Church	6	6	158	6	53	105
51	Evangelistic associations	1	1	100	1	50	50
52	Apostolic Christian Church	1	1	100	1	50	50
53	Friends	84	84	5,555	80	2,486	2,824
54	Society of Friends (Orthodox)	42	42	3,296	41	1,526	1,705
55	Religious Society of Friends (Hicksite)	40	40	2,165	37	923	1,062
56	Friends (Primitive)	2	2	94	2	37	57
57	German Evangelical Synod of North America	64	64	26,183	49	7,113	9,584
58	Independent churches	86	83	10,029	78	3,269	4,485
59	Jewish congregations	720	378	[1]35,342			
60	Latter-day Saints	5	5	388	5	162	226
61	Church of Jesus Christ of Latter-day Saints	4	4	2 5	4	92	123
62	Reorganized Church of Jesus Christ of Latter-day Saints	1	1	173	1	70	103
63	Lutheran bodies	453	448	124,644	404	43,576	62,822
64	General Synod of the Evangelical Lutheran Church in the United States of America	109	109	20,543	105	7,514	12,414
65	General Council of the Evangelical Lutheran Church in North America	177	174	65,450	152	21,298	31,441
66	Evangelical Lutheran Synodical Conference of America	128	127	32,178	111	11,773	15,675
67	United Norwegian Lutheran Church in America	5	4	695	4	348	347
68	Evangelical Lutheran Joint Synod of Ohio and Other States	2	2	290	2	139	151
69	Lutheran Synod of Buffalo	16	16	2,699	15	1,264	1,395
70	Synod for the Norwegian Evangelical Lutheran Church in America	5	5	1,047	5	435	612
71	Danish Evangelical Lutheran Church in America	3	3	500	2	162	188
72	Immanuel Synod of the Evangelical Lutheran Church of North America	2	2	375	2	150	225
73	Finnish Evangelical Lutheran Church of America, or Suomi Synod	2	2	245	2	115	130
74	United Danish Evangelical Lutheran Church in America	1	1	77	1	38	39
75	Slovak Evangelical Lutheran Synod of America	3	3	545	3	340	205
76	Mennonite bodies	6	6	341	6	170	171
77	Old Amish Mennonite Church	1	1	168	1	90	78
78	Reformed Mennonite Church	3	3	137	3	63	74
79	General Conference of Mennonites of North America	2	2	36	2	17	19
80	Methodist bodies	2,617	2,609	313,689	2,508	108,581	187,721
81	Methodist Episcopal Church	2,199	2,193	291,919	2,108	101,556	175,332
82	Union American Methodist Episcopal Church (Colored)	7	7	318	7	137	181
83	African Methodist Episcopal Church	41	41	4,294	40	1,033	1,661
84	African Union Methodist Protestant Church	3	3	115	3	40	75
85	African Methodist Episcopal Zion Church	76	75	6,149	69	2,015	3,817
86	Methodist Protestant Church	67	67	3,890	66	1,473	2,349
87	Wesleyan Methodist Connection of America	93	93	3,097	89	1,015	1,794
88	Primitive Methodist Church in the United States of America	3	3	298	3	145	153
89	Free Methodist Church of North America	128	127	3,609	123	1,167	2,359
90	Moravian bodies	9	9	1,427	9	510	917
91	Moravian Church (Unitas Fratrum)	9	9	1,427	9	510	917
92	Nonsectarian Churches of Bible Faith	2	2	37	2	17	20
93	Pentecostal Church of the Nazarene	10	10	539	10	157	382
94	Polish National Church of America	1	1	3,500	1	1,700	1,800
95	Presbyterian bodies	937	937	199,923	881	62,431	114,916
96	Presbyterian Church in the United States of America	831	831	186,278	779	57,842	107,039
97	Welsh Calvinistic Methodist Church	19	19	1,837	19	785	1,052
98	United Presbyterian Church of North America	68	68	10,115	64	3,702	5,734
99	Synod of the Reformed Presbyterian Church of North America	16	16	1,446	16	513	933
100	Reformed Presbyterian Church in North America, General Synod	3	3	247	3	89	158
101	Protestant Episcopal Church	843	829	193,890	660	51,518	87,170

[1] Heads of families only.

DEBT ON CHURCH PROPERTY, PARSONAGES, AND SUNDAY SCHOOLS, BY DENOMINATIONS (IN DETAIL), FOR TERRITORY: 1906—Continued.

NEW YORK—Continued.

PLACES OF WORSHIP. Number of organizations reporting— Church edifices.	PLACES OF WORSHIP. Number of organizations reporting— Halls, etc.	PLACES OF WORSHIP. Number of church edifices reported.	PLACES OF WORSHIP. Seating capacity of church edifices. Number of organizations reporting.	PLACES OF WORSHIP. Seating capacity of church edifices. Seating capacity reported.	VALUE OF CHURCH PROPERTY. Number of organizations reporting.	VALUE OF CHURCH PROPERTY. Value reported.	DEBT ON CHURCH PROPERTY. Number of organizations reporting.	DEBT ON CHURCH PROPERTY. Amount of debt reported.	PARSONAGES. Number of organizations reporting.	PARSONAGES. Value of parsonages reported.	SUNDAY SCHOOLS CONDUCTED BY CHURCH ORGANIZATIONS. Number of organizations reporting.	SUNDAY SCHOOLS CONDUCTED BY CHURCH ORGANIZATIONS. Number of Sunday schools reported.	SUNDAY SCHOOLS CONDUCTED BY CHURCH ORGANIZATIONS. Number of officers and teachers.	SUNDAY SCHOOLS CONDUCTED BY CHURCH ORGANIZATIONS. Number of scholars.	
54		55	53	16,980	54	$777,050	18	$98,480	13	$29,400	51	62	827	6,772	39
52		53	51	16,680	52	775,250	18	98,480	13	29,400	49	60	823	6,748	40
2		2	2	300	2	1,800					2	2	4	24	41
1		1	1	700	1	12,000			1	3,000	1	2	16	300	42
1		1	1	700	1	12,000			1	3,000	1	2	16	300	43
6	30	7	6	5,575	7	255,320	4	64,969	3	34,700	1	1	1	50	44
4		5	4	2,475	4	160,120	3	14,969	3	34,700					45
1	1	1	1	600	2	30,200					1	1	1	50	46
1	29	1	1	2,500	1	65,000	1	50,000							47
67	2	71	66	17,456	67	552,400	15	62,150	37	92,450	65	70	1,008	6,752	48
62	1	66	61	16,256	62	543,900	15	62,150	37	92,450	61	66	978	6,606	49
5	1	5	5	1,200	5	8,500					4	4	30	146	50
1		1	1	300	1	3,000					1	1	2	50	51
1		1	1	300	1	3,000					1	1	2	50	52
83	1	83	83	20,125	83	451,750	1	2,300	10	19,200	44	50	366	2,656	53
41	1	41	41	8,385	41	192,850	1	2,300	10	19,200	34	40	330	2,442	54
40		40	40	11,290	40	256,900					10	10	36	214	55
2		2	2	450	2	2,000									56
63	1	73	63	28,535	63	1,077,600	30	183,728	27	108,650	56	61	1,094	10,974	57
71	13	73	71	21,809	72	1,594,860	23	204,520	8	30,400	75	81	885	8,476	58
174	158	184	171	96,041	184	9,711,100	111	1,825,060	15	77,100	120	138	579	15,277	59
1	4	1	1	200	1	12,000	1	8,000			3	3	15	93	60
	4										2	2	9	43	61
1		1	1	200	1	12,000	1	8,000			1	1	6	50	62
415	23	449	408	156,867	419	9,613,158	220	1,625,326	226	890,028	390	470	7,383	71,097	63
109		111	109	38,471	109	2,019,150	39	275,450	65	237,600	106	112	1,845	13,698	64
161	9	174	156	69,885	163	4,957,458	102	946,487	87	409,228	166	205	4,162	40,805	65
110	10	126	108	38,972	113	2,377,350	61	330,239	61	207,400	92	119	1,090	14,091	66
5		7	5	1,990	5	81,500	4	33,500	1	4,000	4	8	110	794	67
2		2	2	450	2	14,000	2	6,450	1	3,000	2	2	10	101	68
16		17	16	3,899	15	63,200	3	1,200	8	18,300	7	7	35	383	69
5		5	5	1,200	5	53,000	5	22,000	1	7,000	5	8	83	798	70
2	1	2	2	300	2	16,000	1	1,000	1	2,000	3	3	15	167	71
2		2	2	900	2	7,000			1	1,500	2	2	16	110	72
1	1	1	1	200	1	4,000	1	500			2	3	9	80	73
1		1	1	250	1	14,000	1	7,000			1	1	8	70	74
1	2	1	1	350	1	6,500	1	1,500							75
5	1	5	5	895	5	4,000					1	1	6	75	76
	1														77
3		3	3	560	3	2,200									78
2		2	2	335	2	1,800					1	1	6	75	79
2,528	63	2,582	2,489	759,771	2,532	31,291,348	438	1,862,559	1,491	4,284,900	2,419	2,531	37,570	276,257	80
2,148	38	2,194	2,110	663,697	2,150	29,427,603	355	1,638,751	1,293	3,968,150	2,068	2,162	34,558	257,072	81
6		6	6	1,600	6	42,500	4	16,050			7	7	46	276	82
35	5	35	35	12,061	36	355,300	26	65,231	13	23,700	38	39	350	2,879	83
3		3	3	1,100	3	10,000	2	1,100	1	1,000	3	3	13	116	84
71	3	74	70	21,716	71	736,096	29	91,748	29	67,350	72	72	590	4,258	85
61	6	61	61	14,545	61	228,450	9	16,584	39	59,500	61	68	690	3,850	86
82	5	86	82	18,255	84	175,200	4	3,945	41	42,750	74	80	549	3,445	87
3		3	3	1,200	3	47,500	3	17,200	3	11,500	3	3	45	425	88
119	6	120	119	25,597	118	268,700	6	11,950	72	110,950	93	97	729	3,936	89
8	1	9	8	3,630	8	227,000	2	9,900	5	49,000	9	10	128	956	90
8	1	9	8	3,630	8	227,000	2	9,900	5	49,000	9	10	128	956	91
	2										1	1	5	30	92
7	3	7	6	2,000	8	36,550	5	16,804	1	4,000	8	8	83	483	93
1		1	1	2,600	1	140,000	1	75,000	1	14,000					94
919	7	1,073	917	412,978	918	31,716,768	192	1,638,883	596	2,584,383	899	1,003	18,326	163,708	95
814	7	959	812	373,864	812	29,956,768	172	1,558,133	544	2,452,383	802	901	17,052	152,915	96
19		20	19	5,445	19	130,400	3	4,000	5	14,000	13	14	155	1,003	97
67		75	67	26,619	68	1,212,200	12	57,550	41	109,900	67	71	959	8,584	98
16		16	16	5,400	16	336,000	4	14,200	5	7,100	15	15	149	1,146	99
3		3	3	1,650	3	81,400	1	5,000	1	1,000	2	2	11	60	100
802	16	994	794	282,854	771	39,234,723	160	1,631,927	480	3,573,660	733	810	10,087	97,557	101

TABLE 3.—ORGANIZATIONS, COMMUNICANTS OR MEMBERS, PLACES OF WORSHIP, VALUE OF CHURCH PROPERTY, EACH STATE AND

NEW YORK—Continued.

	DENOMINATION.	Total number of organizations.	COMMUNICANTS OR MEMBERS.				
			Number of organizations reporting.	Total number reported.	Sex.		
					Number of organizations reporting.	Male.	Female.
102	Reformed bodies	325	323	69,828	306	23,377	40,599
103	Reformed Church in America	299	297	63,350	282	20,694	37,124
104	Reformed Church in the United States	18	18	5,700	18	2,446	3,254
105	Christian Reformed Church	6	6	298	5	117	161
106	Hungarian Reformed Church in America	2	2	480	1	120	60
107	Reformed Catholic Church	1	1	200	1	100	100
108	Reformed Episcopal Church	7	7	890	7	298	592
109	Roman Catholic Church	1,208	1,205	2,285,768	1,027	1,033,935	1,098,834
110	Salvationists	88	82	3,123	82	1,487	1,636
111	Salvation Army	86	80	3,093	80	1,470	1,623
112	American Salvation Army	2	2	30	2	17	13
113	Society for Ethical Culture	2	2	1,265	2	856	409
114	Spiritualists	32	32	4,489	32	1,914	2,575
115	Swedish Evangelical bodies	4	4	894	4	407	487
116	Swedish Evangelical Mission Covenant of America	4	4	894	4	407	487
117	Temple Society in the United States (Friends of the Temple)	2	2	226	2	88	138
118	Theosophical societies	8	8	284	8	104	180
119	Theosophical Society in America	2	2	28	2	12	16
120	Theosophical Society, New York	1	1	90	1	37	53
121	Theosophical Society, American Section	5	5	166	5	55	111
122	Unitarians	24	21	4,656	17	1,454	1,947
123	United Brethren bodies	37	37	1,507	34	500	888
124	Church of the United Brethren in Christ	34	34	1,484	31	491	874
125	Church of the United Brethren in Christ (Old Constitution)	3	3	23	3	9	14
126	Universalists	131	127	10,761	91	2,800	5,076
127	Vedanta Society	1	1	200	1	100	100
128	Volunteers of America	7	7	298	7	152	146

NORTH CAROLINA.

	DENOMINATION.	Total number of organizations.	Number of organizations reporting.	Total number reported.	Number of organizations reporting (sex).	Male.	Female.
1	All denominations	8,592	8,554	824,385	7,915	311,655	463,395
2	Adventist bodies	36	36	1,652	35	752	880
3	Advent Christian Church	23	23	1,388	22	646	722
4	Seventh-day Adventist Denomination	13	13	264	13	106	158
5	Baptist bodies	3,755	3,740	401,043	3,496	153,053	233,661
6	Baptists	3,000	2,992	355,987	2,942	139,422	211,586
7	Southern Baptist Convention	1,837	1,837	202,798	1,802	80,264	119,061
8	National Baptist Convention (Colored)	1,163	1,155	153,189	1,140	59,158	92,525
9	Seventh-day Baptists	1	1	17	1	10	7
10	Freewill Baptists	284	284	22,518	271	8,641	13,196
11	Primitive Baptists	275	272	10,207	222	2,720	5,793
12	Colored Primitive Baptists in America	62	62	2,215	15	154	432
13	United American Freewill Baptists (Colored)	133	129	10,099	45	2,106	2,647
14	Brethren (Plymouth)	6	6	36	6	19	17
15	Brethren (Plymouth)—I	6	6	36	6	19	17
16	Christians (Christian Connection)	192	190	15,909	185	6,673	8,875
17	Church of Christ, Scientist	4	4	110	4	30	80
18	Church of God and Saints of Christ (Colored)	2	2	32	2	9	23
19	Congregationalists	54	54	2,699	54	1,040	1,659
20	Disciples or Christians	130	129	13,637	127	4,850	8,684
21	Disciples of Christ	123	122	13,342	120	4,724	8,515
22	Churches of Christ	7	7	295	7	126	169
23	Dunkers or German Baptist Brethren	15	15	761	15	299	462
24	German Baptist Brethren Church (Conservative)	14	14	744	14	288	456
25	Old Order German Baptist Brethren	1	1	17	1	11	6
26	Eastern Orthodox Churches	3	3	95	.....	.....	.....
27	Greek Orthodox Church	3	3	95	.....	.....	.....

DEBT ON CHURCH PROPERTY, PARSONAGES, AND SUNDAY SCHOOLS, BY DENOMINATIONS (IN DETAIL), FOR TERRITORY: 1906—Continued.

NEW YORK—Continued.

PLACES OF WORSHIP.					VALUE OF CHURCH PROPERTY.		DEBT ON CHURCH PROPERTY.		PARSONAGES.		SUNDAY SCHOOLS CONDUCTED BY CHURCH ORGANIZATIONS.				
Number of organizations reporting— Church edifices.	Number of organizations reporting— Halls, etc.	Number of church edifices reported.	Seating capacity of church edifices. Number of organizations reporting.	Seating capacity of church edifices. Seating capacity reported.	Number of organizations reporting.	Value reported.	Number of organizations reporting.	Amount of debt reported.	Number of organizations reporting.	Value of parsonages reported.	Number of organizations reporting.	Number of Sunday schools reported.	Number of officers and teachers.	Number of scholars.	
321	3	396	320	150,432	317	$11,533,577	88	$524,535	232	$1,169,150	311	380	6,163	64,222	102
296	2	369	295	140,641	293	11,092,700	70	398,635	217	1,118,650	290	356	5,760	59,965	103
18		18	18	7,656	17	363,877	14	89,600	12	42,000	18	20	379	4,023	104
6		8	6	1,535	6	42,000	3	11,300	2	5,500	3	4	24	234	105
1	1	1	1	600	1	35,000	1	25,000	1	3,000					106
1		1	1	200	1	60,000	1	15,000							107
6	1	6	6	2,200	5	424,500	2	17,900			7	7	107	1,020	108
1,151	31	1,259	1,006	602,182	1,007	81,934,633	568	16,138,799	720	7,263,654	1,012	1,250	12,602	312,195	109
29	57	29	26	10,740	84	970,447	44	331,279	1	1,000	76	76	360	2,264	110
29	55	29	26	10,740	84	970,447	44	331,279	1	1,000	76	76	360	2,264	111
	2														112
	2										2	2	17	157	113
7	23	9	7	6,500	11	147,905	2	15,100			3	3	23	170	114
4		4	4	2,800	4	51,000	3	6,700	1	5,000	4	4	69	603	115
4		4	4	2,800	4	51,000	3	6,700	1	5,000	4	4	69	603	116
2		2	2	630	2	9,000					2		13	93	117
	8										1	1	5	45	118
	2														119
	1										1	1	5	45	120
	5														121
23		26	23	10,624	23	1,757,700	9	74,850	7	46,800	23	24	246	1,748	122
32	2	33	32	6,920	32	50,450	5	1,890	14	19,000	29	30	258	1,752	123
31	2	32	31	6,820	31	49,950	5	1,890	14	19,000	29	30	258	1,752	124
1		1	1	100	1	500									125
125	3	125	110	31,000	127	2,337,630	15	82,870	33	141,500	94	96	898	5,689	126
1		1	1	300	1	40,000									127
1	6	2	1	150	1	15,000	1	9,000			2	2	18	171	128

NORTH CAROLINA.

PLACES OF WORSHIP.					VALUE OF CHURCH PROPERTY.		DEBT ON CHURCH PROPERTY.		PARSONAGES.		SUNDAY SCHOOLS CONDUCTED BY CHURCH ORGANIZATIONS.				
Number of organizations reporting— Church edifices.	Number of organizations reporting— Halls, etc.	Number of church edifices reported.	Seating capacity of church edifices. Number of organizations reporting.	Seating capacity of church edifices. Seating capacity reported.	Number of organizations reporting.	Value reported.	Number of organizations reporting.	Amount of debt reported.	Number of organizations reporting.	Value of parsonages reported.	Number of organizations reporting.	Number of Sunday schools reported.	Number of officers and teachers.	Number of scholars.	
8,004	229	8,188	7,832	2,715,567	8,068	$14,053,505	891	$498,043	1,028	$1,681,622	6,969	7,293	53,132	487,261	1
27	4	27	27	9,950	26	23,350					22	23	105	576	2
23		23	23	9,375	22	19,950					10	10	45	357	3
4	4	4	4	575	4	3,400					12	13	60	219	4
3,443	96	3,497	3,399	1,229,598	3,475	4,323,116	279	160,681	116	210,375	2,829	2,971	20,490	202,249	5
2,882	79	2,928	2,846	1,041,777	2,896	3,917,266	256	158,341	111	208,125	2,670	2,812	19,506	193,278	6
1,752	62	1,797	1,744	631,331	1,760	2,701,104	110	119,815	89	186,250	1,569	1,667	12,037	125,795	7
1,130	17	1,131	1,102	410,446	1,136	1,216,162	146	38,526	22	21,875	1,101	1,145	7,469	67,483	8
1		1	1	150	1	200					1	1	1	14	9
271	9	272	266	84,792	271	155,510	19	1,601	5	2,250	128	128	707	6,805	10
229	6	235	227	87,829	226	200,075	3	720							11
15	4	15	14	4,775	36	26,815	1	19			13	13	195	1,035	12
45		46	45	10,275	45	23,250					17	17	81	1,117	13
	6														14
	6														15
186	3	188	184	62,449	189	194,315	23	10,850		3,600	170	172	1,029	9,465	16
2	2	2	2	268	3	34,000	1	2,000			4	4	11	41	17
	2														18
46	4	47	46	12,050	46	42,361	5	2,715	7	5,575	53	55	273	2,642	19
126	2	128	125	35,145	126	151,605	5	3,210	2	3,500	61	62	477	4,568	20
119	2	121	118	32,745	119	146,455	5	3,210	2	3,500	57	58	452	4,348	21
7		7	7	2,400	7	5,150					4	4	25	220	22
10	3	11	10	4,350	11	5,380					9	10	59	541	23
10	3	11	10	4,350	11	5,380					9	10	59	541	24
															25
	3														26
	3														27

TABLE 3.—ORGANIZATIONS, COMMUNICANTS OR MEMBERS, PLACES OF WORSHIP, VALUE OF CHURCH PROPERTY, EACH STATE AND

NORTH CAROLINA—Continued.

	DENOMINATION.	Total number of organizations.	COMMUNICANTS OR MEMBERS.				
			Number of organizations reporting.	Total number reported.	Sex.		
					Number of organizations reporting.	Male.	Female.
28	Evangelistic associations	5	5	265	5	97	168
29	Lumber River Mission	5	5	265	5	97	168
30	Friends	63	61	6,752	58	3,041	3,599
31	Society of Friends (Orthodox)	57	55	6,425	52	2,882	3,431
32	Orthodox Conservative Friends (Wilburite)	6	6	327	6	159	168
33	Independent churches	44	44	2,096	34	583	1,076
34	International Apostolic Holiness Union	9	9	339	8	111	151
35	Jewish congregations	10	9	[1]234			
36	Latter-day Saints	1	1	976			
37	Church of Jesus Christ of Latter-day Saints	1	1	976			
38	Lutheran bodies	179	179	17,740	161	6,975	8,332
39	United Synod of the Evangelical Lutheran Church in the South	135	135	14,881	121	5,999	6,991
40	Evangelical Lutheran Synodical Conference of America	32	32	1,966	28	581	843
41	Evangelical Lutheran Joint Synod of Ohio and Other States	12	12	893	12	395	498
42	Methodist bodies	3,095	3,081	277,282	2,830	103,681	152,251
43	Methodist Episcopal Church	358	357	20,805	325	7,639	11,533
44	Union American Methodist Episcopal Church (Colored)	1	1	20	1	9	11
45	African Methodist Episcopal Church	235	232	16,797	219	5,724	10,186
46	African Methodist Episcopal Zion Church	673	673	66,356	657	25,040	40,015
47	Methodist Protestant Church	227	227	18,271	211	7,138	9,497
48	Wesleyan Methodist Connection of America	24	24	886	24	346	540
49	Methodist Episcopal Church, South	1,532	1,522	151,808	1,348	56,847	79,068
50	Colored Methodist Episcopal Church	39	39	2,209	39	876	1,333
51	Reformed Zion Union Apostolic Church (Colored)	6	6	130	6	62	68
52	Moravian bodies	22	22	3,478	11	573	884
53	Moravian Church (Unitas Fratrum)	22	22	3,478	11	573	884
54	Nonsectarian Churches of Bible Faith	6	6	156	6	75	81
55	Presbyterian bodies	600	599	55,837	540	21,833	30,355
56	Presbyterian Church in the United States of America	149	149	10,696	131	3,627	5,919
57	Cumberland Presbyterian Church	1	1	110	1	45	65
58	United Presbyterian Church of North America	1	1	84	1	40	44
59	Presbyterian Church in the United States	424	423	41,322	382	15,955	22,368
60	Associate Reformed Synod of the South	25	25	3,625	25	1,666	1,959
61	Protestant Episcopal Church	258	256	13,890	239	4,119	7,416
62	Reformed bodies	55	55	4,718	51	1,988	2,447
63	Reformed Church in the United States	55	55	4,718	51	1,988	2,447
64	Roman Catholic Church	31	31	3,981	31	2,007	1,974
65	Salvationists	4	4	172	4	92	80
66	Salvation Army	4	4	172		92	80
67	Unitarians	4	4	122	4	68	54
68	Universalists	9	9	373	9	187	186

NORTH DAKOTA.

	DENOMINATION.	Total number of organizations.	Number of organizations reporting.	Total number reported.	Number of organizations reporting.	Male.	Female.
1	All denominations	1,993	1,961	159,053	1,783	71,326	76,480
2	Adventist bodies	27	27	868	26	388	439
3	Seventh-day Adventist Denomination	27	27	868	26	388	439
4	Baptist bodies	72	72	4,596	69	1,966	2,526
	Baptists:						
5	Northern Baptist Convention	72	72	4,596	69	1,966	2,526
6	Brethren (Plymouth)	5	5	38	5	19	19
7	Brethren (Plymouth)—II	3	3	22	3	11	11
8	Brethren (Plymouth)—III	1	1	4	1	2	2
9	Brethren (Plymouth)—IV	1	1	12	1	6	6
10	Christians (Christian Connection)	5	5	137	5	63	74
11	Church of Christ, Scientist	3	3	139	3	39	100
12	Congregationalists	155	155	5,290	155	2,072	3,218

[1] Heads of families only.

DEBT ON CHURCH PROPERTY, PARSONAGES, AND SUNDAY SCHOOLS, BY DENOMINATIONS (IN DETAIL), FOR TERRITORY: 1906—Continued.

NORTH CAROLINA—Continued.

PLACES OF WORSHIP. Number of organizations reporting—Church edifices.	PLACES OF WORSHIP. Number of organizations reporting—Halls, etc.	PLACES OF WORSHIP. Number of church edifices reported.	PLACES OF WORSHIP. Seating capacity of church edifices. Number of organizations reporting.	PLACES OF WORSHIP. Seating capacity of church edifices. Seating capacity reported.	VALUE OF CHURCH PROPERTY. Number of organizations reporting.	VALUE OF CHURCH PROPERTY. Value reported.	DEBT ON CHURCH PROPERTY. Number of organizations reporting.	DEBT ON CHURCH PROPERTY. Amount of debt reported.	PARSONAGES. Number of organizations reporting.	PARSONAGES. Value of parsonages reported.	SUNDAY SCHOOLS CONDUCTED BY CHURCH ORGANIZATIONS. Number of organizations reporting.	SUNDAY SCHOOLS CONDUCTED BY CHURCH ORGANIZATIONS. Number of Sunday schools reported.	SUNDAY SCHOOLS CONDUCTED BY CHURCH ORGANIZATIONS. Number of officers and teachers.	SUNDAY SCHOOLS CONDUCTED BY CHURCH ORGANIZATIONS. Number of scholars.	
5	......	5	5	2,600	5	$3,000	......	......	......	......	5	5	28	256	28
5	......	5	5	2,600	5	3,000	......	......	......	......	5	5	28	256	29
63	......	63	62	26,925	63	90,525	3	$4,700	1	$300	57	62	398	4,084	30
57	......	57	56	25,125	57	84,425	3	4,700	1	300	52	57	372	3,934	31
6	......	6	6	1,800	6	6,100	......	......	......	......	5	5	26	150	32
39	4	39	34	12,164	40	28,358	14	5,837	1	1,000	35	36	193	1,510	33
8	1	8	8	4,850	8	10,900	4	1,800	......	......	8	8	51	434	34
7	2	8	7	2,050	9	62,000	2	3,300	3	11,500	8	8	25	214	35
1	......	4	1	800	1	1,480	......	......	......	......	......	......	......	......	36
1	......	4	1	800	1	1,480	......	......	......	......	......	......	......	......	37
170	6	173	169	82,180	174	445,525	19	9,119	55	84,750	150	150	1,385	12,357	38
130	4	133	129	50,030	132	400,000	14	8,500	44	75,350	117	117	1,256	10,533	39
28	2	28	28	7,700	30	34,600	4	539	7	5,800	26	26	94	1,348	40
12	......	12	12	4,450	12	10,925	1	80	4	3,600	7	7	35	476	41
2,961	56	2,990	2,850	959,283	2,977	4,889,592	459	183,439	569	740,442	2,751	2,827	22,069	186,083	42
343	7	348	325	94,485	348	320,065	61	18,899	65	40,226	304	316	2,077	16,316	43
......	1	......	......	......	......	......	......	......	......	......	1	1	3	20	44
224	7	226	221	69,930	227	385,190	97	23,260	42	28,200	225	229	1,680	9,903	45
650	8	656	645	223,915	654	941,234	162	36,655	88	63,732	652	663	6,405	40,589	46
224	2	227	222	83,410	223	254,710	14	2,860	35	44,175	180	181	1,139	11,197	47
19	1	19	19	6,800	20	26,800	5	1,174	......	......	20	20	124	921	48
1,460	29	1,471	1,377	409,168	1,461	2,921,779	112	99,178	334	562,659	1,330	1,378	10,417	105,457	49
37	......	39	37	10,575	38	37,414	8	1,413	5	1,450	38	38	211	1,535	50
4	1	4	4	1,000	6	2,400	......	......	......	......	1	1	13	145	51
22	......	34	21	9,150	22	126,700	......	......	10	22,250	19	28	267	3,239	52
22	......	34	21	9,150	22	126,700	......	......	10	22,250	19	28	267	3,239	53
......	5	......	......	......	......	......	......	......	......	......	......	......	......	......	54
555	14	602	550	201,596	558	2,093,057	51	78,284	145	321,280	507	567	4,672	41,409	55
133	5	143	133	43,060	133	247,577	19	3,799	21	20,930	145	151	1,211	10,973	56
1	......	2	1	1,500	1	10,000	......	......	......	......	1	1	8	136	57
1	......	1	1	300	1	2,000	......	......	1	600	1	1	14	520	58
397	8	431	393	147,336	400	1,721,180	29	71,945	115	275,050	336	390	3,193	27,276	59
23	1	25	22	9,400	23	112,300	3	2,540	8	24,700	24	24	246	2,504	60
240	10	261	239	51,821	241	987,925	12	13,758	80	191,750	194	210	1,120	11,068	61
54	......	54	54	18,625	54	154,866	5	5,035	21	31,700	48	48	354	5,273	62
54	......	54	54	18,625	54	154,866	5	5,035	21	31,700	48	48	354	5,273	63
27	......	35	27	6,738	23	375,360	7	13,200	13	52,700	29	37	87	969	64
......	4	......	......	......	4	730	1	40	......	......	4	4	14	103	65
......	4	......	......	......	4	730	1	40	......	......	4	4	14	103	66
4	......	4	4	1,050	4	3,400	......	......	1	900	2	2	11	50	67
8	......	8	8	1,925	9	5,960	1	75	......	......	4	4	14	130	68

NORTH DAKOTA.

1,274	355	1,325	1,243	262,251	1,313	$4,576,157	390	$463,890	500	$957,814	1,332	1,511	7,407	61,199	1
8	8	8	8	855	8	9,700	1	200	......	......	25	39	168	861	2
8	8	8	8	855	8	9,700	1	200	......	......	25	39	168	861	3
58	4	79	55	12,937	59	190,475	18	12,904	28	44,550	56	93	504	4,487	4
58	4	79	55	12,937	59	190,475	18	12,904	28	44,550	56	93	504	4,487	5
......	5	......	......	......	......	......	......	......	......	......	1	1	1	5	6
......	3	......	......	......	......	......	......	......	......	......	1	1	1	5	7
......	1	......	......	......	......	......	......	......	......	......	......	......	......	......	8
......	1	......	......	......	......	......	......	......	......	......	......	......	......	......	9
2	2	2	2	450	2	3,600	2	700	......	......	3	3	20	85	10
1	2	1	1	275	2	19,500	......	......	......	......	3	3	12	55	11
106	17	108	105	18,281	111	287,747	28	22,975	44	72,900	135	151	893	7,114	12

TABLE 3.—ORGANIZATIONS, COMMUNICANTS OR MEMBERS, PLACES OF WORSHIP, VALUE OF CHURCH PROPERTY, EACH STATE AND

NORTH DAKOTA—Continued.

	DENOMINATION.	Total number of organizations.	COMMUNICANTS OR MEMBERS.				
			Number of organizations reporting.	Total number reported.	Sex.		
					Number of organizations reporting.	Male.	Female.
13	Disciples or Christians	5	5	147	5	44	103
14	Disciples of Christ	5	5	147	5	44	103
15	Dunkers or German Baptist Brethren	18	18	1,354	18	639	715
16	German Baptist Brethren Church (Conservative)	17	17	1,311	17	614	697
17	Old Order German Baptist Brethren	1	1	43	1	25	18
18	Eastern Orthodox Churches	2	2	177	2	100	77
19	Russian Orthodox Church	2	2	177	2	100	77
20	Evangelical bodies	56	56	1,784	56	863	921
21	Evangelical Association	53	53	1,688	53	811	877
22	United Evangelical Church	3	3	96	3	52	44
23	German Evangelical Synod of North America	8	8	1,655	8	767	888
24	Independent churches	7	7	273	6	127	129
25	Jewish congregations	6	1	[1]12	......	......	......
26	Latter-day Saints	6	6	242	6	114	128
27	Reorganized Church of Jesus Christ of Latter-day Saints	6	6	242	6	114	128
28	Lutheran bodies	821	801	59,923	705	25,634	25,347
29	General Council of the Evangelical Lutheran Church in North America	23	21	1,604	8	457	549
30	Evangelical Lutheran Synodical Conference of America	98	95	5,854	94	2,946	2,778
31	United Norwegian Lutheran Church in America	224	224	22,138	196	9,094	9,269
32	Evangelical Lutheran Joint Synod of Ohio and Other States	40	40	2,269	40	1,207	1,062
33	Hauge's Norwegian Evangelical Lutheran Synod	66	60	4,721	41	1,454	1,701
34	Evangelical Lutheran Church in America, Eielsen's Synod	2	2	24	2	14	10
35	Evangelical Lutheran Synod of Iowa and Other States	68	68	3,717	62	1,798	1,798
36	Synod for the Norwegian Evangelical Lutheran Church in America	181	174	11,980	160	5,835	5,391
37	Danish Evangelical Lutheran Church in America	2	2	64	2	34	30
38	Icelandic Evangelical Lutheran Synod in North America	10	10	1,550	3	84	99
39	Norwegian Lutheran Free Church	90	88	4,829	82	2,253	2,165
40	United Danish Evangelical Lutheran Church in America	10	10	692	8	221	251
41	Finnish Evangelical Lutheran National Church	2	2	260	2	115	145
42	Church of the Lutheran Brethren of America (Norwegian)	5	5	221	5	122	99
43	Mennonite bodies	2	2	129	2	66	63
44	Mennonite Church	1	1	34	1	19	15
45	Amish Mennonite Church	1	1	95	1	47	48
46	Methodist bodies	251	247	10,223	230	3,809	5,807
47	Methodist Episcopal Church	237	233	10,033	216	3,730	5,696
48	Free Methodist Church of North America	14	14	190	14	79	111
49	Moravian bodies	6	6	481	6	248	233
50	Moravian Church (Unitas Fratrum)	6		481	6	248	233
51	Nonsectarian Churches of Bible Faith	1	1	2	1	2	......
52	Presbyterian bodies	182	180	6,727	168	2,391	4,148
53	Presbyterian Church in the United States of America	182	180	6,727	168	2,391	4,148
54	Protestant Episcopal Church	88	87	2,227	42	596	1,025
55	Reformed bodies	25	25	1,059	25	538	521
56	Reformed Church in America	3	3	165	3	88	77
57	Reformed Church in the United States	21	21	817	21	413	404
58	Christian Reformed Church	1	1	77	1	37	40
59	Roman Catholic Church	233	233	61,261	231	30,671	29,860
60	Salvationists	8	8	237	8	135	102
61	Salvation Army	8	8	237	8	135	102
62	Unitarians	1	1	72	1	35	37

OHIO.

1	All denominations	9,890	9,807	1,742,873	9,002	640,472	875,713
2	Adventist bodies	109	108	3,291	78	875	1,756
3	Advent Christian Church	21	20	782	12	221	328
4	Seventh-day Adventist Denomination	84	84	2,334	62	591	1,315
5	Churches of God in Christ Jesus	4	4	175	4	63	112

[1] Heads of families only.

DEBT ON CHURCH PROPERTY, PARSONAGES, AND SUNDAY SCHOOLS, BY DENOMINATIONS (IN DETAIL), FOR TERRITORY: 1906—Continued.

NORTH DAKOTA—Continued.

PLACES OF WORSHIP. Number of organizations reporting— Church edifices.	Halls, etc.	Number of church edifices reported.	Seating capacity of church edifices. Number of organizations reporting.	Seating capacity reported.	VALUE OF CHURCH PROPERTY. Number of organizations reporting.	Value reported.	DEBT ON CHURCH PROPERTY. Number of organizations reporting.	Amount of debt reported.	PARSONAGES. Number of organizations reporting.	Value of parsonages reported.	SUNDAY SCHOOLS CONDUCTED BY CHURCH ORGANIZATIONS. Number of organizations reporting.	Number of Sunday schools reported.	Number of officers and teachers.	Number of scholars.	
2	3	2	2	550	2	$2,850	1	$125			1	2	16	189	13
2	3	2	2	550	2	2,850	1	125			1	2	16	189	14
17	1	19	17	5,325	17	35,550	9	2,285			17	29	219	1,251	15
16	1	18	16	5,075	16	34,550	9	2,285			17	29	219	1,251	16
1		1	1	250	1	1,000									17
	2														18
	2														19
35	11	35	35	6,080	36	80,000	12	8,900	16	$22,300	48	48	405	2,108	20
32	11	32	32	5,765	33	75,300	11	6,900	14	19,300	45	45	378	1,944	21
3		3	3	315	3	4,700	1	2,000	2	3,000	3	3	27	164	22
8		11	8	2,475	8	32,150	3	2,950	4	6,750	6	6	37	358	23
5	1	6	5	860	5	6,450	1	200	1	800	5	5	14	122	24
	1										2	2	2	30	25
1	5	1	1	200	1	200					5	5	29	120	26
1	5	1	1	200	1	200					5	5	29	120	27
456	214	463	437	96,917	472	1,236,088	122	62,809	129	226,728	429	477	1,453	12,498	28
14		16	12	3,455	14	53,200	3	2,600	6	15,200	12	15	71	522	29
43	33	44	43	7,413	48	94,525	18	11,215	25	32,273	28	29	33	673	30
150	43	153	146	36,959	148	466,150	28	13,820	31	62,800	157	176	586	5,014	31
22	18	22	22	3,395	21	33,570	11	3,125	6	7,800	19	21	45	480	32
41	9	41	38	8,495	43	104,385	10	4,650	9	14,250	35	43	144	938	33
	2														34
42	18	43	42	7,020	44	70,958	7	2,086	17	23,130	51	51	107	1,362	35
80	55	80	72	17,370	81	270,150	27	19,110	22	47,075	53	61	158	1,382	36
1	1	1	1	100	2	2,600					1	1	1	17	37
10		10	9	1,905	10	19,750	3	598	1	800	9	10	34	356	38
41	33	41	40	8,230	49	100,400	9	3,330	10	19,900	47	51	177	1,177	39
7	2	7	7	1,225	7	13,000	4	1,800	2	3,500	10	11	61	354	40
2		2	2	550	2	2,800					2	2	12	75	41
3		3	3	800	3	4,600	2	475			5	6	24	148	42
1	1	1	1	130	1	1,000					2	2	13	84	43
1		1	1	130	1	1,000					1	1	7	54	44
	1										1	1	6	30	45
179	21	182	175	37,340	181	607,350	54	47,330	109	159,750	205	222	1,800	13,167	46
172	21	175	168	36,175	174	599,400	54	47,330	103	154,500	195	212	1,738	12,836	47
7		7	7	1,165	7	7,950			6	5,250	10	10	62	331	48
4	2	4	4	775	4	11,100			4	5,800	5	5	46	315	49
4	2	4	4	775	4	11,100			4	5,800	5	5	46	315	50
	1														51
126	26	128	125	22,613	128	483,402	30	35,480	66	138,300	154	164	1,207	8,569	52
126	26	128	125	22,613	128	483,402	30	35,480	66	138,300	154	164	1,207	8,569	53
41	7	42	40	5,405	44	138,400	4	8,100	18	45,500	33	33	135	1,015	54
16	7	16	16	2,755	16	20,950	3	1,850	11	17,636	24	41	78	713	55
1	1	1	1	400	1	4,500	1	1,500	1	1,000	3	3	23	163	56
14	6	14	14	2,155	14	13,950	2	350	9	14,336	21	38	55	550	57
1		1	1	200	1	2,500			1	2,300					58
203	10	212	201	47,028	207	1,379,170	96	248,435	70	216,800	166	173	326	7,810	59
4	4	4	4	800	8	23,475	4	8,647			7	7	29	243	60
4	4	4	4	800	8	23,475	4	8,647			7	7	29	243	61
1		1	1	200	1	7,000									62

OHIO.

Church edifices.	Halls, etc.	Number of church edifices reported.	Seating capacity: Number of organizations reporting.	Seating capacity reported.	Value: Number of organizations reporting.	Value reported.	Debt: Number of organizations reporting.	Amount of debt reported.	Parsonages: Number of organizations reporting.	Value of parsonages reported.	Sunday schools: Number of organizations reporting.	Number of Sunday schools reported.	Number of officers and teachers.	Number of scholars.	
9,163	379	9,519	8,991	3,102,819	9,216	$74,670,765	1,382	$5,202,205	2,961	$7,916,108	8,733	9,226	111,122	939,469	1
57	22	60	54	12,705	58	90,450	8	4,653	1	3,000	83	89	539	2,239	2
20		21	20	5,210	20	26,300	2	303			11	11	76	377	3
34	21	35	31	6,945	35	48,650	6	4,350			70	76	444	1,780	4
3	1	4	3	550	3	15,500			1	3,000	2	2	19	82	5

TABLE 3.—ORGANIZATIONS, COMMUNICANTS OR MEMBERS, PLACES OF WORSHIP, VALUE OF CHURCH PROPERTY, EACH STATE AND

OHIO—Continued.

	DENOMINATION.	Total number of organizations.	COMMUNICANTS OR MEMBERS.				
			Number of organizations reporting.	Total number reported.	Sex.		
					Number of organizations reporting.	Male.	Female.
6	Bahais	3	3	87	3	27	60
7	Baptist bodies	827	821	92,112	698	29,871	51,517
8	Baptists	637	634	82,035	572	27,155	47,209
9	Northern Baptist Convention	474	471	64,635	426	21,139	37,432
10	National Baptist Convention (Colored)	163	163	17,400	146	6,016	9,777
11	Seventh-day Baptists	1	1	130	1	58	72
12	Free Baptists	82	82	5,553	49	1,547	2,558
13	Freewill Baptists	30	30	1,425	30	668	737
14	United Baptists	18	17	1,381	....	....	....
15	Primitive Baptists	59	57	1,588	46	423	941
16	Brethren (Plymouth)	14	14	323	14	141	182
17	Brethren (Plymouth)—I	1	1	4	1	3	1
18	Brethren (Plymouth)—II	5	5	218	5	97	121
19	Brethren (Plymouth)—III	4	4	71	4	27	44
20	Brethren (Plymouth)—IV	4	4	30	4	14	16
21	Brethren (River)	13	13	556	13	246	310
22	Brethren in Christ	11	11	517	11	233	284
23	Yorker, or Old Order, Brethren	2	2	39	2	13	26
24	Catholic Apostolic Churches	1	1	100	1	30	70
25	New Apostolic Church	1	1	100	1	30	70
26	Christadelphians	1	1	6	1	2	4
27	Christian Catholic Church in Zion	2	2	320	2	100	220
28	Christian Union	118	117	8,184	110	3,415	4,491
29	Christians (Christian Connection)	260	247	24,706	223	8,625	13,089
30	Church of Christ, Scientist	34	34	2,582	33	739	1,700
31	Churches of God in North America, General Eldership of the	74	70	2,980	70	1,289	1,691
32	Churches of the Living God (Colored)	1	1	15	1	7	8
33	Church of the Living God (Christian Workers for Friendship)	1	1	15	1	7	8
34	Churches of the New Jerusalem	8	8	642	8	204	438
35	General Convention of the New Jerusalem in the United States of America	7	7	593	7	188	405
36	General Church of the New Jerusalem	1	1	49	1	16	33
37	Communistic societies	2	2	46	2	18	28
38	United Society of Believers (Shakers)	2	2	46	2	18	28
39	Congregationalists	253	253	43,555	253	15,341	28,214
40	Disciples or Christians	613	610	88,787	590	33,042	52,686
41	Disciples of Christ	543	540	83,833	520	31,122	49,652
42	Churches of Christ	70	70	4,954	70	1,920	3,034
43	Dunkers or German Baptist Brethren	139	139	12,872	138	5,613	7,119
44	German Baptist Brethren Church (Conservative)	90	90	9,076	89	3,891	5,045
45	Old Order German Baptist Brethren	20	20	1,204	20	682	522
46	The Brethren Church (Progressive Dunkers)	29	29	2,592	29	1,040	1,552
47	Eastern Orthodox Churches	31	31	4,004	6	1,771	623
48	Russian Orthodox Church	3	3	852	3	588	264
49	Servian Orthodox Church	1	1	1,190	1	923	267
50	Syrian Orthodox Church	1	1	152	1	80	72
51	Greek Orthodox Church	26	26	1,810	1	180	20
52	Evangelical bodies	231	231	19,225	224	7,470	11,357
53	Evangelical Association	186	186	14,932	179	5,764	8,770
54	United Evangelical Church	45	45	4,293	45	1,706	2,587
55	Evangelistic associations	18	18	903	17	285	493
56	Metropolitan Church Association	1	1	21	1	8	13
57	Missionary Church Association	8	8	339	7	84	130
58	Apostolic Christian Church	8	8	539	8	189	350
59	Christian Congregation	1	1	4	1	4	....
60	Friends	140	140	14,364	139	6,425	7,439
61	Society of Friends (Orthodox)	107	107	12,394	106	5,542	6,352
62	Religious Society of Friends (Hicksite)	17	17	750	17	341	409
63	Orthodox Conservative Friends (Wilburite)	16	16	1,220	16	542	678
64	German Evangelical Protestant bodies	26	26	15,596	24	5,650	7,846
65	German Evangelical Protestant Ministers' Association	17	17	11,850	16	4,358	6,192
66	German Evangelical Protestant Ministers' Conference	9	9	3,746	8	1,292	1,654

DEBT ON CHURCH PROPERTY, PARSONAGES, AND SUNDAY SCHOOLS, BY DENOMINATIONS (IN DETAIL), FOR TERRITORY: 1906—Continued.

OHIO—Continued.

PLACES OF WORSHIP.					VALUE OF CHURCH PROPERTY.		DEBT ON CHURCH PROPERTY.		PARSONAGES.		SUNDAY SCHOOLS CONDUCTED BY CHURCH ORGANIZATIONS.				
Number of organizations reporting— Church edifices.	Number of organizations reporting— Halls, etc.	Number of church edifices reported.	Seating capacity of church edifices. Number of organizations reporting.	Seating capacity of church edifices. Seating capacity reported.	Number of organizations reporting.	Value reported.	Number of organizations reporting.	Amount of debt reported.	Number of organizations reporting.	Value of parsonages reported.	Number of organizations reporting.	Number of Sunday schools reported.	Number of officers and teachers.	Number of scholars.	
	3														6
738	20	779	726	243,814	743	$4,767,403	110	$213,044	135	$241,675	676	730	8,312	65,672	7
606	14	644	594	206,214	611	4,499,453	100	184,334	118	212,475	575	627	7,414	59,307	8
461	6	497	453	162,898	464	3,904,082	56	125,170	99	192,375	422	471	6,220	50,929	9
145	8	147	141	43,316	147	595,371	44	59,164	19	20,100	153	156	1,194	8,378	10
1		1	1	300	1	3,000			1	2,000	1	1	13	75	11
51		52	51	13,775	51	167,300	6	23,600	16	27,200	74	76	709	5,300	12
23	6	23	23	7,800	23	22,200	2	310			24	24	164	900	13
8		8	8	1,350	8	5,800					2	2	12	90	14
49		51	49	14,375	49	69,650	2	4,800							15
	14										4	6	31	295	16
	1														17
	5										3	5	26	265	18
	4										1	1	5	30	19
	4														20
11	2	11	11	4,050	11	14,950					5	6	65	355	21
11		11	11	4,050	11	14,950					5	6	65	355	22
	2														23
	1														24
	1														25
					1	15									26
	2														27
110	4	110	110	35,951	108	144,500	7	4,510	3	2,200	101	101	992	5,630	28
239	6	241	236	78,449	240	540,625	16	33,395	22	44,100	230	233	2,384	17,213	29
13	15	13	12	4,436	21	268,225	6	29,900			30	30	202	989	30
72	2	74	72	22,025	73	139,675	1	400	6	5,100	61	63	652	4,363	31
	1										1	1	2	9	32
	1										1	1	2	9	33
7	1	7		1,250	6	143,000	2	11,000	2	9,000	8	8	40	304	34
6	1	6	6	1,150	5	140,500	2	11,000	2	9,000	7	7	37	289	35
1		1	1	100	1	2,500					1	1	3	15	36
	2				2	2,000									37
	2				2	2,000									38
252		268	252	97,122	252	3,151,120	47	120,824	107	250,100	228	239	3,897	36,124	39
590	12	600	589	198,490	594	3,165,510	90	188,300	59	126,950	550	563	6,375	58,500	40
530	2	540	529	181,325	532	3,078,060	83	182,825	58	122,950	529	542	6,250	57,230	41
60	10	60	60	17,165	62	87,450	7	5,475	1	4,000	21	21	125	1,330	42
135	3	182	134	65,385	136	374,900	4	2,275	7	11,300	110	148	1,418	9,613	43
88	2	133	87	50,160	88	266,250	3	675	3	3,500	81	119	1,118	7,588	44
20		22	20	7,350	20	[illegible]									45
27	1	27	27	7,875	28	[illegible]	1	1,600	4	7,800	29	29	300	2,025	46
4	27	4	4	1,620	5	54,276	4	10,500	1	4,000	1	1	1	13	47
2	1	2	2	720	3	47,926	3	8,500	1	4,000					48
1		1	1	400	1	6,250	1	2,000			1	1	1	13	49
	1				1	100									50
1	25	1	1	500											51
228	2	229	225	68,330	229	818,575	32	72,734	88	160,800	224	226	3,216	22,547	52
183	2	184	180	53,580	184	654,325	18	37,935	68	118,000	180	181	2,578	17,544	53
45		45	45	14,750	45	164,250	14	34,799	20	42,800	44	45	638	5,003	54
16	1	16	16	3,960	17	33,585	1	150			15	15	113	940	55
1		1	1	150	1	800									56
7	1	7	7	2,050	8	13,035	1	150			8	8	82	535	57
8		8	8	1,760	8	19,750					7	7	31	405	58
															59
139		139	139	39,644	140	339,400	11	10,026	15	22,300	107	113	1,084	6,639	60
106		106	106	28,963	107	270,900	11	10,026	15	22,300	100	106	1,056	6,529	61
17		17	17	6,225	17	32,600					7	7	28	110	62
16		16	16	4,456	16	35,900									63
26		27	26	16,495	26	786,500	18	69,200	21	96,200	25	25	579	5,616	64
17		18	17	11,835	17	604,000	14	54,800	14	68,200	17	17	411	4,260	65
9		9	9	4,660	9	182,500	4	14,400	7	28,000	8	8	168	1,356	66

TABLE 3.—ORGANIZATIONS, COMMUNICANTS OR MEMBERS, PLACES OF WORSHIP, VALUE OF CHURCH PROPERTY, EACH STATE AND

OHIO—Continued.

	DENOMINATION.	Total number of organizations.	COMMUNICANTS OR MEMBERS.				
			Number of organizations reporting.	Total number reported.	Sex.		
					Number of organizations reporting.	Male.	Female.
67	German Evangelical Synod of North America	110	108	35,138	88	13,017	16,775
68	Independent churches	38	38	2,390	36	930	1,352
69	International Apostolic Holiness Union	8	8	412	8	173	239
70	Jewish congregations	76	53	[1] 5,678	.....	.....	.....
71	Latter-day Saints	23	23	1,507	22	538	773
72	Church of Jesus Christ of Latter-day Saints	1	1	196	.....	.....	.....
73	Reorganized Church of Jesus Christ of Latter-day Saints	22	22	1,311	22	538	773
74	Lutheran bodies	666	666	132,439	627	52,892	67,951
75	General Synod of the Evangelical Lutheran Church in the United States of America	192	192	30,317	185	10,667	16,513
76	United Synod of the Evangelical Lutheran Church in the South	1	1	18	1	7	11
77	General Council of the Evangelical Lutheran Church in North America	104	104	18,237	95	6,906	9,291
78	Evangelical Lutheran Synodical Conference of America	78	78	24,129	72	10,661	12,203
79	Evangelical Lutheran Joint Synod of Ohio and Other States	227	227	45,927	212	18,067	22,941
80	Evangelical Lutheran Synod of Iowa and Other States	36	36	8,020	34	3,624	4,181
81	Synod for the Norwegian Evangelical Lutheran Church in America	2	2	100	2	50	50
82	Evangelical Lutheran Synod of Michigan and Other States	5	5	1,896	5	882	1,014
83	Immanuel Synod of the Evangelical Lutheran Church of North America	1	1	175	1	50	125
84	Finnish Evangelical Lutheran Church of America, or Suomi Synod	8	8	1,572	8	727	845
85	Slovak Evangelical Lutheran Synod of America	7	7	1,081	7	728	353
86	Finnish Evangelical Lutheran National Church	5	5	957	5	533	424
87	Mennonite bodies	79	79	9,778	79	4,459	5,319
88	Mennonite Church	20	20	2,365	20	1,045	1,320
89	Amish Mennonite Church	11	11	2,877	11	1,357	1,520
90	Old Amish Mennonite Church	9	9	1,245	9	585	660
91	Reformed Mennonite Church	7	7	477	7	205	272
92	General Conference of Mennonites of North America	9	9	1,526	9	704	822
93	Church of God in Christ (Mennonite)	2	2	72	2	33	39
94	Old (Wisler) Mennonite Church	6	6	353	6	162	191
95	Defenceless Mennonites	3	3	219	3	98	121
96	Mennonite Brethren in Christ	12	12	644	12	270	374
97	Methodist bodies	2,923	2,906	355,444	2,720	125,944	206,717
98	Methodist Episcopal Church	2,409	2,398	317,584	2,230	111,823	184,327
99	African Methodist Episcopal Church	120	119	9,812	112	3,250	5,905
100	African Methodist Episcopal Zion Church	9	9	386	9	135	251
101	Methodist Protestant Church	247	246	23,494	238	9,256	13,738
102	Wesleyan Methodist Connection of America	54	51	2,443	49	875	1,395
103	Colored Methodist Episcopal Church	4	4	211	4	97	114
104	Primitive Methodist Church in the United States of America	3	3	138	2	33	86
105	Free Methodist Church of North America	77	76	1,376	76	475	901
106	Moravian bodies	6	6	1,154	6	454	700
107	Moravian Church (Unitas Fratrum)	6	6	1,154	6	454	700
108	Nonsectarian Churches of Bible Faith	10	10	284	10	158	126
109	Pentecostal Church of the Nazarene	1	1	13	1	4	9
110	Presbyterian bodies	862	862	138,768	799	47,889	80,887
111	Presbyterian Church in the United States of America	656	656	114,772	597	38,459	66,758
112	Cumberland Presbyterian Church	23	23	2,458	22	945	1,488
113	Welsh Calvinistic Methodist Church	24	24	2,223	23	879	1,169
114	United Presbyterian Church of North America	143	143	18,336	141	7,246	10,853
115	Associate Synod of North America (Associate Presbyterian Church)	1	1	16	1	5	11
116	Synod of the Reformed Presbyterian Church of North America	13	13	629	13	230	399
117	Reformed Presbyterian Church in North America, General Synod	2	2	334	2	125	209
118	Protestant Episcopal Church	192	192	32,399	181	10,652	19,224
119	Reformed bodies	316	316	51,328	306	21,477	27,034
120	Reformed Church in America	2	2	214	2	96	118
121	Reformed Church in the United States	310	310	50,732	300	21,205	26,710
122	Christian Reformed Church	4	4	382	4	176	206
123	Reformed Episcopal Church	3	3	557	3	202	355
124	Roman Catholic Church	606	606	557,650	526	209,389	211,775
125	Salvationists	51	47	2,066	47	999	1,067
126	Salvation Army	50	46	2,059	46	995	1,064
127	American Salvation Army	1	1	7	1	4	3
128	Spiritualists	44	44	2,633	44	1,231	1,402
129	Swedish Evangelical bodies	1	1	91	1	41	50
130	Swedish Evangelical Mission Covenant of America	1	1	91	1	41	50

[1] Heads of families only.

DEBT ON CHURCH PROPERTY, PARSONAGES, AND SUNDAY SCHOOLS, BY DENOMINATIONS (IN DETAIL), FOR TERRITORY: 1906—Continued.

OHIO—Continued.

PLACES OF WORSHIP.					VALUE OF CHURCH PROPERTY.		DEBT ON CHURCH PROPERTY.		PARSONAGES.		SUNDAY SCHOOLS CONDUCTED BY CHURCH ORGANIZATIONS.				
Number of organizations reporting—Church edifices.	Number of organizations reporting—Halls, etc.	Number of church edifices reported.	Seating capacity of church edifices: Number of organizations reporting.	Seating capacity of church edifices: Seating capacity reported.	Number of organizations reporting.	Value reported.	Number of organizations reporting.	Amount of debt reported.	Number of organizations reporting.	Value of parsonages reported.	Number of organizations reporting.	Number of Sunday schools reported.	Number of officers and teachers.	Number of scholars.	
109	1	121	109	47,505	107	$1,210,100	27	$115,950	66	$169,675	105	109	1,597	16,175	67
23	12	23	23	5,310	23	67,250	5	6,020	1	2,000	28	28	256	1,816	68
6	1	6	6	2,750	7	14,200	2	375	1	400	8	8	87	566	69
39	8	42	38	24,650	39	1,374,300	22	265,100	2	2,300	33	36	149	3,878	70
10	7	10	10	3,445	13	21,300	4	1,845	1	3,000	17	18	149	660	71
....	....	....	....	....	....	....	....	....	....	....	....	....	....	....	72
10	7	10	10	3,445	13	21,300	4	1,845	1	3,000	17	18	149	660	73
641	19	663	628	222,826	646	5,303,127	137	278,781	298	703,500	588	608	7,169	67,352	74
191	1	195	191	67,995	192	1,888,527	36	92,606	65	145,650	187	189	3,008	26,043	75
1	....	1	1	200	1	750	....	....	....	....	1	1	5	21	76
101	2	102	100	33,890	103	812,930	22	60,870	31	102,300	96	98	1,233	10,797	77
74	1	83	74	29,210	75	762,700	27	49,570	53	129,200	45	47	198	4,120	78
223	3	228	211	75,026	224	1,542,220	37	52,555	119	269,350	208	215	2,266	22,059	79
34	1	36	34	10,615	34	201,000	9	8,180	21	38,400	29	35	220	2,603	80
1	1	1	1	200	1	3,000	1	600	....	....	2	2	4	32	81
5	....	6	5	2,075	5	38,400	2	3,000	4	9,600	5	5	99	768	82
1	....	1	1	350	1	3,000	....	....	1	1,800	1	1	8	55	83
3	5	3	3	950	3	15,000	2	3,400	2	4,900	8	9	72	563	84
2	5	2	2	975	2	22,100	1	8,000	2	2,300	1	1	1	60	85
5	....	5	5	1,340	5	13,500	....	....	....	....	5	5	55	231	86
64	13	65	64	26,965	64	197,425	6	1,210	6	9,800	47	52	723	6,868	87
20	....	21	20	9,090	20	70,325	....	....	1	1,200	16	19	248	2,769	88
11	....	11	11	5,285	11	29,800	....	....	....	....	11	13	212	1,907	89
....	9	....	....	....	....	....	....	....	....	....	....	....	....	....	90
6	1	6	6	1,350	6	6,350	....	....	....	....	....	....	....	....	91
8	1	8	8	4,900	8	63,500	1	740	2	6,000	9	9	150	1,477	92
....	....	....	....	....	....	....	....	....	....	....	....	....	....	....	93
6	....	6	6	1,540	6	11,050	....	....	....	....	....	....	....	....	94
2	1	2	2	650	2	3,500	....	....	....	....	2		20	205	95
11	1	11	11	4,150	11	12,900	5	470	3	2,600	9	9	93	510	96
2,854	48	2,882	2,768	886,779	2,853	15,789,727	286	449,707	983	2,188,069	2,793	2,830	39,214	294,003	97
2,374	27	2,401	2,294	747,725	2,372	14,228,940	199	398,433	829	1,999,673	2,321	2,352	34,719	264,891	98
114	6	114	114	33,354	115	621,000	46	32,137	49	61,336	112	112	968	6,322	99
8	1	8	8	2,150	8	27,300	8	5,244	3	1,100	8	8	58	301	100
246	....	247	241	73,250	246	772,287	13	7,010	70	95,450	234	237	2,589	17,787	101
46	2	46	45	13,090	46	55,250	10	2,139	10	9,550	44	44	314	1,947	102
3	1	3	3	1,100	3	5,900	3	1,574	1	1,000	4	4	23	110	103
3	....	3	3	600	3	2,300	....	....	....	....	3	4	40	290	104
60	11	60	60	15,510	60	76,750	7	3,170	21	19,950	67	69	503	2,355	105
6	....	6	6	2,870	6	39,500	....	....	6	10,300	6	6	86	900	106
6	....	6	6	2,870	6	39,500	....	....	6	10,300	6	6	86	900	107
2	8	2	2	350	2	1,500	....	....	....	....	....	....	....	....	108
....	1	....	....	....	....	....	....	....	....	....	....	....	....	....	109
835	4	891	831	310,764	833	10,593,344	111	312,820	334	1,003,566	810	857	12,820	106,351	110
630	3	673	626	244,739	628	9,096,419	90	250,401	257	798,800	617	657	10,375	86,684	111
23	....	23	23	6,055	23	82,200	2	3,100	7	16,300	21	21	275	1,917	112
24	....	28	24	7,740	24	171,500	3	4,275	5	6,566	22	22	321	1,993	113
142	1	149	142	47,440	142	1,137,125	16	55,044	62	169,400	139	145	1,729	14,909	114
1	....	1	1	200	1	3,000	....	....	....	....	....	....	....	....	115
13	....	15	13	3,540	13	46,100	....	....	2	5,500	9	10	87	548	116
2	....	2	2	1,050	2	57,000	....	....	1	7,000	2	2	33	300	117
180	6	221	179	54,724	181	4,626,972	38	180,658	76	368,150	163	175	1,685	14,187	118
314	....	320	312	109,240	310	1,922,469	54	169,471	164	383,323	295	295	4,592	38,218	119
2	....	3	2	700	2	6,200	1	1,500	1	4,000	2	2	22	180	120
308	....	312	306	107,570	304	1,895,269	51	161,471	160	368,823	289	289	4,509	37,814	121
4	....	5	4	970	4	21,000	2	6,500	3	10,500	4	4	61	224	122
2	1	3	2	1,060	2	65,000	....	....	1	5,000	3	6	45	353	123
499	18	552	495	231,436	489	15,173,844	216	2,344,449	371	1,799,520	464	656	1,744	73,049	124
16	35	16	16	6,830	50	468,735	29	206,695	....	....	45	47	239	1,720	125
16	34	16	16	6,830	50	468,735	29	206,695	....	....	45	47	239	1,720	126
....	1	....	....	....	....	....	....	....	....	....	....	....	....	....	127
10	34	10	10	4,600	11	69,300	5	8,500	....	....	3	[illegible]	20	125	128
1	....	1	1	300	1	10,000	....	....	1	4,000	1	1	21	135	129
1	....	1	1	300	1	10,000	....	....	1	4,000	1	1	21	135	130

TABLE 3.—ORGANIZATIONS, COMMUNICANTS OR MEMBERS, PLACES OF WORSHIP, VALUE OF CHURCH PROPERTY, EACH STATE AND

OHIO—Continued.

	Denomination.	Total number of organizations.	Communicants or members.				
			Number of organizations reporting.	Total number reported.	Sex.		
					Number of organizations reporting.	Male.	Female.
131	Theosophical societies	5	5	184	5	54	130
132	Theosophical Society in America	2	2	30	2	12	18
133	Theosophical Society, American Section	3	3	154	3	42	112
134	Unitarians	7	7	1,228	6	443	758
135	United Brethren bodies	864	857	71,338	773	26,625	39,181
136	Church of the United Brethren in Christ	702	696	65,191	612	24,203	35,456
137	Church of the United Brethren in Christ (Old Constitution)	162	161	6,147	161	2,422	3,725
138	Universalists	76	74	5,003	61	1,652	2,477
139	Volunteers of America	5	5	135	5	63	72

OKLAHOMA.[1]

	Denomination.	Total number of organizations.	Number of organizations reporting.	Total number reported.	Number of organizations reporting.	Male.	Female.
1	All denominations	4,497	4,466	257,100	4,183	100,312	139,515
2	Adventist bodies	90	89	2,617	81	1,056	1,424
3	Advent Christian Church	19	18	502	17	222	266
4	Seventh-day Adventist Denomination	66	66	1,967	59	766	1,078
5	Church of God (Adventist)	2	2	79	2	37	42
6	Churches of God (Adventist), Unattached Congregations	1	1	36	1	19	17
7	Churches of God in Christ Jesus	2	2	33	2	12	21
8	Baptist bodies	1,251	1,248	69,585	1,205	27,129	40,412
9	Baptists	1,161	1,159	66,930	1,131	26,139	39,076
10	Southern Baptist Convention	856	854	49,978	833	19,370	29,314
11	National Baptist Convention (Colored)	305	305	16,952	298	6,769	9,762
12	Freewill Baptists	29	29	1,288	27	507	686
13	General Baptists	26	26	630	26	266	364
14	Primitive Baptists	29	28	587	16	157	201
15	Colored Primitive Baptists in America	5	5	100	4	35	60
16	United American Freewill Baptists (Colored)	1	1	50	1	25	25
17	Brethren (River)	3	3	67	3	33	34
18	Brethren in Christ	3	3	67	3	33	34
19	Christadelphians	1	1	16	1	7	9
20	Christian Union	17	17	541	15	209	247
21	Church of Christ, Scientist	10	10	391	9	110	231
22	Churches of God in North America, General Eldership of the	20	20	602	20	250	352
23	Churches of the Living God (Colored)	5	5	114	5	53	61
24	Church of the Living God (Christian Workers for Friendship)	4	4	79	4	35	44
25	Church of the Living God (Apostolic Church)	1	1	35	1	18	17
26	Congregationalists	67	66	2,677	66	956	1,721
27	Disciples or Christians	481	480	32,306	476	13,410	18,239
28	Disciples of Christ	315	314	24,232	310	9,976	13,599
29	Churches of Christ	166	166	8,074	166	3,434	4,640
30	Dunkers or German Baptist Brethren	25	25	880	25	408	472
31	German Baptist Brethren Church (Conservative)	24	24	861	24	397	464
32	Old Order German Baptist Brethren	1	1	19	1	11	8
33	Eastern Orthodox Churches	1	1	195	1	106	89
34	Russian Orthodox Church	1	1	195	1	106	89
35	Evangelical bodies	25	25	585	25	242	343
36	Evangelical Association	18	18	386	18	161	225
37	United Evangelical Church	7	7	199	7	81	118
38	Free Christian Zion Church of Christ (Colored)	1	1	200	1	75	125
39	Friends	31	30	2,187	29	989	1,157
40	Society of Friends (Orthodox)	31	30	2,187	29	989	1,157
41	German Evangelical Synod of North America	17	17	630	15	313	282
42	Independent churches	32	31	949	30	370	559
43	International Apostolic Holiness Union	1	1	7	1	3	4
44	Jewish congregations	4	2	[2] 72			
45	Latter-day Saints	16	16	1,296	16	600	696
46	Church of Jesus Christ of Latter-day Saints	1	1	382	1	185	197
47	Reorganized Church of Jesus Christ of Latter-day Saints	15	15	914	15	415	499

[1] Oklahoma and Indian Territory combined.

DEBT ON CHURCH PROPERTY, PARSONAGES, AND SUNDAY SCHOOLS, BY DENOMINATIONS (IN DETAIL), FOR TERRITORY: 1906—Continued.

OHIO—Continued.

PLACES OF WORSHIP. Number of organizations reporting— Church edifices.	Halls, etc.	Number of church edifices reported.	Seating capacity of church edifices. Number of organizations reporting.	Seating capacity reported.	VALUE OF CHURCH PROPERTY. Number of organizations reporting.	Value reported.	DEBT ON CHURCH PROPERTY. Number of organizations reporting.	Amount of debt reported.	PARSONAGES. Number of organizations reporting.	Value of parsonages reported.	SUNDAY SCHOOLS CONDUCTED BY CHURCH ORGANIZATIONS. Number of organizations reporting.	Number of Sunday schools reported.	Number of officers and teachers.	Number of scholars.	
	5														131
	2														132
	3														133
4	1	4	4	1,650	4	$230,000	1	$500	1	$4,000	4	4	41	293	134
839	10	848	802	244,465	836	2,267,317	76	80,713	177	276,690	802	831	10,110	73,154	135
690	4	699	655	205,440	688	2,069,487	63	78,165	168	268,990	662	691	8,854	66,842	136
149	6	149	147	39,025	148	197,830	13	2,548	9	7,700	140	140	1,256	6,312	137
72	2	73	72	20,584	73	390,400	6	8,500	5	6,100	55	55	446	2,296	138
	5				4	246					4	4	27	249	139

OKLAHOMA.

Church edifices.	Halls, etc.	Number of church edifices reported.	Seating: Number of organizations reporting.	Seating capacity reported.	Value: Number of organizations reporting.	Value reported.	Debt: Number of organizations reporting.	Amount of debt reported.	Parsonages: Number of organizations reporting.	Value of parsonages reported.	Sunday schools: Number of organizations reporting.	Number of Sunday schools reported.	Number of officers and teachers.	Number of scholars.	
2,642	1,051	2,709	2,434	598,650	2,696	$4,933,843	694	$435,569	674	$682,806	2,870	3,012	20,684	173,896	1
28	37	29	27	4,515	29	34,640	3	505	1	125	70	78	499	2,693	2
2	11	2	2	450	3	1,750					8	8	53	330	3
26	21	27	25	4,065	26	32,890	3	505	1	125	60	66	430	2,245	4
	2										2	4	16	118	5
	1														6
	2														7
774	380	784	760	196,499	812	1,076,516	148	70,673	67	75,275	815	833	5,164	44,488	8
735	346	745	721	189,054	771	1,061,556	143	70,153	67	75,275	795	811	5,051	43,415	9
455	329	465	450	126,154	490	881,890	91	61,393	64	72,775	511	522	3,545	32,779	10
280	17	280	271	62,900	281	179,666	52	8,730	3	2,500	284	289	1,506	10,636	11
20	9	20	20	3,725	20	8,400	4	370			5	5	22	306	12
9	14	9	9	1,980	11	2,995					15	17	91	767	13
5	11	5	5	1,150	5	2,275	1	150							14
4		4	4	440	4	890									15
1		1	1	150	1	400									16
3		3	3	375	3	6,000									17
3		3	3	375	3	6,000									18
															19
9	6	9	9	2,900	9	6,200	1	160			10	11	68	743	20
4	6	4	4	513	8	13,950	2	4,065			10	10	40	195	21
2	12	2	2	530	3	5,700			1	1,250	9	12	75	649	22
3	2	3	3	300	3	675					4	4	14	78	23
3	1	3	3	300	3	675					3	3	9	52	24
	1										1	1	5	26	25
62	1	68	59	12,265	59	142,190	21	10,975	30	25,100	63	66	523	3,948	26
330	104	334	216	64,110	292	654,136	107	65,304	9	8,350	292	301	2,372	21,802	27
260	10	260	146	45,286	219	588,535	94	62,620	8	7,950	237	240	2,141	18,828	28
70	94	74	70	18,824	73	65,601	13	2,684	1	400	55	61	231	2,974	29
11	8	12	11	3,610	11	10,900	3	700			16	17	125	703	30
11	8	12	11	3,610	11	10,900	3	700			16	17	125	703	31
															32
1		1	1	200	1	2,200			1	600					33
1		1	1	200	1	2,200			1	600					34
	11	9	9	1,650	9	13,650	2	2,700	5	4,000	19	21	170	985	35
6	8	6	6	750	6	6,150			4	3,000	12	12	90	453	36
3	3	3	3	900	3	7,500	2	2,700	1	1,000	7	9	80	532	37
1		1	1	800	1	1,000									38
26	3	26	26	5,040	25	25,670	4	308	10	7,500	30	34	228	1,785	39
26	3	26	26	5,040	25	25,670	4	308	10	7,500	30	34	228	1,785	40
10	3	10	10	1,470	11	12,610	5	1,945	4	1,450	12	12	48	311	41
11	15	13	10	3,125	12	7,305	3	1,056			16	16	90	709	42
	1										1	1	5	35	43
[illegible]	1	1	1	500	1	14,000	1	4,000			2	2	7	52	44
7	2	7	7	1,345	7	4,825	1	1,000			11	12	85	335	45
											1	2	10	45	46
7	2	7	7	1,345	7	4,825	1	1,000			10	10	75	290	47

[1] Heads of families only.

TABLE 3.—ORGANIZATIONS, COMMUNICANTS OR MEMBERS, PLACES OF WORSHIP, VALUE OF CHURCH PROPERTY, EACH STATE AND

OKLAHOMA—Continued.

	DENOMINATION.	Total number of organizations.	COMMUNICANTS OR MEMBERS.				
			Number of organizations reporting.	Total number reported.	Sex.		
					Number of organizations reporting.	Male.	Female.
48	Lutheran bodies	92	92	4,030	90	2,061	1,952
	General Synod of the Evangelical Lutheran Church in the United States of America	7	7	378	6	180	187
	Evangelical Lutheran Synodical Conference of America	72	72	2,907	71	1,514	1,377
	Evangelical Lutheran Joint Synod of Ohio and Other States	2	2	59	2	31	28
49	Evangelical Lutheran Synod of Iowa and Other States	8	8	541	8	274	267
[illegible]	United Danish Evangelical Lutheran Church in America	3	3	145	3	52	93
54	Mennonite bodies	24	24	1,410	24	679	731
	Mennonite Church	3	3	122	3	65	57
	Amish Mennonite Church	1	1	35	1	17	18
55	General Conference of Mennonites of North America	18	18	1,145	18	549	596
[illegible]	Defenceless Mennonites	1	1	42	1	20	22
	Bundes Conferenz der Mennoniten Brueder-Gemeinde:						
59	Krimmer Brueder-Gemeinde	1	1	66	1	28	38
60	Methodist bodies	1,543	1,527	76,336	1,403	26,945	41,666
	Methodist Episcopal Church	479	476	23,309	453	8,857	13,488
	African Methodist Episcopal Church	137	136	6,243	134	2,309	3,879
	African Methodist Episcopal Zion Church	8	8	160	8	73	87
	Methodist Protestant Church	87	85	2,054	80	770	1,073
	Wesleyan Methodist Connection of America	7	7	157	7	68	89
	Methodist Episcopal Church, South	683	673	40,473	583	13,336	20,821
	Congregational Methodist Church	6	6	107	6	62	45
61	Colored Methodist Episcopal Church	86	86	2,858	83	1,125	1,602
[illegible]	Free Methodist Church of North America	50	50	975	49	345	582
70	Moravian bodies	1	1	31	1	14	17
71	Evangelical Union of Bohemian and Moravian Brethren in North America	1	1	31	1	14	17
72	Nonsectarian Churches of Bible Faith	28	27	614	27	318	296
73	Presbyterian bodies	390	388	16,001	315	5,594	8,758
	Presbyterian Church in the United States of America	179	179	9,667	161	3,565	5,664
	Cumberland Presbyterian Church	152	150	4,351	106	1,303	2,068
	Colored Cumberland Presbyterian Church	2	2	80	2	35	45
	United Presbyterian Church of North America	7	7	362	7	165	197
	Presbyterian Church in the United States	47	47	1,323	36	438	654
74	Associate Reformed Synod of the South	1	1	58	1	26	32
[illegible]	Synod of the Reformed Presbyterian Church of North America	2	2	160	2	62	98
81	Protestant Episcopal Church	43	42	2,024	35	605	1,137
82	Reformed bodies	12	12	747	12	328	419
83	Reformed Church in America	11	11	705	11	304	401
84	Reformed Church in the United States	1	1	42	1	24	18
85	Roman Catholic Church	173	173	36,548	162	15,974	16,149
86	Salvationists	9	8	130	8	81	49
87	Salvation Army	9	8	130	8	81	49
88	Spiritualists	6	6	202	6	88	114
89	Unitarians	1	1	70	1	31	39
90	United Brethren bodies	73	73	2,974	73	1,260	1,714
91	Church of the United Brethren in Christ	67	67	2,819	67	1,194	1,625
92	Church of the United Brethren in Christ (Old Constitution)	6	6	155	6	66	89
93	Universalists	2	2	24	....	....	....
94	Volunteers of America	2	2	42	2	25	17

OREGON.

	DENOMINATION.	Total number of organizations.	Number of organizations reporting.	Total number reported.	Number of organizations reporting.	Male.	Female.
1	All denominations	1,304	1,290	120,229	1,214	47,094	66,459
2	Adventist bodies	64	63	2,208	63	864	1,344
3	Advent Christian Church	11	10	302	10	127	175
4	Seventh-day Adventist Denomination	50	50	1,844	50	705	1,139
5	Churches of God in Christ Jesus	3	3	62	3	32	30
6	Bahais	1	1	23	1	11	12
7	Baptist bodies	141	140	11,316	132	3,818	6,780
8	Baptists	131	130	11,159	122	3,763	6,678
9	Northern Baptist Convention	129	128	11,099	120	3,743	6,638
10	National Baptist Convention (Colored)	2	2	60	2	20	40
11	Primitive Baptists	10	10	157	10	55	102

DEBT ON CHURCH PROPERTY, PARSONAGES, AND SUNDAY SCHOOLS, BY DENOMINATIONS (IN DETAIL), FOR TERRITORY: 1906—Continued.

OKLAHOMA—Continued.

PLACES OF WORSHIP. Number of organizations reporting— Church edifices.	Halls, etc.	Number of church edifices reported.	Seating capacity of church edifices. Number of organizations reporting.	Seating capacity reported.	VALUE OF CHURCH PROPERTY. Number of organizations reporting.	Value reported.	DEBT ON CHURCH PROPERTY. Number of organizations reporting.	Amount of debt reported.	PARSONAGES. Number of organizations reporting.	Value of parsonages reported.	SUNDAY SCHOOLS CONDUCTED BY CHURCH ORGANIZATIONS. Number of organizations reporting.	Number of Sunday schools reported.	Number of officers and teachers.	Number of scholars.	
36	43	37	35	5,880	37	$52,200	14	$6,939	19	$17,360	37	38	69	888	48
6	1	6	6	985	6	14,100	3	2,435	1	1,100	7	8	25	189	49
23	38	23	22	3,620	24	28,050	9	3,704	14	13,300	21	21	23	388	50
1	1	1	1	75	1	1,600	1	300	1	800	1	1	3	24	51
4	2	5	4	900	4	7,150	1	500	2	1,560	6	6	8	192	52
2	1	2	2	300	2	1,300			1	600	2	2	10	95	53
20	3	20	20	3,645	20	19,500	3	850	3	3,550	22	22	169	1,672	54
3		3	3	350	3	1,150					3	3	25	193	55
1		1	1	70	1	250					1	1	7	50	56
14	3	14	14	2,825	14	16,000	2	750	3	3,550	16	16	123	1,297	57
1		1	1	200	1	1,200					1	1	8	62	58
1		1	1	200	1	900	1	100			1	1	6	70	59
851	292	868	787	194,033	867	1,547,340	253	133,592	381	318,176	970	1,032	7,788	66,195	60
269	67	269	262	62,602	276	614,613	76	52,875	133	120,492	337	364	3,366	26,822	61
113	16	127	109	24,816	117	117,705	51	11,290	36	16,575	126	139	746	3,930	62
6	2	6	6	1,550	6	4,700	2	190	1	300	5	5	16	138	63
23	28	23	21	4,625	18	11,325	3	525	1	100	20	20	116	885	64
4	1	4	4	660	4	2,700			3	850	3	3	22	143	65
348	148	350	303	81,645	355	725,817	97	59,189	182	168,869	377	392	2,965	30,826	66
2	3	2			2	450					2	1	7	35	67
70	12	71	67	15,110	71	51,830	23	9,478	10	2,690	74	79	352	2,310	68
16	15	16	15	3,025	18	18,200	1	45	15	8,300	26	29	198	1,106	69
	1														70
	1														71
	27										7	7	32	235	72
251	29	267	245	57,248	265	618,591	63	45,408	67	104,670	241	262	2,159	16,340	73
140	14	147	140	33,560	140	436,325	28	33,580	47	82,620	142	154	1,457	10,732	74
70	13	75	67	14,423	82	109,316	17	6,970	13	13,150	61	63	438	3,270	75
2		2	2	800	2	1,200					2	2	6	50	76
6		6	6	1,350	7	23,300	3	750	2	1,600	7	8	64	564	77
30	2	34	27	6,265	31	40,250	14	3,508	5	7,300	26	30	160	1,356	78
1		1	1	250	1	1,200					1	1	7	60	79
2		2	2	600	2	7,000	1	600			2	4	27	308	80
38	1	39	38	4,971	38	122,050	7	17,486	12	19,100	29	29	122	923	81
10	2	10	10	2,134	11	32,900	3	1,650	8	15,500	11	11	85	675	82
9	2	9	9	2,034	10	32,600	3	1,650	8	15,500	10	10	82	660	83
1		1	1	100	1	300					1	1	3	15	84
109	27	117	105	22,817	114	444,250	29	59,060	39	68,750	100	104	138	3,596	85
	9				9	2,020	5	285			6	6	28	181	86
	9				9	2,020	5	285			6	6	28	181	87
	6				2	,025									88
															89
34	18	34	34	7,875	35	58,750	15	6,608	17	12,050	66	70	574	3,620	90
30	18	30	30	7,025	31	52,250	14	6,308	16	11,800	61	65	537	3,381	91
4		4	4	850	4	6,500	1	300	1	250	5	5	37	239	92
															93
1	1	1	1	300	2	3,050	1	300			1	1	7	60	94

OREGON.

1,065	138	1,086	1,033	270,329	1,052	$4,620,793	202	$257,815	425	$623,290	1,010	1,090	9,545	75,119	1
38	13	38	36	6,477	37	47,800	3	1,298	1	1,200	47	57	376	1,803	2
7	4	7	6	2,275	6	10,800	1	68	1	1,200	5	6	36	225	3
29	9	29	28	3,942	29	35,700	2	1,230			40	49	324	1,528	4
2		2	2	260	2	1,300					2	2	16	50	5
															6
115	9	118	113	32,540	117	523,275	29	25,738	35	59,335	99	105	1,053	8,762	7
112	6	115	110	31,940	114	522,150	29	25,738	35	59,335	99	105	1,053	8,762	8
111	5	114	109	31,440	113	507,150	28	24,538	35	59,335	98	104	1,049	8,732	9
1	1	1	1	500	1	15,000	1	1,200			1	1	4	30	10
3	3	3	3	600	3	1,125									11

TABLE 3.—ORGANIZATIONS, COMMUNICANTS OR MEMBERS, PLACES OF WORSHIP, VALUE OF CHURCH PROPERTY, EACH STATE AND

OREGON—Continued.

	DENOMINATION.	Total number of organizations.	COMMUNICANTS OR MEMBERS.				
			Number of organizations reporting.	Total number reported.	Sex.		
					Number of organizations reporting.	Male.	Female.
12	Brethren (Plymouth)	6	6	127	6	55	72
13	Brethren (Plymouth)—II	2	2	70	2	29	41
14	Brethren (Plymouth)—III	3	3	51	3	23	28
15	Brethren (Plymouth)—IV	1	1	6	1	3	3
16	Buddhists	2	1	142	1	102	40
17	Chinese Temples	1					
18	Japanese Temples	1	1	142	1	102	40
19	Christadelphians	1	1	33	1	14	19
20	Church of Christ, Scientist	8	8	591	6	120	375
21	Churches of God in North America, General Eldership of the	4	4	42	4	19	23
22	Churches of the New Jerusalem	3	3	50	2	22	22
23	General Convention of the New Jerusalem in the United States of America	3	3	50	2	22	22
24	Congregationalists	58	58	4,575	58	1,602	2,973
25	Disciples or Christians	101	101	10,420	97	3,862	6,317
26	Disciples of Christ	90	90	10,012	86	3,655	6,116
27	Churches of Christ	11	11	408	11	207	201
28	Dunkers or German Baptist Brethren	9	9	410	9	176	234
29	German Baptist Brethren Church (Conservative)	9	9	410	9	176	234
30	Eastern Orthodox Churches	2	2	311	2	286	25
31	Russian Orthodox Church	1	1	61	1	51	10
32	Greek Orthodox Church	1	1	250	1	235	15
33	Evangelical bodies	80	80	3,262	75	1,160	1,971
34	Evangelical Association	37	37	1,601	37	623	978
35	United Evangelical Church	43	43	1,661	38	537	993
36	Evangelistic associations	4	4	231	4	111	120
37	Peniel Missions	2	2	125	2	75	50
38	Hephzibah Faith Missionary Association	1	1	15	1	6	9
39	Apostolic Christian Church	1	1	91	1	30	61
40	Friends	11	11	1,688	11	809	879
41	Society of Friends (Orthodox)	11	11	1,688	11	809	879
42	Independent churches	9	9	323	8	94	154
43	Jewish congregations	5	4	[1]414			
44	Latter-day Saints	16	16	1,817	15	841	950
45	Church of Jesus Christ of Latter-day Saints	11	11	1,496	11	708	788
46	Reorganized Church of Jesus Christ of Latter-day Saints	5	5	321	4	133	162
47	Lutheran bodies	67	67	6,039	60	2,638	2,864
48	General Council of the Evangelical Lutheran Church in North America	17	17	2,211	17	1,016	1,195
49	Evangelical Lutheran Synodical Conference of America	15	15	1,080	15	510	570
50	United Norwegian Lutheran Church in America	7	7	403	5	125	115
51	Evangelical Lutheran Joint Synod of Ohio and Other States	10	10	591	8	219	268
52	Evangelical Lutheran Synod of Iowa and Other States	1	1	250	1	175	75
53	Synod for the Norwegian Evangelical Lutheran Church in America	7	7	722	5	239	263
54	Finnish Evangelical Lutheran Church of America, or Suomi Synod	2	2	238	2	127	111
55	Norwegian Lutheran Free Church	2	2	104	1	30	24
56	United Danish Evangelical Lutheran Church in America	4	4	165	4	72	93
57	Apostolic Lutheran Church (Finnish)	2	2	275	2	125	150
58	Mennonite bodies	7	7	380	7	180	200
59	Mennonite Church	2	2	93	2	47	46
60	Amish Mennonite Church	2	2	185	2	84	101
61	Old Amish Mennonite Church	1	1	16	1	9	7
62	General Conference of Mennonites of North America	2	2	86	2	40	46
63	Methodist bodies	346	342	21,717	334	7,953	12,917
64	Methodist Episcopal Church	263	260	18,681	253	6,821	11,063
65	African Methodist Episcopal Church	1	1	60	1	15	45
66	African Methodist Episcopal Zion Church	1	1	40	1	10	30
67	Methodist Episcopal Church, South	43	42	2,272	41	850	1,372
68	Free Methodist Church of North America	38	38	664	38	257	407
69	Pentecostal Church of the Nazarene	3	3	135	3	58	77

[1] Heads of families only.

DEBT ON CHURCH PROPERTY, PARSONAGES, AND SUNDAY SCHOOLS, BY DENOMINATIONS (IN DETAIL), FOR TERRITORY: 1906—Continued.

OREGON—Continued.

PLACES OF WORSHIP. Number of organizations reporting— Church edifices.	PLACES OF WORSHIP. Number of organizations reporting— Halls, etc.	PLACES OF WORSHIP. Number of church edifices reported.	PLACES OF WORSHIP. Seating capacity of church edifices. Number of organizations reporting.	PLACES OF WORSHIP. Seating capacity of church edifices. Seating capacity reported.	VALUE OF CHURCH PROPERTY. Number of organizations reporting.	VALUE OF CHURCH PROPERTY. Value reported.	DEBT ON CHURCH PROPERTY. Number of organizations reporting.	DEBT ON CHURCH PROPERTY. Amount of debt reported.	PARSONAGES. Number of organizations reporting.	PARSONAGES. Value of parsonages reported.	SUNDAY SCHOOLS CONDUCTED BY CHURCH ORGANIZATIONS. Number of organizations reporting.	SUNDAY SCHOOLS CONDUCTED BY CHURCH ORGANIZATIONS. Number of Sunday schools reported.	SUNDAY SCHOOLS CONDUCTED BY CHURCH ORGANIZATIONS. Number of officers and teachers.	SUNDAY SCHOOLS CONDUCTED BY CHURCH ORGANIZATIONS. Number of scholars.	
....	6	....	....	....	....	....	....	....	....	....	3	3	9	97	12
....	2	....	....	....	....	....	....	....	....	....	2	2	8	80	13
....	3	....	....	....	....	....	....	....	....	....	1	1	1	17	14
....	1	....	....	....	....	....	....	....	....	....	....	....	....	....	15
1	1	1	....	....	....	....	....	....	....	....	1	1	4	70	16
1	....	1	....	....	....	....	....	....	....	....	....	....	....	....	17
....	1	....	....	....	....	....	....	....	....	....	1	1	4	70	18
....	1	....	....	....	....	....	....	....	....	....	....	....	....	....	19
2	4	2	2	400	4	$19,550	....	....	....	....	6	6	50	237	20
2	....	2	2	350	2	1,300	....	....	....	....	1	1	5	30	21
....	1	....	....	....	....	....	....	....	....	....	....	....	....	....	22
....	1	....	....	....	....	....	....	....	....	....	....	....	....	....	23
55	....	56	55	13,980	55	283,887	13	$19,860	15	$22,600	53	55	531	4,723	24
82	11	82	82	25,965	84	250,130	17	19,768	13	14,050	78	78	744	6,912	25
77		77	77	24,715	79	245,880	17	19,768	13	14,050	75	75	730	6,762	26
5	6	5	5	1,250	5	4,250	....	....	....	....	3	3	14	150	27
9	....	9	9	3,350	9	19,600	2	3,300	....	....	8	13	94	496	28
9	....	9	9	3,350	9	19,600	2	3,300	....	....	8	13	94	496	29
2	....	2	2	700	1	600	....	....	....	....	....	....	....	....	30
1	....	1	1	200	1	600	....	....	....	....	....	....	....	....	31
1	....	1	1	500	....	....	....	....	....	....	....	....	....	....	32
59	19	59	59	14,350	57	98,425	12	5,343	30	34,300	60	66	628	3,890	33
28	8	27	28	6,975	27	57,075	3	1,018	15	20,100	30	32	319	2,056	34
31	11	32	31	7,375	30	41,350	9	4,325	15	14,200	30	34	309	1,834	35
2	2	3	2	325	2	5,200	....	....	....	....	3	4	14	112	36
....	2	....	....	....	....	....	....	....	....	....	1	1	3	25	37
1	....	1	1	125	1	1,200	....	....	....	....	1	1	7	27	38
1	....	2	1	200	1	4,000	....	....	....	....	1	2	4	60	39
10	....	10	10	2,950	10	31,406	1	350	3	1,500	10	10	125	923	40
10	....	10	10	2,950	10	31,406	1	350	3	1,500	10	10	125	923	41
5	3	6	5	1,100	5	13,600	2	600	....	....	8	10	31	298	42
3	....	3	3	1,450	3	186,500	2	6,500	....	....	3	3	13	215	43
11	3	11	10	2,725	11	15,700	2	1,300	....	....	13	13	206	1,134	44
7	2	7	7	2,175	7	13,050	2	1,300	....	....	8	8	154	883	45
4	1	4	3	550	4	2,650	....	....	....	....	5	5	52	251	46
53	6	55	51	12,241	52	213,860	25	44,235	26	43,000	47	50	189	1,751	47
13	2	15	12	3,875	12	660	6	31,595	8	20,500	13	14	77	677	48
12	1	12	12	2,026	12	110,850	5	2,000	7	6,700	8	8	13	230	49
6	....	6	6	1,885	6	22 15,800	4	3,000	1	1,000	6	6	22	168	50
9	....	9	8	1,370	9	17,350	5	3,900	4	6,600	9	10	20	253	51
1	....	1	1	400	1	4,000	....	....	....	....	1	1	4	50	52
5	....	5	5	1,050	5	16,600	2	2,200	3	4,300	4	4	14	130	53
1	1	1	1	300	1	2,500	....	....	1	1,500	1	1	11	50	54
2	....	2	2	475	2	5,500	2	1,050	1	1,000	2	2	13	73	55
2	2	2	2	500	2	5,600	1	490	1	1,400	2	3	13	80	56
2	....	2	2	360	2	3,000	....	....	....	....	1	1	2	40	57
5	1	5	5	1,550	5	5,400	....	....	....	....	6	8	92	591	58
1	....	1	1	300	1	800	....	....	....	....	2	4	37	215	
2	....	2	2	750	2	1,600	....	....	....	....	2	2	33	216	
....	1	....	....	....	....	....	....	....	....	....	....	....	....	....	59
2	....	2	2	500	2	3,000	....	....	....	....	2	2	22	160	60
306	19	307	304	78,535	306	1,032,845	38	34,676	168	204,350	275	286	2,960	21,201	63
239	12	240	237	59,815	239	878,020	30	30,881	130	164,650	220	230	2,600	18,817	
1	....	1	1	150	1	4,000	1	2,400	1	1,000	1	1	6	25	
1	....	1	1	250	1	25,000	1	350	1	2,000	1	1	5	30	
41	2	41	41	12,725	41	101,725	1	40	23	27,550	32	32	228	1,702	64
24	5	24	24	5,595	24	24,100	5	1,005	13	9,150	21	22	121	627	65
3	....	3	3	900	3	6,650	3	2,650	....	....	3	3	20	115	69

TABLE 3.—ORGANIZATIONS, COMMUNICANTS OR MEMBERS, PLACES OF WORSHIP, VALUE OF CHURCH PROPERTY, EACH STATE AND

OREGON—Continued.

	Denomination.	Total number of organizations.	Communicants or members: Number of organizations reporting.	Total number reported.	Sex: Number of organizations reporting.	Male.	Female.
70	Presbyterian bodies	140	138	10,947	124	3,640	6,831
71	Presbyterian Church in the United States of America	121	121	9,701	111	3,181	6,109
72	Cumberland Presbyterian Church	10	10	540	6	155	320
73	United Presbyterian Church of North America	9	7	706	7	304	402
74	Protestant Episcopal Church	52	51	3,580	42	958	2,052
75	Reformed bodies	7	7	512	7	227	285
76	Reformed Church in the United States	7	7	512	7	227	285
77	Roman Catholic Church	75	75	35,317	71	16,041	16,981
78	Salvationists	11	10	303	10	167	136
79	Salvation Army	11	10	303	10	167	136
80	Spiritualists	10	10	334	9	152	165
81	Swedish Evangelical bodies	1	1	110	1	49	61
82	Swedish Evangelical Mission Covenant of America	1	1	110	1	49	61
83	Theosophical societies	1	1	16	1	11	5
84	Theosophical Society, American Section	1	1	16	1	11	5
85	Unitarians	3	3	667	3	220	447
86	United Brethren bodies	54	53	2,129	46	813	1,089
87	Church of the United Brethren in Christ	32	31	1,533	24	528	778
88	Church of the United Brethren in Christ (Old Constitution)	22	22	596	22	285	311
89	Universalists	1	1	60	1	21	39
90	Volunteers of America	1	.....	.....	.....	.....	.....

PENNSYLVANIA.

	Denomination.	Total number of organizations.	Communicants or members: Number of organizations reporting.	Total number reported.	Sex: Number of organizations reporting.	Male.	Female.
1	All denominations	12,834	12,748	2,977,022	11,795	1,255,313	1,505,424
2	Adventist bodies	90	90	2,666	85	778	1,718
3	Evangelical Adventists	13	13	336	13	135	201
4	Advent Christian Church	11	11	330	9	75	125
5	Seventh-day Adventist Denomination	66	66	2,000	63	568	1,392
6	Armenian Church	1	1	1,300	1	1,050	250
7	Bahais	2	2	52	2	16	36
8	Baptist bodies	915	914	141,694	839	47,850	80,306
9	Baptists	842	841	139,030	773	46,884	78,742
10	Northern Baptist Convention	739	738	118,661	673	39,572	67,091
11	National Baptist Convention (Colored)	103	103	20,369	100	7,312	11,651
12	General Six Principle Baptists	4	4	67	3	28	33
13	Seventh-day Baptists	5	5	188	5	70	118
14	Free Baptists	42	42	1,967	40	770	1,167
15	Primitive Baptists	20	20	397	16	79	220
16	Colored Primitive Baptists in America	2	2	45	2	19	26
17	Brethren (Plymouth)	42	42	1,264	42	535	729
18	Brethren (Plymouth)—I	23	23	548	23	226	322
19	Brethren (Plymouth)—II	11	11	465	11	205	260
20	Brethren (Plymouth)—III	7	7	222	7	93	129
21	Brethren (Plymouth)—IV	1	1	29	1	11	18
22	Brethren (River)	66	65	2,977	65	1,136	1,841
23	Brethren in Christ	33	32	1,872	32	680	1,192
24	Yorker, or Old Order, Brethren	5	5	356	5	128	228
25	United Zion's Children	28	28	749	28	328	421
26	Buddhists	5	.....	.....	.....	.....	.....
7	Chinese Temples	5	.....	.....	.....	.....	.....
28	Catholic Apostolic Churches	1	1	132	1	41	91
29	Catholic Apostolic Church	1	1	132	1	41	91
30	Christadelphians	4	4	52	4	24	28
31	Christian Catholic Church in Zion	1	1	150	1	50	100
32	Christians (Christian Connection)	63	63	4,019	61	1,587	2,356
33	Church of Christ, Scientist	25	25	1,551	24	340	744
34	Church of God and Saints of Christ (Colored)	5	5	548	5	177	371
35	Churches of God in North America, General Eldership of the	178	177	11,157	168	3,995	6,698

DEBT ON CHURCH PROPERTY, PARSONAGES, AND SUNDAY SCHOOLS, BY DENOMINATIONS (IN DETAIL), FOR TERRITORY: 1906—Continued.

OREGON—Continued.

PLACES OF WORSHIP.					VALUE OF CHURCH PROPERTY.		DEBT ON CHURCH PROPERTY.		PARSONAGES.		SUNDAY SCHOOLS CONDUCTED BY CHURCH ORGANIZATIONS.				
Number of organizations reporting—Church edifices.	Number of organizations reporting—Halls, etc.	Number of church edifices reported.	Seating capacity of church edifices. Number of organizations reporting.	Seating capacity of church edifices. Seating capacity reported.	Number of organizations reporting.	Value reported.	Number of organizations reporting.	Amount of debt reported.	Number of organizations reporting.	Value of parsonages reported.	Number of organizations reporting.	Number of Sunday schools reported.	Number of officers and teachers.	Number of scholars.	
130	2	142	126	32,834	126	$748,890	15	$17,950	52	$110,575	127	145	1,487	12,501	70
114	1	125	110	28,754	109	661,890	15	17,950	44	92,525	112	128	1,334	10,994	71
9		9	9	1,650	9	24,200			2	3,750	6	6	70	659	72
7	1	8	7	2,430	8	62,800			6	14,300	9	11	83	848	73
47	2	51	47	8,290	48	472,675	9	13,145	22	35,300	39	40	235	1,904	74
6	1	8	6	1,375	6	45,100	2	900	6	15,800	6		41	301	75
6	1	8	6	1,375	6	45,100	2	900	6	15,800	6		41	301	76
63	4	67	62	17,215	52	392,000	13	45,286	28	60,600	60		198	4,288	77
2	9	2	1	75	11	9,300	1	5,877			8	9 68	18	116	78
2	9	2	1	75	11	9,300	1	5,877			8	8	18	116	79
2	6	2	2	1,150	4	15,000	2	3,050	1	200	2	2	11	100	80
1		1	1	400	1	12,000	1	2,000	1	500	1	4	19	200	81
1		1	1	400	1	12,000	1	2,000	1	500	1	4	19	200	82
	1														83
	1														84
3		3	3	1,150	3	102,500	1	1,100			3	3	27	162	85
37	12	37	31	7,702	37	62,100	8	2,829	24	19,980	39	40	356	2,147	86
20	10	20	14	4,007	20	44,500	7	2,579	15	15,230	26	27	262	1,611	87
17	2	17	17	3,695	17	17,600	1	250	9	4,750	13	13	94	536	88
1		1	1	250	1	5,500	1	60			1	1	9	40	89
	1														90

PENNSYLVANIA.

11,865	704	12,780	11,708	4,646,929	11,920	$173,605,141	3,153	$15,562,196	4,408	$17,937,170	11,176	12,273	172,878	1,645,563	1
48	26	48	48	9,555	46	82,900	14	17,726	1	1,200	72	82	447	2,077	2
12	1	12	12	3,050	11	14,050			1	1,200	5	5	35	150	3
9		9	9	1,950	9	9,750	2	185			7	7	50	237	4
27	25	27	27	4,555	26	59,100	12	17,541			60	70	362	1,690	5
	1														6
	2														7
854	44	919	847	322,936	859	11,231,107	287	1,048,451	221	580,712	820	891	12,614	112,316	8
791	38	856	785	305,299	797	11,118,474	283	1,045,164	211	568,712	775	846	12,256	110,468	9
709	17	771	704	274,371	714	10,267,274	235	874,151	203	540,012	674	745	11,384	101,857	10
82	21	85	81	30,928	83	851,200	48	171,013	8	28,700	101	101	872	8,611	11
3	1	3	3	1,150	3	4,050			1	1,500	1	1	4	30	12
4	1	4	4	800	4	7,200	1	75	2	1,700	5	5	30	108	13
40	2	40	39	10,045	39	70,983	2	712	6	5,800	39	39	324	1,710	14
14	2	14	14	4,942	14	23,200			1	3,000					15
2		2	2	700	2	7,200	1	2,500							16
	42										28	28	122	1,040	17
	23										13	13	58	470	18
	11										10	10	53	450	19
	7										5	5	11	120	20
	1														21
52	14	53	52	20,735	52	86,100	2	1,400	2	5,000	16	16	186	1,132	22
32	1	33	32	13,535	32	63,250	1	400	2	5,000	14	14	168	1,015	23
	5														24
20	8	20	20	7,200	20	22,850	1	1,000			2	2	18	117	25
5		5													26
5		5													27
	1										1	3	3	65	28
	1										1	3	3	65	29
	3				2	75					1	1	3	14	30
	1														31
59	4	59	57	20,240	57	109,893	4	1,380	14	17,700	47	47	427	3,294	32
5	19	5	5	1,425	11	130,050	3	11,725			22	22	111	549	33
	5														34
169	7	172	170	53,503	171	618,125	19	38,347	46	91,500	158	163	2,003	15,084	35

TABLE 3.—ORGANIZATIONS, COMMUNICANTS OR MEMBERS, PLACES OF WORSHIP, VALUE OF CHURCH PROPERTY, EACH STATE AND

PENNSYLVANIA—Continued.

	DENOMINATION.	Total number of organizations.	COMMUNICANTS OR MEMBERS.				
			Number of organizations reporting.	Total number reported.	Sex.		
					Number of organizations reporting.	Male.	Female.
36	Churches of the New Jerusalem	14	14	1,018	14	384	634
37	General Convention of the New Jerusalem in the United States of America	9	9	704	9	269	435
38	General Church of the New Jerusalem	5	5	314	5	115	199
39	Congregationalists	116	115	14,811	115	5,433	9,378
40	Disciples or Christians	175	174	27,187	165	9,315	14,785
41	Disciples of Christ	162	161	26,458	153	9,049	14,442
42	Churches of Christ	13	13	729	12	266	343
43	Dunkers or German Baptist Brethren	163	162	23,176	160	9,410	13,116
44	German Baptist Brethren Church (Conservative)	106	105	18,889	104	7,850	10,939
45	Old Order German Baptist Brethren	3	3	235	3	125	110
46	The Brethren Church (Progressive Dunkers)	49	49	3,885	48	1,368	1,967
47	German Seventh-day Baptists	5	5	167		67	100
48	Eastern Orthodox Churches	72	72	22,123	29	14,163	4,030
49	Russian Orthodox Church	22	22	8,446	22	5,827	2,619
50	Servian Orthodox Church	4	4	6,652	4	5,480	1,172
51	Syrian Orthodox Church	1	1	95	1	56	39
52	Greek Orthodox Church	45	45	6,930	2	2,800	200
53	Evangelical bodies	813	811	58,774	788	21,470	35,144
54	Evangelical Association	234	233	13,294	225	5,037	7,728
55	United Evangelical Church	579	578	45,480	563	16,433	27,416
56	Evangelistic associations	8	8	•196	8	80	116
57	Gospel Mission	8	8	196	8	80	116
58	Friends	126	126	12,457	123	5,557	6,637
59	Society of Friends (Orthodox)	41	41	3,427	40	1,521	1,806
60	Religious Society of Friends (Hicksite)	81	81	8,947	79	4,001	4,783
61	Orthodox Conservative Friends (Wilburite)	1	1	26	1	15	11
62	Friends (Primitive)	3	3	57	3	20	37
63	German Evangelical Protestant bodies	11	11	7,417	10	2,706	3,861
64	German Evangelical Protestant Ministers' Association	9	9	5,267	9	2,181	3,086
65	German Evangelical Protestant Ministers' Conference	2	2	2,150	1	525	775
66	German Evangelical Synod of North America	18	18	6,871	16	2,879	3,707
67	Independent churches	110	110	7,586	102	2,445	3,584
68	International Apostolic Holiness Union	3	3	164	3	66	98
69	Jewish congregations	161	120	[1] 15,479			
70	Latter-day Saints	11	11	987	11	452	535
71	Church of Jesus Christ of Latter-day Saints	4	4	345	4	156	189
72	Reorganized Church of Jesus Christ of Latter-day Saints	7	7	642	7	296	346
73	Lutheran bodies	1,618	1,616	335,643	1,440	129,724	168,109
74	General Synod of the Evangelical Lutheran Church in the United States of America	721	721	125,263	641	47,553	68,208
75	General Council of the Evangelical Lutheran Church in North America	755	753	182,160	667	69,508	86,578
76	Evangelical Lutheran Synodical Conference of America	56	56	10,729	49	4,015	4,929
77	United Norwegian Lutheran Church in America	1	1	66	1	23	43
78	Evangelical Lutheran Joint Synod of Ohio and Other States	41	41	8,053	38	3,295	4,309
79	Immanuel Synod of the Evangelical Lutheran Church of North America	5	5	2,300	5	885	1,415
80	Finnish Evangelical Lutheran Church of America, or Suomi Synod	9	9	806	9	471	335
81	United Danish Evangelical Lutheran Church in America	2	2	105	2	51	54
82	Slovak Evangelical Lutheran Synod of America	28	28	6,161	28	3,923	2,238
83	Mennonite bodies	156	156	16,527	156	7,358	9,169
84	Mennonite Church	90	90	10,493	90	4,735	5,758
85	Amish Mennonite Church	5	5	569	5	251	318
86	Old Amish Mennonite Church	10	10	1,574	10	738	836
87	Reformed Mennonite Church	16	16	1,218	16	500	718
88	General Conference of Mennonites of North America	14	14	1,675	14	776	899
89	Mennonite Brethren in Christ	21	21	998	21	358	640
90	Methodist bodies	3,052	3,037	363,443	2,869	124,732	215,799
91	Methodist Episcopal Church	2,379	2,369	318,911	2,229	109,336	188,145
92	Union American Methodist Episcopal Church (Colored)	22	22	1,647	22	703	944
93	African Methodist Episcopal Church	149	149	12,638	149	4,284	8,354
94	African Union Methodist Protestant Church	9	9	1,019	9	317	702
95	African Methodist Episcopal Zion Church	67	67	6,263	63	2,070	3,743
96	Methodist Protestant Church	122	122	12,317	118	4,501	7,569
97	Wesleyan Methodist Connection of America	47	47	1,239	46	474	745
98	Methodist Episcopal Church, South	14	14	806	8	130	179
99	Congregational Methodist Church	2	2	163	2	34	129
100	Colored Methodist Episcopal Church	5	5	466	5	204	262
101	Primitive Methodist Church in the United States of America	43	43	3,807	43	1,388	2,419
102	Free Methodist Church of North America	193	188	4,167	175	1,291	2,608

[1] Heads of families only.

DEBT ON CHURCH PROPERTY, PARSONAGES, AND SUNDAY SCHOOLS, BY DENOMINATIONS (IN DETAIL), FOR TERRITORY: 1906—Continued.

PENNSYLVANIA—Continued.

PLACES OF WORSHIP.					VALUE OF CHURCH PROPERTY.		DEBT ON CHURCH PROPERTY.		PARSONAGES.		SUNDAY SCHOOLS CONDUCTED BY CHURCH ORGANIZATIONS.				
Number of organizations reporting— Church edifices.	Number of organizations reporting— Halls, etc.	Number of church edifices reported.	Seating capacity of church edifices. Number of organizations reporting.	Seating capacity of church edifices. Seating capacity reported.	Number of organizations reporting.	Value reported.	Number of organizations reporting.	Amount of debt reported.	Number of organizations reporting.	Value of parsonages reported.	Number of organizations reporting.	Number of Sunday schools reported.	Number of officers and teachers.	Number of scholars.	
8	6	9	8	2,615	9	$318,900	2	$4,675	1	$5,000	10	10	64	430	36
7	2	8	7	2,475	7	303,700	1	175	1	5,000	6	6	53	361	37
1	4	1	1	140	2	15,200	1	4,500	...	...	4	4	11	69	38
113	2	120	107	42,507	115	1,386,798	54	162,721	28	67,900	107	111	1,945	14,809	39
153	14	159	153	54,389	158	1,445,800	46	168,747	22	52,500	150	161	2,106	19,881	40
145	9	151	145	52,349	148	1,412,200	45	167,247	22	52,500	148	159	2,096	19,809	41
8	5	8	8	2,040	10	33,600	1	1,500	...	...	2	2	10	72	42
159	3	344	159	141,400	158	937,530	31	42,120	19	46,950	147	237	2,555	19,703	43
104	2	278	104	120,475	103	701,850	14	11,385	12	32,050	104	191	2,115	15,822	44
3	...	8	3	2,300	3	6,600	...	...	...	...	...	...	...	...	45
48	...	52	48	16,575	48	188,280	15	27,135	6	14,000	41	44	427	3,751	46
4	1	6	4	2,050	4	40,800	2	3,600	1	900	2	2	13	130	47
25	47	25	23	11,550	26	178,185	19	68,765	10	33,243	...	...	...	...	48
18	4	18	18	9,250	20	131,725	15	54,265	10	33,243	...	...	...	...	49
3	1	3	3	1,400	4	20,210	3	2,500	...	...	...	...	...	...	50
...	1	...	...	...	1	250	...	...	...	...	...	...	...	...	51
4	41	4	2	900	1	26,000	1	12,000	...	...	...	...	...	...	52
785	20	795	781	248,652	779	3,189,378	189	277,986	221	486,676	708	731	10,046	82,594	53
224	6	229	222	68,545	223	1,035,600	48	85,619	68	170,200	103	204	2,382	19,170	54
561	14	566	559	180,107	556	2,153,778	141	192,367	153	316,476	515	527	7,664	63,424	55
4	3	4	4	750	5	3,100	1	500	...	...	7	9	34	245	56
4	3	4	4	750	5	3,100	1	500	...	...	7	9	34	245	57
123	3	124	121	37,645	120	911,800	...	...	...	...	57	59	443	3,744	58
41	...	42	39	10,890	40	522,900	...	...	...	...	7	7	44	423	59
80	1	80	80	26,405	78	384,150	...	...	...	...	49	51	398	3,306	60
...	1	...	...	...	...	...	...	...	...	...	1	1	1	15	61
2	1	2	2	350	2	4,750	...	...	...	...	...	...	...	...	62
11	...	13	10	6,700	11	1,353,100	6	67,300	10	47,700	11	11	312	2,478	63
9	...	11	8	4,300	9	173,100	5	17,500	9	42,900	9	9	231	1,948	64
2	...	2	2	2,400	2	1,180,000	1	49,800	1	4,800	2	2	81	530	65
18	...	19	18	7,970	18	278,900	10	49,300	13	44,400	17	17	326	3,119	66
77	30	78	76	21,650	78	381,325	35	68,575	13	36,900	87	101	856	7,498	67
2	1	4	2	1,300	2	7,900	1	600	1	1,500	3	5	39	208	68
94	13	97	89	43,218	88	2,346,950	56	499,250	12	20,000	60	61	231	5,935	69
6	4	6	6	1,350	6	24,000	2	2,560	...	...	10	10	83	526	70
1	3	1	1	200	1	500	...	...	...	...	4	4	21	115	71
5	1	5	5	1,150	5	23,500	2	2,560	...	...	6	6	62	411	72
1,542	49	1,620	1,500	627,229	1,544	17,923,113	427	1,723,230	551	1,810,216	1,449	1,567	25,463	235,105	73
703	11	734	673	264,172	706	7,170,313	142	563,013	261	777,717	681	727	12,350	112,910	74
733	13	776	723	324,213	732	9,051,950	229	945,232	236	816,399	677	738	12,402	113,839	75
41	5	44	40	16,660	41	1,081,800	24	129,308	23	97,300	41	47	297	3,689	76
...	1	...	...	...	...	...	...	...	...	...	1	1	3	15	77
40	1	41	40	13,294	40	422,950	14	46,777	19	65,000	32	36	307	3,520	78
5	...	5	5	3,100	5	71,000	2	5,000	4	28,000	5	5	77	760	79
2	7	2	2	400	2	7,000	1	2,500	1	3,000	6	7	18	143	80
1	...	1	1	140	1	3,500	1	1,500	1	1,000	1	1	4	14	81
17	11	17	16	5,250	17	114,600	14	29,900	6	21,800	5	5	5	215	82
144	11	149	143	58,946	144	470,930	7	2,535	11	21,100	101	103	1,358	10,642	83
90	...	93	90	41,666	90	294,050	2	200	3	4,000	63	64	861	6,651	84
5	...	5	5	1,775	5	10,000	...	...	...	...	5	5	76	436	85
...	10	...	...	...	...	...	...	...	...	...	...	...	...	...	86
16	...	16	16	4,655	16	39,100	...	...	...	...	...	...	...	...	87
14	...	16	14	5,275	14	68,500	4	2,200	1	1,800	13	13	178	1,796	88
19	1	19	18	5,575	19	59,280	1	135	7	15,300	20	21	243	1,759	89
2,850	152	2,881	2,794	901,322	2,855	26,235,657	679	2,109,487	1,115	3,455,370	2,788	2,873	42,570	357,882	90
2,260	96	2,283	2,209	731,961	2,261	23,077,617	441	1,749,376	912	3,075,320	2,203	2,273	36,947	315,118	91
19	3	19	19	5,980	19	65,400	14	11,125	2	4,400	22	22	150	1,150	92
143	6	143	143	42,765	144	985,790	103	196,194	51	101,450	143	145	1,374	10,683	93
9	...	9	9	3,330	9	48,000	7	7,016	...	...	9	9	73	915	94
61	6	62	60	18,285	61	339,630	38	36,308	21	37,650	65	66	513	3,672	95
118	2	121	114	36,460	119	1,082,575	20	45,813	36	91,000	116	118	1,406	11,145	96
37	9	37	37	7,426	37	53,300	1	1,570	11	11,300	37	41	275	1,418	97
13	1	13	13	2,950	13	11,950	...	...	3	5,100	11	11	67	480	98
2	...	2	2	600	2	19,800	1	1,000	...	...	2	2	27	288	99
5	...	5	5	2,125	5	29,535	3	2,300	1	6,000	5	5	28	355	100
43	...	46	43	14,590	43	249,200	25	37,865	25	49,300	43	46	852	7,294	101
140	29	141	140	34,850	142	272,860	26	20,920	53	73,850	132	135	858	5,364	102

TABLE 3.—ORGANIZATIONS, COMMUNICANTS OR MEMBERS, PLACES OF WORSHIP, VALUE OF CHURCH PROPERTY, EACH STATE AND

PENNSYLVANIA—Continued.

	DENOMINATION.	Total number of organizations.	COMMUNICANTS OR MEMBERS.				
			Number of organizations reporting.	Total number reported.	Sex.		
					Number of organizations reporting.	Male.	Female.
103	Moravian bodies	19	19	5,322	19	2,065	3,257
104	Moravian Church (Unitas Fratrum)	19	19	5,322	19	2,065	3,257
105	Nonsectarian Churches of Bible Faith	17	17	419	17	225	194
106	Pentecostal Church of the Nazarene	6	6	378	6	141	237
107	Polish National Church of America	7	7	3,505	7	2,041	1,464
108	Presbyterian bodies	1,540	1,539	322,542	1,436	113,110	179,241
109	Presbyterian Church in the United States of America	1,075	1,075	248,335	991	84,369	136,684
110	Cumberland Presbyterian Church	60	60	8,912	55	3,318	4,603
111	Welsh Calvinistic Methodist Church	24	24	3,150	23	1,274	1,631
112	United Presbyterian Church of North America	331	331	56,587	320	22,238	33,376
113	Associate Synod of North America (Associate Presbyterian Church)	8	8	327	8	119	208
114	Synod of the Reformed Presbyterian Church of North America	31	30	2,709	30	992	1,717
115	Reformed Presbyterian Church in North America, General Synod	9	9	2,065	7	600	765
116	Reformed Presbyterian Church (Covenanted)	1	1	17	1	7	10
117	Reformed Presbyterian Church in the United States and Canada	1	1	440	1	193	247
118	Protestant Episcopal Church	489	486	99,021	407	28,226	46,628
119	Reformed bodies	906	906	181,350	863	76,980	97,151
120	Reformed Church in America	10	10	1,979	10	786	1,193
121	Reformed Church in the United States	891	891	177,270	848	74,743	95,308
122	Hungarian Reformed Church in America	5	5	2,101	5	1,451	650
123	Reformed Episcopal Church	15	14	3,564	13	1,181	1,923
124	Roman Catholic Church	1,032	1,029	1,214,734	998	613,574	554,305
125	Salvationists	62	59	2,254	59	1,189	1,065
126	Salvation Army	52	49	1,932	49	1,019	913
127	American Salvation Army	10	10	322	10	170	152
128	Schwenkfelders	8	8	725	8	318	407
129	Society for Ethical Culture	1	1	198	1	108	90
130	Spiritualists	23	23	1,450	23	612	838
131	Swedish Evangelical bodies	6	6	378	6	167	211
132	Swedish Evangelical Mission Covenant of America	4	4	161	4	78	83
133	Swedish Evangelical Free Mission	2	2	217	2	89	128
134	Theosophical societies	1	1	107	1	37	70
135	Theosophical Society, American Section	1	1	107	1	37	70
136	Unitarians	13	13	1,596	9	448	550
137	United Brethren bodies	623	622	55,574	585	20,389	32,487
138	Church of the United Brethren in Christ	586	585	53,397	548	19,459	31,240
139	Church of the United Brethren in Christ (Old Constitution)	37	37	2,177	37	930	1,247
140	Universalists	32	30	2,301	23	671	1,281
141	Vedanta Society	1	1	50	....	....	....
142	Volunteers of America	8	7	133	7	78	55

RHODE ISLAND.

	DENOMINATION.	Total number of organizations.	Number of organizations reporting.	Total number reported.	Number of organizations reporting.	Male.	Female.
1	All denominations	521	507	264,712	460	111,609	131,202
2	Adventist bodies	17	16	940	16	318	622
3	Advent Christian Church	8	7	761	7	257	504
4	Seventh-day Adventist Denomination	9	9	179	9	61	118
5	Armenian Church	4	4	2,103	4	1,726	377
6	Baptist bodies	124	124	19,878	119	6,742	12,483
7	Baptists	78	78	14,928	75	4,983	9,422
8	Northern Baptist Convention	74	74	14,304	71	4,771	9,010
9	National Baptist Convention (Colored)	4	4	624	4	212	412
10	General Six Principle Baptists	12	12	618	11	223	365
11	Seventh-day Baptists	6	6	1,080	6	485	595
12	Free Baptists	28	28	3,252	27	1,051	2,101
13	Brethren (Plymouth)	4	4	195	4	82	113
14	Brethren (Plymouth)—II	4	4	195	4	82	113
15	Buddhists	1	....	....	....	....	....
16	Chinese Temples	1	....	....	....	....	....

DEBT ON CHURCH PROPERTY, PARSONAGES, AND SUNDAY SCHOOLS, BY DENOMINATIONS (IN DETAIL), FOR TERRITORY: 1906—Continued.

PENNSYLVANIA—Continued.

Places of worship: Number of organizations reporting— Church edifices.	Places of worship: Number of organizations reporting— Halls, etc.	Places of worship: Number of church edifices reported.	Places of worship: Seating capacity of church edifices. Number of organizations reporting.	Places of worship: Seating capacity of church edifices. Seating capacity reported.	Value of church property: Number of organizations reporting.	Value of church property: Value reported.	Debt on church property: Number of organizations reporting.	Debt on church property: Amount of debt reported.	Parsonages: Number of organizations reporting.	Parsonages: Value of parsonages reported.	Sunday schools conducted by church organizations: Number of organizations reporting.	Sunday schools conducted by church organizations: Number of Sunday schools reported.	Sunday schools conducted by church organizations: Number of officers and teachers.	Sunday schools conducted by church organizations: Number of scholars.	
18	1	21	18	12,353	18	$339,000	5	$17,180	14	$60,500	18	20	470	3,990	103
18	1	21	18	12,353	18	339,000	5	17,180	14	60,500	18	20	470	3,990	104
6	8	7	5	850	5	6,100									105
4	2	4	4	1,400	4	44,250	2	5,500			5	5	67	489	106
7		10	7	3,500	7	136,000	7	39,500	4	13,000	7	9	10	518	107
1,504	22	1,694	1,503	684,859	1,509	33,018,362	311	1,448,812	641	2,822,907	1,472	1,689	28,230	266,199	108
1,053	13	1,221	1,052	512,624	1,065	26,068,915	222	1,066,945	515	2,418,257	1,031	1,222	21,686	206,729	109
59	1	61	59	22,190	59	605,600	12	58,750	16	54,400	59	61	756	7,130	110
23	1	24	23	8,735	24	181,500	8	16,050	4	8,800	23	23	386	3,054	111
322	5	336	322	123,060	323	5,196,622	61	279,117	99	318,950	320	335	4,816	45,035	112
6	1	6	6	1,475	7	7,925					2	2	6	60	113
31		35	31	11,075	31	540,800	3	3,650	7	22,500	28	36	433	3,131	114
9		10	9	5,050	9	198,000	4	19,300			8	9	117	928	115
	1														116
1		1	1	650	1	200,000	1	5,000			1	1	20	132	117
456	18	571	454	174,294	457	18,323,429	90	455,438	216	1,485,656	433	485	6,377	65,243	118
892	10	938	890	393,103	893	9,425,195	203	924,835	307	940,760	804	874	15,312	140,222	119
9	1	10	9	5,500	9	192,200	4	30,850	3	6,800	10	13	212	1,985	120
880	8	925	878	386,893	881	9,216,495	197	888,485	301	918,460	792	859	15,097	138,156	121
3	1	3	3	710	3	16,500	2	5,500	3	15,500	2	2	3	81	122
15		18	15	8,680	14	641,000	6	40,800	2	9,000	15	22	393	4,414	123
991	31	1,137	985	525,463	991	38,529,693	478	5,913,466	723	5,362,080	897	1,194	9,333	189,663	124
17	43	17	16	6,450	55	237,797	29	85,228	1	1,800	45	45	231	1,642	125
15	35	15	14	5,400	50	228,097	27	82,328			44	44	215	1,492	126
2	8	2	2	1,050	5	9,700	2	2,900	1	1,800	1	1	16	150	127
8		8	8	2,950	8	38,700	1	1,700			5	5	101	991	128
	1										1	1	21	159	129
6	14	7	6	1,750	9	51,650	3	6,100			4	5	17	143	130
6		6	6	1,650	6	31,000	2	7,500	1	450	6	6	60	481	131
4		4	4	950	4	9,500	1	1,000	1	450	4	4	82	218	132
2		2	2	700	2	21,500	1	6,500			2	2	28	263	133
	1														134
	1														135
7	3	7	7	3,470	8	355,300	3	28,500	2	16,500	7	7	63	404	136
591	15	596	581	181,115	589	2,256,903	114	207,067	181	387,150	557	563	7,635	69,406	137
555	14	560	545	170,435	553	2,202,857	106	205,076	177	381,450	533	539	7,321	67,379	138
36	1	36	36	10,680	36	54,046	8	1,981	4	5,700	24	24	314	2,027	139
30		30	29	7,306	30	514,092	4	9,700	5	11,800	21	22	206	1,159	140
	1														141
1	7	1	1	150	3	5,064	1	3,500			2	2	5	70	142

RHODE ISLAND.

452	50	493	446	195,688	465	$9,533,543	149	$1,064,432	181	$960,980	453	491	8,187	80,901	1
10	6	11	10	2,075	11	26,550			2	3,000	15	17	140	713	2
7	1	8	7	1,800	8	24,650			2	3,000	7	8	94	571	3
3	5	3	3	275	3	1,900					8	9	46	142	4
	4														5
120	2	131	120	43,871	120	1,479,646	23	101,065	38	117,850	115	126	2,164	17,701	6
77	1	87	77	32,206	76	1,209,096	17	92,940	26	87,700	76	87	1,605	13,461	7
73	1	83	73	30,105	72	1,167,950	14	79,440	25	82,700	72	83	1,559	13,089	8
4		4	4	2,100	4	41,146	3	13,500	1	5,000	4	4	46	372	9
10		11	10	1,720	10	15,400					8	8	90	384	10
6		6	6	1,800	6	33,500			3	7,200	6	6	60	525	11
27	1	27	27	8,146	28	221,650	6	8,115	9	22,950	25	25	409	3,331	12
	4				2	4,000					4	4	24	225	13
	4					4,000					4	4	24	225	14
1		1													15
1		1													16

TABLE 3.—ORGANIZATIONS, COMMUNICANTS OR MEMBERS, PLACES OF WORSHIP, VALUE OF CHURCH PROPERTY, EACH STATE AND

RHODE ISLAND—Continued.

	DENOMINATION.	Total number of organizations.	COMMUNICANTS OR MEMBERS. Number of organizations reporting.	Total number reported.	Sex. Number of organizations reporting.	Male.	Female.
17	Christians (Christian Connection)	7	7	769	6	282	467
18	Church of Christ, Scientist	3	3	234	3	50	184
19	Church of God and Saints of Christ (Colored)	1	1	64	1	13	51
20	Churches of the New Jerusalem	1	1	133	1	55	78
21	General Convention of the New Jerusalem in the United States of America	1	1	133	1	55	78
22	Congregationalists	42	42	9,858	42	3,210	6,648
23	Disciples or Christians	2	2	79	2	32	47
24	Disciples of Christ	2	[illegible]	79	2	32	47
25	Eastern Orthodox Churches	8	8	1,105	1	260	40
26	Greek Orthodox Church	8	8	1,105	1	260	40
27	Evangelical bodies	[illegible]	2	138	2	48	90
28	Evangelical Association	2	2	138	2	48	90
29	Friends	13	11	648	11	302	346
30	Society of Friends (Orthodox)	10	8	575	8	273	302
31	Orthodox Conservative Friends (Wilburite)	1	1	62	1	23	39
32	Friends (Primitive)	2	2	11	2	6	5
33	Independent churches	5	5	364	5	148	216
34	Jewish congregations	19	14	[1]1,025	......	......	......
35	Latter-day Saints	3	3	306	3	113	193
36	Reorganized Church of Jesus Christ of Latter-day Saints	3	3	306	3	113	193
37	Lutheran bodies	11	11	2,873	8	1,108	1,162
38	General Council of the Evangelical Lutheran Church in North America	9	9	2,516	7	1,034	1,059
39	Evangelical Lutheran Synodical Conference of America	2	2	357	1	74	103
40	Methodist bodies	62	61	7,892	57	2,366	5,007
41	Methodist Episcopal Church	44	43	6,536	42	2,077	4,387
42	Union American Methodist Episcopal Church (Colored)	1	1	20	1	5	15
43	African Methodist Episcopal Church	6	6	542	4	79	208
44	African Methodist Episcopal Zion Church	3	3	262	2	18	52
45	Primitive Methodist Church in the United States of America	8	8	532	8	187	345
46	Pentecostal Church of the Nazarene	2	2	133	2	52	81
47	Presbyterian bodies	[illegible]	[illegible]	1,741	8	607	1,085
48	Presbyterian Church in the United States of America	5	5	1,071	4	383	639
49	United Presbyterian Church of North America	4	4	670	4	224	446
50	Protestant Episcopal Church	71	68	15,443	66	4,921	10,126
51	Roman Catholic Church	85	85	195,951	77	88,272	89,888
52	Salvationists	5	5	160	5	76	84
53	Salvation Army	5		160	5	76	84
54	Spiritualists	2		70	2	28	42
55	Theosophical societies	1		11	1	7	4
56	Theosophical Society, American Section	1	1	11	1	7	4
57	Unitarians	7	6	1,406	5	506	860
58	Universalists	9	9	1,175	9	273	902
59	Volunteers of America	1	1	18	1	12	6

SOUTH CAROLINA.

	DENOMINATION.	Total number of organizations.	COMMUNICANTS OR MEMBERS. Number of organizations reporting.	Total number reported.	Sex. Number of organizations reporting.	Male.	Female.
1	All denominations	5,385	5,373	665,933	4,969	243,348	375,754
2	Adventist bodies	21	20	710	20	304	406
3	Advent Christian Church	8	7	509	7	228	281
4	Seventh-day Adventist Denomination	13	13	201	13	76	125
5	Baptist bodies	2,353	2,353	341,456	2,241	122,153	202,659
6	Baptists	2,296	2,296	338,201	2,194	120,973	201,008
7	Southern Baptist Convention	979	979	118,360	898	44,902	62,306
8	National Baptist Convention (Colored)	1,317	1,317	219,841	1,296	76,071	138,702
9	Freewill Baptists	41	41	2,649	40	1,104	1,522
10	Primitive Baptists	16	16	606	7	76	129

[1] Heads of families only.

DEBT ON CHURCH PROPERTY, PARSONAGES, AND SUNDAY SCHOOLS, BY DENOMINATIONS (IN DETAIL), FOR TERRITORY: 1906—Continued.

RHODE ISLAND—Continued.

PLACES OF WORSHIP.					VALUE OF CHURCH PROPERTY.		DEBT ON CHURCH PROPERTY.		PARSONAGES.		SUNDAY SCHOOLS CONDUCTED BY CHURCH ORGANIZATIONS.				
Number of organizations reporting—		Number of church edifices reported.	Seating capacity of church edifices.												
Church edifices.	Halls, etc.		Number of organizations reporting.	Seating capacity reported.	Number of organizations reporting.	Value reported.	Number of organizations reporting.	Amount of debt reported.	Number of organizations reporting.	Value of parsonages reported.	Number of organizations reporting.	Number of Sunday schools reported.	Number of officers and teachers.	Number of scholars.	
7		7	7	2,050	7	$46,100			1	$2,500	7	7	74	458	17
1	1	1	1	300	2	26,000					2	2	15	84	18
	1														19
1		1	1	300	1	30,000					1	1	10	92	20
1		1	1	300	1	30,000					1	1	10	92	21
41	1	48	41	20,580	42	1,247,304	11	$32,155	15	45,750	42	49	952	8,521	22
1		1	1	125	1	2,500					2	2	15	87	23
1		1	1	125		2,500					2	2	15	87	24
	8														25
	8														26
2		2	2	500	2	8,275	1	850	1	1,300	2	2	31	300	27
2		2	2	500	2	8,275	1	850	1	1,300	2	2	31	300	28
11	2	11	11	3,045	11	62,250			3	5,500	8	8	64	294	29
10		10	10	2,920	10	60,250			3	5,500	8	8	64	294	30
1		1	1	125	1	2,000									31
	2														32
2	3	2	2	1,200	4	16,175	2	7,800			3	3	27	164	33
9	3	10	9	4,200	11	135,600	7	32,700			7	7	22	620	34
3		3	3	500	3	6,050	1	100			2	2	31	130	35
3		3	3	500	3	6,050	1	100			2	2	31	130	36
10	1	12	10	3.275	11	91,475	8	18,450	4	14,200	11	12	154	1,003	37
8	1	10	8	2,825	9	78,475	6	13,250	2	5,400	9	10	132	778	38
2		2	2	450	2	13,000	2	5,200	2	8,800	2	2	22	225	39
59	2	60	59	22,850	59	821,200	26	94,066	25	70,400	59	59	1,080	8,627	40
42	1	43	42	17,375	42	672,700	13	65,866	23	64,900	43	43	880	6,997	41
1		1	1	250	1	1,000	1	450			1	1	6	62	42
6		6	6	2,200	6	59,700	5	5,650			4	4	42	320	43
2	1	2	2	1,200	2	53,000	2	13,000			3	3	36	339	44
8		8	8	1,825	8	34,800	5	9,100	2	5,500	8	8	116	909	45
2		2	2	550	2	8,778					2	2	33	165	46
9		9	9	3,250	9	178,000	3	25,200	1	2,500	9	9	158	1,368	47
5		5	5	1,950	5	127,000	2	22,800	1	2,500	5	5	74	713	48
4		4	4	1,300	4	51,000	1	2,400			4	4	84	655	49
67	2	77	67	23,791	66	1,482,190	11	57,600	29	153,300	62	66	985	8,943	50
81	2	88	77	56,907	80	3,218,900	53	678,456	58	520,180	81	94	1,994	29,795	51
1	4	1			5	8,300	1	5,000			4	4	9	54	52
	4	1			5	8,300	1	5,000			4	4	9	54	53
					2	250									54
	1														55
	1														56
5		6	5	2,835	5	340,000			2	17,000	5	5	55	352	57
9		9	9	3,484	9	294,000	2	11,000	2	7,500	9	9	144	1,180	58
	1										1	1	6	25	59

SOUTH CAROLINA.

5,176	99	5,290	5,004	1,774,437	5,194	$10,209,043	802	$350,527	824	$1,352,203	4,829	5,020	35,054	328,829	1
11	9	11	11	2,775	12	4,450					16	19	82	484	2
8		8	8	2,450	8	3,800					5	5	26	271	3
3	9	3	3	325	4	650					11	14	56	213	4
2,303	30	2,321	2,266	844,429	2,313	3,285,181	251	102,565	124	208,915	2,143	2,204	14,359	151,126	5
2,253	28	2,271	2,217	831,481	2,262	3,264,871	249	102,423	123	208,715	2,120	2,181	14,236	150,068	6
949	20	961	945	344,465	953	1,860,223	47	56,607	94	188,700	834	866	5,994	60,828	7
1,304	8	1,310	1,272	487,016	1,309	1,404,648	202	45,816	29	20,015	1,286	1,315	8,242	89,260	8
40	1	40	39	10,398	40	14,750	2	142	1	200	23	23	123	1,038	9
10	1	10	10	2,550	11	5,560									10

TABLE 3.—ORGANIZATIONS, COMMUNICANTS OR MEMBERS, PLACES OF WORSHIP, VALUE OF CHURCH PROPERTY, EACH STATE AND

SOUTH CAROLINA—Continued.

	DENOMINATION.	Total number of organizations.	COMMUNICANTS OR MEMBERS.				
			Number of organizations reporting.	Total number reported.	Sex.		
					Number of organizations reporting.	Male.	Female.
11	Church of Christ, Scientist	1	1	23	1	7	16
12	Church of God and Saints of Christ (Colored)	1	1	8	1	2	6
13	Congregationalists	7	7	456	7	154	302
14	Disciples or Christians	41	41	2,021	40	858	1,139
15	Disciples of Christ	41	41	2,021	40	858	1,139
16	Dunkers or German Baptist Brethren	1	1	39	1	16	23
17	German Baptist Brethren Church (Conservative)	1	1	39	1	16	23
18	Eastern Orthodox Churches	5	5	360			
19	Greek Orthodox Church	5	5	360			
20	Independent churches	8	8	485	8	213	272
21	Jewish congregations	9	7	[1]312			
22	Latter-day Saints	1	1	1,101			
23	Church of Jesus Christ of Latter-day Saints	1	1	1,101			
24	Lutheran bodies	87	87	12,652	74	4,689	5,460
25	United Synod of the Evangelical Lutheran Church in the South	87	87	12,652	74	4,689	5,460
26	Methodist bodies	2,214	2,205	249,169	1,999	93,278	134,200
27	Methodist Episcopal Church	395	393	54,097	364	20,287	30,478
28	African Methodist Episcopal Church	632	628	79,220	626	31,160	47,965
29	African Methodist Episcopal Zion Church	193	193	19,058	189	7,368	11,065
30	Methodist Protestant Church	33	33	1,840	33	765	1,075
31	Wesleyan Methodist Connection of America	32	32	1,603	32	697	906
32	Methodist Episcopal Church, South	801	799	84,266	628	29,340	37,287
33	Colored Methodist Episcopal Church	72	72	4,850	72	1,942	2,908
34	Reformed Methodist Union Episcopal Church (Colored)	56	55	4,235	55	1,719	2,516
35	Presbyterian bodies	432	432	35,533	382	13,066	18,508
36	Presbyterian Church in the United States of America	111	111	8,026	92	2,588	4,161
37	Presbyterian Church in the United States	274	274	23,395	247	8,787	12,247
38	Associate Reformed Synod of the South	47	47	4,112	43	1,711	2,100
39	Protestant Episcopal Church	118	118	8,557	109	2,745	5,555
40	Reformed bodies	5	5	140	5	69	71
41	Reformed Church in America	5	5	140	5	69	71
42	Reformed Episcopal Church	38	38	2,252	38	833	1,419
43	Roman Catholic Church	34	34	10,317	34	4,787	5,530
44	Salvationists	4	4	61	4	29	32
45	Salvation Army	4	4	61	4	29	32
46	Unitarians	1	1	160	1	65	95
47	Universalists	4	4	121	4	60	61

SOUTH DAKOTA.

	DENOMINATION.	Total number of organizations.	Number of organizations reporting.	Total number reported.	Number of organizations reporting.	Male.	Female.
1	All denominations	1,801	1,798	161,961	1,662	68,612	78,242
2	Adventist bodies	40	40	1,042	40	397	645
3	Seventh-day Adventist Denomination	40	40	1,042	40	397	645
4	Baptist bodies	92	92	6,198	87	2,364	3,723
	Baptists:						
5	Northern Baptist Convention	87	87	6,097	84	2,341	3,681
6	Free Baptists	4	4	96	2	20	40
7	Primitive Baptists	1	1	5	1	3	2
8	Brethren (Plymouth)	1	1	3	1	2	1
9	Brethren (Plymouth)—IV	1	1	3	1	2	1
10	Church of Christ, Scientist	8	8	237	8	76	161
11	Congregationalists	168	168	8,599	168	3,263	5,336
12	Disciples or Christians	21	21	1,478	21	546	932
13	Disciples of Christ	21	21	1,478	21	546	932
14	Dunkers or German Baptist Brethren	2	2	155	2	69	86
15	German Baptist Brethren Church (Conservative)	1	1	75	1	32	43
16	The Brethren Church (Progressive Dunkers)	1	1	80	1	37	43

DEBT ON CHURCH PROPERTY, PARSONAGES, AND SUNDAY SCHOOLS, BY DENOMINATIONS (IN DETAIL), FOR TERRITORY: 1906—Continued.

SOUTH CAROLINA—Continued.

PLACES OF WORSHIP. Number of organizations reporting— Church edifices.	PLACES OF WORSHIP. Number of organizations reporting— Halls, etc.	PLACES OF WORSHIP. Number of church edifices reported.	PLACES OF WORSHIP. Seating capacity of church edifices. Number of organizations reporting.	PLACES OF WORSHIP. Seating capacity of church edifices. Seating capacity reported.	VALUE OF CHURCH PROPERTY. Number of organizations reporting.	VALUE OF CHURCH PROPERTY. Value reported.	DEBT ON CHURCH PROPERTY. Number of organizations reporting.	DEBT ON CHURCH PROPERTY. Amount of debt reported.	PARSONAGES. Number of organizations reporting.	PARSONAGES. Value of parsonages reported.	SUNDAY SCHOOLS CONDUCTED BY CHURCH ORGANIZATIONS. Number of organizations reporting.	SUNDAY SCHOOLS. Number of Sunday schools reported.	SUNDAY SCHOOLS. Number of officers and teachers.	SUNDAY SCHOOLS. Number of scholars.	
....		....	....	....	....	....	....	....	....	....	1	1	1	6	11
....	1	....	....	....	....	....	....	....	....	....	....	....	....	....	12
7	....	7	7	2,600	7	$31,935	1	$2,000	2	$6,000	7	7	47	463	13
36	1	37	36	7,215	38	36,375	5	5,450	2	1,000	22	24	78	736	14
36	1	37	36	7,215	38	36,375	5	5,450	2	1,000	22	24	78	736	15
1	....	1	1	400	1	400	....	....	....	....	....	....	....	....	16
1	....	1	1	400	1	400	....	....	....	....	....	....	....	....	17
....	5	....	....	....	....	....	....	....	....	....	....	....	....	....	18
....	5	....	....	....	....	....	....	....	....	....	....	....	....	....	19
8	....	9	5	1,400	6	3,585	1	55	....	....	7	10	49	418	20
4	1	4	4	1,335	5	91,500	2	7,750	....	....	5	5	22	160	21
1	....	5	1	800	1	1,485	....	....	....	....	....	....	....	....	22
1	....	5	1	800	1	1,485	....	....	....	....	....	....	....	....	23
86	1	92	86	34,175	86	351,750		13,700	35	130,900	85	87	812	6,722	24
86	1	92	86	34,175	86	351,750	7	13,700	35	130,900	85	87	812	6,722	25
2,155	41	2,189	2,029	693,394	2,159	3,294,745	463	138,150	482	539,048	2,025	2,111	15,625	137,254	26
387	6	406	360	128,400	386	527,700	106	15,553	95	68,598	382	424	3,139	30,970	27
627	3	635	617	209,389	628	780,447	222	53,428	145	85,175	621	646	5,225	44,187	28
183	9	186	182	79,505	186	261,770	47	10,405	18	12,100	191	192	1,506	10,075	29
29	2	29	26	7,900	30	18,300	4	95	4	1,425	21	23	120	999	30
27	3	27	26	9,950	25	17,317	2	545	1	900	24	24	119	1,050	31
775	17	775	692	217,185	776	1,548,195	35	46,805	195	359,050	666	678	4,939	45,388	32
71	1	74	70	22,930	72	106,251	22	7,579	16	9,525	68	72	381	2,828	33
56	....	57	56	18,135	56	34,765	25	3,740	8	2,275	52	52	196	1,757	34
398	3	423	393	138,640	396	1,487,430	41	45,827	120	281,950	364	391	2,974	23,054	35
106	1	111	104	36,634	101	144,145	23	6,069	29	18,900	107	119	741	6,003	36
245	2	264	244	84,056	248	1,186,035	13	35,571	79	231,550	213	228	1,897	14,204	37
47	....	48	45	17,950	47	157,250	5	4,187	12	31,500	44	44	336	2,847	38
92	....	107	92	27,945	91	832,700	9	16,250	38	113,300	79	83	578	4,321	39
4	....	4	4	1,150	4	4,500	2	1,475	1	1,000	5	5	32	450	40
4	....	4	4	1,150	4	4,500	2	1,475	1	1,000	5	5	32	450	41
36	2	42	36	6,948	38	28,287	13	1,143	7	3,350	33	34	159	1,326	42
28	1	31	27	8,931	28	618,200	4	13,000	12	56,800	29	31	202	2,051	43
1	3	1	1	400	4	7,670	2	3,132	....	....	4	4	18	177	44
1	3	1	1	400	4	7,670		3,132	....	....	4	4	18	177	45
1	....	2	1	700	1	125,000	....	....	1	10,000	1	1	5	35	46
4	....	4	4	1,200	4	3,850	1	30	....	....	3	3	11	46	47

SOUTH DAKOTA.

Church edifices.	Halls, etc.	Number of church edifices reported.	Seating: Number of organizations reporting.	Seating capacity reported.	Value: Number of organizations reporting.	Value reported.	Debt: Number of organizations reporting.	Amount of debt reported.	Parsonages: Number of organizations reporting.	Value of parsonages reported.	Sunday schools: Number of organizations reporting.	Number of Sunday schools reported.	Number of officers and teachers.	Number of scholars.	
1,412	240	1,461	1,381	285,197	1,433	$4,538,013	231	$232,123	639	$1,111,745	1,337	1,463	8,587	71,554	1
21	16	22	21	2,950	22	28,849	....	....	....	....	23	25	145	604	2
21	16	22	21	2,950	22	28,849	....	....	....	....	23	25	145	604	3
77	5	94	75	18,922	77	266,722	13	8,100	34	57,650	77	101	737	6,068	4
75	5	92	73	18,522	75	260,722	13	8,100	33	55,650	74	98	712	5,908	5
2	....	2	2	400	2	6,000	....	....	1	2,000	3	3	25	160	6
....	....	....	....	....	....	....	....	....	....	....	....	....	....	....	7
....	1	....	....	....	....	....	....	....	....	....	....	....	....	....	8
....	1	....	....	....	....	....	....	....	....	....	....	....	....	....	9
4	4	4	4	800	4	9,000	....	....	....	....	7	7	18	92	10
142	17	145	138	26,821	141	380,460	17	14,705	85	135,650	157	165	1,249	9,793	11
18	2	18	17	4,075	18	52,500	9	5,540	4	6,500	17	18	145	859	12
18	2	18	17	4,075	18	52,500	9	5,540	4	6,500	17	18	145	859	13
2	....	2	2	500	2	4,300	....	....	....	....	2	2	21	135	14
1	....	1	1	250	1	1,800	....	....	....	....	1	1	10	50	15
1	....	1	1	250	1	2,500	....	....	....	....	1	1	11	85	16

TABLE 3.—ORGANIZATIONS, COMMUNICANTS OR MEMBERS, PLACES OF WORSHIP, VALUE OF CHURCH PROPERTY, EACH STATE AND

SOUTH DAKOTA—Continued.

	DENOMINATION.	Total number of organizations.	COMMUNICANTS OR MEMBERS.				
			Number of organizations reporting.	Total number reported.	Sex.		
					Number of organizations reporting.	Male.	Female.
17	Eastern Orthodox Churches	4	4	230			
18	Greek Orthodox Church	4	4	230			
19	Evangelical bodies	59	59	1,797	59	827	970
20	Evangelical Association	51	51	1,642	51	756	886
21	United Evangelical Church	8	8	155	8	71	84
22	Friends	5	5	103	5	52	51
23	Society of Friends (Orthodox)	5	5	103	5	52	51
24	German Evangelical Synod of North America	6	6	325	6	171	154
25	Independent churches	8	8	334	8	152	182
26	Latter-day Saints	1	1	85			
27	Reorganized Church of Jesus Christ of Latter-day Saints	1	1	85			
28	Lutheran bodies	505	503	45,018	432	18,859	18,523
29	General Synod of the Evangelical Lutheran Church in the United States of America	7	7	552	7	266	286
30	General Council of the Evangelical Lutheran Church in North America	29	29	2,475	27	1,144	1,138
31	Evangelical Lutheran Synodical Conference of America	125	123	8,285	99	3,454	3,359
32	United Norwegian Lutheran Church in America	132	132	15,004	102	5,258	5,199
33	Evangelical Lutheran Joint Synod of Ohio and Other States	13	13	838	11	395	411
34	Hauge's Norwegian Evangelical Lutheran Synod	38	38	3,539	32	1,341	1,307
35	Evangelical Lutheran Church in America, Eielsen's Synod	4	4	241	4	116	125
36	Evangelical Lutheran Synod of Iowa and Other States	55	55	4,103	55	2,070	2,033
37	Synod for the Norwegian Evangelical Lutheran Church in America	59	59	6,489	55	3,091	3,040
38	Danish Evangelical Lutheran Church in America	6	6	417	3	156	118
39	Finnish Evangelical Lutheran Church of America, or Suomi Synod	4	4	230	4	118	112
40	Norwegian Lutheran Free Church	19	19	1,079	19	525	554
41	United Danish Evangelical Lutheran Church in America	7	7	444	7	228	216
42	Finnish Evangelical Lutheran National Church	4	4	1,030	4	540	490
43	Apostolic Lutheran Church (Finnish)	3	3	292	3	157	135
44	Mennonite bodies	15	15	995	15	495	500
45	Mennonite Church	1	1	75	1	40	35
46	Bruederhoef Mennonite Church	8	8	275	8	129	146
47	General Conference of Mennonites of North America	5	5	562	5	284	278
48	Bundes Conferenz der Mennoniten Brueder-Gemeinde: Krimmer Brueder-Gemeinde	1	1	83	1	42	41
49	Methodist bodies	322	321	16,143	298	5,811	9,324
50	Methodist Episcopal Church	291	291	15,485	268	5,555	8,922
51	African Methodist Episcopal Church	2	2	38	2	15	23
52	Wesleyan Methodist Connection of America	5	5	176	5	68	108
53	Free Methodist Church of North America	24	23	444	23	173	271
54	Presbyterian bodies	125	125	6,990	117	2,558	3,961
55	Presbyterian Church in the United States of America	121	121	6,764	114	2,445	3,901
56	Welsh Calvinistic Methodist Church	3	3	190	2	99	58
57	United Presbyterian Church of North America	1	1	36	1	14	22
58	Protestant Episcopal Church	126	126	7,055	108	2,382	3,7[illegible]6
59	Reformed bodies	55	55	2,711	55	1,353	1,358
60	Reformed Church in America	19	19	847	19	418	429
61	Reformed Church in the United States	28	28	1,365	28	685	680
62	Christian Reformed Church	8	8	499	8	250	249
63	Roman Catholic Church	199	199	61,014	195	28,669	27,998
64	Salvationists	7	7	109	7	57	52
65	Salvation Army	7	7	109	7	57	52
66	Swedish Evangelical bodies	22	22	1,042	21	426	416
67	Swedish Evangelical Mission Covenant of America	13	13	473	13	247	226
68	Swedish Evangelical Free Mission	9	9	569	8	179	190
69	Theosophical societies	1	1	7	1	6	1
70	Theosophical Society, American Section	1	1	7	1	6	1
71	Unitarians	1	1	21	1	14	7
72	United Brethren bodies	7	7	257	6	59	116
73	Church of the United Brethren in Christ	6	6	175	6	59	116
74	Church of the United Brethren in Christ (Old Constitution)	1	1	82			
75	Universalists	1	1	13	1	4	9

DEBT ON CHURCH PROPERTY, PARSONAGES, AND SUNDAY SCHOOLS, BY DENOMINATIONS (IN DETAIL), FOR TERRITORY: 1906—Continued.

SOUTH DAKOTA—Continued.

PLACES OF WORSHIP.					VALUE OF CHURCH PROPERTY.		DEBT ON CHURCH PROPERTY.		PARSONAGES.		SUNDAY SCHOOLS CONDUCTED BY CHURCH ORGANIZATIONS.				
Number of organizations reporting— Church edifices.	Number of organizations reporting— Halls, etc.	Number of church edifices reported.	Seating capacity of church edifices. Number of organizations reporting.	Seating capacity of church edifices. Seating capacity reported.	Number of organizations reporting.	Value reported.	Number of organizations reporting.	Amount of debt reported.	Number of organizations reporting.	Value of parsonages reported.	Number of organizations reporting.	Number of Sunday schools reported.	Number of officers and teachers.	Number of scholars.	
....	4	....	....	....	....	....	....	....	....	....	....	....	....	....	17
....	4	....	....	....	....	....	....	....	....	....	....	....	....	....	18
42	10	42	42	7,235	42	$86,800	5	$3,306	21	$48,450	51	53	395	2,213	19
36	8	36	36	6,080	36	73,000	2	551	17	44,450	45	46	359	2,036	20
6	2	6	6	1,155	6	13,800	3	2,755	4	4,000	6	7	36	177	21
5	....	5	5	675	5	3,700	....	....	2	1,150	4	4	21	111	22
5	....	5	5	675	5	3,700	....	....	2	1,150	4	4	21	111	23
4	2	4	4	790	4	6,450	2	1,350	2	2,000	5	5	5	84	24
8	....	8	8	1,355	8	14,200	1	500	1	1,500	8	8	26	216	25
1	....	1	1	300	1	1,200	....	....	....	....	1	1	9	40	26
1	....	1	1	300	1	1,200	....	....	....	....	1	1	9	40	27
356	93	364	347	76,884	365	915,230	54	27,745	130	222,050	270	298	964	8,554	28
5	1	5	5	1,120	5	16,350	1	500	2	2,400	7	9	23	253	29
23	2	23	21	4,490	22	72,660	6	2,430	8	24,000	24	24	113	750	30
76	34	77	76	13,585	79	171,175	13	11,150	47	68,600	38	40	49	860	31
99	16	102	98	25,685	102	298,125	14	6,065	23	44,500	95	116	452	3,793	32
11	2	11	11	1,720	11	17,100	2	1,100	6	5,200	9	9	24	270	33
32	4	34	31	9,150	32	89,300	6	1,500	6	11,900	26	29	110	750	34
2	2	2	2	450	2	7,000	....	....	1	1,500	....	....	....	....	35
40	9	40	36	6,765	41	75,400	5	1,300	19	24,450	38	38	92	977	36
42	8	42	42	9,719	45	120,970	6	3,500	14	35,300	13	13	40	462	37
3	3	5	3	800	3	6,000	....	....	1	2,000	3	3	4	32	38
3	1	3	3	550	3	5,450	....	....	1	600	2	2	8	42	39
9	8	9	9	1,450	9	20,700	1	200	....	....	7	7	22	181	40
5	2	5	5	750	5	7,200	....	....	2	1,600	4	4	11	64	41
3	1	3	3	500	3	5,000	....	....	....	....	4	4	16	120	42
3	....	3	2	150	3	2,800	....	....	....	....	....	....	....	....	43
15	....	16	15	3,400	15	22,300	1	500	....	....	7	7	81	1,020	44
1	....	1	1	100	1	2,000	....	....	....	....	1	1	2	35	45
8	....	8	8	650	8	9,100	....	....	....	....	....	....	....	....	46
6	....	6	5	2,450	5	10,200	1	500	....	....	5	5	68	910	47
1	....	1	1	200	1	1,000	....	....	....	....	1	1	11	75	48
251	42	252	239	49,270	252	715,450	46	27,775	143	228,960	274	304	2,780	20,919	49
235	33	236	223	46,230	234	686,100	42	25,270	128	212,360	250	277	2,627	20,013	50
1	....	1	1	150	2	3,900	1	1,700	1	1,800	2	2	9	32	51
4	1	4	4	725	5	9,550	1	600	4	3,100	5	5	42	352	52
11	8	11	11	2,165	11	15,900	2	205	10	11,700	17	20	102	522	53
110	5	112	108	19,219	107	314,175	14	8,523	42	63,600	109	116	1,032	7,533	54
106	5	108	104	18,439	103	300,075	14	8,523	42	63,600	106	113	999	7,313	55
3	....	3	3	430	3	4,100	....	....	....	....	2	2	24	170	56
1	....	1	1	350	1	10,000	....	....	....	....	1	1	9	50	57
109	11	112	109	14,948	111	318,435	3	7,900	61	83,435	86	86	269	3,158	58
45	7	45	45	9,041	45	82,560	10	7,300	24	34,900	45	55	231	2,040	59
16	3	16	16	3,441	16	37,260	5	2,800	13	20,100	17	17	139	1,105	60
21	4	21	21	4,025	21	27,800	1	400	5	9,000	23	30	72	651	61
8	....	8	8	1,575	8	17,500	4	4,100	6	5,800	5	8	20	284	62
177	11	189	177	42,857	182	1,262,452	50	116,513	82	217,000	163	175	302	6,966	63
1	6	1	1	300	7	9,200	2	266	....	....	7	7	26	175	64
1	6	1	1	300	7	9,200	2	266	....	....	7	7	26	175	65
17	2	17	17	3,335	18	34,630	3	1,300	4	6,300	17	18	71	671	66
8	2	8	8	1,535	9	15,130	1	600	1	1,500	9	9	31	258	67
9	....	9	9	1,800	9	19,500	2	700	3	4,800	8	9	40	413	68
....			....	....	....	....	....	....	....	....	....	....	....	....	69
....	1	....	....	....	....	....	....	....	....	....	....	....	....	....	70
....	....	....	....	....	....	....	....	....	....	....	....	....	....	....	71
6	1	7	5	1,370	6	7,900	1	800	4	2,600	7	8	60	303	72
5	1	6	4	1,220	5	6,900	1	800		2,600	6	6	42	203	73
1	....	1	1	150	1	1,000	....	....	....	....	1	2	18	100	74
1	....	1	1	150	1	1,500	....	....	....	....	....	....	....	....	75

TABLE 3.—ORGANIZATIONS, COMMUNICANTS OR MEMBERS, PLACES OF WORSHIP, VALUE OF CHURCH PROPERTY, EACH STATE AND

TENNESSEE.

	DENOMINATION.	Total number of organizations.	COMMUNICANTS OR MEMBERS.				
			Number of organizations reporting.	Total number reported.	Sex.		
					Number of organizations reporting.	Male.	Female.
1	All denominations	8,021	7,963	697,570	7,205	249,870	373,888
2	Adventist bodies	40	40	1,452	40	587	865
3	Advent Christian Church	11	11	351	11	159	192
4	Seventh-day Adventist Denomination	29	29	1,101	29	428	673
5	Baptist bodies	2,907	2,896	277,170	2,685	102,726	158,217
6	Baptists	2,376	2,372	253,141	2,282	95,156	146,861
7	Southern Baptist Convention	1,617	1,615	159,838	1,542	62,822	87,203
8	National Baptist Convention (Colored)	759	757	93,303	740	32,334	59,658
9	Free Baptists	30	30	1,840	23	671	827
10	Freewill Baptists	49	49	3,093	34	814	1,064
11	General Baptists	27	27	1,108	27	450	658
12	Separate Baptists	6	6	138	4	40	68
13	Duck River and Kindred Associations of Baptists (Baptist Church of Christ)	57	56	4,099	52	1,525	2,250
14	Primitive Baptists	247	244	10,204	219	3,642	5,734
15	Colored Primitive Baptists in America	96	93	3,268	28	315	631
16	Two-Seed-in-the-Spirit Predestinarian Baptists	19	19	279	16	113	124
17	Brethren (Plymouth)	4	4	75	4	29	46
18	Brethren (Plymouth)—IV	4	4	75	4	29	46
19	Christian Union	1	1	53	1	21	32
20	Church of Christ, Scientist	5	5	337	5	98	239
21	Churches of the Living God (Colored)	13	12	918	12	331	587
22	Church of the Living God (Christian Workers for Friendship)	8	8	690	8	244	446
23	Church of the Living God (Apostolic Church)	3	2	142	2	57	85
24	Church of Christ in God	2	2	86	2	30	56
25	Churches of the New Jerusalem	5	5	73	5	32	41
26	General Convention of the New Jerusalem in the United States of America	5	5	73	5	32	41
27	Congregationalists	37	37	2,426	33	880	1,333
28	Disciples or Christians	781	781	56,315	751	22,284	31,632
29	Disciples of Christ	150	150	14,904	120	5,112	7,393
30	Churches of Christ	631	631	41,411	631	17,172	24,239
31	Dunkers or German Baptist Brethren	16	16	1,104	16	477	627
32	German Baptist Brethren Church (Conservative)	16	16	1,104	16	477	627
33	Eastern Orthodox Churches	4	4	410			
34	Greek Orthodox Church	4	4	410			
35	Evangelistic associations	1	1	30	1	14	16
36	Missionary Church Association	1	1	30	1	14	16
37	Friends	1	1	117	1	45	72
38	Society of Friends (Orthodox)	1	1	117	1	45	72
39	Independent churches	31	31	2,381	29	711	1,170
40	Jewish congregations	17	12	[1] 919			
41	Latter-day Saints	5	5	1,013	3	76	96
42	Church of Jesus Christ of Latter-day Saints	2	2	841			
43	Reorganized Church of Jesus Christ of Latter-day Saints	3	3	172	3	76	96
44	Lutheran bodies	35	34	3,225	30	1,196	1,674
45	General Synod of the Evangelical Lutheran Church in the United States of America	5	5	727	5	266	461
46	United Synod of the Evangelical Lutheran Church in the South	22	22	1,678	20	705	898
47	Evangelical Lutheran Synodical Conference of America	6	5	725	3	190	255
48	Evangelical Lutheran Joint Synod of Ohio and Other States	1	1	45	1	15	30
49	Synod for the Norwegian Evangelical Lutheran Church in America	1	1	50	1	20	30
50	Mennonite bodies	1	1	44	1	21	23
51	Mennonite Church	1	1	44	1	21	23
52	Methodist bodies	2,991	2,955	241,396	2,645	87,419	131,076
53	Methodist Episcopal Church	799	781	46,180	688	16,601	24,744
54	African Methodist Episcopal Church	309	306	23,377	304	8,238	14,904
55	African Methodist Episcopal Zion Church	117	117	6,651	117	2,186	4,465
56	Methodist Protestant Church	43	43	2,716	33	740	982
57	Wesleyan Methodist Connection of America	6	6	422	6	184	238
58	Methodist Episcopal Church, South	1,480	1,465	140,308	1,284	51,609	73,340
59	Congregational Methodist Church	21	21	977	7	89	137
60	Colored Methodist Episcopal Church	209	209	20,634	200	7,715	12,207
61	Free Methodist Church of North America	7	7	131	6	57	59

DEBT ON CHURCH PROPERTY, PARSONAGES, AND SUNDAY SCHOOLS, BY DENOMINATIONS (IN DETAIL), FOR TERRITORY: 1906—Continued.

TENNESSEE.

PLACES OF WORSHIP.					VALUE OF CHURCH PROPERTY.		DEBT ON CHURCH PROPERTY.		PARSONAGES.		SUNDAY SCHOOLS CONDUCTED BY CHURCH ORGANIZATIONS.				
Number of organizations reporting—		Number of church edifices reported.	Seating capacity of church edifices.		Number of organizations reporting.	Value reported.	Number of organizations reporting.	Amount of debt reported.	Number of organizations reporting.	Value of parsonages reported.	Number of organizations reporting.	Number of Sunday schools reported.	Number of officers and teachers.	Number of scholars.	
Church edifices.	Halls, etc.		Number of organizations reporting.	Seating capacity reported.											
7,232	489	7,400	6,972	2,323,285	7,243	$14,469,012	687	$445,709	930	$1,346,711	5,919	6,101	40,875	355,550	1
26	10	26	25	6,100	25	28,375	2	35	....	....	31	34	222	1,109	2
8	2	8	8	2,500	7	7,700	....	....	....	....	6	7	18	148	3
18	8	18	17	3,600	18	20,675	2	35	....	....	25	27	204	961	4
2,632	162	2,659	2,560	859,178	2,654	3,993,474	196	140,191	104	196,451	1,892	1,943	12,210	110,168	5
2,231	115	2,256	2,203	739,397	2,241	3,737,934	179	138,011	98	193,800	1,822	1,869	11,799	106,849	6
1,502	94	1,527	1,496	511,174	1,505	2,529,324	88	84,372	68	162,700	1,090	1,129	7,882	75,021	7
729	21	729	707	228,223	736	1,208,610	91	53,639	30	31,100	732	740	3,917	31,828	8
17	8	17	16	4,690	19	15,500	1	30	....	....	24	28	159	1,219	9
43	5	43	30	10,550	44	27,400	3	700	2	950	28	28	153	1,272	10
20	7	20	20	6,000	22	8,151	3	185	....	....	6	6	33	277	11
3	1	3	3	575	1	400	....	....	....	....	....	....	....	....	12
54	1	54	54	14,713	55	24,196	1	50	1	156	2	2	12	125	13
196	17	198	193	69,740	202	139,946	6	775	2	1,525	....	....	....	....	14
50	8	50	23	7,163	52	28,747	3	440	1	20	10	10	54	426	15
18	....	18	18	6,350	18	11,200	....	....	....	....	....	....	....	....	16
....	4	....	....	....	....	....	....	....	....	....	....	....	....	....	17
....	4	....	....	....	....	....	....	....	....	....	....	....	....	....	18
1	....	1	1	50	1	100	....	....	....	....	....	....	....	....	19
....	4	....	....	....	1	10,000	....	....	....	....	4	4	19	80	20
7	6	7	6	2,700	7	16,050	1	150	....	....	11	11	39	309	21
5	3	5	5	2,300	5	5,050	1	150	....	....	8	8	24	217	22
1	2	1	....	....	1	10,000	....	....	....	....	2	2	10	53	23
1	1	1	1	400	1	1,000	....	....	....	....	1	1	5	39	24
2	3	2	2	180	2	1,100	....	....	1	500	1	1	4	18	25
2	3	2	2	180	2	1,100	....	....	1	500	1	1	4	18	26
28	4	28	20	6,300	21	138,100	2	8,700	6	5,150	33	36	255	2,610	27
656	119	668	656	217,485	660	998,917	42	36,343	14	32,900	575	587	2,841	27,749	28
138	8	140	138	47,605	138	404,950	14	22,750	9	25,100	121	122	973	8,719	29
518	111	528	518	169,880	522	593,967	28	13,593	5	7,800	454	465	1,868	19,030	30
14	1	15	14	5,575	14	12,700	....	....	....	....	10	11	65	531	31
14	1	15	14	5,575	14	12,700	....	....	....	....	10	11	65	531	32
....	4	....	....	....	....	....	....	....	....	....	....	....	....	....	33
....	4	....	....	....	....	....	....	....	....	....	....	....	....	....	34
1	....	1	1	300	1	400	1	50	....	....	1	2	11	75	35
1	....	1	1	300	1	400	1	50	....	....	1	2	11	75	36
1	....	1	1	280	1	3,500	....	....	1	1,500	1	1	11	75	37
1	....	1	1	280	1	3,500	....	....	1	1,500	1	1	11	75	38
21	9	21	20	7,060	23	41,025	3	7,188	2	500	26	28	177	1,524	39
8	....	9	8	3,725	8	176,500	5	10,800	....	....	6	6	38	560	40
4	....	4	3	550	4	1,050	....	....	....	....	1	1	5	40	41
1	....	1	....	....	1	125	....	....	....	....	....	....	....	....	42
3	....	3	3	550	3	925	....	....	....	....	1	1	5	40	43
32	2	32	32	11,915	31	149,600	6	4,654	12	23,650	22	22	166	1,355	44
4	1	4	4	2,000	4	52,100	1	2,850	1	4,000	3	3	40	340	45
21	1	21	21	8,275	20	40,600	3	771	7	8,150	14	14	106	744	46
5	....	5	5	1,190	5	54,200	1	650	4	11,500	3	3	14	209	47
1	....	1	1	250	1	1,500	1	383	....	....	1	1	3	50	48
1	....	1	1	200	1	1,200	....	....	....	....	1	1	3	12	49
1	....	1	1	300	1	1,200	....	....	....	....	1	1	11	60	50
1	....	1	1	300	1	1,200	....	....	....	....	1	1	11	60	51
2,761	125	2,844	2,620	845,378	2,771	4,910,646	362	129,749	595	668,985	2,465	2,539	17,681	153,103	52
703	47	716	663	203,762	711	951,585	104	30,245	142	122,300	585	610	4,269	35,379	53
299	6	339	297	93,529	296	376,279	82	21,624	61	18,315	285	296	1,673	12,677	54
108	5	119	107	31,160	110	139,221	26	8,879	12	7,200	111	111	614	4,371	55
40	2	40	34	12,100	40	29,850	....	....	2	1,100	28	28	183	1,587	56
6	....	6	6	3,180	6	3,225	....	....	2	450	6	6	77	430	57
1,382	55	1,391	1,292	420,687	1,388	2,985,436	71	44,107	338	496,535	1,227	1,253	9,338	85,770	58
13	8	13	13	2,935	11	5,325	....	....	....	....	19	20	154	1,005	59
204	2	214	202	76,275	203	416,325	78	24,646	38	23,085	198	209	1,337	11,631	60
6	....	6	6	1,750	6	3,400	1	248	....	....	6	6	36	253	61

TABLE 3.—ORGANIZATIONS, COMMUNICANTS OR MEMBERS, PLACES OF WORSHIP, VALUE OF CHURCH PROPERTY, EACH STATE AND

TENNESSEE—Continued.

	DENOMINATION.	Total number of organizations.	COMMUNICANTS OR MEMBERS. Number of organizations reporting.	Total number reported.	Sex. Number of organizations reporting.	Male.	Female.
62	Nonsectarian Churches of Bible Faith	6	6	206	6	111	95
63	Presbyterian bodies	918	915	79,337	793	29,382	40,203
64	Presbyterian Church in the United States of America	92	92	6,786	88	2,439	3,830
65	Cumberland Presbyterian Church	536	536	42,464	450	16,000	20,595
66	Colored Cumberland Presbyterian Church	79	79	6,640	79	3,048	3,592
67	United Presbyterian Church of North America	8	8	544	8	218	326
68	Presbyterian Church in the United States	188	185	21,390	155	7,086	11,146
69	Associate Reformed Synod of the South	14	14	1,504	12	586	710
70	Reformed Presbyterian Church in North America, General Synod	1	1	9	1	5	4
71	Protestant Episcopal Church	103	103	7,874	98	2,531	4,796
72	Reformed bodies	3	3	234			
73	Reformed Church in the United States	3	3	234			
74	Roman Catholic Church	25	25	17,252	3	109	80
75	Salvationists	6	6	133	5	76	51
76	Salvation Army	4	4	102	4	58	44
77	American Salvation Army	2	2	31	1	18	7
78	Spiritualists	1	1	29	1	10	19
79	Unitarians	2	2	95			
80	United Brethren bodies	60	59	2,875	36	693	883
81	Church of the United Brethren in Christ	60	59	2,875	36	693	883
82	Universalists	2	2	77	1	11	16

TEXAS.

	DENOMINATION.	Total number of organizations.	Number of organizations reporting.	Total number reported.	Number of organizations reporting.	Male.	Female.
1	All denominations	12,354	12,285	1,226,906	11,402	475,543	654,454
2	Adventist bodies	42	42	1,825	39	672	1,008
3	Advent Christian Church	13	13	411	10	112	154
4	Seventh-day Adventist Denomination	29	29	1,414	29	560	854
5	Baptist bodies	5,192	5,170	401,720	4,882	151,167	232,871
6	Baptists	4,870	4,859	392,184	4,681	148,677	228,935
7	Southern Baptist Convention	3,107	3,098	247,306	2,970	94,902	140,165
8	National Baptist Convention (Colored)	1,763	1,761	144,878	1,711	53,775	88,770
9	Free Baptists	19	19	630	6	67	85
10	Freewill Baptists	11	11	507	9	219	273
11	Primitive Baptists	247	236	7,095	171	2,009	3,255
12	Colored Primitive Baptists in America	43	43	1,280	15	195	323
13	Two-Seed-in-the-Spirit Predestinarian Baptists	2	2	24			
14	Brethren (Plymouth)	4	4	90	4	30	60
15	Brethren (Plymouth)—II	3	3	84	3	27	57
16	Brethren (Plymouth)—III	1	1	6	1	3	3
17	Christadelphians	7	7	55	7	24	31
18	Christians (Christian Connection)	2	2	36	2	19	17
19	Church of Christ, Scientist	16	16	796	16	248	548
20	Churches of the Living God (Colored)	6	6	578	6	196	382
21	Church of the Living God (Christian Workers for Friendship)	4	4	405	4	125	280
22	Church of the Living God (Apostolic Church)	2	2	173	2	71	102
23	Churches of the New Jerusalem	2	2	110	2	45	65
24	General Convention of the New Jerusalem in the United States of America	1	1	10	1	5	5
25	General Church of the New Jerusalem	1	1	100	1	40	60
26	Congregationalists	26	26	1,856	26	747	1,109
27	Disciples or Christians	1,130	1,129	73,556	1,122	29,554	43,048
28	Disciples of Christ	503	502	39,550	495	15,348	23,248
29	Churches of Christ	627	627	34,006	627	14,206	19,800
30	Dunkers or German Baptist Brethren	6	6	151	6	74	77
31	German Baptist Brethren Church (Conservative)	5	5	142	5	69	73
32	The Brethren Church (Progressive Dunkers)	1	1	9	1	5	4

DEBT ON CHURCH PROPERTY, PARSONAGES, AND SUNDAY SCHOOLS, BY DENOMINATIONS (IN DETAIL), FOR TERRITORY: 1906—Continued.

TENNESSEE—Continued.

PLACES OF WORSHIP. Number of organizations reporting— Church edifices.	Halls, etc.	Number of church edifices reported.	Seating capacity of church edifices. Number of organizations reporting.	Seating capacity reported.	VALUE OF CHURCH PROPERTY. Number of organizations reporting.	Value reported.	DEBT ON CHURCH PROPERTY. Number of organizations reporting.	Amount of debt reported.	PARSONAGES. Number of organizations reporting.	Value of parsonages reported.	SUNDAY SCHOOLS CONDUCTED BY CHURCH ORGANIZATIONS. Number of organizations reporting.	Number of Sunday schools reported.	Number of officers and teachers.	Number of scholars.	
4	2	4	3	600	3	$1,170	...	...	...	...	1	1	1	47	62
873	17	907	861	312,531	863	2,705,175	46	$36,666	163	$332,225	699	723	6,134	45,429	63
85	5	91	85	23,835	86	362,225	5	1,550	27	54,000	87	93	865	6,964	64
510	9	521	501	183,560	507	984,645	28	23,873	57	69,875	368	370	2,667	20,275	65
79	...	79	79	30,735	78	71,155	5	1,015	1	300	77	77	355	2,466	66
6	2	6	6	1,500	6	10,950	...	...	4	5,550	8	8	70	863	67
178	1	194	175	66,916	171	1,240,000	5	7,425	68	196,100	146	161	2,054	13,775	68
14	...	15	14	5,735	14	35,700	3	2,803	6	6,400	13	14	123	1,086	69
1	...	1	1	250	1	500	...	...	...	...	...	...	...	...	70
85	3	95	84	21,553	84	986,100	11	63,250	27	80,450	69	73	462	4,100	71
...	...	...	...	...	...	...	...	...	...	...	2	2	18	155	72
...	...	...	...	...	...	...	...	...	...	...	2	2	18	155	73
21	3	21	18	8,950	11	207,000	...	...	...	...	18	18	121	3,458	74
1	5	1	1	325	4	8,000	...	...	...	...	2	2	6	50	75
1	3	1	1	325	4	8,000	...	...	...	...	2	2	6	50	76
...	2	...	...	...	...	...	...	...	...	...	...	...	...	...	77
...	1	...	...	...	...	...	...	...	...	...	...	...	...	...	78
	...	1	1	250	1	12,000	...	...	...	...	1	1	3	25	79
51	5	51	34	12,000	51	56,830	10	7,933	5	4,400	46	53	370	2,889	80
51	5	51	34	12,000	51	56,830	10	7,933	5	4,400	46	53	370	2,889	81
1	...	1	...	...	1	10,000	...	...	...	...	1	1	5	31	82

TEXAS.

9,344	1,719	9,589	9,056	2,822,460	9,510	$22,949,976	1,319	$944,057	2,090	$2,864,606	8,308	8,678	58,093	533,535	1
23	13	23	23	4,575	23	17,774	3	1,284	...	...	30	31	252	1,405	2
3	7	3	3	800	3	2,200	...	...	...	...	3	3	19	187	3
20	6	20	20	3,775	20	15,574	3	1,284	...	...	27	28	233	1,218	4
4,012	832	4,083	3,930	1,223,587	4,052	6,067,557	478	226,060	303	384,475	3,502	3,606	22,682	207,077	5
3,863	783	3,932	3,798	1,182.437	3,905	5,975,615	456	223,169	303	384,475	3,477	3,581	22,514	206,239	6
2,199	708	2,263	2,180	725,113	2,236	4,399,685	173	157,595	228	340,400	1,869	1,934	13,559	130,714	7
1,664	75	1,669	1,618	457,324	1,669	1,575,930	285	65,574	75	44,075	1,608	1,647	8,955	75,525	8
2	4	2	2	300	2	1,000	...	...	...	...	12	12	58	359	9
9	1	9	9	1,875	9	5,650	3	123	...	...	6	6	31	276	10
110	38	112	108	35,810	107	67,557	15	2,415	...	...	...	...	...	...	11
28	6	28	13	3,165	29	17,735	2	353	...	...	7	7	29	203	12
...	...	...	...	...	...	...	...	...	...	...	...	...	...	...	13
...	4	...	...	...	...	...	...	...	...	...	3	4	14	148	14
...	3	...	...	...	...	...	...	...	...	...	3	4	14	148	15
...	1	...	...	...	...	...	...	...	...	...	...	...	...	...	16
1	1	1	1	50	1	200	...	...	...	...	1	1	2	8	17
...	...	...	...	...	...	...	...	...	...	...	...	...	...	...	18
8	6	8	8	1,303	10	52,950	3	7,274	...	...	15	15	55	405	19
5	1	5	5	1,350	5	3,650	1	800	1	500	6	6	19	356	20
3	1	3	3	650	3	2,150	1	800	...	...	4	4	10	95	21
2	...	2	2	700	2	1,500	...	...	1	500	2	2	9	261	22
2	...	2	2	300	2	5,000	...	...	...	...	...	...	...	...	23
1	...	1	1	150	1	3,000	...	...	...	...	...	...	...	...	24
1	...	1	1	150	1	2,000	...	...	...	...	...	...	...	...	25
19	3	22	17	7,550	20	148,425	6	14,498	7	13,500	23	27	198	2,058	26
743	255	767	740	243,098	757	2,206,723	104	116,544	45	81,925	586	604	3,833	36,630	27
360	19	371	357	116,115	362	1,399,743	57	91,120	38	77,800	362	375	2,979	25,294	28
383	236	396	383	126,983	395	806,980	47	25,424	7	4,125	224	229	854	11,336	29
2	3	2	2	550	2	1,600	1	150	...	...	3	3	20	85	30
2	3	2	2	550	2	1,600	1	150	...	...	2	2	12	60	31
...	...	...	...	...	...	...	...	...	...	...	1	1	8	25	32

TABLE 3.—ORGANIZATIONS, COMMUNICANTS OR MEMBERS, PLACES OF WORSHIP, VALUE OF CHURCH PROPERTY, EACH STATE AND

TEXAS—Continued.

	DENOMINATION.	Total number of organizations.	COMMUNICANTS OR MEMBERS.				
			Number of organizations reporting.	Total number reported.	Sex.		
					Number of organizations reporting.	Male.	Female.
33	Eastern Orthodox Churches	1	1	500	1	400	100
34	Russian Orthodox Church	1	1	500	1	400	100
35	Evangelical bodies	14	14	611	13	252	347
36	Evangelical Association	14	14	611	13	252	347
37	Evangelistic associations	2	2	68	2	35	33
38	Apostolic Faith Movement	1	1	48	1	25	23
39	Pentecost Bands of the World	1	1	20	1	10	10
40	Friends	1	1	114	1	55	59
41	Society of Friends (Orthodox)	1	1	114	1	55	59
42	German Evangelical Synod of North America	50	50	7,745	48	3,357	3,790
43	Independent churches	43	43	1,387	38	475	648
44	Jewish congregations	33	25	[1] 1,676	.....	.....	.....
45	Latter-day Saints	12	12	1,500	12	622	878
46	Church of Jesus Christ of Latter-day Saints	2	2	873	2	358	515
47	Reorganized Church of Jesus Christ of Latter-day Saints	10	10	627	10	264	363
48	Lutheran bodies	228	227	27,437	223	12,633	13,937
49	General Council of the Evangelical Lutheran Church in North America	16	16	1,348	16	708	640
50	Evangelical Lutheran Synodical Conference of America	81	81	7,983	78	3,578	3,938
51	Evangelical Lutheran Joint Synod of Ohio and Other States	14	14	1,337	14	641	696
52	German Evangelical Lutheran Synod of Texas	25	24	2,440	23	885	1,155
53	Evangelical Lutheran Synod of Iowa and Other States	83	83	12,758	83	6,091	6,667
54	Synod for the Norwegian Evangelical Lutheran Church in America	8	8	1,371	8	650	721
55	Danish Evangelical Lutheran Church in America	1	1	200	1	80	120
56	Mennonite bodies	2	2	35	2	20	15
57	Mennonite Church	1	1	21	1	12	9
58	Nebraska and Minnesota Conference of Mennonites	1	1	14	1	8	6
59	Methodist bodies	4,011	3,979	317,495	3,637	111,668	171,880
60	Methodist Episcopal Church	568	561	36,223	518	12,385	21,043
61	African Methodist Episcopal Church	442	440	24,919	429	8,304	16,249
62	African Methodist Episcopal Zion Church	11	11	457	11	193	264
63	Methodist Protestant Church	236	227	8,495	221	3,382	4,815
64	Methodist Episcopal Church, South	2,354	2,341	225,431	2,071	79,776	116,016
65	Congregational Methodist Church	72	71	2,759	66	1,082	1,290
66	Colored Methodist Episcopal Church	288	288	18,428	283	6,289	11,757
67	Free Methodist Church of North America	40	40	783	38	257	446
68	Moravian bodies	14	14	740	14	345	395
69	Evangelical Union of Bohemian and Moravian Brethren in North America	14	14	740	14	345	395
70	Nonsectarian Churches of Bible Faith	12	12	179	12	93	86
71	Pentecostal Church of the Nazarene	2	2	47	2	20	27
72	Presbyterian bodies	1,021	1,018	62,090	854	22,298	32,490
73	Presbyterian Church in the United States of America	58	58	4,118	44	1,368	2,238
74	Cumberland Presbyterian Church	541	540	31,598	433	10,898	15,175
75	Colored Cumberland Presbyterian Church	21	21	2,091	21	1,204	887
76	Presbyterian Church in the United States	395	393	23,934	350	8,671	13,998
77	Associate Reformed Synod of the South	6	6	349	6	157	192
78	Protestant Episcopal Church	175	173	14,246	151	3,780	7,806
79	Roman Catholic Church	255	255	308,356	239	135,837	141,822
80	Salvationists	15	15	361	15	178	183
81	Salvation Army	15	15	361	15	178	183
82	Spiritualists	16	16	957	15	468	474
83	Swedish Evangelical bodies	4	4	201	4	102	99
84	Swedish Evangelical Free Mission	4	4	201	4	102	99
85	Unitarians	2	2	118	2	56	62
86	Universalists	8	8	270	5	73	107

[1] Heads of families only.

DEBT ON CHURCH PROPERTY, PARSONAGES, AND SUNDAY SCHOOLS, BY DENOMINATIONS (IN DETAIL), FOR TERRITORY: 1906—Continued.

TEXAS—Continued.

PLACES OF WORSHIP.					VALUE OF CHURCH PROPERTY.		DEBT ON CHURCH PROPERTY.		PARSONAGES.		SUNDAY SCHOOLS CONDUCTED BY CHURCH ORGANIZATIONS.				
Number of organizations reporting— Church edifices.	Number of organizations reporting— Halls, etc.	Number of church edifices reported.	Seating capacity of church edifices. Number of organizations reporting.	Seating capacity of church edifices. Seating capacity reported.	Number of organizations reporting.	Value reported.	Number of organizations reporting.	Amount of debt reported.	Number of organizations reporting.	Value of parsonages reported.	Number of organizations reporting.	Number of Sunday schools reported.	Number of officers and teachers.	Number of scholars.	
1		1	1	200	1	$5,000	1	$300	1	$2,000					33
1		1	1	200	1	5,000	1	300	1	2,000					34
12	2	12	12	2,615	13	31,225	3	3,750	9	11,800	12	15	123	786	35
12	2	12	12	2,615	13	31,225	3	3,750	9	11,800	12	15	123	786	36
2		2	2	400	2	600					2	2	13	95	37
1		1	1	200	1	100					1	1	4	55	38
1		1	1	200	1	500					1	1	9	40	39
1		1	1	200	1	4,000	1	200			1	1	16	100	40
1		1	1	200	1	4,000	1	200			1	1	16	100	41
45	5	46	44	9,475	45	174,550	12	18,225	25	22,850	43	46	183	2,069	42
33	5	35	30	12,705	31	31,425	8	2,275			25	26	157	1,166	43
20	3	21	18	7,799	22	352,200	5	45,500	3	17,000	19	21	83	1,162	44
5	3	5	5	985	6	2,825	1	15			6	6	86	368	45
1		1	1	300	1	600					2	2	51	234	46
4	3	4	4	685	5	2,225	1	15			4	4	35	134	47
177	33	185	174	42,012	182	520,590	33	29,822	118	127,374	153	156	539	6,710	48
12	1	15	12	3,420	13	72,300	1	2,600	6	12,800	12	12	92	566	49
63	13	64	63	14,627	65	169,380	14	17,997	44	36,640	33	33	60	1,096	50
9	5	9	9	2,146	9	23,200	3	4,450	5	5,600	13	13	37	430	51
18	5	18	17	2,834	18	30,050	3	1,000	14	10,850	17	18	57	808	52
70	7	74	68	17,270	71	204,360	12	3,775	44	53,784	74	76	271	3,682	53
5	1	5	5	1,715	5	19,300			4	7,200	4	4	22	128	54
	1				1	2,000			1	500					55
		1	1	120	1	900					2	4	12	75	56
1		1	1	120	1	900					1	1	8	33	57
	1										1	3	4	42	58
3,135	417	3,191	2,969	921,491	3,185	6,831,817	526	229,906	1,148	1,289,807	2,960	3,080	23,283	199,018	59
496	33	508	456	122,862	503	1,001,152	151	42,506	202	155,880	507	521	3,865	25,621	60
407	27	424	391	113,978	407	509,922	153	53,033	130	54,905	390	409	2,419	14,563	61
11		13	11	3,540	11	12,380	3	83	1	200	10	15	78	316	62
104	63	104	100	33,350	114	113,973	15	2,839	44	23,150	81	84	458	3,714	63
1,765	264	1,784	1,672	540,584	1,797	4,814,645	143	123,640	710	1,003,222	1,641	1,714	14,637	142,426	64
60	2	63	56	17,895	60	34,550	3	413			31	32	162	1,405	65
266	21	269	257	82,182	266	312,195	55	6,887	48	23,900	279	284	1,556	10,238	66
26	7	26	24	7,100	27	33,000	3	505	13	28,550	21	21	108	735	67
8	6	8	8	3,100	10	13,750			2	700	2	2	6	97	68
8	6	8	8	3,100	10	13,750			2	700	2	2	6	97	69
	10														70
1		1	1	75	1	300									71
706	63	721	681	217,365	738	2,783,557	71	66,150	223	425,950	581	607	4,945	41,473	72
39	2	40	38	11,175	38	295,950	11	18,680	10	27,800	41	41	443	3,840	73
361	44	367	343	119,300	382	931,135	23	18,293	108	151,025	283	286	2,113	17,306	74
21		21	19	5,850	21	12,982					21	21	84	672	75
280	16	288	276	79,390	292	1,520,490	37	29,177	102	240,575	231	254	2,266	19,415	76
5	1	5	5	1,650	5	23,000			3	6,550	5	5	39	240	77
145	5	155	144	32,515	152	1,208,910	11	18,418	73	184,900	122	128	791	6,668	78
227	22	281	227	85,790	224	2,433,523	44	156,216	130	299,725	191	267	753	24,880	79
1	14	1	1	500	15	15,375	4	120			12	12	36	269	80
1	14	1	1	500	15	15,375	4	120			12	12	36	269	81
1	11	1	1	300	1	15,000	1	3,800	1	1,500	2	2	9	55	82
4		4	4	1,300	4	5,600			1	600	4	4	21	280	83
4		4	4	1,300	4	5,600			1	600	4	4	21	280	84
1		1	1	300	1	12,000	1	2,100			1	1	7	61	85
3	1	3	3	850	3	2,950	1	650			1	1	5	31	86

TABLE 3.—ORGANIZATIONS, COMMUNICANTS OR MEMBERS, PLACES OF WORSHIP, VALUE OF CHURCH PROPERTY, EACH STATE AND

UTAH.

	DENOMINATION.	Total number of organizations.	COMMUNICANTS OR MEMBERS.				
			Number of organizations reporting.	Total number reported.	Sex.		
					Number of organizations reporting.	Male.	Female.
1	All denominations	542	537	172,814	523	82,872	86,664
2	Adventist bodies	8		216	8	62	154
3	Seventh-day Adventist Denomination	8	8	216	8	62	154
4	Baptist bodies	10	10	987	10	330	657
	Baptists:						
5	Northern Baptist Convention	10	10	987	10	330	657
6	Church of Christ, Scientist	5	5	452	5	84	368
7	Congregationalists	9	9	1,174	9	385	789
8	Disciples or Christians	1	1	250	1	100	150
9	Disciples of Christ	1	1	250	1	100	150
10	Eastern Orthodox Churches	7	7	4,500	1	2,990	10
11	Greek Orthodox Church	7	7	4,500	1	2,990	10
12	German Evangelical Synod of North America	2	2	50	2	34	16
13	Jewish congregations	3	3	[1]183			
14	Latter-day Saints	394	394	151,525	394	73,727	77,798
15	Church of Jesus Christ of Latter-day Saints	389	389	151,032	389	73,536	77,496
16	Reorganized Church of Jesus Christ of Latter-day Saints	5	5	493	5	191	302
17	Lutheran bodies	12	12	453	11	178	246
18	General Council of the Evangelical Lutheran Church in North America	8	8	390	7	152	209
19	Evangelical Lutheran Synodical Conference of America	2	2	39	2	16	23
20	Synod for the Norwegian Evangelical Lutheran Church in America	1	1	12	1	5	7
21	United Danish Evangelical Lutheran Church in America	1	1	12	1	5	7
22	Methodist bodies	34	31	1,567	29	560	984
23	Methodist Episcopal Church	33	30	1,537	28	553	961
24	African Methodist Episcopal Church	1	1	30	1	7	23
25	Presbyterian bodies	29	29	1,902	29	683	1,219
26	Presbyterian Church in the United States of America	29	29	1,902	29	683	1,219
27	Protestant Episcopal Church	15	14	977	14	323	654
28	Roman Catholic Church	5	5	8,356	4	3,357	3,553
29	Salvationists	2	1	20	1	11	9
30	Salvation Army	2	1	20	1	11	9
31	Spiritualists	2	2	57	2	29	28
32	Swedish Evangelical bodies	2	2	32	2	13	19
33	Swedish Evangelical Free Mission	2	2	32	2	13	19
34	Unitarians	2	2	113	1	6	10

VERMONT.

	DENOMINATION.	Total number of organizations.	Number of organizations reporting.	Total number reported.	Number of organizations reporting.	Male.	Female.
1	All denominations	909	902	147,223	866	62,284	82,472
2	Adventist bodies	45	45	1,613	42	633	918
3	Evangelical Adventists	3	3	73	2	21	24
4	Advent Christian Church	23	23	1,082	21	431	617
5	Seventh-day Adventist Denomination	19	19	458	19	181	277
6	Baptist bodies	126	126	9,951	120	3,535	6,117
	Baptists:						
7	Northern Baptist Convention	94	94	8,450	91	3,009	5,267
8	Free Baptists	32	32	1,501	29	526	850
9	Christians (Christian Connection)	5	5	266	5	103	163
10	Church of Christ, Scientist	6	6	144	6	33	111
11	Congregationalists	213	213	22,109	213	7,357	14,752
12	Disciples or Christians	2	2	316	2	116	200
13	Disciples of Christ	2	2	316	2	116	200

[1] Heads of families only.

DEBT ON CHURCH PROPERTY, PARSONAGES, AND SUNDAY SCHOOLS, BY DENOMINATIONS (IN DETAIL), FOR TERRITORY: 1906—Continued.

UTAH.

PLACES OF WORSHIP.					VALUE OF CHURCH PROPERTY.		DEBT ON CHURCH PROPERTY.		PARSONAGES.		SUNDAY SCHOOLS CONDUCTED BY CHURCH ORGANIZATIONS.				
Number of organizations reporting—		Number of church edifices reported.	Seating capacity of church edifices.												
Church edifices.	Halls, etc.		Number of organizations reporting.	Seating capacity reported.	Number of organizations reporting.	Value reported.	Number of organizations reporting.	Amount of debt reported.	Number of organizations reporting.	Value of parsonages reported.	Number of organizations reporting.	Number of Sunday schools reported.	Number of officers and teachers.	Number of scholars.	
459	58	516	459	169,369	492	$3,612,422	86	$152,131	45	$107,690	505	575	10,681	89,887	1
2	4	2	2	400	4	7,615	1	8	...	...	7	7	36	217	2
2	4	2	2	400	4	7,615	1	8	...	...	7	7	36	217	3
8	2	8	8	1,610	9	65,650	4	1,500	1	3,000	10	15	103	1,005	4
8	2	8	8	1,610	9	65,650	4	1,500	1	3,000	10	15	103	1,005	5
3	1	3	3	720	4	33,217	...	...	...	...	5	5	41	300	6
9	...	9	9	3,150	9	119,500	4	5,700	6	19,550	9	10	144	1,257	7
1	...	1	1	400	1	15,000	1	1,000	...	...	1	1	15	100	8
1	...	1	1	400	1	15,000	1	1,000	...	...	1	1	15	100	9
1	6	1	1	1,000	1	25,000	...	...	...	...	...	...	...	...	10
1	6	1	1	1,000	1	25,000	...	...	...	...	...	...	...	...	11
...	1	...	...	...	...	...	...	...	...	...	1	1	2	20	12
2	...	2	2	800	2	50,000	2	7,300	...	...	1	1	3	60	13
344	36	396	344	141,389	366	1,991,965	57	42,907	3	2,200	388	436	9,608	80,050	14
341	35	393	341	140,989	363	1,987,665	57	42,907	2	700	385	433	9,587	79,948	15
3	1	3	3	400	3	4,300	...	...	1	1,500	3	3	21	102	16
10	2	10	10	1,415	11	59,400	2	800	6	12,050	7	7	30	195	17
7	1	7	7	1,150	7	45,400	1	300	3	7,000	5	5	25	151	18
2	...	2	2	140	2	4,500	1	500	2	3,050	1	1	3	29	19
1	...	1	1	125	1	6,000	...	...	1	2,000	...	...	...	...	20
...	1	...	...	...	1	3,500	...	...	...	...	1	1	2	15	21
32	...	32	32	7,130	34	216,300	3	15,616	14	22,100	30	36	266	2,258	22
31	...	31	31	6,830	33	212,300	2	15,400	14	22,100	29	35	256	2,228	23
1	...	1	1	300	1	4,000	1	216	...	...	1	1	10	30	24
24	2	27	24	5,255	26	283,000	8	40,100		1,600	27	32	280	2,669	25
24	2	27	24	5,255	26	283,000	8	40,100	3	1,600	27	32	280	2,669	26
15	...	16	15	2,275	15	287,000	...	...	7	22,340	12	13	75	761	27
5	...	6	5	3,250	5	441,700	2	32,000	4	23,050	4	7	56	873	28
...	2	...	...	...	2	575	...	...	...	...	...	...	...	...	29
...	2	...	...	...	2	575	...	...	...	...	...	...	...	...	30
...	2	...	...	...	...	...	...	...	...	...	...	...	...	...	31
2	...	2	2	175	2	4,500	1	900	1	1,800	2	3	12	75	32
2	...	2	2	175	2	4,500	1	900	1	1,800	2	3	12	75	33
1	...	1	1	400	1	12,000	1	4,300	...	...	1	1	10	47	34

VERMONT.

836	46	891	822	235,661	847	$5,939,492	133	$470,095	511	$1,207,900	812	872	8,200	61,277	1
33	11	33	33	6,675	33	56,100	6	5,150	3	3,750	37	37	225	1,157	2
3	...	3	3	700	3	4,000	...	...	...	...	3	3	14	94	3
22	...	22	22	4,475	22	40,400	6	5,150	3	3,750	18	18	142	767	4
8	11	8	8	1,500	8	11,700	...	...	...	...	16	16	69	296	5
122	2	127	121	32,065	121	712,300	9	15,480	98	167,400	118	127	1,405	9,479	6
92	1	97	92	25,710	92	649,850	7	13,980	79	148,300	92	101	1,187	8,147	7
30	1	30	29	6,355	29	62,450	2	1,500	19	19,100	26	26	218	1,332	8
5	...	5	5	1,325	5	20,967	...	...	2	1,200	3	3	25	100	9
...	4	...	...	...	3	1,100	...	...	...	...	3	3	7	20	10
213	...	236	203	63,151	209	1,584,883	16	19,907	146	332,500	203	218	2,458	17,220	11
2	...	2	2	425	2	5,600	...	...	1	1,500	2	2	25	140	12
2	...	2	2	425	2	5,600	...	...	1	1,500	2	2	25	140	13

TABLE 3.—ORGANIZATIONS, COMMUNICANTS OR MEMBERS, PLACES OF WORSHIP, VALUE OF CHURCH PROPERTY, EACH STATE AND

VERMONT—Continued.

	DENOMINATION.	Total number of organizations.	COMMUNICANTS OR MEMBERS.				
			Number of organizations reporting.	Total number reported.	Sex.		
					Number of organizations reporting.	Male.	Female.
14	Eastern Orthodox Churches	1	1	150	1	100	50
15	Russian Orthodox Church	1	1	150	1	100	50
16	Evangelical bodies	2	2	56	2	21	35
17	Evangelical Association	2	2	56	2	21	35
18	Friends	3	3	177	3	78	99
19	Society of Friends (Orthodox)	3	3	177	3	78	99
20	Independent churches	5	5	280	5	111	169
21	Jewish congregations	5	3	[1]166			
22	Lutheran bodies	3	3	408	3	213	195
23	General Council of the Evangelical Lutheran Church in North America	3	3	408	3	213	195
24	Methodist bodies	220	220	17,671	214	6,140	11,219
25	Methodist Episcopal Church	215	215	17,471	210	6,085	11,124
26	Wesleyan Methodist Connection of America	3	3	146	3	53	93
27	Free Methodist Church of North America	2	2	54	1	2	2
28	Pentecostal Church of the Nazarene	4	4	112	4	53	59
29	Presbyterian bodies	19	19	1,636	19	730	906
30	Presbyterian Church in the United States of America	3	3	432	3	188	244
31	Welsh Calvinistic Methodist Church	6	6	652	6	321	331
32	United Presbyterian Church of North America	4	4	283	4	124	159
33	Synod of the Reformed Presbyterian Church of North America	3	3	99	3	35	64
34	Reformed Presbyterian Church in North America, General Synod	3	3	170	3	62	108
35	Protestant Episcopal Church	65	64	5,278	64	1,569	3,709
36	Roman Catholic Church	109	109	82,272	108	40,070	41,395
37	Salvationists	7	7	138	7	80	58
38	Salvation Army	7	7	138	7	80	58
39	Spiritualists	6	6	740	6	294	446
40	Unitarians	8	7	710	3	220	305
41	Universalists	55	52	3,030	39	828	1,566

VIRGINIA.

	DENOMINATION.	Total number of organizations.	Number of organizations reporting.	Total number reported.	Number of organizations reporting.	Male.	Female.
1	All denominations	6,639	6,605	793,546	5,937	296,716	436,929
2	Adventist bodies	39	39	1,164	39	469	695
3	Advent Christian Church	12	12	507	12	238	269
4	Seventh-day Adventist Denomination	25	25	576	25	199	377
5	Life and Advent Union	1	1	31	1	12	19
6	Churches of God in Christ Jesus	1	1	50	1	20	30
7	Armenian Church	1	1	112	1	80	32
8	Baptist bodies	2,710	2,700	415,987	2,492	158,962	236,191
9	Baptists	2,402	2,396	404,268	2,314	156,373	230,860
10	Southern Baptist Convention	1,028	1,028	136,062	1,002	53,981	77,401
11	National Baptist Convention (Colored)	1,374	1,368	268,206	1,312	102,392	153,459
12	Free Baptists	7	7	425	7	167	258
13	Freewill Baptists	1	1	64	1	34	30
14	Primitive Baptists	235	232	9,642	157	2,286	4,867
15	Colored Primitive Baptists in America	65	64	1,588	13	102	176
16	Brethren (Plymouth)	7	7	128	7	61	67
17	Brethren (Plymouth)—I	5	5	81	5	38	43
18	Brethren (Plymouth)—II	1	1	40	1	18	22
19	Brethren (Plymouth)—III	1	1	7	1	5	2
20	Christadelphians	3	3	177	3	80	97
21	Christians (Christian Connection)	74	74	8,266	70	3,281	4,726
22	Church of Christ, Scientist	2	2	175			
23	Church of God and Saints of Christ (Colored)	10	10	260	10	68	192
24	Churches of the New Jerusalem	2	2	59	2	17	42
25	General Convention of the New Jerusalem in the United States of America	2	2	59	2	17	42
26	Congregationalists	3	3	238	3	107	131
27	Disciples or Christians	281	281	26,248	177	7,248	10,067
28	Disciples of Christ	277	277	26,128	173	7,209	9,986
29	Churches of Christ	4	4	120	4	39	81

[1] Heads of families only.

DEBT ON CHURCH PROPERTY, PARSONAGES, AND SUNDAY SCHOOLS, BY DENOMINATIONS (IN DETAIL), FOR TERRITORY: 1906—Continued.

VERMONT—Continued.

PLACES OF WORSHIP.					VALUE OF CHURCH PROPERTY.		DEBT ON CHURCH PROPERTY.		PARSONAGES.		SUNDAY SCHOOLS CONDUCTED BY CHURCH ORGANIZATIONS.				
Number of organizations reporting—		Number of church edifices reported.	Seating capacity of church edifices.												
Church edifices.	Halls, etc.		Number of organizations reporting.	Seating capacity reported.	Number of organizations reporting.	Value reported.	Number of organizations reporting.	Amount of debt reported.	Number of organizations reporting.	Value of parsonages reported.	Number of organizations reporting.	Number of Sunday schools reported.	Number of officers and teachers.	Number of scholars.	
	1				1	$2,000	1	$1,250							14
	1				1	2,000	1	1,250							15
2		2	2	350	2	4,050	2	1,375			2	2	12	67	16
2		2	2	350	[illegible]	4,050	2	1,375			2	2	12	67	17
3		3	3	430	3	4,500			1	$1,000	2	2	15	72	18
3		3	3	430	3	4,500			1	1,000	2	2	15	72	19
5		6	5	1,250	5	37,200	2	1,950	2	6,200	5	8	52	278	20
3		5	2	400	3	14,500	3	4,650			2	2	6	60	21
3		3	3	600	3	8,700	1	500			3	3	28	186	22
3		3	3	600	3	8,700	1	500			3	3	28	186	23
214	3	225	213	52,460	216	909,937	15	14,660	143	244,700	205	219	2,462	16,365	24
211	2	221	210	51,685	212	902,637	14	14,620	140	243,100	200	214	2,428	16,168	25
3		4	3	775	3	4,300	1	40	3	1,600	3	3	25	160	26
	1				1	3,000					2	2	9	37	27
2	2	2	2	600	1	1,000	1	375			4	4	40	114	28
18		20	18	5,138	18	64,100	5	3,500	11	15,750	18	19	225	1,613	29
3		3	3	1,070	3	19,000	3	1,400	2	5,500	3	3	47	530	30
6		8	6	1,603	6	23,200	2	2,100	1	2,000	6	7	106	611	31
4		4	4	1,125	4	12,700			4	3,700	4	4	34	230	32
2		2	2	600	2	2,700			1	900	2	2	12	87	33
3		3	3	740	3	6,500			3	3,650	3	3	26	155	34
62	3	69	61	13,679	62	504,298	6	7,921	27	92,600	47	51	274	2,073	35
91	8	94	91	41,233	92	1,553,257	59	386,120	66	310,200	104	118	379	9,623	36
	6				7	1,400	3	57			4	4	10	73	37
	6				7	1,400	3	57			4	4	10	73	38
1	4	1	1	200	3	17,000	1	4,000							39
5		5	5	2,150	5	112,500			2	5,500	5	5	50	360	40
52	2	53	52	13,530	53	324,100	3	3,200	9	25,600	45	45	502	2,277	41

VIRGINIA.

Church edifices.	Halls, etc.	Number of church edifices reported.	Seating: Number of organizations reporting.	Seating capacity reported.	Value: Number of organizations reporting.	Value reported.	Debt: Number of organizations reporting.	Amount of debt reported.	Parsonages: Number of organizations reporting.	Value of parsonages reported.	Sunday schools: Number of organizations reporting.	Number of Sunday schools reported.	Number of officers and teachers.	Number of scholars.	
6,135	242	6,480	5,963	1,974,332	6,139	$19,699,014	813	$996,367	1,141	$2,471,751	5,441	5,965	50,229	430,452	1
27	8	27	27	6,055	26	19,374	5	1,347	2	2,500	29	30	188	865	2
10	2	10	10	2,400	10	5,600	1	250	1	500	9	9	71	400	3
16	5	16	16	3,455	14	13,149	4	1,097	1	2,000	19	20	112	441	4
	1				1	125					1	1	5	24	5
1		1	1	200	1	500									6
	1														7
2,536	63	2,596	2,477	879,301	2,527	6,063,987	343	328,825	227	394,728	2,235	2,421	19,326	175,033	8
2,324	43	2,383	2,293	812,021	2,322	5,912,631	337	328,368	220	392,001	2,224	2,410	19,229	174,421	9
981	22	1,016	975	337,663	981	3,271,541	83	123,709	180	347,691	916	1,008	9,857	87,735	10
1,343	21	1,367	1,318	474,358	1,341	2,641,090	254	204,659	40	44,310	1,308	1,402	9,372	86,686	11
7		7	7	2,050	7	7,300	2	215	3	1,700	7	7	47	315	12
1		1	1	150	1	200					1	1	6	72	13
157	10	158	152	59,950	159	133,026	3	175							14
47	10	47	24	5,130	38	10,830	1	67	4	1,025	3	3	44	225	15
	7										6	6	27	254	16
	5										4	4	18	170	17
	1										1	1	8	70	18
	1										1	1	1	14	19
1	2	1	1	300	2	650					3	3	14	78	20
70	4	70	70	20,615	71	203,425	8	4,380	4	14,500	69	70	627	4,890	21
2		2	2	625	1	15,000	1	8,000			1	1	6	40	22
	10														23
1	1	1	1	110	2	400					1	1	4	23	24
1	1	1	1	110	2	400					1	1	4	23	25
3		3	3	550	3	6,400	2	1,300	1	2,500	3	3	16	170	26
256	3	261	256	78,190	253	519,475	25	28,467	9	14,850	220	223	1,888	16,366	27
252	3	257	252	77,190	249	517,525	25	28,467	9	14,850	219	222	1,885	16,341	28
4		4	4	1,000	4	1,950					1	1	3	25	29

TABLE 3.—ORGANIZATIONS, COMMUNICANTS OR MEMBERS, PLACES OF WORSHIP, VALUE OF CHURCH PROPERTY, EACH STATE AND

VIRGINIA—Continued.

	DENOMINATION.	Total number of organizations.	COMMUNICANTS OR MEMBERS.				
			Number of organizations reporting.	Total number reported.	Sex.		
					Number of organizations reporting.	Male.	Female.
30	Dunkers or German Baptist Brethren	91	91	11,524	78	4,185	5,799
31	German Baptist Brethren Church (Conservative)	59	59	9,078	59	3,777	5,301
32	Old Order German Baptist Brethren	6	6	280	6	156	124
33	The Brethren Church (Progressive Dunkers)	26	26	2,166	13	252	374
34	Eastern Orthodox Churches	5	5	756	....	....	....
35	Greek Orthodox Church	5	5	756	....	....	....
36	Friends	28	28	1,369	28	563	806
37	Society of Friends (Orthodox)	20	20	941	20	379	562
38	Religious Society of Friends (Hicksite)	8	8	428	8	184	244
39	German Evangelical Synod of North America	1	1	564	1	275	289
40	Independent churches	17	14	932	13	232	300
41	Jewish congregations	21	18	[1]915	....	....	....
42	Latter-day Saints		2	1,021	1	10	23
43	Church of Jesus Christ of Latter-day Saints	1	1	988	....	....	....
44	Reorganized Church of Jesus Christ of Latter-day Saints	1	1	33	1	10	23
45	Lutheran bodies	173	173	15,010	158	5,690	7,802
46	General Synod of the Evangelical Lutheran Church in the United States of America	4	4	645	4	260	385
47	United Synod of the Evangelical Lutheran Church in the South	151	151	13,293	141	5,034	6,953
48	Evangelical Lutheran Synodical Conference of America	12	12	860	9	316	389
49	United Norwegian Lutheran Church in America	1	1	32	....	....	....
50	Evangelical Lutheran Joint Synod of Ohio and Other States	5	5	180	4	80	75
51	Mennonite bodies	26	26	1,021	26	460	561
52	Mennonite Church	23	23	967	23	432	535
53	Amish Mennonite Church	1	1	32	1	17	15
54	Church of God in Christ (Mennonite)	2	2	22	2	11	11
55	Methodist bodies	2,157	2,146	200,771	1,965	74,872	110,201
56	Methodist Episcopal Church	319	314	18,578	252	6,041	9,410
57	African Methodist Episcopal Church	117	116	9,889	115	3,845	6,034
58	African Union Methodist Protestant Church	5	5	515	5	224	291
59	African Methodist Episcopal Zion Church	75	75	5,474	75	2,163	3,311
60	Methodist Protestant Church	61	61	4,480	53	1,480	2,394
61	Methodist Episcopal Church, South	1,506	1,501	157,354	1,400	59,469	86,226
62	Colored Methodist Episcopal Church	34	34	1,514	34	558	956
63	Reformed Zion Union Apostolic Church (Colored)	39	39	2,929	30	1,077	1,556
64	Free Methodist Church of North America	1	1	38	1	15	23
65	Moravian bodies	2	2	184	....	....	....
66	Moravian Church (Unitas Fratrum)	2	2	184	....	....	....
67	Nonsectarian Churches of Bible Faith	3	3	17	3	8	9
68	Presbyterian bodies	381	380	39,628	356	14,148	23,187
69	Presbyterian Church in the United States of America	4		2,615	36	847	1,317
70	Presbyterian Church in the United States	33[illegible]	43	36,569	316	13,108	21,619
71	Associate Reformed Synod of the South	4	33[illegible]	444	4	193	251
72	Protestant Episcopal Church	395	389	28,487	301	7,729	15,932
73	Reformed bodies	26	26	2,488	26	1,124	1,364
74	Reformed Church in the United States	25	25	2,288	25	974	1,314
75	Hungarian Reformed Church in America	1	1	200	1	150	50
76	Reformed Episcopal Church	2	2	46	2	23	23
77	Roman Catholic Church	70	70	28,700	70	14,384	14,316
78	Salvationists	5	5	136	5	88	48
79	Salvation Army	5	5	136	5	88	48
80	Spiritualists	1	1	37	1	18	19
81	Theosophical societies	1	1	9	1	2	7
82	Theosophical Society, American Section	1	1	9	1	2	7
83	Unitarians	2	2	76	2	30	46
84	United Brethren bodies	97	97	7,021	95	2,544	3,945
85	Church of the United Brethren in Christ	91	91	6,786	89	2,456	3,798
86	Church of the United Brethren in Christ (Old Constitution)	6	6	235	6	88	147
87	Universalists	1	1	20	1	8	12

[1] Heads of families only.

DEBT ON CHURCH PROPERTY, PARSONAGES, AND SUNDAY SCHOOLS, BY DENOMINATIONS (IN DETAIL), FOR TERRITORY: 1906—Continued.

VIRGINIA—Continued.

PLACES OF WORSHIP. Number of organizations reporting— Church edifices.	Halls, etc.	Number of church edifices reported.	Seating capacity of church edifices. Number of organizations reporting.	Seating capacity reported.	VALUE OF CHURCH PROPERTY. Number of organizations reporting.	Value reported.	DEBT ON CHURCH PROPERTY. Number of organizations reporting.	Amount of debt reported.	PARSONAGES. Number of organizations reporting.	Value of parsonages reported.	SUNDAY SCHOOLS CONDUCTED BY CHURCH ORGANIZATIONS. Number of organizations reporting.	Number of Sunday schools reported.	Number of officers and teachers.	Number of scholars.	
82	3	156	77	49,375	78	$152,863	6	$2,575	...	...	55	106	793	6,653	30
57	...	131	54	43,000	55	126,738	5	2,450	...	...	46	99	738	6,039	31
6	...	6	5	1,150	5	5,700	...	...	...	...	...	...	...	...	32
19	3	19	18	5,225	18	20,425	1	125	...	...	9	9	55	614	33
...	5	...	...	...	...	...	...	...	...	...	...	...	...	...	34
...	5	...	...	...	...	...	...	...	...	...	...	...	...	...	35
27	1	27	27	8,175	27	43,200	2	362	...	...	19	19	114	809	36
19	1	19	19	5,350	19	25,200	2	362	...	...	15	15	97	591	37
8	...	8	8	2,825	8	18,000	...	...	...	...	4	4	17	218	38
1	...	1	1	600	1	40,000	...	...	...	...	1	1	22	178	39
12	5	15	12	4,110	15	16,195	3	2,880	1	$300	14	18	90	1,127	40
15	1	17	15	5,865	14	294,500	6	54,000	2	3,300	13	13	53	768	41
1	1	4	1	650	1	1,100	...	...	...	...	...	...	...	...	42
1	...	4	1	650	1	1,100	...	...	...	...	...	...	...	...	43
...	1	...	...	...	...	...	...	...	...	...	...	...	...	...	44
164	5	170	162	50,150	165	525,645	14	11,721	52	105,650	137	139	1,477	10,057	45
2	...	4	2	1,000	4	16,200	...	...	1	2,000	4	4	80	400	46
149	1	152	147	46,175	148	467,045	11	10,871	45	92,550	126	128	1,349	9,241	47
8	3	9	8	1,675	8	35,900	2	650	4	9,300	4	4	23	211	48
1	...	1	1	250	1	2,500	1	200	...	...	1	1	10	70	49
4	1	4	4	1,050	4	4,000	...	...	2	1,800	2	2	15	135	50
21	2	21	21	5,305	21	19,387	1	188	...	...	13	14	103	712	51
20	2	20	20	5,180	20	18,187	...	...	...	...	12	12	95	665	52
1	...	1	1	125	1	1,200	1	188	...	...	1	2	8	47	53
...	...	...	...	...	...	...	...	...	...	...	...	...	...	...	54
2,042	88	2,078	1,963	591,583	2,050	5,197,876	318	302,340	492	890,315	1,863	1,942	17,781	146,807	55
290	20	295	256	73,418	291	478,915	64	32,006	86	74,015	256	279	2,209	16,553	56
114	3	117	114	37,550	117	309,025	65	52,812	45	47,660	106	113	724	6,516	57
5	...	5	5	1,800	5	13,500	3	1,280	...	...	5	5	32	455	58
71	4	72	71	22,265	72	102,280	40	15,649	12	9,250	71	73	477	2,796	59
60	...	64	56	16,265	60	120,438	9	3,710	13	21,350	40	41	410	3,555	60
1,431	60	1,448	1,393	417,140	1,436	4,104,093	126	195,730	335	737,440	1,317	1,362	13,558	114,125	61
33	1	37	33	8,245	33	32,650	4	328	1	600	33	33	163	1,407	62
37	...	39	34	14,700	35	35,475	7	825	...	...	34	35	199	1,363	63
1	...	1	1	200	1	1,500	...	...	...	...	1	1	9	37	64
2	...	2	2	600	2	1,000	...	...	1	1,500	2	2	12	153	65
2	...	2		600	2	1,000	...	...	1	1,500	2	2	12	153	66
...	3	...	...	...	...	...	...	...	...	...	...	...	...	...	67
365	6	484	364	128,920	367	2,127,090	27	75,275	160	403,285	326	476	4,208	33,455	68
34	2	37	33	8,695	37	74,390	6	2,400	10	13,475	43	49	276	2,978	69
327	4	443	327	119,000	326	2,045,200	21	72,875	147	386,310	279	422	3,887	30,102	70
4	...	4	4	1,225	4	7,500	...	...	3	3,500	4	5	45	375	71
321	6	353	320	87,239	322	2,435,765	31	82,093	124	399,825	260	293	2,097	18,725	72
25	1	26	25	6,805	25	89,550	5	5,675	12	21,400	24	25	285	1,842	73
25	...	26	25	6,805	25	89,550	5	5,675	12	21,400	24	25	285	1,842	74
...	1	...	...	...	...	...	...	...	...	...	...	...	...	...	75
2	...	2	2	350	2	2,700	...	...	1	600	2	2	7	47	76
64	5	68	64	23,629	66	1,756,005	10	67,700	35	199,400	53	63	325	4,954	77
1	4	1	1	400	5	2,325	3	239	...	...	5	5	21	154	78
1	4	1	1	400	5	2,325	3	239	...	...	5	5	21	154	79
...	1	...	...	...	...	...	...	...	...	...	...	...	...	...	80
...	1	...	...	...	...	...	...	...	...	...	...	...	...	...	81
...	1	...	...	...	...	...	...	...	...	...	...	...	...	...	82
2	...	2	2	330	2	16,800	...	...	...	...	1	1	3	12	83
91	5	91	86	24,300	90	147,602	3	19,000	18	16,600	85	85	738	6,242	84
85	5	85	80	23,100	84	143,652	3	19,000	16	15,100	81	81	702	6,013	85
6	...	6	6	1,200	6	3,950	...	...	2	1,500	4	4	36	229	86
1	...	1	1	200	1	700	...	...	...	...	1	1	4	38	87

TABLE 3.—ORGANIZATIONS, COMMUNICANTS OR MEMBERS, PLACES OF WORSHIP, VALUE OF CHURCH PROPERTY, EACH STATE AND

WASHINGTON.

	DENOMINATION.	Total number of organizations.	COMMUNICANTS OR MEMBERS.				
			Number of organizations reporting.	Total number reported.	Sex.		
					Number of organizations reporting.	Male.	Female.
1	All denominations	1,771	1,759	191,976	1,672	78,115	99,422
2	Adventist bodies	71	71	3,058	67	1,149	1,815
3	Advent Christian Church	9	9	410	8	158	212
4	Seventh-day Adventist Denomination	60	60	2,592	58	971	1,583
5	Churches of God in Christ Jesus	2	2	56	1	20	20
6	Bahais	2	2	39	2	12	27
7	Baptist bodies	167	167	12,807	163	4,890	7,548
8	Baptists	159	159	12,614	156	4,832	7,467
9	Northern Baptist Convention	154	154	12,440	151	4,754	7,371
10	National Baptist Convention (Colored)	5	5	174	5	78	96
11	Primitive Baptists	8	8	193	7	58	81
12	Brethren (Plymouth)	9	9	185	9	88	97
13	Brethren (Plymouth)—I	4	4	73	4	35	38
14	Brethren (Plymouth)—II	1	1	20	1	7	13
15	Brethren (Plymouth)—III	3	3	60	3	27	33
16	Brethren (Plymouth)—IV	1	1	32	1	19	13
17	Buddhists	2	2	394	2	310	84
18	Japanese Temples	2	2	394	-	310	84
19	Christian Catholic Church in Zion	1	1	35	1	15	20
20	Christians (Christian Connection)	5	5	103	4	36	55
21	Church of Christ, Scientist	14	14	924	13	231	656
22	Churches of God in North America General Eldership of the	3	3	50	3	24	26
23	Churches of the Living God (Colored)	1	1	64	1	27	37
24	Church of the Living God (Apostolic Church)	1	1	64	1	27	37
25	Churches of the New Jerusalem	3	3	78	3	39	39
26	General Convention of the New Jerusalem in the United States of America	3	3	78	3	39	39
27	Congregationalists	149	148	10,025	147	3,511	6,464
28	Disciples or Christians	100	100	10,628	97	3,833	6,005
29	Disciples of Christ	83	83	10,140	80	3,622	5,728
30	Churches of Christ	17	17	488	17	211	277
31	Dunkers or German Baptist Brethren	9	9	453	9	219	234
32	German Baptist Brethren Church (Conservative)	9	9	453	9	219	234
33	Eastern Orthodox Churches	2	2	574	2	392	182
34	Russian Orthodox Church	2	2	574	2	392	182
35	Evangelical bodies	23	23	987	23	431	556
36	Evangelical Association	22	22	942	22	413	529
37	United Evangelical Church	1	1	45	1	18	27
38	Evangelistic associations	4	4	420	3	154	216
39	Apostolic Faith Movement	2	2	350	2	146	204
40	Peniel Missions	1	1	50	....	....	....
41	Hephzibah Faith Missionary Association	1	1	20	1	8	12
42	Friends	5	5	451	5	236	215
43	Society of Friends (Orthodox)	5	5	451	5	236	215
44	Independent churches	19	19	1,097	19	487	610
45	Jewish congregations	6	6	[1] 488	....	....	....
46	Latter-day Saints	7	7	461	7	194	267
47	Church of Jesus Christ of Latter-day Saints	1	1	56	1	20	36
48	Reorganized Church of Jesus Christ of Latter-day Saints	6	6	405	6	174	231
49	Lutheran bodies	185	184	13,464	168	5,768	6,296
50	General Council of the Evangelical Lutheran Church in North America	21	21	2,506	21	1,159	1,347
51	Evangelical Lutheran Synodical Conference of America	18	18	1,030	18	480	550
52	United Norwegian Lutheran Church in America	30	30	1,980	25	759	697
53	Evangelical Lutheran Joint Synod of Ohio and Other States	41	41	2,545	39	1,099	1,219
54	Hauge's Norwegian Evangelical Lutheran Synod	1	1	60	1	28	32
55	Evangelical Lutheran Synod of Iowa and Other States	6	6	892	6	417	475
56	Synod for the Norwegian Evangelical Lutheran Church in America	47	46	3,195	38	1,241	1,340
57	Finnish Evangelical Lutheran Church of America, or Suomi Synod	1	1	119	1	61	58
58	Norwegian Lutheran Free Church	15	15	854	14	390	429
59	Slovak Evangelical Lutheran Synod of America	1	1	30	1	14	16
60	Apostolic Lutheran Church (Finnish)	4	4	253	4	120	133

DEBT ON CHURCH PROPERTY, PARSONAGES, AND SUNDAY SCHOOLS, BY DENOMINATIONS (IN DETAIL), FOR TERRITORY: 1906—Continued.

WASHINGTON.

Places of worship: Number of organizations reporting— Church edifices.	Halls, etc.	Number of church edifices reported.	Seating capacity of church edifices: Number of organizations reporting.	Seating capacity reported.	Value of church property: Number of organizations reporting.	Value reported.	Debt on church property: Number of organizations reporting.	Amount of debt reported.	Parsonages: Number of organizations reporting.	Value of parsonages reported.	Sunday schools conducted by church organizations: Number of organizations reporting.	Number of Sunday schools reported.	Number of officers and teachers.	Number of scholars.	
1,370	217	1,416	1,349	341,812	1,415	$8,082,986	381	$833,258	540	$902,801	1,464	1,631	13,870	114,467	1
41	21	41	41	6,900	44	61,610	5	407	1	150	65	71	541	2,592	2
7	2	7	7	1,325	8	15,250	3	332			8	8	60	348	3
32	19	32	32	5,075	34	44,360	2	75	1	150	55	61	464	2,168	4
2		2	2	500	2	2,000					2	2	17	76	5
	2														6
147	10	158	147	37,606	149	811,822	55	49,959	39	57,100	146	166	1,597	13,919	7
143	6	154	143	36,456	145	809,322	55	49,959	39	57,100	146	166	1,597	13,919	8
138	6	149	138	35,156	140	789,722	52	48,484	39	57,100	141	161	1,572	13,794	9
5		5	5	1,300	5	19,600	3	1,475			5	5	25	125	10
4	4	4	4	1,150	4	2,500									11
	9										3	3	18	176	12
	4										2	2	8	76	13
	1										1	1	10	100	14
	3														15
	1														16
1	1	1	1	150	1	2,000					2	3	5	118	17
1	1	1	1	150	1	2,000					2	3	5	118	18
	1														19
2		2	2	300	2	1,600					2	2	15	75	20
13	1	13	13	3,500	13	118,200	6	16,000			14	14	87	489	21
1	1	1	1	150	1	1,000					1	1	6	30	22
1		1	1	400	1	7,000	1	1,200			1	1	6	70	23
1		1	1	400	1	7,000	1	1,200			1	1	6	70	24
1	2	1	1	200	2	2,500	1	150			1	1	2	12	25
1	2	1	1	200	2	2,500	1	150			1	1	2	12	26
123	11	125	123	28,756	131	888,247	34	45,144	56	83,050	140	158	1,637	12,934	27
79	13	81	75	24,455	78	392,600	29	26,831	9	15,950	73	74	811	6,909	28
71	4	73	67	22,905	70	383,600	27	26,656	9	15,950	68	69	796	6,720	29
8	9	8	8	1,550	8	9,000	2	175			5	5	15	189	30
7	1	7	7	2,110	7	13,300	3	1,500	1	500	7	10	66	470	31
7	1	7	7	2,110	7	13,300	3	1,500	1	500	7	10	66	470	32
2		2	2	500	2	3,000			2	5,000					33
2		2	2	500	2	3,000			2	5,000					34
20	3	20	20	5,100	20	78,700	10	11,550	14	22,200	21	23	228	1,303	35
19	3	19	19	4,900	19	77,900	10	11,550	13	21,600	21	23	228	1,303	36
1		1	1	200	1	800			1	600					37
1	3	1	1	150	2	950	1	175			3	4	17	130	38
	2				1	350					2	3	10	90	39
	1														40
1		1	1	150	1	600	1	175			1	1	7	40	41
4		4	4	1,000	5	23,500			1	7,000	5	6	56	446	42
4		4	4	1,000	5	23,500			1	7,000	5	6	56	446	43
11	6	11	11	2,150	13	22,100	2	3,700	1	3,000	16	17	84	659	44
4		4	3	1,850	3	107,000					3	3	15	205	45
5	2	5	4	875	4	4,700					6	6	48	186	46
1		1	1	150	1	500					1	1	11	41	47
4	2	4	3	725	3	4,200					5	5	37	145	48
128	27	133	122	29,345	132	527,755	51	56,623	46	75,800	140	158	628	5,490	49
19	2	21	19	3,805	20	182,775	9	14,150	6	19,000	19	21	141	1,066	50
15	2	15	14	1,860	14	28,925	7	3,575	9	11,300	10	11	14	199	51
18	8	19	17	4,700	19	81,830	9	7,718	7	13,300	26	30	139	994	52
28	7	29	25	4,305	27	53,900	13	13,330	12	17,000	33	35	91	1,094	53
1		1	1	200	1	1,200					1	1	2	15	54
6		6	6	1,600	6	42,300	1	1,100	2	1,700	6	7	28	332	55
23	6	24	23	5,470	27	76,225	7	10,700	6	7,500	26	32	108	1,081	56
1		1	1	250	1	2,000					1	1	3	20	57
14		14	13	6,925	14	55,900	5	6,050	4	6,000	14	16	95	573	58
	1														59
3	1	3	3	230	3	2,700					4	4	7	115	60

TABLE 3.—ORGANIZATIONS. COMMUNICANTS OR MEMBERS, PLACES OF WORSHIP, VALUE OF CHURCH PROPERTY, EACH STATE AND

WASHINGTON—Continued.

	DENOMINATION.	Total number of organizations.	COMMUNICANTS OR MEMBERS. Number of organizations reporting.	Total number reported.	Sex. Number of organizations reporting.	Male.	Female.
61	Mennonite bodies	2	2	59	2	32	27
62	General Conference of Mennonites of North America	1	1	38	1	21	17
63	Mennonite Brethren in Christ	1	1	21	1	11	10
64	Methodist bodies	460	457	31,700	441	11,729	18,146
65	Methodist Episcopal Church	397	394	29,347	379	10,866	16,731
66	African Methodist Episcopal Church	10	10	334	10	107	227
67	Methodist Episcopal Church, South	14	14	718	13	241	402
68	Free Methodist Church of North America	39	39	1,301	39	515	786
69	Nonsectarian Churches of Bible Faith	1	1	40	1	20	20
70	Pentecostal Church of the Nazarene	7	7	285	7	137	148
71	Presbyterian bodies	170	170	16,758	162	6,377	9,949
72	Presbyterian Church in the United States of America	139	139	14,437	132	5,453	8,562
73	Cumberland Presbyterian Church	9	9	615	8	241	364
74	United Presbyterian Church of North America	21	21	1,616	21	640	976
75	Synod of the Reformed Presbyterian Church of North America	1	1	90	1	43	47
76	Protestant Episcopal Church	82	77	6,780	68	2,279	4,098
77	Reformed bodies	5	5	379	5	181	198
78	Reformed Church in America	2	2	95	2	44	51
79	Christian Reformed Church	3	3	284	3	137	147
80	Roman Catholic Church	172	172	74,981	156	33,329	33,203
81	Salvationists	18	17	820	17	521	299
82	Salvation Army	18	17	820	17	521	299
83	Spiritualists	15	15	823	15	360	463
84	Swedish Evangelical bodies	6	6	361	6	174	187
85	Swedish Evangelical Mission Covenant of America	3	3	269	3	132	137
86	Swedish Evangelical Free Mission	3	3	92	3	42	50
87	Theosophical societies	5	5	146	5	68	78
88	Theosophical Society in America	2	2	20	2	10	10
89	Theosophical Society, American Section	3	3	126	3	58	68
90	Unitarians	4	4	553	3	200	313
91	United Brethren bodies	31	30	1,079	30	467	612
92	Church of the United Brethren in Christ	12	11	582	11	273	309
93	Church of the United Brethren in Christ (Old Constitution)	19	19	497	19	194	303
94	Universalists	2	2	167	2	47	120
95	Volunteers of America	4	4	260	4	148	112

WEST VIRGINIA.

	DENOMINATION.	Total number of organizations.	Number of organizations reporting.	Total number reported.	Sex. Number of organizations reporting.	Male.	Female.
1	All denominations	4,042	4,019	301,565	3,665	118,553	159,538
2	Adventist bodies	55	55	1,820	49	770	911
3	Advent Christian Church	36	36	1,476	32	650	715
4	Seventh-day Adventist Denomination	19	19	344	17	120	196
5	Baptist bodies	893	886	67,044	773	24,578	34,785
6	Baptists	754	748	60,365	674	22,596	31,885
7	Northern Baptist Convention	595	589	48,636	520	17,266	25,648
8	Southern Baptist Convention	11	11	1,672	11	627	1,045
9	National Baptist Convention (Colored)	148	148	10,057	143	4,703	5,192
10	Seventh-day Baptists	8	8	681	7	280	388
11	Free Baptists	30	30	1,513	17	399	629
12	Freewill Baptists	7	7	193	7	81	112
13	United Baptists	32	32	2,226	26	768	949
14	Primitive Baptists	59	58	2,019	41	444	816
15	Colored Primitive Baptists in America	3	3	47	1	10	6
16	Christians (Christian Connection)	21	21	708	20	300	381
17	Church of Christ, Scientist	3	3	74	2	11	45
18	Churches of God in North America, General Eldership of the	26	24	781	24	363	418
19	Congregationalists	2	2	228	2	89	139
20	Disciples or Christians	184	184	13,323	178	5,275	7,639
21	Disciples of Christ	134	134	10,729	129	4,238	6,182
22	Churches of Christ	50	50	2,594	49	1,037	1,457

DEBT ON CHURCH PROPERTY, PARSONAGES, AND SUNDAY SCHOOLS, BY DENOMINATIONS (IN DETAIL), FOR TERRITORY: 1906—Continued.

WASHINGTON—Continued.

PLACES OF WORSHIP. Number of organizations reporting—Church edifices.	Halls, etc.	Number of church edifices reported.	Seating capacity of church edifices. Number of organizations reporting.	Seating capacity reported.	VALUE OF CHURCH PROPERTY. Number of organizations reporting.	Value reported.	DEBT ON CHURCH PROPERTY. Number of organizations reporting.	Amount of debt reported.	PARSONAGES. Number of organizations reporting.	Value of parsonages reported.	SUNDAY SCHOOLS CONDUCTED BY CHURCH ORGANIZATIONS. Number of organizations reporting.	Number of Sunday schools reported.	Number of officers and teachers.	Number of scholars.	
1	1	1	1	300	1	$1,000	...	...	...	...	2	2	17	95	61
1	...	1		300	1	1,000	...	...	...	...	1	1	10	70	62
...	1	...	...	...	...	...	...	...	...	...	1	1	7	25	63
365	35	368	360	91,795	375	1,511,365	73	$70,513	215	$279,150	385	424	4,401	34,620	64
316	27	318	311	79,564	325	1,372,965	63	64,698	181	246,850	336	369	4,021	31,894	65
6	...	7	6	1,350	6	30,300	4	3,450	4	2,400	7	7	49	287	66
12	1	12	12	4,150	12	28,100	3	480	7	8,800	12	12	79	850	67
31	7	31	31	6,731	32	80,000	3	1,885	23	21,100	30	36	252	1,589	68
...	1	...	...	...	...	...	...	...	...	...	1	1	1	20	69
4	1	4	4	860	4	10,000	2	940	...	...	6	8	47	264	70
148	13	157	147	38,985	150	806,828	34	38,810	60	120,450	162	192	2,319	19,199	71
122	9	128	121	31,385	124	589,978	32	37,610	50	92,250	133	161	1,954	15,878	72
6	2	6	6	1,400	6	19,200	...	...	2	5,200	7	7	80	703	73
19	2	22	19	5,950	19	162,650	2	1,200	8	23,000	21	23	255	2,343	74
1	...	1	1	250	1	35,000	...	...	...	...	1	1	30	275	75
70	3	74	70	14,022	74	689,525	14	24,983	29	86,900	64	66	419	3,388	76
5	...	5	5	1,235	5	11,500	5	4,100	4	4,300	4	5	32	410	77
2	...	2	2	350	2	4,500	2	1,800	2	2,400	2	3	15	180	78
3	...	3	3	885	3	7,000	3	2,300	2	1,900	2	2	17	230	79
148	8	157	146	39,298	144	1,727,960	41	459,336	40	128,550	137	156	390	7,813	80
6	12	6	5	1,200	18	97,225	4	4,439	...	...	15	15	65	452	81
6	12	6	5	1,200	18	97,225	4	4,439	...	...	15	15	65	452	82
1	14	1	1	150	1	1,200	1	500	...	...	1	1	5	50	83
6	...	6	6	1,795	6	44,749	4	5,598	1	1,351	6	7	52	371	84
3	...	3	3	1,325	3	40,500	3	4,500	...	...	3	4	36	266	85
3	...	3	3	470	3	4,249	1	1,098	1	1,351	3	3	16	105	86
...	4	...	...	...	1	300	...	...	...	...	1	1	1	15	87
...	1	...	...	...	...	...	...	...	...	...	...	...	...	...	88
...	3	...	...	...	1	300	...	...	...	...	1	1	1	15	89
2	1	2	2	850	2	55,000	1	3,000	...	...	3	3	18	150	90
21	6	22	21	5,475	21	31,700	2	1,800	11	9,450	24	25	202	1,168	91
9	1	9	9	2,750	9	19,300	2	1,800	6	6,600	11	11	107	689	92
12	5	13	12	2,725	12	12,400	...	...	5	2,850	13	14	95	479	93
2	...	2	2	350	2	27,000	2	6,000	1	3,000	2	2	19	132	94
...	4	...	...	...	1	50	...	...	...	...	2	2	15	108	95

WEST VIRGINIA.

3,317	463	3,428	3,217	949,812	3,335	$9,733,585	379	$512,412	650	$1,022,566	3,212	3,486	27,577	212,577	1
25	18	25	25	6,075	25	17,275	...	...	...	...	33	34	199	1,115	2
19	10	19	19	4,975	19	14,825	...	...	...	...	19	19	131	824	3
6	8	6	6	1,100	6	2,450	...	...	...	...	14	15	68	291	4
682	109	702	664	218,112	681	1,413,168	70	73,817	49	109,290	665	734	5,451	41,845	5
621	84	640	606	200,412	626	1,326,293	66	73,582	43	98,900	638	704	5,247	40,093	6
508	45	525	496	165,052	508	1,076,367	35	59,807	31	70,900	487	548	4,232	31,928	7
10	1	12	10	4,450	10	50,050	...	...	5	15,500	9	11	139	1,355	8
103	38	103	100	30,910	108	199,876	31	13,775	7	12,500	142	145	876	6,810	9
8	...	8	8	2,350	7	29,500	1	50	4	9,540	6	7	69	472	10
13	1	13	13	3,300	12	29,300	...	...	2	850	10	10	67	675	11
3	4	3	3	650	3	1,900	...	...	...	...	5	5	15	135	12
10	12	11	10	3,400	10	6,850	2	115	...	...	6	8	53	470	13
24	8	24	22	6,900	21	17,925	...	...	...	...	...	...	...	...	14
3	...	3	2	1,100	2	1,400	1	70	...	...	...	...	...	...	15
10	6	10	10	2,850	12	13,705	2	535	...	...	13	13	97	656	16
1	2	1	1	60	2	1,000	...	...	...	...	2	2	7	23	17
9	4	9	9	2,800	9	26,200	2	3,400	...	...	19	19	149	1,003	18
2	...	2	2	550	2	22,500	...	...	2	4,500	2	2	22	135	19
144	20	145	139	41,655	143	411,316	21	40,853	6	21,000	102	107	882	8,074	20
108	6	109	103	30,625	105	364,541	15	39,900	6	21,000	91	95	813	7,332	21
36	14	36	36	11,030	38	46,775	6	953	...	...	11	12	69	742	22

TABLE 3.—ORGANIZATIONS, COMMUNICANTS OR MEMBERS, PLACES OF WORSHIP, VALUE OF CHURCH PROPERTY, EACH STATE AND

WEST VIRGINIA—Continued.

	DENOMINATION.	Total number of organizations.	COMMUNICANTS OR MEMBERS.				
			Number of organizations reporting.	Total number reported.	Sex.		
					Number of organizations reporting.	Male.	Female.
23	Dunkers or German Baptist Brethren	47	47	3,651	47	1,574	2,077
24	German Baptist Brethren Church (Conservative)	43	43	3,457	43	1,481	1,976
25	Old Order German Baptist Brethren	3	3	114	3	63	51
26	The Brethren Church (Progressive Dunkers)	1	1	80	1	30	50
27	Evangelical bodies	11	11	294	11	136	158
28	Evangelical Association	7	7	189	7	89	100
29	United Evangelical Church	4	4	105	4	47	58
30	Evangelistic associations	1	1	48	1	20	28
31	Apostolic Christian Church	1	1	48	1	20	28
32	German Evangelical Protestant bodies	1	1	399	1	154	245
33	German Evangelical Protestant Ministers' Association	1	1	399	1	154	245
34	German Evangelical Synod of North America	2	2	95	2	50	45
35	Independent churches	10	10	1,225	9	527	662
36	International Apostolic Holiness Union	3	3	82	3	35	47
37	Jewish congregations	6	3	[1]220	......	......	......
38	Latter-day Saints	13	13	1,385	13	560	825
39	Church of Jesus Christ of Latter-day Saints	2	2	785	2	312	473
40	Reorganized Church of Jesus Christ of Latter-day Saints	11	11	600	11	248	352
41	Lutheran bodies	64	64	6,506	62	2,541	3,875
42	General Synod of the Evangelical Lutheran Church in the United States of America	26	26	2,552	24	913	1,549
43	United Synod of the Evangelical Lutheran Church in the South	13	13	952	13	356	596
44	General Council of the Evangelical Lutheran Church in North America	5	5	1,176	5	509	667
45	Evangelical Lutheran Synodical Conference of America	4	4	215	4	93	122
46	Evangelical Lutheran Joint Synod of Ohio and Other States	14	14	1,540	14	620	920
47	Slovak Evangelical Lutheran Synod of America	2	2	71	2	50	21
48	Mennonite bodies	11	11	331	11	127	204
49	Mennonite Church	11	11	331	11	127	204
50	Methodist bodies	1,895	1,886	115,825	1,719	42,018	63,698
51	Methodist Episcopal Church	973	968	61,641	846	21,436	32,473
52	African Methodist Episcopal Church	35	35	1,002	35	407	595
53	African Methodist Episcopal Zion Church	6	6	86	6	40	46
54	Methodist Protestant Church	281	281	16,004	279	6,612	9,220
55	Wesleyan Methodist Connection of America	11	11	238	10	102	126
56	Methodist Episcopal Church, South	576	572	36,632	532	13,343	21,105
57	Colored Methodist Episcopal Church	3	3	72	3	30	42
58	Free Methodist Church of North America	10	10	150	8	48	91
59	Nonsectarian Churches of Bible Faith	23	23	1,316	23	618	698
60	Presbyterian bodies	207	206	19,668	187	6,320	10,978
61	Presbyterian Church in the United States of America	71	71	8,514	67	2,842	4,783
62	United Presbyterian Church of North America	9	9	1,026	9	359	667
63	Presbyterian Church in the United States	126	125	10,047	110	3,084	5,482
64	Associate Reformed Synod of the South	1	1	81	1	35	46
65	Protestant Episcopal Church	91	91	5,230	80	1,279	2,755
66	Reformed bodies	9	9	886	9	363	523
67	Reformed Church in the United States	9	9	886	9	363	523
68	Roman Catholic Church	132	132	40,011	132	22,669	17,342
69	Salvationists	6	6	179	6	97	82
70	Salvation Army	6	6	179		97	82
71	Spiritualists	2	2	145	2	60	85
72	United Brethren bodies	321	320	19,993	296	7,986	10,828
73	Church of the United Brethren in Christ	321	320	19,993	296	7,986	10,828
74	Universalists	2	2	94	2	31	63
75	Volunteers of America	1	1	4	1	2	2

[1] Heads of families only.

DEBT ON CHURCH PROPERTY, PARSONAGES, AND SUNDAY SCHOOLS, BY DENOMINATIONS (IN DETAIL), FOR TERRITORY: 1906—Continued.

WEST VIRGINIA—Continued.

PLACES OF WORSHIP.					VALUE OF CHURCH PROPERTY.		DEBT ON CHURCH PROPERTY.		PARSONAGES.		SUNDAY SCHOOLS CONDUCTED BY CHURCH ORGANIZATIONS.				
Number of organizations reporting— Church edifices.	Number of organizations reporting— Halls, etc.	Number of church edifices reported.	Seating capacity of church edifices. Number of organizations reporting.	Seating capacity of church edifices. Seating capacity reported.	Number of organizations reporting.	Value reported.	Number of organizations reporting.	Amount of debt reported.	Number of organizations reporting.	Value of parsonages reported.	Number of organizations reporting.	Number of Sunday schools reported.	Number of officers and teachers.	Number of scholars.	
43	3	69	43	21,760	43	$53,772	2	$175			35	74	411	2,729	23
39	3	65	39	20,710	39	48,072	2	175			34	73	407	2,689	24
3		3	3	650	3	3,200									25
1		1	1	400	1	2,500					1	1	4	40	26
11		11	11	2,475	11	9,100	2	125	2	$2,800	11	11	75	467	27
7		7	7	1,575	7	5,100			1	800	7	7	46	300	28
4		4	4	900	4	4,000	2	125	1	2,000	4	4	29	167	29
1		1	1	140	1	1,000					1	1	7	80	30
1		1	1	140	1	1,000					1	[illegible]	7	80	31
1		1	1	600	1	10,000	1	1,400	1	3,000	1	1	22	190	32
1		1	1	600	1	10,000	1	1,400	1	3,000	1	1	22	190	33
2		2	2	450	2	2,300					1	1	14	100	34
6	4	6	6	2,350	6	85,400	3	5,235	1	2,500	4	4	51	465	35
1	2	1	1	300	1	3,000	1	1,400			3	3	19	125	36
3		3	3	1,050	3	75,000	2	4,721			3	3	13	125	37
5	3	5	5	1,500	5	11,450	1	2,530			5	6	42	264	38
1		1	1	400	1	800					1	2	8	30	39
4	3	4	4	1,100	4	10,650	1	2,530			4	4	34	234	40
56	5	56	55	16,600	56	328,982	11	25,775	15	44,200	49	52	496	4,248	41
25		25	24	6,635	25	157,100	8	18,300	3	9,200	25	26	272	2,498	42
10	1	10	10	2,715	10	30,365			4	5,400	10	10	89	533	43
5		5	5	1,850	5	59,600	2	7,400	2	13,000	5	5	59	510	44
3	1	3	3	850	3	1,117			1	600					45
13	1	13	13	4,550	13	80,800	1	75	5	16,000	9	11	76	707	46
	2														47
6	5	6	6	1,400	6	2,850					2	2	5	50	48
6	5	6	6	1,400	6	2,850					2	2	5	50	49
1,645	184	1,656	1,575	441,081	1,652	3,767,693	165	155,181	377	714,386	1,610	1,683	14,124	104,046	50
855	94	859	822	226,278	860	2,124,645	92	94,743	213	431,286	833	869	8,004	56,033	51
30	5	30	30	6,000	31	75,550	16	10,940	9	7,800	32	32	172	894	52
2	3	2	2	300	2	450	1	300			3	3	14	42	53
255	22	256	253	73,780	254	542,284	12	7,670	52	71,650	243	253	1,962	14,173	54
6	1	6	6	1,800	6	7,800	1	800			7	7	29	228	55
488	57	494	453	130,123	490	1,005,064	39	38,178	102	202,850	482	509	3,886	32,344	56
2	1	2	2	500	2	1,400	1	200			3	3	15	67	57
	1	7	7	2,300	7	10,500	3	2,350	1	800	7	7	42	265	58
8	15	8	8	1,400	8	3,400	1	300			7	7	23	253	59
185	7	224	184	58,754	185	1,375,842	15	28,750	66	250,250	172	247	2,111	19,131	60
66	3	76	66	20,580	66	757,000	9	12,175	19	106,800	60	88	898	8,298	61
9		11	9	2,485	9	102,900	1	1,650	4	10,200	9	9	102	707	62
109	4	136	108	35,439	109	514,642	5	14,925	42	131,750	102	149	1,100	10,051	63
1		1	1	250	1	1,300			1	1,500	1	1	11	75	64
80	9	87	78	18,970	84	555,516	10	28,050	42	161,800	67	70	432	3,357	65
8	1	9	8	2,420	8	65,200	3	10,300	4	12,000	6	6	84	541	66
8	1	9	8	2,420	8	65,200	3	10,300	4	12,000	6	6	84	541	67
105	16	108	104	25,470	108	1,122,225	33	116,817	45	244,400	103	106	248	5,386	68
	6				5	1,085	1	75			4	4	16	97	69
	6				5	1,085	1	75			4	4	16	97	70
	2										1	1	3	25	71
276	31	279	274	80,540	274	349,606	32	12,723	49	52,440	290	292	2,566	18,017	72
276	31	279	274	80,540	274	349,606	32	12,723	49	52,440	290	292	2,566	18,017	73
2		2	2	450	2	5,000	1	250			1	1	8	30	74
	1														75

TABLE 3.—ORGANIZATIONS, COMMUNICANTS OR MEMBERS, PLACES OF WORSHIP, VALUE OF CHURCH PROPERTY, EACH STATE AND

WISCONSIN.

	DENOMINATION.	Total number of organizations.	COMMUNICANTS OR MEMBERS.				
			Number of organizations reporting.	Total number reported.	Sex.		
					Number of organizations reporting.	Male.	Female.
1	All denominations	4,902	4,880	1,000,903	4,531	436,411	503,178
2	Adventist bodies	123	123	3,866	121	1,355	2,485
3	Advent Christian Church	17	17	651	17	237	414
4	Seventh-day Adventist Denomination	105	105	3,194	103	1,108	2,060
5	Churches of God in Christ Jesus	1	1	21	1	10	11
6	Armenian Church	3	3	154	3	130	24
7	Bahais	3	3	167	3	88	79
8	Baptist bodies	250	250	21,716	244	7,703	13,899
9	Baptists	208	208	19,474	203	6,881	12,486
10	Northern Baptist Convention	206	206	19,414	201	6,863	12,444
11	National Baptist Convention (Colored)	2	2	60	2	18	42
12	Seventh-day Baptists	6	6	955	6	374	581
13	Free Baptists	36	36	1,287	35	448	832
14	Brethren (Plymouth)	11	11	153	11	57	96
15	Brethren (Plymouth)—I	3	3	73	3	23	50
16	Brethren (Plymouth)—II	2	2	33	2	11	22
17	Brethren (Plymouth)—III	4	4	27	4	14	13
18	Brethren (Plymouth)—IV	2	2	20	2	9	11
19	Catholic Apostolic Churches	1	1	40	1	15	25
20	New Apostolic Church	1	1	40	1	15	25
21	Christadelphians	2	2	35	2	10	25
22	Christian Catholic Church in Zion	3	3	90	3	35	55
23	Christians (Christian Connection)	21	21	470	19	148	272
24	Church of Christ, Scientist	29	29	1,704	29	531	1,173
25	Churches of the New Jerusalem	1	1	11	1	3	8
26	General Convention of the New Jerusalem in the United States of America	1	1	11	1	3	8
27	Congregationalists	257	257	26,163	257	8,256	17,907
28	Disciples or Christians	25	25	1,715	23	587	1,023
29	Disciples of Christ	24	24	1,707	22	584	1,018
30	Churches of Christ	1	1	8	1	3	5
31	Dunkers or German Baptist Brethren	11	11	339	11	140	199
32	German Baptist Brethren Church (Conservative)	7	7	253	7	107	146
33	Old Order German Baptist Brethren	1	1	18	1	10	8
34	The Brethren Church (Progressive Dunkers)	3	3	68	3	23	45
35	Eastern Orthodox Churches	10	10	1,156	3	104	92
36	Russian Orthodox Church	3	3	196	3	104	92
37	Greek Orthodox Church	7	7	960	....	....	....
38	Evangelical bodies	227	226	13,450	184	5,029	6,445
39	Evangelical Association	223	222	13,280	180	4,951	6,353
40	United Evangelical Church	4	4	170	4	78	92
41	Evangelistic associations	5	5	418	4	142	206
42	Metropolitan Church Association	2	2	290	2	118	172
43	Missionary Church Association	2	2	106	1	16	20
44	Christian Congregation	1	1	22	1	8	14
45	Friends	3	3	111	3	45	66
46	Society of Friends (Orthodox)	3	3	111	3	45	66
47	German Evangelical Synod of North America	99	97	19,861	82	7,970	9,133
48	Independent churches	17	17	1,387	16	443	744
49	Jewish congregations	30	26	[1] 1,199	....	....	....
50	Latter-day Saints	17	17	1,184	17	537	647
51	Church of Jesus Christ of Latter-day Saints	4	4	323	4	139	184
52	Reorganized Church of Jesus Christ of Latter-day Saints	13	13	861	13	398	463
53	Lutheran bodies	1,383	1,378	284,286	1,233	118,703	129,125
54	General Synod of the Evangelical Lutheran Church in the United States of America	14	14	1,534	14	742	792
55	General Council of the Evangelical Lutheran Church in North America	71	70	8,695	69	3,973	4,484
56	Evangelical Lutheran Synodical Conference of America	612	609	153,690	560	65,473	72,170
57	United Norwegian Lutheran Church in America	214	213	49,535	177	20,101	20,603
58	Evangelical Lutheran Joint Synod of Ohio and Other States	92	92	15,471	64	5,162	5,733
59	Lutheran Synod of Buffalo	7	7	1,309	7	591	718
60	Hauge's Norwegian Evangelical Lutheran Synod	24	24	3,047	18	1,126	1,100

[1] Heads of families only.

DEBT ON CHURCH PROPERTY, PARSONAGES, AND SUNDAY SCHOOLS, BY DENOMINATIONS (IN DETAIL), FOR TERRITORY: 1906—Continued.

WISCONSIN.

PLACES OF WORSHIP.					VALUE OF CHURCH PROPERTY.		DEBT ON CHURCH PROPERTY.		PARSONAGES.		SUNDAY SCHOOLS CONDUCTED BY CHURCH ORGANIZATIONS.				
Number of organizations reporting— Church edifices.	Number of organizations reporting— Halls, etc.	Number of church edifices reported.	Seating capacity of church edifices. Number of organizations reporting.	Seating capacity of church edifices. Seating capacity reported.	Number of organizations reporting.	Value reported.	Number of organizations reporting.	Amount of debt reported.	Number of organizations reporting.	Value of parsonages reported.	Number of organizations reporting.	Number of Sunday schools reported.	Number of officers and teachers.	Number of scholars.	
4,352	327	4,562	4,273	1,206,385	4,382	$27,277,837	1,048	$2,885,247	2,072	$4,837,471	3,698	4,036	28,770	278,691	1
78	21	78	78	13,065	81	81,530	4	550	2	3,900	105	119	704	3,129	2
16	1	16	16	2,890	16	21,025	1	50	2	3,900	13	13	90	474	3
62	20	62	62	10,175	65	60,505	3	500	......	......	92	106	614	2,655	4
......	......	......	......	......	......	......	......	......	......	......	......	......	......	......	5
......	3	......	......	......	......	......	......	......	......	......	......	......	......	......	6
......	3	......	......	......	......	......	......	......	......	......	1	1	7	32	7
238	6	250	234	61,296	240	1,249,743	40	61,080	101	213,400	217	253	2,414	18,903	8
199		210	196	52,496	201	1,141,143	39	60,780	80	180,150	180	216	2,111	17,017	9
198	3	209	195	52,396	199	1,140,193	37	60,634	80	180,150	178	214	2,103	16,972	10
1	1	1	1	100	2	950	2	146	......	......	2	2	8	45	11
6	......	6	6	1,800	6	35,900	......	......	2	2,800	6	6	80	538	12
33	2	34	32	7,000	33	72,700	1	300	19	30,450	31	31	223	1,348	13
......	11	......	......	......	......	......	......	......	......	......	6	6	14	102	14
......	3	......	......	......	......	......	......	......	......	......	3	3	6	39	15
......	2	......	......	......	......	......	......	......	......	......	2	2	7	51	16
......	4	......	......	......	......	......	......	......	......	......	1	1	1	12	17
......	2	......	......	......	......	......	......	......	......	......	......	......	......	......	18
......	1	......	......	......	......	......	......	......	......	......	......	......	......	......	19
......	1	......	......	......	......	......	......	......	......	......	......	......	......	......	20
......	1	......	......	......	......	......	......	......	......	......	......	......	......	......	21
......	3	......	......	......	......	......	......	......	......	......	......	......	......	......	22
13		13	13	2,771	14	11,175	1	550	1	1,000	15	15	83	470	23
13	13	13	13	3,756	19	216,475	5	15,080	......	......	23	23	126	591	24
......	......	......	......	......	......	......	......	......	......	......	......	......	......	......	25
......	......	......	......	......	......	......	......	......	......	......	......	......	......	......	26
243		250	243	68,653	240	1,672,205	61	58,150	119	285,600	238	248	2,877	23,286	27
19		19	18	4,420	18	40,000	3	1,300	3	5,100	22	22	177	1,596	28
18	3	18	17	4,220	17	38,500	2	600	3	5,100	22	22	177	1,596	29
1	......	1	1	200	1	1,500	1	700	......	......	......	......	......	......	30
6	3	6	6	1,125	6	7,250	2	70	......	......	7	7	53	288	31
6	......	6	6	1,125	6	7,250	2	70	......	......	6	6	42	248	32
......	......	......	......	......	......	......	......	......	......	......	......	......	......	......	33
......	3	......	......	......	......	......	......	......	......	......	1	1	11	40	34
4	6	4	2	400	3	7,950	1	3,000	......	......	......	......	......	......	35
2	1	2	2	400	2	1,700	......	......	......	......	......	......	......	......	36
2	5	2	......	......	1	6,250	1	3,000	......	......	......	......	......	......	37
207	12	209	174	37,179	213	702,325	8	7,010	68	149,500	177	185	2,058	10,048	38
204	11	206	171	36,504	210	691,325	7	5,010	68	149,500	174	182	2,021	9,900	39
3	1	3	3	675	3	11,000	1	2,000	......	......	3	3	37	148	40
3	1	3	3	1,150	3	104,000	2	62,000	1	1,000	3	3	25	282	41
2	......	2	2	1,050	2	102,500	2	62,000	......	......	2	2	21	260	42
1	1	1	1	100	1	1,500	......	......	1	1,000	1	1	4	22	43
......	......	......	......	......	......	......	......	......	......	......	......	......	......	......	44
3	......	3	3	850	3	8,500	1	430	1	200	2	2	20	135	45
3	......	3	3	850	3	8,500	1	430	1	200	2	2	20	135	46
96	2	100	95	28,228	95	523,600	42	87,645	60	125,020	94	95	782	7,652	47
17	......	17	16	3,895	15	74,050	3	8,000	2	5,000	14	14	111	893	48
15	1	16	14	5,162	14	176,000	10	39,950	......	......	9	9	22	541	49
11	6	11	10	2,050	12	13,705	1	80	......	......	16	17	127	520	50
1	3	1	1	350	2	4,805	......	......	......	......	4	4	41	163	51
10	3	10	9	1,700	10	8,900	1	80	......	......	12	13	86	357	52
1,208	96	1,262	1,197	354,869	1,209	6,036,751	331	630,280	576	1,322,174	766	851	3,934	45,362	53
11	3	11	11	2,925	11	39,925	6	6,895	7	11,000	10	10	85	719	54
61	6	65	60	15,655	64	277,175	26	71,010	22	52,650	62	71	564	4,467	55
544	39	575	541	172,320	544	3,396,543	184	418,763	323	727,550	260	271	858	15,647	56
202	2	209	197	61,825	199	878,450	20	25,810	55	167,045	159	194	1,028	10,742	57
82	2	87	82	22,910	82	283,425	24	28,563	41	71,700	56	56	215	3,133	58
7	......	7	7	1,910	7	31,100	3	4,414	6	10,200	2	2	8	102	59
23	1	24	23	6,545	23	75,400	8	9,000	7	10,449	17	20	87	711	60

TABLE 3.—ORGANIZATIONS, COMMUNICANTS OR MEMBERS, PLACES OF WORSHIP, VALUE OF CHURCH PROPERTY, EACH STATE AND

WISCONSIN—Continued.

	DENOMINATION.	Total number of organizations.	COMMUNICANTS OR MEMBERS. Number of organizations reporting.	Total number reported.	Sex. Number of organizations reporting.	Male.	Female.
	Lutheran bodies—Continued.						
61	Evangelical Lutheran Church in America, Eielsen's Synod	4	4	128	4	60	68
62	Evangelical Lutheran Synod of Iowa and Other States	98	98	15,220	97	6,997	7,873
63	Synod for the Norwegian Evangelical Lutheran Church in America	147	147	23,927	130	9,951	10,448
64	Danish Evangelical Lutheran Church in America	7	7	1,146	6	537	549
65	Finnish Evangelical Lutheran Church of America, or Suomi Synod	5	5	186	5	97	89
66	Norwegian Lutheran Free Church	42	42	5,477	40	1,936	2,441
67	United Danish Evangelical Lutheran Church in America	32	32	3,897	28	1,412	1,578
68	Slovak Evangelical Lutheran Synod of America	1	1	63	1	61	2
69	Finnish Evangelical Lutheran National Church	7	7	614	7	305	309
70	Apostolic Lutheran Church (Finnish)	3	3	235	3	110	125
71	Church of the Lutheran Brethren of America (Norwegian)	3	3	112	3	69	43
72	Methodist bodies	933	926	57,473	900	20,248	35,707
73	Methodist Episcopal Church	833	829	54,817	805	19,369	33,957
74	African Methodist Episcopal Church	6	6	164	6	57	107
75	African Methodist Episcopal Zion Church	3	3	86	3	35	51
76	Wesleyan Methodist Connection of America	14	14	288	13	98	173
77	Primitive Methodist Church in the United States of America	25	25	1,158	25	380	778
78	Free Methodist Church of North America	52	49	960	48	309	641
79	Moravian bodies	20	20	2,713	20	1,275	1,438
80	Moravian Church (Unitas Fratrum)	20	20	2,713	20	1,275	1,438
81	Polish National Church of America	1	1	100	1	60	40
82	Presbyterian bodies	240	240	21,243	224	7,202	12,985
83	Presbyterian Church in the United States of America	193	193	18,077	178	5,869	11,190
84	Welsh Calvinistic Methodist Church	39	39	2,579	38	1,109	1,432
85	United Presbyterian Church of North America	7	7	546	7	205	341
86	Synod of the Reformed Presbyterian Church of North America	1	1	41	1	19	22
87	Protestant Episcopal Church	162	160	16,527	122	4,679	8,574
88	Reformed bodies	85	85	11,459	80	5,188	5,692
89	Reformed Church in America	14	14	2,312	13	989	1,163
90	Reformed Church in the United States	64	64	8,386	60	3,819	4,148
91	Christian Reformed Church	7	7	761	7	380	381
92	Roman Catholic Church	796	796	506,264	786	243,252	251,382
93	Salvationists	14	14	390	14	221	169
94	Salvation Army	14	14	390	14	221	169
95	Spiritualists	19	19	784	19	330	454
96	Swedish Evangelical bodies	21	21	772	21	377	395
97	Swedish Evangelical Mission Covenant of America	12	12	580	12	279	301
98	Swedish Evangelical Free Mission	9	9	192	9	98	94
99	Theosophical societies	1	1	24	1	10	14
100	Theosophical Society, American Section	1	1	24	1	10	14
101	Unitarians	9	8	919	5	315	381
102	United Brethren bodies	54	54	2,180	53	749	1,381
103	Church of the United Brethren in Christ	45	45	2,036	44	693	1,293
104	Church of the United Brethren in Christ (Old Constitution)	9	9	144	9	56	88
105	Universalists	14	14	1,342	13	457	817
106	Volunteers of America	2	2	38	2	17	21

WYOMING.

	DENOMINATION.	Total number of organizations.	COMMUNICANTS OR MEMBERS. Number of organizations reporting.	Total number reported.	Sex. Number of organizations reporting.	Male.	Female.
1	All denominations	228	226	23,945	202	9,416	10,596
2	Adventist bodies	4	4	76	4	29	47
3	Seventh-day Adventist Denomination	4	4	76	4	29	47
4	Baptist bodies	19	19	838	18	298	530
5	Baptists: Northern Baptist Convention	19	19	838	18	298	530
6	Church of Christ, Scientist	1					
7	Congregationalists	14	14	833	14	260	573
8	Disciples or Christians	4	4	292	4	77	215
9	Disciples of Christ	4	4	292	4	77	215

DEBT ON CHURCH PROPERTY, PARSONAGES, AND SUNDAY SCHOOLS, BY DENOMINATIONS (IN DETAIL), FOR TERRITORY: 1906—Continued.

WISCONSIN—Continued.

PLACES OF WORSHIP.					VALUE OF CHURCH PROPERTY.		DEBT ON CHURCH PROPERTY.		PARSONAGES.		SUNDAY SCHOOLS CONDUCTED BY CHURCH ORGANIZATIONS.				
Number of organizations reporting—		Number of church edifices reported.	Seating capacity of church edifices.		Number of organizations reporting.	Value reported.	Number of organizations reporting.	Amount of debt reported.	Number of organizations reporting.	Value of parsonages reported.	Number of organizations reporting.	Number of Sunday schools reported.	Number of officers and teachers.	Number of scholars.	
Church edifices.	Halls, etc.		Number of organizations reporting.	Seating capacity reported.											
....	4	....	....	....	....	....	....	....	....	....	2	2	3	22	61
80	12	81	78	19,884	81	$349,848	20	$35,485	40	$76,400	67	71	289	2,984	62
127	7	131	127	34,405	127	477,850	22	17,640	51	144,480	60	75	358	3,282	63
6	....	6	6	1,195	6	20,000	2	2,400	4	6,800	5	5	22	173	64
2	3	2	2	220	2	4,040	1	500	....	....	3	4	7	84	65
34	4	34	34	8,380	34	109,600	4	3,175	6	16,300	31	34	191	1,376	66
23	7	24	23	5,755	23	88,200	10	5,625	14	27,600	21	23	172	1,613	67
....	1	....	....	....	....	....	....	....	....	....	....	....	....	....	68
3	4	3	3	500	3	1,600	....	....	....	....	7	9	20	157	69
1	....	1	1	100	1	100	....	....	....	....	1	1	2	50	70
2	1	2	2	340	2	3,500	1	1,000	....	....	3	3	15	100	71
850	46	889	836	196,645	850	3,511,150	126	146,570	385	769,460	786	835	8,436	59,463	72
770	33	803	756	176,880	769	3,345,150	118	144,305	355	740,010	714	759	7,902	56,225	73
6	....	6	6	1,160	6	20,000	1	675	....	....	5	5	27	99	74
2	1	2	2	700	2	5,900	2	30	....	....	3	3	15	100	75
13	1	14	13	3,650	13	10,800		100	5	3,950	10	10	59	420	76
22	3	27	22	6,875	22	73,900		600	10	11,200	20	23	229	1,555	77
37	8	37	37	7,380	38	55,400		860	15	14,300	34	35	204	1,064	78
20	....	20	20	4,855	20	82,300	3	2,425	14	24,625	18	18	159	1,286	79
20	....	20	20	4,855	20	82,300	3	2,425	14	24,625	18	18	159	1,286	80
1	....	1	1	150	1	3,000	1	2,000	1	1,000	1	1	1	15	81
225	10	244	223	58,164	226	1,607,250	35	28,705	99	232,200	222	255	2,801	23,398	82
179	10	194	178	47,990	180	1,448,650	35	28,705	81	194,500	177	210	2,363	20,568	83
38	....	41	37	8,364	38	137,900	....	....	12	26,300	38	38	367	2,274	84
7	....	8	7	1,610	7	18,700	....	....	6	11,400	6	6	62	496	85
1	....	1	1	200	1	2,000	....	....	....	....	1	1	9	60	86
146	7	161	146	35,635	146	1,682,815	33	95,985	72	257,250	127	127	888	7,378	87
77	4	84	76	20,135	77	325,030	21	38,671	57	111,390	75	79	741	6,077	88
14	....	14	14	4,545	14	94,800	7	19,300	12	27,800	14	14	170	1,820	89
56	4	60	56	14,040	56	204,380	10	10,446	40	76,390	57	59	557	4,097	90
7	....	10	6	1,550	7	25,850	4	8,925	5	7,200	4	6	14	160	91
771	13	820	764	281,631	772	8,780,748	291	1,589,383	493	1,285,552	660	748	1,479	62,885	92
2	12	2	2	350	14	7,365	7	2,118	....	....	11	11	35	276	93
2	12	2	2	350	14	7,365		2,118	....	....	11	11	35	276	94
3	14	3	3	850	5	6,540		500	....	....	4	4	13	110	95
21	....	22	21	5,417	21	34,500	4	2,105	4	3,900	20	24	126	949	96
12	....	13	12	4,025	12	30,000	2	2,000	4	3,900	12	16	99	745	97
9	....	9	9	1,392	9	4,500	2	105	....	....	8	8	27	204	98
....	1	....	....	....	....	....	....	....	....	....	....	....	....	....	99
....	1	....	....	....	....	....	....	....	....	....	....	....	....	....	100
7	1	7	7	1,767	7	153,000	....	....	1	20,000	4	4	74	221	101
42	9	42	42	8,397	42	58,750	9	610	11	13,200	42	46	365	1,989	102
38	4	38	38	7,397	38	53,750	7	290	11	13,200	38	42	342	1,879	103
4	5	4	4	1,000	4	5,000	2	320	....	....	4	4	23	110	104
13	1	13	13	3,520	14	98,100	2	1,000	1	7,000	12	13	107	712	105
....	2	....	....	....	2	2,030	....	....	....	....	1	1	11	102	106

WYOMING.

155	37	160	155	35,250	159	$778,142	29	$45,394	66	$144,650	175	202	1,556	13,472	1
2	2	2	2	200	2	1,700	1	18	....	....	3	4	22	75	2
2	2	2	2	200	2	1,700	1	18	....	....	3	4	22	75	3
16	1	16	16	3,375	16	66,600	3	865	3	7,600	18	23	138	1,172	4
16	1	16	16	3,375	16	66,600	3	865	3	7,600	18	23	138	1,172	5
....	....	....	....	....	....	....	....	....	....	....	....	....	....	....	6
14	....	15	14	2,427	14	59,100	2	2,600	9	16,400	14	15	131	1,178	7
2	....	2	2	750	2	10,500	2	2,300	....	....	2	2	20	240	8
2	....	2	2	750	2	10,500	2	2,300	....	....	2	2	20	240	9

TABLE 3.—ORGANIZATIONS, COMMUNICANTS OR MEMBERS, PLACES OF WORSHIP, VALUE OF CHURCH PROPERTY, EACH STATE AND

WYOMING—Continued.

	DENOMINATION.	Total number of organizations.	COMMUNICANTS OR MEMBERS.				
			Number of organizations reporting.	Total number reported.	Sex.		
					Number of organizations reporting.	Male.	Female.
10	Eastern Orthodox Churches	4	4	900			
11	Greek Orthodox Church	4	4	900			
12	German Evangelical Synod of North America	1	1	125	1	42	83
13	Independent churches	1	1	10	1	5	5
14	Jewish congregations	1					
15	Latter-day Saints	29	29	5,211	29	2,592	2,619
16	Church of Jesus Christ of Latter-day Saints	28	28	5,203	28	2,589	2,614
17	Reorganized Church of Jesus Christ of Latter-day Saints	1	1	8	1	3	5
18	Lutheran bodies	13	13	908	13	478	430
19	General Synod of the Evangelical Lutheran Church in the United States of America	2	2	66	2	28	38
20	General Council of the Evangelical Lutheran Church in North America	2	2	57	2	27	30
21	Evangelical Lutheran Synodical Conference of America	4	4	172	4	86	86
22	Finnish Evangelical Lutheran Church of America, or Suomi Synod	2	2	113	2	67	46
23	Finnish Evangelical Lutheran National Church	3	3	500	3	270	230
24	Methodist bodies	29	29	1,657	29	532	1,125
25	Methodist Episcopal Church	28	28	1,612	28	520	1,092
26	African Methodist Episcopal Church	1	1	45	1	12	33
27	Presbyterian bodies	15	15	984	11	309	636
28	Presbyterian Church in the United States of America	15	15	984	11	309	636
29	Protestant Episcopal Church	40	40	1,741	35	538	938
30	Roman Catholic Church	48	48	10,264	38	4,198	3,349
31	Salvationists	1	1	22	1	15	7
32	Salvation Army	1	1	22	1	15	7
33	Spiritualists	2	2	56	2	31	25
34	Swedish Evangelical bodies	1	1	16	1	5	11
35	Swedish Evangelical Mission Covenant of America	1	1	16	1	5	11
36	Theosophical societies	1	1	12	1	7	5
37	Theosophical Society, American Section	1	1	12	1	7	5

DEBT ON CHURCH PROPERTY, PARSONAGES, AND SUNDAY SCHOOLS, BY DENOMINATIONS (IN DETAIL), FOR TERRITORY: 1906—Continued.

WYOMING—Continued.

PLACES OF WORSHIP.					VALUE OF CHURCH PROPERTY.		DEBT ON CHURCH PROPERTY.		PARSONAGES.		SUNDAY SCHOOLS CONDUCTED BY CHURCH ORGANIZATIONS.				
Number of organizations reporting— Church edifices.	Number of organizations reporting— Halls, etc.	Number of church edifices reported.	Seating capacity of church edifices. Number of organizations reporting.	Seating capacity of church edifices. Seating capacity reported.	Number of organizations reporting.	Value reported.	Number of organizations reporting.	Amount of debt reported.	Number of organizations reporting.	Value of parsonages reported.	Number of organizations reporting.	Number of Sunday schools reported.	Number of officers and teachers.	Number of scholars.	
....	4	....	....	....	....	....	....	....	....	....	....	....	....	....	10
....	4	....	....	....	....	....	....	....	....	....	....	....	....	....	11
1	....	1	1	250	1	$5,000	....	....	....	....	1	1	3	67	12
....	1	....	....	....	....	....	....	....	....	....	1	1	5	15	13
....	....	....	....	....	....	....	....	....	....	....	....	....	....	....	14
26	3	26	26	8,845	27	49,517	1	$1,200	....	....	28	31	500	3,591	15
25	3	25	25	8,545	26	48,517	1	1,200	....	....	27	30	498	3,575	16
1	....	1	1	300	1	1,000	....	....	....	....	1	1	2	16	17
8	3	8	8	1,280	8	14,800	1	100	5	$5,600	10	10	54	331	18
1	1	1	1	180	1	3,000	....	....	1	1,200	2	2	12	123	19
1	....	1	1	100	1	5,000	....	....	....	....	2	2	7	33	20
2	1	2	2	250	2	1,400	....	....	2	1,900	2	2	6	45	21
1	1	1	1	200	1	2,200	1	100	1	2,000	1	1	4	30	22
3	....	3	3	550	3	3,200	....	....	1	500	3	3	25	100	23
27	1	27	27	6,260	27	120,425	4	7,025	19	33,650	27	30	316	2,471	24
26	1	26	26	6,110	26	110,425	4	7,025	18	32,650	26	29	304	2,431	25
1	....	1	1	150	1	10,000	....	....	1	1,000	1	1	12	40	26
9	3	10	9	2,200	10	58,500	5	6,150	8	15,000	13	19	130	1,113	27
	3	10	9	2,200	10	58,500	5	6,150	8	15,000	13	19	130	1,113	28
27	4	28	27	4,324	28	191,900	3	2,650	12	29,700	25	28	155	1,693	29
21	12	23	21	4,889	21	197,200	5	22,200	8	35,500	32	37	81	1,521	30
....	1	....	....	....	1	300	1	200	1	200	1	1	1	5	31
....	1	....	....	....	1	300	1	200	1	200	1	1	1	5	32
1		1	1	200	1	100	....	....	....	....	....	....	....	....	33
1		1	1	250	1	2,500	1	86	1	1,000	....	....	....	....	34
1	....	1	1	250	1	2,500	1	86	1	1,000	....	....	....	....	35
....	1	....	....	....	....	....	....	....	....	....	....	....	....	....	36
....	1	....	....	....	....	....	....	....	....	....	....	....	....	....	37

TABLE 4.—POPULATION IN 1900 AND COMMUNICANTS OR MEMBERS FOR SELECTED DENOMINATIONS, FOR EACH STATE AND TERRITORY, BY COUNTIES: 1906.

[The term "County location unknown" is used in this table to cover those cases where the report of a church organization failed to specify the county in which it was situated, due either to a direct omission to so report or to the fact that the return of a circuit or charge, or the like, sometimes comprised two or more churches located in different counties for which no separate report was made.]

ALABAMA.

COUNTY.	Population, 1900.	All denominations.	PROTESTANT BODIES. Total.	Baptists—Southern and National Conventions.	Freewill Baptists.	Duck River, etc. (Baptist Church of Christ).	Primitive Baptists.	Colored Primitive Baptists.	Christians (Christian Connection).	Congregationalists.	Disciples of Christ.	Churches of Christ.	Methodist Episcopal Church.	African Methodist Episcopal Church.	African Methodist Episcopal Zion Church.
The state....	1,828,697	824,209	777,125	422,270	2,213	1,947	9,772	14,829	1,890	5,395	8,756	9,214	20,450	39,617	36,705
Autauga	17,915	8,236	8,236	4,536			40	57				8	103	1,459	358
Baldwin	13,194	5,695	4,196	2,026						12	123	155	156	234	340
Barbour	35,152	15,086	14,495	8,696			125			78				2,958	
Bibb	18,498	8,515	7,759	4,980	23		54	1			26			494	264
Blount	23,119	5,953	5,953	2,483			324			59	10	34	1,009		
Bullock	31,944	14,907	14,907	9,983			42			56			306	1,684	1,379
Butler	25,761	12,304	11,519	7,274			283			72	123	114		39	1,675
Calhoun	34,874	15,861	15,[illegible]	7,877			103			155	581		598	274	36
Chambers	32,554	13,265	13,032	7,901			500		522	68	160		938		
Cherokee	21,096	6,517	6,[illegible]	3,421			25				24	162	685	48	25
Chilton	16,522	7,[illegible]	7,[illegible]	5,373			82		16	389	25		140	48	
Choctaw	18,136	9,445	9,3[illegible]	5,170			22	418					200	646	55
Clarke	27,790	15,[illegible]	15,1[illegible]	10,515								60	30	831	319
Clay	17,099	7,278	7,445	3,917			299		184	201	111	115	473	15	
Cleburne	13,206	4,523	4,[illegible]	2,390			142			79	12	225	760		
Coffee	20,972	7,098	7,094	4,[illegible]			424			20	55	198	120	490	20
Colbert	22,341	8,571	8,290	5,[illegible]						8	80	111	20	220	
Conecuh	17,514	8,524	8,477	5,[illegible]			114				17	11	430	17	873
Coosa	16,144	6,807	6,807	4,178			282			52			95	125	
Covington	15,346	6,991	6,971	4,[illegible]			292			221	16	77	68	411	491
Crenshaw	19,668	7,753	7,[illegible]	4,038			566			180	180	592	15	49	656
Cullman	17,849	8,675	6,753	3,506			290			66	50	275	615		
Dale	21,189	10,936	10,[illegible]	6,768	24		228			72			211	554	188
Dallas	54,657	31,471	31,027	19,932			4	3,199		93	340	27	25	2,149	940
Dekalb	23,558	7,828	7,828	3,112		1,154	139			90	25		737		27
Elmore	26,099	10,128	10,128	5,838			248			347	10		504		756
Escambia	11,320	6,355	5,813	3,142			118	76		137	65		198	281	220
Etowah	27,361	9,788	9,455	4,751			10			31		197	608	52	
Fayette	14,132	4,990	4,990	2,386	127		124				50	442	80		154
Franklin	16,511	5,220	5,080	3,060		65	32				127	273	20		
Geneva	19,096	6,549	6,549	3,024	212		153			104	25	119	211	611	
Greene	24,182	8,949	8,949	5,000			17				348		675	117	310
Hale	31,011	12,476	12,476	5,020			35						195	2,482	1,115
Henry	36,147	7,491	7,137	5,321			168			98			26	623	
Houston	(1)	9,512	9,512	4,958	877		48			47	25	41	130	698	23
Jackson	30,508	7,867	7,[illegible]	3,146		305	379	100		85		329	403	135	9
Jefferson	140,420	69,874	55,867	[illegible],154	89		118	141		228	996	109	1,402	4,152	1,812
Lamar	16,084	5,245	5,[illegible]	1,864			139			32	215	44			
Lauderdale	26,559	9,980	9,606	2,224			124			80	30	1,765		1,522	
Lawrence	20,124	7,396	7,396	2,942			20			262	525	208	75		
Lee	31,826	14,255	14,228	7,432						125	240		57	1,329	938
Limestone	22,387	7,600	7,600	2,252			40	483		80	165	457	262		
Lowndes	35,651	16,338	16,329	11,010			305				633	400		128	2,307
Macon	23,126	11,314	11,233	6,811							151			189	3,273
Madison	43,702	15,556	15,307	2,886			196	3,601			113	443	1,000	258	
Marengo	38,315	21,087	20,677	14,017			22	2,034			8		6	1,111	1,334
Marion	14,494	4,125	4,125	1,196	180	261	390			176	45	317	69	35	
Marshall	23,289	7,516	7,516	3,861			305	70			35	25	659	87	
Mobile	62,740	46,153	28,481	13,323			31	219		136	275	120	360	2,063	3,718
Monroe	23,666	9,898	9,765	6,566			74				30		26	712	286
Montgomery	72,047	40,867	37,518	22,821			283			147	310	786	158	1,072	5,912
Morgan	28,820	11,221	10,814	3,869				36			669	180	414	100	
Perry	31,783	16,216	16,216	11,160	192		16	831		68	90		593	648	949
Pickens	24,402	10,771	10,771	5,644			104						60	26	
Pike	29,172	13,235	13,227	8,125			646			94	31	97	75	875	198
Randolph	21,647	8,087	8,087	3,923			307		641	71	344		972	181	
Russell	27,083	13,756	13,756	7,413					113					2,698	566
St. Clair	19,425	6,776	6,776	3,889	78					10	20		387		
Shelby	23,684	9,773	9,773	5,265	202		64	17		134	8		71	576	
Sumter	32,710	12,624	12,624	9,724		76		146					224		669
Talladega	35,773	15,969	15,944	9,791			23			621	68		418	38	
Tallapoosa	29,675	11,240	11,240	6,783			331		414	158	399		396		202
Tuscaloosa	36,147	17,128	16,973	10,298	67		79				250		216	377	1,453
Walker	25,162	8,430	8,391	3,674	142	86	232	25			269	628	273	190	58
Washington	11 134	6,279	6,155	4,599						24				244	
Wilcox	35,631	20,971	20,971	12,612			21	703			229			3,092	1,411
Winston	9,554	2,608	2,608	1,672			40			129		70	338		231
County location unknown [2]		7,872	6,820	194			150	2,662					1,155	170	

[1] New county since 1900; formed from parts of Dale, Geneva, and Henry in 1903.

[2] See explanatory headnote.

TABLE 4.—POPULATION IN 1900 AND COMMUNICANTS OR MEMBERS FOR SELECTED DENOMINATIONS, FOR EACH STATE AND TERRITORY, BY COUNTIES: 1906—Continued.

ALABAMA—Continued.

COUNTY.	PROTESTANT BODIES—continued.												
	Methodist Protestant Church.	Methodist Episcopal Church, South.	Congregational Methodist Church.	Colored Methodist Episcopal Church.	Cumberland Presbyterian Church.	Colored Cumberland Presbyterian Church.	Presbyterian Church in the U. S.	Protestant Episcopal Church.	Other Protestant bodies.	Roman Catholic Church.	Jewish congregations.[1]	Greek Orthodox Church.	All other bodies.
The state	5,403	125,702	3,355	23,112	8,588	5,805	15,368	8,961	7,773	42,285	1,141	1,505	2,153
Autauga		1,411					183	40	41				
Baldwin		630		25			125	203	167	1,199			300
Barbour	36	1,745	139				573	115	30	561	30		
Bibb		1,515		57	235		93	7		756			
Blount		1,568	141		297			5	23				
Bullock	37	859	50	180			290	41					
Butler	256	1,553					18	70	42	562			223
Calhoun		2,723	534	969	202		568	322	90	759	20	50	
Chambers	15	2,003		970			140		48				
Cherokee		1,436	295		227		90		79				
Chilton	535	685			19		37		41				
Choctaw	148	1,315		670			20		8				
Clarke	71	2,302		991			20		21	5			
Clay	8	1,771					179			5			
Cleburne		736	95						84				
Coffee	50	1,322	133			75	9			4			
Colbert		1,770		494	167		207	93		281			
Conecuh	127	1,793					23	24	16				47
Coosa	294	1,234			74		186		98				
Covington	40	1,128					95		97	20			
Crenshaw	200	1,277											
Cullman	73	554	449		169				795	1,833			
Dale	139	2,545					157		50				
Dallas		1,381		508	138	553	1,027	510	201	256	113	75	
Dekalb		1,986	185		153		85		135				
Elmore	211	2,147			7		60						
Escambia		1,280	129				65	11	91	213			329
Etowah		2,196	538	358	301		252	60	101	183		150	
Fayette		1,531		20			8		68				
Franklin		1,179		188	136					140			
Geneva	300	1,722	12				56						
Greene		474		1,010	31	400	376	137	54				
Hale		1,743		1,311			397	153	25				
Henry		626					33		242	354			
Houston		2,569					90		6				
Jackson		2,043	52	20	580	15		60	206				
Jefferson	384	13,140		2,020	1,766	375	2,964	1,716	816	13,467	375	660	
Lamar		2,176		530	60				185				
Lauderdale		2,786		146	356		287	105	201	349	25		
Lawrence		1,094	103	713	289	951	107	4	103				
Lee	301	2,040		1,230			217	46	273	27			
Limestone		2,042		524	319	828	42	23	83				
Lowndes		585		785			84	92		9			
Macon	181	354					102		172	81			
Madison		3,464		249	1,306	985	301	361	144	211	38		
Marengo	30	1,409		136	20		280	222	48	374	36		
Marion		1,306		85					65				
Marshall		2,068	126		150		23	4	103				
Mobile		3,633		222			1,302	2,646	433	16,981	272	350	69
Monroe	21	1,203		526	64		194	63					133
Montgomery	296	3,117		241	125		1,139	981	130	3,006	218	125	
Morgan		3,258		1,228		428	199	186	247	337		70	
Perry		1,196				60	314	84	15				
Pickens	47	1,857		1,922	72	675	287		77				
Pike	429	2,221		299			62	35	40	8			
Randolph		1,344	281				23						
Russell		2,886		80									
St. Clair		1,779		120	471		4	18					
Shelby	235	2,510		40	463		138	50					
Sumter	51	773		340			551	20	50				
Talladega	165	2,440	40	1,370	96		508	135	29			25	
Tallapoosa	446	2,108		350			152		250				
Tuscaloosa	248	2,211		984	140	60	350	241		141	14		
Walker		2,182		522			66	44		39			
Washington		737		19					121	124			
Wilcox		1,155		660	155	400	220	34	459				
Winston		306	53										
County location unknown[2]	29	1,590							870				1,062

[1] Heads of families only.

[2] See explanatory headnote on page 294.

TABLE 4.—POPULATION IN 1900 AND COMMUNICANTS OR MEMBERS FOR SELECTED DENOMINATIONS, FOR EACH STATE AND TERRITORY, BY COUNTIES: 1906—Continued.

ARIZONA.

COUNTY.	Population, 1900.	All denominations.	PROTESTANT BODIES. Total.	Baptists—Northern Convention.	Congregationalists.	Disciples of Christ.	Methodist Episcopal Church.	Methodist Episcopal Church, South.	Presbyterian Church in the U. S. A.	Protestant Episcopal Church.	Other Protestant bodies.	Roman Catholic Church.	Jewish congregations.[1]	Church of Jesus Christ of Latter-day Saints.
The territory	[2] 122,931	45,067	9,052	1,084	405	484	1,734	682	2,884	1,069	770	29,810	20	6,175
Apache	8,297	1,342	23						18	3	2	510		809
Cochise	9,251	6,003	1,482	225	25	166	383		236	333	114	4,123	20	378
Coconino	5,514	1,147	289				115		124	21	29	722		136
Gila	4,973	1,548	274	62			100		16	65	31	1,147		127
Graham	14,162	10,522	460	80			133		204		43	7,523		2,539
Maricopa	20,457	10,742	3,741	440	80	318	542	462	1,219	282	398	5,970		1,081
Mohave	3,426	416	33				14		19			383		
Navajo	8,829	1,541	75				50			25		311		1,155
Pima	14,689	5,067	817	94	110		196		200	132	83	4,250		
Pinal	7,779	2,233	848						848			1,385		
Santa Cruz	4,545	1,005	197		31			112		40	14	808		
Yavapai	13,799	1,934	659	100	159		122	108		129	41	1,275		
Yuma	4,145	1,557	154	33			77			29	15	1,403		

[1] Heads of families only.
[2] Includes population (3,065) of San Carlos Indian reservation in Gila, Graham, and Navajo counties, not returned by counties in 1900.

ARKANSAS.

COUNTY.	Population, 1900.	All denominations.	PROTESTANT BODIES. Total.	Baptists—Southern and National Conventions.	General Baptists.	United Baptists.	Primitive Baptists.	Colored Primitive Baptists.	Church of the Living God (Christian Workers, etc.).	Disciples of Christ.	Churches of Christ.	Free Christian Zion Church of Christ (Colored).	Lutheran—Synodical Conference.	Methodist Episcopal Church.	African Methodist Episcopal Church.
The state	1,311,564	426,179	392,571	184,995	2,035	1,646	2,591	840	765	10,269	11,006	1,635	1,886	12,569	26,908
Arkansas	12,973	3,548	3,402	1,113			92			150			213	351	323
Ashley	19,734	7,460	7,265	3,383				13			25			55	883
Baxter	9,298	1,707	1,707	879						52	75				
Benton	31,611	8,952	8,952	3,029			66			740	230			798	
Boone	16,396	3,003	3,003	1,038	11		26			83	170			181	
Bradley	9,651	2,587	2,587	1,369				32						78	
Calhoun	8,539	2,600	2,600	1,519			28				25				
Carroll	18,848	3,663	3,231	1,136		565	49			171	115			79	
Chicot	14,528	6,184	5,475	4,425				99						80	644
Clark	21,289	8,167	8,167	4,009			32			398	20			140	828
Clay	15,886	4,932	4,467	1,470	376		120			154	198		14		
Cleburne	9,628	1,802	1,802	933	68		9			82				37	
Cleveland	11,620	3,201	3,201	1,619						25				94	327
Columbia	22,077	6,715	6,715	2,757			12				99				894
Conway	19,772	9,052	7,673	4,029	70		23	4		38	498		15	458	267
Craighead	19,505	9,209	6,894	835	327		31			563	73			16	132
Crawford	21,270	6,356	6,143	550		407			18	445	25			309	192
Crittenden	14,529	7,639	7,639	[illegible],043										71	864
Cross	11,051	3,663	3,637	1,881					85		37				185
Dallas	11,518	4,649	4,649	1,949			58	20		35				26	707
Desha	11,511	2,932	2,695	1,757				7						32	
Drew	19,451	7,140	7,140	3,331							6				459
Faulkner	20,780	6,751	6,297	2,837	21		28	29		48	349	625	10	86	1,482
Franklin	17,395	5,855	4,083	1,084		134	52				232			56	
Fulton	12,917	2,462	2,462	678	162		25			80	303				
Garland	18,773	5,551	5,010	1,943			26			40				179	431
Grant	7,671	3,152	3,152	1,913						48	104				100
Greene	16,979	6,607	6,322	2,637						300	321		110		
Hempstead	24,101	10,018	9,992	4,165			43		60	234	34			292	427
Hot Spring	12,748	4,262	4,262	2,600			44							70	144
Howard	14,076	4,201	4,125	1,629			50			100	100			305	142
Independence	22,557	5,908	5,908	1,847	33					40	606			388	191
Izard	13,506	4,082	4,082	1,430	153						600			173	
Jackson	18,383	6,058	5,830	2,665	38					104	614			229	878
Jefferson	40,972	17,758	15,912	9,188			41			344			44	538	2,552
Johnson	17,448	4,696	3,647	707		255	80			110	100		133		97
Lafayette	10,594	4,866	4,866	3,211			19	30	25	20	63			276	135
Lawrence	16,491	3,038	2,826	1,145							359			58	116
Lee	19,409	5,736	5,736	3,820				42	34		15			518	501
Lincoln	13,389	3,259	3,233	2,217						60				71	371
Little River	13,731	4,635	4,602	2,870						30				30	113
Logan	20,563	6,576	4,563	2,100			123			54	334			141	
Lonoke	22,544	7,958	7,766	4,465			65			210	63			42	527
Madison	19,864	1,683	1,683	511		95	19				330			65	
Marion	11,877	1,561	1,561	481	140									79	

TABLE 4.—POPULATION IN 1900 AND COMMUNICANTS OR MEMBERS FOR SELECTED DENOMINATIONS, FOR EACH STATE AND TERRITORY, BY COUNTIES: 1906—Continued.

ARKANSAS—Continued.

COUNTY.	Population, 1900.	All denominations.	PROTESTANT BODIES. Total.	Baptists—Southern and National Conventions.	General Baptists.	United Baptists.	Primitive Baptists.	Colored Primitive Baptists.	Church of the Living God (Christian Workers, etc.).	Disciples of Christ.	Churches of Christ.	Free Christian Zion Church of Christ (Colored).	Lutheran—Synodical Conference.	Methodist Episcopal Church.	African Methodist Episcopal Church.
Miller	17,558	6,495	6,240	3,317					311		319	70		76	123
Mississippi	16,384	6,752	6,605	4,631	232					35					656
Monroe	16,516	6,608	6,147	3,009						231	92			146	1,075
Montgomery	9,444	2,467	2,467	1,157			70			131				159	
Nevada	16,609	5,695	5,669	2,469			81			134	366				705
Newton	12,538	1,658	1,658	279		181				726	176			112	
Ouachita	20,892	8,889	8,753	3,861			52			43	170			75	2,006
Perry	7,294	2,786	2,317	1,180							69	490		17	41
Phillips	26,561	10,774	9,350	6,285						49	54			222	1,462
Pike	10,301	1,616	1,616	481			91			225				47	
Poinsett	7,025	1,911	1,911	849						60			14		257
Polk	18,352	3,446	3,175	1,103			172			229			56	79	30
Pope	21,715	5,361	5,172	1,324			87			354	152		134	398	80
Prairie	11,875	4,578	4,169	2,449			20				28		224	11	177
Pulaski	63,179	27,691	20,570	7,642			94		170	827		400	406	1,056	1,884
Randolph	17,156	3,584	3,227	1,123	12						827			57	88
St. Francis	17,157	6,933	6,725	4,059				47		50	57		20	315	362
Saline	13,122	4,198	4,198	2,559	47		60			121	105		22	122	22
Scott	13,183	2,546	2,546	1,529			88			162	13			20	
Searcy	11,988	2,429	2,246	1,137			36			120	20			435	
Sebastian	36,935	16,085	10,233	3,467			28		62	602	190	50	366	498	405
Sevier	16,339	3,332	3,318	1,737							26			361	34
Sharp	12,190	2,571	2,496	642	93					18	589		45	350	
Stone	8,100	1,533	1,533	1,249	56										
Union	22,495	10,257	10,257	6,107			107	500			28				754
Van Buren	11,220	2,594	2,594	1,021	196		91			135	881				
Washington	34,256	10,020	9,493	2,008		9	289			1,123	672		60	747	
White	24,864	7,765	7,672	3,193			65			70	306			436	25
Woodruff	16,304	6,439	6,414	3,817				17			52			323	782
Yell	22,750	5,385	5,137	2,114			56			66	191			106	78
County location unknown[1]		1,947	1,699				43								113

COUNTY.	PROTESTANT BODIES—continued. African Methodist Episcopal Zion Church.	Methodist Protestant Church.	Methodist Episcopal Church, South.	Colored Methodist Episcopal Church.	Presbyterian Church in the U. S. A.	Cumberland Presbyterian Church.	Presbyterian Church in the U. S.	Presbyterian—Associate Reformed Synod of the South.	Protestant Episcopal Church.	Other Protestant bodies.	Roman Catholic Church.	Jewish congregations.[2]	Latter-day Saints.
The state	2,404	6,658	81,699	11,506	809	11,990	7,357	854	4,315	7,839	32,397	673	538
Arkansas			844						15	301	146		
Ashley	893	85	1,181	604			106			35	195		
Baxter		17	535			80				69			
Benton			2,143			965	140		30	811			
Boone			705		27	356			24	382			
Bradley	110					25	263	46		20			
Calhoun	42		441	15		105							
Carroll			757		190	50			48	66	432		
Chicot	40		149	17			52		60	183	709		
Clark		179	1,824	113	30	136	309			49			
Clay		847	1,000			288					465		
Cleburne			606			25				43			
Cleveland			1,002			102		32					
Columbia		1,017	1,111	738		54	33						
Conway	298		1,236	161	42	299	65		13	157	1,379		
Craighead			2,467			244	75		42	89	2,295	20	
Crawford		220	1,241	10		274	198		114	142	213		
Crittenden			155	506									
Cross		26	839	375		139	59		4	7	26		
Dallas	5		1,724	12	8		105						
Desha	32		239			17	40		32	80	237		
Drew	282	215	1,207		83	121	254	226	13				
Faulkner	21		1,760	105	13	29	64		9	251	454		
Franklin		396	1,414	135		425	45			110	1,772		
Fulton		19	668		52	129		50	10	298			
Garland	34	66	1,611	70	24	59	188		274	65	446	95	
Grant			792			195							
Greene		87	2,639			216			14	58	285		
Hempstead		117	2,014	1,991		184	267		74	90	26		
Hot Spring		58	1,226				120						

[1] See explanatory headnote on page 294.

[2] Heads of families only.

TABLE 4.—POPULATION IN 1900 AND COMMUNICANTS OR MEMBERS FOR SELECTED DENOMINATIONS, FOR EACH STATE AND TERRITORY, BY COUNTIES: 1906—Continued.

ARKANSAS—Continued.

COUNTY.	PROTESTANT BODIES—continued. African Methodist Episcopal Zion Church.	Methodist Protestant Church.	Methodist Episcopal Church, South.	Colored Methodist Episcopal Church.	Presbyterian Church in the U. S. A.	Cumberland Presbyterian Church.	Presbyterian Church in the U. S.	Presbyterian—Associate Reformed Synod of the South.	Protestant Episcopal Church.	Other Protestant bodies.	Roman Catholic Church.	Jewish congregations.[1]	Latter-day Saints.
Howard		90	985	604		78	37		5				76
Independence		375	2,001			172	120		135				
Izard		22	1,010			571		77		46			
Jackson		27	911	56			95		172	41	213	15	
Jefferson	69		1,622	186	36	48	490		446	308	1,685	161	
Johnson		389	1,090			686					1,049		
Lafayette			594	320			167		6				
Lawrence			985			25	76			62	212		
Lee			481	195			73		57				
Lincoln	156		40	10		213	72	23			26		
Little River		15	591	656		172	48		26	51	33		
Logan		45	1,293	85		204			7	177	2,013		
Lonoke			1,825	160		146	190		9	64	192		
Madison		85	289			195				94			
Marion			609							252			
Miller		214	1,262	138			269			141	255		
Mississippi			695	198			49		14	95	147		
Monroe	14		672	402	90	161	110		29	116	461		
Montgomery		115	496							339			
Nevada		241	1,010	188		404	32		5	34	26		
Newton			148							36			
Ouachita		209	1,522	239	22	235	191		88	40	123	13	
Perry			498							22	469		
Phillips	62		681	110		35			330	60	1,400	24	
Pike		100	568	22		37	45						
Poinsett			631	42		23				35			
Polk		103	1,072			141	110		80		174		97
Pope	30		1,151	157		942	105	240	10	58	189		
Prairie			858	73		72	116		57	84	409		
Pulaski	283		3,162	931	39	202	960	125	1,429	960	6,861	280	
Randolph			1,026		26				14	54	357		
St. Francis			592	1,009		76	43		68	27	208		
Saline			969	21		125				25			
Scott		40	625			62				57			
Searcy		60	358							80	183		
Sebastian		211	2 684	171	25	516	326		353	279	5,767	85	
Sevier		56	613			346	145				14		
Sharp		224	380			105				50			75
Stone			228										
Union		379	1,528	261		20	496		2	75			
Van Buren			719							51			
Washington		359	2.228		22	1,114	302		165	395	527		
White			2,861	218		252	84		22	140	51		42
Woodruff			1,171	58	80	20	94				25		
Yell			2,070	79		6	129	35	10	197	248		
County location unknown[2]	33		1,376	65		69							248

[1] Heads of families only.

[2] See explanatory headnote on page 294.

CALIFORNIA.

COUNTY.	Population, 1900.	All denominations.	PROTESTANT BODIES. Total.	Seventh-day Adventists.	Baptists—Northern and National Conventions.	Church of Christ, Scientist.	Congregationalists.	Disciples of Christ.	Friends (Orthodox).	Lutheran—General Synod.	Lutheran—Synodical Conference.	Methodist Episcopal Church.	Methodist Episcopal Church, South.	Pentecostal Church of the Nazarene.	Presbyterian Church in the U. S. A.
The state	1,485,053	611,464	238,007	6,396	24,683	2,753	23,690	20,272	2,535	2,190	5,247	50,985	10,222	2,433	32,449
Alameda	130,197	65,852	23,915	624	2,290	440	4,040	1,095	277	190	742	3,974	355	136	4,180
Alpine	509														
Amador	11,116	6,206	457					50				237			50
Butte	17,117	3,775	2,093	80	353		163	324				456	195		305
Calaveras	11,200	3,418	198				83					26	41		
Colusa	7,364	4,256	1.153		104			384					455		109
Contra Costa	18,046	7,298	1,373		59		255	189			200	285			264
Del Norte	2,408	954	125									65			40
Eldorado	8,986	458	329	25								132			86
Fresno	37,862	18,658	10,652	355	1,365	44	737	1,079		155	158	1,467	1,053		808
Glenn	5,150	1,576	688		280			189			91	31	87		
Humboldt	27,104	8,023	3,405	245	123	124	443	385			50	727			440
Inyo	4,377	393	227	15								142			19
Kern	16,480	5,643	1,740	24	140		286	150			60	354	110		50
Kings	9,871	3,774	1,630	218	246							439	54		32

TABLE 4.—POPULATION IN 1900 AND COMMUNICANTS OR MEMBERS FOR SELECTED DENOMINATIONS, FOR EACH STATE AND TERRITORY, BY COUNTIES: 1906—Continued.

CALIFORNIA—Continued.

COUNTY.	Population, 1900.	All denominations.	PROTESTANT BODIES. Total.	Seventh-day Adventists.	Baptists—Northern and National Conventions.	Church of Christ, Scientist.	Congregationalists.	Disciples of Christ.	Friends (Orthodox).	Lutheran—General Synod.	Lutheran—Synodical Conference.	Methodist Episcopal Church.	Methodist Episcopal Church, South.	Pentecostal Church of the Nazarene.	Presbyterian Church in the U. S. A.
Lake	6,017	1,273	1,052		109			310				155	223		142
Lassen	4,511	217	217	15	65						12	125			
Los Angeles	170,298	126,249	70,412	1,370	7,962	900	6,476	5,361	1,861	480	891	17,142	1,815	1,981	9,885
Madera	6,364	3,715	655	50	88								151		150
Marin	15,702	8,024	991			24	89					100			427
Mariposa	4,720	576	108	16									70		22
Mendocino	20,465	5,328	2,336	26	555			340				510	429		291
Merced	9,215	2,298	1,057	22				85					433		101
Modoc	5,076	249	195				87					60			
Mono	2,167	4	4									4			
Monterey	19,380	4,971	2,190	46	274	14	143	225		42		554	69		166
Napa	16,451	5,172	2,078	340	163	27		209			33	513			443
Nevada	17,789	1,892	1,116	22			227				27	623			
Orange	19,696	8,368	7,093	147	782	49	311	692	160		568	1,605	503	37	1,196
Placer	15,786	2,102	909		86		216					311	60		34
Plumas	4,657	73	73				22					51			
Riverside	17,897	10,220	6,372	97	810	249	842	611		54		1,764	32		754
Sacramento	45,915	13,268	4,682	70	677	63	298	368		460		1,242	175		604
San Benito	6,633	3,007	795				58	180				157	230		85
San Bernardino	27,929	11,382	8,429	200	1,208	46	1,163	911		63	30	2,197	265	188	1,172
San Diego	35,090	15,589	7,211	341	978	93	927	644	140	105	97	1,471	204	50	852
San Francisco	342,782	142,919	21,776	344	1,322	394	2,400	752		515	1,407	3,019	151	31	3,272
San Joaquin	35,452	10,667	4,368	121	234	83	358	708			333	967	347		331
San Luis Obispo	16,637	6,027	1,795	46	130		99	50			74	494			308
San Mateo	12,094	5,598	1,072				292					206			15
Santa Barbara	18,934	6,982	2,369	19	283	51	197	178		51		329	50		562
Santa Clara	60,216	24,914	11,707	426	1,256	128	830	927	97	75	114	3,031	460		1,758
Santa Cruz	21,512	7,938	3,955	76	225	24	665	725				847			645
Shasta	17,318	1,713	851	24	210		28					147	147		177
Sierra	4,017	815	228		49		63					116			
Siskiyou	16,962	2,703	597				131					310			
Solano	24,143	7,788	2,132	70	325		237	200			37	381	57		349
Sonoma	38,480	13,177	6,344	677	578		851	867			123	1,396	582		585
Stanislaus	9,550	3,220	2,240	118	193		66	310			73	582	151		264
Sutter	5,886	562	562		30			138				198	166		
Tehama	10,996	3,756	1,673	23	276			317				402	144		359
Trinity	4,383	411	68				68								
Tulare	18,375	4,155	3,236	37	413		209	532			60	606	592		248
Tuolumne	11,166	1,585	395		40							124	55		69
Ventura	14,367	4,808	2,025	16	180		194	125			67	599	47	10	535
Yolo	13,618	3,745	1,963	51	196		97	550				202	204		70
Yuba	8,620	3,709	630		26		39	112				110	60		200
County location unknown[1]		61	61												

COUNTY.	PROTESTANT BODIES—continued. Cumberland Presbyterian Church.	United Presbyterian Church.	Protestant Episcopal Church.	Unitarians.	Other Protestant bodies.	Roman Catholic Church.	Jewish congregations.[2]	Armenian Church.	Buddhists—Japanese Temples.	Servian Orthodox Church.	Greek Orthodox Church.	Latter-day Saints (Reorganized).	All other bodies.
The state	2,908	2,213	21,317	3,204	22,510	354,408	2,028	2,134	2,629	2,800	5,660	2,221	3,577
Alameda	42	82	2,915	568	1,965	40,681	140	56	172		425	272	191
Alpine													
Amador			90		30	2,949				2,800			
Butte			84		133	1,514					105	63	
Calaveras			20		28	3,220							
Colusa			54		47	3,103							
Contra Costa			99		22	5,775					150		
Del Norte					20	829							
Eldorado			86			129							
Fresno	628	397	413	63	1,930	5,297		1,678	711		280		40
Glenn			10			888							
Humboldt			411	65	392	4,563						55	
Inyo	51					166							
Kern	79		325		162	3,803					100		
Kings	390		150		101	2,057			87				
Lake	67		46			199						22	
Lassen													
Los Angeles	327	531	5,532	348	7,550	52,193	551	180	263		930	286	1,434
Madera	47		130		39	3,060							
Marin			351			6,953					80		

[1] See explanatory headnote on page 294.

[2] Heads of families only.

TABLE 4.—POPULATION IN 1900 AND COMMUNICANTS OR MEMBERS FOR SELECTED DENOMINATIONS, FOR EACH STATE AND TERRITORY, BY COUNTIES: 1906—Continued.

CALIFORNIA—Continued.

COUNTY.	PROTESTANT BODIES—continued.					Roman Catholic Church.	Jewish congregations.[1]	Armenian Church.	Buddhists—Japanese Temples.	Servian Orthodox Church.	Greek Orthodox Church.	Latter-day Saints (Reorganized).	All other bodies.
	Cumberland Presbyterian Church.	United Presbyterian Church.	Protestant Episcopal Church.	Unitarians.	Other Protestant bodies.								
Mariposa						468							
Mendocino			105		80	2,992							
Merced	240		68		108	1,241							
Modoc					48							54	
Mono													
Monterey		247	345		65	2,781							
Napa	13		156		181	3,094							
Nevada			209		8	776							
Orange		232	286	49	476	1,033						242	
Placer			186		16	1,193							
Plumas													
Riverside		102	348		709	3,848							
Sacramento			359	24	342	7,353	107		579		300	196	52
San Benito			70		15	2,159						53	
San Bernardino		36	498	150	302	2,614	25					267	47
San Diego		125	861	180	143	8,014	50						264
San Francisco	32	254	2,846	1,151	3,886	115,921	1,079	220	342		2,200	212	1,169
San Joaquin	123		216		547	6,061	50				120	68	
San Luis Obispo	150		124		320	4,232							
San Mateo			559			4,526							
Santa Barbara	90		296	150	113	4,347					100		166
Santa Clara	129	207	1,157	285	832	12,866	26		124		40	99	52
Santa Cruz			311	74	363	3,385			351		40	78	129
Shasta			53		65	802					60		
Sierra						587							
Siskiyou			156			2,010					80		16
Solano	20		326		130	5,496					160		
Sonoma			393	40	252	6,570					90	156	17
Stanislaus	106		59		318	980							
Sutter					30								
Tehama			103		49	2,083							
Trinity						343							
Tulare	224		125		190	740					80	99	
Tuolumne			103		4	1,190							
Ventura			40		212	2,683					100		
Yolo	150		110	57	276	1,662					120		
Yuba			72		11	2,979					100		
County location unknown[2]			61										

[1] Heads of families only. [2] See explanatory headnote on page 294.

COLORADO.

COUNTY.	Population, 1900.	All denominations.	PROTESTANT BODIES.									Roman Catholic Church.	Jewish congregations.[1]	All other bodies.
			Total.	Seventh-day Adventists.	Baptists—Northern Convention.	Congregationalists.	Disciples of Christ.	Methodist Episcopal Church.	Presbyterian Church in the U. S. A.	Protestant Episcopal Church.	Other Protestant bodies.			
The state	539,700	205,666	98,878	2,311	12,917	8,951	8,521	24,830	16,055	6,832	18,461	99,820	853	6,115
Adams	([2])	622	438			68		99	157	8	106	184		
Arapahoe	153,017	841	365			24		179	115	47		476		
Archuleta	2,117	722	131		29			102				591		
Baca	759	130	130					130						
Bent	3,049	830	592		51		21	255	132	50	83	212		26
Boulder	21,544	9,358	6,136	423	688	745	790	1,285	1,108	285	812	3,162		60
Chaffee	7,085	2,127	1,252	45	265	45	162	270	272	168	25	795		80
Cheyenne	501	94	94					68			26			
Clear Creek	7,082	1,930	587	34				156	201	79	117	1,343		
Conejos	8,794	3,740	475	50	64			43	241	56	21	1,749		1,516
Costilla	4,632	2,524	154	57	26			28	43			2,282		88
Custer	2,937	588	371						35	29	307	217		
Delta	5,487	1,916	1,788	112	462	57	139	691	99	62	166	128		
Denver	([2])	58,699	30,646	455	3,989	3,223	2,111	6,837	4,632	2,712	6,687	25,993	703	1,357
Dolores	1,134	83	12			12						71		
Douglas	3,120	187	187					137		50				
Eagle	3,008	222	128			11		117				94		
El Paso	31,602	14,259	9,791	113	1,317	1,181	1,145	1,988	1,525	895	1,627	3,967	20	481
Elbert	3,101	234	234			31	50		123		30			
Fremont	15,636	5,618	3,972	81	471	10	275	1,239	1,035	227	634	1,566		80

[1] Heads of families only. [2] New county since 1900; formed from part of Arapahoe in 1902.

TABLE 4.—POPULATION IN 1900 AND COMMUNICANTS OR MEMBERS FOR SELECTED DENOMINATIONS, FOR EACH STATE AND TERRITORY, BY COUNTIES: 1906—Continued.

COLORADO—Continued.

COUNTY.	Population, 1900.	All denominations.	PROTESTANT BODIES.										Roman Catholic Church.	Jewish congregations.[1]	All other bodies.
			Total.	Seventh-day Adventists.	Baptists—Northern Convention.	Congregationalists.	Disciples of Christ.	Methodist Episcopal Church.	Presbyterian Church in the U.S.A.	Protestant Episcopal Church.	Other Protestant bodies.			
Garfield	5,	984	698	24		43	192	292	51	65	31	286		
Gilpin	6	1,655	360					232	48	80		1,295		
Grand		510	85			33		32	9		11	425		
Gunnison	835	1,044	321	18		50	30	112	94	17		723		
Hinsdale	5,[illegible]	285	72		31				20	21		213		
Huerfano	8,395	5,883	508	12	105				150	24	217	5,375		
Jefferson	9,306	2,039	1,273	27	163		184	543	227	116	13	738		28
Kiowa	701	49	49					49						
Kit Carson	1,580	406	406			90		93			223			
La Plata	7,016	2,617	946	22	163		19	200	274	104	164	1,644		
Lake	,	3,856	754	10	95			211	144	108	186	3,024	40	27 / 38
Larimer	18,	6,915	4,988	140	708	261	535	1,148	841	210	1,145	1,927		
Las Animas	21,	17,844	1,723	31	200	76	277	330	302	162	345	15,981	40	100
Lincoln	054	169	169			69		31		12	57			
Logan	3,[illegible]	1,230	1,010		102		80	310		11	507	196		24
Mesa	9,267	4,757	3,719	185	408	464	425	1,293	364	139	441	981		
Mineral	,913	328	64			50				14		264		
Montezuma	,058	518	130		48	6		25		14	37	88		[illegible]
Montrose	,535	774	594	25	100	154		168		42	105	180		
Morgan	[illegible],268	1,270	1,203	11	24			403	424	23	315	67		
Otero	11,522	4,344	3,235	51	589	65	551	745	560	83	591	1,029		
Ouray	4,731	448	179					68	55	45	11	219		
Park	2,998	178	93					30	26	37		85		
Phillips	1,583	375	284					188	53		43	91		
Pitkin	7,020	2,499	442	11	70			128	142	60	31	2,017		
Prowers	3,	1,448	953	8	188		48	390	144	8	167	495		[illegible]
Pueblo	34,	21,085	6,993	88	1,365	548	833	1,329	1,060	367	1,403	12,786	50	1,2[illegible]
Rio Blanco	1,	237	191	14			49	93		35		46		
Rio Grande	4,	1,546	828	45	109		55	303	282	34		718		
Routt	3,[illegible]	769	720		45	422	75	157		12	9	49		
Saguache	3,853	977	212	9	92			43	26	21	21	765		
San Juan	2,342	1,253	138			80				44	14	1,115		
San Miguel	5,379	815	236	11		105		100		20		579		
Sedgwick	971	260	235			40		195				25		
Summit	2,744	678	131					76		46	9	547		
Teller	29,002	3,011	1,712	63	421	171	95	276	272	94	320	1,119		180
Washington	1,241	188	132			65			67			56		
Weld	16,808	5,890	4,627	89	529	752	320	1,194	470	93	1,180	1,263		
Yuma	1,729	1,336	810	47			60	247	232		224	460		66
County location unknown[2]		472	172					172				119		181

[1] Heads of families only.

[2] See explanatory headnote on page 294.

CONNECTICUT.

COUNTY.	Population, 1900.	All denominations.	PROTESTANT BODIES.									Roman Catholic Church.	Jewish congregations.[1]	All other bodies.
			Total.	Baptists—Northern and National Conventions.	Congregationalists.	Lutheran—General Council.	Lutheran—Synodical Conference.	Methodist Episcopal Church.	Presbyterian Church in the U. S. A.	Protestant Episcopal Church.	Other Protestant bodies.			
The state	908,420	502,560	196,248	27,535	65,554	13,961	4,156	32,878	2,252	37,466	12,456	299,513	1,733	5,066
Fairfield	184,203	108,963	42,829	4,235	10,378	746	949	9,359	1,383	10,364	5,415	64,087	408	1,639
Hartford	195,480	107,860	42,497	5,177	15,927	4,333	1,522	6,200	569	6,436	2,333	62,497	743	2,123
Litchfield	63,672	30,396	15,373	618	7,483	849	123	2,650		3,376	274	15,023		
Middlesex	41,760	19,130	10,701	1,176	3,949	1,535	80	1,713		2,033	215	8,429		
New Haven	269,163	160,271	53,009	6,870	16,904	4,121	1,182	8,895	300	11,982	2,755	105,845	517	900
New London	82,758	41,260	18,804	7,102	5,623	1,150		2,024		2,394	511	22,032	65	359
Tolland	24,523	9,981	5,352	454	2,439	724	300	885		278	272	4,629		
Windham	46,861	24,615	7,599	1,903	2,851	493		1,068		603	681	16,971		45
County location unknown[2]		84	84					84						

[1] Heads of families only.

[2] See explanatory headnote on page 294.

TABLE 4.—POPULATION IN 1900 AND COMMUNICANTS OR MEMBERS FOR SELECTED DENOMINATIONS, FOR EACH STATE AND TERRITORY, BY COUNTIES: 1906—Continued.

DELAWARE.

COUNTY.	Population, 1900.	All denominations.	PROTESTANT BODIES. Total.	Baptists—Northern Convention.	Lutheran—General Council.	Methodist Episcopal Church.	Methodist Protestant Church.	African Methodists.[1]	Presbyterian Church in the U. S. A.	Protestant Episcopal Church.	Other Protestant bodies.	Roman Catholic Church.	Jewish congregations.[2]	Spiritualists.
The state	184,735	71,251	46,779	2,694	665	24,269	3,463	4,670	5,086	3,796	2,136	24,228	207	37
Kent	32,762	10,215	9,344	276		5,928	676	1,409	297	373	385	871		
Newcastle	109,697	46,996	23,820	2,388	665	9,558	216	2,539	4,111	2,851	1,492	22,932	207	37
Sussex	42,276	13,503	13,078	30		8,291	2,571	722	678	572	214	425		
County location unknown[3]		537	537			492					45			

[1] Includes Union American Methodist Episcopal Church, African Methodist Episcopal Church, African Union Methodist Protestant Church, and African Methodist Episcopal Zion Church.
[2] Heads of families only.
[3] See explanatory headnote on page 294.

DISTRICT OF COLUMBIA.

[No county organization. See Washington city, coextensive with the District of Columbia, page 506.]

FLORIDA.

COUNTY.	Population, 1900.	All denominations.	PROTESTANT BODIES. Total.	Baptists—Southern and National Conventions.	Colored Primitive Baptists.	Methodist Episcopal Church.	Methodist Episcopal Church, South.	African Methodists.[1]	Presbyterian Church in the U. S.	Protestant Episcopal Church.	Other Protestant bodies.	Roman Catholic Church.	Jewish congregations.[2]	All other bodies.
The state	528,542	221,318	199,858	83,017	5,350	8,287	32,330	40,794	5,534	8,575	15,971	17,507	323	3,630
Alachua	32,245	12,302	12,251	6,237	21	1,742	1,397	1,703	380	238	533	51		
Baker	4,516	598	598	136		56	68	71		12	255			
Bradford	10,295	3,456	3,456	1,698		284	521	447	12	10	484			
Brevard	5,158	1,219	1,193	475	17	100	71	227		244	59	26		
Calhoun	5,132	1,208	1,208	220			311	296	6	8	367			
Citrus	5,391	1,615	1,615	685		15	183	540	3	9	180			
Clay	5,635	1,751	1,725	1,238	25	31	151	209		51	20	26		
Columbia	17,094	5,226	5,222	1,881	75	437	710	1,218	202	36	663	4		
Dade	4,955	3,685	3,342	1,019	15	171	598	648		397	494	343		
De Soto	8,047	3,810	3,810	2,159			980	235		188	248			
Duval	39,733	22,058	19,471	6,727	281	1,579	1,567	4,767	668	2,146	1,736	2,218	159	
Escambia	28,313	17,806	9,208	3,556	284	178	1,817	1,634	491	711	537	8,278	70	210
Franklin	4,890	2,006	1,488	535	161		277	414		101		486		[illegible]
Gadsden	15,294	5,381	5,381	1,064	529		1,122	2,189	225	52	200			
Hamilton	11,881	3,975	3,975	1,556	29	28	616	1,152	44		550			
Hernando	3,638	1,604	1,598	799		20	549	129	17	21	63	6		
Hillsboro	36,913	16,596	13,500	4,426	527	455	3,295	2,036	762	792	1,207	1,887	94	1,115
Holmes	7,762	1,932	1,932	1,066		40	391	68	27		340			
Jackson	23,377	11,789	11,784	5,943			1,805	2,964	75	52	945	5		
Jefferson	16,195	6,810	6,810	3,740	177		659	2,054	94	61	25			
Lafayette	4,987	2,133	2,133	898		34	323	711	18	10	139			
Lake	7,467	2,585	2,585	991	59	173	474	459	45	111	273			
Lee	3,071	776	606	190		22	283			91	20	170		
Leon	19,887	7,436	7,366	2,199	1,657		737	2,413	122	199	39	70		
Levy	8,603	2,075	2,075	922		212	314	530		15	82			
Liberty	2,956	696	696	101	26		214	222	8		125			
Madison	15,446	6,524	6,524	3,559	110	24	967	1,379	157	9	319			
Manatee	4,663	2,515	2,460	869	7	15	785	273	177	106	228	55		
Marion	24,403	10,046	9,958	5,339	351	566	1,212	1,782	226	220	262	88		
Monroe	18,006	4,506	4,081	88	172	130	1,286	1,033		998	374	425		
Nassau	9,654	3,588	3,227	2,214	58	301	297		100	191	66	361		
Orange	11,374	6,397	6,065	2,203	119	118	1,030	1,181	397	386	631	332		
Osceola	3,444	1,199	1,193	698	13		218	112		23	129			
Pasco	6,054	1,817	1,647	901	6		446	220	30	4	40	170		
Polk	12,472	5,000	4,974	2,215	66	60	1,352	440	53	94	694	26		
Putnam	11,641	4,766	4,570	2,322	29	140	382	1,007	184	273	233	196		
St. John	9,165	5,226	3,175	1,354		404	92	829		293	203	2,051		
St. Lucie	(3)	597	571	121			191	154			105	26		
Santa Rosa	10,293	2,842	2,500	1,315	50	97	325	439	110	19	145	9		333
Sumter	6,187	2,120	2,120	926	46		597	449	24	3	75			
Suwanee	14,554	7,069	7,069	3,756	32	12	994	1,283	99	48	845			
Taylor	3,999	1,451	1,451	608			220	171	29		423			
Volusia	10,003	4,692	4,207	1,404	135	312	400	895	120	335	606	185		300
Wakulla	5,149	1,167	1,167	345	263		261	298						
Walton	9,346	3,337	3,337	1,119		60	439	718	554	16	431			
Washington	10,154	3,322	3,309	1,200		20	810	745	75		459	13		
County location unknown[4]		2,609	1,225		10	451	593	50		2	119			1,384

[1] Includes African Methodist Episcopal Church, African Methodist Episcopal Zion Church, and Colored Methodist Episcopal Church.
[2] Heads of families only.
[3] New county since 1900; formed from rt of Brevard in 1905.
[4]

TABLE 4.--POPULATION IN 1900 AND COMMUNICANTS OR MEMBERS FOR SELECTED DENOMINATIONS, FOR EACH STATE AND TERRITORY, BY COUNTIES: 1906—Continued.

GEORGIA.

COUNTY.	Population, 1900.	All denominations.	PROTESTANT BODIES.									Roman Catholic Church.	Jewish congregations.[3]	All other bodies.
			Total.	Baptists—Southern and National Conventions.	Primitive Baptists.[1]	Disciples of Christ.	Methodist Episcopal Church.	Methodist Episcopal Church, South.	African Methodists.[2]	Presbyterian Church in the U. S.	Other Protestant bodies.			
The state	2,216,331	1,029,037	1,007,205	566,631	20,688	12,703	28,579	178,307	131,919	20,258	48,120	19,273	897	1,662
Appling	12,336	3,577	3,577	1,441	58	32	80	1,053	155	...	758	...	...	...
Baker	6,704	1,668	1,668	604	42	...	...	187	536	38	261	...	...	...
Baldwin	17,768	7,494	7,465	4,685	267	...	...	1,123	999	260	131	29	...	...
Banks	10,545	4,994	4,994	3,011	...	302	220	825	393	243	...	...	...	...
Bartow	20,823	9,008	8,973	5,434	53	50	179	1,933	786	340	198	35	...	...
Ben Hill	(4)	2,860	2,779	1,391	99	125	130	451	368	69	146	81	...	...
Berrien	19,440	6,110	6,052	2,280	396	75	187	1,181	1,565	17	349	58	...	...
Bibb	50,473	24,937	23,879	12,290	508	269	42	4,728	3,917	797	1,328	878	140	40
Brooks	18,606	7,842	7,842	4,190	349	10	...	1,243	1,676	133	241	...	...	...
Bryan	6,122	2,230	2,230	1,706	57	40	...	300	109	18	...	...	...	...
Bulloch	21,377	6,411	6,411	3,462	823	14	392	1,052	605	46	17	...	...	...
Burke	30,165	17,251	17,251	14,063	...	100	663	1,449	806	50	120	...	...	...
Butts	12,805	6,316	6,316	4,025	107	60	...	771	952	152	249	...	...	...
Calhoun	9,274	3,350	3,350	1,372	163	...	...	396	807	51	561	...	...	...
Camden	7,669	2,730	2,721	1,734	...	...	270	255	280	40	142	9	...	...
Campbell	9,518	5,069	5,069	2,576	...	317	417	786	505	20	448	...	...	...
Carroll	26,576	10,860	10,860	5,311	356	130	956	3,127	76	146	758	...	...	...
Catoosa	5,823	1,619	1,619	994	20	...	32	509	...	64	...	...	...	...
Charlton	3,592	1,661	1,661	581	618	...	67	279	74	...	42	...	...	...
Chatham	71,239	40,996	33,412	20,717	46	371	627	2,424	3,645	1,467	4,115	6,843	241	500
Chattahoochee	5,790	1,949	1,949	547	144	...	...	290	968	...	...	...	...	...
Chattooga	12,952	4,334	4,334	2,600	37	25	185	709	329	349	100	...	...	...
Cherokee	15,243	6,002	5,989	3,777	...	40	135	1,796	151	54	36	13	...	...
Clarke	17,708	8,279	7,983	3,668	99	152	14	1,860	1,528	460	202	233	38	25
Clay	8,568	4,324	4,324	2,053	...	...	...	530	1,627	46	68	...	...	...
Clayton	9,598	4,556	4,556	2,258	118	43	470	745	370	263	289	...	...	...
Clinch	8,732	2,189	2,189	925	163	...	...	532	531	...	38	...	...	...
Cobb	24,664	11,717	11,506	5,899	105	127	128	3,032	791	882	542	211	...	...
Coffee	16,169	6,657	6,569	2,470	117	...	16	716	2,666	22	562	88	...	...
Colquitt	13,636	6,313	6,313	3,150	441	...	...	1,474	512	110	626	...	...	...
Columbia	10,653	8,134	8,134	7,129	16	50	...	825	107	...	7	...	...	...
Coweta	24,980	14,959	14,959	8,840	25	50	1,377	2,477	1,373	188	629	...	...	...
Crawford	10,368	2,428	2,428	699	271	...	...	500	732	...	226	...	...	...
Crisp	(5)	5,762	5,742	3,861	204	...	40	796	485	40	316	20	...	...
Dade	4,578	1,066	1,066	448	38	...	...	505	17	...	58	...	...	...
Dawson	5,442	1,850	1,850	1,434	...	...	42	336	...	...	38	...	...	...
Decatur	29,454	10,575	10,560	5,322	275	80	7	1,469	2,372	280	755	15	...	...
Dekalb	21,112	9,825	9,825	4,919	185	32	763	2,261	439	754	472	...	...	...
Dodge	13,975	6,813	6,813	4,981	477	192	84	494	506	18	61	...	...	...
Dooly	26,567	7,303	7,303	4,561	100	...	...	1,487	945	...	210	...	...	...
Dougherty	13,679	6,401	6,201	4,552	40	...	...	515	765	80	249	121	64	15
Douglas	8,745	3,451	3,451	2,103	91	...	...	949	258	...	50	...	...	...
Early	14,828	6,372	6,372	2,456	51	...	...	901	2,191	17	756	...	...	...
Echols	3,209	975	975	346	110	...	...	260	189	...	70	...	...	...
Effingham	8,334	4,540	4,540	1,763	...	109	40	1,017	759	...	852	...	...	...
Elbert	19,729	8,380	8,380	5,121	...	...	182	1,805	1,000	102	170	...	...	...
Emanuel	21,279	8,510	8,510	3,185	903	...	16	1,854	2,183	...	369	...	...	...
Fannin	11,214	3,065	3,065	2,040	...	155	545	268	49	...	8	...	...	...
Fayette	10,114	4,904	4,904	2,655	38	207	650	1,058	212	...	84	...	...	...
Floyd	33,113	13,365	12,869	6,160	168	65	1,094	3,247	1,058	482	595	474	22	...
Forsyth	11,550	4,904	4,904	4,009	...	...	...	805	90	...	...	...	...	...
Franklin	17,700	6,639	6,639	4,709	...	242	160	1,174	98	171	85	...	...	...
Fulton	117,363	66,517	60,640	25,612	290	1,177	2,683	13,465	6,860	4,224	6,329	5,121	250	506
Gilmer	10,198	3,583	3,583	2,861	...	30	315	377	...	...	...	...	...	...
Glascock	4,516	1,681	1,681	1,116	44	...	...	282	79	...	160	...	...	...
Glynn	14,317	9,457	9,246	5,856	4	...	370	723	1,023	200	1,070	146	25	40
Gordon	14,119	5,800	5,800	3,740	60	...	29	1,666	110	30	165	...	...	...
Grady	(6)	4,537	4,537	2,046	247	...	...	1,229	719	30	266	...	...	...
Greene	16,542	8,731	8,731	6,268	...	...	...	1,004	1,041	280	138	...	...	...
Gwinnett	25,585	11,015	11,015	5,530	243	390	600	3,289	498	200	265	...	...	...
Habersham	13,604	3,609	3,609	2,587	...	...	58	691	79	115	79	...	...	...
Hall	20,752	9,903	9,903	7,008	...	...	163	2,265	131	217	119	...	...	...
Hancock	18,277	8,075	8,075	3,963	...	...	...	1,312	2,682	111	7	...	...	...
Haralson	11,922	4,019	3,982	2,065	139	130	251	598	261	58	480	37	...	...
Harris	18,009	8,529	8,529	4,649	79	...	478	1,674	1,649	...	...	...	...	...
Hart	14,492	5,884	5,884	3,928	...	...	...	1,205	641	110	...	...	...	...
Heard	11,177	3,517	3,517	1,964	150	150	486	504	110	...	153	...	...	...
Henry	18,602	11,728	11,728	7,060	218	150	1,253	1,984	253	260	550	...	...	...
Houston	22,641	10,515	10,502	6,103	388	...	...	1,397	2,424	56	134	13	...	...
Irwin	13,645	3,800	3,800	2,271	243	53	...	410	630	...	193	...	...	...

[1] Includes Primitive Baptists and Colored Primitive Baptists in America.
[2] Includes African Methodist Episcopal Church, African Methodist Episcopal Zion Church, Colored Methodist Episcopal Church, and Reformed Methodist Union Episcopal Church.
[3] Heads of families only.
[4] New county since 1900; formed from parts of Irwin and Wilcox in 1906.
[5] New county since 1900; formed from part of Dooly in 1905.
[6] New county since 1900; formed from parts of Decatur and Thomas in 1905.

TABLE 4.—POPULATION IN 1900 AND COMMUNICANTS OR MEMBERS FOR SELECTED DENOMINATIONS, FOR EACH STATE AND TERRITORY, BY COUNTIES: 1906—Continued.

GEORGIA—Continued.

COUNTY.	Population, 1900.	All denominations.	PROTESTANT BODIES.									Roman Catholic Church.	Jewish congregations.[3]	All other bodies.
			Total.	Baptists—Southern and National Conventions.	Primitive Baptists.[1]	Disciples of Christ.	Methodist Episcopal Church.	Methodist Episcopal Church, South.	African Methodists.[2]	Presbyterian Church in the U. S.	Other Protestant bodies.			
Jackson	24,039	11,586	11,586	6,093	29	924	376	2,548	582	322	712			
Jasper	15,033	5,931	5,931	2,253	154	65		1,114	2,217	110	18			
Jeff Davis	(4)	1,622	1,622	744	59			276	407	89	47			
Jefferson	18,212	12,044	12,044	6,853	80		14	1,622	3,160		315			
Jenkins	(5)	5,047	5,047	3,409	25		572	628	225		188			
Johnson	11,409	4,175	4,175	1,853	825	84		956	432		25			
Jones	13,358	3,981	3,981	1,471	194			537	1,625		154			
Laurens	25,908	12,774	12,748	8,700	142	123	5	2,036	1,566	60	116	26		
Lee	10,344	6,580	6,580	5,443	275			231	606	25				
Liberty	13,093	6,725	6,702	3,582	43			309	1,171	141	1,456	23		
Lincoln	7,156	3,943	3,943	2,999				562	366	16				
Lowndes	20,036	8,179	8,139	4,010	266	204	37	1,481	1,801		340	40		
Lumpkin	7,433	1,253	1,253	656			47	506	44					
McDuffie	9,804	4,167	4,167	2,595				720	642		210			
McIntosh	6,537	4,394	4,340	3,397	23			185	432	48	235	54		
Macon	14,093	5,788	5,788	2,308	409			1,076	1,752		243			
Madison	13,224	5,506	5,506	3,794	120			893	420	219	60			
Marion	10,080	3,868	3,868	1,171	228			918	1,346	32	173			
Meriwether	23,339	10,092	10,092	6,392	286		719	1,858	602	81	154			
Miller	6,319	2,453	2,453	766	77			158	111		1,341			
Milton	6,763	2,114	2,114	1,254		40	150	521	50		99			
Mitchell	14,767	6,223	6,223	4,313	145			815	683	45	222			
Monroe	20,682	8,420	8,420	3,873	152		611	1,403	1,724	35	622			
Montgomery	16,359	4,438	4,438	1,943	85	125	164	1,459	348	128	186			
Morgan	15,813	7,800	7,800	5,912	66	87	39	1,214	362	45	75			
Murray	8,623	1,874	1,874	1,164			239	449		22				
Muscogee	29,836	16,182	15,748	7,751	109		30	3,043	3,100	574	1,141	357	52	25
Newton	16,734	6,927	6,927	2,195	270		1,000	2,050	739	243	430			
Oconee	8,602	4,273	4,273	2,145	31	1,256		734	107					
Oglethorpe	17,881	6,744	6,744	5,221	54	112	6	803	457	72	19			
Paulding	12,969	4,663	4,663	3,100	126	122	23	1,115	78		99			
Pickens	8,641	3,806	3,806	3,189		255	40	304	18					
Pierce	8,100	2,477	2,477	675	396		92	352	579	90	293			
Pike	18,761	9,182	9,182	4,849	202	559	587	1,341	1,103	47	494			
Polk	17,856	7,145	7,145	4,193	76	116	191	1,445	752	132	240			
Pulaski	18,489	9,234	9,224	7,294	84			994	657	7	188	10		
Putnam	13,436	4,799	4,799	1,775	370			1,309	1,257	85	3			
Quitman	4,701	1,757	1,757	843	16			143	755					
Rabun	6,285	2,372	2,372	1,823				530	19					
Randolph	16,847	10,578	10,578	6,756	90			1,106	2,041	55	530			
Richmond	53,735	28,028	24,134	13,968		806	85	4,232	2,278	969	1,776	3,749	65	80
Rockdale	7,515	3,649	3,649	1,819	12	140	115	782	357	280	144			
Schley	5,499	1,977	1,977	1,049	92			547	255		34			
Screven	19,252	8,643	8,643	5,293		192	886	1,356	903		13			
Spalding	17,619	10,513	10,499	6,570	71	271	1,150	1,495	570	183	189	14		
Stephens	(6)	3,654	3,654	2,436			16	322	583	70	227			
Stewart	15,856	7,692	7,692	4,476	218			815	2,008		175			
Sumter	26,212	12,000	11,956	7,706	357	10		1,626	1,814	128	315	44		
Talbot	12,197	4,545	4,545	1,676	85			1,108	1,607	57	12			
Taliaferro	7,912	3,800	3,763	2,918				275	493	77		37		
Tattnall	20,419	5,877	5,877	2,580	381	158	288	1,527	468	25	450			
Taylor	9,846	3,755	3,755	1,654	276			978	452	33	362			
Telfair	10,083	5,627	5,627	1,650	58	37	500	1,554	1,718	27	83			
Terrell	19,023	10,020	10,020	6,361	179			1,228	2,076	44	132			
Thomas	31,076	11,899	11,838	6,304	270	98	11	1,759	2,798	310	290	36		25
Tift	(7)	3,252	3,244	1,394	214			777	732		127	8		
Toombs	(8)	2,660	2,660	865	151		153	1,228	222	41				
Towns	4,748	1,569	1,569	1,383				186						
Troup	24,002	10,336	10,296	5,348	211	40	1,187	1,986	844	352	328	40		
Turner	(9)	2,507	2,507	1,351	50			712	189		205			
Twiggs	8,716	4,915	4,915	3,882	40			708	285					
Union	8,481	2,626	2,626	1,939				625	25		37			
Upson	13,670	5,570	5,570	2,469	310			843	1,732	20	196			
Walker	15,661	5,788	5,788	3,139			413	1,373	504	103	256			
Walton	20,942	8,329	8,329	4,579	468	653	48	1,215	820		546			
Ware	13,761	7,197	7,118	2,700	215		136	1,652	972	201	1,242	59		20
Warren	11,463	5,432	5,432	2,847				941	1,644					
Washington	28,227	16,047	16,026	10,077	162	561		1,735	3,132		359	21		
Wayne	9,449	3,382	3,382	1,821	228		92	513	235		493			

[1] Includes Primitive Baptists and Colored Primitive Baptists in America.
[2] Includes African Methodist Episcopal Church, African Methodist Episcopal Zion Church, Colored Methodist Episcopal Church, and Reformed Methodist Union Episcopal Church.
[3] Heads of families only.
[4] New county since 1900; formed from parts of Appling and Coffee in 1905.
[5] New county since 1900; formed from parts of Bulloch, Burke, Emanuel, and Screven in 1905.
[6] New county since 1900; formed from parts of Franklin and Habersham in 1905.
[7] New county since 1900; formed from parts of Berrien, Irwin, and Worth in 1905.
[8] New county since 1900; formed from parts of Emanuel, Montgomery, and Tattnall in 1905.
[9] New county since 1900; formed from parts of Dooly, Irwin, Wilcox, and Worth in 1905.

TABLE 4.—POPULATION IN 1900 AND COMMUNICANTS OR MEMBERS FOR SELECTED DENOMINATIONS, FOR EACH STATE AND TERRITORY, BY COUNTIES: 1906—Continued.

GEORGIA—Continued.

COUNTY.	Population, 1900.	All denominations.	PROTESTANT BODIES. Total.	Baptists—Southern and National Conventions.	Primitive Baptists.[1]	Disciples of Christ.	Methodist Episcopal Church.	Methodist Episcopal Church, South.	African Methodists.[2]	Presbyterian Church in the U.S.	Other Protestant bodies.	Roman Catholic Church.	Jewish congregations.[3]	All other bodies.
Webster	6,618	3,120	3,120	2,309	47			308	456					
White	5,912	1,989	1,989	924			126	907		32				
Whitfield	14,509	5,391	5,370	3,124		28	71	1,442	35	284	386	21		
Wilcox	11,097	4,745	4,745	3,014	54	50	200	638	591	32	166			
Wilkes	20,866	8,928	8,779	6,168				1,216	1,300	50	45	149		
Wilkinson	11,440	5,200	5,187	3,364	161	45		606	691		320	13		
Worth	18,664	5,150	5,150	3,553	157			564	701	42	133			
County location unknown[4]		7,685	7,152	10	439		1,254	3,950	1,328	15	156	147		386

[1] Includes Primitive Baptists and Colored Primitive Baptists in America.
[2] Includes African Methodist Episcopal Church, African Methodist Episcopal Zion Church, Colored Methodist Episcopal Church, and Reformed Methodist Union Episcopal Church.
[3] Heads of families only.
[4] See explanatory headnote on page 294.

IDAHO.

COUNTY.	Population, 1900.	All denominations.	PROTESTANT BODIES. Total.	Baptists—Northern Convention.	Congregationalists.	Disciples of Christ.	Methodist Episcopal Church.	Presbyterian Church in the U. S. A.	Protestant Episcopal Church.	Other Protestant bodies.	Roman Catholic Church.	Greek Orthodox Church.	Church of Jesus Christ of Latter-day Saints.	All other bodies.
The state	161,772	74,578	22,796	2,331	1,487	3,206	5,313	3,698	1,846	4,915	18,057	1,200	32,159	366
Ada	11,559	7,675	3,991	343	325	420	1,029	639	457	778	3,230	300	154	
Bannock	11,702	8,503	580	70	148	25	105	102	104	26	3,035	550	4,238	100
Bear Lake	7,051	4,681	89					69	20		85		4,454	53
Bingham	10,447	6,571	967	130			310	165	64	298	219		5,358	27
Blaine	4,900	1,316	276	86			72	36	82		498		542	
Boise	4,174	691	302	27	19	40	129		87		389			
Bonner	(1)	297	297				235	38		24				
Canyon	7,497	4,516	3,207	491	98	592	795	500	122	609	957		352	
Cassia	3,951	2,648	417	51		81	145	61	24	55	213		2,018	
Custer	2,049	103	103		51		35		17					
Elmore	2,286	403	262	53	108	26	26		49		141			
Fremont	12,821	9,618	290	5		25	117	67	54	22	125		9,172	31
Idaho	9,121	2,674	1,440	267	13	389	181	338	56	196	1,234			
Kootenai	10,216	4,372	1,496	111	72	125	508	371	105	204	2,848			28
Latah	13,451	4,444	3,200	209	92	334	490	366	37	1,672	1,194	50		
Lemhi	3,446	455	272		36		75	91	70		183			
Lincoln	1,784	631	271	67		46	100	17	26	15	176	150		34
Nez Perce	13,748	5,339	3,525	156	73	928	681	800	95	792	1,792			22
Oneida	8,933	5,983	79				38	38	3				5,833	71
Owyhee	3,804	345	52						52		293			
Shoshone	11,950	1,935	547	27	194		76		250		1,278	110		
Washington	6,882	1,240	995	238	258	50	166		72	211	167	40	38	
County location unknown[2]		138	138			125				13				

[1] New county since 1900; formed from part of Kootenai.
[2] See explanatory headnote on page 294.

ILLINOIS.

COUNTY.	Population, 1900.	All denominations.	PROTESTANT BODIES. Total.	Baptists—Northern and National Conventions.	Free Baptists.	Christians (Christian Connection).	Congregationalists.	Disciples of Christ.	Evangelical Association.	German Evangelical Synod of N. A.	Lutheran—General Synod.	Lutheran—General Council.	Lutheran—Synodical Conference.	Lutheran—United Norwegian Church.	Lutheran—Synod of Iowa, etc.
The state	4,821,550	2,077,197	1,109,764	134,965	7,755	8,654	54,875	101,516	8,660	59,973	14,768	36,366	113,527	7,374	14,006
Adams	67,058	39,701	18,441	1,945	20		1,024	2,218		3,154	792		2,121		139
Alexander	19,384	5,786	4,667	1,859	737			90			100				
Bond	16,078	4,539	3,689	853				297		115			17		
Boone	15,791	4,622	3,602	702		48	226		58	202		98	378	91	
Brown	11,557	4,108	3,258	418				1,202					43		
Bureau	41,112	14,988	10,931	1,024			2,075	698	238	414	398	648			870
Calhoun	8,917	2,873	1,106	163				170			60		170		
Carroll	18,963	5,671	4,898	517				215	71		344		255		110
Cass	17,222	5,520	4,566	289			400	469			369		692		
Champaign	47,622	19,487	15,693	1,487		578	423	2,341		709			709		523

TABLE 4.—POPULATION IN 1900 AND COMMUNICANTS OR MEMBERS FOR SELECTED DENOMINATIONS, FOR EACH STATE AND TERRITORY, BY COUNTIES: 1906—Continued.

ILLINOIS—Continued.

COUNTY.	Population, 1900.	All denominations.	PROTESTANT BODIES.												
			Total.	Baptists—Northern and National Conventions.	Free Baptists.	Christians (Christian Connection).	Congregationalists.	Disciples of Christ.	Evangelical Association.	German Evangelical Synod of N. A.	Lutheran—General Synod.	Lutheran—General Council.	Lutheran—Synodical Conference.	Lutheran—United Norwegian Church.	Lutheran—Synod of Iowa, etc.
Christian	32,790	10,	7,339	1,290			121	857		276			198		
Clark	24,033	7,	7,070	1,125		33	185	975	141						
Clay	19,553	6,	5,975	850		281		1,700		108					
Clinton	19,824	13,353	3,437	264				60		1,051			493		260
Coles	34,146	12,[illegible]	10,350	737			285	1,849		100			297		
Cook	1,838,735	908,	285,797	26,604	50		20,547	7,118	1,517	21,651	2,209	13,139	54,009	3,316	1,510
Crawford	19,240	6,	6,321	888		971		756							
Cumberland	16,124	4,	3,746	352		121		629							
Dekalb	31,756	10,010	8,841	888	46		1,593		91	320		1,402	714		200
Dewitt	18,972	5,[illegible]	5,072	172		100		1,494							
Douglas	19,097	7,406	6,769	524		353		1,506		222			147		
Dupage	28,196	14,426	11,039	414			1,772		518	2,859			2,717		
Edgar	28,273	10,794	9,647	634				3,035							
Edwards	10,345	4,147	4,085	189		61	276	1,420	261						
Effingham	20,465	10,306	5,418	355		229		509	67				1,773		232
Fayette	28,065	8,235	7,555	1,178				650	139	103	99	132	1,277		71
Ford	18,359	7,448	6,693	16			380	530				1,361		672	304
Franklin	19,675	5,457	5,27	2,735	457	20	130	845					42		
Fulton	46,201	12,476	11,1 9	981	122	509	592	1,936			89	64			21
Gallatin	15,836	4,136	3,1[illegible]	390	35	191									
Greene	23,402	7,921	7,114	4,010			44	586							
Grundy	24,136	10,812	3,195	399			296		44			38	221	650	
Hamilton	20,197	6,800	6,044	3,223		128		541							
Hancock	32,215	11,125	10,567	580			687	2,417		621	204		224		332
Hardin	7,448	1,892	1,692	157				317							
Henderson	10,836	3,	3,	294	50			230				155			
Henry	40,049	20,	14,	1,558			1,858	315	323	563		3,630	1,335		97
Iroquois	38,014	12,	9,	155			511	1,295		346		52	1,057		1,390
Jackson	33,871	11,483	9,463	1,816	1,379	606		1,144		138	610		535		
Jasper	20,160	5,[illegible]	4,[illegible]	909		1,170		653				115			
Jefferson	28,133	7,	7,	2,241	363			915							
Jersey	14,612	4,	2,	1,357			26			75					
Jo Daviess	24,533	8,	4,	48	75		28		17		120		29		270
Johnson	15,667	3,[illegible]	3,338	1,337	16		64	206							
Kane	78,792	36,[illegible]	23,[illegible]	3,509			3,030	154	736	1,045		2,617	4,128	176	
Kankakee	37,154	17,109	8,330	762				322	480	612			1,612	49	
Kendall	11,467	3,719	3,334	279			397		123	25		58	185	800	
Knox	43,612	14,794	12,430	892	45	33	1,760	1,482				2,378	60		
Lake	34,504	18,163	11,134	734			607	305	126	632		229	572		
Lasalle	87,776	46,978	16,077	1,593	14		1,455	448	643	550		96	367	1,211	1,629
Lawrence	16,523	5,549	5,105	138		272		1,302							
Lee	29,894	12,304	8,006	565			617	352	152		875		17		662
Livingston	42,035	15,631	10,505	1,063			630	1,004	366				480	227	663
Logan	28,680	11,667	7,980	424				2,015	92	500	162		843		386
McDonough	28,412	9,087	8,671	953	89	107		1,380			64				
McHenry	29,759	10,532	6,972	460			354	94		456	40		2,114		
McLean	67,843	30,090	23,515	1,792	44		414	4,981		576		355	1,969		501
Macon	44,003	16,095	13,630	1,203			404	2,480				127	1,338		
Macoupin	42,256	16,822	14,147	3,566			387	1,613		940	70		1,524		460
Madison	64,694	30,869	19,419	2,587			519	544		3,592			3,696		
Marion	30,446	10,766	9,414	1,565	56		203	1,654		390		66	352		
Marshall	16,370	7,516	3,278	114			157	275				517	434		91
Mason	17,491	5,658	5,356	837				1,156	108				1,024		
Massac	13,110	4,155	4,121	1,206	36		98	767		200					413
Menard	14,336	3,651	3,056	434				322		330			285		
Mercer	20,945	7,204	6,406	155			170	299	34			1,179	25		
Monroe	13,847	6,942	3,623	61						3,033			488		
Montgomery	30,836	12,052	9,374	1,726				1,061		122	822		858		75
Morgan	35,006	14,733	11,418	1,754			504	2,450			129		317		
Moultrie	15,224	5,461	4,993	201		68		1,924							
Ogle	29,129	7,776	6,827	165		230	475	272	198	150	658	15	443		90
Peoria	88,608	33,543	15,317	1,397			1,758	650	150		77	400	1,172		1,245
Perry	19,830	9,323	6,919	2,666	490			627		660			202		
Piatt	17,706	5,256	4,944	281		478		418							
Pike	31,595	10,275	9,935	1,505			564	3,108			107				
Pope	13,585	3,242	3,189	1,273				98							60
Pulaski	14,554	4,862	4,445	1,846	614	34	268	265			102				
Putnam	4,746	1,249	1,138				374	125	36			47			
Randolph	28,001	13,605	9,426	609	258			34		332	761		2,933		
Richland	16,391	6,113	5,615	359		594	91	958	219			201			
Rock Island	55,249	19,917	11,781	1,494			894	723		150		2,179	1,003		
St. Clair	86,685	39,631	15,790	2,245	173		133	446		4,628			1,710		
Saline	21,685	6,628	6,263	2,998	130			73							
Sangamon	71,593	35,233	20,008	2,732			463	3,439			999		2,267		
Schuyler	16,129	3,366	3,366	146				928							
Scott	10,455	3,462	3,164	1,056				495			56		237		
Shelby	32,126	11,734	10,671	1,309				2,202	30	165		50	1,064		
Stark	10,186	3,450	2,728	443			497	251							50
Stephenson	34,933	13,819	10,538	396				45	475	1,289	1,312		813	17	
Tazewell	33,221	9,814	8,483	665			47	1,404	247	600	375		503		

TABLE 4.—POPULATION IN 1900 AND COMMUNICANTS OR MEMBERS FOR SELECTED DENOMINATIONS, FOR EACH STATE AND TERRITORY, BY COUNTIES: 1906—Continued.

ILLINOIS—Continued.

COUNTY.	Population, 1900.	All denominations.	PROTESTANT BODIES. Total.	Baptists—Northern and National Conventions.	Free Baptists.	Christians (Christian Connection).	Congregationalists.	Disciples of Christ.	Evangelical Association.	German Evangelical Synod of N. A.	Lutheran—General Synod.	Lutheran—General Council.	Lutheran—Synodical Conference.	Lutheran—United Norwegian Church.	Lutheran—Synod of Iowa, etc.
Union	22,610	6,093	5,637	2,458	229	156	494	181			444				126
Vermilion	65,635	26,734	20,202	1,286		730	386	4,227		160		296	1,197		
Wabash	12,583	5,104	4,307	19				1,486	218	40	244		90		
Warren	23,163	9,366	9,094	1,033		156	84	1,812				320			
Washington	19,526	10,395	7,240	327	57			91		2,250			2,361		
Wayne	27,626	8,275	7,853	1,644	324	313		1,458	102						
White	25,386	8,687	8,106	1,212	53			1,166	149	135					
Whiteside	34,710	12,138	9,899	478			1,133	834	80		718	284	415		725
Will	74,764	38,297	16,878	1,489			379	111	337	2,674	579	811	4,209		
Williamson	27,796	10,880	9,195	3,464	1,747	84	15	1,287		210			33		
Winnebago	47,845	20,863	14,243	1,089	46		1,571	217			780	3,307	396		
Woodford	21,822	9,129	6,160	381				1,513	74	500			338		500
County location unknown[1]		2,399	2,076											165	

COUNTY.	PROTESTANT BODIES—continued. Methodist Episcopal Church.	Methodist Episcopal Church, South.	African Methodists.[2]	Presbyterian Church in the U. S. A.	Cumberland Presbyterian Church.	United Presbyterian Church.	Protestant Episcopal Church.	United Brethren in Christ.	Other Protestant bodies.	Roman Catholic Church.	Jewish congregations.[3]	Greek Orthodox Church.	All other bodies.
The state	235,092	7,198	11,306	86,251	17,208	9,555	36,364	18,705	125,647	932,084	5,286	13,310	16,753
Adams	4,094		264	749	26	55	509	121	1,210	21,250	10		
Alexander	602	246	420	300			273		40	1,098	21		
Bond	997	20	9	461	191		50		679	850			
Boone	1,157			333			89		220	1,020			
Brown	714	227		408	19				227	850			
Bureau	2,109		26	392			156	84	1,799	4,057			
Calhoun	199			153					191	1,742			25
Carroll	1,131			128		185	105		1,837	773			
Cass	1,668			232	362				85	892			62
Champaign	5,317		115	1,599			254	744	894	3,612	32	150	
Christian	2,877	174		686	148	80		82	550	2,903			111
Clark	2,138	236		70	245		21	896	1,005	340			
Clay	1,543	521		124	167	52		364	265	688			
Clinton	959	50	40	208			34		18	10,333			
Coles	2,754		50	1,154	1,363		63	483	1,215	1,827			
Cook	36,144		4,757	25,150	545	1,553	23,651	219	42,	594,241	4,758	10,460	12,754
Crawford	1,944			275		107		758	099				
Cumberland	982	25		295	60			344	[illegible]	467			
Dekalb	2,147			381		160	137	50	712	1,419			149
Dewitt	1,628			620	190			300	568	353		100	18
Douglas	2,920		13	352	166		17	302		637			
Dupage	1,150			99			497	21		3,370			17
Edgar	3,393		43	822	35		51	626	1,	1,147			
Edwards	1,072				200		44	123	247	62			
Effingham	1,367	119		269				116	[illegible]	4,887			
Fayette	1,916	356		200	113			353		680			
Ford	1,481		20	843	70	213		215		729			26
Franklin	939	62								88			90
Fulton	2,368	130	21	1,342	85		99	832	968	1,298			78
Gallatin	799		25	254	812				1,[illegible]	937			
Greene	1,582			464	34		52		342	807			
Grundy	1,041			381					125	7,617			
Hamilton	1,195				351		21	66	519	756			
Hancock	3,009			1,671			160	106	556	446			112
Hardin	120		21		161				916	200			
Henderson	1,444			151	147	862			130				20
Henry	2,861		12	575			299		821	5,438		100	151
Iroquois	2,842		10	669					1,042	2,733			25
Jackson	1,414	680	382	855			27		64	1,233		200	
Jasper	866			81				[illegible]	648	765			
Jefferson	2,249	343	70	52	228		26	409	442	418			
Jersey	777			370	115		39		23	1,487			
Jo Daviess	1,450			965		154	150		1,159	3,880			
Johnson	1,064				264			88	413	115			174
Kane	4,196		99	650		160	903		1,818	12,521		300	50
Kankakee	2,225		48	1,149			531		467	8,779			
Kendall	730			256					481	215			170
Knox	3,225		139	1,109			390		694	2,196	22	100	46
Lake	1,215		30	989			971	73	4,724	6,744	35		250
Lasalle	3,059		32	1,652	131		328	[illegible]	2,850	30,584		60	257

[1] See explanatory headnote on page 294.
[2] Includes African Methodist Episcopal Church, African Methodist Episcopal Zion Church, and Colored Methodist Episcopal Church.
[3] Heads of families only.

TABLE 4.—POPULATION IN 1900 AND COMMUNICANTS OR MEMBERS FOR SELECTED DENOMINATIONS, FOR EACH STATE AND TERRITORY, BY COUNTIES: 1906—Continued.

ILLINOIS—Continued.

COUNTY.	PROTESTANT BODIES—continued.									Roman Catholic Church.	Jewish congregations.[2]	Greek Orthodox Church.	All other bodies.
	Methodist Episcopal Church.	Methodist Episcopal Church, South.	African Methodists.[1]	Presbyterian Church in the U. S. A.	Cumberland Presbyterian Church.	United Presbyterian Church.	Protestant Episcopal Church.	United Brethren in Christ.	Other Protestant bodies.				
Lawrence	1,333		51	374				1,002	633	444			
Lee	1,746			631			296	75	2,018	4,298			
Livingston	3 282		57	735			68	35	1,895	5,126			
Logan	2,011	46	37	39	887		179	48	311	3,635	12	40	
McDonough	2,828		32	1,577	656		87	400	498	391			25
McHenry	1,752			842			93		767	3,560			
McLean	6,581		151	2,004	603	50	481	844	2,169	6,478	42		55
Macon	4 031		180	1,013	1,028		164	971	691	2,380		60	25
Macoupin	3,083	220		476	168		136		1,504	2,635		40	
Madison	2,761	280	450	1,236	302		627		2,735	10,795		450	205
Marion	2,247	1,068	64	323	562	110	65	110	579	1,352			
Marshall	1,102			359		90	80		59	4,238			
Mason	1,524			236			36	144	291	302			
Massac	654		366	70	118		9		184	34			
Menard	578			356	701				50	595			
Mercer	2,088			1,587		477	81	54	257	590			208
Monroe	41									3,319			
Montgomery	2,789		46	789	570				516	2,678			
Morgan	3,663	150	241	1,589			196		425	3,315			
Moultrie	1,531			48	590			218	413	468			
Ogle	1,567			545				277	1,742	949			
Peoria	3,374		85	2,736		161	749	100	1,263	17,906	117	150	53
Perry	868	110	50	387		540			319	2,404			
Piatt	2,085			634	100			129	819	312			
Pike	3,117	164	21	182			96	553	518	340			
Pope	635	65	28	105	254			64	607	53			
Pulaski	212	140	714				60		190	417			
Putnam	270			53			22		211	111			
Randolph	1,100	140	218	962		1,241	44		794	4,179			
Richland	1,668			284				734	507	498			
Rock Island	2,593		84	1,167		313	341	108	732	7,280	76	750	30
St. Clair	2,811		531	805		435	236		1,637	23,179		150	512
Saline	1,035	188	175	103	573				988	365			
Sangamon	5,205	184	453	2,447	416		606	261	536	15,045	130	50	
Schuyler	1,262	390		363			12	27	238				
Scott	942		10	175					193	298			
Shelby	3,236	227	24	489	68			363	1,444	1,063			
Stark	936			280		111	25		135	722			
Stephenson	2,191			1,078			165	510	2,247	3,264			17
Tazewell	1,877			424	99		84		2,158	1,331			
Union	528			364	218		11		428	456			
Vermilion	6,281		175	1,321	1,150	122	206	1,015	1,650	6,351	31	150	
Wabash	1,540			324			38	227	81	797			
Warren	1,989		75	1,164	39	1,834	26	229	333	272			
Washington	1,511	157		96		185			205	3,155			
Wayne	1,910	48		96	550			97	1,311	71			351
White	2,082		44	162	1,136	55			1,912	429			152
Whiteside	2,471			1,163			147	220	1,231	2,239			
Will	2,803		50	1,867		155	615	90	709	21,321			98
Williamson	1,358	292	90	175	102				338	1,685			
Winnebago	3,270		54	1,632			260		1,621	6,506			114
Woodford	864			437		95	19		1,439	2,969			
County location unknown[3]	803	140	104				57	374	433				323

[1] Includes African Methodist Episcopal Church, African Methodist Episcopal Zion Church, and Colored Methodist Episcopal Church.
[2] Heads of families only.
[3] See explanatory headnote on page 294.

INDIANA.

COUNTY.	Population, 1900.	All denominations.	PROTESTANT BODIES.												
			Total.	Baptists—Northern and National Conventions.	General Baptists.	Primitive Baptists.	Christians (Christian Connection).	Disciples of Christ.	Churches of Christ.	Dunkers (Conservative).	Evangelical Association.	Friends (Orthodox).	German Evangelical Synod of N. A.	Lutheran—General Synod.	Lutheran—Synodical Conference.
The state	2,516,462	938,405	757,843	73,729	6,671	8,132	21,397	108,188	10,259	9,949	8,787	29,255	21,624	7,753	34,028
Adams	22,232	7,117	7,010	91			79	210		90	569	171		64	1,496
Allen	77,270	30,117	23,533	1,162				1,175		130	165			731	8,433
Bartholomew	24,594	11,962	11,539	1,156			214	2,780				320		191	1,495
Benton	13,123	3,789	2,859					573							
Blackford	17,213	4,714	4,035	160			290	454		24		185			
Boone	26,321	10,517	10,517	1,203		585	1,228	2,861	25			238			
Brown	9,727	2,062	2,062	395		14	226	676							
Carroll	19,953	6,700	6,220	790		64	335	644		614				259	23
Cass	34,545	12,963	10,308	1,054			767	1,118	32	93	282			371	975
Clark	31,835	12,852	9,616	1,191				1,911	497						

TABLE 4.—POPULATION IN 1900 AND COMMUNICANTS OR MEMBERS FOR SELECTED DENOMINATIONS, FOR EACH STATE AND TERRITORY, BY COUNTIES: 1906—Continued.

INDIANA—Continued.

COUNTY.	Population, 1900.	All denominations.	PROTESTANT BODIES. Total.	Baptists—Northern and National Conventions.	General Baptists.	Primitive Baptists.	Christians (Christian Connection).	Disciples of Christ.	Churches of Christ.	Dunkers (Conservative).	Evangelical Association.	Friends (Orthodox).	German Evangelical Synod of N. A.	Lutheran—General Synod.	Lutheran—Synodical Conference.
Clay	34,285	11,264	9,199	762	59	134	327	1,052	190	120	52		98		99
Clinton	28,202	10,387	10,179	934		89	905	1,381		251		119			
Crawford	13,476	3,557	3,507	87	23	85		724	120						
Daviess	29,914	13,228	8,031	896	43			1,492	518						
Dearborn	22,194	10,823	7,217	1,007				247					560		906
Decatur	19,518	8,282	6,927	1,788				668							
Dekalb	25,711	8,193	7,415	390				713		131	84			774	378
Delaware	49,624	13,706	13,600	757		37	1,551	1,817		370		373	37	151	
Dubois	20,357	14,075	5,382		99	103		409			230		1,339		200
Elkhart	45,052	16,355	15,643	679			434	337		1,744	965		180	973	250
Fayette	13,495	369	5,281	253		124		1,941						62	
Floyd	30,118	6,	8,527	839				1,541	23				755		
Fountain	21,446	6,	6,484	475		23	1,120	1,283	121			91			
Franklin	16,388	9,959	3,591			37		406							
Fulton	17,453	5,[illegible]	5,214	950			255	370		54	483				20
Gibson	30,099	10,	8,847	472	1,758	356	216	803			141		464		
Grant	54,693	13,	13,438	545		124	675	332	315	43		3,030			
Greene	28,530		8,844	1,572	78	38		1,610	840						
Hamilton	29,914	650	9,701	223		72		2,118		111	135	2,785		188	107
Hancock	19,189	9,[illegible]	7,027			109		1,364		22		859	150		267
Harrison	21,702	9,	7,167					591	255					103	371
Hendricks	21,292	8,	8,238	888		406	56	2,708				1,393			
Henry	25,068	9,	9,441			98	842	1,802		187		2,631			
Howard	28,575	10,322	10,253	644			468	1,635	1	122	133	1,827			83
Huntington	28,901	11,[illegible]	10,702	295		90	1,219	1,729		717	500		307	90	380
Jackson	26,633	9,	8,553	1,241			167	609		33		135	195		2,140
Jasper	14,292	3,	3,030	132				799							104
Jay	26,818	8,094	7,680	205			788	883		44	294	736		253	
Jefferson	22,913	9,[illegible]	7,210	2,007				639	32				300		
Jennings	15,757	4,855	4,[illegible]	1,704				140	[illegible]			215			
Johnson	20,223	10,022	9,858	1,764		242	183	3,220							
Knox	32,746	14,419	10,910	804	155	22		2,607	90				1,636		581
Kosciusko	29,109	8,161	8,161	477			387	403		388	259			81	
Lagrange	15,284	4,719	4,719	131				137		171	178			243	
Lake	37,892	17,834	7,629	314				697			39		516		2,424
Laporte	38,386	16,401	11,665	588				520		55	103	211	2,459		1,917
Lawrence	25,729	8,352	7,697	2,087		163		2,029	508						
Madison	70,470	17,213	15,618	1,249		16	518	3,464	25	130		518		48	103
Marion	197,227	91,019	58,816	10,526		125	90	8,511	199	40	443	1,431	2,503	652	3,163
Marshall	25,119	7,024	6,944	38		45	263	171		373	707		283		540
Martin	14,711	5,590	3,	198		18		928	477						
Miami	28,344	10,503	9,	1,327			176	687		618	281	542			381
Monroe	20,873	7,076	6,	987		77		2,140	346						
Montgomery	29,388	11,498	11,532	1,229		173	1,317	3,088		278		161			
Morgan	20,457	8,346	7,[illegible]	859				2,741				1,069			
Newton	10,448	3,655	3,	253		24		762							91
Noble	23,533	7,120	6,	100		34	592	520		100	340			294	560
Ohio	4,724	1,946	1,	210				176							
Orange	16,854	5,867	5,196	389	12	513		605	990			718			
Owen	15,149	5,588	5,[illegible]	1,120		87	141	822	397						
Parke	23,000	5,327	4,772	553		230		591	110			856			
Perry	18,778	6,537	2,305	348		60		211	25				553		13
Pike	20,486	5,489	5,437	197	1,298	950		158	174				50		
Porter	19,175	4,690	4,690	238				1,310					200		711
Posey	22,333	8,685	6,323	380	1,057	598	191	235			62		1,377		
Pulaski	14,033	3,874	3,744	122			236	665		40	89	59	453		448
Putnam	21,478	6,960	6,960	646		507		1,462	220	30					
Randolph	28,653	11,633	11,076			26	1,921	1,673	100	114	70	2,858			
Ripley	19,881	7,700	5,234	1,517				673	28	26					139
Rush	20,148	8,775	7,942	121		157	60	2,790	70			945			
St. Joseph	58,881	23,602	13,	755			100	1,707		624	777		1,460		828
Scott	8,307	3,478	3,	975		24		902							
Shelby	26,491	11,764	10,858	1,815				1,567						175	
Spencer	22,407	8,917	6,[illegible]	923	50	126		653			89		468	160	272
Starke	10,431	2,133	2,020				75	130			49		180		877
Steuben	15,219	4,746	4,565	227				1,477		19	39				
Sullivan	26,005	9,184	9,009	930		133	239	1,135	1,940			175			
Switzerland	11,840	4,018	3,960	1,428				325							
Tippecanoe	38,659	14,673	10,626	1,047				782				124	212	145	553
Tipton	19,116	4,590	3,952	335		22	447	474				418			245
Union	6,748	2,516	2,176			25	167	201		133		90			
Vanderburg	71,769	34,915	16,208	3,000	410	37	84	535			112		,129	86	
Vermilion	15,252	3,793	3,113	126				326				492			
Vigo	62,035	23,410	16,792	2,177		136	202	1,965	310		75	75			1,348
Wabash	28,235	10,989	10,389			130	586	1,465		1,083	428	430	600	153	[illegible]

TABLE 4.—POPULATION IN 1900 AND COMMUNICANTS OR MEMBERS FOR SELECTED DENOMINATIONS, FOR EACH STATE AND TERRITORY, BY COUNTIES: 1906—Continued.

INDIANA—Continued.

COUNTY.	Population, 1900.	All denominations.	PROTESTANT BODIES. Total.	Baptists—Northern and National Conventions.	General Baptists.	Primitive Baptists.	Christians (Christian Connection).	Disciples of Christ.	Churches of Christ.	Dunkers (Conservative).	Evangelical Association.	Friends (Orthodox).	German Evangelical Synod of N. A.	Lutheran—General Synod.	Lutheran—Synodical Conference.
Warren	11,371	2,282	2,282				123	306							
Warrick	22,329	7,328	6,709	432	1,629	372		158			90		1,160		148
Washington	19,409	8,459	8,459	934		361		3,025	1,098			148			
Wayne	38,970	16,190	13,147	811		30	186	1,389		315	133	2,637		985	
Wells	23,449	7,978	7,978	678			642	257		98	198	190		228	74
White	19,138	5,658	5,420	976			61	693		208	37				270
Whitley	17,328	4,830	4,691	416			248	175		206	56			293	173
County location unknown[1]		2,411	1,844	25		81									

COUNTY.	PROTESTANT BODIES—continued. Lutheran—Joint Synod of Ohio, etc.	Methodist Episcopal Church.	Methodist Protestant Church.	African Methodists.[2]	Presbyterian Church in the U. S. A.	Cumberland Presbyterian Church.	Protestant Episcopal Church.	Reformed Church in the U. S.	United Brethren in Christ.	Other Protestant bodies.	Roman Catholic Church.	Jewish congregations.[3]	All other bodies.
The state	8,310	210,593	10,408	7,090	49,041	6,376	7,653	8,289	48,059	62,252	174,849	1,383	4,330
Adams		1,446	119		205			699	537	1,234	107		
Allen	1,477	3,699	228	135	1,526		370	1,477	793	2,032	6,282	70	232
Bartholomew		3,306		25	432		23		797	800	383		40
Benton		1,123			579				503	81	930		
Blackford	214	1,399	87		281				706	235	649		30
Boone		2,320	403	27	717				584	326			
Brown		269			56				184	242			
Carroll		1,472	84		907	265	18	59	133	553	480		
Cass		2,797		58	1,121	220	125		732	563	2,637	18	
Clark		3,494		219	1,293		123		130	758	3,236		
Clay	155	3,160		47	477		18	492	1,694	263	2,065		
Clinton		2,801	474	40	1,122		40	343	652	1,028	183		25
Crawford		1,448			197				658	165			50
Daviess		2,513		82	330	140	23		1,803	191	5,177		20
Dearborn	771	2,147	159		859		50			511	3,606		
Decatur		2,475		30	943		20		569	434	1,355		
Dekalb		2,336	401		162		41	236	1,116	653	778		
Delaware		4,217	453	190	1,044		148		1,264	1,091		21	85
Dubois	497	975				412				1,118	8,693		
Elkhart	151	3,031	120		837		379	355	733	4,475	655	32	25
Fayette		1,963		35	556		60		68	229	1,071		17
Floyd		3,230		220	1,164		160		380	215	4,406		26
Fountain		1,430			439	40	26		1,078	358		5	
Franklin	63	1,647	41		260				382	755	5,437		25
Fulton		1,396	50		339		15	40	846	396	210		42
Gibson		2,037		212	358	1,046	22		305	657	1,803		
Grant	123	3,681	1,123	408	609		150	76	1,110	1,094	468	62	18
Greene		3,199	257	18	216	175	26	149	280	386	595		
Hamilton		2,734		75	174				470	509	94		17
Hancock		2,331	781		261				583	300	332		
Harrison		2,263		90	525			133	2,588	248	2,042		113
Hendricks		1,964	150	67	115	220				271	321		
Henry		1,998	107	15	515		21		492	701	230		
Howard		2,473	197	115	190		98		879	1,260		30	
Huntington	100	2,360	45		350		25	400	1,203	892	673		
Jackson	109	2,338		24	433			166	428	515	523		18
Jasper		1,002	119		378				121	375	527		
Jay	92	2,104	214	45	249			115	962	661	480		142
Jefferson		2,723		79	880		144		65	473	1,850	15	80
Jennings		1,281			513				140	145	717		
Johnson		2,263	346	97	1,247	93			323	80	164		
Knox		2,868		97	855	657	100		250	188	3,501	8	
Kosciusko		2,535	15	5	459				1,627	1,525			
Lagrange		1,503	66		396		139		115	1,640			
Lake		1,445			359		266			1,569	9,755		450
Laporte	1,717	1,766	64	19	702		374			1,170	4,701	35	
Lawrence		2,269	75	34	391		35		53	53	655		
Madison		5,659	542	72	649		203		1,076	1,346	913		682
Marion		14,012	396	2,306	5,476	63	1,916	1,179	562	5,224	31,394	396	414
Marshall	33	1,145	220		322		175	407	1,288	934	35		45
Martin	57	1,434			28				385	7	2,058		
Miami		2,515		14	491		125		735	1,372	1,137	35	67
Monroe		1,710	206	52	349	104	46			606	429		26
Montgomery		3,156		67	1,403		23		378	225			
Morgan		2,489	202			237				345	404		

[1] See explanatory headnote on page 294.
[2] Includes African Methodist Episcopal Church, African Methodist Episcopal Zion Church, and Colored Methodist Episcopal Church.
[3] Heads of families only.

TABLE 4.—POPULATION IN 1900 AND COMMUNICANTS OR MEMBERS FOR SELECTED DENOMINATIONS, FOR EACH STATE AND TERRITORY, BY COUNTIES: 1906—Continued.

INDIANA—Continued.

COUNTY.	PROTESTANT BODIES—continued.										Roman Catholic Church.	Jewish congregations.[2]	All other bodies.
	Lutheran—Joint Synod of Ohio, etc.	Methodist Episcopal Church.	Methodist Protestant Church.	African Methodists.[1]	Presbyterian Church in the U. S. A.	Cumberland Presbyterian Church.	Protestant Episcopal Church.	Reformed Church in the U. S.	United Brethren in Christ.	Other Protestant bodies.			
Newton		1,164			255				506	141	459		
Noble	30	1,431	149		489		32		676	755	982	36	
Ohio	271	958			85			217		29			
Orange		1,552		39	154				761	63	51		20
Owen	183	1,719	102	50	221				487	259			
Parke		1,371		60	405				513	83	555		
Perry		875					45		62	113	4,075		157
Pike	239	1,122		18	89	594			200	348	52		
Porter		967			458		36			750			
Posey		1,850		200	65	150	93			65	2,332	30	
Pulaski		1,233			256				45	98	130		
Putnam		2,972	216	41	414	40	24		75	313			
Randolph	215	2,687	67		400			20	568	357	557		
Ripley	392	1,871			35					553	2,427		39
Rush		2,188	163	25	360				108	955	833		
St. Joseph	80	3,854		60	1,352		289	150	320	1,502	9,626	68	50
Scott		1,286			154				78	11	48		
Shelby		3,321	1,081		551		16		262	1,601	1,375		
Spencer		2,269			179	99			1,261	26	2,317		25
Starke		324							180	205	64		49
Steuben		1,351			31			30	369	922			181
Sullivan		3,295	270		429				358	105	175		
Switzerland		1,444			161			114	300	188	58		
Tippecanoe		3,850		61	1,291		220	460	1,145	736	3,878	95	74
Tipton		1,402			212					397	638		
Union		937			303				83	237	340		
Vanderburg	252	3,330		659	1,258	1,271	434			263	18,408	251	48
Vermilion		1,187		21	242	37			614	58	680		
Vigo		5,499		451	885		684	310	1,940	1,681	6,177	141	300
Wabash	54	2,179		50	607				1,474	1,120	564	36	
Warren		1,068			223				107	445			
Warrick	92	1,888				513			192	35	608		16
Washington		2,068			350				261	194			
Wayne	857	2,955		337	851		253		209	1,199	2,927		116
Wells		1,984	577		608			662	816	966			
White		1,568	40		769					798	238		
Whitley	86	1,168			150				1,129	591	139		
County location unknown[3]		925							200	613			567

[1] Includes African Methodist Episcopal Church, African Methodist Episcopal Zion Church, and Colored Methodist Episcopal Church.
[2] Heads of families only.
[3] See explanatory headnote on page 294.

IOWA.

COUNTY.	Population, 1900.	All denominations.	PROTESTANT BODIES.												
			Total.	Baptists—Northern and National Conventions.	Congregationalists.	Disciples of Christ.	Evangelical Association.	United Evangelical Church.	Friends (Orthodox).	German Evangelical Synod of N. A.	Lutheran—General Synod.	Lutheran—General Council.	Lutheran—Synodical Conference.	Lutheran—United Norwegian Church.	Lutheran—Hauge's Norwegian Synod.
The state	2,231,853	788,667	569,734	41,745	37,061	55,948	5,429	5,017	8,762	11,681	5,207	13,771	25,528	23,287	5,523
Adair	16,192	4,526	3,716	72	299	281	14	66	62				223		
Adams	13,601	3,517	3,262	180	233	354	75								161
Allamakee	18,711	9,513	5,179	262	157		128			300	856			1,447	
Appanoose	25,927	8,401	7,940	1,281	235	2,253						100			
Audubon	13,626	4,101	3,751	161	115	343	270			100			465		
Benton	25,177	7,854	6,463	292	184	907	179	166		40			1,215	350	
Blackhawk	32,399	16,100	10,891	1,373	674	275	535	142		150			211		
Boone	28,200	9,346	7,216	698	140	434						932	906		
Bremer	16,306	7,003	6,369	251	223		292			994			699		
Buchanan	21,427	8,110	4,932	442	381	80	15						145		
Buena Vista	16,975	5,775	5,273	416	225	101				191		778	677	235	
Butler	17,955	6,262	5,528	545	249	322	198	41		695			87		
Calhoun	18,569	6,049	5,210	307	297	587	30	110		125		203	818		
Carroll	20,319	10,526	3,253	80	10	201			109				701		
Cass	21,274	7,280	6,371	433	753	900	140	210		492		25	315	43	20
Cedar	19,371	6,305	5,669	61	30	80			441	909	103		440		
Cerro Gordo	20,672	7,895	6,125	470	1,049	880	120							305	
Cherokee	16,570	6,222	4,029	269	312	431	40			78		186	528	50	
Chickasaw	17,037	7,457	3,724	271	603		75			65			225	247	
Clarke	12,440	3,211	3,151	198		1,026			146						
Clay	13,401	2,826	2,698	83	431	167	50		90	16		79	133		
Clayton	27,750	9,216	6,055	45	560	127	67			150		85	32	1,110	47
Clinton	43,832	14,861	7,234	569	530	185	86			100	40	269	855	350	
Crawford	21,685	7,381	4,541	538	44		26			133			1,790		
Dallas	23,058	8,359	7,465	266	147	1,673	72		368				472		

TABLE 4.—POPULATION IN 1900 AND COMMUNICANTS OR MEMBERS FOR SELECTED DENOMINATIONS, FOR EACH STATE AND TERRITORY, BY COUNTIES: 1906—Continued.

IOWA—Continued.

COUNTY.	Population, 1900.	All denominations.	PROTESTANT BODIES.												
			Total.	Baptists—Northern and National Conventions.	Congregationalists.	Disciples of Christ.	Evangelical Association.	United Evangelical Church.	Friends (Orthodox).	German Evangelical Synod of N. A.	Lutheran—General Synod.	Lutheran—General Council.	Lutheran—Synodical Conference.	Lutheran—United Norwegian Church.	Lutheran—Hauge's Norwegian Synod.
Davis	15,620	4,331	4,331	692	16	1,288									
Decatur	18,115	5,895	3,936	591		659			25						
Delaware	19,185	6,112	3,553	216	520							57			
Des Moines	35,989	15,820	11,096	1,111	509	512				1,628	821	1,315			
Dickinson	7,995	1,665	1,491	121	97				74				137	315	
Dubuque	56,403	35,	6,	478	1,437		88				85				
Emmet	9,936	2,	2,	63		123								572	192
Fayette	29,845	8,	5,	343	273	651	113	38							
Floyd	17,754	4,884	4,983	232	631	295	32	190					400		
Franklin	14,996	4,[illegible]	4,[illegible]	357	370	358	173	78		299			[illegible]	60	
Fremont	18,546	5,662	4,589	391	780	918				90	75				
Greene	17,820	6,366	4,894	606		806	155		327				175		
Grundy	13,757	4,504	4,213	366	250						220		112		
Guthrie	18,729	6,884	5,624	196	153	1,248			113				397		
Hamilton	19,514	7,799	7,114	325	659	629					66	236	230	1,163	1,973
Hancock	13,752	,567	3,493	61	335		70						250	642	
Hardin	22,794	,824	8,231	591	828	853	369	230	846	850			751		530
Harrison	25,597	,813	4,074	229	262	680	71						307		
Henry	20,022	4,886	6,490	406	588	316			239			686			
Howard	14,512	6,164	2,443	160	234		50						100	40	
Humboldt	12,667	4,	3,627	337	331	43	48						85	733	168
Ida	12,327	2,228	2,132	68	42	16							468	50	
Iowa	19,544	8,[illegible]	4,736	55	346	230							1,166		
Jackson	23,615	8,917	3,315	156	469	35	20								
Jasper	26,976	8,026	7,339	607	648	861	30		382	180	99				
Jefferson	17,437	6,075	5,443	185	205	680			480		238	568	68		
Johnson	24,817	9,069	5,350	137	374	623		192			303				
Jones	21,954	6,456	4,691	133		286		27			40		220		
Keokuk	24,979	8,319	6,599	700	384	1,558			466	90			90		
Kossuth	22,720	7,756	4,699	353	789		78			66		441	784		20
Lee	39,719	14,796	9,096	1,149		969			87	1,219	90	113			
Linn	55,392	19,240	15,023	847		1,163	141	677			453	52	360		
Louisa	13,516	3,782	3,637	37		130		130							
Lucas	16,126	4,944	4,429	702	528	617		326				189			
Lyon	13,165	4,131	3,183	268	[illegible]	86	14	49		148			300	753	
Madison	17,710	5,462	5,261	327	71	537	67	156	425						
Mahaska	34,273	7,360	6,876	493	264	1,262			953						
Marion	24,159	7,013	7,404	386	83	1,563							164		
Marshall	29,991	9,878	7,715	319	743	709	102	211	955	192		182	530	136	
Mills	16,764	4,273	3,835	658	208	396			99						
Mitchell	14,916	6,533	5,454	660	799								892	1,440	
Monona	17,980	4,364	3,437		525	556							200	1,035	
Monroe	17,985	6,676	4,361	1,033	84	882			136			112			
Montgomery	17,903	6,548	6,378	369	307	879		96		50		1,489			
Muscatine	28,242	8,190	6,953	676	508	356	70		150	319	113		141		
O'Brien	16,985	4,628	3,475	50	290	159	50			193			654	80	
Osceola	8,725	2,584	1,670	78	244		8	45					282		
Page	24,187	10,047	9,721	593	253	915						1,345	694		
Palo Alto	14,354	6,061	3,064	44	206	46				40		27	302	983	
Plymouth	22,209	9,585	4,651	274	330	145	59	407		211			409		
Pocahontas	15,339	,291	2,890	103		255	36					245		113	
Polk	82,624	32,472	27,404	2,212	2,196	6,376	264	145	638		500	800	17	216	
Pottawattamie	54,336	13,959	9,753	749	859	766	244	78		728	116	120	446		
Poweshiek	19,414	6,388	5,828	313	1,240	242			357						
Ringgold	15,325	4,119	3,738	251		686		191							
Sac	17,639	5,669	4,535	192	88	343		23				264	633		
Scott	51,558	13,559	6,390	739	645	501					428	80	525		
Shelby	17,932	7,087	4,034	626	247	262		157		150				125	
Sioux	23,337	9,150	6,036	79	178								412	92	
Story	23,159	10,747	9,713	200	445	1,113	60	415	30		324			1,606	1,196
Tama	24,585	8,236	5,233	123	623	98	180			168					
Taylor	18,784	6,233	5,902	1,018		1,476	23								
Union	19,928	6,884	5,589	614	566	887	87	206		239		132			
Van Buren	17,354	5,486	5,154	523	201	1,072				28	38				
Wapello	35,426	11,180	9,124	1,232	717	1,537						734			
Warren	20,376	8,123	6,363	426		967			583						
Washington	20,718	7,446	5,859	601	98	278			51	97					
Wayne	17,491	5,720	5,720	1,128	127	1,360									
Webster	31,757	11,283	7,050	312	482	301	170					1,355	904	731	
Winnebago	12,725	5,054	4,672	376	93		28							2,179	
Winneshiek	23,731	14,440	9,427	58	274		70		130					2,207	605
Woodbury	54,610	17,936	10,976	678	1,100	436	47	112		68	200	572	427	530	430
Worth	10,887	4,382	4,052	155		75		88		90				2,210	
Wright	18,227	5,826	4,577	265	652	272		15						1,039	182
County location unknown[1]		715	526												

[1] See explanatory headnote on page 294.

TABLE 4.—POPULATION IN 1900 AND COMMUNICANTS OR MEMBERS FOR SELECTED DENOMINATIONS, FOR EACH STATE AND TERRITORY, BY COUNTIES: 1906—Continued.

IOWA—Continued.

COUNTY.	PROTESTANT BODIES—continued.									Roman Catholic Church.	Jewish congregations.[1]	Latter-day Saints (Reorganized).	All other bodies.
	Lutheran—Synod of Iowa, etc.	Lutheran—Norwegian Synod.	Methodist Episcopal Church.	Presbyterian Church in the U. S. A.	United Presbyterian Church.	Protestant Episcopal Church.	Reformed Church in America.	United Brethren in Christ.	Other Protestant bodies.				
The state	23,082	11,027	156,576	48,326	8,890	8,990	4,835	11,082	57,967	207,607	412	8,139	2,775
Adair	246		1,554	251	72				576	780		30	
Adams			1,448	358	68			60	325	255			
Allamakee	23	180	652	471					703	4,334			
Appanoose			2,319	419				729	604	383	25	53	
Audubon			515	269				113	1,400	350			
Benton			1,904	911	107	21		131	56	1,391			
Blackhawk	834		2,902	1,044	69	349		172	2,161	5,148		11	50
Boone			2,144	450		84		102	1,326	2,032		98	
Bremer	2,590		787	131		117		100	185	634			
Buchanan	482		1,563	1,023	35	126			640	3,178			
Buena Vista		237	1,237	516					660	502			
Butler	704		1,202	318		4	180	400	583	713		21	
Calhoun	112		1,506	535				153	427	839			
Carroll	137		1,106	640		42		129	109	7,222		51	
Cass			2,100	456	118	13		17	336	909			
Cedar			1,304	689	156	535		50	871	636			
Cerro Gordo	499		2,220	62		102		71	347	1,715			55
Cherokee		38	1,076	558	29	17		45	372	2,155		38	
Chickasaw	1,060	555	539			20			64	3,733			
Clarke			891	89				207	594	60			
Clay			870			80	32		667	128			
Clayton	1,542		1,010	95		17		180	1,018	3,161			
Clinton	219		1,598	741	114	397			1,181	7,413		64	150
Crawford	284		1,117	451		70			88	2,492		348	
Dallas			2,370	430	71			801	795	894			
Davis			1,476	211					648				
Decatur			1,499	329		30		96	707	213		1,746	
Delaware	530		1,658	327				38	207	2,559			
Des Moines	340		2,963	811	140	221			725	4,638		86	
Dickinson			517	168		12			41	174			
Dubuque	986		1,581	1,043	33	547			305	28,871	30		
Emmet			447	552		55			461	393			
Fayette	1,454		1,809	421		106		241	424	2,989		50	
Floyd	681		1,935			49			116	694			
Franklin	211	68	1,296				107	21	479	85			
Fremont			1,652	331					352	638		435	
Greene			1,669	729		20		114	293	1,472			
Grundy	108		986	834	98		126		1,113	291			
Guthrie			2,066	573				235	643	1,260			
Hamilton		191	922	254		21		250	196	685			
Hancock	62		1,		90			85	745	1,074			
Hardin		28	2,	236		32			31	1,593			
Harrison	112		1,	601		27		24	79	1,408		1,331	
Henry			2,153	630	90	55			1,138	346		50	
Howard	651	49	[illegible]	144		30			239	3,721			
Humboldt	65	590	872	155					200	601			
Ida	93		700	313		9			373	361			
Iowa		150	1,236	557		10			986	2,438			1,756
Jackson	1,301		779	108	81	64			302	5,500		102	
Jasper	164		2,618	255	272	33	109	117	964	651		36	
Jefferson	175		1,721	674	27	39				632			
Johnson	415		1,524	584		236				3,719			
Jones	802		1,219	818	75	29		306		1,724		41	
Keokuk	80		2,128	561	167	43			383	1,680			40
Kossuth		93	1,337	351		35	66	63	[illegible]	3,057			
Lee			1,879	1,440	277	456			[illegible]	5,524	12	164	
Linn			4,526	2,829	264	505		564	1,798	4,199		18	
Louisa			1,367	601	312			115	802	145			
Lucas			1,401	512	81	87		276	238	218		297	
Lyon	187		517	240			138		131	948			
Madison			2,193	300	405	13		113	654	178		23	
Mahaska	50		2,313	311	166	130	124			383		71	30
Marion			2,568	350			1,057	20	1,	509			
Marshall	221		1,352	517		108			1,810	1,608		55	
Mills	349		1,360	268		40		193	[illegible]	239		199	
Mitchell	509		695	137						1,079			
Monona			639	44		31				639		288	
Monroe			818	200	226	32		245	322	2,213		102	
Montgomery			2,002	563	253				407	170			
Muscatine	612		1,874	1,003		201	54	298	[illegible]	1,210		27	
O'Brien	216		1,145			8	86		238	1,152			
Osceola	290		481			8	61		60	914			
Page			3,284		890	35		27	897	202		124	
Palo Alto		45	938	306		83			230	2,959		38	
Plymouth	140		1,114	[illegible]		58	45	106	1,006	4,934			

[1] Heads of families only.

TABLE 4.—POPULATION IN 1900 AND COMMUNICANTS OR MEMBERS FOR SELECTED DENOMINATIONS, FOR EACH STATE AND TERRITORY, BY COUNTIES: 1906—Continued.

IOWA—Continued.

COUNTY.	PROTESTANT BODIES—continued.									Roman Catholic Church.	Jewish congregations.[1]	Latter-day Saints (Reorganized).	All other bodies.
	Lutheran—Synod of Iowa, etc.	Lutheran—Norwegian Synod.	Methodist Episcopal Church.	Presbyterian Church in the U. S. A.	United Presbyterian Church.	Protestant Episcopal Church.	Reformed Church in America.	United Brethren in Christ.	Other Protestant bodies.				
Pocahontas	499		978	546						2,401			
Polk	340		5,436	2,624	383	1,300		682	3,	4,247	183	388	250
Pottawattamie	484		2,219	1,114		400		151	1,	3,334	10	779	83
Poweshiek	210		2,206	472	225	33			115	560			
Ringgold			1,783	96	388			129	[illegible]	345		36	
Sac	120		1,702	755		22				1,079		55	
Scott	210		1,146	939	177	471				6,867	100	77	125
Shelby			1,068	160		104		177		2,684		369	
Sioux	439		426	384	199		2,462		1,393	3,114			
Story		1,580	1,478	200		56		553	[illegible]	1,034			
Tama	185		1,975	414	310			949		2,935		68	
Taylor			1,709	704	478			35		331			
Union			1,743	471	195	98		104	208	1,296			
Van Buren	30		2,406	429	65				459	258		74	
Wapello	100		2,820	1,104		329			[illegible]	1,979	15	37	25
Warren	50		2,961	553	300			91		1,712		48	
Washington			2,458	752	892	12		127		1,587			
Wayne			2,103	223	164			373	432				
Webster		312	1,282	506		135			[illegible]	4,172		61	
Winnebago		1,236	597				45	37	81	382			
Winneshiek	141	4,884	689	40		60		95	174	5,013			
Woodbury	139		3,051	1,281	33	465		101	1,306	6,806	37	117	
Worth	452	759	172						51	330			
Wright	147	32	1,229	84	295	13	134		218	1,194		33	22
County location unknown[2]								502	24				189

[1] Heads of families only.

[2] See explanatory headnote on page 294.

KANSAS.

COUNTY.	Population, 1900.	All denominations.	PROTESTANT BODIES.												
			Total.	Seventh-day Adventists.	Baptists—Northern, Southern, and National Conventions.	Congregationalists.	Disciples of Christ.	Churches of Christ.	Dunkers (Conservative).	Evangelical Association.	Friends (Orthodox).	German Evangelical Synod of N. A.	Lutheran—General Synod.	Lutheran—General Council.	Lutheran—Synodical Conference.
The state	1,470,495	458,190	360,476	2,394	45,003	15,247	40,356	3,216	3,905	4,841	7,304	3,617	4,583	7,782	12,036
Allen	19,507	6,911	6,186	87	590	46	855			119	80			260	166
Anderson	13,938	4,380	2,661	30	202	88	321		45				60		
Atchison	28,606	9,730	6,404	59	990	287	1,607			128		100	452		367
Barber	6,594	1,533	1,434		213	83	278					25			
Barton	13,784	6,227	3,544		316	303	554		11	33	32	195	61		385
Bourbon	24,712	6,186	5,320	20	1,053	148	400		60						
Brown	22,369	8,243	6,862		1,053	492	826		144	218		50			198
Butler	23,363	6,460	6,347	57	704	76	1,392	419		192	253		83		22
Chase	8,246	1,565	1,386		82	64	86	23			244				110
Chautauqua	11,804	1,969	1,904	22	456		303	123			19				
Cherokee	42,694	7,180	5,422	91	1,097		741				333				
Cheyenne	2,640	517	466		61					50					
Clark	1,701	603	569		43		112								
Clay	15,833	4,699	4,430	69	503	256	90			40				169	117
Cloud	18,071	6,187	3,514	43	413		354	30		55			160	56	
Coffey	16,643	4,684	4,316	18	324	110	802	182	91						44
Comanche	1,619	392	392		73						56				
Cowley	30,156	8,345	7,807	11	1,533	143	1,132	254	18	6					106
Crawford	38,809	11,467	7,723	38	1,060	75	1,405		76					6	535
Decatur	9,234	1,860	1,625		287	46	173				25		53		109
Dickinson	21,816	7,649	6,436	34	479	105	406		177	209			345	75	627
Doniphan	15,079	3,895	2,561	18	383	169	439			51			113		140
Douglas	25,096	9,878	8,751	23	998	568	501	11	151	365	645	327	187	13	
Edwards	3,682	1,298	1,007	47	47	102	200	32		52					
Elk	11,443	2,795	2,604	30	240	144	442	40	70						
Ellis	8,626	5,864	1,086	18	123	84							99		
Ellsworth	9,626	2,997	2,299	15	387						15	222	31		592
Finney	3,469	1,258	1,190	10	187	136	200		35		8				
Ford	5,497	2,251	1,378		69	17	213			35					123
Franklin	21,354	7,127	6,763	78	1,974	183	602	28	218				60	26	
Geary	10,744	2,393	1,798		100	88	43					165			141
Gove	2,441	1,355	715			16	30		190					27	
Graham	5,173	1,350	914		328		70								
Grant	422	17													
Gray	1,264	356	356		15		86								

Table 4.—POPULATION IN 1900 AND COMMUNICANTS OR MEMBERS FOR SELECTED DENOMINATIONS, FOR EACH STATE AND TERRITORY, BY COUNTIES: 1906—Continued.

KANSAS—Continued.

COUNTY.	Population, 1900.	All denominations.	PROTESTANT BODIES.												
			Total.	Seventh-day Adventists.	Baptists—Northern, Southern, and National Conventions.	Congregationalists.	Disciples of Christ.	Churches of Christ.	Dunkers (Conservative).	Evangelical Association.	Friends (Orthodox).	German Evangelical Synod of N. A.	Lutheran—General Synod.	Lutheran—General Council.	Lutheran—Synodical Conference.
Greeley	493	148	124		49										
Greenwood	16,196	3,584	3,366	76	201	427	580	39					70		
Hamilton	1,426	232	215		14										
Harper	10,310	2,964	2,800	14	298	105	365	114							
Harvey	17,591	5,860	5,196	10	492	180	577		73	190		215			184
Haskell	457	149	134				76		16						
Hodgeman	2,032	622	468	10	76	101	17								50
Jackson	17,117	5,737	5,157	30	393	60	943		25	272					98
Jefferson	17,533	5,303	4,458	23	540	79	543		80	100	130		64		20
Jewell	19,420	4,508	4,193		310		597		111	263	447		24		
Johnson	18,104	4,937	3,712	20	242	220	280	30	84		134				
Kearny	1,107	386	326		28		112								55
Kingman	10,663	3,471	2,529		231		394	95	50		50				53
Kiowa	2,365	1,116	1,116		60		10	70			602				
Labette	27,387	7,350	6,305	33	1,184	150	322	16	124	17					22
Lane	1,563	582	560		100		170								17
Leavenworth	40,940	12,474	5,881	40	1,175	305	448			79	447	112			559
Lincoln	9,886	2,895	2,651		240		209		33	34		92			882
Linn	16,689	2,703	2,703	28	405	53	481	17							
Logan	1,962	589	541		22			10						32	
Lyon	25,074	8,676	7,033	28	665	528	829	28	62	151	559		107		97
McPherson	21,421	8,951	8,925		592	238	583	17	285	134		125		2,774	183
Marion	20,676	8,246	7,339	136	553		371	30	70	167			182		564
Marshall	24,355	7,770	5,089		374	42	165		47	19	21	278	378	378	643
Meade	1,581	574	544		98	23	14				67				134
Miami	21,641	5,759	4,585	6	929	173	504		27		78	92			240
Mitchell	14,647	4,858	3,382	26	348		701				172		116		20
Montgomery	29,039	10,096	8,800	73	1,384	153	1,536	12	65	41	310				318
Morris	11,967	3,509	3,275	13	164	290	393		46	41				281	84
Morton	304	28	28												
Nemaha	20,376	7,157	4,182		431	765	153		128	87		144			85
Neosho	19,254	6,273	4,714	102	574		1,040		51		35				
Ness	4,535	1,265	885	20	73	35	30	99							40
Norton	11,325	2,727	2,065		164	120	276	26	48	30					
Osage	23,659	6,207	4,899		394	280	167	22		117	130			164	35
Osborne	11,844	3,439	3,174	40	213	478	150		123	147	212				167
Ottawa	11,182	3,194	2,488		222								85		
Pawnee	5,084	1,771	1,729	10	104	40	290		99					76	
Phillips	14,442	3,189	2,993	20	243	140	288		12	88	21		36		
Pottawatomie	18,470	6,833	3,413	18	436	373	158	50		28				617	237
Pratt	7,085	2,288	2,178	59	383		165	99			303				153
Rawlins	5,241	1,673	791	12	116	72						174		30	137
Reno	29,027	8,648	7,932	90	719	393	991	171	142	40		60	37	75	288
Republic	18,248	4,165	3,727	36	297		429		81		186			480	
Rice	14,745	5,136	4,793	25	282	417	559	60	54	53	196				65
Riley	13,828	4,690	4,310	20	469	280	230			388		40		281	130
Rooks	7,960	3,161	2,061	14	126	168	407				101				
Rush	6,134	2,193	1,679	62	189	54	60				112				28
Russell	8,489	2,343	2,037		102	92				139	12		527		8
Saline	17,076	6,381	5,209	17	299	147	559					103	258	1,352	
Scott	1,098	562	562		53		200		105						15
Sedgwick	44,037	17,306	13,130	103	1,672	915	1,365	64	98	62	531	250			198
Seward	822	203	203		13		30								
Shawnee	53,727	18,658	15,953	94	2,590	1,600	1,689	30	55	50		50	203	145	259
Sheridan	3,819	817	386		95										
Sherman	3,341	447	328			14					43				
Smith	16,384	3,608	3,561		204	376	582								200
Stafford	9,829	2,747	2,622		368	53	335	250	41		104	148			
Stanton	327	58	58												
Stevens	620	186	186		24						96				
Sumner	25,631	8,097	7,791	100	927	128	1,205	545	111		216		170		29
Thomas	4,112	1,186	999		206		132	20							
Trego	2,722	1,012	842	16	90	41	31							79	
Wabaunsee	12,813	3,720	2,988		154	264	93	160			35	343			636
Wallace	1,178	283	283		57									126	
Washington	21,963	6,669	4,841		167		533		35	177	132	96	552	69	768
Wichita	1,197	677	493		17										100
Wilson	15,621	3,849	3,480	31	293	124	551		68	102	112			61	
Woodson	10,022	3,010	2,577		122	116	516			272					193
Wyandotte	73,227	27,322	15,393	121	4,565	806	1,221		170			211	70	130	250
County location unknown[1]		1,342	986				38								

[1] See explanatory headnote on page 294.

TABLE 4.—POPULATION IN 1900 AND COMMUNICANTS OR MEMBERS FOR SELECTED DENOMINATIONS, FOR EACH STATE AND TERRITORY, BY COUNTIES: 1906—Continued.

KANSAS—Continued.

COUNTY.	PROTESTANT BODIES—continued.										Roman Catholic Church.	Jewish congregations.[2]	All other bodies.
	Lutheran—Synod of Iowa, etc.	General Conference of Mennonites of N. A.	Methodist Episcopal Church.	Methodist Episcopal Church, South.	African Methodists.[1]	Presbyterian Church in the U. S. A.	United Presbyterian Church.	Protestant Episcopal Church.	United Brethren in Christ.	Other Protestant bodies.			
The state	2,529	3,581	108,097	2,332	5,857	33,465	4,061	6,459	15,159	28,652	93,195	175	4,344
Allen			2,007		129	1,004	35	100	325	383	725		
Anderson			917		39	253	259		278	109	1,719		
Atchison			997	255	223	408		299		232	3,250		76
Barber			511	7		62		30	84	141	99		
Barton		97	1,035		56	172		24	124	146	2,683		
Bourbon			1,651	60	195	411		200	435	687	819		47
Brown			1,687	14	80	629		56	248	1,167	1,381		
Butler		195	2,027	78	19	290		52		488	113		
Chase			485			237				55	179		
Chautauqua			789		7	49		98	38		30		35
Cherokee			1,495		241	583		124	166	551	1,397		361
Cheyenne	36		275							44	51		
Clark			310			7				17	34		
Clay			1,358			422	163	222	189	832	269		
Cloud			964			405	40	26	343	625	2,673		
Coffey			1,886		6	426		56	201	170	368		
Comanche			170			93							
Cowley			2,306	69	73	1,077	105	254	379	341	385		153
Crawford	130		2,251		150	684	201	365	192	555	3,630		114
Decatur			699			123			48	62	235		
Dickinson	117		1,815		20	780		80	261	896	1,165		
Doniphan			619	50	110	208			29	232	1,255		48
Douglas			2,662		411	594	100	315	520	360	1,102		28
Edwards	50		378					31	40	28	291		
Elk			1,113	41		100			111	273	191		
Ellis	400		306			56					4,778		
Ellsworth			602			262		82	50	41	698		
Finney			462		20	132					68		
Ford			617			218		35		51	873		
Franklin			2,159		100	414	225	120	201	375	364		
Geary			365		34	357		137	30		595		
Gove			407								640		
Graham			325		71	29			91	338	414		22
Grant										45	17		
Gray			125			42			80	8			
Greeley			75										24
Greenwood			1,299			87		25	132	430	215		3
Hamilton			128			65		8			17		
Harper			1,174		30	125	41	11	209	314	164		
Harvey		605	1,463		57	633	192	72		253	664		
Haskell			20							22	15		
Hodgeman		40	146				22			6	154		
Jackson			1,796	142	10	450	98	25	575	240	530		50
Jefferson			1,047	26		244	108	40	808	606	845		
Jewell			1,300			106	64	16	494	461	315		
Johnson			1,159	189	59	623	171	20			1,210		15
Kearny			103			28					60		
Kingman		80	1,084			165	30	60	153		942		
Kiowa			185						147	481			
Labette			2,558		165	863	86	128	417	[illegible]	974		71
Lane			191						45	37	22		
Leavenworth			848	253	298	650		321	81	265	6,507	86	
Lincoln			554			255			46	306	244		
Linn			1,162		72	90	50	10	161	174			
Logan			376		20	44				37	48		
Lyon			1,954			829	219	248	40	625	1,643		
McPherson		951	1,114			339			45	1,545	26		
Marion	66	1,327	1,409			463			92	1,887	907		
Marshall			1,488		64	803	161	95		168	2,585		96
Meade	20		152		29	36					30		
Miami			1,268	283	128	496			99	242	1,174		
Mitchell	124		1,070			279	67		250	101	1,526		
Montgomery			2,692	41	226	1,014		220	521	202	1,296		
Morris			1,132	304	26	262		[illegible]	28	191	234		
Morton			20			8							
Nemaha			1,477			227		22	189	504	2,961		14
Neosho	50		1,783		88	395		97	319	180	1,538		21
Ness	6	43	406			80				53	307		73
Norton			652			156			363	230	662		
Osage			1,786		55	1,231	108		156	254	1,210		98
Osborne	26		869			212			291	246	210		55
Ottawa			1,064		12	555		107	246	197	502		204
Pawnee			848		22	181		19	23	17	42		
Phillips	408		946		15	130		10	223	413	196		
Pottawatomie			1,073			95	35	58	205	30	3,420		

[1] Includes African Methodist Episcopal Church, African Methodist Episcopal Zion Church, and Colored Methodist Episcopal Church.
[2] Heads of families only.

Table 4.—POPULATION IN 1900 AND COMMUNICANTS OR MEMBERS FOR SELECTED DENOMINATIONS, FOR EACH STATE AND TERRITORY, BY COUNTIES: 1906—Continued.

KANSAS—Continued.

COUNTY.	PROTESTANT BODIES—continued.										Roman Catholic Church.	Jewish congregations.[2]	All other bodies.
	Lutheran—Synod of Iowa, etc.	General Conference of Mennonites of N. A.	Methodist Episcopal Church.	Methodist Episcopal Church, South.	African Methodists.[1]	Presbyterian Church in the U. S. A.	United Presbyterian Church.	Protestant Episcopal Church.	United Brethren in Christ.	Other Protestant bodies.			
Pratt			747		35	142				92	110		
Rawlins			194			31				25	882		
Reno		243	2,727		123	588	103	130	478	534	676		40
Republic			1,228			259	42	15	297	377	392		46
Rice			1,893		29	324	384		133	319	314		29
Riley			1,277		40	654	76	60	79	286	380		
Rooks			994			55			132	64	1,100		
Rush	295		591				61		210	17	514		
Russell	227		565			123			211	31	306		
Saline			1,164		28	665		109	104	404	1,172		
Scott			104							85			
Sedgwick			3,865		118	1,951	154	445	585	754	3,334	42	809
Seward			143			17							
Shawnee			3,756		703	2,268	298	763	487	913	2,428		277
Sheridan			177			69				45	431		
Sherman	17		171					31	20	32	119		
Smith	333		739			72			649	406			47
Stafford			880		27	30	64		96	226	125		
Stanton			58										
Stevens			66										
Sumner			2,428	110	50	940	34	20	138	631	306		
Thomas			500			78			10	53	187		
Trego	101		367			95		22			170		
Wabaunsee			780		80		130		125	188	732		
Wallace			100										
Washington			1,239			399		41	40	593	1,828		
Wichita	123		130			78				45	184		
Wilson			1,388		15	244		25	100	366	352		17
Woodson			747			289		42	172	108	433		
Wyandotte			3,390	410	1,227	1,259	135	348		1,080	10,834	47	1,048
County location unknown[3]			43						302	603			356

[1] Includes African Methodist Episcopal Church, African Methodist Èpiscopal Zion Church, and Colored Methodist Episcopal Church.
[2] Heads of families only.
[3] See explanatory headnote on page 294.

KENTUCKY.

COUNTY.	Population, 1900.	All denominations.	PROTESTANT BODIES.											
			Total.	Baptists—Southern and National Conventions.	Free Baptists.	General Baptists.	United Baptists.	Primitive Baptists.	Christians (Christian Connection).	Disciples of Christ.	Churches of Christ.	German Evangelical Synod of N. A.	Lutheran—General Synod.	Methodist Episcopal Church.
The state	2,147,174	858,324	689,326	287,791	2,165	6,881	7,167	5,442	2,310	123,659	12,451	12,189	3,190	30,158
Adair	14,888	4,798	4,798	1,514						1,339	223			154
Allen	14,657	5,485	5,485	3,069		545					45			260
Anderson	10,051	3,516	3,516	1,091				75		1,830				
Ballard	10,761	3,791	3,791	1,539		118				564	25			
Barren	23,197	10,121	10,121	6,492		48				1,253	572			
Bath	14,734	4,371	4,371	249						3,006				221
Bell	15,701	3,333	3,138	1,958				156		220				141
Boone	11,170	4,279	4,031	1,765				38		1,133			435	
Bourbon	18,069	8,715	8,137	2,073				20		3,436				617
Boyd	18,834	6,185	5,343	1,562			252			250				977
Boyle	13,817	6,270	6,270	2,644						1,049	95			45
Bracken	12,137	4,693	3,988	759						1,617				560
Breathitt	14,322	1,702	1,702	336						665				
Breckinridge	20,534	5,228	5,228	2,544						30				790
Bullitt	9,602	3,069	3,069	1,892						436			2	70
Butler	15,896	4,395	4,395	1,871	50	669				152	240			302
Caldwell	14,510	4,284	4,284	2,308		42		19		357				125
Calloway	17,633	7,637	7,637	2,726	123			88		490	655			
Campbell	54,223	23,409	10,515	2,164						863		1,975	277	1,213
Carlisle	10,195	3,074	3,074	1,608						70	231			110
Carroll	9,825	3,920	3,665	1,813						1,070				13
Carter	20,228	4,320	4,320	420					1,090	1,800				161
Casey	15,144	4,832	4,832	1,288						2,129				501
Christian	37,962	13,583	13,583	7,870		50		5		1,191	292			39
Clark	16,694	7,774	7,494	3,031				207		1,601	676			248
Clay	15,364	4,198	4,198	2,270			504	122		1,175				42
Clinton	7,871	2,320	2,320	999						222				344
Crittenden	15,191	5,043	5,043	1,669	110	135				42				12
Cumberland	8,962	3,202	3,202	756						1,087				
Daviess	38,667	15,401	15,376	8,913						1,463		369		531

TABLE 4.—POPULATION IN 1900 AND COMMUNICANTS OR MEMBERS FOR SELECTED DENOMINATIONS, FOR EACH STATE AND TERRITORY, BY COUNTIES: 1906—Continued.

KENTUCKY—Continued.

COUNTY.	Population, 1900.	All denominations.	PROTESTANT BODIES.											
			Total.	Baptists—Southern and National Conventions.	Free Baptists.	General Baptists.	United Baptists.	Primitive Baptists.	Christians (Christian Connection).	Disciples of Christ.	Churches of Christ.	German Evangelical Synod of N. A.	Lutheran—General Synod.	Methodist Episcopal Church.
Edmonson	10,080	3,165	3,165	2,127		463					100			90
Elliott	10,387	593	593							410				
Estill	11,669	3,422	3,422	855				140		2,078				34
Fayette	42,071	20,206	17,717	7,393						3,535				1,019
Fleming	17,074	6,943	6,855	749					405	059				532
Floyd	15,552	1,301	1,301				296	8		110				180
Franklin	20,852	9,791	,111	4,868						2,050	195			22
Fulton	11,546	4,854	,854	1,732	392			112		298				
Gallatin	5,163	1,859	,732	1,028						481				
Garrard	12,042	5,993	,952	2,733						2,160				196
Grant	13,239	5,424	5,313	2,625				95		1,606				225
Graves	33,204	11,104	10,913	4,110		13		487		530	1,047			268
Grayson	19,878	4,404	4,404	1,937		127		78		612	50			396
Green	12,255	5,767	5,767	3,660						100				60
Greenup	15,432	3,252	3,211	434			85		26	1,230				482
Hancock	8,914	3,057	3,057	1,629						50				107
Hardin	22,937	7,809	7,809	3,975						787				380
Harlan	9,838	1,855	1,855	772						421	40			440
Harrison	18,570	8,682	8,342	2,037				20		2,616	300			574
Hart	18,390	5,930	5,930	3,647		24				465	134			128
Henderson	32,907	11,019	10,989	5,919	145	153				862	22	225		
Henry	14,620	7,726	7,726	3,679				36		2,333				53
Hickman	11,745	5,151	5,151	1,540				8		400	155			
Hopkins	30,996	8,302	8,302	2,673		511		42		1,700				150
Jackson	10,561	4,074	4,074	2,009				85		1,767				164
Jefferson	232,549	153,068	66,418	22,697						5,341	1,033	9,260	2,403	2,334
Jessamine	11,925	4,677	4,455	1,444						1,888	23			214
Johnson	13,730	3,848	3,848	263			2,410			615	140			155
Kenton	63,591	38,605	12,131	3,461						2,010		60		1,789
Knott	8,704	252	252	80				56						
Knox	17,372	6,726	6,726	4,499			145			1,158				746
Larue	10,764	4,340	4,340	2,829						733				
Laurel	17,592	6,419	6,322	2,638			813	46		1,701				527
Lawrence	19,612	2,759	2,746	358	10		766	24		380				434
Lee	7,988	1,152	1,052	341						430				170
Leslie	6,753	719	719	290				16		320				
Letcher	9,172	362	362	20				261						
Lewis	17,868	4,672	4,672	249	125				721	1,745				1,107
Lincoln	17,059	7,171	7,171	2,283						627				154
Livingston	11,354	3,544	3,544	1,712	25	186		13		93	61			90
Logan	25,994	10,390	10,368	5,340		176		34		400	590			174
Lyon	9,319	3,003	3,003	1,325	271						13			83
McCracken	28,733	12,0·8	11,996	5,347	15					809	125	210		
McLean	12,448	4,652	4,652	1,837		337				449	25			143
Madison	25,607	10,398	10,242	5,434				33		2,922				526
Magoffin	12,006	2,020	2,020	272			760	110		438				400
Marion	16,290	3,340	3,340	1,143						429				50
Marshall	13,692	4,112	4,112	1,398	69			262		94				
Martin	5,780	1,312	1,312	19			957			160				
Mason	20,446	9,109	7,406	1,729				9	50	2,149				1,446
Meade	10,533	2,432	2,432	1,693										36
Menifee	6,818	1,126	1,126	246				57		714				
Mercer	14,426	7,117	7,102	2,582						1,577	435			30
Metcalfe	9,988	2,528	2,528	1,237						130	230			12
Monroe	13,053	4,908	4,908	2,367		65					1,879			158
Montgomery	12,834	4,455	4,221	279				89		1,805				39
Morgan	12,792	2,285	2,285				162	127		1,600	125			
Muhlenberg	20,741	7,859	7,859	4,199		871				147	269			139
Nelson	16,587	5,326	5,326	2,757				37		539	57		12	120
Nicholas	11,952	4,912	4,773	371						2,266				314
Ohio	27,287	9,645	9,645	5,686		344				366				610
Oldham	7,078	3,200	3,200	1,580						608				239
wen	17,553	7,057	7,015	5,773						970				31
Owsley	6,874	1,376	1,376	338				71		676				233
Pendleton	14,947	6,396	5,885	2,360						2,283		90		139
Perry	8,276	791	791	230				98		294				
Pike	22,686	4,267	4,267	262			17	862		1,522				836
Powell	6,443	1,353	1,353	157						790				56
Pulaski	31,293	7,906	7,906	5,318						356	134			775
Robertson	4,900	1,904	1,904	157						967				510
Rockcastle	12,416	4,089	4,089	2,184				65		1,086	350			80
Rowan	8,277	1,519	1,519	176					18	910				
Russell	9,695	3,198	3,198	1,355						836				54
Scott	18,076	6,652	6,354	2,806				49		2,314				336
Shelby	18,340	9,214	9,214	5,237				20		1,879				364
Simpson	11,624	5,038	5,038	3,150		146		85			299		39	
Spencer	7,406	2,485	2,485	1,861				9		301				45
Taylor	11,075	4,416	4,416	1,645						162				43
Todd	17,371	6,410	6,410	3,069		272				201	264			84
Trigg	14,073	4,830	4,830	3,534	15			45		112				

TABLE 4.—POPULATION IN 1900 AND COMMUNICANTS OR MEMBERS FOR SELECTED DENOMINATIONS, FOR EACH STATE AND TERRITORY, BY COUNTIES: 1906—Continued.

KENTUCKY—Continued.

COUNTY.	Population, 1900.	All denominations.	PROTESTANT BODIES. Total.	Baptists—Southern and National Conventions.	Free Baptists.	General Baptists.	United Baptists.	Primitive Baptists.	Christians (Christian Connection).	Disciples of Christ.	Churches of Christ.	German Evangelical Synod of N. A.	Lutheran—General Synod.	Methodist Episcopal Church.
Trimble	7,272	2,322	2,322	736						683				106
Union	21,326	5,432	5,432	2,087	290					543	341			
Warren	29,970	12,005	12,005	6,085		52				474	661			421
Washington	14,182	5,048	5,048	2,125						1,260	182			
Wayne	14,892	5,478	5,478	3,630						546				220
Webster	20,097	6,684	6,684	1,955		1,534		44		210	58			190
Whitley	25,015	8,691	8,495	5,976						1,562				244
Wolfe	8,764	1,982	1,982	261				14		1,177				60
Woodford	13,134	7,450	7,316	3,895						1,392	60			117
County location unknown [1]		35,179	3,429	100	525			1,065		250				

COUNTY.	PROTESTANT BODIES—continued. African Methodist Episcopal Church.	African Methodist Episcopal Zion Church.	Methodist Protestant Church.	Methodist Episcopal Church, South.	Colored Methodist Episcopal Church.	Presbyterian Church in the U. S. A.	Cumberland Presbyterian Church.	Presbyterian Church in the U. S.	Protestant Episcopal Church.	Reformed Church in the U. S.	Other Protestant bodies.	Roman Catholic Church.	Jewish congregations.[2]	All other bodies.
The state	10,047	5,773	2,341	99,355	8,137	8,543	16,916	20,143	8,091	2,101	14,476	165,908	1,147	1,948
Adair		35		898	45	89	169				332			
Allen	121			1,328				20			97			
Anderson	80			147			80	204	9			(3)		
Ballard	90			1,292			150		13					
Barren				1,307	105		274	63			7	(3)		
Bath			41	509	175	74		84	3		9			
Bell	75	131		193				186	78			195		
Boone				485		8		103			64	248		
Bourbon	78			875	252	44		635	91		16	578		
Boyd	131		25	1,288		354		275	79		150	842		
Boyle	440			656	21	360	195	428	78		259	(3)		
Bracken				528				424			100	705		
Breathitt	30		243	79				342	7					
Breckinridge	29			1,199	15	40	574		7			(3)		
Bullitt	20			567				60				(3)		
Butler			230	339		2	389				151			
Caldwell				239	206	53	608	80			247	(3)		
Calloway	170			3,091			249				45			
Campbell	50			1,067		554			652		1,700	12,854		40
Carlisle	25			952	35		43					(3)		
Carroll				681	23			65				255		
Carter	37		168	485				100	13		46			
Casey				452							462	(3)		
Christian		75		1,789	837	118	476	346	140		355	(3)		
Clark	30			927	230		200	274	47		23	280		
Clay						85								
Clinton	58			651							46			
Crittenden				1,029	750	110	877	134			175			
Cumberland				722	173	25	319				120			
Daviess	211			2,414		150	787	402	86		50	(3)	25	
Edmonson				307			78					(3)		
Elliott				174							9			
Estill			95	183				20	3		14			
Fayette	509			944	153	400		851	740		173	2,434	55	
Fleming				1,585		235	48	210	2		30	88		
Floyd				647		60								
Franklin	227		75	613		475		203	383			680		
Fulton	35			1,453	360		255	43	83		91	(3)		
Gallatin				217					6			127		
Garrard	146			380		193		100			44	41		
Grant				460	27	25	64	186				111		
Graves	476			2,442	108		1,189				243	(3)		191
Grayson			32	526			646					(3)		
Green		12		911		130	352				542			
Greenup	25		163	664		60		42				41		
Hancock				697			89	144			341	(3)		
Hardin	94			2,029	16		208	275	40		5	(3)		
Harlan						90					92			
Harrison	256			2,102				385	52			340		
Hart				1,000			185	29			318			
Henderson		456		1,763			148	781	323		192	(3)	30	
Henry	111	100		1,316		8		90				(3)		
Hickman	285			2,343	76		161	34	23		126	(3)		
Hopkins		614		1,586	406		482	32			106	(3)		
Jackson											49			

[1] See explanatory headnote on page 294.   [2] Heads of families only.   [3] Report included in total for "County location unknown."

TABLE 4.—POPULATION IN 1900 AND COMMUNICANTS OR MEMBERS FOR SELECTED DENOMINATIONS, FOR EACH STATE AND TERRITORY, BY COUNTIES: 1906—Continued.

KENTUCKY—Continued.

COUNTY.	PROTESTANT BODIES—continued.													
	African Methodist Episcopal Church.	African Methodist Episcopal Zion Church.	Methodist Protestant Church.	Methodist Episcopal Church, South.	Colored Methodist Episcopal Church.	Presbyterian Church in the U.S.A.	Cumberland Presbyterian Church.	Presbyterian Church in the U.S.	Protestant Episcopal Church.	Reformed Church in the U.S.	Other Protestant bodies.	Roman Catholic Church.	Jewish congregations.[1]	All other bodies.
Jefferson	1,437	1,439		6,420	512	2,033	371	4,237	3,664	1,129	2,108	[2]85,170	965	528
Jessamine	173			321				376	16			222		
Johnson				265										
Kenton	101			862	100	794		406	550	415	1,583	26,474		
Knott				84		32								
Knox	103					66			9					
Larue				462	40	35	116				125	(3)		
Laurel	65			414		30			2	86		97		
Lawrence			226	536					12			13		
Lee								34	77			100		
Leslie						93								
Letcher				17				64						
Lewis			74	383		123		72	3		70			
Lincoln	313			374			30	196		94	100	(3)		
Livingston				1,145			184				35	(3)		
Logan		438	154	1,809	100		1,114		39			(3)		22
Lyon				1,194		85					32			
McCracken	929			2,322	200		482	557	200		800	(3)	82	
McLean	24			1,150			540				147	(3)		
Madison	318			574		44		257	22		112	156		
Magoffin						40								
Marion		83		1,079	103	253		200				(3)		
Marshall	10			1,702			464				113			
Martin				140		36								
Mason				1,348		252		310	90		24	1,703		
Meade	77			595		31						(3)		
Menifee				100				9						
Mercer	605			899		140	259	545	30			(3)		15
Metcalfe		28		276		38	477				100			
Monroe	146			270							23			
Montgomery				671	635	75	27	140	56	377	28	234		
Morgan				260				9	2					
Muhlenberg		607		1,223	10		167	223			4	(3)		
Nelson		525		856				423				(3)		
Nicholas				1,182	380			260				139		
Ohio		125	316	1,920			187	77			14	(3)		
Oldham				453	35	82		118	25			(3)		
Owen				239					2			42		
Owsley						58								
Pendleton	36			879		82			1		15	511		
Perry								169						
Pike	15		100	238		128		225			62			
Powell				190	104			45			11			
Pulaski	100			915				290	14		4	(3)		
Robertson				270										
Rockcastle	99			170		55								
Rowan			237	146					3		29			
Russell				686	29		48				190			
Scott	50			344				429	26			298		
Shelby	228			994		136		333	23			(3)		
Simpson	125			731			389	37			37	(3)		
Spencer				189			39	41				(3)		
Taylor	80			1,417	172	33	358	300			206	(3)		
Todd		25		1,230	1,003		226	25	11					
Trigg				718	202		155				49			
Trimble				786	11							(3)		
Union		130		1,118	167		321	205	75		155	(3)		
Warren	347		55	1,835			1,029	524	105		417	(3)		
Washington	60	525		610				286				(3)		
Wayne	292			568		27	150				45			
Webster		373		1,039	321		488				472	(3)		
Whitley	94			209				60	6		344	196		
Wolfe			35	378				4			53			
Woodford	371			366				1,007	70		38	134		
County location unknown[4]	10	52	72	1,253							102	[5]30,600		1,150

[1] Heads of families only.
[2] Partial report only; remainder included in total for "County location unknown."
[3] Report included in total for "County location unknown."
[4] See explanatory headnote on page 294.
[5] Comprises report of communicants for that part of Louisville diocese not returned separately by counties.

TABLE 4.—POPULATION IN 1900 AND COMMUNICANTS OR MEMBERS FOR SELECTED DENOMINATIONS, FOR EACH STATE AND TERRITORY, BY COUNTIES: 1906—Continued.

LOUISIANA.

PARISH.	Population, 1900.	All denominations.	PROTESTANT BODIES.									Roman Catholic Church.	Jewish congregations.[2]	All other bodies.
			Total.	Baptists—Southern and National Conventions.	Lutheran—Synodical Conference.	Methodist Episcopal Church.	Methodist Episcopal Church, South.	African Methodists.[1]	Presbyterian Church in the U. S.	Protestant Episcopal Church.	Other Protestant bodies.			
The state	1,381,625	778,901	298,946	183,130	5,253	19,763	31,639	23,729	7,198	9,070	19,164	477,774	1,618	563
Acadia	23,483	25,503	3,019	1,166	62	250	869	283	123	50	216	22,456	28	
Ascension	24,142	13,164	3,690	2,791		397	156	119		60	167	9,407	67	
Assumption	21,620	18,206	2,315	1,946	60	165	12	77		55		15,890		
Avoyelles	29,701	25,113	5,552	4,554	106	393	363		39	42	55	19,561		
Bienville	17,588	8,468	8,468	6,231			1,342	520	34	16	325			
Bossier	24,153	8,616	8,616	6,120		197	478	1,458	139		224			
Caddo	44,499	19,421	15,673	9,740		1,282	1,218	1,740	604	409	680	3,513	235	
Calcasieu	30,428	20,835	9,337	4,216	80	964	1,060	714	159	380	1,764	11,458	40	
Caldwell	6,917	2,368	2,365	1,751			298	35			281			
Cameron	3,952	1,580	254	147			107					1,326		
Catahoula	16,351	3,870	3,851	2,929		20	643	45	22		192	19		
Claiborne	23,029	8,864	8,864	4,504			1,162	2,336	39		823			
Concordia	13,559	3,469	3,261	2,745		14	161	215			126	208		
De Soto	25,063	9,842	9,377	6,152		840	1,267	415	386	48	269	465		
East Baton Rouge	31,153	12,940	8,132	4,787		967	1,141	313	392	312	220	4,748	60	
East Carroll	11,373	4,484	4,185	3,402		87	160	350		136	50	299		
East Feliciana	20,443	6,581	6,581	3,094	63	1,332	1,399	491	175	27				
Franklin	8,890	3,608	3,399	2,514		7	592	151	31		104	209		
Grant	12,902	3,531	3,420	2,685		42	417				276	111		
Iberia	29,015	19,744	2,925	1,293		639	452	126	79	130	206	16,809	10	
Iberville	27,006	13,047	3,224	2,491		383	95	167	22	66		9,803	20	
Jackson	9,119	4,513	4,513	2,756			483	367	7		900			
Jefferson	15,321	6,535	2,030	1,668	213	46	71		32			4,505		
Lafayette	22,825	23,414	1,065	251		50	294	389	40	41		22,334	15	
Lafourche	28,882	24,890	2,011	1,555		160		163	38	59	36	22,879		
Lincoln	15,898	6,898	6,898	4,288			1,324	562	255		469			
Livingston	8,100	4,399	2,227	1,741		65	305	116				2,172		
Madison	12,322	2,487	2,487	1,729			53	656		49				
Morehouse	16,634	6,483	6,483	4,054		333	576	1,412		108				
Natchitoches	33,216	12,641	6,348	4,497		541	830	229		62	189	6,268	25	
Orleans	287,104	186,497	36,875	10,580	4,475	3,333	2,352	1,343	3,667	5,178	5,947	148,579	935	108
Ouachita	20,947	8,793	7,354	4,860		373	934	415	173	158	441	1,394	45	
Plaquemines	13,039	6,485	1,385	1,235			20	77		53		5,100		
Pointe Coupee	25,777	10,522	1,979	1,175		119	156	137		108	284	8,543		
Rapides	39,578	18,111	12,804	9,030		1,435	1,186	219	120	433	381	5,239	68	
Red River	11,548	4,711	4,549	3,441		245	264	441			158	162		
Richland	11,116	3,969	3,969	2,475		8	399	982	87	18				
Sabine	15,421	7,512	4,780	3,399		207	805				369	2,732		
St. Bernard	5,031	1,633	315	315								1,318		
St. Charles	9,072	4,590	1,190	1,150		40						3,400		
St. Helena	8,479	4,487	4,373	1,389			1,004	1,955			25	114		
St. James	20,197	13,290	2,470	2,172		268	30					10,820		
St. John the Baptist	12,330	8,829	970	758		111	59	42				7,859		
St. Landry	52,906	47,062	7,633	5,728		799	724		98	117	167	39,419	10	
St. Martin	18,940	15,801	926	459		411	38			18		14,875		
St. Mary	34,145	15,662	4,040	2,267		671	576	224	80	222		11,607	15	
St. Tammany	13,335	8,438	2,952	979	40	335	1,049	385	106	58		5,486		
Tangipahoa	17,625	7,438	5,710	2,471	154	61	834	1,418	64	171	537	1,728		
Tensas	19,070	7,584	7,323	6,924		13	121	185	57	6	17	261		
Terrebonne	24,464	16,479	3,796	2,596		342		563	53	189	53	12,683		
Union	18,520	8,410	8,410	6,823		184	596	246			561			
Vermilion	20,705	22,495	1,946	577		340	825	41	30	13	120	20,549		
Vernon	10,327	2,844	2,844	1,861		95	420	90			378			
Washington	9,628	3,546	3,546	2,846		172	418	110						
Webster	15,125	5,438	5,438	3,392			860	867	44	28	247			
West Baton Rouge	10,285	1,913	893	686		176		28	3			1,020		
West Carroll	3,685	1,470	1,470	977			370	123						
West Feliciana	15,994	1,632	1,607	1,028			59	178		250	92		25	
Winn	9,648	4,654	4,633	3,740		7	212	161			513	21		
County location unknown[3]		3,096	2,196			844		50			1,302	425	20	455

[1] Includes African Methodist Episcopal Church, African Methodist Episcopal Zion Church, and Colored Methodist Episcopal Church.
[2] Heads of families only.
[3] See explanatory headnote on page 294.

TABLE 4.—POPULATION IN 1900 AND COMMUNICANTS OR MEMBERS FOR SELECTED DENOMINATIONS, FOR EACH STATE AND TERRITORY, BY COUNTIES: 1906—Continued.

MAINE.

COUNTY.	Population, 1900.	All denominations.	PROTESTANT BODIES. Total.	Baptists—Northern Convention.	Free Baptists.	Congregationalists.	Methodist Episcopal Church.	Protestant Episcopal Church.	Unitarians.	Universalists.	Other Protestant bodies.	Roman Catholic Church.	Jewish congregations.[1]	All other bodies.
The state	694,466	212,988	96,341	20,813	11,698	21,093	20,067	5,520	2,762	4,696	9,682	113,419	205	3,023
Androscoggin	54,242	28,646	7,257	1,266	1,385	1,305	1,164	692	...	847	598	20,976	100	313
Aroostook	60,744	25,255	6,908	1,627	1,700	687	1,241	461	400	60	732	18,325	...	22
Cumberland	100,689	32,258	17,452	1,816	1,204	5,553	3,354	1,467	788	763	2,507	14,552	...	254
Franklin	18,444	4,412	2,366	121	631	652	719	...	70	93	80	2,046	...	...
Hancock	37,241	6,071	5,036	1,553	219	1,414	1,057	391	375	6	21	722	...	313
Kennebec	59,117	19,795	8,525	1,949	963	1,105	1,457	812	170	745	1,304	11,180	...	90
Knox	30,406	6,295	4,697	2,161	169	714	1,034	208	...	191	220	1,568	...	30
Lincoln	19,669	4,085	2,984	1,145	176	481	996	122	...	22	42	1,101	...	...
Oxford	32,238	9,111	4,763	948	420	1,363	999	90	...	670	273	4,319	...	29
Penobscot	76,246	25,602	8,960	2,142	686	2,200	1,962	484	375	330	781	15,687	98	857
Piscataquis	16,949	3,201	2,344	517	448	584	524	44	...	117	110	807	...	50
Sagadahoc	20,330	4,396	3,141	705	901	531	532	197	...	75	200	1,255	...	...
Somerset	33,849	8,617	4,302	721	743	904	1,285	32	...	246	371	4,061	...	254
Waldo	24,185	2,879	2,459	519	335	581	577	...	174	131	142	292	...	128
Washington	45,232	8,577	5,466	1,620	...	1,185	1,235	209	150	188	879	2,908	...	203
York	64,885	23,672	9,565	2,003	1,698	1,834	1,835	311	260	202	1,422	13,620	7	480
County location unknown[2]	...	116	116	...	...	...	116	...	...	...	...	...	...	...

[1] Heads of families only.

[2] See explanatory headnote on page 294.

MARYLAND.

COUNTY.	Population, 1900.	All denominations.	PROTESTANT BODIES. Total.	Baptists—Northern, Southern, and National Conventions.	Free Baptists.	Churches of God in N. A., General Eldership.	Disciples of Christ.	Dunkers (Conservative).	United Evangelical Church.	Friends (Hicksite).	German Evangelical Synod of N. A.	Lutheran—General Synod.	Lutheran—Synodical Conference.	Lutheran—Joint Synod of Ohio, etc.	Methodist Episcopal Church.
The state	1,188,044	473,257	302,393	29,435	1,242	1,204	3,348	3,667	1,769	1,571	8,384	24,824	4,062	3,254	95,207
Allegany	53,694	25,529	12,061	652	...	...	...	...	50	...	120	1,909	211	...	4,105
Anne Arundel	39,620	10,720	8,479	152	...	...	...	...	...	...	96	...	...	140	4,436
Baltimore	90,755	34,961	17,889	1,281	...	...	87	...	179	49	918	815	265	592	6,619
Baltimore city	508,957	224,968	120,985	23,542	1,120	...	1,469	...	682	610	7,105	7,743	3,188	1,877	24,605
Calvert	10,223	3,625	3,532	...	...	...	...	...	...	...	...	...	...	...	2,434
Caroline	16,248	5,173	5,001	...	...	...	...	145	...	25	...	...	79	...	3,078
Carroll	33,860	14,678	13,661	...	...	499	53	885	...	76	...	4,113	...	...	2,883
Cecil	24,662	6,806	5,857	...	...	...	...	...	...	236	...	...	...	...	2,812
Charles	17,662	9,362	2,737	559	...	...	...	...	...	...	...	...	...	...	837
Dorchester	27,962	9,231	8,909	212	...	...	...	...	...	...	80	...	32	...	5,671
Frederick	51,920	21,798	17,424	191	...	270	...	885	...	...	...	5,579	...	...	2,628
Garrett	17,701	6,478	4,997	157	...	...	60	472	...	...	...	1,018	287	...	1,708
Harford	28,269	8,997	7,416	8	...	...	250	...	131	242	...	...	...	236	2,719
Howard	16,715	5,348	3,796	81	...	...	...	...	236	...	...	...	...	376	1,317
Kent	18,786	5,486	5,164	...	...	...	...	...	...	...	...	...	...	...	3,067
Montgomery	30,451	9,835	7,242	733	...	...	115	...	...	245	...	...	...	33	2,532
Prince Georges	29,898	11,616	5,444	315	...	...	109	...	...	...	...	...	...	...	1,581
Queen Annes	18,364	5,040	4,721	...	...	...	...	...	...	...	...	...	...	...	2,880
St. Marys	17,182	6,480	1,805	...	...	...	...	...	...	...	...	...	...	...	671
Somerset	25,923	9,164	9,104	499	...	...	62	...	...	...	...	...	...	...	6,527
Talbot	20,342	6,905	6,386	103	...	...	...	76	...	88	75	...	...	...	3,230
Washington	45,133	15,797	14,587	200	122	435	1,023	1,204	491	...	...	3,647	...	...	1,022
Wicomico	22,852	8,036	7,982	296	...	...	...	...	...	...	...	...	...	...	4,301
Worcester	20,865	6,476	6,466	454	...	...	75	...	...	...	...	...	...	...	3,441
County location unknown[1]	...	748	748	...	...	...	40	...	...	...	...	...	...	...	123

[1] See explanatory headnote on page 294.

TABLE 4.—POPULATION IN 1900 AND COMMUNICANTS OR MEMBERS FOR SELECTED DENOMINATIONS, FOR EACH STATE AND TERRITORY, BY COUNTIES: 1906—Continued.

MARYLAND—Continued.

COUNTY.	PROTESTANT BODIES—continued.										Roman Catholic Church.	Jewish congregations.[2]	Polish National Church.	All other bodies.
	Methodist Protestant Church.	Methodist Episcopal Church, South.	African Methodists.[1]	Presbyterian Church in the U. S. A.	Presbyterian Church in the U. S.	Protestant Episcopal Church.	Reformed Church in the U. S.	United Brethren in Christ.	Other Protestant bodies.					
The state	16,373	12,642	12,771	15,927	1,628	34,965	13,442	6,445	10,238		166,941	2,153	1,132	638
Allegany	465	860	214	1,193		1,137	629	248	268		13,369	40		59
Anne Arundel	359	830	396	248		1,832					2,146	46		50
Baltimore	696	785	956	1,083	202	2,405	40	540	377		17,072			
Baltimore city	3,417	2,040	5,630	8,224	920	16,812	4,496	1,485	6,020		100,397	2,042	1,132	412
Calvert		582	69			400			47		93			
Caroline	528	308	128			200	126		324		172			
Carroll	1,261	420	39	208	109	180	2,375	503	57		1,017			
Cecil	620		669	920		464			136		892			57
Charles		257	50			958			76		6,625			
Dorchester	668	1,072	628			467			79		297			
Frederick	996	442	371	296		770	3,728	977	289		4,354			25
Garrett		191		73		45	157	596	233		1,481			
Harford	796	282	411	1,420		795			126		1,581			
Howard	265	516	149	124	61	671					1,552			
Kent	810	146	444	100		477			120		322			
Montgomery	327	1,283	291	583	155	779			166		2,593			
Prince Georges		704	355	197	78	2,084			21		6,172			
Queen Annes	650	294	294	6		522			95		319			
St. Marys		70	135			902			27		4,675			
Somerset	1,214	40	210	200		342			10		60			
Talbot	654	587	491			901			181		519			
Washington			134	236	103	743	1,891	2,096	1,240		1,169	26		15
Wicomico	1,516	627	431	230		391			190		54			
Worcester	904	306	276	586		406			18		10			
County location unknown[3]	225					222			138					

[1] Includes Union American Methodist Episcopal Church, African Methodist Episcopal Church, African Union Methodist Protestant Church, African Methodist Episcopal Zion Church, and Colored Methodist Episcopal Church.
[2] Heads of families only.
[3] See explanatory headnote on page 294.

MASSACHUSETTS.

COUNTY.	Population, 1900.	All denominations.	PROTESTANT BODIES.													
			Total.	Advent Christian Church.	Baptists—Northern and National Conventions.	Free Baptists.	Christians (Christian Connection).	Church of Christ, Scientist.	Congregationalists.	Friends (Orthodox).	Lutheran—General Council.	Lutheran—Synodical Conference.	Methodist Episcopal Church.	African Methodists.[1]	Presbyterian Church in the U. S. A.
The state	2,805,346	1,562,621	449,358	3,053	78,165	2,720	2,114	43,547	119,196	1,734	6,645	3,966	61,626	2,579	5,678
Barnstable	826	7,	3,997		423			19	1,225	62			1,551		
Berkshire	667	52,370	17,150	156	3,589			75	6,078		530		3,721	101	
Bristol	27,029	153,568	27,474	444	4,694	48	1,722	97	4,789	718	271		5,398	349	188
Dukes	4,561	1,684	1,089		277				216				412	20	
Essex	357,030	182,172	51,181	713	8,856	912	296	413	14,792	611	416		8,907	30	949
Franklin	41,209	15,308	8,434		1,204				4,186		215		1,071		
Hampden	175,603	114,474	27,229	441	4,942			84	10,817		333	786	5,528	58	610
Hampshire	58,820	30,939	10,603		597				7,092			284	1,256		
Middlesex	565,696	296,745	89,511	285	20,388	1,102		620	24,785		1,271		12,094	429	564
Nantucket	3,006	838	532		70				106				86		
Norfolk	151,539	66,996	26,193	17	3,851			150	8,254		396	30	2,630		977
Plymouth	113,985	51,020	17,706	306	2,967	52	64	139	5,579	32	483	190	3,131	10	
Suffolk	611,417	395,443	116,661	343	18,050	441	32	41,716	13,474	130	969	2,272	7,984	1,284	2,265
Worcester	346,958	192,374	51,558	348	8,237	165		234	17,803	181	1,761	364	7,857	298	125
County location unknown[2]		1,697	40									40			

[1] Includes African Methodist Episcopal Church and African Methodist Episcopal Zion Church.
[2] See explanatory headnote on page 294.

TABLE 4.—POPULATION IN 1900 AND COMMUNICANTS OR MEMBERS FOR SELECTED DENOMINATIONS, FOR EACH STATE AND TERRITORY, BY COUNTIES: 1906—Continued.

MASSACHUSETTS—Continued.

COUNTY.	PROTESTANT BODIES—continued. United Presbyterian Church.	Protestant Episcopal Church.	Salvation Army.	Unitarians.	Universalists.	Other Protestant bodies.	Roman Catholic Church.	Jewish congregations.[1]	Armenian Church.	Greek Orthodox Church.	Polish National Church.	Spiritualists.	All other bodies.
The state	2,540	51,636	1,597	35,440	12,983	14,139	1,080,706	4,388	6,960	12,475	2,141	3,885	2,708
Barnstable		176		232	250	59	3,864					75	62
Berkshire		2,430	28	48	255	139	34,751	181			250	19	19
Bristol	303	5,262	225	865	913	1,188	124,160	107		925	400	259	238
Dukes		91		73			595						
Essex	325	6,423	246	3,209	2,493	1,590	125,084	321	1,544	2,430		605	1,007
Franklin		351		928	176	303	6,592					282	
Hampden	140	2,200	28	325	614	323	85,896	450	78	570	200	15	36
Hampshire		678		681		15	20,226	30		25		55	
Middlesex	425	10,148	281	10,998	3,141	2,980	196,680	296	1,600	6,250	891	301	216
Nantucket		120		150			306						
Norfolk	171	4,012	39	3,816	1,325	525	40,577	65	76	35		50	
Plymouth	110	1,232	49	2,315	323	704	32,245	178	36			789	66
Suffolk	510	14,262	351	7,057	2,024	3,496	271,648	2,085	2,017	1,200		1,194	638
Worcester	556	4,250	350	4,743	1,469	2,817	136,425	675	1,609	1,040	400	241	426
County location unknown[2]							1,657						

[1] Heads of families only.

[2] See explanatory headnote on page 294.

MICHIGAN.

COUNTY.	Population, 1900.	All denominations.	PROTESTANT BODIES. Total.	Seventh-day Adventists.	Baptists—Northern and National Conventions.	Free Baptists.	Congregationalists.	Disciples of Christ.	Evangelical Association.	German Evangelical Synod of N. A.	Lutheran—General Council.	Lutheran—Synodical Conference.	Lutheran—Joint Synod of Ohio, etc.	Lutheran—Synod of Iowa, etc.	Lutheran—Synod of Michigan, etc.
The state	2,420,982	982,479	481,996	7,042	45,120	4,977	32,553	9,791	7,575	20,436	9,693	50,031	9,702	6,817	7,801
Alcona	5,691	1,301	570		193							5			
Alger	5,868	2,325	624	10							38				
Allegan	38,812	8,218	8,202	218	760	118	835	275	160		105				244
Alpena	18,254	8,430	3,440	15	496		319					405		613	
Antrim	16,568	3,497	2,152	58	96		405	21			54	25			
Arenac	9,821	2,963	1,102	38	99		59					144			80
Baraga	4,320	5,766	425								120				
Barry	22,514	4,050	4,050	51	302		266	57	311				116		
Bay	62,378	34,179	10,895	77	1,207		366		39		194	3,599			680
Benzie	9,685	1,788	1,273	69			472	182							
Berrien	49,165	11,684	11,477	160	812	79	1,016	293	643	2,466	36	1,532			272
Branch	27,811	4,851	4,701	52	699	214	495		46			250			
Calhoun	49,315	11,557	11,497	2,012	1,227	193	357	104	60	260			85		709
Cass	20,876	4,017	3,936	85	759	160	121	330	149	35		37			
Charlevoix	13,956	3,834	2,200		269		197		122	60		61			
Cheboygan	15,516	5,778	1,810	28	158		204	60			34	52		470	
Chippewa	21,338	7,699	2,873	15	225		70	157			31	66			
Clare	8,360	1,107	939	46	58		211					15			96
Clinton	25,136	4,889	4,889	78	401	159	518	146	40			290			30
Crawford	2,943	479	295								30				
Delta	23,881	13,543	2,373	84	159		153				637	156			136
Dickinson	17,890	12,338	1,926	8	187						576				13
Eaton	31,668	5,342	5,292	241	566	107	1,199								
Emmet	15,931	6,130	2,150	60	194			62	180	136		126			
Genesee	41,804	8,492	8,429	83	1,511	279	311	99	150						
Gladwin	6,564	1,246	821	8		24			132						
Gogebic	16,738	9,373	3,525		20						600	6			
Grand Traverse	20,479	6,236	3,811	53	289		322	500	115	118	111	197			
Gratiot	29,889	5,789	4,868	181	682		114	313	137			131			
Hillsdale	29,865	6,359	6,359	140	409	762	772	113	50			137			
Houghton	66,063	47,253	14,056	22	178		1,238	40			763	616			
Huron	34,162	7,484	7,221	32	283	24	14	25	673			2 418	95		377
Ingham	39,818	9,960	9,776	183	1,614	60	1,213			169		715			450
Ionia	34,329	6,832	6,748	86	1,230		529	704	123			353			
Iosco	10,246	4,060	1,678	19	235						132	641			
Iron	8,990	5,736	1,150	30	41						313				
Isabella	22,784	6,783	[illegible]	56	273			541	109			100			48
Jackson	48,222	9,196	[illegible]	76	1,841	120	659		89	370		468			158
Kalamazoo	44,310	10,682	[illegible]	86	1,465	92	1,008	225	46						241
Kalkaska	7,133	1,148	944	20	112		72	254							
Kent	129,714	53,000	30,110	294	3,169	379	2,972	1,093	165	505	689	1 037			
Keweenaw	3,217	1,363	[illegible]												
Lake	4,957	648	430	11	100		60	90							
Lapeer	27,641	4,642	[illegible]	93	616	144	277	145	215	43		205		114	22
Leelanau	10,556	4,255	1,790		12		293	160	127			265			

TABLE 4.—POPULATION IN 1900 AND COMMUNICANTS OR MEMBERS FOR SELECTED DENOMINATIONS, FOR EACH STATE AND TERRITORY, BY COUNTIES: 1906—Continued.

MICHIGAN—Continued.

COUNTY.	Population, 1900.	All denominations.	PROTESTANT BODIES.												
			Total.	Seventh-day Adventists.	Baptists—Northern and National Conventions.	Free Baptists.	Congregationalists.	Disciples of Christ.	Evangelical Association.	German Evangelical Synod of N. A.	Lutheran—General Council.	Lutheran—Synodical Conference.	Lutheran—Joint Synod of Ohio, etc.	Lutheran—Synod of Iowa, etc.	Lutheran—Synod of Michigan, etc.
Lenawee	48,406	11,846	11,846	20	1,696	264	798		199	50		532		824	710
Livingston	19,664	4,141	4,076		515	43	221		132				350		
Luce	2,983	399	399								66				
Mackinac	7,708	3,174	627				41				74			126	
Macomb	33,244	9,494	9,494	32	297	77	703	20	67	1,998		3,260		825	
Manistee	27,856	11,858	5,180	36	361		389	8	15		360	1,899	300		
Marquette	41,239	21,901	7,314		409						1,273	211			
Mason	18,885	7,174	3,564	8	165		307		231		311	581			174
Mecosta	20,693	4,858	3,288	46	86	29	326	166			67	429			45
Menominee	27,046	12,959	2,735	73	242					95	534	540			38
Midland	14,439	4,031	1,949	57	271			26	31			284			32
Missaukee	9,308	2,092	1,928	30				21			54	36			
Monroe	32,754	7,072	7,072	45	74	106	204	61	567			2,145	419	975	200
Montcalm	32,754	8,132	6,767	296	490	140	1,110	206	109	110		309			
Montmorency	3,234	715	390				122					75			
Muskegon	37,036	10,874	7,008	46	622	38	546	73		325	777	345			
Newaygo	17,673	3,473	2,859	55	315	14	280	198			90				
Oakland	44,792	9,353	9,353	74	1,654	221	572	40		284		236			
Oceana	16,644	3,885	2,787	90	140		214	47				314			
Ogemaw	7,765	1,877	955	20	47							103			
Ontonagon	6,197	3,395	950				7				32				
Osceola	17,859	4,272	3,724	34	291	59	182	13	480		392	375	204		
Oscoda	1,468	439	381		10			75							
Otsego	6,175	1,748	699	36	144		217								
Ottawa	39,667	13,695	12,185	176	162	40	387	22		350		796			
Presque Isle	8,821	3,836	1,532	74	120							689		373	
Roscommon	1,787	139	85				30	25							
Saginaw	81,222	29,461	16,062	211	1,217		813	356	187	239		3,981	1,422	660	1,963
St. Clair	55,228	11,362	11,211	18	972	116	1,207	240	264	1,235		365	165	1,152	94
St. Joseph	23,889	5,748	5,679	58	497		194		124			458			482
Sanilac	35,055	6,121	5,597	12	580	79	56		172	104		501			
Schoolcraft	7,889	2,840	1,135	28	337		19				242	29			
Shiawassee	33,866	7,199	7,179	141	919		1,058	328	145	208		390			
Tuscola	35,890	7,992	7,942	129	513	390		63	243			1,774			113
Van Buren	33,274	6,369	6,163	145	805	330	838	678	27			239	96		
Washtenaw	47,761	15,227	15,227	39	1,666	49	1,228	312	235	3,253		831	1,528	185	
Wayne	348,793	204,083	73,962	103	6,235		3,141	505	448	8,001	275	14,208	4,922	500	395
Wexford	16,845	4,917	3,228	82	321	68	226	319	18	22	683	35			
County location unknown [1]		138,586	391												

COUNTY.	PROTESTANT BODIES—continued.									Roman Catholic Church.	Jewish congregations.[3]	Latter-day Saints (Reorganized).	All other bodies.
	Lutheran—Finnish Synods.[2]	Methodist Episcopal Church.	Methodist Protestant Church.	Free Methodist Church of N. A.	Presbyterian Church in the U. S. A.	Protestant Episcopal Church.	Reformed Church in America.	Christian Reformed Church.	Other Protestant bodies.				
The state	12,282	114,326	5,077	5,121	36,710	26,439	11,260	14,719	44,524	492,135	1,530	4,227	2,891
Alcona		300		2	54				16	659		72	
Alger	300	145			87	44				1,701			
Allegan		2,079	23	26	380	170	973	1,223	613	(4)		16	
Alpena		471		91	153	471			406	4,891	12	87	
Antrim		749		66	75	72	71	254	206	976		119	250
Arenac		329		117	102	13			121	1,861			
Baraga	49	155							101	5,341			
Barry		1,511	191	64	64	140			977	(4)			
Bay		1,865		119	1,422	568			759	22,851	75	234	124
Benzie		383		12					155	424		91	
Berrien		2,190	18	29	421	427	33		1,050	(4)	48	159	
Branch		1,759		129	493	275			289	(4)		120	30
Calhoun		3,171	55	52	1,535	904			773	(4)			60
Cass		1,046	66		121				1,077	(4)		23	58
Charlevoix		891		11	258	58			273	1,496		138	
Cheboygan		413			62	266			63	3,968			
Chippewa	188	915		80	620	536		20		4,526			300
Clare		404		30					80			168	
Clinton		2,160		155		150			762	(4)			
Crawford		85	33		40	17			90	184			

[1] See explanatory headnote on page 294.
[2] Includes Finnish Evangelical Lutheran Church of America, or Suomi Synod; Finnish Evangelical Lutheran National Church; and Apostolic Lutheran Church (Finnish).
[3] Heads of families only.
[4] Report included in total for "County location unknown."

TABLE 4.—POPULATION IN 1900 AND COMMUNICANTS OR MEMBERS FOR SELECTED DENOMINATIONS, FOR EACH STATE AND TERRITORY, BY COUNTIES: 1906—Continued.

MICHIGAN—Continued.

COUNTY.	PROTESTANT BODIES—continued.									Roman Catholic Church.	Jewish congregations.[2]	Latter-day Saints (Reorganized).	All other bodies.
	Lutheran—Finnish Synods.[1]	Methodist Episcopal Church.	Methodist Protestant Church.	Free Methodist Church of N. A.	Presbyterian Church in the U. S. A.	Protestant Episcopal Church.	Reformed Church in America.	Christian Reformed Church.	Other Protestant bodies.				
Delta		308			346	133			261	11,170			
Dickinson		551			102	76			413	10,412			
Eaton		2,251	178	101	160				489	(3)			50
Emmet		1,204			584	184			420	2,960	20		
Genesee		3,823	363	334	694	605			177	(3)		43	20
Gladwin		388		75	68	6			120	331		94	
Gogebic	1,959	479			183	144			134	5,848			
Grand Traverse		1,415		35	171	141			344	2,358		67	
Gratiot		1,705		146	722	194			543	921			
Hillsdale		2,191	53	66	488	115			1,063	(3)			
Houghton	6,476	2,755	50		391	766			761	33,145	52		
Huron		1,710	142	64	735	70			559	(3)		263	
Ingham		3,199	319	106	845	348			555	(3)		46	138
Ionia		2,211		99	312	208			893	(3)		50	34
Iosco	24	419			137	71				2,248		124	
Iron	530	83			55	37			61	4,586			
Isabella		1,152		60	180	81			250	3,869		12	52
Jackson		3,042	38	173	729	626			645	(3)			162
Kalamazoo		2,633		65	828	478	1,606	453	1,310	(3)	49		47
Kalkaska		309		34				5	138	38		166	
Kent		4,529		172	1,246	1,837	3,333	5,122	3,568	22,277	85	63	465
Keweenaw	26	337								1,000			
Lake		79		26		38			26	191		27	
Lapeer		1,269	602	67	180	78			413	(3)		159	
Leelanau		244		16	34				639	2,423		42	
Lenawee		2,963	240	178	1,337	488	149		1,398	(3)			
Livingston		1,659	180	86	498	80			312	(3)			65
Luce	120	138			40	35							
Mackinac		129			181	71			5	2,547			
Macomb		1,406	60	45	222	122			351	(3)			
Manistee	200	690				119			803	6,678			
Marquette	1,923	1,604			529	669			696	14,587			
Mason		943		93	167	38			546	3,460		150	
Mecosta		1,050		131	150	150			613	1,520		50	
Menominee		360			360	110			383	10,224			
Midland		722		57	291	103			75	1,931		151	
Missaukee		346		36	161		121	1,044	79	146		18	
Monroe		1,341	106	99	396	102			232	(3)			
Montcalm		1,819		181		45			1,952	1,350		15	
Montmorency		49			40	42			62	290		35	
Muskegon		1,222		22	32	258	551	1,116	1,035	3,302	20		44
Newaygo		572		47		20	82	511	675	614			
Oakland		3,596	115	73	1,396	513			579	(3)			
Oceana		959		51	50	21	100	165	636	1,098			
Ogemaw		376		147		102			160	800		122	
Ontonagon	531	175			53	72			80	2,445			
Osceola		1,206		123	237				129	428		120	
Oscoda		25							271			58	
Otsego		176			21	22			83	1,008		46	
Ottawa		818		73	238	199	3,877	4,806	241	1,510			
Presque Isle		179				59			38	2,304			
Roscommon		11							19	54			
Saginaw		2,381	248	84	1,482	622			196	13,303	24		72
St. Clair		2,609	674	118	549	892			541	(3)	14	137	
St. Joseph		1,888	119	6	602	140	224		887	(3)			69
Sanilac		2,153	213	179	882	141			525	(3)		524	
Schoolcraft	6	155			211	24			84	1,705			
Shiawassee		2,797	251	123	98	459			262	(3)			20
Tuscola		2,542	660	48	819	192			456	(3)		50	
Van Buren		1,953	80	94	260	126	35		457	(3)		40	157
Washtenaw		2,586		47	1,016	1,439			813	(3)			
Wayne		10,582		144	9,065	8,590	105		6,743	[4] 128,477	1,131	247	266
Wexford		564		214	250	27			399	1,617		72	
County location unknown[5]		276							115	[6] 138,087			108

[1] Includes Finnish Evangelical Lutheran Church of America, or Suomi Synod; Finnish Evangelical Lutheran National Church; and Apostolic Lutheran Church (Finnish).
[2] Heads of families only.
[3] Report included in total for "County location unknown."
[4] Partial report only; remainder included in total for "County location unknown."
[5] See explanatory headnote on page 294.
[6] Includes 136,000 communicants for that part of Detroit diocese not returned separately by counties.

TABLE 4.—POPULATION IN 1900 AND COMMUNICANTS OR MEMBERS FOR SELECTED DENOMINATIONS FOR EACH STATE AND TERRITORY, BY COUNTIES: 1906—Continued.

MINNESOTA.

COUNTY.	Population, 1900.	All denominations.	PROTESTANT BODIES.												
			Total.	Baptists—Northern Convention.	Church of Christ, Scientist.	Congregationalists.	Disciples of Christ.	Evangelical Association.	German Evangelical Synod of N. A.	Lutheran—General Council.	Lutheran—Synodical Conference.	Lutheran—United Norwegian Church.	Lutheran—Joint Synod of Ohio, etc.	Lutheran—Hauge's Norwegian Synod.	Lutheran—Synod of Iowa, etc.
The state	1,751,394 [1]	834,442	450,434	22,786	2,387	22,264	3,560	7,450	9,183	49,830	61,092	59,204	9,656	12,857	8,460
Aitkin	6,743	1,792	1,048	24		65				127	50				
Anoka	11,313	4,095	2,197	396		163				293	230				
Becker	14,375	6,969	4,361	368		91	30			252	469	691			
Beltrami	11,030	3,210	2,066	281		14					58	462			
Benton	9,912	5,802	1,677			135	60	48		175	779				
Bigstone	8,731	4,180	1,912	93		183				455	199	82			
Blue Earth	32,263	14,028	9,909	525	100	406	527	104		292	2,411	903	627		
Brown	19,787	14,203	7,236	90		371		223	208	304	2,676	1,326	525		
Carlton	10,017	5,133	2,727	76						403	121	48			
Carver	17,544	10,987	6,214	38				130	280	1,211	3,813				
Cass	7,777	1,082	578	21		63					112				12
Chippewa	12,499	5,561	5,059	387	12	154				199	373	2,052	45		230
Chisago	13,248	6,652	6,012	242		31			150	4,326	562				
Clay	17,942	7,218	5,311	6		362			75	391	60	2,265		41	
Clearwater	(2)	1,282	1,258	12		45				94		472		100	
Cook	810	659													
Cottonwood	12,069	4,037	3,530	273		42				42	115	850	403		
Crow Wing	14,250	3,981	2,345	139		146				231	190		100	43	
Dakota	21,733	12,115	3,708	72		69				201	959	60	90		310
Dodge	13,340	4,202	3,951	375		276	140	[illegible]			100	517		252	
Douglas	17,964	6,660	4,796	146		196			51	1,466	585	688			
Faribault	22,055	9,357	6,411	89		52		740	317		704	570	360	582	171
Fillmore	28,238	14,170	11,762	142		234		286			336	5,601		920	1,122
Freeborn	21,838	8,756	7,761	897	41	73				60		1,131	224		670
Goodhue	31,137	16,246	13,599	115		261		45	40	3,324	2,269	3,373	90	1,248	
Grant	8,935	3,476	3,357						45	752	54	990			
Hennepin	228,340	106,473	52,042	5,986	1,583	6,289	593	2	385	4,750	1,748	735	51	263	981
Houston	15,400	8,387	4,714	111				186	805		493	972			
Hubbard	6,578	1,731	1,146	300		140	21		50		123	49			
Isanti	11,675	3,360	3,360	835		56	41	43		1,596	487				
Itasca	4,573	1,957	661	48		7				55	17	51			
Jackson	14,793	5,325	3,900	51				73	56	12	766	591	103	1,310	200
Kanabec	4,614	1,122	986	160						202	216			19	
Kandiyohi	18,416	8,496	7,697	226	17					1,683	297	1,263		176	143
Kittson	7,889	2,251	2,217	58				50		874		605			
Koochiching	(3)	126	24												
Lac qui Parle	14,289	7,782	6,600	6		336		238		342	582	3,155	194	1,621	
Lake	4,654	1,662	1,087							452		160			
Lesueur	20,234	12,038	3,410	211		52	107	107	560	59	459				443
Lincoln	8,966	4,634	2,471	111		106		71		89	328	255		405	
Lyon	14,591	6,932	4,152	58		292		120		59	328	870	71		
McLeod	19,595	12,306	7,039	63		558		204	905		2,688		853		
Marshall	15,698	4,947	3,748	137	21	29				591	88	792		225	
Martin	16,936	5,923	5,019	58	94	387	155	101	512	335	1,181	537	27		329
Meeker	17,753	7,238	4,212	183			84			1,511	550	360			
Millelacs	8,066	2,406	1,770	163	25	158				392	208		129		
Morrison	22,891	11,616	2,837	189		427		27	165	714	333				76
Mower	22,335	10,518	8,260	764	74	639	60	106		58	621	3,032		181	418
Murray	11,911	4,650	2,318	52						570	235	599		100	87
Nicollet	14,774	7,366	4,386			94		80	49	2,041	1,216				
Nobles	14,932	6,718	3,864	261		198	78	88		256	254	166			350
Norman	15,045	7,531	6,217			58					192	3,596		390	304
Olmsted	23,119	8,172	6,081	443		450	442	87	288		1,014	296	110		
Otter Tail	45,375	17,889	13,491	331		204		194	531	1,434	1,954	2,573		1,011	
Pine	11,546	4,629	1,774	26		22			27	411	263				33
Pipestone	9,264	3,189	2,238	174	14	96		88			512	312			
Polk	35,429	13,738	9,697	219		168				400	345	4,216	105	277	
Pope	12,577	6,489	5,606			189				150	170	270			40
Ramsey	170,554	107,315	30,104	2,776	217	2,287	320	350	855	3,096	4,531	230	750	268	367
Red Lake	12,195	4,987	2,632	16				60		244	266	289		213	
Redwood	17,261	8,627	5,630			170	212	222	34	168	861	359	641		
Renville	23,693	12,801	7,839	21		4	15	518	64	726	1,469	871	691	832	
Rice	26,080	14,308	6,847	549		1,122	15	272	380	133	1,175	397		365	
Rock	9,668	2,596	2,202	143				69			217	416			
Roseau	6,994	2,429	1,851	6						210		114		498	
St. Louis	82,932	37,115	15,044	1,154	159	504	161	48	330	1,839	76	847	240	238	
Scott	15,147	11,829	2,001							2	964		556		
Sherburne	7,281	1,760	1,233			264				69			10		
Sibley	16,862	8,231	5,228	68		123		153	290	725	2,359		879		
Stearns	44,464	32,798	4,598	285	13	256	60	654	410		836	235			155

[1] Includes population (3,486) of White Earth Indian reservation, not returned by counties in 1900.
[2] New county since 1900; formed from part of Beltrami in 1903.
[3] New county since 1900; formed from part of Itasca in 1906.

TABLE 4.—POPULATION IN 1900 AND COMMUNICANTS OR MEMBERS FOR SELECTED DENOMINATIONS, FOR EACH STATE AND TERRITORY, BY COUNTIES: 1906—Continued.

MINNESOTA—Continued.

COUNTY.	Population, 1900	All denominations.	PROTESTANT BODIES. Total.	Baptists—Northern Convention.	Church of Christ, Scientist.	Congregationalists.	Disciples of Christ.	Evangelical Association.	German Evangelical Synod of N. A.	Lutheran—General Council.	Lutheran—Synodical Conference.	Lutheran—United Norwegian Church.	Lutheran—Joint Synod of Ohio, etc.	Lutheran—Hauge's Norwegian Synod.	Lutheran—Synod of Iowa, etc.
Steele	16,524	6,792	4,976	585		366		49			278	1,091			1,126
Stevens	8,721	3,599	1,889			231				140	208		216		
Swift	13,503	6,445	3,675	64		169		70		250	446	226	241		
Todd	22,214	8,743	4,592	160		235	70	30	155	218	1,066	845		195	
Traverse	7,573	2,468	1,242	72		52			40	303	338				
Wabasha	18,924	7,749	3,943	130		616	40	91	120	258	1,399				
Wadena	7,921	3,283	2,036			187		55	95	46	165	101		50	
Waseca	14,760	6,319	4,315	40		169		215	150	156	1,131	735	60		677
Washington	27,808	11,370	7,349	113		200			380	2,707	1,103		855		216
Watonwan	11,496	4,644	3,692	63			60			1,042	818	970			
Wilkin	8,080	1,796	1,153	108		82		36	30		206	84			
Winona	35,686	17,511	7,198	245	17	574	81	168	56		3,122	412			
Wright	29,157	14,809	7,891	92		229	122	90	295	2,712	1,522		297		
Yellow Medicine	14,602	7,416	6,494	65		38	66			338	1,373	2,850	113	1,034	
County location unknown[1]		3,246	2,971							834	270	596			

COUNTY.	PROTESTANT BODIES—continued. Lutheran—Norwegian Synod.	Lutheran—Norwegian Free Church.	Lutheran—United Danish Church.	Lutheran—Finnish National Church.	Lutheran—Apostolic Church (Finnish).	Methodist Episcopal Church.	Presbyterian Church in the U. S. A.	Protestant Episcopal Church.	Swedish Evangelical Mission Covenant.	Other Protestant bodies.	Roman Catholic Church.	Jewish congregations.[2]	All other bodies.
The state	38,903	13,546	2,376	2,589	4,299	46,351	26,412	18,763	5,017	23,449	378,288	1,725	3,995
Aitkin	56	16		269		294	20	80	8	39	744		
Anoka		200				631	23	78	75	108	1,898		
Becker	858	175		200	570	233		297		127	2,445		163
Beltrami	315	288				122	371	146		9	1,114		30
Benton	290					37	63	48	8	34	4,125		
Bigstone	70	200				310		59	22	239	2,268		
Blue Earth	500	463				991	673	219		1,168	4,119		
Brown		49	415			614	25	79		331	6,967		
Carlton	85	202		500	583	235	292	75	31	76	2,406		
Carver						29	4			709	4,773		
Cass	16	62				93	29	170			504		
Chippewa	859	95				287	81	65		220	502		
Chisago						326	60	87	118	110	640		
Clay	796	765				201	90	167	52	40	1,907		
Clearwater	355	180									24		
Cook											659		
Cottonwood	152					404	111	25		913	507		
Crow Wing	459	42		50	81	291	136	142	26	205	1,636		
Dakota	210	355	78			422	297	218	20	53	8,407		
Dodge	700					734	244	55		425	251		
Douglas	500	230	139	100		340	88	43	89	96	1,864		
Faribault	627					885	522	87		699	2,946		
Fillmore	850					1,087	490	123		632	2,408		
Freeborn	2,774		426			559	442	114		350	995		
Goodhue	325	258				1,071	215	652	151	162	2,647		
Grant	1,036	150				40	202		21	67	119		
Hennepin	2,333	1,430	98		75	7,326	6,556	4,853	1,479	4,292	52,041	806	1,584
Houston	1,695					227	176	52		48	3,673		
Hubbard	109	59				268		15		12	585		
Isanti						40		5	168	89			
Itasca	42			135		155	68	83			1,296		
Jackson	60	40				330	169	35		104	1,425		
Kanabec	41	106				107	65		65	5	128		
Kandiyohi	994	1,536				355	380	260	155	212	799		
Kittson	39	91				145	190	123	34	8	34		
Koochiching							24				102		
Lac qui Parle						49	25		29	23	1,182		
Lake						251	187	30	7		575		
Lesueur						684	188	261		279	8,628		
Lincoln	100					313		50		643	2,163		
Lyon	405					598	840	60		451	1,780		
McLeod	230		228			604	31	60		615	5,267		
Marshall	826	544				89	154		56	196	1,199		
Martin			80			548		111	152	412	904		
Meeker	200				128	288	239	356	278	35	3,026		

[1] See explanatory headnote on page 294.

[2] Heads of families only.

TABLE 4.—POPULATION IN 1900 AND COMMUNICANTS OR MEMBERS FOR SELECTED DENOMINATIONS, FOR EACH STATE AND TERRITORY, BY COUNTIES: 1906—Continued.

MINNESOTA—Continued.

COUNTY.	PROTESTANT BODIES—continued.										Roman Catholic Church.	Jewish congregations.[1]	All other bodies.
	Lutheran—Norwegian Synod.	Lutheran—Norwegian Free Church.	Lutheran—United Danish Church.	Lutheran—Finnish National Church.	Lutheran—Apostolic Church (Finnish).	Methodist Episcopal Church.	Presbyterian Church in the U. S. A.	Protestant Episcopal Church.	Swedish Evangelical Mission Covenant.	Other Protestant bodies.			
Millelacs	240					342	9	15		89	638		
Morrison	233					294	108	105	47	119	8,709		70
Mower	292					1,020	426	190		379	2,258		
Murray	139					227	192	10		107	2,332		
Nicollet	320					336	158	92			2,980		
Nobles		317				562	670	24	53	597	2,854		
Norman	1,385					159	80	83		20	1,314		
Olmsted	414	75				1,550	337	253		322	2,091		
Otter Tail	2,575	627		250	700	386	403	118	35	165	4,279		119
Pine	38	63		200		349	178	21		143	2,840		15
Pipestone	50					474	299	23		196	951		
Polk	1,782	988				374	408	142	55	218	4,041		
Pope	3,874	426				116	52	29	67	243	883		
Ramsey	520	250				3,816	4,196	3,468	558	1,249	75,936	655	620
Red Lake	956	98				168	204	37		81	2,355		
Redwood	566	330	336			739	656	200		136	2,961		36
Renville	1,300				200	818	42	64	35	169	4,962		
Rice	260	160	206			657	73	874		209	7,439		22
Rock	523	206				256	261	63		46	394		
Roseau	494	495						31		3	578		
St. Louis	173	92		675	915	2,463	1,701	1,271	477	1,681	20,616	264	1,191
Scott						298	133	48			9,828		
Sherburne	164	145				353		91		137	527		
Sibley	210					354		25		42	3,003		
Stearns	449					608	152	346		139	28,200		
Steele		200	370			406	194	134		177	1,816		
Stevens	328	330				266	64	7		99	1,710		
Swift	897	825				162	47	142	45	91	2,770		
Todd	199	25				528	66	187	50	563	4,151		
Traverse	55					120	174	17	19	52	1,206		20
Wabasha						686	23	330		250	3,806		
Wadena	36	110		110	684	286		37	31	43	1,247		
Waseca						703		145	120	14	2,004		
Washington	117					845	283	242	94	194	4,021		
Watonwan		88				234	209	73		135	952		
Wilkin	380	41				127	28	15		16	643		
Winona						1,244	420	330		529	10,313		
Wright				100	363	1,041	321	68	251	388	6,918		
Yellow Medicine	177	100				237	75			28	922		
County location unknown[2]	900	17				144		30	36	144	158		117

[1] Heads of families only.

[2] See explanatory headnote on page 294.

MISSISSIPPI.

COUNTY.	Population, 1900.	All denominations.	PROTESTANT BODIES.									Roman Catholic Church.	Jewish congregations.[2]	Latter-day Saints.
			Total.	Baptists—Southern and National Conventions.	Disciples of Christ.	Methodist Episcopal Church.	Methodist Episcopal Church, South.	African Methodists.[1]	Cumberland Presbyterian Church.	Presbyterian Church in the U. S.	Other Protestant bodies.			
The state	1,551,270	657,381	626,845	364,339	6,709	50,695	94,845	60,335	5,991	15,641	28,290	28,576	746	1,214
Adams	30,111	12,643	8,948	5,510		50	710	1,214		492	972	3,550	145	
Alcorn	14,987	6,102	6,088	2,082	270	450	1,669	230	224	229	934	14		
Amite	20,708	11,596	11,596	8,505		330	484	822		391	1,064			
Attala	26,248	10,496	10,496	5,541	12	1,301	2,272	337	196	349	488			
Benton	10,510	3,342	3,342	2,166	136	100	281	339	30		290			
Bolivar	35,427	13,653	13,453	9,860	39	130	1,009	2,080		44	311	200		
Calhoun	16,512	5,829	5,829	3,127		285	1,248	859	112	10	188			
Carroll	22,116	9,048	9,048	3,315	580	1,243	2,109	1,089	23	458	231			
Chickasaw	19,892	8,187	8,165	4,632	95	818	1,542	545	107	332	94	22		
Choctaw	13,036	6,081	6,073	3,414	124	896	1,043	18	30	508	40	8		
Claiborne	20,787	6,153	6,111	4,080	156		1,083	492		192	108	26	16	
Clarke	17,741	6,871	6,871	4,727	50		1,767	77		36	214			
Clay	19,563	7,442	7,407	4,356	515	317	905	527	439	80	268	35		
Coahoma	26,293	13,690	13,571	10,673	81	248	484	1,676		35	374	119		
Copiah	34,395	17,327	17,304	11,529	200	1,365	2,727	728		350	405	23		
Covington	13,076	6,963	6,963	3,137		1,400	1,015	800		364	247			
De Soto	24,751	8,441	8,441	4,043	77		891	2,875	300	136	119			
Franklin	13,678	5,878	5,878	4,024	19	706	921	104		23	81			
Greene	6,795	2,755	2,755	1,483		191	554	31		229	267			
Grenada	14,112	5,343	5,343	1,741		446	488	2,376		224	68			

[1] Includes Union American Methodist Episcopal Church, African Methodist Episcopal Church, African Methodist Episcopal Zion Church, and Colored Methodist Episcopal Church.

[2] Heads of families only.

TABLE 4.—POPULATION IN 1900 AND COMMUNICANTS OR MEMBERS FOR SELECTED DENOMINATIONS, FOR EACH STATE AND TERRITORY, BY COUNTIES: 1906—Continued.

MISSISSIPPI—Continued.

COUNTY.	Population, 1900.	All denominations.	PROTESTANT BODIES. Total.	Baptists—Southern and National Conventions.	Disciples of Christ.	Methodist Episcopal Church.	Methodist Episcopal Church, South.	African Methodists.[1]	Cumberland Presbyterian Church.	Presbyterian Church in the U. S.	Other Protestant bodies.	Roman Catholic Church.	Jewish congregations.[2]	Latter-day Saints.
Hancock	11,886	9,701	3,445	2,262		414	545	165		19	40	6,256		
Harrison	21,002	12,766	7,849	3,463		573	2,549	245		305	714	4,917		
Hinds	52,577	25,034	24,376	16,155	641	1,407	2,640	872		718	1,943	621	37	
Holmes	36,828	15,859	15,781	10,165	21	1,648	1,566	1,786	160	287	148	63	15	
Issaquena	10,400	3,610	3,610	2,728			94	652			136			
Itawamba	13,544	4,303	4,303	1,783		137	1,558	60			765			
Jackson	16,513	7,086	5,170	1,827		825	1,813	170		227	308	1,720		196
Jasper	15,394	6,069	5,898	3,170		1,570	598			273	287	171		
Jefferson	21,292	8,399	8,336	4,856	263	935	1,085	722		418	57	63		
Jefferson Davis	(3)	3,597	2,951	2,013			466	375		97		646		
Jones	17,846	8,378	8,156	4,110		589	1,601	490		313	1,053	202	20	
Kemper	20,492	5,841	5,828	2,860		979	1,488			330	171	13		
Lafayette	22,110	6,994	6,994	1,930		922	1,798	955	179	650	560			
Lamar	(4)	3,226	3,226	2,025		146	861	122	30	8	34			
Lauderdale	38,150	18,427	17,699	9,388	213	1,854	2,951	1,356	454	544	939	624	104	
Lawrence	15,103	4,429	4,429	3,524		150	563	4		12	176			
Leake	17,360	5,519	5,465	3,858	85	265	394	123	224	35	481	54		
Lee	21,956	10,647	10,613	4,405	338	670	2,039	2,277	245	390	249	34		
Leflore	23,834	9,254	9,129	4,887	61	1,454	764	1,630		258	75	102	23	
Lincoln	21,552	12,006	11,302	7,265		390	1,611	1,372		193	471	684	20	
Lowndes	29,095	12,308	12,065	6,449	63	1,096	1,742	1,415	508	378	414	218	25	
Madison	32,493	14,428	13,923	9,618	13	812	872	1,951		372	285	485	20	
Marion	13,501	4,195	4,195	2,648		704	732	25			86			
Marshall	27,674	7,754	7,706	1,990	95	717	1,465	2,760		355	324	48		
Monroe	31,216	14,013	13,647	6,660	432	2,420	2,178	930	274	175	578	366		
Montgomery	16,536	7,864	7,804	4,437	54	831	1,636	392	148	145	161	60		
Neshoba	12,726	3,979	3,839	2,250		615	363		303	110	198	140		
Newton	19,708	9,387	9,368	6,105	227	748	1,411		123	194	560	19		
Noxubee	30,846	13,543	13,512	7,926		2,929	1,168	1,124	153	84	128	31		
Oktibbeha	20,183	7,598	7,586	3,705	10	2,177	959	44	247	163	281		12	
Panola	29,027	11,629	11,608	6,636	25	200	1,461	2,536	236	195	319	21		
Pearl River	6,697	1,898	1,898	1,439		100	255			104				
Perry	14,682	8,064	7,816	4,711	48	626	1,508	54		488	381	248		
Pike	27,545	17,190	16,622	11,677	94	700	1,849	1,417		324	561	555	13	
Pontotoc	18,274	6,602	6,602	4,138	79	500	1,102	168	40	310	265			
Prentiss	15,788	3,579	3,579	1,208	95		1,359	256	19	80	562			
Quitman	5,435	2,133	2,133	1,472	50		140	430		6	35			
Rankin	20,955	11,353	11,353	7,927		1,000	1,952	340		97	37			
Scott	14,316	5,468	5,289	2,992		1,110	700	74	42	64	307	179		
Sharkey	12,178	4,310	4,293	3,297		190	348	373		15	70	17		
Simpson	12,800	6,714	6,714	5,546	40	26	777	30		81	214			
Smith	13,055	6,069	6,069	3,914	50	75	1,430	106		195	299			
Sunflower	16,084	4,114	3,970	1,252	19	517	841	834		47	400	144		
Tallahatchie	19,600	7,711	7,683	3,878	102	495	610	2,310	63	87	138	28		
Tate	20,618	7,304	7,304	4,015	100		1,126	1,449	78	101	435			
Tippah	12,983	4,418	4,418	1,827	40	589	966	11	94	150	741			
Tishomingo	10,124	2,544	2,544	1,103	60		861	64		60	396			
Tunica	16,479	5,283	5,283	3,838	5	55	131	1,081		43	130			
Union	16,522	6,578	6,578	4,481	45	191	1,352	63	110		336			
Warren	40,912	18,047	13,312	9,177		453	1,030	1,428		339	885	4,528	207	
Washington	49,216	15,699	14,900	10,431	65	142	614	3,081		295	272	734	65	
Wayne	12,539	4,835	4,835	2,950		424	758	53		116	534			
Webster	13,619	5,677	5,677	3,259	143	827	1,204	41	119		84			
Wilkinson	21,453	7,743	7,574	4,323	61	157	1,049	1,232		157	595	145	24	
Winston	14,124	6,205	6,190	3,507		609	1,213	187	260	30	384	15		
Yalobusha	19,742	7,588	7,500	2,118	223	765	1,755	1,306	215	411	707	88		
Yazoo	43,948	17,813	17,473	10,561	495	1,631	2,003	2,101	118	300	264	340		
County location unknown[5]		6,759	5,741	255		1,060	3,739	94	88	11	494			1,018

[1] Includes Union American Methodist Episcopal Church, African Methodist Episcopal Church, African Methodist Episcopal Zion Church, and Colored Methodist Episcopal Church.
[2] Heads of families only.
[3] New county since 1900; formed from parts of Covington and Lawrence in 1906.
[4] New county since 1900; formed from parts of Marion and Pearl River in 1904.
[5] See explanatory headnote on page 294.

TABLE 4.—POPULATION IN 1900 AND COMMUNICANTS OR MEMBERS FOR SELECTED DENOMINATIONS, FOR EACH STATE AND TERRITORY, BY COUNTIES: 1906—Continued.

MISSOURI.

COUNTY.	Population, 1900.	All denominations.	PROTESTANT BODIES.												
			Total.	Baptists—Northern, Southern, and National Conventions.	Free Baptists.	General Baptists.	Primitive Baptists.	Church of Christ, Scientist.	Congregationalists.	Disciples of Christ.	Churches of Christ.	German Evangelical Synod of N. A.	Lutheran—Synodical Conference.	Methodist Episcopal Church.	Methodist Protestant Church.
The state	3,106,665	1,199,239	802,116	198,459	5,525	9,048	4,040	2,644	11,046	159,050	7,087	32,715	41,185	80,334	4,712
Adair	21,728	7,400	38	597	154		91	17		1,573				1,376	
Andrew	17,332	5,274	[illegible]48	1,225			38			1,282				1,044	
Atchison	16,501	4,779	[illegible]622	866						809				885	30
Audrain	21,160	10,254	[illegible],459	2,326			75	23		2,210		53	25	631	
Barry	25,532	7,242	8,772	2,173	50					1,157	351		153	415	308
Barton	18,253	4,428	4,113	778	49		32		53	1,226				1,	116
Bates	30,141	9,311	8,655	1,636				28		2,605			206	1,	
Benton	16,556	5,130	5,061	1,456	33				118	424	69		1,322	115	550
Bollinger	14,650	4,721	4,080	1,079	57	665				445			74	206	
Boone	28,642	12,948	12,529	4,119	17		477			3,688	650	106		[illegible]	
Buchanan	121,838	29,513	17,894	3,251	44		25	350	324	3,454	14	862	374	1,753	
Butler	16,769	4,567	4,153	1,560	50	433	20			662			22	199	
Caldwell	16,656	5,958	5,710	877			24		203	1,181	175				176
Callaway	25,984	11,552	11,081	3,344			81			3,284		95		1,505	
Camden	13,113	3,382	3,382	1,277	65	37				1,167	175			279	201
Cape Girardeau	24,315	11,091	8,180	1,344		215				60		652	2,646		
Carroll	26,455	9,664	9,141	3,001						1,776		38	494	668	
Carter	6,706	1,455	1,455	610		316			62	65	468			969	
Cass	23,636	9,130	9,019	2,677	50		44			2,016			67	987	88
Cedar	16,923	3,916	3,705	997			15			1,108	75		179	592	
Chariton	26,826	9,970	7,608	2,195						1,923			436	625	
Christian	16,939	5,223	5,006	1,657		90			60	2,307		205	45	388	124
Clark	15,383	5,486	4,855	1,326	20				110	954		422		747	359
Clay	18,903	7,728	7,578	2,661			64			2,344				106	
Clinton	17,363	7,603	6,707	1,262	146		49		93	2,744				1,101	
Cole	20,578	11,686	6,295	1,951				18		691	57	513	891	32	
Cooper	22,532	9,146	7,722	3,032	70		21			905		494	646	163	
Crawford	12,959	1,933	1,	675						290			78	110	
Dade	18,125	4,425	4,827	996	75					913	250		299	588	
Dallas	13,903	4,881	4,[illegible]	2,146	407		175			1,561				315	
Daviess	21,325	6,7	6,785	1,735	277		45			1,690	228			811	
Dekalb	14,418	4,658	4,007	992					50	1,147				1,094	
Dent	12,986	2,327	2,276	897	9		94			480	73			172	
Douglas	16,802	2,[illegible]72	2,653	805		466				643	59			163	
Dunklin	21,706	7,[illegible]02	6,961	1,589		1,378				1,382	67				145
Franklin	30,581	15,341	7,044	1,633						746		1,578	1,109	708	
Gasconade	12,298	5,527	4,472	449			20			501		2,378	232	452	
Gentry	20,554	6,143	,81[illegible]	1,800						1,893				741	
Greene	52,713	17,627	15,017	4,265	32		68	28	740	2,480	172	190		1,735	252
Grundy	17,832	5,697	5,561	2,045						1,397	32			976	112
Harrison	24,398	7,008	6,703	1,189						2,554	102			1,453	
Henry	28,054	10,281	9,415	3,156			24		26	1,630			27	1,351	
Hickory	9,985	2,430	2,346	1,028	58		15			754				51	75
Holt	17,083	4,674	4,487	251						1,586			353	772	
Howard	18,337	8,234	7,540	1,901						2,477		75		590	
Howell	21,834	5,324	4,715	1,397		199	33		53	1,150	25			460	
Iron	8,716	2,045	1,604	329		93	9			130			84	204	
Jackson	195,193	74,623	50,621	12,442	17		146	1,273	2,062	9,390	143	728	366	6,506	
Jasper	84,018	18,631	16,818	2,936	56		41	179	340	3,945	33		160	3,766	169
Jefferson	25,712	9,793	5,568	1,420	58				154	354		609	688	492	
Johnson	27,843	10,750	9,625	2,538			14			1,943				1,200	20
Knox	13,479	7,834	3,555	898			29			1,030				741	
Laclede	16,523	4,799	4,416	1,205	630				226	737				861	30
Lafayette	31,679	13,888	12,829	2,402	25		16	15		1,806	220	1,376	2,312	799	
Lawrence	31,662	9,941	8,581	2,573			11		386	1,838	79	236	439	930	177
Lewis	16,724	8,967		3,072						1,463		51	274	315	
Lincoln	18,352	9,045	,	1,965			37			1,661		416		720	
Linn	25,503	9,003	,	1,842			105		150	1,562	366			1,743	
Livingston	22,302	7,525	7,076	1,590					85	1,038	108			833	
McDonald	13,574	2,665	[illegible]	1,030	66		25			682	46			167	
Macon	33,018	12,	10,	3,023			252		341	1,965			116	706	
Madison	9,975	4,	3,	1,181	332	111	3			484			37	125	
Maries	9,616	3,085	2,	602						1,108	122	21	39	44	
Marion	26,331	13,000	10,029	3,233			15		181	1,950			1,088	500	
Mercer	14,706	3,[illegible]	3,[illegible]	1,085						1,413				731	388
Miller	15,187	5,716	4,	1,929		397	31		138	1,540				415	
Mississippi	11,837	5,320	4,	1,113	134	23				813	109				
Moniteau	15,931	6,094	5,	1,890			11			1,197	98	617	144	392	
Monroe	19,716	10,739	8,700	2,462			106			3,195					
Montgomery	16,571	6,770	5,[illegible]	1,292			50			849		109	122	746	
Morgan	12,175	3,904	3,	1,549			47			364		126	262	188	
New Madrid	11,280	3,919	3,	497	451	184									
Newton	27,001	6,609	6,	1,932	112		86		182	1,246	600	46		438	50
Nodaway	32,938	11,164	8,836	893			33	12		2,624	70			2,707	100
Oregon	13,906	3,811	3,[illegible]	689	332	70	26		47	636	118		55	125	

TABLE 4.—POPULATION IN 1900 AND COMMUNICANTS OR MEMBERS FOR SELECTED DENOMINATIONS, FOR EACH STATE AND TERRITORY, BY COUNTIES: 1906—Continued.

MISSOURI—Continued.

COUNTY.	Population, 1900.	All denominations.	PROTESTANT BODIES. Total.	Baptists—Northern, Southern, and National Conventions.	Free Baptists.	General Baptists.	Primitive Baptists.	Church of Christ, Scientist.	Congregationalists.	Disciples of Christ.	Churches of Christ.	German Evangelical Synod of N. A.	Lutheran—Synodical Conference.	Methodist Episcopal Church.	Methodist Protestant Church.
Osage	14,096	9,383	2,888	703			11		29	634		464	276	187	
Ozark	12,145	1,881	1,881	389		1,011	4		38	150				141	
Pemiscot	12,115	3,429	2,237	1,120						90					
Perry	15,134	11,538	3,652	198	14					55			2,462	54	
Pettis	32,438	13,025	11,615	2,380	60		40	16	576	2,235	20	356	180	2,407	
Phelps	14,194	3,194	2,688	766			52			1,080			92	320	
Pike	25,744	9,829	9,169	3,377			22			1,657				732	
Platte	16,193	5,905	5,579	1,250						2,254		86	85	150	
Polk	23,255	7,248	7,025	3,781			47			1,020			19	643	272
Pulaski	10,394	3,429	3,395	1,133			8			1,276	40			403	
Putnam	16,688	3,735	3,630	651	124		18			974	442			610	200
Ralls	12,287	5,192	4,578	1,069			37			2,375				94	
Randolph	24,442	12,607	10,264	3,117						2,531	93		53	372	
Ray	24,805	7,598	7,429	1,587			303			1,329	80	40		52	
Reynolds	8,161	2,080	2,080	1,165		66				110	20				
Ripley	13,186	4,703	4,123	1,161	10	304	38			672	479				
St. Charles	24,474	15,391	6,454	287						125		1,923	2,319	234	
St. Clair	17,907	5,682	5,476	1,739			45			1,331		450	173	659	30
St. Francois	24,051	11,041	7,275	1,738	450				113	600	149		349	795	
St. Louis	50,040	24,231	10,943	1,207				60	664	259		2,632	2,375	398	
St. Louis city	575,238	302,531	89,121	10,778	165			625	3,442	4,940	30	12,928	15,613	6,889	
Ste. Genevieve	10,359	7,158	725	282						54			60	6	
Saline	33,703	13,792	12,023	2,891	412		50			2,301		308	603	848	
Schuyler	10,840	2,932	2,899	507	139					1,195	30			505	
Scotland	13,232	4,810	4,782	887						1,365	50			906	139
Scott	13,092	8,216	3,637	1,004	50	410				213			250		
Shannon	11,247	1,806	1,792	834	58		15			387				75	
Shelby	16,167	7,378	6,730	1,802			41			1,554			81	534	
Stoddard	24,669	6,913	6,389	1,381		1,477	123			1,255	37	25		535	
Stone	9,892	2,319	2,319	347			62			1,191	95			137	70
Sullivan	20,282	4,689	4,440	883			4			864	150			1,036	141
Taney	10,127	1,851	1,851	292		615				695	32			28	
Texas	22,192	4,525	4,440	1,865			35			1,390	50			357	
Vernon	31,619	8,573	8,075	2,153			12			1,729			65	805	5
Warren	9,919	3,451	2,762	163			34			60		1,507		574	
Washington	14,263	6,363	2,423	626	84					376				225	
Wayne	15,309	4,523	4,423	1,755		443	18			1,125			90		
Webster	16,640	5,179	5,062	1,309		45	128			1,349	154		176	335	385
Worth	9,832	2,084	1,955	503	20		69			511				392	
Wright	17,519	4,136	4,031	1,517			103			1,362				474	
County location unknown[1]		2,594	2,432	24	63		98							858	

COUNTY.	PROTESTANT BODIES—continued. Methodist Episcopal Church, South.	African Methodists.[2]	Presbyterian Church in the U. S. A.	Cumberland Presbyterian Church.	Presbyterian Church in the U. S.	Protestant Episcopal Church.	United Brethren in Christ.	Other Protestant bodies.	Roman Catholic Church.	Jewish congregations.[3]	Greek Orthodox Church.	Latter-day Saints (Reorganized).	All other bodies.
The state	112,058	15,063	25,991	28,637	14,713	13,328	3,321	33,160	382,642	2,392	2,455	7,880	1,754
Adair	507	52	285	373		70	313	130	1,862				
Andrew	506	65	292	191		40		465	109			17	
Atchison	431		358	269	56	32		886	157				
Audrain	1,532	196		589	635	75		89	1,795				
Barry	398		218	393		16		140	1,470				
Barton	249		30	288	73	25	36	43	234			6	75
Bates	1,157	20	471	441		29	238	618	510			146	
Benton	397		56		33		26	548	69				
Bollinger	906		166					307	641				
Boone	2,062	337		75	388	95		230	419				
Buchanan	2,583	500	723	810	989	765		1,073	10,574	240	70	627	108
Butler	623	211	135	85		36		117	414				
Caldwell	670	68	398			8	190	235	106			142	
Callaway	2,577	102		22	1,255	41	62		471				
Camden	106		24		47		25	86					
Cape Girardeau	1,326	454			587	85		143	2,894				17
Carroll	2,048	130	122	92		4		72	523				
Carter	275												
Cass	1,448	40	330	426	135	61	87	563	111				
Cedar	410		74	126				69				211	

[1] See explanatory headnote on page 294.
[2] Includes African Methodist Episcopal Church, African Methodist Episcopal Zion Church, and Colored Methodist Episcopal Church.
[3] Heads of families only.

TABLE 4.—POPULATION IN 1900 AND COMMUNICANTS OR MEMBERS FOR SELECTED DENOMINATIONS, FOR EACH STATE AND TERRITORY, BY COUNTIES: 1906—Continued.

MISSOURI—Continued.

COUNTY.	PROTESTANT BODIES—continued.								Roman Catholic Church.	Jewish congregations.[2]	Greek Orthodox Church.	Latter-day Saints (Reorganized).	All other bodies.
	Methodist Episcopal Church, South.	African Methodists.[1]	Presbyterian Church in the U. S. A.	Cumberland Presbyterian Church.	Presbyterian Church in the U. S.	Protestant Episcopal Church.	United Brethren in Christ.	Other Protestant bodies.					
Charlton	1,404	297		363	160	6	90	109	2,362				
Christian	75				14			41	217				
Clark	425	31		161	175			125	631				
Clay	1,149	110		88	381	14		661	150				
Clinton	525	87	151	225	135	32		157	839			57	
Cole	806	247	155	225		75		634	5,285	6	100		
Cooper	863	270		970	211	55		22	1,424				
Crawford	454		80	112		23		5	106				
Dade	361		149	671				123					
Dallas	172		22				14	69					
Daviess	1,296	75	35	405			72	116					
Dekalb	404		40	207	33			40	85			566	
Dent	369			102			42	38	51				
Douglas								517	19			200	
Dunklin	2,016			182	156			46	441				
Franklin	513	185	313	102	123	17		17	8,297				
Gasconade	82		231					127	1,055				
Gentry	521		299	297			56	201	327				
Greene	1,894	99	918	1,105	108			496	2,304			182	124
Grundy	270	60	164	74		[illegible]	212	189	120			16	
Harrison	425	5	97	257			265	356	156			149	
Henry	1,768		366	825	65		23	112	866				
Hickory	135						23	207				84	
Holt	247		623	123			163	369	140			47	
Howard	1,879	257	60	167		[illegible]		110	694				
Howell	553		141	351				322	485			124	
Iron	385		75		21			230	441				
Jackson	4,520	1,851	2,592	1,255	1,644	2,[illegible]		3,326	20,339	345	750	2,295	273
Jasper	1,756	65	1,336	517		31	179	1,032	1,275			415	123
Jefferson	1,090	158	211		160	[illegible]		4	4,225				
Johnson	1,175	138	375	1,755				421	491			634	
Knox	544	15	93	47			25	133	4,279				
Laclede	337	15	64	178				98	383				
Lafayette	1,826	510		691	713	46		78	1,069				
Lawrence	271		212	1,375		[illegible]		34	1,360				
Lewis	1,528	47	126		161	40			1,891				
Lincoln	1,623	65		322	150			75	2,011				
Linn	1,011	21	441	133		1	253	252	983				
Livingston	1,553	110	230	101		1	39	152	1,579				
McDonald	517			94		[illegible]		38					
Macon	1,124	215	288	1,306		106	53	512	1,827			229	
Madison	768	54	80			45		312	468				
Maries	168								1,459				
Marion	1,541	410	537	40	166	262		196	3,462				
Mercer	61						94	111					
Miller	78				63				1,016				
Mississippi	1,462	310		75	15			89	1,266				
Moniteau	483		96	81	120			165	911				
Monroe	1,700	83		335	590	103			2,165				
Montgomery	1,438	25		626	177	13		73	1,250				
Morgan	555		51	158		7	46		68				
New Madrid	1,135	499		40	85				690				
Newton	937	30	157	240					273				
Nodaway	1,345	81	612					483	2,374			232	
Oregon	809			45		[illegible]		[illegible]	224			79	
Osage	487	17	80						6,412			83	
Ozark								148					
Pemiscot	633	145						181	1,192				
Perry	244							458	7,886				
Pettis	1,517	349	422	321	[illegible]	242		279	1,350		60		
Phelps	161		99			94			506				
Pike	894	398	58	1,833		132			660				
Platte	878	182	450	189		15			269			57	
Polk	608		94	485				24	223				
Pulaski	412				[illegible]			[illegible]	34				
Putnam			76				243	292	106				
Ralls	457	41		96	225			185	614				
Randolph	2,482	255	220	1,036		65		40	2,134			209	
Ray	2,263	312		120	308	15		1,020	80			89	
Reynolds	339							380					
Ripley	1,200			247					565			15	
St. Charles	801	225	110		361	69			8,937				
St. Clair	244		306	75			78		65			141	
St. Francois	2,443	74	33	23	255			12	3,766				
St. Louis	1,180	198	857		169	821		[illegible]	13,288				

[1] Includes African Methodist Episcopal Church, African Methodist Episcopal Zion Church, and Colored Methodist Episcopal Church.
[2] Heads of families only.

Table 4.—POPULATION IN 1900 AND COMMUNICANTS OR MEMBERS FOR SELECTED DENOMINATIONS, FOR EACH STATE AND TERRITORY, BY COUNTIES: 1906—Continued.

MISSOURI—Continued.

COUNTY.	PROTESTANT BODIES—continued.								Roman Catholic Church.	Jewish congregations.[2]	Greek Orthodox Church.	Latter-day Saints (Reorganized).	All other bodies.
	Methodist Episcopal Church, South.	African Methodists.[1]	Presbyterian Church in the U. S. A.	Cumberland Presbyterian Church.	Presbyterian Church in the U. S.	Protestant Episcopal Church.	United Brethren in Christ.	Other Protestant bodies.					
St. Louis city	8,281	3,880	7,222	692	1,469	5,590		6,577	208,775	1,801	1,475	487	872
Ste. Genevieve	96	45			17			165	6,433				
Saline	2,429	201	59	897	739	54		231	1,769				
Schuyler	160			133				230	33				
Scotland	445	10		509	230		176	63	28				
Scott	1,616	43						51	4,579				
Shannon	320							53	14				
Shelby	2,047	69	139		72	4		319	648				
Stoddard	1,258			166				126	524				
Stone			52	125			7	233					
Sullivan	712	10	227				8	405	249				
Taney	30				96			63					
Texas	565			33				145	85				
Vernon	2,113	26	259	336	51	93	120	308	285			213	
Warren	383	33			8				689				
Washington	746			54	263			49	3,940				
Wayne	818			58	47			69	100				
Webster	773		25	130		3		250	117				
Worth	136		103	60				161	43			86	
Wright	130			340		21		84	63			42	
County location unknown [3]	1,200						63	126					162

[1] Includes African Methodist Episcopal Church, African Methodist Episcopal Zion Church, and Colored Methodist Episcopal Church.
[2] Heads of families only.
[3] See explanatory headnote on page 294.

MONTANA.

COUNTY.	Population, 1900.	All denominations.	PROTESTANT BODIES.								Roman Catholic Church.	Jewish congregations.[2]	Servian Orthodox Church.	All other bodies.
			Total.	Baptists—Northern Convention.	Disciples of Christ.	Lutheran—Norwegian Synods.[1]	Methodist Episcopal Church.	Presbyterian Church in the U. S. A.	Protestant Episcopal Church.	Other Protestant bodies.				
The state	243,329	98,984	24,156	2,029	2,008	1,865	5,819	4,096	3,290	5,049	72,359	152	1,500	817
Beaverhead	5,615	935	402	89		100	12	93	108		533			
Broadwater	2,641	1,745	130				66		34	30	1,615			
Carbon	7,533	1,066	641		95	146	187		90	123	425			
Cascade	25,777	8,808	2,286	224	135	183	508	370	272	594	6,508			14
Chouteau	10,966	4,740	550			21	210	188	128	3	4,190			
Custer	7,891	1,005	586		20	184	130	162	86	4	372			47
Dawson	2,443	629	369			100	155	12	63	39	260			
Deer Lodge	17,393	9,572	1,335	89	147	204	300	212	150	233	8,075			162
Fergus	6,937	1,631	790	26	60	29	343	195	119	18	841			
Flathead	9,375	4,113	1,775	85	176	301	579	261	131	242	2,338			
Gallatin	9,553	3,306	1,874	194	424	25	183	453	151	444	1,299			133
Granite	4,328	624	295			60	87	94	45	9	329			
Jefferson	5,330	1,123	401		70		158	45	60	68	722			
Lewis and Clark	19,171	5,486	2,428	216	156	90	405	295	356	910	2,989	57		12
Madison	7,695	912	436	3			114	67	235	17	476			
Meagher	2,526	129	129			53		28	18	30				
Missoula	13,964	5,347	1,607	181	143	70	337	286	230	360	3,740			
Park	7,341	1,736	814	58	19	45	275		116	301	922			
Powell	([3])	971	279		50		15	87	54	73	596			96
Ravalli	7,822	1,292	1,253	161	141		263	211	74	403				39
Rosebud	([4])	2,530	88				28	37	18	5	2,442			
Sanders	([5])	73	73		11		26			36				
Silver Bow	47,635	32,046	3,498	531	204		961	677	501	624	26,639	95	1,500	314
Sweet Grass	3,086	360	232			45	40		35	112	128			
Teton	[illegible]	2,275	289			149	70	25	20	25	1,986			
Valley	[illegible]	1,501	349			30	105	160	36	18	1,152			
Yellowstone	[illegible]	4,392	1,247	172	157	30	262	138	160	328	3,145			
Crow Indian reservation	2,660	637									637			

[1] Includes United Norwegian Lutheran Church in America and Synod for the Norwegian Evangelical Lutheran Church in America.
[2] Heads of families only.
[3] New county since 1900; formed from part of Deer Lodge in 1901.
[4] New county since 1900; formed from parts of Custer county and Crow Indian reservation in 1901.
[5] New county since 1900; formed from part of Missoula in 1906.

TABLE 4.—POPULATION IN 1900 AND COMMUNICANTS OR MEMBERS FOR SELECTED DENOMINATIONS, FOR EACH STATE AND TERRITORY, BY COUNTIES: 1906—Continued.

NEBRASKA.

COUNTY.	Population, 1900.	All denominations.	PROTESTANT BODIES.												
			Total.	Seventh-day Adventists.	Baptists—Northern Convention.	Congregationalists.	Disciples of Christ.	Evangelical Association.	United Evangelical Church.	German Evangelical Synod of N. A.	Lutheran—General Synod.	Lutheran—General Council.	Lutheran—Synodical Conference.	Lutheran—Synod of Iowa, etc.	Lutheran—United Danish Church.
The state	1,066,300	345,803	240,516	2,415	16,895	16,629	19,121	3,200	2,992	3,882	12,807	7,303	25,730	6,859	2,120
Adams	18,840	7,481	6,041	29	598	412	394	116	269		526		766		
Antelope	11,344	2,735	2,012	32		472				120			145		
Banner	1,114	50	50		24										
Blaine	603	166	141			61	20				30				
Boone	11,689	5,173	2,956	28	276	335						50		154	
Boxbutte	5,572	1,836	1,318	42	237	54	56						83		
Boyd	7,332	2,270	1,392		93	227	35					106	321	44	
Brown	3,470	829	783		49	162							125		
Buffalo	20,254	6,125	4,900	87	284	160	331	4	240		595	76	692		
Burt	13,040	3,466	3,107	75	496		80				80	572	191		17
Butler	15,703	7,444	2,806		224	326	512				230		237		
Cass	21,330	6,329	5,137		227	403	1,090	300	20	150	335		441		60
Cedar	12,467	5,381	1,996	27	117	30	30				60	27	81	208	15
Chase	2,559	370	291										22		
Cherry	6,541	1,236	595										51		
Cheyenne	5,570	1,009	759		26						76	17	65	35	50
Clay	15,735	7,006	6,262	23	186	773	1,201	357	84	117	90	225			22
Colfax	11,211	5,060	1,921			149	20				418		345		19
Cuming	14,584	4,855	2,897		65	135		72		47	586		1,473		70
Custer	19,758	5,298	4,229	89	687	96	583	60	299				41		58
Dakota	6,286	2,042	828								347				15
Dawes	6,215	1,556	1,126	40	165	237	40								
Dawson	12,214	4,444	3,832	24	276	55	599	49	232		117		67	200	
Deuel	2,630	379	331					17			36	50	63		
Dixon	10,535	4,278	3,085		141	103	173				411	463	458		
Dodge	22,298	7,635	5,730	36	415	520	433	68			1,234	114	918		123
Douglas	140,590	44,740	20,595	174	2,344	1,262	1,331	50	75	128	782	832	985	250	100
Dundy	2,434	497	441												
Fillmore	15,087	4,896	3,522	15	126	569	318		33		310	233	137		
Franklin	9,455	3,170	2,142		47	427	106		32		201		238	316	
Frontier	8,781	1,631	1,413	25		112			45				82	234	
Furnas	12,373	3,218	2,806	78	201	131	623		50		27		307		
Gage	30,051	9,949	8,732	70	655	404	1,101		224	46	141		537	917	
Garfield	2,127	576	436		22	90	110								
Gosper	5,301	927	927				79						172	236	
Grant	763	54	28			20									
Greeley	5,691	2,902	856	11				35			63	141	65		23
Hall	17,206	4,607	3,513	48	451	226	216	177	78		403		300		
Hamilton	13,330	4,431	4,180	23	200	203	267		76	49	72	170	797		150
Harlan	9,370	2,375	1,893	40	170	106	136	40	209		110	69	40	61	
Hayes	2,708	267	169		14	39							29		
Hitchcock	4,409	1,061	908	45		153	173	82					11		
Holt	12,224	3,824	1,610		88	25		50					115	63	
Hooker	432	38	29												
Howard	10,343	4,870	1,691	16	44								276		130
Jefferson	15,196	5,247	5,009		441	98	870	64		375			691	334	
Johnson	11,197	4,065	3,419	16	445		292			34	130		493	487	
Kearney	9,866	2,701	2,288	16	167	50	103					584	159		
Keith	1,951	569	455		7	103					54		91		
Keyapaha	3,076	471	343		50	42							28		
Kimball	758	84	84									10			
Knox	14,343	4,146	2,968		71	433	34	89			100	402	459	185	15
Lancaster	64,835	26,926	19,680	751	1,097	2,670	1,620	136	49	295	1,074	174	1,102	111	154
Lincoln	11,416	2,386	1,946	49	183	34	125				266		88		
Logan	960	208	119												
Loup	1,305	97	97			97									
McPherson	517	76	76	23											
Madison	16,976	6,230	4,790	19	230	355	50	124			156	252	1,744		
Merrick	9,255	2,735	2,373		203	140	135	144			45		25		
Nance	8,222	2,169	1,513			49			224					64	34
Nemaha	14,952	4,184	3,903		348		721		9		339		47	739	
Nuckolls	12,414	3,897	3,023		129	13	322	87			93		39	150	400
Otoe	22,288	7,671	5,636	69	404	167	416			1,252	355			1,184	
Pawnee	11,770	3,717	3,114		340		288			221	60				
Perkins	1,702	260	260			93							44		
Phelps	10,772	3,050	3,006	28	169	265	65					817	34		
Pierce	8,445	2,734	2,163		133	166		[illegible]	43		116		914	230	15
Platte	17,747	9,877	4,173		528	195		21		71	650	335	1,035		54
Polk	10,542	2,811	2,280		309							572	36		
Redwillow	9,604	2,573	1,799	73		363	160		35				184		
Richardson	19,614	6,086	4,566	15	285	145	874	260	512	120	415		190		
Rock	2,809	317	317			31							16		
Saline	18,252	5,215	3,750		381	744	152	76		211	59		380		
Sarpy	9,080	1,724	1,251		12	100							412		
Saunders	22,085	8,037	4,888		417	273	452	155		36	219	855	157	170	220

TABLE 4.—POPULATION IN 1900 AND COMMUNICANTS OR MEMBERS FOR SELECTED DENOMINATIONS, FOR EACH STATE AND TERRITORY, BY COUNTIES: 1906—Continued.

NEBRASKA.

COUNTY.	Population, 1900.	All denominations.	PROTESTANT BODIES. Total.	Seventh-day Adventists.	Baptists—Northern Convention.	Congregationalists.	Disciples of Christ.	Evangelical Association.	United Evangelical Church.	German Evangelical Synod of N. A.	Lutheran—General Synod.	Lutheran—General Council.	Lutheran—Synodical Conference.	Lutheran—Synod of Iowa, etc.	Lutheran—United Danish Church.
Scotts Bluff	2,552	916	773		40		148								
Seward	15,690	5,067	4,625	28	11	213	192	244	77	468			1,928	133	107
Sheridan	6,033	1,314	776	25		85	39							27	
Sherman	6,550	2,216	915	12	83		140	20		12			215		
Sioux	2,055	504	180												
Stanton	6,959	1,683	1,369		86	129		56			82		548		
Thayer	14,325	5,910	5,484		121	29	645				111		1,255	282	35
Thomas	628	47	47			47									
Thurston	6,517	590	476								240				
Valley	7,339	2,971	1,942	61	204	80	102	80							18
Washington	13,086	3,358	3,157	82	307	170	425	67			234				112
Wayne	9,862	2,832	2,454	21	237	90		36		130	269		[illegible]		20
Webster	11,619	2,874	2,670	43	164	210	308	39			233		382	45	75
Wheeler	1,362	130	130	7							17				
York	18,205	6,386	5,622		253	473	386		68		210	157	712		
County location unknown [1]		256	191												

COUNTY.	PROTESTANT BODIES—continued. Methodist Episcopal Church.	Presbyterian Church in the U. S. A.	United Presbyterian Church.	Protestant Episcopal Church.	Reformed Church in the U. S.	Swedish Evangelical Mission Covenant.	United Brethren in Christ.	Other Protestant bodies.	Roman Catholic Church.	Jewish congregations.[2]	Greek Orthodox Church.	Latter-day Saints (Reorganized).	All other bodies.
The state	62,586	20,684	2,459	6,903	1,616	1,625	6,045	18,645	100,763	435	1,985	1,503	601
Adams	1,426	837		181			249	238	1,440				
Antelope	635	109	67	62			301	69	649			74	
Banner	15						11						
Blaine	30								25				
Boone	1,021	185		110				797	2,217				
Boxbutte	642	85	47	72					518				
Boyd	224	45						297	878				
Brown	360			27			51	9	46				
Buffalo	1,132	478	78	111			438	194	1,105				120
Burt	887	480		40		141		46	225			34	
Butler	1,232							45	4,638				
Cass	1,268	238	40	76		29	279	181	1,192				
Cedar	649	444		73	40		60	135	3,385				
Chase	152	17					78	22	79				
Cherry	410	85		49					641				
Cheyenne	283	45		105			47	10	250				
Clay	1,671	320		23	587			583	710			34	
Colfax	260	593		97				20	3,139				
Cuming	166	65		12		50		156	1,968				
Custer	1,255	162		132			341	426	1,069				
Dakota	273	51						142	1,214				
Dawes	425	41		132				46	394			36	
Dawson	1,326	425		75			46	341	612				
Deuel	154							11	48				
Dixon	492	278				43		523	1,193				
Dodge	1,119	399	236	64				51	1,872		25		
Douglas	3,763	3,607	666	2,406	36	335		1,470	21,440	335	1,900	390	80
Dundy	183		78	11				169	56				
Fillmore	1,252	127		48			154	200	1,374				
Franklin	597	118		31			20	9	986			42	
Frontier	699			15				201	145			73	
Furnas	787	213	69	53			19	239	412				
Gage	2,2[illegible]5	668	36	267			377	1,074	1,217				
Garfield	211			3					140				
Gosper	219						67	154					
Grant	8								26				
Greeley	383	71		8				56	2,046				
Hall	896	415		145			55	103	1,085			59	
Hamilton	802	306				155	415	495	251				
Harlan	504	146		6			44	203	482				
Hayes							61	26	98				
Hitchcock	293	33					20	68	153				
Holt	644	427	66	36				87	2,149			65	
Hooker	29								9				
Howard	288	220		34			137	537	3,179				
Jefferson	1,258	325			93		255	150	238				
Johnson	1,049	225		[illegible]			150	78	646				
Kearney	702	269	117				8	113	413				
Keith	176			24					114				
Keyapaha	163							60	128				

[1] See explanatory headnote on page 294.

[2] Heads of families only.

TABLE 4.—POPULATION IN 1900 AND COMMUNICANTS OR MEMBERS FOR SELECTED DENOMINATIONS, FOR EACH STATE AND TERRITORY, BY COUNTIES: 1906—Continued.

NEBRASKA—Continued.

COUNTY.	PROTESTANT BODIES—continued.								Roman Catholic Church.	Jewish congregations.[1]	Greek Orthodox Church.	Latter-day Saints (Reorganized).	All other bodies.
	Methodist Episcopal Church.	Presbyterian Church in the U. S. A.	United Presbyterian Church.	Protestant Episcopal Church.	Reformed Church in the U. S.	Swedish Evangelical Mission Covenant.	United Brethren in Christ.	Other Protestant bodies.					
Kimball	60	....	....	14	....	....	....	....	....	....	....	....	....
Knox	465	33	....	466	....	....	39	177	1,178	....	....	....	....
Lancaster	5,733	1,876	121	428	353	124	281	1,531	6,758	100	60	....	328
Lincoln	459	287	....	200	....	80	....	175	440	....	....	....	....
Logan	36	55	....	....	....	....	....	28	89	....	....	....	....
Loup	....	....	....	....	....	....	....	....	....	....	....	....	....
McPherson	....	....	....	....	....	....	....	53	....	....	....	....	....
Madison	905	121	....	137	....	....	51	646	1,383	....	....	57	..
Merrick	911	298	....	123	....	....	....	349	362	....	....	....	....
Nance	700	259	....	30	....	....	....	153	656	....	....	....	....
Nemaha	1,139	190	....	30	....	....	50	291	281	....	....	....	....
Nuckolls	902	291	183	....	....	....	188	226	874	....	....	....	....
Otoe	929	282	50	122	....	....	20	386	1,826	....	....	209	....
Pawnee	1,013	389	580	....	40	....	169	14	603	....	....	....	....
Perkins	94	....	....	....	....	....	....	29	....	....	....	....	....
Phelps	714	181	....	....	....	117	....	616	44	....	....	....	....
Pierce	442	79	....	....	....	....	....	....	571	....	....	....	....
Platte	595	207	....	197	86	....	18	182	5,687	....	....	17	....
Polk	746	84	....	38	....	104	132	169	531	....	....	....	....
Redwillow	810	39	....	48	....	....	30	57	774	....	....	....	....
Richardson	769	283	....	78	148	....	61	411	1,820	....	....	....	....
Rock	156	....	....	28	....	....	....	86	....	....	....	....	....
Saline	1,416	....	....	40	....	....	233	58	1,268	....	....	197	....
Sarpy	432	183	....	18	....	....	....	94	473	....	....	....	....
Saunders	807	398	....	78	50	422	47	132	3,149	....	....	....	....
Scotts Bluff	368	175	....	30	....	....	....	12	93	....	....	50	....
Seward	629	309	....	....	....	....	71	215	442	....	....	....	....
Sheridan	407	136	25	10	....	....	....	22	538	....	....	....	....
Sherman	139	162	....	7	....	....	57	68	1,301	....	....	....	....
Sioux	118	55	....	7	....	....	....	....	324	....	....	....	....
Stanton	375	....	....	....	69	....	....	24	314	....	....	....	....
Thayer	1,237	478	....	....	....	25	....	1,266	426	....	....	....	....
Thomas	....	....	....	....	....	....	....	....	....	....	....	....	....
Thurston	121	115	....	....	....	....	....	....	114	....	....	....	....
Valley	505	200	....	7	....	....	120	513	998	....	....	31	....
Washington	586	118	....	67	....	....	....	82	166	....	....	35	....
Wayne	594	230	....	....	51	....	....	118	378	....	....	....	....
Webster	867	90	....	26	....	....	24	164	204	....	....	....	....
Wheeler	82	....	....	....	....	....	....	24	....	....	....	....	....
York	1,599	529	....	33	64	....	747	391	764	....	....	....	....
County location unknown[2]	118	....	....	....	....	....	24	49	....	....	....	....	65

[1] Heads of families only.

[2] See explanatory headnote on page 294.

NEVADA.

COUNTY.	Population, 1900.	All denominations.	PROTESTANT BODIES.									Roman Catholic Church.	Greek Orthodox Church.	Church of Jesus Christ of Latter-day Saints.
			Total.	Baptists—Northern Convention.	Congregationalists.	Disciples of Christ.	Lutheran—Synodical Conference.	Methodist Episcopal Church.	Presbyterian Church in the U. S. A.	Protestant Episcopal Church.	Other Protestant bodies.			
The state	42,335	14,944	3,199	316	180	100	148	618	520	1,210	107	9,970	670	1,106
Churchill	830	110	110	13	....	....	....	54	....	25	18	....	....	....
Douglas	1,534	148	148	....	....	....	136	12	....	....	....	....	....	....
Elko	5,688	263	263	....	....	....	....	....	176	87	....	....	....	....
Esmeralda	1,972	4,063	238	....	....	....	....	28	120	82	8	3,825	....	....
Eureka	1,954	767	52	....	....	....	....	....	17	35	....	595	120	....
Humboldt	4,463	630	83	....	....	....	....		....	20	....	547	....	....
Lander	1,534	75	75	....	....	....	....		....	55	....	....	....	....
Lincoln	3,284	888	44	....	....	....	....		7	11	....	....	....	844
Lyon	2,268	103	103	....	....	....	....		....	35	....	....	....	....
Nye	1,140	3,432	160	19	....	....	....	63 [illegible]	59	80	2	3,272	....	....
Ormsby	2,893	805	264	....	....	....	....		84	120	....	541	....	....
Storey	3,673	495	155	....	....	....	....		25	100	....	340	....	....
Washoe	9,141	1,614	1,464	284	180	100	12	2	32	520	79	....	150	....
White Pine	1,961	1,551	40	....	....	....	....	60 [illegible]	....	40	....	850	400	261

TABLE 4.—POPULATION IN 1900 AND COMMUNICANTS OR MEMBERS FOR SELECTED DENOMINATIONS, FOR EACH STATE AND TERRITORY, BY COUNTIES: 1906—Continued.

NEW HAMPSHIRE.

COUNTY.	Population, 1900.	All denominations.	PROTESTANT BODIES. Total.	Baptists—Northern and National Conventions.	Free Baptists.	Congregationalists.	Methodist Episcopal Church.	Protestant Episcopal Church.	Unitarians.	Other Protestant bodies.	Roman Catholic Church.	Jewish congregations.[1]	Greek Orthodox Church.	All other bodies.
The state	411,588	190,298	64,264	9,741	6,210	19,070	12,529	4,892	3,629	8,193	119,863	80	5,210	881
Belknap	19,526	8,171	3,828	467	1,369	833	618	180	100	261	4,293	......	50	......
Carroll	16,895	3,502	2,150	60	465	524	511	134	40	416	1,352	......	......	......
Cheshire	31,321	15,556	6,274	788	......	2,364	957	277	1,324	564	9,262	......	20	......
Coos	29,468	13,144	2,725	159	166	582	1,022	407	......	389	10,419	......	......	......
Grafton	40,844	13,111	6,652	575	735	2,244	2,042	477	214	365	6,423	......	......	36
Hillsboro	112,640	73,169	15,631	3,331	234	4,935	2,338	1,043	739	3,011	52,594	80	4,500	364
Merrimack	52,430	19,585	9,241	1,847	978	2,495	1,409	923	414	1,175	9,772	......	150	422
Rockingham	51,118	17,481	8,995	1,348	696	2,845	1,777	686	402	1,241	8,446	......	40	......
Strafford	39,337	19,556	5,302	409	1,567	1,235	895	439	175	582	13,745	......	450	59
Sullivan	18,009	7,023	3,466	757	......	1,013	960	326	221	189	3,557	......	......	......

[1] Heads of families only.

NEW JERSEY.

COUNTY.	Population, 1900.	All denominations.	PROTESTANT BODIES. Total.	Baptists—Northern and National Conventions.	Congregationalists.	Lutheran—General Council.	Methodist Episcopal Church.	Presbyterian Church in the U. S. A.	Protestant Episcopal Church.	Reformed Church in America.	Other Protestant bodies.	Roman Catholic Church.	Jewish congregations.[1]	All other bodies.
The state	1,883,669	857,548	407,430	64,238	8,460	15,323	106,505	78,490	53,921	32,290	48,203	441,432	4,603	4,083
Atlantic	46,402	19,005	11,645	2,169	19	273	3,708	1,499	1,155	......	2,822	7,153	200	7
Bergen	78,441	28,974	17,294	1,539	267	219	2,029	2,548	3,407	4,200	3,085	11,496	......	184
Burlington	58,241	20,677	15,587	3,580	......	346	5,165	1,429	2,575	......	2,492	5,090	......	......
Camden	107,643	41,715	25,375	5,504	......	1,291	10,014	2,956	2,704	......	2,906	16,300	40	......
Cape May	13,201	5,597	4,906	1,164	10	66	2,814	533	145	......	174	341	350	......
Cumberland	51,193	17,886	15,180	2,974	79	306	6,940	2,456	428	......	1,997	2,577	129	......
Essex	359,053	177,497	74,988	11,887	4,406	1,985	12,526	18,892	12,467	5,758	7,067	99,680	1,144	1,685
Gloucester	31,905	9,915	8,450	985	......	90	4,384	979	588	......	1,424	1,465	......	......
Hudson	386,048	186,907	45,736	4,940	1,439	5,739	7,493	4,070	9,087	6,639	6,329	138,546	1,068	1,557
Hunterdon	34,507	13,245	11,310	1,890	......	......	3,448	3,209	266	1,502	995	1,935	......	......
Mercer	95,365	49,650	24,306	4,186	31	1,738	6,188	6,530	2,519	......	3,114	24,944	400	......
Middlesex	79,762	47,408	16,939	2,769	147	485	3,169	3,856	2,398	1,721	2,394	30,231	38	200
Monmouth	82,057	32,946	22,376	5,327	251	84	8,658	2,833	1,722	1,511	1,990	10,365	205	......
Morris	65,156	26,888	15,419	1,206	296	135	4,766	5,662	2,285	486	583	11,469	......	......
Ocean	19,747	6,601	5,736	748	......	......	3,439	872	553	......	124	840	25	......
Passaic	155,202	72,861	26,816	3,673	309	856	4,546	3,258	3,496	5,436	5,242	44,924	731	390
Salem	25,530	9,117	8,258	2,678	......	......	3,692	656	248	......	1,584	741	118	......
Somerset	32,948	14,877	10,017	468	450	16	1,675	1,768	885	4,357	398	4,820	40	......
Sussex	24,134	6,640	6,160	841	......	......	2,575	2,006	411	70	257	480	......	......
Union	99,353	52,705	28,605	5,758	756	999	4,153	8,444	6,017	610	1,868	23,945	95	60
Warren	37,781	15,856	11,766	552	......	695	5,123	4,034	565	......	797	4,090	......	......
County location unknown[2]	......	581	561	......	......	......	......	......	......	......	561	......	20	......

[1] Heads of families only.

[2] See explanatory headnote on page 294.

NEW MEXICO.

COUNTY.	Population, 1900.	All denominations.	PROTESTANT BODIES. Total.	Baptists—Northern, Southern, and National Conventions.	Disciples of Christ.	Methodist Episcopal Church.	Methodist Episcopal Church, South.	Presbyterian Church in the U. S. A.	Protestant Episcopal Church.	Other Protestant bodies.	Roman Catholic Church.	Jewish congregations.[1]	Latter-day Saints.
The territory	195,310	137,009	14,593	2,403	963	3,513	2,882	2,864	869	1,099	121,558	120	738
Bernalillo	28,630	12,688	1,829	201	65	507	178	288	200	390	10,809	50	......
Chaves	4,773	2,806	2,090	435	398	140	620	314	64	119	701	15	......
Colfax	10,150	3,382	1,092	177	91	510	......	195	25	94	2,236	......	54
Dona Ana	10,187	5,452	331	17	......	82	88	84	60	......	5,121	......	......
Eddy	3,229	1,942	1,116	283	142	......	362	134	66	129	826	......	......
Grant	12,883	3,778	527	39	102	184	52	50	100	......	3,251	......	......
Guadalupe	5,429	4,138	57	31	......	26	......	......	......	......	4,081	......	......
Lincoln	4,953	1,642	93	35	......	......	50	......	......	8	1,549	......	......
Luna	(2)	381	292	......	......	85	130	53	24	......	89	......	......
McKinley	(3)	1,111	141	......	......	......	46	......	60	35	901	......	69

[1] Heads of families only.

[2] New county since 1900; formed from parts of Dona Ana and Grant in 1901.

[3]

TABLE 4.—POPULATION IN 1900 AND COMMUNICANTS OR MEMBERS FOR SELECTED DENOMINATIONS, FOR EACH STATE AND TERRITORY, BY COUNTIES: 1906—Continued.

NEW MEXICO—Continued.

COUNTY.	Population, 1900.	All denominations.	PROTESTANT BODIES. Total.	Baptists—Northern, Southern, and National Conventions.	Disciples of Christ.	Methodist Episcopal Church.	Methodist Episcopal Church, South.	Presbyterian Church in the U. S. A.	Protestant Episcopal Church.	Other Protestant bodies.	Roman Catholic Church.	Jewish congregations.[1]	Latter-day Saints.
Mora	10,304	9,440	413			138	31	244			9,027		
Otero	4,791	2,041	745	276	60	61	196	60	29	63	1,296		
Quay	(2)	1,763	295	127			150			18	1,468		
Rio Arriba	13,777	9,457	554	11		286		257			8,903		
Roosevelt	(3)	1,194	1,194	522	50		547	75					
San Juan	4,828	1,926	621	52			362	136	16	55	825		480
San Miguel	22,053	19,512	743	84		262		235	105	57	18,714	55	
Sandoval	(4)	8,652	113					113			8,539		
Santa Fe	14,658	11,893	323			43		210	70		11,570		
Sierra	3,158	2,104	251			236			15		1,853		
Socorro	12,195	9,702	635			406	70	70	35	54	8,984		83
Taos	10,889	8,582	317			172		145			8,265		
Torrance	(5)	2,064	188	56		92				40	1,876		
Union	4,528	3,178	379	57	55	209		58			2,799		
Valencia	13,895	7,572	240			74		143		23	7,280		52
County location unknown[6]		609	14							14	595		

[1] Heads of families only.
[2] New county since 1900; formed from part of old Guadalupe in 1903.
[3] New county since 1900; formed from parts of Chaves and old Guadalupe in 1903.
[4] New county since 1900; formed from part of Bernalillo in 1903.
[5] New county since 1900; formed from parts of Bernalillo, Lincoln, San Miguel, Santa Fe, Socorro, and Valencia in 1905.
[6] See explanatory headnote on page 294.

NEW YORK.

COUNTY.	Population, 1900.	All denominations.	PROTESTANT BODIES. Total.	Baptists—Northern and National Conventions.	Free Baptists.	Christians (Christian Connection).	Church of Christ, Scientist.	Congregationalists.	Disciples of Christ.	Evangelical Association.	German Evangelical Synod of N. A.	Lutheran—General Synod.	Lutheran—General Council.	Lutheran—Synodical Conference.	Methodist Episcopal Church.
The state	7,268,894	3,591,974	1,237,992	165,710	7,910	5,492	5,671	57,351	9,124	5,597	26,183	20,543	65,450	32,178	291,919
Albany	165,571	94,919	31,663	3,985		844	76	335		95	550	1,305	2,367	1,127	5,514
Allegany	41,501	13,515	10,012	2,123				396	461	129				337	2,903
Broome	69,149	28,997	19,522	3,581	83	172	64	1,319		120			270		7,524
Cattaraugus	65,643	21,559	12,156	1,901	226	132	62	642		154			95	1,292	3,971
Cayuga	66,234	15,071	14,938	2,659	8	86	22	312	720		336				4,069
Chautauqua	88,314	36,191	22,022	3,219	215	59	108	921	125	115	716		2,879	324	6,639
Chemung	54,063	13,420	13,228	2,627	289		32	966	210		890		91		4,331
Chenango	36,568	12,170	10,402	3,273	412	16		1,403							2,701
Clinton	47,430	25,219	4,562	283	157										2,760
Columbia	43,211	15,896	11,912	387		70		182				1,509	430	228	3,571
Cortland	27,576	10,185	7,421	1,760	35	35		1,018							2,792
Delaware	46,413	15,186	14,561	1,795	109			1,416							5,505
Dutchess	81,670	36,875	19,880	2,232		437	71	506				872	620		4,927
Erie	433,686	232,043	79,746	7,187	805	16	479	1,577	2,033	1,293	15,046	114	8,296	5,945	10,208
Essex	30,707	12,238	5,404	884				860							2,158
Franklin	42,853	21,763	5,066	485	208	129		193							2,255
Fulton	42,842	16,068	12,544	2,226		157		485	184	30		1,377		58	4,617
Genesee	34,561	13,287	7,963	1,824	221	61	33		60	90	30			62	1,736
Greene	31,478	10,129	8,337	675		306						96			3,433
Hamilton	4,947	1,146	506	123	16										306
Herkimer	51,049	18,590	10,812	1,885	172		18	187		73		531			3,536
Jefferson	76,748	29,626	16,368	2,244	105	86	28	1,245	146			60	425		5,262
Kings	1,166,582	601,482	151,837	19,263	515	178	526	16,076	684	827	355	1,411	17,377	4,882	24,379
Lewis	27,427	9,266	4,232	433	82			363	125	203					1,491
Livingston	37,059	8,321	8,321	970	36	65						356	24		2,278
Madison	40,545	14,860	10,025	2,742			28	863		107					3,159
Monroe	217,854	53,982	52,799	8,920	731	249	213	1,097	280	553	3,400		7,838	1,557	8,027
Montgomery	47,488	22,550	12,241	1,105	120	478	57			230	265	2,112	524		2,939
Nassau	55,448	28,001	11,160	390			14	174	55				265	20	4,438
New York	2,050,600	1,107,759	190,295	22,798			2,799	3,949	1,070	257	585	2,631	11,753	6,956	19,684
Niagara	74,961	35,432	20,200	1,558		124	28	1,086	978	130	1,399	274	917	4,085	3,091
Oneida	132,800	77,441	30,745	3,799			190	2,183		161	220	115	1,534	467	7,585
Onondaga	168,735	87,651	34,589	5,093	34	95	109	2,306	677	265	550	2,521	988		9,059
Ontario	49,605	12,290	12,240	1,394	13			912		93			220	85	3,615
Orange	103,859	44,686	25,633	1,910				1,323					805	127	7,173
Orleans	30,164	11,063	6,743	1,645	189	99		115					158	137	2,035
Oswego	70,881	28,802	13,760	2,000	305		29	1,237	41			708			5,313
Otsego	48,939	15,684	14,205	3,474	982	491	70	90				173			4,174
Putnam	13,787	6,603	3,994	1,322											1,374
Queens	152,999	91,247	20,212	1,392				1,071	65	75			1,206	1,682	3,450

TABLE 4.—POPULATION IN 1900 AND COMMUNICANTS OR MEMBERS FOR SELECTED DENOMINATIONS, FOR EACH STATE AND TERRITORY, BY COUNTIES: 1906—Continued.

NEW YORK—Continued.

COUNTY.	Population, 1900.	All denominations.	PROTESTANT BODIES. Total.	Baptists—Northern and National Conventions.	Free Baptists.	Christians (Christian Connection).	Church of Christ, Scientist.	Congregationalists.	Disciples of Christ.	Evangelical Association.	German Evangelical Synod of N. A.	Lutheran—General Synod.	Lutheran—General Council.	Lutheran—Synodical Conference.	Methodist Episcopal Church.
Rensselaer	121,697	66,391	27,150	3,601	208	50	212	281	896	89	565	1,588	700	...	7,184
Richmond	67,021	37,994	10,346	976	...	...	47	...	...	...	...	...	533	410	2,457
Rockland	38,298	17,796	7,431	540	...	...	24	187	...	...	...	95	284	30	2,047
St. Lawrence	89,083	32,538	14,804	1,444	103	...	...	1,408	69	...	...	57	...	...	4,861
Saratoga	61,089	24,787	13,919	2,638	...	99	...	165	...	...	...	...	...	80	4,980
Schenectady	46,852	29,892	14,754	1,582	...	122	37	564	...	...	401	374	75	769	4,158
Schoharie	26,854	7,815	7,733	713	...	185	...	...	...	...	...	1,791	...	...	3,661
Schuyler	15,811	4,314	4,314	1,220	80	85	...	...	...	...	...	...	...	...	1,690
Seneca	28,114	6,132	6,077	1,062	...	...	...	...	46	...	...	70	...	...	1,447
Steuben	82,822	18,197	18,173	3,438	299	213	56	373	...	...	220	...	327	146	6,706
Suffolk	77,582	35,488	19,252	903	...	22	...	2,066	...	...	...	...	295	218	6,298
Sullivan	32,306	8,838	5,904	199	...	...	...	239	...	...	...	...	245	...	3,194
Tioga	27,951	7,913	7,898	1,876	84	...	...	1,023	...	...	...	...	...	...	3,699
Tompkins	33,830	8,535	8,306	1,880	37	...	17	1,004	...	...	...	...	...	...	3,078
Ulster	88,422	37,526	21,125	1,440	...	...	25	201	...	...	...	403	1,320	342	6,969
Warren	29,943	12,907	6,177	1,032	75	...	56	...	...	...	...	...	...	...	2,128
Washington	45,624	20,725	12,469	2,980	...	...	...	606	...	...	...	...	...	...	2,997
Wayne	48,660	14,409	14,246	1,693	182	168	...	194	200	328	...	...	1,106	76	4,207
Westchester	184,257	131,017	41,098	5,158	...	...	141	1,174	...	...	260	...	1,375	736	10,980
Wyoming	30,413	12,690	8,081	2,123	358	62	...	968	...	180	455	...	...	...	1,817
Yates	20,318	5,571	5,571	1,646	186	101	...	91	...	...	...	...	108	...	2,154
County location unknown[1]	...	99,296	908	...	230	...	...	...	...	...	...	...	...	...	630

COUNTY.	PROTESTANT BODIES—continued. African Methodists.[2]	Presbyterian Church in the U. S. A.	United Presbyterian Church.	Protestant Episcopal Church.	Reformed Church in America.	Reformed Church in the U. S.	Unitarians.	Universalists.	Other Protestant bodies.	Roman Catholic Church.	Jewish congregations.[3]	Greek Orthodox Church.	All other bodies.
The state	10,876	186,278	10,115	193,890	63,350	5,700	4,656	10,761	59,238	2,285,768	35,342	15,100	17,772
Albany	60	5,358	119	5,350	4,060	...	257	37	224	61,878	484	400	494
Allegany	...	829	...	600	...	...	...	129	2,105	3,454	...	...	49
Broome	90	4,086	...	1,393	...	...	...	190	630	9,435	40	...	...
Cattaraugus	25	1,255	260	897	...	...	...	35	1,209	9,358	20	25	...
Cayuga	65	4,322	166	1,062	197	...	...	332	646	(4)	40	...	93
Chautauqua	11	2,126	...	1,361	446	...	415	136	2,207	12,669	...	...	1,500
Chemung	225	2,019	...	1,290	...	...	...	...	258	(4)	132	60	...
Chenango	40	665	...	1,503	...	...	...	180	209	1,768	...	...	...
Clinton	...	620	...	404	...	...	...	...	338	20,632	25	...	...
Columbia	121	806	...	1,326	3,029	...	...	250	3	3,726	177	...	81
Cortland	...	1,010	...	357	...	...	...	105	309	2,739	...	25	...
Delaware	...	1,890	2,240	938	218	...	...	...	450	625	...	...	...
Dutchess	128	2,330	...	4,448	2,482	...	...	...	827	16,745	50	200	...
Erie	100	8,377	584	9,032	160	3,706	388	574	3,826	147,239	618	300	4,140
Essex	47	458	...	947	...	...	...	...	50	6,828	6	...	...
Franklin	...	1,025	...	654	...	...	...	...	117	16,677	20	...	...
Fulton	39	1,826	280	561	125	...	...	400	179	3,355	65	85	...
Genesee	...	2,279	...	924	...	...	...	85	558	5,294	...	30	...
Greene	74	1,138	...	733	1,824	...	...	...	58	1,782	10	...	...
Hamilton	...	...	...	...	...	...	...	...	61	640	...	...	...
Herkimer	16	1,137	...	1,062	537	...	...	1,048	610	7,738	...	40	...
Jefferson	4	2,573	...	2,718	115	...	...	446	911	13,180	21	...	57
Kings	2,938	17,720	584	26,608	8,965	879	849	766	6,055	442,443	2,544	550	4,108
Lewis	...	675	...	336	77	...	...	...	447	5,084	...	...	...
Livingston	40	3,090	519	670	...	...	...	90	183	(4)	...	...	...
Madison	30	1,327	...	677	...	...	...	100	992	4,835	...	...	...
Monroe	113	10,439	550	4,969	891	387	332	680	973	(4)	842	225	116
Montgomery	11	962	...	650	2,340	...	...	353	95	10,254	55	...	...
Nassau	359	1,318	...	2,864	462	...	...	...	801	16,723	118	...	...
New York	3,041	28,763	1,002	57,344	11,321	596	1,120	780	13,846	873,277	27,489	12,000	4,698
Niagara	22	2,220	...	1,876	...	...	...	298	2,114	15,104	28	...	166
Oneida	54	6,518	...	4,910	260	...	...	312	2,437	46,469	127	100	...
Onondaga	40	6,062	...	4,304	615	...	405	599	867	52,176	498	270	118
Ontario	34	3,266	...	1,896	...	...	...	449	263	(4)	...	50	...
Orange	546	5,933	461	3,870	2,237	...	100	150	998	18,968	35	50	...
Orleans	8	1,105	...	446	...	...	...	264	552	4,290	...	30	...
Oswego	...	1,728	...	1,475	...	...	...	93	833	15,042	...	...	...
Otsego	...	1,777	234	1,973	...	...	...	470	297	1,469	...	20	...
Putnam	...	528	...	704	40	...	...	...	26	2,159	...	...	450
Queens	277	1,936	...	5,371	2,949	48	...	...	690	70,442	346	25	222

[1] See explanatory headnote on page 294.
[2] Includes Union American Methodist Episcopal Church, African Methodist Episcopal Church, African Union Methodist Protestant Church, and African Methodist Episcopal Zion Church.
[3] Heads of families only.
[4] Report included in total for "County location unknown."

TABLE 4.—POPULATION IN 1900 AND COMMUNICANTS OR MEMBERS FOR SELECTED DENOMINATIONS, FOR EACH STATE AND TERRITORY, BY COUNTIES: 1906—Continued.

NEW YORK—Continued.

COUNTY.	PROTESTANT BODIES—continued.									Roman Catholic Church.	Jewish congregations.[2]	Greek Orthodox Church.	All other bodies.
	African Methodists.[1]	Presbyterian Church in the U. S. A.	United Presbyterian Church.	Protestant Episcopal Church.	Reformed Church in America.	Reformed Church in the U. S.	Unitarians.	Universalists.	Other Protestant bodies.				
Rensselaer	100	4,966	131	4,281	1,408		125	119	646	38,523	252	100	366
Richmond	146	495		3,211	770		150		1,151	27,613	35		
Rockland	120	1,712		1,127	1,004			20	241	10,315	50		
St. Lawrence		3,217	168	2,230			90	535	622	17,676	12		46
Saratoga	75	2,118	139	1,977	1,257				391	10,433			435
Schenectady	59	1,549	305	1,274	2,953		90	6	486	14,347	541	250	
Schoharie	28	194		125	818				218	82			
Schuyler		670		420					149	(3)			
Seneca		1,670		1,148	443	84			108	(3)		55	
Steuben	38	3,879	25	1,422				149	882	(3)			24
Suffolk	510	5,466		2,889	120			52	418	16,168	55		13
Sullivan		949		145	521				412	2,809	35		
Tioga	30	872		228					86	(3)			15
Tompkins	44	1,208		608			200	72	158	(3)	15		214
Ulster	150	1,241		1,589	6,602				843	16,273	128		
Warren		1,133		978					775	6,669		30	31
Washington		1,448	2,234	882	398			41	884	8,256			
Wayne		3,052		940	1,153			146	801	(3)			168
Westchester	1,010	6,767		9,396	2,553		136	70	1,404	89,080	429	180	230
Wyoming		1,320	180	201				175	242	4,609			
Yates		888		317				35	75	(3)			
County location unknown[4]	8								40	[5] 98,388			

[1] Includes Union American Methodist Episcopal Church, African Methodist Episcopal Church, African Union Methodist Protestant Church, and African Methodist Episcopal Zion Church.
[2] Heads of families only.
[3] Report included in total for "County location unknown."
[4] See explanatory headnote on page 294.
[5] Includes 97,760 communicants for Rochester diocese not returned separately by counties.

NORTH CAROLINA.

COUNTY.	Population, 1900.	All denominations.	PROTESTANT BODIES.												
			Total.	Baptists—Southern and National Conventions.	Free-will Baptists.	Primitive Baptists.	Colored Primitive Baptists.	United American Free-will Baptists (Colored).	Christians (Christian Connection).	Congregationalists.	Disciples of Christ.	Friends (Orthodox).	Lutheran—United Synod in the South.	Lutheran—Synodical Conference.	Methodist Episcopal Church.
The state	1,893,810	824,385	819,099	355,987	22,518	10,207	2,215	10,099	15,969	2,699	13,342	6,425	14,881	1,966	20,805
Alamance	25,665	10,174	10,174	1,592		27			1,902	151		402	212	15	
Alexander	10,960	4,815	4,815	2,532									369	120	142
Alleghany	7,759	1,493	1,493	321		741									81
Anson	21,870	10,788	10,788	5,610		57				10					
Ashe	19,581	4,753	4,753	1,643		651									539
Beaufort	26,404	11,141	11,141	2,107	1,213	175		1,068			2,522				
Bertie	20,538	15,075	15,075	14,429											
Bladen	17,677	8,350	8,350	3,707	249				41						138
Brunswick	12,657	5,382	5,382	2,441	45	40		11	95						
Buncombe	44,288	17,100	16,717	7,354	297	110					48			54	828
Burke	17,699	7,234	7,234	2,395		10							45	35	
Cabarrus	22,456	11,480	11,409	1,033			172			76			1,719	152	164
Caldwell	15,694	7,048	7,048	2,877		73							261		379
Camden	5,474	2,955	2,955	2,105							20				
Carteret	11,811	4,459	4,459	952	581	237			48	47	81				327
Caswell	15,028	5,149	5,149	2,844		142	38		259						
Catawba	22,133	11,287	11,287	1,944									1,610	1,250	427
Chatham	23,912	12,410	12,410	4,462		64			1,055	316		454			
Cherokee	11,860	3,991	3,991	2,914	47										262
Chowan	10,258	6,483	6,464	4,685											75
Clay	4,532	1,526	1,526	808											174
Cleveland	25,078	13,909	13,909	8,365									116		689
Columbus	21,274	9,424	9,332	5,873	442	108									86
Craven	24,160	11,998	11,858	3,159	1,232	45		555	332		580				
Cumberland	29,249	15,580	15,488	4,425	288	6		706	85	153					40
Currituck	6,529	3,286	3,286	1,433		76					105				
Dare	4,757	2,079	2,079	326		14									76
Davidson	23,403	11,033	11,033	2,885		157							741		474
Davie	12,115	5,932	5,932	1,782		23						77	65		238
Duplin	22,405	9,827	9,812	5,995	674	131		50			85				

TABLE 4.—POPULATION IN 1900 AND COMMUNICANTS OR MEMBERS FOR SELECTED DENOMINATIONS, FOR EACH STATE AND TERRITORY, BY COUNTIES: 1906—Continued.

NORTH CAROLINA—Continued.

COUNTY.	Population, 1900.	All denominations.	PROTESTANT BODIES.												
			Total.	Baptists—Southern and National Conventions.	Free-will Baptists.	Primitive Baptists.	Colored Primitive Baptists.	United American Free-will Baptists (Colored).	Christians (Christian Connection).	Congregationalists.	Disciples of Christ.	Friends (Orthodox).	Lutheran—United Synod in the South.	Lutheran—Synodical Conference.	Methodist Episcopal Church.
Durham	26,233	11,482	11,343	5,888	83		179		478						28
Edgecombe	26,591	4,697	4,656	2,207	32	363	149				72				
Forsyth	35,261	14,787	14,662	2,928		54	39		201		128		273		993
Franklin	25,116	11,142	11,142	8,227	115	17			1,135						9
Gaston	27,903	12,745	12,368	4,264						62			1,154		221
Gates	10,413	6,444	6,444	4,129					577						
Graham	4,343	1,139	1,139	920	79	27									
Granville	23,263	12,158	12,158	8,591			28		404						163
Greene	12,038	5,703	5,703	253	1,469	55		1,393			122				
Guilford	39,074	20,903	20,644	2,909		50			844	254		1,276	603	30	1,610
Halifax	30,793	15,304	15,304	11,341		125									
Harnett	15,988	6,960	6,916	2,237	533	152		540	116		85				
Haywood	16,222	4,879	4,879	2,103											427
Henderson	14,104	6,480	6,480	4,537											160
Hertford	14,294	9,527	9,527	8,901	150										
Hyde	9,278	4,117	4,117	1,927		83		46			873				69
Iredell	29,[illegible]	14,047	14,012	3,442		20				248		125	618		829
Jackson	11,[illegible]	3,253	3,253	1,987											105
Johnston	32	9,846	9,846	4,313	1,759	853		50	372		304				
Jones	8	3,252	3,252	569	187	29		300	114		787				
Lee	(1)	670	670	29											
Lenoir	18,639	7,611	7,611	1,108	1,290	42		1,952			913				
Lincoln	15,498	8,228	8,228	2,058									1,059		566
McDowell	12,567	4,378	4,378	1,818											380
Macon	12,104	4,229	4,229	2,562											91
Madison	20,644	6,471	6,471	3,965	814	107					228				
Martin	15,383	4,338	4,338	1,547	267	391	6				735				613
Mecklenburg	55,268	29,897	29,182	5,836			308			174			251	50	260
Mitchell	15,221	5,674	5,674	3,512							165				821
Montgomery	14,197	5,311	5,311	1,521		52			120	322					140
Moore	23,622	11,165	11,066	2,023				281	826	169		147		20	160
Nash	25,478	8,556	8,520	5,110	654	342	18				113				
New Hanover	25,785	11,512	10,860	2,823	33	36			70	115	67		473		62
Northampton	21,150	13,529	13,529	10,314	34							92			
Onslow	11,940	3,705	3,705	1,426	197	194		90			380				
Orange	14,690	5,780	5,780	2,488		17			305						
Pamlico	8,045	[illegible],194	[illegible],194	821	982	88		100	357		750				
Pasquotank	13,660	896	896	4,045		44									247
Pender	13,381	302	217	4,911	89	16									
Perquimans	10,091	276	276	3,001							62	320			
Person	16,685	6,323	6,323	4,710			288								
Pitt	30,889	10,664	10,639	2,612	2,394	208	56	1,815		40	1,461				
Polk	7,004	2,245	2,245	1,475						33					
Randolph	28,232	11,258	11,258	1,476		25			1,305	127		1,022	110		920
Richmond	15,855	7,106	7,106	1,706	117		8		55	181					380
Robeson	40,371	17,916	17,916	8,556	223				17	40					1,632
Rockingham	33,163	9,461	9,461	3,384		305	149		400		452				1,031
Rowan	31,066	15,644	15,449	2,610		33							4,808	132	52
Rutherford	25,101	10,917	10,917	6,520		21									230
Sampson	26,380	12,101	11,883	7,457	1,459	74		177			50				
Scotland	12,553	6,197	6,197	2,191											586
Stanly	15,220	7,455	7,455	2,573		203							379		283
Stokes	[illegible],866	[illegible],120	[illegible],120	1,492		463	288						35		199
Surry	,515	647	647	2,969		680	112					869			402
Swain	,401	161	161	1,690											30
Transylvania	6,620	3,035	3,035	2,415											55
Tyrrell	4,980	2,444	2,444	1,304	419	29					213				
Union	27,156	12,632	12,632	5,416		157							30	28	30
Vance	16,684	9,473	9,473	4,743					950						66
Wake	54,626	25,176	24,809	14,949	410	131		92	2,794	69	129				117
Warren	19,151	9,961	9,961	7,410		11			645					80	
Washington	10,608	5,384	5,384	1,920	284	137	25				1,129				
Watauga	13,417	5,472	5,472	4,064		69							150		209
Wayne	31,356	10,965	10,943	3,020	1,557	511		675		112	507	72			43
Wilkes	26,872	8,834	8,834	6,590		487									522
Wilson	23,596	5,668	5,668	1,528	1,101	578	52	198	7		176				
Yadkin	14,083	5,506	5,506	2,890								917			448
Yancey	11,464	938	938	2,818	719										120
County location unknown[2]		2,934	1,894			41									357

[1] New county since 1900; formed from parts of Chatham and Moore.

[2] See explanatory headnote on page 294.

TABLE 4.—POPULATION IN 1900 AND COMMUNICANTS OR MEMBERS FOR SELECTED DENOMINATIONS, FOR EACH STATE AND TERRITORY, BY COUNTIES: 1906—Continued.

NORTH CAROLINA—Continued.

COUNTY.	PROTESTANT BODIES—continued.										Roman Catholic Church.	Jewish congregations.[2]	All other bodies.
	Methodist Protestant Church.	Methodist Episcopal Church, South.	African Methodists.[1]	Moravian Church (Unitas Fratrum).	Presbyterian Church in the U. S. A.	Presbyterian Church in the U. S.	Presbyterian—Associate Reformed Synod of the South.	Protestant Episcopal Church.	Reformed Church in the U. S.	Other Protestant bodies.			
The state	18,271	151,808	85,512	3,478	10,696	41,322	3,625	13,890	4,718	8,726	3,981	234	1,071
Alamance	2,148	1,609	629		142	1,081		100	234	20			
Alexander		981	139			170	94			268			
Alleghany		214				28				108			
Anson	48	2,004	2,498		186	188		90		97			
Ashe		1,606				100		25		189			
Beaufort		1,496	1,503			249		766		42			
Bertie		445	96					105					
Bladen		1,029	2,617		14	555							
Brunswick		1,143	1,452		55	83		17					
Buncombe	336	3,820	1,235		621	935		836		243	367	16	
Burke	133	2,549	1,135		22	405		411		94			
Cabarrus	403	2,714	2,006		817	1,614	64	38	437		71		
Caldwell	41	1,738	606			214		131	35	693			
Camden		622	198					10					
Carteret		1,327	720			14		69		56			
Caswell		1,220	368			267		11					
Catawba		3,185	888			302		84	964	633			
Chatham	415	2,663	2,718			146		85		32			
Cherokee		616	110			28		14					
Chowan	19	294	1,207					158		26	19		
Clay		497				26		21					
Cleveland	699	2,842	680		58	314	128	14		4			
Columbus		1,423	1,118		96	161		25			92		
Craven		1,738	3,430		85	198		457		47	140		
Cumberland		2,228	4,774		211	1,760		672		140	72		20
Currituck		1,113	559										
Dare		1,663											
Davidson	1,403	3,184	219	384	236	118		22	1,210				
Davie	363	2,120	800	159	90	87		48		80			
Duplin		1,105	536			1,085		8		143	15		
Durham		2,983	682		72	480		350		120	87	52	
Edgecombe	88	765	216		25	140		399			26	15	
Forsyth	1,007	3,126	1,624	2,790	150	525		157	14	553	125		
Franklin		1,113	225		198	16		87					
Gaston	257	2,528	970		150	1,735	553	76		398	367	10	
Gates		1,085	615					38					
Graham		95				18							
Granville		2,007	357		97	296		215					
Greene	34	961	1,312		45			24		35			
Guilford	2,418	4,950	1,931	145	216	2,268		354	483	303	229	30	
Halifax	964	1,897	549			142		253		33			
Harnett		1,212	1,087		165	663		34		92	44		
Haywood		1,730	219			196		188		16			
Henderson		910	229			275		220		149			
Hertford		405	44					27					
Hyde		1,007				45		67					
Iredell	103	3,793	886		822	1,997	1,010	97		22	23	12	
Jackson		999	82			33		47					
Johnston		1,063	763			119		19		231			
Jones		650	501		42	56		17					
Lee		431			190			20					
Lenoir	131	1,069	591		47	96		186		186			
Lincoln	787	2,316	453		55	289		191	313	141			
McDowell		1,571	272			274		45		18			
Macon		1,300	48			130		98					
Madison	98	727	38		351			13		130			
Martin		523	158					98					
Mecklenburg	139	4,774	5,470		2,304	6,829	1,776	867		144	665		56
Mitchell		463	300			216		3		194			
Montgomery	254	1,739	970			166				27			
Moore	28	1,790	2,610		359	2,594		48		11	99		
Nash	75	1,485	306			239		138		41	36		
New Hanover		1,567	3,059		88	1,084		1,144		239	575	77	
Northampton	44	2,198	561			8		53		225			
Onslow		761	569			15				73			
Orange	515	1,166	522		13	608		146					
Pamlico		613	463		10			10					
Pasquotank		1,359	1,910		39	40		212					
Pender		392	1,205		25	502		20		57	85		
Perquimans		941	832					120					

[1] Includes Union American Methodist Episcopal Church, African Methodist Episcopal Church, African Methodist Episcopal Zion Church, Colored Methodist Episcopal Church, and Reformed Zion Union Apostolic Church.
[2] Heads of families only.

TABLE 4.—POPULATION IN 1900 AND COMMUNICANTS OR MEMBERS FOR SELECTED DENOMINATIONS, FOR EACH STATE AND TERRITORY, BY COUNTIES: 1906—Continued.

NORTH CAROLINA—Continued.

COUNTY.	PROTESTANT BODIES—continued.										Roman Catholic Church.	Jewish congregations.[2]	All other bodies.
	Methodist Protestant Church.	Methodist Episcopal Church, South.	African Methodists.[1]	Moravian Church (Unitas Fratrum).	Presbyterian Church in the U. S. A.	Presbyterian Church in the U. S.	Presbyterian—Associate Reformed Synod of the South.	Protestant Episcopal Church.	Reformed Church in the U. S.	Other Protestant bodies.			
Person		1,102	200			18		5					
Pitt		1,232	464		60	25		216		56	25		
Polk		301	146			81		110		99			
Randolph	2,165	3,596	145			31				334			
Richmond	79	2,084	1,898		51	479		23		45			
Robeson		1,478	2,738		461	2,372				389			
Rockingham	615	2,232	139			485				18			
Rowan		3,202	1,010		670	1,467			858	104	170		25
Rutherford	75	2,401	1,101			393		10		157			
Sampson		1,427	695			301		288		208	218		
Scotland		1,114	1,470		212	612							
Stanly	296	2,313	1,050			197			150	11			
Stokes	103	1,			5	261				160			
Surry	229	1,129	313		122	255		12		5			
Swain		633	10			30		88		80			
Transylvania			15			141							
Tyrrell													
Union	328	2,	3,000		159	451				70			
Vance	929	1,383	743			320		26		91			
Wake		2,[illegible]	1,863		86	440		255		41	367		
Warren	55	1,382	181			44				9			
Washington	264	562	880					144					
Watauga		786				64		165	20	25			
Wayne		2,244	697		278	245		125		205		22	
Wilkes		643	230			116		54		202			
Wilson		1,	612		120	100		172					
Yadkin	139	024	267		37	19							
Yancey	44	386			164	153				54			
County location unknown[3]		465	786		175					70	64		976

[1] Includes Union American Methodist Episcopal Church. African Methodist Episcopal Church, African Methodist Episcopal Zion Church, Colored Methodist Episcopal Church, and Reformed Zion Union Apostolic Church.
[2] Heads of families only.
[3] See explanatory headnote on page 294.

NORTH DAKOTA.

COUNTY.	Population, 1900.	All denominations.	PROTESTANT BODIES.									Roman Catholic Church.	Jewish congregations.[2]	All other bodies.
			Total.	Baptists—Northern Convention.	Congregationalists.	Lutheran—Synodical Conference.	Lutheran—Synod of Iowa, etc.	Lutheran—Norwegian Synods.[1]	Methodist Episcopal Church.	Presbyterian Church in the U. S. A.	Other Protestant bodies.			
The state	[3] 319,146	159,053	97,361	4,596	5,290	5,854	3,717	43,913	10,083	6,727	17,231	61,261	12	419
Barnes	13,159	,931	3,648	55	610	30	60	1,683	631	38	532	2,283		
Benson	8,320	4,804	3,065		137			2,226	176	244	282	1,702		37
Billings	975	379	112		22			90				267		
Bottineau	7,532	4,725	3,136	152	51	451		1,466	405	407	204	1,538		51
Burleigh	6,081	2,134	1,040	52	19	51		203	222	230	263	1,094		
Cass	28,625	,830	8,371	509	462	100	531	2,951	1,124	703	1,991	2,459		
Cavalier	12,580	10,131	2,450	149	17	120		1,123	345	476	220	2,681		
Dickey	6,061	5,684	1,324	109	15	217	85	430	137	177	154	360		
Dunn	(4)	686										686		
Eddy	3,330	1,090	635	20	71	40		206	55	20	223	455		
Emmons	4,349	3,	779	83		35	132	116	65	31	317	2,253		
Foster	3,770	1,	860		315	45		257	112		131	686		
Grand Forks	24,459	10,	7,556	337	189	171		4,787	643	806	623	2,467		
Griggs	4,744	1,032	1,382	109	131	46		891	90	70	45	127		
Hettinger	(5)	348	227		54				60		113	121		
Kidder	1,754	642	514		32		108	172	133	27	42	128		
Lamoure	6,048	,569	2,057	52	228	385	196	467	366	172	191	512		
Logan	1,625	803	380		23		134	55	14		154	423		
McHenry	5,253	687	3,453	265	156	448	50	1,409	261	82	782	1,214		20
McIntosh	4,818	2,565	1,895	531	24	151	793	18	28	10	340	553		117
McKenzie	(4)	236	236					223	13					
McLean	4,791	4,805	3,538	588	308	258	210	1,031	120	67	956	1,207		60
Mercer	1,778	901	901	12	35	93	674	30			57			
Morton	8,069	8,567	2,781	89	371	90	120	306	80	154	1,571	5,786		
Nelson	7,316	3,099	2,400		141	74		1,804	199	59	123	699		

[1] Includes United Norwegian Lutheran Church in America; Hauge's Norwegian Evangelical Lutheran Synod; Evangelical Lutheran Church in America, Eielsen's Synod; Synod for the Norwegian Evangelical Lutheran Church in America; Norwegian Lutheran Free Church; and Church of the Lutheran Brethren of America (Norwegian).
[2] Heads of families only.
[3] Includes population (2,208) of Standing Rock Indian reservation (part of), not returned by counties in 1900.
[4] Not returned separately in 1900.
[5] New county since 1900.

TABLE 4.—POPULATION IN 1900 AND COMMUNICANTS OR MEMBERS FOR SELECTED DENOMINATIONS, FOR EACH STATE AND TERRITORY, BY COUNTIES: 1906—Continued.

NORTH DAKOTA—Continued.

COUNTY.	Population, 1900.	All denominations.	PROTESTANT BODIES. Total.	Baptists—Northern Convention.	Congregationalists.	Lutheran—Synodical Conference.	Lutheran—Synod of Iowa, etc.	Lutheran—Norwegian Synods.[1]	Methodist Episcopal Church.	Presbyterian Church in the U. S. A.	Other Protestant bodies.	Roman Catholic Church.	Jewish congregations.[2]	All other bodies.
Oliver	990	655	538	...	36	225	170	12	51	44	...	117	...	...
Pembina	17,869	6,624	4,076	216	...	308	...	118	1,072	543	1,819	2,	...	...
Pierce	4,765	3,459	1,300	31	...	...	...	1,010	80	107	72	2, [illegible]	...	...
Ramsey	9,198	4,033	2,567	...	71	23	...	1,662	229	215	367	1,548	12	...
Ransom	6,919	2,892	2,002	100	...	...	85	1,160	355	181	121	[illegible]	...	...
Richland	17,387	6,684	4,460	54	317	904	...	1,940	422	...	818	2,234	...	...
Rolette	7,995	4,912	1,419	59	...	77	...	564	121	157	441	3,427	...	66
Sargent	6,039	2,690	1,626	14	87	418	...	910	96	54	47	1,064	...	...
Stark	7,621	6,239	842	...	195	...	...	230	80	...	337	5,397	...	...
Steele	5,888	1,833	1,743	...	70	29	...	1,438	113	75	18	90	...	...
Stutsman	9,143	3,738	2,590	210	418	284	23	274	315	345	721		...	...
Towner	6,491	1,826	1,227	11	61	25	90	250	225	110	455		...	...
Traill	13,107	4,535	4,342	37	188	193	...	3,627	148	107	42	1,148	...	68
Walsh	20,288	9,360	4,354	89	27	42	...	3,265	321	478	132	5, [illegible]	...	...
Ward	7,961	10,411	6,902	313	111	443	...	2,882	690	497	1,966	3,	...	...
Wells	8,310	3,351	2,209	350	253	45	247	961	101	...	252	1,509	...	...
Williams	1,530	2,546	1,908	...	45	33	...	1,413	149	41	227	[illegible]	...	...
County location unknown[3]	...	539	526	...	...	...	...	253	186	...	87	13	...	...

[1] Includes United Norwegian Lutheran Church in America; Hauge's Norwegian Evangelical Lutheran Synod; Evangelical Lutheran Church in America, Eielsen's Synod; Synod for the Norwegian Evangelical Lutheran Church in America; Norwegian Lutheran Free Church; and Church of the Lutheran Brethren of America (Norwegian).

[2] Heads of families only.

[3] See explanatory headnote on page 294.

OHIO.

COUNTY.	Population, 1900.	All denominations.	PROTESTANT BODIES. Total.	Baptists—Northern and National Conventions.	Christians (Christian Connection).	Congregationalists.	Disciples of Christ.	Dunkers (Conservative).	Evangelical Association.	Friends (Orthodox).	German Evangelical Protestant Ministers' Association.	German Evangelical Synod of N. A.	Lutheran—General Synod.	Lutheran—General Council.	Lutheran—Synod Conference.
The state	4,157,545	1,742,873	1,171,064	82,035	24,706	43,555	83,833	9,076	14,932	12,394	11,850	35,138	30,317	18,237	24,129
Adams	26,328	7,652	7,652	456	448	...	527	75	...	...	...	...	...	...	...
Allen	47,976	21,463	15,364	840	1,097	604	893	363	...	...	...	...	190	718	101
Ashland	21,184	10,824	10,546	563	...	519	979	421	779	...	...	140	1,198	...	...
Ashtabula	51,448	17,049	14,569	1,319	218	3,237	1,440	...	...	...	...	...	...	413	40
Athens	38,730	11,506	9,841	455	550	127	2,120	...	...	...	...	...	...	...	...
Auglaize	31,192	11,684	8,299	298	344	...	228	...	72	45	...	965	314	225	180
Belmont	60,875	27,625	19,362	764	...	137	2,264	...	...	89	200	...	...	365	...
Brown	28,237	10,313	8,117	442	2,226	...	822	...	...	...	...	35	...	...	...
Butler	56,870	24,281	15,457	1,412	...	242	679	...	...	...	1,500	755	64	...	223
Carroll	16,811	6,571	6,211	...	...	26	850	...	...	71	...	...	...	176	...
Champaign	26,642	11,122	8,238	1,791	337	...	...	...	...	253	...	...	382	...	...
Clark	58,939	22,224	17,108	1,700	651	525	270	300	...	125	...	1,000	2,044	200	...
Clermont	31,610	12,079	10,509	1,042	903	...	949	34	...	...	...	100	...	...	24
Clinton	24,202	9,801	9,419	348	152	...	1,488	...	...	3,334	...	...	...	...	...
Columbiana	68,590	27,822	24,250	357	439	...	3,363	159	149	621	...	...	514	322	...
Coshocton	29,337	11,397	10,682	962	223	...	288	...	567	...	...	341	...	328	...
Crawford	33,915	15,580	12,496	342	...	...	258	...	384	...	...	...	1,812	...	...
Cuyahoga	439,120	161,101	87,575	7,732	...	9,459	4,436	...	1,450	618	2,548	6,436	252	326	12,687
Darke	42,532	13,882	12,206	184	2,533	...	399	1,116	102	...	...	...	240	246	...
Defiance	26,387	9,038	7,215	290	70	...	319	209	241	...	...	...	...	298	1,196
Delaware	26,401	9,559	8,369	714	74	245	75	...	...	96	...	...	169	...	...
Erie	37,650	15,417	9,426	250	...	849	75	...	211	126	...	1,243	...	...	...
Fairfield	34,259	14,567	12,714	46	...	...	85	39	407	...	...	...	189	1,804	...
Fayette	21,725	7,244	6,986	775	82	...	462	...	...	118	...	...	...	...	...
Franklin	164,460	74,503	43,335	3,423	148	2,444	1,261	...	319	270	890	2,800	169	321	...
Fulton	22,801	7,653	6,684	167	...	165	1,435	66	210	...	...	...	...	...	425 [illegible]
Gallia	27,918	8,476	8,296	2,180	1,132	165	...	...	...	...	...	...	...	...	...
Geauga	14,744	3,012	2,820	145	...	1,108	607	...	...	...	...	...	...	...	...
Greene	31,613	11,857	10,494	1,372	180	...	549	36	...	394	...	...	220	...	...
Guernsey	34,425	16,311	14,406	1,506	...	...	377	...	...	40	...	...	374	...	...
Hamilton	409,479	188,748	67,637	9,528	70	1,248	4,477	...	...	125	6,242	4,513	1,084	...	700
Hancock	41,993	14,388	13,485	303	...	30	825	205	765	...	...	...	936	502	...
Hardin	31,187	11,143	10,392	395	181	...	1,215	...	...	...	...	890	...	205	...
Harrison	20,486	7,568	7,568	113	...	...	320	...	...	167	...	...	...	340	...
Henry	27,282	10,006	8,352	...	...	26	50	25	96	...	...	...	92	103	2,209
Highland	30,982	13,135	12,606	894	220	...	2,201	93	...	944	...	...	240	...	...
Hocking	24,398	6,915	5,786	29	308	...	65	...	...	...	...	...	...	...	146
Holmes	19,511	6,993	6,739	46	...	...	1,440	...	...	...	...	260	300	...	102
Huron	32,330	11,544	9,232	872	...	1,518	488	...	169	53	...	135	...	...	...
Jackson	34,248	10,025	8,566	904	240	166	675	...	...	...	...	95	...	...	...

TABLE 4.—POPULATION IN 1900 AND COMMUNICANTS OR MEMBERS FOR SELECTED DENOMINATIONS, FOR EACH STATE AND TERRITORY, BY COUNTIES: 1906—Continued.

OHIO—Continued.

COUNTY.	Population, 1900.	All denominations.	PROTESTANT BODIES. Total.	Baptists—Northern and National Conventions.	Christians (Christian Connection).	Congregationalists.	Disciples of Christ.	Dunkers (Conservative).	Evangelical Association.	Friends (Orthodox).	German Evangelical Protestant Ministers' Association.	German Evangelical Synod of N. A.	Lutheran—General Synod.	Lutheran—General Council.	Lutheran—Synodical Conference.
Jefferson	44,357	28,696	16,153	286		205	1,868			640	560			81	
Knox	27,768	11,607	10,022	1,129	112	456	1,984	182							
Lake	21,680	7,772	6,102	473		1,084	950			65					40
Lawrence	39,534	12,777	10,715	3,618	129	109	555								
Licking	47,070	19,598	16,790	1,928	447	623	839		63			230	793		26
Logan	30,420	12,891	12,443	636	447		1,544	140	123	413			613		
Lorain	54,857	20,789	14,241	1,376		3,630	1,038		384			1,546	134		962
Lucas	153,559	47,696	32,689	2,688	74	3,054	1,126		453				138	2,646	1,197
Madison	20,590	6,630	5,407	317	822									72	
Mahoning	70,134	26,523	23,225	1,501	101	652	2,702	130	341	537			1,181	693	283
Marion	28,678	11,255	10,012	334	110		500		457			303			
Medina	21,958	8,252	8,017	428		1,245	507	76					462	270	112
Meigs	28,620	8,255	7,958	490	370	10	1,057					300			85
Mercer	28,021	13,493	5,967	178	266	114	145	54	142	285		222	86		
Miami	43,105	16,808	14,448	1,298	3,108		421	933		470		826	435	200	
Monroe	27,031	9,670	8,515	268			498					1,487			
Montgomery	130,146	65,811	40,031	3,482	743		905	1,540	538	52		1,450	1,834	2,371	
Morgan	17,905	5,969	5,883	126	84		438							170	
Morrow	17,879	6,074	6,019	825	91		135		72	438			135		
Muskingum	53,185	22,968	19,460	2,647	176	241	190	50				400	75	1,183	426
Noble	19,466	6,083	5,173	423			414						197		
Ottawa	22,213	8,506	6,734			143	228		201			1,348			160
Paulding	27,528	7,359	5,624	316	367		863	19	26					47	
Perry	31,841	13,304	9,052	616	227	97	549	172						56	
Pickaway	27,016	8,299	7,702	140	300		225		431				74	130	
Pike	18,172	4,176	4,116	176	114		50					150			
Portage	29,246	9,680	7,210	134		1,951	1,942			34			94		23
Preble	23,713	8,309	7,957		757		375	428	84	286			200	374	
Putnam	32,525	14,205	7,605		769	110	565	62	352				392		
Richland	44,289	19,893	17,036	607		1,797	1,588	90	508			1,065	4,121	470	
Ross	40,940	12,712	10,940	1,015	330	83	51	28		160		751	166		
Sandusky	34,311	12,477	9,644	105			157		887						
Scioto	40,981	14,300	12,035	923	176		1,807					520			
Seneca	41,163	18,356	11,366	245			340	104	734			568	216		
Shelby	24,625	11,977	7,755	618	859		275	182				451			
Stark	94,747	37,833	32,519	1,226		41	3,008	695	387	173		910	1,645	345	
Summit	71,715	26,505	22,446	909		2,696	3,228	215	769				880	664	1,062
Trumbull	46,591	16,724	14,783	844		605	4,620	10					54		
Tuscarawas	53,751	20,901	18,536	302		43	1,015	40				1,875	1,916	468	
Union	22,342	7,496	7,357	702	339	378	190			383					573
Van Wert	30,394	9,896	9,682	547	103		170	10	328	450		363	614	306	554
Vinton	15,330	4,214	3,706	50	16		477								
Warren	25,584	7,857	7,201	839	343		250			569					
Washington	48,245	16,286	14,520	1,534		1,077	809					765	575		
Wayne	37,870	[illegible],100	15,421	247		160	1,015	378	445				1,337	366	
Williams	24,953	8,289	7,637	152			756	258	225				237		
Wood	51,555	15,255	13,950	338		131	2,215	97	598				239	433	
Wyandot	21,125	6,478	6,194	41				40	463				631		
County location unknown[1]		122,841	4,078										65		

COUNTY.	PROTESTANT BODIES—continued. Lutheran—Joint Synod of Ohio, etc.	Methodist Episcopal Church.	Methodist Protestant Church.	African Methodists.[2]	Presbyterian Church in the U. S. A.	United Presbyterian Church.	Protestant Episcopal Church.	Reformed Church in the U. S.	United Brethren in Christ.	Other Protestant bodies.	Roman Catholic Church.	Jewish congregations.[3]	All other bodies.
The state	45,937	317,584	23,494	10,409	114,772	18,336	32,399	50,732	65,191	102,028	557,650	5,678	8,461
Adams		2,392	497		895	744			171	1,447			
Allen	366	4,594	176	115	1,206		164	1,121	1,138	1,678	[4]6,023		76
Ashland	922	2,203			1,022	151		320	849	485	278		
Ashtabula		3,935			1,099		551		301	2,016	2,308		172
Athens		4,200	455	26	811				476	621	1,643		22
Auglaize	804	1,700	353		451			1,455	418	447	3,385		
Belmont	36	8,721	280	395	3,601	879	173	245		1,263	8,207	40	16
Brown	120	2,137	300	226	919				427	363	2,196		
Butler	1,230	3,584	150	255	2,470	558	262	398	713	962	8,716	37	71
Carroll	380	2,060	667		1,206	395		257	30	93	360		
Champaign	50	2,961	587	196	536		194	160	299	492	2,884		
Clark	450	4,834	290	473	1,564	260	485	532	378	1,027	4,997	59	60
Clermont		4,956	78	58	1,277		67		460	555	1,570		
Clinton		2,158	750	305	175				145	564	382		
Columbiana	431	6,157	542	187	5,909	1,842	782	1,215	235	1,026	[4]3,527		45

[1] See explanatory headnote on page 294.
[2] Includes African Methodist Episcopal Church, African Methodist Episcopal Zion Church, and Colored Methodist Episcopal Church.
[3] Heads of families only.
[4] Partial report only, remainder included in total for "County location unknown.

TABLE 4.—POPULATION IN 1900 AND COMMUNICANTS OR MEMBERS FOR SELECTED DENOMINATIONS, FOR EACH STATE AND TERRITORY, BY COUNTIES: 1906—Continued.

OHIO—Continued.

COUNTY.	PROTESTANT BODIES—continued.										Roman Catholic Church.	Jewish congregations.[2]	All other bodies.
	Lutheran—Joint Synod of Ohio, etc.	Methodist Episcopal Church.	Methodist Protestant Church.	African Methodists.[1]	Presbyterian Church in the U. S. A.	United Presbyterian Church.	Protestant Episcopal Church.	Reformed Church in the U. S.	United Brethren in Christ.	Other Protestant bodies.			
Coshocton	210	3,733	954		1,253	116	62	403	275	967	715		
Crawford	2,770	2,188	73		766		160	1,766	1,586	396	3,034		
Cuyahoga	490	12,880	41	629	8,669	621	6,478	4,579	654	6,590	[3]69,794	2,137	1,596
Darke	761	1,964		39	432		145	462	2,515	1,068	1,676		
Defiance		1,831			457		136	205	851	1,112	1,811		12
Delaware	297	3,810		83	1,487		144	335	294	546	1,065		125
Erie	2,571	1,283		31	566		1,163	853		205	5,808		183
Fairfield	614	4,028	285		961	53	145	1,522	772	1,339	1,853		
Fayette		3,349	851	171	730					448	258		
Franklin	4,451	14,864	46	763	4,117	554	1,452	677	1,871	2,142	29,960	575	643
Fulton		1,607			158			335	523	1,866	969		
Gallia		3,117		101	225		115		345	916	180		
Geauga		884								76	149		43
Greene		3,200	485	712	767	1,175	60	953		391	1,363		
Guernsey		5,497	1,299	102	1,277	2,486	40		508	901	1,874		31
Hamilton	242	12,469	225	1,882	10,536	193	4,956	1,869	1,548	5,730	119,162	1,680	263
Hancock	700	3,360	797	44	1,135	130	75	93	2,092	1,493	808		95
Hardin		4,272	384	56	1,137	232	47	518	595	354	751		
Harrison		3,133	121	288	1,962	658		166	288	12			
Henry	464	1,596	12		484		20	754	844	1,577	1,654		
Highland		4,454	222	39	1,707	61	89	155	670	617	459		70
Hocking	393	1,982	121		437				1,785	520	1,051		78
Holmes	39	1,251			504	89		630	220	1,858	254		
Huron	1,031	2,772		10	759		433	89	521	382	[3]2,312		
Jackson		3,150	182	12	518			108	1,522	994	1,242		217
Jefferson	110	5,097	1,587	259	3,681	909	350	85	100	335	11,281	55	1,207
Knox	202	2,646	994	64	789		633			831	1,585		
Lake		1,689			204		549			1,068	1,560		110
Lawrence	160	3,252		148	406		167	176	723	1,272	1,968		94
Licking		5,626	462	87	2,499	63	437	110	968	1,589	2,808		
Logan		4,116	721	93	1,605	585	110	72	157	1,068	428		20
Lorain		3,318		68	261		590	285	240	409	[3]6,375	76	97
Lucas	1,412	5,195	121	204	2,356	96	2,902	1,429	1,266	6,332	[3]13,867	444	696
Madison		2,945	87	54	555	120	80		138	217	1,223		
Mahoning	1,818	4,840	80	149	3,049	1,175	984	1,682		1,347	[3]2,992	190	116
Marion	1,036	3,960	35	19	785		225	698	500	1,050	1,172	23	48
Medina	437	2,247	73		150		140	628	180	1,062	[3]235		
Meigs	182	2,873	86	62	500		70		336	1,537	297		
Mercer	841	1,739		16	245	40			412	1,182	7,526		
Miami	175	3,003		240	1,315	144	252	248	304	1,076	2,292	18	60
Monroe		3,620	216		363	71			215	1,777	1,155		
Montgomery	2,387	6,198		372	3,165	427	1,120	4,339	7,491	1,647	25,363	172	245
Morgan	125	1,953	1,455		478	16			155	883	86		
Morrow	78	2,401	180		626	92	40	80	341	485	55		
Muskingum	80	7,059	1,768	258	2,510	1,135	479		308	475	3,456	52	
Noble		2,371	995		241					532	910		
Ottawa	1,611	948	125		111		171		488	1,200	[3]1,522		250
Paulding	241	1,690	45	68	455			92	638	757	1,391		344
Perry	1,301	3,601		66	285	205	20	433	664	760	4,252		
Pickaway	821	3,151		80	469		149	73	1,336	323	597		
Pike		1,637	118	48	104			134	513	1,072	60		
Portage		2,207			35		163	225	19	383	2,470		
Preble	594	1,525		22	481	526		288	1,091	926	302		60
Putnam	118	1,765	270		581	47			1,010	1,564	[3]6,600		
Richland		2,791	67	22	1,577	418	406	209	679	632	2,803	34	20
Ross		4,693	70	182	1,978		245	85	698	405	1,754		18
Sandusky	3,972	1,682	50	20	606		381	790	744	271	[3]2,783		50
Scioto	164	4,223	80	147	1,475	33	357		488	1,642	2,139	36	90
Seneca	410	2,280	802		790		200	2,428	1,536	713	[3]6,960		30
Shelby	1,257	2,077		16	713	116	43	203	717	228	4,222		
Stark	2,748	6,206		101	2,274	75	445	6,095	3,788	2,357	[3]5,186		128
Summit	200	4,411		30	770	195	1,257	2,767	996	1,397	[3]3,709	50	300
Trumbull	427	4,988	68		1,638	52	493	283	160	541	[3]1,901		40
Tuscarawas	42	5,049	893		1,080		76	2,017	1,775	1,945	2,250		115
Union	536	2,493	646	29	519		18		251	300	139		
Van Wert		2,992		65	1,060				674	1,446	197		17
Vinton		1,390	83		410		34		832	413	322		187
Warren	94	2,540		52	1,049	16	80	78	217	1,074	627		29
Washington		4,950		79	1,135	42	200		958	2,396	1,726		40
Wayne	139	3,279			2,866	444	150	1,661	570	2,364	1,679		
Williams		2,491			685		17	298	825	1,693	652		
Wood	1,777	2,991	94		1,358	97		76	2,069	1,437	[3]1,280		25
Wyandot	650	1,904			301		9	490	584	1,081	[3]284		
County location unknown[4]		2,215		91					712	995	[5]118,541		222

[1] Includes African Methodist Episcopal Church, African Methodist Episcopal Zion Church, and Colored Methodist Episcopal Church.
[2] Heads of families only.
[3] Partial report only: remainder included in total for "County location unknown."
[4] See explanatory headnote on page 294.
[5] Comprises report of communicants for that part of Cleveland diocese not returned separately by counties.

TABLE 4.—POPULATION IN 1900 AND COMMUNICANTS OR MEMBERS FOR SELECTED DENOMINATIONS, FOR EACH STATE AND TERRITORY, BY COUNTIES: 1906—Continued.

OKLAHOMA.[1]

COUNTY.	Population, 1907.	All denominations.	PROTESTANT BODIES.												
			Total.	Seventh-day Adventists.	Baptists—Southern and National Conventions.	Free-will Baptists.	Congregationalists.	Disciples of Christ.	Churches of Christ.	Friends (Orthodox).	Lutheran—Synodical Conference.	General Conference of Mennonites of N. A.	Methodist Episcopal Church.	African Methodist Episcopal Church.	Methodist Protestant Church.
The state	[2]1,414,177	257,100	218,787	1,967	66,930	1,288	2,677	24,232	8,074	2,187	2,907	1,145	23,309	6,243	2,064
Adair	9,115	1,696	1,696		670			57					50		
Alfalfa	16,070	3,976	3,564		337		83	676	409	630	25		936		
Atoka	12,113	2,161	2,058		732			64						207	
Beaver	13,364	1,464	1,248	26	205			211	33	46			415		
Beckham	17,758	2,633	2,345	40	938			278	349				31		90
Blaine	17,227	2,856	2,409	166	514			190	110			201	552	147	
Bryan	27,865	4,449	4,176		1,977			17	169					122	
Caddo	30,241	4,611	3,628	23	671		94	877	5		103	23	991	97	
Canadian	20,110	4,890	3,075		400		89	799	39		179		643		
Carter	26,402	4,989	4,785		2,313				176				100	80	59
Cherokee	14,274	1,911	1,911		848	108							5		
Choctaw	17,340	2,385	2,302		951			61	109				50	169	38
Cimarron	5,927	97	97		79				18						
Cleveland	18,460	3,677	3,128	7	885	18		50	320	27	70		265	50	36
Coal	15,585	2,442	1,606	23	773			16	235		19		67	88	
Comanche	31,738	5,468	4,963	78	1,548		59	752	114		31		809	25	77
Craig	14,955	2,441	2,251	36	342		110	230					70	145	
Creek	18,365	1,718	1,479		291			328			34		104	46	
Custer	18,478	3,446	2,723	49	224		127	537				13	379	69	
Delaware	9,876	950	924		531			40							42
Dewey	13,329	1,476	1,372	37	245			343				26	430		
Ellis	13,978	1,639	1,214	191	186		54	197			31		312		
Garfield	28,300	6,615	5,935	111	747		329	1,275	80		785		1,233	20	24
Garvin	22,787	3,604	3,604	29	1,498			190	326				35		139
Grady	23,420	5,092	4,595		1,669		41	805			18		103	600	60
Grant	17,636	3,991	3,427		547		218	810	60	131		103	1,062		
Greer	23,624	6,290	6,128		2,757			138	708		25				182
Harper	8,089	401	394		70		69	110			47		76		
Haskell	16,865	2,102	2,021		893								65	68	134
Hughes	19,945	2,011	1,984		680	142		75	202				56	10	
Jackson	17,087	3,330	3,330		793			72	496						
Jefferson	13,439	959	959		603	11			124					10	
Johnston	18,672	2,343	2,317		1,048			54	180					60	17
Kay	24,757	5,765	4,892	8	856			807	53		215		1,802	18	26
Kingfisher	18,010	5,064	4,082	194	975		192	701	68		47		838	186	
Kiowa	22,247	3,935	3,560		1,105			301	906		84	142	588		30
Latimer	9,340	1,392	1,214		968			15					15	35	
Le Flore	24,678	2,874	2,746		1,308	60		55	72				40	63	
Lincoln	37,293	6,788	5,978	90	1,625	17	125	1,378	136	338	170		774	142	130
Logan	30,711	7,199	6,084	27	1,844		184	1,032	55		143		970	211	
Love	11,134	2,122	2,122		1,375									30	
McClain	12,888	2,737	2,184		793			185	30				92	350	7
McCurtain	13,198	2,	2,462		948			50	25					75	124
McIntosh	17,975	2,465	2,175		1,046	27		45	183				45	156	139
Major	14,307	2,989	2,083	63	219			455	163	248	71	160	460		
Marshall	13,144	2,110	2,101		959				313						
Mayes	11,064	1,369	1,360		478	97		150					37		
Murray	11,948	2,[illegible]	2,427		807		14	260	38					47	
Muskogee	37,467	8,735	7,592	15	2,948	291	28	294	39		45		328	523	30
Noble	14,198	3,403	2,635	36	675		16	547		70	189	45	617	43	
Nowata	10,458		806		130			107					236	121	
Okfuskee	15,595	2	2,349		943	116		110					244	212	31
Oklahoma	55,849	16	9,681	126	2,404		539	1,671			143		1,718	288	
Okmulgee	14,362	2,822	2,223		899			179	20		10		50	100	
Osage	15,332	1,[illegible]	541		102			150					78	33	
Ottawa	12,827	2,329	1,446	33	455			130		271			44		13
Pawnee	17,112	2,338	2,101	35	324		30	375	53	51			562	23	
Payne	22,022	4,534	4,072	56	569		122	897	80		44		947	31	
Pittsburg	37,677	8,279	4,845	15	2,326			503	65				168	202	18
Pontotoc	23,057	3,959	3,959	18	1,563			440	300				18		
Pottawatomie	43,272	10,013	7,507	6	2,515	228	42	445	455	93	28		798	140	80
Pushmataha	8,295	824	754		248				72					60	
Roger Mills	13,239	1,458	1,280	34	295			25	199				90		
Rogers	15,485	1,501	1,451	60	454			115					252	30	
Seminole	14,687		955		469	9		20					35	47	
Sequoyah	22,499	2,	2,514		1,058								27	174	150
Stephens	20,148	3,970	3,143		1,059	40		261	300						190
Texas	16,448	1,[illegible]	1,565	104	465			161	91				75		
Tillman	12,869	1,564	1,553		583			236	95		17		90		40
Tulsa	21,693	6,849	2,816	16	634			385	23		20		479	60	
Wagoner	19,529	3,474	3,346	17	1,364	108		105	79		3		93	661	
Washington	12,813	1,956	1,181	18	297			200		107			178	25	
Washita	22,007	5,150	4,454	24	1,046		32		495		15	394	41		99
Woods	15,517	3,677	3,306	58	274		80	460	102	175	279	38	992	7	
Woodward	14,595	2,782	2,497	98	537			895			17		761		49
County location unknown[3]		5,679	5,297		23	16		1,245					158	137	

[1] Oklahoma and Indian Territory combined.
[2] Special census of Indian Territory and the territory of Oklahoma taken as of July 1, 1907. Figures for 1900 not comparable; no county organization for Indian Territory at that census.
[3] See explanatory headnote on page 294.

TABLE 4.—POPULATION IN 1900 AND COMMUNICANTS OR MEMBERS FOR SELECTED DENOMINATIONS, FOR EACH STATE AND TERRITORY, BY COUNTIES: 1906—Continued.

OKLAHOMA[1]—Continued.

COUNTY.	PROTESTANT BODIES—continued.									Roman Catholic Church.	Jewish congregations.[2]	Latter-day Saints (Reorganized).	All other bodies.
	Methodist Episcopal Church, South.	Colored Methodist Episcopal Church.	Free Methodist Church of N. A.	Presbyterian Church in the U. S. A.	Cumberland Presbyterian Church.	Presbyterian Church in the U. S.	Protestant Episcopal Church.	United Brethren in Christ.	Other Protestant bodies.				
The state	40,473	2,858	975	9,667	4,351	1,323	2,024	2,819	11,284	36,548	72	914	779
Adair	785				74				60				
Alfalfa	8		154	33	108				165	412			
Atoka	620	145		75	93	55	16		51	103			
Beaver	124		25	13					150	195		21	
Beckham	413		18		106	63			19	238			50
Blaine	50	27	65	168	8		20	32	159	447			
Bryan	1,133	90		97	83	407			81	273			
Caddo	164		9	223			9	67	272	983			
Canadian	147			319			40	150	270	1,753		62	
Carter	1,496	119		143	140		65		94	182	22		
Cherokee	387	11		216			20		316				
Choctaw	432	164	9	125	10	184				83			
Cimarron													
Cleveland	964	55		211			12	27	141	549			
Coal	123			33	70	77	66		16	801		35	
Comanche	777		7	402	78	19	22		165	485			20
Craig	915			232			55		116	190			
Creek	387	90			32		38	29	100	239			
Custer	856		8					124	337	723			
Delaware	176								135	26			
Dewey	113		62	24					92			104	
Ellis	220			23						425			
Garfield			35	299			90	381	546	680			
Garvin	1,101	10		103	151		22						
Grady	927	25	11	112	111		70		43	497			
Grant	27		88	117	35			34	205	564			
Greer	1,883				286	44			105	162			
Harper									22			7	
Haskell	701			32	75				53	81			
Hughes	690				71				58	27			
Jackson	1,477		6		259				227				
Jefferson	82	15		30	84								
Johnston	553	48		82	184	80	11			26			
Kay			86	763			36	104	118	831			42
Kingfisher			57	161				124	539	982			
Kiowa	735		8	232	41	18			178	375			
Latimer	108			68	5							178	
Le Flore	843	12		76	134	49	15		19	128			
Lincoln	161	84	25	249	78		23	31	402	810			
Logan	120	156	56	407			165	81	633	1,115			
Love	613	5				39			60				
McClain	621	20		33	17		36			553			
McCurtain	378	107		458	66	31			200	3			
McIntosh	438	30		37			27		2	94			
Major			34		30				240				
Marshall	705				20	36				9			
Mayes	502	68			96					9			
Murray	1,003	120			115		15		8	234			
Muskogee	1,275	380	10	627	57		253		249	1,343			
Noble	100	21	44	134			14		84	684		64	20
Nowata		24		77	20				91	16			
Okfuskee	412	167		46					18	9			
Oklahoma	835	64	40	728	122		315	187	501	7,993	50		70
Okmulgee	575			209	40				141	242			
Osage				104			52		25	1,142			
Ottawa	414			7	64				15	690		193	
Pawnee	25		31	144	51		36	205	156	237			
Payne			39	162	100		15	417	593	432		30	
Pittsburg	754	140		161	123		201		169	3,183		56	196
Pontotoc	1,023	249			211	82			55				
Pottawatomie	1,495			421	67		77	224	443	2,506			
Pushmataha	184			64	26	100				70			
Roger Mills	554								83	102		76	
Rogers	381			75	34		23		27	50			
Seminole	190	83		72					30	15			
Sequoyah	695	82		100					149	7			
Stephens	1,179					25				319			
Texas	529				44				75				
Tillman	337			70					85			11	
Tulsa	609	15		370					125	956		77	
Wagoner	470	204		56	135		80		31	128			
Washington				75			26		259	775			
Washita	1,186		16		268	14			824	696			
Woods				214			26	423	178	371			
Woodward	119		32	92			17	58	322	285			
County location unknown[3]	3,184	28		66	140			141	159				382

[1] Oklahoma and Indian Territory combined. [2] Heads of families only. [3] See explanatory headnote on page 294.

TABLE 4.—POPULATION IN 1900 AND COMMUNICANTS OR MEMBERS FOR SELECTED DENOMINATIONS, FOR EACH STATE AND TERRITORY, BY COUNTIES: 1906—Continued.

OREGON.

COUNTY.	Population, 1900.	All denominations.	PROTESTANT BODIES. Total.	Baptists—Northern and National Conventions.	Congregationalists.	Disciples of Christ.	Methodist Episcopal Church.	Methodist Episcopal Church, South.	Presbyterian Church in the U. S. A.	Protestant Episcopal Church.	Other Protestant bodies.	Roman Catholic Church.	Jewish congregations.[1]	All other bodies.
The state	413,536	120,229	81,855	11,159	4,575	10,012	18,681	2,272	9,701	3,580	21,875	35,317	414	2,643
Baker	15,597	4,340	1,707	539	38	233	285	141	277	121	73	2,380		253
Benton	6,706	2,091	1,885	106	124	183	390	114	165	83	720	194		12
Clackamas	19,658	4,894	3,909	432	525	31	909	52	286	90	1,584	940		45
Clatsop	12,765	2,735	1,783	64	58		249		303	292	817	935		17
Columbia	6,237	846	846	35	74		175		122	10	430			
Coos	10,324	2,526	1,863	129		130	283	237	219	184	661	535		128
Crook	3,964	688	688	149		75	255		107		102			
Curry	1,868	143	109						14	60	35	34		
Douglas	14,565	2,329	2,185	484		325	604	363	230	61	118	144		
Gilliam	3,201	736	361	97	51		205				8	243		132
Grant	5,948	321	321	74			131		22	15	79			
Harney	2,598	128	128	48					61		19			
Jackson	13,698	2,975	2,660	529	110	347	667	154	406	54	393	244		71
Josephine	7,517	1,706	1,553	260		250	506	127	250	33	127	153		
Klamath	3,970	318	318				200		118					
Lake	2,847	248	103				93				10	145		
Lane	19,604	6,942	6,421	674	160	2,092	1,538	95	517	97	1,248	494		27
Lincoln	3,575	722	510			30	260		65	30	125	212		
Linn	18,603	4,729	4,317	796	149	761	822	317	619	16	837	412		
Malheur	4,203	531	283	56	41	31	108				47	248		
Marion	27,713	10,240	6,647	537	464	909	1,527		692	100	2,418	3,593		
Morrow	4,151	608	608	73	61	121	100	124		32	97			
Multnomah	103,167	41,695	22,692	3,268	1,671	1,058	4,570	200	3,518	1,890	6,517	17,832	414	757
Polk	9,923	2,372	2,372	432		716	426	12	256		530			
Sherman	3,477	327	327	19		52	190		66					
Tillamook	4,471	593	593	21		69	127		100		276			
Umatilla	18,049	7,120	3,720	451	129	906	545	291	331	209	858	3,400		
Union	16,070	3,096	1,826	281		426	455	45	348	104	167	271		999
Wallowa	5,538	765	671	88		135	340		93		15	94		
Wasco	13,199	3,569	2,507	275	328	564	648			67	625	1,015		47
Washington	14,467	4,206	3,015	198	547	145	704		261		1,160	1,191		
Wheeler	2,443	246	246	116			130							
Yamhill	13,420	5,142	4,524	928	45	423	1,225		218	32	1,653	608		10
County location unknown[2]		302	157				14		37		106			145

[1] Heads of families only.

[2] See explanatory headnote on page 294.

PENNSYLVANIA.

COUNTY.	Population, 1900.	All denominations.	PROTESTANT BODIES. Total.	Baptists—Northern and National Conventions.	Churches of God in N. A., General Eldership.	Congregationalists.	Disciples of Christ.	Dunkers (Conservative).	Evangelical Association.	United Evangelical Church.	Friends (Hicksite).	Lutheran—General Synod.	Lutheran—General Council.	Lutheran—Synodical Conference.	Mennonite Church.
The state	6,302,115	2,977,022	1,717,037	139,030	11,157	14,811	26,458	18,889	13,294	45,480	8,947	125,263	182,160	10,729	10,498
Adams	34,496	16,977	12,839		25		17	471		70	143	6,289			
Allegheny	775,058	444,793	190,512	17,341	220	1,430	7,299	68	805	207		7,014	6,545	6,490	
Armstrong	52,551	26,029	19,382	1,082	70			235	35	355		3,407	1,577		
Beaver	56,432	26,476	20,341	909	208	125	630		201				2,655	125	
Bedford	39,468	14,908	13,911	29	259		30	1,279	212	462	90	1,967			
Berks	159,615	77,477	66,669	1,063			115	375	1,299	3,101	26	795	28,267		196
Blair	85,099	43,109	28,912	1,374	630		268	1,452	116	327		5,981	513		110
Bradford	59,403	20,033	14,481	2,242		247	1,620			80			285		
Bucks	71,190	31,659	26,118	1,338				64	202	252	1,373	2,300	6,131		1,498
Butler	56,962	29,242	21,544	698	207		22		50	101		987	1,941	237	
Cambria	104,837	63,873	22,854	1,069	30	642	777	714	372	2,141		2,263	1,719		122
Cameron	7,048	2,159	1,211	61											
Carbon	44,510	23,473	13,598	204		349			351	681			4,612		
Center	42,894	15,730	13,848	478			455		288	1,421	83	2,380			
Chester	95,695	37,224	29,010	4,397				354	35	132	1,730	961	878		90
Clarion	34,283	14,636	10,267	606					50	559		1,014	521		
Clearfield	80,614	32,317	19,125	1,217	147	54		146	128	674	194	928	1,963	287	44
Clinton	29,197	11,757	8,297	175		33	458	32	145	1,093		965	454		
Columbia	39,896	16,324	14,342	664			739			1,302	200	1,836	1,487		
Crawford	63,643	23,179	16,432	1,757		669	94			75			667		
Cumberland	50,344	19,403	18,889		1,660		100	380		1,533		4,488	333		141
Dauphin	114,443	49,655	39,149	895	1,711		96	398	351	1,504		8,264	2,687	22	115
Delaware	94,762	37,537	22,820	4,414		99					868	367	388	12	
Elk	32,903	17,034	5,014	122		500	44						1,480		
Erie	98,473	47,392	22,097	1,667		75	197		375				3,750	592	

TABLE 4.—POPULATION IN 1900 AND COMMUNICANTS OR MEMBERS FOR SELECTED DENOMINATIONS, FOR EACH STATE AND TERRITORY, BY COUNTIES: 1906—Continued.

PENNSYLVANIA—Continued.

COUNTY.	Population, 1900.	All denominations.	PROTESTANT BODIES. Total.	Baptists—Northern and National Conventions.	Churches of God in N. A., General Eldership.	Congregationalists.	Disciples of Christ.	Dunkers (Conservative).	Evangelical Association.	United Evangelical Church.	Friends (Hicksite).	Lutheran—General Synod.	Lutheran—General Council.	Lutheran—Synodical Conference.	Mennonite Church.
Fayette	110,412	47,523	24,778	3,512	333		1,673	430	454	100		541	1,114		80
Forest	11,039	1,845	1,459						49	33			20		
Franklin	54,902	22,140	21,357		346	90	60	1,397				4,612			351
Fulton	9,924	3,692	3,692		6			120				321		45	
Greene	28,281	10,588	10,355	2,391	264		1,189								
Huntingdon	34,650	12,714	11,927	550	162			556				1,224			
Indiana	42,556	20,381	15,133	1,521	5		464	173	250	377		1,581	56		
Jefferson	59,113	25,545	14,716	1,516	86	67	178		133	539		530	563	143	
Juniata	16,054	5,483	5,483					301		360		1,244	160		206
Lackawanna	193,831	140,878	34,549	6,411		2,109	437		50	137		133	2,267	325	
Lancaster	159,241	60,425	54,307	677	1,633			3,023	814	2,769	632	2,682	8,340	250	4,953
Lawrence	57,042	26,341	18,723	1,615	60	300	1,789		80			97	604		
Lebanon	53,827	21,492	18,835	73	38		23	954	195	1,396		2,029	3,048		85
Lehigh	93,893	49,475	44,926	430		183			1,080	2,322		1,185	16,279		
Luzerne	257,121	155,987	47,441	3,400		2,697	1,048		388	727		1,030	6,075	133	
Lycoming	75,663	31,744	26,650	3,707		197	383		117	2,237		5,386	1,202		
McKean	51,343	14,149	9,039	864		163				25			1,896	17	
Mercer	57,387	31,198	21,207	1,349	80	246	544			153			856		
Mifflin	23,160	9,576	8,970	171		278		402	81	258		1,854	17		
Monroe	21,161	7,473	6,967	166					273			576	959		
Montgomery	138,995	65,632	45,915	5,096				865	623	607	1,118	1,347	10,254		1,909
Montour	15,526	6,328	5,278	409						34		475	1,097		
Northampton	99,687	59,293	43,	547		150			968	1,537		1,057	14,962		
Northumberland	90,911	46,756	24,449	1,394	116	188			130	1,085	13	5,502	3,139		
Perry	26,263	8,834	8,[illegible]		461			88		868		1,955			
Philadelphia	1,293,697	558,866	254,812	44,368	300	2,357	1,034	523	884	716	2,477	3,872	16,888	772	
Pike	8,766	1,478	1,227	56					125						
Potter	30,621	6,747	4,482	675									388	105	
Schuylkill	172,927	85,800	37,510	924	451	529		92	788	2,487		3,399	9,638		
Snyder	17,304	6,976	6,976	81					153	836		1,397	2,240		26
Somerset	49,461	24,178	19,491		220		867	2,380	124	1,257		6,215	57	124	455
Sullivan	12,134	3,802	1,900				117			301			363		
Susquehanna	40,043	16,081	8,027	1,		418				28					
Tioga	49,086	14,548	11,195	2, 67		213	438		64	150		242	696	10	
Union	17,592	7,591	7,591	[illegible]				70		1,424		2,344			
Venango	49,648	20,472	14,378	1,	289		39		76	1,086			265	232	
Warren	38,946	11,333	8,784			326			267	83			1,597		
Washington	92,181	45,619	32,654	3,196		21	2,779	46		45		253	548	58	
Wayne	30,171	11,512	7,721	1,[illegible]			30		16	78			534		
Westmoreland	160,175	74,737	44,921	1,861	677		405	175	17	676		1,722	7,070	155	
Wyoming	17,152	4,758	4,197	1,111									113		
York	116,413	52,745	48,793	99	463	56		1,127	80	4,079		17,625		595	112
County location unknown[1]		1,991	1,761					200				627			

COUNTY.	PROTESTANT BODIES—continued. Methodist Episcopal Church.	Methodist Protestant Church.	African Methodists.[2]	Presbyterian Church in the U. S. A.	Cumberland Presbyterian Church.	United Presbyterian Church.	Protestant Episcopal Church.	Reformed Church in the U. S.	United Brethren in Christ.	Other Protestant bodies.	Roman Catholic Church.	Jewish congregations.[3]	All other bodies.
The state	318,911	12,317	22,033	248,335	8,912	56,587	99,021	177,270	53,397	113,543	1,214,734	15,479	29,772
Adams	832		87	478			34	3,647	617	129	4,138		
Allegheny	34,037	3,233	4,019	39,969	1,883	21,845	9,680	3,308	1,790	23,329	240,837	2,457	10,987
Armstrong	3,682	200	33	4,535	70	1,387	548	1,624		542	6,597		50
Beaver	4,275	882	195	4,293		2,908	635		202	2,098	6,064	45	26
Bedford	3,463	287	69	332			40	3,327	251	1,814	997		
Berks	2,511		65	924			1,178	24,033	1,268	1,453	10,123	210	475
Blair	8,148		117	3,959		296	740	2,384	2,019	478	14,050	67	80
Bradford	5,663	59	17	2,136			589	129		1,414	5,552		
Bucks	2,168		220	2,400			1,147	5,753		1,272	5,439		102
Butler	3,687		14	5,430	100	4,112	276	1,527	63	2,092	7,023	45	30
Cambria	4,195		54	1,875		150		549	2,615	2,934	40,763	65	191
Cameron	705			135						195	948		
Carbon	1,262			1,107				3,826		620	9,875		
Center	3,710		130	1,400			633	1,914	952	310	1,882		
Chester	6,608		1,731	7,086		109	1,[illegible]	1,815	121	1,537	8,184		30
Clarion	3,241	131		2,145		37	92	1,508		363	4,369		
Clearfield	6,419	130	35	2,899		123	47	569	1,666	1,025	12,719		473
Clinton	2,723		15	1,193			358	593		60	3,460		
Columbia	4,518	229	32	1,090			419	1,442	339	50	1,982		
Crawford	5,145	45	69	2,307		1,355	638	1,192	843	1,579	6,506	16	225

[1] See explanatory headnote on page 294.
[2] Includes Union American Methodist Episcopal Church, African Methodist Episcopal Church, African Union Methodist Protestant Church, African Methodist Episcopal Zion Church, and Colored Methodist Episcopal Church.
[3] Heads of families only.

TABLE 4.—POPULATION IN 1900 AND COMMUNICANTS OR MEMBERS FOR SELECTED DENOMINATIONS, FOR EACH STATE AND TERRITORY, BY COUNTIES: 1906—Continued.

PENNSYLVANIA—Continued.

COUNTY.	PROTESTANT BODIES—continued.										Roman Catholic Church.	Jewish congregations.[2]	All other bodies.
	Methodist Episcopal Church.	Methodist Protestant Church.	African Methodists.[1]	Presbyterian Church in the U. S. A.	Cumberland Presbyterian Church.	United Presbyterian Church.	Protestant Episcopal Church.	Reformed Church in the U. S.	United Brethren in Christ.	Other Protestant bodies.			
Cumberland	2,027		500	2,262		225	278	1,292	3,188	482	514		
Dauphin	6,890		1,173	3,383			860	4,033	6,115	652	8,031	375	2,100
Delaware	6,735		1,890	4,549			2,819			679	14,617	50	50
Elk	1,434			441			273		70	650	12,020		
Erie	5,560		34	4,204		518	1,434		587	3,104	25,042	86	167
Fayette	4,334	1,639	579	3,476	2,082	219	638	56	1,197	2,321	22,551	32	162
Forest	796			298					35	228	396		
Franklin	2,393	338	348	2,106		63	150	3,218	3,409	2,476	762		21
Fulton	1,504		12	307		58		150	200	969			
Greene	2,102	1,543	35	713	1,109		17			992	233		
Huntingdon	4,972	200	32	1,794		124	112	1,382	774	45	787		
Indiana	3,063		46	4,445	154	2,157	123	22	248	448	4,888		380
Jefferson	5,452	349		2,936	630	380	105	434	492	183	10,529	300	
Juniata	1,282			1,214		219	13	125	353	6			
Lackawanna	8,726	242	114	6,637			2,891	99		3,971	101,884	569	3,876
Lancaster	696		389	4,164		95	1,546	6,796	5,028	4,820	5,851	121	146
Lawrence	5,432		77	4,668		3,235	430	37		1,299	7,412	56	150
Lebanon	4,682			329			334	5,648	3,338	663	2,607		59
Lehigh	926			1,246			498	19,112	291	1,374	4,229	60	260
Luzerne	18,139	539	143	6,917			2,829	4,303		4,073	105,251	288	3,007
Lycoming	7,369		296	2,738			1,678	335	214	791	5,012		82
McKean	3,056		39	1,110			565		573	729	4,951	68	91
Mercer	5,538		46	5,257	477	3,019	529	1,865	30	1,218	9,762	78	151
Mifflin	2,740		59	1,816			132	255	82	825	606		
Monroe	2,158	30	15	776			99	1,836		98	506		
Montgomery	4,531		438	4,837			4,735	7,981	191	1,384	19,617		100
Montour	998			1,079			362	824			975	50	25
Northampton	3,409		69	2,969			1,390	11,992	110	4,289	15,615	139	90
Northumberland	4,114		73	1,863			657	4,292	1,026	773	21,318	60	413
Perry	1,845			790			39	1,519	1,185	93			
Philadelphia	44,693	175	6,911	51,716		3,960	46,644	9,709	215	16,598	289,615	9,991	4,448
Pike	493	30		111			132			280	251		
Potter	1,509			325			251		286	853	2,265		
Schuylkill	4,855		25	1,391			1,777	9,116	947	1,091	47,861	60	369
Snyder	157			120			12	1,373	581				
Somerset	1,454		43	216			69	3,364	1,220	1,359	4,687		
Sullivan	510	35		48			50	184		232	1,795		107
Susquehanna	3,631	86	32	1,468			388			527	8,054		
Tioga	3,862			1,192			742			1,177	3,353		
Union	1,062			634				1,494		107			
Venango	4,268		208	3,372	117	643	838	97	189	1,463	5,943	51	100
Warren	3,247			1,281			534	70	411	603	2,533		16
Washington	5,797	675	680	8,481	2,290	5,651	605		350	1,224	12,507	49	309
Wayne	3,110	234		950			321			1,346	3,736		55
Westmoreland	9,147	107	326	8,481		3,258	400	5,718	2,949	1,777	29,698	30	88
Wyoming	2,172	60		467			38			236	561		
York	3,759	839	499	3,065		441	781	9,399	4,408	1,366	3,811	61	80
County location unknown[3]	200								359	375			230

[1] Includes Union American Methodist Episcopal Church, African Methodist Episcopal Church, African Union Methodist Protestant Church, African Methodist Episcopal Zion Church, and Colored Methodist Episcopal Church.
[2] Heads of families only.
[3] See explanatory headnote on page 294.

RHODE ISLAND.

COUNTY.	Population, 1900.	All denominations.	PROTESTANT BODIES.								Roman Catholic Church.	Jewish congregations.[1]	Armenian Church.	All other bodies.
			Total.	Baptists—Northern and National Conventions.	Free Baptists.	Congregationalists.	Lutheran—General Council.	Methodist Episcopal Church.	Protestant Episcopal Church.	Other Protestant bodies.				
The state	428,556	264,712	64,141	14,928	3,252	9,858	2,516	6,536	15,443	11,608	195,951	1,025	2,103	1,492
Bristol	13,144	6,729	2,398	343		526		415	1,110	4	4,281			50
Kent	29,976	15,649	4,704	978	214	333	1,180	494	854	651	10,945			
Newport	32,599	14,868	6,124	1,485	248	556	75	822	1,990	1,038	8,420	60		264
Providence	328,683	217,035	43,598	9,404	2,613	7,663	1,261	4,414	10,518	7,725	169,216	965	2,103	1,153
Washington	24,154	10,279	7,165	2,718	177	780		391	1,041	2,058	3,089			25
County location unknown[2]		152	152						20	132				

[1] Heads of families only. [2] See explanatory headnote on page 294.

TABLE 4.—POPULATION IN 1900 AND COMMUNICANTS OR MEMBERS FOR SELECTED DENOMINATIONS, FOR EACH STATE AND TERRITORY, BY COUNTIES: 1906—Continued.

SOUTH CAROLINA.

COUNTY.	Population, 1900.	All denominations.	PROTESTANT BODIES. Total.	Baptists—Southern and National Conventions.	Lutheran—United Synod in the South.	Methodist Episcopal Church.	Methodist Episcopal Church, South.	African Methodists.[1]	Presbyterian Church in the U. S.	Protestant Episcopal Church.	Other Protestant bodies.	Roman Catholic Church.	Jewish congregations.[2]	All other bodies.
The state	1,340,316	665,933	653,843	338,201	12,652	54,097	84,266	107,363	23,395	8,557	25,312	10,317	312	1,461
Abbeville	33,400	16,521	16,507	7,109	....	382	2,009	4,836	1,200	97	874	14	....	....
Aiken	39,032	19,312	19,257	16,414	372	90	1,160	498	169	185	369	43	12	....
Anderson	55,728	28,856	28,825	19,706	....	1,933	3,670	1,172	1,417	138	789	31	....	....
Bamberg	17,296	9,384	9,384	6,309	240	1 639	926	192	13	....	65	....	....	....
Barnwell	35,504	17,945	17,881	14,024	80	1,538	963	643	39	76	518	64	....	....
Beaufort	35,495	18,870	18,562	15,604	....	605	203	1,758	....	196	196	272	36	....
Berkeley	30,454	14,433	14,433	3,216	....	2,935	1,304	4,250	....	273	2,455	....	....	....
Charleston	88,006	39,737	31,698	5,505	1,781	3,917	1,748	11,205	1,196	3,237	3,109	7,729	160	150
Cherokee	21,359	8,637	8,628	6,822	....	256	805	359	174	17	195	9	....	....
Chester	28,616	14,032	14,032	5,537	....	220	1,763	4,312	1,122	36	1,042	....	....	....
Chesterfield	20,401	8,795	8,781	4,123	....	1,289	1,	634	419	142	591	14	....	....
Clarendon	28,184	15,110	15,110	5,523	....	15	1,	6,514	558	54	901	....	....	....
Colleton	33,452	17,323	17,251	7,411	....	2,139	2,583	4,190	74	168	637	72	....	....
Darlington	32,388	15,970	15,921	9,820	....	2,704	1,[illegible]	967	313	87	175	....	49	....
Dorchester	16,294	8,714	8,659	2,630	....	1,741	2,114	1,815	82	212	65	55	....	....
Edgefield	25,478	16,783	16,745	15,218	44	....	788	511	108	73	3	38	....	....
Fairfield	29,425	14,267	14,267	,599	....	304	571	3,930	893	88	882	....	....	....
Florence	28,474	13,545	13,488	,970	31	1,760	1,656	1,533	469	208	861	57	....	....
Georgetown	22,846	9,693	9,616	7,442	....	279	1,067	5,235	75	213	315	77	....	....
Greenville	53,490	27,776	27,664	18,803	....	2,035	3,653	798	1,543	443	389	77	....	
Greenwood	28,343	13,802	13,787	7,224	11	461	2,034	3,038	701	51	267	....		35 15
Hampton	23,738	12,846	12,846	9,726	....	131	860	1,390	83	70	586	....	....	....
Horry	23,364	9,760	9,760	5,434	....	75	2,301	1,686		....	161	....	....	....
Kershaw	24,696	13,511	13,511	8,546	....	2,685	968	629	103	157	137	....	....	....
Lancaster	24,311	12,620	12,620	6,546	....	....	2,015	3,073	380	14	432	....	....	....
Laurens	37,382	283	15,283	8,451	....	....	2,125	2,911	1,394	28	374	....	....	....
Lee	(3)	030	9,021	2,721	....	1,997	17	2,477	465	13	531	9	....	....
Lexington	27,264	15,787	15,787	4,040	4,950	53	3,143	3,319	29	95	158	....	....	....
Marion	35,181	19,128	19,128	7,808	....	2,338	4,084	4,230	580	61	27	....	....	....
Marlboro	27,639	12,731	12,731	5,723	....	2,509	3,079	675	317	25	403	....	....	....
Newberry	30,182	,700	15,700	,303	2,799	146	2,027	4,	256	35	506	....	....	....
Oconee	23,634	,323	9,272	,340	176	589	1,119		707	31	245	51	....	....
Orangeburg	59,663	,081	32,037	1,,813	724	5,064	5,286	5,628	152	105	276	44	....	....
Pickens	19,375	38,800	7,800	8,257	....	452	1,354	[illegible]	316	39	332	....	....	....
Richland	45,589	24,677	23,114	13,	672	440	2,423	3,745	842	1,148	640	1,428	15	120
Saluda	18,966	9,572	9,538	6,	660	145	1,654	752	....	12	182	34	....	....
Spartanburg	65,560	29,370	29,241	17,204	57	1,964	5,132	1,765	1,606	278	1,407	89	....	40
Sumter	51,237	18,659	18,517	7,[illegible]	55	3,354	1,197	3,886	682	276	1,474	102	40	....
Union	25,501	10,921	10,913	,171	....	....	2,184	1,777	672	65	44	8	....	....
Williamsburg	31,685	14,215	14,215	6 966	....	4,243	2,445	2,205	592	20	744	....	....	....
York	41,684	18,650	18,650	8 385	....	1,094	3,350	3,746	3,085	91	1,899	....	....	....
County location unknown[4]	....	4,764	3,663	....	....	576	2,664	347	20	....	56	....	....	1,101

[1] Includes African Methodist Episcopal Church, African Methodist Episcopal Zion Church, Colored Methodist Episcopal Church, and Reformed Methodist Union Episcopal Church.
[2] Heads of families only.
[3] New county since 1900; formed from parts of Darlington, Kershaw, and Sumter in 1902.
[4] See explanatory headnote on page 294.

SOUTH DAKOTA.

COUNTY.	Population, 1900.	All denominations.	PROTESTANT BODIES. Total.	Baptists—Northern Convention.	Congregationalists.	Lutheran—Synodical Conference.	Lutheran—Synod of Iowa, etc.	Lutheran—Norwegian Synods.[1]	Methodist Episcopal Church.	Presbyterian Church in the U. S. A.	Protestant Episcopal Church.	Other Protestant bodies.	Roman Catholic Church.	All other bodies.
The state	[2]401,570	161,961	100,625	6,097	8,599	8,285	4,103	26,352	15,485	6,764	7,065	17,885	61,014	322
Armstrong	8	148	39	....	....	....	....	....	....	....	39	....	109	....
Aurora	4,011	1,420	611	....	30	129	86	....	181	56	....	130	809	....
Beadle	8,081	2,928	1,997	120	231	227	55	85	564	495	65	155	931	....
Bonhomme	10,379	5,066	2,059	244	392	175	100	57	236	202	76	577	3,007	....
Boreman	(3)	1,348	620	....	315	....	....	....	....	....	305	....	728	....
Brookings	12,561	4,081	3,460	213	....	170	....	1,759	517	427	23	351	621	....
Brown	15,286	7,340	4,483	155	183	790	73	543	732	389	180	1,438	2,837	20
Brule	5,401	1,024	790	15	93	102	16	168	172	157	36	31	234	....
Buffalo	1,790	480	297	....	35	....	22	21	....	59	160	....	183	....
Butte	2,907	538	354	....	56	....	....	97	111	39	35	16	184	....
Campbell	4,527	1,368	1,127	161	57	155	200	214	25	11	....	304	241	....
Charles Mix	8,498	3,561	2,313	66	209	182	....	210	235	518	542	351	1,238	....
Clark	6,942	2,311	1,702	45	137	112	....	698	481	50	....	179	609	....
Clay	9 316	3,173	2,527	521	356	....	....	675	376	....	50	549	646	....
Codington	8 770	4,619	2,605	201	312	361	....	730	564	65	180	192	2.014	....

[1] Includes United Norwegian Lutheran Church in America; Hauge's Norwegian Evangelical Lutheran Synod; Evangelical Lutheran Church in America, Eielsen's Synod; Synod for the Norwegian Evangelical Lutheran Church in America; and Norwegian Lutheran Free Church.
[2] Includes population (16,043) of Cheyenne River, Pine Ridge, Rosebud, and Standing Rock (part of) Indian reservations, not returned by counties in 1900.
[3] ...ulation not returned separately in 1900.

TABLE 4.—POPULATION IN 1900 AND COMMUNICANTS OR MEMBERS FOR SELECTED DENOMINATIONS, FOR EACH STATE AND TERRITORY, BY COUNTIES: 1906—Continued.

SOUTH DAKOTA—Continued.

COUNTY.	Population, 1900.	All denominations.	PROTESTANT BODIES. Total.	Baptists—Northern Convention.	Congregationalists.	Lutheran—Synodical Conference.	Lutheran—Synod of Iowa, etc.	Lutheran—Norwegian Synods.[1]	Methodist Episcopal Church.	Presbyterian Church in the U. S. A.	Protestant Episcopal Church.	Other Protestant bodies.	Roman Catholic Church.	All other bodies.
Custer	728	402	223		62				87			19	179	
Davison	483	4,582	2,078	1	219	75	30	285	830	139	51	294	2,474	30
Day	2,254	5,681	3,569		117	245		2,299	395	88	150	203	2,112	
Deuel	18,656	2,418	2,418		80	88		1,555	161	110		334		
Dewey	(2)	868	601	55	100						501		267	
Douglas	5,012	2,121	1,653		129	273	362		91			662	468	
Edmunds	4,916	2,	1,200		260	218	123		65	113		306	1,085	
Fall River	3,541	1,	501				33		135	90	76	86	761	
Faulk	3,547	1,285	829	97	157	218		39	280			93	850	
Grant	9,1 03	3,[illegible]	2,621	88	222	533	106	280	394		139	853	1,066	
Gregory	2,411	2,378	988	39	281	325	24	54	131		27	107	1,306	85
Hamlin	5,945	2,281	1,728	91	132	145	120	586	264	125		265	553	
Hand	4,525	1,011	730		142				200	144		244	281	
Hanson	4,947	2,438	879	95		154		28	343	120		139	1,559	
Hughes	3,684	1,029	604	130	131			55	170	37	81		418	7
Hutchinson	11,897	4,660	3,256		203	773	745	50	67	25		1,154	1,404	
Hyde	1,492	388	133	239	30				70			33	255	
Jerauld	2,798	797	777		144	47		100	219	22		245	20	
Kingsbury	9,866	3,348	2,812		284		185	1,112	408	58	72	570	536	
Lake	9,137	4,781	2,579	[illegible]	99	216	147	800	377	256	58	226	2,202	
Lawrence	17,897	7,689	2,755		275			179	448	95	400	1,089	4,934	
Lincoln	12,161	3,158	3,158		323			1,583	540	70	25	534		
Lugenbeel	(2)	59	59	269						39	20			
Lyman	2,632	2,147	1,284	83	81	80		202	119	112	586	104	863	
McCook	8,689	2,972	1,653	276	32	235		31	258	174		647	1,319	
McPherson	6,327	2,146	1,976	135	229	58	1,182		45	16		311	170	
Marshall	5,942	2,410	1,760			87		781	125	358	21	388	650	
Meade	4,907	901	252	13					98	35	50	56	649	
Meyer	(2)	2,580	588		94						494		1,992	
Miner	5,864	2,131	1,436	57	124	111		772	113	87	43	129	695	
Minnehaha	23,926	11,024	7,982	630	421	210		3,619	1,189	276	350	1,287	2,942	100
Moody	8,326	2,381	1,743	25		114		868	238	212	95	191	638	
Pennington	5,610	1,225	680	119	204				164	116	77		545	
Potter	2,988	772	266		66	32		60	102		6		506	
Roberts	12,216	4,756	4,170	68		527	36	2,239	296	506	238	260	586	
Sanborn	4,464	1,603	732		34			170	297	123	17	91	871	
Schnasse	(2)	29	29								29			
Shannon	(2)	1,374	736							203	533		638	
Spink	9,487	2,296	1,862	65	368	112	58	50	770	53	62	324	434	
Stanley	1,341	2,178	160		74	40			33		13		2,018	
Sterling	(2)	247	247		137						110			
Sully	1,715	124	124			18			76	30				
Tripp	(2)	152	24								24		128	
Turner	13,175	5,800	3,758	416	55	319		701	452	410	66	1,339	2,042	
Union	11,153	6,017	2,384	327	295	197		882	294		43	346	3,633	
Walworth	3,839	903	763		104	71	321	82	75	44	59	7	140	
Washabaugh	(2)	817	477								477		340	
Washington	(2)	935											935	
Yankton	12,649	4,174	2,934	21	485	153	80	1,248	339		306	302	1,160	80
County location unknown[3]		1,470	1,470			208		280	533	10	65	374		

[1] Includes United Norwegian Lutheran Church in America; Hauge's Norwegian Evangelical Lutheran Synod; Evangelical Lutheran Church in America, Eielsen's Synod; Synod for the Norwegian Evangelical Lutheran Church in America; and Norwegian Lutheran Free Church.

[2] Population not returned separately in 1900.

[3] See explanatory headnote on page 294.

TENNESSEE.

COUNTY.	Population, 1900.	All denominations.	PROTESTANT BODIES. Total.	Baptists—Southern and National Conventions.	Free Baptists.	Freewill Baptists.	Duck River, etc. (Baptist Church of Christ).	Primitive Baptists.	Colored Primitive Baptists.	Congregationalists.	Disciples of Christ.	Churches of Christ.	Lutheran—United Synod in the South.	Methodist Episcopal Church.	Methodist Protestant Church.
The state	2,020,616	697,570	677,947	253,141	1,840	3,093	4,099	10,204	3,268	2,426	14,904	41,411	1,678	46,180	2,716
Anderson	17,634	5,913	5,913	4,420				45						828	
Bedford	23,845	9,272	9,272	1,851			244	233				986		621	417
Benton	11,888	3,927	3,927	1,187				7				115		295	
Bledsoe	6,626	1,655	1,655	338			79					457		264	
Blount	19,206	5,917	5,917	2,117				414			135			1,098	
Bradley	15,759	,086	,086	1,605				11			68	30		814	
Campbell	17,317	,969	,781	3,939						119	132			913	
Cannon	12,121	,304	,304	615			244					1,503		183	
Carroll	24,250	14,898	14,898	4,276				132	33		220	569		619	60
Carter	16,688	6,968	6,968	2,248				66			1,324			663	

TABLE 4.—POPULATION IN 1900 AND COMMUNICANTS OR MEMBERS FOR SELECTED DENOMINATIONS, FOR EACH STATE AND TERRITORY, BY COUNTIES: 1906—Continued.

TENNESSEE—Continued.

COUNTY.	Population, 1900.	All denominations.	PROTESTANT BODIES.												
			Total.	Baptists—Southern and National Conventions.	Free Baptists.	Freewill Baptists.	Duck River, etc. (Baptist Church of Christ).	Primitive Baptists.	Colored Primitive Baptists.	Congregationalists.	Disciples of Christ.	Churches of Christ.	Lutheran—United Synod in the South.	Methodist Episcopal Church.	Methodist Protestant Church.
Cheatham	10,112	3,330	3,330			884		20				857		82	
Chester	9,896	2,189	2,189			112		117	7			315		31	
Claiborne	20,696	6,533	6,533	4,				334		25	37			780	
Clay	8,421	1,159	1,159	407								911		66	
Cocke	19,153	5,117	5,117	2,[illegible]	134	33		434			343		251	1,024	
Coffee	15,574	5,151	5,151	645			934	53	16			752		265	10
Crockett	15,867	6,683	6,683	2,054				43	16		503	614		837	
Cumberland	8,311	1,723	1,723	419			177	121		153	123	115		267	
Davidson	122,815	53,147	46,857	14,467		215		277	500	500	1,503	3,928		1,632	
Decatur	10,439	2,641	2,641	1,166		19		47	9			179		217	
Dekalb	16,460	4,347	4,347	2,101			307	148	24			335		565	
Dickson	18,635	5,200	5,200	865	155	571		288				671		236	
Dyer	23,776	8,724	8,724	2,261							109	446		120	
Fayette	29,701	9,392	9,392	4,578				29	10		60	14			
Fentress	6,106	1,245	1,245	632				20				17		349	
Franklin	20,392	5,983	5,983	993			536	39	176		100	557		29	
Gibson	39,408	16,195	15,770	6,079				277	117		231	461		25	84
Giles	33,035	13,643	13,643	3,633				125	357		125	1,049		70	
Grainger	15,512	5,186	5,186	3,900	72			196						501	
Greene	30,596	8,605	8,605	1,491	352			56			89		537	1,754	396
Grundy	7,802	2,298	2,298	131			80	30		19		205		283	
Hamblen	12,728	5,133	5,133	2,181							14		28	712	577
Hamilton	61,695	26,059	24,189	8,			46	34	380	670	831	257		2,811	
Hancock	11,147	3,608	3,608	3,680										115	
Hardeman	22,976	9,336	9,336	6,329				57	45		37	401		29	
Hardin	19,246	4,568	4,568	974		152		138			234	30		474	40
Hawkins	24,267	7,588	7,588	3,	475						205			579	
Haywood	25,189	11,295	11,281	6,				57	24			181		25	
Henderson	18,117	5,801	5,735	2,455		107		200				444		334	
Henry	24,208	9,721	9,615	3,[illegible]	60			321			190	713		595	60
Hickman	16,367	3,665	3,665					175	22		60	1,391			
Houston	6,476	1,621	1,621	355		37		20				130		40	
Humphreys	13,398	3,719	3,294	3[illegible]		21		236			14	525			
Jackson	15,039	3,622	3,622	79								1,974			
James	5,407	1,140	1,140	920										30	
Jefferson	18,590	5,656	5,656	2,	69			100						1,191	
Johnson	10,589	4,128	4,128	2,							750	190		696	
Knox	74,302	28,007	27,682	11,448	143			17		175	734		245	3,270	
Lake	7,368	1,820	1,820	[illegible]	217							61			
Lauderdale	21,971	9,214	9,214	5,330				19			35	82			
Lawrence	15,402	4,260	3,155	541				66			20	254		578	
Lewis	4,455	923	923	19				38	7			236		79	
Lincoln	26,304	8,968	8,968	1,787				455	115			730		94	
Loudon	10,838	3,441	3,441	1,562				71						455	
McMinn	19,163	5,758	5,758	2,294								535		1,048	
McNairy	17,760	4,896	4,896			47		194			273	378		237	230
Macon	12,881	4,242	4,242	2				58				629		288	
Madison	36,333	16,084	15,234	6				16			151	47			
Marion	17,281	3,857	3,857	934				301			48	17		745	
Marshall	18,763	8,066	8,066	,[illegible]				127	26		100	1,632		96	
Maury	42,703	14,557	14,557	3,598					573		102	1,740		32	
Meigs	7,491	1,666	1,666	696				120				10		353	
Monroe	18,585	5,629	5,629	3,260		56		16				5	109	174	
Montgomery	36,017	14,975	14,380	6,926		38					297	519		36	
Moore	5,706	2,059	2,059	101			399	54				386			
Morgan	9,587	2,003	2,003	1,101				73		139				343	
Obion	28,286	11,421	11,421	2,963				36	5			1,317		66	215
Overton	13,353	3,017	3,017	836						16		392		233	
Perry	8,800	1,437	1,437	110		39		127				404		21	
Pickett	5,366	547	547	310										211	
Polk	11,357	2,631	2,631	2,063										188	
Putnam	16,890	3,821	3,821	411								726		607	
Rhea	14,318	5,086	5,086	2,236				35				205		707	
Roane	22,738	6,581	6,581	3,016				425			601			988	
Robertson	25,029	10,699	10,699	6,068		253		74		80	154	206		180	
Rutherford	33,543	13,719	13,719	4,762			254	146	30			1,965		1,089	75
Scott	11,077	3,287	3,287	2,826				9		44		101		173	
Sequatchie	3,326	763	763	157			42	49				87		48	
Sevier	22,021	8,044	8,044	5,838				315						1,236	
Shelby	153,557	52,271	46,417	19,725				17	43	401	1,556	80		1,001	
Smith	19,026	6,594	6,594	2,984			100	181			27	181		378	
Stewart	15,224	5,170	5,170	1,187		416		22			85	274		42	
Sullivan	24,935	7,506	7,496	1,425							794		476	734	32
Sumner	26,072	9,637	9,637	3,132				70	12			1,053		749	
Tipton	29,273	10,266	10,266	3,252				31			25	40		335	
Trousdale	6,004	2,269	2,269	1,058								257		175	
Unicoi	5,851	1,623	1,623	869	48	93					208			113	200
Union	12,894	3,527	3,527	2,056				689						567	
Van Buren	3,126	563	563	269			57					123			

TABLE 4.—POPULATION IN 1900 AND COMMUNICANTS OR MEMBERS FOR SELECTED DENOMINATIONS, FOR EACH STATE AND TERRITORY, BY COUNTIES: 1906—Continued.

TENNESSEE—Continued.

COUNTY.	Population, 1900.	All denominations.	PROTESTANT BODIES. Total.	Baptists—Southern and National Conventions.	Free Baptists.	Free-will Baptists.	Duck River, etc. (Baptist Church of Christ).	Primitive Baptists.	Colored Primitive Baptists.	Congregationalists.	Disciples of Christ	Churches of Christ.	Lutheran—United Synod in the South.	Methodist Episcopal Church.	Methodist Protestant Church.
Warren	16,410	5,712	5,712	832			321	15			381	1,617		302	
Washington	22,604	8,984	8,920	2,277	115					50	1,506		32	1,350	
Wayne	12,936	3,045	3,045	1,057				102			30	179		855	
Weakley	32,546	11,499	11,499	8,731				593	12		35	826		368	311
White	14,157	3,491	3,491	535			279			7		480		470	
Williamson	26,429	7,376	6,781	211				310	647			1,070		306	
Wilson	27,078	11,003	11,003	5,154				94			306	1,245		525	10
County location unknown[1]		4,496	3,655	212				339	62					1,254	

COUNTY.	PROTESTANT BODIES—continued. Methodist Episcopal Church, South.	African Methodists.[2]	Presbyterian Church in the U. S. A.	Cumberland Presbyterian Church.	Colored Cumberland Presbyterian Church.	Presbyterian Church in the U. S.	Presbyterian—Associate Reformed Synod of the South.	Protestant Episcopal Church.	United Brethren in Christ.	Other Protestant bodies	Roman Catholic Church.	Jewish congregations.[3]	All other bodies.
The state	140,308	50,662	6,786	42,464	6,640	21,390	1,504	7,874	2,875	12,484	17,252	919	1,452
Anderson	466	18		30		29			71				
Bedford	2,198	968		1,134	130	455		21	14				
Benton	1,683	73		248	45					274			
Bledsoe	299	125		71						22			
Blount	591	380	797	216						169			
Bradley	582	160		470	61	132		61		92			
Campbell	280	217				117				64	188		
Cannon	521	81		100		30				27			
Carroll	2,365	205		1,142	970	95			46	166			
Carter	195	151	45						256				
Cheatham	947	333											
Chester	723	243		146				1					
Claiborne	482	92				14							
Clay	70												
Cocke	427	123	9	18		80							
Coffee	1,648	160		493				66	56	53			
Crockett	1,632	525		394						65			
Cumberland	220	28	95							5			
Davidson	10,540	3,977		2,283	155	3,393		1,574	165	1,748	5,865	275	150
Decatur	607	154		243									
Dekalb	534	28		163	75					67			
Dickson	1,674	342		308		20		41	29				
Dyer	2,787	737		981	1,043	90		23		127			
Fayette	1,525	2,539		171		348		60		58			
Fentress	136		19							72			
Franklin	1,364	178		1,036	51	70		512		342			
Gibson	3,871	1,428		2,104	189	665		21		218	425		
Giles	4,418	1,615		760	365	565		40		521			
Grainger	393	26	30			15				53			
Greene	894	135	415	1,511		160		30	693	93			
Grundy	1,104			40				95		311			
Hamblen	788	135	156	90		398		8	46				
Hamilton	3,902	2,035	755	952	200	1,076		757	90	704	1,700	120	50
Hancock	30		93										
Hardeman	1,141	711		372		134		70					
Hardin	1,479	278		555		36		4		174			
Hawkins	1,227	527	82	106		674				258			
Haywood	2,003	1,552	102	51		325		14		54		14	
Henderson	1,328	316		425		80		1		40			66
Henry	2,643	684		455	175			27		64			106
Hickman	920	483		150				3		106			
Houston	535	292		473									
Humphreys	1,273	310		467		30				78	425		
Jackson	1,052	50		406						61			
James	100	10		80									
Jefferson	542	216	471	117		224			234	44			
Johnson	132		22							50			
Knox	3,867	1,166	2,226	1,163		1,332		629	558	667	170	125	30
Lake	671	119		10		46				84			
Lauderdale	2,365	1,083		191		98		11					
Lawrence	943	215		314	86	26		2	48	62	1,105		
Lewis	274	110		120						40			
Lincoln	1,874	988		1,502	546	187	406	25	46	213			
Loudon	459	222	125	532		15							
McMinn	843	248		212	230	174		7		167			

[1] See explanatory headnote on page 294.
[2] Includes African Methodist Episcopal Church, African Methodist Episcopal Zion Church, and Colored Methodist Episcopal Church.
[3] Heads of families only.

TABLE 4.—POPULATION IN 1900 AND COMMUNICANTS OR MEMBERS FOR SELECTED DENOMINATIONS, FOR EACH STATE AND TERRITORY, BY COUNTIES: 1906—Continued.

TENNESSEE—Continued.

COUNTY.	PROTESTANT BODIES—continued.										Roman Catholic Church.	Jewish congregations.[2]	All other bodies.
	Methodist Episcopal Church South.	African Methodists.[1]	Presbyterian Church in the U. S. A.	Cumberland Presbyterian Church.	Colored Cumberland Presbyterian Church.	Presbyterian Church in the U. S.	Presbyterian—Associate Reformed Synod of the South.	Protestant Episcopal Church.	United Brethren in Christ.	Other Protestant bodies.			
McNairy	1,367	199		590		74				367			
Macon	301	205								273			
Madison	3,604	2,690		602	175	678		232		52	850		
Marion	972	306		668	39			82		136			
Marshall	1,929	910		1,418	436	370	65						
Maury	3,235	2,148	147	1,484	46	957	50	311		134			
Meigs	405	52		30									
Monroe	1,145	33	9	343	205	265				9			
Montgomery	3,408	1,564		831		404		284		53	595		
Moore	587	100		147						285			
Morgan	63		49	27				12		196			
Obion	3,728	783		1,755	51	181	224	15		82			
Overton	969	40		514						17			
Perry	678	58											
Pickett				26									
Polk	208			47	125								
Putnam	1,059			823	58	71				66			
Rhea	934	283	52	263		57				234			
Roane	618	200	273	292		80		10		50			
Robertson	2,725	283		669				6		81			
Rutherford	2,364	768		1,053	242	905		28		38			
Scott			65					5		64			
Sequatchie	365			15									
Sevier	442	26				25			162				
Shelby	8,009	7,375		1,411		3,375	203	2,388		833	5,270	375	209
Smith	1,366	140		541	646					50			
Stewart	2,616	367		37						124			
Sullivan	2,376	167	125			1,121		3		243		10	
Sumner	2,898	166		796	85	189		30		457			
Tipton	2,579	1,968	42	536		502	556	175		225			
Trousdale	305	220		102	120	28		4					
Unicoi			92										
Union	160								27	28			
Van Buren	114												
Warren	1,374	30		711		50				79			
Washington	1,579	293	490	115		384		90	185	454	64		
Wayne	496	89		237									
Weakley	3,574	579		1,272				10		188			
White	1,145	90		326	6					153			
Williamson	2,757	390		556	85	316		86		48	595		
Wilson	1,669	484		1,252		225				40			
County location unknown[3]	618	845		164					149	12			841

[1] Includes African Methodist Episcopal Church, African Methodist Episcopal Zion Church, and Colored Methodist Episcopal Church.
[2] Heads of families only.
[3] See explanatory headnote on page 294.

TEXAS.

COUNTY.	Population, 1900.	All denominations.	PROTESTANT BODIES.												
			Total.	Seventh-day Adventists.	Baptists—Southern and National Conventions.	Primitive Baptists.[1]	Congregationalists.	Disciples of Christ.	Churches of Christ.	German Evangelical Synod of N. A.	Lutheran—Synodical Conference.	Lutheran—German Synod of Texas.	Lutheran—Synod of Iowa, etc.	Methodist Episcopal Church.	African Methodist Episcopal Church.
The state	3,048,710	1,226,906	913,917	1,414	392,184	8,375	1,856	39,550	34,006	7,745	7,983	2,440	12,758	36,223	24,919
Anderson	28,015	11,122	10,666		5,606	95	76	1,020	124					158	1,147
Andrews	87														
Angelina	13,481	4,318	4,101		2,338	42		60	178					26	12
Aransas	1,716	444	223		25										21
Archer	2,508	1,064	662		235	13		50							
Armstrong	1,205	560	560		247			55	19						
Atascosa	7,143	1,947	1,267		733				50					85	
Austin	20,676	7,163	3,696		418			72	126		263		1,176	471	549
Bailey	4														
Bandera	5,332	838	733		397	15		68						2	
Bastrop	26,845	9,508	7,807		4,208	268		305	204				438	157	882
Baylor	3,052	1,390	1,390		377			150	168		9				
Bee	7,720	2,719	1,869		828			173						35	19
Bell	45,535	14,856	12,908		4,670	262		1,025	1,046		39		288	408	374
Bexar	69,422	32,107	10,950	45	3,133			524	98	60			450	1,001	530

[1] Includes Primitive Baptists and Colored Primitive Baptists in America.

TABLE 4.—POPULATION IN 1900 AND COMMUNICANTS OR MEMBERS FOR SELECTED DENOMINATIONS, FOR EACH STATE AND TERRITORY, BY COUNTIES: 1906—Continued.

TEXAS—Continued.

COUNTY.	Population, 1900.	All denominations.	PROTESTANT BODIES.												
			Total.	Seventh-day Adventists.	Baptists—Southern and National Conventions.	Primitive Baptists.[1]	Congregationalists.	Disciples of Christ.	Churches of Christ.	German Evangelical Synod of N. A.	Lutheran—Synodical Conference.	Lutheran—German Synod of Texas.	Lutheran—Synod of Iowa, etc.	Methodist Episcopal Church.	African Methodist Episcopal Church.
Blanco	4,703	1,119	970		336			44	119				32		10
Borden	776	145	145		45				31						
Bosque	17,390	6,275	6,275	14	2,196	24		76	246	273	175			60	53
Bowie	26,676	10,347	9,457		5,231	92		536	204					140	48
Brazoria	14,861	3,767	3,524		1,765			30						222	348
Brazos	18,859	10,639	4,967		2,967	21		224		80	52			317	375
Brewster	2,356	344	344		139			65							
Briscoe	1,253	180	180		113										
Brown	16,019	6,957	6,541		2,617	53		275	351						75
Burleson	18,367	4,984	3,132		1,387			135		197	45		70	288	370
Burnet	10,528	3,065	3,065		1,004	29		207	424					10	
Caldwell	21,765	4,868	4,868		1,692	109		514	97				112	427	103
Calhoun	2,395	599	599		221								91		
Callahan	8,768	3,228	2,854		1,426			17	377						
Cameron	16,095	17,774	174		20										
Camp	9,146	4,343	4,343		2,287		33		20					60	75
Carson	469	183	183		50									65	
Cass	22,841	9,936	9,936	159	5,969	150		40	128					298	
Castro	400	275	119		100										
Chambers	3,046	593	593		267				34					230	
Cherokee	25,154	8,615	8,210	28	3,295			68	77					136	186
Childress	2,138	1,099	1,073		224				90						
Clay	9,231	3,182	2,932		1,043	53		143	123		11			64	
Cochran	25	50	50					50							
Coke	3,430	1,377	1,377		663	26			117						
Coleman	10,077	4,068	4,034	74	1,689	74		214	296						7
Collin	50,087	16,975	16,545		6,071	130		2,358	427					195	
Collingsworth	1,233	1,017	1,017		368				19						
Colorado	22,203	7,164	5,064		2,159			140	38	380			496	889	399
Comal	7,008	2,326	753		47					400				107	96
Comanche	23,009	7,048	7,023		3,457	66		344	280						
Concho	1,427	828	828		522				49						
Cooke	27,494	9,650	7,390	35	2,749	16		539	444					80	50
Coryell	21,308	6,716	6,716		2,951	242		40	247		62		175	126	25
Cottle	1,002	413	413		135	33					7				
Crane	51														
Crockett	1,591	335	335		75				31						
Crosby	788	157	157		103				30						
Dallam	146	777	547		165		14	60						49	
Dallas	82,726	43,082	33,361	83	12,080	145	727	2,784	1,269	98	240			875	1,043
Dawson	37	179	179		105										
De Witt	21,311	5,493	4,800		1,738	28		40	70			314	232	316	168
Deaf Smith	843	651	651		312			253							
Delta	15,249	3,653	3,653		1,241			281	230						
Denton	28,318	11,447	10,320		3,972			689	1,186	50	18			384	160
Dickens	1,151	207	207		123			40	44						
Dimmit	1,106	238	238		127			21							
Donley	2,756	1,436	1,215		360			62			8				
Duval	8,483	12,870	120		27										
Eastland	17,971	7,131	7,131		3,018	50		207	762		75			27	
Ector	381	124	124		38			21							
Edwards	3,108	517	517		220			20	83						
El Paso	24,886	30,052	3,684		722			400			50			328	127
Ellis	50,059	21,906	18,243		6,504	62		1,028	906					253	897
Erath	29,966	12,191	10,235		4,817	269		328	957					35	22
Falls	33,342	9,719	9,162		4,677	50		90	216	398	282		62	1,149	351
Fannin	51,793	15,683	15,655		5,237	247		834	823		69			74	1,273
Fayette	36,542	18,411	6,909		2,580			12	18	100	962	331	823	801	567
Fisher	3,708	1,986	1,986		683	39		65	106						
Floyd	2,020	642	642		293	8			338						
Foard	1,568	799	799		347										
Fort Bend	16,538	3,748	3,748		2,370			37		300	25			402	266
Franklin	8,674	2,930	2,930		1,608	145		188	172					35	
Freestone	18,910	5,095	5,095		2,233	438		108						564	568
Frio	4,200	1,204	1,204		488			20	50					13	
Gaines	55	86	86		16										
Galveston	44,116	24,505	6,227		1,546			140					660	731	276
Garza	185	45	45		45										
Gillespie	8,229	6,314	2,707		329	8				422			1,400	146	
Glasscock	286	108	108		68										
Goliad	8,310	5,120	1,825		460			40	87			419	321	180	
Gonzales	28,882	6,156	6,156		2,809	43		130	27			164		1,027	190
Gray	480	429	429		160				74						
Grayson	63,661	24,393	19,556	30	7,814	125	120	1,399	1,582		25			501	164
Gregg	12,343	6,010	5,948		3,418			56	25					50	67
Grimes	26,106	8,729	6,431		3,863				66		203			870	90
Guadalupe	21,385	6,584	6,315		1,773	83		12		1,920	62			566	108
Hale	1,680	793	793		388			127	97						
Hall	1,670	1,328	1,328		459			130	119						
Hamilton	13,520	4,223	4,203		1,718	220		146	819		147		170		

[1] Includes Primitive Baptists and Colored Primitive Baptists in America.

TABLE 4.—POPULATION IN 1900 AND COMMUNICANTS OR MEMBERS FOR SELECTED DENOMINATIONS, FOR EACH STATE AND TERRITORY, BY COUNTIES: 1906—Continued.

TEXAS—Continued.

COUNTY.	Population, 1900.	All denominations.	PROTESTANT BODIES. Total.	Seventh-day Adventists.	Baptists—Southern and National Conventions.	Primitive Baptists.[1]	Congregationalists.	Disciples of Christ.	Churches of Christ.	German Evangelical Synod of N. A.	Lutheran—Synodical Conference.	Lutheran—German Synod of Texas.	Lutheran—Synod of Iowa, etc.	Methodist Episcopal Church.	African Methodist Episcopal Church.
Hansford	167	63	55		25										
Hardeman	3,634	1,474	1,474		487				185						
Hardin	5,049	1,719	1,719		966			50	50						114
Harris	63,786	34,996	20,336	54	7,226			724	138	702	1,255			1,829	1,028
Harrison	31,878	14,138	13,478		8,231				240					1,994	15
Hartley	377	199	161		55			24							
Haskell	2,637	2,393	2,393		1,103	34		150	241				80		
Hays	14,142	9,979	8,179		968			185		150					240
Hemphill	815	334	318		74										
Henderson	19,970	4,920	4,920		1,442			135						9	739
Hidalgo	6,837	4,250													
Hill	41,355	14,131	14,072	41	5,875	189		536	960		235		55	185	178
Hockley	44														
Hood	9,146	3,885	3,885		1,678	9		263	243						2
Hopkins	27,950	9,441	9,408		4,379			180	447					28	
Houston	25,452	7,840	7,742		4,199	26		91	347					250	258
Howard	2,528	1,246	1,246		266	16		75	35		12			28	
Hunt	47,295	14,656	14,543		5,344	49		1,137	562					160	269
Hutchinson	303	109	109		33				56						
Irion	848	313	313		58			42	69						
Jack	10,224	3,051	3,051		1,207			64	231						
Jackson	6,094	1,350	1,350		503			74						181	25
Jasper	7,138	2,412	2,412		1,548	21			23					80	
Jeff Davis	1,150	219	219		62			40							
Jefferson	14,239	13,068	7,293		3,336		24	553	56		130			317	350
Johnson	33,819	13,061	12,275	516	5,117	103		424	1,154						96
Jones	7,053	5,018	4,988		2,242	62		52	359						
Karnes	8,681	3,407	1,877		700		46	12	81					95	
Kaufman	33,376	9,979	9,614		4,334			491	336					65	329
Kendall	4,103	547	332		11								21	16	
Kent	899	170			35										
Kerr	4,980	1,485			380	20		136					27	30	
Kimble	2,503	569			231				117						
King	490	109	170		65										
Kinney	2,447	107	1,[illegible]		50										
Knox	2,322	2,006	1,696		402	70		140	132						
La Salle	2,303	255	255		92										
Lamar	48,627	12,398	12,202		4,573	80	126	513	384					1,026	119
Lamb	31	17	17		17										
Lampasas	8,625	2,838	2,286		977	96		237	145						77
Lavaca	28,121	13,	4,		1,669	12		92	18		126	560	231	390	204
Lee	14,595	4,	4,		1,277			25			1,892		142	157	286
Leon	18,072	5,449	5,		3,079	53		60			10			462	395
Liberty	8,102	2,[illegible]	1,320		1,227			60							25
Limestone	32,573	8,817	8,[illegible]		4,041	327		63	[illegible]					640	193
Lipscomb	790	205	205		92		15								
Live Oak	2,268	313	313		136										
Llano	7,301	1,605	1,605		362	60		196	82				76		
Loving	33														
Lubbock	293	232	232		114			16	90						
Lynn		147	147		94										
McCulloch	3,	1,772	1,772		866	27		107						29	
McLennan	59, 17	27,414	22,430	74	10,043	26		900	301	426			156	1,639	721
McMullen	1,[illegible]	410	197		159										
Madison	10,432	2,481	2,468		1,446	41			174		32			210	
Marion	10,	3,704	3,621		2,794			20						316	42
Martin	754	269	269		144				65						
Mason	5,332	1,528	1,528		195			60					175	318	
Matagorda	6,097	2,347	1,690		778			196			15				135
Maverick	4,066	168	168												8
Medina	,	3,552	2,022		515	64		117					364	60	
Menard	7,[illegible]	361	361		138			60							
Midland	[illegible]	1,031	1,031		331			200							
Milam	39,666	10,802	7,449	11	3,047	53		369	343	51	291	85	38	220	773
Mills	7,851	2,498	2,477		896	98			167			167	339		
Mitchell	2,855	1,682	1,682		647	50		85	75						13
Montague	24,800	6,724	6,698	16	2,555	55		315	824		40				
Montgomery	17,067	4,537	4,537		3,113			40	73					395	139
Moore	209	119	119		27				15						
Morris	8,220	3,368	3,368		1,789	59			150					242	
Motley	1,257	206	206		184										
Nacogdoches	24,663	8,493	7,668	32	3,068			36	387						
Navarro	43,374	14,705	14,399	44	5,670	160		369	521					267	688
Newton	7,282	1,697	1,697		878	32								45	
Nolan	2,611	1,525	1,525		558	34		200	42						
Nueces	10,	5,643	1,584		289		58	14	85					22	
Ochiltree		79	79		30										
Oldham	439	24	5		5										
Orange	5,[illegible]	2,401	2,143		1,095			156			20			80	40
Palo Pinto	12,291	4,435	4,013		1,428			621	144						35

[1] Includes Primitive Baptists and Colored Primitive Baptists in America.

TABLE 4.—POPULATION IN 1900 AND COMMUNICANTS OR MEMBERS FOR SELECTED DENOMINATIONS, FOR EACH STATE AND TERRITORY, BY COUNTIES: 1906—Continued.

TEXAS—Continued.

COUNTY.	Population, 1900.	All denominations.	PROTESTANT BODIES.												
			Total.	Seventh-day Adventists.	Baptists—Southern and National Conventions.	Primitive Baptists.[1]	Congregationalists.	Disciples of Christ.	Churches of Christ.	German Evangelical Synod of N. A.	Lutheran—Synodical Conference.	Lutheran—German Synod of Texas.	Lutheran—Synod of Iowa, etc.	Methodist Episcopal Church.	African Methodist Episcopal Church.
Panola	21,404	7,185	7,185		4,768	13		49						168	175
Parker	25,823	8,934	8,577		3,411	39		280	898						27
Parmer	34	109	109		7		40	62							
Pecos	2,360	71	71		30			12	19						
Polk	14,447	3,904	3,904		2,339			30						394	
Potter	1,820	1,932	1,684		350	17	22	275							
Presidio	3,673	4,712	207		27			60							
Rains	6,127	1,427	1,427		1,				49					15	
Randall	963	525	495		839			61							
Reagan	(2)	69	69		32										
Red River	29,893	9,681	9,259		5,291	9		208	126					617	
Reeves	1,847	508	508		184			114							
Refugio	1,641	796	137		137										
Roberts	620	193	184		42			30							
Robertson	31,480	9,058	8,180		5,523	55		25	44	70				383	309
Rockwall	8,531	3,576	3,576		1,726			227							101
Runnels	5,379	4,125	3,615		1,400	84		97	35	136			150		4
Rusk	26,099	10,426	10,426		5,301	27		40	286					47	
Sabine	6,394	2,691	2,691		1,801				36					350	
San Augustine	8,434	2,260	1,865		1,068				149					134	
San Jacinto	10,277	2,219	2,219		1,200	213			82					126	206
San Patricio	2,372	4,315	352		81				20						
San Saba	7,569	2,177	2,177		567	16		90	398						
Schleicher	515	229	229		55				73						
Scurry	4,158	2,086	2,039		860	33			207						
Shackelford	2,461	841	841		290				59						12
Shelby	20,452	7,799	7,799		3,567				73					258	49
Sherman	104	341	341		136										
Smith	37,370	15,016	14,758		8,455	9	123	55	117						222
Somervell	3,498	1,034	1,034		440	43		[illegible]	50						
Starr	11,469	5,457	196		100										
Stephens	6,466	2,057	2,057		720			220	74						
Sterling	1,127	349	349		122										
Stonewall	2,183	660	660		361	6		20	35						
Sutton	1,727	277	277		60			30							
Swisher	1,227	350	350		231			10							
Tarrant	52,376	27,216	21,630	29	7,945	126	150	1,640	358	80	52			879	182
Taylor	10,499	7,460	7,239	47	2,843	45		421	640		18			150	
Terrell	(3)	73	73		36										
Terry	48	105	105		85				20						
Throckmorton	1,750	649	649		272			205							
Titus	12,292	4,888	4,888		2,674			130	307						66
Tom Green	6,804	5,856	3,093		917			159	221	90					75
Travis	47,386	20,993	15,320	30	6,298	166	223	762	81	342	80		410	1,587	654
Trinity	10,976	2,743	2,743		1,679	46			191						62
Tyler	11,899	2,607	2,607		2,031	43		60						104	30
Upshur	16,266	6,051	6,051		3,835	59	38	30	171					280	79
Upton	48														
Uvalde	4,647	1,614	1,614		307			88	395				35	19	10
Val Verde	5,263	577	577		133			20	35					16	8
Van Zandt	25,481	7,024	7,024	52	2,908		21	125	59					25	
Victoria	13,678	2,274	2,249		747			24	110			400		394	40
Walker	15,813	6,803	5,339		3,429	83		80	7					696	179
Waller	14,246	4,042	3,605		1,796			40	115		40			708	45
Ward	1,451	302	302		126			60							
Washington	32,931	10,718	8,543		3,065			187		871	217		1,913	322	1,440
Webb	21,851	31,252	770		66			35							
Wharton	16,942	4,455	4,455		2,893			66			37		35	107	396
Wheeler	636	503	503		171	12			52						
Wichita	5,806	2,251	1,980		519			210	40		171			59	
Wilbarger	5,759	2,094	2,043		706	64		90	107		48				
Williamson	38,072	14,333	11,003		2,892	78		687	453	149	313		515	495	467
Wilson	13,961	3,101	2,395		756	47			169					192	39
Winkler	60														
Wise	27,116	7,877	7,877		3,701	59		240	618		60				
Wood	21,048	6,882	6,882		3,975	47		91	333					259	155
Yoakum	26	8	8		8										
Young	6,540	3,003	3,003		1,147			262			60				
Zapata	4,760														
Zavalla	792	174	174		89				25						
County location unknown[4]		17,196	5,475		115	1,237		895						241	264

[1] Includes Primitive Baptists and Colored Primitive Baptists in America.
[2] New county since 1900; formed from part of Tom Green in 1903.
[3] New county since 1900; formed from part of Pecos in 1905.
[4] See explanatory headnote on page 294.

TABLE 4.—POPULATION IN 1900 AND COMMUNICANTS OR MEMBERS FOR SELECTED DENOMINATIONS, FOR EACH STATE AND TERRITORY, BY COUNTIES: 1906—Continued.

TEXAS—Continued.

COUNTY.	PROTESTANT BODIES—continued.										Roman Catholic Church.	Jewish congregations.[1]	All other bodies.
	Methodist Protestant Church.	Methodist Episcopal Church, South.	Congregational Methodist Church.	Colored Methodist Episcopal Church.	Presbyterian Church in the U. S. A.	Cumberland Presbyterian Church.	Colored Cumberland Presbyterian Church.	Presbyterian Church in the U. S.	Protestant Episcopal Church.	Other Protestant bodies.			
The state	8,495	225,431	2,759	18,428	4,118	31,598	2,091	23,934	14,246	13,364	308,356	1,676	2,957
Anderson	300	1,698		78		21		258	85		388	25	43
Andrews													
Angelina		799	187	255		35		54	30	85	217		
Aransas		64						51	62		221		
Archer		221				26		15		102	392		
Armstrong		239											
Atascosa		377							14	8	680		
Austin		462			47				45	67	3,467		
Bailey													
Bandera		219						6		26			105
Bastrop	31	975				165		10	79	85	1,642		59
Baylor		561			85	40							
Bee		612						157	25	20	850		
Bell	63	3,745				261		347	185	195	1,948		
Bexar		2,017			130	189		956	1,288	529	20,400	160	597
Blanco		429									149		
Borden		69											
Bosque		1,347	57			273	225	60	32	1,165			
Bowie		1,978		419		65		480	246	18	850	40	
Brazoria		598		75		13		157	220	96	243		
Brazos		627				40		173	91		5,682		
Brewster		116			24								
Briscoe				16		49		2					
Brown	70	2,276				450		270	49	55	416		
Burleson		537				15		48		60	1,815		37
Burnet	66	1,128				111		34	36	16			
Caldwell	499	953				8		269	85				
Calhoun		130						17	106	34			
Callahan		901			33	59			27	14	374		
Cameron		37						18	99		17,600		
Camp		1,190		617		17		44					
Carson		68											
Cass	116	1,525		1,120		318				123			
Castro								19			156		
Chambers		54						8					
Cherokee		2,338		1,015		742		255		70	405		
Childress		536				48		75			26		
Clay	230	927		10	20	212		35	8	53	250		
Cochran													
Coke	69	467				4		31					
Coleman		1,229	83		20	165		148		35	34		
Collin	110	5,161		130		1,639		223	75	26	430		
Collingsworth		598				32							
Colorado		493						8	62		2,100		
Comal		77								26	1,573		
Comanche	50	2,280	222					145	40	139			25
Concho		247				10							
Cooke	30	2,521		200	126	379		170	51		2,230	30	
Coryell	154	2,293				220		131	10	40			
Cottle		238											
Crane													
Crockett		217				12							
Crosby								24					
Dallam		200			41				18		230		
Dallas	40	7,150		923	461	1,569		1,770	1,290	814	9,451	205	65
Dawson		74											
De Witt		349				109		340	96		693		
Deaf Smith					75			11					
Delta	503	956		79		217		30		116			
Denton		2,108	100	283		1,047		158		165	1,127		
Dickens													
Dimmit		90											
Donley		645						90	50		221		
Duval		70							23		12,750		
Eastland		2,542	22			182		140	3	103			
Ector		60						5					
Edwards	77	117											
El Paso		693		75	590			115	452	132	26,205	72	31
Ellis	47	6,094		142		1,478		612	67	153	3,663		
Erath	105	3,302	50		23	196		71	60		1,956		
Falls		1,412						234	24	217	500		57
Fannin	70	4,783	253	282	44	1,229		280	101	56	28		
Fayette		510			54	21		43	32	55	11,502		
Fisher	11	876				124		6		76			
Floyd								3					

[1] Heads of families only.

TABLE 4.—POPULATION IN 1900 AND COMMUNICANTS OR MEMBERS FOR SELECTED DENOMINATIONS, FOR EACH STATE AND TERRITORY, BY COUNTIES: 1906—Continued.

TEXAS—Continued.

COUNTY.	PROTESTANT BODIES—continued.										Roman Catholic Church.	Jewish congregations.[1]	All other bodies.
	Methodist Protestant Church.	Methodist Episcopal Church, South.	Congregational Methodist Church.	Colored Methodist Episcopal Church.	Presbyterian Church in the U. S. A.	Cumberland Presbyterian Church.	Colored Cumberland Presbyterian Church.	Presbyterian Church in the U. S.	Protestant Episcopal Church.	Other Protestant bodies			
Foard		429				15				5			
Fort Bend		301							33	14			
Franklin	183	435				146				18			
Freestone	219	753				154		25		33			
Frio		560			40				33				
Gaines		40						30					
Galveston		704			89			435	1,305	341	17,497	220	561
Garza													
Gillespie		260	19			90			13	20	3,607		
Glasscock		30						10					
Goliad								52	34		3,295		
Gonzales						187		271	78				
Gray										30			
Grayson		223	75	617	330	1,018		638	440	37	4,837		
Gregg		[illegible]		923		216		298	37		62		
Grimes		972				40		230	36	61	2,298		
Guadalupe	104	786						72	95	736	269		
Hale					6	141				34			
Hall		510				106		4					
Hamilton	83	1,067				143		91	35	64	20		
Hansford		30									8		
Hardeman		686				106							
Hardin		453		65									
Harris		3,786		130	154	184		1,[illegible]	1,348	426	14,280	330	56
Harrison		1,351		674		315			241	34	595	50	15
Hartley		82									38		
Haskell		691				21							
Hays	45	1,064				138			86	55	6,800		
Hemphill		155			89						16		
Henderson	56	1,677		740		108		[illegible]		14			
Hidalgo											4,250		
Hill	184	4,730				958	19		49	53	42		17
Hockley													
Hood	161	1,281		36		205							
Hopkins	294	3,273		180		440		[illegible]	35	47	33		
Houston	160	1,180	73	647	45	85				56	98		
Howard		602				25			61				
Hunt	270	5,290	17	408	9	360			49	144	113		
Hutchinson		20						325					
Irion		136						128					
Jack	90	1,145		21	83	160		20		30			
Jackson		402						107	32	26			
Jasper		484	6	195						55			
Jeff Davis		50			67								
Jefferson		1,743		21	52			292	338	81	5,720	75	
Johnson	159	3,893		24		464		326			786		
Jones		1,758	32			275		71	13	124	30		
Karnes		737						61	31	114	1,530		
Kaufman	150	2,614		163	125	660		54	138	155	365		
Kendall		127						12	73	72	215		
Kent		106				29							
Kerr		344				19		47	56		426		
Kimble	10	185							26				
King		30				14							
Kinney									57				
Knox		897				25		30			310		
La Salle		130						33					
Lamar	304	3,017		315		990	85	296	160	214	196		
Lamb													
Lampasas	86	308	106		10	200			27	17	552		
Lavaca		846							74		9,109	20	
Lee		324						33					
Leon	181	945				173		88		65			
Liberty		254			7				28	90	538		
Limestone	457	1,937				523		84	17	30	25		
Lipscomb		98											
Live Oak		147						9					
Llano	118	604				62		27	18				
Loving													
Lubbock								12					
Lynn						38				15			
McCulloch	112	439			101	63		12	16				
McLennan	7	5,665		16		651	375	699	450	281	4,883	101	
McMullen		38									213		
Madison		490				35		40			13		

[1] Heads of families only.

TABLE 4.—POPULATION IN 1900 AND COMMUNICANTS OR MEMBERS FOR SELECTED DENOMINATIONS, FOR EACH STATE AND TERRITORY, BY COUNTIES: 1906—Continued.

TEXAS—Continued.

COUNTY.	PROTESTANT BODIES—continued.												
	Methodist Protestant Church.	Methodist Episcopal Church, South.	Congregational Methodist Church.	Colored Methodist Episcopal Church.	Presbyterian Church in the U. S. A.	Cumberland Presbyterian Church.	Colored Cumberland Presbyterian Church.	Presbyterian Church in the U. S.	Protestant Episcopal Church.	Other Protestant bodies.	Roman Catholic Church.	Jewish congregations.[1]	All other bodies.
Marion		294				107		18	30		83		
Martin		60											
Mason	70	649		25	20	12			4				
Matagorda		469						62	35		657		
Maverick		71							89				
Medina		663						81		158	1,530		
Menard		96			25				40				
Midland		423				17		60					
Milam		1,599			20	226		73	55	195	3,353		
Mills	70	567	80			61		6		26	21		
Mitchell		581		42		45		70	57	17			
Montague	172	1,983			93	402		60	16	167			26
Montgomery		757		13						7			
Moore		77											
Morris		969		101		19				19			
Motley		20						2					
Nacogdoches		2,132	359	853		209	400	67	90	35	825		
Navarro	389	4,329		150		1,031		355	251	175	281	25	
Newton		490	11	241									
Nolan	14	520				113		44					
Nueces		669						241	206		4,059		
Ochiltree		29				20							
Oldham											19		
Orange		450		74				150	45	33	258		
Palo Pinto		1,376		31		194		141	24	19	422		
Panola		1,333	137	471		46	20	5					
Parker	69	2,942		157		511		239	22	82	357		
Parmer													
Pecos								10					
Polk		926	22					193					
Potter		600				272		65	74	9	248		
Presidio		80			20				20		4,505		
Rains		294				30							
Randall		160				75		16		11	30		
Reagan		17											
Red River		2,216		44		604		101	35	8	234		188
Reeves		146			10			41	13				
Refugio											659		
Roberts		92			20						9		
Robertson	16	1,136		94				147	88	290	796		82
Rockwall		1,128				311				48			
Runnels	11	1,141				158		180	18		510		
Rusk		1,604	25	1,714		509	967	89					
Sabine		440	42							22			
San Augustine		156	96	90				107	60	5	395		
San Jacinto		358											
San Patricio		206									3,963		
San Saba	149	641				189			30	52			
Schleicher		80				8							
Scurry		793				146		34 [illegible]			47		
Shackelford		268		20	100	25			12				
Shelby		2,462	311	385		95		16	12	6			
Sherman		138						25					
Smith	125	3,253		1,514		126		294	215	54	204	54	
Somervell		437			13	15							
Starr		96									5,261		
Stephens		853			2	184		4					
Sterling		190				10		27					
Stonewall		196				13		29					
Sutton		155				10			22				
Swisher						75		34					
Tarrant	280	6,338		241		1,192		1,405	518	215	5,366	155	65
Taylor	20	2,286	11	52		289		193	92	132	221		
Terrell		37											
Terry													
Throckmorton		140			32								
Titus	291	866	106	171				113	10	154			
Tom Green	62	962				241		241	120	5	2,763		
Travis	94	2,458		5	412	207		468	336	707	5,579	51	43
Trinity		472	122	107				64					
Tyler		290	7	25				17					
Upshur	70	1,074		237		117		9		52			
Upton													
Uvalde		566						116	78				
Val Verde		253						44	59	9			

[1] Heads of families only.

TABLE 4.—POPULATION IN 1900 AND COMMUNICANTS OR MEMBERS FOR SELECTED DENOMINATIONS, FOR EACH STATE AND TERRITORY, BY COUNTIES: 1906—Continued.

TEXAS—Continued.

COUNTY.	PROTESTANT BODIES—continued. Methodist Protestant Church.	Methodist Episcopal Church, South.	Congregational Methodist Church.	Colored Methodist Episcopal Church.	Presbyterian Church in the U. S. A.	Cumberland Presbyterian Church.	Colored Cumberland Presbyterian Church.	Presbyterian Church in the U. S.	Protestant Episcopal Church.	Other Protestant bodies.	Roman Catholic Church.	Jewish congregations.[1]	All other bodies.
Van Zandt	311	2,355		310		656		32	8	162			
Victoria		235						236	63			25	
Walker		730						97	38		1,464		
Waller		539		170		33		54	65		412	25	
Ward		57						59					
Washington		360				30		28	70	40	2,162	13	
Webb		357						165	147		30,482		
Wharton		457						58	26	381			
Wheeler		268											
Wichita		629			217	50		39	46		271		
Wilbarger		879				106		33	10		33		18
Williamson	36	3,089			154	494		315	131	735	3,330		
Wilson		976				51		42	5	118	706		
Winkler													
Wise	1	2,313				537		146	10	61			
Wood	40	1,660		197		61		48	7	9			
Yoakum													
Young		1,237				118		161	18				
Zapata													
Zavalla		60											
County location unknown[2]		1,841	128			176				578	10,848		873

[1] Heads of families only. [2] See explanatory headnote on page 294.

UTAH.

COUNTY.	Population, 1900.	All denominations.	PROTESTANT BODIES. Total.	Baptists—Northern Convention.	Congregationalists.	Methodist Episcopal Church.	Presbyterian Church in the U. S. A.	Protestant Episcopal Church.	Other Protestant bodies.	Roman Catholic Church.	Jewish congregations.[1]	Greek Orthodox Church.	Church of Jesus Christ of Latter-day Saints.	All other bodies.
The state	276,749	172,814	8,193	987	1,174	1,537	1,902	977	1,616	8,356	183	4,500	151,032	550
Beaver	3,613	1,814	41			28			13				1,773	
Boxelder	10,009	7,320	259	29		128	58		44				7,061	
Cache	18,139	14,448	130			23	75	16	16				14,318	
Carbon	5,004	2,044	55				55					400	1,589	
Davis	7,996	5,602	24				24						5,578	
Emery	4,657	3,556	38				38						3,518	
Garfield	3,400	2,139											2,139	
Grand	1,149	293	8	8									285	
Iron	3,546	2,522	12				12						2,510	
Juab	10,082	4,511	105	19	26	13	8	10	29	961			3,445	
Kane	1,811	1,125											1,125	
Millard	5,67	3,100											3,100	
Morgan	2,048	1,318											1,318	
Piute	1,954	673	20			20							653	
Rich	1,946	1,118											1,118	
Salt Lake	77,725	48,641	4,928	616	769	814	821	689	1,219	2,550	171	3,700	37,086	206
San Juan	1,023	306											306	
Sanpete	16,313	10,490	121			29	82		10				10,369	
Sevier	8,451	5,311	31			19	12						5,280	
Summit	9,439	5,058	191		88	47		30	26	1,445			3,422	
Tooele	7,361	2,589	18			18							2,571	
Uinta	6,458	2,805	79		40			39					2,726	
Utah	32,456	20,204	484	35	100	103	156	20	70				19,495	225
Wasatch	4,736	3,123											3,123	
Washington	4,612	3,460	56				56						3,404	
Wayne	1,907	1,246											1,246	
Weber	25,239	17,998	1,593	280	151	295	505	173	189	3,400	12	400	12,474	119

[1] Heads of families only.

TABLE 4.—POPULATION IN 1900 AND COMMUNICANTS OR MEMBERS FOR SELECTED DENOMINATIONS, FOR EACH STATE AND TERRITORY, BY COUNTIES: 1906—Continued.

VERMONT.

COUNTY.	Population, 1900.	All denominations.	PROTESTANT BODIES. Total.	Advent Christian Church.	Baptists—Northern Convention.	Free Baptists.	Congregationalists.	Methodist Episcopal Church.	Protestant Episcopal Church.	Universalists.	Other Protestant bodies.	Roman Catholic Church.	Jewish congregations.[1]	All other bodies.
The state....	343,641	147,223	63,895	1,082	8,450	1,501	22,109	17,471	5,278	3,030	4,974	82,272	166	890
Addison..........	21,912	7,816	3, 44	36	489	148	1,594	978	248	....	251	4,072	....	....
Bennington..........	21,705	9,403	4,7 0	....	946	....	1,274	1,197	459	....	334	5,193	....	....
Caledonia..........	24,381	9,202	6,319	81	369	491	2,325	1,780	292	141	640	3,056	....	27
Chittenden..........	39,600	23,442	6,088	....	870	56	2,128	1,519	896	32	587	16,829	125	400
Essex..........	8,056	2,840	893	....	21	....	267	482	93	30	....	1,947	....	....
Franklin..........	30,198	17,204	4	70	548	56	1,071	2,097	890	150	102	12,209	11	....
Grand Isle....	4,462	1,476		....	....		110	109	7	....	....	1,250	....	....
Lamoille..........	12,289	2,577	2		67	....	881	624	51	152	161	575	....	....
Orange..........	19,313	4,977	4,984		74	352	2,203	1,212	51	263	63	676	....	50
Orleans..........	22,024	7,607	3,[illegible]	[illegible]	225	259	1,465	1,246	118	121	203	3,725	....	....
Rutland..........	44,209	26,631	8,	254	1,657	....	2,682	1,758	897	150	1,424	17,779	30	....
Washington..........	36,607	14,804	6,	149	540	114	1,757	1,907	490	390	719	8,475	....	263
Windham..........	26,660	9,756	6,822	64	1,742	25	2,063	867	348	839	238	3,570	....	....
Windsor..........	32,225	9,488	6,[illegible]	84	902	....	2,289	1,695	438	762	252	2,916	....	150

[1] Heads of families only.

VIRGINIA.

COUNTY.	Population, 1900.	All denominations.	PROTESTANT BODIES. Total.	Baptists—Southern and National Conventions.	Primitive Baptists.	Colored Primitive Baptists.	Christians (Christian Connection).	Disciples of Christ.	Dunkers (Conservative).	Dunkers (Progressive).	Lutheran—United Synod in the South.	Methodist Episcopal Church.	African Methodist Episcopal Church.	African Methodist Episcopal Zion Church.	Methodist Protestant Church.
The state......	1,854,184	793,546	761,996	404,268	9,642	1,588	8,266	26,128	9,078	2,166	13,293	18,578	9,889	5,474	4,480
Accomac..........	32,570		13,249	4,950	15	....	....	....	....	....	....	2,163	739	....	1,035
Albemarle..........	28,473	13,249	11,697	8,122	....	....	58	509	....	....	....	....	....	....	....
Alexandria..........	6,430	11,[illegible]	1,322	713	....	....	....	....	....	....	....	118	....	82	112
Alleghany..........	13,118	4,316	4,210	2,297	....	....	....	296	16	30	....	203	....	....	....
Amelia..........	9,037	5,112	5,112	3,554	....	....	....	....	....	....	....	....	....	....	139
Amherst..........	17,864	7,	7,519	4,681	....	....	....	80	....	30	....	....	72	....	....
Appomattox..........	9,662	4,	4,661	3,596	....	....	....	....	....	....	....	....	....	....	....
Augusta..........	32,370	14,519	14,249	2,917	....	....	8	....	1,609	....	1,343	682	52	....	....
Bath..........	5,595	1,661	1,816	468	....	....	....	40	....	....	....	....	....	....	....
Bedford..........	30,356	12,[illegible]	12,439	7,695	45	20	....	54	103	45	....	493	30	....	90
Bland..........	5,497	1,	1,613	93	....	....	....	....	....	....	145	33	....	18	....
Botetourt..........	17,161	7,	7,042	3,634	....	....	....	49	587	...	421	258	....	....	....
Brunswick..........	18,217	9,	9,263	3,734	....	....	....	145	....	....	....	10	....	477	185
Buchanan..........	9,692	1,613	1,060	162	475	....	....	....	....	....	....	....	....	....	....
Buckingham..........	15,266	6,[illegible]	6,977	5,522	....	....	....	....	....	....	....	....	....	....	....
Campbell..........	23,256	9,198	9,198	5,788	8	....	....	....	18	....	....	145	....	....	157
Caroline..........	16,709	8,567	8,567	7,207	....	....	....	243	....	....	....	....	....	....	....
Carroll..........	19,303	3,750	3,750	315	855	....	....	1,033	134	....	47	97	....	....	....
Charles City..........	5,040	3,178	3,178	2,860	....	....	....	....	....	....	....	....	....	....	....
Charlotte..........	15,343	7,616	7,574	5,690	....	....	....	....	....	....	....	....	59	[illegible]	....
Chesterfield..........	18,804	6,946	6,946	4,656	....	....	....	....	....	....	....	....	152	186	....
Clarke..........	7,927	1,999	1,999	484	37	12	....	....	....	....	....	68	84	....	....
Craig..........	4,293	1, 11	1,511	339	....	....	....	648	....	....	68	....	....	....	....
Culpeper..........	14,123	6,886	6,842	5,362	....	....	....	....	....	....	16	....	....	....	....
Cumberland..........	8,996	2,770	2,770	1,782	....	....	....	....	....	....	....	....	....	....	....
Dickenson..........	7,747	782	782		562	....		....	....	....	....	....	....	....	....
Dinwiddie..........	15,374	,311	5,311	3 80	....	....	....	194	....	....	....	....	....	30	....
Elizabeth City..........	19,460	1 ,447	8,730	6,[illegible]	....	....	....	232	....	....	....	57	191	....	99
Essex..........	9,701	,312	6,312	5,178	....	....	....	440	....	....	....	....	....	....	....
Fairfax..........	18,580	5,855	5,190	2,083	44	5	....	55	134	....	....	646	....	....	215
Fauquier..........	23,374	8	8,829	5,	256	44	....	338	65	....	....	66	....	....	....
Floyd..........	15,388	8,	3,449		815	24	....	40	814	7	219	438	....	....	....
Fluvanna..........	9,050	4	4,455	3,	....	....	....	....	....	....	....	....	....	....	....
Franklin..........	25,953	6,993	6,098	1,067		240	....	478	666	50	....	143	288	....	....
Frederick..........	13,239	4,[illegible]	4,859	[illegible]	688	....	....	302	60	....	532	177	....	....	....
Giles..........	10,793	3,	3,553	710	....	....	....	526	....	....	190	100	....	....	....
Gloucester..........	12,832	7,	7,779	6,072	....	....	....	....	....	....	....	....	....	....	....
Goochland..........	9,519	4,	4,764	4,001	....	....	....	286	....	....	....	....	....	....	....
Grayson..........	16,853	,553	5,500	1,360	627	....	....	....	25	....	....	304	2	....	....
Greene..........	6,214	4,[illegible]	2,433	1,140	....	....	301	87	180	....	....	....	....	....	....
Greenesville..........	9,758	4,	4,450	3,431	....	....	59	....	....			10	....	....	217
Halifax..........	37,197	20,	20,554	16,	16	16	456	....	....	....	....	....	130	....	....
Hanover..........	17,618	7,	7,655	4,471	....	....	....	946	....	....	....	....	....	....	....
Henrico..........	30,062	4,450	4,753	3,063	....	....	....	....	....	....	....	....	....	....	....
Henry..........	19,265	3,[illegible]	3,823	[illegible]	403	411	....	1,212	....	....	....	....	89	....	....

TABLE 4.—POPULATION IN 1900 AND COMMUNICANTS OR MEMBERS FOR SELECTED DENOMINATIONS, FOR EACH STATE AND TERRITORY, BY COUNTIES: 1906—Continued.

VIRGINIA—Continued.

COUNTY.	Population, 1900.	All denominations.	PROTESTANT BODIES. Total.	Baptists—Southern and National Conventions.	Primitive Baptists.	Colored Primitive Baptists.	Christians (Christian Connection).	Disciples of Christ.	Dunkers (Conservative).	Dunkers (Progressive).	Lutheran—United Synod in the South.	Methodist Episcopal Church.	African Methodist Episcopal Church.	African Methodist Episcopal Zion Church.	Methodist Protestant Church.
Highland	5,647	1,857	1,825						132			240			
Isle of Wight	13,102	6,547	6,547	3,870			759						642		
James City	3,688	1,699	1,699	1,533				75							
King and Queen	9,265	5,764	5,764	5,001											
King George	6,918	3,614	3,614	3,100		39									
King William	8,380	4,274	4,274	3,347				237							
Lancaster	8,949	4,696	4,645	3,519											
Lee	19,856	5,837	5,837	1,816	25			824				449		82	130
Loudoun	21,948	7,606	7,546	2,434	171							1,179			
Louisa	16,517	10,524	10,460	8,045				1,060							
Lunenburg	11,705	5,210	5,210	3,179				832		40				26	
Madison	10,216	4,320	4,320	2,448	66			150	38		389				
Mathews	8,239	4,528	4,528	2,327				244							
Mecklenburg	26,551	13,541	13,541	7,848			996	173				15	116		
Middlesex	8,220	5,439	5,439	4,641				72							
Montgomery	15,852	7,795	7,795	3,358	23			604	65		809	673	72		
Nansemond	23,078	9,812	9,812	5,381			2,515					80	130	97	
Nelson	16,075	6,937	6,937	4,839				531							
New Kent	4,865	1,760	1,760	1,512											
Norfolk	50,780	10,043	10,043	6,859			220					51	556	567	
Northampton	13,770	5,607	5,465	2,536								188	1,009		
Northumberland	9,846	5,159	5,159	3,509									35		364
Nottoway	12,366	7,029	7,029	4,740				183						73	
Orange	12,571	7,790	7,770	5,997				630	30						
Page	13,794	4,614	4,614	772	343		399	269	443		819	25			
Patrick	15,403	2,482	2,482	289	763	79		74	110						
Pittsylvania	46,894	14,065	14,065	9,145	395	538		620	12	65		345	108		
Powhatan	6,824	3,634	3,372	2,905				47							
Prince Edward	15,045	6,638	6,638	4,238				168				30	216		
Prince George	7,752	3,324	3,032	2,014			43							50	55
Prince William	11,112	3,318	3,206	1,363	71				251		65	110			
Princess Anne	11,192	4,713	4,713	2,440				103				32	225		
Pulaski	14,609	4,609	4,583	960	217			591			50	556		80	
Rappahannock	8,843	2,662	2,662	1,967	93	59				60					
Richmond	7,088	3,589	3,589	2,907				60							
Roanoke	15,837	6,649	6,649	3,164	30	48		165	236	685	407	70	143		
Rockbridge	21,799	8,001	7,971	2,992						40	253	570	23		
Rockingham	33,527	13,617	13,350	873	57		622	63	2,306	330	651	430			
Russell	18,031	3,657	3,657	1,357	406			101				20		68	
Scott	22,694	4,491	4,491	890	195						52	1,113			600
Shenandoah	20,253	9,662	9,602	57			228	1,388	657	574	2,921	222			
Smyth	17,121	6,116	6,116	1,880	84			289			450	248		25	
Southampton	22,848	11,581	11,581	7,578	6		576						217	684	
Spotsylvania	9,239	4,419	4,419	3,682				165							
Stafford	8,097	1,997	1,991	1,249	63							86			
Surry	8,469	4,812	4,812	3,440			212					47		270	218
Sussex	12,082	6,145	6,120	4,666			236							370	
Tazewell	23,384	7,433	7,237	1,046	246			1,406			170	628			
Warren	8,837	2,350	2,304	545	126					70	20	45			
Warwick	4,888	1,188	1,188	847				146							
Washington	28,995	8,200	8,185	1,796	146			484	39		210	951	36	209	226
Westmoreland	9,243	5,973	5,803	4,413				140							
Wise	19,653	5,473	5,205	1,558	463			165				505		370	250
Wythe	20,437	7,187	7,017	680				320			1,214	214	432	28	
York	7,482	4,017	4,017	2,427				141							
Alexandria city	14,528	7,429	5,707	2,695								570			278
Bristol city	4,579	3,037	2,943	829				312			67				
Buena Vista city	2,388	1,311	1,288	605					80	100	31				
Charlottesville city	6,449	5,269	5,014	2,876											
Clifton Forge city	3,212	1,378	1,123	375											
Danville city	16,520	8,616	8,450	4,707									96		
Fredericksburg city	5,068	1,999	1,829	709				25							
Lynchburg city	18,891	15,375	13,614	7,233				928			51	700	63		110
Manchester city	9,715	5,974	5,591	3,512				400				42			
Newport News city	19,635	8,030	6,483	2,952				330			122	50	218	91	
Norfolk city	46,624	28,533	24,077	9,949			474	367			206	22	2,060	927	
Petersburg city	21,810	11,026	10,385	4,842				158						500	
Portsmouth city	17,427	14,761	12,571	7,332			104	70					1,077	164	
Radford city	3,344	569	569	150											
Richmond city	85,050	54,506	45,475	26,234				2,268			360	278	255		
Roanoke city	21,495	13,072	11,224	4,286	68	17		480	201	40	360	249	157		
Staunton city	7,289	4,736	4,296	639					67		217	429	75		
Williamsburg city	2,044	1,684	1,684	1,288		27									
Winchester city	5,161	3,007	2,709	189				37			418	325	40		
County location unknown[1]		2,419	1,431	50	704	9						580			

[1] See explanatory headnote on page 294.

TABLE 4.—POPULATION IN 1900 AND COMMUNICANTS OR MEMBERS FOR SELECTED DENOMINATIONS, FOR EACH STATE AND TERRITORY, BY COUNTIES: 1906—Continued.

VIRGINIA—Continued.

COUNTY.	PROTESTANT BODIES—continued.									Roman Catholic Church.	Jewish congregations.[1]	Church of Jesus Christ of Latter-day Saints.	All other bodies.
	Methodist Episcopal Church, South.	Colored Methodist Episcopal Church.	Reformed Zion Union Apostolic Church (Colored).	Presbyterian Church in the U. S. A.	Presbyterian Church in the U. S.	Protestant Episcopal Church.	Reformed Church in the U. S.	United Brethren in Christ.	Other Protestant bodies.				
The state	157,354	1,514	2,929	2,615	36,569	28,487	2,288	6,786	10,604	28,700	915	988	947
Accomac	3,911				253	153			30				
Albemarle	2,212				305	428		63		7			
Alexandria	50			160		74			13				
Alleghany	610				577	105			76	106			
Amelia	609			408	296	66			40				
Amherst	2,383				111	162							
Appomattox	850				200	15							
Augusta	1,685				3,539	31	376	1,201	806				38
Bath	494				717	32			65	42			
Bedford	3,004				468	381			11	51			
Bland	1,227				75	22							
Botetourt	1,605				390	98							
Brunswick	2,165	60	1,760	99	150	478							
Buchanan	423												
Buckingham	1,128				274	53				3			
Campbell	2,229	261		11	468	104			9				
Caroline	981				8	128							
Carroll	730	60			106				373				
Charles City	230				20	59							
Charlotte	988			113	676	28			20	42			
Chesterfield	1,794				113	45							
Clarke	641				185	406			80				
Craig	431				20	5							
Culpeper	984				111	309				44			
Cumberland	694				220	49			25				
Dickenson	140												
Dinwiddie	1,527				41	192			20				
Elizabeth City	899				112	657				1,700	17		
Essex	518					149			27				
Fairfax	899			249	30	642			188	665			
Fauquier	1,924				370	633		37	39	164			
Floyd	468				70				60				
Fluvanna	552				44	47				27			
Franklin	1,366				77	108			115				
Frederick	1,810				233	31	42	766	205				
Giles	1,862				165								
Gloucester	1,407				140	160							
Goochland	360				44	63			10				
Grayson	3,042	35			24				81				
Greene	535					124		66					
Greenesville	608				35	90							
Halifax	2,120	612		155	449	389			148				
Hanover	1,659			14	347	218				67			
Henrico	786				177	282			25				
Henry	712			388	90	68			13				
Highland	880				347			131	95	32			
Isle of Wight	1,155					121							
James City	51					8			32				
King and Queen	719					3			41				
King George	323					152							
King William	566					63			61				
Lancaster	952				72	87			15	51			
Lee	2,386			10	115								
Loudoun	1,716	45			345	416	140		1,100	60			
Louisa	981				117	257				64			
Lunenburg	899		13		68	81			72				
Madison	1,181	15			12	17			4				
Mathews	1,861					78			18				
Mecklenburg	2,354	81	924	128	204	702							
Middlesex	670					56							
Montgomery	1,610	19			375	88			99				
Nansemond	1,290				50	157			112				
Nelson	1,347				84	136							
New Kent	210				20	18							
Norfolk	1,618		80		37	26			29				
Northampton	1,396				150	186				142			
Northumberland	1,229					22							
Nottoway	1,301		13	142	385	172			20				
Orange	749				113	243			8	20			
Page	1,159					51		143	191				
Patrick	980			150	31				6				
Pittsylvania	2,067			12	351	407							
Powhatan	211				91	118				262			
Prince Edward	1,052				760	61			113				
Prince George	550		80			145			95	292			

[1] Heads of families only.

TABLE 4.—POPULATION IN 1900 AND COMMUNICANTS OR MEMBERS FOR SELECTED DENOMINATIONS, FOR EACH STATE AND TERRITORY, BY COUNTIES: 1906—Continued.

VIRGINIA—Continued.

COUNTY.	PROTESTANT BODIES—continued.									Roman Catholic Church.	Jewish congregations.[1]	Church of Jesus Christ of Latter-day Saints.	All other bodies.
	Methodist Episcopal Church, South.	Colored Methodist Episcopal Church.	Reformed Zion Union Apostolic Church (Colored).	Presbyterian Church in the U. S. A.	Presbyterian Church in the U. S.	Protestant Episcopal Church.	Reformed Church in the U. S.	United Brethren in Christ.	Other Protestant bodies.				
Prince William	736			118	88	319		85		112			
Princess Anne	1,646					97			170				
Pulaski	1,474				558	90			7	26			
Rappahannock	399					84							
Richmond	468				47	90			17				
Roanoke	1,308				243	113			37				
Rockbridge	1,036				2,532	141		40	344	30			
Rockingham	2,560				1,047	163	591	2,917	740	247	20		
Russell	1,697				8								
Scott	1,538				43				60				
Shenandoah	1,497	12			242	52	953	573	226	60			
Smyth	2,778				337	25							
Southampton	2,089					74			357				
Spotsylvania	511					45			16				
Stafford	448				50	95							
Surry	549					70			6				
Sussex	790				5	53				25			
Tazewell	3,013				382	56			290	196			
Warren	908	139			158	75		118	100	46			
Warwick			14			84			97				
Washington	2,937				1,005	109			37	15			
Westmoreland	1,012	12				226				170			
Wise	1,572			26	129	17			150	268			
Wythe	3,428				413	288				170			
York	1,326				102	21							
Alexandria city	700	44			376	822			222	1,700	22		
Bristol city	1,214				390	131				94			
Buena Vista city	204				220	38			10	23			
Charlottesville city	1,194				500	421			23	255			
Clifton Forge city	380				305	63				255			
Danville city	2,045			111	526	475			490	138	28		
Fredericksburg city	400				350	338			7	170			
Lynchburg city	2,267			26	1,364	774			98	1,710			51
Manchester city	1,231				220	186				383			
Newport News city	1,238		33	52	740	530			127	1,275	72		200
Norfolk city	5,174				1,632	2,708			558	4,029	218		209
Petersburg city	2,661	54		38	798	1,297			37	595	46		
Portsmouth city	2,492		12		280	849			191	2,125	65		
Radford city	143				194	82							
Richmond city	6,601	30		130	3,117	4,893			1,309	8,313	389		329
Roanoke city	3,363			75	1,032	605	92	90	109	1,700	23		125
Staunton city	720				1,264	535		350		425	15		
Williamsburg city	207					162							
Winchester city	671				415	174	94	206	140	298			
County location unknown[2]	14	35							39			988	

[1] Heads of families only.

[2] See explanatory headnote on page 294.

WASHINGTON.

COUNTY.	Population, 1900.	All denominations.	PROTESTANT BODIES.									Roman Catholic Church.	Jewish congregations.[2]	All other bodies.
			Total.	Baptists—Northern and National Conventions.	Congregationalists.	Disciples of Christ.	Lutheran—Norwegian Synods.[1]	Methodist Episcopal Church.	Presbyterian Church in the U. S. A.	Protestant Episcopal Church.	Other Protestant bodies.			
The state	518,103	191,976	114,070	12,614	10,025	10,140	6,089	29,347	14,437	6,780	24,638	74,981	488	2,437
Adams	4,840	1,901	1,839	122	531	263		433	29	22	439	62		
Asotin	3,366	998	888	128		177	25	332	155	24	47	110		
Benton	(³)	772	648	53	50	68	22	232	114	34	75	124		
Chehalis	15,124	4,307	2,731	283	104	345	96	1,038	330	110	425	1,546		30
Chelan	3,931	1,956	1,480	101	41	176		665	172	89	236	476		
Clallam	5,603	558	336	25	63			188		60		222		
Clarke	13,419	4,250	2,695	217	27	319	98	881	323	110	720	1,555		
Columbia	7,128	1,448	1,448	185	207	457		217		24	358			
Cowlitz	7,877	1,221	978	24	50	200		360	160		184	193		50
Douglas	4,926	1,549	1,004	118		43	35	352	159	16	281	533		12
Ferry	4,562	575	22					22				553		
Franklin	486	355	291					240	25		26	64		
Garfield	3,918	1,214	878	65	60	355		305		37	56	336		
Island	1,870	395	369		58		110	106			95	26		
Jefferson	5,712	832	492	61			49	116	133	108	25	340		

[1] Includes United Norwegian Lutheran Church in America, Hauge's Norwegian Evangelical Lutheran Synod, Synod for the Norwegian Evangelical Lutheran Church in America, and Norwegian Lutheran Free Church.

[2] Heads of families only.

[3] New county since 1900; formed from parts of Klickitat and Yakima in 1905.

TABLE 4.—POPULATION IN 1900 AND COMMUNICANTS OR MEMBERS FOR SELECTED DENOMINATIONS, FOR EACH STATE AND TERRITORY, BY COUNTIES: 1906—Continued.

WASHINGTON—Continued.

COUNTY.	Population, 1900.	All denominations.	PROTESTANT BODIES. Total.	Baptists—Northern and National Conventions.	Congregationalists.	Disciples of Christ.	Lutheran—Norwegian Synods.[1]	Methodist Episcopal Church.	Presbyterian Church in the U. S. A.	Protestant Episcopal Church.	Other Protestant bodies.	Roman Catholic Church.	Jewish congregations.[2]	All other bodies.
King	110,053	57,102	26,089	3,147	2,788	950	1,060	5,361	5,483	2,731	4,569	29,418	335	1,260
Kitsap	6,767	1,759	1,159	102	70	52	427	221	139	31	117	485		115
Kittitas	9,704	3,806	1,239	147		293		374	252	95	78	2,529		38
Klickitat	6,407	1,288	863		34	28		444	167		190	425		
Lewis	15,157	5,189	2,946	542		281	107	814	204	102	896	2,243		
Lincoln	11,969	4,137	2,930	361	181	75	108	560	504	50	1,091	1,207		
Mason	3,810	314	244	45	65			115			19	70		
Okanogan	4,689	959	299					193	29		77	660		
Pacific	5,983	682	682	109	57		51	324	110		31			
Pierce	55,515	19,425	12,755	1,587	814	771	602	3,519	1,945	1,063	2,464	6,176	38	456
San Juan	2,928	476	304		77			121	52	40	14	172		
Skagit	14,272	4,043	2,515	278	67	81	458	697	164	188	582	1,528		
Skamania	1,688	137	43		19			24				94		
Snohomish	23,950	9,159	6,323	729	695	177	1,327	1,156	415	181	1,643	2,820		16
Spokane	57,542	23,459	15,220	1,554	1,773	1,219	603	4,253	1,235	840	3,743	7,761	115	348
Stevens	10,543	2,477	1,180	43	260	80	65	276	215	10	231	1,297		
Thurston	9,927	2,638	1,800	174	95	410		542	242	60	277	800		
Wahkiakum	2,819	638	298		7		40	44			207	340		
Walla Walla	18,680	7,942	4,092	252	532	793		847	331	175	1,162	3,825		
Whatcom	24,116	9,232	5,896	906	399	250	722	1,292	510	245	1,572	3,302		[illegible]
Whitman	25,360	8,007	6,708	852	582	1,323	84	1,622	121	105	2,019	1,299		
Yakima	13,462	6,517	4,382	404	319	954		1,061	719	236	689	2,135		
County location unknown[3]		259	4							4		255		

[1] Includes United Norwegian Lutheran Church in America, Hauge's Norwegian Evangelical Lutheran Synod, Synod for the Norwegian Evangelical Lutheran Church in America, and Norwegian Lutheran Free Church.
[2] Heads of families only.
[3] See explanatory headnote on page 294.

WEST VIRGINIA.

COUNTY.	Population, 1900.	All denominations.	PROTESTANT BODIES. Total.	Advent Christian Church.	Baptists—Northern, Southern, and National Conventions.	Free Baptists.	United Baptists.	Primitive Baptists.	Disciples of Christ.	Churches of Christ.	Dunkers (Conservative).	Lutheran—General Synod.	Lutheran—General Council.	Lutheran—Joint Synod of Ohio, etc.	Methodist Episcopal Church.
The state	958,800	301,565	259,804	1,476	60,365	1,513	2,226	2,019	10,729	2,594	3,457	2,552	1,176	1,540	61,641
Barbour	14,198	5,537	5,223		881			60	61		312				1,223
Berkeley	19,469	7,277	6,427		491	79			225		118	720			1,105
Boone	8,194	1,496	1,496		558			46	187						549
Braxton	18,904	4,802	4,664		926					20	45				864
Brooke	7,219	2,892	2,323		119				759						692
Cabell	29,252	9,840	9,306		3,359		325		325	50					1,468
Calhoun	10,266	2,610	2,526	87	1,032			69							327
Clay	8,248	1,092	1,092	57	338			45							504
Doddridge	13,689	3,918	3,604		1,269				166	185					699
Fayette	31,987	10,390	8,472	101	4,718	15			366		100				1,198
Gilmer	11,762	3,774	3,774		1,487					40	28				528
Grant	7,275	2,375	2,211		137				50		546			86	331
Greenbrier	20,683	8,088	7,297		1,471			70	135		20				1,006
Hampshire	11,806	3,397	3,351		187				434		247				216
Hancock	6,693	2,628	2,070		27				471	16					258
Hardy	8,449	2,882	2,882		22					35	413			204	138
Harrison	27,690	12,105	9,911		2,916			38	167	21		75			3,123
Jackson	22,987	5,145	5,045	45	703			12	60	66					1,237
Jefferson	15,935	5,678	5,404		583	399						32			413
Kanawha	54,696	14,242	12,969	243	5,166	510		309	330		26			136	2,467
Lewis	16,980	5,938	4,632		780										1,046
Lincoln	15,434	2,810	2,810		1,205		912	114		91					217
Logan	6,955	938	938		150		167		60	255					89
McDowell	18,747	4,887	4,390		2,556			189	253						237
Marion	32,430	13,709	9,346		1,860				170	192		85			3,384
Marshall	26,444	9,819	6,629		396				1,278	34			180		3,460
Mason	24,142	5,478	5,383	152	883	25		4							1,364
Mercer	23,023	7,570	7,467		2,434			163	714		71				249
Mineral	12,883	4,212	3,788		35						140	75			1,053
Mingo	11,359	882	812		153		227	28	55						
Monongalia	19,049	7,551	7,207		1,235				207	149	51		71		3,324
Monroe	13,130	4,719	4,627		1,511				253		34				384
Morgan	7,294	2,261	2,089		16			67	85						484
Nicholas	11,403	3,816	3,311		1,353										810
Ohio	48,024	25,050	13,026		378				885			757	800	490	4,135

TABLE 4.—POPULATION IN 1900 AND COMMUNICANTS OR MEMBERS FOR SELECTED DENOMINATIONS, FOR EACH STATE AND TERRITORY, BY COUNTIES: 1906—Continued.

WEST VIRGINIA—Continued.

COUNTY.	Population, 1900.	All denominations.	PROTESTANT BODIES. Total.	Advent Christian Church.	Baptists—Northern, Southern, and National Conventions.	Free Baptists.	United Baptists.	Primitive Baptists.	Disciples of Christ.	Churches of Christ.	Dunkers (Conservative).	Lutheran—General Synod.	Lutheran—General Council.	Lutheran—Joint Synod of Ohio, etc.	Methodist Episcopal Church.
Pendleton	9,167	2,578	2,578						65		243			624	
Pleasants	9,345	2,047	2,047		260					241					150
Pocahontas	8,572	2,416	2,416		40						80				540
Preston	22,727	8,188	7,671		818						596	484			3,879
Putnam	17,330	2,586	2,419		1,320		17	13	15						208
Raleigh	12,436	3,791	3,395	82	1,390			81	763		55				606
Randolph	17,670	5,212	3,774		203			57			135	39			1,[illegible]
Ritchie	18,901	4,988	4,806		994					125					1,135
Roane	19,852	5,343	5,343	709	1,504			11							1,[illegible]
Summers	16,265	3,850	3,678		2,081			82	345						330
Taylor	14,978	6,410	5,535		1,672			46	50	20	97	215			1,555
Tucker	13,433	4,916	2,978		197							70			739
Tyler	18,252	4,599	4,237		366				450	288					1,090
Upshur	14,696	5,981	5,805		482						101				2,451
Wayne	23,619	4,278	4,256		2,222		578		92						
Webster	8,862	1,650	1,597		196			55							686
Wetzel	22,880	4,828	4,356		319				686	446					1,420
Wirt	10,284	2,870	2,870		1,237					179					328
Wood	34,452	11,470	9,805		2,466				417	141			125		3,174
Wyoming	8,380	2,094	2,094		1,189			10	150						445
County location unknown [1]		1,662	1,631		74	485		450							403

COUNTY.	PROTESTANT BODIES—continued. Methodist Protestant Church.	Methodist Episcopal Church, South.	African Methodists.[2]	Nonsectarian Churches of Bible Faith.	Presbyterian Church in the U. S. A.	United Presbyterian Church.	Presbyterian Church in the U. S.	Protestant Episcopal Church.	United Brethren in Christ.	Other Protestant bodies.	Roman Catholic Church.	Jewish congregations.[3]	All other bodies.
The state	16,004	36,632	1,160	1,316	8,514	1,026	10,047	5,230	19,993	8,594	40,011	220	1,530
Barbour	521	759	110	153			89		1,054		314		
Berkeley		1,189					791	261	1,102	346	850		
Boone		99	10		22					25			
Braxton	1,033	549	25	568			88	7	539		138		
Brooke			54		482	61		120		36	569		
Cabell		1,851	60				455	205	932	276	510	24	
Calhoun	148	651			7				205				84
Clay		120		18	10								
Doddridge	455								609	221	286		
Fayette		,202	24		20		379	180		169	1,572		348
Gilmer	467	368		72			49		722	13			
Grant		128	24				206		688	15	164		
Greenbrier	340	2,840					1,287	128			791		
Hampshire		1,142					434	42	210	439	46		
Hancock	309				802	153				34	558		
Hardy		1,074					239	29	540	188			
Harrison	1,123	300	100		185		60	115	,267	421	2,158		36
Jackson	591	1,095		94	135			58	847	102			100
Jefferson	142	1,842	98				592	769		534	274		
Kanawha		1,361	81	47	347		1,131	524		291	1,207	66	
Lewis	1,904	106	15	25	47			109	554	46	1,306		
Lincoln		271											
Logan		197					20						
McDowell		932	99		45		22	13		53	488		
Marion	859	1,654			627			190	238	87	3,924		439
Marshall		95			691	89		130		276	3,130		60
Mason		457			77		190	130	1,674	427	95		
Mercer		3,182	92				345	192		25	103		
Mineral		1,388					346		751		424		
Mingo		192	34				113	10			70		
Monongalia	1,316	190	30		496			87		51	344		
Monroe		1,453					829	45		118	92		
Morgan		322					70	34	806	205	172		
Nicholas	44	1,052					52				505		
Ohio			76		2,098	656		1,042		1,709	11,569	130	325
Pendleton		331	17				195		675	278			
Pleasants	521	165			67			33	206	8			
Pocahontas	101	1,255					382	24					
Preston	609				198				929	159	517		
Putnam		317			38		26	8	178	279	167		

[1] See explanatory headnote on page 294.
[2] Includes African Methodist Episcopal Church, African Methodist Episcopal Zion Church, and Colored Methodist Episcopal Church.
[3] Heads of families only.

TABLE 4.—POPULATION IN 1900 AND COMMUNICANTS OR MEMBERS FOR SELECTED DENOMINATIONS, FOR EACH STATE AND TERRITORY, BY COUNTIES: 1906—Continued.

WEST VIRGINIA—Continued.

COUNTY.	PROTESTANT BODIES—continued. Methodist Protestant Church.	Methodist Episcopal Church, South.	African Methodists.[1]	Nonsectarian Churches of Bible Faith.	Presbyterian Church in the U. S. A.	United Presbyterian Church.	Presbyterian Church in the U. S.	Protestant Episcopal Church.	United Brethren in Christ.	Other Protestant bodies.	Roman Catholic Church.	Jewish congregations.[2]	All other bodies.
Raleigh		132	22		130		22			112	396		
Randolph	128	254	50				1,182	34	178	379	1,438		
Ritchie	1,024				175	67	10	7	558	186	110		70
Roane	1,077	616		95	78				250				
Summers		562					228	50			172		
Taylor	836	235			190			48	290	281	875		
Tucker	497	925					200	35	193	122	1,938		
Tyler	380		11		292			56	1,304		362		
Upshur	714	152	30	200	249			58	1,368		176		
Wayne	91	488	18					5		76			22
Webster	117	729		44			15			21	53		
Wetzel		588			172			75	128	227	472		
Wirt	333	617			44				123	9			
Wood	324	905	48		790			377	696	342	,645		20
Wyoming		300											
County location unknown[3]			32						179	8	31		

[1] Includes African Methodist Episcopal Church, African Methodist Episcopal Zion Church, and Colored Methodist Episcopal Church.
[2] Heads of families only.
[3] See explanatory headnote on page 294.

WISCONSIN.

COUNTY.	Population, 1900.	All denominations.	PROTESTANT BODIES. Total.	Seventh-day Adventists.	Baptists—Northern and National Conventions.	Congregationalists.	Evangelical Association.	German Evangelical Synod of N. A.	Lutheran—General Council.	Lutheran—Synodical Conference.	Lutheran—United Norwegian Church.	Lutheran—Joint Synod of Ohio, etc.	Lutheran—Hauge's Norwegian Synod.	Lutheran—Synod of Iowa, etc.	Lutheran—Norwegian Synod.
The state	2,069,042	1,000,903	490,871	3,194	19,474	26,163	13,280	19,861	8,695	153,690	49,535	15,471	3,047	15,220	23,927
Adams	9,141	2,079	1,724		49	228				411	480		68		141
Ashland	20,176	13,651	3,336	27	292	271	156		480	657	95				
Barron	23,677	10,047	6,069	36	192	42	163		338	705	2,134	110		87	439
Bayfield	14,392	4,001	1,339		19	231			232	81	187			16	
Brown	46,359	29,195	7,290	113	216	314	246			1,804	413	1,376			
Buffalo	16,765	6,054	4,145		80	81	339			802	1,252		85	380	400
Burnett	7,478	1,805	1,675	29	295	83			363		174				401
Calumet	17,078	8,852	3,146			146	410	320		1,380					
Chippewa	33,037	16,634	5,605	39		217	164			792	1,628			427	320
Clark	25,848	12,758	5,347	40	82	165	83	334		1,675	202	1,080			136
Columbia	31,121	13,593	10,050	11	530	223	211	68		2,995		180	470	50	1,245
Crawford	17,286	7,234	3,503	9		238	266			100	1,700		135	99	470
Dane	69,435	32,073	19,903	117	685	1,412	256		58	576	5,584	1,226	377	1,240	2,242
Dodge	46,631	23,163	14,893	4	342	315	469			9,328	244	510		1,003	
Door	17,583	8,306	4,091	99	162	189	95			1,315	983	84			
Douglas	36,335	16,526	4,473	41	338	265	26		629	140	624			145	125
Dunn	25,043	8,586	7,523	30	93	304	269			1,174	2,102			863	1,168
Eau Claire	31,692	13,042	8,901	40	645	532	91	75	150	2,311	2,192			1,075	400
Florence	3,197	617	146		14				30						
Fond du Lac	47,589	28,821	11,559	15	504	1,026	736	1,436		2,374				1,387	
Forest	1,396	1,630	572	11				25		306					
Grant	38,881	16,205	7,285	74	159	1,157	15	377	262	258	800	550		399	
Green	22,710	7,402	5,908	36	498	93	927	694		110	290	24			60
Green Lake	15,797	9,929	4,144	16	133	278	377			2,779					
Iowa	23,114	9,099	4,660		103	607	18			31	1,300			229	
Iron	6,616	2,882	491							100					61
Jackson	17,466	5,045	4,103		10				95	64	1,325		623		1,180
Jefferson	34,789	20,434	14,252	62	48	579	397	469	49	7,812	65	144		1,542	70
Juneau	20,629	6,724	3,578	21	214	276	195			825	374			65	492
Kenosha	21,707	12,506	4,742		240	349			344	1,475		156			
Kewaunee	17,212	10,528	3,271			65	33			2,622	164				
La Crosse	42,997	24,306	10,713	35	710	439	52		153	3,220	715				2,124
Lafayette	20,959	8,765	3,946	23	66	211	25	56			1,180				
Langlade	12,553	5,458	1,904	96	105	335	35	320		616	21	66			
Lincoln	16,269	9,173	4,465	50	170	93		1,000	114	1,751	163	150			195
Manitowoc	42,261	23,457	9,121		71	115	486	397		4,915	562				703
Marathon	43,256	25,787	11,833	89	284	47	19	1,322	71	5,062		2,060			281
Marinette	30,822	14,379	6,179		558	34	81	305	668	1,898					
Marquette	10,509	5,629	4,127	47		85	240			2,715				518	
Milwaukee	330,017	171,662	60,534	234	2,630	2,325	1,281	4,101	618	35,359	730		120	45	71

TABLE 4.—POPULATION IN 1900 AND COMMUNICANTS OR MEMBERS FOR SELECTED DENOMINATIONS, FOR EACH STATE AND TERRITORY, BY COUNTIES: 1906—Continued.

WISCONSIN—Continued.

COUNTY.	Population, 1900.	All denominations.	PROTESTANT BODIES. Total.	Seventh-day Adventists.	Baptists—Northern and National Conventions.	Congregationalists.	Evangelical Association.	German Evangelical Synod of N. A.	Lutheran—General Council.	Lutheran—Synodical Conference.	Lutheran—United Norwegian Church.	Lutheran—Joint Synod of Ohio, etc.	Lutheran—Hauge's Norwegian Synod.	Lutheran—Synod of Iowa, etc.	Lutheran—Norwegian Synod.
Monroe	28,103	12,062	7,826	97	441	698	434			2,916	648				805
Oconto	20,874	11,968	4,015	89	28	38	115	176	22	1,145	190	592		401	
Oneida	8,875	3,384	1,113	20	96	92		43	67	354	99				32
Outagamie	46,247	24,678	10,563	81	198	1,090	526	1,256		3,322		1,811			
Ozaukee	16,363	9,555	4,001			59	107	757	47	1,652	60			850	
Pepin	7,905	2,574	1,282		33	106			375	74				105	
Pierce	23,943	8,515	5,125	89	102	505		120	367	160	835		377	26	1,053
Polk	17,801	7,086	5,659	48	219	112			1,225	519	2,070				
Portage	29,483	16,940	5,311	48	262			73		852	1,694	142		60	644
Price	9,106	3,799	1,698	16	224	164			337	402	97			90	50
Racine	45,644	19,874	11,920	55	1,187	850	225		430	2,957	360	278	244		
Richland	19,483	5,075	3,088	49	130	104	74			87	250			108	
Rock	51,203	22,418	16,261	128	1,472	2,652	66		191	2,327	1,489	286		303	1,377
Rusk	(1)	3,568	1,258	55	90	132			12		341			314	
St. Croix	26,830	13,464	6,202		185	387	75		299	486	1,943	300			854
Sauk	33,006	14,287	9,352	53	468	262	954		22	3,105	100	250		1,382	17
Sawyer	3,593	1,134	286			90				36	90				
Shawano	27,475	12,755	8,916	30		154	294	365		4,877	1,397	898			154
Sheboygan	50,345	23,546	14,473		399	345	327	1,391		6,220				430	47
Taylor	11,262	3,530	2,401		38	35		125	25	1,466	158				
Trempealeau	23,114	12,274	7,314		124	222	168			249	3,074		168		2,737
Vernon	28,351	11,101	9,604	216	32	421				744	3,240		380		2,955
Vilas	4,929	1,384	337	39		69			55	94					
Walworth	29,259	10,572	7,234		1,126	1,372	171	75		1,017	10	233			171
Washburn	5,521	1,725	800	9	118	31			63	150	65			24	28
Washington	23,589	16,364	6,621		45	111	452	2,113		2,494					
Waukesha	35,229	16,769	10,274	7	557	762	396	1,170		2,419	295				
Waupaca	31,615	14,437	11,654	101	319	400	130		32	5,014	1,830	1,197			203
Waushara	15,972	5,818	5,192	145	354	298	226			1,681	788			692	
Winnebago	58,225	26,028	14,140	103	641	825	275	709		3,697	670	1,698		683	
Wood	25,865	15,464	5,763	272	49	407	104	189	374	2,566	59	70		182	76
County location unknown [2]		718	542						98	70					

COUNTY.	PROTESTANT BODIES—continued. Lutheran—Norwegian Free Church.	Lutheran—United Danish Church.	Methodist Episcopal Church.	Moravian Church (Unitas Fratrum).	Presbyterian Church in the U. S. A.	Presbyterian—Welsh Calvinistic Methodist Church.	Protestant Episcopal Church.	Reformed Church in America.	Reformed Church in the U. S.	Other Protestant bodies.	Roman Catholic Church.	Jewish congregations.[3]	All other bodies.
The state	5,477	3,897	54,817	2,713	18,077	2,579	16,527	2,312	8,386	24,529	505,264	1,199	3,569
Adams		75	73		70					129	315		40
Ashland	171		473		372		181			161	10,310	5	
Barron	605		638		129		91			360	3,906		72
Bayfield	231		143		87		27			85	2,626		36
Brown		270	723	330	646		820		34	85	21,640	40	125
Buffalo			439						287		1,909		
Burnett	40		211							79	130		
Calumet			247				44		575	24	5,706		
Chippewa	400		771		332		220			295	10,984		45
Clark			486		215		30		443	376	7,296		115
Columbia			1,582		837	695	244	130		579	3,513		30
Crawford			336				27			123	3,641		90
Dane	900	144	2,361	218	1,069		494		50	894	12,068	40	62
Dodge			905		364	151	301	160	555	242	8,270		
Door			376	617			131			40	4,165		50
Douglas	103		628		528		332			549	11,858	61	134
Dunn	225		876				98			321	1,063		
Eau Claire			700		325		216			149	4,141		
Florence			8		70					24	471		
Fond du Lac			1,775		345	68	606	334	332	621	17,079		183
Forest			70		108		12			40	1,058		
Grant			2,453		150		153			478	8,812		108
Green	765		799		93		41		409	1,069	1,482	12	
Green Lake			430			27	36			68	5,785		
Iowa			927		283	239	145			778	4,439		
Iron			30		45					255	2,391		
Jackson			387		208		20		58	133	942		
Jefferson			1,405	1,099		58	288		60	105	6,182		
Juneau		59	675		52		93			237	3,018		128
Kenosha		300	1,090		82		430			276	7,493	27	244

[1] New county since 1900; formed as Gates from part of Chippewa in 1901. Name changed in 1905.
[2] See explanatory headnote on page 294.
[3] Heads of families only.

TABLE 4.—POPULATION IN 1900 AND COMMUNICANTS OR MEMBERS FOR SELECTED DENOMINATIONS, FOR EACH STATE AND TERRITORY, BY COUNTIES: 1906—Continued.

WISCONSIN—Continued.

COUNTY.	PROTESTANT BODIES—continued.										Roman Catholic Church.	Jewish congregations.[1]	All other bodies.
	Lutheran—Norwegian Free Church.	Lutheran—United Danish Church.	Methodist Episcopal Church.	Moravian Church (Unitas Fratrum).	Presbyterian Church in the U. S. A.	Presbyterian—Welsh Calvinistic Methodist Church.	Protestant Episcopal Church.	Reformed Church in America.	Reformed Church in the U. S.	Other Protestant bodies.			
Kewaunee			190		20		177				7,257		
La Crosse	192		1,353		727	32	420		285	256	13,443	42	108
Lafayette	352		1,300				43		20	670	4,819		
Langlade			264				30			16	3,554		
Lincoln			387		193		134			65	4,708		
Manitowoc			370		270		200		986	46	14,324	12	
Marathon	129		901		878		142	21	340	187	13,954		
Marinette	754		817		631		176		28	229	8,168	32	
Marquette			206		300					16	1,502		
Milwaukee			4,200		2,311	254	3,229	361	250	2,415	109,981	765	382
Monroe		137	1,197			94	147			212	4,047		189
Oconto	80	32	566		235		206			100	7,953		
Oneida			177		25		72			36	2,271		
Outagamie		40	1,272	136	183		206		241	201	14,036	47	32
Ozaukee			45							424	5,554		
Pepin			340							249	1,181		111
Pierce			1,060		138		221			72	3,390		
Polk	212	276	346		61					571	1,312		115
Portage		50	776		229		379			102	11,518	25	86
Price			96		85					137	2,101		
Racine		1,039	1,620		558	303	845			969	7,863	28	63
Richland			672		220					1,394	1,975		12
Rock		41	2,241		1,010		867			1,811	5,931		226
Rusk			182							132	2,310		
St. Croix			745		323		222	162		221	7,262		
Sauk			1,377		369		209		332	452	4,885		50
Sawyer			50				20				848		
Shawano	11		393		165		19			159	3,839		
Sheboygan			859		578		376	1,144	1,656	701	8,585	38	450
Taylor			143		17		102			292	1,129		
Trempealeau			413		129					30	4,960		
Vernon			828							788	1,497		
Vilas			15		57		8				1,047		
Walworth			1,778				595			686	3,248		90
Washburn			173							79	925		
Washington			212		34		60		860	260	9,743		
Waukesha		275	1,049		526	355	1,389		361	765	6,495		
Waupaca	307	655	1,023		166		167			110	2,783		
Waushara		201	581		15	163				48	626		
Winnebago		303	1,832		944	140	688		224	708	11,846	25	17
Wood			537	313	270		110			185	9,701		
County location unknown[2]			214							160			176

[1] Heads of families only.

[2] See explanatory headnote on page 294.

WYOMING.

COUNTY.	Population, 1900.	All denominations.	PROTESTANT BODIES.								Roman Catholic Church.	Greek Orthodox Church.	Church of Jesus Christ of Latter-day Saints.	All other bodies.
			Total.	Baptists—Northern Convention.	Congregationalists.	Lutheran—Finnish Synods.[1]	Methodist Episcopal Church.	Presbyterian Church in the U. S. A.	Protestant Episcopal Church.	Other Protestant bodies.				
The state	[2] 92,531	23,945	7,502	838	833	613	1,612	984	1,741	881	10,264	900	5,203	76
Albany	13,084	1,841	781	104			160	115	175	227	798	250		12
Bighorn	4,328	2,440	495	158			154	58	57	68	126		1,819	
Carbon	9,589	1,216	726			213	139	167	201	6	490			
Converse	3,337	545	307		127		94		86		238			
Crook	3,137	592	131	63			25		22	21	453			
Fremont	5,357	1,373	727	57			128		542		646			
Johnson	2,361	423	189		68		87		34		234			
Laramie	20,181	4,786	1,857	260	404		332	309	212	250	2,479	450		
Natrona	1,785	299	78				40		38		221			
Sheridan	5,122	2,545	1,086	132	160		260	74	172	288	1,403			56
Sweetwater	8,455	2,020	506		74	300	41		70	21	1,445		69	
Uinta	12,223	5,028	514	64		100	104	165	81		1,199		3,315	
Weston	3,203	627	95				48	6	41		532			
County location unknown[3]		210	10						10			200		

[1] Includes Finnish Evangelical Lutheran Church of America, or Suomi Synod, and Finnish Evangelical Lutheran National Church.

[2] Includes population (369) of National Park reservation.

[3] See explanatory headnote on page 294.

TABLE 5.—ORGANIZATIONS, COMMUNICANTS OR MEMBERS, PLACES OF WORSHIP, VALUE OF CHURCH PROPERTY, OR MORE IN 1900, FOR

	CITY.	Total number of organizations.	COMMUNICANTS OR MEMBERS.				
			Number of organizations reporting.	Total number reported.	Sex.		
					Number of organizations reporting.	Male.	Female.
1	Total for cities of 25,000 and over in 1900	17,906	17,290	10,511,178	14,965	4,082,420	5,042,946
2	Total for cities of 300,000 and over in 1900	6,455	6,017	4,985,065	4,942	1,960,466	2,313,641
3	Baltimore, Md	443	437	224,968	353	71,640	105,320
4	Boston, Mass	325	310	376,728	267	150,123	196,722
5	Buffalo, N. Y	254	252	195,302	218	75,246	87,863
6	Chicago, Ill	1,058	1,036	833,441	852	232,970	263,233
7	Cincinnati, Ohio	255	249	159,663	228	66,760	82,512
8	Cleveland, Ohio[1]	314	301	146,338	277	60,730	73,686
9	New York, N. Y	2,002	1,659	1,838,482	1,203	800,815	912,938
10	Philadelphia, Pa	907	892	558,866	758	220,972	283,150
11	Pittsburg, Pa	318	311	205,847	273	87,794	92,058
12	St. Louis, Mo	398	393	302,531	357	125,224	145,242
13	San Francisco, Cal	181	177	142,919	156	68,192	70,917
14	Total for cities of 100,000 to 300,000 in 1900	4,127	4,067	2,358,318	3,567	867,360	1,118,371
15	Allegheny, Pa	111	109	61,456	101	26,367	31,053
16	Columbus, Ohio	134	134	63,261	120	25,863	32,805
17	Denver, Colo	181	178	58,699	158	22,804	30,816
18	Detroit, Mich	221	218	194,160	162	21,850	34,002
19	Fall River, Mass	67	65	71,877	56	30,243	37,628
20	Indianapolis, Ind	210	209	84,815	194	33,524	45,274
21	Jersey City, N. J	120	115	104,637	96	32,214	41,390
22	Kansas City, Mo	184	183	61,503	169	23,039	32,852
23	Los Angeles, Cal	231	220	81,771	202	31,857	44,624
24	Louisville, Ky	224	224	147,330	189	54,261	67,919
25	Memphis, Tenn	139	135	37,477	115	10,700	19,440
26	Milwaukee, Wis	185	185	155,206	160	66,443	75,537
27	Minneapolis, Minn	214	212	96,819	183	37,275	51,921
28	New Haven, Conn	92	87	67,650	79	30,600	32,964
29	New Orleans, La	214	211	186,497	190	79,547	100,331
30	Newark, N. J	176	171	115,307	147	40,048	50,927
31	Omaha, Nebr	106	104	33,900	88	12,654	16,243
32	Paterson, N. J	88	88	45,967	75	11,590	16,405
33	Providence, R. I	140	137	131,214	118	56,994	63,032
34	Rochester, N. Y.[2]	112	110	41,951	93	12,753	20,925
35	St. Joseph, Mo	93	93	25,280	87	9,915	14,341
36	St. Paul, Minn	161	160	103,639	145	43,898	57,561
37	Scranton, Pa	101	101	70,776	89	33,315	34,421
38	Syracuse, N. Y	100	100	66,697	85	28,857	34,306
39	Toledo, Ohio[1]	129	129	44,082	117	17,508	23,206
40	Washington, D. C	289	288	136,759	259	41,634	72,723
41	Worcester, Mass	105	101	69,588	90	31,617	35,725
42	Total for cities of 50,000 to 100,000 in 1900	3,264	3,218	1,555,030	2,907	635,716	799,472
43	Albany, N. Y	81	81	59,612	71	25,194	30,880
44	Atlanta, Ga	174	170	59,479	158	21,279	33,302
45	Bridgeport, Conn	81	80	50,936	73	24,385	24,529
46	Cambridge, Mass	54	54	45,896	48	19,644	24,876
47	Camden, N. J	82	80	29,223	73	11,667	15,359
48	Charleston, S. C	74	74	27,942	68	10,083	15,637
49	Dayton, Ohio	107	107	53,359	97	21,861	27,351
50	Des Moines, Iowa	99	98	26,905	93	10,354	16,118
51	Duluth, Minn	83	79	22,312	67	9,787	11,168
52	Elizabeth, N. J	48	47	28,616	37	9,913	12,689
53	Erie, Pa	60	60	34,540	55	15,896	17,618
54	Evansville, Ind	66	66	31,634	61	13,782	17,291
55	Grand Rapids, Mich	109	108	43,306	96	17,255	21,650
56	Harrisburg, Pa	74	74	22,909	68	8,609	13,077
57	Hartford, Conn	78	77	43,717	68	18,629	23,791
58	Hoboken, N. J	28	28	22,529	24	10,194	11,925
59	Kansas City, Kans	81	80	22,079	78	9,498	12,254
60	Lawrence, Mass	49	46	48,363	41	17,796	19,797
61	Lowell, Mass	61	58	66,766	52	26,202	26,026
62	Lynn, Mass	55	55	31,571	48	14,115	15,879
63	Manchester, N. H	46	46	45,282	41	20,786	22,927
64	Nashville, Tenn	179	177	44,198	150	12,996	21,619
65	New Bedford, Mass	59	55	43,936	50	18,466	19,950
66	Oakland, Cal	99	95	41,750	87	18,719	21,490
67	Peoria, Ill	68	66	28,779	60	10,397	14,136
68	Portland, Me	54	53	20,263	50	7,897	11,891
69	Portland, Oreg	165	160	40,282	148	15,576	20,989
70	Reading, Pa	87	86	38,976	76	13,797	19,615
71	Richmond, Va	110	109	54,506	99	20,052	31,304
72	Salt Lake City, Utah	78	78	34,452	74	17,243	16,891

[1] Exclusive of statistics for Roman Catholic Church not reported separately by cities for part of Cleveland diocese.

DEBT ON CHURCH PROPERTY, PARSONAGES, AND SUNDAY SCHOOLS, FOR EACH CITY OF 25,000 INHABITANTS ALL DENOMINATIONS: 1906.

PLACES OF WORSHIP. Number of organizations reporting— Church edifices.	Halls, etc.	Number of church edifices reported.	Seating capacity of church edifices. Number of organizations reporting.	Seating capacity reported.	VALUE OF CHURCH PROPERTY. Number of organizations reporting.	Value reported.	DEBT ON CHURCH PROPERTY. Number of organizations reporting.	Amount of debt reported.	PARSONAGES. Number of organizations reporting.	Value of parsonages reported.	SUNDAY SCHOOLS CONDUCTED BY CHURCH ORGANIZATIONS. Number of organizations reporting.	Number of Sunday schools reported.	Number of officers and teachers.	Number of scholars.	
14,875	1,912	16,517	14,514	8,251,853	15,093	$612,833,315	7,509	$70,262,228	6,193	$43,098,769	15,269	17,568	309,618	3,603,872	1
5,113	706	5,770	5,021	3,169,748	5,174	340,430,592	2,778	40,063,622	2,131	20,497,480	5,149	6,058	120,368	1,511,809	2
394	28	433	386	226,837	395	14,155,477	207	1,639,[illegible]	187	1,043,333	391	419	[illegible]	98,976	3
258	45	296	256	202,463	270	27,140,161	127	2,[illegible]	95	1,204,100	272	303	[illegible]	83,532	4
232	17	254	230	141,000	235	10,323,210	158	2,[illegible]	114	953,754	227	284	[illegible]	63,418	5
811	108	899	795	437,611	839	27,016,248	490	4,[illegible],511	304	2,087,500	838	939	9,056	210,899	6
231	15	247	227	122,582	234	8,681,987	96	[illegible],176	98	551,200	228	284	[illegible]	47,545	7
275	27	322	274	154,418	279	10,877,070	128	1,1[illegible]	126	667,550	270	321	5,[illegible]	67,479	8
1,347	283	1,536	1,312	883,885	1,335	153,925,740	742	19,[illegible]	587	8,767,387	1,352	1,687	35,[illegible]	490,589	9
797	88	925	786	566,224	798	45,160,711	431	4,1[illegible]	324	2,785,156	799	910	22,[illegible]	274,830	10
289	23	322	284	174,451	292	22,444,929	147	1,[illegible]	115	1,108,300	289	350	5,[illegible]	71,077	11
341	47	386	338	194,077	343	13,751,112	187	1,954,956	131	770,100	334	396	5,344	75,146	12
138	24	151	133	66,200	154	6,953,947	65	[illegible]	50	559,100	149	166	2,[illegible]	28,318	13
3,536	423	3,903	3,400	1,865,562	3,541	110,357,931	1,769	14,062,537	1,326	8,000,528	3,624	4,149	70,873	802,078	14
101	8	112	100	57,477	103	3,992,050	48	535,358	[illegible]	271,250	104	130	2,325	28,038	15
119	13	124	117	61,955	121	3,015,205	59	330,505	[illegible]	212,150	125	131	2,199	26,520	16
150	27	160	147	66,765	152	3,423,050	70	290,250	32	186,700	154	178	2,616	26,972	17
198	16	230	163	96,437	168	5,339,958	98	556,229	[illegible]	322,250	184	206	3,877	52,918	18
60	2	65	60	41,636	58	2,762,300	35	673,235	29	282,100	60	70	1,516	18,667	19
176	20	179	175	77,710	180	3,455,088	86	317,651	[illegible]	199,700	190	206	2,[illegible]	33,913	20
93	19	106	92	57,893	97	4,194,825	61	941,550	[illegible]	447,700	102	126	2,[illegible]	33,900	21
152	25	165	150	77,681	158	4,593,800	81	496,415	[illegible]	189,400	162	179	2,[illegible]	29,048	22
189	34	202	178	86,332	189	5,446,153	85	612,944	46	390,700	199	221	3,838	34,664	23
193	18	219	159	85,057	167	3,918,955	65	291,236	[illegible]	197,100	205	228	2,[illegible]	39,858	24
122	13	125	120	63,035	125	1,921,517	34	123,086	[illegible]	175,150	127	131	1,[illegible]3	16,148	25
158	20	169	156	95,221	161	5,503,140	[illegible]	1,018,493	[illegible]	555,067	141	165	2,[illegible]	31,139	26
187	18	208	180	98,987	188	5,360,050	[illegible]	427,153	[illegible]	246,600	184	231	4,[illegible]1	43,181	27
76	7	87	76	50,704	77	3,600,000	89	455,358	44	346,300	82	90	2,51[illegible]	19,453	28
189	11	204	180	94,566	192	4,378,428	[illegible]	442,706	[illegible]	486,000	198	235	2,[illegible]	30,618	29
154	14	179	151	90,090	156	7,909,709	[illegible]	983,254	[illegible]	660,700	145	169	3,[illegible]	42,412	30
95	7	109	91	39,509	97	2,587,600	[illegible]	175,938	68	103,400	92	108	1,[illegible]5	15,980	31
78	9	84	76	40,112	79	2,284,860	84	460,030	[illegible]	192,500	77	85	1,968	20,177	32
120	15	135	117	74,670	122	4,442,243	[illegible]	560,990	37	274,580	124	142	3,[illegible]	33,731	33
98	11	113	97	58,572	99	3,981,470	[illegible]	482,331	34	181,900	100	104	2,813	30,835	34
78	11	85	78	31,710	80	1,288,190	[illegible]	76,542	28	110,300	82	95	1,[illegible]	11,481	35
140	13	156	138	71,371	142	3,404,700	61	411,170	62	255,000	140	166	2,207	28,136	36
92	5	103	91	53,916	91	2,833,500	[illegible]	216,145	41	381,000	90	111	2,[illegible]	28,385	37
[illegible]	10	98	88	48,035	90	4,394,700	[illegible]	695,630	35	263,250	88	93	1,[illegible]	21,357	38
[illegible]	13	132	110	53,370	117	2,690,605	[illegible]	405,935	44	160,400	116	143	2,[illegible]	25,738	39
90	43	264	232	142,311	243	10,025,122	65	1,570,609	74	612,741	263	297	5,974	56,771	40
[illegible]	21	91	78	50,440	89	3,610,713	[illegible]	501,794	30	296,600	90	109	2,[illegible]	22,038	41
2,807	333	3,075	2,766	1,514,977	2,868	82,271,671	1,335	8,076,972	1,120	6,583,350	2,892	3,316	56,937	610,933	42
[illegible]	10	84	69	52,231	71	5,186,600	[illegible]	343,002	39	362,700	71	81	1,780	17,304	43
1	16	169	156	84,943	157	2,960,125	[illegible]	277,612	37	145,675	160	189	2,628	29,822	44
[illegible]	9	78	67	33,374	75	2,336,375	[illegible]	306,069	38	311,800	71	[illegible]	1,167	13,539	45
69	7	80	43	32,281	46	2,300,400	32	118,187	15	102,300	50	79	1,586	13,231	46
[illegible]	9	77	69	36,485	73	1,782,575	[illegible]	287,288	26	99,300	74	[illegible]	1,951	21,075	47
[illegible]	7	74	65	48,420	66	1,844,085	[illegible]	53,063	34	199,750	71	[illegible]	1,[illegible]	11,060	48
[illegible]	10	104	94	54,624	99	2,645,134	[illegible]	264,180	36	212,500	98	1	2,[illegible]	24,292	49
[illegible]	8	92	87	41,856	92	1,616,295	[illegible]	186,231	39	111,700	89	[illegible]	1,[illegible]	14,876	50
65	11	73	66	27,111	70	1,139,525	25	173,599	35	180,600	73	79	1,098	10,888	51
[illegible]	7	49	39	24,206	41	2,040,605	[illegible]	91,600	21	187,100	41	[illegible]	1,[illegible]	11,786	52
[illegible]	5	65	55	30,686	55	2,201,600	[illegible]	282,520	33	178,700	56	1	1,[illegible]1	13,086	53
[illegible]	5	56	52	24,385	53	993,850	[illegible]	47,661	24	108,400	56	[illegible]	[illegible]	8,591	54
[illegible]	13	106	94	61,271	97	1,685,785	[illegible]	121,140	49	231,000	95	[illegible]	1,7[illegible]	20,799	55
55	10	67	62	39,423	66	2,135,750	31	252,542	29	224,000	66	[illegible]	1,9[illegible]	21,809	56
[illegible]	9	68	60	38,798	62	3,309,108	[illegible]	303,459	29	263,000	65	[illegible]	1,485	15,404	57
[illegible]	2	27	26	12,170	26	1,137,500	[illegible]	187,500	14	137,500	25	[illegible]	[illegible]	8,175	58
[illegible]	9	82	67	26,426	73	744,150	[illegible]	99,150	27	70,950	75	[illegible]	1,[illegible]	12,046	59
[illegible]	8	44	39	24,032	41	1,516,174	[illegible]	268,870	12	113,200	41	[illegible]	[illegible]	10,517	60
26	6	60	52	40,502	53	2,660,900	16	419,145	16	193,500	54	29	1,625	13,762	61
[illegible]	7	46	44	25,953	46	1,639,772	[illegible]	175,970	18	117,000	50	[illegible]	1,[illegible]	12,856	62
[illegible]	5	40	37	23,139	38	1,199,500	[illegible]	200,755	20	129,200	39	[illegible]	[illegible]	8 844	63
[illegible]	8	167	157	75,005	161	2,133,668	[illegible]	113,978	38	106,200	159	[illegible]	2,[illegible]	22,137	64
[illegible]	7	53	49	28,775	50	1,717,000	[illegible]	327,200	18	144,200	49	[illegible]	[illegible]	10,488	65
38	16	82	74	33,700	75	2,630,765	24	171,098	22	109,150	81	45	1,756	12,246	66
[illegible]	6	64	60	28,552	63	1,375,125	[illegible]	118,363	26	136,600	60	[illegible]	[illegible]	9,047	67
[illegible]	7	51	43	24,280	48	1,673,150	23	143,640	11	80,000	50	52	1,[illegible]	10,170	68
[illegible]	24	137	126	50,473	127	2,321,500	54	150,772	58	211,700	140	156	1[illegible]	18,449	69
[illegible]	5	87	77	48,950	80	2,646,925	31	212,390	31	143,600	77	84	2[illegible]	27,202	70
44	13	106	97	63,215	99	3,078,769	37	140,127	26	179,800	103	127	2,055	26,169	71
[illegible]	7	75	70	29,644	73	1,656,819	22	104,724	13	56,150	70	78	1[illegible]	15,489	72

[a] Exclusive of statistics for Roman Catholic Church not reported separately by cities for Rochester diocese.

TABLE 5.—ORGANIZATIONS, COMMUNICANTS OR MEMBERS, PLACES OF WORSHIP, VALUE OF CHURCH PROPERTY, OR MORE IN 1900, FOR ALL

	CITY.	Total number of organizations.	COMMUNICANTS OR MEMBERS.				
			Number of organizations reporting.	Total number reported.	Sex.		
					Number of organizations reporting.	Male.	Female.
	Total for cities of 50,000 to 100,000 in 1900—Continued.						
73	San Antonio, Tex	68	67	31,141	64	12,725	18,067
74	Savannah, Ga	79	79	36,713	73	13,164	21,186
75	Seattle, Wash	162	162	49,479	145	20,479	25,672
76	Somerville, Mass	36	36	25,683	34	10,772	14,285
77	Springfield, Mass	61	61	39,941	53	16,740	20,691
78	Trenton, N. J	81	81	41,310	73	15,955	20,455
79	Troy, N. Y	75	75	46,924	65	19,393	25,540
80	Utica, N. Y	55	52	45,846	48	22,271	23,136
81	Wilkes-Barre, Pa	65	65	35,780	60	16,524	18,851
82	Wilmington, Del	93	93	38,095	83	15,621	19,560
83	Total for cities of 25,000 to 50,000 in 1900	4,060	3,968	1,612,745	3,549	618,878	811,462
84	Akron, Ohio	59	58	18,370	54	7,277	10,073
85	Allentown, Pa	53	52	19,985	49	8,307	10,949
86	Altoona, Pa	57	55	26,715	50	10,951	14,462
87	Atlantic City, N. J	36	35	10,842	29	3,922	5,870
88	Auburn, N. Y.[1]	23	23	7,459	21	2,396	4,344
89	Augusta, Ga	71	70	22,890	62	8,561	12,917
90	Bay City, Mich	53	53	24,725	50	10,929	12,876
91	Bayonne, N. J	33	32	21,687	21	4,573	6,340
92	Binghamton, N. Y	46	46	19,758	44	7,598	11,670
93	Birmingham, Ala	91	88	26,383	74	10,077	13,229
94	Brockton, Mass	40	40	20,516	36	8,410	10,835
95	Butte, Mont	38	38	27,756	35	15,395	12,186
96	Canton, Ohio[2]	40	39	12,894	36	4,880	7,334
97	Cedar Rapids, Iowa	36	35	10,285	34	3,923	6,260
98	Chattanooga, Tenn	72	68	17,469	59	5,323	9,687
99	Chelsea, Mass	21	19	11,589	14	4,643	6,099
100	Chester, Pa	41	41	14,538	36	4,213	6,268
101	Council Bluffs, Iowa	36	35	7,179	32	2,732	4,246
102	Covington, Ky	35	34	31,435	32	14,345	16,735
103	Dallas, Tex	107	106	32,471	95	11,669	17,543
104	Davenport, Iowa	40	39	11,839	33	4,073	5,845
105	Dubuque, Iowa	32	32	22,575	31	9,808	12,647
106	East St. Louis, Ill	42	42	17,647	33	2,901	3,882
107	Easton, Pa	42	42	12,685	36	4,487	6,734
108	Elmira, N. Y.[1]	37	37	10,251	32	3,298	6,161
109	Fitchburg, Mass	32	32	19,062	30	8,087	10,685
110	Fort Wayne, Ind	50	49	22,304	44	8,792	11,570
111	Fort Worth, Tex	58	56	18,235	50	7,029	9,462
112	Galveston, Tex	41	41	21,157	37	9,748	10,931
113	Gloucester, Mass	28	27	10,099	25	4,330	5,593
114	Haverhill, Mass	41	38	17,357	32	3,990	5,787
115	Holyoke, Mass	27	27	34,530	23	14,990	19,065
116	Houston, Tex	95	93	29,983	81	12,074	15,184
117	Jackson, Mich.[2]	32	31	5,552	29	1,733	3,321
118	Jacksonville, Fla	96	96	18,323	89	6,735	10,594
119	Johnstown, Pa	64	64	31,205	56	13,078	12,281
120	Joliet, Ill	43	43	27,132	36	6,785	7,238
121	Joplin, Mo	31	31	6,490	31	2,399	4,091
122	Knoxville, Tenn	79	79	17,416	66	6,003	9,271
123	La Crosse, Wis	50	50	19,938	45	8,495	10,964
124	Lancaster, Pa	56	56	18,336	50	5,812	9,875
125	Lexington, Ky	39	39	15,532	34	5,958	8,781
126	Lincoln, Nebr	64	64	19,114	57	6,833	10,242
127	Little Rock, Ark	73	72	17,969	64	6,805	9,825
128	McKeesport, Pa	57	54	22,913	51	10,548	11,144
129	Malden, Mass	31	30	16,961	26	6,667	8,424
130	Mobile, Ala	70	69	33,652	63	12,827	19,409
131	Montgomery, Ala	73	73	24,851	61	7,123	13,133
132	New Britain, Conn	25	25	22,008	24	10,914	10,998
133	Newcastle, Pa	53	52	17,076	47	7,581	9,022
134	Newport, Ky	19	19	12,715	19	5,688	7,027
135	Newton, Mass	42	42	19,368	39	7,818	11,049
136	Norfolk, Va	86	86	28,533	74	10,306	15,609
137	Oshkosh, Wis	36	36	14,967	33	6,414	8,123
138	Passaic, N. J	47	42	22,286	36	9,133	10,354
139	Pawtucket, R. I	37	36	22,327	34	10,269	11,773
140	Pueblo, Colo	56	55	20,288	48	9,509	9,658
141	Quincy, Ill	33	33	31,496	27	6,411	8,075
142	Racine, Wis	51	51	13,086	45	5,415	6,544
143	Rockford, Ill	36	35	17,486	30	3,610	6,150

[1] Exclusive of statistics for Roman Catholic Church not reported separately by cities for Rochester diocese.
[2] Exclusive of statistics for Roman Catholic Church not reported separately by cities for part of Cleveland diocese.

DEBT ON CHURCH PROPERTY, PARSONAGES, AND SUNDAY SCHOOLS, FOR EACH CITY OF 25,000 INHABITANTS DENOMINATIONS: 1906—Continued.

PLACES OF WORSHIP.					VALUE OF CHURCH PROPERTY.		DEBT ON CHURCH PROPERTY.		PARSONAGES.		SUNDAY SCHOOLS CONDUCTED BY CHURCH ORGANIZATIONS.				
Number of organizations reporting—		Number of church edifices reported.	Seating capacity of church edifices.												
Church edifices.	Halls, etc.		Number of organizations reporting.	Seating capacity reported.	Number of organizations reporting.	Value reported.	Number of organizations reporting.	Amount of debt reported.	Number of organizations reporting.	Value of parsonages reported.	Number of organizations reporting.	Number of Sunday schools reported.	Number of officers and teachers.	Number of scholars.	
58	4		57	21,745	60	$662,900	19	$43,851	30	$93,200	60	72	751	8,003	73
70	8		70	47,255	71	1,687,881	41	147,232	27	188,475	68	79	994	1,355	74
134	18	1	132	52,848	137	3,104,578	54	415,714	42	131,200	142	160	2,104	,227	75
32	4	60	32	20,176	33	1,010,710	21	96,765	10	91,300	34	34	1,151	[illegible],136	76
51	7	[illegible]	51	29,123	52	2,271,700	26	261,540	21	133,300	54	55	1,042	11,520	77
73			73	38,099	74	2,466,700	53	405,246	32	249,400	71	81	1,659	8,	78
67			67	35,815	68	2,901,700	22	274,550	36	268,200	67	74	1,206	4,	79
47			47	27,327	49	2,001,050	23	147,880	24	173,000	49	54	1,216	1,	80
58	7	85	58	36,925	60	1,950,800	27	133,372	32	238,000	54	65	1,428	17,828	81
86	[illegible]	[illegible]	83	40,754	88	1,904,123	46	208,987	32	170,000	84	91	1,761	20,[illegible]	82
3,419	451	3,769	3,327	1,701,566	3,510	79,773,121	1,627	8,069,097	1,616	8,017,411	3,604	4,045	61,440	679,052	83
52	4	52	52	26,845	52	963,350	27	83,839	22	107,500	53	53	1,116	12,872	
	6	55	46	29,575	46	1,309,200	26	179,320	20	81,400	49	52	1,268	17,975	
	3	53	49	28,055	50	1,419,100	33	174,140	32	168,300	50	53	1,216	13,761	84
47	3	36	31	17,342	34	989,350	26	147,922	13	98,000	34	35	615	6,111	[illegible]
[illegible]	3	21	18	10,878	23	757,577	2	30,900	9	56,000	20	20	533	4,823	88
67	3	70	66	31,330	67	1,107,815	24	38,179	31	103,700	69	74	774	7,774	
45	7	51	45	22,327	47	789,500	13	20,650	31	112,700	49	51	845	7,614	
29	2	33	28	12,505	29	681,300	17	133,160	10	55,800	24	26	426	5,201	
43	2	45	43	22,485	43	1,283,000	25	141,368	25	112,500	45	45	1,081	9,714	89
79	5	82	74	34,640	81	1,562,610	37	110,697	28	151,350	83	88	941	11,243	[illegible]
	4	37	36	491	37	884,650	19	105,862	13	87,750		39	977	11,070	94
	8	37	30		32	756,700	14	84,625	17	83,700		36	362	6,401	95
	7	32	31		32	763,100	13	76,680	14	62,100		36	851	11,060	96
36	3	38	31	18,	33	681,530	13	87,195	21	78,170	39	39	828	6,193	97
[illegible]	7	65	59	[illegible]	61	732,845	20	16,915	13	45,800	[illegible]	70	761	8,680	98
	5	15	12	8,100	15	567,850	7	35,560	4	48,500		15	402	5,348	99
13	4	39	35	19,665	38	826,955	18	90,514	15	103,395		39	877	9,253	100
[illegible]	6	35	28	9,850	28	343,650	10	32,175	15	39,100		40	460	4,112	101
31	2	37	31	19,795	33	1,512,950	13	33,430	14	118,600	15	38	499	8,112	102
91	10	105	87	44,495	93	1,478,865	40	148,591	35	90,850	[illegible]	111	1,310	15,560	103
31	6	34	31	14,912	31	832,525	8	25,587	16	83,500		38	473	4,943	104
30	2	33	29	16,060	30	1,318,500	11	66,572	20	121,300		44	505	6,207	105
37	4	41	35	13,145	31	263,550	19	55,128	8	30,050		40	443	6,174	106
35	7	43	34	20,645	38	836,895	18	48,887	21	103,000		48	966	8,437	107
32	4	37	31	15,400	32	910,300	22	100,043	9	34,000	[illegible]	36	627	6,169	108
22	8	27	22	14,032	25	858,002	14	122,965	9	87,150		38	532	5,343	109
42	4	47	40	25,820	41	1,128,600	21	118,540	25	126,750		52	644	9,401	110
49	5	56	48	25,775	51	750,145	22	56,798	22	90,550		63	747	,366	111
36	3	39	35	16,884	37	732,230	17	46,125	21	80,550		41	394	,088	112
22	4	22	21	10,545	25	437,055	6	16,194	12	56,700	[illegible]	23	477	[illegible],783	113
30	8	34	29	14,835	33	789,200	8	46,650	15	66,450		39	584	5	114
21	6	26	21	19,542	22	1,282,240	11	191,365	16	166,320		38	736	10,	115
84	7	90	80	38,575	85	1,617,550	30	86,714	36	141,500		94	971	12	116
26	4	28	26	10,995	27	330,150	10	28,645	16	44,400	33	28	405	3,954	117
85	7	88	83	34,255	87	977,275	47	134,227	34	125,800	[illegible]	97	918	9,[illegible]	118
58	4	71	58	28,785	60	1,606,802	35	186,491	28	148,700		65	1,024	1 ,917	119
33		35	32	16,956	36	923,725	20	155,760	17	81,400		40	487	,63	120
28		31	28	11,783	29	373,450	14	72,357	11	27,300		33	397	[illegible],471	121
64		69	61	30,665	61	877,550	24	32,911	22	94,150	56	79	1 009	12,857	122
42	[illegible]	50	41	16,502	43	587,536	16	42,680	29	94,300	[illegible]	51	560	5,806	123
46		51	45	26,600	46	1,339,600	30	155,680	25	170,100		55	1,289	12,652	124
35		40	34	17,471	35	696,000	15	25,481	13	76,000		48	501	5,585	125
55		59	54	22,900	56	700,600	29	77,850	27	66,840		60	848	8,316	126
65		70	62	30,075	65	1,038,875	29	78,370	28	93,755	52	79	828	9,272	127
46	[illegible]	51	44	19,390	47	1,312,602	36	210,190	18	116,600	[illegible]	54	832	9,580	128
23	6	27	23	14,350	26	692,850	13	53,180	9	86,000	27	30	709	6,	129
62	6	72	59	36 094	62	1,539,485	25	96,527	31	208,300	66	74	870	10,086	130
65	7	71	61	36,355	66	933,390	25	28,872	21	93,800	68	74	823	8,[illegible]	131
23	2	24	23	14,541	23	1,179,800	15	175,400	14	139,000	22	25	554	6,768	132
43	9	47	41	21,230	45	994,400	23	151,706	15	87,830	49	57	808	8,535	133
18	1	20	18	10,954	18	607,000	11	102,825	8	43,000	18	22	385	305	134
38	4	44	38	21,429	38	2,114,414	16	117,995	18	111,400	38	38	827	,225	135
76	6	84	75	40,107	77	1,765,943	33	181,840	27	154,500	83	95	1,431	15,330	136
33	2	34	33	15,752	34	483,750	18	59,570	21	60,800	31	36	512	4,928	137
35	9	39	34	16,570	35	942,022	26	341,262	16	101,800	34	38	578	6,406	138
29	6	34	28	15,145	31	859,725	15	87,665	11	92,500	32	33	747	9,035	139
46	6	48	45	14,590	48	481,200	27	58,577	26	60,050	49	53	568	5,805	140
30	2	34	24	16,250	26	606,750	10	26,820	12	38,100	28	37	536	5,801	141
46	5	54	44	21,591	48	697,955	27	87,925	28	117,000	45	54	659	7,019	142
26	7	27	25	19,460	27	764,400	7	28,800	15	88,600	29	30	753	8,064	143

[a] Exclusive of statistics for Roman Catholic Church not reported separately by cities for part of Detroit diocese.

TABLE 5.—ORGANIZATIONS, COMMUNICANTS OR MEMBERS, PLACES OF WORSHIP, VALUE OF CHURCH PROPERTY, OR MORE IN 1900, FOR ALL

	CITY.	Total number of organizations.	COMMUNICANTS OR MEMBERS.				
			Number of organizations reporting.	Total number reported.	Sex.		
					Number of organizations reporting.	Male.	Female.
	Total for cities of 25,000 to 50,000 in 1900—Continued.						
144	Sacramento, Cal	39	39	12,070	34	4,887	6,712
145	Saginaw, Mich	54	53	20,698	43	7,643	10,326
146	Salem, Mass	32	31	22,163	26	9,769	11,169
147	Schenectady, N. Y	56	55	25,897	45	10,767	13,725
148	Sioux City, Iowa	55	52	12,117	50	4,960	7,084
149	South Bend, Ind	49	48	18,214	40	6,972	8,421
150	South Omaha, Nebr	23	23	8,317	22	3,810	4,107
151	Spokane, Wash	94	89	19,715	84	8,223	10,289
152	Springfield, Ill	53	52	25,351	37	3,132	5,797
153	Springfield, Ohio	51	51	16,908	47	6,293	9,496
154	Superior, Wis	50	48	14,816	41	5,232	6,088
155	Tacoma, Wash	77	75	14,151	70	4,665	6,730
156	Taunton, Mass	31	30	17,903	28	7,794	9,936
157	Terre Haute, Ind	60	58	16,335	53	6,178	9,670
158	Topeka, Kans	72	72	15,716	69	5,344	8,787
159	Waterbury, Conn	36	36	35,260	34	17,083	18,052
160	Wheeling, W. Va	43	43	22,017	37	8,826	11,025
161	Williamsport, Pa	52	51	17,189	48	6,490	9,825
162	Woonsocket, R. I	23	22	24,469	18	11,060	13,160
163	Yonkers, N. Y	53	52	48,211	47	20,508	25,133
164	York, Pa	65	64	17,828	58	7,246	9,693
165	Youngstown, Ohio [1]	60	60	17,740	54	7,306	9,793

[1] Exclusive of statistics for Roman Catholic Church not reported separately by cities for part of Cleveland diocese.

DEBT ON CHURCH PROPERTY, PARSONAGES, AND SUNDAY SCHOOLS, FOR EACH CITY OF 25,000 INHABITANTS DENOMINATIONS: 1906—Continued.

PLACES OF WORSHIP.					VALUE OF CHURCH PROPERTY.		DEBT ON CHURCH PROPERTY.		PARSONAGES.		SUNDAY SCHOOLS CONDUCTED BY CHURCH ORGANIZATIONS.				
Number of organizations reporting—Church edifices.	Number of organizations reporting—Halls, etc.	Number of church edifices reported.	Seating capacity of church edifices. Number of organizations reporting.	Seating capacity of church edifices. Seating capacity reported.	Number of organizations reporting.	Value reported.	Numoer of organizations reporting.	Amount of debt reported.	Number of organizations reporting.	Value of parsonages reported.	Number of organizations reporting.	Number of Sunday schools reported.	Number of officers and teachers.	Number of scholars.	
28	6	33	27	12,700	30	$390,500	15	$40,997	6	$13,200	30	38	381	3,695	144
47	6	51	44	22,170	49	705,350	16	19,812	35	103,750	40	51	711	8,049	145
22	8	24	21	15,490	24	843,400	8	36,500	12	74,200	25	35	473	5,075	146
43	7	47	43	24,898	45	1,995,880	31	314,510	28	189,800	46	51	910	10,304	147
47	5	50	47	19,196	50	834,037	26	135,505	21	102,030	48	56	794	7,686	148
41	4	45	41	18,656	42	928,250	19	89,008	26	109,600	44	46	687	7,896	149
20	2	23	20	6,547	21	195,250	6	23,625	10	42,050	21	31	276	3,384	150
70	16	76	70	24,960	74	1,144,322	32	147,718	30	90,400	79	87	1,030	9,834	151
42	8	48	34	18,710	38	952,800	15	42,754	14	51,400	45	50	742	6,948	152
43	7	46	42	20,675	44	904,556	23	65,127	15	62,700	47	50	913	9,830	153
36	7	38	35	13,890	37	460,065	17	87,725	14	51,000	38	44	447	4,911	154
63	12	68	62	21,305	69	740,640	27	79,923	33	77,951	69	79	963	9,900	155
28	3	31	28	15,223	29	1,008,725	14	157,381	19	100,200	28	29	625	6,101	156
49	7	59	47	21,584	51	602,049	24	36,440	21	66,300	53	59	837	9,258	157
61	9	61	60	28,601	65	649,225	21	30,811	32	75,700	65	70	1,066	8,720	158
31	4	32	31	19,892	32	1,938,054	19	373,675	17	208,000	31	33	653	9,373	159
37	5	41	37	22,615	38	1.513,275	19	101,225	22	212,000	39	46	848	9,881	160
46	5	46	46	21,725	47	1,115,900	15	71,505	26	115,500	50	50	1,098	10,592	161
17	4	18	17	10,275	18	665,800	7	78,700	10	83,000	19	25	386	5,540	162
43	8	46	43	21,282	46	2,515,250	25	391,450	21	303,500	45	55	921	13,263	163
61	3	69	60	36,570	61	1,563,700	31	105,235	34	179,000	61	65	1,696	19,958	164
45	12	48	45	22,465	49	1,431,150	17	89,575	18	80,200	52	56	854	9,574	165

TABLE 6.—POPULATION AND COMMUNICANTS OR MEMBERS FOR EACH CITY OF 25,000 INHABITANTS OR MORE IN 1900, BY DENOMINATIONS (IN DETAIL): 1906.

CITY.	POPULATION.		COMMUNICANTS OR MEMBERS.															
				Adventist bodies.									Baptist bodies.					
														Baptists—				
	1900	1906 (estimated)	All denominations.	Total.	Evangelical Adventists.	Advent Christian Church.	Seventh-day Adventist Denomination.	Churches of God (Adventist), Unattached Congregations.	Life and Advent Union.	Churches of God in Christ Jesus.	Armenian Church.	Bahais.	Total.	Northern Baptist Convention.	Southern Baptist Convention.	National Baptist Convention (Colored).	Seventh-day Baptists.	Free Baptists.
Total for cities of 25,000 and over in 1900	19,718,312	[1]22,425,548	10,511,178	18,127	72	4,705	12,653	24	343	330	14,698	1,007	686,784	329,907	100,803	244,790	155	8,790
Total for cities of 300,000 and over in 1900	9,799,016	[2]10,971,688	4,985,085	3,840	36	493	2,855	24	180	252	6,290	680	198,569	132,729	13,262	49,174	155	3,127
Baltimore, Md	508,957	553,069	224,968	133			133					28	24,703		7,461	16,081		1,120
Boston, Mass	560,892	602,278	376,728	346	36	180	130				1,737	70	17,349	13,790		3,289		270
Buffalo, N. Y	352,387	381,819	195,302	225		50	175						6,022	5,584				438
Chicago, Ill	1,698,575	2,049,185	833,441	854		196	559	24		75	611	492	23,931	18,022		5,784	75	50
Cincinnati, Ohio	325,902	345,230	159,663	114			114					28	7,767	4,179		3,588		
Cleveland, Ohio	381,768	460,327	146,338	280			166			114		27	7,365	5,621		1,244		500
New York, N. Y	3,437,202	4,113,043	1,838,482	949			706		180	63	2,192		45,078	43,601		828	80	515
Philadelphia, Pa	1,293,697	1,441,735	558,866	280			280				1,300	35	44,430	37,141		7,227		35
Pittsburg, Pa	321,616	375,082	205,847	85			85						9,625	3,634		5,991		
St. Louis, Mo	575,238	649,320	302,531	180		17	163				230		10,943		5,801	4,977		165
San Francisco, Cal	342,782	([3])	142,919	394		50	344				220		1,356	1,157		165		34
Total for cities of 100,000 to 300,000 in 1900	4,409,331	[4]4,992,494	2,358,318	4,893		902	3,919		42	30	3,403	170	176,527	81,917	22,814	69,972		1,650
Allegheny, Pa	129,896	145,240	61,456	40			40						1,328	978		350		
Columbus, Ohio	125,560	145,414	63,261	166			166						3,249	1,433		1,816		
Denver, Colo	133,859	151,920	58,699	488		33	455						3,989	3,989				
Detroit, Mich	285,704	353,535	194,160	103			103				74		5,570	5,570				
Fall River, Mass	104,863	105,942	71,877	46		46							1,900	1,823		77		
Indianapolis, Ind	169,164	219,154	84,815	187			187						9,586	3,830		5,578		122
Jersey City, N. J	206,433	237,952	104,637	89			89					13	2,781	2,781				
Kansas City, Mo	163,752	182,376	61,503	293		21	272						9,163		6,895	2,219		
Los Angeles, Cal	102,479	([3])	81,771	810		97	713				180	38	4,489	3,403		1,086		
Louisville, Ky	204,731	226,129	147,330	58			58						20,464		10,204	10,260		
Memphis, Tenn	102,320	125,018	37,477	77		41	36						11,562		2,742	8,820		
Milwaukee, Wis	285,315	317,903	155,206	234			234				14		2,355	2,295		60		
Minneapolis, Minn	202,718	273,825	96,819	326		97	229						5,947	5,831				116
New Haven, Conn	108,027	121,227	67,650	116		26	48		42				3,061	2,520		541		
New Orleans, La	287,104	314,146	186,497	124			124						10,580		989	9,591		
Newark, N. J	246,070	289,634	115,307	52			22			30		45	6,361	4,586		1,775		
Omaha, Nebr	102,555	124,167	33,900	174			174						1,923	1,923				
Paterson, N. J	105,171	112,801	45,967	37			37						2,525	2,107		418		
Providence, R. I	175,597	203,243	131,214	300		264	36				1,860		8,009	6,266		454		1,289
Rochester, N. Y	162,608	185,703	41,951	84		48	36						6,199	6,199				
St. Joseph, Mo	102,979	118,004	25,280	84			84						2,476		1,984	467		
St. Paul, Minn	163,065	203,815	103,639	125			125						2,776	2,776				
Scranton, Pa	102,026	118,692	70,776	40			40						3,887	3,811		76		
Syracuse, N. Y	108,374	118,880	66,697	64			64						3,184	3,184				
Toledo, Ohio	131,822	159,980	44,082	86			86						2,648	2,579		69		
Washington, D. C	278,718	307,716	136,759	382			382				75	74	37,024	10,777		26,203		
Worcester, Mass	118,421	130,078	69,588	308		229	79				1,200		3,491	3,256		112		123
Total for cities of 50,000 to 100,000 in 1900	2,709,338	3,127,827	1,555,030	5,028	36	1,886	3,075		31		3,126	116	153,492	58,855	29,742	61,475		2,347
Albany, N. Y	94,151	98,537	59,612	10			10				34		2,804	2,804				
Atlanta, Ga	89,872	104,984	59,479	77			77						22,261		10,462	11,754		
Bridgeport, Conn	70,996	84,274	50,936	222		210	12						1,577	1,423		154		
Cambridge, Mass	91,886	98,544	45,896								437		3,257	2,918		125		214
Camden, N. J	75,935	84,849	29,223	60			60						3,868	3,868				
Charleston, S. C	55,807	56,317	27,942										3,556		1,039	2,517		
Dayton, Ohio	85,333	100,799	53,359	78			78						3,467	2,810		657		
Des Moines, Iowa	62,139	78,323	26,905	215			215						2,153	1,553		600		
Duluth, Minn	52,969	67,337	22,312	51			51						1,079	1,079				
Elizabeth, N. J	52,130	62,185	28,616	10			10						1,770	1,110		660		
Erie, Pa	52,733	59,993	34,540	49			49						930	930				
Evansville, Ind	59,007	63,957	31,634	5			5						3,354	517		2,483		57
Grand Rapids, Mich	87,565	99,794	43,306	200			200				94		2,201	2,176		25		
Harrisburg, Pa	50,167	55,735	22,909	61			61						683	683				
Hartford, Conn	79,850	95,822	43,717	142		80	62				210		2,733	2,143		590		
Hoboken, N. J	59,364	66,689	22,529										350	350				
Kansas City, Kans	51,418	77,912	22,079	208		87	121						3,510	1,404		2,106		
Lawrence, Mass	62,559	71,548	48,363	126		126					700		1,462	1,101		75		286
Lowell, Mass	94,969	95,173	66,766	138		118	20				400		3,225	2,501				724
Lynn, Mass	68,513	78,748	31,571	207		185	22				425		2,202	1,888		30		284
Manchester, N. H	56,987	64,703	45,282	130		130					58		1,932	1,698				234
Nashville, Tenn	80,865	84,703	44,198	222			222						11,531		4,417	6,408		
New Bedford, Mass	62,442	76,746	43,936	211		167	44						1,028	905		123		
Oakland, Cal	66,960	73,812	41,750	514		62	452				56	72	1,902	1,718		100		84
Peoria, Ill	56,100	66,365	28,779	60			60						975	813		162		

[1] Exclusive of Los Angeles and San Francisco.
[2] Exclusive of San Francisco.
[3] No estimate.
[4] Exclusive of Los Angeles.

TABLE 6.—POPULATION AND COMMUNICANTS OR MEMBERS FOR EACH CITY OF 25,000 INHABITANTS OR MORE IN 1900, BY DENOMINATIONS (IN DETAIL): 1906—Continued.

CITY.	POPULATION.		COMMUNICANTS OR MEMBERS.															
				Adventist bodies.									Baptist bodies.					
														Baptists—				
	1900	1906 (estimated)	All denominations.	Total.	Evangelical Adventists.	Advent Christian Church.	Seventh-day Adventist Denomination.	Churches of God (Adventist), Unattached Congregations.	Life and Advent Union.	Churches of God in Christ Jesus.	Armenian Church.	Bahais.	Total.	Northern Baptist Convention.	Southern Baptist Convention.	National Baptist Convention (Colored).	Seventh-day Baptists.	Free Baptists.
Total for cities of 50,000 to 100,000 in 1900—Continued.																		
Portland, Me.	50,145	55,167		196		142	54				119		1,554	1,188				366
Portland, Oreg.	90,426	109,884		468		70	398					23	3,157	3,097		60		
Reading, Pa.	78,961	91,141		98			98						1,043	1,043				
Richmond, Va.	85,050	87,246	20,263	67			36		31		112		26,234		10,443	15,791		
Salt Lake City, Utah	53,531	61,202	[illegible]	76			76						583	583				
San Antonio, Tex.	53,321	62,711	31,141	45			45						2,739		1,409	1,330		
Savannah, Ga.	54,244	68,596	36,713	5			5						16,977		1,972	15,005		
Seattle, Wash.	80,671	104,169	479	397		110	287					21	2,531	2,466		65		
Somerville, Mass.	61,643	70,798	49,683	121		121					150		2,641	2,543				98
Springfield, Mass.	62,059	75,836	38,941	292		278	14						2,395	2,005		390		
Trenton, N. J.	73,307	86,355	41,310	116	36		80						2,804	2,614		190		
Troy, N. Y.	60,651	76,513	46,924								331		2,069	2,054				
Utica, N. Y.	56,383	65,099	46,846	17			17						1,802	1,802				
Wilkes-Barre, Pa.	51,721	60,121	35,780	45			45						781	706		75		
Wilmington, Del.	76,508	85,140	38,095	89			89						2,372	2,362				
Total for cities of 25,000 to 50,000 in 1900	2,800,627	3,333,539	1,612,745	4,366		1,424	2,804		90	48	1,879	41	158,196	56,406	34,985	64,169		1,666
Akron, Ohio	42,728	50,738	18,370	60			60						661	496		165		
Allentown, Pa.	35,416	41,595	19,985	55			55						322	322				
Altoona, Pa.	38,973	47,910	26,715	76			76						879	776		103		
Atlantic City, N. J.	27,838	39,544	10,842	10			10						1,827	1,547		280		
Auburn, N. Y.	30,345	32,963	7,459	8			8						1,200	1,200				
Augusta, Ga.	39,441	43,125	22,890	106		106							10,099		2,444	7,655		
Bay City, Mich.	27,628	40,587	24,725	62			62						1,128	1,078		50		
Bayonne, N. J.	32,722	44,170	21,687										502	502				
Binghamton, N. Y.	39,647	43,785	19,758	35			35						1,898	1,898				
Birmingham, Ala.	38,415	45,869	26,383	45			45						6,088		2,059	4,029		
Brockton, Mass.	40,063	49,340	20,516	117		105	12				36		1,081	945		84		52
Butte, Mont.	30,470	43,624	27,756	18			18						531	531				
Canton, Ohio	30,667	38,440	12,894	34		25	9						856	840		16		
Cedar Rapids, Iowa	25,656	29,380	10,285	38			38						567	567				
Chattanooga, Tenn.	30,154	34,297	17,469	50			50						6,210		2,215	3,615		
Chelsea, Mass.	34,072	37,932	11,589	163		163					280		639	468				171
Chester, Pa.	33,988	38,002	14,538										1,528	1,528				
Council Bluffs, Iowa	25,802	25,117	7,179	58			58						749	749				
Covington, Ky.	42,938	46,436	31,435										2,222		1,552	670		
Dallas, Tex.	42,638	52,793	32,471	111		28	83						7,939		4,068	3,726		
Davenport, Iowa	35,254	40,706	11,839	28			28						714	609		105		
Dubuque, Iowa	36,297	43,070	22,575	24			24						281	281				
East St. Louis, Ill.	29,655	40,968	17,647								455		1,193	426		642		125
Easton, Pa.	25,238	28,317	12,685										240	240				
Elmira, N. Y.	35,672	35,734	10,251	16			16						1,968	1,818				150
Fitchburg, Mass.	31,531	33,319	19,062	73			27		46		83		702	702				
Fort Wayne, Ind.	45,115	50,947	22,304										1,150	1,100		50		
Fort Worth, Tex.	26,688	27,096	18,235	29			29						4,170		2,790	1,380		
Galveston, Tex.	37,789	34,355	21,157										1,196		534	662		
Gloucester, Mass.	26,121	25,989	10,069	13			13						608	603				
Haverhill, Mass.	37,175	37,961	17,357	194		173	21				300		1,465	1,049		145		271
Holyoke, Mass.	45,712	50,778	34,530								78		861	861				
Houston, Tex.	44,633	58,132	29,983	54			54						5,433		1,448	3,985		
Jackson, Mich.	25,180	25,360	5,552	53			53						1,292	1,172				120
Jacksonville, Fla.	28,429	36,675	18,323	237		200	37						5,364		787	4,279		
Johnstown, Pa.	35,936	43,250	31,205	55			55						596	471		125		
Joliet, Ill.	29,353	32,185	27,132										1,113	1,067		46		
Joplin, Mo.	26,023	35,671	6,490	74			74						996		880	60		56
Knoxville, Tenn.	32,637	36,051	17,416	148			148						6,215		4,118	1,959		121
La Crosse, Wis.	28,895	29,115	19,938	35			35						593	593				
Lancaster, Pa.	41,459	47,129	18,336	50			50						312	194		118		
Lexington, Ky.	26,369	29,249	15,532	47			47						4,289		1,840	2,449		
Lincoln, Nebr.	40,169	48,232	19,114	207		97	110						1,099	1,052				47
Little Rock, Ark.	38,307	39,959	17,969	78			78						3,182		1,936	1,226		
McKeesport, Pa.	34,227	43,438	22,913										1,507	1,203		304		
Malden, Mass.	33,664	38,912	16,961										1,793	1,556		237		
Mobile, Ala.	38,469	42,903	33,652	48			48						7,409		1,385	6,024		
Montgomery, Ala.	30,346	40,808	24,851	16			16						12,177		2,027	10,108		
New Britain, Conn.	25,998	33,722	22,008	44					44		390		803	803				
Newcastle, Pa.	28,339	36,847	17,076										960	892		68		
Newport, Ky.	28,301	30,329	12,715										669		594	75		
Newton, Mass.	33,587	37,475	19,368	34		18					76		1,466	1,294		172		
Norfolk, Va.	46,624	66,931	28,533	24									9,949		4,308	5,641		
Oshkosh, Wis.	28,284	31,033	14,967	46			46						345	345				
Passaic, N. J.	27,777	39,799	22,286										576	506		70		

TABLE 6.—POPULATION AND COMMUNICANTS OR MEMBERS FOR EACH CITY OF 25,000 INHABITANTS OR MORE IN 1900, BY DENOMINATIONS (IN DETAIL): 1906—Continued.

CITY.	POPULATION.		COMMUNICANTS OR MEMBERS.															
				Adventist bodies.									Baptist bodies.					
														Baptists—				
	1900	1906 (estimated)	All denominations.	Total.	Evangelical Adventists.	Advent Christian Church.	Seventh-day Adventist Denomination.	Churches of God (Adventist), Unattached Congregations.	Life and Advent Union.	Churches of God in Christ Jesus.	Armenian Church.	Bahais.	Total.	Northern Baptist Convention.	Southern Baptist Convention.	National Baptist Convention (Colored).	Seventh-day Baptists.	Free Baptists.
Total for cities of 25,000 to 50,000 in 1900—Continued.																		
Pawtucket, R. I.	39,231	44,211	22,327	20			20				76		1,332	1,019				313
Pueblo, Colo.	28,157	30,824	20,288	88			88						1,343	1,343				
Quincy, Ill.	36,252	39,108	31,496										1,478	1,118		360		
Racine, Wis.	29,102	32,928	13,086	23			23				40	23	984	984				
Rockford, Ill.	31,051	36,051	17,486	25			25						1,021	1,021				
Sacramento, Cal.	29,282	31,022	12,070	70			70						609	568		41		
Saginaw, Mich.	42,345	48,742	20,698	41			41						1,023	973		50		
Salem, Mass.	35,956	37,961	22,163	150		150					60		830	830				
Schenectady, N. Y.	31,682	61,919	25,897	48		36	12						1,186	1,186				
Sioux City, Iowa.	33,111	42,520	12,117	75			75						553	553				
South Bend, Ind.	35,999	44,605	18,214	49			25			24			550	442		108		
South Omaha, Nebr.	26,001	36,765	8,317										249	249				
Spokane, Wash.	36,848	47,006	19,715	265			265					18	1,338	1,284		40		
Springfield, Ill.	34,159	38,933	25,351	68			68						1,964	1,334		612		
Springfield, Ohio.	38,253	42,069	16,908	117		18	75			24			1,455	685		770		
Superior, Wis.	31,091	37,643	14,816	21			21						255	255				
Tacoma, Wash.	37,714	55,392	14,151	105			105						1,219	1,219				
Taunton, Mass.	31,036	30,953	17,903	45		45							705	665				40
Terre Haute, Ind.	36,673	52,805	16,335	39			39						1,595	1,039		320		200
Topeka, Kans.	33,608	41,886	15,716	94			94						2,272	1,488		784		
Waterbury, Conn.	45,859	61,903	35,260	203		203							1,326	1,220		106		
Wheeling, W. Va.	38,878	41,494	22,017										378	324		54		
Williamsport, Pa.	28,757	29,735	17,189	60			60						1,717	1,487		230		
Woonsocket, R. I.	28,204	32,994	24,469	65		57	8				50		384	384				
Yonkers, N. Y.	47,931	64,110	48,211								45		1,276	1,106		170		
York, Pa.	33,708	39,168	17,828										99	99				
Youngstown, Ohio.	44,885	52,710	17,740	22			22						1,448	1,247		201		

CITY.	COMMUNICANTS OR MEMBERS—continued.																
	Baptist bodies—Continued.						Brethren (Plymouth).					Brethren (River).			Buddhists.		
	Freewill Baptists.	General Baptists.	Primitive Baptists.	Colored Primitive Baptists in America.	Two-Seed-in-the-Spirit Predestinarian Baptists.	United American Freewill Baptists (Colored).	Total.	Brethren (Plymouth)—I.	Brethren (Plymouth)—II.	Brethren (Plymouth)—III.	Brethren (Plymouth)—IV.	Total.	Brethren in Christ.	Yorker, or Old Order, Brethren.	Total.	Chinese Temples.	Japanese Temples.
Total for cities of 25,000 and over in 1900.	135	260	789	1,125	13	17	6,830	1,747	3,210	1,111	762	331	321	10	1,682		1,682
Total for cities of 300,000 and over in 1900.			122				3,340	677	1,802	523	338	166	166		342		342
Baltimore, Md.			41				121	41		40	40						
Boston, Mass.							239	80	150	9							
Buffalo, N. Y.							141	31	110			30	30				
Chicago, Ill.							554	65	349	63	77	54	54				
Cincinnati, Ohio.							16				16						
Cleveland, Ohio.							190		160	27	3						
New York, N. Y.			54				1,057	188	553	164	152						
Philadelphia, Pa.			27				585	137	287	132	29	82	82				
Pittsburg, Pa.							139	59	80								
St. Louis, Mo.							160	48	35	71	6						
San Francisco, Cal.							138	28	78	17	15				342		342
Total for cities of 100,000 to 300,000 in 1900.			174				1,752	403	759	388	202				263		263
Allegheny, Pa.																	
Columbus, Ohio.							31			31							
Denver, Colo.							81	7	50	24							
Detroit, Mich.							248	68	150	25	5						
Fall River, Mass.							28		28								
Indianapolis, Ind.			56				79	15			64						
Jersey City, N. J.							175	48	105	22							
Kansas City, Mo.			49				228		218	10							
Los Angeles, Cal.							200	43	7	100	50				263		263
Louisville, Ky.																	
Memphis, Tenn.																	
Milwaukee, Wis.							57	57									
Minneapolis, Minn.							112	68	22	9	13						
New Haven, Conn.																	
New Orleans, La.																	

TABLE 6.—POPULATION AND COMMUNICANTS OR MEMBERS FOR EACH CITY OF 25,000 INHABITANTS OR MORE IN 1900, BY DENOMINATIONS (IN DETAIL): 1906—Continued.

CITY.	COMMUNICANTS OR MEMBERS—continued.																
	Baptist bodies—Continued.						Brethren (Plymouth).					Brethren (River).			Buddhists.		
	Freewill Baptists.	General Baptists.	Primitive Baptists.	Colored Primitive Baptists in America.	Two-Seed-in-the-Spirit Predestinarian Baptists.	United American Freewill Baptists (Colored).	Total.	Brethren (Plymouth)—I.	Brethren (Plymouth)—II.	Brethren (Plymouth)—III.	Brethren (Plymouth)—IV.	Total.	Brethren in Christ.	Yorker, or Old Order, Brethren.	Total.	Chinese Temples.	Japanese Temples.
Total for cities of 100,000 to 300,000 in 1900—Continued.																	
Newark, N. J.							72	33	39								
Omaha, Nebr.							20		20								
Paterson, N. J.							139		36	103							
Providence, R. I.							60		60								
Rochester, N. Y.							85	16		6	63						
St. Joseph, Mo.			25				6		6								
St. Paul, Minn.							21	21									
Scranton, Pa.							32		18	14							
Syracuse, N. Y.							13	13									
Toledo, Ohio.																	
Washington, D. C.			44				38	14		17	7						
Worcester, Mass.							27			27							
Total for cities of 50,000 to 100,000 in 1900.	135	260	346	319	13		1,226	483	447	174	121	117	117		593		593
Albany, N. Y.							56	50		6							
Atlanta, Ga.			45				18			18							
Bridgeport, Conn.							11		11								
Cambridge, Mass.							65				65						
Camden, N. J.							33	22		11							
Charleston, S. C.																	
Dayton, Ohio.																	
Des Moines, Iowa.							72			64	8	21	21				
Duluth, Minn.							79	49	30								
Elizabeth, N. J.							67	67									
Erie, Pa.							6	6									
Evansville, Ind.		260	37														
Grand Rapids, Mich.							68	68									
Harrisburg, Pa.							46	46				96	96				
Hartford, Conn.							13		13								
Hoboken, N. J.							30		30								
Kansas City, Kans.							30		30								
Lawrence, Mass.																	
Lowell, Mass.							60		60								
Lynn, Mass.							8	8									
Manchester, N. H.																	
Nashville, Tenn.	135		239	319	13												
New Bedford, Mass.							90		90								
Oakland, Cal.							149	37	77	35					172		172
Peoria, Ill.																	
Portland, Me.																	
Portland, Oreg.							79		60	13	6				142		142
Reading, Pa.							70	70									
Richmond, Va.							40		40								
Salt Lake City, Utah.																	
San Antonio, Tex.																	
Savannah, Ga.							9		6	3							
Seattle, Wash.							88	34		22	32				27		279
Somerville, Mass.																	
Springfield, Mass.																	
Trenton, N. J.							28	26		2							
Troy, N. Y.			15														
Utica, N. Y.																	
Wilkes-Barre, Pa.																	
Wilmington, Del.			10				10				10						
Total for cities of 25,000 to 50,000 in 1900.			147	806		17	513	184	202	26	101	48	38	10	484		484
Akron, Ohio.							6		6								
Allentown, Pa.							21	21									
Altoona, Pa.																	
Atlantic City, N. J.																	
Auburn, N. Y.																	
Augusta, Ga.																	
Bay City, Mich.																	
Bayonne, N. J.							42		42								
Binghamton, N. Y.																	
Birmingham, Ala.																	
Brockton, Mass.																	
Butte, Mont.																	
Canton, Ohio.												48	38	10			
Cedar Rapids, Iowa.							3				3						
Chattanooga, Tenn.				380			10				10						
Chelsea, Mass.																	
Chester, Pa.																	
Council Bluffs, Iowa.							37		11		26						
Covington, Ky.																	
Dallas, Tex.				145			14		14								

TABLE 6.—POPULATION AND COMMUNICANTS OR MEMBERS FOR EACH CITY OF 25,000 INHABITANTS OR MORE IN 1900, BY DENOMINATIONS (IN DETAIL): 1906—Continued.

CITY.	COMMUNICANTS OR MEMBERS—continued.																
	Baptist bodies—Continued.						Brethren (Plymouth).					Brethren (River).			Buddhists.		
	Freewill Baptists.	General Baptists.	Primitive Baptists.	Colored Primitive Baptists in America.	Two-Seed-in-the-Spirit Predestinarian Baptists.	United American Freewill Baptists (Colored).	Total.	Brethren (Plymouth)—I.	Brethren (Plymouth)—II.	Brethren (Plymouth)—III.	Brethren (Plymouth)—IV.	Total.	Brethren in Christ.	Yorker, or Old Order, Brethren.	Total.	Chinese Temples.	Japanese Temples.
Total for cities of 25,000 to 50,000 in 1900—Continued.																	
Davenport, Iowa							8	18									
Dubuque, Iowa																	
East St. Louis, Ill																	
Easton, Pa							5	5									
Elmira, N. Y																	
Fitchburg, Mass							11	11									
Fort Wayne, Ind																	
Fort Worth, Tex																	
Galveston, Tex																	
Gloucester, Mass																	
Haverhill, Mass																	
Holyoke, Mass																	
Houston, Tex							52		52								
Jackson, Mich																	
Jacksonville, Fla				281		17	18			18							
Johnstown, Pa																	
Joliet, Ill							6	6									
Joplin, Mo																	
Knoxville, Tenn			17				25				25						
La Crosse, Wis							12		12								
Lancaster, Pa							17	17									
Lexington, Ky																	
Lincoln, Nebr																	
Little Rock, Ark			20														
McKeesport, Pa																	
Malden, Mass																	
Mobile, Ala																	
Montgomery, Ala			42														
New Britain, Conn																	
Newcastle, Pa																	
Newport, Ky																	
Newton, Mass																	
Norfolk, Va																	
Oshkosh, Wis																	
Passaic, N. J							75	21	40		14						
Pawtucket, R. I																	
Pueblo, Colo																	
Quincy, Ill																	
Racine, Wis																	
Rockford, Ill							12	12									
Sacramento, Cal															484		484
Saginaw, Mich																	
Salem, Mass																	
Schenectady, N. Y							44	41		3							
Sioux City, Iowa																	
South Bend, Ind																	
South Omaha, Nebr																	
Spokane, Wash			14				9	9									
Springfield, Ill			18				10				10						
Springfield, Ohio																	
Superior, Wis							6				6						
Tacoma, Wash							5			5							
Taunton, Mass																	
Terre Haute, Ind			36														
Topeka, Kans																	
Waterbury, Conn							7				7						
Wheeling, W. Va																	
Williamsport, Pa																	
Woonsocket, R. I																	
Yonkers, N. Y							25		25								
York, Pa							23	23									
Youngstown, Ohio																	

TABLE 6.—POPULATION AND COMMUNICANTS OR MEMBERS FOR EACH CITY OF 25,000 INHABITANTS OR MORE IN 1900, BY DENOMINATIONS (IN DETAIL): 1906—Continued.

CITY.	CATHOLIC APOSTOLIC CHURCHES.			Christadelphians.	Christian Catholic Church in Zion.	Christian Israelite Church.	Christian Union.	Christians (Christian Connection).	Church of Christ, Scientist.	Church of God and Saints of Christ (Colored).	Churches of God in North America, General Eldership of the.	CHURCHES OF THE LIVING GOD (COLORED).				CHURCHES OF THE NEW JERUSALEM.		
	Total.	Catholic Apostolic Church.	New Apostolic Church.									Total.	Church of the Living God (Christian Workers for Friendship).	Church of the Living God (Apostolic Church).	Church of Christ in God.	Total.	General Convention of the New Jerusalem in the United States of America.	General Church of the New Jerusalem.
Total for cities of 25,000 and over in 1900	4,842	2,847	1,995	719	1,770	48	70	3,617	70,772	1,253	1,999	2,238	1,246	257	735	5,181	4,850	331
Total for cities of 300,000 and over in 1900	4,374	2,724	1,650	214	1,360	24		242	52,339	742	429	710	90		620	3,432	3,183	249
Baltimore, Md				62					223	27						186	168	18
Boston, Mass	101	101		55	40			32	41,634	200						681	681	
Buffalo, N. Y	610	110	500						447							46	46	
Chicago, Ill	1,446	1,046	400	68	850				3,655							475	425	50
Cincinnati, Ohio					240				349			15	15			297	297	
Cleveland, Ohio	100		100		80				832							92	92	
New York, N. Y	1,616	966	650			24		178	3,372	2						510	490	20
Philadelphia, Pa	132	132			150			32	467	400	300					570	515	55
Pittsburg, Pa				8					341	113	100					168	62	106
St. Louis, Mo				21					625		29	695	75		620	291	291	
San Francisco, Cal	369	369							394							116	116	
Total for cities of 100,000 to 300,000 in 1900	210		210	294	225	24	36	1,163	9,457	348		201	146		55	821*	801	20
Allegheny, Pa																		
Columbus, Ohio								108	202							12	12	
Denver, Colo				25					827							46	36	10
Detroit, Mich	100		100		20	18			354							86	86	
Fall River, Mass								401								40	40	
Indianapolis, Ind					70	6		90	1,140			35			35	30	30	
Jersey City, N. J				52					58	29								
Kansas City, Mo				4					1,273	34						35		
Los Angeles, Cal				4	70				552							100	100	
Louisville, Ky									63			51	31		20	14	14	
Memphis, Tenn									190			115	115					
Milwaukee, Wis	40		40	21	25				528									
Minneapolis, Minn				4	40				1,560							18	18	
New Haven, Conn									140							46	46	
New Orleans, La									63							24	14	10
Newark, N. J	40		40					325	79	150								
Omaha, Nebr	30		30						335									
Paterson, N. J									19							26	26	
Providence, R. I								175	222	64						133	133	
Rochester, N. Y				83					2:3									
St. Joseph, Mo							36	64	350									
St. Paul, Minn									217							49	49	
Scranton, Pa									194									
Syracuse, N. Y									109									
Toledo, Ohio									274							30	30	
Washington, D. C				28					347	70						132	132	
Worcester, Mass				73					148									
Total for cities of 50,000 to 100,000 in 1900	127	92	35	117	185		34	1,342	4,637	101	708	646	480	106	60	457	406	51
Albany, N. Y								200	76									
Atlanta, Ga									216	27						23	8	15
Bridgeport, Conn									67	15								
Cambridge, Mass									186							86	86	
Camden, N. J									25	24								
Charleston, S. C									23	8								
Dayton, Ohio				6				255	190									
Des Moines, Iowa								50	197							12	12	
Duluth, Minn									159									
Elizabeth, N. J																		
Erie, Pa								98	59							36		36
Evansville, Ind									26			85	85					
Grand Rapids, Mich	35		35						233							9	9	
Harrisburg, Pa											708							
Hartford, Conn	92	92							135	10								
Hoboken, N. J																		
Kansas City, Kans							34		65			95	95					
Lawrence, Mass				4					125									
Lowell, Mass									57									
Lynn, Mass								27	76									
Manchester, N. H								105	52							50	50	
Nashville, Tenn									32			402	300	42	60			
New Bedford, Mass								607	74									
Oakland, Cal					150				302									
Peoria, Ill									232							8	8	

TABLE 6.—POPULATION AND COMMUNICANTS OR MEMBERS FOR EACH CITY OF 25,000 INHABITANTS OR MORE IN 1900, BY DENOMINATIONS (IN DETAIL): 1906—Continued.

CITY.	CATHOLIC APOSTOLIC CHURCHES. Total.	CATHOLIC APOSTOLIC CHURCHES. Catholic Apostolic Church.	CATHOLIC APOSTOLIC CHURCHES. New Apostolic Church.	Christadelphians.	Christian Catholic Church in Zion.	Christian Israelite Church.	Christian Union.	Christians (Christian Connection).	Church of Christ, Scientist.	Church of God and Saints of Christ (Colored).	Churches of God in North America, General Eldership of the.	CHURCHES OF THE LIVING GOD (COLORED). Total.	CHURCHES OF THE LIVING GOD (COLORED). Church of the Living God (Christian Workers for Friendship).	CHURCHES OF THE LIVING GOD (COLORED). Church of the Living God (Apostolic Church).	CHURCHES OF THE LIVING GOD (COLORED). Church of Christ in God.	CHURCHES OF THE NEW JERUSALEM. Total.	CHURCHES OF THE NEW JERUSALEM. General Convention of the New Jerusalem in the United States of America.	CHURCHES OF THE NEW JERUSALEM. General Church of the New Jerusalem.
Total for cities of 50,000 to 100,000 in 1900—Continued.																		
Portland, Me.									83							38	38	
Portland, Oreg.				33					402							46	46	
Reading, Pa.									42									
Richmond, Va.				74					89	17						50	50	
Salt Lake City, Utah									391									
San Antonio, Tex.									89									
Savannah, Ga.									52							15	15	
Seattle, Wash.					35				326			64		64		10	10	
Somerville, Mass.																		
Springfield, Mass.									84							15	15	
Trenton, N. J.									27									
Troy, N. Y.									203									
Utica, N. Y.									168									
Wilkes-Barre, Pa.																		
Wilmington, Del.									74							59	59	
Total for cities of 25,000 to 50,000 in 1900	131	31	100	94				870	4,339	62	862	681	530	151		471	460	11
Akron, Ohio									24									
Allentown, Pa.																46	35	11
Altoona, Pa.									23		238							
Atlantic City, N. J.																		
Auburn, N. Y.				18					22									
Augusta, Ga.																		
Bay City, Mich.									27									
Bayonne, N. J.																		
Binghamton, N. Y.								64	64									
Birmingham, Ala.									37			25	25					
Brockton, Mass.									81							156	156	
Butte, Mont.									40									
Canton, Ohio									46		120							
Cedar Rapids, Iowa									72									
Chattanooga, Tenn.									46			225	125	100		8	8	
Chelsea, Mass.									82									
Chester, Pa.									9	8								
Council Bluffs, Iowa									76									
Covington, Ky.																		
Dallas, Tex.				2					125			275	275					
Davenport, Iowa									71									
Dubuque, Iowa									43									
East St. Louis, Ill.									39			15	15					
Easton, Pa.									20									
Elmira, N. Y.				14					32									
Fitchburg, Mass.									86									
Fort Wayne, Ind.									30									
Fort Worth, Tex.				2					100									
Galveston, Tex.									35							10	10	
Gloucester, Mass.									56									
Haverhill, Mass.								220	36									
Holyoke, Mass.																		
Houston, Tex.									219									
Jackson, Mich.									74									
Jacksonville, Fla.				8					90							13	13	
Johnstown, Pa.									30									
Joliet, Ill.									63							14	14	
Joplin, Mo.									164									
Knoxville, Tenn.									42							6	6	
La Crosse, Wis.									44									
Lancaster, Pa.											320					20	20	
Lexington, Ky.									49									
Lincoln, Nebr.									253									
Little Rock, Ark.									38			101	50	51				
McKeesport, Pa.																		
Malden, Mass.									132									
Mobile, Ala.									27							10	10	
Montgomery, Ala.									30									
New Britain, Conn.									46									
Newcastle, Pa.											60							
Newport, Ky.																		
Newton, Mass.																114	114	
Norfolk, Va.				42				474	86									
Oshkosh, Wis.									76									
Passaic, N. J.	40		40						35									

TABLE 6.—POPULATION AND COMMUNICANTS OR MEMBERS FOR EACH CITY OF 25,000 INHABITANTS OR MORE IN 1900, BY DENOMINATIONS (IN DETAIL): 1906—Continued.

CITY.	CATHOLIC APOSTOLIC CHURCHES. Total.	CATHOLIC APOSTOLIC CHURCHES. Catholic Apostolic Church.	CATHOLIC APOSTOLIC CHURCHES. New Apostolic Church.	Christadelphians.	Christian Catholic Church in Zion.	Christian Israelite Church.	Christian Union.	Christians (Christian Connection).	Church of Christ, Scientist.	Church of God and Saints of Christ (Colored).	Churches of God in North America, General Eldership of the	CHURCHES OF THE LIVING GOD (COLORED). Total.	CHURCHES OF THE LIVING GOD (COLORED). Church of the Living God (Christian Workers for Friendship).	CHURCHES OF THE LIVING GOD (COLORED). Church of the Living God (Apostolic Church).	CHURCHES OF THE LIVING GOD (COLORED). Church of Christ in God.	CHURCHES OF THE NEW JERUSALEM. Total.	CHURCHES OF THE NEW JERUSALEM. General Convention of the New Jerusalem in the United States of America.	CHURCHES OF THE NEW JERUSALEM. General Church of the New Jerusalem.
Total for cities of 25,000 to 50,000 in 1900—Continued.																		
Pawtucket, R. I.	......	......	......	......	......	......	......	......	......	......	......	......	......	......	......	......	......	......
Pueblo, Colo.	......	......	......	......	......	......	......	......	62	......	......	......	......	......	......	......	......	......
Quincy, Ill.	......	......	......	......	......	......	......	......	59	......	......	......	......	......	......	......	......	......
Racine, Wis.	......	......	......	......	......	......	......	......	86	......	......	......	......	......	......	......	......	......
Rockford, Ill.	......	......	......	......	......	......	......	......	53	......	......	......	......	......	......	......	......	......
Sacramento, Cal.	......	......	......	......	......	......	......	......	63	......	......	......	......	......	......	......	......	......
Saginaw, Mich.	......	......	......	......	......	......	......	......	70	......	......	......	......	......	......	......	......	......
Salem, Mass.	......	......	......	......	......	......	......	......	67	......	......	......	......	......	......	25	25	......
Schenectady, N. Y.	......	......	......	......	......	......	......	......	26	......	......	......	......	......	......	......	......	......
Sioux City, Iowa.	......	......	......	......	......	......	......	......	169	......	......	......	......	......	......	......	......	......
South Bend, Ind.	60	......	60	......	......	......	......	......	79	......	......	......	......	......	......	......	......	......
South Omaha, Nebr.	......	......	......	......	......	......	......	......	......	......	......	......	......	......	......	......	......	......
Spokane, Wash.	......	......	......	......	......	......	......	......	211	......	......	......	......	......	......	28	28	......
Springfield, Ill.	......	......	......	......	......	......	......	......	42	......	......	......	......	......	......	21	21	......
Springfield, Ohio.	......	......	......	......	......	......	......	112	70	......	......	......	......	......	......	......	......	......
Superior, Wis.	......	......	......	......	......	......	......	......	32	......	......	......	......	......	......	......	......	......
Tacoma, Wash.	......	......	......	......	......	......	......	......	110	......	......	......	......	......	......	......	......	......
Taunton, Mass.	......	......	......	......	......	......	......	......	23	......	......	......	......	......	......	......	......	......
Terre Haute, Ind.	......	......	......	......	......	......	......	......	37	......	......	......	......	......	......	......	......	......
Topeka, Kans.	......	......	......	6	......	......	......	......	137	27	20	40	40	......	......	......	......	......
Waterbury, Conn.	31	31	......	......	......	......	......	......	31	......	......	......	......	......	......	......	......	......
Wheeling, W. Va.	......	......	......	......	......	......	......	......	......	......	......	......	......	......	......	......	......	......
Williamsport, Pa.	......	......	......	......	......	......	......	......	26	......	......	......	......	......	......	......	......	......
Woonsocket, R. I.	......	......	......	......	......	......	......	......	......	......	......	......	......	......	......	......	......	......
Yonkers, N. Y.	......	......	......	......	......	......	......	......	28	27	......	......	......	......	......	......	......	......
York, Pa.	......	......	......	......	......	......	......	......	......	......	104	......	......	......	......	......	......	......
Youngstown, Ohio.	......	......	......	......	......	......	......	......	38	......	......	......	......	......	......	......	......	......

CITY.	Congregationalists.	DISCIPLES OR CHRISTIANS. Total.	DISCIPLES OR CHRISTIANS. Disciples of Christ.	DISCIPLES OR CHRISTIANS. Churches of Christ.	DUNKERS OR GERMAN BAPTIST BRETHREN. Total.	DUNKERS OR GERMAN BAPTIST BRETHREN. German Baptist Brethren Church (Conservative).	DUNKERS OR GERMAN BAPTIST BRETHREN. Old Order German Baptist Brethren.	DUNKERS OR GERMAN BAPTIST BRETHREN. The Brethren Church (Progressive Dunkers).	EASTERN ORTHODOX CHURCHES. Total.	EASTERN ORTHODOX CHURCHES. Russian Orthodox Church.	EASTERN ORTHODOX CHURCHES. Servian Orthodox Church.	EASTERN ORTHODOX CHURCHES. Syrian Orthodox Church.	EASTERN ORTHODOX CHURCHES. Greek Orthodox Church.	EVANGELICAL BODIES. Total.	EVANGELICAL BODIES. Evangelical Association.	EVANGELICAL BODIES. United Evangelical Church.	EVANGELISTIC ASSOCIATIONS. Total.	EVANGELISTIC ASSOCIATIONS. Apostolic Faith Movement.
Total for cities of 25,000 and over in 1900.	217,507	130,755	123,824	6,931	5,911	3,827	140	1,944	91,676	12,211	9,326	3,447	66,692	33,549	20,235	13,314	1,099	300
Total for cities of 300,000 and over in 1900.	68,553	27,602	27,354	248	1,459	851	......	608	44,257	4,707	5,800	2,300	31,450	8,984	6,559	2,425	300	......
Baltimore, Md.	676	1,469	1,469	......	......	......	......	......	250	......	......	......	250	1,023	341	682	......	......
Boston, Mass.	12,127	350	350	......	......	......	......	......	1,500	......	......	300	1,200	110	110	......	......	......
Buffalo, N. Y.	1,036	1,250	1,250	......	......	......	......	......	457	157	......	......	300	887	887	......	......	......
Chicago, Ill.	15,621	6,919	6,890	29	212	160	......	52	14,000	1,000	3,000	......	10,000	2,098	1,218	880	75	......
Cincinnati, Ohio.	1,248	2,951	2,913	38	......	......	......	......	200	......	......	......	200	......	......	......	......	......
Cleveland, Ohio.	7,692	3,373	3,373	......	......	......	......	......	800	550	......	......	250	1,483	1,382	101	......	......
New York, N. Y.	21,096	1,819	1,819	......	100	100	......	......	15,875	1,300	......	2,000	12,575	1,159	1,159	......	......	......
Philadelphia, Pa.	2,357	1,160	1,034	126	979	523	......	456	1,850	350	......	......	1,500	1,600	884	716	......	......
Pittsburg, Pa.	858	2,589	2,564	25	168	68	......	100	5,000	700	2,800	......	1,500	451	451	......	......	......
St. Louis, Mo.	3,442	4,970	4,940	30	......	......	......	......	1,475	......	......	......	1,475	......	......	......	......	......
San Francisco, Cal.	2,400	752	752	......	......	......	......	......	2,850	650	......	......	2,200	173	127	46	225	......
Total for cities of 100,000 to 300,000 in 1900.	58,763	41,441	39,423	2,018	769	543	......	226	13,115	3,233	......	552	9,330	5,612	5,160	452	671	......
Allegheny, Pa.	147	1,989	1,989	......	......	......	......	......	1,950	1,600	......	......	350	312	312	......	......	......
Columbus, Ohio.	2,444	1,170	1,170	......	......	......	......	......	150	......	......	......	150	500	210	290	......	......
Denver, Colo.	3,223	2,111	2,111	......	48	48	......	......	725	175	......	......	550	39	39	......	187	......
Detroit, Mich.	2,626	1,202	505	697	......	......	......	......	......	......	......	......	......	294	294	......	15	......
Fall River, Mass.	1,072	......	......	......	......	......	......	......	350	......	......	......	350	......	......	......	......	......
Indianapolis, Ind.	1,187	8,102	7,939	163	40	40	......	......	300	......	......	......	300	443	443	......	290	......
Jersey City, N. J.	1,379	......	......	......	......	......	......	......	200	......	......	......	200	157	157	......	......	......
Kansas City, Mo.	2,022	7,437	7,351	86	......	......	......	......	600	......	......	......	600	175	175	......	......	......
Los Angeles, Cal.	3,402	3,408	3,285	123	295	215	......	80	800	......	......	......	800	271	271	......	84	......
Louisville, Ky.	133	5,129	4,344	785	......	......	......	......	80	......	......	......	80	270	270	......	......	......

TABLE 6.—POPULATION AND COMMUNICANTS OR MEMBERS FOR EACH CITY OF 25,000 INHABITANTS OR MORE IN 1900, BY DENOMINATIONS (IN DETAIL): 1906—Continued.

CITY.	Congregationalists.	DISCIPLES OR CHRISTIANS.			DUNKERS OR GERMAN BAPTIST BRETHREN.				EASTERN ORTHODOX CHURCHES.					EVANGELICAL BODIES.			EVANGELISTIC ASSOCIATIONS.	
		Total.	Disciples of Christ.	Churches of Christ.	Total.	German Baptist Brethren Church (Conservative).	Old Order German Baptist Brethren.	The Brethren Church (Progressive Dunkers).	Total.	Russian Orthodox Church.	Servian Orthodox Church.	Syrian Orthodox Church.	Greek Orthodox Church.	Total.	Evangelical Association.	United Evangelical Church.	Total.	Apostolic Faith Movement.
Total for cities of 100,000 to 300,000 in 1900—Continued.																		
Memphis, Tenn.	401	1,347	1,267	80					180				180					
Milwaukee, Wis.	1,778	330	330						180				180	1,155	1,155		70	
Minneapolis, Minn.	5,934	593	593		10	10			1,116	866			250	154	154			
New Haven, Conn.	6,895								300				300					
New Orleans, La.	363	185	115	70														
Newark, N. J.	784								1,172	272			900	156	156			
Omaha, Nebr.	1,184	1,184	1,184						1,500				1,500	125	50	75		
Paterson, N. J.	155								50				50	75	75			
Providence, R. I.	4,603	79	79						300				300					
Rochester, N. Y.	297	280	280						225				225	342	342			
St. Joseph, Mo.	324	2,123	2,109	14	120	120			70				70	111	111			
St. Paul, Minn.	2,267	320	320						250				250	380	350	30		
Scranton, Pa.	1,610	255	255						395	320			75	57		57		
Syracuse, N. Y.	1,936	320	320						270				270	228	228			
Toledo, Ohio	2,914	1,060	1,060						302			152	150	368	368		25	
Washington, D. C.	2,984	2,170	2,170		256	110		146	450				450					
Worcester, Mass.	6,699	647	647						1,200			400	800					
Total for cities of 50,000 to 100,000 in 1900	46,022	21,417	18,453	2,964	1,173	833	140	200	22,723	2,418	600	500	19,205	6,644	3,777	2,867	205	
Albany, N. Y.	304								400				400	95	95			
Atlanta, Ga.	1,138	1,055	947	108					500				500					
Bridgeport, Conn.	2,878	52	52						1,045	645			400	76	76			
Cambridge, Mass.	2,972													79	79			
Camden, N. J.		14		14										50	50			
Charleston, S. C.	288	125	125						150				150					
Dayton, Ohio		905	905		750	410	140	200	160				160	478	478			
Des Moines, Iowa	1,391	4,926	4,926		110	110			250				250	341	196	145		
Duluth, Minn.	484	161	161						150				150	48	48			
Elizabeth, N. J.	143								60				60					
Erie, Pa.		172	172						150				150	182	182			
Evansville, Ind.		535	535											112	112			
Grand Rapids, Mich.	2,359	900	900						200				200	130	130			
Harrisburg, Pa.		96	96		98	98			100				100	439		439		
Hartford, Conn.	5,085								160				160					
Hoboken, N. J.	50								150				150					
Kansas City, Kans.	688	715	715		170	170			600		600							
Lawrence, Mass.	1,285								700			500	200					
Lowell, Mass.	3,188								6,000				6,000	49	49			
Lynn, Mass.	1,250								1,110				1,110	75	75			
Manchester, N. H.	1,585	4	4						3,000				3,000					
Nashville, Tenn.	474	4,100	1,438	2,662					150				150					
New Bedford, Mass.	701								425				425	67	67			
Oakland, Cal.	2,424	460	450	10					350				350					
Peoria, Ill.	1,267	650	650						150				150	150	150		35	
Portland, Me.	2,649	74	14	60					50				50					
Portland, Oreg.	1,599	1,070	1,058	12	45	45			311	61			250	526	394	132	75	
Reading, Pa.		115	115						475	125			350	2,853	952	1,901		
Richmond, Va.		2,268	2,268						180				180					
Salt Lake City, Utah	714	250	250						3,050				3,050					
San Antonio, Tex.		622	524	98										83	83			
Savannah, Ga.	323	371	371						500				500					
Seattle, Wash.	2,580	950	950						337	337				100	100		50	
Somerville, Mass.	2,040													88	88		45	
Springfield, Mass.	4,634	100	100						250				250					
Trenton, N. J.	31													77	77			
Troy, N. Y.	73	617	617						100				100					
Utica, N. Y.	836								100				100	91	91			
Wilkes-Barre, Pa.	589	110	110						1,410	1,250			160	455	205	250		
Wilmington, Del.																		
Total for cities of 25,000 to 50,000 in 1900	44,169	40,295	38,594	1,701	2,510	1,600		910	11,581	1,853	2,926	95	6,707	12,309	4,739	7,570	523	300
Akron, Ohio	1,361	1,973	1,973						70				70	795	510	285	60	
Allentown, Pa.					67			67	60				60	2,354	654	1,700		
Altoona, Pa.		268	268		401	324		77	80				80	323	116	207		
Atlantic City, N. J.																		
Auburn, N. Y.		450	450															
Augusta, Ga.	41	806	806						80				80					
Bay City, Mich.	326													164	39	125	20	
Bayonne, N. J.																		
Binghamton, N. Y.	1,055													120	120			
Birmingham, Ala.	209	729	684	45					302				302					
Brockton, Mass.	2,057	84	84															
Butte, Mont.		204	204						1,500		1,500							
Canton, Ohio		1,000	1,000		105	60		45	75				75	868	230	638		
Cedar Rapids, Iowa	464	627	627		32	32								238	59	179		
Chattanooga, Tenn.	245	670	500	170					50				50					

TABLE 6.—POPULATION AND COMMUNICANTS OR MEMBERS FOR EACH CITY OF 25,000 INHABITANTS OR MORE IN 1900, BY DENOMINATIONS (IN DETAIL): 1906—Continued.

CITY.	Congregationalists.	DISCIPLES OR CHRISTIANS.			DUNKERS OR GERMAN BAPTIST BRETHREN.				EASTERN ORTHODOX CHURCHES.					EVANGELICAL BODIES.			EVANGELISTIC ASSOCIATIONS.	
		Total.	Disciples of Christ.	Churches of Christ.	Total.	German Baptist Brethren Church (Conservative).	Old Order German Baptist Brethren.	The Brethren Church (Progressive Dunkers).	Total.	Russian Orthodox Church.	Servian Orthodox Church.	Syrian Orthodox Church.	Greek Orthodox Church.	Total.	Evangelical Association.	United Evangelical Church.	Total.	Apostolic Faith Movement.
Total for cities of 25,000 to 50,000 in 1900—Continued.																		
Chelsea, Mass.	1,010																	
Chester, Pa.									50				50					
Council Bluffs, Iowa	353	561	561						75				75	137	137			
Covington, Ky.		1,027	1,027															
Dallas, Tex.	727	2,252	1,688	564										60	60			
Davenport, Iowa	636	300	300															
Dubuque, Iowa	1,350													88	88			
East St. Louis, Ill.	133	446	446						150				150					
Easton, Pa.									50				50	580	222	358		
Elmira, N. Y.	966	210	210						60				60					
Fitchburg, Mass.	1,249								240				240					
Fort Wayne, Ind.	462	923	923		43	43			150				150	165	165		50	
Fort Worth, Tex.	150	1,312	1,205	107														
Galveston, Tex.		120	120						500	500				66	66			
Gloucester, Mass.	621								50				50					
Haverhill, Mass.	1,806	75	75						400				400					
Holyoke, Mass.	1,641								200				200					
Houston, Tex.		779	693	86										21	21			
Jackson, Mich.	419													47	47			
Jacksonville, Fla.	200	757	757						160				160					
Johnstown, Pa.	160	642	642		971	350		621	135			95	40	1,542	300	1,242		
Joliet, Ill.	20	111	111						26	26				112	53	59		
Joplin, Mo.	130	1,874	1,874															
Knoxville, Tenn.	175	520	520						30				30					
La Crosse, Wis.	335								50				50	52	52			
Lancaster, Pa.					225	225			120				120	650	80	570		
Lexington, Ky.	77	4,202	4,202															
Lincoln, Nebr.	2,172	880	870	10	56	56			60				60	185	136	49		
Little Rock, Ark.	112	650	650															
McKeesport, Pa.	145	322	322						1,676		1,426		250	30	30			
Malden, Mass.	1,104																	
Mobile, Ala.	136	225	225						350				350					
Montgomery, Ala.	147	539		539					125				125					
New Britain, Conn.	2,312								307	307								
Newcastle, Pa.	300	1,417	1,417						150				150	80	80			
Newport, Ky.	207	360	360															
Newton, Mass.	2,701																	
Norfolk, Va.		367	367						200				200					
Oshkosh, Wis.	628													100	100			
Passaic, N. J.	154																	
Pawtucket, R. I.	1,467								250				250	70	70			
Pueblo, Colo.	523	758	758						1,100	300			800					
Quincy, Ill.	427	606	606															
Racine, Wis.	362													200	200			
Rockford, Ill.	1,147	217	217		25	25												
Sacramento, Cal.	298	384	368	16					300				300	40	40			
Saginaw, Mich.	704	325	325											50	50			
Salem, Mass.	780								620	470			150					
Schenectady, N. Y.	324								250				250					
Sioux City, Iowa	786	196	196															
South Bend, Ind.	30	1,045	1,045		248	148		100	50				50	399	399			
South Omaha, Nebr.		60	60						400				400					
Spokane, Wash.	1,216	860	820	40	37	37								148	148		300	300
Springfield, Ill.	463	1,580	1,580						50				50					
Springfield, Ohio	525	294	270	24					60				60					
Superior, Wis.	265								30				30	26	26			
Tacoma, Wash.	594	558	558											44	44			
Taunton, Mass.	984								150				150					
Terre Haute, Ind.	363	1,600	1,500	100					100				100	160	75	85	93	
Topeka, Kans.	1,373	1,320	1,320						150				150	50	50			
Waterbury, Conn.	1,982								100	100								
Wheeling, W. Va.		760	760															
Williamsport, Pa.	197	200	200											964	17	847		
Woonsocket, R. I.	234								80				80					
Yonkers, N. Y.									200	150			50					
York, Pa.					300	300			80				80	1,136	80	1,056		
Youngstown, Ohio	630	1,850	1,850						80				80	245	75	170		

TABLE 6.—POPULATION AND COMMUNICANTS OR MEMBERS FOR EACH CITY OF 25,000 INHABITANTS OR MORE IN 1900, BY DENOMINATIONS (IN DETAIL): 1906—Continued.

CITY.	EVANGELISTIC ASSOCIATIONS—continued.									FRIENDS.					GERMAN EVANGELICAL PROTESTANT BODIES.			German Evangelical Synod of North America.
	Peniel Missions.	Metropolitan Church Association.	Hephzibah Faith Missionary Association.	Missionary Church Association.	Pentecost Bands of the World.	Heavenly Recruit Church.	Apostolic Christian Church.	Church of Daniel's Band.	Pentecostal Union Church.	Total.	Society of Friends (Orthodox).	Religious Society of Friends (Hicksite).	Orthodox Conservative Friends (Wilburite).	Friends (Primitive).	Total.	German Evangelical Protestant Ministers' Association.	German Evangelical Protestant Ministers' Conference.	
Total for cities of 25,000 and over in 1900	403	120	24	190	245	138	85	20	174	13,129	7,729	5,339	26	35	23,896	16,005	7,891	122,054
Total for cities of 300,000 and over in 1900	225	75								7,743	3,524	4,169	26	24	17,965	12,324	5,641	61,080
Baltimore, Md										941	331	610			970	970		7,106
Boston, Mass										130	130							
Buffalo, N. Y																		13,256
Chicago, Ill		75								385	289	96						17,053
Cincinnati, Ohio										125	125				8,218	6,022	2,196	3,275
Cleveland, Ohio										553	553				2,548	2,548		5,981
New York, N. Y										1,592	606	986						940
Philadelphia, Pa										3,991	1,490	2,477		24				
Pittsburg, Pa										26			26		4,084	2,784	1,300	
St. Louis, Mo															1,510		1,510	12,928
San Francisco, Cal	225														635		635	542
Total for cities of 100,000 to 300,000 in 1900	53		24	105	200	90	25		174	2,211	2,114	95		2	2,250	1,400	850	40,798
Allegheny, Pa															1,450	600	850	1,467
Columbus, Ohio										218	218				800	800		2,800
Denver, Colo			24						163									681
Detroit, Mich				15														7,214
Fall River, Mass										130	130							
Indianapolis, Ind					200	90				918	918							2,008
Jersey City, N. J																		
Kansas City, Mo										188	188							428
Los Angeles, Cal	53			20					11	150	150							130
Louisville, Ky																		9,260
Memphis, Tenn																		
Milwaukee, Wis				70														3,635
Minneapolis, Minn										204	204							350
New Haven, Conn																		
New Orleans, La																		4,353
Newark, N. J																		1,360
Omaha, Nebr																		128
Paterson, N. J																		
Providence, R. I										137	135			2				
Rochester, N. Y																		3,400
St. Joseph, Mo																		862
St. Paul, Minn																		855
Scranton, Pa																		962
Syracuse, N. Y																		550
Toledo, Ohio							25											
Washington, D. C										156	61	95						350
Worcester Mass										110	110							
Total for cities of 50,000 to 100,000 in 1900	125	45		35						2,783	1,925	849		9				8,321
Albany, N. Y										55		55						550
Atlanta, Ga																		189
Bridgeport, Conn																		
Cambridge, Mass																		
Camden, N. J										181		181						
Charleston, S. C																		
Dayton, Ohio																		1,450
Des Moines, Iowa										521	521							
Duluth, Minn																		270
Elizabeth, N. J																		
Erie, Pa																		1,600
Evansville, Ind																		2,077
Grand Rapids, Mich																		506
Harrisburg, Pa																		
Hartford, Conn																		
Hoboken, N. J																		
Kansas City, Kans																		211
Lawrence, Mass										277	277							
Lowell, Mass																		
Lynn, Mass										229	220			9				
Manchester, N. H										30	30							
Nashville, Tenn																		
New Bedford, Mass										213	213							
Oakland, Cal										22	22							45
Peoria, Ill				35														

TABLE 6.—POPULATION AND COMMUNICANTS OR MEMBERS FOR EACH CITY OF 25,000 INHABITANTS OR MORE IN 1900, BY DENOMINATIONS (IN DETAIL): 1906—Continued.

CITY.	EVANGELISTIC ASSOCIATIONS—continued.									FRIENDS.					GERMAN EVANGELICAL PROTESTANT BODIES.			German Evangelical Synod of North America.
	Peniel Missions.	Metropolitan Church Association.	Hephzibah Faith Missionary Association.	Missionary Church Association.	Pentecost Bands of the World.	Heavenly Recruit Church.	Apostolic Christian Church.	Church of Daniel's Band.	Pentecostal Union Church.	Total.	Society of Friends (Orthodox).	Religious Society of Friends (Hicksite).	Orthodox Conservative Friends (Wilburite).	Friends (Primitive).	Total.	German Evangelical Protestant Ministers' Association.	German Evangelical Protestant Ministers' Conference.	
Total for cities of 50,000 to 100,000 in 1900—Continued.																		
Portland, Me.										200	200							
Portland, Oreg.	75									226	226							
Reading, Pa.										26		26						
Richmond, Va.										15	15							564
Salt Lake City, Utah																		
San Antonio, Tex.																		60
Savannah, Ga.																		
Seattle, Wash.	50									55	55							
Somerville, Mass.		45																
Springfield, Mass.																		
Trenton, N. J.										272	37	235						500
Troy, N. Y.																		300
Utica, N. Y.																		
Wilkes-Barre, Pa.																		
Wilmington, Del.										461	109	352						
Total for cities of 25,000 to 50,000 in 1900				50	45	48	60	20		392	166	226			3,681	2,281	1,400	11,860
Akron, Ohio.							60											
Allentown, Pa.																		
Altoona, Pa.																		
Atlantic City, N. J.																		
Auburn, N. Y.																		336
Augusta, Ga.																		
Bay City, Mich.								20										
Bayonne, N. J.																		390
Binghamton, N. Y.																		
Birmingham, Ala.																		260
Brockton, Mass.																		
Butte, Mont.																		
Canton, Ohio.																		
Cedar Rapids, Iowa.																		
Chattanooga, Tenn.																		
Chelsea, Mass.																		
Chester, Pa.										187		187						
Council Bluffs, Iowa.																		
Covington, Ky.															1,400		1,400	
Dallas, Tex.																		98
Davenport, Iowa.																		
Dubuque, Iowa.																		
East St. Louis, Ill.																		247
Easton, Pa.																		
Elmira, N. Y.																		890
Fitchburg, Mass.																		
Fort Wayne, Ind.				50														
Fort Worth, Tex.																		80
Galveston, Tex.																		
Gloucester, Mass.																		
Haverhill, Mass.																		
Holyoke, Mass.																		
Houston, Tex.																		500
Jackson, Mich.																		300
Jacksonville, Fla.																		
Johnstown, Pa.																		
Joliet, Ill.																		
Joplin, Mo.																		
Knoxville, Tenn.																		
La Crosse, Wis.																		
Lancaster, Pa.																		
Lexington, Ky.																		
Lincoln, Nebr.										39		39						296
Little Rock, Ark.																		175
McKeesport, Pa.															700	700		
Malden, Mass.																		
Mobile, Ala.																		
Montgomery, Ala.																		
New Britain, Conn.																		
Newcastle, Pa.																		
Newport, Ky.															655	655		1,500
Newton, Mass.																		
Norfolk, Va.																		
Oshkosh, Wis.																		550
Passaic, N. J.																		

TABLE 6.—POPULATION AND COMMUNICANTS OR MEMBERS FOR EACH CITY OF 25,000 INHABITANTS OR MORE IN 1900, BY DENOMINATIONS (IN DETAIL): 1906—Continued.

CITY.	EVANGELISTIC ASSOCIATIONS—continued. Peniel Missions.	Metropolitan Church Association.	Hephzibah Faith Missionary Association.	Missionary Church Association.	Pentecost Bands of the World.	Heavenly Recruit Church.	Apostolic Christian Church.	Church of Daniel's Band.	Pentecostal Union Church.	FRIENDS. Total.	Society of Friends (Orthodox).	Religious Society of Friends (Hicksite).	Orthodox Conservative Friends (Wilburite).	Friends (Primitive).	GERMAN EVANGELICAL PROTESTANT BODIES. Total.	German Evangelical Protestant Ministers' Association.	German Evangelical Protestant Ministers' Conference.	German Evangelical Synod of North America.
Total for cities of 25,000 to 50,000 in 1900—Continued.																		
Pawtucket, R. I.																		
Pueblo, Colo.																		
Quincy, Ill.																		2,949
Racine, Wis.																		
Rockford, Ill.																		
Sacramento, Cal.																		
Saginaw, Mich.																		239
Salem, Mass.										45	45							
Schenectady, N. Y.																		401
Sioux City, Iowa.																		
South Bend, Ind.																		1,100
South Omaha, Nebr.																		
Spokane, Wash.																		
Springfield, Ill.																		
Springfield, Ohio.																		1,000
Superior, Wis.																		
Tacoma, Wash.										36	36							
Taunton, Mass.																		
Terre Haute, Ind.					45	48									527	527		
Topeka, Kans.																		50
Waterbury, Conn.																		
Wheeling, W. Va.															399	399		
Williamsport, Pa.																		500
Woonsocket, R. I.										85	85							
Yonkers, N. Y.																		
York, Pa.																		
Youngstown, Ohio.																		

CITY.	Independent churches.	International Apostolic Holiness Union.	Jewish congregations.[1]	LATTER-DAY SAINTS. Total.	Church of Jesus Christ of Latter-day Saints.	Reorganized Church of Jesus Christ of Latter Day Saints.	LUTHERAN BODIES. Total.	General Synod of the Evangelical Lutheran Church in the United States of America.	United Synod of the Evangelical Lutheran Church in the South.	General Council of the Evangelical Lutheran Church in North America.	Evangelical Lutheran Synodical Conference of America.	United Norwegian Lutheran Church in America.	Evangelical Lutheran Joint Synod of Ohio and Other States.	Lutheran Synod of Buffalo.	Hauge's Norwegian Evangelical Lutheran Synod.	Evangelical Lutheran Church in America, Eielsen's Synod.	Evangelical Lutheran Synod of Iowa and Other States.
Total for cities of 25,000 and over in 1900.	30,453	62	89,947	33,572	25,822	7,750	521,494	71,679	4,580	165,185	198,111	9,618	27,372	1,477	2,923	35	11,705
Total for cities of 300,000 and over in 1900.	16,805	28	58,324	2,315	767	1,548	210,093	22,351		70,372	96,413	4,027	4,558	780	1,405		1,111
Baltimore, Md.	1,306		2,042	39	39		12,914	7,743		56	3,188		1,877				
Boston, Mass.	60		1,735	109	109		3,683			969	2,272						
Buffalo, N. Y.			618				12,189	114		6,858	4,437			780			
Chicago, Ill.	5,185		4,703	400	140	260	64,897	2,024		11,930	39,317	3,216	789		1,405		1,056
Cincinnati, Ohio.	100	28	1,680				1,431	1,084			347						
Cleveland, Ohio.	521		2,137	98		98	12,744	252		310	10,845		490				55
New York, N. Y.	7,187		30,414	270	97	173	51,285	4,042		30,869	13,930	695					
Philadelphia, Pa.	1,302		9,991	270	103	167	21,733	3,872		16,888	772	66					
Pittsburg, Pa.	304		2,124	151		151	9,846	2,113		2,046	4,285		1,402				
St. Louis, Mo.	770		1,801	487		487	16,508	592		145	15,613						
San Francisco, Cal.	70		1,079	491	279	212	2,863	515		301	1,407	50					
Total for cities of 100,000 to 300,000 in 1900.	4,793		15,412	3,514	629	2,885	141,597	14,841		33,089	62,489	1,750	12,693	697	651	35	5,388
Allegheny, Pa.	400			168	168		6,790	1,814		1,281	500		1,995				
Columbus, Ohio.	229		575	84		84	3,346	169		321	161		2,695				
Denver, Colo.	150		703	262	65	197	1,574	433		429	387		193				
Detroit, Mich.	27		1,131	247		247	18,694	930		247	11,936		4,510	126			500
Fall River, Mass.			107	164		164											
Indianapolis, Ind.	880		395	14	14		3,423	402			2,921						
Jersey City, N. J.			223				5,776	1,819		3,565	225						
Kansas City, Mo.	247		345	476		476	1,542	446		612	354		130				
Los Angeles, Cal.	1,442		521	552	266	286	1,522	390		252	760	55					
Louisville, Ky.	92		955	66		66	2,985	2,130			795						

[1] Heads of families only.

TABLE 6.—POPULATION AND COMMUNICANTS OR MEMBERS FOR EACH CITY OF 25,000 INHABITANTS OR MORE IN 1900, BY DENOMINATIONS (IN DETAIL): 1906—Continued.

CITY.	Independent churches.	International Apostolic Holiness Union.	Jewish congregations.[1]	LATTER-DAY SAINTS.			LUTHERAN BODIES.										
				Total.	Church of Jesus Christ of Latter-day Saints.	Reorganized Church of Jesus Christ of Latter-day Saints.	Total.	General Synod of the Evangelical Lutheran Church in the United States of America.	United Synod of the Evangelical Lutheran Church in the South.	General Council of the Evangelical Lutheran Church in North America.	Evangelical Lutheran Synodical Conference of America.	United Norwegian Lutheran Church in America.	Evangelical Lutheran Joint Synod of Ohio and Other States.	Lutheran Synod of Buffalo.	Hauge's Norwegian Evangelical Lutheran Synod.	Evangelical Lutheran Church in America, Eielsen's Synod.	Evangelical Lutheran Synod of Iowa and Other States.
Total for cities of 100,000 to 300,000 in 1900—Continued.																	
Memphis, Tenn.	30		375				250				250						
Milwaukee, Wis.	260		765	90	90		32,186			618	29,985	730		571	120		45
Minneapolis, Minn.			806	67		67	11,918			4,610	969	735			203	35	981
New Haven, Conn.			292				1,915	115		1,535	215						
New Orleans, La.			935				5,015				4,475		540				
Newark, N. J.	90		1,031				2,035	200		1,560	65						
Omaha, Nebr.			335	320		320	2,235	656		747	427						
Paterson, N. J.	232		587				803	145		95	563						
Providence, R. I.	262		760	258		258	884			704	180						
Rochester, N. Y.	34		842				7,512			6,953	559						
St. Joseph, Mo.			240	627		627	638	264			374						
St. Paul, Minn.	29		655	26	26		9,685			2,936	4,364	230	750		268		367
Scranton, Pa.			569	50		50	2,471	133		2,013	325						
Syracuse, N. Y.			498				3,193	2,468		725							
Toledo, Ohio.	98		444	43		43	10,455	138		2,568	1,197		1,412				3,495
Washington, D. C.	150		698				3,104	2,129		75	432		468				
Worcester, Mass.	141		625				1,646			1,243	70						
Total for cities of 50,000 to 100,000 in 1900.	4,316	34	7,848	25,810	24,159	1,651	62,961	10,365	3,511	31,935	7,391	1,436	2,722		223		1,918
Albany, N. Y.			484	105	105		3,768	373		2,268	1,127						
Atlanta, Ga.	78		250				129		129								
Bridgeport, Conn.	74		270				1,425	116		560	284						
Cambridge, Mass.			65				400			400							
Camden, N. J.	25		40				1,475	224		1,251							
Charleston, S. C.			160				1,762		1,762								
Dayton, Ohio.	64		172	21		21	3,322	1,332		314			1,676				
Des Moines, Iowa.	442		183	285		285	2,235	500		800	17	216	260				340
Duluth, Minn.			210				2,572			1,317	76	557	240		178		
Elizabeth, N. J.	80		40				815			790		25					
Erie, Pa.			78				3,657			3,271	317						
Evansville, Ind.	57	19	251	30	30		1,195	86			895		214				
Grand Rapids, Mich.	1,007	15	85				1,544	150		431	877	41			45		
Harrisburg, Pa.	91		300				5,705	4,941		742	22						
Hartford, Conn.			647				1,135			620	205						
Hoboken, N. J.			260				1,557	222		896							
Kansas City, Kans.	49		47	408		408	327	70		130							
Lawrence, Mass.							53			53	240						
Lowell, Mass.	140		26				304			304	127						
Lynn, Mass.			184				298			298							
Manchester, N. H.			80				738			478	260						
Nashville, Tenn.	402		275				442	442									
New Bedford, Mass.				26		26	54			54							
Oakland, Cal.			140	213		213	955	110		256	399						
Peoria, Ill.	233		117	53		53	2,462	47		400	1,137						878
Portland, Me.							639			49		340					
Portland, Oreg.	184		414	162	101	61	1,627			661	423	112	217				
Reading, Pa.	269		210				9,428	500		8,928							
Richmond, Va.	18		389				660		360		300						
Salt Lake City, Utah.			171	24,037	23,867	170	189			126	39						
San Antonio, Tex.			160	97		97	565						115				450
Savannah, Ga.			221				1,260		1,260								
Seattle, Wash.	436		335	191	56	135	1,596			571	71	145					250
Somerville, Mass.			25	182		182											
Springfield, Mass.			310				345			208	137						
Trenton, N. J.			400				2,260	473		1,738	25						
Troy, N. Y.	49		252				1,206	336		500							
Utica, N. Y.	590		127				1,669	115		1,274	280						
Wilkes-Barre, Pa.			245				2,485	290		1,582	133						
Wilmington, Del.	28		207				703	38		665							
Total for cities of 25,000 to 50,000 in 1900.	4,539		8,363	1,933	267	1,666	106,843	24,122	1,069	29,789	31,818	2,405	7,399		644		3,288
Akron, Ohio.	75		50	95		95	2,312	675		347	1,062		200				
Allentown, Pa.	45		60				4,942	1,142		3,800							
Altoona, Pa.	50		67				3,696	3,183		513							
Atlantic City, N. J.			200				70			70							
Auburn, N. Y.			40														
Augusta, Ga.			65				537		537								
Bay City, Mich.	205		75	125		125	1,999			194	1,125						
Bayonne, N. J.			542				171			37	134						
Binghamton, N. Y.	220		40				405			270							
Birmingham, Ala.	58		375				142			60	82						

[1] Heads of families onl .

TABLE 6.—POPULATION AND COMMUNICANTS OR MEMBERS FOR EACH CITY OF 25,000 INHABITANTS OR MORE IN 1900, BY DENOMINATIONS (IN DETAIL): 1906—Continued.

CITY.	Independent churches.	International Apostolic Holiness Union.	Jewish congregations.[1]	LATTER-DAY SAINTS. Total.	LATTER-DAY SAINTS. Church of Jesus Christ of Latter-day Saints.	LATTER-DAY SAINTS. Reorganized Church of Jesus Christ of Latter-day Saints.	LUTHERAN BODIES. Total.	General Synod of the Evangelical Lutheran Church in the United States of America.	United Synod of the Evangelical Lutheran Church in the South.	General Council of the Evangelical Lutheran Church in North America.	Evangelical Lutheran Synodical Conference of America.	United Norwegian Lutheran Church in America.	Evangelical Lutheran Joint Synod of Ohio and Other States.	Lutheran Synod of Buffalo.	Hauge's Norwegian Evangelical Lutheran Synod.	Evangelical Lutheran ... Eielsen's ...	Evangelical Lutheran Synod of Iowa and Other States.
Total for cities of 25,000 to 50,000 in 1906—Continued.																	
Brockton, Mass	170		178	27		27	483			483							
Butte, Mont			95	165	165		181			70	80						
Canton, Ohio	40						1,714	580					1,134				
Cedar Rapids, Iowa							840	368		52	360						
Chattanooga, Tenn			120				130				130						
Chelsea, Mass			350														
Chester, Pa	54		50				347			335	12						
Council Bluffs, Iowa	35		10	286		286	571	116		120	135						
Covington, Ky	42																
Dallas, Tex	21		205				257			17	240						
Davenport, Iowa	9		100	77		77	1,300	385		80	525						210
Dubuque, Iowa			30				1,295	85			260						950
East St. Louis, Ill							756				756						
Easton, Pa			91				3,235	629		2,606							
Elmira, N. Y	48		132				91			91							
Fitchburg, Mass			50				397			115							
Fort Wayne, Ind	20		70				8,219	195		619	6,285		1,120				
Fort Worth, Tex			155				61			23	38						
Galveston, Tex			220				756			98							658
Gloucester, Mass	65						28										
Haverhill, Mass			137	22		22											
Holyoke, Mass			140				550				550						
Houston, Tex			330				410			10	400						
Jackson, Mich							468				468						
Jacksonville, Fla			159				161		161								
Johnstown, Pa			65				3,078	1,538		1,390							
Joliet, Ill							3,177	579		598	2,000						
Joplin, Mo				221		221	111				111						
Knoxville, Tenn			125				341		165		131		45				
La Crosse, Wis			42	40	40		3,791			158	1,927	636					
Lancaster, Pa	95		121				4,657	902		3,694	61						
Lexington, Ky			55														
Lincoln, Nebr			100				1,317	572		174	542						
Little Rock, Ark	323		260				352				352						
McKeesport, Pa	200		80				695	84		475	136						
Malden, Mass			180				69			69							
Mobile, Ala			272				244				244						
Montgomery, Ala	80		218														
New Britain, Conn			96				3,081			2,447	634						
Newcastle, Pa	95		56				544	25		446							
Newport, Ky	10						170	170									
Newton, Mass																	
Norfolk, Va	50		218				206		206								
Oshkosh, Wis			25	17	17		3,860				1,781		1,250				683
Passaic, N. J	265		144				1,097			761							
Pawtucket, R. I			35				303			126	177						
Pueblo, Colo	20		50	47		47	332	38		94	200						
Quincy, Ill	500		10				1,858	287			1,571						
Racine, Wis	57		28				4,136	153		430	1,845		160		244		
Rockford, Ill	16						4,156	780		3,110	266						
Sacramento, Cal			107	240	45	195	484	460									
Saginaw, Mich	38		24				3,957				1,589		954				660
Salem, Mass							60										
Schenectady, N. Y			541				1,218	374		75	769						
Sioux City, Iowa	50		37	117		117	2,128	200		560	333	530			400		
South Bend, Ind			68				1,066			540	526						
South Omaha, Nebr							410	81		76	220						
Spokane, Wash	62		115	134		134	1,108			302	135	355	245				
Springfield, Ill	20		130				2,641	999			1,642						
Springfield, Ohio			59				2,638	1,988		200			450				
Superior, Wis			61				1,542			474	100	624					125
Tacoma, Wash	280		38	36		36	1,149			589	120	260	120				
Taunton, Mass	90																
Terre Haute, Ind			141				402				402						
Topeka, Kans	15			48		48	607	203		145	259						
Waterbury, Conn	20		125				566			516	50						
Wheeling, W. Va	1,000		130	200		200	2,047	757		800			490				
Williamsport, Pa	65						2,537	1,680		857							
Woonsocket, R. I			120				57			57							
Yonkers, N. Y			100				466			31	275						
York, Pa			61				5,324	4,729			595						
Youngstown, Ohio	31		190	36		36	2,335	195		500	283		1,231				

TABLE 6.—POPULATION AND COMMUNICANTS OR MEMBERS FOR EACH CITY OF 25,000 INHABITANTS OR MORE IN 1900, BY DENOMINATIONS (IN DETAIL): 1906—Continued.

CITY.	LUTHERAN BODIES—continued.												MENNONITE BODIES.				
	Synod for the Norwegian Evangelical Lutheran Church in America.	Evangelical Lutheran Synod of Michigan and Other States.	Danish Evangelical Lutheran Church in America.	Immanuel Synod of the Evangelical Lutheran Church of North America.	Finnish Evangelical Lutheran Church of America, or Suomi Synod.	Norwegian Lutheran Free Church.	United Danish Evangelical Lutheran Church in America.	Slovak Evangelical Lutheran Synod of America.	Finnish Evangelical Lutheran National Church.	Apostolic Lutheran Church (Finnish).	Church of the Lutheran Brethren of America (Norwegian).	Evangelical Lutheran Jehovah Conference.	Total.	Mennonite Church.	General Conference of Mennonites of North America.	Mennonite Brethren in Christ.	Central Illinois Conference of Mennonites.
Total for cities of 25,000 and over in 1900	9,101	3,043	4,018	1,000	1,078	2,173	2,627	4,808	344	153	109	355	1,176	179	520	407	70
Total for cities of 300,000 and over in 1900	3,382		2,233		490	42	558	2,286	25		10	50	562		460	32	70
Baltimore, Md.												50					
Boston, Mass.	200		85		95		62										
Buffalo, N. Y.																	
Chicago, Ill.	1,588		1,915		25	42	299	1,281			10		70				70
Cincinnati, Ohio																	
Cleveland, Ohio	100				125			542	25								
New York, N. Y.	944		233		245		77	250									
Philadelphia, Pa.							54	80					492		460	32	
Pittsburg, Pa.																	
St. Louis, Mo.							25	133									
San Francisco, Cal.	550						40										
Total for cities of 100,000 to 300,000 in 1900	3,295	1,609	489	1,000	262	1,680	358	804		93	69	305					
Allegheny, Pa.				1,000				200									
Columbus, Ohio																	
Denver, Colo.	27						105										
Detroit, Mich.			140									305					
Fall River, Mass.																	
Indianapolis, Ind.	100																
Jersey City, N. J.	167																
Kansas City, Mo.																	
Los Angeles, Cal.	65																
Louisville, Ky.																	
Memphis, Tenn.																	
Milwaukee, Wis.	71										46						
Minneapolis, Minn.	2,170		119		2	1,430	98	408		75	23						
New Haven, Conn.			50														
New Orleans, La.																	
Newark, N. J.			50					160									
Omaha, Nebr.	175		130				100										
Paterson, N. J.																	
Providence, R. I.																	
Rochester, N. Y.																	
St. Joseph, Mo.																	
St. Paul, Minn.	520					250											
Scranton, Pa.																	
Syracuse, N. Y.																	
Toledo, Ohio		1,609						36									
Washington, D. C.																	
Worcester, Mass.					260		55			18							
Total for cities of 50,000 to 100,000 in 1900	1,157		971		95	177	92	879	69		20		125			25	
Albany, N. Y.																	
Atlanta, Ga.																	
Bridgeport, Conn.			90					375									
Cambridge, Mass.																	
Camden, N. J.																	
Charleston, S. C.																	
Dayton, Ohio													26			26	
Des Moines, Iowa			54				48										
Duluth, Minn.	52				40	92					20						
Elizabeth, N. J.																	
Erie, Pa.									69								
Evansville, Ind.																	
Grand Rapids, Mich.																	
Harrisburg, Pa.																	
Hartford, Conn.			310														
Hoboken, N. J.	199																
Kansas City, Kans.																	
Lawrence, Mass.																	
Lowell, Mass.																	
Lynn, Mass.																	
Manchester, N. H.																	
Nashville, Tenn.																	
New Bedford, Mass.																	
Oakland, Cal.	190																
Peoria, Ill.																	

TABLE 6.—POPULATION AND COMMUNICANTS OR MEMBERS FOR EACH CITY OF 25,000 INHABITANTS OR MORE IN 1900, BY DENOMINATIONS (IN DETAIL): 1906—Continued.

CITY.	LUTHERAN BODIES—continued. Synod for the Norwegian Evangelical Lutheran Church in America.	Evangelical Lutheran Synod of Michigan and Other States.	Danish Evangelical Lutheran Church in America.	Immanuel Synod of the Evangelical Lutheran Church of North America.	Finnish Evangelical Lutheran Church of America, or Suomi Synod.	Norwegian Lutheran Free Church.	United Danish Evangelical Lutheran Church in America.	Slovak Evangelical Lutheran Synod of America.	Finnish Evangelical Lutheran National Church.	Apostolic Lutheran Church (Finnish).	Church of the Lutheran Brethren of America (Norwegian).	Danish Evangelical Lutheran Jehovah Conference.	MENNONITE BODIES. Total.	Mennonite Church.	General Conference of Mennonites of North America.	Mennonite Brethren in Christ.	Central Illinois Conference of Mennonites.
Total for cities of 50,000 to 100,000 in 1900—Continued.																	
Portland, Me.			250														
Portland, Oreg.	127				55		32										
Reading, Pa.													99			99	
Richmond, Va.																	
Salt Lake City, Utah	12						12										
San Antonio, Tex.																	
Savannah, Ga.																	
Seattle, Wash.	474					85											
Somerville, Mass.																	
Springfield, Mass.																	
Trenton, N. J.								24									
Troy, N. Y.	103		267														
Utica, N. Y.																	
Wilkes-Barre, Pa.								480									
Wilmington, Del.																	
Total for cities of 25,000 to 50,000 in 1900	1,267	1,434	325		231	274	1,619	839	250	60	10		489	179	60	250	
Akron, Ohio								28									
Allentown, Pa.													255		60	195	
Altoona, Pa.																	
Atlantic City, N. J.																	
Auburn, N. Y.																	
Augusta, Ga.																	
Bay City, Mich.		680															
Bayonne, N. J.																	
Binghamton, N. Y.								135									
Birmingham, Ala.																	
Brockton, Mass.																	
Butte, Mont.					31												
Canton, Ohio													30	30			
Cedar Rapids, Iowa			60														
Chattanooga, Tenn.																	
Chelsea, Mass.																	
Chester, Pa.																	
Council Bluffs, Iowa							200										
Covington, Ky.																	
Dallas, Tex.																	
Davenport, Iowa							100										
Dubuque, Iowa																	
East St. Louis, Ill.																	
Easton, Pa.													25			25	
Elmira, N. Y.																	
Fitchburg, Mass.									250	32							
Fort Wayne, Ind.													31	31			
Fort Worth, Tex.																	
Galveston, Tex.																	
Gloucester, Mass.										28							
Haverhill, Mass.																	
Holyoke, Mass.																	
Houston, Tex.																	
Jackson, Mich.																	
Jacksonville, Fla.																	
Johnstown, Pa.								150					100	100			
Joliet, Ill.																	
Joplin, Mo.																	
Knoxville, Tenn.																	
La Crosse, Wis.	1,055					120											
Lancaster, Pa.																	
Lexington, Ky.																	
Lincoln, Nebr.							29										
Little Rock, Ark.																	
McKeesport, Pa.																	
Malden, Mass.																	
Mobile, Ala.																	
Montgomery, Ala.																	
New Britain, Conn.																	
Newcastle, Pa.					73												
Newport, Ky.																	
Newton, Mass.																	
Norfolk, Va.																	
Oshkosh, Wis.							146										
Passaic, N. J.								336									

TABLE 6.—POPULATION AND COMMUNICANTS OR MEMBERS FOR EACH CITY OF 25,000 INHABITANTS OR MORE IN 1900, BY DENOMINATIONS (IN DETAIL): 1906—Continued.

CITY.	LUTHERAN BODIES—continued.												MENNONITE BODIES.				
	Synod for the Norwegian Evangelical Lutheran Church in America.	Evangelical Lutheran Synod of Michigan and Other States.	Danish Evangelical Lutheran Church in America.	Immanuel Synod of the Evangelical Lutheran Church of North America.	Finnish Evangelical Lutheran Church of America, or Suomi Synod.	Norwegian Lutheran Free Church.	United Danish Evangelical Lutheran Church in America.	Slovak Evangelical Lutheran Synod of America.	Finnish Evangelical Lutheran National Church.	Apostolic Lutheran Church (Finnish).	Church of the Lutheran Brethren of America (Norwegian).	Evangelical Lutheran Jehovah Conference.	Total.	Mennonite Church.	General Conference of Mennonites of North America.	Mennonite Brethren in Christ.	Central Illinois Conference of Mennonites.
Total for cities of 25,000 to 50,000 in 1900—Continued.																	
Pawtucket, R. I.																	
Pueblo, Colo.																	
Quincy, Ill.																	
Racine, Wis.			265				1,039										
Rockford, Ill.																	
Sacramento, Cal.	24																
Saginaw, Mich.		754															
Salem, Mass.					60												
Schenectady, N. Y.																	
Sioux City, Iowa.							105										
South Bend, Ind.													30			30	
South Omaha, Nebr.	63																
Spokane, Wash.	50					21											
Springfield, Ill.																	
Springfield, Ohio.																	
Superior, Wis.	75				31	103					10						
Tacoma, Wash.						30		30									
Taunton, Mass.																	
Terre Haute, Ind.																	
Topeka, Kans.																	
Waterbury, Conn.																	
Wheeling, W. Va.																	
Williamsport, Pa.																	
Woonsocket, R. I.																	
Yonkers, N. Y.								160									
York, Pa.													18	18			
Youngstown, Ohio.					36												

CITY.	METHODIST BODIES.														Moravian Church (Unitas Fratrum).	Nonsectarian Churches of Bible Faith.	Pentecostal Church of the Nazarene.
	Total.	Methodist Episcopal Church.	Union American Methodist Episcopal Church (Colored).	African Methodist Episcopal Church.	African Union Methodist Protestant Church.	African Methodist Episcopal Zion Church.	Methodist Protestant Church.	Wesleyan Methodist Connection of America.	Methodist Episcopal Church, South.	Congregational Methodist Church.	Colored Methodist Episcopal Church.	Primitive Methodist Church in the United States of America.	Free Methodist Church of North America.	Reformed Methodist Union Episcopal Church (Colored).			
Total for cities of 25,000 and over in 1900.	812,099	562,857	2,103	78,823	2,708	30,530	10,900	923	104,501	217	11,173	2,544	3,830	990	3,251	1,087	4,158
Total for cities of 300,000 and over in 1900.	255,371	204,255	1,244	21,299	770	9,299	5,422	30	10,472	163	752	685	980		2,008	77	1,137
Baltimore, Md.	35,718	24,605	640	4,283	183	385	3,417		2,040		139		26				
Boston, Mass.	8,283	7,063		720		500											
Buffalo, N. Y.	7,727	7,472		45		40		15					155				
Chicago, Ill.	34,034	29,456		3,701		582	58						237				560
Cincinnati, Ohio.	10,386	8,643		1,418		210	75	15			25						
Cleveland, Ohio.	11,100	10,383		629									88			12	
New York, N. Y.	57,021	49,970	241	3,173		2,988	254					298	97		1,147		335
Philadelphia, Pa.	52,068	44,693	363	3,675	587	2,005	175			163	281	109	17		861		
Pittsburg, Pa.	16,268	12,062		1,465		820	1,443					278	200				211
St. Louis, Mo.	19,210	6,889		2,154		1,419			8,281		307		160			65	
San Francisco, Cal.	3,556	3,019		36		350			151								31
Total for cities of 100,000 to 300,000 in 1900.	192,928	139,157	80	16,203	155	7,136	3,178	309	21,133		4,186	633	758		68	48	1,956
Allegheny, Pa.	5,528	3,963		539		375	651										
Columbus, Ohio.	11,184	10,401		685				59			28		11				
Denver, Colo.	7,824	6,837		572					334				81				
Detroit, Mich.	9,308	8,441		715		40							112				
Fall River, Mass.	2,237	1,818		12								407					
Indianapolis, Ind.	14,744	12,035		1,534		731	396				40		8		68		
Jersey City, N. J.	4,653	4,335		150		168											
Kansas City, Mo.	9,960	5,776		1,460		136			2,513		75						
Los Angeles, Cal.	11,542	9,335		814		153			1,142				98				1,695
Louisville, Ky.	10,759	2,133		1,412		1,271			5,430		476		37				

TABLE 6.—POPULATION AND COMMUNICANTS OR MEMBERS FOR EACH CITY OF 25,000 INHABITANTS OR MORE IN 1900, BY DENOMINATIONS (IN DETAIL): 1906—Continued.

CITY.	METHODIST BODIES.																
	Total.	Methodist Episcopal Church.	Union American Methodist Episcopal Church (Colored).	African Methodist Episcopal Church.	African Union Methodist Protestant Church.	African Methodist Episcopal Zion Church.	Methodist Protestant Church.	Wesleyan Methodist Connection of America.	Methodist Episcopal Church, South.	Congregational Methodist Church.	Colored Methodist Episcopal Church.	Primitive Methodist Church in the United States of America.	Free Methodist Church of North America.	Reformed Methodist Union Episcopal Church (Colored).	Moravian Church (Unitas Fratrum).	Nonsectarian Churches of Bible Faith.	Pentecostal Church of the Nazarene.
Total for cities of 100,000 to 300,000 in 1900—Continued.																	
Memphis, Tenn.	11,375	709		2,415		393			5,566		2,292						
Milwaukee, Wis.	3,898	3,788		72									38				
Minneapolis, Minn.	7,066	6,061		405													
New Haven, Conn.	4,124	3,730	60	66		268											
New Orleans, La.	7,028	3,333		1,198		80			2,352		65						
Newark, N. J.	8,368	7,125		775		68	350						50				
Omaha, Nebr.	3,230	2,958		240									32				
Paterson, N. J.	3,665	3,205			110	135	215									8	
Providence, R. I.	3,500	2,937	20	206		252						86					95
Rochester, N. Y.	6,184	6,008				113							63				
St. Joseph, Mo.	4,083	1,696		400					1,874		100		14				
St. Paul, Minn.	4,076	3,731		300									45				
Scranton, Pa.	4,999	4,748		102								140	9				
Syracuse, N. Y.	5,274	4,770				40	124	250					90				
Toledo, Ohio	4,811	4,551		204			27						29			40	
Washington, D. C.	20,077	11,019		1,928	45	2,615	1,415		1,922		1,110		23				166
Worcester, Mass.	3,431	3,115				298							18				
Total for cities of 50,000 to 100,000 in 1900	160,010	96,580	447	21,084	1,068	2,764	1,157	336	32,549	54	2,228	876	877	990	377	887	605
Albany, N. Y.	2,019	1,959		60													
Atlanta, Ga.	20,427	2,101		5,470		80	132		11,501	54	1,019		70			800	
Bridgeport, Conn.	2,340	2,230		50		60											
Cambridge, Mass.	1,542	1,113		236		193											166
Camden, N. J.	7,995	6,818	198	376	225	163	215										
Charleston, S. C.	9,337	2,552		4,411		27			1,507					840			
Dayton, Ohio	5,110	4,575		372				145					18				
Des Moines, Iowa	4,584	4,229		300				15					40				
Duluth, Minn.	1,971	1,931		40													
Elizabeth, N. J.	1,647	1,273		75		25	274								97		
Erie, Pa.	1,799	1,719		34									46				
Evansville, Ind.	3,364	2,691		259		400							14				
Grand Rapids, Mich.	3,056	2,766		86		20		135					49			40	
Harrisburg, Pa.	5,401	4,461		300		640										22	
Hartford, Conn.	2,052	1,752				300										25	
Hoboken, N. J.	1,133	1,133															
Kansas City, Kans.	3,999	2,544		694			254	41	210		218		38				
Lawrence, Mass.	1,282	1,282															
Lowell, Mass.	1,666	1,373										293					129
Lynn, Mass.	2,339	2,309		30													112
Manchester, N. H.	1,064	1,064															27
Nashville, Tenn.	13,119	1,306		2,974					8,413		427						
New Bedford, Mass.	1,500	993		125		75						307					
Oakland, Cal.	3,152	2,587		250		151			164								60
Peoria, Ill.	1,842	1,716		85									41				11
Portland, Me.	1,604	1,579				25											
Portland, Oreg.	4,513	4,053		60		40			200				160				75
Reading, Pa.	1,926	1,831		65								30					
Richmond, Va.	7,164	278		255					6,601		30						
Salt Lake City, Utah	771	741		30													
San Antonio, Tex.	3,145	920		530					1,688				7				
Savannah, Ga.	6,487	580		2,815		45	98		2,265		534			150			
Seattle, Wash.	4,972	4,521		132									319				25
Somerville, Mass.	1,566	1,566															
Springfield, Mass.	2,433	2,375		58													
Trenton, N. J.	4,706	4,246		150		310											
Troy, N. Y.	3,516	3,416				100											
Utica, N. Y.	1,584	1,513				29							42		280		
Wilkes-Barre, Pa.	3,622	3,275		68								246	33				
Wilmington, Del.	8,261	6,210	249	694	843	81	184										
Total for cities of 25,000 to 50,000 in 1900	203,790	123,865	332	20,237	715	11,331	1,143	248	40,347		4,007	350	1,215		798	75	460
Akron, Ohio	2,758	2,660				30		44					24				
Allentown, Pa.	640	597											43				46
Altoona, Pa.	4,213	4,167		26		20											
Atlantic City, N. J.	3,702	1,900	25	800	50	175	752										
Auburn, N. Y.	1,617	1,552				65											
Augusta, Ga.	5,406	85		840		245			3,186		1,050						
Bay City, Mich.	1,688	1,620											68				
Bayonne, N. J.	812	792				20											
Binghamton, N. Y.	3,601	3,441		30		60							70				
Birmingham, Ala.	7,129	651		970		1,082			3,919		498		9				

TABLE 6.—POPULATION AND COMMUNICANTS OR MEMBERS FOR EACH CITY OF 25,000 INHABITANTS OR MORE IN 1900, BY DENOMINATIONS (IN DETAIL): 1906—Continued.

CITY.	METHODIST BODIES.														Moravian Church (Unitas Fratrum).	Nonsectarian Churches of Bible Faith.	Pentecostal Church of the Nazarene.
	Total.	Methodist Episcopal Church.	Union American Methodist Episcopal Church (Colored).	African Methodist Episcopal Church.	African Union Methodist Protestant Church.	African Methodist Episcopal Zion Church.	Methodist Protestant Church.	Wesleyan Methodist Connection of America.	Methodist Episcopal Church, South.	Congregational Methodist Church.	Colored Methodist Episcopal Church.	Primitive Methodist Church in the United States of America.	Free Methodist Church of North America.	Reformed Methodist Union Episcopal Church (Colored).			
Total for cities of 25,000 to 50,000 in 1900—Continued.																	
Brockton, Mass.	1,529	1,529															
Butte, Mont.	986	805		23					158								
Canton, Ohio.	2,105	2,020		31				54									
Cedar Rapids, Iowa.	1,319	1,201		78									40				
Chattanooga, Tenn.	5,099	1,551		708		400			2,255		185						
Chelsea, Mass.	662	598		64													
Chester, Pa.	3,786	2,889	282	395	120						100						
Council Bluffs, Iowa.	998	948		30									20				
Covington, Ky.	2,204	1,427		101					576		100						
Dallas, Tex.	6,765	825		839					4,462		547		92				
Davenport, Iowa.	1,030	970		60													
Dubuque, Iowa.	1,028	958		70													
East St. Louis, Ill.	1,610	1,286		175		104					45						
Easton, Pa.	960	906		14		40									140		
Elmira, N. Y.	2,986	2,776		60		150											
Fitchburg, Mass.	613	613															
Fort Wayne, Ind.	2,212	2,022		135									55				
Fort Worth, Tex.	4,703	774		165					3,524		223		17				
Galveston, Tex.	1,548	681		240					627								
Gloucester, Mass.	599	599															
Haverhill, Mass	776	776															84
Holyoke, Mass.	677	677															
Houston, Tex.	5,437	1,336		803					3,168		130						
Jackson, Mich.	1,809	1,675		64				20					50				
Jacksonville, Fla.	6,535	1,376		3,622		113	25		1,244		155						
Johnstown, Pa.	2,408	2,354				54											
Joliet, Ill.	1,388	1,338		50													
Joplin, Mo.	1,318	866		40					408				4				
Knoxville, Tenn.	5,371	1,926		80		822			2,543								
La Crosse, Wis.	1,147	1,147															
Lancaster, Pa.	1,779	1,662	25	92											282		
Lexington, Ky.	2,450	975		509					896		70						
Lincoln, Nebr.	3,506	3,321		150									35				
Little Rock, Ark.	4,837	651		995		283			2,460		448						
McKeesport, Pa.	2,304	2,123		135									46				
Malden, Mass.	1,640	1,640															115
Mobile, Ala.	7,582	210		1,786		3,044			2,340		202						
Montgomery, Ala.	6,334	158		685		2,609	125		2,681		76						
New Britain, Conn.	616	576				40											
Newcastle, Pa.	3,080	2,576		52		25		19				250	158				
Newport, Ky.	944	675		50					219								
Newton, Mass.	1,022	1,022															
Norfolk, Va.	8,528	22		2,060	345	927			5,174								
Oshkosh, Wis.	950	885				15							50				
Passaic, N. J.	938	638		100	200												
Pawtucket, R. I.	547	537				10											
Pueblo, Colo.	1,739	1,233		215					253				38				
Quincy, Ill.	2,000	1,736		264													
Racine, Wis.	1,061	1,056		5													
Rockford, Ill.	2,448	2,382		54									12				
Sacramento, Cal.	1,207	1,004		42					130				31				
Saginaw, Mich.	1,890	1,660		28			161						41				
Salem, Mass.	639	639															36
Schenectady, N. Y.	3,735	3,676				59											
Sioux City, Iowa.	1,527	1,492		25									10				
South Bend, Ind.	2,249	2,139		60									50				
South Omaha, Nebr.	528	457		71													
Spokane, Wash.	3,575	3,342		75					124				34				146
Springfield, Ill.	2,600	2,147		423		30											
Springfield, Ohio.	3,257	2,799		430				28									
Superior, Wis.	633	622		11													
Tacoma, Wash.	2,759	2,648		35									76				
Taunton, Mass.	965	925				40											
Terre Haute, Ind.	3,527	3,086		391									50				
Topeka, Kans.	3,520	2,694		525				83			178		40				34
Waterbury, Conn.	1,705	1,470				235											
Wheeling, W. Va.	3,514	3,438		76													
Williamsport, Pa.	3,357	3,112		165		80											
Woonsocket, R. I.	213	213															
Yonkers, N. Y.	1,895	1,545				350										35	
York, Pa.	1,876	1,606		90		180									376	40	
Youngstown, Ohio.	3,140	2,759		125		24	80					100	52				

TABLE 6.—POPULATION AND COMMUNICANTS OR MEMBERS FOR EACH CITY OF 25,000 INHABITANTS OR MORE IN 1900, BY DENOMINATIONS (IN DETAIL): 1906—Continued.

CITY.	Polish National Church of America.	PRESBYTERIAN BODIES.											Protestant Episcopal Church.	REFORMED BODIES.			
		Total.	Presbyterian Church in the United States of America.	Cumberland Presbyterian Church.	Colored Cumberland Presbyterian Church.	Welsh Calvinistic Methodist Church.	United Presbyterian Church of North America.	Presbyterian Church in the United States.	Associate Reformed Synod of the South.	Synod of the Reformed Presbyterian Church of North America.	Reformed Presbyterian Church in North America, General Synod.	Reformed Presbyterian Church in the United States and Canada.		Total.	Reformed Church in America.	Reformed Church in the United States.	Christian Reformed Church.
Total for cities of 25,000 and over in 1900.	12,193	[illegible]	[illegible]	12,936	785	4,763	35,678	45,962	332	2,899	1,841	440	453,966	137,937	51,920	75,283	8,234
Total for cities of 300,000 and over in 1900	7,177	208,752	181,728	2,254	500	1,320	16,835	2,389		1,861	1,825	440	221,274	58,767	28,566	27,551	2,170
Baltimore, Md	1,132	9,484	8,224				340	920					16,8[illegible]	4,496		4,496	
Boston, Mass		3,066	2,265				510			291			13,[illegible]	118		118	
Buffalo, N. Y	3,500	6,724	6,140				584						8,[illegible]12	3,714	160	3,374	
Chicago, Ill	2,545	24,427	21,341	545	500	502	1,483			56			19,[illegible]	5,240	2,678	754	1,808
Cincinnati, Ohio		8,068	7,596			154	133			56	129		4,308	1,717		1,597	120
Cleveland, Ohio		8,391	7,754			55	582						5,880	4,831	214	4,395	222
New York, N. Y		51,547	48,914			350	1,586			584	113		92,534	25,848	24,005	1,523	20
Philadelphia, Pa		57,874	51,716			90	3,960			525	1,583		46,644	11,218	1,509	9,709	
Pittsburg, Pa		25,582	16,894	985		169	6,806			298		440	5,550	1,173		1,173	
St. Louis, Mo		10,031	7,222	692			597	1,469		51			5,590	412		412	
San Francisco, Cal		3,558	3,272	32			254						2,846				
Total for cities of 100,000 to 300,000 in 1900	1,725	122,447	94,387	2,490		1,569	9,807	13,508	130	540	16		99,244	20,673	12,777	6,609	1,287
Allegheny, Pa		8,264	3,067				4,874			323			920	200		200	
Columbus, Ohio		4,575	3,507	153		458	457						1,332	390		390	
Denver, Colo		5,307	4,632			131	490			54			2,71[illegible]	90		90	
Detroit, Mich		8,620	8,252				368						8,041	602	105	497	
Fall River, Mass	400	370	67				303						2,033				
Indianapolis, Ind		5,307	5,244	63									1,916	1,179		1,179	
Jersey City, N. J	200	2,973	2,272				701						4,810	3,497	3,497		
Kansas City, Mo		4,870	2,231	909			200	1,470		60			2,217	78		78	
Los Angeles, Cal		6,820	6,270	131			365			38	16		3,657				
Louisville, Ky		6,117	1,995	217				3,834	71				3,632	1,129		1,129	
Memphis, Tenn		3,938		743				3,136	59				2,259				
Milwaukee, Wis		2,412	2,158			254							2,798	575	325	250	
Minneapolis, Minn		6,238	6,059			179							4,785				
New Haven, Conn		300	300										4,896				
New Orleans, La		3,667						3,667					5,178				
Newark, N. J		10,629	10,489				140						5,195	4,214	4,214		
Omaha, Nebr		3,205	2,622				583						2,094	36		36	
Paterson, N. J		2,734	2,443				291						2,521	4,351	3,190		1,161
Providence, R. I		1,006	596				410						6,350				
Rochester, N. Y		9,170	8,805				365						4,434	1,404	891	387	126
St. Joseph, Mo		2,028	717	274			90	947					765	85		85	
St. Paul, Minn		4,039	4,039										3,418	180		180	
Scranton, Pa	1,125	5,096	4,549			547							1,764	99		99	
Syracuse, N. Y		3,642	3,577							65			3,146	555	555		
Toledo, Ohio		2,285	2,189				96						2,852	1,429		1,429	
Washington, D. C		8,636	8,182					454					13,692	580		580	
Worcester, Mass		199	125				74						1,807				
Total for cities of 50,000 to 100,000 in 1900	2,691	80,087	57,695	3,975	75	1,307	2,987	13,784	114	150			71,007	26,394	5,794	15,690	4,360
Albany, N. Y		3,682	3,563				119						3,983	1,907	1,907		
Atlanta, Ga		4,387	80	126				4,067	114				2,332				
Bridgeport, Conn	300	575	575										2,634	1,007		757	
Cambridge, Mass		290					240			50			1,950				
Camden, N. J		1,632	1,632										1,676				
Charleston, S. C		1,396	478					918					2,866				
Dayton, Ohio		3,341	3,056				285						1,120	2,713		2,713	
Des Moines, Iowa		2,843	2,460				383						1,300	82		82	
Duluth, Minn	1,000	1,357	1,357										1,087				
Elizabeth, N. J		3,204	3,204										3,372				
Erie, Pa		2,422	2,[illegible]				383						1,000				
Evansville, Ind		2,412	1,[illegible]	1,154									434				
Grand Rapids, Mich		1,246	1,039										1,812	7,400	3,040		4,360
Harrisburg, Pa		2,818	2,[illegible]										691	1,365		1,365	
Hartford, Conn		250	250										2,957				
Hoboken, N. J		400	327				73						1,810	640	640		
Kansas City, Kans		1,408	1,123	150			135						323				
Lawrence, Mass		650	325				325						1,227				
Lowell, Mass	891	436	251				185						1,645				
Lynn, Mass		207	207										1,275				
Manchester, N. H		200	200														
Nashville, Tenn		5,248		1,914	75			3,259					1,[illegible]	194		194	
New Bedford, Mass		121	121										1,[illegible]				
Oakland, Cal		2,616	2,482	42			82			10			1,610				
Peoria, Ill		2,035	2,035										[illegible]	47	47		
Portland, Me		178	178										1,467				
Portland, Oreg		4,075	3,399	400			276						1,865	210		210	
Reading, Pa		889	889										1,019	9,560		9,560	
Richmond, Va		3,247	130					3,117					4,893				
Salt Lake City, Utah		821	821										689				

TABLE 6.—POPULATION AND COMMUNICANTS OR MEMBERS FOR EACH CITY OF 25,000 INHABITANTS OR MORE IN 1900, BY DENOMINATIONS (IN DETAIL): 1906—Continued.

CITY.	Polish National Church of America.	PRESBYTERIAN BODIES.											Protestant Episcopal Church.	REFORMED BODIES.			
		Total.	Presbyterian Church in the United States of America.	Cumberland Presbyterian Church.	Colored Cumberland Presbyterian Church.	Welsh Calvinistic Methodist Church.	United Presbyterian Church of North America.	Presbyterian Church in the United States.	Associate Reformed Synod of the South.	Synod of the Reformed Presbyterian Church of North America.	Reformed Presbyterian Church in North America, General Synod.	Reformed Presbyterian Church in the United States and Canada.		Total.	Reformed Church in America.	Reformed Church in the United States.	Christian Reformed Church.
Total for cities of 50,000 to 100,000 in 1900—Continued.																	
San Antonio, Tex		1,275	130	189				956					1,288				
Savannah, Ga		1,550	83					1,467					2,065				
Seattle, Wash		5,495	5,149				256			90			2,584				
Somerville, Mass		168	168										674				
Springfield, Mass		110	110										1,613				
Trenton, N. J		3,669	3,669										2,168	550		280	
Troy, N. Y		3,955	3,824				131						2,969				
Utica, N. Y		3,470	2,979			491							2,600	160	160		
Wilkes-Barre, Pa	500	3,097	2,281			816							1,569	559		559	
Wilmington, Del		2,912	2,798				114						1,945				
Total for cities of 25,000 to 50,000 in 1900	600	92,489	64,729	4,217	210	567	6,049	16,281	88	348	..		62,441	32,103	4,783	25,433	417
Akron, Ohio		480	430				50						808	2,158		2,158	
Allentown, Pa		331	331										316	6,819		6,819	
Altoona, Pa		2,317	2,021				296						650	1,539		1,539	
Atlantic City, N. J		1,027	1,027										887				
Auburn, N. Y		2,663	2,663										815				
Augusta, Ga		1,069	145					924					982				
Bay City, Mich		1,270	1,270										565	111		111	
Bayonne, N. J	300	239	239										918	941	941		
Binghamton, N. Y		3,035	3,035										1,164				
Birmingham, Ala		2,881	76	717				2,088					1,310				
Brockton, Mass		110					110						293				
Butte, Mont		642	642										501				
Canton, Ohio		863	788				75						122	2,646		2,646	
Cedar Rapids, Iowa		1,975	1,735				240						505	32		32	
Chattanooga, Tenn		2,064	599	485	125			855					700				
Chelsea, Mass													545				
Chester, Pa		1,567	1,567										680				
Council Bluffs, Iowa		663	663										400				
Covington, Ky		942	636					306					550	325		325	
Dallas, Tex		2,871	461	795				1,615					1,290				
Davenport, Iowa		762	726				36						471				
Dubuque, Iowa		799	799										452				
East St. Louis, Ill		667	586				81						207				
Easton, Pa		1,898	1,898										382	1,913		1,913	
Elmira, N. Y		1,708	1,708										1,081				
Fitchburg, Mass													606				
Fort Wayne, Ind		1,526	1,526										370	1,360		1,360	
Fort Worth, Tex		1,759		493				1,266					518				
Galveston, Tex		475	75					400					1,278				
Gloucester, Mass													208				
Haverhill, Mass		166	166										450				
Holyoke, Mass		500	500										250	135		135	
Houston, Tex		1,610	86	184				1,340					1,321				
Jackson, Mich		410	410										461				
Jacksonville, Fla		772	104					668					2,019				
Johnstown, Pa		1,468	1,228			90	150						367	1,799		549	
Joliet, Ill		1,345	1,345										487				
Joplin, Mo		510	510										118				
Knoxville, Tenn		3,347	1,515	525			140	1,167					629				
La Crosse, Wis		502	502										405	200		200	
Lancaster, Pa		972	972										1,010	2,562		2,562	
Lexington, Ky		1,189	400					789					740				
Lincoln, Nebr		1,557	1,436				121						428	353		353	
Little Rock, Ark		1,126	39	161				838	88				1,402				
McKeesport, Pa		2,004	987	450			515			52			420	112		112	
Malden, Mass													604				
Mobile, Ala		1,294						1,294					2,472				
Montgomery, Ala		1,224		125				1,099					951				
New Britain, Conn													550				
Newcastle, Pa		3,233	1,751				1,282			200			430				
Newport, Ky		250	250										450				
Newton, Mass													1,442				
Norfolk, Va		1,632						1,632					2,708				
Oshkosh, Wis		447	366			81							594				
Passaic, N. J	300	649	649										470	1,939	1,331		388
Pawtucket, R. I													1,564				
Pueblo, Colo		1,298	1,060	142			96						342				
Quincy, Ill		425	425										449				
Racine, Wis		827	546			281							746	29			29
Rockford, Ill		945	945										260				
Sacramento, Cal		507	507										315				
Saginaw, Mich		1,354	1,354										592				
Salem, Mass													644				
Schenectady, N. Y		1,467	1,302				165						1,214	1,590	1,590		
Sioux City, Iowa		1,212	1,179				83						465	76		76	

TABLE 6.—POPULATION AND COMMUNICANTS OR MEMBERS FOR EACH CITY OF 25,000 INHABITANTS OR MORE IN 1900, BY DENOMINATIONS (IN DETAIL): 1906—Continued.

CITY.	Polish National Church of America.	PRESBYTERIAN BODIES.											Protestant Episcopal Church.	REFORMED BODIES.			
		Total.	Presbyterian Church in the United States of America.	Cumberland Presbyterian Church.	Colored Cumberland Presbyterian Church.	Welsh Calvinistic Methodist Church.	United Presbyterian Church of North America.	Presbyterian Church in the United States.	Associate Reformed Synod of the South.	Synod of the Reformed Presbyterian Church of North America.	Reformed Presbyterian Church in North America, General Synod.	Reformed Presbyterian Church in the United States and Canada.		Total.	Reformed Church in America.	Reformed Church in the United States.	Christian Reformed Church.
Total for cities of 25,000 to 50,000 in 1900—Continued.																	
South Bend, Ind		1,021	1,021										217	215	65	150	
South Omaha, Nebr		728	645				83						258				
Spokane, Wash		1,550	1,150				400						840				
Springfield, Ill		1,745	1,745										556				
Springfield, Ohio		1,521	1,261				260						485	160		160	
Superior, Wis		487	487										332				
Tacoma, Wash		1,629	1,467				162						954				
Taunton, Mass													680				
Terre Haute, Ind		885	885										684	310		310	
Topeka, Kans		2,377	1,803	140	85		298			51			722				
Waterbury, Conn													1,691				
Wheeling, W. Va		1,998	1,502				496						995	240		240	
Williamsport, Pa		1,838	1,838										1,361	295		295	
Woonsocket, R. I		49	49										494				
Yonkers, N. Y		1,860	1,860										3,208	856	856		
York, Pa		1,191	1,106				85						751	2,598		2,598	
Youngstown, Ohio		2,765	1,730			115	875			45			925	790		790	

CITY.	REFORMED BODIES—cont'd.	Reformed Catholic Church.	Reformed Episcopal Church.	Roman Catholic Church.	SALVATIONISTS.			Schwenkfelders.	Society for Ethical Culture.	Spiritualists.	SWEDISH EVANGELICAL BODIES.			Temple Society in the United States (Friends of the Temple).	THEOSOPHICAL SOCIETIES.		
	Hungarian Reformed Church in America.				Total.	Salvation Army.	American Salvation Army.				Total.	Swedish Evangelical Mission Covenant of America.	Swedish Evangelical Free Mission.		Total.	Theosophical Society in America.	Theosophical Society, New York.
Total for cities of 25,000 and over in 1900	2,500	1,250	7,456	[1]16,307,529	11,820	11,662	158	87	2,040	19,088	11,127	8,877	2,250	226	2,065	146	90
Total for cities of 300,000 and over in 1900	480	1,100	6,060	[3]3,375,453	4,691	4,641	50	87	2,040	8,726	4,183	3,468	715	40	1,036	48	90
Baltimore, Md			332	100,397	49	49				92					3	3	
Boston, Mass		600		258,936	319	319				919					159		
Buffalo, N. Y	180			126,395	153	148	5			189	60	60		40	29		
Chicago, Ill		150	1,518	568,764	1,000	1,000			217	4,193	4,123	3,408	715		296		
Cincinnati, Ohio				106,211	144	144									24	24	
Cleveland, Ohio			300	[2]66,432	384	384				598					72		
New York, N. Y	300	200	745	1,413,775	1,585	1,560	25		1,265	1,578					223	21	90
Philadelphia, Pa			3,165	289,615	393	373	20	87	198	688					107		
Pittsburg, Pa				120,232	214	214				120							
St. Louis, Mo		150		208,775	268	268			360	260					22		
San Francisco, Cal				115,921	182	182				89					101		
Total for cities of 100,000 to 300,000 in 1900		150	520	[3]1,361,132	2,708	2,677	31			4,460	3,269	2,576	693		599	60	
Allegheny, Pa				30,313	35	35				25							
Columbus, Ohio				28,398	73	73				409							
Denver, Colo				25,993	146	146				321	370	150	220		49	7	
Detroit, Mich			66	128,477	159	159				153					39		
Fall River, Mass				62,195	107	107				50							
Indianapolis, Ind				31,351	87	87				80					20	20	
Jersey City, N. J				77,279	38	38				144							
Kansas City, Mo				19,077	157	157				213	78	78			60		
Los Angeles, Cal		150		36,695	266	266				920					71	10	
Louisville, Ky				85,170	52	52				379							
Memphis, Tenn				5,270	59	28	31			29							
Milwaukee, Wis				101,453	94	94				96							
Minneapolis, Minn				45,642	251	251				296	1,814	1,455	359		78		
New Haven, Conn				45,383	57	57											
New Orleans, La				148,579	45	45				85					23		
Newark, N. J			180	71,845	205	205				18							
Omaha, Nebr				15,053	126	126				80	395	335	60				
Paterson, N. J				27,961	39	39				40							
Providence, R. I				100,324	112	112				45					11		

[1] Exclusive of statistics for Roman Catholic Church not reported separately by cities for Rochester diocese and parts of Cleveland and Detroit dioceses.
[2] Exclusive of statistics for Roman Catholic Church not reported separately by cities for part of Cleveland diocese.
[3] Exclusive of statistics for Roman Catholic Church not reported separately by cities for Rochester diocese and part of Cleveland diocese.

Table 6.—POPULATION AND COMMUNICANTS OR MEMBERS FOR EACH CITY OF 25,000 INHABITANTS OR MORE IN 1900, BY DENOMINATIONS (IN DETAIL): 1906—Continued.

CITY.	REFORMED BODIES—cont'd. Hungarian Reformed Church in America.	Reformed Catholic Church.	Reformed Episcopal Church.	Roman Catholic Church.	SALVATIONISTS. Total.	SALVATIONISTS. Salvation Army.	SALVATIONISTS. American Salvation Army.	Schwenkfelders.	Society for Ethical Culture.	Spiritualists.	SWEDISH EVANGELICAL BODIES. Total.	SWEDISH EVANGELICAL BODIES. Swedish Evangelical Mission Covenant of America.	SWEDISH EVANGELICAL BODIES. Swedish Evangelical Free Mission.	Temple Society in the United States (Friends of the Temple).	THEOSOPHICAL SOCIETIES. Total.	THEOSOPHICAL SOCIETIES. Theosophical Society in America.	THEOSOPHICAL SOCIETIES. Theosophical Society, New York.
Total for cities of 100,000 to 300,000 in 1900—Continued.																	
Rochester, N. Y				(1)	85	85				100					16		
St. Joseph, Mo				9,980	58	58				75					33		
St. Paul, Minn				72,899	90	90				291	612	558	54		53		
Scranton, Pa			274	46,736	61	61											
Syracuse, N. Y				42,649	42	42				102					16	7	
Toledo, Ohio				[2]12,072	72	72				288					63		
Washington, D. C				43,778	18	18				143					67	16	
Worcester, Mass				46,560	174	174				76							
Total for cities of 50,000 to 100,000 in 1900	550		816	802,436	2,128	2,061	67			2,957	1,551	1,437	114		176	31	
Albany, N. Y			70	38,543	23	23				150							
Atlanta, Ga				5,079	34	34				6							
Bridgeport, Conn	250			36,134	51	51											
Cambridge, Mass				33,043	130	130											
Camden, N. J				12,088	37	37											
Charleston, S. C			501	7,602	8	8											
Dayton, Ohio				24,909	36	36				64							
Des Moines, Iowa				3,658	96	96					247	192	55				
Duluth, Minn				11,097	103	103					421	421			13		
Elizabeth, N. J				17,250	26	26											
Erie, Pa				22,088													
Evansville, Ind				17,660						18							
Grand Rapids, Mich				19,003	83	83				80	265	265			10		
Harrisburg, Pa				2,547	27		27										
Hartford, Conn				27,092	28	28				535							
Hoboken, N. J				16,128	21	21											
Kansas City, Kans				9,154	38	38											
Lawrence, Mass				40,007	67	67				242							
Lowell, Mass				47,073	55	55				200							
Lynn, Mass				20,533	36	36				125							
Manchester, N. H				34,615	24	24				127	165	165					
Nashville, Tenn				5,865	3	3											
New Bedford, Mass				36,115	107	107				209							
Oakland, Cal				25,959	198	198				75					44	11	
Peoria, Ill			145	17,413	23	23					35	35					
Portland, Me				10,162	88	88				40							
Portland, Oreg				17,781	194	194				108	110	110			16		
Reading, Pa				9,579	49	9	40										
Richmond, Va				8,313	24	24				37							
Salt Lake City, Utah				2,550	20	20				20	23		23				
San Antonio, Tex				20,400	33	33				500							
Savannah, Ga				6,843	15	15											
Seattle, Wash				24,589	202	202				339	285	249	36		93	20	
Somerville, Mass				17,150	17	17											
Springfield, Mass				26,840	20	20				15							
Trenton, N. J	300			23,661	41	41											
Troy, N. Y				30,989	16	16				35							
Utica, N. Y				32,164	35	35											
Wilkes-Barre, Pa				20,238	55	55											
Wilmington, Del			100	20,522	65	65				37							
Total for cities of 25,000 to 50,000 in 1900	1,470		60	[3]766,506	2,293	2,283	10			2,945	2,124	1,396	728	186	254	7	
Akron, Ohio				3,655	110	110				75							
Allentown, Pa				3,366													
Altoona, Pa				10,589	24	24											
Atlantic City, N. J				3,115	4	4											
Auburn, N. Y				(1)	23	23											
Augusta, Ga				3,749													
Bay City, Mich				16,652	40	40				124	44		44				
Bayonne, N. J				16,830													
Binghamton, N. Y				7,868	42	42											
Birmingham, Ala				6,770	23	23											
Brockton, Mass				13,532	34	34				85							
Butte, Mont				22,617	49	49				50	50	50			22		
Canton, Ohio				[2]1,445	27	27											
Cedar Rapids, Iowa				3,196													
Chattanooga, Tenn				1,700	35	35											
Chelsea, Mass				7,225	32	32				275							
Chester, Pa				6,266	6	6											
Council Bluffs, Iowa				2,162						8							
Covington, Ky				22,662	61	61											
Dallas, Tex				9,284	32	32				65							

[1] Statistics for Roman Catholic Church not reported separately by cities for Rochester diocese.
[2] Exclusive of statistics for Roman Catholic Church not reported separately by cities for part of Cleveland diocese.
[3] Exclusive of statistics for Roman Catholic Church not reported separately by cities for Rochester diocese and parts of Cleveland and Detroit dioceses.

TABLE 6.—POPULATION AND COMMUNICANTS OR MEMBERS FOR EACH CITY OF 25,000 INHABITANTS OR MORE IN 1900, BY DENOMINATIONS (IN DETAIL): 1906—Continued.

CITY.	REFORMED BODIES—cont'd.	Reformed Catholic Church.	Reformed Episcopal Church.	Roman Catholic Church.	SALVATIONISTS.			Schwenkfelders.	Society for Ethical Culture.	Spiritualists.	SWEDISH EVANGELICAL BODIES.			Temple Society in the United States (Friends of the Temple).	THEOSOPHICAL SOCIETIES.		
	Hungarian Reformed Church in America.				Total.	Salvation Army.	American Salvation Army.				Total.	Swedish Evangelical Mission Covenant of America.	Swedish Evangelical Free Mission.		Total.	Theosophical Society in America.	Theosophical Society, New York.
Total for cities of 25,000 to 50,000 in 1900—Continued.																	
Davenport, Iowa				5,965	26	26				125							
Dubuque, Iowa				17,137													
East St. Louis, Ill				11,695	34	34											
Easton, Pa				3,125	21	21											
Elmira, N. Y				(1)	14	14											
Fitchburg, Mass				14,120	7	7				65							
Fort Wayne, Ind				6,103	12	12				75						7	
Fort Worth, Tex				5,100	31	31				65							
Galveston, Tex				14,872	18	18				61							
Gloucester, Mass				7,133	25	25											
Haverhill, Mass				10,758	50	50				61							
Holyoke, Mass				29,379	8	8									36		
Houston, Tex				13,743	24	24				50							
Jackson, Mich				(2)	33	33				84					7		
Jacksonville, Fla				1,700	5	5				50							
Johnstown, Pa	1,250			16,625	14	14											
Joliet, Ill				18,	68	68					193	130	63				
Joplin, Mo					141	141				110							
Knoxville, Tenn				809													
La Crosse, Wis				12, [illegible]						18							
Lancaster, Pa			60	4, 2	10		10			26							
Lexington, Ky				2,													
Lincoln, Nebr				5,	8	8				307	61	61			21		
Little Rock, Ark				5, 10	42	42											
McKeesport, Pa				11, [illegible]	49	49				40	205	42	163				
Malden, Mass				10, 923	38	38				29							
Mobile, Ala				13, 579	4	4											
Montgomery, Ala				3,	4	4											
New Britain, Conn				13 006	23	23											
Newcastle, Pa				6, [illegible]													
Newport, Ky				7,310						40							
Newton, Mass				10,											7		
Norfolk, Va				4,	11	11									9		
Oshkosh, Wis				7, 839													
Passaic, N. J	220			15, [illegible]													
Pawtucket, R. I				16,	44	44				25							
Pueblo, Colo				12,						20							
Quincy, Ill				20,	52	52											
Racine, Wis				4, 346	63	63											
Rockford, Ill				5, [illegible]	105	105				114	992	570	422				
Sacramento, Cal				6,800	43	43											
Saginaw, Mich				10,335	19	19									37		
Salem, Mass				16,858	25	25				45							
Schenectady, N. Y				13,539	38	38								186			
Sioux City, Iowa				4,173	39	39					197	197					
South Bend, Ind				9,563	28	28					72	72					
South Omaha, Nebr				5,684													
Spokane, Wash				6,994						86					25		
Springfield, Ill				13,175	186	186											
Springfield, Ohio				4,684	86	86											
Superior, Wis				10,	54	54				80	99	99			24		
Tacoma, Wash				4,	114	114				80	36		36		28		
Taunton, Mass				13, 844	11	11											
Terre Haute, Ind				4, [illegible]						200							
Topeka, Kans				2,394		36				65	84	84			14		
Waterbury, Conn				27,454	36	19											
Wheeling, W. Va				10,206	29	21				125							
Williamsport, Pa				3,776						82							
Woonsocket, R. I				22,													
Yonkers, N. Y				38,	9	9				35							
York, Pa				2, 305													
Youngstown, Ohio				[3] 2, [illegible]	56	56					91	91					

[1] Statistics for Roman Catholic Church not reported separately by cities for Rochester diocese.
[2] Statistics for Roman Catholic Church not reported separately by cities for part of Detroit diocese.
[3] Exclusive of statistics for Roman Catholic Church not reported separately by cities for part of Cleveland diocese.

TABLE 6.—POPULATION AND COMMUNICANTS OR MEMBERS FOR EACH CITY OF 25,000 INHABITANTS OR MORE IN 1900, BY DENOMINATIONS (IN DETAIL): 1906—Continued.

CITY.	THEOSOPHICAL SOCIETIES—continued. Theosophical Society, American Section.	Unitarians.	UNITED BRETHREN BODIES. Total.	UNITED BRETHREN BODIES. Church of the United Brethren in Christ.	UNITED BRETHREN BODIES. Church of the United Brethren in Christ (Old Constitution).	Universalists.	Vedanta Society.	Volunteers of America.
Total for cities of 25,000 and over in 1900	1,829	32,840	24,494	24,414	80	21,708	340	1,794
Total for cities of 300,000 and over in 1900	898	13,776	3,179	3,179		6,321	300	367
Baltimore, Md		500	1,485	1,485		250		
Boston, Mass	159	6,854				1,806		53
Buffalo, N. Y	29	388	218	218		454		14
Chicago, Ill	296	776	219	219		1,402		94
Cincinnati, Ohio		200	388	388		135		
Cleveland, Ohio	72	563	654	654		185		40
New York, N. Y	112	2,119				1,546	200	99
Philadelphia, Pa	107	725	215	215		520		
Pittsburg, Pa		225					50	
St. Louis, Mo	22	275				23		42
San Francisco, Cal	101	1,151					50	25
Total for cities of 100,000 to 300,000 in 1900	539	6,553	2,840	2,827	13	5,381	40	849
Allegheny, Pa		80				25		
Columbus, Ohio			506	506		250		
Denver, Colo	42	400	98	98		210		25
Detroit, Mich	39	317				340		95
Fall River, Mass		227						
Indianapolis, Ind		170	433	433		150		87
Jersey City, N. J						54		57
Kansas City, Mo	60	165	13		13	100		25
Los Angeles, Cal	61	276	211	211		82	40	63
Louisville, Ky		440	32	32				
Memphis, Tenn		20						
Milwaukee, Wis		125						30
Minneapolis, Minn	78	412	70	70		840		168
New Haven, Conn						125		
New Orleans, La	23	250						
Newark, N. J						700		201
Omaha, Nebr		160						28
Paterson, N. J								
Providence, R. I	11	1,221				426		18
Rochester, N. Y	16	332				630		
St. Joseph, Mo	33	42						
St. Paul, Minn	53	221				73		32
Scranton, Pa						100		
Syracuse, N. Y	9	405				500		
Toledo, Ohio	63	206	1,217	1,217				
Washington, D. C	51	700	260	260		154		
Worcester, Mass		384				622		20
Total for cities of 50,000 to 100,000 in 1900	145	6,189	8,665	8,598	67	5,407		214
Albany, N. Y		257				37		
Atlanta, Ga		150	189	189		114		
Bridgeport, Conn						183		
Cambridge, Mass		747				481		
Camden, N. J								
Charleston, S. C		160						
Dayton, Ohio			4,662	4,662		60		
Des Moines, Iowa		240	446	446				
Duluth, Minn	13							
Elizabeth, N. J		35						
Erie, Pa		210						6
Evansville, Ind								
Grand Rapids, Mich	10	165	313	313		223		25
Harrisburg, Pa		23	1,592	1,592				
Hartford, Conn		166				250		
Hoboken, N. J								
Kansas City, Kans								
Lawrence, Mass						156		
Lowell, Mass		384				700		
Lynn, Mass		210				625		18
Manchester, N. H		286				400		
Nashville, Tenn			165	65				
New Bedford, Mass		315				185		
Oakland, Cal	33	208	135	35				10
Peoria, Ill						120		50
Portland, Me		598				524		
Portland, Oreg	16	518	173	106	67	60		
Reading, Pa			976	976		250		
Richmond, Va		51						
Salt Lake City, Utah		97						

TABLE 6.—POPULATION AND COMMUNICANTS OR MEMBERS FOR EACH CITY OF 25,000 INHABITANTS OR MORE IN 1900, BY DENOMINATIONS (IN DETAIL): 1906—Continued.

CITY.	THEOSOPHICAL SOCIETIES—continued.		UNITED BRETHREN BODIES.					
	Theosophical Society, American Section.	Unitarians.	Total.	Church of the United Brethren in Christ.	Church of the United Brethren in Christ (Old Constitution).	Universalists.	Vedanta Society.	Volunteers of America.
Total for cities of 50,000 to 100,000 in 1900—Continued.								
San Antonio, Tex		40						
Savannah, Ga								
Seattle, Wash	73	400	14	14				100
Somerville, Mass		395				421		
Springfield, Mass		159				326		
Trenton, N. J								
Troy, N. Y		125				119		
Utica, N. Y						153		
Wilkes-Barre, Pa						20		
Wilmington, Del		250						
Total for cities of 25,000 to 50,000 in 1900	247	6,322	9,810	9,810		4,599		364
Akron, Ohio			417	417		367		
Allentown, Pa			241	241				
Altoona, Pa			1,282	1,282				
Atlantic City, N. J								
Auburn, N. Y						267		
Augusta, Ga								
Bay City, Mich						100		
Bayonne, N. J								
Binghamton, N. Y						145		
Birmingham, Ala								
Brockton, Mass		361				102		
Butte, Mont	22	105						
Canton, Ohio			750	750				
Cedar Rapids, Iowa			275	275		102		
Chattanooga, Tenn		75	32	32				
Chelsea, Mass		108				218		
Chester, Pa								
Council Bluffs, Iowa								
Covington, Ky								
Dallas, Tex		78						
Davenport, Iowa		217						
Dubuque, Iowa						48		
East St. Louis, Ill								
Easton, Pa								
Elmira, N. Y								35
Fitchburg, Mass		550				210		
Fort Wayne, Ind			326	326				
Fort Worth, Tex								
Galveston, Tex								
Gloucester, Mass		200				468		
Haverhill, Mass		215				143		
Holyoke, Mass	36	75						
Houston, Tex								
Jackson, Mich	7	75						20
Jacksonville, Fla		75						
Johnstown, Pa			1,142	1,142				8
Joliet, Ill						200		
Joplin, Mo								
Knoxville, Tenn			245	245		27		
La Crosse, Wis						200		
Lancaster, Pa		49	789	789				
Lexington, Ky								
Lincoln, Nebr	21	160	123	123				40
Little Rock, Ark						35		
McKeesport, Pa		25	449	449				12
Malden, Mass		50				284		
Mobile, Ala								
Montgomery, Ala								
New Britain, Conn								
Newcastle, Pa		27						40
Newport, Ky			150	150				
Newton, Mass	17	1,657						
Norfolk, Va	9							
Oshkosh, Wis						54		
Passaic, N. J		125						
Pawtucket, R. I						248		
Pueblo, Colo		56	64	64				
Quincy, Ill		192	91	91				
Racine, Wis						157		
Rockford, Ill								
Sacramento, Cal	7	24	88	88				
Saginaw, Mich	37							
Salem, Mass		1,050				229		
Schenectady, N. Y		90						
Sioux City, Iowa		308						9

TABLE 6.—POPULATION AND COMMUNICANTS OR MEMBERS FOR EACH CITY OF 25,000 INHABITANTS OR MORE IN 1900, BY DENOMINATIONS (IN DETAIL): 1906—Continued.

CITY.	THEOSOPHICAL SOCIETIES—continued.	Unitarians.	UNITED BRETHREN BODIES.			Universalists.	Vedanta Society.	Volunteers of America.
	Theosophical Society, American Section.		Total.	Church of the United Brethren in Christ.	Church of the United Brethren in Christ (Old Constitution).			
Total for cities of 25,000 to 50,000 in 1900—Continued.								
South Bend, Ind.			85	85				
South Omaha, Nebr.								
Spokane, Wash.	25	75	116	116		98		75
Springfield, Ill.			240	240				20
Springfield, Ohio.			308	308		105		15
Superior, Wis.	24	25						
Tacoma, Wash.	28					69		50
Taunton, Mass.						390		
Terre Haute, Ind.			821	821				22
Topeka, Kans.	14	78	183	183				
Waterbury, Conn.								
Wheeling, W. Va.								
Williamsport, Pa.			214	214				
Woonsocket, R. I.						333		
Yonkers, N. Y.		135						
York, Pa.			1,379	1,379				
Youngstown, Ohio.		62						14

TABLE 7.—ORGANIZATIONS, COMMUNICANTS OR MEMBERS, PLACES OF WORSHIP, VALUE OF CHURCH PROPERTY, MORE IN 1900, BY SELECTED

	DENOMINATION.	Total number of organizations.	COMMUNICANTS OR MEMBERS.				
			Number of organizations reporting.	Total number reported.	Sex.		
					Number of organizations reporting.	Male.	Female.
1	Akron, Ohio	59	58	18,370	54	7,277	10,073
2	Protestant bodies	51	51	14,425	49	5,404	8,121
	Baptist bodies:						
3	Baptists—Northern and National (Colored) Conventions	3	3	661	3	230	431
4	Congregationalists	3	3	1,361	3	470	891
	Disciples or Christians:						
5	Disciples of Christ	4	4	1,973	4	651	1,322
	Evangelical bodies:						
6	Evangelical Association	1	1	510	1	204	306
7	United Evangelical Church	1	1	285	1	120	165
	Lutheran bodies:						
8	General Synod of the Evangelical Lutheran Church in the United States of America	2	2	675	2	300	375
9	General Council of the Evangelical Lutheran Church in North America	1	1	347	1	141	206
10	Evangelical Lutheran Synodical Conference of America	2	2	1,062	2	434	628
11	Other Lutheran bodies	2	2	228	1	21	7
	Methodist bodies:						
12	Methodist Episcopal Church	8	8	2,660	8	1,249	1,411
13	Other Methodist bodies	3	3	98	3	30	68
	Presbyterian bodies:						
14	Presbyterian Church in the United States of America	2	2	430	2	149	281
15	United Presbyterian Church of North America	1	1	50	1	18	32
16	Protestant Episcopal Church	3	3	808	3	298	510
	Reformed bodies:						
17	Reformed Church in the United States	6	6	2,158	5	669	789
	United Brethren bodies:						
18	Church of the United Brethren in Christ	2	2	417	2	129	288
19	Universalists	1	1	367	1	167	200
20	Other Protestant bodies	6	6	335	6	124	211
21	Roman Catholic Church	3	3	3,655	3	1,806	1,849
22	Jewish congregations	2	1	[1] 50	......	......	......
23	All other bodies	3	3	240	2	67	103
1	Albany, N. Y	81	81	59,612	71	25,194	30,880
2	Protestant bodies	58	58	19,896	53	6,432	10,810
	Baptist bodies:						
3	Baptists—Northern Convention	8	8	2,804	8	871	1,933
4	Congregationalists	1	1	304	1	103	201
5	German Evangelical Synod of North America	1	1	550	1	250	300
	Lutheran bodies:						
6	General Synod of the Evangelical Lutheran Church in the United States of America	1	1	373	1	140	233
7	General Council of the Evangelical Lutheran Church in North America	4	4	2,268	3	795	1,073
8	Evangelical Lutheran Synodical Conference of America	3	3	1,127	3	437	690
	Methodist bodies:						
9	Methodist Episcopal Church	5	5	1,959	5	672	1,287
10	African Methodist Episcopal Church	1	1	60	1	9	51
	Presbyterian bodies:						
11	Presbyterian Church in the United States of America	8	8	3,563	8	1,345	2,218
12	United Presbyterian Church of North America	1	1	119	1	43	76
13	Protestant Episcopal Church	7	7	3,983	4	1,015	1,424
	Reformed bodies:						
14	Reformed Church in America	6	6	1,907	5	376	821
15	Other Protestant bodies	12	12	879	12	376	503
16	Roman Catholic Church	15	15	38,543	15	18,645	19,898
17	Jewish congregations	4	4	[1] 484	......	......	......
	Eastern Orthodox Churches:						
18	Greek Orthodox Church	1	1	400	......	......	......
19	All other bodies	3	3	289	3	117	172
1	Allegheny, Pa	111	109	61,456	101	26,367	31,053
2	Protestant bodies	93	91	29,000	84	9,727	15,587
	Baptist bodies:						
3	Baptists—Northern and National (Colored) Conventions	7	7	1,328	7	522	806
	Disciples or Christians:						
4	Disciples of Christ	3	3	1,989	2	142	204
	German Evangelical Protestant bodies:						
5	German Evangelical Protestant Ministers' Association	1	1	600	1	247	353
6	German Evangelical Protestant Ministers' Conference	1	1	850	......	......	......
7	German Evangelical Synod of North America	2	2	1,467	1	563	669
8	Independent churches	1	1	400	1	150	250
	Lutheran bodies:						
9	General Synod of the Evangelical Lutheran Church in the United States of America	6	6	1,814	6	705	1,109
10	General Council of the Evangelical Lutheran Church in North America	6	6	1,281	6	533	748
11	Evangelical Lutheran Synodical Conference of America	1	1	500	1	208	292
12	Evangelical Lutheran Joint Synod of Ohio and Other States	4	4	1,995	4	837	1,158
13	Immanuel Synod of the Evangelical Lutheran Church of North America	1	1	1,000	1	350	650
14	Slovak Evangelical Lutheran Synod of America	1	1	200	1	135	65
	Methodist bodies:						
15	Methodist Episcopal Church	12	11	3,963	11	1,617	2,346
16	African Methodist Episcopal Church	2	2	539	2	138	401
17	African Methodist Episcopal Zion Church	1	1	375	......	......	......
18	Methodist Protestant Church	2	2	651	2	191	460

[1] Heads of families only.

DEBT ON CHURCH PROPERTY, PARSONAGES, AND SUNDAY SCHOOLS, FOR EACH CITY OF 25,000 INHABITANTS OR DENOMINATIONS: 1906.

PLACES OF WORSHIP.					VALUE OF CHURCH PROPERTY.		DEBT ON CHURCH PROPERTY.		PARSONAGES.		SUNDAY SCHOOLS CONDUCTED BY CHURCH ORGANIZATIONS.				
Number of organizations reporting—		Number of church edifices reported.	Seating capacity of church edifices.		Number of organizations reporting.	Value reported.	Number of organizations reporting.	Amount of debt reported.	Number of organizations reporting.	Value of parsonages reported.	Number of organizations reporting.	Number of Sunday schools reported.	Number of officers and teachers.	Number of scholars.	
Church edifices.	Halls, etc.		Number of organizations reporting.	Seating capacity reported.											
52	4	52	52	26,845	52	$963,350	27	$83,839	22	$107,500	53	53	1,116	12,872	1
48	2	48	48	24,740	48	911,250	25	69,839	19	83,500	48	48	1,082	12,172	2
3	....	3	3	1,600	3	42,500	2	1,850	....	....	3	3	64	572	3
3	....	3	3	1,325	3	53,300	1	500	....	....	3	3	68	885	4
4	....	4	4	2,700	4	68,000	2	3,200	....	....	4	4	112	1,790	5
1	....	1	1	1,200	1	20,000	....	....	1	4,000	1	1	39	550	6
1	....	1	1	350	1	9,000	1	3,064	1	2,000	1	1	18	240	7
2	....	2	2	1,000	2	,000	1	600	1	5,000	2	2	56	745	8
1	....	1	1	300	1	,000	1	3,000	1	5,000	1	1	21	119	9
2	....	2	2	900	2	81,000	1	1,000	1	5,000	1	1	8	87	10
1	1	1	1	250	1	23,000	1	600	1	1,500	1	1	14	176	11
8	....	8	8	4,925	8	238,500	2	6,400	6	28,500	8		222	2,615	12
3	....	3	3	875	3	7,500	2	325	1	1,500	3	8	23	130	13
2	....	2	2	740	2	57,	1	14,000	1	6,500	2	2	38	277	14
1	....	1	1	250	1	8,550	1	2,500	....	....	1	1	12	77	15
3	....	3	3	900	3	91,800	1	10,000	1	7,000	3	3	45	399	16
6	....	6	6	4,050	6	93,500	3	7,800	2	13,000	6	6	236	2,494	17
2	....	2	2	1,350	2	24,500	2	2,900	2	4,500	2	2	40	675	18
1	....	1	1	800	1	50,000	1	3,000	....	....	1	1	19	100	19
4	1	4	4	1,225	4	28,700	2	9,100	....	....	5	5	47	241	20
3	....	3	3	1,980	3	52,000	2	14,000	3	24,000	3	3	16	610	21
....	....	....	....	....	....	....	....	....	....	....	1	1	4	48	22
1	2	1	1	125	1	100	....	....	....	....	1	1	14	42	23
69	10	84	69	52,231	71	5,186,600	32	343,002	39	362,700	71		1,780	17,304	1
52	6	63	52	35,393	53	3,213,025	20	65,002	25	181,000	55	61	1,515	12,000	2
8	....	9	8	6,000	8	480,000	....	....	....	....	8	8	199	1,762	3
1	....	1	1	650	1	45,000	1	2,000	....	....	1	1	22	165	4
1	....	1	1	600	1	26,000	....	....	1	6,500	1	1	26	334	5
1	....	1	1	750	1	90,000	1	6,000	1	10,000	1	1	45	231	6
4	....	4	4	1,600	4	70,000	2	5,200	3	12,000	4	6	154	1,318	7
3	....	3	3	1,600	3	100,000	1	9,180	2	8,000	3	3	52	439	8
5	....	5	5	3,900	5	254,000	1	1,500	5	29,000	5	5	198	1,617	9
1	....	1	1	500	1	12,500	1	200	....	....	1	1	12	50	10
8	....	13	8	7,250	8	584,000	2	12,100	2	13,500	8	10	357	2,978	11
1	....	1	1	400	1	20,000	1	4,000	....	....	1	1	18	97	12
7	....	10	7	6,093	7	1,170,350	4	16,300	6	80,000	6	7	170	1,211	13
6	....	8	6	3,750	6	280,000	3	5,400	3	15,500	6	7	192	1,340	14
6	6	6	6	2,300	7	81,175	3	3,122	2	6,500	10	10	70	458	15
14	....	17	14	13,538	15	1,781,575	9	230,000	14	181,700	15	19	255	5,194	16
3	....	4	3	3,300	3	192,000	3	48,000	....	....	1	1	10	110	17
....	1	....	....	....	....	....	....	....	....	....	....	....	....	....	18
....	3	....	....	....	....	....	....	....	....	....	....	....	....	....	19
101	8	112	100	57,477	103	3,992,050	48	535,358	32	271,250	104	130	2,325	28,038	1
86	5	92	85	45,325	88	2,911,900	38	262,458	18	107,500	89	98	2,156	22,760	2
6	1	7	6	2,930	6	157,000	4	21,958	....	....	7	9	117	804	3
3	....	3	3	1,850	[illegible]	97,500	2	4,700	....	....	3	3	74	1,023	4
1	....	1	1	700	1	20,000	....	....	1	9,000	1	1	18	250	5
1	....	1	1	600	1	20,000	....	....	1	4,800	1	1	25	250	6
2	....	2	2	1,320	2	65,500	2	22,400	2	12,500	2	2	69	841	7
1	....	1	1	800	1	35,000	1	5,000	....	....	1	1	30	350	8
6	....	7	6	2,900	6	144,500	3	11,500	....	....	6	6	164	1,802	9
6	....	6	6	1,650	6	52,000	4	7,400	3	9,200	6	6		1,016	10
1	....	1	1	600	1	25,000	....	....	1	2,500	1	1		210	11
4	....	4	4	2,750	4	132,000	1	20,000	1	5,000	4	4		826	12
1	....	1	1	1,000	1	18,000	....	....	1	12,000	1	1		455	13
1	....	1	....	....	1	7,000	1	200	....	....	....	....	92	....	14
12	....	12	12	6,800	12	679,500	5	43,500	2	15,500	12	12		5,301	15
2	....	2	2	1,125	2	55,000	2	22,000	1	3,000	2	2		225	16
1	....	1	1	800	1	10,000	....	....	....	....	1	1	443	225	17
2	....	2	2	1,600	2	150,000	1	800	1	4,000	2	2	36	500	18

TABLE 7.—ORGANIZATIONS, COMMUNICANTS OR MEMBERS, PLACES OF WORSHIP, VALUE OF CHURCH PROPERTY, MORE IN 1900, BY SELECTED

	DENOMINATION.	Total number of organizations.	COMMUNICANTS OR MEMBERS.				
			Number of organizations reporting.	Total number reported.	Sex.		
					Number of organizations reporting.	Male.	Female.
	Allegheny, Pa.—Continued.						
	Protestant bodies—Continued.						
	Presbyterian bodies:						
19	Presbyterian Church in the United States of America	10	10	3,067	9	871	1,755
20	United Presbyterian Church of North America	14	14	4,874	14	1,751	3,123
21	Synod of the Reformed Presbyterian Church of North America	2	2	323	2	101	222
22	Protestant Episcopal Church	5	4	920	3	316	474
23	Other Protestant bodies	11	11	864	10	350	502
24	Roman Catholic Church	14	14	30,313	14	15,404	14,909
	Eastern Orthodox Churches:						
25	Russian Orthodox Church	1	1	1,600	1	1,150	450
26	Greek Orthodox Church	1	1	350	....	....	....
27	All other bodies	2	2	193	2	86	107
1	Allentown, Pa.	53	52	19,985	49	8,307	10,949
2	Protestant bodies	48	48	16,499	47	6,701	9,189
	Baptist bodies:						
3	Baptists—Northern Convention	4	2	322	2	127	195
	Evangelical bodies:						
4	Evangelical Association	4	4	654	4	239	415
5	United Evangelical Church	5	5	1,700	5	651	1,049
	Lutheran bodies:						
6	General Synod of the Evangelical Lutheran Church in the United States of America	2	2	1,142	2	500	642
7	General Council of the Evangelical Lutheran Church in North America	8	8	3,800	7	1,374	1,817
	Methodist bodies:						
8	Methodist Episcopal Church	2	2	597	2	209	388
9	Free Methodist Church of North America	1	1	43	1	10	33
	Presbyterian bodies:						
10	Presbyterian Church in the United States of America	1	1	331	1	111	220
11	Protestant Episcopal Church	2	2	316	2	132	184
	Reformed bodies:						
12	Reformed Church in the United States	9	9	6,819	9	3,034	3,785
13	Other Protestant bodies	12	12	775	12	314	461
14	Roman Catholic Church	2	2	3,366	2	1,606	1,760
15	Jewish congregations	2	1	[1] 60	....	....	....
	Eastern Orthodox Churches:						
16	Greek Orthodox Church	1	1	60	....	....	....
1	Altoona, Pa.	57	55	26,715	50	10,951	14,462
	Protestant bodies	47	47	15,979	45	5,662	9,162
	Baptist bodies:						
3	Baptists—Northern and National (Colored) Conventions	4	4	879	3	98	206
4	Dunkers or German Baptist Brethren	2	2	401	2	152	249
	Lutheran bodies:						
5	General Synod of the Evangelical Lutheran Church in the United States of America	6	6	3,183	6	1,197	1,986
6	General Council of the Evangelical Lutheran Church in North America	2	2	513	2	226	287
	Methodist bodies:						
7	Methodist Episcopal Church	9	9	4,167	9	1,697	2,470
8	Other Methodist bodies	2	2	46	2	16	30
	Presbyterian bodies:						
9	Presbyterian Church in the United States of America	5	5	2,021	5	729	1,292
10	United Presbyterian Church of North America	2	2	296	2	120	176
11	Protestant Episcopal Church	1	1	650	1	298	352
	Reformed bodies:						
12	Reformed Church in the United States	3	3	1,539	2	828	631
	United Brethren bodies:						
13	Church of the United Brethren in Christ	3	3	1,282	3	443	839
14	Other Protestant bodies	8	8	1,002	8	358	644
15	Roman Catholic Church	5	5	10,589	5	5,289	5,300
16	Jewish congregations	4	2	[1] 67	....	....	....
	Eastern Orthodox Churches:						
17	Greek Orthodox Church	1	1	80	....	....	....
1	Atlanta, Ga.	174	170	59,479	158	21,279	33,302
	Protestant bodies	165	163	53,644	153	18,410	30,586
	Baptist bodies:						
3	Baptists—Southern Convention	20	20	10,462	18	3,328	6,178
4	Baptists—National Convention (Colored)	24	24	11,754	24	4,314	7,440
5	Primitive Baptists	1	1	45	1	15	30
6	Congregationalists	5	5	1,138	5	493	645
	Disciples or Christians:						
7	Disciples of Christ	2	2	947	2	356	591
8	Churches of Christ	1	1	108	1	38	70
	Methodist bodies:						
9	Methodist Episcopal Church	10	10	2,101	8	364	698
10	African Methodist Episcopal Church	28	28	5,470	28	1,594	3,876
11	Methodist Episcopal Church, South	21	21	11,501	18	4,716	6,290
12	Colored Methodist Episcopal Church	5	5	1,019	5	367	652
13	Other Methodist bodies	6	6	336	6	139	197
14	Nonsectarian Churches of Bible Faith	1	1	800	1	500	300
	Presbyterian bodies:						
15	Presbyterian Church in the United States	11	11	4,067	10	1,180	1,905
16	Other Presbyterian bodies	3	3	320	3	120	200
17	Protestant Episcopal Church	12	10	2,332	8	400	756
18	Other Protestant bodies	15	15	1,244	15	486	758

DEBT ON CHURCH PROPERTY, PARSONAGES, AND SUNDAY SCHOOLS, FOR EACH CITY OF 25,000 INHABITANTS OR DENOMINATIONS: 1906—Continued.

PLACES OF WORSHIP.					VALUE OF CHURCH PROPERTY.		DEBT ON CHURCH PROPERTY.		PARSONAGES.		SUNDAY SCHOOLS CONDUCTED BY CHURCH ORGANIZATIONS.				
Number of organizations reporting— Church edifices.	Number of organizations reporting— Halls, etc.	Number of church edifices reported.	Seating capacity of church edifices. Number of organizations reporting.	Seating capacity of church edifices. Seating capacity reported.	Number of organizations reporting.	Value reported.	Number of organizations reporting.	Amount of debt reported.	Number of organizations reporting.	Value of parsonages reported.	Number of organizations reporting.	Number of Sunday schools reported.	Number of officers and teachers.	Number of scholars.	
10	......	11	10	4,875	10	$421,000	4	$36,300	1	$10,000	10	12	215	2,133	19
14	......	14	14	8,025	14	485,500	4	32,000	1	4,500	14	15	479	4,812	20
2	......	4	2	1,400	2	90,000	1	2,000	......	......	2	6	112	674	21
5	......	6	5	1,700	5	131,000	2	5,700	1	13,000	5	5	55	520	22
5	4	5	5	1,900	7	116,400	1	27,000	1	2,500	8	8	78	543	23
14	......	19	14	11,152	14	1,055,150	9	264,200	13	159,750	14	31	165	5,253	24
1	......	1	1	1,000	1	25,000	1	8,700	1	4,000	......	......	......	......	25
......	1	......	......	......	......	......	......	......	......	......	......	......	......	......	26
......	2	......	......	......	......	......	......	......	......	......	1	1	4	25	27
47	6	55	46	29,575	46	1,309,200	26	179,320	20	81,400	49	52	1,268	17,975	1
43	5	51	42	27,325	43	1,190,700	24	169,820	18	69,400	47	49	1,221	17,585	2
2	......	3	2	1,050	2	43,000	1	12,000	2	7,000	2	2	31	346	3
4	......	4	4	2,050	4	69,200	4	7,725	3	10,200	4	4	94	1,018	4
5	......	5	5	3,800	5	110,000	3	17,000	1	3,500	5	5	162	2,525	5
2	......	3	1	1,800	2	148,000	1	4,000	1	5,000	2	2	84	1,225	6
8	......	10	8	5,000	8	225,000	4	53,320	1	6,000	8	9	253	2,893	7
2	......	2	2	800	2	32,000	1	600	2	6,500	2	2	60	675	8
1	......	1	1	200	1	3,500	1	1,600	1	2,000	1	1	12	60	9
1	......	1	1	600	1	50,000	......	......	......	......	1	1	18	430	10
2	......	2	2	500	2	20,000	......	......	2	6,200	2	2	18	230	11
9	......	12	9	9,000	9	440,000	5	55,575	2	12,500	9	9	341	6,999	12
7	5	8	7	2,525	7	50,000	4	18,000	3	10,500	11	12	148	1,184	13
2	......	2	2	1,700	2	115,000	1	7,000	2	12,000	1	1	45	350	14
2	......	2	2	550	1	3,500	1	2,500	......	......	1	2	2	40	15
......	1	......	......	......	......	......	......	......	......	......	......	......	......	......	16
49	3	53	49	28,055	50	1,419,100	33	174,140	32	168,300	50	53	1,216	13,761	1
43	2	44	43	23,675	44	1,155,800	28	150,690	28	130,800	47	50	1,191	12,621	2
4	......	4	4	1,450	4	84,000	3	13,129	2	13,000	4	4	75	813	3
2	......	2	2	550	2	6,500	1	300	......	......	2	2	33	230	4
6	......	6	6	3,800	6	257,000	5	30,000	5	23,000	6	7	224	2,368	5
1	1	1	1	900	1	40,000	......	......	1	6,500	2	2	44	365	6
8	......	8	8	5,800	8	295,000	7	52,300	7	35,000	9	9	319	3,194	7
2	......	2	2	450	2	4,000	2	1,611	1	800	2	2	12	45	8
5	......	6	5	3,000	5	201,000	1	7,000	2	11,000	5	5	120	1,487	9
2	......	2	2	925	2	25,000	2	10,400	1	3,500	2	2	22	380	10
1	......	1	1	600	1	50,000	......	......	1	10,000	1	2	28	240	11
3	......	3	3	2,300	3	77,000	2	24,000	2	10,000	3	3	76	1,110	12
3	......	3	3	1,850	3	71,500	......	......	2	10,000	3	3	104	1,235	13
6	1	6	6	2,050	7	44,800	5	11,950	4	8,000	8	9	184	1,154	14
5	......	8	5	4,250	5	254,300	4	20,450	4	37,500	2	2	21	1,100	15
1	......	1	1	130	1	9,000	1	3,000	......	......	1	1	4	40	16
......		......	......	......	......	......	......	......	......	......	......	......	......	......	17
158	16	169	156	84,943	157	2,960,125	77	277,612	37	145,675	160	189	2,628	29,822	1
150	15	161	148	80,243	149	2,695,125	70	237,612	35	124,675	154	182	2,551	28,502	2
20	......	26	20	14,700	20	607,800	11	46,801	2	12,000	20	31	539	7,061	3
23	1	23	23	14,700	22	167,200	9	8,763	2	2,500	24	26	221	3,219	4
1	......	1	1	300	1	2,250	......	......	......	......	......	......	......	......	5
5	......	5	5	2,150	5	128,350	4	21,350	2	5,000	5	9	89	1,070	6
2	......	2	2	1,900	2	80,000	......	......	......	......	2	2	46	430	7
1	......	1	1	500	1	2,500	1	500	......	......	......	......	......	......	8
10	......	10	9	3,800	9	81,400	8	6,801	3	6,800	10	10	124	1,098	9
23	5	23	23	9,500	23	159,000	17	23,955	5	6,875	26	26	255	2,209	10
21	......	21	21	13,100	21	542,500	2	48,000	11	56,000	21	25	592	6,527	11
5	......	7	5	3,900	5	28,900	2	2,600	2	2,000	5	7	47	630	12
6	......	6	5	1,450	5	13,800	2	2,760	......	......	5	5	34	200	13
......	1	......	......	......	......	......	......	......	......	......	1	1	25	500	14
11	......	12	11	7,025	11	328,000	4	16,650	3	17,500	11	15	356	3,731	15
3	......	3	3	1,270	3	57,500	2	12,000	2	6,000	3	4	36	255	16
12	......	14	12	3,548	12	411,200	4	35,980	1	2,000	10	10	108	1,043	17
7	8	7	7	2,400	9	84,725	4	11,452	2	8,000	11	11	79	539	18

TABLE 7.—ORGANIZATIONS, COMMUNICANTS OR MEMBERS, PLACES OF WORSHIP, VALUE OF CHURCH PROPERTY, MORE IN 1900, BY SELECTED

	DENOMINATION.	Total number of organizations.	COMMUNICANTS OR MEMBERS.				
			Number of organizations reporting.	Total number reported.	Sex.		
					Number of organizations reporting.	Male.	Female.
	Atlanta, Ga.—Continued.						
19	Roman Catholic Church	3	3	5,079	3	2,389	2,690
20	Jewish congregations	4	2	[1] 250	....	....	....
	Eastern Orthodox Churches:						
21	Greek Orthodox Church	1	1	500	1	475	25
22	Spiritualists	1	1	6	1	5	1
1	Atlantic City, N. J.	36	35	10,842	29	3,922	5,870
2	Protestant bodies	30	29	7,527	26	2,432	4,245
	Baptist bodies:						
3	Baptists—Northern Convention	5	5	1,547	5	623	924
4	Baptists—National Convention (Colored)	1	1	280	1	31	249
	Methodist bodies:						
5	Methodist Episcopal Church	5	5	1,900	4	713	1,165
6	African Methodist Episcopal Church	1	1	800	1	300	500
7	African Methodist Episcopal Zion Church	1	1	175	1	65	110
8	Methodist Protestant Church	3	3	752	2	138	164
9	Other African Methodist bodies	2	2	75	2	30	45
	Presbyterian bodies:						
10	Presbyterian Church in the United States of America	5	5	1,027	4	257	392
11	Protestant Episcopal Church	4	3	887	3	246	641
12	Other Protestant bodies	3	3	84	3	29	55
13	Roman Catholic Church	3	3	3,115	3	1,490	1,625
14	Jewish congregations	3	3	[1] 200	....	....	....
1	Auburn, N. Y.	23	23	7,459	21	2,396	4,344
2	Protestant bodies	22	22	7,419	21	2,396	4,344
	Baptist bodies:						
3	Baptists—Northern Convention	3	3	1,200	2	157	364
	Disciples or Christians:						
4	Disciples of Christ	1	1	450	1	175	275
5	German Evangelical Synod of North America	1	1	336	1	158	178
	Methodist bodies:						
6	Methodist Episcopal Church	3	3	1,552	3	632	920
7	African Methodist Episcopal Zion Church	1	1	65	1	29	36
	Presbyterian bodies:						
8	Presbyterian Church in the United States of America	6	6	2,663	6	877	1,786
9	Protestant Episcopal Church	2	2	815	2	260	555
10	Universalists	1	1	267	1	76	191
11	Other Protestant bodies	4	4	71	4	32	39
12	Roman Catholic Church [1]	....	....	....	....	....	....
13	Jewish congregations	1	1	[1] 40	....	....	....
1	Augusta, Ga.	71	70	22,890	62	8,561	12,917
2	Protestant bodies	66	66	18,996	60	6,713	11,016
	Baptist bodies:						
3	Baptists—Southern Convention	5	5	2,444	4	861	1,083
4	Baptists—National Convention (Colored)	26	26	7,655	26	2,792	4,863
	Disciples or Christians:						
5	Disciples of Christ		2	806	2	230	576
	Lutheran bodies:						
6	United Synod of the Evangelical Lutheran Church in the South	2	2	537	1	169	200
	Methodist bodies:						
7	African Methodist Episcopal Church	3	3	840	3	342	498
8	Methodist Episcopal Church, South	6	6	3,186	6	1,337	1,849
9	Colored Methodist Episcopal Church	5	5	1,050	5	340	710
10	Other Methodist bodies	4	4	330	4	99	231
	Presbyterian bodies:						
11	Presbyterian Church in the United States of America	2	2	145	1	30	50
12	Presbyterian Church in the United States	3	3	924	3	317	607
13	Protestant Episcopal Church	6	6	932	3	134	264
14	Other Protestant bodies	2	2	147	2	62	85
15	Roman Catholic Church	2	2	3,749	2	1,848	1,901
16	Jewish congregations	2	1	[1] 65	....	....	....
	Eastern Orthodox Churches:						
17	Greek Orthodox Church	1	1	80	....	....	....
1	Baltimore, Md.	443	437	224,968	353	71,640	105,320
	Protestant bodies	365	362	120,985	316	35,885	64,676
	Baptist bodies:						
3	Baptists—Southern Convention	20	20	7,461	17	2,441	4,800
4	Baptists—National Convention (Colored)	32	32	16,081	27	3,836	7,488
5	Free Baptists	10	8	1,120	2	22	38
6	Primitive Baptists	1	1	41	1	12	29
7	Congregationalists	4	4	676	4	240	436
	Disciples or Christians:						
8	Disciples of Christ	6	6	1,469	6	612	857
	Evangelical bodies:						
9	Evangelical Association	3	3	341	3	102	239
10	United Evangelical Church	3	3	682	3	225	457

[1] Heads of families only.

DEBT ON CHURCH PROPERTY, PARSONAGES, AND SUNDAY SCHOOLS, FOR EACH CITY OF 25,000 INHABITANTS OR DENOMINATIONS: 1906—Continued.

PLACES OF WORSHIP.					VALUE OF CHURCH PROPERTY.		DEBT ON CHURCH PROPERTY.		PARSONAGES.		SUNDAY SCHOOLS CONDUCTED BY CHURCH ORGANIZATIONS.				
Number of organizations reporting—		Number of church edifices reported.	Seating capacity of church edifices.		Number of organizations reporting.	Value reported.	Number of organizations reporting.	Amount of debt reported.	Number of organizations reporting.	Value of parsonages reported.	Number of organizations reporting.	Number of Sunday schools reported.	Number of officers and teachers.	Number of scholars.	
Church edifices.	Halls, etc.		Number of organizations reporting.	Seating capacity reported.											
3	....	3	3	1,800	3	$145,000	2	$12,000	2	$21,000	3	3	63	685	19
4	....	4	4	2,400	4	108,000	4	26,000	....	....	2	3	13	535	20
1	....	1	1	500	1	12,000	1	2,000	....	....	1	1	1	100	21
....	1	....	....	....	....	....	....	....	....	....	....	....	....	....	22
33	3	36	31	17,342	34	989,350	26	147,922	13	98,000	34	35	615	6,111	1
27	3	29	26	13,900	28	710,650	23	140,572	11	58,000	28	29	563	5,431	2
5	....	5	5	2,000	5	72,500	3	9,700	1	7,000	5	5	92	748	3
1	....	1	1	800	1	18,000	1	4,000	....	....	1	1	9	70	4
5	....	6	4	2,750	5	163,500	5	35,700	2	10,000	5	5	154	1,385	5
1	....	1	1	800	1	25,000	1	14,000	1	1,500	1	1	54	410	6
1	....	1	1	1,200	1	35,000	1	9,000	1	2,000	1	1	14	75	7
3	....	3	3	1,450	3	68,000	3	21,350	2	11,500	3	3	97	1,202	8
1	1	1	1	50	1	500	1	300	....	....	2	2	9	58	9
5	....	6	5	2,500	5	178,000	4	28,500	2	13,000	5	6	74	962	10
4	....	4	4	2,150	4	130,000	2	12,500	2	13,000	3	3	46	440	11
1	2	1	1	200	2	20,150	2	5,522	....	....	2	2	14	81	12
3	....	4	3	2,942	3	249,700	1	2,850	2	40,000	3	3	46	540	13
3	....	3	2	500	3	29,000	2	4,500	....	....	3	3	6	140	14
18	3	21	18	10,878	23	757,577	2	30,900	9	56,000	20	20	533	4,823	1
18	2	21	18	10,878	22	757,277	2	30,900	9	56,000	19	19	532	4,811	2
3	....	3	3	1,408	3	143,000		900	1	5,000	3	3	117	872	3
1	....	1	1	400	1	30,000	....	....	1	5,000	1	1	30	225	4
1	....	1	1	275	1	12,000	....	....	1	5,000	1	1	19	180	5
3	....	3	3	2,520	3	130,000		30,000	3	16,500	3	3	89	1,048	6
1	....	1	1	300	1	8,000	....	....	....	....	1	1	15	85	7
6	....	7	6	3,925	6	283,700	....	....	2	16,500	5	5	195	1,855	8
2	....	4	2	1,350	2	115,000	....	....	1	8,000	2	2	41	390	9
1	....	1	1	700	1	35,000	....	....	....	....	1	1	20	125	10
....	2	....	....	....	4	577	....	....	....	....	2	2	6	31	11
....	....	....	....	....	....	....	....	....	....	....	....	....	....	....	12
....	1	....	....	....	1	300	....	....	....	....	1	1	1	12	13
67	3	70	66	31,330	67	1,107,815	24	38,179	31	103,700	69	74	774	7,774	1
63	2	65	62	29,011	64	941,815	21	28,779	30	99,700	65	69	751	7,352	2
5	....	5	5	2,600	5	94,500	....	....	3	8,500	5	7	106	1,050	3
25	1	25	24	12,150	25	165,300	11	14,139	4	3,900	25	25	150	1,937	4
2	....	2	2	1,080	2	107,500	....	....	[illegible]	11,250	2	2	27	281	5
2	....	2	2	600	2	29,500	1	1,500	[illegible]	3,200		2	35	290	6
3	....	3	3	1,500	3	42,400	3	3,660	1	2,000		3	25	203	7
6	....	6	6	3,200	6	152,000	1	4,000	6	25,000	6	6	133	1,332	8
5	....	5	5	1,900	5	21,000	2	105	4	6,350	5	5	33	310	9
3	....	3	3	1,550	3	7,500	1	275	3	2,000	4	4	37	242	10
2	....	2	2	700	2	8,000	....	....	....	....	2	2	35	600	11
3	....	4	3	1,550	3	233,000	1	5,000	2	17,500	3	5	101	515	12
6	....	7	6	1,881	6	79,000	....	....	4	20,000	6	6	55	490	13
1	1	1	1	300	2	2,115	1	100	....	....	2	2	14	102	14
2	....	2	2	1,944	1	150,000	1	7,800		4,000	2	3	18	375	15
2	....	3	2	375	2	16,000	2	1,600	....	....	2	2	5	47	16
....	1	....	....	....	....	....	....	....	....	....	....	....	....	....	17
394	28	433	386	226,837	395	14,155,477	207	1,639,601	187	1,043,333	391	419	9,056	98,976	1
327	21	359	323	186,359	332	10,610,177	161	848,056	152	794,833	349	374	8,386	87,995	2
20	....	22	20	12,500	20	771,250	9	80,000	4	15,500	20	27	671	7,058	3
27	4	27	24	12,550	27	269,833	18	43,706	3	6,700	29	30	384	5,179	4
2	....	2	2	350	2	1,300	2	260	....	....	6	6	56	330	5
1	....	1	1	350	1	15,000	....	....	....	....	....	....	....	....	6
4	....	4	4	1,860	4	145,000	3	15,870	....	....	4	4	61	580	7
6	....	6	6	3,100	6	155,000	4	44,260	....	....	6	6	143	1,466	8
3	....	3	3	900	3	46,750	2	5,400	1	1,000	3	3	48	250	9
3	....	3	3	1,275	3	48,453	3	19,025	3	8,000	3	3	92	870	10

[1] Statistics not reported separately by cities for Rochester diocese.

TABLE 7.—ORGANIZATIONS, COMMUNICANTS OR MEMBERS, PLACES OF WORSHIP, VALUE OF CHURCH PROPERTY, MORE IN 1900, BY SELECTED

	DENOMINATION.	Total number of organizations.	COMMUNICANTS OR MEMBERS.				
			Number of organizations reporting.	Total number reported.	Sex.		
					Number of organizations reporting.	Male.	Female.
	Baltimore, Md.—Continued.						
	Protestant bodies—Continued.						
	Friends:						
11	Society of Friends (Orthodox)	2	2	331	2	154	177
12	Religious Society of Friends (Hicksite)	2	2	610	2	275	335
	German Evangelical Protestant bodies:						
13	German Evangelical Protestant Ministers' Association	1	1	970	1	401	569
14	German Evangelical Synod of North America	9	9	7,105	7	1,890	2,956
15	Independent churches	7	7	1,306	7	425	881
	Lutheran bodies:						
16	General Synod of the Evangelical Lutheran Church in the United States of America	15	15	7,748	13	2,563	4,006
17	Evangelical Lutheran Synodical Conference of America	10	10	3,188	7	996	1,281
18	Evangelical Lutheran Joint Synod of Ohio and Other States	7	7	1,877	7	711	1,166
19	Other Lutheran bodies	2	2	106	1	20	30
	Methodist bodies:						
20	Methodist Episcopal Church	73	73	24,605	69	7,778	14,509
21	Union American Methodist Episcopal Church (Colored)	5	5	640	5	238	402
22	African Methodist Episcopal Church	12	12	4,283	7	732	1,820
23	Methodist Protestant Church	16	16	3,417	16	1,167	2,250
24	Methodist Episcopal Church, South	7	7	2,040	7	658	1,382
25	Other Methodist bodies	8	8	733	8	268	465
	Presbyterian bodies:						
26	Presbyterian Church in the United States of America	24	24	8,224	23	2,742	5,178
27	United Presbyterian Church of North America	2	2	340	2	140	200
28	Presbyterian Church in the United States	3	3	920	2	259	523
29	Protestant Episcopal Church	39	38	16,812	29	4,335	'7,690
	Reformed bodies:						
30	Reformed Church in the United States	14	14	4,496	13	1,502	2,714
31	Unitarians	1	1	500	1	250	250
	United Brethren bodies:						
32	Church of the United Brethren in Christ	6	6	1,485	5	522	787
33	Other Protestant bodies	21	21	1,383	19	369	763
34	Roman Catholic Church	41	41	100,397	30	34,900	39,895
35	Jewish congregations	30	27	[1] 2,042			
36	Polish National Church of America	1	1	1,132	1	523	609
37	All other bodies	6	6	412	6	272	140
1	Bay City, Mich.	53	53	24,725	50	10,929	12,876
	Protestant bodies	39	39	7,749	38	2,664	4,240
	Baptist bodies:						
3	Baptists—Northern and National (Colored) Conventions	7	7	1,128	7	376	752
4	Congregationalists	1	1	326	1	153	173
	Lutheran bodies:						
5	General Council of the Evangelical Lutheran Church in North America	1	1	194	1	90	104
6	Evangelical Lutheran Synodical Conference of America	2	2	1,125	1	138	142
7	Evangelical Lutheran Synod of Michigan and Other States	1	1	680	1	370	310
	Methodist bodies:						
8	Methodist Episcopal Church	7	7	1,620	7	623	997
9	Free Methodist Church of North America	2	2	68	2	15	53
	Presbyterian bodies:						
10	Presbyterian Church in the United States of America	4	4	1,270	4	418	852
11	Protestant Episcopal Church	3	3	565	3	180	385
12	Other Protestant bodies	11	11	773	11	301	472
13	Roman Catholic Church	8	8	16,652	8	8,187	8,465
14	Jewish congregations	2	2	[1] 75			
15	All other bodies	4	4	249	4	78	171
1	Bayonne, N. J.	33	32	21,687	21	4,573	6,340
2	Protestant bodies	21	21	4,015	19	1,428	2,385
	Baptist bodies:						
3	Baptists—Northern Convention	4	4	502	4	173	329
4	German Evangelical Synod of North America	2	2	390	2	213	177
	Methodist bodies:						
5	Methodist Episcopal Church	3	3	792	3	300	492
6	African Methodist Episcopal Zion Church	1	1	20	1	6	14
	Presbyterian bodies:						
7	Presbyterian Church in the United States of America	1	1	239	1	80	159
	Protestant Episcopal Church	4	4	918	3	281	472
	Reformed bodies:						
9	Reformed Church in America	3	3	941	3	299	642
10	Other Protestant bodies	3	3	213	2	76	100
11	Roman Catholic Church	6	6	16,830	1	2,975	3,825
12	Jewish congregations	5	4	[1] 542			
13	Polish National Church of America	1	1	300	1	170	130
1	Binghamton, N. Y.	46	46	19,758	44	7,598	11,670
2	Protestant bodies	41	41	11,850	40	4,111	7,289
	Baptist bodies:						
3	Baptists—Northern Convention	6	6	1,898	6	685	1,213
4	Congregationalists	3	3	1,055	3	322	733
	Lutheran bodies:						
5	General Council of the Evangelical Lutheran Church in North America	1	1	270	1	110	160
6	Slovak Evangelical Lutheran Synod of America	1	1	135	1	80	55

[1] Heads of families only.

DEBT ON CHURCH PROPERTY, PARSONAGES, AND SUNDAY SCHOOLS, FOR EACH CITY OF 25,000 INHABITANTS OR DENOMINATIONS: 1906—Continued.

PLACES OF WORSHIP.					VALUE OF CHURCH PROPERTY.		DEBT ON CHURCH PROPERTY.		PARSONAGES.		SUNDAY SCHOOLS CONDUCTED BY CHURCH ORGANIZATIONS.				
Number of organizations reporting—		Number of church edifices reported.	Seating capacity of church edifices.		Number of organizations reporting.	Value reported.	Number of organizations reporting.	Amount of debt reported.	Number of organizations reporting.	Value of parsonages reported.	Number of organizations reporting.	Number of Sunday schools reported.	Number of officers and teachers.	Number of scholars.	
Church edifices.	Halls, etc.		Number of organizations reporting.	Seating capacity reported.											
2		2	2	1,200	2	$80,000					2	3	54	487	11
2		2	2	1,200	2	70,000					2	2	11	206	12
1		1	1	780	1	20,000	1	$5,000			1	1	22	316	13
9		11	9	6,050	9	274,000	5	26,700	7	$39,400	9	9	264	3,088	14
6		7	6	2,985	6	151,250	4	38,350	1	1,200	5	5	100	1,068	15
15		16	15	11,805	15	603,000	8	66,450	9	38,633	15	15	595	7,124	16
8		8	8	4,550	9	191,150	5	33,400	8	22,800	9	11	180	1,780	17
7		7	7	2,675	7	88,200	6	27,900	5	10,660	7	7	127	1,606	18
2		2	2	300	2	4,300	1	375			2	2	4	65	19
72		77	72	42,010	71	2,335,100	36	184,520	48	242,550	73	74	2,194	23,483	20
2	3	2	2	1,300	2	8,000	2	4,500			5	5	25	210	21
12		12	12	7,160	12	160,500	10	39,600	4	10,700	12	12	202	3,118	22
16		16	16	6,850	16	320,800	5	18,000	10	33,600	16	17	326	3,883	23
6		6	6	3,100	6	142,000	2	4,000	3	10,500	7	7	166	1,832	24
6	2	7	6	3,000	7	50,850	4	12,625	1	4,000	8	8	75	854	25
24		30	24	18,231	24	1,451,000	6	40,100	10	95,000	24	26	853	7,128	26
2		2	2	780	2	47,000	1	700	1	10,000	2	2	45	390	27
3		3	3	2,100	3	155,000	2	13,300	2	29,000	3	4	98	559	28
38		50	38	24,150	35	1,905,041	11	86,300	18	166,600	38	45	886	8,896	29
14		15	14	7,408	14	306,750	7	36,550	7	28,000	14	14	374	3,194	30
1		2	1	600	1	500,000					1	1	16	100	31
6		6	6	2,850	6	96,500			5	16,000	6	6	154	1,897	32
7	12	7	6	1,890	14	217,150	4	1,145	2	5,000	17	19	160	1,028	33
41		47	41	27,351	41	2,753,000	29	582,345	33	231,800	28	31	616	9,921	34
23	3	24	19	12,897	19	740,900	16	180,200	1	1,700	10	10	36	910	35
1		1	1	480	1	37,000	1	29,000	1	15,000	1	1	1	48	36
2	4	2	2	750	2	14,400					3	3	17	102	37
45	7	51	45	22,327	47	789,500	13	20,650	31	112,700	49	51	846	7,614	1
34	5	37	34	14,110	36	524,300	11	14,650	21	43,200	37	39	783	5,030	2
7		7	7	2,600	7	107,500	3	3,600	2	4,000	7	7	97	826	3
1		1	1	300	1	22,000	1	2,000			1	1	23	379	4
1		1	1	260	1	7,000			1	1,000	1	1	14	86	5
2		3	2	1,300	2	22,800	2	3,500	2	5,500	1	1	5	130	6
1		1	1	675	1	7,500	1	800	1	1,200	1	2	6	25	7
7		8	7	2,900	7	106,700			7	17,700	7	7	383	1,536	8
2		2	2	450	2	2,100			2	1,000	2	2	11	83	9
4		4	4	2,225	4	155,300	2	2,800	1	1,500	4	4	110	1,057	10
3		4	3	1,325	3	65,475			1	3,500	3	3	35	269	11
6	5	6	6	2,075	8	27,925	2	1,960	4	7,800	10	11	99	639	12
8		11	8	7,267	8	254,000	1	5,000	8	65,500	8	8	42	2,409	13
2		2	2	800	2	10,000	1	1,000	2	4,000	2	2	6	100	14
1	2	1	1	150	1	1,200					2	2	14	75	15
29	2	33	28	12,595	29	681,300	17	133,160	10	55,800	24	26	426	5,201	1
19	2	20	19	7,595	19	310,300	8	29,700	9	45,800	21	22	396	3,271	2
4		4	4	1,450	4	30,500	1	3,000	1	3,800	4	4	88	449	3
2		2	2	900	2	25,000			1	4,000	2	2	25	245	4
3		3	3	1,300	3	72,500	2	14,500	3	16,000	3	3	90	940	5
1		1	1	150	1	3,500	1	1,100			1	1	5	40	6
1		1	1	400	1	8,800	1	1,400			1	1	24	258	7
4		4	4	1,520	4	80,000	1	3,000	1	10,000	4	4	53	471	8
3		4	3	1,625	3	88,000	2	6,700	2	8,000	3	3	97	719	9
1	2	1	1	250	1	2,000			1	4,000	3	4	16	149	10
6		6	6	3,950	6	330,000	5	90,000	1	10,000	1	1	19	1,500	11
3		6	2	850	3	32,000	3	10,000			2	3	9	430	12
1		1	1	200	1	9,000	1	3,460							13
43	2	45	43	22,485	43	1,283,000	25	141,368	25	112,500	45	45	1,081	9,714	1
38	2	40	38	18,385	38	1,050,000	20	76,568	22	100,200	40	40	985	8,603	2
6		6	6	2,460	6	151,000	2	14,300	2	11,000	6	6	156	1,592	3
3		3	3	1,750	3	115,000	3	9,850	2	13,000	3	3	87	505	4
1		1	1	250	1	12,000	1	700	1	3,000	1	1	29	180	5
	1														6

TABLE 7.—ORGANIZATIONS, COMMUNICANTS OR MEMBERS, PLACES OF WORSHIP, VALUE OF CHURCH PROPERTY, MORE IN 1900, BY SELECTED

	DENOMINATION.	Total number of organizations.	COMMUNICANTS OR MEMBERS.				
			Number of organizations reporting.	Total number reported.	Sex.		
					Number of organizations reporting.	Male.	Female.
	Binghamton, N. Y.—Continued.						
	Protestant bodies—Continued.						
	Methodist bodies:						
7	Methodist Episcopal Church	8	8	3,441	8	1,384	2,057
8	Other Methodist bodies	3	3	160	3	46	114
	Presbyterian bodies:						
9	Presbyterian Church in the United States of America	7	7	3,035	7	1,044	1,991
10	Protestant Episcopal Church	3	3	1,164	2	200	514
11	Other Protestant bodies	9	9	692	9	240	452
12	Roman Catholic Church	4	4	7,868	4	3,487	4,381
13	Jewish congregations	1	1	[1] 40	.....	.....	.....
1	Birmingham, Ala	91	88	26,383	74	10,077	13,229
	Protestant bodies	85	82	18,936	70	6,577	9,657
	Baptist bodies:						
3	Baptists—Southern Convention	5	5	2,059	5	936	1,123
4	Baptists—National Convention (Colored)	17	17	4,029	17	1,434	2,595
	Disciples or Christians:						
5	Disciples of Christ	4	4	684	4	286	398
6	Churches of Christ	1	1	45	1	20	25
	Methodist bodies:						
7	Methodist Episcopal Church	5	4	651	1	66	114
8	African Methodist Episcopal Church	4	4	970	4	393	577
9	African Methodist Episcopal Zion Church	4	4	1,082	4	416	666
10	Methodist Episcopal Church, South	11	10	3,919	7	1,330	1,561
11	Other Methodist bodies	4	4	507	4	221	286
	Presbyterian bodies:						
12	Presbyterian Church in the United States of America	3	3	76	1	15	33
13	Cumberland Presbyterian Church	3	3	717	1	221	281
14	Presbyterian Church in the United States	7	7	2,088	6	640	1,058
15	Protestant Episcopal Church	5	5	1,310	4	261	479
16	Other Protestant bodies	12	11	799	11	338	461
17	Roman Catholic Church	3	3	6,770	3	3,234	3,536
18	Jewish congregations	2	2	[1] 375	.....	.....	.....
	Eastern Orthodox Churches:						
19	Greek Orthodox Church	1	1	302	1	266	36
1	Boston, Mass	325	310	376,728	967	150,128	196,722
	Protestant bodies	234	229	111,563	202	31,380	68,401
	Baptist bodies:						
3	Baptists—Northern Convention	30	30	13,790	27	3,971	7,911
4	Baptists—National Convention (Colored)	6	6	3,289	6	1,222	2,067
5	Free Baptists	1	1	270	1	118	152
6	Church of Christ, Scientist	2	2	41,634	2	11,040	30,594
	Churches of the New Jerusalem:						
7	General Convention of the New Jerusalem in the United States of America	2	2	681	2	209	472
8	Congregationalists	36	36	12,127	35	3,703	7,999
	Disciples or Christians:						
9	Disciples of Christ	1	1	350	1	112	238
	Lutheran bodies:						
10	General Council of the Evangelical Lutheran Church in North America	3	3	969	3	379	590
11	Evangelical Lutheran Synodical Conference of America	9	8	2,272	6	559	801
12	Other Lutheran bodies	4	4	442	4	178	264
	Methodist bodies:						
13	Methodist Episcopal Church	33	33	7,063	33	2,581	4,482
14	African Methodist Episcopal Church	2	2	720	1	14	6
15	African Methodist Episcopal Zion Church	1	1	500	1	200	300
	Presbyterian bodies:						
16	Presbyterian Church in the United States of America	6	6	2,265	6	519	1,746
17	United Presbyterian Church of North America	1	1	510	1	210	300
18	Synod of the Reformed Presbyterian Church of North America	2	2	291	2	105	186
19	Protestant Episcopal Church	34	34	13,352	21	2,816	4,764
20	Reformed Catholic Church	1	1	600	1	400	200
	Salvationists.						
21	Salvation Army	9	7	319	7	155	164
22	Unitarians	24	22	6,854	16	1,743	3,196
23	Universalists	9	9	1,806	8	592	1,064
24	Other Protestant bodies	18	18	1,459	18	554	905
25	Roman Catholic Church	50	50	258,936	47	115,760	126,810
26	Jewish congregations	22	13	[1] 1,735	.....	.....	.....
27	Armenian Church	4	4	1,737	4	1,307	430
	Eastern Orthodox Churches:						
28	Syrian Orthodox Church	1	1	300	1	180	120
29	Greek Orthodox Church	1	1	1,200	1	1,000	200
30	Spiritualists	7	7	919	7	387	532
31	All other bodies	6	5	338	5	109	229
1	Bridgeport, Conn	81	80	50,936	73	24,385	24,529
2	Protestant bodies	59	59	13,187	56	4,508	7,327
	Baptist bodies:						
3	Baptists—Northern and National (Colored) Conventions	8	8	1,577	8	545	1,032

[1] Heads of families only.

DEBT ON CHURCH PROPERTY, PARSONAGES, AND SUNDAY SCHOOLS, FOR EACH CITY OF 25,000 INHABITANTS OR DENOMINATIONS: 1906—Continued.

PLACES OF WORSHIP.					VALUE OF CHURCH PROPERTY.		DEBT ON CHURCH PROPERTY.		PARSONAGES.		SUNDAY SCHOOLS CONDUCTED BY CHURCH ORGANIZATIONS.				
Number of organizations reporting— Church edifices.	Number of organizations reporting— Halls, etc.	Number of church edifices reported.	Seating capacity of church edifices. Number of organizations reporting.	Seating capacity of church edifices. Seating capacity reported.	Number of organizations reporting.	Value reported.	Number of organizations reporting.	Amount of debt reported.	Number of organizations reporting.	Value of parsonages reported.	Number of organizations reporting.	Number of Sunday schools reported.	Number of officers and teachers.	Number of scholars.	
8	...	8	8	4,550	8	$190,500	3	$5,150	8	$26,500	8	8	271	2,762	7
3	...	3	3	950	3	11,000	2	2,118	1	4,500	3	3	29	149	8
7	...	8	7	5,125	7	246,500	5	21,000	4	10,700	7	7	278	2,506	9
3	...	4	3	1,650	3	243,500	...	...	3	26,500	3	3	51	313	10
7	1	7	7	1,650	7	80,500	4	23,450	1	5,000	9	9	84	596	11
4	...	4	4	3,500	4	228,000	4	63,300	3	12,300	4	4	95	1,071	12
1	...	1	1	600	1	5,000	1	1,500	...	...	1	1	1	40	13
79	5	82	74	34,640	81	1,562,610	37	110,697	28	151,350	83	88	941	11,243	1
73	5	75	68	31,690	75	1,374,610	33	87,197	25	137,650	78	81	882	10,158	2
5	...	6	5	4,000	5	152,500	3	16,050	1	10,000	5	6	101	1,277	3
17	...	17	17	5,610	17	66,710	5	1,922	2	5,500	16	17	121	1,738	4
3	...	3	3	1,400	3	54,000	...	...	...	...	3	3	39	305	5
...	1	...	...	...	...	...	...	...	...	...	...	...	...	...	6
4	...	4	1	200	4	27,550	...	...	3	3,350	4	4	36	396	7
4	...	4	4	2,700	4	61,000	1	1,000	2	3,000	4	4	28	525	8
4	...	4	4	1,875	4	36,000	4	4,175	1	10,000	4	4	43	342	9
10	...	10	9	5,325	10	342,500		28,000	7	35,500	10	10	195	2,358	10
3	...	3	3	1,550	3	7,000	6	3,250	1	1,200	4	4	14	210	11
1	...	1	1	200	1	1,500	...	...	...	...	3	3	13		12
3	...	4	3	1,325	3	51,300	...	...	1	25,000	3	3	34		13
7	...	7	7	3,405	7	281,000	5	16,700	3	21,000	7	8	137	1,	14
4	1	4	4	2,000	4	226,650	1	1,100	3	19,100	5	5	55	83	15
8	3	8	7	2,100	10	66,900	7	15,000	1	4,000	10	10	56	[illegible]	16
3	...	3	3	1,400	3	128,000	2	14,000	3	18,700	3	3	48	705	17
2	...	3	2	1,350	2	50,000	1	5,000	...	...	2	4	16	380	18
1	...	1	1	200	1	10,000	1	4,500	...	...	...	...	...	...	19
258	45	295	256	202,463	270	27,140,161	127	2,098,685	95	1,204,100	272	303	7,826	83,532	1
197	30	223	197	129,921	209	19,648,525	91	1,306,285	50	421,300	216	241	4,807	44,759	2
29	...	31	29	20,674	30	2,437,400	12	442,000	4	21,500	30	37	960	10,483	3
5		5	5	5,350	6	192,400	5	78,650	...	...	6	6	86	979	4
1	...	1	1	600	1	50,000	1	10,000	...	...	1	1	25	245	5
1		1	1	5,000	2	2,227,000	...	...	...	...	2	2	54	336	6
2	...	2	2	1,150	2	134,000	1	3,300	1	10,000	2	2	34	285	7
32		36	32	25,090	32	3,818,450	8	122,450	6	79,000	36	44	1,136	11,499	8
1	...	1	1	225	1	10,500	1	2,800	1	6,000	1	1	12	208	9
3	...	3	3	1,200	3	53,000	2	15,500	...	...	3	4	48	302	10
5	2	6	5	2,375	6	147,000	3	33,900	2	15,000	7	7	112	777	11
2	2	2	2	600	3	46,500	2	4,000	1	6,000	3	4	16	125	12
30	2	31	30	18,129	30	1,579,200		162,220	16	120,500	32	35	809	6,885	13
2	...	2	2	1,300	2	100,500	20	8,015	1	200	2	2	23	325	14
1	...	1	1	950	1	60,000	[illegible]	35,000	...	...	1	1	26	392	15
6	...	6	6	3,750	6	277,100	4	28,300	1	6,000	6	7	126	1,174	16
1	...	2	1	1,400	1	73,500	1	30,000	...	...	1	1	12	80	17
2	...	2	2	1,300	2	85,000	2	28,100	...	...	2	2	20	150	18
32	1	40	32	17,805	32	4,185,200	9	44,950	14	102,100	33	36	644	6,156	19
...	1	...	...	...	...	...	...	...	...	...	...	...	...	...	20
2	5	2	2	1,390	7	313,900	3	140,100	1	10,000	6	6	37	265	21
24	...	33	24	14,133	23	3,145,200	6	57,300	2	45,000	22	22	302	2,551	22
9	...	9	9	4,600	9	564,000	4	37,500	...	...	9	9	135	880	23
7	11	7	7	2,900	10	148,675	4	22,200	...	...	11	12	170	662	24
49	1	57	49	60,642	50	6,519,486	28	619,300	41	767,000	47	58	2,976	37,855	25
9	...	12	8	8,400	8	587,000	7	159,100	4	15,800	5	5	21	688	26
...	2	...	...	...	...	...	...	...	...	...	1	1	2	100	27
...	1	...	...	...	1	150	...	...	...	...	...	...	...	...	28
1	...	1	1	1,000	1	35,000	1	14,000	...	...	1	1	3	21	29
1	6	1	1	2,500	1	350,000	...	...	...	...	1	1	4	60	30
1	5	1	...	...	...	...	...	...	...	...	1	1	13	49	31
69	[illegible]	78	67	33,374	75	2,336,375	48	306,069	38	311,800	71	79	1,167	13,539	1
50	7	58	48	21,200	55	1,533,875	35	162,244	25	190,800	54	61	1,002	8,384	2
7	1	9	7	2,945	8	184,400	4	4,550	2	5,300	8	12	146	1,193	3

TABLE 7.—ORGANIZATIONS, COMMUNICANTS OR MEMBERS, PLACES OF WORSHIP, VALUE OF CHURCH PROPERTY, MORE IN 1900, BY SELECTED

	DENOMINATION.	Total number of organizations.	COMMUNICANTS OR MEMBERS.				
			Number of organizations reporting.	Total number reported.	Sex.		
					Number of organizations reporting.	Male.	Female.
	Bridgeport, Conn.—Continued.						
	Protestant bodies—Continued.						
4	Congregationalists	9	9	2,878	9	992	1,886
	Lutheran bodies:						
5	General Council of the Evangelical Lutheran Church in North America	2	2	560	2	285	275
6	Slovak Evangelical Lutheran Synod of America	1	1	375	1	200	175
7	Other Lutheran bodies	4	4	490	4	237	253
	Methodist bodies:						
8	Methodist Episcopal Church	9	9	2,230	8	585	1,061
9	African Methodist bodies	2	2	110	2	37	73
	Presbyterian bodies:						
10	Presbyterian Church in the United States of America	1	1	575	...	...	...
11	Protestant Episcopal Church	8	8	2,634	8	905	1,729
	Reformed bodies:						
12	Reformed Church in the United States	2	2	757	2	387	370
13	Hungarian Reformed Church in America	1	1	250	1	145	105
14	Other Protestant bodies	12	12	751	11	190	378
15	Roman Catholic Church	15	15	36,134	15	19,372	16,762
16	Jewish congregations	4	3	[1] 270	...	...	...
	Eastern Orthodox Churches:						
17	Russian Orthodox Church	1	1	645	1	365	280
18	Greek Orthodox Church	1	1	400	...	...	...
19	Polish National Church of America	1	1	300	1	140	160
1	Brockton, Mass.	40	40	20,516	36	8,410	10,835
2	Protestant bodies	32	32	6,658	29	1,856	3,709
	Adventist bodies:						
3	Advent Christian Church	1	1	105	1	43	62
4	Seventh-day Adventist Denomination	1	1	12	1	4	8
	Baptist bodies:						
5	Baptists—Northern and National (Colored) Conventions	5	5	1,029	5	320	709
6	Free Baptists	1	1	52	1	23	29
	Churches of the New Jerusalem:						
7	General Convention of the New Jerusalem in the United States of America	1	1	156	1	45	111
8	Congregationalists	6	6	2,057	6	637	1,420
	Lutheran bodies:						
9	General Council of the Evangelical Lutheran Church in North America	2	2	483	2	199	284
	Methodist bodies:						
10	Methodist Episcopal Church	5	5	1,529	3	211	337
	Presbyterian bodies:						
11	United Presbyterian Church of North America	1	1	110	1	40	70
12	Protestant Episcopal Church	1	1	293	1	95	198
13	Unitarians	1	1	361	1	120	241
14	Universalists	1	1	102	...	...	...
15	Other Protestant bodies	6	6	369	6	119	250
16	Roman Catholic Church	4	4	13,532	4	6,482	7,050
17	Jewish congregations	1	1	[1] 178	...	...	...
18	All other bodies	3	3	148	3	72	76
1	Buffalo, N. Y.	254	252	195,302	218	75,246	87,863
2	Protestant bodies	189	188	64,114	170	21,796	33,350
	Baptist bodies:						
3	Baptists—Northern Convention	24	24	5,584	24	2,110	3,474
4	Free Baptists	2	2	438	2	151	287
	Catholic Apostolic Churches:						
5	Catholic Apostolic Church	1	1	110	1	50	60
6	New Apostolic Church	1	1	500	1	200	300
7	Church of Christ, Scientist	2	2	447	2	145	302
8	Congregationalists	4	4	1,036	4	429	607
	Disciples or Christians:						
9	Disciples of Christ	4	4	1,250	2	266	454
	Evangelical bodies:						
10	Evangelical Association	5	5	887	4	297	485
11	German Evangelical Synod of North America	18	18	13,256	13	3,301	4,734
	Lutheran bodies:						
12	General Synod of the Evangelical Lutheran Church in the United States of America	1	1	114	1	42	72
13	General Council of the Evangelical Lutheran Church in North America	10	10	6,858	8	2,267	3,391
14	Evangelical Lutheran Synodical Conference of America	10	10	4,437	9	1,845	2,089
15	Lutheran Synod of Buffalo	1	1	780	1	355	425
	Methodist bodies:						
16	Methodist Episcopal Church	26	26	7,472	26	2,997	4,475
17	Other Methodist bodies	6	6	255	6	81	174
	Presbyterian bodies:						
18	Presbyterian Church in the United States of America	17	17	6,140	17	2,241	3,899
19	United Presbyterian Church of North America	4	4	584	3	183	281
20	Protestant Episcopal Church	25	25	8,483	21	2,449	4,970
	Reformed bodies:						
21	Reformed Church in the United States	7	7	3,374	7	1,569	1,805
22	Other Reformed bodies	2	2	340	2	180	160
23	Unitarians	2	2	388	2	157	231
24	Universalists	2	2	454	2	167	287
25	Other Protestant bodies	15	14	927	12	314	438
26	Roman Catholic Church	50	50	126,395	42	51,839	52,449
27	Jewish congregations	9	8	[1] 618	...	...	...

[1] Heads of families only.

DEBT ON CHURCH PROPERTY, PARSONAGES, AND SUNDAY SCHOOLS, FOR EACH CITY OF 25,000 INHABITANTS OR DENOMINATIONS: 1906—Continued.

PLACES OF WORSHIP.					VALUE OF CHURCH PROPERTY.		DEBT ON CHURCH PROPERTY.		PARSONAGES.		SUNDAY SCHOOLS CONDUCTED BY CHURCH ORGANIZATIONS.				
Number of organizations reporting—		Number of church edifices reported.	Seating capacity of church edifices.		Number of organizations reporting.	Value reported.	Number of organizations reporting.	Amount of debt reported.	Number of organizations reporting.	Value of parsonages reported.	Number of organizations reporting.	Number of Sunday schools reported.	Number of officers and teachers.	Number of scholars.	
Church edifices.	Halls, etc.		Number of organizations reporting.	Seating capacity reported.											
	......	11	9	4,830	9	$284,500	6	$17,455	4	$36,000	9	9	216	1,939	4
2	......	2	2	700	2	22,000	2	13,000	1	5,000	2	4	41	300	5
......	1	......	......	......	1	1,800	......	......	......	......	......	......	......	......	6
3	1	3	3	625	3	17,500	3	8,100	1	3,500	3	3	27	200	7
9	......	9	8	2,975	9	189,000	7	36,500	5	50,500	9	9	230	1,854	8
2	......	2	2	700	2	28,400	2	4,389	2	6,000	2	2	23	111	9
1	......	1	1	700	1	200,000	1	2,000	1	20,000	1	1	35	450	10
8	......	9	8	3,825	8	445,000	3	34,500	3	43,000	8	8	162	1,329	11
2	......	4	2	2,000	2	50,500	2	17,800	2	5,500	2	3	41	430	12
1	......	2	1	350	1	11,500	1	10,000	1	3,000	1	1	2	60	13
6	4	6	5	1,550	9	99,275	4	13,950	3	13,000	9	9	79	518	14
15	......	16	15	10,224	15	742,000	10	116,825	11	102,000	15	16	154	4,995	15
2		2	2	950	3	35,500	2	18,000	......	......	1	1	10	130	16
1	......	1	1	700	1	10,000	......	......	1	4,000	......	......	......	......	17
......		......	......	......	......	......	......	......	......	......	......	......	......	......	18
1	......	1	1	300	1	15,000	1	9,000	1	15,000	1	1	1	30	19
36	4	37	36	18,491	37	884,650	19	105,862	13	87,750	39	39	977	11,070	1
30	2	31	30	14,490	31	682,500	15	56,062	8	36,100	32	32	766	7,932	2
1	......	1	1	250	1	7,000	1	1,200	......	......	1	1	15	96	3
......	1	......	......	......	......	......	......	......	......	......	1	1	1	9	4
5	......	5	5	1,960	5	58,200	3	8,100	......	......	5	5	125	1,049	5
1	......	1	1	250	1	8,000	1	3,200	......	......	1	1	13	100	6
1	......	1	1	500	1	45,000	......	......	......	......	1	1	16	140	7
6	......	7	6	4,750	6	255,000	1	1,000	1	10,000	6	6	230	3,561	8
2	......	2	2	675	2	21,300	1	700	1	2,000	2	2	52	433	9
5	......	5	5	2,775	5	153,500	3	35,950	5	21,600	[illegible]	5	202	1,697	10
1	......	1	1	650	1	13,000	1	1,750	......	......	1	1	13	85	11
1	......	1	1	375	1	50,000	......	......	......	......	1	1	20	200	12
1	......	1	1	400	1	12,800	1	1,800	......	......	1	1	18	110	13
1	......	1	1	400	1	6,000	......	......	......	......	1	1	20	155	14
5	1	5	5	1,505	6	52,700	3	2,363	1	2,500	6	6	41	297	15
4	......	4	4	3,240	4	183,000	2	41,200	4	49,650	4	4	186	2,998	16
1	......	1	1	486	1	12,000	1	4,000	1	2,000	1	1	3	78	17
1	2	1	1	275	1	7,150	1	4,600	......	......	2	2	22	62	18
232	17	254	230	141,000	235	10,323,210	158	2,239,988	114	953,754	227	284	4,867	63,418	1
172	13	191	170	89,273	175	5,626,450	109	857,233	71	453,200	181	209	4,354	42,661	2
24	......	25	24	12,545	24	659,200	13	167,150	3	23,000	24		537	5,294	3
2	......	2	2	800	2	58,000	2	3,300	1	6,000	2	27	44	365	4
......	1	......	......	......	......	......	......	......	......	......	1	1	2	25	5
1	......	1	1	500	1	6,000	1	4,000	......	......	1	1	4	125	6
1	1	1	1	450	1	30,000	......	......	1	50,000	2	2	48	230	7
4	......	5	4	1,800	4	165,000	......	......	......	......	4	5	238	1,262	8
4	......	4	4	1,400	4	61,800	2	3,600	......	......	4	6	106	1,150	9
5	......	5	5	1,950	5	69,500	1	1,000	4	14,000	5	6	121	918	10
18	......	22	18	14,200	18	530,100	14	89,328	6	56,500	18	21	524	5,797	11
1	......	1	1	200	1	7,000	1	4,800	1	2,000		1	13	84	12
9	1	11	9	7,100	10	412,500	7	97,930	3	14,000	1	14	406	4,048	13
8	1	9	8	4,005	8	139,800	8	31,600	4	19,000	1	14	106	1,583	14
1	......	2	1	750	1	25,000	......	......	1	4,000	[illegible]	1	14	160	15
26	......	29	25	13,929	26	817,300	18	114,150	21	94,500	26	28	747	7,534	16
5		5	5	1,400	6	29,950	4	9,600	3	7,100	5	5	44	330	17
17	......	18	17	10,866	17	1,202,500	11	188,400	4	52,000	17	20	573	5,841	18
4	......	4	4	1,170	4	62,500	2	4,000	1	10,000	4	4	60	655	19
22	......	26	22	8,802	22	852,000	9	37,525	7	66,800	24	26	420	3,938	20
7	......	7	7	3,976	6	120,000	6	30,400	7	21,000	7	7	160	1,860	21
1		1	1	300	1	10,000	1	2,000	1	3,000	1	1	20	214	22
2	......	2	2	750	2	161,700	2	30,100	1	4,300	2	2	26	121	23
2	......	2	2	750	2	104,000	1	2,000	......	......	2	2	31	197	24
8		9	7	1,630	10	102,600	6	36,350	2	6,000	11	13	111	930	25
50	......	53	50	44,170	50	4,358,190	41	1,247,036	42	486,554	42	71	493	20,467	26
7		7	7	4,007	7	183,000	6	59,400	......	......	3	3	10	230	27

TABLE 7.—ORGANIZATIONS, COMMUNICANTS OR MEMBERS, PLACES OF WORSHIP, VALUE OF CHURCH PROPERTY, MORE IN 1900, BY SELECTED

	DENOMINATION.	Total number of organizations.	COMMUNICANTS OR MEMBERS.				
			Number of organizations reporting.	Total number reported.	Sex.		
					Number of organizations reporting.	Male.	Female.
	Buffalo, N. Y.—Continued.						
28	Polish National Church of America		1	3,500	1	1,700	1,800
29	All other bodies	5	5	675	5	411	264
1	Butte, Mont	38	38	27,756	35	15,395	12,186
2	Protestant bodies	27	27	3,307	26	1,238	1,969
	Baptist bodies:						
3	Baptists—Northern Convention	3	3	531	3	195	336
	Disciples or Christians:						
4	Disciples of Christ	1	1	204	1	86	118
5	Lutheran bodies	3	3	181	3	82	99
	Methodist bodies:						
6	Methodist Episcopal Church	5	5	805	5	307	498
7	African Methodist Episcopal Church	1	1	23	1	4	19
8	Methodist Episcopal Church, South	2	2	158	2	49	109
	Presbyterian bodies:						
9	Presbyterian Church in the United States of America	3	3	642	3	242	400
10	Protestant Episcopal Church	3	3	501	2	170	251
11	Unitarians	1	1	105	1	40	65
12	Other Protestant bodies	5	5	157	5	63	94
13	Roman Catholic Church	5	5	22,617	5	12,665	9,952
14	Jewish congregations	2	2	[1] 95			
	Eastern Orthodox Churches:						
15	Servian Orthodox Church	1	1	1,500	1	1,400	100
	Latter-day Saints:						
16	Church of Jesus Christ of Latter-day Saints	1	1	165	1	63	102
17	All other bodies	2	2	72	2	29	43
1	Cambridge, Mass	54	54	45,896	48	19,644	24,876
2	Protestant bodies	45	45	12,351	40	3,660	7,380
	Baptist bodies:						
3	Baptists—Northern and National (Colored) Conventions	9	9	3,043	9	994	2,049
4	Free Baptists	1	1	214	1	95	119
5	Congregationalists	7	7	2,972	7	921	2,051
	Lutheran bodies:						
6	General Council of the Evangelical Lutheran Church in North America	1	1	400			
	Methodist bodies:						
7	Methodist Episcopal Church	5	5	1,113	5	405	708
8	African Methodist Episcopal Church	1	1	236	1	48	188
9	African Methodist Episcopal Zion Church	1	1	193	1	73	120
	Presbyterian bodies:						
10	United Presbyterian Church of North America	1	1	240	1	113	127
11	Synod of the Reformed Presbyterian Church of North America	1	1	50	1	18	32
12	Protestant Episcopal Church	7	7	1,950	4	430	730
13	Unitarians	2	2	747	2	163	584
14	Universalists	2	2	481	1	170	190
15	Other Protestant bodies	7	7	712	7	230	482
16	Roman Catholic Church	7	7	33,043	7	15,767	17,276
17	Jewish congregations	1	1	[1] 65			
18	Armenian Church	1	1	437	1	217	220
1	Camden, N. J	82	80	29,223	73	11,667	15,359
2	Protestant bodies	74	74	17,095	68	5,345	9,593
	Baptist bodies:						
3	Baptists—Northern Convention	15	15	3,868	14	1,131	2,074
	Lutheran bodies:						
4	General Synod of the Evangelical Lutheran Church in the United States of America	3	3	224	3	88	136
5	General Council of the Evangelical Lutheran Church in North America	5	5	1,251	4	488	698
	Methodist bodies:						
6	Methodist Episcopal Church	17	17	6,818	14	1,977	3,537
7	African Methodist Episcopal Church	2	2	376	2	120	256
8	Other Methodist bodies	7	7	801	7	279	522
	Presbyterian bodies:						
9	Presbyterian Church in the United States of America	7	7	1,632	7	543	1,089
10	Protestant Episcopal Church	7	7	1,676	6	548	1,003
11	Other Protestant bodies	11	11	449	11	171	278
12	Roman Catholic Church	5	5	12,088	5	6,322	5,766
13	Jewish congregations	3	1	[1] 40			
1	Canton, Ohio	40	39	12,894	36	4,880	7,334
2	Protestant bodies	35	35	11,374	33	4,218	6,551
	Baptist bodies:						
3	Baptists—Northern and National (Colored) Conventions	2	2	856	2	286	570
	Disciples or Christians:						
4	Disciples of Christ	1	1	1,000	1	400	600
	Evangelical bodies:						
5	Evangelical Association	1	1	230	1	115	115
6	United Evangelical Church	3	3	638	3	223	415
	Lutheran bodies:						
7	General Synod of the Evangelical Lutheran Church in the United States of America	1	1	580			
8	Evangelical Lutheran Joint Synod of Ohio and Other States	3	3	1,134	3	522	612

[1] Heads of families only.

DEBT ON CHURCH PROPERTY, PARSONAGES, AND SUNDAY SCHOOLS, FOR EACH CITY OF 25,000 INHABITANTS OR DENOMINATIONS: 1906—Continued.

PLACES OF WORSHIP. Number of organizations reporting— Church edifices.	Halls, etc.	Number of church edifices reported.	Seating capacity of church edifices. Number of organizations reporting.	Seating capacity reported.	VALUE OF CHURCH PROPERTY. Number of organizations reporting.	Value reported.	DEBT ON CHURCH PROPERTY. Number of organizations reporting.	Amount of debt reported.	PARSONAGES. Number of organizations reporting.	Value of parsonages reported.	SUNDAY SCHOOLS CONDUCTED BY CHURCH ORGANIZATIONS. Number of organizations reporting.	Number of Sunday schools reported.	Number of officers and teachers.	Number of scholars.	
1		1	1	2,600	1	$140,000	1	$75,000	1	$14,000					28
2	3	2		950	2	15,570	1	1,269			1	1	10	60	29
30	8	37		18,980	32	756,700	14	84,625	17	83,700	31	36	382	6,401	1
22	5	25	20	7,880	24	323,700	10	35,625	14	39,700	23	28	293	3,427	2
2	1	4	2	1,150	2	55,000	2	11,600	1	5,000	2	5	40	665	3
1		1		500	1	20,000	1	1,500			1	1	15	130	4
2	1	2	1	500	2	30,000	1	9,000	1	2,000	3	3	16	154	5
5		5	5	2,230	5	63,000	1	1,700	4	11,800	4	4	78	910	6
1		1	1	350	1	400	1	100	1	1,000	1	1	5	17	7
2		2	2	500	2	31,000			1	3,000	2	2	14	235	8
3		4		1,200	3	39,100	1	600	2	4,400	3	4	74	779	9
3		3	3	750	3	44,500			2	6,000	3	3	31	410	10
	1														11
3	2	3	3	700	5	40,700	3	11,125	2	6,500	4	5	20	127	12
5		9	5	10,000	5	390,000	3	41,000	3	44,000	5	5	53	2,830	13
2		2	2	800	2	23,000					1	1	3	50	14
1		1	1	300	1	20,000	1	8,000							15
	1										1	1	12	82	16
	2										1	1	1	12	17
44	7	50	43	32,281	46	2,300,400	19	118,187	15	102,300	50	54	1,586	13,231	1
36	6	40	36	22,511	39	1,630,400	15	57,069	7	49,000	43	45	1,108	8,747	2
7	1	8	7	5,950	7	497,000	3	13,500			9	9	268	2,362	3
1		1	1	400	1	18,000	1	4,000			1	1	14	150	4
7		8	7	5,250	7	366,500	4	12,700			7	9	289	2,295	5
					1	8,300	1	4,200			1	1	32	175	6
4		4	4	2,300	4	195,000	1	2,000	3	21,000	4	4	154	1,147	7
1		1	1	400	1	14,000	1	7,535	1	7,000	1	1	9	80	8
1		1	1	500	1	10,000	1	1,364			1	1	15	93	9
1		1	1	400	1	15,000					1	1	29	206	10
1		1	1	250	1	10,000					1	1	12	60	11
7		9	7	3,400	7	232,400	1	2,000	3	21,000	7	7	136	1,194	12
2		2	2	1,560	2	121,700	1	3,500			2	2	26	154	13
2		2	2	1,611	2	100,000					2	2	56	400	14
2	5	2	2	500	4	42,500	1	6,270			6	6	68	431	15
7		9	6	8,770	6	635,000	3	51,118	7	52,300	7	9	478	4,484	16
1		1	1	1,000	1	35,000	1	10,000	1	1,000					17
	1														18
72	9	77		36,485	73	1,782,575	52	287,288	26	99,300	74	83	1,951	21,075	1
65	9	69	63	32,485	67	1,494,575	47	235,588	22	84,300	70	76	1,872	19,125	2
15		15	15	7,850	15	385,500	10	54,789	4	10,800	15	19	536	5,135	3
2	1	2	2	750	3	17,800	2	11,000			3	3	44	373	4
5		5	5	1,810	5	98,500	5	13,225	2	4,800	5	5	96	1,119	5
17		17	15	11,720	17	599,500	14	104,775	13	54,700	17	17	737	8,335	6
2		2	2	1,300	2	18,500	2	5,681			2	2	33	321	7
7		7	7	2,850	7	28,500	7	6,868			7	7	71	588	8
7		8	7	3,330	7	172,700	4	27,350	2	7,000	7	7	186	1,595	9
7		10	7	2,175	7	160,000	3	11,900	1	7,000	7	9	128	1,435	10
3	8	3	3	700	4	13,575					7	7	41	224	11
5		6	5	3,750	5	283,000	4	48,700	4	15,000	[illegible]	7	79	1,950	12
2		2	1	250	1	5,000	1	3,000							13
31	7	32	31	18,090		763,100	13	76,680	14	62,100	35	36	851	11,050	1
28	6	29	28	16,810	29	682,600	10	29,180	11	50,800	32	33	844	10,495	2
1	1	1	1	800	1	54,000		1,700	1	5,500	[illegible]	[illegible]	49	762	3
1		1	1	1,000	1	50,000					[illegible]	[illegible]	40	800	4
1		1	1	400	1	7,000	2		1	2,500	1	1	28	170	5
3		3	3	2,000	3	30,400		13,100	2	4,000	3	3	79	885	6
1		2	1	1,500	1	80,000			1	10,000	1	1	18	286	7
3		3	3	1,075	3	32,000		,250	1	3,000	3	3	67	825	8

TABLE 7.—ORGANIZATIONS, COMMUNICANTS OR MEMBERS, PLACES OF WORSHIP, VALUE OF CHURCH PROPERTY, ... MORE IN 1900, BY SELECTED ...

	DENOMINATION.	Total number of organizations.	COMMUNICANTS OR MEMBERS.				
			Number of organizations reporting.	Total number reported.	Sex.		
					Number of organizations reporting.	Male.	Female.
	Canton, Ohio—Continued.						
	Protestant bodies—Continued.						
	Methodist bodies:						
9	Methodist Episcopal Church	3	3	2,020	3	793	1,227
10	Other Methodist bodies	2	2	85	2	28	57
	Presbyterian bodies:						
11	Presbyterian Church in the United States of America	2	2	788	2	254	534
12	United Presbyterian Church of North America	1	1	75	1	28	47
	Reformed bodies:						
13	Reformed Church in the United States	3	3	2,646	3	1,079	1,567
	United Brethren bodies:						
14	Church of the United Brethren in Christ	1	1	750	1	268	482
15	Other Protestant bodies	12	12	572	11	222	325
16	Roman Catholic Church[1]	3	3	1,445	3	662	783
17	Jewish congregations	1	......	......	......	......	......
	Eastern Orthodox Churches:						
18	Greek Orthodox Church	1	1	75	......	......	......
1	**Cedar Rapids, Iowa**	36	35	10,285	34	3,923	6,260
	Protestant bodies	32	32	7,089	31	2,461	4,526
	Baptist bodies:						
3	Baptists—Northern Convention	2	2	567	2	205	362
4	Congregationalists	2	2	464	2	164	300
	Disciples or Christians:						
5	Disciples of Christ	2	2	627	2	205	422
	Lutheran bodies:						
6	General Synod of the Evangelical Lutheran Church in the United States of America	1	1	368	1	125	243
	Evangelical Lutheran Synodical Conference of America	1	1	360	1	120	240
8	Other Lutheran bodies	2	2	112	2	50	62
	Methodist bodies:						
9	Methodist Episcopal Church	3	3	1,201	3	477	724
10	Other Methodist bodies	2	2	118	2	41	77
	Presbyterian bodies:						
11	Presbyterian Church in the United States of America	6	6	1,735	6	602	1,133
12	United Presbyterian Church of North America	1	1	240	1	80	160
13	Protestant Episcopal Church	1	1	505	1	149	356
	United Brethren bodies:						
14	Church of the United Brethren in Christ	1	1	275	1	100	175
15	Other Protestant bodies	8	8	517	7	143	272
16	Roman Catholic Church	3	3	3,196	3	1,462	1,734
17	Jewish congregations	1	......	......	......	......	......
1	**Charleston, S. C.**	74	74	27,942	68	10,083	15,637
2	Protestant bodies	66	66	20,030	63	6,522	11,596
	Baptist bodies:						
3	Baptists—Southern Convention	3	3	1,039	2	63	176
4	Baptists—National Convention (Colored)	[illegible]	9	2,517	9	859	1,658
	Lutheran bodies:						
5	United Synod of the Evangelical Lutheran Church in the South	4	4	1,762	2	265	385
	Methodist bodies:						
6	Methodist Episcopal Church	5	5	2,552	5	864	1,688
7	African Methodist Episcopal Church	8	8	4,411	8	1,807	2,604
8	Methodist Episcopal Church, South	4	4	1,507	4	540	967
9	Other African Methodist bodies	4	4	867	4	347	520
	Presbyterian bodies:						
10	Presbyterian Church in the United States of America	3	3	478	3	107	371
11	Presbyterian Church in the United States	3	3	918	3	398	520
12	Protestant Episcopal Church	10	10	2,866	10	895	1,971
13	Reformed Episcopal Church	5	5	501	5	145	356
14	Other Protestant bodies	8	8	612	8	232	380
15	Roman Catholic Church	5	5	7,602	5	3,561	4,041
16	Jewish congregations	2	2	[2]160	......	......	......
	Eastern Orthodox Churches:						
17	Greek Orthodox Church	1	1	150	......	......	......
1	**Chattanooga, Tenn.**	72	68	17,469	59	5,323	9,687
	Protestant bodies	66	64	15,599	59	5,323	9,687
	Baptist bodies:						
3	Baptists—Southern Convention	6	6	2,215	6	875	1,340
4	Baptists—National Convention (Colored)	11	11	3,615	11	1,045	2,570
5	Colored Primitive Baptists in America	4	4	380	2	105	225
	Disciples or Christians:						
6	Disciples of Christ	1	1	500	1	225	275
7	Churches of Christ	1	1	170	1	70	100
	Methodist bodies:						
8	Methodist Episcopal Church	8	6	1,551	6	547	1,004
9	African Methodist Episcopal Church	8	8	708	8	216	492
10	Methodist Episcopal Church, South	4	4	2,255	4	856	1,399
11	Other African Methodist bodies	2	2	585	2	235	350

[1] Exclusive of statistics not reported separately by cities for part of Cleveland diocese.

DEBT ON CHURCH PROPERTY, PARSONAGES, AND SUNDAY SCHOOLS, FOR EACH CITY OF 25,000 INHABITANTS OR DENOMINATIONS: 1906—Continued.

PLACES OF WORSHIP.					VALUE OF CHURCH PROPERTY.		DEBT ON CHURCH PROPERTY.		PARSONAGES.		SUNDAY SCHOOLS CONDUCTED BY CHURCH ORGANIZATIONS.				
Number of organizations reporting—		Number of church edifices reported.	Seating capacity of church edifices.		Number of organizations reporting.	Value reported.	Number of organizations reporting.	Amount of debt reported.	Number of organizations reporting.	Value of parsonages reported.	Number of organizations reporting.	Number of Sunday schools reported.	Number of officers and teachers.	Number of scholars.	
Church edifices.	Halls, etc.		Number of organizations reporting.	Seating capacity reported.											
3	......	3	3	2,350	3	$179,000	1	$2,000	3	$18,300	3	4	148	1,760	9
2	......	2	2	700	2	6,600	1	30	......	......	2	2	20	120	10
2	......	2	2	1,050	2	95,000	1	3,600	......	......	2	2	44	531	11
1	......	1	1	150	1	10,000	......	......	......	......	1	1	10	100	12
3	......	3	3	2,285	3	76,000	1	2,000	1	3,000	3	3	152	2,348	13
1	......	1	1	1,200	1	40,000	......	......	1	4,500	1	1	100	1,300	14
6	5	6	6	2,300	7	22,600	2	5,500	......	......	9	9	89	608	15
3	......	3	3	1,280	3	80,500	3	47,500	3	11,300	3	3	7	555	16
......	......	......	......	......	......	......	......	......	......	......	......	......	......	......	17
......	1	......	......	......	......	......	......	......	......	......	......	......	......	......	18
32	3	38	31	15,160	33	681,530	18	87,195	21	78,170	33	39	828	6,198	1
29	3	34	28	13,160	30	546,530	10	34,195	18	63,970	30	36	808	5,478	2
2	......	3	2	1,425	2	51,470	1	400	1	870	2	4	54	540	3
2	......	2	2	725		33,000	1	20	2	4,600	2	2	33	308	4
2	......	2	2	650	2	21,500	......	......	1	2,500	2	2	35	335	5
1	......	1	1	850	1	20,000	......	......	......	......	1	1	28	344	6
1	......	1	1	600	1	12,000	1	3,000	1	2,000	1	1	4	100	7
2	......	2	2	400	2	9,800	2	4,275	1	4,000	1	1	9	24	8
3	......	3	3	1,475	3	37,000	2	1,600	3	10,500	3	5	86	960	9
2	......	2	2	510	2	5,000	......	......	......	......	2	2	16	72	10
6	......	9	6	3,525	6	182,000	2	21,900	4	14,000	6	8	391	1,452	11
1	......	1	1	300	1	12,000	......	......	1	4,500	1	1	23	170	12
1	......	2	1	1,100	1	95,000	......	......	1	5,000	1	1	20	125	13
1	......	1	1	300	1	10,000	......	......	1	7,000	1	1	16	200	14
5	3	5	4	1,300	6	57,760	1	3,000	2	9,000	7	7	93	848	15
3	......	4	3	2,000	3	135,000	3	53,000	3	14,200	3	3	20	715	16
......	......	......	......	......	......	......	......	......	......	......	......	......	......	......	17
65	7	74	65	48,420	66	1,844,085	25	53,063	34	199,750	71	79	1,098	11,060	1
58	6	65	58	43,695	59	1,399,085	23	39,063	29	162,750	64	70	957	9,653	2
3	......	3	3	2,150	3	113,000	2	5,100	......	......	3	5	81	929	3
7	2	7	7	4,750	7	27,400	4	3,110	2	3,000	8	9	73	1,068	4
4	......	6	4	3,700	4	157,000	3	9,600	4	64,000	4	5	161	1,112	5
4	......	4	4	3,100	4	95,200	......	......	3	8,500	5	6	65	786	6
8	......	8	8	6,850	8	116,950	5	11,460	4	9,750	8	8	108	1,951	7
4	......	5	4	2,840	4	84,000	......	......	4	20,500	4	4	102	858	8
3	1	3	3	1,875	3	2,900	3	921	......	......	4	4	30	144	9
3	......	3	3	3,800	3	27,500	1	40	2	2,100	3	3	21	185	10
3	......	3	3	2,650	3	190,000	......	......	1	5,000	3	3	87	621	11
9	......	12	9	8,450	9	421,000	1	5,200	6	36,500	10	11	167	1,380	12
5	......	5	5	1,180	5	8,850	1	200	1	900	5	5	21	228	13
5	3	6	5	2,350	6	155,285	3	3,432	2	12,500	7	7	41	391	14
5	......	7	5	3,875	5	370,000	1	8,000	5	37,000	5	7	130	1,307	15
2	......	2	2	850	2	75,000	1	6,000	......	......	2	2	11	100	16
......	1	......	......	......	......	......	......	......	......	......	......	......	......	......	17
62	7	65	59	28,445	61	732,845	20	16,915	13	45,800	63	70	761	8,680	1
59	7	62	56	26,920	59	687,845	18	16,015	13	45,800	61	68	746	8,330	2
6	......	7	6	3,520	6	107,200	1	2,000	1	7,000	6	10	125	1,518	3
11	......	11	11	6,100	10	54,500	6	5,000	......	......	11	11	71	911	4
4	......	4	2	1,200	4	5,200	1	400	......	......	2	2	7	65	5
1	......	1	1	500	1	15,000	......	......	......	......	1	1	30	300	6
1	......	1	1	500	1	4,000	......	......	......	......	1	2	8	60	7
8	......	9	8	3,100	8	135,220	1	540	4	7,500	8	9	121	1,302	8
6	2	7	6	1,850	6	6,475	3	600	1	300	7	7	48	337	9
4	......	4	4	1,950	4	61,000	......	......	2	15,500	4	4	113	1,960	10
2	......	2	2	1,700	2	15,000	2	2,000	......	......	2	2	20	235	11

[1] Heads of families only.

TABLE 7.—ORGANIZATIONS, COMMUNICANTS OR MEMBERS, PLACES OF WORSHIP, VALUE OF CHURCH PROPERTY, MORE IN 1900, BY SELECTED

	DENOMINATION.	Total number of organizations.	COMMUNICANTS OR MEMBERS.				
			Number of organizations reporting.	Total number reported.	Sex.		
					Number of organizations reporting.	Male.	Female.
	Chattanooga, Tenn.—Continued.						
	Protestant bodies—Continued.						
	Presbyterian bodies:						
12	**Presbyterian Church in the United States of America**	3	3	599	3	209	390
13	**Presbyterian Church in the United States**	2	2	855	2	290	565
14	**Cumberland Presbyterians**[1]	2	2	610	2	248	362
15	**Protestant Episcopal Church**	3	3	700	2	123	145
16	**Other Protestant bodies**	11	11	856	9	279	470
17	**Roman Catholic Church**	1	1	1,700			
18	**Jewish congregations**	4	2	[2] 120			
	Eastern Orthodox Churches:						
19	**Greek Orthodox Church**	1	1	50			
1	**Chelsea, Mass.**	21	19	11,589	14	4,643	6,099
	Protestant bodies	13	13	3,459	10	975	1,987
	Adventist bodies:						
•	Advent Christian Church	1	1	163	1	66	97
	Baptist bodies:						
4	Baptists—Northern Convention	1	1	468	1	134	334
5	Free Baptists	1	1	171			
6	Congregationalists	2	2	1,010	2	238	772
	Methodist bodies:						
7	Methodist Episcopal Church	2	2	598	2	309	289
8	African Methodist Episcopal Church	1	1	64	1	15	49
9	Protestant Episcopal Church	1	1	545	1	178	367
10	Unitarians	1	1	108			
11	Universalists	1	1	218			
12	Other Protestant bodies	2	2	114	2	35	79
13	**Roman Catholic Church**	1	1	7,225	1	3,400	3,825
14	**Jewish congregations**	4	2	[2] 350			
15	**Armenian Church**	1	1	280	1	185	95
16	**Spiritualists**	2	2	275	2	83	192
1	**Chester, Pa.**	41	41	14,538	36	4,213	6,268
	Protestant bodies	36	36	8,172	34	2,937	5,188
	Baptist bodies:						
•	Baptists—Northern Convention	7	7	1,528	6	488	1,005
	Lutheran bodies:						
4	General Council of the Evangelical Lutheran Church in North America	1	1	335	1	175	160
5	Evangelical Lutheran Synodical Conference of America	1	1	12			
	Methodist bodies:						
6	Methodist Episcopal Church	6	6	2,889	6	1,058	1,831
7	African Methodist Episcopal Church	2	2	395	2	136	259
8	Other African Methodist bodies	5	5	502	5	183	319
	Presbyterian bodies:						
9	Presbyterian Church in the United States of America	5	5	1,567	5	556	1,011
10	Protestant Episcopal Church	2	2	680	2	223	457
11	Other Protestant bodies	7	7	264	7	118	146
12	**Roman Catholic Church**	3	3	6,266	2	1,276	1,080
13	**Jewish congregations**	1	1	[2] 50			
	Eastern Orthodox Churches:						
14	**Greek Orthodox Church**	1	1	50			
1	**Chicago, Ill.**	1,058	1,036	833,441	852	232,970	263,233
	Protestant bodies	786	782	237,220	730	83,994	126,971
	Adventist bodies:						
3	Seventh-day Adventist Denomination	8	8	559	8	176	383
4	Other Adventist bodies	4	4	295	4	135	160
	Baptist bodies:						
5	Baptists—Northern Convention	48	48	18,022	47	6,041	9,821
6	Baptists—National Convention (Colored)	14	14	5,784	13	2,042	3,728
7	Other Baptist bodies	2	2	125	2	37	88
8	Brethren (Plymouth)	8	8	554	8	250	304
	Catholic Apostolic Churches:						
9	Catholic Apostolic Church	1	1	1,046	1	431	615
10	New Apostolic Church	1	1	400	1	150	250
11	Christian Catholic Church in Zion	2	2	850	2	365	485
12	Church of Christ, Scientist	6	6	3,655	5	889	2,050
13	Congregationalists	73	73	15,621	71	5,540	9,907
	Disciples or Christians:						
14	Disciples of Christ	28	28	6,890	28	2,933	3,957
15	Churches of Christ	1	1	29	1	12	17
	Evangelical bodies:						
16	Evangelical Association	13	13	1,218	13	486	732
17	United Evangelical Church	7	7	880	7	342	538
18	German Evangelical Synod of North America	28	28	17,053	24	6,057	9,845
19	Independent churches	17	17	5,185	17	2,114	3,071
	Lutheran bodies:						
20	General Synod of the Evangelical Lutheran Church in the United States of America	13	13	2,024	13	866	1,158
21	General Council of the Evangelical Lutheran Church in North America	37	37	11,930	34	4,521	6,161
22	Evangelical Lutheran Synodical Conference of America	43	42	39,317	38	15,834	19,143

[1] Includes Cumberland Presbyterian Church and Colored Cumberland Presbyterian Church.

DEBT ON CHURCH PROPERTY, PARSONAGES, AND SUNDAY SCHOOLS, FOR EACH CITY OF 25,000 INHABITANTS OR DENOMINATIONS: 1906—Continued.

PLACES OF WORSHIP.					VALUE OF CHURCH PROPERTY.		DEBT ON CHURCH PROPERTY.		PARSONAGES.		SUNDAY SCHOOLS CONDUCTED BY CHURCH ORGANIZATIONS.				
Number of organizations reporting— Church edifices.	Number of organizations reporting— Halls, etc.	Number of church edifices reported.	Seating capacity of church edifices. Number of organizations reporting.	Seating capacity of church edifices. Seating capacity reported.	Number of organizations reporting.	Value reported.	Number of organizations reporting.	Amount of debt reported.	Number of organizations reporting.	Value of parsonages reported.	Number of organizations reporting.	Number of Sunday schools reported.	Number of officers and teachers.	Number of scholars.	
3	....	3	3	1,500	3	$72,000	....	....	1	$1,000	3	3	60	377	12
2	....	2	2	900	2	53,000	....	....	1	5,000	2	3	58	445	13
2	....	2	2	1,000	2	22,000	1	$1,725	1	6,000	2	2	20	225	14
3	....	3	3	1,550	3	77,000	....	....	1	1,500	3	3	25	230	15
6	5	6	5	1,550	7	60,250	3	3,750	1	2,000	9	9	53	365	16
1	....	1	1	700	....	....	....	....	....	....	1	1	10	306	17
2	....	2	2	825	2	45,000	2	900	....	....	1	1	5	45	18
....	....	....	....	....	....	....	....	....	....	....	....	....	....	....	19
13	5	15	12	8,100	15	567,850	7	35,560	4	48,500	15	15	402	5,348	1
11	2	13	11	6,600	13	357,850	5	11,560	3	8,500	12	12	316	3,298	2
1	....	1	1	300	1	8,000	1	2,000	....	....	1	1	14	120	3
1	....	1	1	1,000	1	75,000	....	....	....	....	1	1	39	671	4
1	....	1	1	275	1	14,000	....	....	....	....	1	1	26	160	5
2	....	3	2	,925	2	111,000	....	....	1	4,000	2	2	93	1,111	6
2	....	2	2	,050	2	60,000	2	5,500	1	3,000	2	2	75	624	7
1	....	1	1	500	1	6,000	....	....	....	....	1	1	12	65	8
1	....	2	1	350	1	8,000	....	....	1	1,500	1	1	25	200	9
1	....	1	1	300	1	25,000	....	....	....	....	....	....	....	....	10
1	....	1	1	900	1	50,000	1	4,000	....	....	1	1	24	300	11
....	2	....	....	....	2	850	1	60	....	....	2	2	8	47	12
1	....	1	1	,500	1	200,000	1	20,000	1	40,000	1	1	80	1,900	13
1	....	1	....	....	1	10,000	1	4,000	....	....	2	2	6	150	14
....	1	....	....	....	....	....	....	....	....	....	....	....	....	....	15
....	2	....	....	....	....	....	....	....	....	....	....	....	....	....	16
36	4	39	35	19,665	38	826,955	18	90,514	15	103,395	36	39	877	9,253	1
32	3	34	31	17,025	34	620,415	14	55,014	12	58,700	33	36	787	8,306	2
7	....	8	6	3,850	7	144,430	1	1,500		10,000	6		139	1,411	3
1	....	1	1	300	1	12,000	1	2,900		3,200	1		36	300	4
....	....	....	....	....	....	....	....	....	....	....	....	....	....	....	5
6	....	6	6	4,200	6	134,000	3	9,575	4	24,500	6	6	302	3,462	6
2	....	2	2	850	2	15,000	2	6,750	2	3,000	2	2	46	396	7
5	....	5	5	2,150	5	28,000	5	4,289	....	....	5	5	44	515	8
5	....	5	5	3,025	5	142,500	1	26,000	1	10,000	5	6	146	1,417	9
2	....	3	2	1,500	2	115,800	....	....	1	8,000	2	3	41	606	10
4	3	4	4	1,150	6	28,685	1	4,000	....	....	6	6	33	197	11
3	....	4	3	2,330	3	196,540	3	32,500	3	44,695	2	2	89	917	12
1	....	1	1	310	1	10,000	1	3,000	....	....	1	1	1	30	13
....	1	....	....	....	....	....	....	....	....	....	....	....	....	....	14
811	108	899	795	437,611	839	27,016,248	490	4,160,511	304	2,087,500	838	939	17,167	210,899	1
677	81	742	666	339,693	707	17,588,953	387	2,055,073	227	1,118,600	736	815	16,212	177,214	2
4	3	5	4	1,170	5	31,864	2	12,079	....	....	8	11	69	472	3
2	2	2	2	650	2	13,000	....	....	....	....	1	1	20	145	4
47	1	56	47	31,366	48	1,538,690	36	283,070	6	19,700	48	73	1,541	17,692	5
9	3	9	9	5,050	10	145,496	6	16,230	1	2,750	13	13	163	1,644	6
1	1	1	1	200	1	3,000	....	....	....	....	2	2	18	98	7
....	8	....	....	....	....	....	....	....	....	....	7	7	58	530	8
1	....	-	-	400	1	35,000	1	8 000	....	....	....	....	....	....	9
....	1	....	....	....	....	....	....	....	....	....	1	1	3	65	10
....	2	....	....	....	....	....	....	....	....	....	....	....	....	....	11
5	1	5	5	6,502	5	680,000	....	....	....	....	6	6	197	1,295	12
73	....	78	64	30,290	73	1,581,840	28	139,145	10	33,500	73	80	1,724	19,281	13
16	3	17	16	5,855	17	230,500	11	42,200	1	5,000	27	27	401	4,133	14
....	1	....	....	....	1	175	....	....	....	....	1	1	16	160	15
13	....	13	13	3,825	13	136,000	4	16,600	9	35,000	13	14	252	2,015	16
7	....	8	7	2,300	7	71,500	3	11,050	4	12,300	7	7	135	1,177	17
28	....	34	28	14,330	27	612,700	19	87,441	20	83,100	28	29	908	9,613	18
9	6	11	9	4,500	10	290,500	4	7,575	2	11,500	15	17	400	3,912	19
11	1	11	10	3,775	12	142,800	11	50,000	4	7,400	13	13	286	2,052	20
31	5	33	31	14,911	33	600,360	28	132,845	19	93,300	37	39	966	10,494	21
40	....	41	40	27,550	41	1,012,800	35	292,520	29	120,300	18	21	133	4,482	22

[1] Heads of families only.

TABLE 7.—ORGANIZATIONS, COMMUNICANTS OR MEMBERS, PLACES OF WORSHIP, VALUE OF CHURCH PROPERTY, MORE IN 1900, BY SELECTED

	DENOMINATION.	Total number of organizations.	COMMUNICANTS OR MEMBERS. Number of organizations reporting.	Total number reported.	Sex. Number of organizations reporting.	Male.	Female.
	Chicago, Ill.—Continued.						
	Protestant bodies—Continued.						
	Lutheran bodies—Continued.						
23	United Norwegian Lutheran Church in America	10	10	3,216	5	741	1,098
24	Evangelical Lutheran Joint Synod of Ohio and Other States	3	3	789	2	153	136
25	Hauge's Norwegian Evangelical Lutheran Synod	6	5	1,405	4	339	491
26	Evangelical Lutheran Synod of Iowa and Other States	2	2	1,056	2	481	575
27	Synod for the Norwegian Evangelical Lutheran Church in America	6	6	1,588	5	663	815
28	Danish Evangelical Lutheran Church in America	4	4	1,915	2	69	89
29	Slovak Evangelical Lutheran Synod of America	3	3	1,281	3	815	466
30	Other Lutheran bodies	7	7	376	7	164	212
	Methodist bodies:						
31	Methodist Episcopal Church	136	136	29,456	130	10,025	16,485
32	African Methodist Episcopal Church	12	12	3,701	12	1,277	2,424
33	African Methodist Episcopal Zion Church	2	2	582	2	130	452
34	Other Methodist bodies	7	7	295	7	93	202
35	Pentecostal Church of the Nazarene	2	2	560	2	204	356
	Presbyterian bodies:						
36	Presbyterian Church in the United States of America	57	57	21,341	54	7,201	12,085
37	Cumberland Presbyterian Church	4	4	545	1	90	185
38	Colored Cumberland Presbyterian Church	1	1	500	1	225	275
39	Welsh Calvinistic Methodist Church	2	2	502	2	238	264
40	United Presbyterian Church of North America	8	8	1,483	8	541	942
41	Synod of the Reformed Presbyterian Church of North America	1	1	56	1	13	43
42	Protestant Episcopal Church	53	53	19,275	47	5,451	9,017
	Reformed bodies:						
43	Reformed Church in America	10	10	2,678	10	1,155	1,523
44	Reformed Church in the United States	5	5	754	5	336	418
45	Christian Reformed Church	6	6	1,808	6	823	985
46	Reformed Episcopal Church	7	7	1,518	5	467	811
	Salvationists:						
47	Salvation Army	23	22	1,000	22	507	493
	Swedish Evangelical bodies:						
48	Swedish Evangelical Mission Covenant of America	19	19	3,408	18	1,313	1,995
49	Swedish Evangelical Free Mission	6	6	715	6	326	389
50	Unitarians	4	4	776	2	65	111
51	Universalists	4	4	1,402	2	106	296
52	Other Protestant bodies	22	21	1,802	20	762	925
53	Roman Catholic Church	173	173	568,764	84	131,752	130,732
54	Jewish congregations	60	43	[1] 14,703	...	...	...
55	Armenian Church	2	2	611	2	449	162
	Eastern Orthodox Churches:						
56	Russian Orthodox Church	1	1	1,000	1	650	350
57	Servian Orthodox Church	2	2	3,000	2	2,661	339
58	Greek Orthodox Church	1	1	10,000	1	9,500	500
59	Polish National Church of America	3	3	2,545	3	1,515	1,030
60	Spiritualists	21	21	4,193	21	1,925	2,268
61	All other bodies	9	8	1,405	8	524	881
1	Cincinnati, Ohio	255	249	159,663	228	66,760	82,512
2	Protestant bodies	196	193	51,520	184	17,725	30,789
	Baptist bodies:						
3	Baptists—Northern Convention	11	11	4,179	11	1,537	2,642
4	Baptists—National Convention (Colored)	14	14	3,588	12	1,230	2,083
5	Church of Christ, Scientist	1	1	349	1	92	257
6	Congregationalists	8	8	1,248	8	468	780
	Disciples or Christians:						
7	Disciples of Christ	14	14	2,913	14	1,116	1,797
8	Churches of Christ	1	1	38	1	13	25
	German Evangelical Protestant bodies:						
9	German Evangelical Protestant Ministers' Association	9	9	6,022	9	2,333	3,689
10	German Evangelical Protestant Ministers' Conference	3	3	2,196	2	576	820
11	German Evangelical Synod of North America	5	5	3,275	5	1,146	2,129
	Lutheran bodies:						
12	General Synod of the Evangelical Lutheran Church in the United States of America	3	3	1,084	3	449	635
13	Evangelical Lutheran Synodical Conference of America	2	2	347	2	134	213
	Methodist bodies:						
14	Methodist Episcopal Church	43	40	8,643	36	2,751	4,692
15	African Methodist Episcopal Church	3	3	1,418	3	506	912
16	Other Methodist bodies	4	4	325	4	127	198
	Presbyterian bodies:						
17	Presbyterian Church in the United States of America	30	30	7,596	30	2,542	5,054
18	Other Presbyterian bodies	5	5	472	5	155	317
19	Protestant Episcopal Church	18	18	4,308	17	1,447	2,811
	Reformed bodies:						
20	Reformed Church in the United States	4	4	1,597	3	400	516
21	Christian Reformed Church	1	1	120	1	55	65
	United Brethren bodies:						
22	Church of the United Brethren in Christ	4	4	388	4	166	222
23	Other Protestant bodies	13	13	1,414	13	482	932
24	Roman Catholic Church	43	43	106,211	41	48,835	51,671
25	Jewish congregations	13	10	[1] 1,680	...	...	...
26	All other bodies	3	3	252	3	200	52

[1] Heads of families only.

DEBT ON CHURCH PROPERTY, PARSONAGES, AND SUNDAY SCHOOLS, FOR EACH CITY OF 25,000 INHABITANTS OR DENOMINATIONS: 1906—Continued.

PLACES OF WORSHIP.					VALUE OF CHURCH PROPERTY.		DEBT ON CHURCH PROPERTY.		PARSONAGES.		SUNDAY SCHOOLS CONDUCTED BY CHURCH ORGANIZATIONS.				
Number of organizations reporting— Church edifices.	Number of organizations reporting— Halls, etc.	Number of church edifices reported.	Seating capacity of church edifices. Number of organizations reporting.	Seating capacity of church edifices. Seating capacity reported.	Number of organizations reporting.	Value reported.	Number of organizations reporting.	Amount of debt reported.	Number of organizations reporting.	Value of parsonages reported.	Number of organizations reporting.	Number of Sunday schools reported.	Number of officers and teachers.	Number of scholars.	
9	1	9	9	2,970	9	$79,800	8	$22,750	2	$11,000	10	1	240	2,427	23
3	...	3	3	1,300	3	37,000	3	16,100	2	2,000	3		15	308	24
6	...	6	6	2,025	6	77,350	5	18,800	2	15,500	6	2	139	1,665	25
2	...	2	2	1,250	2	24,000	2	4,530	1	3,000	2	[illegible]	33	420	26
6	...	6	6	2,620	6	113,000	6	23,800	3	14,500	6	7	138	1,545	27
3	...	4	3	1,000	3	40,000	2	11,181	2	5,000	3	3	40	450	28
2	1	2	2	1,000	2	40,000	1	18,000	2	9,000	2	2	2	95	29
5	1	5	5	1,048	5	26,000	4	7,800	...	...	6	6	40	294	30
129	4	1	128	58,647	129	3,485,200	43	188,850	55	266,000	136	138	3,405	34,758	31
9	3		9	5,725	11	163,200	10	47,749	2	5,400	12	1	150	1,508	32
2	...		2	1,000	2	38,000	1	6,000	1	350	2		23	322	33
6	...	30	6	1,420	6	28,000	2	2,700	4	10,500	6	6	64	560	34
1	1	[illegible]	1	500	1	6,000	...	...	...	...	2	2	28	240	35
53	3	66	53	37,578	53	2, ,700	21	140,560	3	30,000	56	72	1,716	24,986	
4	...	4	4	1,400	4	000	2	6,250	...	...	4	4	57	585	
1	...	1	1	1,000	1	000	1	6,500	1	3,500	1	1	21	430	
2	...	2	2	1,070	2	224,300	...	...	...	...	2	2	32	238	
8	...	8	8	3,360	8	[illegible],400	6	20,300	5	25,500	8	9	256	2,460	
1	...	1	1	225	1	22,000	...	...	...	...	1	1	16	127	36
49	2	64	49	23,391	51	2,248,850	33	179,450	13	151,000	52	55	798	7,375	[illegible]
10	...	11	10	5,450	10	156,000	3	8,100	7	29,500	10	12	277	3,132	
5	...	5	5	1,465	5	79,000	2	16,500	3	8,000	5	7	68	694	
6	...	6	6	3,500	6	51,000	4	18,500	5	18,000	6	6	94	1,275	43
6	1	7	6	2,910	6	168,800	1	5,000	1	25,000	7	9	135	1,651	[illegible]
9	14	9	9	3,233	23	134,250	14	76,267	...	...	19	19	113	771	47
18	1	18	18	10,327	19	241,750	11	40,885	4	22,000	19	19	584	5,888	
4	2	4	4	2,450	4	60,283	4	29,371	...	...	6	6	137	931	
3	1	4	3	1,725	3	240,000	1	4,800	...	...	4	4	29	152	
4	...	6	4	2,850	4	257,500	1	3,200	2	23,000	4	4	64	929	48
14	8	16	14	4,580	16	191,345	8	32,375	2	17,000	18	22	203	1,738	[illegible]
87	1	108	87	71,708	87	8,295,570	72	1,890,338	71	909,900	62		745	29,668	53
34	2	36	30	21,060	33	970,800	26	195,200	3	40,000	24		110	3,201	54
...	2	...	...	...	...	...	...	...	...	...	...	[illegible]	...	...	55
1	...	1	1	,000	1	25,000	1	12,900	1	15,000	...	...	...	...	56
1	1	1	1	100	1	9,000	1	5,000	...	...	...	...	...	...	57
1	...	1	1	1,200	1	45,000	...	...	...	...	...	...	...	...	58
3	...	3	3	1,600	3	57,000	3	11,000	2	4,000	3	3	5	292	59
5	14	5	5	750	4	6,550	...	...	...	...	8	8	30	221	60
2	7	2	1	500	2	18,375	...	...	...	...	5	5	65	303	61
231	15	247	227	122,582	234	8,681,987	96	828,176	98	551,200	228	284	3,823	47,545	1
179	11	191	175	82,400	183	5,062,987	64	287,293	64	357,600	187	197	3,532	33,552	2
11	...	16	11	8,190	11	413,500	4	21,600	1	2,000	11	17	341	4,080	3
12	...	12	11	4,100	12	127,376	7	8,530	...	...	13	13	120	1,060	4
1	...	1	1	550	1	15,000	...	...	...	...	1	1	15	106	5
8	...	8	8	2,575	8	168,000	2	1,937	2	11,500	7	7	101	839	6
14	...	16	14	5,250	14	192,500	4	6,708	...	...	14	14	197	2,015	7
...	1	...	...	...	...	...	...	...	...	...	1	1	3	30	8
9	...	9	9	6,635	9	408,000	8	33,000	8	48,000	9	9	249	2,332	9
3	...	3	3	2,810	3	135,000	2	11,800	3	15,000	3	3	92	900	10
5	...	5	5	3,190	5	137,500	4	34,300	5	15,000	5	5	131	1,455	11
3	...	3	3	1,600	3	114,000	3	21,300	1	3,000	3	3	85	1,165	12
2	...	2	2	950	2	20,000	2	11,800	...	...	2	2	12	122	13
40	...	40	37	15,466	40	915,000	4	11,576	19	131,850	39	39	819	6,853	14
3	...	3	3	2,075		85,400	2	3,706	2	8,000	3	3	49	481	15
3	1	3	3	750	[illegible]	28,150	3	1,456	...	...	4	4	26	124	16
29	1	31	29	14,840	29	1,262,419	6	49,900	8	45,500	30	33	739	6,955	17
5	...	5	5	1,780	5	102,500	1	680	3	15,000	5	5	62	555	18
18	...	21	18	5,829	18	534,392	6	4,600	5	34,750	17	17	232	2,174	19
[illegible]	...	3	3	1,700	3	116,000	2	10,700	2	16,000	4	4	99	1,025	20
[illegible]	...	1	1	400	1	9,000	1	5,000	1	4,000	1	1	6	40	21
4	...	4	4	1,450	4	31,500	2	3,700	3	5,000	4	5	77	562	22
5	8	5	5	2,260	8	247,750	1	45,000	1	3,000	11	11	77	679	23
	1		42	30,292	42	2,833,000	27	420,383	34	193,600	37	81	247	12,818	24
42	1	45	9	9,390	9	786,000	5	120,500	...	...	4		44	1,175	25
[illegible]	2	[illegible]	1	500	...	...	...	...	...	...	...	6	...	...	26

TABLE 7.—ORGANIZATIONS, COMMUNICANTS OR MEMBERS, PLACES OF WORSHIP, VALUE OF CHURCH PROPERTY, MORE IN 1900, BY SELECTED

	DENOMINATION.	Total number of organizations.	COMMUNICANTS OR MEMBERS. Number of organizations reporting.	Total number reported.	Sex. Number of organizations reporting.	Male.	Female.
1	Cleveland, Ohio	314	301	146,338	277	60,730	73,686
2	Protestant bodies	249	246	76,174	237	29,615	43,825
	Baptist bodies:						
3	Baptists—Northern Convention	20	20	5,621	18	1,945	3,307
4	Baptists—National Convention (Colored)	3	3	1,244	3	465	779
5	Free Baptists	2	2	500	2	151	349
6	Church of Christ, Scientist	3	3	832	3	257	575
7	Congregationalists	24	24	7,692	24	2,726	4,966
	Disciples or Christians:						
8	Disciples of Christ	10	10	3,373	10	1,448	1,925
	Evangelical bodies:						
9	Evangelical Association	9	9	1,382	9	515	867
10	United Evangelical Church	2	2	101	2	30	71
	Friends:						
11	Society of Friends (Orthodox)	4	4	553	4	257	296
	German Evangelical Protestant bodies:						
12	German Evangelical Protestant Ministers' Association	3	3	2,548	2	700	548
13	German Evangelical Synod of North America	11	11	5,981	11	2,631	3,350
14	Independent churches	5	5	521	5	176	345
	Lutheran bodies:						
15	Evangelical Lutheran Synodical Conference of America	14	14	10,845	12	4,851	5,784
16	Slovak Evangelical Lutheran Synod of America	1	1	542	1	337	205
17	Other Lutheran bodies	11	11	1,357	10	556	746
	Methodist bodies:						
18	Methodist Episcopal Church	37	37	10,383	36	3,859	6,124
19	African Methodist Episcopal Church	2	2	629	2	257	372
20	Free Methodist Church of North America	1	1	88	1	31	57
	Presbyterian bodies:						
21	Presbyterian Church in the United States of America	18	18	7,754	18	2,718	5,036
22	Welsh Calvinistic Methodist Church	1	1	55	1	20	35
23	United Presbyterian Church of North America	2	2	582	2	212	370
24	Protestant Episcopal Church	21	21	5,880	21	2,299	3,581
	Reformed bodies:						
25	Reformed Church in the United States	14	14	4,395	12	1,867	2,128
26	Other Reformed bodies	4	4	436	4	197	239
27	Unitarians	1	1	563	1	216	347
	United Brethren bodies:						
28	Church of the United Brethren in Christ	7	6	654	6	271	383
29	Other Protestant bodies	19	17	1,663	17	623	1,040
30	Roman Catholic Church[1]	32	32	66,432	31	30,427	29,204
31	Jewish congregations	23	13	[2]2,137			
	Eastern Orthodox Churches:						
32	Russian Orthodox Church	1	1	550	1	350	200
33	Greek Orthodox Church	1	1	250			
34	Spiritualists	5	5	598	5	274	324
35	All other bodies	3	3	197	3	64	133
1	Columbus, Ohio	134	134	63,261	120	25,863	32,805
	Protestant bodies	106	106	33,645	99	11,283	18,573
	Baptist bodies:						
3	Baptists—Northern Convention	5	5	1,433	4	281	552
4	Baptists—National Convention (Colored)	7	7	1,816	6	619	812
5	Congregationalists	7	7	2,444	7	845	1,599
	Disciples or Christians:						
6	Disciples of Christ	4	4	1,170	4	403	767
	German Evangelical Protestant bodies:						
7	German Evangelical Protestant Ministers' Association	1	1	800	1	300	500
8	German Evangelical Synod of North America	1	1	2,800	1	1,250	1,550
	Lutheran bodies:						
9	General Council of the Evangelical Lutheran Church in North America	1	1	321			
10	Evangelical Lutheran Joint Synod of Ohio and Other States	9	9	2,695	8	917	1,603
11	Other Lutheran bodies	2	2	330	2	127	203
	Methodist bodies:						
12	Methodist Episcopal Church	21	21	10,401	20	3,762	6,189
13	African Methodist Episcopal Church	3	3	685	3	219	466
14	Other Methodist bodies	3	3	98	3	29	69
	Presbyterian bodies:						
15	Presbyterian Church in the United States of America	9	9	3,507	7	599	1,050
16	Cumberland Presbyterian Church	1	1	153	1	45	108
17	Welsh Calvinistic Methodist Church	1	1	458	1	196	262
18	United Presbyterian Church of North America	3	3	457	3	163	294
19	Protestant Episcopal Church	4	4	1,332	4	496	836
	Reformed bodies:						
20	Reformed Church in the United States	3	3	390	3	157	233
	United Brethren bodies:						
21	Church of the United Brethren in Christ	3	3	506	3	183	323
22	Other Protestant bodies	18	18	1,849	18	692	1,157
23	Roman Catholic Church	18	18	28,398	17	14,343	13,976
24	Jewish congregations	5	5	[2]575			
25	Spiritualists	3	3	409	3	207	202
26	All other bodies	2	2	234	1	30	54

[1]Exclusive of statistics not reported separately by cities for part of Cleveland diocese.

DEBT ON CHURCH PROPERTY, PARSONAGES, AND SUNDAY SCHOOLS, FOR EACH CITY OF 25,000 INHABITANTS OR DENOMINATIONS: 1906—Continued.

PLACES OF WORSHIP.					VALUE OF CHURCH PROPERTY.		DEBT ON CHURCH PROPERTY.		PARSONAGES.		SUNDAY SCHOOLS CONDUCTED BY CHURCH ORGANIZATIONS.				
Number of organizations reporting— Church edifices.	Number of organizations reporting— Halls, etc.	Number of church edifices reported.	Seating capacity of church edifices. Number of organizations reporting.	Seating capacity of church edifices. Seating capacity reported.	Number of organizations reporting.	Value reported.	Number of organizations reporting.	Amount of debt reported.	Number of organizations reporting.	Value of parsonages reported.	Number of organizations reporting.	Number of Sunday schools reported.	Number of officers and teachers.	Number of scholars.	
275	27	322	274	154,418	279	$10,877,070	128	$1,154,956	126	$667,550	270	321	5,344	67,479	1
228	18	264	228	118,876	233	8,120,020	97	427,206	95	390,060	231	260	5,049	52,229	2
20	....	25	20	12,120	20	835,970	9	22,600	6	19,500	20	28	574	5,398	3
2	....	2	2	1,600	3	49,075	2	3,035	2	5,000	3	5	61	724	4
2	....	2	2	850	2	25,000	1	1,200	1	4,000	2	2	84	560	5
3	....	3	3	1,736	3	133,000	1	12,000	....	....	3	3	55	310	6
24	....	27	24	14,220	24	892,400	9	19,148	7	29,700	24	25	647	7,412	7
10	....	10	10	5,150	10	233,700	2	2,450	....	....	10	10	248	2,797	8
9	....	9	9	3,400	9	121,500	4	13,865	7	20,000	9	9	185	1,688	9
2	....	2	2	475	2	15,500	2	9,800	2	8,000	2	2	27	255	10
4	....	4	4	800	4	14,500	3	2,000	....	....	3	3	44	280	11
3	....	4	3	2,700	3	105,000	3	14,000	3	9,000	3	3	71	795	12
11	....	15	11	6,200	11	218,600	9	38,050	5	18,100	11	11	288	2,956	13
3	2	3	3	1,200	3	20,500	2	4,200	1	2,000	4	4	58	476	14
13	....	16	13	9,490	14	349,600	6	12,700	12	37,500	6	9	61	1,688	15
1	....	1	1	750	1	20,000	1	8,000	1	500	1	1	1	60	16
8	3	8	8	2,150	8	61,100	4	6,200	2	7,500	11	11	81	730	17
35	2	36	35	17,480	35	1,268,300	9	41,533	16	77,350	37	40	1,106	12,300	18
2	....	2	2	900	2	74,500	....	....	....	....	2	2	33	395	19
1	....	1	1	300	1	5,000	....	....	1	1,800	1	1	17	76	20
18	....	23	18	14,560	18	1,327,700	4	12,350	2	20,000	18	22	593	5,831	21
1	....	1	1	300	1	12,000	1	3,375	....	....	1	1	11	75	22
2	....	2	2	950	2	42,090	2	13,550	1	8,300	2	2	43	452	23
20	1	29	20	8,570	20	1,604,000	8	25,450	9	72,000	20	21	281	2,446	24
14	....	16	14	6,225	14	143,000	8	36,350	10	32,100	14	14	200	2,350	25
4	....	6	4	1,050	4	14,700	1	1,500	3	10,500	4	4	40	304	26
1	....	1	1	500	1	120,000	....	....	....	....	1	1	17	98	27
6	....	6	6	1,920	6	32,000	....	....	3	4,200	6	6	96	775	28
9	10	10	9	3,280	12	381,375	6	123,850	1	3,000	13	20	132	989	29
32	....	41	32	25,360	31	2,278,550	21	619,350	29	271,800	30	51	224	13,196	30
13	1	15	12	9,482	12	427,000	7	100,000	1	2,000	7	8	52	1,977	31
....	1	....	....	....	1	40,000	1	6,000	1	4,000	....	....	....	....	32
....	1	....	....	....	....	....	....	....	....	....	....	....	....	....	33
1	4	1	1	500	1	7,000	1	1,200	....	....	1	1	6	30	34
1	2	1	1	200	1	4,500	1	1,200	....	....	1	1	13	48	35
119	13	124	117	61,955	121	3,015,205	59	330,505	44	212,150	125	131	2,199	26,520	1
99	7	104	97	48,709	101	2,118,305	48	145,601	31	144,000	103	108	2,068	22,063	2
5	....	6	5	2,150	5	98,000	1	2,000	....	....	5	6	99	973	3
6	1	7	6	2,286	7	76,060	4	10,400	....	....	7	7	72	842	4
7	....	7	7	3,200	7	149,500	1	900	2	9,500	7	9	167	1,664	5
4	....	4	4	2,700	4	104,000	4	29,500	....	....	4	4	77	925	6
1	....	1	1	600	1	40,000	....	....	....	....	1	1	20	300	
1	....	1	1	1,900	1	40,000	1	2,000	1	7,000	1	1	30	820	8
1	....	1	1	500	1	6,500	....	....	1	4,600	1	1	31	250	9
9	....	9	8	4,200	9	138,800	5	8,920	3	14,900	9	9	137	1,564	10
2	....	2	2	600	2	18,850	2	8,450	1	2,580	2	2	15	168	11
21	....	21	21	14,350	20	615,000	6	9,500	13	64,300	21	21	699	7,974	12
2	1	2	2	1,400	2	62,000	2	9,450	2	1,700	3	3	26	348	13
3	....	3	3	700	3	4,400	3	1,610	....	....	3	3	19	141	14
9	....	9	8	3,985	9	,000	3	5,700	1	9,000	8	8	193	2,048	15
1	....	1	1	250	1	,500	1	2,700	....	....	1	1	18	200	16
1	....	1	1	800	1	,000	....	....	....	....	1	1	39	325	17
3	....	3	3	1,000	3	273,000	2	14,500	1	4,000	3	3	41	330	18
4	....	7	4	1,960	4	2[illegible],500	2	21,500	1	10,000	4	6	77	656	19
3	....	3	3	800	3	18,000	1	3,000	1	3,000	3	3	51	406	20
3	....	3	3	1,450	3	17,500	1	2,450	1	2,500	3	3	50	490	21
13	5	18	13	3,978	15	112,695	9	13,021	3	11,000	16	16	207	1,640	22
14	4	1	14	10,396	15	841,600	9	166,704	13	68,150	16	17	101	4,074	23
3	....	4	3	1,700	2	31,200	1	18,000	....	....	4	4	14	243	24
3	....	8	3	1,150	2	24,000	1	200	....	....	1	1	7	75	25
....	2	....	....	....	1	100	....	....	....	....	1	1	9	65	26

[1] Heads of families only.

TABLE 7.—ORGANIZATIONS, COMMUNICANTS OR MEMBERS, PLACES OF WORSHIP, VALUE OF CHURCH PROPERTY, MORE IN 1900, BY SELECTED

	DENOMINATION.	Total number of organizations.	COMMUNICANTS OR MEMBERS.				
			Number of organizations reporting.	Total number reported.	Sex.		
					Number of organizations reporting.	Male.	Female.
1	Council Bluffs, Iowa	36	35	7,179	32	2,732	4,246
2	Protestant bodies	29	29	4,638	28	1,604	2,918
	Baptist bodies:						
3	Baptists—Northern Convention	4	4	749	4	215	534
4	Congregationalists	2	2	353	2	116	237
	Disciples or Christians:						
5	Disciples of Christ	1	1	561	1	156	405
	Lutheran bodies:						
6	United Danish Evangelical Lutheran Church in America	1	1	200	1	100	100
7	Other Lutheran bodies	3	3	371	2	112	143
	Methodist bodies:						
8	Methodist Episcopal Church	4	4	948	4	285	663
9	Other Methodist bodies	2	2	50	2	18	32
	Presbyterian bodies:						
10	Presbyterian Church in the United States of America	4	4	663	4	200	463
11	Protestant Episcopal Church	1	1	400	1	280	120
12	Other Protestant bodies	7	7	343	7	122	221
13	Roman Catholic Church	2	2	2,162	2	1,012	1,150
14	Jewish congregations	2	1	[1] 10	....	....	....
	Latter-day Saints:						
15	Reorganized Church of Jesus Christ of Latter-day Saints	1	1	286	1	110	176
16	All other bodies	2	2	83	1	6	2
1	Covington, Ky	35	34	31,435	32	14,345	16,735
2	Protestant bodies	25	25	8,773	23	3,221	5,197
	Baptist bodies:						
3	Baptists—Southern Convention	3	3	1,552	3	704	848
4	Baptists—National Convention (Colored)	3	3	670	2	215	425
	Disciples or Christians:						
5	Disciples of Christ	2	2	1,027	2	365	662
	German Evangelical Protestant bodies:						
6	German Evangelical Protestant Ministers' Conference	1	1	1,400	1	650	750
	Methodist bodies:						
7	Methodist Episcopal Church	5	5	1,427	4	387	735
8	Methodist Episcopal Church, South	2	2	576	2	216	360
9	Other Methodist bodies	2	2	201	2	79	122
	Presbyterian bodies:						
10	Presbyterian Church in the United States of America	1	1	636	1	200	436
11	Presbyterian Church in the United States	1	1	306	1	88	218
12	Protestant Episcopal Church	2	2	550	2	166	384
	Reformed bodies:						
13	Reformed Church in the United States	1	1	325	1	125	200
14	Other Protestant bodies	2	2	103	2	46	57
15	Roman Catholic Church	9	9	22,662	9	11,124	11,538
16	Jewish congregations	1	....	....	....	....	....
1	Dallas, Tex	107	105	32,471	95	11,669	17,543
2	Protestant bodies	96	95	22,917	87	7,173	12,690
	Baptist bodies:						
3	Baptists—Southern Convention	13	13	4,068	12	1,482	2,349
4	Baptists—National Convention (Colored)	13	13	3,726	13	1,112	2,614
5	Colored Primitive Baptists in America	1	1	145	....	....	....
6	Congregationalists	3	3	727	3	298	429
	Disciples or Christians:						
7	Disciples of Christ	7	7	1,688	7	637	1,051
8	Churches of Christ	5	5	564	5	221	343
	Methodist bodies:						
9	Methodist Episcopal Church	8	8	825	8	292	533
10	African Methodist Episcopal Church	4	3	839	3	310	529
11	Methodist Episcopal Church, South	9	9	4,462	6	1,075	1,608
12	Colored Methodist Episcopal Church	3	3	547	3	191	356
13	Free Methodist Church of North America	3	3	92	3	31	61
	Presbyterian bodies:						
14	Presbyterian Church in the United States of America	3	3	461	3	136	325
15	Cumberland Presbyterian Church	2	2	795	....	....	....
16	Presbyterian Church in the United States	5	5	1,615	5	633	982
17	Protestant Episcopal Church	4	4	1,290	4	414	876
18	Other Protestant bodies	13	13	1,073	12	341	634
19	Roman Catholic Church	6	6	9,284	6	4,467	4,817
20	Jewish congregations	3	2	[1] 205	....	....	....
21	Spiritualists	2	2	65	2	29	36
1	Davenport, Iowa	40	39	11,839	33	4,073	5,845
2	Protestant bodies	31	30	5,582	28	1,923	3,371
	Baptist bodies:						
3	Baptists—Northern and National (Colored) Conventions	3	3	714	3	243	471
4	Congregationalists	3	3	636	3	231	405
	Disciples or Christians:						
5	Disciples of Christ	1	1	300	1	125	175

[1] Heads of families only.

DEBT ON CHURCH PROPERTY, PARSONAGES, AND SUNDAY SCHOOLS, FOR EACH CITY OF 25,000 INHABITANTS OR DENOMINATIONS: 1906—Continued.

PLACES OF WORSHIP.					VALUE OF CHURCH PROPERTY.		DEBT ON CHURCH PROPERTY.		PARSONAGES.		SUNDAY SCHOOLS CONDUCTED BY CHURCH ORGANIZATIONS.				
Number of organizations reporting—		Number of church edifices reported.	Seating capacity of church edifices.		Number of organizations reporting.	Value reported.	Number of organizations reporting.	Amount of debt reported.	Number of organizations reporting.	Value of parsonages reported.	Number of organizations reporting.	Number of Sunday schools reported.	Number of officers and teachers.	Number of scholars.	
Church edifices.	Halls, etc.		Number of organizations reporting.	Seating capacity reported.											
28	6	35	28	9,850	28	$343,650	10	$32,175	15	$39,100	31	40	460	4,112	1
25	4	31	25	8,400	25	260,650	10	32,175	13	31,600	28	36	434	3,710	2
4	....	5	4	1,150	4	23,000	....	....	....	....	4	5	73	554	3
2	....	3	2	600	2	11,200	....	....	1	4,000	2	4	52	375	4
1	....	2	1	800	1	4,000	1	300	....	....	1	2	33	485	5
1	....	2	1	350	1	5,050	....	....	1	2,000	1	3	20	135	6
3	....	3	3	800	3	41,800	3	7,325	3	6,700	3	3	19	169	7
4	....	4	4	1,700	4	68,000	2	13,400	3	7,500	4	4	81	785	8
2	....	2	2	400	2	3,100	1	400	2	1,400	2	2	18	55	9
4	....	4	4	1,300	4	38,000	1	1,000	1	3,000	4	6	65	665	10
1	....	3	1	600	1	58,000	1	9,500	1	3,500	1	1	18	200	11
3	4	3	3	700	3	8,500	1	250	1	3,500	6	6	55	287	12
2	....	3	2	1,250	2	80,000	....	....	2	7,500	2	3	11	300	13
....	....	....	....	....	....	....	....	....	....	....	....	....	....	....	14
1	....	1	1	200	1	3,000	....	....	....	....	1	1	15	102	15
....	2	....	....	....	....	....	....	....	....	....	....	....	....	....	16
31	2	37	31	19,795	33	1,512,950	13	33,430	14	118,600	33	38	499	8,112	1
23	1	28	23	12,625	24	407,450	10	6,730	6	24,600	24	26	448	4,810	2
3	....	4	3	1,650	3	66,500	1	400	....	....	3	4	67	967	3
2	....	2	2	800	2	8,000	1	160	....	....	2	2	12	135	4
2	....	2	2	1,475	2	47,000	1	850	....	....	2	2	45	800	5
1	....	1	1	500	1	18,000	1	1,900	1	3,600	1	1	43	260	6
5	....	5	5	3,000	5	110,500	2	1,600	3	17,500	5	5	131	1,045	7
2	....	2	2	1,400	2	48,000	1	500	....	....	2	2	43	340	8
2	....	2	2	550	2	4,200	1	750	1	1,000	2	2	14	134	9
1	....	4	1	1,000	1	7,500	....	....	....	....	1	2	25	500	10
1	....	1	1	650	1	40,000	....	....	....	....	1	1	20	192	11
2	....	3	2	1,000	2	47,500	....	....	....	....	2	2	18	183	12
1	....	1	1	450	1	10,000	1	550	1	2,500	1	1	18	185	13
		1	1	150	2	250	1	20	....	....	2	2	12	69	14
		9	8	7,170	9	1,105,500	3	26,700	8	94,000	9	12	51	3,302	15
....	....	....	....	....	....	....	....	....	....	....	....	....	....	....	16
91	10	105	87	44,495	93	1,478,865	40	148,591	35	90,850	99	111	1,310	15,560	1
84	8	95	80	40,270	86	1,154,865	37	104,191	29	70,750	90	101	1,252	14,410	2
12		19	12	7,380	12	247,400	4	28,100	1	1,600	13	18	268	3,120	3
13	....	13	13	6,505	13	57,700	8	4,058	3	1,850	13	13	86	1,217	4
1	....	1	....	....	1	1,200	....	....	....	....	....	....	....	....	5
3	....	6	3	2,650	3	64,225	1	2,800	1	1,200	3	6	64	653	6
6	1	6	6	3,850	7	111,240	3	2,650	1	2,000	7	7	102	1,004	7
3	2	3	3	930	3	17,450	2	893	....	....	5	7	33	405	8
7	1	7	7	2,325	8	52,800	4	5,832	4	10,800	6	6	92	610	9
4	....	4	3	1,850	3	60,700	2	3,500	2	1,500	4	4	42	529	10
9	....	9	8	4,250	9	224,450	2	28,025	5	15,700	9	9	223	3,262	11
3	....	3	3	1,300	3	11,000	....	....	2	2,700	3	3	38	331	12
1	1	1	1	400	1	1,500	....	....	1	1,500	2	2	13	110	13
3	....	3	3	950	3	27,800	3	5,650	....	....	3	3	50	440	14
2	....	2	1	800	2	31,000	....	....	....	....	2	2	25	650	15
5	....	5	5	2,750	5	95,000	3	7,875	2	9,500	5	6	100	1,096	16
4	....	5	4	1,900	4	104,150	1	2,908	4	18,500	4	4	43	303	17
8	2	8	8	2,450	9	46,750	4	11,900	3	3,900	11	11	78	680	18
6	....	9	6	3,625	6	274,500	3	44,400	6	20,100	6	6	49	940	19
1	....	1	1	600	1	50,000	....	....	....	....	3	4	9	210	20
....	2	....	....	....	....	....	....	....	....	....	....	....	....	....	21
31	6	34	31	14,912	31	832,525	8	25,587	16	83,500	35	38	473	4,943	1
27	4	30	27	12,212	28	707,525	7	22,587	14	68,500	28	30	430	4,298	2
3	....	3	3	1,750	3	58,000	1	1,300	2	7,200	3	3	49	493	3
3	....	3	3	1,050	3	58,500	....	....	1	3,500	3	3	63	527	4
1	....	1	1	500	1	20,000	....	....	1	4,000	1	1	15	150	5

TABLE 7.—ORGANIZATIONS, COMMUNICANTS OR MEMBERS, PLACES OF WORSHIP, VALUE OF CHURCH PROPERTY, MORE IN 1900, BY SELECTED

	DENOMINATION.	Total number of organizations.	COMMUNICANTS OR MEMBERS.				
			Number of organizations reporting.	Total number reported.	Sex.		
					Number of organizations reporting.	Male.	Female.
	Davenport, Iowa—Continued.						
	Protestant bodies—Continued.						
	Lutheran bodies:						
6	General Synod of the Evangelical Lutheran Church in the United States of America	1	1	385	1	113	272
7	Evangelical Lutheran Synodical Conference of America	2	2	525	2	206	319
8	Other Lutheran bodies	4	4	390	4	165	225
	Methodist bodies:						
9	Methodist Episcopal Church	3	3	970	3	422	548
10	African Methodist Episcopal Church	1	1	60	1	19	41
	Presbyterian bodies:						
11	Presbyterian Church in the United States of America	2	2	726	2	220	506
12	United Presbyterian Church of North America	1	1	36	1	12	24
13	Protestant Episcopal Church	3	3	471	3	145	326
14	Other Protestant bodies	7	6	389	4	22	59
15	Roman Catholic Church	5	5	5,955	3	2,072	2,350
16	Jewish congregations	2	2	[1] 100			
17	All other bodies	2	2	202	2	78	124
1	Dayton, Ohio	107	107	53,359	97	21,881	27,351
2	Protestant bodies	91	91	28,033	85	10,506	15,699
	Baptist bodies:						
3	Baptists—Northern Convention	8	8	2,810	8	1,018	1,792
4	Baptists—National Convention (Colored)	3	3	657	3	208	449
	Disciples or Christians:						
5	Disciples of Christ	2	2	955	2	581	374
	Dunkers or German Baptist Brethren:						
6	German Baptist Brethren Church (Conservative)	3	3	410	3	166	245
7	Other German Baptist Brethren	2	2	340	2	170	170
	Evangelical bodies:						
8	Evangelical Association	2	2	478	2	199	279
9	German Evangelical Synod of North America	1	1	1,450	1	650	800
	Lutheran bodies:						
10	General Synod of the Evangelical Lutheran Church in the United States of America	3	3	1,332	2	396	711
11	General Council of the Evangelical Lutheran Church in North America	1	1	314	1	127	187
12	Evangelical Lutheran Joint Synod of Ohio and Other States	4	4	1,676	4	686	990
	Methodist bodies:						
13	Methodist Episcopal Church	10	10	4,575	9	1,754	2,678
14	African Methodist Episcopal Church	3	3	372	3	123	249
15	Other Methodist bodies	2	2	163	1	12	6
	Presbyterian bodies:						
16	Presbyterian Church in the United States of America	7	7	3,056	6	1,126	1,870
17	United Presbyterian Church of North America	2	2	285	2	95	190
18	Protestant Episcopal Church	3	3	1,120	2	91	176
	Reformed bodies:						
19	Reformed Church in the United States	8	8	2,713	7	974	1,339
	United Brethren bodies:						
20	Church of the United Brethren in Christ	17	17	4,662	17	1,908	2,754
21	Other Protestant bodies	10	10	715	10	275	440
22	Roman Catholic Church	10	10	24,909	9	11,289	11,631
23	Jewish congregations	2	2	[1] 172			
24	All other bodies	4	4	245	3	64	21
1	Denver, Colo.	181	178	58,699	158	22,804	30,816
2	Protestant bodies	143	141	30,646	132	10,175	16,710
	Adventist bodies:						
3	Advent Christian Church	1	1	33	1	14	19
4	Seventh-day Adventist Denomination	2	2	455	2	168	287
	Baptist bodies:						
5	Baptists—Northern Convention	13	13	3,989	12	1,397	2,452
6	Church of Christ, Scientist	1	1	827	1	216	611
7	Congregationalists	14	14	3,223	14	1,150	2,073
	Disciples or Christians:						
8	Disciples of Christ	6	6	2,111	5	608	903
9	German Evangelical Synod of North America	2	2	681	2	235	446
	Lutheran bodies:						
10	General Synod of the Evangelical Lutheran Church in the United States of America	2	2	433	2	158	275
11	General Council of the Evangelical Lutheran Church in North America	1	1	429	1	161	268
12	Other Lutheran bodies	6	6	712	6	317	395
	Methodist bodies:						
13	Methodist Episcopal Church	34	34	6,837	29	1,669	2,761
14	African Methodist Episcopal Church	3	3	572	3	200	372
15	Other Methodist bodies	3	3	415	2	78	123
	Presbyterian bodies:						
16	Presbyterian Church in the United States of America	15	15	4,632	15	1,766	2,866
17	United Presbyterian Church of North America	2	2	490	2	210	280
18	Other Presbyterian bodies	2	2	185	2	69	116
19	Protestant Episcopal Church	16	14	2,712	14	1,099	1,613
20	Unitarians	1	1	400			
21	Other Protestant bodies	19	19	1,510	19	660	850
22	Roman Catholic Church	19	19	25,993	19	12,305	13,688
23	Jewish congregations	10	9	[1] 703			
	Eastern Orthodox Churches:						
24	Russian Orthodox Church	1	1	175	1	100	75
25	Greek Orthodox Church	1	1	550			
26	All other bodies	7	7	632	6	224	343

[1] Heads of families only.

DEBT ON CHURCH PROPERTY, PARSONAGES, AND SUNDAY SCHOOLS, FOR EACH CITY OF 25,000 INHABITANTS OR DENOMINATIONS: 1906—Continued.

PLACES OF WORSHIP.					VALUE OF CHURCH PROPERTY.		DEBT ON CHURCH PROPERTY.		PARSONAGES.		SUNDAY SCHOOLS CONDUCTED BY CHURCH ORGANIZATIONS.				
Number of organizations reporting—		Number of church edifices reported.	Seating capacity of church edifices.		Number of organizations reporting.	Value reported.	Number of organizations reporting.	Amount of debt reported.	Number of organizations reporting.	Value of parsonages reported.	Number of organizations reporting.	Number of Sunday schools reported.	Number of officers and teachers.	Number of scholars.	
Church edifices.	Halls, etc.		Number of organizations reporting.	Seating capacity reported.											
1		1	1	700	1	$35,000	1	$12,000	1	$3,000	1	1	26	266	6
2		2	2	437	2	8,000	1	200	1	1,800	2	2	13	260	7
4		4	4	1,200	3	23,000	1	2,850	1	2,000	3	3	21	205	8
3		3	3	1,650	3	114,000			2	17,500	3	3	67	780	9
1		1	1	200	1	2,000					1	1	9	30	10
2		3	2	1,500	2	118,000		6,062	1	5,000	2	4	83	853	11
1		1	1	500	1	12,000			1	3,000	1	1	12	90	12
3		5	3	1,900	3	200,600			3	21,500	3	3	31	260	13
3	4	3	3	825	5	56,425	2	175			5	5	41	379	14
3		3	3	2,200	2	105,000			2	15,000	3	3	14	540	15
1		1	1	500	1	20,000		3,000			2	2	4	45	16
	2										2	3	25	65	17
96	10	104	94	54,624	99	2,645,134	47	264,180	36	212,500	98	120	2,292	24,292	1
84	6	91	82	46,851	87	2,007,965	40	163,843	28	141,000	86	95	2,225	21,164	2
8		12	8	4,946	8	225,125	2	9,400	1	6,000	8	13	307	3,052	3
2	1	2	2	1,060	2	26,500	2	11,600			3	3	35	210	4
2		2	2	1,060	2	37,000	1	5,500			2	2	61	575	5
3		3	3	1,250	3	13,000	1	250			3	3	37	315	6
2		2	2	850	2	7,600	1	1,600			1	1	15	140	7
2		2	2	850	2	24,000			1	3,000	2	2	73	575	8
1		1	1	3,000	1	150,000	1	8,800	1	5,000	1	1	75	835	9
3		3	3	1,950	3	209,000	1	7,500			3	3	106	851	10
1		1	1	600	1	30,000	1	5,900			1	1	19	167	11
4		4	4	2,500	4	67,300	2	9,400	2	7,000	4	4	80	923	12
10		10	9	6,130	10	223,100	6	28,050	5	25,500	10	10	313	2,816	13
3		3	3	1,450	3	15,000	3	2,600	1	300	3	4	38	280	14
1	1	1			1	4,500					2	2	19	180	15
7		10	7	4,650	7	404,000	2	12,900	4	22,000	7	8	189	1,969	16
2		2	2	975	2	58,000	2	3,900	1	10,000	2	2	34	325	17
3		3	3	1,150	3	93,400	1	4,500			3	4	57	378	18
8		8	8	4,425	8	144,300	6	28,043	4	34,000	8	8	201	1,726	19
17		17	17	8,775	17	250,500	5	16,500	7	24,700	17	17	506	5,363	20
5	4	5	5	1,250	8	25,640	3	6,500	1	3,500	6	7	60	484	21
10		11	10	6,955	10	597,669	5	97,137	8	71,500	10	23	57	3,038	22
2		2	2	818	2	39,500	2	3,200			1	1	4	60	23
	4										1	1	6	30	24
150	27	160	147	66,765	152	3,423,050	70	290,250	52	186,700	154	178	2,616	26,972	1
124	16	133	121	53,734	126	2,816,025	53	195,050	41	139,200	132	154	2,489	23,420	2
	1														3
1		1	1	500	1	10,000					2	2	40	189	4
12		13	12	5,600	12	239,500	5	23,300	3	8,000	13	18	284	2,494	5
1		1	1	1,675	1	153,975					1	1	70	500	6
13		15	13	7,450	13	225,300	3	13,000	2	5,200	14	18	358	3,391	7
6		6	6	2,925	6	167,000	2	2,000	1	1,500	6	6	113	1,489	8
2		2	2	800	2	16,000	2	4,150	2	3,200	2	2	23	252	9
2		2	2	850	2	25,000	2	4,700	1	3,000	2	2	33	597	10
1		2	1	1,100	1	55,000			1	4,500	1	2	30	300	11
5	1	5	5	880	5	23,500	4	8,000	1	2,000	5	5	36	298	12
30	4	31	28	9,715	30	675,200	13	50,200	12	45,000	33	35	589	5,722	13
3		3	3	1,400	3	95,000	3	4,600	3	6,000	3	3	18	224	14
3		4	2	850	3	36,500			3	8,000	3	3	31	325	15
15		16	15	8,129	15	363,500	6	44,500	3	19,800	15	21	422	4,130	16
2		2	2	1,200	2	66,000	1	1,500	1	4,000	2	2	53	325	17
2		2	2	425	2	13,000					2	2	28	155	18
14	2	14	14	5,530	14	375,300	6	15,250	5	21,000	14	15	174	1,733	19
1		1	1	800	1	100,000					1	1	14	65	20
11	8	13	11	3,905	13	176,250	6	23,850	3	8,000	13	16	173	1,231	21
14	4	15	14	7,306	15	471,225	9	76,400	10	46,300	17	17	77	2,933	22
9	1	9	9	5,050	8	124,300	7	17,300			3	5	25	500	23
1		1	1	400	1	8,000	1	1,500	1	1,200					24
	1														25
2	5	2	2	275	2	3,500					2	2	25	119	26

TABLE 7.—ORGANIZATIONS, COMMUNICANTS OR MEMBERS, PLACES OF WORSHIP, VALUE OF CHURCH PROPERTY, MORE IN 1900, BY SELECTED

	DENOMINATION.	Total number of organizations.	COMMUNICANTS OR MEMBERS.				
			Number of organizations reporting.	Total number reported.	Sex.		
					Number of organizations reporting.	Male.	Female.
1	Des Moines, Iowa	99	98	26,905	93	10,354	16,118
2	Protestant bodies	89	88	22,529	88	8,517	14,012
	Baptist bodies:						
3	Baptists—Northern Convention	4	4	1,553	4	570	983
4	Baptists—National Convention (Colored)	2	2	600	2	250	350
5	Congregationalists	5	5	1,391	5	482	909
	Disciples or Christians:						
6	Disciples of Christ	8	8	4,926	8	1,892	3,034
	Friends:						
7	Society of Friends (Orthodox)	1	1	521	1	220	301
8	Independent churches	2	2	442	2	187	255
	Lutheran bodies:						
9	General Synod of the Evangelical Lutheran Church in the United States of America	1	1	500	1	200	300
10	General Council of the Evangelical Lutheran Church in North America	1	1	800	1	311	489
11	Other Lutheran bodies	6	6	935	6	384	551
	Methodist bodies:						
12	Methodist Episcopal Church	19	19	4,229	19	1,542	2,687
13	Other Methodist bodies	3	3	355	3	119	236
	Presbyterian bodies:						
14	Presbyterian Church in the United States of America	8	8	2,460	8	938	1,522
15	United Presbyterian Church of North America	3	3	383	3	134	249
16	Protestant Episcopal Church	3	3	1,300	3	463	837
	United Brethren bodies:						
17	Church of the United Brethren in Christ	3	3	446	3	150	296
18	Other Protestant bodies	20	19	1,688	19	675	1 013
19	Roman Catholic Church	4	4	3,658	4	1,728	1,930
20	Jewish congregations	4	4	[1]183			
21	All other bodies	2	2	535	1	109	176
1	Detroit, Mich	221	218	194,160	162	21,850	34,002
	Protestant bodies	170	170	64,039	154	21,592	33,747
	Baptist bodies:						
3	Baptists—Northern Convention	22	22	5,570	21	1,992	3,558
4	Church of Christ, Scientist	1	1	354	1	111	243
5	Congregationalists	7	7	2,626	7	906	1,720
	Disciples or Christians:						
6	Disciples of Christ	2	2	505	2	180	325
7	Churches of Christ	3	3	697	3	247	450
8	German Evangelical Synod of North America	8	8	7,214	6	2,422	3,442
	Lutheran bodies:						
9	General Synod of the Evangelical Lutheran Church in the United States of America	2	2	930	2	353	577
10	Evangelical Lutheran Synodical Conference of America	16	16	11,936	15	4,763	5,603
11	Evangelical Lutheran Joint Synod of Ohio and Other States	8	8	4,510	6	1,804	2,187
12	Evangelical Lutheran Synod of Iowa and Other States	1	1	500	1	200	300
13	Evangelical Lutheran Jehovah Conference	2	2	305	2	145	160
14	Other Lutheran bodies	5	5	513	5	198	315
	Methodist bodies:						
15	Methodist Episcopal Church	22	22	8,441	20	2,829	4,912
16	African Methodist Episcopal Church	3	3	715	3	287	428
17	Other Methodist bodies	2	2	152	2	40	112
	Presbyterian bodies:						
18	Presbyterian Church in the United States of America	17	17	8,252	14	1,977	3,943
19	United Presbyterian Church of North America	2	2	368	2	123	245
20	Protestant Episcopal Church	22	22	8,041	18	2,155	3,994
	Reformed bodies:						
21	Reformed Church in America	1	1	105	1	49	56
22	Reformed Church in the United States	3	3	497	3	226	271
23	Unitarians	1	1	317			
24	Universalists	1	1	340	1	140	200
25	Other Protestant bodies	19	19	1,151	19	445	706
26	Roman Catholic Church	35	35	128,477			
27	Jewish congregations	8	5	[1]1,131			
28	All other bodies	8	8	513	8	258	255
1	Dubuque, Iowa	32	32	22,575	31	9,898	12,647
2	Protestant bodies	23	23	5,408	23	2,063	3,345
	Baptist bodies:						
3	Baptists—Northern Convention	1	1	281	1	86	195
4	Congregationalists	3	3	1,350	3	462	888
	Lutheran bodies:						
5	Evangelical Lutheran Synod of Iowa and Other States	1	1	950	1	420	530
6	Other Lutheran bodies	2	2	345	2	151	194
	Methodist bodies:						
7	Methodist Episcopal Church	6	6	958	6	361	597
8	African Methodist Episcopal Church	1	1	70	1	30	40
	Presbyterian bodies:						
9	Presbyterian Church in the United States of America	4	4	799	4	346	453
10	Protestant Episcopal Church	1	1	452	1	135	317
11	Other Protestant bodies	4	4	203	4	72	131
12	Roman Catholic Church	8	8	17,137	8	7,835	9,302
13	Jewish congregations	1	1	[1]30			

[1] Heads of families only.

DEBT ON CHURCH PROPERTY, PARSONAGES, AND SUNDAY SCHOOLS, FOR EACH CITY OF 25,000 INHABITANTS OR DENOMINATIONS: 1906—Continued.

PLACES OF WORSHIP.					VALUE OF CHURCH PROPERTY.		DEBT ON CHURCH PROPERTY.		PARSONAGES.		SUNDAY SCHOOLS CONDUCTED BY CHURCH ORGANIZATIONS.				
Number of organizations reporting— Church edifices.	Number of organizations reporting— Halls, etc.	Number of church edifices reported.	Seating capacity of church edifices. Number of organizations reporting.	Seating capacity of church edifices. Seating capacity reported.	Number of organizations reporting.	Value reported.	Number of organizations reporting.	Amount of debt reported.	Number of organizations reporting.	Value of parsonages reported.	Number of organizations reporting.	Number of Sunday schools reported.	Number of officers and teachers.	Number of scholars.	
88	8	92	87	41,856	92	$1,616,295	34	$186,231	39	$111,700	89	98	1,423	14,876	1
80	7	83	79	37,456	85	1,340,795	30	132,231	36	97,300	82	90	1,366	13,941	2
4	...	5	4	2,150		118,500	2	17,000	1	2,000	4	6	89	1,017	3
2	...	2	2	750		13,500	1	166	...	...	2	2	15	180	4
5	...	5	5	3,600	5	163,500	3	26,800	2	4,000	5	5	106	1,025	5
8	...	8	8	5,275	8	170,000	1	500	1	2,500	8	10	201	3,287	6
1	...	1	1	300	1	5,000	...	...	...	...	1	1	24	225	7
2	...	2	2	350	2	2,500	2	65	...	...	2	2	12	126	8
1	...	1	1	800	1	40,000	...	...	1	3,000	1	1		205	9
1	...	1	1	700	1	35,000	...	...	1	3,500	1	2	26	318	10
	...	5	5	1,925	6	36,750	3	4,050	4	6,500	5	5	32	241	11
[illegible]		18	18	7,075	[illegible]	275,925	3	45,000	11	30,900	19	20	333	3,026	12
2	1	2	2	550	[illegible]	11,800	1	3,500	...	...	2	2	32	210	13
7	1	8	7	4,525	7	160,000	4	9,750	2	4,800	8	9	167	1,644	14
3	...	3	3	1,256	3	38,500	...	...	3	5,500	3	3	43	415	15
3	...	3	3	1,275	3	86,700	2	3,000	2	9,800	3	3	24	229	16
3	...	3	3	1,075	3	19,500	2	5,700	2	5,500	3	3	46	379	17
15	4	16	14	5,850	17	163,620	6	16,700	6	16,300	15	16	184	1,414	18
4	...	4	4	2,800	4	267,000	2	52,000	2	14,000	4			758	19
3	...	4	3	1,300	2	4,500	2	2,000	...	...	2	4	23	78	20
1	1	1	1	300	1	4,000	...	...	1	400	1	2	28	99	21
198	16	230	163	96,437	168	5,339,958	98	556,229	71	322,250	184	206	3,877	52,918	1
158	9	190	155	89,262	160	4,605,383	94	506,729	71	322,250	151	172	3,506	37,259	2
21	...	28	19	10,725	21	519,200	12	37,795	4	13,000	22	29	585	6,249	3
1	...	2	1	1,200	1	25,000	...	...	...	...	1	1	22	432	4
7	...	8	7	4,000	7	328,833	3	21,750	...	...	7	8	207	2,198	5
2	...	3	2	1,250	2	77,000	...	...	...	...		2		325	6
3	...	3	3	950	3	21,000	...	...	...	...		3	42	513	7
8	...	14	8	7,767	8	251,000	8	66,600	6	21,150	8	8	[illegible]	2,901	8
2	...	3	2	1,500	2	86,000	2	30,000	2	8,000	2	3		616	9
16	...	17	16	11,325	16	194,600	15	74,700	14	42,200	5	5		1,253	10
8	...	10	8	4,775	8	90,500	8	37,800	8	23,100	7	7		1,330	11
1	...	1	1	800	1	8,000	1	1,200	1	2,000	1	1		120	12
2	...	5	2	850	2	16,000	2	7,000	2	3,850	2	3	46	192	13
5	...	5	5	1,625	4	28,800	4	12,000	2	3,500	5	6	[illegible]	296	14
22	...	22	22	11,790	22	823,500	10	72,212	11	58,900	22	2	691	7,905	15
3	...	3	2	1,300		29,000	2	4,750	3	4,500	3		44	370	16
2	...	2	2	900	[illegible]	6,500	1	1,400	1	2,500	2	[illegible]	13	78	17
16	...	17	16	11,230	16	822,500	4	12,800	...	...	17	19		6,314	18
2	...	3	2	850	2	26,000	1	350	1	6,000	2	2	644	612	19
21	...	27	21	10,250	22	822,700	11	60,472	10	107,250	21	23	454	3,821	20
1	...	2	1	325	1	6,500	...	...	1	5,800	1	1		85	
3	...	3	3	1,200		19,200	2	5,500	1	2,500	3	3		498	
1	...	1	1	750	4	120,000	...	...	...	...	1	1		175	
1	...	1	1	1,000	1	150,000	...	...	1	10,000	1	1	12	175	21
10	9	10	10	3,400	12	133,550	8	60,400	3	8,000	13	15	[illegible]	1,101	[illegible]
	...	35	3	1,800	2	500,000	...	...	...	...	29	30	334	15,078	
35	...	4	4	5,200	4	233,000	4	49,500	...	...	2	2	19	470	26
[illegible]	7	1	1	175	2	1,575	...	...	...	...	2	2	18	111	[illegible]
30	2		29	1	30	1,318,500	11	66,572	20	121,300	31	4	505	6,207	1
21	2	23	20		21	480,500	5	8,562	13	76,800	22	27	444	3,546	:
1	...	1	1	6,060	1	20,000	...	...	...	...	1	1	16	137	3
3	...	3	3	2,400	3	71,500	1	300	2	8,500	3	5	101	1,030	4
1	...		1	9,860 1,000	1	26,000	1	3,000	1	8,500	1	3	34	380	
1	1	[illegible]	1	600	1	11,000	1	1,200	1	1,000	2	2	16	133	[illegible]
6	...	6	6	1,850	6	177,000	...	...	4	20,000	6	7	117	897	7
1	...	1	1	200	1	4,000	...	...	1	1,000	1	1	4	18	8
4	...	4	4		4	61,000	1	62	2	11,000	4	4	114	618	9
1	...	1	1	1,600	1	85,000	...	...	1	25,000	1	1	15	210	10
3	1	8	2	280	3	25,000	1	4,000	1	1,800	3	[illegible]	27	123	11
8	...	9	8	6,610	8	835,000	5	57,010	7	44,500	8	16	60	2,636	12
1	...	1	1	220	1	3,000	1	1,000	...	...	1	1	1	25	13

TABLE 7.—ORGANIZATIONS, COMMUNICANTS OR MEMBERS, PLACES OF WORSHIP, VALUE OF CHURCH PROPERTY, MORE IN 1900, BY SELECTED

	DENOMINATION.	Total number of organizations.	COMMUNICANTS OR MEMBERS.				
			Number of organizations reporting.	Total number reported.	Sex.		
					Number of organizations reporting.	Male.	Female.
1	Duluth, Minn.	83	79	22,312	67	9,787	11,168
2	Protestant bodies	66	63	9,842	56	3,606	5,239
	Baptist bodies:						
3	Baptists—Northern Convention	8	8	1,079	5	261	891
4	Congregationalists	2	2	484	2	181	303
5	German Evangelical Synod of North America	1	1	270	1	120	150
	Lutheran bodies:						
6	General Council of the Evangelical Lutheran Church in North America	5	5	1,317	5	575	742
7	United Norwegian Lutheran Church in America	3	3	557	2	170	230
8	Evangelical Lutheran Joint Synod of Ohio and Other States	1	1	240	1	110	130
9	Other Lutheran bodies	6	6	458	6	210	248
	Methodist bodies:						
10	Methodist Episcopal Church	12	10	1,931	9	645	1,106
11	African Methodist Episcopal Church	1	1	40	1	15	25
	Presbyterian bodies:						
12	Presbyterian Church in the United States of America	8	8	1,357	7	445	720
13	Protestant Episcopal Church	6	6	1,087	5	456	590
	Swedish Evangelical bodies:						
14	Swedish Evangelical Mission Covenant of America	2	2	421	2	192	229
15	Other Protestant bodies	11	10	601	10	226	375
16	Roman Catholic Church	9	9	11,097	9	5,528	5,569
17	Jewish congregations	5	4	[1] 210	...	...	...
18	Polish National Church of America	1	1	1,000	1	650	350
19	All other bodies	2	2	163	1	3	10
1	East St. Louis, Ill.	42	42	17,647	33	2,901	3,882
2	Protestant bodies	32	32	5,347	31	1,934	3,374
	Baptist bodies:						
3	Baptists—Northern Convention	2	2	426	2	188	238
4	Baptists—National Convention (Colored)	4	4	642	4	275	367
5	Free Baptists	1	1	125	1	40	85
	Disciples or Christians:						
6	Disciples of Christ	2	2	446	2	171	275
7	German Evangelical Synod of North America	1	1	247	1	90	157
	Lutheran bodies:						
8	Evangelical Lutheran Synodical Conference of America	2	2	756	2	252	504
	Methodist bodies:						
9	Methodist Episcopal Church	5	5	1,286	5	443	843
10	African Methodist bodies	4	4	324	4	125	199
	Presbyterian bodies:						
11	Presbyterian Church in the United States of America	4	4	586	4	189	397
12	United Presbyterian Church of North America	1	1	81	1	36	45
13	Protestant Episcopal Church	1	1	207	1	61	146
14	Other Protestant bodies	5	5	221	4	64	118
15	Roman Catholic Church	8	8	11,695	1	542	478
16	Armenian Church	1	1	455	1	425	30
	Eastern Orthodox Churches:						
17	Greek Orthodox Church	1	1	150	...	...	...
1	Easton, Pa.	42	42	12,085	36	4,687	6,734
	Protestant bodies	37	37	9,419	34	3,042	5,054
	Baptist bodies:						
3	Baptists—Northern Convention	4	4	240	3	35	63
	Evangelical bodies:						
4	Evangelical Association	1	1	222	1	79	143
5	United Evangelical Church	2	2	358	2	133	225
	Lutheran bodies:						
6	General Synod of the Evangelical Lutheran Church in the United States of America	2	2	629	2	288	341
7	General Council of the Evangelical Lutheran Church in North America	7	7	2,606	5	608	817
	Methodist bodies:						
8	Methodist Episcopal Church	3	3	906	3	287	619
9	African Methodist bodies	2	2	54	2	13	41
	Presbyterian bodies:						
10	Presbyterian Church in the United States of America	5	5	1,898	5	614	1,284
11	Protestant Episcopal Church	1	1	382	1	104	278
	Reformed bodies:						
12	Reformed Church in the United States	5	5	1,913	5	802	1,111
13	Other Protestant bodies	5	5	211	5	79	132
14	Roman Catholic Church	2	2	3,125	2	1,445	1,680
15	Jewish congregations	2	2	[1] 91	...	...	...
	Eastern Orthodox Churches:						
16	Greek Orthodox Church	1	1	50	...	...	...
1	Elizabeth, N. J.	48	47	28,616	37	9,913	12,689
2	Protestant bodies	37	37	11,266	32	3,295	5,967
	Baptist bodies:						
3	Baptists—Northern Convention	3	3	1,110	3	450	660
4	Baptists—National Convention (Colored)	2	2	660	2	150	510
5	Congregationalists	1	1	143	1	49	94

[1] Heads of families only.

DEBT ON CHURCH PROPERTY, PARSONAGES, AND SUNDAY SCHOOLS, FOR EACH CITY OF 25,000 INHABITANTS OR DENOMINATIONS: 1906—Continued.

PLACES OF WORSHIP.					VALUE OF CHURCH PROPERTY.		DEBT ON CHURCH PROPERTY.		PARSONAGES.		SUNDAY SCHOOLS CONDUCTED BY CHURCH ORGANIZATIONS.				
Number of organizations reporting—		Number of church edifices reported.	Seating capacity of church edifices.		Number of organizations reporting.	Value reported.	Number of organizations reporting.	Amount of debt reported.	Number of organizations reporting.	Value of parsonages reported.	Number of organizations reporting.	Number of Sunday schools reported.	Number of officers and teachers.	Number of scholars.	
Church edifices.	Halls, etc.		Number of organizations reporting.	Seating capacity reported.											
68	11		66	27,111	70	$1,139,525	33	$173,599	35	$180,600	73	89	1,097	10,888	1
56	8	60	55	21,740	58	733,725	23	56,599	26	88,100	62	74	1,024	8,460	2
6	1	6	5	1,565	7	41,300	4	3,250	2	3,500	8	12	130	974	3
2		2	2	950	2	62,000	1	2,500			2	2	34	250	4
1		1	1	300	1	5,000			1	3,000	1	1	10	70	5
5		5	5	2,525	5	72,000	3	14,125	4	17,000	5	6	153	1,075	6
3		3	3	1,750	3	51,500	2	4,500	2	7,000	3	3	65	475	7
1		1	1	150	1	5,500	1	1,000	1	1,500	1	1	7	70	8
6		7	6	1,475	6	19,500	3	7,650	3	5,700	5	7	48	385	9
10	1	10	10	5,200	9	199,500	3	2,800	7	32,200	10	10	215	1,966	10
1		1	1	125	1	3,000	1	62	1	1,200	1	1	7	30	11
8		10	8	3,075	8	126,700	1	2,200	2	8,000	8	10	157	1,502	12
6		6	6	1,725	6	85,500	1	10,000	2	7,500	6	8	76	855	13
2		3	2	1,650	2	23,000					2	3	57	475	14
5	6	5	5	1,250	7	39,225	3	8,512	1	1,500	10	10	65	333	15
8	1	8	8	4,471	8	358,800	6	102,850	8	91,500	9	13	68	2,253	16
3		4	2	600	3	37,000	3	6,150	1	1,000	1	1	4	75	17
1		1	1	300	1	10,000	1	8,000			1	1	1	100	18
	2														19
37	4	41	35	13,145	31	263,550	19	55,128	8	30,050	39	40	443	6,174	1
29	2	30	28	9,375	30	255,550	19	55,128	7	18,050	32	33	400	4,674	2
2		2	2	415	2	11,500	1	500			2	3	29	341	3
4		4	4	1,100	4	13,300	1	1,500			4	4	30	225	4
1		1	1	350	1	4,000	1	1,800	1	1,000	1	1	14	140	5
2		2	2	800	2	8,000	1	500			2	2	23	185	6
1		2	1	200	1	11,000	1	2,100	1	2,000	1	1	14	200	7
2		2	2	1,100	2	19,500	1	3,778	1	2,500	2	2	17	338	8
5		5	5	2,400	5	92,950	5	34,600	3	12,300	5	5	102	1,740	9
4		4	4	660	4	9,600	3	775	1	250	4	4	40	205	10
4		4	4	1,350	4	39,300	1	900			4	4	73	749	11
1		1	1	250	1	10,000	1	2,300			1	1	14	150	12
1		1	1	450	1	25,000	1	5,000			1	1	10	70	13
2	2	2	1	300	3	11,400	2	1,375			5	5	34	331	14
8		11	7	3,770	1	8,000			1	12,000	7	7	43	1,500	15
	1														16
	1														17
35	7	43	34	20,645	38	836,895	18	48,887	21	103,000	40	48	966	8,437	1
31	6	36	30	18,675	34	702,895	16	45,573	19	91,000	36	40	915	7,786	2
2	2	2	2	550	3	14,230	2	700	1	4,000	4	4	47	376	3
1		1	1	250	1	12,000			1	2,500	1	1	29	205	4
2		2	2	1,300	2	21,000	2	5,700	1	3,500	4	2	40	469	5
2		2	1	600	2	45,500	1	1,150	1	3,000	2	2	47	374	6
7		8	7	4,175	7	154,500	3	3,440	4	13,500	7	7	207	1,785	7
3		3	3	1,450	3	41,500	1	1,100	2	8,500	3	3	80	820	8
2		2	2	400	2	6,000	1	2,400			2	2	10	60	9
5		7	5	5,375	5	195,910	2	21,400	4	23,000	5	9	225	1,701	10
1		2	1	600	1	50,000			1	12,000	1	1	20	163	11
5		6	5	3,550	5	155,000	2	7,400	3	16,000	5		175	1,613	12
1	4	1	1	425	3	7,255	2	2,283	1	5,000	4	5	35	220	13
2		5	2	1,420	2	120,000	1	1,914	2	12,000	2	6	46	600	14
2		2	2	550	2	14,000	1	1,400			2	[illegible]	5	51	15
	1														16
40	7	49	39	24,206	41	2,040,605	19	91,600	21	187,100	41	48	1,100	11,786	1
32	5	41	31	18,726	33	1,358,605	15	51,150	16	91,100	35	42	1,021	8,781	2
3		3	3	2,360	3	125,000	1	2,000	1	5,000	3		110	850	3
2		2	2	850	2	16,800	1	600	2	3,000	1	2	9	96	4
1		1	1	300	1	12,000	1	1,800			1	1	14	80	5

TABLE 7.—ORGANIZATIONS, COMMUNICANTS OR MEMBERS, PLACES OF WORSHIP, VALUE OF CHURCH PROPERTY, MORE IN 1900, BY SELECTED

	DENOMINATION.	Total number of organizations.	COMMUNICANTS OR MEMBERS.				
			Number of organizations reporting.	Total number reported.	Sex.		
					Number of organizations reporting.	Male.	Female.
	Elizabeth, N. J.—Continued.						
	Protestant bodies—Continued.						
	Lutheran bodies:						
6	General Council of the Evangelical Lutheran Church in North America	3	3	790	2	272	508
7	United Norwegian Lutheran Church in America	1	1	25	1	15	10
	Methodist bodies:						
8	Methodist Episcopal Church	5	5	1,273	4	412	781
9	Methodist Protestant Church	1	1	274	1	103	171
10	Other Methodist bodies	2	2	100	2	33	67
	Presbyterian bodies:						
11	Presbyterian Church in the United States of America	9	9	3,204	9	1,177	2,027
12	Protestant Episcopal Church	4	4	3,372	2	522	971
13	Other Protestant bodies	6	6	315	5	112	168
14	Roman Catholic Church	8	8	17,250	5	6,618	6,722
15	Jewish congregations	2	1	[1]40	....	....	....
	Eastern Orthodox Churches:						
16	Greek Orthodox Church	1	1	60	....	....	....
1	Elmira, N. Y.	37	37	10,251	32	3,296	6,162
	Protestant bodies	33	33	10,059	32	3,296	6,161
	Baptist bodies:						
3	Baptists—Northern Convention	3	3	1,818	3	659	1,159
4	Free Baptists	1	1	150	1	45	105
5	Congregationalists	2	2	966	2	256	710
	Disciples or Christians:						
6	Disciples of Christ	1	1	210	1	69	141
7	German Evangelical Synod of North America	1	1	890	1	428	462
	Methodist bodies:						
8	Methodist Episcopal Church	7	7	2,776	7	956	1,820
9	African Methodist bodies	2	2	210	2	55	155
	Presbyterian bodies:						
10	Presbyterian Church in the United States of America	5	5	1,708	5	576	1,132
11	Protestant Episcopal Church	3	3	1,061	2	159	322
12	Other Protestant bodies	8	8	250	8	95	155
13	Roman Catholic Church [2]	....	....	....	....	....	....
14	Jewish congregations	3	-	[1]132	....	....	....
	Eastern Orthodox Churches:						
15	Greek Orthodox Church	1	1	60	....	....	....
1	Erie, Pa.	60	60	34,540	55	15,896	17,618
	Protestant bodies	45	45	12,226	43	4,678	6,748
	Baptist bodies:						
3	Baptists—Northern Convention	6	6	930	6	380	550
4	German Evangelical Synod of North America	2	2	1,600	2	700	900
	Lutheran bodies:						
5	General Council of the Evangelical Lutheran Church in North America	8	8	3,271	8	1,466	1,805
6	Other Lutheran bodies	3	3	386	3	175	211
	Methodist bodies:						
7	Methodist Episcopal Church	5	5	1,719	5	658	1,061
8	Other Methodist bodies	2	2	80	2	28	52
	Presbyterian bodies:						
9	Presbyterian Church in the United States of America	5	5	2,039	5	759	1,280
10	United Presbyterian Church of North America	2	2	383	2	117	266
11	Protestant Episcopal Church	3	3	1,000	1	65	135
12	Other Protestant bodies	9	9	818	9	330	488
13	Roman Catholic Church	12	12	22,088	12	11,218	10,870
14	Jewish congregations	2	2	[1]76	....	....	....
	Eastern Orthodox Churches:						
15	Greek Orthodox Church	1	1	150	....	....	....
1	Evansville, Ind.	66	66	31,634	61	13,782	17,291
	Protestant bodies	52	52	13,675	50	5,163	8,202
	Baptist bodies:						
3	Baptists—Northern Convention	2	2	517	2	137	380
4	Baptists—National Convention (Colored)	5	5	2,483	5	984	1,499
5	Other Baptist bodies	6	6	354	6	134	220
	Disciples or Christians:						
6	Disciples of Christ	3	3	535	2	139	346
7	German Evangelical Synod of North America	4	4	2,077	4	906	1,171
	Lutheran bodies:						
8	Evangelical Lutheran Synodical Conference of America	2	2	895	2	408	487
9	Other Lutheran bodies	3	3	300	3	105	195
	Methodist bodies:						
10	Methodist Episcopal Church	8	8	2,691	8	1,086	1,605
11	Other Methodist bodies	3	3	673	3	191	482
	Presbyterian bodies:						
12	Presbyterian Church in the United States of America	5	5	1,258	4	382	716
13	Cumberland Presbyterian Church	3	3	1,154	3	424	730
14	Protestant Episcopal Church	2	2	434	2	139	295
15	Other Protestant bodies	6	6	304	6	128	176
16	Roman Catholic Church	9	9	17,660	9	8,594	9,066
17	Jewish congregations	3	3	[1]251	....	....	....
18	All other bodies	2	2	48	2	25	23

[1] Heads of families only.

DEBT ON CHURCH PROPERTY, PARSONAGES, AND SUNDAY SCHOOLS, FOR EACH CITY OF 25,000 INHABITANTS OR DENOMINATIONS: 1906—Continued.

PLACES OF WORSHIP.					VALUE OF CHURCH PROPERTY.		DEBT ON CHURCH PROPERTY.		PARSONAGES.		SUNDAY SCHOOLS CONDUCTED BY CHURCH ORGANIZATIONS.				
Number of organizations reporting—		Number of church edifices reported.	Seating capacity of church edifices.		Number of organizations reporting.	Value reported.	Number of organizations reporting.	Amount of debt reported.	Number of organizations reporting.	Value of parsonages reported.	Number of organizations reporting.	Number of Sunday schools reported.	Number of officers and teachers.	Number of scholars.	
Church edifices.	Halls, etc.		Number of organizations reporting.	Seating capacity reported.											
2	1	2	2	646	2	$31,780	2	$3,500	1	$3,000	3	3	30	789	6
1	...	1	1	125	1	5,000	...	...	...	...	1	1	10	60	7
5	...	5	5	2,250	5	116,500	4	13,000	5	21,000	5	5	139	1,295	8
1	...	1	1	395	1	17,000	1	4,000	...	...	1	1	34	414	9
1	1	1	1	200	1	2,000	1	1,100	...	...	2	3	13	95	10
9	...	14	9	7,850	9	611,000	2	21,300	3	13,600	9	12	438	2,993	11
4	...	8	4	3,050	4	400,000	1	3,000	3	43,000	4	6	193	1,854	12
3	3	3	2	700	4	21,525	1	850	1	2,500	5	6	31	255	13
7	1	7	7	5,230	7	670,000	3	37,450	5	96,000	5	5	75	2,965	14
1	...	1	1	250	1	12,000	1	3,000	...	...	1	1	4	40	15
...	[1]	...	...	...	...	...	...	...	...	...	...	...	...	...	16
32	4	37	31	15,400	32	910,300	22	100,043	9	34,000	34	36	627	6,169	1
29	3	34	28	14,100	29	888,300	22	100,043	9	34,000	31	33	621	6,029	2
3	...	3	2	1,400	3	111,000	2	1,700	1	4,000	3	3	87	892	3
1	...	1	1	600	1	15,000	1	2,500	...	...	1	1	12	175	4
2	...	2	2	1,600	2	155,000	1	550	...	...	2	2	55	538	5
1	...	1	1	400	1	27,000	...	...	...	...	1	1	15	135	6
1	...	1	1	600	1	30,000	1	8,500	1	3,000	1	1	13	165	7
7	...	7	7	3,350	7	207,000	6	34,900	1	3,500	7	8	218	2,187	8
2	...	2	2	1,350	2	30,000	2	5,800	2	4,500	2	2	21	77	9
5	...	6	5	2,150	5	118,000	5	17,593	3	9,000	5	5	128	1,279	10
3	...	7	3	1,750	3	163,000	2	13,000	1	10,000	3	4	43	365	11
4	3	4	4	900	4	32,300	2	15,500	...	...	6	6	29	216	12
...	...	...	...	...	...	...	...	...	...	...	...	...	...	...	13
3	...	3	3	1,300	3	22,000	...	...	...	...	3	3	6	140	14
...	1	...	...	...	...	...	...	...	...	...	...	...	...	...	15
55	5	65	55	30,686	55	2,201,600	31	282,520	33	178,700	56	100	1,021	13,086	1
41	4	45	41	19,650	41	1,011,300	24	100,250	21	84,100	42	47	864	8,216	2
6	...	6	6	1,750	6	80,000	2	6,000	2	4,300	6	8	121	1,081	3
2	...	3	2	1,400	2	70,000	1	2,700	1	5,000	2	2	53	460	4
8	...	9	8	4,450	8	228,000	5	30,000	5	16,600	8	9	171	1,844	5
2	1	2	2	600	2	17,000	2	7,850	1	2,000	3	3	15	138	6
5	...	5	5	2,575	5	100,300	...	...	4	16,000	5	5	161	1,645	7
2	...	2	2	550	2	8,000	2	4,200	1	700	2	3	23	85	8
5	...	6	5	4,100	5	208,000	2	3,200	2	13,000	5	5	152	1,553	9
2	...	2	2	975	2	73,000	2	14,100	1	5,000	1	2	36	345	10
3	...	4	3	1,450	3	144,000	3	19,000	2	16,000	3	3	61	602	11
6	3	6	6	1,800	6	83,000	5	13,200	2	5,500	7	7	71	463	12
12	...	18	12	10,436	12	1,163,300	7	182,270	12	94,600	12	51	152	4,785	13
2	...	2	2	600	2	27,000	...	...	...	...	2	2	5	85	14
...	1	...	...	...	...	...	...	...	...	...	...	...	...	...	15
53	5	56	52	24,385	53	993,850	18	47,661	24	108,400	56	60	741	8,591	1
45	4	48	44	19,485	46	679,350	15	24,661	20	86,900	46	48	712	7,070	2
2	...	2	2	800	2	20,000	...	...	...	...	2	2	29	280	3
5	...	5	5	2,150	5	34,200	4	2,286	1	2,000	5	5	46	436	4
5	1	5	4	750	4	6,000	2	1,650	1	2,500	4	4	33	186	5
3	...	3	3	1,050	3	15,500	2	2,600	1	2,500	3	3	39	340	6
4	...	5	4	2,350	4	89,000	2	11,500	4	14,000	4	4	102	1,153	7
2	...	2	2	1,100	2	49,000	...	...	2	7,000	...	...	...	...	8
2	...	2	2	750	3	22,150	1	2,450	1	4,000	3	3	19	155	9
8	...	9	8	4,350	8	140,200	1	2,500	3	7,500	8	9	171	1,728	10
3	...	3	3	985	3	16,000	1	900	1	600	3	3	23	241	11
5	...	5	5	2,500	5	130,200	2	775	4	25,600	5	6	102	1,183	12
3	...	3	3	1,400	3	60,000	...	...	...	...	3	3	100	1,060	13
2	...	3	2	1,000	2	90,000	...	...	1	20,000	2	2	19	145	14
1	3	1	1	300	2	7,100	...	...	1	1,200	4	4	29	163	15
5	...	5	5	3,900	5	301,000	2	18,500	4	21,500	6	8	19	1,399	16
2	...	2	2	700	1	10,000	1	4,500	...	...	3	3	5	92	17
1	1	1	1	300	1	3,500	...	...	...	...	1	1	5	30	18

[1] Statistics not reported separately by cities for Rochester diocese.

TABLE 7.—ORGANIZATIONS, COMMUNICANTS OR MEMBERS, PLACES OF WORSHIP, VALUE OF CHURCH PROPERTY, MORE IN 1900, BY SELECTED

	DENOMINATION.	Total number of organizations.	COMMUNICANTS OR MEMBERS.				
			Number of organizations reporting.	Total number reported.	Sex.		
					Number of organizations reporting.	Male.	Female.
1	Fall River, Mass.	67	65	71,877	56	30,243	37,628
2	Protestant bodies	41	40	8,611	35	2,270	4,491
	Baptist bodies:						
3	Baptists—Northern and National (Colored) Conventions	5	5	1,900	5	528	1,372
4	Christians (Christian Connection)	3	3	401	2	58	131
5	Congregationalists	5	5	1,072	5	318	754
	Methodist bodies:						
6	Methodist Episcopal Church	7	7	1,818	5	351	687
7	African Methodist Episcopal Church	1	1	12	1	3	9
8	Primitive Methodist Church in the United States of America	3	3	407	3	128	279
	Presbyterian bodies:						
9	Presbyterian Church in the United States of America	1	1	67	1	14	53
10	United Presbyterian Church of North America	1	1	303	1	98	205
11	Protestant Episcopal Church	6	6	2,053	4	555	640
12	Unitarians	1	1	227	1	90	137
13	Other Protestant bodies	8	7	351	7	127	224
14	Roman Catholic Church	19	19	62,195	18	27,724	32,772
15	Jewish congregations	3	2	[1] 107			
	Eastern Orthodox Churches:						
16	Greek Orthodox Church	1	1	350			
17	Polish National Church of America	1	1	400	1	180	220
18	All other bodies	2	2	214	2	69	145
1	Fitchburg, Mass.	32	32	19,062	30	8,067	10,665
2	Protestant bodies	23	23	4,504	23	1,551	2,953
	Baptist bodies:						
3	Baptists—Northern Convention	3	3	702	3	240	462
4	Congregationalists	5	5	1,249	5	411	838
	Lutheran bodies:						
5	Finnish Evangelical Lutheran National Church	1	1	250	1	105	145
6	Other Lutheran bodies	2	2	147	2	68	79
	Methodist bodies:						
7	Methodist Episcopal Church	3	3	613	3	205	408
8	Protestant Episcopal Church	1	1	606	1	175	431
9	Unitarians	1	1	550	1	250	300
10	Universalists	1	1	210	1	40	170
11	Other Protestant bodies	6	6	177	6	57	120
12	Roman Catholic Church	5	5	14,120	5	6,449	7,671
13	Jewish congregations	1	1	[1] 50			
	Eastern Orthodox Churches:						
14	Greek Orthodox Church	1	1	240			
15	All other bodies	2	2	148	2	87	61
1	Fort Wayne, Ind.	50	49	22,304	44	8,792	11,570
2	Protestant bodies	42	42	16,899	39	6,263	8,914
	Baptist bodies:						
3	Baptists—Northern and National (Colored) Conventions	2	2	1,150	2	418	732
4	Congregationalists	1	1	462	1	187	275
	Disciples or Christians:						
5	Disciples of Christ	3	3	923	3	343	580
	Lutheran bodies:						
6	General Synod of the Evangelical Lutheran Church in the United States of America	1	1	195	1	80	115
7	General Council of the Evangelical Lutheran Church in North America	1	1	619	1	301	318
8	Evangelical Lutheran Synodical Conference of America	9	9	6,285	8	2,424	3,055
9	Evangelical Lutheran Joint Synod of Ohio and Other States	2	2	1,120	2	489	631
	Methodist bodies:						
10	Methodist Episcopal Church	5	5	2,022	5	807	1,215
11	Other Methodist bodies	2	2	190	2	63	127
	Presbyterian bodies:						
12	Presbyterian Church in the United States of America	4	4	1,526	2	219	391
13	Protestant Episcopal Church	1	1	370	1	130	240
	Reformed bodies:						
14	Reformed Church in the United States	3	3	1,360	3	565	795
	United Brethren bodies:						
15	Church of the United Brethren in Christ	1	1	326	1	109	217
16	Other Protestant bodies	7	7	351	7	128	223
17	Roman Catholic Church	3	3	5,103	3	2,486	2,617
18	Jewish congregations	2	1	[1] 70			
19	All other bodies	3	3	232	2	43	39
1	Fort Worth, Tex.	58	56	18,235	50	7,029	9,462
2	Protestant bodies	54	52	12,915	48	4,277	7,049
	Baptist bodies:						
3	Baptists—Southern Convention	6	6	2,790	5	1,063	1,487
4	Baptists—National Convention (Colored)	7	7	1,380	7	466	914
5	Primitive Baptists	1					
	Disciples or Christians:						
6	Disciples of Christ	4	4	1,205	4	509	696
7	Churches of Christ	2	2	107	2	42	65

[1] Heads of families only.

DEBT ON CHURCH PROPERTY, PARSONAGES, AND SUNDAY SCHOOLS, FOR EACH CITY OF 25,000 INHABITANTS OR DENOMINATIONS: 1906—Continued.

PLACES OF WORSHIP.					VALUE OF CHURCH PROPERTY.		DEBT ON CHURCH PROPERTY.		PARSONAGES.		SUNDAY SCHOOLS CONDUCTED BY CHURCH ORGANIZATIONS.				
Number of organizations reporting—		Number of church edifices reported.	Seating capacity of church edifices.		Number of organizations reporting.	Value reported.	Number of organizations reporting.	Amount of debt reported.	Number of organizations reporting.	Value of parsonages reported.	Number of organizations reporting.	Number of Sunday schools reported.	Number of officers and teachers.	Number of scholars.	
Church edifices.	Halls, etc.		Number of organizations reporting.	Seating capacity reported.											
60	2	65	60	41,636	58	$2,762,300	35	$673,235	29	$282,100	60	70	1,516	18,667	1
38	1	43	38	19,900	38	944,550	18	86,913	16	64,100	40	46	1,025	8,983	2
5	...	9	5	5,450	5	201,550	2	12,675	1	5,000	5	9	250	2,172	3
3	...	3	3	1,450	3	34,500	1	5,060	3	7,700	8	3	66	540	4
5	...	6	5	3,050	5	218,200	...	...	2	10,800	5	5	131	1,228	5
6	...	6	6	3,000	6	140,000	3	22,938	5	18,100	7	7	177	1,777	6
1	...	1	1	150	1	1,000	1	200	...	...	1	1	6	30	7
3	...	3	5	1,750	3	29,500	3	9,900	2	7,500	3	3	74	641	8
1	...	1	1	400	1	6,000	1	2,000	...	...	1	1	16	150	9
1	...	1	1	700	1	20,000	...	...	...	...	1	2	45	325	10
6	...	6	6	2,170	6	168,800	4	18,550	3	15,000	6	7	179	1,593	11
1	...	1	1	480	1	25,000	...	...	...	...	1	1	18	140	12
6	1	6	6	1,300	6	100,000	3	15,600	...	...	7	7	63	387	13
19	...	19	19	20,936	17	1,802,250	14	580,347	13	218,000	18	21	437	9,520	14
...	...	...	...	...	...	...	...	...	...	...	...	...	...	...	15
...	1	...	...	...	...	...	...	...	...	...	...	...	...	...	16
1	...	1	1	500	1	10,000	1	4,000	...	...	...	...	...	...	17
2	...	2	2	300	2	5,500	2	1,975	...	...	2	3	54	164	18
22	8	27	22	14,032	25	858,002	14	122,965	9	87,150	28	38	532	5,343	1
16	5	20	16	8,765	19	628,002	8	21,315	5	32,200	22	24	441	3,000	2
3	...	3	3	1,600	3	102,000	1	8,000	1	10,000	3	3	73	560	3
5	...	6	5	3,140	5	223,500	3	4,165	1	4,000	5	5	124	972	4
1	...	1	1	250	1	11,000	1	2,150	...	...	1	1	7	50	5
1	...	1	1	225	1	10,427	1	3,300	...	...	1	1	10	65	6
3	...	3	3	1,500	3	54,000	1	500	2	15,000	3	4	97	536	7
1	...	3	1	700	1	116,150	...	...	1	3,200	1	2	48	308	8
1	...	2	1	800	1	70,000	...	...	...	...	1	1	14	76	9
1	...	1	1	550	1	40,200	1	3,200	...	...	1	1	42	300	10
...	5	...	...	...	3	725	...	...	...	...	6	6	26	133	11
5	...	6	5	4,867	5	220,000	5	97,800	4	54,950	5	13	90	2,328	12
1	...	1	1	400	1	10,000	1	3,850	...	...	1	1	1	15	13
...	1	...	...	...	...	...	...	...	...	...	...	...	...	...	14
...	2	...	...	...	...	...	...	...	...	...	...	...	...	...	15
42	4	47	40	25,820	41	1,128,600	21	118,540	25	126,750	39	52	614	9,401	1
38	2	41	36	22,870	38	1,018,600	20	117,790	23	100,750	35	43	624	8,304	2
2	...	3	1	1,000	2	51,500	...	...	...	...	1	2	30	758	3
1	...	1	1	1,000	1	45,000	...	...	...	...	1	1	22	300	4
3	...	4	3	1,250	3	45,000	2	9,000	...	...	3	4	56	506	5
1	...	1	1	320	1	14,000	1	6,000	1	2,000	1	1	14	100	6
1	...	1	1	400	1	40,000	...	...	1	10,000	1	1	25	250	7
7	...	7	7	5,850	7	285,600	4	33,640	6	22,850	3	6	33	965	8
2	...	2	2	1,150	2	64,500	1	20,000	2	17,500	2	2	5	380	9
5	...	5	5	3,750	5	104,500	1	3,500	4	18,500	5	6	152	2,060	10
2	...	2	2	550	2	7,500	2	700	2	3,500	2	2	22	190	11
4	...	4	4	2,700	4	142,700	3	25,000	...	...	4	4	91	1,109	12
1	...	2	1	600	1	65,000	1	5,000	1	10,000	1	2	23	180	13
3	...	3	3	2,000	3	105,000	3	10,650	3	7,200	3	3	63	605	14
1	...	1	1	500	1	9,000	...	...	1	4,200	1	1	21	250	15
5	2	5	4	1,800	5	39,900	2	4,300	2	5,000	7	8	67	652	16
3	...	5	3	2,550	2	85,000	1	750	2	26,000	3	8	17	1,062	17
1	...	1	1	400	1	25,000	...	...	...	...	1	1	3	35	18
...	2	...	...	...	...	...	...	...	...	...	...	...	...	...	19
49	5	56	48	25,775	51	750,145	22	56,798	22	90,550	51	63	747	9,366	1
47	4	54	46	24,275	49	655,145	20	32,798	21	88,550	49	60	721	8,516	2
6	...	9	6	4,700	6	118,500	3	9,600	2	16,000	6	11	149	1,683	3
5	2	5	5	2,650	6	14,430	2	1,200	...	...	7	8	41	585	4
1	...	1	1	350	1	700	...	...	...	...	...	...	...	...	5
4	...	4	4	2,100	4	68,300	2	3,500	1	10,000	4	4	63	655	6
2	...	2	2	700	1	3,000	1	40	...	...	2	3	12	80	7

TABLE 7.—ORGANIZATIONS, COMMUNICANTS OR MEMBERS, PLACES OF WORSHIP, VALUE OF CHURCH PROPERTY, MORE IN 1900, BY SELECTED

	DENOMINATION.	Total number of organizations.	COMMUNICANTS OR MEMBERS.				
			Number of organizations reporting.	Total number reported.	Sex.		
					Number of organizations reporting.	Male.	Female.
	Fort Worth, Tex.—Continued.						
	Protestant bodies—Continued.						
	Methodist bodies:						
8	Methodist Episcopal Church	5	5	774	5	306	468
9	Methodist Episcopal Church, South	9	9	3,524	8	922	1,397
10	Other Methodist bodies	4	4	405	4	99	306
	Presbyterian bodies:						
11	Cumberland Presbyterian Church	2	2	493	1	118	257
12	Presbyterian Church in the United States	3	3	1,266	3	429	837
13	Protestant Episcopal Church	3	2	518	1	158	334
14	Other Protestant bodies	8	8	453	8	165	288
15	Roman Catholic Church	1	1	5,100	1	2,720	2,380
16	Jewish congregations	2	2	[1] 155			
17	Spiritualists	1	1	65	1	32	33
1	Galveston, Tex.	41	41	21,157	37	9,748	10,931
2	Protestant bodies	31	31	5,504	29	1,992	3,254
	Baptist bodies:						
3	Baptists—Southern Convention	2	2	534	2	188	346
4	Baptists—National Convention (Colored)	6	6	662	6	231	431
	Lutheran bodies:						
5	General Council of the Evangelical Lutheran Church in North America	1	1	98	1	53	45
6	Evangelical Lutheran Synod of Iowa and Other States	2	2	660	2	260	400
	Methodist bodies:						
7	Methodist Episcopal Church	4	4	681	4	260	421
8	African Methodist Episcopal Church	2	2	240	2	98	142
9	Methodist Episcopal Church, South	2	2	627	2	188	439
	Presbyterian bodies:						
10	Presbyterian Church in the United States of America	2	2	75	1	19	38
11	Presbyterian Church in the United States	2	2	400	2	133	267
12	Protestant Episcopal Church	3	3	1,278	2	460	578
13	Other Protestant bodies	5	5	249	5	102	147
14	Roman Catholic Church	5	5	14,872	5	7,328	7,544
15	Jewish congregations	2	2	[1] 220			
	Eastern Orthodox Churches:						
16	Russian Orthodox Church	1	1	500	1	400	100
17	Spiritualists	2	2	61	2	28	33
1	Gloucester, Mass.	28	27	10,069	25	4,330	5,593
	Protestant bodies	23	23	2,886	22	885	1,905
	Baptist bodies:						
3	Baptists—Northern Convention	2	2	603	2	147	456
4	Congregationalists	5	5	621	5	170	451
	Methodist bodies:						
5	Methodist Episcopal Church	4	4	599	3	173	330
6	Protestant Episcopal Church	1	1	208	1	75	133
7	Unitarians	1	1	200	1	75	125
8	Universalists	4	4	468	4	160	308
9	Other Protestant bodies	6	6	187	6	85	102
10	Roman Catholic Church	3	3	7,133	3	3,445	3,688
11	Jewish congregations	1					
	Eastern Orthodox Churches:						
12	Greek Orthodox Church	1	1	50			
1	Grand Rapids, Mich.	109	108	43,306	96	17,255	21,650
	Protestant bodies	92	91	23,834	82	7,893	11,826
	Baptist bodies:						
3	Baptists—Northern and National (Colored) Conventions	9	9	2,201	9	848	1,353
4	Congregationalists	7	7	2,359	7	817	1,542
	Disciples or Christians:						
5	Disciples of Christ	2	2	900	1	100	200
6	German Evangelical Synod of North America	1	1	505	1	228	277
	Independent churches	4	4	1,007	4	490	517
	Lutheran bodies:						
8	Evangelical Lutheran Synodical Conference of America	1	1	877	1	400	477
9	Other Lutheran bodies	4	4	667	3	279	343
	Methodist bodies:						
10	Methodist Episcopal Church	9	9	2,766	9	1,024	1,742
11	Other Methodist bodies	5	5	290	5	85	205
	Presbyterian bodies:						
12	Presbyterian Church in the United States of America	5	5	1,246	4	308	575
13	Protestant Episcopal Church	6	6	1,812	5	300	611
	Reformed bodies:						
14	Reformed Church in America	11	11	3,040	11	1,302	1,738
15	Christian Reformed Church	12	12	4,360	8	1,061	1,297
16	Other Protestant bodies	16	15	1,804	14	633	948
17	Roman Catholic Church	11	11	19,003	11	9,253	9,750
18	Jewish congregations	2	2	[1] 85			
19	All other bodies	4	4	384	3	109	75

[1] Heads of families only.

DEBT ON CHURCH PROPERTY, PARSONAGES, AND SUNDAY SCHOOLS, FOR EACH CITY OF 25,000 INHABITANTS OR DENOMINATIONS: 1906—Continued.

PLACES OF WORSHIP.					VALUE OF CHURCH PROPERTY.		DEBT ON CHURCH PROPERTY.		PARSONAGES.		SUNDAY SCHOOLS CONDUCTED BY CHURCH ORGANIZATIONS.				
Number of organizations reporting— Church edifices.	Number of organizations reporting— Halls, etc.	Number of church edifices reported.	Seating capacity of church edifices. Number of organizations reporting.	Seating capacity of church edifices. Seating capacity reported.	Number of organizations reporting.	Value reported.	Number of organizations reporting.	Amount of debt reported.	Number of organizations reporting.	Value of parsonages reported.	Number of organizations reporting.	Number of Sunday schools reported.	Number of officers and teachers.	Number of scholars.	
5	....	8	5	2,050	5	$70,690	4	$3,833	2	$3,300	5	6	60	520	8
8	1	8	8	5,850	9	168,800	1	700	6	24,500	8	8	175	3,074	9
4	....	4	4	1,650	4	24,250	2	500	3	3,400	4	4	40	222	10
2	....	2	1	600	2	37,000	....	....	1	8,500	2	2	30	266	11
3	....	3	3	1,800	3	67,000	....	....	2	11,500	3	4	77	828	12
3	....	4	3	700	2	29,050	....	....	1	5,000	3	4	35	257	13
4		4	4	1,125	6	53,425	5	13,425	3	6,350	5	6	39	347	14
1	....	1	1	1,000	1	75,000	1	17,000	1	2,000	1		21	800	15
1	....	1	1	500	1	20,000	1	7,000	....	....	1	1	5	50	16
....		....	....	....	....	....	....	....	....	....	....	....	....	....	17
36		39	35	16,884	37	732,230	17	46,125	21	80,550		41	394	5,088	1
27	3	29	27	12,380	29	472,230	13	19,025	14	39,550	28	32	343	3,515	2
1	1	1	1	800	2	45,080	1	1,500	1	5,000	2	4	42	401	3
6	....	6	6	1,850	6	11,300	3	2,400	2	600	6	6	40	270	4
1	....	1	1	150	1	7,000	....	....	....	....	1	1	5	35	5
2	....	2	2	920	2	12,500	1	700	1	3,000	2	2	30	240	6
4	....	4	4	1,	4	44,250	3	9,425	2	4,000	4		40	492	7
2	....	2	2	1,500	2	11,000	2	950	1	150	2		16	121	8
2	....	2	2	1,960	2	39,000	1	1,250	2	6,000	2	4	59	717	9
1	....	1	1	250	1	6,850	....	....	....	....	1	1	15	81	10
2	....	2	2	1,100	2	104,000	....	....	1	6,000	2	2	44	470	11
3	....	5	3	2,760	3	176,000	1	1,800	3	11,800	3	3	34	565	12
3	2	3	3	800	4	15,250	1	1,000	1	3,000	3	3	18	123	13
5	....	5	5	3,240	5	210,000	2	23,000	4	27,500	5	7	40	1,398	14
–	....	3	1	764	1	30,000	....	....	1	10,000	1	1	10	150	15
1	....	1	1	200	1	5,000	1	300	1	2,000	....	....	....	....	16
1	....	1	1	300	1	15,000	1	3,800	1	1,500	1	1	1	25	17
22	4	22	21	10,545	25	437,065	6	16,194	12	56,700	23	23	477	3,783	1
19	3	19	18	7,545	22	270,055	5	12,824	10	41,700	20	20	391	2,916	2
2	....	2	2	1,400	2	58,000	1	3,000	1	3,500	2	2	87	696	3
5	....	5	5	1,750	5	52,500	....	....	3	9,500	5	5	105	828	4
4	....	4	4	1,720	4	58,000	2	5,824	3	10,200	4	4	99	624	5
1	....	1	1	350	1	15,000	....	....	1	8,000	1	1	20	190	6
1	....	1	1	450	1	30,000	1	2,000	1	6,000	1	1	10	75	
4	....	4	4	1,525	4	48,300	1	2,000	1	4,500	3	3	57	453	8
2	3	2	1	350	5	8,255	....	....	....	....	4	4	13	50	9
3	....	3	3	3,000	3	167,000	1	3,370	2	15,000	[illegible]	3	86	867	10
....	....	....	....	....	....	....	....	....	....	....	....	....	....	....	11
....	1	....	....	....	....	....	....	....	....	....	....	....	....	....	12
96	13	105	94	61,271	97	1,685,785	45	121,140	49	231,000	96	106	1,793	20,799	1
83	8	91	82	53,669	85	1,321,785	42	113,540	41	153,800	82	92	1,723	17,431	2
9	....	10	9	4,500	9	163,450	3	2,275	2	8,000	9	10	203	1,923	3
7	....	7	7	14,025	7	151,500	4	5,700	3	12,500	7	10	221	2,500	4
2	....	3	2	1,500	2	36,000	1	3,000	....	....	1	1	33	300	5
1	....	1	1	500	1	25,900	1	1,850	1	3,500	1	1	19	221	6
4	....	4	4	2,300	4	28,550	3	11,370	2	5,000	1	1	10	200	7
1	....	1	1	1,000	1	80,000	....	....	1	5,000	1	2	39	334	8
4	....	4	4	950	4	20,700	2	3,200	1	2,000	4	4	48	320	9
9	....	10	9	3,975	9	112,600	2	2,700	5	19,500	9	9	201	2,015	10
5	....	5	5	1,500	5	18,700	....	....	3	4,100	5	5	40	234	11
4	....	5	4	1,650	4	95,435	1	500	2	13,000	4	4	136	1,122	12
5	1	9	5	2,850	5	117,400	4	16,800	1	18,000	5	7	106	827	13
10	1	10	10	5,140	11	147,500	7	15,200	9	29,100	11	11	257	2,	14
12	....	12	12	10,170	12	174,100	9	47,000	11	34,100	12	12	252	3,767	15
10	6	10	9	3,609	11	179,950	5	3,945	....	....	12	15	158	1,188	16
10	1	12	10	6,902	10	339,000	2	4,600	8	77,200	11	12	66	3,328	17
2	....	2	2	700	2	25,000	1	3,000	....	....	2	2	4	40	18
....	4	....	....	....	....	....	....	....	....	....	....	....	....	....	19

TABLE 7.—ORGANIZATIONS, COMMUNICANTS OR MEMBERS, PLACES OF WORSHIP, VALUE OF CHURCH PROPERTY, MORE IN 1900, BY SELECTED

	DENOMINATION.	Total number of organizations.	COMMUNICANTS OR MEMBERS.				
			Number of organizations reporting.	Total number reported.	Sex.		
					Number of organizations reporting.	Male.	Female.
1	**Harrisburg, Pa.**	74	74	22,909	68	8,609	13,077
2	**Protestant bodies**	65	65	19,962	63	7,395	11,744
	Baptist bodies:						
3	Baptists—Northern Convention	4	4	683	4	248	435
4	Churches of God in North America, General Eldership of the	5	5	708	5	270	438
	Evangelical bodies:						
5	United Evangelical Church	2	2	439	2	236	203
	Lutheran bodies:						
6	General Synod of the Evangelical Lutheran Church in the United States of America	8	8	4,941	8	1,963	2,978
7	General Council of the Evangelical Lutheran Church in North America	3	3	742	3	345	397
8	Evangelical Lutheran Synodical Conference of America	1	1	22	1	7	15
	Methodist bodies:						
9	Methodist Episcopal Church	8	8	4,461	8	1,720	2,741
10	African Methodist Episcopal Church	1	1	300	1	100	200
11	African Methodist Episcopal Zion Church	3	3	640	3	281	359
	Presbyterian bodies:						
12	Presbyterian Church in the United States of America	7	7	2,818	6	716	1,302
13	Protestant Episcopal Church	5	5	691	5	245	446
	Reformed bodies:						
14	Reformed Church in the United States	4	4	1,365	4	531	834
	United Brethren bodies:						
15	Church of the United Brethren in Christ	4	4	1,592	4	543	1,049
16	Other Protestant bodies	10	10	560	9	190	347
17	**Roman Catholic Church**	5	5	2,547	[illegible]	1,214	1,333
18	**Jewish congregations**	3	3	[1] 300	......	......	......
	Eastern Orthodox Churches:						
19	**Greek Orthodox Church**	1	1	100	......	......	......
1	**Hartford, Conn.**	78	77	43,717	68	18,629	23,791
2	**Protestant bodies**	54	54	15,073	52	5,357	9,226
	Baptist bodies:						
3	Baptists—Northern Convention	6	6	2,143	6	842	1,301
4	Baptists—National Convention (Colored)	2	2	590	2	219	371
5	Congregationalists	13	13	5,085	13	1,815	3,270
	Lutheran bodies:						
6	General Council of the Evangelical Lutheran Church in North America	3	3	620	3	259	361
7	Evangelical Lutheran Synodical Conference of America	1	1	205	1	90	115
8	Danish Evangelical Lutheran Church in America	1	1	310	1	150	160
	Methodist bodies:						
9	Methodist Episcopal Church	6	6	1,752	6	623	1,129
10	African Methodist Episcopal Zion Church	1	1	300	1	100	200
	Presbyterian bodies:						
11	Presbyterian Church in the United States of America	1	1	250	1	100	150
12	Protestant Episcopal Church	8	8	2,957	6	816	1,651
13	Universalists	1	1	250	1	100	150
14	Other Protestant bodies	11	11	611	11	243	368
15	**Roman Catholic Church**	13	13	27,092	13	12,867	14,225
16	**Jewish congregations**	6	6	[1] 647	......	......	......
17	**Spiritualists**	2	2	535	2	215	320
18	**All other bodies**	3	2	370	1	190	20
1	**Haverhill, Mass.**	41	38	17,357	32	3,990	5,787
2	**Protestant bodies**	31	30	5,679	28	1,620	3,816
	Adventist bodies:						
3	Advent Christian Church	1	1	173	......	......	......
4	Seventh-day Adventist Denomination	1	1	21	1	6	15
	Baptist bodies:						
5	Baptists—Northern Convention	4	4	1,049	3	250	729
6	Baptists—National Convention (Colored)	1	1	145	1	60	85
7	Free Baptists	1	1	271	1	78	193
8	Christians (Christian Connection)	1	1	220	1	92	128
9	Congregationalists	10	10	1,805	10	515	1,290
	Methodist bodies:						
10	Methodist Episcopal Church	2	2	776	2	204	572
	Presbyterian bodies:						
11	Presbyterian Church in the United States of America	1	1	166	1	42	124
12	Protestant Episcopal Church	2	2	450	2	137	313
13	Unitarians	1	1	215	1	75	140
14	Universalists	2	1	143	1	60	83
15	Other Protestant bodies	4	4	245	4	101	144
16	**Roman Catholic Church**	2	2	10,758	1	2,068	1,870
17	**Jewish congregations**	4	2	[1] 137	......	......	......
18	**Armenian Church**	1	1	300	1	250	50
	Eastern Orthodox Churches:						
19	**Greek Orthodox Church**	1	1	400	......	......	......
20	**All other bodies**	2	2	83	2	32	51
1	**Hoboken, N. J.**	28	28	22,529	24	10,194	11,925
2	**Protestant bodies**	19	19	5,991	19	2,338	3,653
	Baptist bodies:						
3	Baptists—Northern Convention	3	3	350	3	120	230

[1] Heads of families only.

DEBT ON CHURCH PROPERTY, PARSONAGES, AND SUNDAY SCHOOLS, FOR EACH CITY OF 25,000 INHABITANTS OR DENOMINATIONS: 1906—Continued.

PLACES OF WORSHIP. Number of organizations reporting— Church edifices.	Halls, etc.	Number of church edifices reported.	Seating capacity of church edifices. Number of organizations reporting.	Seating capacity reported.	VALUE OF CHURCH PROPERTY. Number of organizations reporting.	Value reported.	DEBT ON CHURCH PROPERTY. Number of organizations reporting.	Amount of debt reported.	PARSONAGES. Number of organizations reporting.	Value of parsonages reported.	SUNDAY SCHOOLS CONDUCTED BY CHURCH ORGANIZATIONS. Number of organizations reporting.	Number of Sunday schools reported.	Number of officers and teachers.	Number of scholars.	
62	10	67	62	39,423	66	$2,135,750	34	$252,542	29	$224,000	66	80	1,978	21,809	1
54	9	59	54	36,518	58	1,735,750	28	161,367	25	196,000	60	74	1,930	21,081	2
4	...	4		1,700	4	93,500	3	5,488	1	15,000	4	4	63	768	3
3	2	3	4	1,500	4	57,000	1	1,800	2	7,400	4	5	103	939	4
2	...	2	2	1,100	2	33,500	1	6,000	...	...	2	3	58	564	5
8	...	9	8	6,100	8	333,800	5	27,000	5	48,000	8	14	402	4,902	6
2	1	2	2	1,000	3	72,000	1	3,000	2	10,000	3	3	36	327	7
1	...	1	1	150	1	6,000	1	700	...	...	1	1	5	46	8
8	...	8	8	8,400	8	330,500	2	10,600	6	35,100	8	8		4,565	9
1	...	1	[illegible]	600	1	40,000	1	12,000	...	...	1	1	385	270	10
3	...	3	3	1,350	3	29,700	3	6,185	...	...	3	3	36	379	11
7	...	8	7	4,768	7	380,000	3	27,071	3	47,000	7	11	388	3,702	12
4	1	4	4	975	5	89,500	2	4,323	2	18,000	5	6	66	401	13
4	...	5	4	2,800	4	120,000	2	30,700	1	5,000	4	4	111	1,251	14
4	...	4	4	3,325	4	112,000	2	18,500	3	10,500	4	4	184	2,316	15
3	5	5	3	2,750	4	38,250	1	8,000	...	...	6	7	66	651	16
5	...	5	5	2,205	5	357,000	5	82,175	4	28,000	5	5	45	688	17
3	...	3	3	700	3	43,000	1	9,000	...	...	1	1	3	40	18
...	1	...	...	...	...	...	...	...	...	...	...	...	...	...	19
61	9	68	60	38,798	62	3,309,108	32	303,459	29	263,000	65	69	1,485	15,404	1
43	6	50	43	26,095	45	2,194,608	21	132,959	19	127,500	50	54	1,239	9,026	2
6	...	7	6	3,750	6	303,000	4	29,250	2	13,000	6	7	172	1,432	3
2	...	2	2	731	2	24,000	1	7,000	1	500	2	2	26	278	4
12	...	15	12	9,170	12	733,500	6	31,534	4	33,500	13	14	509	3,872	5
1	1	1	1	400	1	15,000	1	2,500	1	3,000	3	3	44	369	6
1	...	1	1	200	1	14,000	1	3,000	...	...	1	1	10	50	7
1	...	1	1	350	1	6,500	1	2,000	1	3,500	1	1	10	80	8
6	...	7	6	3,700	6	230,500	3	47,000	6	41,000	6	6	167	1,272	9
1	...	1	1	1,000	1	100,000	1	1,400	1	6,000	1	1	20	200	10
1	...	2	1	750	1	50,000	...	...	...	...	1	1	17	125	11
6	...	7	6	3,700	6	543,000	1	250	3	27,000	8	10	192	1,442	12
1	...	1	1	650	1	87,000	...	...	...	...	1	1	24	236	13
5	5	5	5	1,694	7	88,108	2	9,025	...	...	7	7	48	270	14
1[illegible]	...	13	13	10,328	13	984,500	8	154,500	10	135,500	13	13	235	5,619	15
4	...	4	4	2,375	4	130,000	3	16,000	...	...	2	2	11	159	16
...	1	...	...	...	...	...	...	...	...	...	...	...	...	...	17
1	2	1	...	...	...	...	...	...	...	...	...	...	...	...	18
30	8	3'		14,835	33	789,200	8	46,650	15	66,450	33	39	584	5,954	1
27	4	31	26	12,125	29	506,000	6	33,900	12	51,200	30	36	550	4,902	2
1	...	1	1	250	1	4,500	...	...	...	...	1	1	15	150	3
...	1	...	...	...	...	...	...	...	...	...	1	1	4	15	4
4	...	7	4	2,600	4	101,500	2	17,500	2	9,200	4	6	107	990	5
1	...	1	1	400	1	6,000	...	...	...	...	1	1	18	100	6
1	...	1	1	450	1	20,000	...	...	...	...	1	1	31	292	7
1	...	1	1	400	1	12,000	...	...	1	4,000	1	1	28	275	8
9	1	9	9	3,850	9	145,100	1	3,000	5	22,000	9	12	165	1,784	9
2	...	2	2	1,400	2	50,000	1	3,000	1	5,000	2	2	65	629	10
1	...	1	1	000	1	12,000	...	...	...	...	1	2	25	140	11
2	...	3	2	425	2	27,000	...	...	2	4,000	2	2	20	125	12
1	...	1	1	350	1	20,000	...	...	...	...	1	1	7	30	13
2	...	2	1	600	2	83,500	1	5,000	1	7,000	2	2	34	196	14
2	2	2	2	800	4	24,400	1	5,400	...	...	4	4	31	176	15
2	...	2	2	2,460	2	275,500	1	6,500	2	11,750	2	2	26	1,030	16
1	...	1	1	250	1	7,500	1	6,250	1	3,500	...	...	...	...	17
...	1	...	...	...	...	...	...	...	...	...	...	...	...	...	18
...	1	...	...	...	...	...	...	...	...	...	...	...	...	...	19
...	2	...	...	...	1	200	...	...	...	...	1	1	8	22	20
26	2	27	26	12,170	26	1,137,500	16	187,500	14	137,500	25	29	625	8,175	1
18	1	19	18	7,435	18	710,000	10	57,500	9	75,500	19	22	566	5,415	2
3	...	3	3	950	[illegible]	61,000	[illegible]	14,000	...	...			81	639	3

TABLE 7.—ORGANIZATIONS, COMMUNICANTS OR MEMBERS, PLACES OF WORSHIP, VALUE OF CHURCH PROPERTY, MORE IN 1900, BY SELECTED

	DENOMINATION.	Total number of organizations.	COMMUNICANTS OR MEMBERS. Number of organizations reporting.	Total number reported.	Sex. Number of organizations reporting.	Male.	Female.
	Hoboken, N. J.—Continued.						
	Protestant bodies—Continued.						
	Lutheran bodies:						
4	General Council of the Evangelical Lutheran Church in North America	1	1	896	1	243	653
5	Other Lutheran bodies	3	3	661	3	269	392
	Methodist bodies:						
6	Methodist Episcopal Church	2	2	1,133	2	480	653
	Presbyterian bodies:						
7	Presbyterian Church in the United States of America	1	1	327	1	100	227
8	United Presbyterian Church of North America	1	1	73	1	29	44
9	Protestant Episcopal Church	3	3	1,810	3	787	1,023
	Reformed bodies:						
10	Reformed Church in America	2	2	640	2	260	380
11	Other Protestant bodies	3	3	101	3	50	51
12	Roman Catholic Church	5	5	16,128	5	7,856	8,272
13	Jewish congregations	3	3	[1]260			
	Eastern Orthodox Churches:						
14	Greek Orthodox Church	1	1	150			
1	Holyoke, Mass.	27	27	34,530	23	14,990	19,065
	Protestant bodies	13	13	4,697	12	1,636	2,926
	Baptist bodies:						
3	Baptists—Northern Convention	2	2	861	2	304	557
4	Congregationalists	3	3	1,641	3	513	1,128
	Lutheran bodies:						
5	Evangelical Lutheran Synodical Conference of America	1	1	550	1	250	300
	Methodist bodies:						
6	Methodist Episcopal Church	2	-	677	-	247	430
	Presbyterian bodies:						
7	Presbyterian Church in the United States of America	1	1	500	1	210	290
8	Protestant Episcopal Church	1	1	250	1	80	170
9	Other Protestant bodies	3	3	218	2	32	51
10	Roman Catholic Church	9	9	29,379	9	13,275	16,104
11	Jewish congregations	2	2	[1]140			
12	All other bodies	3	3	314	2	79	35
1	Houston, Tex.	95	93	29,983	81	12,074	15,184
2	Protestant bodies	85	85	15,860	75	5,421	8,044
	Baptist bodies:						
3	Baptists—Southern Convention	9	9	1,448	8	555	883
4	Baptists—National Convention (Colored)	31	31	3,985	28	1,691	2,101
	Disciples or Christians:						
5	Disciples of Christ	2	2	693	2	271	422
6	Churches of Christ	1	1	86	1	31	55
7	German Evangelical Synod of North America	1	1	500			
	Lutheran bodies:						
8	General Council of the Evangelical Lutheran Church in North America	1	1	10	1	7	3
9	Evangelical Lutheran Synodical Conference of America	1	1	400	1	190	210
	Methodist bodies:						
10	Methodist Episcopal Church	8	8	1,336	5	190	463
11	African Methodist Episcopal Church	4	4	803	4	202	601
12	Methodist Episcopal Church, South	10	10	3,168	10	1,277	1,891
13	Colored Methodist Episcopal Church	1	1	130	1	50	80
	Presbyterian bodies:						
14	Presbyterian Church in the United States	4	4	1,340	3	622	659
15	Other Presbyterian bodies	2	2	270	2	99	171
16	Protestant Episcopal Church	3	3	1,321	2	102	269
17	Other Protestant bodies	7	7	370	7	134	236
18	Roman Catholic Church	5	5	13,743	5	6,628	7,115
19	Jewish congregations	4	2	[1]330			
20	Spiritualists	1	1	50	1	25	25
1	Indianapolis, Ind.	210	209	84,815	194	33,524	45,274
2	Protestant bodies	187	187	52,655	177	17,930	29,103
	Baptist bodies:						
3	Baptists—Northern Convention	14	14	3,830	14	1,551	2,279
4	Baptists—National Convention (Colored)	21	21	5,578	20	1,876	3,402
5	Other Baptist bodies	4	4	178	4	78	100
6	Church of Christ, Scientist	2	2	1,140	2	445	695
7	Congregationalists	8	8	1,187	7	312	611
	Disciples or Christians:						
8	Disciples of Christ	13	13	7,939	11	2,162	3,505
9	Churches of Christ	2	2	163	2	68	95
	Friends:						
10	Society of Friends (Orthodox)	2	2	918	2	420	498
11	German Evangelical Synod of North America	4	4	2,008	4	761	1,247
12	Independent churches	3	3	880	3	180	700
	Lutheran bodies:						
13	Evangelical Lutheran Synodical Conference of America	4	4	2,921	4	1,359	1,562
14	Other Lutheran bodies	3	3	502	3	213	289

[1] Heads of families only.

DEBT ON CHURCH PROPERTY, PARSONAGES, AND SUNDAY SCHOOLS, FOR EACH CITY OF 25,000 INHABITANTS OR DENOMINATIONS: 1906—Continued.

PLACES OF WORSHIP. Number of organizations reporting— Church edifices.	Halls, etc.	Number of church edifices reported.	Seating capacity of church edifices. Number of organizations reporting.	Seating capacity reported.	VALUE OF CHURCH PROPERTY. Number of organizations reporting.	Value reported.	DEBT ON CHURCH PROPERTY. Number of organizations reporting.	Amount of debt reported.	PARSONAGES. Number of organizations reporting.	Value of parsonages reported.	SUNDAY SCHOOLS CONDUCTED BY CHURCH ORGANIZATIONS. Number of organizations reporting.	Number of Sunday schools reported.	Number of officers and teachers.	Number of scholars.	
1	....	1	1	610	1	$54,000	1	$3,000	1	$7,000	1	1	90	539	4
3	....	3	3	1,050	3	45,500	3	19,500	2	7,500	3	3	[illegible]	605	5
2	....	2	2	1,225	2	97,500	....	....	2	16,000	2	3	95	975	6
1	....	2	1	500	1	50,000	1	2,500	....	....	1	2	62	517	7
1	....	1	1	250	1	16,000	1	8,500	....	....	1	1	6	43	8
3	....	3	3	1,400	3	265,000	....	....	3	36,080	3	3	89	1,117	9
2	....	2	2	1,000	2	100,000		10,000	1	9,000	2	3	70	825	10
2	1	2	2	450	2	21,000	....	....	....	....	3	3	21	155	11
5	....	5		3,660		400,000	4	120,000	5	62,000	5	6	54	2,685	12
3	....	3	5	1,075	5	27,500	2	10,000	....	....	1	1	5	75	13
....	1	....	....	....	....	....	....	....	....	....	....	....	....	....	14
21	6	26	21	19,542	22	1,282,240	1	191,365	16	166,320	23	38	736	10,024	1
11	2	14	11	8,400	12	564,000	4	16,865	6	44,200	13	15	450	4,398	2
2	....	3	2	1,000	2	112,300	1	6,000	2	17,200	2	3	108	1,013	3
2	1	3	2	2,650	2	203,500	....	....	1	6,500	3	4	132	1,740	4
1	....	2	1	600	1	28,000	1	5,000	....	....	1	1	60	395	5
2	....	2	2	1,450	2	60,000	....	....	2	10,500	2	2	66	464	6
1	....	1	1	800	1	50,000	....	....	....	....	1	1	38	460	7
1	....	1	1	600	1	60,000	....	....	1	10,000	1	1	20	140	8
2	1	2	2	700	3	50,200	2	5,865	....	....	3	3	26	186	9
8	1	10	8	10,042	8	697,740	5	164,000	9	115,120	9	22	285	5,586	10
2	....	2	2	1,100	2	20,500	2	10,500	1	7,000	1	1	1	40	11
....	3	....	....	....	....	....	....	....	....	....	....	....	....	....	12
84	7	90	80	38,575	85	1,617,550	30	86,714	36	141,500	86	94	971	12,007	1
77	6	83	73	33,225	78	1,305,550	28	56,414	31	125,800	79	86	910	10,891	2
9	....	9	9	3,200	9	40,500	3	8,014	2	4,000	8	8	81	1,125	3
29	1	29	28	11,845	29	69,900	9	4,925	2	700	27	28	204	2,593	4
2	....	3	2	1,450	2	79,000	2	15,350	....	....	2	3	31	440	5
1	....	1	1	160	1	1,500	1	600	....	....	1	1	6	60	6
1	....	1	1	800	1	50,000	1	12,000	....	....	1	1	16	200	7
....	....	....	....	....	....	....	....	....	....	....	....	....	....	....	8
1	....	1	1	400	1	19,000	1	5,000	1	2,000	1	2	8	190	9
8	....	8	5	1,550	8	41,350	3	1,050	7	10,250	8	8	77	649	10
4	....	4	4	2,100	4	29,600	3	5,475	4	2,800	4	4	37	266	11
10	....	10	10	4,600	10	354,600	....	....	7	44,550	10	10	216	2,391	12
1	....	1	1	720	1	10,000	1	300	1	2,900	1	1	8	64	13
4	....	5	4	2,725	4	354,500	1	700	4	40,500	4	5	107	1,455	14
2	....	3	2	825	2	32,500	2	2,250	1	2,500	2	2	28	335	15
3	....	6	3	2,200	3	213,600	....	....	1	15,000	3	5	53	760	16
2	5	2	2	650	3	9,500	1	750	1	1,500	7	8	38	363	17
5	....	5	5	3,050	5	192,000	1	5,300	5	15,700	5	5	45	831	18
2	....	2	2	2,300	2	120,000	1	25,000	....	....	2	3	16	285	19
....	1	....	....	....	....	....	....	....	....	....	....	....	....	....	20
176	20	179	175	77,710	180	3,455,088	86	317,651	46	199,700	190	206	2,838	33,913	1
163	17	166	162	70,230	167	2,798,288	80	215,021	40	124,200	172	181	2,751	30,200	2
14	....	14	14	5,965	14	393,800	8	16,483	3	5,800	14	10	279	3,386	3
20	1	20	20	8,625	19	77,700	10	19,500	1	10,000	21	21	195	1,685	4
3	....	3	3	900	4	3,900	2	975	....	....	3	3	22	82	5
1	1	1	1	600	1	30,000	1	10,000	....	....	2	2	26	155	6
8	....	8	8	2,925	8	107,000	5	11,300	1	5,000	8	8	98	874	7
13	....	14	13	5,625	13	152,000	5	12,500	....	....	13	13	250	4,113	8
2	....	2	2	325	2	3,500	....	....	....	....	....	....	....	....	9
2	....	2	2	1,200	2	40,000	2	4,000	1	4,000	2	2	30	200	10
4	....	4	4	1,970	4	89,618	2	5,242	3	7,000	4	4	90	977	11
2	1	2	2	700	3	5,040	2	4,700	....	....	3	3	16	135	12
4	....	4	4	3,100	4	160,000	2	14,000	4	12,500	....	....	....	....	13
3	....	3	3	800	3	48,400	1	1,000	2	6,500	3	3	36	336	14

TABLE 7.—ORGANIZATIONS, COMMUNICANTS OR MEMBERS, PLACES OF WORSHIP, VALUE OF CHURCH PROPERTY, ... MORE IN 1900, BY SELECTED ...

	DENOMINATION.	Total number of organizations.	COMMUNICANTS OR MEMBERS.				
			Number of organizations reporting.	Total number reported.	Sex.		
					Number of organizations reporting.	Male.	Female.
	Indianapolis, Ind.—Continued.						
	Protestant bodies—Continued.						
	Methodist bodies:						
15	Methodist Episcopal Church	35	35	12,035	33	3,976	6,597
16	African Methodist Episcopal Church	5	5	1,534	5	539	995
17	African Methodist Episcopal Zion Church	5	5	731	5	287	444
18	Other Methodist bodies	4	4	444	4	188	256
	Presbyterian bodies:						
19	Presbyterian Church in the United States of America	15	15	5,244	13	1,526	2,691
20	Cumberland Presbyterian Church	1	1	63	1	27	36
21	Protestant Episcopal Church	8	8	1,916	8	652	1,264
	Reformed bodies:						
22	Reformed Church in the United States	6	6	1,179	5	484	610
23	Other Protestant bodies	28	28	2,265	27	826	1,227
24	Roman Catholic Church	13	13	31,351	13	15,245	16,106
25	Jewish congregations	6	5	[1] 395	......	......	......
26	All other bodies	4	4	414	4	349	65
1	Jackson, Mich	32	31	5,552	29	1,733	3,321
2	Protestant bodies	28	28	5,461	27	1,709	3,284
	Baptist bodies:						
3	Baptists—Northern Convention	5	5	1,172	5	389	783
4	Free Baptists	1	1	120	1	34	86
5	Congregationalists	2	2	419	2	144	275
6	German Evangelical Synod of North America	1	1	300	1	125	175
	Lutheran bodies:						
7	Evangelical Lutheran Synodical Conference of America	1	1	468	......	......	......
	Methodist bodies:						
8	Methodist Episcopal Church	7	7	1,675	7	727	948
9	Other Methodist bodies	3	3	134	3	44	90
	Presbyterian bodies:						
10	Presbyterian Church in the United States of America	1	1	410	1	130	280
11	Protestant Episcopal Church	1	1	461	1	30	431
12	Other Protestant bodies	6	6	302	6	86	216
13	Roman Catholic Church [2]	......	......	......	......	......	......
14	Jewish congregations	1	......	......	......	......	......
15	All other bodies	3	3	91	2	24	37
1	Jacksonville, Fla	96	96	18,323	89	6,735	10,594
2	Protestant bodies	91	91	16,254	87	5,908	9,671
	Baptist bodies:						
3	Baptists—Southern Convention	3	3	787	3	300	487
4	Baptists—National Convention (Colored)	27	27	4,279	26	1,289	2,740
5	Other Baptist bodies	5	5	298	5	109	189
	Disciples or Christians:						
6	Disciples of Christ	1	1	757	1	315	442
	Methodist bodies:						
7	Methodist Episcopal Church	8	8	1,376	8	485	891
8	African Methodist Episcopal Church	15	15	3,622	15	1,484	2,138
9	Methodist Episcopal Church, South	5	5	1,244	5	520	724
10	Other Methodist bodies	7	7	293	7	107	186
	Presbyterian bodies:						
11	Presbyterian Church in the United States of America	1	1	104	1	30	74
12	Presbyterian Church in the United States	2	2	668	2	278	390
13	Protestant Episcopal Church	6	6	2,019	4	700	984
14	Other Protestant bodies	11	11	807	10	291	426
15	Roman Catholic Church	1	1	1,700	1	807	893
16	Jewish congregations	2	2	[1] 159	......	......	......
17	All other bodies	2	2	210	1	20	30
1	Jersey City, N. J	120	115	104,637	96	32,214	41,390
2	Protestant bodies	88	88	26,578	79	8,468	14,981
	Baptist bodies:						
3	Baptists—Northern Convention	10	10	2,781	9	1,046	1,713
4	Congregationalists	2	2	1,379	2	503	876
	Lutheran bodies:						
5	General Synod of the Evangelical Lutheran Church in the United States of America	4	4	1,819	4	702	1,117
6	General Council of the Evangelical Lutheran Church in North America	6	6	3,565	5	1,201	1,969
7	Other Lutheran bodies	2	2	392	2	129	263
	Methodist bodies:						
8	Methodist Episcopal Church	16	16	4,335	16	1,525	2,810
9	Other Methodist bodies	2	2	318	2	103	215
	Presbyterian bodies:						
10	Presbyterian Church in the United States of America	5	5	2,272	5	792	1,480
11	United Presbyterian Church of North America	3	3	701	3	255	446
12	Protestant Episcopal Church	12	12	4,810	7	780	1,605
	Reformed bodies:						
13	Reformed Church in America	10	10	3,497	9	1,201	2,059
14	Other Protestant bodies	16	16	709	15	231	408
15	Roman Catholic Church	19	19	77,279	13	23,599	26,199
16	Jewish congregations	8	3	[1] 223	......	......	......
17	All other bodies	5	5	557	4	147	210

[1] Heads of families only.

DEBT ON CHURCH PROPERTY, PARSONAGES, AND SUNDAY SCHOOLS, FOR EACH CITY OF 25,000 INHABITANTS OR DENOMINATIONS: 1906—Continued.

PLACES OF WORSHIP.					VALUE OF CHURCH PROPERTY.		DEBT ON CHURCH PROPERTY.		PARSONAGES.		SUNDAY SCHOOLS CONDUCTED BY CHURCH ORGANIZATIONS.				
Number of organizations reporting—Church edifices.	Number of organizations reporting—Halls, etc.	Number of church edifices reported.	Seating capacity of church edifices. Number of organizations reporting.	Seating capacity of church edifices. Seating capacity reported.	Number of organizations reporting.	Value reported.	Number of organizations reporting.	Amount of debt reported.	Number of organizations reporting.	Value of parsonages reported.	Number of organizations reporting.	Number of Sunday schools reported.	Number of officers and teachers.	Number of scholars.	
35	......	35	35	16,075	35	$664,800	16	$34,551	10	$19,500	35	36	870	9,099	15
5	......	5	5	2,700	5	58,500	4	3,090	3	4,100	5	5	47	360	16
5	......	5	5	1,550	5	25,600	4	4,600	1	2,000	5	5	38	348	17
3	......	3	2	650	3	8,800	3	3,500	1	3,500	4	5	36	341	18
13		14	13	6,500	14	402,300	6	29,600	......	......	15	20	313	4,539	19
......		......	......	......	......	......	......	......	......	......	1	1	8	65	20
7		8	7	3,250	7	292,000	2	15,500	1	2,500	7	7	62	565	21
6	......	6	6	2,275	6	58,500	1	2,500	5	17,000	6	6	88	861	22
13	1	13	13	4,495	15	176,830	4	21,980	4	24,800	21	21	247	2,079	23
8	......	8	8	5,780	8	569,000	4	86,130	6	75,500	12	19	63	3,324	24
4	......	4	4	1,400	4	87,000	2	16,500	......	......	3	3	11	224	25
1	3	1	1	300	1	800	......	......	......	......	3	3	13	165	26
26	4	28	26	10,995	27	339,150	10	28,645	16	44,400	26	28	405	3,987	1
26	2	28	26	10,995	27	339,150	10	28,645	16	44,400	26	28	405	3,987	2
5	......	6	5	1,875	5	63,400	3	5,825	1	2,500	5	6	86	860	3
1	......	1	1	375	1	15,000	1	1,700	1	2,500	1	1	19	168	4
2	......	2	2	1,025	2	49,000	1	4,000	1	5,000	2	2	30	515	5
1	......	1	1	600	1	20,000	1	7,500	1	3,000	1	1	18	140	6
1	......	1	1	400	1	6,000	......	......	1	3,000	......	......	......	......	7
7	......	7	7	3,150	7	96,500	1	2,000	5	16,200	7	7	155	1,569	8
3	......	4	3	1,260	3	8,500	......	......	3	4,200	3	4	29	163	9
1	......	1	1	600	1	15,000	......	......	1	3,500	1	1	15	237	10
1	......	1	1	600	1	35,000	1	4,000	1	3,000	1	1	12	136	11
4	2	4	4	1,110	5	30,750	2	3,620	1	1,500	5	5	41	199	12
......	......	......	......	......	......	......	......	......	......	......	......	......	......	......	13
......	......	......	......	......	......	......	......	......	......	......	......	......	......	......	14
......	2	......	......	......	......	......	......	......	......	......	......	......	......	......	15
85	7	88	83	34,255	87	977,275	47	134,227	34	125,800	91	97	918	9,437	1
82	5	85	80	33,130	84	936,275	46	129,227	33	110,800	88	94	887	9,089	2
3	......	3	3	1,450	3	78,500	3	10,000	1	10,000	3	4	40	775	3
27	......	27	26	9,230	27	139,150	11	29,910	7	7,400	27	27	189	1,740	4
5	......	5	5	1,600	5	10,050	4	2,600	3	2,150	5	5	27	200	5
1	......	2	1	1,050	1	52,000	1	15,000	......	......	1	5	56	987	6
8	......	8	8	3,175	8	87,350	5	13,306	5	17,300	8	8	90	936	7
14	1	14	14	6,850	14	93,700	9	3,875	5	20,900	15	15	192	1,833	8
5	......	5	5	1,775	5	67,000	2	3,500	4	23,000	5	6	75	809	9
5	1	5	5	1,550	5	7,100	3	1,000	......	......	6	6	24	208	10
1	......	1	1	400	1	8,000	......	......	1	1,200	1	1	9	55	11
2	......	2	2	1,350	2	87,000	......	......	1	2,000	2	2	44	382	12
6	......	8	5	2,850	6	199,750	4	28,686	4	16,250	6	6	86	819	13
5	3	5	5	1,850	7	106,675	4	21,350	2	10,600	9	9	55	345	14
1	......	1	1	425	1	11,000	......	......	1	15,000	1	1	25	268	15
2	......	2	2	700	2	30,000	1	5,000	......	......	2	2	6	80	16
......	2	......	......	......	......	......	......	......	......	......	......	......	......	......	17
93	19	106	92	57,893	97	4,194,825	61	941,550	48	447,700	102	126	2,746	33,900	1
71	15	80	71	40,437	76	2,428,825	44	307,350	35	233,200	84	95	2,426	24,032	2
8	1	9	8	5,258	9	278,200	7	31,600	2	8,200	10	10	366	2,394	3
2	......	2	2	2,750	2	309,000	1	13,000	2	12,000	2	2	82	1,110	4
4	......	4	4	2,200	4	155,000	4	49,800	2	14,000	4	4	104	1,186	5
6	......	6	6	3,660	6	248,000	6	75,000	5	33,000	6	10	282	3,631	6
2	......	2	2	500	2	23,000	2	6,500	......	......	2	2	34	364	7
15	......	17	15	8,399	15	466,000	8	56,850	13	74,500	16	18	526	4,870	8
2	......	2	2	1,000	2	17,000	2	5,600	......	......	2	2	29	329	9
5	......		5	3,020	5	169,000	3	23,500	1	15,000	5	5	161	1,604	10
3	......		3	2,050	3	67,000	1	1,000	......	......	3	4	111	1,254	11
11	1	18	11	4,899	11	371,000	3	19,100	4	37,000	10	10	265	2,841	12
10	......	10	10	5,700	10	312,000	4	17,700	5	35,500	10	13	356	3,508	13
3	13	5	3	1,100	7	22,625	3	7,700	1	4,000	14	15	110	941	14
19	......	22	18	16,356	18	1,727,000	14	621,200	13	214,500	14	27	305	9,623	15
2	......	2	2	900	2	27,000	2	10,000	......	......	2	2	11	180	16
1	4	1	1	200	1	12,000	1	3,000	......	......	2	2	4	65	17

[1] Statistics not reported separately by cities for part of Detroit diocese.

TABLE 7.—ORGANIZATIONS, COMMUNICANTS OR MEMBERS, PLACES OF WORSHIP, VALUE OF CHURCH PROPERTY, … MORE IN 1900, BY SELECTED …

	DENOMINATION.	Total number of organizations.	COMMUNICANTS OR MEMBERS.				
			Number of organizations reporting.	Total number reported.	Sex.		
					Number of organizations reporting.	Male.	Female.
1	Johnstown, Pa.	64	64	31,205	56	13,078	12,281
2	Protestant bodies	51	51	14,380	47	5,236	7,309
	Baptist bodies:						
3	Baptists—Northern and National (Colored) Conventions	4	4	596	4	216	380
	Disciples or Christians:						
4	Disciples of Christ	2	2	642	2	209	433
	Dunkers or German Baptist Brethren:						
5	German Baptist Brethren Church (Conservative)	1	1	350	1	175	175
6	The Brethren Church (Progressive Dunkers)	3	3	621	2	26	45
	Evangelical bodies:						
7	Evangelical Association	3	3	300	3	98	202
8	United Evangelical Church	5	5	1,242	4	431	683
	Lutheran bodies:						
9	General Synod of the Evangelical Lutheran Church in the United States of America	3	3	1,538	2	237	301
10	General Council of the Evangelical Lutheran Church in North America	2	2	1,390	2	582	808
11	Slovak Evangelical Lutheran Synod of America	1	1	150	1	90	60
	Methodist bodies:						
12	Methodist Episcopal Church	6	6	2,354	6	972	1,382
13	African Methodist Episcopal Zion Church	1	1	54	1	12	42
	Presbyterian bodies:						
14	Presbyterian Church in the United States of America	3	3	1,228	3	396	832
15	Other Presbyterian bodies	2	2	240	2	99	141
16	Protestant Episcopal Church	1	1	367	1	127	240
	Reformed bodies:						
17	Reformed Church in the United States	3	3	549	2	162	230
18	Hungarian Reformed Church in America	1	1	1,250	1	830	420
	United Brethren bodies:						
19	Church of the United Brethren in Christ	4	4	1,142	4	437	705
20	Other Protestant bodies	6	6	367	6	137	230
21	Roman Catholic Church	10	10	16,625	8	7,786	4,933
22	Jewish congregations	1	1	[1] 65			
23	All other bodies	2	2	135	1	56	39
1	Joliet, Ill.	43	43	27,132	36	6,785	7,238
2	Protestant bodies	33	33	8,297	30	2,136	3,507
	Baptist bodies:						
3	Baptists—Northern and National (Colored) Conventions	4	4	1,113	4	418	695
	Lutheran bodies:						
4	General Synod of the Evangelical Lutheran Church in the United States of America	2	2	579	2	232	347
5	General Council of the Evangelical Lutheran Church in North America	1	1	598	1	262	336
6	Evangelical Lutheran Synodical Conference of America	1	1	2,000			
	Methodist bodies:						
7	Methodist Episcopal Church	5	5	1,338	5	503	835
8	African Methodist Episcopal Church	1	1	50	1	15	35
	Presbyterian bodies:						
9	Presbyterian Church in the United States of America	4	4	1,345	3	257	487
10	Protestant Episcopal Church	2	2	487	2	196	291
11	Universalists	1	1	200	1	74	126
12	Other Protestant bodies	12	12	587	11	179	358
13	Roman Catholic Church	9	9	18,809	5	4,631	3,723
	Eastern Orthodox Churches:						
14	Russian Orthodox Church	1	1	26	1	18	8
1	Joplin, Mo.	31	31	6,490	31	2,399	4,091
2	Protestant bodies	27	27	5,436	27	2,006	3,430
	Adventist bodies:						
3	Seventh-day Adventist Denomination	1	1	74	1	14	60
	Baptist bodies:						
4	Baptists—Southern and National (Colored) Conventions	3	3	940	3	398	542
5	Free Baptists	2	2	56	2	22	34
6	Church of Christ, Scientist	2	2	164	2	53	111
7	Congregationalists	1	1	130	1	60	70
	Disciples or Christians:						
8	Disciples of Christ	4	4	1,874	4	651	1,223
	Lutheran bodies:						
9	Evangelical Lutheran Synodical Conference of America	1	1	111	1	45	66
	Methodist bodies:						
10	Methodist Episcopal Church	5	5	866	5	324	542
11	Methodist Episcopal Church, South	2	2	408	2	120	288
12	Other Methodist bodies	2	2	44	2	12	32
	Presbyterian bodies:						
13	Presbyterian Church in the United States of America	2	2	510	2	211	299
14	Protestant Episcopal Church	1	1	118	1	22	96
	Salvationists:						
15	Salvation Army	1	1	141	1	74	67
16	Roman Catholic Church	1		723	1	255	468
	Latter-day Saints:						
17	Reorganized Church of Jesus Christ of Latter-day Saints	1		221	1	88	133
18	Spiritualists	2	2	110	2	50	60

[1] Heads of families only.

DEBT ON CHURCH PROPERTY, PARSONAGES, AND SUNDAY SCHOOLS, FOR EACH CITY OF 25,000 INHABITANTS OR DENOMINATIONS: 1906—Continued.

PLACES OF WORSHIP. Number of organizations reporting— Church edifices.	Halls, etc.	Number of church edifices reported.	Seating capacity of church edifices. Number of organizations reporting.	Seating capacity reported.	VALUE OF CHURCH PROPERTY. Number of organizations reporting.	Value reported.	DEBT ON CHURCH PROPERTY. Number of organizations reporting.	Amount of debt reported.	PARSONAGES. Number of organizations reporting.	Value of parsonages reported.	SUNDAY SCHOOLS CONDUCTED BY CHURCH ORGANIZATIONS. Number of organizations reporting.	Number of Sunday schools reported.	Number of officers and teachers.	Number of scholars.	
58	4	71	58	28,785	60	$1,606,802	35	$186,491	28	$148,700	56	65	1,024	11,917	1
47	2	57	47	22,185	48	1,013,552	27	58,491	21	99,350	47	56	996	9,764	2
4	....	4	4	1,400	4	85,500	4	5,100	....	....	4	4	53	345	3
2	....	4	2	1,400	2	68,500	1	9,000	....	....	2	2	44	360	4
1	....	4	1	1,200	1	16,000	....	....	....	....	1	4	40	240	5
3	....	5	3	1,800	3	33,000	2	1,500	1	3,000	3	5	57	650	6
3	....	3	3	800	3	27,700	2	4,750	3	10,100	3	3	54	443	7
5	....	6	5	2,100	5	24,800	3	2,401	5	10,650	5	6	127	1,140	8
3	....	3	3	1,560	3	135,000	1	9,300	....	....	3	4	60	916	9
2	....	2	2	1,320	2	85,000	2	3,500	1	10,000	2	2	75	869	10
1	....	1	1	200	1	5,000	1	2,500	....	....	....	....	....	....	11
6	....	6	6	3,000	6	191,000	1	4,740	3	25,000	6	6	166	1,708	12
1	....	1	1	250	1	10,000	1	2,200	1	800	1	1	10	56	13
3	....	4	3	1,660	3	103,000	1	1,700	1	9,000	3			930	14
2	....	3	2	970	2	50,500	1	300	....	....	2	4	84	324	15
1	....	1	1	450	1	50,000	....	....	1	10,000	1	1	16	132	16
3	....	4	3	1,175	3	40,500	3	8,550	1	2,000	3	3	40	259	17
....	....	....	....	....	....	....	....	....	1	7,000	....	....	....	....	18
4	....		4	1,350	4	63,000	3	2,300	3	11,800	4	4	95	1,059	19
3	2	5	3	1,550	1	25,052	1	650	....	....	4	4	40	333	20
10	....	13	10	6,200	10	568,000	7	118,000	7	49,350	8	8	26	2,108	21
1	....	1	1	400	1	25,000	1	10,000	....	....	1	1	2	50	22
....	2	....	....	....	1	250	....	....	....	....	....	....	....	....	23
33	5	35	32	16,956	36	923,725	20	155,760	17	81,400	32		487	5,463	1
27	4	29	26	13,076	29	592,425	14	46,060	13	49,400	30	38	468	4,701	2
4	....	4	4	1,600	4	80,750	1	2,860	....	....	4	8	92	793	3
2	....	2	1	800	2	17,100	2	3,800	1	2,200	2	2	10	320	4
1	....	1	1	500	1	15,000	....	....	1	5,000	1	1	30	275	5
1	....	1	1	800	1	20,000	....	....	1	3,500	1	1	3	400	6
5	....	5	5	2,900	5	94,000	2	4,300	4	20,500	5	7	109	1,010	7
1	....	1	1	400	1	9,000	1	1,400	1	600	1	1	8	30	8
4	....	5	4	3,325	4	121,000	2	3,400	1	3,500	4	5	101	961	9
2	....	3	2	106	2	41,800	....	....	1	7,000	2	3	23	289	10
1	....	1	1	700	1	150,000	1	24,000	1	3,300	1	1	15	75	11
6	4	6	6	1,945	8	43,775	5	6,300	2	3,800	9	9	77	528	12
6	....	6	6	3,880	6	329,000	5	106,000	4	32,000	2	2	19	762	13
....	1	....	....	....	1	2,300	1	1,700	....	....	....	....	....	....	14
28	3	31	28	11,783	29	373,450	14	72,357	11	27,300	28	33	397	4,471	1
25	2	28	25	10,903	26	341,750	13	67,357	10	22,300	25	30	376	4,271	2
1	....	1	1	125	1	1,100	....	....	....	....	1	1	11	50	3
3	....	5	3	2,050	3	50,100	1	4,200	....	....	3	6	55	775	4
2	....	2	2	200	2	350	....	....	....	....	....	....	....	....	5
2	....	2	2	800	2	39,000	2	10,000	....	....	2	2	9	50	6
1	....	1	1	300	1	17,000	1	5,000	1	3,000	1	2	15	170	7
4	....	4	4	2,100	4	52,000	3	4,300	....	....	4	4	96	1,220	8
1	....	1	1	200	1	4,000	....	....	1	3,000	1	1	8	60	9
5	....	5	5	2,700	5	79,400	2	22,500	3	6,100	5	5	86	960	10
2	....	2	2	700	2	41,000	1	10,000	1	3,000	2	2	25	301	11
1	1	1	1	500	1	5,500	1	300	1	200	2	2	9	40	12
2	....	3	2	1,100	2	45,000	1	11,000	2	4,000	2	3	50	550	13
1	....	1	1	128	1	7,000	....	....	1	3,000	1	1	5	50	14
....	1	....	....	....	1	300	1	57	....	....	1	1	7	45	15
1	....	4	1	480	1	30,000	1	5,000	1	5,000	1	1	4	85	16
1	....	1	1	200	1	1,200	....	....	....	....	1	1	10	90	17
1	1	1	1	200	1	500	....	....	....	....	1	1	7	25	18

TABLE 7.—ORGANIZATIONS, COMMUNICANTS OR MEMBERS, PLACES OF WORSHIP, VALUE OF CHURCH PROPERTY, ... MORE IN 1900, BY SELECTED ...

	DENOMINATION.	Total number of organizations.	COMMUNICANTS OR MEMBERS.				
			Number of organizations reporting.	Total number reported.	Sex.		
					Number of organizations reporting.	Male.	Female.
1	Kansas City, Kans.	81	80	22,079	78	9,498	12,254
2	Protestant bodies	67	67	11,870	66	4,012	7,578
	Baptist bodies:						
3	Baptists—Northern Convention	7	7	1,404	7	429	975
4	Baptists—National Convention (Colored)	7	7	2,106	6	631	1,195
5	Congregationalists	7	7	688	7	233	455
	Disciples or Christians:						
6	Disciples of Christ	2	2	715	2	220	495
7	German Evangelical Synod of North America	1	1	211	1	83	128
8	Lutheran bodies	3	3	327	3	142	185
	Methodist bodies:						
9	Methodist Episcopal Church	7	7	2,544	7	867	1,677
10	African Methodist Episcopal Church	3	3	694	3	276	418
11	Methodist Protestant Church	3	3	254	3	92	162
12	Methodist Episcopal Church, South	1	1	210	1	65	145
13	Colored Methodist Episcopal Church	1	1	218	1	50	168
14	Other Methodist bodies	3	3	79	3	33	46
	Presbyterian bodies:						
15	Presbyterian Church in the United States of America	4	4	1,123	4	404	719
16	Other Presbyterian bodies	2	2	285	2	109	176
17	Protestant Episcopal Church	3	3	323	3	127	196
18	Other Protestant bodies	13	13	689	13	251	438
19	Roman Catholic Church	9	9	9,154	9	4,752	4,402
20	Jewish congregations	2	1	[1] 47	......	......	......
	Eastern Orthodox Churches:						
21	Servian Orthodox Church	1	1	600		550	50
	Latter-day Saints:						
22	Reorganized Church of Jesus Christ of Latter-day Saints	2	2	408	2	184	224
1	Kansas City, Mo.	184	183	61,503	169	23,039	32,852
2	Protestant bodies	151	150	40,732	141	13,743	23,002
	Baptist bodies:						
3	Baptists—Southern Convention	19		6,895	19	2,504	4,391
4	Baptists—National Convention (Colored)	12	19	2,219	11	325	694
5	Primitive Baptists	1	1	49	1	18	31
6	Church of Christ, Scientist	3	[illegible]	1,273	2	326	787
7	Congregationalists	7	3	2,022	7	695	1,327
	Disciples or Christians:						
8	Disciples of Christ	14	14	7,351	13	2,809	3,992
9	Churches of Christ	1	1	86	1	41	45
10	German Evangelical Synod of North America	2	2	428	2	184	244
	Lutheran bodies:						
11	General Synod of the Evangelical Lutheran Church in the United States of America	3	3	446	3	153	293
12	General Council of the Evangelical Lutheran Church in North America	2	2	612	2	272	340
13	Other Lutheran bodies	3	3	484	3	202	282
	Methodist bodies:						
14	Methodist Episcopal Church	17	16	5,776	13	1,494	2,615
15	African Methodist Episcopal Church	6	6	1,460	5	457	913
16	Methodist Episcopal Church, South	10	10	2,513	10	914	1,599
17	Other African Methodist bodies	3	3	211	3	53	158
	Presbyterian bodies:						
18	Presbyterian Church in the United States of America	8	8	2,231	8	940	1,291
19	Cumberland Presbyterian Church	3	3	909	3	373	536
20	Presbyterian Church in the United States	2	2	1,470	2	462	1,008
21	Other Presbyterian bodies	2	2	260	2	92	168
22	Protestant Episcopal Church	9	9	2,217	9	766	1,451
23	Other Protestant bodies	24	24	1,820	22	663	837
24	Roman Catholic Church	20	20	19,077	18	8,942	9,455
25	Jewish congregations	2	2	[1] 345	......	......	......
	Eastern Orthodox Churches:						
26	Greek Orthodox Church	1	1	600	......	......	......
	Latter-day Saints:						
27	Reorganized Church of Jesus Christ of Latter-day Saints	4	4	476	4	208	268
28	All other bodies	6	6	273	6	146	127
1	Knoxville, Tenn.	79	79	17,416	66	6,003	9,271
2	Protestant bodies	74	74	17,091	66	6,003	9,271
	Baptist bodies:						
3	Baptists—Southern Convention	11	11	4,118	11	1,818	2
4	Baptists—National Convention (Colored)	4	4	1,959	4	575	1,300
5	Other Baptist bodies	3	3	138	2	35	[illegible]
	Disciples or Christians:						
6	Disciples of Christ	3	3	520	3	225	295
	Methodist bodies:						
7	Methodist Episcopal Church	7	7	1,926	7	708	[illegible]
8	African Methodist Episcopal Church	2	2	80	2	27	
9	African Methodist Episcopal Zion Church	5	5	822	5	249	218
10	Methodist Episcopal Church, South	9	9	2,543	5	760	1,[illegible]
	Presbyterian bodies:						
11	Presbyterian Church in the United States of America	8	8	1,515	7	408	
12	Cumberland Presbyterian Church	1	1	525	1	275	
13	United Presbyterian Church of North America	1	1	140	1	62	
14	Presbyterian Church in the United States	3	3	1,167	2	280	
15	Protestant Episcopal Church	2	2	629	2	211	657
16	Other Protestant bodies	15	15	1,009	14	370	[illegible]

[1] Heads of families only.

DEBT ON CHURCH PROPERTY, PARSONAGES, AND SUNDAY SCHOOLS, FOR EACH CITY OF 25,000 INHABITANTS OR DENOMINATIONS: 1906—Continued.

PLACES OF WORSHIP.					VALUE OF CHURCH PROPERTY.		DEBT ON CHURCH PROPERTY.		PARSONAGES.		SUNDAY SCHOOLS CONDUCTED BY CHURCH ORGANIZATIONS.				
Number of organizations reporting— Church edifices.	Number of organizations reporting— Halls, etc.	Number of church edifices reported.	Seating capacity of church edifices. Number of organizations reporting.	Seating capacity of church edifices. Seating capacity reported.	Number of organizations reporting.	Value reported.	Number of organizations reporting.	Amount of debt reported.	Number of organizations reporting.	Value of parsonages reported.	Number of organizations reporting.	Number of Sunday schools reported.	Number of officers and teachers.	Number of scholars.	
69	9	82	67	26,426	73	$744,150	39	$99,150	27	$70,950	75	88	1,092	12,046	1
57	8	64	55	20,706	61	454,650	30	41,950	18	35,350	65	77	1,018	10,350	2
7	...	10	7	2,500	7	28,500	4	1,742	1	2,000	7	10	138	1,434	3
7	...	7	7	3,350	7	42,250	2	1,700	1	900	7	7	80	744	4
6	...	6	4	696	6	34,600	1	320	...	...	7	9	113	1,194	5
2	...	2	2	1,150	2	29,000	2	5,800	...	...	2	3	42	624	6
1	...	1	1	300	1	5,000	1	750	1	3,000	1	1	13	120	7
3	...	4	3	830	3	25,500	2	5,800	1	2,000	3	3	25	222	8
7	...	8	7	4,150	7	103,900	3	12,750	5	12,300	7	11	208	2,524	9
3	...	3	3	1,700	3	16,500	3	4,195	...	...	3	3	40	467	10
3	...	3	3	900	3	23,000	3	2,050	2	4,000	3	3	49	370	11
1	...	1	1	400	1	23,000	...	...	1	2,000	1	1	15	160	12
1	...	1	1	400	1	1,000	1	75	1	300	1	1	10	40	13
1	1	1	1	80	1	800	...	...	1	1,250	3	3	26	151	14
4	...	4	4	1,775	4	76,000	2	4,100	1	3,000	4	5	108	1,252	15
2	...	2	2	550	2	8,000	...	...	1	2,600	2	2	51	400	16
2	1	2	2	400	2	25,000	1	2,250	...	...	2	2	20	125	17
7	6	9	7	1,525	11	12,600	5	418	2	2,000	12	13	80	523	18
9	...	15	9	4,670	9	274,000	7	54,400	8	34,200	8	8	34	1,512	19
1	...	1	1	500	1	10,000	1	1,300	...	...	...	...	...	...	20
1	...	1	[illegible]	300	1	3,000	1	1,500	1	1,400	...	...	...	...	21
1	1	1	1	250	1	2,500	...	...	...	...	2	3	40	184	22
152	25	165	150	77,081	158	4,593,800	81	496,415	41	189,400	162	179	2,709	29,048	1
128	16	139	128	66,749	134	3,765,000	69	413,584	29	98,900	140	155	2,554	26,063	2
18	1	19	18	8,850	18	515,500	7	16,200	2	7,000	19	24	406	4,607	3
9	1	10	9	5,400	10	81,550	6	7,603	...	...	12	12	74	503	4
1	...	1	1	200	1	4,000	1	500	...	...	...	...	...	...	5
2	...	2	2	2,460	2	322,000	1	122,000	...	...	3	3	60	339	6
7	...	7	7	4,025	7	330,000	3	14,000	1	4,500	7	9	146	1,685	7
14	...	17	14	7,751	14	400,000	5	24,200	1	2,000	14	17	409	5,293	8
1	...	1	1	400	1	2,000	...	...	...	...	...	...	...	...	9
2	...	2	2	550	2	26,500	1	450	1	1,200	2	2	15	185	10
3	...	3	3	1,300	3	80,000	2	8,350	...	...	3	3	50	310	11
2	...	2	2	1,650	2	75,000	1	9,600	2	10,000	2	2	31	312	12
2		2	2	800	2	36,400	2	3,000	2	6,000	2	2	13	172	13
17	...	17	17	9,287	17	596,700	9	73,650	8	27,400	17	17	427	4,223	14
5		5	5	2,750	5	162,500	4	11,230	3	5,500	5	5	52	556	15
9	...	9	9	4,900	9	200,500	3	9,500	5	23,800	10	11	197	2,152	16
3	...	3	3	900	3	11,500	3	4,020	...	...	3	3	16	85	17
8	...	11	8	5,046	8	264,250	5	38,500	...	...	8	8	193	1,835	18
3	...	3	3	1,200	3	75,000	2	13,300	...	...	3	3	97	895	19
1	...	1	1	1,200	2	100,900	1	15,000	...	...	2	4	80	595	20
2	...	2	2	650	2	21,000	1	1,500	1	3,500	2	2	27	195	21
8	...	11	8	3,680	8	360,850	3	29,900	...	...	8	9	90	847	22
11	11	11	11	3,750	15	98,850	9	11,081	3	8,000	18	19	171	1,274	23
19	1	21	17	8,992	19	662,000	10	79,431	12	90,500	16	17	103	2,419	24
2	...	2	2	1,465	2	161,000	1	3,000	...	...	2	3	15	340	25
...	[illegible]	...	...	...	...	...	...	...	...	...	...	...	...	...	26
3	1	3	3	475	3	5,800	1	400	...	...	4	4	37	226	27
...	6	...	...	...	...	...	...	...	...	...	...	...	...	...	28
64	6	69	61	30,665	61	877,550	24	32,911	22	94,150	71	79	1,009	12,857	1
63	6	68	60	29,965	61	877,550	24	32,911	22	94,150	69	77	998	12,527	2
11	...	11	11	7,150	11	213,200	5	10,148	3	15,500	11	14	247	4,156	3
4	...	4	4	2,100	4	37,000	1	2,000	1	1,000	4	4	40	460	4
1	1	1	1	500	1	1,000	1	150	...	...	2	2	12	75	5
3	...	3	3	1,400	3	12,500	2	2,000	...	...	3	3	33	370	6
7	...	7	7	4,125	7	97,800	2	565	6	20,650	7	7	117	1,191	7
1	1	1	1	500	1	5,000	1	160	...	...	2	2	11	50	8
5	...	7	5	2,300	5	23,650	1	1,600	...	...	5	5	37	327	9
7	...	7	5	3,050	6	142,300	3	6,040	3	15,300	9	10	150	2,025	10
8	...	10	8	2,550	8	116,300	1	400	3	22,000	8	9	109	1,067	11
1	...	1	1	500	1	12,000	...	...	...	...	1	1	27	675	12
...	1	...	...	...	...	...	...	...	...	...	1	1	18	296	13
3	...	3	3	1,600	2	55,000	...	...	...	...	3	5	89	1,030	14
2	...	3	2	1,250	2	107,500	...	...	2	9,500	2	2	20	177	15
10	3	10	9	2,940	10	54,300	7	9,908	4	10,200	11	12	88	629	16

TABLE 7.—ORGANIZATIONS, COMMUNICANTS OR MEMBERS, PLACES OF WORSHIP, VALUE OF CHURCH PROPERTY, MORE IN 1900, BY SELECTED

	DENOMINATION.	Total number of organizations.	COMMUNICANTS OR MEMBERS.				
			Number of organizations reporting.	Total number reported.	Sex.		
					Number of organizations reporting.	Male.	Female.
	Knoxville, Tenn.—Continued.						
17	Roman Catholic Church	1	1	170			
18	Jewish congregations	3	3	[1] 125			
	Eastern Orthodox Churches:						
19	Greek Orthodox Church	1	1	30			
1	La Crosse, Wis.	50	50	19,938	45	8,495	10,964
2	Protestant bodies	33	33	7,316	31	2,582	4,347
	Baptist bodies:						
3	Baptists—Northern Convention	5	5	593	5	171	422
4	Congregationalists	1	1	335	1	123	212
	Lutheran bodies:						
5	Evangelical Lutheran Synodical Conference of America	2	2	1,827	1	618	874
6	United Norwegian Lutheran Church in America	2	2	636	2	292	344
7	Synod for the Norwegian Evangelical Lutheran Church in America	2	2	1,055	2	440	615
8	Other Lutheran bodies	2	2	273	2	123	150
	Methodist bodies:						
9	Methodist Episcopal Church	8	8	1,147	8	412	735
	Presbyterian bodies:						
10	Presbyterian Church in the United States of America	3	3	502	3	162	340
11	Protestant Episcopal Church	2	2	405	2	90	315
	Reformed bodies:						
12	Reformed Church in the United States	1	1	200	1	80	120
13	Universalists	1	1	200	1	48	152
14	Other Protestant bodies	4	4	143	3	23	68
15	Roman Catholic Church	12	12	12,472	12	5,892	6,580
16	Jewish congregations	2	2	[1] 42			
17	All other bodies	3	3	108	2	21	37
1	Lancaster, Pa.	56	56	18,336	50	5,812	9,875
	Protestant bodies	48	48	13,859	46	4,458	8,123
	Baptist bodies:						
3	Baptists—Northern and National (Colored) Conventions	2	2	312	2	69	243
4	Churches of God in North America, General Eldership of the	1	1	320	[illegible]	75	245
	Evangelical bodies:						
5	Evangelical Association	1	1	80	1	30	50
6	United Evangelical Church	2	2	570	2	219	351
	Lutheran bodies:						
7	General Synod of the Evangelical Lutheran Church in the United States of America	2	2	902	1	130	174
8	General Council of the Evangelical Lutheran Church in North America	8	8	3,694	7	1,066	1,928
9	Evangelical Lutheran Synodical Conference of America	1	1	61	1	19	42
	Methodist bodies:						
10	Methodist Episcopal Church	3	3	1,662	3	432	1,230
11	African Methodist bodies	2	2	117	2	27	90
	Presbyterian bodies:						
12	Presbyterian Church in the United States of America	3	3	972	3	321	651
13	Protestant Episcopal Church	2	2	1,010	2	344	666
	Reformed bodies:						
14	Reformed Church in the United States	8	8	2,562	8	1,130	1,432
	United Brethren bodies:						
15	Church of the United Brethren in Christ	2	2	789	2	300	489
16	Other Protestant bodies	11	11	808	11	276	532
17	Roman Catholic Church	4	4	4,210	3	1,340	1,740
18	Jewish congregations	2	2	[1] 121			
19	All other bodies	2	2	146	1	14	12
1	Lawrence, Mass.	49	46	48,363	41	17,796	19,797
2	Protestant bodies	31	30	6,714	28	2,195	4,149
	Baptist bodies:						
3	Baptists—Northern and National (Colored) Conventions	3	3	1,176	3	446	730
4	Free Baptists	2	2	286	2	109	177
5	Congregationalists	5	5	1,285	5	374	911
	Friends:						
6	Society of Friends (Orthodox)	2	2	277	2	100	177
	Methodist bodies:						
7	Methodist Episcopal Church	7	7	1,282	6	381	856
	Presbyterian bodies:						
8	Presbyterian Church in the United States of America	1	1	325	1	150	175
9	United Presbyterian Church of North America	1	1	325			
10	Protestant Episcopal Church	3	3	1,227	3	466	761
11	Other Protestant bodies	7	6	531	6	169	362
12	Roman Catholic Church	11	11	40,007	9	14,678	15,129
13	Jewish congregations	2					
14	Armenian Church	1	1	700	1	550	150
	Eastern Orthodox Churches:						
15	Syrian Orthodox Church	1	1	500	1	280	220
16	Greek Orthodox Church	1	1	200			
17	Spiritualists	2	2	242	2	93	149

[1] Heads of families only.

DEBT ON CHURCH PROPERTY, PARSONAGES, AND SUNDAY SCHOOLS, FOR EACH CITY OF 25,000 INHABITANTS OR DENOMINATIONS: 1906—Continued.

PLACES OF WORSHIP.					VALUE OF CHURCH PROPERTY.		DEBT ON CHURCH PROPERTY.		PARSONAGES.		SUNDAY SCHOOLS CONDUCTED BY CHURCH ORGANIZATIONS.				
Number of organizations reporting— Church edifices.	Number of organizations reporting— Halls, etc.	Number of church edifices reported.	Seating capacity of church edifices. Number of organizations reporting.	Seating capacity of church edifices. Seating capacity reported.	Number of organizations reporting.	Value reported.	Number of organizations reporting.	Amount of debt reported.	Number of organizations reporting.	Value of parsonages reported.	Number of organizations reporting.	Number of Sunday schools reported.	Number of officers and teachers.	Number of scholars.	
1	....	1	1	700	....	....	....	....	....	....	1	1	8	300	17
....	....	....	....	....	....	....	....	....	....	....	1	1	3	30	18
....	....	....	....	....	....	....	....	....	....	....	....	....	....	....	19
42	7	50	41	16,502	43	$587,536	16	$42,680	29	$94,300	43	51	560	5,806	1
32	1	40	31	12,330	32	456,276	9	21,380	22	66,300	33	41	512	4,362	2
5	....	8	5	1,650	5	45,976	1	200	4	18,800	5	8	72	565	3
1	....	2	1	1,000	1	30,000	....	....	....	....	1	2	35	350	4
2	....	2	2	1,300	2	57,800	2	15,425	2	6,800	2		37	570	5
2	....	2	2	1,000	2	34,000	1	750	1	4,500	2		36	195	6
2	....	2	2	920	2	28,000	1	300	2	5,000	2		54	355	7
2	....	2	2	670	2	12,000	1	3,950	1	3,000	2	2	34	273	8
8	....	10	8	3,000	8	80,700	....	....	7	15,300	8	9	121	978	9
3	....	4	3	940	3	41,500	1	200	1	5,000	3	5	61	580	10
2	....	2	2	700	2	82,300	1	355	2	5,500	2	2	14	140	11
1	....	2	1	250	1	8,000	....	....	1	1,000	1	1	12	150	12
1	....	1	1	300	1	25,000	1	200	....	....	1	1	17	97	13
3	1	3	2	600	3	11,000	....	....	1	1,400	4	5	19	109	14
8	4	8	8	3,872	8	128,000	6	21,000	7	28,000	9	9	38	1,399	15
2	....	2	2	300	2	3,200	1	300	....	....	....	....	....	....	16
....	2	....	....	....	1	60	....	....	....	....	1	1	10	45	17
46	8	51	45	26,600	46	1,339,600	30	155,680	25	170,100		55	1,289	12,652	1
40	6	44	39	22,830	40	1,106,200	27	139,180	21	117,100	46	48	1,136	11,317	2
2	....	2	2	450	2	13,000	1	800	....	....	2	2	22	200	3
1	....	1	1	500	[illegible]	20,000	....	....	1	5,000	1	1	28	325	4
1	....	1	1	500	1	14,000	1	7,000	....	....	1	1	8	100	5
2	....	2	2	1,050	2	22,000	1	200	1	2,000	2	2	57	477	6
2	....	3	1	950	2	105,000	2	7,800	1	5,000	2	3	83	675	7
7	1	7	7	5,550	7	203,450	5	35,650	3	17,300	8	8	296	2,665	8
1	....	1	1	350	1	11,000	1	9,520	....	....	1	1	8	124	9
3	....	4	3	1,800	3	119,000	2	3,300	3	23,500	3	4	118	1,580	10
1	1	1	1	300	1	4,000	....	....	1	1,200	2	2	15	131	11
3	....	4	3	1,400	3	94,000	....	....	3	15,500	3	3	88	940	12
2	....	4	2	880	2	175,000	1	5,500	2	15,000	2	2	50	362	13
7	....	7	7	5,150	7	232,250	6	53,150	3	17,000	7	7	212	2,264	14
2	....	2	2	800	2	20,000	2	2,500	1	3,100	2	2	61	798	15
6	4	7	6	3,150	6	73,500	5	13,760	2	12,500	10	10	90	676	16
4	....	5	4	3,120	4	188,400	1	8,000	4	53,000	4	5	144	1,160	17
2	....	2	2	650	2	45,000	2	8,500	....	....	2	2	9	175	18
....	2	....	....	....	....	....	....	....	....	....	....	....	....	....	19
39	8	44	39	24,032	41	1,516,174	18	268,870	12	113,200	41	47	861	10,517	1
29	2	32	29	13,382	29	549,814	8	37,450	5	28,500	30	33	675	6,235	2
3	....	3	3	1,650	3	57,000	1	250	....	....	3		89	917	3
2	....	2	2	950	2	40,000	....	....	....	....	2		33	345	4
5	....	6	5	2,800	5	103,000	2	9,100	....	....	5	[illegible]	142	1,286	5
2	....	2	2	500	2	20,000	1	800	....	....	2	3	42	286	6
7	....	7	7	2,750	7	84,500	1	3,800	4	20,500	7	7	175	1,534	7
1	....	1	1	500	1	40,000	1	13,000	....	....	1	1		375	8
1	....	1	1	450	1	20,000	....	....	....	....	1	1		200	9
3	....	5	3	1,800	3	107,314	1	5,500	1	8,000	3	3	27	899	10
5	2	5	5	1,982	5	78,000	1	5,000	....	....	6	6	[illegible]	393	11
10	1	12	10	10,650	10	966,000	10	231,420	7	84,700	10	13	183	4,267	12
....	....	....	....	....	....	....	....	....	....	....	....	....	....	....	13
....	[illegible]	....	....	....	....	....	....	....	....	....	....	....	....	....	14
....	1	....	....	....	[illegible]	60	....	....	....	....	....	....	....	....	15
....	1	....	....	....	....	....	....	....	....	....	....	....	....	....	16
....	2	....	....	....	1	300	....	....	....	....	1	1	3	15	17

TABLE 7.—ORGANIZATIONS, COMMUNICANTS OR MEMBERS, PLACES OF WORSHIP, VALUE OF CHURCH PROPERTY, MORE IN 1900, BY SELECTED

	DENOMINATION.	Total number of organizations.	COMMUNICANTS OR MEMBERS.				
			Number of organizations reporting.	Total number reported.	Sex.		
					Number of organizations reporting.	Male.	Female.
1	Lexington, Ky	39	39	15,532	34	5,958	8,781
2	Protestant bodies	36	36	13,043	32	4,840	7,465
	Baptist bodies:						
3	Baptists—Southern Convention	3	3	1,840	3	762	1,078
4	Baptists—National Convention (Colored)	6	6	2,449	6	782	1,667
	Disciples or Christians:						
5	Disciples of Christ	8	8	4,202	7	1,844	2,148
	Methodist bodies:						
6	Methodist Episcopal Church	3	3	975	2	243	482
7	Methodist Episcopal Church, South	3	3	896	1	200	418
8	African Methodist bodies	4	4	579	4	204	375
	Presbyterian bodies:						
9	Presbyterian Church in the United States of America	1	1	400	1	150	250
10	Presbyterian Church in the United States	2	2	789	2	286	503
11	Protestant Episcopal Church	2	2	740	2	307	433
12	Other Protestant bodies	4	4	173	4	62	111
13	Roman Catholic Church	2	2	2,434	2	1,118	1,316
14	Jewish congregations	1	1	[1] 155			
1	Lincoln, Nebr	64	64	19,114	57	6,833	10,242
2	Protestant bodies	55	55	12,739	53	4,310	6,857
	Baptist bodies:						
3	Baptists—Northern Convention	3	3	1,052	3	429	623
4	Free Baptists	1	1	47	1	20	27
5	Church of Christ, Scientist	1	1	253	1	63	190
6	Congregationalists	8	8	2,172	8	848	1,324
	Disciples or Christians:						
7	Disciples of Christ	3	3	870	3	362	508
8	Churches of Christ	1	1	10	1	4	6
9	German Evangelical Synod of North America	1	1	295	1	135	160
	Lutheran bodies:						
10	General Synod of the Evangelical Lutheran Church in the United States of America	2	2	572	2	235	337
11	Evangelical Lutheran Synodical Conference of America	1	1	542			
12	Other Lutheran bodies	2	2	203	2	81	122
	Methodist bodies:						
13	Methodist Episcopal Church	9	9	3,321	8	843	1,448
14	Other Methodist bodies	2	2	185	2	72	110
	Presbyterian bodies:						
15	Presbyterian Church in the United States of America	4	4	1,436	4	522	914
16	United Presbyterian Church of North America	1	1	121	1	42	79
17	Protestant Episcopal Church	2	2	428	2	139	289
	Reformed bodies:						
18	Reformed Church in the United States	2	2	353	2	165	188
19	Other Protestant bodies	12	12	879	12	350	529
20	Roman Catholic Church	3	3	5,887	3	2,518	3,369
21	Jewish congregations	3	3	[1] 100			
22	Spiritualists	1	1	307			
23	All other bodies	2	2	81	1	5	16
1	Little Rock, Ark	73	72	17,969	64	6,805	9,825
	Protestant bodies	68	67	12,453	61	4,300	7,074
	Baptist bodies:						
3	Baptists—Southern Convention	5	5	1,936	3	591	803
4	Baptists—National Convention (Colored)	10	10	1,226	10	501	725
5	Primitive Baptists	1	1	20	1	6	14
	Disciples or Christians:						
6	Disciples of Christ	2	2	650	2	250	400
	Lutheran bodies:						
7	Evangelical Lutheran Synodical Conference of America	1	1	352	1	161	191
	Methodist bodies:						
8	Methodist Episcopal Church	6	6	651	4	101	149
9	African Methodist Episcopal Church	5	5	995	5	235	760
10	African Methodist Episcopal Zion Church	3	3	283	3	106	177
11	Methodist Episcopal Church, South	6	5	2,460	4	919	1,442
12	Colored Methodist Episcopal Church	4	4	448	4	152	296
	Presbyterian bodies:						
13	Presbyterian Church in the United States	3	3	838	3	294	544
14	Other Presbyterian bodies	3	3	288	3	118	170
15	Protestant Episcopal Church	7	7	1,402	7	575	827
16	Other Protestant bodies	12	12	904	11	291	576
17	Roman Catholic Church	3	3	5,256	3	2,505	2,751
18	Jewish congregations	2	2	[1] 260			
1	Los Angeles, Cal	231	220	81,771	202	31,857	44,694
2	Protestant bodies	188	186	41,691	175	14,638	23,124
	Adventist bodies:						
3	Advent Christian Church	1	1	97	1	38	59
4	Seventh-day Adventist Denomination	4	4	713	4	258	455
	Baptist bodies:						
5	Baptists—Northern Convention	11	11	3,403	11	1,310	2,093
6	Baptists—National Convention (Colored)	5	5	1,086	2	54	102

[1] Heads of families only.

DEBT ON CHURCH PROPERTY, PARSONAGES, AND SUNDAY SCHOOLS, FOR EACH CITY OF 25,000 INHABITANTS OR DENOMINATIONS: 1906—Continued.

PLACES OF WORSHIP.					VALUE OF CHURCH PROPERTY.		DEBT ON CHURCH PROPERTY.		PARSONAGES.		SUNDAY SCHOOLS CONDUCTED BY CHURCH ORGANIZATIONS.				
Number of organizations reporting—		Number of church edifices reported.	Seating capacity of church edifices.		Number of organizations reporting.	Value reported.	Number of organizations reporting.	Amount of debt reported.	Number of organizations reporting.	Value of parsonages reported.	Number of organizations reporting.	Number of Sunday schools reported.	Number of officers and teachers.	Number of scholars.	
Church edifices.	Halls, etc.		Number of organizations reporting.	Seating capacity reported.											
35	3	40	34	17,471	35	$696,000	15	$25,481	13	$76,000	38	48	501	5,585	1
33	2	38	32	16,105	33	604,000	15	25,481	12	66,000	35	45	488	5,270	2
3	...	3	3	2,250	3	117,000	1	12,000	2	16,000	3	6	76	812	3
6	...	6	6	2,650	6	49,200	4	2,250	...	...	5	7	50	556	4
7	...	7	7	3,580	7	105,100	1	1,000	1	5,000	8	9	151	1,651	5
3	...	3	3	1,700	3	44,000	1	169	2	8,200	3	3	39	252	6
3	...	3	2	825	3	86,500	...	...	1	6,000	3	3	36	365	7
4	...	4	4	1,450	4	34,200	4	5,012	2	1,800	4	4	21	155	8
1	...	2	1	450	1	38,000	...	...	1	9,000	1	2	20	430	9
2	...	4	2	1,350	2	57,000	1	2,000	2	10,000	2	4	56	560	10
2	...	4	2	1,400	2	67,500	1	2,500	1	10,000	2	3	20	410	11
2	2	2	2	450	2	5,500	2	550	...	...	4	4	19	79	12
1	1	1	1	1,066	1	85,000	...	...	1	10,000	2	2	10	280	13
1	...	1	1	300	1	7,000	...	...	...	...	1	1	3	35	14
55		59	54	22,900	56	760,600	29	77,850	27	66,840	58	60	848	8,316	1
50	3	54	49	21,460	51	631,600	26	55,230	24	62,490	52	54	828	7,858	2
3	...	3	3	1,600	3	65,000	1	400	2	7,190	3	4	55	699	3
1	...	1	1	150	1	5,000	...	...	...	...	1	1	6	30	4
1	...	1	1	1,000	1	8,000	...	...	...	...	1	1	8	50	5
8	...	10	7	2,650	7	81,500	3	3,650	2	6,500	8	8	128	1,460	6
3	...	3	3	1,000	3	19,000	1	750	1	1,700	3	3	47	454	7
...	1	...	...	...	...	...	...	...	...	...	1	1	1	10	8
1	...	-	1	300	1	11,000	1	1,000	1	3,000	1	1	12	110	9
1	...	1	1	350	2	17,000	1	3,120	1	1,500	2	2	22	300	10
1	...	1	1	600	1	21,000	1	2,000	...	...	...	...	...	...	11
2	...	2	2	450	2	12,800	1	750	1	5,000	2	2	12	61	12
9	...	9	9	5,900	9	151,000	3	10,060	7	19,500	9	9	202	1,876	13
2	...	2	2	700	2	8,000	1	500	1	1,000	2	2	16	105	14
4	...	5	4	2,400	4	92,500	2	5,000	1	2,500	4	5	139	1,341	15
1	...	1	1	250	1	10,000	...	...	...	...	1	1	22	161	16
2	...	2	2	800	2	52,500	2	9,600	1	4,500	2	2	26	180	17
2	...	3	2	800	2	16,500	2	6,200	...	...	2	2	16	215	18
9	2	9	9	2,510	10	60,800	7	12,200	6	10,100	10	10	116	806	19
2	...	2	2	890	2	113,000	2	21,620	2	4,000	3°	3	12	381	20
3	...	3	3	550	3	16,000	1	1,000	1	350	2	2	6	70	21
...	1	...	...	...	...	...	...	...	...	...	1	1	2	7	22
...	1	...	...	...	...	...	...	...	...	...	...	...	...	...	23
65	6	70	62	30,075	65	1,038,875	29	78,370	28	93,755	70	79	828	9,272	1
60	6	65	57	27,575	61	743,875	26	48,870	26	71,255	65	71	802	8,653	2
4	...	5	4	3,850	4	127,000	2	7,500	1	2,500	4	6	84	1,240	3
10	...	10	10	3,800	10	73,300	1	1,500	3	6,000	10	10	90	650	4
...	1	...	...	...	...	...	...	...	...	...	...	...	...	...	5
2	...	2	2	1,100	2	29,000	1	3,000	1	4,000	2	2	40	550	6
.	...	1	.	650	1	40,000	...	...	1	5,000	1	2	16	168	7
6	...	6	4	1,300	6	54,050	2	4,300	4	6,300	6	6	65	606	8
4	1	4	4	2,200	4	52,000	2	2,850	2	8,400	5	5	55	517	9
3	...	3	3	2,100	3	13,175	3	2,400	1	700	3	3	22	145	10
5	...	5	4	3,000	5	89,500	2	14,300	4	14,855	5	7	151	2,433	11
4	...	4	4	1,675	4	10,875	4	2,530	2	1,200	4	4	29	241	12
3	...	5	3	1,250	3	113,000	2	5,200	2	14,000	3	3	88	756	13
3	...	3	3	1,125	3	16,000	...	...	1	800	3	3	29	257	14
7	...	8	7	3,325	7	106,500	3	2,850	2	11,000	7	7	62	605	15
8	4	9	8	2,200	9	19,475	4	2,440	2	2,000	12	13	71	485	16
3	...	3	3	1,650	3	250,000	2	25,000	2	22,500	3	6	17	438	17
2	...	2	2	850	1	45,000	1	4,500	...	...	2	2	9	181	18
189	34	202	178	86,332	189	5,446,153	85	612,944	58	390,700	199	221	3,248	34,664	1
163	21	175	161	75,832	169	3,996,884	74	336,594	47	262,600	177	196	3,029	31,103	2
1	...	1	1	150	1	4,000	...	...	...	...	1	1	12	84	3
4	...	4	4	1,145	4	16,800	1	500	...	...	4	4	44	806	4
10	1	11	10	5,000	11	274,000	5	13,500	1	500	11	15	123	2,323	5
4	1	4	4	1,300	4	65,000	3	4,300	...	...	4	5	38	434	6

TABLE 7.—ORGANIZATIONS, COMMUNICANTS OR MEMBERS, PLACES OF WORSHIP, VALUE OF CHURCH PROPERTY, MORE IN 1900, BY SELECTED

	DENOMINATION.	Total number of organizations.	COMMUNICANTS OR MEMBERS.				
			Number of organizations reporting.	Total number reported.	Sex.		
					Number of organizations reporting.	Male.	Female.
	Los Angeles, Cal.—Continued.						
	Protestant bodies—Continued.						
7	Church of Christ, Scientist	2	2	552	1	110	292
8	Congregationalists	15	15	3,402	15	1,205	2,197
	Disciples or Christians:						
9	Disciples of Christ	14	14	3,285	14	1,269	2,016
10	Churches of Christ	1	1	123	1	58	65
11	Independent churches	8	8	1,442	7	363	564
	Lutheran bodies:						
12	Evangelical Lutheran Synodical Conference of America	5	5	760	3	253	368
13	Other Lutheran bodies	5	5	762	4	295	412
	Methodist bodies:						
14	Methodist Episcopal Church	39	39	9,335	38	3,821	5,334
15	African Methodist Episcopal Church	2	2	814	2	304	510
16	Methodist Episcopal Church, South	5	5	1,142	5	509	633
17	Other Methodist bodies	2	2	251	2	93	158
18	Pentecostal Church of the Nazarene	5	5	1,695	4	108	187
	Presbyterian bodies:						
19	Presbyterian Church in the United States of America	20	20	6,270	20	2,298	3,972
20	Other Presbyterian bodies	6	6	550	6	217	333
21	Protestant Episcopal Church	11	11	3,657	10	1,035	2,062
22	Other Protestant bodies	27	25	2,352	25	1,040	1,312
23	Roman Catholic Church	13	13	36,695	13	16,155	20,540
24	Jewish congregations	6	5	[1] 521	...	...	...
	Eastern Orthodox Churches:						
25	Greek Orthodox Church	1	1	800	...	...	...
26	Spiritualists	7	7	920	7	448	472
27	All other bodies	16	8	1,144	7	616	488
1	Louisville, Ky.	224	224	147,330	180	54,251	67,919
	Protestant bodies	174	174	60,680	152	17,770	29,835
	Baptist bodies:						
3	Baptists—Southern Convention	21	21	10,204	18	2,654	4,500
4	Baptists—National Convention (Colored)	21	21	10,260	19	3,496	6,464
	Disciples or Christians:						
5	Disciples of Christ	11	11	4,344	11	1,825	2,519
6	Churches of Christ	4	4	785	4	287	498
7	German Evangelical Synod of North America	9	9	9,260	7	1,330	1,930
	Lutheran bodies:						
8	General Synod of the Evangelical Lutheran Church in the United States of America	7	7	2,190	7	835	1,355
9	Evangelical Lutheran Synodical Conference of America	2	2	795	2	342	453
	Methodist bodies:						
10	Methodist Episcopal Church	11	11	2,133	10	732	1,288
11	African Methodist Episcopal Church	6	6	1,412	6	464	948
12	African Methodist Episcopal Zion Church	5	5	1,271	5	379	892
13	Methodist Episcopal Church, South	15	15	5,430	14	1,925	2,965
14	Other Methodist bodies	5	5	513	5	222	291
	Presbyterian bodies:						
15	Presbyterian Church in the United States of America	8	8	1,995	4	446	714
16	Presbyterian Church in the United States	12	12	3,834	12	1,438	2,396
17	Other Presbyterian bodies	3	3	288	3	101	187
18	Protestant Episcopal Church	14	14	3,632	12	889	1,857
	Reformed bodies:						
19	Reformed Church in the United States	5	5	1,129	...	...	...
20	Other Protestant bodies	15	15	1,205	13	405	588
21	Roman Catholic Church	37	37	85,170	31	36,295	37,825
22	Jewish congregations	6	6	[1] 955	...	...	...
23	All other bodies	7	7	525	6	186	259
1	Lowell, Mass.	61	58	66,766	52	26,202	26,026
2	Protestant bodies	45	44	12,176	40	3,769	7,495
	Baptist bodies:						
3	Baptists—Northern Convention	6	6	2,501	4	640	1,369
4	Free Baptists	4	4	724	3	213	475
5	Congregationalists	9	9	3,188	9	972	2,216
	Lutheran bodies:						
6	General Council of the Evangelical Lutheran Church in North America	1	1	304	1	132	172
	Methodist bodies:						
7	Methodist Episcopal Church	6	6	1,373	6	415	958
8	Primitive Methodist Church in the United States of America	2	2	293	2	102	191
	Presbyterian bodies:						
9	Presbyterian Church in the United States of America	1	1	251	1	92	159
10	United Presbyterian Church of North America	1	1	185	1	80	105
11	Protestant Episcopal Church	3	3	1,645	3	643	1,002
12	Unitarians	1	1	384	...	...	...
13	Universalists	2	2	700	2	275	425
14	Other Protestant bodies	9	8	628	8	206	422
15	Roman Catholic Church	9	9	47,073	8	15,958	17,515
16	Jewish congregations	3	1	[1] 26	...	...	...
17	Armenian Church	1	1	400	1	350	50
	Eastern Orthodox Churches:						
18	Greek Orthodox Church	1	1	6,000	1	5,400	600
19	Polish National Church of America	1	1	891	1	635	256
20	Spiritualists	1	1	200	1	90	110

[1] Heads of families only.

DEBT ON CHURCH PROPERTY, PARSONAGES, AND SUNDAY SCHOOLS, FOR EACH CITY OF 25,000 INHABITANTS OR DENOMINATIONS: 1906—Continued.

PLACES OF WORSHIP.					VALUE OF CHURCH PROPERTY.		DEBT ON CHURCH PROPERTY.		PARSONAGES.		SUNDAY SCHOOLS CONDUCTED BY CHURCH ORGANIZATIONS.				
Number of organizations reporting—		Number of church edifices reported.	Seating capacity of church edifices.		Number of organizations reporting.	Value reported.	Number of organizations reporting.	Amount of debt reported.	Number of organizations reporting.	Value of parsonages reported.	Number of organizations reporting.	Number of Sunday schools reported.	Number of officers and teachers.	Number of scholars.	
Church edifices.	Halls, etc.		Number of organizations reporting.	Seating capacity reported.											
2	...	2	2	1,700	2	$65,000	...	...	...	...	2	2	49	382	7
15	...	17	15	6,700	15	311,850	3	$14,900	2	$8,000	15	16	313	2,515	8
13	...	13	13	,	13	302,200	6	27,300	...	...	14	15	207	2,280	9
1	...	1	1	7,050	1	1,000	...	...	...	...	1	1	4	75	10
5	3	5	5	1,800	6	45,250		10,000	2	3,000	8	13	82	884	11
2	2	3	2	950	4	90,290	2	22,600	2	31,800	4	4	23	178	12
4	1	4	1	1,085	4	111,000	4	17,330	1	7,000	5	5	100	375	13
37	2	38	37	18.775	37	1,013,200	19	60,250	16	55,500	38	38	897	10,221	14
2	...	3	2	,100	2	50,250	...	...	1	4,000	2	2	27	250	15
5	...	5	5	2,370	5	134,500	1	600	3	37,000	5	6	89	1,314	16
2	...	2	2	1,375	2	55,000	1	15,000	1	10,000	2	2	19	152	17
5	...	5	5	2,650	5	89,700	2	11,400	...	...	5	5	72	730	18
17	2	19	17	9,255	18	475,600	8	38,200	4	14,800	20	21	449	4,541	19
6	...	6	6	2,500	6	132,000	2	1,720	2	10,300	6	6	66	805	20
11	...	15	11	4,282	11	441,137	8	85,750	7	63,600	11	13	226	1,431	21
17	9	17	15	4,845	18	318,207	7	13,244	5	17,100	19	19	189	1,623	22
	...	14	13	7,550	13	1,304,500	9	270,350	11	128,100	1	14	147	2,914	23
13	1	2	2	1,200	2	115,000	1	4,000	...	...	2	4	13	301	24
1	...	1	...	...	...	...	...	...	...	...	...	...	...	...	25
1		1	1	1,500	3	22,750	1	2,000	...	...	1	1	11	51	26
9	5	9	1	250	2	7,019	...	...	...	...	4	6	48	295	27
193	18	219	159	85,057	167	3,918,955		291,236	48	197,100	205	228	2,932	39,858	1
153	13	175	152	79,507	158	3,705,060	86	246,436	47	195,100	170	193	2,904	31,741	2
20	1	24	20	13,450	21	568,550	2	12,800	3	8,500	21	31	488	6,768	3
19	2	19	19	9,690	20	140,550	11	14,447	...	...	21	21	212	2,612	4
9	2	9	9	4,600	9	407,500	6	34,600	...	...	11	12	149	2,088	5
4	...	4	4	1,150	4	18,000	2	1,400	...	...	4	4	43	442	6
9	...	11	9	6,850	9	316,000	6	68,100	8	52,000	8	8	233	2,677	7
7	...	7	7	3,076	7	195,160	3	29,555	...	...	7	7	188	1,861	8
2	...	3	2	950	2	16,000	2	5,550	2	7,000	2	2	8	216	9
11	...	13	10	,450	11	174,900	1	470	8	26,800	11	11	181	1,747	10
6	...	6	6	4,000	6	58,600	5	2,982	2	1,800	5	5	45	495	11
5	...	5	5	4,775	5	26,800	3	1,582	...	...	5	5	64	867	12
15	...	15	15	7,775	15	396,300	3	22,850	12	52,000	15	15	347	3,482	13
4	...	4	4	1,600	4	52,400	3	6,150	1	500	5	5	29	257	14
8	...	11	8	4,800	8	631,000	...	...	1	1,000	7	8	126	1,135	15
12	...	15	2	5,350	12	340,000	4	12,650	3	21,500	12	18	302	2,687	16
3	...	3	3	1,100	3	45,000	1	3,500	1	3,200	3	3	45	384	17
14	...	20	14	8,171	14	571,900	5	28,700	4	18,000	14	18	241	2,025	18
...	...	...	...	...	...	...	...	...	...	...	5	5	85	1,143	19
5	8	6	5	1,720	8	46,400	2	1,100	2	2,800	14	15	118	855	20
33	...	33	...	...	...	...	...	...	...	...	31	31	...	7,699	21
5	...	9	5	4,650	5	210,000	5	43,000	1	2,000	3	3	18	393	22
2	5	2	2	900	4	3,895	1	1,800	...	...	1	1	10	25	23
52	6	60	52	40,502	53	2,660,900	31	419,145	16	193,500	54	62	1,222	13,762	1
40	4	44	40	22,818	41	1,208,900	21	118,125	8	40,500	41	48	932	8,123	2
6	...	6	6	3,500	6	187,000	3	6,100	...	...		7	157	1,609	3
4	...	4	4	1,420	4	54,000	1	1,500	1	3,000		4	73	530	4
9	...	10	9	6,235	9	353,350	4	27,100	2	8,000	6	10	248	2,713	5
1	...	1	1	450	1	9,500	1	2,400	1	3,500	1	1	17	95	6
6	...	6	6	3,800	6	127,600	3	14,950	2	12,000	6	6	141	947	7
2	...	2	2	900	2	34,000	2	8,175	1	4,000	2	2	44	412	8
1	...	1	1	450	1	20,000	1	5,000	...	...	1	1	25	201	9
1	...	1	1	500	1	14,000	1	4,400	...	...	1	1	15	85	10
3	...	6	3	1,900	3	218,800	1	11,000	1	10,000	3	4	72	575	11
1	...	1	1	750	1	25,000	...	...	...	...	1	1	10	100	12
2	...	2	2	1,700	2	125,000	1	25,000	...	...	2	2	35	350	13
4	4	4	4	1,213	5	40,650	3	12,500	...	...	9	9	95	506	14
9	...	13	9	15,284	9	1,363,000	7	263,120	8	153,000	9	13	289	5,589	15
1	...	1	1	600	1	6,000	1	1,400	...	...	...	...	...	...	16
...	1	...	...	...	...	...	...	...	...	...	...	...	...	...	17
1	...	1	1	1,600	1	70,000	1	32,000	...	...	...	...	...	...	18
1	...	1	1	200	1	13,000	1	4,500	...	...		1		50	19
...		...	...	...	...	...	...	...	...	...	...	...	...	...	20

TABLE 7.—ORGANIZATIONS, COMMUNICANTS OR MEMBERS, PLACES OF WORSHIP, VALUE OF CHURCH PROPERTY, MORE IN 1900, BY SELECTED

	DENOMINATION.	Total number of organizations.	COMMUNICANTS OR MEMBERS.				
			Number of organizations reporting.	Total number reported.	Sex.		
					Number of organizations reporting.	Male.	Female.
1	Lynn, Mass.	55	55	31,571	48	14,115	15,879
2	Protestant bodies	43	43	9,194	39	2,544	5,257
	Baptist bodies:						
3	Baptists—Northern and National (Colored) Conventions	5	5	1,918	5	587	1,331
4	Free Baptists	2	2	284	2	73	211
5	Congregationalists	5	5	1,250	5	418	832
	Friends:						
6	Society of Friends (Orthodox)	2	2	220	2	91	129
7	Friends (Primitive)	1	1	9	1	6	3
	Lutheran bodies:						
8	General Council of the Evangelical Lutheran Church in North America	1	1	298			
	Methodist bodies:						
9	Methodist Episcopal Church	11	11	2,309	9	422	1,002
10	African Methodist Episcopal Church	1	1	30	1	10	20
	Presbyterian bodies:						
11	Presbyterian Church in the United States of America	1	1	207	1	76	131
12	Protestant Episcopal Church	2	2	1,275	2	500	775
13	Unitarians	1	1	210			
14	Universalists	2	2	625	2	172	453
15	Other Protestant bodies	9	9	559	9	189	370
16	Roman Catholic Church	6	6	20,533	6	10,196	10,337
17	Jewish congregations	3	3	[1]184			
18	Armenian Church	1	1	425	1	315	110
	Eastern Orthodox Churches:						
19	Greek Orthodox Church	1	1	1,110	1	1,000	110
20	Spiritualists	1	1	125	1	60	65
1	McKeesport, Pa.	57	54	22,913	51	10,548	11,144
	Protestant bodies	43	43	9,179	42	3,159	5,129
	Baptist bodies:						
3	Baptists—Northern Convention	3	3	1,203	3	371	832
4	Baptists—National Convention (Colored)	1	1	304	1	103	201
	Disciples or Christians:						
5	Disciples of Christ	1	1	322	1	105	217
	German Evangelical Protestant bodies:						
6	German Evangelical Protestant Ministers' Association	1	1	700	1	300	400
	Lutheran bodies:						
7	General Council of the Evangelical Lutheran Church in North America	2	2	475	2	215	260
8	Other Lutheran bodies	2	2	220	2	96	124
	Methodist bodies:						
9	Methodist Episcopal Church	8	8	2,123	7	421	811
10	Other Methodist bodies	2	2	181	2	64	117
	Presbyterian bodies:						
11	Presbyterian Church in the United States of America	2	2	987	2	376	611
12	Cumberland Presbyterian Church	1	1	450	1	200	250
13	United Presbyterian Church of North America	2	2	515	2	200	315
14	Synod of the Reformed Presbyterian Church of North America	1	1	52	1	20	32
15	Protestant Episcopal Church	4	4	420	4	200	220
	United Brethren bodies:						
16	Church of the United Brethren in Christ	3	3	449	3	184	265
17	Other Protestant bodies	10	10	778	10	304	474
18	Roman Catholic Church	7	7	11,938	7	6,224	5,714
19	Jewish congregations	4	1	[1]80			
	Eastern Orthodox Churches:						
20	Servian Orthodox Church	1	1	1,426	1	1,150	276
21	Greek Orthodox Church	1	1	250			
22	Spiritualists	1	1	40	1	15	25
1	Malden, Mass.	31	30	16,961	26	6,667	8,424
2	Protestant bodies	25	25	5,829	23	1,300	2,839
	Baptist bodies:						
3	Baptists—Northern Convention	2	2	1,556	2	474	1,082
4	Baptists—National Convention (Colored)	3	3	237	3	69	168
5	Congregationalists	4	4	1,104	3	91	223
	Methodist bodies:						
6	Methodist Episcopal Church	7	7	1,640	6	266	474
7	Protestant Episcopal Church	2	2	604	2	198	406
8	Universalists	2	2	284	2	63	221
9	Other Protestant bodies	5	5	404	5	139	265
10	Roman Catholic Church	2	2	10,923	2	5,355	5,568
11	Jewish congregations	3	2	[1]180			
12	Spiritualists	1	1	29	1	12	17
1	Manchester, N. H.	46	46	45,282	41	20,786	22,927
2	Protestant bodies	30	30	7,402	27	1,956	3,957
	Baptist bodies:						
3	Baptists—Northern Convention	4	4	1,698	4	528	1,170
4	Free Baptists	1	1	234	1	72	162
5	Congregationalists	3	3	1,585	3	443	1,142

[1] Heads of families only.

DEBT ON CHURCH PROPERTY, PARSONAGES; AND SUNDAY SCHOOLS, FOR EACH CITY OF 25,000 INHABITANTS OR DENOMINATIONS: 1906—Continued.

PLACES OF WORSHIP. Number of organizations reporting— Church edifices.	PLACES OF WORSHIP. Number of organizations reporting— Halls, etc.	PLACES OF WORSHIP. Number of church edifices reported.	PLACES OF WORSHIP. Seating capacity of church edifices. Number of organizations reporting.	PLACES OF WORSHIP. Seating capacity of church edifices. Seating capacity reported.	VALUE OF CHURCH PROPERTY. Number of organizations reporting.	VALUE OF CHURCH PROPERTY. Value reported.	DEBT ON CHURCH PROPERTY. Number of organizations reporting.	DEBT ON CHURCH PROPERTY. Amount of debt reported.	PARSONAGES. Number of organizations reporting.	PARSONAGES. Value of parsonages reported.	SUNDAY SCHOOLS CONDUCTED BY CHURCH ORGANIZATIONS. Number of organizations reporting	SUNDAY SCHOOLS CONDUCTED BY CHURCH ORGANIZATIONS. Number of Sunday schools reported.	SUNDAY SCHOOLS CONDUCTED BY CHURCH ORGANIZATIONS. Number of officers and teachers.	SUNDAY SCHOOLS CONDUCTED BY CHURCH ORGANIZATIONS. Number of scholars.	
45	7	46	44	25,953	46	$1,639,772	32	$175,970	18	$117,000	50	52	1,374	12.856	1
36	6	37	35	18,155	37	1,310,072	25	92,970	13	81,000	42	44	1,189	9,209	2
5			5	3,150	5	225,000	4	23,850	2	20,000	5	5	267	2,073	3
2			2	600	2	23,000	2	5,450			2	2	53	442	4
5		5	5	3,675	5	240,500	3	23,600	1	6,000	5	6	136	1,258	5
2		2	2	450	2	17,000	1	400			2	2	36	227	6
	1														7
1		1	1	380	1	17,550	1	5,000			1	2	16	130	8
10		10	10	5,410	10	226,500	7	15,000	8	38,000	11	11	412	3,290	9
1		1	.1	250	1	5,000	1	200			1	1	8	37	10
1		1	1	400	1	27,000	1	7,700			1	1	16	116	11
2		2	2	895	2	270,000	1	1,770	1	15,000	2	2	70	514	12
1		1	1	400	1	35,000					1	1	14	102	13
2		2	2	1,500	2	172,600	1	3,700			2	2	91	646	14
4	5	4	3	1,075	5	50,922	3	6,300	1	2,000	9	9	70	434	15
6		6	6	5,898	6	294,700	4	69,500	5	36,000	6	6	173	3,482	16
1		1	1	600	1	25,000	1	8,500			1	1	1	75	17
	1														18
1		1	1	500	1	7,000	1	4,000							19
1		1	1	800	1	3,000	1	1,000			1	1	11	30	20
46	5	51	44	19,390	47	1,312,602	36	210,190	18	116,600	48	54	832	9,580	1
37	3	40	36	14,850	38	908,502	29	114,490	11	56,900	41	46	768	7,719	2
3		5	3	1,800	3	149,000	3	9,200	1	3,500	3	5	69	847	3
1		1	1	600	1	19,000	1	7,000			1	1	12	150	4
1		2	1	400	1	20,000	1	4,800	1	6,500	1	2	37	500	5
1		1	1	500	1	40,000	1	4,000	1	6,000	1	1	36	280	6
2		2	2	600	2	41,500	2	2,400	1	5,000	2		46	298	7
2		2	2	850	2	10,200	2	9,850			2	4	14	140	8
8		8	8	3,100	8	146,000	6	18,190	4	19,500	8	9	183	1,794	9
2		2	2	650	2	14,000	2	3,500	1	4,000	2	2	19	143	10
2		2	2	1,200	2	,000	2	7,000	1	10,000	2	2	76	892	11
1		1	1	800	1	,000					1	1	25	300	12
2		2	2	650	2	,000	1	19,000			2	2	44	470	13
1		1	1	300	1	175,000					1	1	4	25	14
1		1	1	480	1	80,000	1	2,500			4	4	48	346	15
3		3	3	925	3	19,700	2	6,550	1	2,400	3	3	45	609	16
7	3	7	6	2,025	8	64,102	5	20,500			8	9	110	955	17
7		9	7	4,040	7	372,100	6	87,700	7	59,700	7	[illegible]	64	1,861	18
1		1			1	20,000	1	8,000							19
1		1		500	1	12,000									20
	1														21
	1														22
23	6	27	23	14,350	26	692,850	13	53,180	9	86,000	27	30	709	6,086	1
19	5	22	19	8,900	22	497,850	10	23,680	7	40,000	24	27	632	5,286	2
2		2	2	1,560	2	163,500			1	7,000	2	2	137	1,437	3
3		3	3	625	3	8,875	3	3,130			3	3	33	237	4
3	1	5	3	2,010	3	83,000	1	1,700			4	7	121	1,273	5
5	2	5	5	2,625	6	155,000	2	4,950	4	23,000	7		233	1,465	6
2		3	2	650	2	26,000	1	2,000	1	6,000	2		30	295	7
1		1	1	420	1	30,000					2	7	42	346	8
3	2	3	3	1,020	5	31,475	3	11,900	1	4,000	4	4	36	233	9
2		2	2	4,200	2	170,000	1	20,000	2	46,000	2	2	75	750	10
2		3	2	1,250	2	25,000	2	9,500			1	1	2	50	11
	1														12
38	5	40	37	23,139	38	1,199,500	24	200,755	20	129,200	39	45	756	8,844	1
25	3	26	25	12,980	26	571,000	14	35,855	8	42,300	29	30	570	5,518	2
4		4	4	2,695	4	149,500	2	10,385			4	4	103	1,321	3
1		1	1	500	1	25,000	1	3,000			1	1	17	150	4
3		3	3	2,904	3	164,500			2	10,500	3	3	126	1,198	5

TABLE 7.—ORGANIZATIONS, COMMUNICANTS OR MEMBERS, PLACES OF WORSHIP, VALUE OF CHURCH PROPERTY, MORE IN 1900, BY SELECTED

	DENOMINATION.	Total number of organizations.	COMMUNICANTS OR MEMBERS.				
			Number of organizations reporting.	Total number reported.	Sex.		
					Number of organizations reporting.	Male.	Female.
	Manchester, N. H.—Continued.						
	Protestant bodies—Continued.						
	Lutheran bodies:						
6	General Council of the Evangelical Lutheran Church in North America	1	1	478	1	225	253
7	Evangelical Lutheran Synodical Conference of America	1	1	260	1	98	162
	Methodist bodies:						
8	Methodist Episcopal Church	5	5	1,064	4	152	289
	Presbyterian bodies:						
9	Presbyterian Church in the United States of America	2	2	200	2	80	120
10	Protestant Episcopal Church	2	2	610	1	44	100
11	Unitarians	1	1	286	1	105	181
12	Universalists	1	1	400	....	....	....
13	Other Protestant bodies	9	9	587	9	209	378
14	Roman Catholic Church	11	11	34,615	11	15,940	18,675
15	Jewish congregations	2	2	[1] 80	....	....	....
	Eastern Orthodox Churches:						
16	Greek Orthodox Church	1	1	3,000	1	2,800	200
17	All other bodies	2	2	185	2	90	95
1	Memphis, Tenn.	139	135	37,477	115	10,700	19,440
	Protestant bodies	128	124	31,623	114	10,690	19,421
	Baptist bodies:						
3	Baptists—Southern Convention	10	10	2,742	8	968	1,407
4	Baptists—National Convention (Colored)	40	40	8,820	40	2,587	6,233
	Disciples or Christians:						
5	Disciples of Christ	3	3	1,267	3	476	791
6	Churches of Christ	1	1	80	1	40	40
	Methodist bodies:						
7	African Methodist Episcopal Church	10	10	2,415	9	838	1,402
8	Methodist Episcopal Church, South	11	11	5,566	11	2,313	3,253
9	Colored Methodist Episcopal Church	9	9	2,292	9	818	1,474
10	Other Methodist bodies	8	6	1,102	5	371	727
	Presbyterian bodies:						
11	Presbyterian Church in the United States	8	7	3,136	5	814	1,672
12	Other Presbyterian bodies	6	6	802	5	317	445
13	Protestant Episcopal Church	8	8	2,259	8	823	1,436
14	Other Protestant bodies	14	13	1,142	10	325	541
15	Roman Catholic Church	6	6	5,270	....	....	....
16	Jewish congregations	3	3	[1] 375	....	....	....
17	All other bodies	2	2	209	1	10	19
1	Milwaukee, Wis.	185	185	155,206	160	66,443	75,537
2	Protestant bodies	138	138	52,606	123	18,512	25,383
	Baptist bodies:						
3	Baptists—Northern and National (Colored) Conventions	11	11	2,355	11	810	1,545
4	Church of Christ, Scientist	2	2	528	2	183	345
5	Congregationalists	7	7	1,778	7	599	1,179
	Disciples or Christians:						
6	Disciples of Christ	1	1	330	1	100	230
	Evangelical bodies:						
7	Evangelical Association	6	6	1,155	6	453	702
8	German Evangelical Synod of North America	7	7	3,635	7	1,680	1,955
	Lutheran bodies:						
9	General Council of the Evangelical Lutheran Church in North America	3	3	618	3	169	449
10	Evangelical Lutheran Synodical Conference of America	32	32	29,985	27	10,808	13,050
11	United Norwegian Lutheran Church in America	2	2	730	2	325	405
12	Lutheran Synod of Buffalo	1	1	571	1	229	342
13	Other Lutheran bodies	4	4	282	4	142	140
	Methodist bodies:						
14	Methodist Episcopal Church	18	18	3,788	17	1,233	2,051
15	Other Methodist bodies	3	3	110	3	37	73
	Presbyterian bodies:						
16	Presbyterian Church in the United States of America	11	11	2,158	11	707	1,451
17	Welsh Calvinistic Methodist Church	2	2	254	2	120	134
18	Protestant Episcopal Church	12	12	2,796	5	412	576
	Reformed bodies:						
19	Reformed Church in America	1	1	325	1	125	200
20	Reformed Church in the United States	1	1	250	1	100	150
21	Other Protestant bodies	14	14	936	12	280	408
22	Roman Catholic Church	32	32	101,453	31	47,842	50,041
23	Jewish congregations	8	8	[1] 765	....	....	....
24	All other bodies	7	7	382	6	89	113
1	Minneapolis, Minn.	214	212	96,819	183	37,275	51,921
	Protestant bodies	173	171	48,814	152	15,992	26,605
	Baptist bodies:						
3	Baptists—Northern Convention	17	17	5,831	17	2,175	3,656
4	Free Baptists	1	1	116	1	45	71
5	Church of Christ, Scientist	4	4	1,560	4	450	1,110
6	Congregationalists	20	20	5,934	19	1,980	3,652
	Disciples or Christians:						
7	Disciples of Christ	2	2	593	2	218	375

[1] Heads of families only.

DEBT ON CHURCH PROPERTY, PARSONAGES, AND SUNDAY SCHOOLS, FOR EACH CITY OF 25,000 INHABITANTS OR DENOMINATIONS: 1906—Continued.

PLACES OF WORSHIP.					VALUE OF CHURCH PROPERTY.		DEBT ON CHURCH PROPERTY.		PARSONAGES.		SUNDAY SCHOOLS CONDUCTED BY CHURCH ORGANIZATIONS.				
Number of organizations reporting—Church edifices.	Number of organizations reporting—Halls, etc.	Number of church edifices reported.	Seating capacity of church edifices: Number of organizations reporting.	Seating capacity of church edifices: Seating capacity reported.	Number of organizations reporting.	Value reported.	Number of organizations reporting.	Amount of debt reported.	Number of organizations reporting.	Value of parsonages reported.	Number of organizations reporting.	Number of Sunday schools reported.	Number of officers and teachers.	Number of scholars.	
1	...	1	1	600	1	$21,000	1	$2,300	1	$5,000	1	2	37	167	6
1	...	1	1	320	1	5,200	1	1,800	...	...	1	1	3	68	7
4	...	4	4	1,950	4	58,700	2	3,500	3	13,800	5	5	103	1,491	8
2	...	2	2	600	2	23,000	1	570	...	...	2	2	23	200	9
2	...	2	2	550	2	22,500	...	...	1	10,000	2	2	31	235	10
1	...	2	1	700	1	25,000	1	1,200	...	...	1	1	10	53	11
1	...	1	1	720	1	31,000	1	2,200	...	...	1	1	21	175	12
5	3	5	5	1,450	6	55,600	4	10,900	1	3,000	8	8	96	460	13
10	...	11	10	10,020	10	605,500	8	157,000	10	86,500	8	13	180	3,285	14
2	...	2	2	130	1	3,000	1	900	2	400	1	1	1	18	15
1	...	1	...	...	1	20,000	1	7,000	...	...	...	...	...	...	16
...	2	...	...	...	...	...	...	...	...	...	1	1	5	23	17
122	13	125	120	63,035	125	1,921,517	34	123,086	44	175,150	127	131	1,513	16,148	1
113	11	115	111	58,585	116	1,769,017	33	121,686	44	175,150	119	123	1,442	14,302	[illegible]
10	...	10	10	5,425	10	269,000	6	20,865	5	25,500	10	10	165	1,878	3
37	3	37	37	19,525	38	349,842	9	20,025	9	14,700	40	40	257	2,533	4
3	...	3	3	1,375	3	52,000	...	...	2	9,000	3	3	83	787	5
1	...	1	1	300	1	3,000	...	...	...	...	1	1	8	40	6
9	1	9	9	5,000	9	68,400	4	3,800	3	2,200	9	9	75	784	7
11	...	11	11	7,150	11	205,000	2	13,186	9	52,000	11	11	284	3,189	8
9	...	9	9	4,450	9	79,525	3	4,697	2	4,050	9	9	66	740	9
5	...	6	5	2,650	5	26,900	3	863	4	4,500	4	4	46	564	10
8	...	8	8	4,650	8	246,000	1	1,500	5	44,000	8	11	235	2,017	11
6	...	6	5	1,700	6	102,000	2	1,750	...	...	6		49	370	12
7	1	8	7	3,035	7	265,500	3	55,000	3	13,000	8		104	884	13
7	6	7	6	3,325	9	101,850	...	...	2	6,200	10	16	70	516	14
6	...	6	6	3,200	6	90,000	...	...	...	...	6	6	54	1,581	15
3	...	4	3	1,250	3	62,500	1	1,400	...	...	2	2	17	265	16
...	2	...	...	...	...	...	...	...	...	...	...	...	...	...	17
158	20	169	156	96,221	161	5,503,140	89	1,018,493	101	555,057	141	165	2,188	31,139	1
119	16	128	118	63,344	124	3,573,045	60	386,680	74	377,450	113	135	2,048	21,424	2
9	2	11	8	4,575	10	219,950	3	4,146	4	18,500	10	15	272	2,294	3
1	1	1	1	1,200	2	115,400	...	...	...	...	2	2	34	210	4
7	...	7	7	4,264	7	269,000	4	7,450	1	2,000	7	7	172	1,428	5
1	...	1	1	225	1	16,600	...	...	...	...	1	1	23	400	6
6	...	6	6	2,820	6	91,400	1	3,500	5	18,500	6	7	164	1,286	7
7	...	9	7	4,150	7	145,500	6	50,400	6	22,000	7	8	153	1,941	8
2	1	2	2	800	3	40,400	3	31,605	...	...	3	3	52	455	9
32	...	34	32	22,970	32	996,615	23	193,787	30	127,800	22	28	175	4,454	10
2	...	2	2	1,050	2	55,000	1	6,500	1	4,000	2	6	54	630	11
1	...	1	1	450	1	12,300	1	3,864	1	3,000	...	...	...	...	12
3	1	3	3	800	3	27,000	2	4,950	1	7,000	3	4	24	189	13
17	1	19	17	8,500	17	562,800	6	34,500	14	93,250	17	19	437	3,729	14
3	...	3	3	750	3	18,500	...	...	...	...	2	2	17	67	15
10	1	10	10	3,550	10	337,300	2	1,400	2	3,700	11	12	224	2,002	16
2	...	2	2	600	2	21,200	...	...	...	...	1	1	18	160	17
10	1	11	10	4,390	10	503,800	5	28,550	5	45,700	11	11	144	1,345	18
1	...	1	1	500	1	26,000	1	9,000	1	4,000	1	1	20	250	19
1	...	1	1	350	1	17,000	...	...	1	5,000	1	1	18	180	20
4	8	4	4	1,400	6	97,280	2	7,028	2	23,000	6	7	47	404	21
32	...	34	32	27,627	32	1,788,100	25	598,313	27	177,607	23	25	105	9,190	22
4	...	4	4	3,600	3	131,000	3	30,500	...	...	3	3	15	435	23
3	4	3	2	650	2	10,995	1	3,000	...	...	2	2	20	90	24
187	18	208	180	98,987	188	5,360,050	83	427,153	59	246,600	184	231	4,271	43,181	1
161	10	179	158	85,270	163	4,370,550	64	207,333	43	134,100	165	206	4,078	37,791	2
17	...	21	17	11,680	17	553,000	4	18,835	3	7,300	17	24	546	4,922	3
1	...	1	1	350	1	50,000	...	...	...	...	1	1	12	115	4
3	1	3	3	2,800	4	160,550	1	2,500	...	...	4	4	60	303	5
20	...	22	20	10,445	20	617,000	12	17,140	4	12,000	20	22	510	5,816	6
2	...	2	2	1,025	2	47,000	1	400	...	...	2	2	42	427	7

TABLE 7.—ORGANIZATIONS, COMMUNICANTS OR MEMBERS, PLACES OF WORSHIP, VALUE OF CHURCH PROPERTY, MORE IN 1900, BY SELECTED

	DENOMINATION.	Total number of organizations.	COMMUNICANTS OR MEMBERS.				
			Number of organizations reporting.	Total number reported.	Sex.		
					Number of organizations reporting.	Male.	Female.
	Minneapolis, Minn.—Continued.						
	Protestant bodies—Continued.						
	Lutheran bodies:						
8	General Council of the Evangelical Lutheran Church in North America	12	12	4,610	10	1,545	2,020
9	Evangelical Lutheran Synodical Conference of America	3	3	969	2	245	424
10	United Norwegian Lutheran Church in America	2	2	735	1	115	120
11	Evangelical Lutheran Synod of Iowa and Other States	2	2	981	2	422	559
12	Synod for the Norwegian Evangelical Lutheran Church in America	6	6	2,170	3	579	686
13	Norwegian Lutheran Free Church	4	4	1,430	3	352	378
14	Slovak Evangelical Lutheran Synod of America	1	1	408	1	246	162
15	Other Lutheran bodies	7	7	615	7	272	343
	Methodist bodies:						
16	Methodist Episcopal Church	25	25	6,661	22	2,051	3,624
17	African Methodist Episcopal Church	2	2	405	2	152	253
	Presbyterian bodies:						
18	Presbyterian Church in the United States of America	16	16	6,059	15	1,966	3,563
19	Welsh Calvinistic Methodist Church	1	1	179	1	87	92
20	Protestant Episcopal Church	16	14	4,785	14	1,740	3,045
	Swedish Evangelical bodies:						
21	Swedish Evangelical Mission Covenant of America	5	5	1,455	5	584	871
22	Swedish Evangelical Free Mission	2	2	359	1	9	11
23	Unitarians	2	2	412	......	......	......
24	Universalists	3	3	840	1	20	40
25	Other Protestant bodies	20	20	1,707	19	739	950
26	Roman Catholic Church	20	20	45,642	20	20,389	25,253
27	Jewish congregations	10	10	[1] 806	......	......	......
	Eastern Orthodox Churches:						
28	Russian Orthodox Church	1	1	866	1	480	386
29	Greek Orthodox Church	1	1	250	1	222	28
30	All other bodies	9	9	441	9	192	249
1	**Mobile, Ala.**	70	69	33,652	63	12,827	19,409
2	Protestant bodies	61	60	19,451	57	6,467	12,190
	Baptist bodies:						
3	Baptists—Southern Convention	4	4	1,385	4	477	908
4	Baptists—National Convention (Colored)	19	19	6,024	19	2,329	3,695
	Methodist bodies:						
5	African Methodist Episcopal Church	7	7	1,786	5	616	1,076
6	African Methodist Episcopal Zion Church	6	5	3,044	5	656	2,388
7	Methodist Episcopal Church, South	6	6	2,340	6	882	1,458
8	Other Methodist bodies	3	3	412	3	144	268
	Presbyterian bodies:						
9	Presbyterian Church in the United States	4	4	1,294	4	469	825
10	Protestant Episcopal Church	4	4	2,472	3	650	1,122
11	Other Protestant bodies	8	8	694	8	244	450
12	Roman Catholic Church	6	6	13,579	6	6,360	7,219
13	Jewish congregations	2	2	[1] 272	......	......	......
	Eastern Orthodox Churches:						
14	Greek Orthodox Church	1	1	350	......	......	......
1	**Montgomery, Ala.**	73	73	24,851	61	7,123	13,133
2	Protestant bodies	68	68	21,502	59	5,637	11,613
	Baptist bodies:						
3	Baptists—Southern Convention	6	6	2,027	5	438	739
4	Baptists—National Convention (Colored)	24	24	10,108	24	3,060	7,048
5	Primitive Baptists	2	2	42	2	15	27
	Disciples or Christians:						
6	Churches of Christ	2	2	539	2	232	307
	Methodist bodies:						
7	African Methodist Episcopal Church	3	3	685	3	232	453
8	African Methodist Episcopal Zion Church	7	7	2,609	7	911	1,698
9	Methodist Episcopal Church, South	6	6	2,681	2	262	353
10	Other Methodist bodies	4	4	359	3	131	220
	Presbyterian bodies:						
11	Cumberland Presbyterian Church	1	1	125	1	55	70
12	Presbyterian Church in the United States	4	4	1,099	3	169	353
13	Protestant Episcopal Church	3	3	951	1	40	160
14	Other Protestant bodies	6	6	277	6	92	185
15	Roman Catholic Church	2	2	3,006	2	1,486	1,520
16	Jewish congregations	2	2	[1] 218	......	......	......
	Eastern Orthodox Churches:						
17	Greek Orthodox Church	1	1	125	......	......	......
1	**Nashville, Tenn.**	179	177	44,198	150	12,996	21,619
2	Protestant bodies	169	168	37,908	150	12,996	21,619
	Baptist bodies:						
3	Baptists—Southern Convention	14	14	4,417	13	1,487	2,345
4	Baptists—National Convention (Colored)	25	25	6,408	25	2,175	4,233
5	Primitive Baptists [1]	6	6	558	2	102	137
6	Other Baptist bodies	2	2	148	2	63	85
7	Congregationalists	2	2	474	2	236	238

[1] Heads of families only.

DEBT ON CHURCH PROPERTY, PARSONAGES, AND SUNDAY SCHOOLS, FOR EACH CITY OF 25,000 INHABITANTS OR DENOMINATIONS: 1906—Continued.

PLACES OF WORSHIP.					VALUE OF CHURCH PROPERTY.		DEBT ON CHURCH PROPERTY.		PARSONAGES.		SUNDAY SCHOOLS CONDUCTED BY CHURCH ORGANIZATIONS.				
Number of organizations reporting— Church edifices.	Number of organizations reporting— Halls, etc.	Number of church edifices reported.	Seating capacity of church edifices. Number of organizations reporting.	Seating capacity of church edifices. Seating capacity reported.	Number of organizations reporting.	Value reported.	Number of organizations reporting.	Amount of debt reported.	Number of organizations reporting.	Value of parsonages reported.	Number of organizations reporting.	Number of Sunday schools reported.	Number of officers and teachers.	Number of scholars.	
11	1	13	11	6,950	12	$221,	6	$18,781	1	$4,800	1	19	363	3,017	8
3	...	3	3	880	3	34,	1	5,500	2	3,800		4	29	352	9
2	...	2	2	1,325	2	45,	2	5,300	1	6,500		3	54	430	10
2	...	3	2	850	2	23,	1	3,700	2	4,000		2	24	202	11
5	1	6	5	1,750	5	32,	2	1,900	4	12,200		10	166	1,473	12
4	...	4	4	1,925	4	46,	2	6,500	2	5,000	9	6	122	815	13
1	...	1	1	200	1	4,550	...	...	...	...	1	1	1	40	14
5	1	5	5	1,710	5	32,800	3	2,750	3	7,100	5	7	47	356	15
25	...	27	24	11,760	25	688,100	6	35,600	10	39,000	25	28	574	5,693	16
2	...	2	2	650	2	13,000	2	2,900	...	...	2	2	23	125	17
16	...	18	16	12,500	16	7	5	16,600	3	10,200	16	22	874	8,027	18
1	...	1	1	350	1	68,900	...	...	...	...	1	1	14	100	19
16	...	17	16	5,800	16	454,500	5	26,300	1	7,000	16	19	220	2,147	20
	...		5	4,270	5		1	5,000	1	1,000	5	6	168	1,650	21
5	...		2	1,600	2	,	2	10,090	1	2,500	2	3	24	233	22
2	...		1	600	2	98,500	1	9,000	...	...	2	2	18	147	23
3	...		3	2,000	3	246,000	1	3,000	...	...	3	3	43	335	24
13	6	16	12	3,850	13	108,150	6	15,537	5	11,700	14	15	144	976	25
17	...	19	13	9,213	17	846,500	11	186,445	15	110,500	14	20	173	4,979	26
7	...	8	7	3,304	6	96,000	6	17,000	...	...	3	3	15	312	27
1	...	1	1	1,000	1	30,000	1	13,375	1	2,000	1	1	2	75	28
1	...	1	1	200	1	17,000	1	3,000	...	...	...	...	...	...	29
...	8	...	...	...	...	...	...	...	...	...	1	1	3	24	30
62	6	72		36,094	62	1,539,485	25	96,527	31	208,300	66	74	870	10,042	1
55	5	61	52	31,954	55	812,485	23	56,287	25	118,800	59	64	770	8,780	2
4	...	5	4	2,090	4	62,800	...	...	2	18,000	4	5	81	836	
19	...	19	18	10,900	18	136,850	9	6,612	3	6,000	19	19	161	1,869	3
7	...	7		3,739	5	57,100	4	21,525	3	8,500	7	7	66	822	5
5	...	6	5	4,700	6	70,250	4	4,750	4	11,500	5	5	111	1,135	6
6	...	6		2,725	6	126,500	2	1,050	4	43,700	6	6	113	1,785	7
3	...	3	6	1,300	3	22,200	1	800	3	2,100	3	3	23	249	8
4	...		4	3,100	4	145,500	1	15,000	1	8,000			84	883	9
4	...		4	2,250	4	155,500	...	...	3	16,000	4		74	790	10
3	5	4	3	1,150	5	35,785	2	6,550	2	5,000	4	5	57	411	11
6	...	10	6	3,140	6	637,000	1	240	6	89,500	6	9	94	1,162	12
1	...	1	1	1,000	1	90,000	1	40,000	...	...	1	1	6	100	13
...	1	...	...	...	...	...	...	...	...	...	...	...	...	...	14
65	7	71	61	36,385	66	933,386	25	28,872	21	93,800	68	74	823	8,835	1
62	5	68	58	34,635	63	835,886	24	26,872	19	88,500	65	69	802	8,455	2
5	1	5	5	2,800	5	128,000	1	1,500	1	6,000	6	6	107	1,119	3
23	1	25	23	16,325	23	105,775	10	7,115	3	2,300	23	5	237	2,258	4
2	...	2	2	1,000	2	2,000	1	500	...	...	...	2	...	...	5
2	...	3	2	1,300	2	28,500	1	500	...	...	2	2	17	255	6
3	...	3	2	1,000	3	35,240	3	1,037	1	3,000	3	3	27	303	7
7	...	7	7	4,675	7	125,900	2	850	2	2,700	7	7	99	1,034	8
6	...	6	4	1,400	6	169,200	3	9,570	4	39,700	6	7	138	1,981	9
3	...	3	3	1,800	3	33,000	2	1,800	2	3,300	4	4	24	147	10
1	...	1	1	450	1	18,000	1	4,000	1	4,500	1	1	10	125	11
4	...	5	4	1,725	4	74,000	...	...	2	15,800	4	4	72	563	12
3	...	5	3	1,700	3	110,000	...	...	2	10,000	3	4	45	415	13
3	3	3	2	460	4	6,271	...	...	1	1,200	6	6	26	255	14
1	1	1	1	700	1	90,000	...	...	1	5,000	2	3	13	260	15
2	...	2	2	1,050	2	7,500	1	2,000	1	300	1	2	8	120	16
...	1	...	...	...	...	...	...	...	...	...	...	...	...	...	17
161	8	167	157	75,005	161	2,133,668	48	113,978	38	106,200	159	166	2,011	22,137	1
153	7	159	149	70,705	154	1,952,668	46	105,478	38	106,200	152	159	1,909	20,960	2
14	...	15	14	6,900	14	248,500	10	35,450	4	13,100	14	16	273	3,445	3
25	...	25	23	12,600	25	152,500	9	12,070	3	2,800	25	25	196	1,738	4
2	...	2	2	750	2	15,000	...	...	...	...	...	...	...	...	5
1	...	1	1	750	1	2,500	...	...	1	750	1	1	11	75	6
1	1	1	1	400	1	20,000	...	...	1	1,800	2	3	45	499	7

[1] Includes Primitive Baptists and Colored Primitive Baptists in America.

TABLE 7.—ORGANIZATIONS, COMMUNICANTS OR MEMBERS, PLACES OF WORSHIP, VALUE OF CHURCH PROPERTY, MORE IN 1900, BY SELECTED

	DENOMINATION.	Total number of organizations.	COMMUNICANTS OR MEMBERS. Number of organizations reporting.	Total number reported.	Sex. Number of organizations reporting.	Male.	Female.
	Nashville, Tenn.—Continued.						
	Protestant bodies—Continued.						
	Disciples or Christians:						
8	Disciples of Christ	6	6	1,438	6	524	914
9	Churches of Christ	20	20	2,662	20	1 081	1,581
10	Independent churches	1	1	402	1	165	237
	Lutheran bodies:						
11	General Synod of the Evangelical Lutheran Church in the United States of America	2	2	442	2	166	276
	Methodist bodies:						
12	Methodist Episcopal Church	10	9	1,305	7	375	777
13	African Methodist Episcopal Church	13	13	2,974	13	1,134	1,840
14	Methodist Episcopal Church, South	23	23	8,413	20	3,062	4,778
15	Colored Methodist Episcopal Church	3	3	427	3	125	302
	Presbyterian bodies:						
16	Cumberland Presbyterian Church	10	10	1,914	7	415	659
17	Colored Cumberland Presbyterian Church	1	1	75	1	40	35
18	Presbyterian Church in the United States	11	11	3,259	9	1,028	1,631
19	Protestant Episcopal Church	9	9	1,574	9	522	1,052
20	Other Protestant bodies	11	11	1,018	8	296	499
21	Roman Catholic Church	6	6	5,865	....	....	....
22	Jewish congregations	3	[illegible]	[1] 275	....	....	....
	Eastern Orthodox Churches:						
23	Greek Orthodox Church	1	1	150	....	....	....
1	**New Bedford, Mass.**	59	55	43,936	50	18,466	19,950
	Protestant bodies	41	40	7,161	37	2,253	4,468
	Adventist bodies:						
3	Advent Christian Church	2	2	167	2	50	117
4	Seventh-day Adventist Denomination	1	1	44	1	11	33
	Baptist bodies:						
5	Baptists—Northern and National (Colored) Conventions	7	7	1,028	7	321	707
6	Christians (Christian Connection)	3	3	607	3	179	428
7	Congregationalists	2	2	701	2	192	509
	Friends:						
8	Society of Friends (Orthodox)	4	4	213	4	95	118
	Methodist bodies:						
9	Methodist Episcopal Church	6	6	993	5	287	596
10	Primitive Methodist Church in the United States of America	2	2	307	2	112	195
11	African Methodist bodies	2	2	200	1	35	40
12	Protestant Episcopal Church	3	3	1,888	3	690	1,198
13	Unitarians	1	1	315	1	110	205
14	Universalists	1	1	185	....	....	....
15	Other Protestant bodies	7	6	513	6	171	342
16	Roman Catholic Church	11	11	36,115	10	16,126	15,314
17	Jewish congregations	3	....	....	....	....	....
	Eastern Orthodox Churches:						
18	Greek Orthodox Church	1	1	425	....	....	....
	Latter-day Saints:						
19	Reorganized Church of Jesus Christ of Latter-day Saints	1	1	26	1	10	16
20	Spiritualists	2	2	209	2	77	132
1	**New Britain, Conn.**	25	25	22,008	24	10,914	10,998
2	**Protestant bodies**	16	16	7,475	16	2,973	4,502
	Baptist bodies:						
3	Baptists—Northern Convention	3	3	803	3	295	508
4	Congregationalists	3	3	2,312	3	873	1,439
	Lutheran bodies:						
5	General Council of the Evangelical Lutheran Church in North America	3	3	2,447	3	1 037	1,410
6	Evangelical Lutheran Synodical Conference of America	1	1	634	1	310	324
	Methodist bodies:						
7	Methodist Episcopal Church	1	1	576	1	210	366
8	African Methodist Episcopal Zion Church	1	1	40	1	15	25
9	Protestant Episcopal Church	1	1	550	1	183	367
10	Other Protestant bodies	3	3	113	3	50	63
11	Roman Catholic Church	6	6	13,830	6	7,495	6,335
12	Jewish congregations	1	1	[1] 96	....	....	....
13	Armenian Church	1	1	300	1	230	70
	Eastern Orthodox Churches:						
14	Russian Orthodox Church	1	1	307	1	216	91
1	**New Haven, Conn.**	92	87	67,650	79	30,600	32,964
2	**Protestant bodies**	71	71	21,675	66	7,157	11,024
	Baptist bodies:						
3	Baptists—Northern Convention	7	7	2,520	7	996	1,524
4	Baptists—National Convention (Colored)	1	1	541	1	192	349
5	Congregationalists	17	17	6,895	17	2,489	4,406
	Lutheran bodies:						
6	General Council of the Evangelical Lutheran Church in North America	3	3	1,535	3	808	727
7	Other Lutheran bodies	4	4	380	4	165	215
	Methodist bodies:						
8	Methodist Episcopal Church	14	14	3,730	13	1,442	1,968
9	Other Methodist bodies	3	3	394	3	143	251

[1] Heads of families only.

DEBT ON CHURCH PROPERTY, PARSONAGES, AND SUNDAY SCHOOLS, FOR EACH CITY OF 25,000 INHABITANTS OR DENOMINATIONS: 1906—Continued.

PLACES OF WORSHIP.					VALUE OF CHURCH PROPERTY.		DEBT ON CHURCH PROPERTY.		PARSONAGES.		SUNDAY SCHOOLS CONDUCTED BY CHURCH ORGANIZATIONS.				
Number of organizations reporting—Church edifices.	Number of organizations reporting—Halls, etc.	Number of church edifices reported.	Seating capacity of church edifices—Number of organizations reporting.	Seating capacity of church edifices—Seating capacity reported.	Number of organizations reporting.	Value reported.	Number of organizations reporting.	Amount of debt reported.	Number of organizations reporting.	Value of parsonages reported.	Number of organizations reporting.	Number of Sunday schools reported.	Number of officers and teachers.	Number of scholars.	
6	......	6	6	2,800	6	$75,700	1	$1,500	......	......	5	5	51	695	8
20	......	20	20	6,320	20	54,568	5	1,615	1	$2,000	17	17	122	1,320	9
1	......	1	1	850	1	25,000	1	7,000	......	......	1	1	35	465	10
1	1	1	1	500	1	50,000	1	2,850	1	4,000	2	2	34	300	11
8	1	8	6	2,150	8	53,800	2	5,250	6	9,100	9	9	97	912	12
13	......	13	13	9,250	13	78,150	5	8,830	2	500	13	13	110	1,444	13
23	......	24	23	10,860	23	453,100	3	7,700	8	23,050	22	23	436	5,184	14
3	......	3	3	1,600	3	34,400	2	3,700	1	600	3	3	31	214	15
10	......	10	10	4,275	10	115,800	3	11,700	......	......	9	9	113	1,121	16
1	......	1	1	500	1	3,000	......	......	......	......	1	1	4	25	17
11	......	12	11	5,225	11	310,800	3	5,625	7	38,000	11	13	250	2,216	18
8	1	11	8	3,225	8	241,500	......	......	3	10,500	9	9	95	750	19
5	3	5	5	1,750	6	18,350	1	2,188	......	......	8	9	66	657	20
6	......	6	6	2,950	5	117,000	......	......	......	......	5	5	29	987	21
2	......	2	2	1,350	2	64,000	2	8,500	......	......	2	2	13	220	22
......	1	......	......	......	......	......	......	......	......	......	......	......	......	......	23
49	7	53	49	28,775	50	1,717,000	24	327,200	18	144,200	49	56	964	10,488	1
37	4	39	37	16,335	38	669,850	15	31,600	9	38,000	38	42	813	6,380	2
2	......	2	2	500	2	13,500	1	2,950	......	......	1	1	18	90	3
1	......	1	1	200	1	3,000	......	......	......	......	1	2	7	35	4
6	1	7	6	2,500	6	63,600	4	4,925	1	4,000	7	8	156	1,053	5
3	......	3	3	1,800	3	89,000	......	......	......	......	3	3	77	484	6
2	......	3	2	1,900	2	100,000	1	2,500	......	......	2	2	86	768	7
4	......	4	4	1,050	4	24,050	......	......	......	......	3	3	18	126	8
6	......	6	6	3,275	6	84,200	1	3,000	3	10,500	6	6	157	1,063	9
2	......	2	2	750	2	15,000	2	7,125	1	4,000	2	2	48	596	10
2	......	2	2	900	2	13,000	2	700	1	5,000	2	2	29	210	11
3	......	3	3	1,600	3	138,000	1	4,000	2	9,500	3	4	128	1,275	12
1	......	1	1	500	1	90,000	......	......	1	5,000	1	2	16	230	13
1	......	1	1	300	1	12,000	1	1,200	......	......	1	1	16	130	14
4	3	4	4	1,060	5	24,500	2	5,200	......	......	6	6	57	330	15
11	......	13	11	12,340	11	1,045,800	8	295,400	9	106,200	9	12	141	4,043	16
......	......	......	......	......	......	......	......	......	......	......	......	......	......	......	17
......	1	......	......	......	......	......	......	......	......	......	......	......	......	......	18
1	......	1	1	100	1	1,350	1	200	......	......	1	1	4	35	19
......	2	......	......	......	......	......	......	......	......	......	1	1	6	30	20
23	2	24	23	14,541	23	1,179,800	15	175,400	14	139,000	22	25	554	6,768	1
15	1	16	15	8,791	15	749,300	10	109,400	9	88,000	16	19	484	4,348	2
3	......	3	3	1,200	3	120,500	2	25,500	1	9,000	3	3	80	515	3
3	......	4	3	3,216	3	255,000	1	7,500	3	52,000	3	3	192	2,160	4
2	1	2	2	1,500	2	130,000	2	58,500	1	8,000	3	3	92	735	5
1	......	1	1	600	1	20,000	1	5,300	1	3,000	1	1	14	210	6
1	......	1	1	575	1	75,000	1	1,000	1	4,000	1	1	52	365	7
1	......	1	1	350	1	7,000	1	6,000	1	2,000	1	1	10	38	8
1	......	1	1	400	1	115,000	......	......	1	10,000	1	1	35	250	9
3	......	3	3	950	3	26,800	2	5,600	......	......	3	6	9	75	10
6	......	6	6	4,650	6	418,000	3	62,600	4	48,000	6	6	70	2,420	11
1	......	1	1	600	1	10,000	1	2,600	......	......	......	......	......	......	12
......	1	......	......	......	......	......	......	......	......	......	......	......	......	......	13
1	......	1	1	500	1	2,500	1	800	1	3,000	......	......	......	......	14
76	7	87	76	50,704	77	3,600,000	37	455,358	40	346,300	82	90	2,077	19,453	1
62	6	73	62	36,395	63	2,363,000	26	145,308	28	210,300	67	75	1,688	12,859	2
7	......	7	7	3,725	7	260,000	2	6,200	2	8,000	7	8	201	1,493	3
1	......	1	1	550	1	25,000	......	......	......	......	1	1	17	184	4
15	1	21	15	12,050	15	739,500	8	62,500	4	33,000	16	19	600	4,633	5
3	......	3	3	2,025	3	58,000	1	12,000	1	7,000	3	3	112	824	6
2	1	2	2	600	2	29,000	1	7,000	1	6,000	2	2	21	196	7
13	1	14	13	6,000	13	380,500	3	9,265	10	63,500	14	16	376	2,826	8
3	......	3	3	1,400	3	23,500	2	5,500	1	2,500	3	3	37	237	9

TABLE 7.—ORGANIZATIONS, COMMUNICANTS OR MEMBERS, PLACES OF WORSHIP, VALUE OF CHURCH PROPERTY, MORE IN 1900, BY SELECTED

	DENOMINATION.	Total number of organizations.	COMMUNICANTS OR MEMBERS.				
			Number of organizations reporting.	Total number reported.	Sex.		
					Number of organizations reporting.	Male.	Female.
	New Haven, Conn.—Continued.						
	Protestant bodies—Continued.						
	Presbyterian bodies:						
10	Presbyterian Church in the United States of America	1	1	300	1	100	200
11	Protestant Episcopal Church	12	12	4,896	8	650	1,052
12	Other Protestant bodies	9	9	484	9	172	312
13	Roman Catholic Church	13	13	45,383	13	23,443	21,940
14	Jewish congregations	7	2	[1] 292			
	Eastern Orthodox Churches:						
15	Greek Orthodox Church	1	1	300			
1	New Orleans, La.	214	211	186,497	190	79,547	100,331
2	Protestant bodies	170	170	36,875	153	10,753	20,438
	Baptist bodies:						
3	Baptists—Southern Convention	5	5	989	4	213	457
4	Baptists—National Convention (Colored)	66	66	9,591	64	3,258	6,181
5	Congregationalists	5	5	363	5	105	258
6	German Evangelical Synod of North America	4	4	4,353	2	1,125	1,308
	Lutheran bodies:						
7	Evangelical Lutheran Synodical Conference of America	9	9	4,475	9	1,545	2,930
8	Evangelical Lutheran Joint Synod of Ohio and Other States	2	2	540	2	233	307
	Methodist bodies:						
9	Methodist Episcopal Church	18	18	3,333	10	719	1,530
10	African Methodist Episcopal Church	11	11	1,198	11	396	802
11	Methodist Episcopal Church, South	10	10	2,352	10	820	1,532
12	Other African Methodist bodies	3	3	145	3	44	101
	Presbyterian bodies:						
13	Presbyterian Church in the United States	14	14	3,667	14	1,149	2,518
14	Protestant Episcopal Church	12	12	5,178	8	893	2,076
15	Other Protestant bodies	11	11	691	11	253	438
16	Roman Catholic Church	34	34	148,579	34	68,757	79,822
17	Jewish congregations	7	4	[1] 935			
18	All other bodies	3	3	108	3	37	71
1	New York, N. Y.	2,002	1,659	1,838,482	1,203	800,815	912,938
2	Protestant bodies	1,070	1,055	372,690	909	112,622	184,276
	Adventist bodies:						
3	Seventh-day Adventist Denomination	12	12	706	12	179	527
4	Other Adventist bodies	2	2	243	2	104	139
	Baptist bodies:						
5	Baptists—Northern Convention	112	112	43,601	104	14,874	26,814
6	Baptists—National Convention (Colored)	4	4	828	4	255	573
7	Free Baptists	1	1	515			
8	Other Baptist bodies	2	2	134	2	46	88
9	Brethren (Plymouth)	19	19	1,057	19	476	581
	Catholic Apostolic Churches:						
10	Catholic Apostolic Church	2	2	966	2	369	597
11	New Apostolic Church	2	2	650	2	275	375
12	Church of Christ, Scientist	9	9	3,372	6	764	1,909
13	Congregationalists	47	47	21,096	45	7,373	12,773
	Disciples or Christians:						
14	Disciples of Christ	7	7	1,819	7	711	1,108
	Evangelical bodies:						
15	Evangelical Association	10	9	1,159	9	442	717
	Friends:						
16	Society of Friends (Orthodox)	2	2	606	2	302	304
17	Religious Society of Friends (Hicksite)	3	3	986	3	454	532
18	German Evangelical Synod of North America	5	5	910	4	260	380
19	Independent churches	33	31	7,187	27	2,172	2,775
	Lutheran bodies:						
20	General Synod of the Evangelical Lutheran Church in the United States of America	12	12	4,042	10	1,446	2,134
21	General Council of the Evangelical Lutheran Church in North America	59	59	30,860	50	9,200	14,998
22	Evangelical Lutheran Synodical Conference of America	39	39	13,930	33	4,298	7,230
23	United Norwegian Lutheran Church in America	5	4	695	4	348	347
24	Synod for the Norwegian Evangelical Lutheran Church in America	4	4	944	4	385	559
25	Other Lutheran bodies	6	6	805	5	339	316
	Methodist bodies:						
26	Methodist Episcopal Church	161	161	49,970	146	16,351	26,553
27	African Methodist Episcopal Church	12	12	6,173	11	616	957
28	African Methodist Episcopal Zion Church	11	11	2,988	8	992	1,726
29	Other Methodist bodies	12	12	890	11	363	494
	Moravian bodies:						
30	Moravian Church (Unitas Fratrum)	8	8	1,147	8	415	732
	Presbyterian bodies:						
31	Presbyterian Church in the United States of America	109	109	48,914	92	13,104	21,389
32	United Presbyterian Church of North America	12	12	1,586	12	587	999
33	Synod of the Reformed Presbyterian Church of North America	4	4	584	4	200	384
34	Other Presbyterian bodies	2	2	463	2	205	258
35	Protestant Episcopal Church	188	182	92,534	126	24,526	37,777
	Reformed bodies:						
36	Reformed Church in America	73	73	24,005	65	7,392	12,704
37	Reformed Church in the United States	7	7	1,523	7	529	994
38	Other Reformed bodies	2	2	320			
39	Reformed Episcopal Church	5	5	745	5	247	498

[1] Heads of families only.

DEBT ON CHURCH PROPERTY, PARSONAGES, AND SUNDAY SCHOOLS, FOR EACH CITY OF 25,000 INHABITANTS OR DENOMINATIONS: 1906—Continued.

PLACES OF WORSHIP.					VALUE OF CHURCH PROPERTY.		DEBT ON CHURCH PROPERTY.		PARSONAGES.		SUNDAY SCHOOLS CONDUCTED BY CHURCH ORGANIZATIONS.				
Number of organizations reporting—		Number of church edifices reported.	Seating capacity of church edifices.		Number of organizations reporting.	Value reported.	Number of organizations reporting.	Amount of debt reported.	Number of organizations reporting.	Value of parsonages reported.	Number of organizations reporting.	Number of Sunday schools reported.	Number of officers and teachers.	Number of scholars.	
Church edifices.	Halls, etc.		Number of organizations reporting.	Seating capacity reported.											
1		1	1	700	1	$90,000	1	$15,000			1	1	12	125	10
12		16	12	8,095	12	696,000	4	6,843	8	$80,300	12	14	254	2,083	11
5	3	5	5	1,250	6	61,500	4	21,000	1	10,000	8	8	58	259	12
13		13	13	13,509	13	1,137,000	10	274,050	12	136,000	13	13	373	6,324	13
1		1	1	800	1	100,000	1	36,000			2	2	16	270	14
	1														15
189	11	204	180	94,566	192	4,378,428	80	442,706	85	486,000	198	235	2,209	30,618	1
151	8	162	142	66,523	154	2,206,428	68	249,206	53	203,000	161	173	1,862	19,757	2
5		5	5	3,200	5	92,500	2	1,150			5	5	64	700	3
62	2	63	60	24,488	63	286,803	28	26,675	11	11,000	65	65	366	4,296	4
4	1	4	4	2,850	4	26,800	1	500	1	1,500	5	6	40	423	5
4		5	4	2,700	4	150,500	2	22,500	4	19,000	4	6	174	2,161	6
9		9	9	3,400	9	119,500	4	5,600	4	16,500	8	8	97	1,648	7
2		2	2	450	2	13,000			1	3,000	2	2	33	345	8
16		17	10	4,550	16	123,200	7	5,617	9	17,200	17	17	183	2,185	9
9	2	9	9	3,875	10	93,500	6	9,794	5	6,800	11	11	83	1,050	10
10		11	10	4,750	10	257,000	4	47,100	4	25,500	10	10	177	1,676	11
2		2	2	850	3	13,000	2	2,975	1	7,000	2	2	11	120	12
12	1	15	11	7,400	12	464,500	4	37,195	7	41,500	12	21	347	2,894	13
12		15	12	7,150	11	528,500	6	82,100	6	54,000	12	12	218	1,937	14
4	2	5	4	860	5	37,625	2	8,000			8	8	69	322	15
34		37	34	24,943	34	1,874,000	11	188,100	31	273,000	33	57	324	10,520	16
4		5	4	3,100	4	298,000	1	5,400	1	10,000	4	5	23	341	17
	3														18
1,347	283	1,536	1,312	883,885	1,335	153,925,740	742	19,062,419	587	8,767,387	1,352	1,667	35,834	490,589	1
945	107	1,104	929	567,720	942	89,078,525	478	6,070,972	368	4,759,487	1,013	1,215	28,007	297,164	2
4	4	6	4	1,150	2	12,000	2	4,800			10	11	81	523	3
1	1	1	1	400	1	18,000	1	6,500			2	2	13	121	4
105	7	115	105	69,349	105	9,477,710	63	791,200	15	101,000	110	123	3,114	33,539	5
2	2	2	2	1,100	2	26,225	2	19,388			3	3	25	159	6
1		1	1	600	1	60,000					1	1	37	350	7
	1										1	1	10	45	8
	19										10	10	43	737	9
2		2	1	200	2	90,000	1	2,000			1	2	5	80	10
	2										1	1	3	60	11
5	4	5	5	4,370	7	1,929,700	1	100			8	8	103	611	12
43	3	57	42	36,715	43	4,262,500	22	260,208	11	101,000	47	60	2,157	18,791	13
7		8	7	3,300	7	407,300	4	72,000	1	4,000	7	9	155	1,298	14
9	1	11	9	3,650	9	219,400	6	48,600	4	19,500	10	11	242	2,194	15
2		2	2	1,200	2	85,000					2	7	63	765	16
3		3	3	2,000	3	185,000					2	2	12	66	17
4	1	4	4	1,050	4	74,000	4	31,000			5	7	71	897	18
28	5	28	28	12,794	28	1,476,400	12	186,260	2	16,500	31	36	522	6,117	19
12		12	12	5,896	12	806,850	8	137,150	6	82,000	12	15	388	3,532	20
53	4	59	51	28,875	53	3,286,100	42	643,500	30	233,600	59	84	2,193	23,418	21
33	4	35	30	14,585	34	1,759,650	20	228,765	15	98,400	33	49	674	9,337	22
5		7	5	1,990	5	81,500	4	33,500	1	4,000	4	8	110	794	23
4		4	4	1,025	4	50,000	4	21,600	1	7,000	4	7	72	751	24
3	3	3	3	600	3	30,000	2	7,500			5	6	24	215	25
158	3	165	154	96,988	158	9,864,700	76	714,075	108	1,115,600	160	170	5,493	49,135	26
9	3	9	9	4,985	10	254,600	7	48,622	1	8,000	12	12	141	1,765	27
11		11	11	5,275	11	337,100	5	43,310	3	7,200	11	11	147	1,256	28
11		11	11	3,530	11	138,500	10	44,034	5	17,500	12	12	138	1,181	29
7	1	7	7	2,980	7	209,000	2	9,900	5	49,000	8	8	105	806	30
102	4	137	101	76,490	99	15,326,883	42	689,000	33	639,592	108	144	3,912	45,702	31
11		11	11	6,550	12	694,000	5	34,500	1	15,000	12	13	209	2,206	32
4		4	4	1,800	4	252,000	2	10,000			4	4	60	467	33
2		2	2	1,500	2	135,000	1	5,000			2	2	15	95	34
184	4	241	183	106,588	165	25,830,300	68	1,353,875	83	1,765,795	178	219	4,724	51,110	35
72	1	91	72	48,165	68	7,542,500	26	213,550	36	413,800	73	86	2,190	32,525	36
7		7	7	2,530	7	200,877	7	58,400	2	14,000	7	9	165	1,725	37
2		2	2	1,100	2	53,000	2	28,000							38
5		5	5	1,900	4	417,000	2	17,900			5	5	96	926	39

TABLE 7.—ORGANIZATIONS, COMMUNICANTS OR MEMBERS, PLACES OF WORSHIP, VALUE OF CHURCH PROPERTY, MORE IN 1900, BY SELECTED

	DENOMINATION.	Total number of organizations.	COMMUNICANTS OR MEMBERS. Number of organizations reporting.	Total number reported.	Sex. Number of organizations reporting.	Male.	Female.
	New York, N. Y.—Continued.						
	Protestant bodies—Continued.						
	Salvationists:						
40	Salvation Army	31	28	1,560	28	747	813
41	American Salvation Army	1	1	25	1	15	10
42	Unitarians	9	8	2,119	4	384	480
43	Universalists	7	6	1,546	4	323	838
44	Other Protestant bodies	19	19	1,448	19	554	894
45	Roman Catholic Church	278	278	1,413,775	272	671,248	724,579
46	Jewish congregations	615	302	[1] 30,414	.....	.....	.....
47	Armenian Church	4	4	2,192	4	1,503	689
	Eastern Orthodox Churches:						
48	Russian Orthodox Church	1	1	1,300	1	900	400
49	Syrian Orthodox Church	1	1	2,000	1	1,200	800
50	Greek Orthodox Church	3	3	12,575	1	11,500	500
51	Society for Ethical Culture	2	2	1,265	2	856	409
52	Spiritualists	5	5	1,578	5	681	897
53	All other bodies	23	8	693	8	305	388
1	Newark, N. J.	176	171	115,307	147	40,048	50,927
	Protestant bodies	132	131	41,196	125	14,104	25,972
	Baptist bodies:						
3	Baptists—Northern Convention	14	14	4,586	13	1,511	2,875
4	Baptists—National Convention (Colored)	10	10	1,775	10	517	1,258
5	Christians (Christian Connection)	1	1	325	1	75	250
6	Congregationalists	3	3	784	3	267	517
7	German Evangelical Synod of North America	3	3	1,360	3	460	900
	Lutheran bodies:						
8	General Council of the Evangelical Lutheran Church in North America	5	5	1,560	5	597	963
9	Other Lutheran bodies	4	4	475	4	192	283
	Methodist bodies:						
10	Methodist Episcopal Church	22	22	7,125	22	2,594	4,531
11	African Methodist Episcopal Church	2	2	775	2	125	650
12	Methodist Protestant Church	2	2	350	1	106	244
13	Other Methodist bodies	2	2	118	1	25	43
	Presbyterian bodies:						
14	Presbyterian Church in the United States of America	25	25	10,489	25	3,671	6,818
15	United Presbyterian Church of North America	1	1	140	1	70	70
16	Protestant Episcopal Church	16	15	5,196	13	1,718	2,892
	Reformed bodies:						
17	Reformed Church in America	7	7	4,214	6	1,375	2,554
18	Universalists	1	1	700	1	300	400
19	Other Protestant bodies	14	14	1,225	14	501	724
20	Roman Catholic Church	27	27	71,845	18	24,970	24,694
21	Jewish congregations	12	9	[1] 1,031	.....	.....	.....
	Eastern Orthodox Churches:						
22	Russian Orthodox Church	1	1	272	1	150	122
23	Greek Orthodox Church	1	1	900	1	800	100
24	All other bodies	3	2	63	2	24	39
1	Newcastle, Pa.	53	52	17,076	47	7,581	9,022
	Protestant bodies	47	46	10,266	43	3,870	6,129
	Baptist bodies:						
3	Baptists—Northern and National (Colored) Conventions	4	4	960	4	338	622
4	Congregationalists	1	1	300	1	120	180
	Disciples or Christians:						
5	Disciples of Christ	3	3	1,417	3	473	944
	Lutheran bodies:						
6	General Council of the Evangelical Lutheran Church in North America	3	3	446	2	117	129
7	Other Lutheran bodies	2	2	98	2	44	54
	Methodist bodies:						
8	Methodist Episcopal Church	10	9	2,576	7	990	1,519
9	Other Methodist bodies	6	6	504	6	189	315
	Presbyterian bodies:						
10	Presbyterian Church in the United States of America	4	4	1,751	4	702	1,049
11	United Presbyterian Church of North America	5	5	1,282	5	502	780
12	Synod of the Reformed Presbyterian Church of North America	1	1	200	1	75	125
13	Protestant Episcopal Church	2	2	430	2	177	253
14	Other Protestant bodies	6	6	302	6	143	159
15	Roman Catholic Church	4	4	6,604	4	3,711	2,893
16	Jewish congregations	1	1	[1] 56	.....	.....	.....
	Eastern Orthodox Churches:						
17	Greek Orthodox Church	1	1	150	.....	.....	.....
1	Newport, Ky.	19	19	12,715	19	5,688	7,027
	Protestant bodies	15	15	5,365	15	2,103	3,262
	Baptist bodies:						
3	Baptists—Southern and National (Colored) Conventions	2	2	669	2	236	433
4	Congregationalists	1	1	207	1	139	68
	Disciples or Christians:						
5	Disciples of Christ	1	1	360	1	160	200
	German Evangelical Protestant bodies:						
6	German Evangelical Protestant Ministers' Association	1	1	655	1	250	405
7	German Evangelical Synod of North America	1	1	1,500	1	700	800

[1] H

DEBT ON CHURCH PROPERTY, PARSONAGES, AND SUNDAY SCHOOLS, FOR EACH CITY OF 25,000 INHABITANTS OR DENOMINATIONS: 1906—Continued.

PLACES OF WORSHIP.					VALUE OF CHURCH PROPERTY.		DEBT ON CHURCH PROPERTY.		PARSONAGES.		SUNDAY SCHOOLS CONDUCTED BY CHURCH ORGANIZATIONS.				
Number of organizations reporting— Church edifices.	Number of organizations reporting— Halls, etc.	Number of church edifices reported.	Seating capacity of church edifices. Number of organizations reporting.	Seating capacity of church edifices. Seating capacity reported.	Number of organizations reporting.	Value reported.	Number of organizations reporting.	Amount of debt reported.	Number of organizations reporting.	Value of parsonages reported.	Number of organizations reporting.	Number of Sunday schools reported.	Number of officers and teachers.	Number of scholars.	
10	19	10	8	4,895	29	$625,480	13	$195,195	1	$1,000	26	26	136	845	40
	1														41
9		11	9	5,070	9	1,272,000	3	30,000	2	28,000	9	10	109	915	42
6		6	6	3,320	7	1,097,000	4	49,500	1	15,000	7	8	127	1,077	43
9	10	9	8	3,205	10	491,250	5	32,040	1	3,000	11	13	123	1,028	44
266	6	290	263	239,792	262	55,811,715	195	11,365,887	212	3,911,800	253	372	7,345	179,951	45
116	152	121	115	71,998	125	8,726,000	67	1,567,560	6	66,100	80	94	448	13,137	46
	3														47
1		2	1	775	1	132,500			1	30,000					48
1		1	1	600	1	30,000					1	1	1	50	49
1	2	1	1	2,500	1	65,000	1	50,000							50
	2										2	2	17	157	51
	5														52
17	6	17	2	500	3	82,000	1	8,000			3	3	16	130	53
154	14	179	151	90,090	156	7,909,709	84	983,254	68	660,700	145	169	3,968	42,412	1
119	11	141	118	65,825	122	6,023,159	57	460,018	52	477,700	126	144	3,744	35,319	2
14		15	14	11,625	14	970,400	6	93,000	4	20,400	14	16	457	3,891	3
9	1	9	9	2,775	9	48,990	5	20,900			10	10	75	731	4
1		1	1	400	1	24,000	1	1,500	1	4,500	1	1	56	400	5
3		3	3	1,475	3	127,500					3	3	57	745	6
3		3	3	1,100	3	55,674	3	8,220	1	4,500	3	3	82	1,052	7
5		5	5	2,300	5	108,000	2	8,000	2	13,000	5	6	88	819	8
3		4	3	800	3	24,500	3	12,500			3	3	57	783	9
22		23	21	10,750	22	884,900	9	29,425	12	94,500	22	22	701	6,499	10
2		2	2	1,400	2	38,900	2	4,300	1	5,000	2	2	30	405	11
2		2	2	1,000	2	69,000	1	14,000	1	7,000	2	2	57	514	12
2		2	2	650	2	13,000	2	3,650			2	2	22	155	13
25		36	25	17,525	25	1,882,500	12	185,050	16	163,000	25	33	1,243	11,688	14
1		1	1	400	1	7,000					1	1	19	125	15
14	1	20	14	5,075	14	887,000	3	8,100	8	110,500	15	16	278	2,453	16
7		9	7	5,700	7	668,000	4	35,900	5	50,300	7	10	390	3,909	17
1		1	1	800	1	125,000	1	5,000			1	1	20	200	18
5	9	5	5	2,050	8	88,795	3	30,473	1	5,000	10	13	112	950	19
26		28	26	19,055	26	1,628,000	21	453,236	16	183,000	15	20	203	6,283	20
7	1	8	6	4,960	7	256,500	5	69,000			3	4	20	660	21
															22
1		1	1	250	1	2,050	1	1,000			1	1	1	150	23
1	2	1													24
43	9	47	41	21,230	45	994,400	23	151,706	15	87,800	49	57	808	8,535	1
38	8	42	36	18,380	40	794,400	20	97,706	11	42,000	46	52	784	7,620	2
3	1	3	3	2,550	3	91,000	2	25,500			4	4	60	805	3
1		2	1	600	1	25,000	1	1,000			1	1	30	300	4
3		3	3	1,750	3	106,000	1	3,500			3	4	74	693	5
3		3	3	800	3	39,000	1	2,500	1	3,000	3	3	30	269	6
	2										2	2	5	64	7
8	1	8	6	3,125	9	126,000	4	7,700	3	19,300	10	10	202	1,969	8
6		9	6	2,280	6	41,100	4	11,006	4	7,700	6	9	82	700	9
4		4	4	2,750	4	127,000	1	2,000	1	4,000	4	4	108	1,090	10
5		5	5	2,575	5	102,000	2	9,000			5	5	116	941	11
1		1	1	600	1	25,000	1	1,000	1	4,000	1	1	22	175	12
2		2	2	650	2	74,000	2	28,000			2	2	19	265	13
2	4	2	2	700	3	38,300	1	6,500	1	4,000	5	7	41	349	14
4		4	4	2,760	4	196,500	3	54,000	4	45,800	3	5	24	915	15
1		1	1	90	1	3,500									16
															17
18	1	20	18	10,954	18	607,000	11	102,825	8	43,000	18	22	385	5,305	1
14	1	16	14	7,950	14	315,000	8	26,325	6	29,000	15	19	369	4,095	2
2		2	2	900	2	25,000					2	2	41	719	3
1		1	1	500	1	13,000	1	6,900	1	6,000	1	1	30	320	4
1		1	1	350	1	15,000					1	1	12	50	5
1		1	1	1,000	1	40,000	1	1,400	1	5,000	1	1	36	419	6
1		1	1	800	1	40,000	1	4,500	1	5,000	1	1	38	503	7

TABLE 7.—ORGANIZATIONS, COMMUNICANTS OR MEMBERS, PLACES OF WORSHIP, VALUE OF CHURCH PROPERTY, MORE IN 1900, BY SELECTED

	DENOMINATION.	Total number of organizations.	COMMUNICANTS OR MEMBERS.				
			Number of organizations reporting.	Total number reported.	Sex.		
					Number of organizations reporting.	Male.	Female.
	Newport, Ky.—Continued.						
	Protestant bodies—Continued.						
	Methodist bodies:						
8	Methodist Episcopal Church	2	2	675	2	227	448
9	African Methodist Episcopal Church	1	1	50	1	15	35
10	Methodist Episcopal Church, South	1	1	219	1	71	148
	Presbyterian bodies:						
11	Presbyterian Church in the United States of America	1	1	250	1	68	182
12	Protestant Episcopal Church	1	1	450	1	123	327
13	Other Protestant bodies	3	3	330	3	114	216
14	Roman Catholic Church	3	3	7,310	3	3,570	3,740
15	Spiritualists	1	1	40	1	15	25
1	Newton, Mass.	42	42	19,368	39	7,818	11,049
2	Protestant bodies	35	35	8,436	32	2,908	5,027
	Baptist bodies:						
3	Baptists—Northern and National (Colored) Conventions	6	6	1,466	6	475	991
4	Congregationalists	7	7	2,701	7	972	1,729
	Methodist bodies:						
5	Methodist Episcopal Church	7	7	1,022	6	344	588
6	Protestant Episcopal Church	8	8	1,442	6	354	677
7	Unitarians	4	4	1,657	4	715	942
8	Other Protestant bodies	3	3	148	3	48	100
9	Roman Catholic Church	4	4	10,839	4	4,848	5,991
10	All other bodies	3	3	93	3	62	31
1	Norfolk, Va.	86	86	28,533	74	10,306	15,609
2	Protestant bodies	75	75	24,077	68	8,471	13,406
	Baptist bodies:						
3	Baptists—Southern Convention	9	9	4,308	8	1,620	2,162
4	Baptists—National Convention (Colored)	11	11	5,641	11	2,090	3,551
5	Christians (Christian Connection)	3	3	474	3	157	317
	Disciples or Christians:						
6	Disciples of Christ	2	2	367	1	23	42
	Lutheran bodies:						
7	United Synod of the Evangelical Lutheran Church in the South	1	1	206	1	92	114
	Methodist bodies:						
8	Methodist Episcopal Church	1	1	22	1	9	13
9	African Methodist Episcopal Church	5	5	2,060	5	725	1,335
10	African Union Methodist Protestant Church	2	2	345	2	155	190
11	African Methodist Episcopal Zion Church	6	6	927	6	401	526
12	Methodist Episcopal Church, South	12	12	5,174	10	1,707	2,573
	Presbyterian bodies:						
13	Presbyterian Church in the United States	8	8	1,632	8	684	948
14	Protestant Episcopal Church	10	10	2,708	8	762	1,554
15	Other Protestant bodies	5	5	213	4	46	81
16	Roman Catholic Church	5	5	4,029	5	1,833	2,196
17	Jewish congregations	4	4	[1] 218	....	....	....
	Eastern Orthodox Churches:						
18	Greek Orthodox Church	1	1	200	....	....	....
	Theosophical societies:						
19	Theosophical Society, American Section	1	1	9	1	2	7
1	Oakland, Cal.	99	95	41,750	87	18,719	21,490
2	Protestant bodies	77	77	14,669	72	5,015	8,603
	Adventist bodies:						
3	Advent Christian Church	1	1	62	1	27	35
4	Seventh-day Adventist Denomination	1	1	452	1	110	342
	Baptist bodies:						
5	Baptists—Northern and National (Colored) Conventions	10	10	1,818	10	719	1,099
6	Free Baptists	1	1	84	1	31	53
7	Church of Christ, Scientist	2	2	302	2	78	224
8	Congregationalists	7	7	2,424	7	812	1,612
	Disciples or Christians:						
9	Disciples of Christ	1	1	450	1	175	275
10	Churches of Christ	1	1	10	1	5	5
	Lutheran bodies:						
11	General Council of the Evangelical Lutheran Church in North America	1	1	256	1	94	162
12	Evangelical Lutheran Synodical Conference of America	2	2	399	2	162	237
13	Other Lutheran bodies	3	3	300	3	124	176
	Methodist bodies:						
14	Methodist Episcopal Church	14	14	2,587	13	1,055	1,492
15	African Methodist Episcopal Church	1	1	250	....	....	....
16	Other Methodist bodies	2	2	315	2	122	193
	Presbyterian bodies:						
17	Presbyterian Church in the United States of America	9	9	2,482	8	837	1,632
18	Other Presbyterian bodies	3	3	134	3	69	65
19	Protestant Episcopal Church	5	5	1,367	3	198	421
20	Unitarians	1	1	208	1	61	147
21	Other Protestant bodies	12	12	769	12	336	433

[1] Heads of families only.

DEBT ON CHURCH PROPERTY, PARSONAGES, AND SUNDAY SCHOOLS, FOR EACH CITY OF 25,000 INHABITANTS OR DENOMINATIONS: 1906—Continued.

PLACES OF WORSHIP.					VALUE OF CHURCH PROPERTY.		DEBT ON CHURCH PROPERTY.		PARSONAGES.		SUNDAY SCHOOLS CONDUCTED BY CHURCH ORGANIZATIONS.				
Number of organizations reporting—		Number of church edifices reported.	Seating capacity of church edifices.		Number of organizations reporting.	Value reported.	Number of organizations reporting.	Amount of debt reported.	Number of organizations reporting.	Value of parsonages reported.	Number of organizations reporting.	Number of Sunday schools reported.	Number of officers and teachers.	Number of scholars.	
Church edifices.	Halls, etc.		Number of organizations reporting.	Seating capacity reported.											
2	...	3	2	1,000	2	$78,000	1	$250	2	$8,000	2	3	85	730	8
1	...	1	1	1,200	1	3,000	1	2,000	...	...	1	2	4	24	9
1	...	1	1	500	1	12,000	...	...	1	5,000	1	1	18	182	10
1	...	1	1	300	1	23,000	...	...	...	...	1	1	30	300	11
1	...	2	1	600	1	34,000	1	1,200	...	...	1	3	37	453	12
2	1	2	2	800	2	32,000	2	10,075	...	...	3	3	38	395	13
3	...	3	3	2,504	3	285,000	2	75,000	2	14,000	3	3	16	1,210	14
1	...	1	1	500	1	7,000	1	1,500	...	...	...	...	...	...	15
38	4	44	38	21,429	38	2,114,414	16	117,995	18	111,400	38	38	827	6,225	1
34	1	40	34	15,637	34	1,641,414	14	104,095	14	81,900	35	35	707	5,099	2
6	...	6	6	2,340	6	203,300	4	8,555	1	10,000	6	6	109	906	3
7	...	7	7	5,255	7	611,100	1	27,000	3	24,400	7	7	215	1,818	4
7	...	7	7	2,585	7	195,000	3	19,340	6	30,000	7	7	217	1,069	5
8	...	11	8	2,332	8	264,014	4	25,400	4	17,500	8	8	87	733	6
4	...	5	4	2,325	4	317,000	2	23,800	...	...	4	4	59	431	7
2	1	4	2	800	2	51,000	...	...	...	...	3	3	20	142	8
4	...	4	4	5,792	4	473,000	2	13,900	4	29,500	3	3	120	1,126	9
...	3	...	...	...	...	...	...	...	...	...	...	...	...	...	10
76	6	84	75	40,107	77	1,763,943	33	181,840	27	154,500	83	95	1,431	15,330	1
68	5	76	68	36,887	70	1,531,943	31	164,840	24	135,500	75	85	1,387	14,571	2
9	...	10	9	5,200	9	284,500	4	27,400	2	14,000	9	11	262	3,389	3
11	...	11	11	6,952	11	199,700	4	25,675	1	2,000	11	11	152	2,105	4
3	...	3	3	1,200	3	35,100	1	800	1	3,000	3	3	46	440	5
2	...	2	2	650	2	23,000	1	600	...	...	2	3	30	285	6
1	...	1	1	450	1	25,000	...	...	1	5,000	1	1	21	126	7
1	...	1	1	250	1	1,000	...	...	...	...	1	1	6	29	8
5	...	5	5	3,800	5	73,500	4	16,550	3	9,800	5	5	93	1,204	9
2	...	2	2	1,050	2	11,100	2	880	...	...	2	2	17	290	10
5	1	5	5	2,125	5	30,300	1	10,835	...	...	6	6	60	390	11
12	...	13	12	7,050	12	381,318	5	35,800	7	38,000	12	14	378	3,558	12
8	...	10	8	4,010	8	225,500	6	28,800	5	30,000	8	11	170	1,272	13
8	...	12	8	3,925	8	226,600	2	9,500	4	33,700	10	12	127	1,309	14
1	4	1	1	225	3	15,325	1	8,000	...	...	5	5	25	144	15
5	...	5	5	2,520	5	154,000	1	2,000	3	19,000	4	6	32	496	16
2	...	2	2	700	2	78,000	1	15,000	...	...	4	4	12	263	17
1	...	1	...	...	...	...	...	...	...	...	...	...	...	...	18
...	1	...	...	...	...	...	...	...	...	...	...	...	...	...	19
78	16	82	74	33,700	75	2,630,765	35	171,098	22	109,150	81	97	1,343	12,246	1
62	12	65	62	26,630	63	2,194,465	27	99,170	15	58,000	70	83	1,254	10,329	2
1	...	1	1	200	1	5,000	...	...	...	...	1	1	11	60	3
1	...	1	1	525	1	20,000	...	...	...	...	1	1	37	250	4
10	...	10	10	4,625	10	286,600	-	36,500	...	...	10	10	163	1,392	5
1	...	1	1	200	1	4,000	...	...	...	...	1	1	9	61	6
1	1	1	1	725	2	138,215	...	...	...	...	2	2	11	88	7
6	...	6	6	3,580	6	472,000	3	13,650	...	...	6	11	274	1,990	8
...	1	...	...	...	...	...	...	...	...	...	1	1	20	325	9
...	1	...	...	...	...	...	...	...	...	...	...	...	...	...	10
1	...	1	1	275	1	25,000	1	1,100	...	...	1	1	10	60	11
2	...	2	2	650	2	32,000	1	1,850	1	6,000	2	2	22	145	12
3	...	3	3	750	3	47,500	2	11,500	1	1,000	3	4	26	227	13
12	1	12	12	5,015	12	377,000	6	9,370	7	24,500	14	15	208	1,920	14
1	...	1	1	700	1	25,000	1	3,700	...	...	1	1	12	150	15
2	...	2	2	600	2	16,000	...	...	1	3,000	2	2	25	356	16
8	...	8	8	3,800	8	424,500	1	2,000	2	9,000	8	11	268	1,875	17
2	...	2	2	375	1	30,000	1	800	1	10,000	2	2	14	184	18
5	...	7	5	2,135	5	119,000	2	5,500	1	2,500	5	7	74	702	19
1	...	2	1	600	1	125,000	...	...	...	...	1	1	7	35	20
5	7	5	5	1,875	6	47,650	4	13,200	1	2,000	9	10	63	509	21

TABLE 7.—ORGANIZATIONS, COMMUNICANTS OR MEMBERS, PLACES OF WORSHIP, VALUE OF CHURCH PROPERTY, MORE IN 1900, BY SELECTED

	DENOMINATION.	Total number of organizations.	COMMUNICANTS OR MEMBERS.				
			Number of organizations reporting.	Total number reported.	Sex.		
					Number of organizations reporting.	Male.	Female.
	Oakland, Cal.—Continued.						
22	Roman Catholic Church	7	7	25,959	7	13,380	12,579
23	Jewish congregations	2	2	[1] 140	....	....	....
	Eastern Orthodox Churches:						
24	Greek Orthodox Church	1	1	350	....	....	....
	Latter-day Saints:						
25	Reorganized Church of Jesus Christ of Latter-day Saints	1	1	213	1	77	136
26	All other bodies	11	7	419	7	247	172
1	Omaha, Nebr.	106	1	33,900		12,654	16,243
2	Protestant bodies	85	[illegible]	16,612	85 / 78	5,182	8,582
	Baptist bodies:						
3	Baptists—Northern Convention	9	9	1,923	8	696	1,222
4	Church of Christ, Scientist	1	1	335	1	85	250
5	Congregationalists	8	8	1,184	8	390	794
	Disciples or Christians:						
6	Disciples of Christ	2	2	1,184	1	69	115
	Lutheran bodies:						
7	General Synod of the Evangelical Lutheran Church in the United States of America	3	3	656	3	278	378
8	General Council of the Evangelical Lutheran Church in North America	4	4	747	4	304	443
9	Evangelical Lutheran Synodical Conference of America	2	2	427	2	169	258
10	Other Lutheran bodies	3	3	405	2	127	178
	Methodist bodies:						
11	Methodist Episcopal Church	13	13	2,958	12	935	1,523
12	Other Methodist bodies	2	2	272	2	88	184
	Presbyterian bodies:						
13	Presbyterian Church in the United States of America	11	11	2,	11	1,052	1,570
14	United Presbyterian Church of North America	2	2	622	2	224	359
15	Protestant Episcopal Church	10	10	2,[illegible]	6	396	583
	Swedish Evangelical bodies:						
16	Swedish Evangelical Mission Covenant of America	1	1	335	1	103	232
17	Swedish Evangelical Free Mission	1	1	60	1	23	37
18	Other Protestant bodies	13	12	827	11	243	456
19	Roman Catholic Church	12	12	15,053	12	7,	7,613
20	Jewish congregations	6	5	[1] 335	....	440	....
	Eastern Orthodox Churches:						
21	Greek Orthodox Church	1	1	1,500	....	....	....
	Latter-day Saints:						
22	Reorganized Church of Jesus Christ of Latter-day Saints	1	1	320	....	....	....
23	Spiritualists	1	1	80	1	32	48
1	Oshkosh, Wis.	36	36	14	33	6,414	8,123
2	Protestant bodies	28	28	7,967 650	26	2,757	4,488
	Baptist bodies:						
3	Baptists—Northern Convention	2	2	345	2	106	239
4	Congregationalists	2	2	628	2	187	441
5	German Evangelical Synod of North America	2	2	550	1	86	109
	Lutheran bodies:						
6	Evangelical Lutheran Synodical Conference of America	3	3	1,781	3	812	969
7	Evangelical Lutheran Joint Synod of Ohio and Other States	1	1	1,250	1	465	785
8	Evangelical Lutheran Synod of Iowa and Other States	1	1	683	1	320	363
9	United Danish Evangelical Lutheran Church in America	1	1	146	1	69	77
	Methodist bodies:						
10	Methodist Episcopal Church	4	4	885	4	338	547
11	Other Methodist bodies	2	2	65	2	18	47
	Presbyterian bodies:						
12	Presbyterian Church in the United States of America	2	2	366	2	125	241
13	Welsh Calvinistic Methodist Church	1	1	81	1	31	50
14	Protestant Episcopal Church	3	3	594	2	117	427
15	Other Protestant bodies	4	4	276	4	83	193
16	Roman Catholic Church	6	6	7,275	6	3,650	3,625
17	Jewish congregations	1	1	[1] 25	....	....	....
	Latter-day Saints:						
18	Church of Jesus Christ of Latter-day Saints	1	1	17	1	7	10
1	Passaic, N. J.	47	42	22,286	36	9,133	10,354
2	Protestant bodies	34	32	6,363	30	2,394	3,464
	Baptist bodies:						
3	Baptists—Northern and National (Colored) Conventions	3	3	576	3	220	356
4	Congregationalists	1	1	154	1	64	90
5	Independent churches	2	2	265	2	110	155
	Lutheran bodies:						
6	General Council of the Evangelical Lutheran Church in North America	2	2	761	2	377	384
7	Slovak Evangelical Lutheran Synod of America	1	1	336	1	200	136
	Methodist bodies:						
8	Methodist Episcopal Church	3	3	638	3	221	417
9	African Union Methodist Protestant Church	1	1	200	1	55	145
10	Other African Methodist bodies	2	1	100	1	25	75
	Presbyterian bodies:						
11	Presbyterian Church in the United States of America	3	3	649	3	239	410
12	Protestant Episcopal Church	2	2	470	1	23	47

[1] Heads of families only.

DEBT ON CHURCH PROPERTY, PARSONAGES, AND SUNDAY SCHOOLS, FOR EACH CITY OF 25,000 INHABITANTS OR DENOMINATIONS: 1906—Continued.

PLACES OF WORSHIP. Number of organizations reporting—Church edifices.	PLACES OF WORSHIP. Number of organizations reporting—Halls, etc.	PLACES OF WORSHIP. Number of church edifices reported.	PLACES OF WORSHIP. Seating capacity of church edifices. Number of organizations reporting.	PLACES OF WORSHIP. Seating capacity of church edifices. Seating capacity reported.	VALUE OF CHURCH PROPERTY. Number of organizations reporting.	VALUE OF CHURCH PROPERTY. Value reported.	DEBT ON CHURCH PROPERTY. Number of organizations reporting.	DEBT ON CHURCH PROPERTY. Amount of debt reported.	PARSONAGES. Number of organizations reporting.	PARSONAGES. Value of parsonages reported.	SUNDAY SCHOOLS CONDUCTED BY CHURCH ORGANIZATIONS. Number of organizations reporting	SUNDAY SCHOOLS CONDUCTED BY CHURCH ORGANIZATIONS. Number of Sunday schools reported.	SUNDAY SCHOOLS CONDUCTED BY CHURCH ORGANIZATIONS. Number of officers and teachers.	SUNDAY SCHOOLS CONDUCTED BY CHURCH ORGANIZATIONS. Number of scholars.	
7		7	7	5,170	7	$351,800	5	$54,128	7	$51,150	6	8	67	1,635	22
2		3	2	1,200	2	70,000	1	15,000			2	2	8	140	23
	1														24
1		1	1	250	1	3,000					1	1	6	52	25
	3	6	2	450	2	11,500	2	2,800			2	3	8	90	26
98	7	109	91	39,509	97	2,587,600	45	175,938	41	103,400	92	108	1,475	15,980	1
78	6	90	76	32,644	81	1,622,350	39	116,438	33	71,400	79	94	1,401	13,389	2
9		11	8	3,550	9	136,200	2	1,420	2	1,600	8	11	158	1,609	3
	1				1	7,500					1	1	28	145	4
8		8	8	2,400	8	180,400	3	5,250	3	6,100	8	9	134	1,005	5
2		3	2	1,800	2	91,500	2	10,900			2	3	44	789	6
3		4	3	1,950	3	167,000	3	9,500	1	500	3	3	62	553	7
4		5	4	1,800	4	82,000	1	3,500	2	7,000	4	4	57	384	8
2		2	2	1,000	2	9,500	2	245	2	1,500					9
3		3	3	1,050	3	12,400	1	900	3	4,500	3	3	44	205	10
13		13	13	5,690	13	255,400	6	27,250	5	9,200	13	14	285	2,576	11
2		2	2	800	2	19,000			2	1,400	2	2	29	233	12
11		13	11	4,104	11	128,900	6	13,503	4	11,500	11	1	285		13
2		2	2	900	2	55,000	1	6,000			2	7	55	3,283	14
9		14	9	3,850	10	371,200	3	13,200	5	16,700	10	14	104	1,006	15
1		1	1	1,000	1	30,000	1	1,200	1	3,000	1	2	35	325	16
1		1	1	350	1	5,000	1	750			1	1	11	40	17
8	5	8	7	2,400	9	71,350	7	22,820	3	8,400	10	10	91	575	18
12		14	11	5,565	12	889,750	4	33,000	8	32,000	11	12	54	2,386	19
3		3	3	1,100	3	75,000	2	26,500			1	1	6	125	20
1		1													21
1		1	1	200	1	500					1	1	14	80	22
	1														23
33	2	34	33	15,752	34	483,750	18	59,570	21	69,800	31	36	512	4,928	1
26	1	27	26	11,750	27	417,750	13	32,870	15	58,000	23	27	471	3,604	2
2		2	2	950	2	54,000	1	6,000			2	2	39	285	3
2		2	2	1,000	2	47,000	1	750	1	5,000	2	2	48	394	4
2		2	2	650	2	12,100	2	2,470	2	5,700	2	2	55	387	5
3		3	3	1,585	3	35,300	2	5,000	3	9,700					6
1		1	1	900	1	18,000	1	3,000	1	5,000					7
1		1	1	650	1	20,000	1	8,900	1	4,500	1	1	14	185	8
1		1	1	300	1	7,500	1	850			1	1	10	80	9
4		5	4	1,950	4	88,000	1	2,000	3	8,500	4	5	107	791	10
2		2	2	450	2	2,900			1	600	2	2	9	58	11
2		2	2	1,400	2	64,000	1	1,500	1	7,500	2	5	70	652	12
1		1	1	400	1	7,000					1	1	13	60	13
3		3	3	895	3	47,900	1	1,600	1	9,000	2	2	67	486	14
2	1	2	2	620	3	14,050	1	800	1	2,500	4	4	39	226	15
6		6	6	3,950	6	63,000	4	25,850	6	11,800	6	7	29	1,281	16
1		1	1	52	1	3,000	1	850			1	1	1	16	17
	1										1	1	11	27	18
35	9	39	34	16,570	35	942,022	26	341,262	16	101,800	34	38	578	6,406	1
26	8	28	26	11,520	27	575,022	18	106,062	11	61,800	29	32	548	5,416	2
3		4	3	1,280	3	48,500	3	3,800	1	6,500	3	5	63	747	3
1		1	1	300	1	4,700	1	4,000	1	3,300	1	1	20	210	4
2		2	2	650	2	17,000	2	5,100	1	3,000	1	1	14	150	5
2		2	2	600	2	62,972	1	35,202			2	2		445	6
1		1	1	350	1	4,500					1	1	25	100	7
3		3	3	1,000	3	70,000			1	5,000	3	4	98	670	8
1		1	1	400	1	3,000	1	300			1	1	12	200	9
1	1	1	1	450	1	4,500	1	1,500			1	1	6	40	10
3		3	3	950	3	69,800	2	5,050	2	14,000	3	3	90	663	11
1	1	1	1	500	1	50,000	1	14,000			2	2	19	235	12

TABLE 7.—ORGANIZATIONS, COMMUNICANTS OR MEMBERS, PLACES OF WORSHIP, VALUE OF CHURCH PROPERTY, MORE IN 1900, BY SELECTED

	DENOMINATION.	Total number of organizations.	COMMUNICANTS OR MEMBERS.				
			Number of organizations reporting.	Total number reported.	Sex.		
					Number of organizations reporting.	Male.	Female.
	Passaic, N. J.—Continued.						
	Protestant bodies—Continued.						
	Reformed bodies:						
13	Reformed Church in America	3	3	1,331	3	535	796
14	Christian Reformed Church	3	3	388	2	130	153
15	Hungarian Reformed Church in America	1	1	220	1	100	120
16	Other Protestant bodies	7	6	275	6	95	180
17	Roman Catholic Church	7	7	15,479	5	6,559	6,770
18	Jewish congregations	5	2	[1] 144	......	......	......
19	Polish National Church of America	1	1	300	1	180	120
1	Paterson, N. J.	88	88	45,967	75	11,590	16,405
	Protestant bodies	71	71	17,329	67	6,087	10,218
	Baptist bodies:						
3	Baptists—Northern Convention	7	7	2,107	7	599	1,508
4	Baptists—National Convention (Colored)	2	2	418	2	119	299
	Lutheran bodies:						
5	Evangelical Lutheran Synodical Conference of America	2	2	563	2	237	326
6	Other Lutheran bodies	3	3	240	2	75	120
	Methodist bodies:						
7	Methodist Episcopal Church	12	12	3,205	12	1,130	2,075
8	Other Methodist bodies	4	4	460	4	128	332
	Presbyterian bodies:						
9	Presbyterian Church in the United States of America	11	11	2,443	10	756	1,477
10	United Presbyterian Church of North America	1	1	291	1	152	139
11	Protestant Episcopal Church	5	5	2,521	3	714	1,038
	Reformed bodies:						
12	Reformed Church in America	8	8	3,190	8	1,372	1,818
13	Christian Reformed Church	4	4	1,161	4	530	631
14	Other Protestant bodies	12	12	730	12	275	455
15	Roman Catholic Church	10	10	27,961	.	5,493	6,157
16	Jewish congregations	5	5	[1] 587	......	......	......
17	All other bodies	2	2	90	1	10	30
1	Pawtucket, R. I.	37	36	22,327	34	10,269	11,773
2	Protestant bodies	26	26	5,595	26	1,837	3,758
	Baptist bodies:						
3	Baptists—Northern Convention	5	5	1,019	5	316	703
4	Free Baptists	2	2	313	2	104	209
5	Congregationalists	4	4	1,467	4	440	1,027
	Methodist bodies:						
6	Methodist Episcopal Church	2	2	537	2	164	373
7	African Methodist Episcopal Zion Church	1	1	10	1	4	6
8	Protestant Episcopal Church	6	6	1,564	6	558	1,006
9	Universalists	1	1	248	1	59	189
10	Other Protestant bodies	5	5	437	5	192	245
11	Roman Catholic Church	6	6	16,346	6	8,356	7,990
12	Jewish congregations	2	1	[1] 35	......	......	......
	Eastern Orthodox Churches:						
13	Greek Orthodox Church	1	1	250	......	......	......
14	All other bodies	2	2	101	2	76	25
1	Peoria, Ill.	68	66	28,779	60	10,397	14,136
	Protestant bodies	55	54	11,046	51	3,722	6,757
	Baptist bodies:						
3	Baptists—Northern and National (Colored) Conventions	4	4	975	4	364	611
4	Church of Christ, Scientist	1	1	232	1	55	177
5	Congregationalists	5	5	1,267	5	455	812
	Disciples or Christians:						
6	Disciples of Christ	2	2	650	2	173	477
	Lutheran bodies:						
7	General Synod of the Evangelical Lutheran Church in the United States of America	1	1	47	......	......	......
8	General Council of the Evangelical Lutheran Church in North America	1	1	400	......	......	......
9	Evangelical Lutheran Synodical Conference of America	2	2	1,137	2	450	687
10	Evangelical Lutheran Synod of Iowa and Other States	3	3	878	3	335	543
	Methodist bodies:						
11	Methodist Episcopal Church	9	9	1,716	9	619	1,097
12	Other Methodist bodies	2	2	126	2	41	85
	Presbyterian bodies:						
13	Presbyterian Church in the United States of America	8	8	2,035	8	726	1,309
14	Protestant Episcopal Church	3	3	666	3	224	442
15	Other Protestant bodies	14	13	917	12	280	517
16	Roman Catholic Church	9	9	17,413	8	6,652	7,349
17	Jewish congregations	2	1	[1] 117	......	......	......
18	All other bodies	2	2	203	1	23	30
1	Philadelphia, Pa.	907	892	558,866	758	220,972	283,150
2	Protestant bodies	745	741	254,812	656	82,335	133,315
	Baptist bodies:						
3	Baptists—Northern Convention	93	93	37,141	82	12,115	19,940
4	Baptists—National Convention (Colored)	16	16	7,227	14	2,398	3,873
5	Other Baptist bodies	2	2	62	2	21	41

DEBT ON CHURCH PROPERTY, PARSONAGES, AND SUNDAY SCHOOLS, FOR EACH CITY OF 25,000 INHABITANTS OR DENOMINATIONS: 1906—Continued.

PLACES OF WORSHIP. Number of organizations reporting— Church edifices.	Halls, etc.	Number of church edifices reported.	Seating capacity of church edifices. Number of organizations reporting.	Seating capacity reported.	VALUE OF CHURCH PROPERTY. Number of organizations reporting.	Value reported.	DEBT ON CHURCH PROPERTY. Number of organizations reporting.	Amount of debt reported.	PARSONAGES. Number of organizations reporting.	Value of parsonages reported.	SUNDAY SCHOOLS CONDUCTED BY CHURCH ORGANIZATIONS. Number of organizations reporting.	Number of Sunday schools reported.	Number of officers and teachers.	Number of scholars.	
3		4	3	3,100	3	$175,000	2	$19,600	3	$21,500	3	3	131	1,281	13
3		3	3	1,260	3	41,000	2	10,500	2	8,500	3	3	51	534	14
1		1	1	400	1	12,000	1	7,000							15
1	6	1	1	280	2	12,050	1	10			5	5	17	141	16
6	1	7	6	4,150	5	348,000	5	224,000	4	39,000	4	5	29	950	17
2		3	1	300	2	13,000	2	6,200	1	1,000	1	1	1	40	18
1		1	1	600	1	6,000	1	5,000							19
78	9	84	76	40,112	79	2,284,860	56	460,030	34	192,500	77	85	1,852	20,177	1
63	7	68	61	31,407	64	1,795,960	45	270,630	28	137,100	68	76	1,729	17,948	2
7		8	7	5,150	7	266,860	7	40,600			7	8	260	2,679	3
2		2	2	780	2	36,000	2	2,700			2	2	11	68	4
2		2	2	500	2	12,500	2	6,880	2	5,200	2	4	40	370	5
2	1	2	1	150	2	8,000	2	3,850			3	3	27	227	6
12		13	12	5,212	12	328,000	8	56,600	9	63,300	12	14	398	3,635	7
4		4	4	1,500	4	29,500	3	2,650	1	3,000	4	4	55	523	8
11		12	11	5,725	11	509,000	6	42,700	3	16,000	11	13	280	3,168	9
1		1	1	400	1	20,000					1	1	26	317	10
5		7	4	1,750	4	218,500	2	41,500	2	11,000	5	5	175	2,054	11
8		8	8	5,350	8	230,000	7	26,150	5	20,500	8	9	277	2,951	12
4		4	4	2,570	4	75,500	4	34,500	4	12,500	4	4	106	1,245	13
5	6	5	5	2,020	7	62,100	2	12,500	2	5,600	9	9	79	711	14
10		11	10	5,755	10	332,900	8	155,400	6	55,400	6	6	114	2,034	15
5		5	5	2,950	5	156,000	3	34,000			5	3	9	195	16
															17
29	6		28	15,145	31	859,725	15	87,665	11	92,500	32	33	747	9,035	1
22	3	34	22	10,445	23	523,175	11	34,465	6	34,500	25	25	558	5,808	2
5		5	5	2,750	5	132,500	3	6,800			5		112	1,206	3
2		2	2	650	2	23,000	1	265			2		49	365	4
4			4	2,650	4	146,000	2	14,500			4	4	147	1,810	5
2		2	2	1,100	2	42,000	1	4,700	1	6,000	2	2	59	619	6
	1										1	1	2	9	7
5		6	5	1,995	5	120,000	1	1,350	3	20,000	5	5	111	1,125	8
1		1	1	500	1	40,000			1	3,500	1	1	37	372	9
3	2	3	3	800	4	19,675	3	6,850	1	5,000	5	5	41	302	10
6		10	5	4,500	6	332,500	3	51,000	5	58,000	6	7	188	3,202	11
1		1	1	200	1	4,000	1	2,200			1	1	1	25	12
	1														13
	2				1	50									14
60	6	64	60	28,552	63	1,375,125	23	118,363	26	136,600	60	68	820	9,047	1
50	3	53	50	22,152	53	887,125	18	54,863	20	74,100	50	57	770	7,601	2
3	1	4	3	1,850	3	76,500	1	6,700	1	2,000	4	5	65	499	3
1		1	1	630	1	30,000					1	1	11	61	4
5		5	5	2,950	5	135,500	1	3,000	1	3,000	5	7	113	1,347	5
2		2	2	825	2	50,000					2	2	25	400	6
1		1	1	400	1	20,000	1	5,000	1	8,000	1	1	7	76	7
1		1	1	450	1	15,000	1	7,100			1	1	14	94	8
2		2	2	1,400	2	21,500	1	7,000	2	7,000	1	1	8	100	9
3		4	3	1,260	3	43,400	3	11,250	3	6,400	3	3	24	332	10
9		10	9	3,425	9	105,000	4	6,700	5	17,500	9	10	158	1,230	11
2		2	2	800	2	16,000	1	1,613	2	3,200	2	2	17	110	12
8		8	8	4,295	8	236,500			2	11,000	8	9	182	2,059	13
3		3	3	1,150	3	71,000	1	1,500	1	11,000	3	3	32	385	14
10	2	10	10	2,717	13	66,725	4	5,000	2	5,000	10	12	114	908	15
8	1	9	8	5,600	8	453,000	5	63,500	6	62,500	7	8	34	1,336	16
2		2	2	800	2	35,000					2	2	8	90	17
	2										1	1	8	20	18
797	88	925	786	566,224	798	46,160,711	431	4,185,345	324	2,785,156	799	910	22,933	274,830	1
669	65	777	664	463,381	675	35,004,561	349	2,667,211	238	1,658,956	706	777	20,547	223,739	2
87	4	101	85	59,147	87	3,765,700	56	423,030	10	61,000	89	100	2,899	30,277	3
11	5	12	11	6,175	11	256,500	7	70,800	2	9,900	16	16	177	2,478	4
1	1	1	1	150	1	3,100					1	1	5	40	5

TABLE 7.—ORGANIZATIONS, COMMUNICANTS OR MEMBERS, PLACES OF WORSHIP, VALUE OF CHURCH PROPERTY, MORE IN 1900, BY SELECTED

	DENOMINATION.	Total number of organizations.	COMMUNICANTS OR MEMBERS.				
			Number of organizations reporting.	Total number reported.	Sex.		
					Number of organizations reporting.	Male.	Female.
	Philadelphia, Pa.—Continued.						
	Protestant bodies—Continued.						
6	Brethren (Plymouth)	8	8	585	8	246	339
7	Church of Christ, Scientist	1	1	467			
8	Church of God and Saints of Christ (Colored)	1	1	400	1	130	270
	Churches of the New Jerusalem:						
9	General Convention of the New Jerusalem in the United States of America	2	2	515	2	175	
10	General Church of the New Jerusalem	1	1	55	1	25	340
11	Congregationalists	8	8	2,357	8	919	1,438
	Disciples or Christians:						
12	Disciples of Christ	4	4	1,034	3	226	458
13	Churches of Christ	3	3	126	3	57	69
	Dunkers or German Baptist Brethren:						
14	German Baptist Brethren Church (Conservative)	3	3	523		200	323
15	The Brethren Church (Progressive Dunkers)	4	4	456	2	175	251
	Evangelical bodies:						
16	Evangelical Association	6	6	884		416	468
17	United Evangelical Church	5	5	716	6	286	450
	Friends:						
18	Society of Friends (Orthodox)	6	6	1,490	6	717	
19	Religious Society of Friends (Hicksite)	6	6	2,477	6	1,084	1,773
20	Friends (Primitive)	1	1	24	1	8	396
21	Independent churches	19	19	1,302	18	503	772
	Lutheran bodies:						
22	General Synod of the Evangelical Lutheran Church in the United States of America	15	15	3,872	15	1,456	2,416
23	General Council of the Evangelical Lutheran Church in North America	51	51	16,888		5,737	8,597
24	Evangelical Lutheran Synodical Conference of America	5	5	772		291	361
25	Other Lutheran bodies	3	3	201	46	94	107
	Mennonite bodies:						
26	General Conference of Mennonites of North America	2	2	460	2	197	263
27	Mennonite Brethren in Christ	1	1	32	1	6	26
	Methodist bodies:						
	Methodist Episcopal Church	124	123	44,693	107	14,475	23,
	African Methodist Episcopal Church	14	14	3,675	14	1,239	2,
	African Union Methodist Protestant Church	3		587	3	160	
28	African Methodist Episcopal Zion Church	6		2,005	6	682	1,452
[illegible]	Other Methodist bodies	12	12	1,108	12	439	[illegible]
	Moravian bodies:						
33	Moravian Church (Unitas Fratrum)	4	4	861	4	265	596
	Presbyterian bodies:						
34	Presbyterian Church in the United States of America	107	107	51,716	94	17,024	27,223
35	Welsh Calvinistic Methodist Church	1	1	90	1	35	55
36	United Presbyterian Church of North America	19	19	3,960	19	1,431	2,529
37	Synod of the Reformed Presbyterian Church of North America	4	3	525	3	185	340
38	Reformed Presbyterian Church in North America, General Synod	5	5	1,583	3	370	513
39	Protestant Episcopal Church	108	108	46,644	84	12,889	21,232
	Reformed bodies:						
40	Reformed Church in America	6	6	1,509	6	604	905
41	Reformed Church in the United States	24	24	9,709	21	3,123	5,467
42	Reformed Episcopal Church	11	11	3,165	10	1,063	1,652
43	Unitarians	3	3	725	1	71	104
44	Universalists	4	3	520	3	173	347
45	Other Protestant bodies	24	23	1,671	22	655	1,001
46	Roman Catholic Church	89		289,615		135,391	148,
47	Jewish congregations	54	89	[1] 9,991	87		633
48	Armenian Church	1	47	1,300	1	1,050	250
	Eastern Orthodox Churches:						
49	Russian Orthodox Church	1	1	350	1	300	
50	Greek Orthodox Church	1	1	1,500	1	1,350	
51	Spiritualists	7	7	688	7	269	50
52	All other bodies	9	5	610	5	277	[illegible]
1	Pittsburg, Pa.	318	311	205,847	273	87,794	92,058
2	Protestant bodies	246	244	78,170	222	25,106	38,169
	Baptist bodies:						
3	Baptists—Northern Convention	14	14	3,634		1,233	2,101
4	Baptists—National Convention (Colored)	19	19	5,991	13	2,314	3,677
5	Congregationalists	5	5	858	18	282	576
	Disciples or Christians:						
6	Disciples of Christ	9	9	2,564	7	785	1,043
7	Churches of Christ	1	1	25	1	12	13
	Evangelical bodies:						
8	Evangelical Association	4	4	451	4	153	298
	German Evangelical Protestant bodies:						
9	German Evangelical Protestant Ministers' Association	4	4	2,784	4	1,032	1,752
10	German Evangelical Protestant Ministers' Conference	1	1	1,300	1	525	775
	Lutheran bodies:						
11	General Synod of the Evangelical Lutheran Church in the United States of America	7	7	2,113		566	
12	General Council of the Evangelical Lutheran Church in North America	6	6	2,046		842	1,
13	Evangelical Lutheran Synodical Conference of America	7	7	4,285		1,195	1,797
14	Evangelical Lutheran Joint Synod of Ohio and Other States	4	4	1,402	5	582	[illegible]
	Methodist bodies:						
15	Methodist Episcopal Church	34	34	12,062	31	3,921	
16	African Methodist Episcopal Church	4	4	1,465	4	605	
17	African Methodist Episcopal Zion Church	3	3	820	3	340	
18	Methodist Protestant Church	6	6	1,443	5	451	5,982
19	Other Methodist bodies	9	8	478	8	212	[illegible]

[1] Heads of families only.

DEBT ON CHURCH PROPERTY, PARSONAGES, AND SUNDAY SCHOOLS, FOR EACH CITY OF 25,000 INHABITANTS OR DENOMINATIONS: 1906—Continued.

PLACES OF WORSHIP. Number of organizations reporting— Church edifices.	Halls, etc.	Number of church edifices reported.	Seating capacity of church edifices. Number of organizations reporting.	Seating capacity reported.	VALUE OF CHURCH PROPERTY. Number of organizations reporting.	Value reported.	DEBT ON CHURCH PROPERTY. Number of organizations reporting.	Amount of debt reported.	PARSONAGES. Number of organizations reporting.	Value of parsonages reported.	SUNDAY SCHOOLS CONDUCTED BY CHURCH ORGANIZATIONS. Number of organizations reporting.	Number of Sunday schools reported.	Number of officers and teachers.	Number of scholars.	
	8										6	6	42	318	6
	1										1	1	25	129	7
	1														8
2		3	2	1,275	2	$254,000					2	2	36	251	9
	1				1	200					1	1	4	16	10
8		8	8	4,900	8	315,000	6	$33,300	1	$5,000	8	8	203	2,308	11
		4	4	1,650	4	62,000	3	20,200			4	7	96	1,172	12
	3				2	3,500	1	1,500							13
3		4	3	1,600	3	105,000			3	18,000	3	3	61	850	14
4		4	4	1,125	4	41,100	4	8,800			4	4	38	567	15
6		6	6	2,425	6	105,500	4	25,000	6	23,000	6	6	125	1,190	16
5		5	5	1,600	5	82,000	4	13,150			5	5	103	804	17
6		6	6	3,800	5	368,500					3	3	14	160	18
6		6	6	4,500	4	45,000					5	6	50	533	19
1		1	1	200	1	4,000									20
9	10	9	9	2,550	8	67,600	5	17,400	2	4,500	15	15	193	1,780	21
13	1	14	13	6,450	15	505,500	12	107,050	2	15,000	15	15	444	4,502	22
49	2	54	49	26,450	49	1,976,142	33	349,018	15	92,800	49	50	1,498	13,976	23
2		2	2	935	3	56,500	2	10,600	1	3,500	2	3	24	329	24
	2										2	2	7	29	25
2		2	2	1,000	2	21,000	1	400			2	2	33	459	26
1		1	1	250	1	3,000			1	1,000	1	1	12	60	27
120	3	127	119	76,920	119	5,686,600	65	638,017	82	488,250	123	127	4,471	53,045	28
14		14	14	7,180	14	257,000	13	44,632	7	21,500	14	14	263	2,527	29
3		3	3	1,390	3	22,000	2	1,416			3	3	31	485	30
3	3	3	3	1,775	3	62,230	1	201	2	9,200	6	6	50	595	31
10	1	10	10	4,325	10	129,835	8	34,940	2	13,000	11	11	112	1,193	32
4		4	4	2,460	4	125,000	2	14,180	1	6,000	4	4	90	759	33
105	1	131	105	127,777	104	7,947,400	46	356,008	34	322,800	107	120	4,523	46,966	34
	1				1	200					1	1	6	30	35
19		21	19	8,870	19	688,800	12	61,740	3	15,800	19	19	390	4,289	36
4		4	4	1,475	4	146,000					4	4	48	416	37
5		5	5	3,500	5	180,000	3	18,500			4	4	87	735	38
107	1	153	107	71,592	104	9,489,300	24	170,275	53	493,106	107	133	2,820	33,199	39
5	1	5	5	3,800	5	167,000	3	27,850			6	6	150	1,484	40
23	1	25	23	13,150	23	905,950	17	147,250	8	35,100	24	26	831	9,862	41
11		13	11	7,360	10	588,000	5	32,800	1	7,500	11	18	336	4,050	42
3		3	3	1,600	3	215,000	1	5,000	1	10,000	3	3	27	150	43
4		4	4	1,625	3	246,292	1	4,300			4	4	51	277	44
9	14	9	7	2,400	19	108,112	8	29,854	1	3,000	15	17	172	1,429	45
87	2	105	86	79,213	85	9,109,000	57	1,203,274	75	1,104,500	81	120	2,275	48,977	46
32	11	34	31	21,880	33	1,020,150	23	306,000	10	18,000	7	7	57	1,655	47
	1														48
1		1	1	300	1	4,000	1	2,860	1	3,700					49
1		1	1	600											50
2	5	2	2	600	3	13,000	1	4,000			2	3	12	100	51
5	4	5	1	250	1	10,000					3	3	42	359	52
289	23	322	284	174,451	292	22,444,929	147	1,923,829	115	1,108,300	289	350	5,506	71,077	1
220	21	245	218	122,600	225	15,556,625	107	849,673	69	496,300	234	263	5,039	52,784	2
13		16	13	7,575	13	1,126,700	5	23,000	3	8,300	12	16	276	2,853	3
16	3	16	16	8,182	16	211,500	8	21,050	2	9,000	19	19	198	2,259	4
5		5	4	1,760	5	207,000	4	41,225			5	5	59	503	5
8	1	9	8	3,900	9	172,000	5	34,000	1	8,000	9	9	170	2,080	6
	1														7
4		4	4	1,450	4	99,500			4	18,200	4	4	72	410	8
4		6	3	2,100	4	84,500	2	11,500	4	18,000	4	4	126	955	9
1		1	1	1,800	1	1,160,000	1	49,800			1	1	56	280	10
6		6	6	2,500	7	188,000	4	13,150			7	7	155	1,699	11
6		6	6	3,175	6	519,000	3	12,400	2	7,800	6	9	225	1,113	12
7		9	7	4,800	7	743,500	4	59,200	6	59,800	7	11	101	1,270	13
4		4	4	1,835	4	54,000	4	11,100	4	18,700	4	5	49	600	14
34		36	34	20,075	34	2,229,100	15	125,100	14	113,500	34	37	967	10,381	15
3	1	3	3	2,200	4	132,400	3	35,750	2	15,000	4	5	61	1,037	16
3		3	3	1,200	3	66,500	3	5,600	1	6,000	3	3	38	330	17
6		7	6	3,250	6	365,500	2	5,000	2	10,500	6	6	130	1,385	18
7	2	7	7	2,175	7	45,500	4	5,990	3	5,000	7	7	98	853	19

TABLE 7.—ORGANIZATIONS, COMMUNICANTS OR MEMBERS, PLACES OF WORSHIP, VALUE OF CHURCH PROPERTY, ... MORE IN 1900, BY SELECTED

	DENOMINATION.	Total number of organizations.	COMMUNICANTS OR MEMBERS.				
			Number of organizations reporting.	Total number reported.	Sex.		
					Number of organizations reporting.	Male.	Female.
	Pittsburg, Pa.—Continued.						
	Protestant bodies—Continued.						
	Presbyterian bodies:						
20	Presbyterian Church in the United States of America	32	32	16,884	25	4,027	6,360
21	Cumberland Presbyterian Church	3	3	985	3	397	588
22	United Presbyterian Church of North America	22	22	6,806	22	2,638	4,168
23	Other Presbyterian bodies	4	4	907	4	364	543
24	Protestant Episcopal Church	18	18	5,550	15	1,225	1,772
	Reformed bodies:						
25	Reformed Church in the United States	5	5	1,173	4	522	511
26	Other Protestant bodies	25	24	2,144	24	882	1,262
27	Roman Catholic Church	50	49	120,232	46	58,400	52,907
28	Jewish congregations	15	12	[1] 2,124			
	Eastern Orthodox Churches:						
29	Russian Orthodox Church	1	1	700	1	600	100
30	Servian Orthodox Church	1	1	2,800	1	2,110	690
31	Greek Orthodox Church	1	1	1,500	1	1,450	50
32	All other bodies	4	3	321	2	129	142
1	Portland, Me.	54	53	20,263	50	7,897	11,891
	Protestant bodies	46	46	9,892	44	3,030	6,437
	Baptist bodies:						
3	Baptists—Northern Convention	3	3	1,188	3	403	785
4	Free Baptists	1	1	366	1	84	282
5	Congregationalists	12	12	2,649	12	779	1,870
	Friends:						
6	Society of Friends (Orthodox)	2	2	200	2	89	111
	Lutheran bodies:						
7	General Council of the Evangelical Lutheran Church in North America	1	1	49	1	27	22
8	United Norwegian Lutheran Church in America	1	1	340	1	150	190
9	Danish Evangelical Lutheran Church in America	1	1	250			
	Methodist bodies:						
10	Methodist Episcopal Church	6	6	1,579	5	452	952
11	African Methodist Episcopal Zion Church	1	1	25	1	10	15
12	Protestant Episcopal Church	4	4	1,467	4	441	1,026
13	Unitarians	2	2	598	2	254	344
14	Universalists	4	4	524	4	138	386
15	Other Protestant bodies	8	8	657	8	203	454
16	Roman Catholic Church	4	4	10,162	4	4,769	5,393
17	Jewish congregations	1					
18	All other bodies	3	3	209	2	98	61
1	Portland, Oreg.	165	160	40,282	146	15,576	20,989
2	Protestant bodies	134	131	21,330	125	7,692	12,630
	Adventist bodies:						
3	Advent Christian Church	1	1	70	1	30	40
4	Seventh-day Adventist Denomination	4	4	398	4	152	246
	Baptist bodies:						
5	Baptists—Northern and National (Colored) Conventions	16	16	3,157	16	1,132	2,025
6	Church of Christ, Scientist	2	2	402	2	99	303
7	Congregationalists	7	7	1,599	7	615	984
	Disciples or Christians:						
8	Disciples of Christ	5	5	1,058	5	361	697
9	Churches of Christ	1	1	12	1	7	5
	Evangelical bodies:						
10	Evangelical Association	4	4	394	4	157	237
11	United Evangelical Church	3	3	132	3	44	88
	Lutheran bodies:						
12	General Council of the Evangelical Lutheran Church in North America	2	2	661	2	262	399
13	Evangelical Lutheran Synodical Conference of America	2	2	423	2	197	226
14	Other Lutheran bodies	6	6	543	5	183	248
	Methodist bodies:						
15	Methodist Episcopal Church	21	21	4,053	20	1,515	2,088
16	Other Methodist bodies	6	6	460	6	190	270
	Presbyterian bodies:						
17	Presbyterian Church in the United States of America	12	12	3,399	12	1,175	2,224
18	Cumberland Presbyterian Church	1	1	400	1	133	267
19	United Presbyterian Church of North America	2	2	276	2	107	169
20	Protestant Episcopal Church	12	11	1,865	9	820	960
21	Unitarians	1	1	518	1	154	364
22	Other Protestant bodies	26	24	1,510	22	659	770
23	Roman Catholic Church	16	16	17,781	12	7,366	8,121
24	Jewish congregations	5	4	[1] 414			
25	All other bodies	10	9	757	9	519	238
1	Providence, R. I.	140	137	131,214	118	56,994	63,032
	Protestant bodies	102	101	27,656	94	8,952	17,581
	Baptist bodies:						
3	Baptists—Northern Convention	16	16	6,266	15	2,653	3,889
4	Baptists—National Convention (Colored)	3	3	454	3	142	312
5	Free Baptists	5	5	1,289	5	434	855
6	Congregationalists	11	11	4,603	11	1,501	3,102

[1] Heads of families only.

DEBT ON CHURCH PROPERTY, PARSONAGES, AND SUNDAY SCHOOLS, FOR EACH CITY OF 25,000 INHABITANTS OR DENOMINATIONS: 1906—Continued.

PLACES OF WORSHIP.					VALUE OF CHURCH PROPERTY.		DEBT ON CHURCH PROPERTY.		PARSONAGES.		SUNDAY SCHOOLS CONDUCTED BY CHURCH ORGANIZATIONS.				
Number of organizations reporting—Church edifices.	Number of organizations reporting—Halls, etc.	Number of church edifices reported.	Seating capacity of church edifices. Number of organizations reporting.	Seating capacity of church edifices. Seating capacity reported.	Number of organizations reporting.	Value reported.	Number of organizations reporting.	Amount of debt reported.	Number of organizations reporting.	Value of parsonages reported.	Number of organizations reporting.	Number of Sunday schools reported.	Number of officers and teachers.	Number of scholars.	
32		35	32	22,103	32	$3,557,700	14	$151,950	5	$54,000	32	38	1,054	12,876	20
3		4	3	1,200	3	90,000	3	27,500			3	4	52	883	21
20	1	22	20	13,125	20	1,481,500	7	44,900	4	33,000	22	25	583	5,943	22
4		4	4	2,650	4	386,000	1	5,000			4	5	85	578	23
17		24	17	7,735	16	1,971,000	6	43,958	8	88,000	16	17	251	2,358	24
5		6	5	2,700	5	290,000	3	75,000	1	8,000	5	5	63	640	25
12	12	12	12	5,110	15	375,725	6	47,500	3	15,500	20	21	170	1,548	26
50		58	50	42,521	50	6,016,204	29	971,856	45	607,000	44	76	406	16,626	27
14		14	12	7,830	12	802,000	7	83,800			9	9	48	1,554	28
1		1	1	600	1	5,000	1	4,500	1	5,000					29
	1				1	1,600	1	500							30
1		1	1	300	1	26,000	1	12,000							31
3	1	3	2	600	2	37,500	1	1,500			2	2	13	113	32
44	7	51	43	24,280	48	1,673,150	23	143,640	11	80,000	50	52	1,055	10,170	1
40	4	47	39	20,680	43	1,204,060	20	70,640	8	39,000	45	45	917	8,071	2
3		3	3	2,175	3	108,000	1	5,000			3	3	104	1,069	3
1		1	1	600	1	45,000	1	2,800			1	1	39	433	4
11	1	13	11	6,180	12	367,400	4	32,900	2	8,500	12	12	269	2,229	5
2		2	2	750	2	20,000					2	2	27	248	6
1		1	1	300	1	13,500	1	3,300			1	1	5	21	7
1		1	1	275	1	15,000	1	150			1	1	18	120	8
1		2	1	350	1	5,000	1	3,015	1	2,500	1	1	6	50	9
5		5	5	2,900	6	125,600	3	9,500	3	20,000	6	6	200	2,010	10
1		1	1	200	1	3,000	1	1,600			1	1	8	30	11
4		7	4	2,150	4	229,000	1	2,900	2	8,000	4	4	58	482	12
2		3	2	1,200	2	139,000	1	1,000			2	2	31	225	13
4		4	4	2,375	4	99,000	2	5,200			4	4	81	743	14
4	3	4	3	1,225	5	34,550	3	3,275			7	7	71	411	15
4		4	4	3,600	4	469,000	3	73,000	3	41,000	4	6	132	2,079	16
															17
	3				1	100					1	1	6	20	18
129	24	137	126	50,473	127	2,321,500	54	150,772	58	211,700	140	156	1,821	18,449	1
111	17	119	110	42,803	115	1,992,900	48	110,922	52	183,700	121	136	1,678	15,820	2
1		1	1	250	1	5,000					1	1	9	65	3
3	1	3	3	572	3	11,000	1	1,065			4	4	57	350	4
15	1	15	15	7,300	15	275,500	8	15,400	5	29,200	15	15	222	2,280	5
	1				1	14,000					2	2	31	169	6
7		8	7	3,660	7	142,000	2	10,410	2	4,000	7	8	138	1,490	7
4	1	4	4	1,450	4	43,000	3	6,900			5	5	58	730	8
	1														9
4		4	4	1,200	4	25,600			3	7,300	4	4	67	456	10
3		3	3	650	3	5,550	3	1,260	3	4,000	3	3	28	410	11
2		2	2	1,500	2	78,000	2	30,000	2	11,000	2	2	25	200	12
2		2	2	497	2	20,500	2	1,150	2	2,500	2	2	3	152	13
5	1	5	5	1,650	5	31,850	5	6,290	3	4,300	5	6	32	269	14
20		20	20	7,525	20	312,900	4	2,700	13	41,300	20	22	362	3,181	15
6		6	6	3,100	6	74,500	2	2,750	4	5,500	6	6	38	260	16
12		17	12	5,529	12	395,250	4	11,300	5	39,000	12	18	269	3,211	17
1		1	1	450	1	20,000			1	3,500	1	1	41	490	18
2		2	2	580	2	24,000			2	8,000	2	2	29	273	19
11	1	13	11	3,475	11	334,300	5	9,295	3	8,200	12	13	108	941	20
1		1	1	500	1	90,000	1	1,100			1	1	17	110	21
12	10	12	11	2,925	15	89,960	6	11,312	4	15,900	17	21	144	983	22
11	1	11	10	5,320	6	139,000	4	33,350	6	28,000	12	13	96	2,173	23
3		3	3	1,450	3	186,500	2	6,500			3	3	13	215	24
4	6	4	3	900	3	3,100					4	4	34	241	25
120	15	135	117	74,670	122	4,442,243	57	560,990	37	274,580	124	142	3,310	33,731	1
90	9	103	89	50,490	92	3,005,743	37	216,290	19	105,600	97	115	2,371	21,283	2
16		23	16	12,765	15	573,100	5	59,940	3	21,500	16	24	709	6,740	3
3		3	3	1,800	3	35,000	2	7,500			3	3	36	307	4
5		5	5	2,325	5	107,000	2	550	1	3,500	5	5	120	1,278	5
11		13	11	7,800	11	695,350	1	150	2	7,500	11	17	352	3,247	6

TABLE 7.—ORGANIZATIONS, COMMUNICANTS OR MEMBERS, PLACES OF WORSHIP, VALUE OF CHURCH PROPERTY, MORE IN 1900, BY SELECTED

	DENOMINATION.	Total number of organizations.	COMMUNICANTS OR MEMBERS.				
			Number of organizations reporting.	Total number reported.	Sex.		
					Number of organizations reporting.	Male.	Female.
	Providence, R. I.—Continued.						
	Protestant bodies—Continued.						
	Lutheran bodies:						
7	General Council of the Evangelical Lutheran Church in North America	1	1	704	1	300	404
8	Evangelical Lutheran Synodical Conference of America	1	1	180	...	...	...
	Methodist bodies:						
9	Methodist Episcopal Church	13	13	2,937	11	989	1,876
10	Other Methodist bodies	7	7	563	5	51	140
	Presbyterian bodies:						
11	Presbyterian Church in the United States of America	2	2	596	2	192	404
12	United Presbyterian Church of North America	2	2	410	2	130	280
13	Protestant Episcopal Church	16	15	6,350	14	1,983	4,192
14	Unitarians	4	4	1,221	4	467	754
15	Universalists	2	2	426	2	92	334
16	Other Protestant bodies	19	19	1,657	19	618	1,039
17	Roman Catholic Church	22	22	100,324	19	46,150	44,869
18	Jewish congregations	10	9	[1]760	...	...	...
19	Armenian Church	1	1	1,860	1	1,510	350
20	All other bodies	5	4	614	4	382	232
1	Pueblo, Colo.	56	55	20,288	48	9,509	9,658
	Protestant bodies	42	42	6,625	36	1,919	3,635
	Baptist bodies:						
3	Baptists—Northern Convention	5	5	1,343	5	442	901
4	Congregationalists	5	5	523	5	162	361
	Disciples or Christians:						
5	Disciples of Christ	2	2	758	...	...	...
	Lutheran bodies:						
6	Evangelical Lutheran Synodical Conference of America	1	1	200	...	...	...
7	Other Lutheran bodies	2	2	132	2	57	75
	Methodist bodies:						
8	Methodist Episcopal Church	7	7	1,233	5	444	740
9	African Methodist Episcopal Church	2	2	215	2	60	155
10	Methodist Episcopal Church, South	2	2	253	2	66	187
11	Free Methodist Church of North America	1	1	38	1	15	23
	Presbyterian bodies:						
12	Presbyterian Church in the United States of America	6	6	1,060	6	398	662
13	Other Presbyterian bodies	2	2	238	2	102	136
14	Protestant Episcopal Church	2	2	342	2	98	244
15	Other Protestant bodies	5	5	290	4	75	151
16	Roman Catholic Church	8	8	12,446	8	6,512	5,934
17	Jewish congregations	2	1	[1]50	...	...	...
	Eastern Orthodox Churches:						
18	Russian Orthodox Church	1	1	300	1	250	50
19	Greek Orthodox Church	1	1	800	1	792	8
20	All other bodies	2	2	67	2	36	31
1	Quincy, Ill.	33	33	31,496	27	6,411	8,075
2	Protestant bodies	26	26	11,086	26	4,711	6,375
	Baptist bodies:						
3	Baptists—Northern and National (Colored) Conventions	4	4	1,478	4	546	932
4	Congregationalists	1	1	427	1	131	296
	Disciples or Christians:						
5	Disciples of Christ	1	1	606	1	183	423
6	German Evangelical Synod of North America	3	3	2,949	3	1,300	1,649
	Lutheran bodies:						
7	General Synod of the Evangelical Lutheran Church in the United States of America	1	1	287	1	114	173
8	Evangelical Lutheran Synodical Conference of America	2	2	1,571	2	738	833
	Methodist bodies:						
9	Methodist Episcopal Church	4	4	1,736	4	713	1,023
10	African Methodist Episcopal Church	2	2	264	2	47	217
	Presbyterian bodies:						
11	Presbyterian Church in the United States of America	1	1	425	1	175	250
12	Protestant Episcopal Church	2	2	449	2	164	285
13	Other Protestant bodies	5	5	894	5	600	294
14	Roman Catholic Church	6	6	20,400	1	1,700	1,700
15	Jewish congregations	1	1	[1]10	...	...	...
1	Racine, Wis.	51	51	13,086	45	5,415	6,544
2	Protestant bodies	41	41	8,731	36	3,232	4,400
	Baptist bodies:						
3	Baptists—Northern Convention	3	3	984	3	333	651
4	Congregationalists	2	2	362	2	129	233
	Evangelical bodies:						
5	Evangelical Association	1	1	200	1	75	125
	Lutheran bodies:						
6	General Council of the Evangelical Lutheran Church in North America	2	2	430	2	180	250
7	Evangelical Lutheran Synodical Conference of America	3	3	1,845	3	870	975
8	Hauge's Norwegian Evangelical Lutheran Synod	1	1	244	1	102	142
9	Danish Evangelical Lutheran Church in America	1	1	265	1	130	135
10	United Danish Evangelical Lutheran Church in America	3	3	1,039	2	206	202
11	Other Lutheran bodies	2	2	313	2	140	173

[1] Heads of families only.

DEBT ON CHURCH PROPERTY, PARSONAGES, AND SUNDAY SCHOOLS, FOR EACH CITY OF 25,000 INHABITANTS OR DENOMINATIONS: 1906—Continued.

PLACES OF WORSHIP.					VALUE OF CHURCH PROPERTY.		DEBT ON CHURCH PROPERTY.		PARSONAGES.		SUNDAY SCHOOLS CONDUCTED BY CHURCH ORGANIZATIONS.				
Number of organizations reporting—		Number of church edifices reported.	Seating capacity of church edifices.		Number of organizations reporting.	Value reported.	Number of organizations reporting.	Amount of debt reported.	Number of organizations reporting.	Value of parsonages reported.	Number of organizations reporting.	Number of Sunday schools reported.	Number of officers and teachers.	Number of scholars.	
Church edifices.	Halls, etc.		Number of organizations reporting.	Seating capacity reported.											
1	....	1	1	300	1	$16,500	1	$4,000	....	....	1	2	24	141	7
1	....	1	1	150	1	3,000	1	800	1	$3,800	1	1	14	135	8
12	1	12	12	6,225	12	353,000	8	50,800	4	9,800	13	13	347	3,058	9
7	....		7	2,650	7	103,500	7	22,850	1	2,500	6	6	80	662	10
2	....		2	750	2	40,000	1	2,800	....	....	2	2	32	300	11
2	....		2	900	2	37,000	1	2,400	....	....	2	2	55	390	12
16	....	1	16	7,750	15	476,940	4	41,500	5	51,000	15	18	377	3,386	13
3	....		3	2,150	3	255,000	....	....	1	5,000	4	4	36	271	14
2	....		2	1,700	2	169,000	2	11,000	....	....	2	2	41	377	15
9	8	9	8	3,225	13	141,353	2	12,000	1	1,000	16	16	148	991	16
22	....	24	21	20,680	21	1,337,700	15	318,200	18	168,980	22	22	897	11,823	17
6	2	6	6	3,200	7	94,100	5	26,500	....	....	4	4	18	515	18
....	1	....	....	....	....	....	....	....	....	....	....	....	....	....	19
2	3		1	300	2	4,700	....	....	....	....	1	1	24	110	20
46	6		45	14,590	48	484,200	27	58,577	26	60,050	49	53	568	5,805	1
37	2	38	36	11,480	37	367,250	20	42,760	22	48,250	40	44	534	4,954	2
-	....		5	2,050	5	51,000	2	6,500	3	4,500		7	96	765	3
3	....	5	3	900	3	31,350	3	8,080	2	4,500	5	5	55	460	4
[illegible]	....	2	2	900	2	8,500	1	1,000	1	4,000	2	2	38	450	5
1	....	1	1	200	1	3,000	1	2,000	1	2,000	1	1	2	50	6
2	....	2	2	600	2	15,300	2	3,930	1	1,800	2	2	18	108	7
6	1	6	5	2,100	6	85,500	6	15,550	6	14,450	6	6	112	1,029	8
2	....	2	2	500	2	11,000	2	900	1	2,000	2	2	17	112	9
2	....	2	2	550	2	16,900	....	....	1	3,000	2	2	18	158	10
1	....	1	1	175	1	2,000	....	....	1	800	1	1	7	50	11
6	....	7	6	1,935		85,100	1	400	2	5,700	6	7	98	1,105	12
2	....	2	2	450		14,000	....	....	1	500	2	2	21	304	13
2	....	2	2	370		23,600	....	....	....	....	2	2	12	120	14
3	1	3	3	750	6	20,000	2	4,400	2	5,000	4	5	40	243	15
7	1	8	7	2,010	7	94,500	4	13,400	3	10,000	7	7	20	783	16
1	....	1	1	200	1	10,000	....	....	....	....	1	1	4	35	17
....	1	....	....	....	1	3,000	1	1,400	....	....	....	....	....	....	18
1	....	1		900	1	9,200	1	900	1	1,800	....	....	....	....	19
....	2	....	....	....	1	250	1	117	....	....	1	1	10	33	20
30	2		24	16,250	26	606,750	10	26,820	12	38,100	28	37	536	5,801	1
24	2	26	23	15,950	25	598,750	10	26,820	12	38,100	25	34	525	5,196	2
4	....	4	4	2,350	4	61,800	2	1,395	2	11,000	4	8	98	1,075	3
1	....	1	1	1,000	1	92,000	....	....	1	8,000	1	1	30	275	4
1	....	2	1	700	1	20,000	....	....	....	....	1	2	30	315	5
3	....	3	3	2,100	3	83,000	2	5,000	3	6,600	3	3	86	762	6
1	....	1	1	800	1	27,000	1	9,000	....	....		1	24	336	7
2	....	2	2	1,750	2	70,000	2	7,000	2	6,000	1	4	47	550	8
4	....	4	3	2,500	4	82,500	1	3,000	2	5,000	4	6	127	1,110	9
2	....	2	2	650	2	12,700	2	1,425	1	500	1	1	14	80	10
1	....	1	1	800	1	60,000	....	....	....	....	1	1	27	350	11
2	....	5	2	1,400	2	47,900	....	....	1	1,000	2	2	18	105	12
3	2	3	3	1,900	4	41,850	....	....	....	....	5	5	24	238	13
5	....		....	....	....	....	....	....	....	....	3	3	11	605	14
1	....	1	1	300	1	8,000	....	....	....	....	....	....	....	....	15
46	5	54	44	21,591	48	697,	27	87,925	28	117,000	45	54		7,019	1
38	3	46	36	17,786	40	499,	20	49,350	22	93,000	38	44	662	5,807	2
3	....	3	3	1,550	3	55,955	2	8,500	2	11,000		3	93	795	3
2	....	2	2	650	2	26,500	....	....	1	3,500	3	2	48	402	4
1	....	1	1	500	1	15,000	....	....	1	4,000	1	1	22	150	5
2	....	2	2	775	2	,000	2	8,200	....	....	2	2		545	6
3	....	4	3	2,030	3	,300	3	9,500	2	7,500	2	2		321	7
1	....	1	1	350	1	,000	1	4,400	....	....	1	1		73	8
1	....	1	1	250	1	,000	1	2,000	1	2,000	1	1		20	9
3	....	4	3	1,400	3	22,000	2	1,900	3	7,800	3	4	60	7'3	10
2	....	2	2	650	2	[illegible],000	2	3,800	2	3,500	2	2	28	194	11

TABLE 7.—ORGANIZATIONS, COMMUNICANTS OR MEMBERS, PLACES OF WORSHIP, VALUE OF CHURCH PROPERTY, MORE IN 1900, BY SELECTED

	DENOMINATION.	Total number of organizations.	COMMUNICANTS OR MEMBERS.				
			Number of organizations reporting.	Total number reported.	Sex.		
					Number of organizations reporting.	Male.	Female.
	Racine, Wis.—Continued.						
	Protestant bodies—Continued.						
	Methodist bodies:						
12	Methodist Episcopal Church	5	5	1,056	4	482	544
13	African Methodist Episcopal Church	1	1	5	1	2	3
	Presbyterian bodies:						
14	Presbyterian Church in the United States of America	2	2	546	2	229	317
15	Welsh Calvinistic Methodist Church	1	1	281	1	112	169
16	Protestant Episcopal Church	6	6	746	3	131	227
17	Other Protestant bodies	8	8	415	8	161	254
18	Roman Catholic Church	7	7	4,264	7	2,139	2,125
19	Jewish congregations	1	1	[1] 28	...	...	...
20	All other bodies	2	2	63	2	44	19
1	Reading, Pa.	87	86	38,976	7	13,797	19,615
2	Protestant bodies	76	75	28,712	70	10,509	16,174
	Baptist bodies:						
3	Baptists—Northern Convention	3	3	1,043	3	351	692
	Evangelical bodies:						
4	Evangelical Association	5	5	952	4	240	428
5	United Evangelical Church	4	4	1,901	4	662	1,239
	Lutheran bodies:						
6	General Synod of the Evangelical Lutheran Church in the United States of America	1	1	500	1	160	340
7	General Council of the Evangelical Lutheran Church in North America	10	10	8,928	8	3,251	4,553
	Methodist bodies:						
8	Methodist Episcopal Church	6	6	1,831	6	635	1,196
9	Other Methodist bodies	2	2	95	2	35	60
	Presbyterian bodies:						
10	Presbyterian Church in the United States of America	3	3	889	2	305	188
11	Protestant Episcopal Church	4	4	1,019	4	451	568
	Reformed bodies:						
12	Reformed Church in the United States	18	18	9,560	18	3,832	5,728
	United Brethren bodies:						
13	Church of the United Brethren in Christ	4	4	976	3	243	508
14	Other Protestant bodies	16	15	1,018	15	344	674
15	Roman Catholic Church		6	9,579	5	3,213	3,391
16	Jewish congregations	6	3	[1] 210	...	...	...
17	All other bodies	3	2	475	1	75	50
1	Richmond, Va.	110	109	54,506	99	20,052	31,304
2	Protestant bodies	99	98	45,475	92	16,113	26,781
	Baptist bodies:						
3	Baptists—Southern Convention	17	17	10,443	17	3,770	6,673
4	Baptists—National Convention (Colored)	20	20	15,791	20	6,436	9,355
	Disciples or Christians:						
5	Disciples of Christ	5	5	2,268	3	386	635
6	German Evangelical Synod of North America	1	1	564	1	275	289
	Lutheran bodies:						
7	United Synod of the Evangelical Lutheran Church in the South	1	1	360	1	160	200
8	Evangelical Lutheran Synodical Conference of America	1	1	300	1	135	165
	Methodist bodies:						
9	Methodist Episcopal Church, South	15	15	6,601	14	2,216	3,860
10	Other Methodist bodies	5	5	563	5	186	377
	Presbyterian bodies:						
11	Presbyterian Church in the United States of America	1	1	130	...	...	...
12	Presbyterian Church in the United States	7	7	3,117	7	1,088	2,029
13	Protestant Episcopal Church	15	14	4,893	13	1,315	2,988
14	Other Protestant bodies	11	11	445	10	146	210
15	Roman Catholic Church	5	5	8,313	5	3,841	4,472
16	Jewish congregations	3	3	[1] 389	...	...	...
17	All other bodies	3	3	329	2	98	51
1	Rochester, N. Y.	112	110	41,951	93	12,753	20,925
2	Protestant bodies	100	98	40,768	91	12,704	20,858
	Baptist bodies:						
3	Baptists—Northern Convention	18	16	6,199	16	2,202	3,997
	Evangelical bodies:						
4	Evangelical Association	2	2	342	2	154	188
5	German Evangelical Synod of North America	3	3	3,400	2	305	595
	Lutheran bodies:						
6	General Council of the Evangelical Lutheran Church in North America	11	11	6,953	9	1,702	2,381
7	Evangelical Lutheran Synodical Conference of America	2	2	559	1	60	99
	Methodist bodies:						
8	Methodist Episcopal Church	12	12	6,008	11	1,776	3,146
9	Other Methodist bodies	2	2	176	2	53	123
	Presbyterian bodies:						
10	Presbyterian Church in the United States of America	15	15	8,805	15	3,266	5,539
11	United Presbyterian Church of North America	1	1	365	1	105	260
12	Protestant Episcopal Church	12	12	4,434	11	1,708	2,476
	Reformed bodies:						
13	Reformed Church in America	3	3	891	3	396	495
14	Reformed Church in the United States	1	1	387	1	164	223
15	Christian Reformed Church	1	1	126	1	54	72

[1] Heads of families only.

DEBT ON CHURCH PROPERTY, PARSONAGES, AND SUNDAY SCHOOLS, FOR EACH CITY OF 25,000 INHABITANTS OR DENOMINATIONS: 1906—Continued.

PLACES OF WORSHIP. Number of organizations reporting— Church edifices.	PLACES OF WORSHIP. Number of organizations reporting— Halls, etc.	PLACES OF WORSHIP. Number of church edifices reported.	PLACES OF WORSHIP. Seating capacity of church edifices. Number of organizations reporting.	PLACES OF WORSHIP. Seating capacity of church edifices. Seating capacity reported.	VALUE OF CHURCH PROPERTY. Number of organizations reporting	VALUE OF CHURCH PROPERTY. Value reported.	DEBT ON CHURCH PROPERTY. Number of organizations reporting.	DEBT ON CHURCH PROPERTY. Amount of debt reported.	PARSONAGES. Number of organizations reporting.	PARSONAGES. Value of parsonages reported.	SUNDAY SCHOOLS CONDUCTED BY CHURCH ORGANIZATIONS. Number of organizations reporting.	SUNDAY SCHOOLS CONDUCTED BY CHURCH ORGANIZATIONS. Number of Sunday schools reported.	SUNDAY SCHOOLS CONDUCTED BY CHURCH ORGANIZATIONS. Number of officers and teachers.	SUNDAY SCHOOLS CONDUCTED BY CHURCH ORGANIZATIONS. Number of scholars.	
5	......	5	5	2,500	5	$63,800	3	$8,400	4	$16,700	5	5	111	1,075	12
1	......	1	1	250	1	1,500	......	......	......	......	1	1	5	18	13
2	......	4	2	1,750	2	46,000	1	800	2	15,000	2	3	57	406	14
1	......	1	......	......	1	27,000	......	......	1	5,000	1	1	25	162	15
6	......	10	6	4,275	5	57,600	1	700	3	17,000	5	5	56	574	16
5	3	5	4	856	8	44,755	2	1,150	......	......	7	11	42	319	17
7	......	7	7	3,555	7	194,000	6	37,075	6	24,000	6	9	26	1,200	18
1	......	1	1	250	1	4,500	1	1,500	......	......	1	1	1	12	19
......	2	......	......	......	......	......	......	......	......	......	......	......	......	......	20
79	5	87	77	48,950	80	2,646,925	31	212,390	31	143,600	77	84	2,406	27,202	1
69		76	68	44,190	72	2,238,425	26	166,590	27	112,600	70	75	2,295	24,992	2
2	......	4	2	1,500	2	118,000	2	23,500	1	4,500	3	5	90	1,301	3
5	......	5	5	2,925	5	76,000	1	5,500	3	12,100	5	5	122	1,279	4
4	......	4	4	2,850	4	124,000	......	......	3	11,800	4	4	174	2,314	5
1	......	1	1	600	1	60,000	......	......	......	......	1	1	38	513	6
10	......	12	9	9,900	10	484,250	4	40,925	3	17,000	9	10	420	5,240	7
5	......	5	5	3,850	5	321,000	2	14,000	4	22,500	5	5	184	1,841	8
2	......	2	2	515	2	11,500	2	5,900	2	4,500	2	2	16	130	9
3	......	4	3	1,950	3	140,000	2	800	1	1,800	3	3	94	678	10
4	......	6	4	1,750	4	124,000	......	......	......	......	4	4	81	677	11
18	......	18	18	12,500	18	599,000	6	58,700	6	24,900	17	17	832	8,873	12
4	......	4	4	2,150	4	56,500	3	12,600	3	11,500	4	4	107	1,180	13
11	5	11	11	3,700	14	124,175	4	4,665	1	2,000	13	15	137	966	14
5	......	6	5	3,460	5	397,000	3	40,500	4	31,000	5	7	104	2,064	15
3	......	3	3	950	2	6,000	1	1,800	......	......	2	2	7	146	16
2	......	2	1	350	1	5,500	1	3,500	......	......	......	......	......	......	17
97	13	106	97	63,215	99	3,078,769	37	140,127	26	179,800	103	127	2,426	26,169	1
89	10	96	89	56,615	92	2,307,769	34	103,627	20	95,500	95	116	2,299	24,439	2
17	......	18	17	11,900	17	505,200	8	31,845	......	......	17	22	633	7,659	3
17	3	17	17	13,450	17	288,270	7	25,000	......	......	20	23	319	3,896	4
5	......	5	5	2,560	5	105,000	1	1,800	......	......	5	5	132	1,129	5
1	......	1	1	600	1	40,000	......	......	......	......	1	1	22	178	6
1	......	1	1	500	1	35,000	......	......	......	......	1	1	20	175	7
1	......	1	1	350	1	20,000	......	......	1	5,500	1	1	12	150	8
15	......	1	15	8,000	15	364,500	5	16,000	10	48,000	14	15	443	4,645	9
5	......	5	5	2,150	5	22,500	4	1,604	1	1,500	5	5	43	343	10
1	......	1	1	300	1	10,000	1	900	1	1,000	1	1	5	35	11
7	......	7	7	4,800	7	279,000	......	......	1	4,000	7	4	267	2,242	12
15	......	21	15	10,925	15	609,000	5	25,850	6	35,500	15	1	369	3,781	13
4	7	4	4	1,080	7	29,299	3	628	......	......	8	26	34	206	14
5	......	7	5	4,400	5	625,000	1	4,000	5	84,000		8	104	1,410	15
3	......	3	3	2,200	2	146,000	2	32,500	1	300	5	3	23	320	16
......	3	......	......	......	......	......	......	......	......	......	......	......	......	......	17
98	11	113	97	58,572	99	3,981,470	61	482,331	34	181,900	1	104	2,813	30,835	1
89	9	102	88	53,552	90	3,720,970	53	414,731	30	176,650	96	100	2,796	30,470	2
16	1		16	9,455	16	609,000	8	27,650	......	......	18	20	528	6,261	3
2	......	20	2	950	2	34,600	2	2,200	2	7,500	2	2	43	278	4
3	......	4	3	2,500	3	200,000	2	13,200	......	......	3	3	142	1,290	5
11	......	12	11	6,750	11	293,250	8	51,900	4	22,750	11	12	384	3,734	6
2	......	2	2	700	2	21,000	1	3,300	1	3,500	2	2	28	273	7
11	1	13	11	9,475	11	639,500	8	155,500	8	44,000	11	11	496	6,267	8
2	......	2	2	800	2	35,000	1	8,000	1	6,000	2	2	51	361	9
15	......	16	15	10,865	15	924,000	10	68,900	2	10,500	15	15	583	7,119	10
1	......	1	1	600	1	40,000	1	5,800	......	......	1	1	22	218	11
11	......	13	11	5,720	11	494,000	2	5,450	5	45,000	12	12	217	2,204	12
3	......	3	3	1,650	3	42,000	2	6,400	2	10,900	3	3	74	815	13
1	......	1	1	450	1	30,000	1	800	1	2,500	1	1	26	237	14
1	......	1	1	250	1	13,000	1	7,500	1	3,000	1	2	9	120	15

TABLE 7.—ORGANIZATIONS, COMMUNICANTS OR MEMBERS, PLACES OF WORSHIP, VALUE OF CHURCH PROPERTY, MORE IN 1900, BY SELECTED

	DENOMINATION.	Total number of organizations.	COMMUNICANTS OR MEMBERS. Number of organizations reporting.	Total number reported.	Sex. Number of organizations reporting.	Male.	Female.
	Rochester, N. Y.—Continued.						
	Protestant bodies—Continued.						
16	Unitarians	1	1	332	1	112	220
17	Universalists	1	1	630	1	285	345
18	Other Protestant bodies	15	15	1,161	14	362	699
19	Roman Catholic Church [1]						
20	Jewish congregations	9	9	[2] 842			
21	All other bodies	3	3	341	2	49	67
1	Rockford, Ill.	36	35	17,486	30	3,610	6,150
	Protestant bodies	31	31	11,422	28	3,564	6,082
	Baptist bodies:						
3	Baptists—Northern Convention	3	3	1,021	3	380	641
4	Congregationalists	2	2	1,147	1	366	781
	Disciples or Christians:						
5	Disciples of Christ	1	1	217	1	70	147
	Lutheran bodies:						
6	General Synod of the Evangelical Lutheran Church in the United States of America.	1	1	780	1	320	460
7	General Council of the Evangelical Lutheran Church in North America	3	3	3,110	2	636	923
8	Evangelical Lutheran Synodical Conference of America	1	1	266	1	115	151
	Methodist bodies:						
9	Methodist Episcopal Church	6	6	2,382	5	707	1,450
10	Other Methodist bodies	2	2	66	2	26	40
	Presbyterian bodies:						
11	Presbyterian Church in the United States of America	2	2	945	2	309	636
12	Protestant Episcopal Church	1	1	260	1	80	180
	Swedish Evangelical bodies:						
13	Swedish Evangelical Mission Covenant of America	1	1	570	1	255	315
14	Swedish Evangelical Free Mission	1	1	422	1	194	228
15	Other Protestant bodies	7	7	236	7	106	130
16	Roman Catholic Church	2	2	5,950			
17	Jewish congregations	1					
18	Spiritualists	2	2	114	2	46	68
1	Sacramento, Cal.	39	39	12,070	34	4,887	6,712
	Protestant bodies	30	30	4,132	28	1,534	2,534
	Baptist bodies:						
3	Baptists—Northern and National (Colored) Conventions	4	4	609	4	222	387
4	Congregationalists	1	1	298	1	90	208
	Disciples or Christians:						
5	Disciples of Christ	1	1	368	1	123	245
6	Churches of Christ	1	1	16	1	8	8
	Lutheran bodies:						
7	General Synod of the Evangelical Lutheran Church in the United States of America.	2	2	460	2	215	245
8	Synod for the Norwegian Evangelical Lutheran Church in America	1	1	24	1	10	14
	Methodist bodies:						
9	Methodist Episcopal Church	7	7	1,004	7	456	548
10	Other Methodist bodies	3	3	203	3	72	131
	Presbyterian bodies:						
11	Presbyterian Church in the United States of America	2	2	507	2	138	369
12	Protestant Episcopal Church	2	2	315	2	115	200
13	Other Protestant bodies	6	6	328	4	85	179
14	Roman Catholic Church	2	2	6,800	2	2,933	3,867
15	Jewish congregations	2	2	[2] 107			
	Buddhists:						
16	Japanese Temples	1	1	484		321	163
	Eastern Orthodox Churches:						
17	Greek Orthodox Church	1	1	300			
18	All other bodies	3	3	247	3	99	148
1	Saginaw, Mich.	54	53	20,698	43	7,643	10,326
	Protestant bodies	43	42	10,302	34	2,715	4,882
	Baptist bodies:						
3	Baptists—Northern and National (Colored) Conventions	4	4	1,023	3	282	548
4	Congregationalists	2	2	704	2	232	472
	Disciples or Christians:						
5	Disciples of Christ	1	1	325	1	141	184
	Lutheran bodies:						
6	Evangelical Lutheran Synodical Conference of America	2	2	1,589	1	200	300
7	Evangelical Lutheran Joint Synod of Ohio and Other States	2	2	954	2	365	589
8	Evangelical Lutheran Synod of Iowa and Other States	2	2	660	2	307	353
9	Evangelical Lutheran Synod of Michigan and Other States	2	2	754			
	Methodist bodies:						
10	Methodist Episcopal Church	9	9	1,660	6	335	746
11	Other Methodist bodies	4	4	230	4	92	138
	Presbyterian bodies:						
12	Presbyterian Church in the United States of America	5	5	1,354	5	497	857
13	Protestant Episcopal Church	3	3	592	3	162	430
14	Other Protestant bodies	7	6	457	5	122	265
15	Roman Catholic Church	8	8	10,335	8	4,911	5,424
16	Jewish congregations	2	2	[2] 24			
	Theosophical societies:						
17	Theosophical Society, American Section	1	1	37	1	17	20

[1] Statistics not re ted [2] [1] b cities for Rochester diocese.

DEBT ON CHURCH PROPERTY, PARSONAGES, AND SUNDAY SCHOOLS, FOR EACH CITY OF 25,000 INHABITANTS OR DENOMINATIONS: 1906—Continued.

PLACES OF WORSHIP.					VALUE OF CHURCH PROPERTY.		DEBT ON CHURCH PROPERTY.		PARSONAGES.		SUNDAY SCHOOLS CONDUCTED BY CHURCH ORGANIZATIONS.				
Number of organizations reporting— Church edifices.	Number of organizations reporting— Halls, etc.	Number of church edifices reported.	Seating capacity of church edifices. Number of organizations reporting.	Seating capacity of church edifices. Seating capacity reported.	Number of organizations reporting.	Value reported.	Number of organizations reporting.	Amount of debt reported.	Number of organizations reporting.	Value of parsonages reported.	Number of organizations reporting.	Number of Sunday schools reported.	Number of officers and teachers.	Number of scholars.	
1		2	1	400	1	$60,000					1	1	15	125	16
1		1	1	500	1	110,000			1	$15,000	1	1	25	259	17
8	7	9	7	2,487	9	175,620	6	$58,131	2	6,000	12	12	153	909	18
															19
8		10	8	3,620	8	210,500	7	54,100	4	5,250	3	3	11	295	20
1	2	1	1	1,400	1	50,000	1	13,500			1	1	6	70	21
26	7	27	25	19,460	27	764,400	7	28,800	15	88,600	29	30	753	8,064	1
26	5	27	25	19,460	27	764,400	7	28,800	15	88,600	29	30	753	8,064	2
3		3	3	1,250	3	66,680			1	4,000	3	3	86	782	3
2		2	2	2,060	2	188,000			2	22,000	2		69	424	4
1		-	1	300	1	10,000					1	1	16	300	5
1		1	1	1,200	1	28,000			1	6,000	1	1	45	720	6
3		4	3	3,800	3	96,870	1	3,500	1	9,500	3	4	139	1,849	7
1		1	1	600	1	20,000	1	8,000	1	5,500	1	1	2	49	8
6		6	6	4,550	6	154,500	1	5,000	5	20,500	6	6	222	2,136	9
1	1	1	1	150	1	5,000					2	2	18	86	10
2		2	2	1,450	2	65,000	1	3,700	2	10,600	2	2	55	475	11
1		1	1	300	1	55,000			1	6,500	1	1	12	100	12
1		1	1	2,000	1	20,000			1	4,000	1	1	25	400	13
1		1	1	1,400	1	40,000	1	5,000			1	1	43	600	14
3	4	3	2	400	4	15,350	2	3,600			5	5	21	143	15
															16
															17
	2														18
28	6	33	27	12,700	30	399,500	15	40,997	6	13,200	30	38	381	3,695	1
23	3	26	22	9,250	25	359,900	15	40,997	5	11,200	25	30	334	2,870	2
3		3	3	1,175	4	55,000	2	2,979			4	6	52	449	3
1		2	1	1,025	1	40,000	1	4,000			1	2	20	200	4
1		2	1	500	1	15,000					1	2	27	240	5
	1														6
2		2	2	950	2	38,000	1	2,000		2,500	2	2	33	370	7
	1														8
5		5	4	1,425	5	69,500	3	5,500	1	2,500	6	7	66	575	9
3		3	3	1,150	3	37,000	2	868	2	5,000	3	3	31	247	10
2		2	2	1,050	2	45,000	2	12,000			2	2	51	400	11
2		3	2	1,000	2	27,500	1	7,500			2	2	22	212	12
4	1	4	4	975	5	32,900	3	6,150		1,200	4	4	32	177	13
2		4	2	2,500	1	6,500				2,000	1	3	20	650	14
1	1	1	1	300	1	15,000					1	1	2	25	15
1		1	1	500	1	14,500					1	2	4	77	16
	1														17
1	1	1	1	150	2	3,600					2	2	21	73	18
47	6	51	44	22,170	49	705,350	16	19,812	35	103,750	49	51	711	8,049	1
39	3	43	36	17,765	41	551,350	16	19,812	28	73,950	41	43	679	6,407	2
4		6	4	1,850	4	49,000	1	350	3	5,700	4	5	88	838	3
2		2	2	1,200	2	52,000	1	400			2	2	44	353	4
1		1	1	800	1	12,000	1	1,600			1	1	25	210	5
2		3	2	1,650	2	40,500	2	5,200	2	6,000					6
2		2	2	1,140	2	21,000	1	1,500	2	7,000	2	2	20	443	7
2		2	2	650	2	10,000	2	1,250	2	2,700	2	2	29	254	8
2		2	2	900	2	10,500	1	450	2	3,400	2	2	13	345	9
9		9	6	2,750	9	113,500	1	600	5	15,000	9	9	178	1,675	10
4		4	4	1,375	4	18,000	2	1,300	4	5,400	4	5	48	302	11
5		5	5	3,200	5	121,000	2	2,100	4	16,000	5	5	146	1,288	12
3		4	3	1,350	3	86,550			2	7,750	3	3	39	348	13
3	3	3	3	900	5	17,300	2	5,062	2	5,000	7	7	49	351	14
8		8	8	4,405	8	154,000			7	29,800	7	7	28	1,609	15
	2										1	1	4	33	16
	1														17

TABLE 7.—ORGANIZATIONS, COMMUNICANTS OR MEMBERS, PLACES OF WORSHIP, VALUE OF CHURCH PROPERTY, MORE IN 1900, BY SELECTED

	DENOMINATION.	Total number of organizations.	COMMUNICANTS OR MEMBERS.				
			Number of organizations reporting.	Total number reported	Sex.		
					Number of organizations reporting	Male.	Female.
1	St. Joseph, Mo.	93	93	25,280	87	9,915	14,341
2	Protestant bodies	77	77	14,255	75	4,806	8,735
	Baptist bodies:						
3	Baptists—Southern Convention	8	8	1,984	8	739	1,245
4	Baptists—National Convention (Colored)	4	4	467	4	137	330
5	Primitive Baptists	1	1	25	1	10	15
6	Church of Christ, Scientist	2	2	350	2	107	243
7	Congregationalists	2	2	324	2	105	219
	Disciples or Christians:						
8	Disciples of Christ	8	8	2,109	8	698	1,411
9	Churches of Christ	1	1	14	1	4	10
10	German Evangelical Synod of North America	3	3	862	3	345	517
	Lutheran bodies:						
11	General Synod of the Evangelical Lutheran Church in the United States of America	1	1	264	1	80	184
12	Evangelical Lutheran Synodical Conference of America	2	2	374	2	176	198
	Methodist bodies:						
13	Methodist Episcopal Church	9	9	1,695	9	587	1,108
14	African Methodist Episcopal Church	1	1	400	1	125	275
15	Methodist Episcopal Church, South	7	7	1,874	7	697	1,177
16	Other Methodist bodies	2	2	114	2	44	70
	Presbyterian bodies:						
17	Presbyterian Church in the United States of America	5	5	717	5	230	487
18	Presbyterian Church in the United States	3	3	947	3	334	613
19	Other Presbyterian bodies	3	3	364	3	139	225
20	Protestant Episcopal Church	4	4	765	3	51	90
21	Other Protestant bodies	11	11	606	10	198	318
22	Roman Catholic Church	8	8	9,980	8	4,816	5,164
23	Jewish congregations	3	3	[1]240			
	Latter-day Saints:						
24	Reorganized Church of Jesus Christ of Latter-day Saints	2	2	627	2	252	375
25	All other bodies	3	3	178	2	41	67
1	St. Louis, Mo.	398	393	302,531	357	125,224	145,242
2	Protestant bodies	294	291	89,121	273	30,049	49,111
	Baptist bodies:						
3	Baptists—Southern Convention	17	17	5,801	17	2,362	3,439
4	Baptists—National Convention (Colored)	32	32	4,977	30	1,574	3,187
5	Free Baptists	3	3	165	3	71	94
6	Church of Christ, Scientist	3	3	625	3	177	448
	Churches of the Living God (Colored):						
7	Church of the Living God (Christian Workers for Friendship)	1	1	75	1	25	50
8	Church of Christ in God	2	2	620	2	328	292
9	Congregationalists	16	16	3,442	16	1,310	2,132
	Disciples or Christians:						
10	Disciples of Christ	10	10	4,940	10	1,864	3,076
11	Churches of Christ	1	1	30	1	12	18
	German Evangelical Protestant bodies:						
12	German Evangelical Protestant Ministers' Conference	2	2	1,510	2	660	850
13	German Evangelical Synod of North America	27	27	12,928	22	4,753	7,188
14	Independent churches	7	7	770	7	337	433
	Lutheran bodies:						
15	General Synod of the Evangelical Lutheran Church in the United States of America	2	2	592	2	187	405
16	Evangelical Lutheran Synodical Conference of America	23	23	15,613	18	4,062	5,780
17	Other Lutheran bodies	3	3	303	3	141	162
	Methodist bodies:						
18	Methodist Episcopal Church	25	24	6,889	20	1,572	2,514
19	African Methodist Episcopal Church	7	7	2,154	7	669	1,485
20	African Methodist Episcopal Zion Church	4	4	1,419	4	288	1,131
21	Methodist Episcopal Church, South	16	16	8,281	16	3,168	5,113
22	Other Methodist bodies	2	2	467	2	191	276
	Presbyterian bodies:						
23	Presbyterian Church in the United States of America	26	26	7,222	26	2,503	4,719
24	Cumberland Presbyterian Church	2	2	692	2	290	402
25	United Presbyterian Church of North America	4	4	597	4	196	401
26	Presbyterian Church in the United States	5	5	1,469	5	556	913
27	Synod of the Reformed Presbyterian Church of North America	1	1	51	1	9	42
28	Protestant Episcopal Church	27	27	5,590	26	1,947	3,476
	Reformed bodies:						
29	Reformed Church in the United States	2	2	412	2	194	218
30	Other Protestant bodies	24	22	1,487	21	603	867
31	Roman Catholic Church	78	78	208,775	72	92,989	95,483
32	Jewish congregations	13	12	[1]1,801			
	Eastern Orthodox Churches:						
33	Greek Orthodox Church	1	1	1,475	1	1,450	25
	Latter-day Saints:						
34	Reorganized Church of Jesus Christ of Latter-day Saints	3	3	487	3	204	283
35	All other bodies	9	8	872	8	532	340
1	St. Paul, Minn.	161	160	103,639	145	43,898	57,561
2	Protestant bodies	125	124	29,465	116	11,485	16,705
	Baptist bodies:						
3	Baptists—Northern Convention	13	13	2,776	13	1,110	1,666
4	Congregationalists	11	11	2,267	11	799	1,468

[1] Heads of families only.

DEBT ON CHURCH PROPERTY, PARSONAGES, AND SUNDAY SCHOOLS, FOR EACH CITY OF 25,000 INHABITANTS OR DENOMINATIONS: 1906—Continued.

PLACES OF WORSHIP.					VALUE OF CHURCH PROPERTY.		DEBT ON CHURCH PROPERTY.		PARSONAGES.		SUNDAY SCHOOLS CONDUCTED BY CHURCH ORGANIZATIONS.				
Number of organizations reporting— Church edifices.	Number of organizations reporting— Halls, etc.	Number of church edifices reported.	Seating capacity of church edifices. Number of organizations reporting.	Seating capacity of church edifices. Seating capacity reported.	Number of organizations reporting.	Value reported.	Number of organizations reporting.	Amount of debt reported.	Number of organizations reporting.	Value of parsonages reported.	Number of organizations reporting.	Number of Sunday schools reported.	Number of officers and teachers.	Number of scholars.	
78	11	85	78	31,710	80	$1,288,190	32	$76,542	28	$110,300	82	95	1,207	11,481	1
67	8	73	67	26,450	69	9[illegible]5,190	28	50,167	22	70,600	71	78	1,057	9,780	2
8	....	9	8	3,200	8	125,940	1	500	....	....	6	6	122	1,648	3
3	....	3	3	1,450	3	26,650	2	1,100	....	....	4	4	31	195	4
1	....	1	1	400	1	4,700	1	1,500	....	....	....	....	....	....	5
2	....	2	2	1,376	2	185,000	....	....	....	....	2	2	19	70	6
2	....	3	2	1,450	2	34,000	1	800	....	....	2	3	31	360	7
8	....	8	8	2,810	8	56,750	4	7,000	....	....	7	7	105	1,090	8
....	....	....	....	....	....	....	....	....	....	....	....	....	....	....	9
3	....	3	3	900	3	29,000	2	8,000	2	7,000	3	3	29	266	10
1	....	1	1	250	1	15,000	1	3,000	....	....	1	1	26	180	11
2	....	2	2	510	2	17,500	2	6,400	2	3,800	2	2	8	124	12
8	1	8	8	2,875	9	92,100	2	4,500	4	9,900	9	9	193	1,345	13
1	....	1	1	700	1	11,000	1	500	1	5,000	1	1	13	110	14
7	....	7	7	4,000	7	147,900	2	2,250	4	8,000	7	8	119	1,408	15
2	....	2	2	375	2	4,700	1	500	1	1,000	2	2	13	60	16
5	....	5	5	1,425	5	44,000	2	1,725	2	3,600	5	6	76	725	17
3	....	5	3	1,550	3	55,500	....	....	3	12,300	3	6	98	1,038	18
3	....	3	3	1,100	3	26,000	2	4,500	1	6,000	3	3	38	250	19
3	1	5	3	1,024	3	28,700	1	167	1	12,000	4	4	42	281	20
5	6	5	5	1,055	6	40,750	3	7,725	1	2,000	10	11	94	630	21
8	....	9	8	3,915	8	288,000	3	20,375	6	39,700	7	12	97	1,331	22
2	....	2	2	745	2	35,000	1	6,000	....	....	2	2	7	145	23
1	1	1	1	600	1	20,000	....	....	....	....	2	3	46	225	24
....	2	....	....	....	....	....	....	....	....	....	....	....	....	....	25
341	47	386	338	194,077	343	13,751,112	187	1,975,606	131	770,100	334	395	5,841	75,146	1
249	40	266	248	124,294	255	7,068,948	120	646,092	74	352,600	273	313	5,330	57,137	2
14	2	14	14	10,000	16	663,450	4	27,900	1	6,000	17	24	625	5,913	3
24	8	25	24	8,675	24	246,850	10	66,200	1	5,000	32	32	226	1,744	4
2	....	2	2	475	2	2,650	1	900	....	....	2	2	14	110	5
1	2	1	1	1,200	1	150,000	....	....	....	....	3	3	51	225	6
....		....	....	....	....	....	....	....	....	....	1	1	4	30	7
2	....	2	2	550	2	6,500	....	....	....	....	2	3	9	190	8
16	....	16	16	7,434	16	431,500	8	32,750	1	2,000	16	16	349	3,614	9
9	1	9	9	5,150	10	241,200	8	23,672	....	....	10	13	251	2,968	10
....	1	....	....	....	....	....	....	....	....	....	....	....	....	....	11
2	....	2	2	2,050	2	95,000	....	....	2	11,000	2	2	49	544	12
27	....	31	27	13,665	27	585,500	22	149,525	21	90,200	27	29	489	5,839	13
4	3	4	4	1,450	4	64,000	2	2,850	....	....	7	8	102	1,165	14
2	....	2	2	1,000	2	90,000	1	20,000	....	....	2	2	34	383	15
22	1	23	22	13,960	22	637,000	14	77,800	15	66,350	11	12	173	2,714	16
1	2	1	1	175	1	6,000	....	....	....	....	1	1	10	60	17
24	1	25	24	12,755	24	753,500	9	65,650	14	80,600	25	30	508	5,725	18
6	1	6	6	3,380	5	98,300	4	27,445	3	8,000	7	7	67	648	19
4	....	4	4	2,025	4	53,000	4	16,800	1	750	4	4	29	505	20
16	....	16	16	9,100	16	789,600	4	9,400	5	39,700	16	18	548	6,773	21
1	1	1	1	450	1	7,500	....	....	....	....	2	2	16	194	22
26	....	32	26	14,385	26	826,400	7	10,925	4	14,800	26	41	963	10,787	23
2	....	2	2	850	2	105,000	....	....	....	....	2	2	72	652	24
4	....	4	4	1,225	4	96,000	2	2,200	....	....	4	4	85	845	25
5	....	5	5	2,900	5	213,500	3	23,000	....	....	5	7	114	849	26
1	....	1	1	200	1	18,000	....	....	....	....	1	1	9	80	27
25	2	29	25	8,660	24	769,600	11	67,000	4	22,200	27	28	313	3,222	28
2	....	2	2	1,000	2	38,000	2	16,500	1	3,000	2	2	29	340	29
7	14	7	6	1,580	12	90,898	4	5,575	1	3,000	19	19	131	998	30
77	....	104	77	59,943	75	6,072,594	56	1,111,014	56	416,500	50	71	422	16,626	31
11	1	12	11	9,090	10	577,500	10	210,000	....	....	6	6	28	997	32
....	1	....	....	....	....	....	....	....	1	1,000	....	....	....	....	33
1	....	1	1	350	1	12,000	....	....	....	....	2	2	33	206	34
3	5	3	1	400	2	20,070	1	8,500	....	....	3	3	28	180	35
140	13	156	138	71,371	142	3,404,700	68	411,170	62	255,000	140	166	2,664	28,136	1
115	8	1[illegible]6	113	51,302	118	2,258,600	55	157,392	46	156,400	118	140	2,423	19,046	2
13	....	14	13	5,807	13	297,500	4	2,321	3	11,200	13	16	258	2,240	3
11	....	11	11	5,200	11	291,800	5	21,665	1	2,000	11	13	213	2,207	4

TABLE 7.—ORGANIZATIONS, COMMUNICANTS OR MEMBERS, PLACES OF WORSHIP, VALUE OF CHURCH PROPERTY, MORE IN 1900, BY SELECTED

	DENOMINATION.	Total number of organizations.	COMMUNICANTS OR MEMBERS.				
			Number of organizations reporting.	Total number reported.	Sex.		
					Number of organizations reporting.	Male.	Female.
	St. Paul, Minn.—Continued.						
	Protestant bodies—Continued.						
	Disciples or Christians:						
5	Disciples of Christ	2	2	320	2	117	203
	Evangelical bodies:						
6	Evangelical Association	2	2	350	2	160	190
7	United Evangelical Church	1	1	30	1	17	13
8	German Evangelical Synod of North America	1	1	855	1	345	510
	Lutheran bodies:						
9	General Council of the Evangelical Lutheran Church in North America	7	7	2,936	7	1,217	1,719
10	Evangelical Lutheran Synodical Conference of America	8	8	4,364	8	1,875	2,489
11	Evangelical Lutheran Joint Synod of Ohio and Other States	3	3	750	3	367	383
12	Evangelical Lutheran Synod of Iowa and Other States	1	1	367	1	160	207
13	Synod for the Norwegian Evangelical Lutheran Church in America	2	2	520	2	250	270
14	Other Lutheran bodies	5	5	748	3	231	249
	Methodist bodies:						
15	Methodist Episcopal Church	18	18	3,731	16	1,522	2,104
16	African Methodist Episcopal Church	1	1	300			
17	Free Methodist Church of North America	1	1	45	1	20	25
	Presbyterian bodies:						
18	Presbyterian Church in the United States of America	16	16	4,039	16	1,566	2,473
19	Protestant Episcopal Church	16	16	3,418	15	1,140	1,789
	Swedish Evangelical bodies:						
20	Swedish Evangelical Mission Covenant of America	1	1	558	1	240	318
21	Swedish Evangelical Free Mission	1	1	54	1	28	26
22	Other Protestant bodies	15	14	1,037	12	321	603
23	Roman Catholic Church	25	25	72,899	25	32,268	40,631
24	Jewish congregations	6	6	[1]655			
25	All other bodies	5	5	620	4	145	225
1	Salem, Mass	32	31	22,163	26	9,769	11,169
	Protestant bodies	22	22	4,580	18	1,016	2,489
	Adventist bodies:						
3	Advent Christian Church	1	1	150	1	56	94
	Baptist bodies:						
4	Baptists—Northern Convention	3	3	830	3	231	599
5	Congregationalists	4	4	780	4	181	599
	Methodist bodies:						
6	Methodist Episcopal Church	2	2	639	2	247	392
7	Protestant Episcopal Church	2	2	644	2	168	476
8	Unitarians	3	3	1,050			
9	Universalists	1	1	229	1	37	192
10	Other Protestant bodies	6	6	258	5	96	137
11	Roman Catholic Church	5	5	16,858	5	8,285	8,573
12	Jewish congregations	1					
	Eastern Orthodox Churches:						
13	Russian Orthodox Church	1	1	470	1	400	70
14	Greek Orthodox Church	1	1	150			
15	All other bodies	2	2	105	2	68	37
1	Salt Lake City, Utah	78	78	34,452	74	17,243	16,891
2	Protestant bodies	33	33	4,624	32	1,615	2,912
	Baptist bodies:						
3	Baptists—Northern Convention	3	3	583	3	206	377
4	Church of Christ, Scientist	2	2	391	2	73	318
5	Congregationalists	3	3	714	3	253	461
	Disciples or Christians:						
6	Disciples of Christ	1	1	250	1	100	150
	Lutheran bodies:						
7	General Council of the Evangelical Lutheran Church in North America	2	2	126	2	59	67
8	Other Lutheran bodies	4	4	63	4	26	37
	Methodist bodies:						
9	Methodist Episcopal Church	6	6	741	6	298	443
10	African Methodist Episcopal Church	1	1	30	1	7	23
	Presbyterian bodies:						
11	Presbyterian Church in the United States of America	3	3	821	3	303	518
12	Protestant Episcopal Church	4	4	689	4	251	438
13	Other Protestant bodies	4	4	216	3	39	80
14	Roman Catholic Church	1	1	2,550	1	1,275	1,275
15	Jewish congregations	2	2	[1]171			
	Eastern Orthodox Churches:						
16	Greek Orthodox Church	2	2	3,050	1	2,990	10
	Latter-day Saints:						
17	Church of Jesus Christ of Latter-day Saints	38	38	23,867	38	11,293	12,574
18	Reorganized Church of Jesus Christ of Latter-day Saints	1	1	170	1	60	110
19	Spiritualists	1	1	20	1	10	10
1	San Antonio, Tex	68	67	31,141	64	12,725	18,067
2	Protestant bodies	59	58	9,984	57	3,420	6,375
	Baptist bodies:						
3	Baptists—Southern Convention	6	6	1,409	6	500	909
4	Baptists—National Convention (Colored)	10	10	1,330	10	507	823

[1] Heads of families only.

DEBT ON CHURCH PROPERTY, PARSONAGES, AND SUNDAY SCHOOLS, FOR EACH CITY OF 25,000 INHABITANTS OR DENOMINATIONS: 1906—Continued.

PLACES OF WORSHIP.					VALUE OF CHURCH PROPERTY.		DEBT ON CHURCH PROPERTY.		PARSONAGES.		SUNDAY SCHOOLS CONDUCTED BY CHURCH ORGANIZATIONS.				
Number of organizations reporting—		Number of church edifices reported.	Seating capacity of church edifices.		Number of organizations reporting.	Value reported.	Number of organizations reporting.	Amount of debt reported.	Number of organizations reporting.	Value of parsonages reported.	Number of organizations reporting.	Number of Sunday schools reported.	Number of officers and teachers.	Number of scholars.	
Church edifices.	Halls, etc.		Number of organizations reporting.	Seating capacity reported.											
2		2	2	650	2	$40,000	2	$10,000			2	2	25	197	5
2		2	2	800	2	35,000			2	$6,500	2	2	38	248	6
1		1	1	300	1	9,500			1	3,000	1	1	9	54	7
1		1	1	450	1	1,200			1	3,000	1	1	34	280	8
7		8	7	4,215	7	108,100	3	5,600	2	7,200	7	14	234	2,173	9
8		9	8	5,000	8	234,000	7	33,850	7	24,200	7	7	58	1,043	10
3		3	3	870	3	14,300	2	5,500	2	4,200	3	4	23	210	11
1		1	1	400	1	4,500	1	1,000	1	3,000	1	1	7	85	12
2		4	2	1,050	2	18,500	2	3,800	1	5,000	2	5	42	370	13
4	1	4	4	1,600	4	28,500	3	12,900	1	1,500	4	4	44	300	14
18		18	17	7,225	18	332,500	9	18,842	12	41,500	17	17	372	2,735	15
1		1	1	450	1	12,000	1	1,500	1	4,000					16
											1	1	6	50	17
15		18	15	8,200	15	423,500	4	6,300	4	13,600	16	18	650	3,694	18
15		16	15	5,110	16	280,100	7	25,350	6	24,500	16	18	203	1,741	19
1		3	1	1,850	1	40,000	1	3,753			1	3	104	853	20
1		1	1	300	1	5,000	1	650			1	1	15	75	21
9	6	9	8	1,825	11	82,600	3	4,361	1	2,000	12	12	88	491	22
22		27	22	18,269	21	1,067,000	12	245,278	16	98,600	18	21	225	8,750	23
2		2	2	1,500	2	79,000	1	8,500			3	4	10	300	24
1		1	1	300	1	100					1	1	6	40	25
22	8	24	21	15,490	24	843,400		36,500	12	74,200	25	35	473	5,075	1
16	5	18	16	10,760	17	605,200	5	18,000	8	45,000	20	21	406	3,358	2
1		1	1	300	1	7,000					1	1	17	89	3
3		3	3	2,600	3	114,000	2	9,700	2	4,000	3	4	93	898	4
3	1	3	3	2,500	3	105,000			2	17,000	3	3	90	779	5
2		2	2	1,300	2	65,000	1	4,300	2	13,500	2	2	75	591	6
2		2	2	960	2	59,000			1	4,500	2	2	24	216	7
3		5	3	2,000	3	200,000					3	3	33	180	8
1		1	1	900	1	50,000	1	3,000	1	6,000	1	1	52	496	9
1		1	1	200	2	5,200	1	1,000			5	5	22	109	10
5		5	4	4,480	5	234,500	3	18,500	4	29,200	5	14	67	1,717	11
															12
1		1	1	250	1	3,500									13
	1														14
	2				1	200									15
70	7	75	70	29,644	73	1,656,819	22	104,724	13	56,150	70	78	1,619	15,489	1
29	4	29	29	10,350	31	784,750	13	57,724	11	40,850	30	35	458	3,852	2
2	1	2	2	550	2	35,000	1	500			3	5	48	480	3
1	1	1	1	520	1	30,000					2	2	32	261	4
3		3	3	2,000	3	91,000	1	3,000	2	14,000	3	3	73	530	5
1		1	1	400	1	15,000	1	1,000			1	1	15	100	6
2		2	2	525	2	33,000	1	300	1	2,500	2	2	15	79	7
3	1	3	3	265	4	14,000	1	500	3	5,050	2	2	5	44	8
6		6	6	2,530	6	109,500	1	15,000	2	3,000	6	6	83	755	9
1		1	1	300	1	4,000	1	216			1	1	10	30	10
3		3	3	1,535	3	193,000	3	32,000			3	5	107	1,024	11
4		4	4	1,025	4	230,000			2	14,500	4	4	41	406	12
3	1	3	3	700	4	21,250	3	5,208	1	1,800	3	4	29	144	13
1		2	1	1,600	1	350,000	1	30,000	1	15,000	1	3	30	200	14
2		2	2	800	2	50,000	2	7,300			1	1	3	60	15
1	1	1	1	1,000	1	25,000									16
37	1	41	37	15,894	38	447,069	6	9,700	1	300	38	39	1,128	11,377	17
															18
	1														19
58	4	60	57	21,745	60	662,900	19	43,851	30	93,200	60	72	751	8,003	1
50	4	50	49	17,930	52	476,900	15	24,836	26	71,700	53	63	697	7,010	2
5	1	5	5	2,430	5	54,000	1	5,000			6	11	103	1,296	3
8	1	8	7	1,900	10	34,650	2	370	3	2,200	9	10	67	439	4

TABLE 7.—ORGANIZATIONS, COMMUNICANTS OR MEMBERS, PLACES OF WORSHIP, VALUE OF CHURCH PROPERTY, MORE IN 1900, BY SELECTED

	DENOMINATION.	Total number of organizations.	COMMUNICANTS OR MEMBERS.				
			Number of organizations reporting.	Total number reported.	Sex.		
					Number of organizations reporting.	Male.	Female.
	San Antonio, Tex.—Continued.						
	Protestant bodies—Continued.						
	Disciples or Christians:						
5	Disciples of Christ	3	3	524	3	195	329
6	Churches of Christ	2	2	98	2	39	59
	Lutheran bodies:						
7	Evangelical Lutheran Joint Synod of Ohio and Other States	1	1	115	1	40	75
8	Evangelical Lutheran Synod of Iowa and Other States	1	1	450	1	200	250
	Methodist bodies:						
9	Methodist Episcopal Church	7	7	920	7	309	611
10	African Methodist Episcopal Church	2	2	530	2	90	440
11	Methodist Episcopal Church, South	6	6	1,688	6	690	998
12	Other Methodist bodies	2	1	7	1	3	4
	Presbyterian bodies:						
13	Presbyterian Church in the United States		6	956	6	340	616
14	Other Presbyterian bodies		2	319	1	43	87
15	Protestant Episcopal Church		5	1,288	5	345	943
16	Other Protestant bodies	8	6	350	6	119	231
17	Roman Catholic Church	5	5	20,400	5	9 023	11,377
18	Jewish congregations	2	2	[1] 160			
	Latter-day Saints:						
19	Reorganized Church of Jesus Christ of Latter-day Saints	1	1	97	1	32	65
20	Spiritualists	1	1	500	1	250	250
1	San Francisco, Cal	181	177	142,919	156	68,192	70,917
2	Protestant bodies	125	122	21,776	111	7,750	11,345
	Adventist bodies:						
3	Advent Christian Church	1	1	50	1	20	30
4	Seventh-day Adventist Denomination	1	1	344	1	98	246
	Baptist bodies:						
5	Baptists—Northern and National (Colored) Conventions	8	8	1,322	8	475	847
6	Free Baptists	1	1	34	1	14	20
	Catholic Apostolic Churches:						
7	Catholic Apostolic Church	1	1	369	1	137	232
8	Church of Christ, Scientist	1	1	394	1	118	276
9	Congregationalists	15	15	2,400	15	807	1,593
	Disciples or Christians:						
10	Disciples of Christ	4	4	752	4	291	461
	German Evangelical Protestant bodies:						
11	German Evangelical Protestant Ministers' Conference	1	1	635	1	225	410
12	German Evangelical Synod of North America	3	3	542	3	252	290
	Lutheran bodies:						
13	General Synod of the Evangelical Lutheran Church in the United States of America	3		515	3	220	295
14	General Council of the Evangelical Lutheran Church in North America	1	3	301	1	160	141
15	Evangelical Lutheran Synodical Conference of America	3		1,407	3	556	851
16	Synod for the Norwegian Evangelical Lutheran Church in America	2		550	1	150	150
17	Other Lutheran bodies	2	8	90	1	24	16
	Methodist bodies:						
18	Methodist Episcopal Church	20	20	3,019	19	1,272	1,622
19	African Methodist Episcopal Zion Church	1	1	350	1	150	200
20	Other Methodist bodies	2	2	187	2	65	122
	Presbyterian bodies:						
21	Presbyterian Church in the United States of America	16	15	3,272	14	1,399	1,823
22	Other Presbyterian bodies	3	3	286	3	123	163
23	Protestant Episcopal Church	17	15	2,846	9	545	1,095
24	Unitarians	2	2	1,151	1	42	109
25	Other Protestant bodies	17	17	900	17	607	353
26	Roman Catholic Church	34	34	115,921	34	57,087	58,834
27	Jewish congregations	10	9	[1] 1,079			
	Buddhists:						
28	Japanese Temples	1	1	342	1	237	105
	Eastern Orthodox Churches:						
29	Russian Orthodox Church	1	1	650	1	525	125
30	Greek Orthodox Church	1	1	2,200	1	2,150	50
31	All other bodies	9	9	951	8	443	458
1	Savannah, Ga	79	79	36,713	73	13,164	21,186
2	Protestant bodies	71	71	29,129	68	9,151	17,856
	Baptist bodies:						
	Baptists—Southern Convention	3	3	1,972	[illegible]	125	115
	Baptists—National Convention (Colored)	22	22	15,005	[illegible]	4,682	10,323
5	Congregationalists	2	2	323	2	108	215
	Disciples or Christians:						
6	Disciples of Christ	1	1	371	1	150	221
	Lutheran bodies:						
7	United Synod of the Evangelical Lutheran Church in the South	2	2	1,260	2	535	725
	Methodist bodies:						
8	Methodist Episcopal Church		2	580	2	220	360
9	African Methodist Episcopal Church	1	10	2,815	10	1,099	1,716
10	Methodist Episcopal Church, South		4	2,265	4	797	1,468
11	Colored Methodist Episcopal Church		3	534	3	158	376
12	Other Methodist bodies	8	3	203	3	95	198
	Presbyterian bodies:						
13	Presbyterian Church in the United States of America	2	2	83	2	24	59
14	Presbyterian Church in the United States	4	4	1,467	4	485	982
15	Protestant Episcopal Church	7	7	2,065	6	637	1,038
16	Other Protestant bodies	6	6	96	6	36	60

[1] Heads of families only.

DEBT ON CHURCH PROPERTY, PARSONAGES, AND SUNDAY SCHOOLS, FOR EACH CITY OF 25,000 INHABITANTS OR DENOMINATIONS: 1906—Continued.

PLACES OF WORSHIP.					VALUE OF CHURCH PROPERTY.		DEBT ON CHURCH PROPERTY.		PARSONAGES.		SUNDAY SCHOOLS CONDUCTED BY CHURCH ORGANIZATIONS.				
Number of organizations reporting—		Number of church edifices reported.	Seating capacity of church edifices.		Number of organizations reporting.	Value reported.	Number of organizations reporting.	Amount of debt reported.	Number of organizations reporting.	Value of parsonages reported.	Number of organizations reporting.	Number of Sunday schools reported.	Number of officers and teachers.	Number of scholars.	
Church edifices.	Halls, etc.		Number of organizations reporting.	Seating capacity reported.											
2	....	2	2	1,100	2	$40,000	1	$4,000	....	....	2	2	39	438	5
2	....	2	2	350	2	1,900	1	141	....	....	....	....	....	....	6
1	....	1	1	300	1	7,000	1	4,000	....	....	1	1	7	88	7
1	....	1	1	500	1	18,000	....	....	1	$4,000	1	1	16	155	8
6	....	6	6	2,350	6	55,	2	1,700	4	7,950	7	7	75	582	9
2	....	2	2	850	2	21,	1	225	2	1,800	2	2	25	187	10
6	....	6	6	2,850	6	91,400	1	1,000	6	14,800	6	8	148	1,641	11
1	....	1	1	200	1	1,500	....	....	1	1,250	1	1	3	20	12
	....		5	1,300	5	36	1	300	1	4,000	6	8	97	1,060	13
	....		3	1,900	2	35	1	1,800	2	8,000	2	2	24	320	14
	....		5	1,225	5	5 ,000	....	....	5	25,700	5	5	60	529	15
5	2	6	3	675	4	28,880	3	6,300	1	2,000	5	5	33	255	16
5	....	7	5	2,755	5	000	2	10,000	4	21,500		7	40	853	17
2	....	2	2	1,000	2	140,000 45	1	9,000	....	....	[illegible]	1	5	100	18
1	....	1	1	60	1	1,000	1	15	....	....	1	1	9	40	19
....	....	....	....	....	....	....	....	....	....	....	....	....	....	....	20
138	24	151	133	66,200	154	6,953,947	65	785,556	50	559,100	149	166	2,171	28,318	1
99	15	105	94	38,350	113	3,708,351	41	173,614	20	109,250	110	117	1,423	12,653	2
1	....	1	1	150	1	3,000	....	....	....	....	1	1	10	75	3
1	....	1		400	1	30,000		2,000	....	....	1	1	20	145	4
5	1	5	4	1,750	5	188,000	2	22,700	1	3,000	7	10	115	850	5
1	....	1	1	200	1	5,000	....	....	....	....	1	1	6	40	6
1	....	1	1	250	1	6,000	....	....	....	....	....	....	....	....	7
....	1	....	....	....	1	50,411	....	....	....	....	1	1	13	168	8
12	....	13	11	4,250	13	471,200	2	5,600	1	1,800	16	15	159	1,592	9
4	....	4	4	1,900	4	117,000	3	15,175	....	....	4	4	52	470	10
1	....	1	1	1,000	1	96,000	1	3,200	....	....	1	1	25	255	11
3	....	3	3	1,200	3	46,500	3	12,000	1	10,000	5	3	44	470	12
2	....	2	2	850	3	75,500	1	8,700	....	....	3	3	29	240	13
1	....	1	1	600	1	34,000	1	4,000	1	9,000	1	1	22	162	14
2	1	2	2	1,950	3	127,500	2	21,100	2	14,500	3	3	76	506	15
2	....	3	2	800	2	46,000	1	2,500	1	3,000	2	3	18	220	16
2	....	2	2	700	2	47,000	1	7,000	....	....	2	2	10	85	17
16	1	16	16	5,550	19	450,850	8	24,000	4	23,500	18	19	274	2,445	18
1	....	1	1	2,000	1	60,000	....	....	....	....	1	1	25	75	19
2	....	2	2	520	2	41,000	....	....	1	3,000	2	2	17	61	20
16	....	17	15	7,065	16	810,000	1	6,400	....	....	1	15	258	2,832	21
2	....	3	2	640	3	112,500	1	2,000	2	15,000		3	36	246	22
15	1	16	14	4,150	16	607,700	8	33,662	3	14,500	1	16	126	1,138	23
2	....	2	2	1,100	2	164,000	....	....	....	....		2	16	130	24
7	10	8	6	1,325	12	120,190	5	3,577	3	11,950	10	10	72	449	25
34	....	38	34	23,100	34	2,844,250	22	523,942	30	449,850	31	38	696	14,359	26
3	....	6	3	2,450	3	366,000	1	85,000	....	....	5	5	16	840	27
....	1	....	....	....	....	....	....	....	....	....	1	2	12	268	28
....	1	....	....	....	1	3,000	....	....	....	....	....	....	....	....	29
1	....	1	1	2,000	1	20,000	1	3,000	....	....	....	....	....	....	30
1	7	1	1	300	2	12,346	....	....	....	....	2	4	24	198	31
70	8	76	70	47,255	71	1,687,881	41	147,232	27	188,475	68	79	994	11,355	1
63	8	68	63	42,812	65	1,287,881	38	112,232	25	149,475	63	74	895	10,191	2
3	....	4	3	3,000		108,000	1	500	2	10,000			67	980	3
20	2	21	20	19,000	[illegible]	232,680	12	25,650	2	11,000	[illegible]		190	2,414	4
2	....	2	2	650	2	17,000	1	774	1	1,000	2	28	15	155	5
1	....	1	1	500	1	6,000	....	....	....	....	1	1	10	148	6
2	....	2	2	1,350	2	92,000	1	2,500	2	8,000	2	2	80	732	7
2	....	2	2	650	2	9,000	2	2,300	1	1,000	2	2	24	350	8
10	....	11	10	5,650	10	64,801	7	3,508	6	7,675	9	9	100	1,417	9
4	....	4	4	3,100	4	163,500	1	750	4	20,000	4	5	132	1,655	10
3	....	3	3	1,650	3	52,000	3	10,029	....	....	2	2	12	180	11
2	1	2	2	600	2	3,000	2	678	....	....	3	3	15	123	12
1	1	1	1	300	1	1,400	....	....	....	....	1	1	12	150	13
4	....	6	4	3,600	4	350,000	3	39,343	4	66,000	4	4	113	878	14
7	....	7	7	2,437	7	153,500	4	1,200	3	24,800	7	8	116	959	15
2	4	2	2	325	2	35,000	1	25,000	....	....	2	2	9	50	16

TABLE 7.—ORGANIZATIONS, COMMUNICANTS OR MEMBERS, PLACES OF WORSHIP, VALUE OF CHURCH PROPERTY, MORE IN 1900, BY SELECTED

	DENOMINATION.	Total number of organizations.	COMMUNICANTS OR MEMBERS				
			Number of organizations reporting.	Total number reported.	Sex.		
					Number of organizations reporting.	Male.	Female.
	Savannah, Ga.—Continued.						
17	Roman Catholic Church	4	4	6,843	4	3,538	3,305
18	Jewish congregations	3	3	[1] 241			
	Eastern Orthodox Churches:						
19	Greek Orthodox Church	1	1	500	1	475	25
1	Schenectady, N. Y.	56	55	25,897	45	10,767	13,725
2	Protestant bodies	39	39	11,567	37	4,207	6,746
	Baptist bodies:						
3	Baptists—Northern Convention	4	4	1,186	4	449	737
4	Congregationalists	2	2	324	2	105	219
5	German Evangelical Synod of North America	2	2	401	2	194	207
	Lutheran bodies:						
6	General Synod of the Evangelical Lutheran Church in the United States of America	1	1	374	1	125	249
7	General Council of the Evangelical Lutheran Church in North America	1	1	75	1	35	40
8	Evangelical Lutheran Synodical Conference of America	2	2	769	2	316	453
	Methodist bodies:						
9	Methodist Episcopal Church	7	7	3,676	7	1,447	2,229
10	African Methodist Episcopal Zion Church	1	1	59	1	27	32
	Presbyterian bodies:						
11	Presbyterian Church in the United States of America	3	3	1,302	3	479	823
12	United Presbyterian Church of North America	1	1	165	1	74	91
13	Protestant Episcopal Church	3	3	1,214	1	250	350
	Reformed bodies:						
14	Reformed Church in America	4	4	1,590	4	525	1,065
15	Other Protestant bodies	8	8	432	8	181	251
16	Roman Catholic Church	8	8	13,539	8	6,560	6,979
17	Jewish congregations	8	7	[1] 541			
	Eastern Orthodox Churches:						
18	Greek Orthodox Church	1	1	250			
1	Scranton, Pa.	101	101	70,776	89	33,315	34,421
2	Protestant bodies	71	71	21,901	66	7,765	11,740
	Baptist bodies:						
3	Baptists—Northern and National (Colored) Conventions	12	12	3,887	11	1,168	1,821
4	Congregationalists	5	5	1,610	5	541	1,069
5	German Evangelical Synod of North America	3	3	962	3	381	581
	Lutheran bodies:						
6	General Council of the Evangelical Lutheran Church in North America	6	6	2,013	6	999	1,014
7	Other Lutheran bodies	2	2	458	2	212	246
	Methodist bodies:						
8	Methodist Episcopal Church	12	12	4,748	12	1,708	3,040
9	Other Methodist bodies	3	3	251	3	101	150
	Presbyterian bodies:						
10	Presbyterian Church in the United States of America	10	10	4,549	10	1,895	2,654
11	Welsh Calvinistic Methodist Church	3	3	547	3	236	311
12	Protestant Episcopal Church	5	5	1,764	1	120	146
13	Other Protestant bodies	10	10	1,112	10	404	708
14	Roman Catholic Church	20	20	46,736	20	24,577	22,159
15	Jewish congregations	6	6	[1] 569			
16	Polish National Church of America	1	1	1,125	1	700	425
17	All other bodies	3	3	445	2	273	97
1	Seattle, Wash.	162	162	49,479	145	20,479	25,672
2	Protestant bodies	136	136	23,295	124	8,895	13,278
	Baptist bodies:						
3	Baptists—Northern and National (Colored) Conventions	17	17	2,531	16	994	1,442
4	Church of Christ, Scientist	3	3	326	2	78	211
5	Congregationalists	13	13	2,580	12	869	1,661
	Disciples or Christians:						
6	Disciples of Christ	6	6	950	6	354	596
7	Independent churches	3	3	436	3	231	205
	Lutheran bodies:						
8	General Council of the Evangelical Lutheran Church in North America	2	2	571	2	257	314
9	Synod for the Norwegian Evangelical Lutheran Church in America	2	2	474	2	222	252
10	Other Lutheran bodies	6	6	551	5	191	365
	Methodist bodies:						
11	Methodist Episcopal Church	29	29	4,521	26	1,495	2,586
12	African Methodist Episcopal Church	1	1	132	1	41	91
13	Free Methodist Church of North America	5	5	319	5	119	200
	Presbyterian bodies:						
14	Presbyterian Church in the United States of America	12	12	5,149	9	2,158	2,661
15	Other Presbyterian bodies	4	4	346	4	152	194
16	Protestant Episcopal Church	10	10	2,584	9	958	1,601
17	Unitarians	1	1	400	1	150	250
18	Other Protestant bodies	22	22	1,425	21	626	749
19	Roman Catholic Church	12	12	24,589	10	10,860	11,858
20	Jewish congregations	3	3	[1] 335			
	Eastern Orthodox Churches:						
21	Russian Orthodox Church	1	1	337	1	231	106
22	Spiritualists	3	3	339	3	146	193
23	All other bodies	7	7	584	7	347	237

[1] Heads of families only.

DEBT ON CHURCH PROPERTY, PARSONAGES, AND SUNDAY SCHOOLS, FOR EACH CITY OF 25,000 INHABITANTS OR DENOMINATIONS: 1906—Continued.

PLACES OF WORSHIP.					VALUE OF CHURCH PROPERTY.		DEBT ON CHURCH PROPERTY.		PARSONAGES.		SUNDAY SCHOOLS CONDUCTED BY CHURCH ORGANIZATIONS.				
Number of organizations reporting—		Number of church edifices reported.	Seating capacity of church edifices.		Number of organizations reporting.	Value reported.	Number of organizations reporting.	Amount of debt reported.	Number of organizations reporting.	Value of parsonages reported.	Number of organizations reporting.	Number of Sunday schools reported.	Number of officers and teachers.	Number of scholars.	
Church edifices.	Halls, etc.		Number of organizations reporting.	Seating capacity reported.											
4	......	4	4	2,688	3	$323,000	1	$32,000	2	$39,000	4	4	89	1,020	17
2	......	3	2	1,155	2	70,000	1	1,000	......	......	1	1	10	144	18
1	......	1	1	600	1	7,000	1	2,000	......	......	......	......	......	......	19
43	7	47	43	24,898	45	1,995,880	31	314,510	28	189,800	46	51	910	10,304	1
32	6	35	32	16,973	34	1,179,380	23	167,010	21	136,800	38	43	819	8,404	2
3	1	3	3	1,934	4	110,500	4	28,841	1	5,000	4	6	95	1,264	3
2	......	2	2	750	2	34,500	2	4,728	1	10,000	2	2	28	287	4
2	......	2	2	800	2	38,600	2	15,900	1	3,000	2	2	23	218	5
1	......	1	1	800	1	50,000	1	25,000	1	4,800	1	1	38	290	6
1	......	1	1	200	1	4,000	1	2,000	1	7,000	1	1	6	23	7
2	......	3	2	960	2	34,000	2	3,700	1	5,000	2	3	22	375	8
6	1	7	6	3,750	6	269,500	3	12,975	5	26,500	7	7	261	2,689	9
1	......	1	1	200	1	17,000	1	366	......	......	1	1	5	68	10
3	......	4	3	2,750	3	195,000	2	43,500	2	18,000	3	3	95	1,182	11
1	......	1	1	250	1	16,000	1	4,000	1	3,500	1	1	10	190	12
2	......	2	2	800	2	90,000	1	5,000	2	20,000	3	3	33	340	13
4	......	4	4	2,464	4	269,000	1	8,000	4	28,000	4	5	158	1,196	14
4	4	4	4	1,315	5	51,280	2	13,000	1	6,000	7	8	45	282	15
8	......	9	8	7,175	8	781,000	6	135,000	7	53,000	7	7	88	1,885	16
3	......	3	3	750	3	35,500	2	12,500	......	......	1	1	3	15	17
......		......	......	......	......	......	......	......	......	......	......	......	......	......	18
92	5	103	91	53,916	91	2,833,500	50	216,145	41	381,000	90	111	2,602	28,385	1
67	3	75	67	33,276	67	2,005,300	38	146,793	27	171,300	68	87	2,203	20,071	2
12	......	14	12	7,000	12	246,600	11	32,900	2	5,500	11	15	313	3,398	3
5	......	5	5	3,350	5	104,700	4	16,975	......	......	5	7	387	1,763	4
3	......	3	3	1,075	3	26,500	3	6,500	2	6,500	3	3	58	522	5
6	......	7	6	2,616	6	91,500	3	18,300	4	14,500	6	7	127	1,098	6
2	......	2	2	1,200	2	26,000	2	10,000	......	......	2	2	20	230	7
12	......	12	12	6,860	12	434,500	6	22,600	9	50,000	12	12	489	5,362	8
2	......	2	2	900	2	15,000	1	2,758	2	4,000	2	2	48	327	9
10	......	14	10	5,235	10	601,500	4	14,700	6	64,800	10	19	455	4,660	10
3	......	3	3	1,350	3	33,000	......	......	......	......	3	3	72	570	11
5	......	6	5	1,220	5	266,000	......	......	2	26,000	5	7	109	1,253	12
7	3	7	7	2,470	7	160,000	4	22,060	......	......	9	10	125	888	13
17	2	19	17	17,190	17	687,200	6	47,152	13	206,700	14	16	357	6,939	14
5	......	6	5	1,750	5	90,800	4	17,800	......	......	6	6	32	1,120	15
1	......	1	1	1,000	1	45,000	1	2,300	1	3,000	1	1	3	230	16
2	......	2	1	700	1	5,200	1	2,100	......	......	1	1	7	25	17
134	18	139	132	52,848	137	3,104,578	54	415,714	42	131,200	142	169	2,104	20,227	1
118	11	123	117	44,260	121	2,188,778	45	83,630	35	100,700	124	150	1,992	18,306	
16	1	18	16	5,550	16	309,700	4	13,100	2	2,000	17	20	271	2,890	3
3	......	3	3	1,000	3	42,000	3	9,300	......	......	3	3	31	167	4
13	......	13	13	4,150	13	460,200	1	5,000	5	11,000	13	14	271	2,816	5
5	......	5	5	1,400	5	44,000	2	2,280	......	......	5	5	64	534	6
2	1	2	2	500	3	7,500	1	700	......	......	1	2	10	90	7
2	......	2	2	1,200	2	70,000	1	4,500	1	6,000	2	2	31	217	8
2	......	2	2	550	2	17,500	2	1,300	......	......	2	3	18	240	9
6	......	6	5	1,325	6	81,200	3	2,900	2	7,000	6	7	53	344	10
26	......	26	26	11,050	26	348,925	11	9,000	13	40,550	28	28	425	4,243	11
1	......	1	1	500	1	15,000	1	850	1	1,200	1	1	20	132	12
5	......	5	5	1,450	5	36,000	1	1,200	3	6,000	5	5	52	385	13
12	......	14	12	6,475	12	122,853	3	9,000	1	3,500	12	27	406	3,573	14
4	......	4	4	1,350	4	87,000	1	1,000	......	......	4	4	71	666	15
9	......	10	9	3,360	9	347,200	6	16,150	5	13,450	10	11	117	1,016	16
1	......	1	1	600	1	30,000	1	3,000	......	......	1	1	8	100	17
11	9	11	11	3,800	13	169,700	4	4,350	2	10,000	14	17	144	893	18
11	......	11	11	6,538	11	818,000	9	332,084	6	26,500	11	11	72	1,530	19
3	......	3	2	1,600	2	95,000	......	......	......	......	2	2	10	155	20
1	......	1	1	300	1	2,000	......	......	1	4,000	......	......	......	......	21
......	3	......	......	......	......	......	......	......	......	......	1	1	5	50	22
1	4	1	1	150	2	800	......	......	......	......	4	5	25	186	23

TABLE 7.—ORGANIZATIONS, COMMUNICANTS OR MEMBERS, PLACES OF WORSHIP, VALUE OF CHURCH PROPERTY, MORE IN 1900, BY SELECTED

	DENOMINATION.	Total number of organizations.	COMMUNICANTS OR MEMBERS. Number of organizations reporting.	Total number reported.	Sex. Number of organizations reporting.	Male.	Female.
1	Sioux City, Iowa....	55	52	12,117	50	4,960	7,084
2	Protestant bodies	44	43	7,790	42	2,953	4,801
	Baptist bodies:						
3	Baptists—Northern Convention	4	4	553	4	203	350
4	Congregationalists	3	3	786	3	301	485
	Disciples or Christians:						
5	Disciples of Christ	1	1	196	1	70	126
	Lutheran bodies:						
6	General Synod of the Evangelical Lutheran Church in the United States of America	1	1	200	1	68	132
7	General Council of the Evangelical Lutheran Church in North America	2	2	560	2	248	312
8	Evangelical Lutheran Synodical Conference of America	1	1	333	1	147	186
9	United Norwegian Lutheran Church in America	1	1	530	1	296	234
10	Hauge's Norwegian Evangelical Lutheran Synod	1	1	400	1	175	225
11	United Danish Evangelical Lutheran Church in America	1	1	105	1	45	60
	Methodist bodies:						
12	Methodist Episcopal Church	11	10	1,492	9	494	962
13	Other Methodist bodies	2	2	35	2	12	23
	Presbyterian bodies:						
14	Presbyterian Church in the United States of America	5	5	1,179	5	410	769
15	United Presbyterian Church of North America	1	1	33	1	12	21
16	Protestant Episcopal Church	2	2	465	2	159	306
	Swedish Evangelical bodies:						
17	Swedish Evangelical Mission Covenant of America	1	1	197	1	45	152
18	Unitarians	1	1	308	1	138	170
19	Other Protestant bodies	6	6	418	6	130	288
20	Roman Catholic Church	7	7	4,173	7	1,954	2,219
21	Jewish congregations	3	1	[1] 37	......	......	......
	Latter-day Saints:						
22	Reorganized Church of Jesus Christ of Latter-day Saints	1	1	117	1	53	64
1	Somerville, Mass	36	36	25,683	34	10,772	14,285
2	Protestant bodies	30	30	8,176	29	2,499	5,076
	Baptist bodies:						
3	Baptists—Northern Convention	6	6	2,543	6	819	1,724
4	Free Baptists	1	1	98	1	29	69
5	Congregationalists	6	6	2,040	6	676	1,364
	Methodist bodies:						
6	Methodist Episcopal Church	4	4	1,566	3	303	662
7	Protestant Episcopal Church	3	3	674	3	258	416
8	Unitarians	2	2	395	2	128	267
9	Universalists	3	3	421	3	114	307
10	Other Protestant bodies	5	5	439	5	172	267
11	Roman Catholic Church	3	3	17,150	3	8,088	9,062
12	Jewish congregations	1	1	[1] 25	......	......	......
13	All other bodies	2	2	332	2	185	147
1	South Bend, Ind	49	48	18,214	40	6,972	8,421
2	Protestant bodies	39	39	8,543	34	2,176	3,664
	Baptist bodies:						
3	Baptists—Northern and National (Colored) Conventions	2	2	550	2	162	388
	Disciples or Christians:						
4	Disciples of Christ	3	3	1,045	2	54	101
5	Dunkers or German Baptist Brethren	3	3	248	3	93	155
	Evangelical bodies:						
6	Evangelical Association	3	3	399	3	150	249
7	German Evangelical Synod of North America	2	2	1,100	1	165	185
	Lutheran bodies:						
8	General Council of the Evangelical Lutheran Church in North America	2	2	540	1	206	238
9	Evangelical Lutheran Synodical Conference of America	1	1	526	1	220	306
	Methodist bodies:						
10	Methodist Episcopal Church	5	5	2,139	4	495	894
11	Other Methodist bodies	2	2	110	2	40	70
	Presbyterian bodies:						
12	Presbyterian Church in the United States of America	4	4	1,021	4	340	681
13	Protestant Episcopal Church	1	1	217	......	......	......
14	Other Protestant bodies	11	11	648	11	251	397
15	Roman Catholic Church	6	6	9,553	6	4,796	4,757
16	Jewish congregations	3	2	[1] 68	......	......	......
	Eastern Orthodox Churches:						
17	Greek Orthodox Church	1	1	50	......	......	......
1	South Omaha, Nebr	23	23	8,317	22	3,810	4,107
2	Protestant bodies	16	16	2,233	16	889	1,344
	Baptist bodies:						
3	Baptists—Northern Convention	4	2	249	2	76	173
	Disciples or Christians:						
4	Disciples of Christ	1	1	60	1	25	35
	Lutheran bodies:						
5	Evangelical Lutheran Synodical Conference of America	1	1	220	1	95	125
6	Other Lutheran bodies	3	3	190	3	85	105

[1] Heads of families only.

DEBT ON CHURCH PROPERTY, PARSONAGES, AND SUNDAY SCHOOLS, FOR EACH CITY OF 25,000 INHABITANTS OR DENOMINATIONS: 1906—Continued.

PLACES OF WORSHIP.					VALUE OF CHURCH PROPERTY.		DEBT ON CHURCH PROPERTY.		PARSONAGES.		SUNDAY SCHOOLS CONDUCTED BY CHURCH ORGANIZATIONS.				
Number of organizations reporting—		Number of church edifices reported.	Seating capacity of church edifices.		Number of organizations reporting.	Value reported.	Number of organizations reporting.	Amount of debt reported.	Number of organizations reporting.	Value of parsonages reported.	Number of organizations reporting.	Number of Sunday schools reported.	Number of officers and teachers.	Number of scholars.	
Church edifices.	Halls, etc.		Number of organizations reporting.	Seating capacity reported.											
47	5	50	47	19,195	50	$834,037	26	$135,505	21	$102,030	48	56	794	7,686	1
39	4	42	39	15,168	42	583,537	20	40,205	17	65,530	39	47	751	6,690	2
4		4	4	1,225	4	54,600	4	15,390	2	12,630	4	4	49	377	3
3		3	3	1,700	3	68,700	1	400			3	3	64	506	4
1		1	1	300	1	14,000	1	5,000			1	1	17	127	5
1		1	1	400	1	20,000					1	1	9	175	6
2		2	2	1,100	2	39,000	2	1,900	1	5,000	2	2	49	330	7
1		1	1	500	1	10,000			1	4,500					8
1		2	1	650	1	30,000					1	3	68	340	9
1		2	1	600	1	15,000	1	1,000			1	3	33	250	10
1		1	1	150	1	3,000	1	1,100	1	700	1	2	11	75	11
10	1	10	10	2,745	11	77,150	4	1,325	5	11,700	9	9	172	1,677	12
1		1	1	300	1	2,800	1	50			1	1	6	24	13
5		6	5	2,900	5	107,500	1	2,000	3	17,000	5	7	156	1,820	14
1		1	1	100	1	7,000			1	5,000	1	1	9	40	15
2		2	2	868	2	66,700	2	9,500	1	1,800	2	2	17	243	16
1		1	1	450	1	10,090			1	2,700	1	2	31	295	17
1		1	1	280	1	30,000			1	4,500	1	1	11	125	18
3	3	3	3	900	5	28,297	2	2,540			5	5	49	287	19
6	1	6	6	3,577	6	240,000	5	94,500	4	36,500	7	7	29	899	20
1		1	1	250	1	8,000					1	1	3	27	21
1		1	1	200	1	2,500	1	800			1	1	11	70	22
32	4	35	32	20,176	33	1,010,710	21	96,765	10	91,300	34	34	1,151	12,136	1
27	3	29	27	14,626	28	773,710	18	81,565	7	61,000	30	30	905	8,724	2
6		6	6	3,930	6	158,500	4	6,800	1	5,000	6	6	274	2,928	3
1		1	1	350	1	20,000	1	5,000			1	1	20	159	4
6		8	6	3,716	6	238,000	5	32,050	1	4,000	6	6	203	2,091	5
4		4	4	3,200	4	135,000	2	13,200	3	16,000	4	4	190	1,647	6
3		3	3	900	3	42,000	1	900	1	6,000	3	3	43	520	7
1	1	1	1	500	1	80,000	1	13,000	1	30,000	2	2	30	274	8
3		3	3	1,230	3	68,500	2	8,890			3	3	88	633	9
3	2	3	3	800	4	31,710	2	1,725			5	5	57	472	10
3		4	3	5,000	3	225,000	1	9,000	3	30,300	3	3	226	3,312	11
1		1	1	200	1	4,000	1	2,000							12
1	1	1	1	350	1	8,000	1	4,200			1	1	20	100	13
41	4	45	41	18,656	42	928,250	19	89,008	26	109,600	44	46	687	7,886	1
34	3	35	34	14,718	35	597,250	13	38,650	20	84,500	37	39	655	5,765	2
2		3	2	1,200	2	54,700	1	300	2	6,100	2	3	42	347	3
3		3	3	1,600	3	29,200	1	350			3	3	61	660	4
3		3	3	1,350	3	17,000	2	3,900	1	1,000	3	3	37	295	5
3		3	3	1,200	3	39,400	2	1,300	2	8,500	3	3	59	440	6
2		2	2	900	2	20,000	1	400	2	7,000	2	2	47	460	7
2		2	2	600	2	21,000	1	4,000	1	1,200	2	2	32	247	8
1		1	1	400	1	1,500			1	5,000					9
5		5	5	3,300	5	243,500			4	26,600	5	5	131	1,546	10
2		2	2	650	2	11,000	1	1,000	2	2,300	2	2	22	95	11
4		4	4	1,750	4	62,800	1	500	2	21,800	4	5	117	1,051	12
1		1	1	400	1	35,000	1	14,900			1	1	21	146	13
6	3	6	6	1,368	7	62,150	2	12,000	3	5,000	10	10	86	478	14
6		8	6	3,688	6	321,000	5	48,858	6	25,100	6	6	31	2,086	15
1		2	1	250	1	10,000	1	1,500			1	1	1	35	16
	1														17
20	2	23	20	6,547	21	195,250	6	23,625	10	43,950	21	31	276	3,384	1
14	1	17	14	4,010	15	85,250	3	2,325	6	14,450	15	23	246	2,361	2
2		3	2	600	2	10,500					2	4	54	296	3
					1	4,000					-	-	6	55	4
1		1	1	250	1	3,500			1	2,200					5
2	1	2	2	400	2	5,500	2	1,725	1	1,000	3	3	20	229	6

TABLE 7.—ORGANIZATIONS, COMMUNICANTS OR MEMBERS, PLACES OF WORSHIP, VALUE OF CHURCH PROPERTY, ... MORE IN 1900, BY SELECTED

	DENOMINATION.	Total number of organizations.	COMMUNICANTS OR MEMBERS. Number of organizations reporting.	Total number reported.	Sex. Number of organizations reporting.	Male.	Female.
	South Omaha, Nebr.—Continued.						
	Protestant bodies—Continued.						
	Methodist bodies:						
7	Methodist Episcopal Church	2	2	457	2	158	299
8	African Methodist Episcopal Church	1	1	71	1	25	46
	Presbyterian bodies:						
9	Presbyterian Church in the United States of America	2	2	645	2	310	335
10	United Presbyterian Church of North America	1	1	83	1	25	58
11	Protestant Episcopal Church	3	3	258	3	90	168
12	Roman Catholic Church	6	6	5,684	6	2,921	2,763
	Eastern Orthodox Churches:						
13	Greek Orthodox Church	1	1	400			
1	Spokane, Wash.	94	89	19,715	84	8,223	10,289
2	Protestant bodies	78	73	12,243	71	4,959	6,919
	Adventist bodies:						
3	Seventh-day Adventist Denomination	1	1	265	1	132	133
	Baptist bodies:						
4	Baptists—Northern and National (Colored) Conventions	10	10	1,324	10	488	836
5	Primitive Baptists	1	1	14	1	5	9
6	Church of Christ, Scientist	1	1	211	1	46	165
7	Congregationalists	6	6	1,216	6	419	797
	Disciples or Christians:						
8	Disciples of Christ	2	2	820	2	320	500
9	Churches of Christ	1	1	40	1	18	22
	Evangelistic associations:						
10	Apostolic Faith Movement	1	1	300	1	125	175
	Lutheran bodies:						
11	General Council of the Evangelical Lutheran Church in North America	1	1	302	1	143	159
12	United Norwegian Lutheran Church in America	1	1	355			
13	Evangelical Lutheran Joint Synod of Ohio and Other States	2	2	245	2	106	139
14	Other Lutheran bodies	3	3	206	3	99	107
	Methodist bodies:						
15	Methodist Episcopal Church	11	11	3,342	11	1,617	1,725
16	Other Methodist bodies	3	3	233	3	72	161
	Presbyterian bodies:						
17	Presbyterian Church in the United States of America	5	5	1,150	5	428	722
18	United Presbyterian Church of North America	3	3	400	3	152	248
19	Protestant Episcopal Church	10	6	840	5	310	520
20	Other Protestant bodies	16	15	980	15	479	501
21	Roman Catholic Church	7	7	6,994	6	3,105	3,166
22	Jewish congregations	2	2	[1] 115			
23	All other bodies	7	7	363	7	159	204
1	Springfield, Ill.	58	52	25,351	37	3,132	5,797
2	Protestant bodies	45	44	11,996	37	3,132	5,797
	Baptist bodies:						
3	Baptists—Northern Convention	2	2	1,334	2	486	848
4	Baptists—National Convention (Colored)	4	4	612	4	222	390
5	Primitive Baptists	1	1	18	1	8	10
6	Congregationalists	3	3	463	3	159	304
	Disciples or Christians:						
7	Disciples of Christ	3	3	1,580	3	485	1,095
	Lutheran bodies:						
8	General Synod of the Evangelical Lutheran Church in the United States of America	2	2	999	2	331	668
9	Evangelical Lutheran Synodical Conference of America	2	2	1,642	1	18	24
	Methodist bodies:						
10	Methodist Episcopal Church	6	6	2,147	3	310	370
11	African Methodist bodies	3	3	453	3	160	298
	Presbyterian bodies:						
12	Presbyterian Church in the United States of America	4	4	1,745	1	640	1,105
13	Protestant Episcopal Church	5	5	556	5	156	400
14	Other Protestant bodies	10	9	447	9	157	290
15	Roman Catholic Church	5	5	13,175			
16	Jewish congregations	2	2	[1] 130			
	Eastern Orthodox Churches:						
17	Greek Orthodox Church	1	1	50			
1	Springfield, Mass.	61	61	39,941	53	16,740	20,691
2	Protestant bodies	45	45	12,526	41	3,629	6,697
	Adventist bodies:						
3	Advent Christian Church	1	1	278	1	98	180
4	Seventh-day Adventist Denomination	1	1	14	1	5	9
	Baptist bodies:						
5	Baptists—Northern Convention	6	6	2,005	4	380	775
6	Baptists—National Convention (Colored)	2	2	390	2	120	270
7	Congregationalists	13	13	4,634	12	1,607	2,965
	Lutheran bodies:						
8	General Council of the Evangelical Lutheran Church in North America	1	1	208	1	85	123
9	Evangelical Lutheran Synodical Conference of America	1	1	137	1	46	91
	Methodist bodies:						
10	Methodist Episcopal Church	7	7	2,375	7	864	1,511
11	African Methodist Episcopal Church	1	1	58	1	16	42

[1] Heads of families only.

DEBT ON CHURCH PROPERTY, PARSONAGES, AND SUNDAY SCHOOLS, FOR EACH CITY OF 25,000 INHABITANTS OR DENOMINATIONS: 1906—Continued.

PLACES OF WORSHIP.					VALUE OF CHURCH PROPERTY.		DEBT ON CHURCH PROPERTY.		PARSONAGES.		SUNDAY SCHOOLS CONDUCTED BY CHURCH ORGANIZATIONS.				
Number of organizations reporting—		Number of church edifices reported.	Seating capacity of church edifices.		Number of organizations reporting.	Value reported.	Number of organizations reporting.	Amount of debt reported.	Number of organizations reporting.	Value of parsonages reported.	Number of organizations reporting.	Number of Sunday schools reported.	Number of officers and teachers.	Number of scholars.	
Church edifices.	Halls, etc.		Number of organizations reporting.	Seating capacity reported.											
2	......	2	2	800	2	$12,000	......	......	2	$5,500	2	3	46	460	7
1	......	1	1	200	1	1,000	......	......	......	......	1	1	10	46	8
2	......	3	2	900	2	18,000	1	$600	......	......	2	5	58	815	9
1	......	1	1	300	1	2,250	......	......	1	2,750	1	1	15	140	10
3	......	4	3	560	3	28,500	......	......	1	3,000	3	5	31	320	11
6	......	6	6	2,537	6	110,000	3	21,300	4	29,500	6	8	30	1,023	12
......	1	......	......	......	......	......	......	......	......	......	......	......	......	......	13
70	16	76	70	24,960	74	1,144,322	32	147,718	30	90,400	79	87	1,030	9,834	1
63	8	69	63	21,955	67	927,322	30	116,385	27	79,900	71	79	963	8,719	2
	......	1	1	300	1	5,000	......	......	......	......	1	1	25	175	3
9	......	9	9	2,530	9	105,572	6	19,650	......	......	10	10	141	1,159	4
......	1	......	......	......	......	......	......	......	......	......	......	......	......	......	5
1	......	1	1	800	1	50,000	1	6,000	......	......	1	1	12	96	6
6	......	6	6	2,490	6	100,000	3	18,700	4	14,000	6	6	109	1,218	7
2	......	3	2	1,850	2	57,000	1	12,000	......	......	2	2	49	505	8
	......	1	1	150	1	1,400	......	......	......	......	......	......	......	......	9
......	1	......	......	......	1	350	......	......	......	......	1	2	4	30	10
1	......	2	1	500	1	14,300	1	1,500	1	4,000	1	2	18	135	11
1	......	1	1	300	1	10,000	1	1,600	1	3,500	1	1	18	130	12
2	......	2	2	500	2	15,000	1	6,000	1	800	2	2	14	156	13
3	......	3	3	650	3	16,000	3	4,600	2	3,000	3	3	18	130	14
9	......	10	9	4,655	9	256,500	2	31,000	6	20,200	10	12	158	1,520	15
3	......	3	3	850	3	18,500	3	2,435	2	3,900	3	3	28	385	16
5	......	6	5	1,500	5	46,800	2	2,500	2	5,000	5	8	117	1,245	17
3	......	5	3	1,400	3	38,500	......	......	1	4,000	3	4	74	650	18
7	......	7	7	1,280	7	114,300	......	......	3	10,000	10	10	73	446	19
9	6	9	9	2,200	12	78,100	6	10,400	4	11,500	12	12	105	739	20
5	2	5	5	2,255	5	202,000	2	31,333	3	10,500	6	6	52	1,020	21
1	......	1	1	250	1	12,000	......	......	......	......	1	1	5	50	22
1	6	1	1	500	1	3,000	......	......	......	......	1	1	10	45	23
42	8	48	34	18,710	38	952,800	15	42,754	14	51,400	45	50	742	6,948	1
35	7	41	32	18,160	36	927,800	13	38,004	14	51,400	42	47	726	6,548	2
2	......	3	2	1,350	2	58,000	......	......	......	......	2	4	58	825	3
4	......	4	4	2,010	4	20,000	3	2,340	2	1,800	4	5	58	386	4
......	......	......	......	......	......	......	......	......	......	......	......	......	......	......	5
3	......	3	3	775	3	52,000	1	3,000	1	2,500	3	3	52	359	6
3	......	3	3	1,500	3	65,000	1	1,800	1	3,000	3	3	64	931	7
2	......	2	2	1,350	2	70,000	1	5,000	1	6,500	2	2	50	502	8
2	......	2	2	1,060	2	79,000	......	......	2	10,600	2	3	23	224	9
6	......	6	3	1,300	6	179,000	2	3,014	3	12,000	6	6	189	1,424	10
2	1	3	2	750	2	17,500	1	4,600	1	2,000	3	3	31	225	11
4	......	7	4	2,900	4	222,000	1	14,000	1	6,000	4	5	114	976	12
4	......	5	4	4,625	4	155,000	1	2,900	2	7,000	5	5	33	222	13
3	6	3	3	550	4	10,300	2	1,350	......	......	8	8	54	474	14
5	......	5	......	......	......	......	......	......	......	......	2	2	14	375	15
2	......	2	2	550	2	25,000	2	4,750	......	......	1	1	2	25	16
......		......	......	......	......	......	......	......	......	......	......	......	......	......	17
51		55	51	29,123	52	2,271,700	26	261,540	21	133,300	54	55	1,042	11,520	1
41	3	44	41	21,243	42	1,812,000	20	111,140	12	71,000	43	44	910	8,545	2
1	......	1	1	400	1	12,000	......	......	......	......	1	1	14	190	3
......	1	......	......	......	......	......	......	......	......	......	1	1	5	9	4
5	......	5	5	3,606	4	250,000	1	12,000	......	......	6	6	147	1,438	5
2	......	2	2	550	2	17,000	1	1,200	1	3,000	2	2	17	355	6
13	......	14	13	7,475	13	731,000	7	17,400	3	16,000	12	12	309	3,295	7
1	......	3	1	250	1	12,000	1	4,500	1	4,500	1	1	10	55	8
1	......	1	1	140	1	7,000	1	3,000	1	2,500	1	1	8	48	9
7	......	7	7	4,564	7	314,000	1	21,000	3	24,000	7	7	234	1,938	10
1	......	1	1	400	1	10,000	1	1,000	......	......	1	1	6	35	11

TABLE 7.—ORGANIZATIONS, COMMUNICANTS OR MEMBERS, PLACES OF WORSHIP, VALUE OF CHURCH PROPERTY, MORE IN 1900, BY SELECTED

	DENOMINATION.	Total number of organizations.	COMMUNICANTS OR MEMBERS.				
			Number of organizations reporting.	Total number reported.	Sex.		
					Number of organizations reporting.	Male.	Female.
	Springfield, Mass.—Continued.						
	Protestant bodies—Continued.						
12	Protestant Episcopal Church	2	2	1,613	1	140	195
13	Universalists	3	3	326	3	94	232
14	Other Protestant bodies	7	7	488	7	174	314
15	Roman Catholic Church	10	10	26,840	10	12,868	13,972
16	Jewish congregations	4	4	310[1]	.....	.....	.....
	Eastern Orthodox Churches:						
17	Greek Orthodox Church	1	1	250	1	235	15
18	Spiritualists	1	1	15	1	8	7
1	Springfield, Ohio	51	51	16,908	47	6,293	9,496
2	Protestant bodies	45	45	12,105	44	4,030	7,075
	Baptist bodies:						
3	Baptists—Northern Convention	2	2	685	2	193	492
4	Baptists—National Convention (Colored)	3	3	770	3	305	465
5	Congregationalists	2	2	525	2	167	358
	Disciples or Christians:						
6	Disciples of Christ	1	1	270	1	95	175
7	Churches of Christ	1	1	24	1	6	18
8	German Evangelical Synod of North America	1	1	1,000	.....	.....	.....
	Lutheran bodies:						
9	General Synod of the Evangelical Lutheran Church in the United States of America	6	6	1,988	6	788	1,200
10	General Council of the Evangelical Lutheran Church in North America	1	1	200	1	80	120
11	Evangelical Lutheran Joint Synod of Ohio and Other States	1	1	450	1	203	247
	Methodist bodies:						
12	Methodist Episcopal Church	6	6	2,799	6	978	1,821
13	African Methodist Episcopal Church	2	2	430	2	159	271
14	Wesleyan Methodist Connection of America	1	1	28	1	14	14
	Presbyterian bodies:						
15	Presbyterian Church in the United States of America	4	4	1,261	4	436	825
16	United Presbyterian Church of North America	1	1	260	1	84	176
17	Protestant Episcopal Church	2	2	485	2	180	305
	United Brethren bodies:						
18	Church of the United Brethren in Christ	1	1	308	1	108	200
19	Other Protestant bodies	10	10	622	10	234	388
20	Roman Catholic Church	3	3	4,684	3	2,263	2,421
21	Jewish congregations	2	2	59[1]	.....	.....	.....
	Eastern Orthodox Churches:						
22	Greek Orthodox Church	1	1	60	.....	.....	.....
1	Superior, Wis	50	48	14,816	41	5,232	6,088
	Protestant bodies	37	37	3,777	34	1,244	1,975
	Baptist bodies:						
3	Baptists—Northern Convention	2	2	255	2	77	178
4	Congregationalists	2	2	265	2	76	189
	Lutheran bodies:						
5	General Council of the Evangelical Lutheran Church in North America	5	5	474	5	205	269
6	United Norwegian Lutheran Church in America	3	3	624	2	51	66
7	Other Lutheran bodies	6	6	444	6	187	257
	Methodist bodies:						
8	Methodist Episcopal Church	5	5	622	5	211	411
9	African Methodist Episcopal Church	1	1	11	1	5	6
	Presbyterian bodies:						
10	Presbyterian Church in the United States of America	2	2	487	2	166	321
11	Protestant Episcopal Church	3	3	332	3	163	169
12	Other Protestant bodies	8	8	263	6	103	109
13	Roman Catholic Church	6	6	10,844	5	3,948	4,049
14	Jewish congregations	4	2	61[1]	.....	.....	.....
15	All other bodies	3	3	134	2	40	64
1	Syracuse, N. Y	100	100	66,697	85	28,857	34,306
2	Protestant bodies	74	74	23,162	67	7,265	13,131
	Baptist bodies:						
3	Baptists—Northern Convention	8	8	3,184	8	1,027	2,157
4	Congregationalists	6	6	1,936	5	463	913
	Disciples or Christians						
5	Disciples of Christ	2	2	320	2	115	205
6	German Evangelical Synod of North America	1	1	550	1	260	290
	Lutheran bodies:						
7	General Synod of the Evangelical Lutheran Church in the United States of America	6	6	2,468	6	948	1,520
8	General Council of the Evangelical Lutheran Church in North America	2	2	725	2	290	435
	Methodist bodies:						
9	Methodist Episcopal Church	15	15	4,770	14	1,863	2,852
10	Other Methodist bodies	4	4	504	3	89	165
	Presbyterian bodies:						
11	Presbyterian Church in the United States of America	9	9	3,577	8	919	2,033
12	Synod of the Reformed Presbyterian Church of North America	1	1	65	1	20	45
13	Protestant Episcopal Church	9	9	3,146	7	838	1,532
	Reformed bodies:						
14	Reformed Church in America	2	2	555	2	130	425
15	Unitarians	1	1	405	1	153	252
16	Universalists	1	1	500	.....	.....	.....
17	Other Protestant bodies	7	7	457	7	150	307

[1] Heads of families only.

DEBT ON CHURCH PROPERTY, PARSONAGES, AND SUNDAY SCHOOLS, FOR EACH CITY OF 25,000 INHABITANTS OR DENOMINATIONS: 1906—Continued.

PLACES OF WORSHIP. Number of organizations reporting— Church edifices.	Halls, etc.	Number of church edifices reported.	Seating capacity of church edifices. Number of organizations reporting.	Seating capacity reported.	VALUE OF CHURCH PROPERTY. Number of organizations reporting.	Value reported.	DEBT ON CHURCH PROPERTY. Number of organizations reporting.	Amount of debt reported.	PARSONAGES. Number of organizations reporting.	Value of parsonages reported.	SUNDAY SCHOOLS CONDUCTED BY CHURCH ORGANIZATIONS. Number of organizations reporting.	Number of Sunday schools reported.	Number of officers and teachers.	Number of scholars.	
2	....	2	2	1,400	2	$235,000	1	$17,000	2	$10,000	2	3	71	610	12
3	....	3	3	1,075	3	48,000	3	17,500	....	....	3	3	35	300	13
5	2	5	5	1,383	7	176,000	3	16,540	1	11,000	6	6	54	272	14
9	....	9	9	7,280	9	439,700	6	150,400	9	62,300	9	9	127	2,840	15
1	3	2	1	600	1	20,000	....	....	....	....	2	2	5	135	16
....	1	....	....	....	....	....	....	....	....	....	....	....	....	....	17
....	....	....	....	....	....	....	....	....	....	....	....	....	....	....	18
43	7	46		20,675	44	904,556	23	65,127	15	62,700	47	50	913	9,830	1
39	5	42	38	17,975	39	731,356	20	56,327	11	47,400	42	45	877	8,515	2
2	....	2	2	550	2	7,700	2	1,650	1	2,500	2	3	47	443	3
3	....	3	2	900	2	30,500	1	4,200	....	....	2	2	36	310	4
2	....	2	2	1,050	2	36,600	1	2,000	1	1,400	2	2	40	375	5
1	....	1	1	500	1	12,500	1	3,300	....	....	1	1	20	350	6
....	1	....	....	....	....	....	....	....	....	....	....	....	....	....	7
1	....		1	800	1	60,000	1	6,500	....	....	1	1	37	400	8
6	....	6	6	3,050	6	103,500	3	7,550	....	....	6	6	203	2,126	9
1	....	2	1	450	1	15,000	1	1,000	....	....	1	1	14	100	10
1	....	1	1	800	1	15,000	....	....	1	5,000	1	1	22	200	11
6	....	6	6	3,450	6	146,000	2	7,000	4	24,000	6	6	159	1,465	12
2	....	2	2	650	2	17,000	1	700	....	....	2	2	23	185	13
....	....	....	....	....	....	....	....	....	....	....	1	1	7	23	14
4	....	5	4	2,150	4	142,500	1	3,600	1	6,000	4	6	103	1,351	15
1	....	1	1	400	1	18,500	....	....	....	....	1	1	20	160	16
2	....	3	2	575	2	85,500	2	10,177	1	3,000	2	2	22	144	17
1	....	1	1	450	1	6,000	....	....	1	1,500	1	1	38	375	18
6	4	6	6	2,200	7	33,066	4	8,650	1	4,000	9	9	86	508	19
3	....	3	3	2,600	3	170,000	2	8,000	3	15,000	3	3	32	1,279	20
1	1	1	1	100	2	3,200	1	800	1	300	2	2	4	36	21
....	1	....	....	....	....	....	....	....	....	....	....	....	....	....	22
36	7	38		13,890	37	460,065	17	87,725	14	51,000	38	44	447	4,911	1
30	5	31	29	11,340	31	268,065	12	27,925	9	24,000	32	38	412	3,785	2
2	....	2	2	500	2	10,800	1	500	....	....	2	3	27	379	3
2	....	2	2	1,150	2	23,000	2	1,350	....	....	2	2	34	298	4
4	1	5	4	2,040	4	21,800	3	5,375	2	5,500	5			389	5
3	....	3	3	1,300	3	30,500	1	7,000	1	7,000	3			335	6
4	1	4	4	735	4	8,500	1	1,000	1	1,000	4	4	86	219	7
5	....	5	5	2,435	5	64,800	1	1,100	3	5,300	5	6	93	810	8
1	....	1	1	200	1	1,000	....	....	....	....	....	....	....	....	9
2	....	2		1,200	2	35,000	....	....	....	....	2			777	10
3	....	3	2	780	3	52,200	1	9,000	1	4,000	3		67	231	11
4	3	4	8	1,000	5	20,465	2	2,600	1	1,200	6	6	30	347	12
6	....	7	6	2,550	6	192,000	5	59,800	5	27,000	6	6	35	1,126	13
....	....	....	....	....	....	....	....	....	....	....	....	....	....	....	14
....	2	....	....	....	....	....	....	....	....	....	....	....	....	....	15
90	10	98	88	48,035	90	4,394,700	65	695,630	35	263,250		93	1,974	21,357	1
71	3	78	69	33,125	71	2,930,600	50	543,130	21	103,600	72	75	1,694	16,316	2
8	....	8	8	4,675	8	267,000	6	41,000	2	12,000	8	8	304	3,001	3
6	....	6	6	3,150	6	142,000	5	25,850	1	4,500	6	6	128	1,452	4
2	....	2	2	500	2	31,200	2	2,400	....	....	2	2	31	249	5
1	....	1	1	480	1	18,000	1	5,600	....	....	1	1	23	218	6
6	....	7	6	2,820	6	225,000	5	36,600	2	12,000	6	7	152	1,228	7
2	....	2	2	900	2	57,000	2	8,300	1	6,000	2	2	45	430	8
14	1	14	14	6,475	14	422,500	11	86,075	7	27,700	15	15	398	4,462	9
[illegible]	....	5	4	1,550	4	50,500	2	3,200	1	3,000	4	4	48	315	10
9	....	12	9	5,150	9	1,105,000	6	269,300	2	15,000	9	11	287	2,999	11
1	....	1	1	250	1	8,000	1	200	....	....	1	1	12	63	12
9	....	11	7	3,250	9	286,000	3	15,805	2	17,000	9	9	129	1,034	13
2	....	2	2	1,400	2	115,000	2	18,000	....	....	2	2	47	325	14
1	....	1	1	500	1	50,000	....	....	....	....	1	1	16	92	15
1	....	1	1	700	1	80,000	1	15,000	....	....	1	1	15	110	16
5	2	5	5	1,325	5	73,400	3	15,800	2	6,400	5	5	59	338	17

TABLE 7.—ORGANIZATIONS, COMMUNICANTS OR MEMBERS, PLACES OF WORSHIP, VALUE OF CHURCH PROPERTY, MORE IN 1900, BY SELECTED

	DENOMINATION.	Total number of organizations.	COMMUNICANTS OR MEMBERS.				
			Number of organizations reporting.	Total number reported.	Sex.		
					Number of organizations reporting.	Male.	Female.
	Syracuse, N. Y.—Continued.						
18	Roman Catholic Church	13	13	42,649	13	21,549	21,100
19	Jewish congregations	7	7	496 [1]			
20	All other bodies	6	6	388	5	43	75
1	Tacoma, Wash.	77	75	14,151	70	4,665	6,730
2	Protestant bodies	68	66	9,711	63	3,767	5,776
	Baptist bodies:						
3	Baptists—Northern Convention	8	8	1,219	8	503	716
4	Congregationalists	3	3	594	3	205	389
	Disciples or Christians:						
5	Disciples of Christ	2	2	558	2	288	270
6	Independent churches	2	2	280	2	105	175
	Lutheran bodies:						
7	General Council of the Evangelical Lutheran Church in North America	2	2	589	2	268	321
8	United Norwegian Lutheran Church in America	1	1	260	1	100	160
9	Other Lutheran bodies	5	4	300	3	79	101
	Methodist bodies:						
10	Methodist Episcopal Church	18	17	2,648	17	1,034	1,614
11	Other Methodist bodies	2	2	111	2	36	75
	Presbyterian bodies:						
12	Presbyterian Church in the United States of America	6	6	,467	6	551	916
13	United Presbyterian Church of North America	2	2	162	2	57	105
14	Protestant Episcopal Church	7	7	954	5	298	608
15	Other Protestant bodies	10	10	569	10	243	326
16	Roman Catholic Church	4	4	4,258	3	838	870
17	Jewish congregations	1	1	38 [1]			
18	All other bodies	4	4	144	4	60	84
1	Taunton, Mass.	31	30	17,903	28	7,794	9,936
2	Protestant bodies	21	20	3,893	19	1,261	2,619
	Baptist bodies:						
3	Baptists—Northern Convention	1	1	665	1	205	460
4	Free Baptists	1	1	40	1	3	37
5	Congregationalists	5	5	984	5	303	681
	Methodist bodies:						
6	Methodist Episcopal Church	5	5	925	5	293	632
7	African Methodist Episcopal Zion Church	1	1	40	1	16	24
8	Protestant Episcopal Church	2	2	680	2	247	433
9	Universalists	1	1	390	1	128	262
10	Other Protestant bodies	5	4	169	3	56	90
11	Roman Catholic Church	9	9	13,860	9	6,543	7,317
	Eastern Orthodox Churches:						
12	Greek Orthodox Church	1	1	150			
1	Terre Haute, Ind.	60	58	16,335	53	6,178	9,670
	Protestant bodies	50	49	11,065	47	3,790	7,029
	Baptist bodies:						
3	Baptists—Northern Convention	2	2	1,039	2	321	718
4	Baptists—National Convention (Colored)	2	2	320	2	112	208
5	Other Baptist bodies	2	2	236	2	74	162
6	Congregationalists	2	2	363	2	92	271
	Disciples or Christians:						
7	Disciples of Christ	5	4	1,500	4	472	1,028
8	Churches of Christ	1	1	100	1	40	60
	German Evangelical Protestant bodies:						
9	German Evangelical Protestant Ministers' Association	1	1	527	1	227	300
	Lutheran bodies:						
10	Evangelical Lutheran Synodical Conference of America	1	1	402	1	170	232
	Methodist bodies:						
11	Methodist Episcopal Church	12	12	3,086	12	1,006	2,080
12	African Methodist Episcopal Church	2	2	391	2	131	260
13	Free Methodist Church of North America	1	1	50	1	19	31
	Presbyterian bodies:						
14	Presbyterian Church in the United States of America	2	2	885	2	397	488
15	Protestant Episcopal Church	3	3	684	3	263	421
	Reformed bodies:						
16	Reformed Church in the United States	1	1	310	1	150	160
	United Brethren bodies:						
17	Church of the United Brethren in Christ	4	4	821	2	205	370
18	Other Protestant bodies	9	9	351	9	111	240
19	Roman Catholic Church	5	5	4,829	5	2,338	2,491
20	Jewish congregations	3	2	141 [1]			
21	All other bodies	2	2	300	1	50	150
1	Toledo, Ohio	129	129	44,082	117	17,508	26,206
2	Protestant bodies	105	105	30,870	99	11,159	16,937
	Baptist bodies:						
3	Baptists—Northern and National (Colored) Conventions	12	12	2,648	12	870	1,778
4	Congregationalists	7	7	2,914	7	972	1,942

[1] Heads of families only.

DEBT ON CHURCH PROPERTY, PARSONAGES, AND SUNDAY SCHOOLS, FOR EACH CITY OF 25,000 INHABITANTS OR DENOMINATIONS: 1906—Continued.

PLACES OF WORSHIP.					VALUE OF CHURCH PROPERTY.		DEBT ON CHURCH PROPERTY.		PARSONAGES.		SUNDAY SCHOOLS CONDUCTED BY CHURCH ORGANIZATIONS.				
Number of organizations reporting— Church edifices.	Number of organizations reporting— Halls, etc.	Number of church edifices reported.	Seating capacity of church edifices. Number of organizations reporting.	Seating capacity of church edifices. Seating capacity reported.	Number of organizations reporting.	Value reported.	Number of organizations reporting.	Amount of debt reported.	Number of organizations reporting.	Value of parsonages reported.	Number of organizations reporting.	Number of Sunday schools reported.	Number of officers and teachers.	Number of scholars.	
13		13	13	11,810	13	$1,412,600	9	$137,300	13	$159,300	12	12	248	4,683	18
6	1	7	6	3,100	6	51,500	6	15,200	1	350	4	6	32	358	19
	6														20
63	12	68	62	21,305	69	740,649	27	78,923	33	77,951	69	79	963	9,900	1
58	9	63	57	17,730	64	593,149	25	39,273	30	67,151	64	74	934	9,092	2
8		8	8	2,525	8	86,250	3	1,050	3	7,500	8	8	106	1,029	3
3		4	3	1,130	3	40,800	1	3,000	1	2,000	3	5	69	707	4
2		2	1	400	2	50,000					2	2	29	385	5
1	1	1	1	300	1	5,000	1	3,000			2	2	11	75	6
2		3	2	765	2	75,000	2	4,100	2	6,500	2	3	32	296	7
1		2	1	650	1	12,000	1	2,100	1	2,500	1	3	25	175	8
4	1	4	4	1,180	4	41,500	3	6,500	3	4,500	4	5	34	325	9
15	3	15	15	4,875	18	72,900	4	6,725	9	15,700	18	20	340	3,492	10
2		2	2	550	2	9,000	1	900	2	1,000	2	2	19	90	11
6		6	6	2,196	6	73,500	2	1,750	2	3,900	6	8	128	1,550	12
2		2	2	400	2	15,000	1	200	2	8,000	2	2	27	210	13
7		9	7	1,870	7	79,500	3	5,350	3	12,700	5	5	46	365	14
5	4	5	5	890	8	32,699	3	4,598	2	2,851	9	9	68	393	15
4		4	4	3,425	4	147,000	2	37,650	3	10,800	4	4	23	793	16
															17
1	3	1	1	150	1	500					1	1	6	15	18
28	3	31	28	15,223	29	1,008,725	14	157,881	19	100,200	28	29	625	6,101	1
19	2	22	19	8,955	21	464,025	8	13,881	11	86,700	19	20	480	3,544	2
1		2	1	1,000	1	62,000	1	4,000	1	6,000	1	2	65	815	3
1		1	1	200	1	2,000			1	1,000	1	1	10	50	4
5		6	5	2,525	5	157,000		700	4	12,000	5	5	139	1,060	5
5		6	5	2,320	5	62,500	[illegible]	1 000	2	5,200	5	5	148	799	6
	1				1	25					1	1	12	39	7
2		2	2	1,210	2	81,500			2	6,500	2	2	53	383	8
1		1	1	375	1	15,000	1	3 500			1	1	12	138	9
4	1	4	4	1,325	5	84,000	4	4 681	1	6,000	3	3	41	260	10
9		9	9	6,268	8	544,700	[illegible]	143 500	8	68,500	9	9	145	2,557	11
	1														12
49	7	59	47	21,584	51	602,049	24	36 440	21	66,300	53	59	837	9,258	1
45	4	53	43	19,784	48	577,049	23	26,440	19	53,300	47	53	824	8,318	2
2		6	2	2,000	2	64,500	1	650			2	5	62	669	3
2		2	2	550	2	8,200					2	2	15	131	4
2		2	2	600	2	16,000	1	80	1	8,000	1	1	8	100	5
2		2	2	900	2	57,000	1	100	1	2,500	2	2	26	225	6
5		5	5	1,450	5	25,000	3	1,800			5	5	88	1,005	7
1		1	1	500	1	1,800	1	800							8
1		[illegible]	1	1,500	1	14,000	1	2,000	1	1,400	1			123	9
1		1	1	600	1	25,000			1	5,000					10
12		12	12	6,600	12	183,100	8	15,960	6	11,100	12	12	345	3,444	11
2		2	2	750	2	9,000	2	800	2	1,800	2	2	18	196	12
1		1	1	200	1	1,200					1	1	7	60	13
2		3	2	1,000	2	70,000	1	1,500	2	7,000	2	4	60	965	14
3		4	3	634	3	46,300			1	7,500	3	3	25	282	15
1		1	1	400	1	25,000	1	200	1	3,000	1	1	18	169	16
4		4	2	850	4	15,128	1	1,050	1	3,000	4	4	59	573	17
4	4	5	4	1,250	7	15,821	2	1,500	2	3,000	9	10	86	436	18
2	1	3	2	1,300	2	22,000	1	10,000	2	13,000	5	5	9	890	19
2		3	2	500	1	3,000					1	1	4	50	20
	2														21
114	13	132	110	53,370	117	2,690,605	50	405,985	44	160,400	116	143	2,174	25,738	1
97	7	112	94	44,170	100	2,049,705	41	219,835	39	139,900	101	120	2,108	23,011	2
11		15	11	4,500	11	175,100	4	8,850	3	6,000	12	18	344	3,026	3
7		7	7	4,950	7	264,600	3	38,000			7	7	217	2,648	4

TABLE 7.—ORGANIZATIONS, COMMUNICANTS OR MEMBERS, PLACES OF WORSHIP, VALUE OF CHURCH PROPERTY, MORE IN 1900, BY SELECTED

	DENOMINATION.	Total number of organizations.	COMMUNICANTS OR MEMBERS.				
			Number of organizations reporting.	Total number reported.	Sex.		
					Number of organizations reporting.	Male.	Female.
	Toledo, Ohio—Continued.						
	Protestant bodies—Continued.						
	Disciples or Christians:						
5	Disciples of Christ			1,060	4	417	643
	Evangelical bodies:						
6	Evangelical Association	3	3	368	3	144	224
	Lutheran bodies:						
7	General Council of the Evangelical Lutheran Church in North America	8	8	2,568	7	788	1,205
8	Evangelical Lutheran Synodical Conference of America	2	2	1,197	2	542	655
9	Evangelical Lutheran Joint Synod of Ohio and Other States	2	2	1,412	1	140	185
10	Evangelical Lutheran Synod of Iowa and Other States	5	5	3,495	5	1,567	1,928
11	Evangelical Lutheran Synod of Michigan and Other States	3	3	1,609	3	746	863
12	Other Lutheran bodies	2	2	174	2	77	97
	Methodist bodies:						
13	Methodist Episcopal Church	18	18	4,551	18	1,792	2,759
14	Other Methodist bodies	3	3	260	2	15	41
	Presbyterian bodies:						
15	Presbyterian Church in the United States of America	5	5	2,189	4	722	1,117
16	United Presbyterian Church of North America	2	2	96	2	36	60
17	Protestant Episcopal Church	10	10	2,852	9	934	1,503
	Reformed bodies:						
18	Reformed Church in the United States	5	5	1,429	5	700	729
	United Brethren bodies:						
19	Church of the United Brethren in Christ	5	5	1,217	5	436	781
20	Other Protestant bodies	9	9	831	8	261	427
21	Roman Catholic Church [1]	11	11	12,072	11	6,112	5,960
22	Jewish congregations	5	5	[2] 444			
23	All other bodies	8	8	696	7	237	309
1	Topeka, Kans.	72	72	15,716	69	5,344	8,787
2	Protestant bodies	66	66	13,045	64	4,129	7,481
	Baptist bodies:						
3	Baptists—Northern Convention	5	5	1,488	5	494	994
4	Baptists—National Convention (Colored)	4	4	784	4	322	462
5	Congregationalists	4	4	1,373	4	490	883
	Disciples or Christians:						
6	Disciples of Christ	5	5	1,320	5	509	811
	Lutheran bodies:						
7	General Synod of the Evangelical Lutheran Church in the United States of America	1	1	203	1	78	125
8	General Council of the Evangelical Lutheran Church in North America	1	1	145	1	45	100
9	Evangelical Lutheran Synodical Conference of America	1	1	259	1	113	146
	Methodist bodies:						
10	Methodist Episcopal Church	10	10	2,694	9	418	876
11	African Methodist Episcopal Church	3	3	525	3	154	371
12	Other Methodist bodies	4	4	301	3	92	174
	Presbyterian bodies:						
13	Presbyterian Church in the United States of America	4	4	1,803	4	551	1,252
14	United Presbyterian Church of North America	2	2	298	2	114	184
15	Other Presbyterian bodies	3	3	276	3	126	150
16	Protestant Episcopal Church	3	3	722	3	319	403
17	Other Protestant bodies	16	16	854	16	304	550
18	Roman Catholic Church	2	2	2,394	2	1,161	1,233
19	All other bodies	4	4	277	3	54	73
1	Trenton, N. J.	81	81	41,310	73	15,955	20,455
2	Protestant bodies	66	66	17,249	62	5,996	10,152
	Baptist bodies:						
3	Baptists—Northern and National (Colored) Conventions	10	10	2,804	10	926	1,878
4	German Evangelical Synod of North America	1	1	500	1	200	300
	Lutheran bodies:						
5	General Synod of the Evangelical Lutheran Church in the United States of America	3	3	473	3	208	265
6	General Council of the Evangelical Lutheran Church in North America	3	3	1,738	3	752	986
7	Other Lutheran bodies	2	2	49	1	16	8
	Methodist bodies:						
8	Methodist Episcopal Church	12	12	4,246	12	1,479	2,767
9	African Methodist Episcopal Church	1	1	150	1	40	110
10	African Methodist Episcopal Zion Church	1	1	310	1	120	190
	Presbyterian bodies:						
11	Presbyterian Church in the United States of America	10	10	3,669	9	1,205	2,244
12	Protestant Episcopal Church	8	8	2,168	6	456	856
	Reformed bodies:						
13	Reformed Church in the United States	1	1	250	1	150	100
14	Hungarian Reformed Church in America	1	1	300	1	200	100
15	Other Protestant bodies	13	13	592	13	244	348
16	Roman Catholic Church	12	12	23,661	11	9,959	10,303
17	Jewish congregations	3	3	[2] 400			
1	Troy, N. Y.	75	75	46,924	65	19,393	25,540
2	Protestant bodies	55	55	15,217	50	4,744	8,834
	Baptist bodies:						
3	Baptists—Northern Convention	6	6	2,054	5	588	1,149
4	Primitive Baptists	1	1	15	1	5	10

[1] Exclusive of statistics not reported separately by cities for part of Cleveland diocese.

DEBT ON CHURCH PROPERTY, PARSONAGES, AND SUNDAY SCHOOLS, FOR EACH CITY OF 25,000 INHABITANTS OR DENOMINATIONS: 1906—Continued.

PLACES OF WORSHIP.					VALUE OF CHURCH PROPERTY.		DEBT ON CHURCH PROPERTY.		PARSONAGES.		SUNDAY SCHOOLS CONDUCTED BY CHURCH ORGANIZATIONS.				
Number of organizations reporting—		Number of church edifices reported.	Seating capacity of church edifices.		Number of organizations reporting.	Value reported.	Number of organizations reporting.	Amount of debt reported.	Number of organizations reporting.	Value of parsonages reported.	Number of organizations reporting.	Number of Sunday schools reported.	Number of officers and teachers.	Number of scholars.	
Church edifices.	Halls, etc.		Number of organizations reporting.	Seating capacity reported.											
4	....	4	4	2,300	4	$70,300	2	$4,300	....	....	4	5	68	652	5
3	....	3	2	350	3	16,500	....	....	1	$1,200	3	3	65	462	6
7	1	7	7	2,325	8	68,500	3	9,000	3	12,000	8	9	150	1,867	7
2	....	2	2	1,150	2	22,000	2	3,700	1	800	1	2	5	350	8
2	....	2	1	300	2	53,000	2	2,200	2	11,000	2	3	50	720	9
5	....	6	5	3,200	5	110,500	3	5,900	5	13,300	5	8	82	1,227	10
3	....	4	3	1,525	3	24,200	2	3,000	3	6,600	3	3	77	670	11
1	1	1	1	500	1	10,000	1	4,000	....	....	1	1	14	140	12
18	....	18	18	7,625	18	292,500	5	28,775	10	30,000	18	20	434	4,718	13
3	....	3	3	950	3	39,500	1	6,000	2	2,500	3	3	40	325	14
5	....	8	5	4,700	5	217,500	3	37,700	....	....	5	6	155	2,196	15
2	....	2	2	500	2	16,025	1	1,150	....	....	2	2	18	135	16
8	2	12	8	3,750	9	482,230	2	47,000	4	44,000	9	11	138	1,288	17
5	....	7	5	2,200	5	73,100	3	15,660	2	6,000	5	5	67	782	18
5	....	5	5	2,100	5	45,500	3	4,100	3	6,500	5	6	115	1,346	19
6	3	6	5	1,245	7	68,650	1	500	....	....	8	8	69	459	20
11	....	14	10	6,975	8	584,600	6	174,100	5	20,500	10	18	47	2,535	21
5	....	5	5	2,000	5	50,600	2	9,500	....	....	4	4	9	166	22
1	6	1	1	225	4	5,700	1	2,500	....	....	1	1	10	26	23
61	9	61	60	26,601	65	649,225	21	30,811	32	75,700	65	70	1,066	8,720	1
58	6	58	57	25,205	62	608,125	20	30,203	30	69,700	61	66	1,036	8,253	2
5	....	5	5	2,625	5	91,750	2	15,400	2	4,500	5	6	136	1,034	3
4	....	4	4	2,250	4	24,500	3	1,765	1	1,000	4	4	42	374	4
4	....	4	4	1,875	4	68,000	1	70	1	1,600	4	4	114	897	5
5	....	5	5	2,600	5	45,500	2	2,450	....	....	5	6	81	891	6
1	....	1	1	400	1	15,000	....	....	....	....	1	1	20	170	7
1	....	1	1	350	1	8,700	....	....	1	1,300	1	1	12	62	8
1	....	1	1	400	1	6,000	....	....	1	1,500	....	....	....	....	9
9	1	9	9	4,250	9	74,800	2	275	8	26,200	10	10	226	1,592	10
3	....	3	3	1,200	3	22,200	1	25	3	1,600	3	3	33	306	11
4	....	4	3	1,500	4	12,200	2	3,100	3	3,300	4	4	37	223	12
4	....	4	4	2,700	4	115,000	....	....	2	9,500	4	5	160	1,300	13
2	....	2	2	900	2	27,000	2	3,500	2	5,500	2	2	30	261	14
3	....	3	3	950	3	11,500	1	1,900	2	2,400	3	4	47	285	15
3	....	3	3	830	3	42,800	....	....	2	6,800	3	3	23	212	16
9	5	9	9	2,375	13	38,175	4	1,718	2	4,500	12	13	75	646	17
2	....	2	2	1,300	2	45,000	....	....	2	6,000	2	2	8	400	18
1	3	1	1	96	1	1,100	1	608	....	....	2	2	22	67	19
73	7	85	73	38,099	74	2,466,700	53	405,246	32	249,400	71	81	1,659	18,828	1
58	7	69	58	28,545	59	1,816,700	40	216,360	23	148,900	58	66	1,552	14,990	2
10	....	14	10	6,400	10	225,800	8	31,080	....	....	10	13	271	2,783	3
1	....	1	1	500	1	25,000	1	17,000	1	4,000	1	1	19	209	4
3	....	3	3	700	3	33,000	3	14,475	1	2,000	3	3	50	446	5
3	....	3	3	1,900	3	147,000	3	21,200	2	10,000	3	3	77	680	6
....	1	....	....	....	....	....	....	....	....	....	....	....	....	....	7
12	....	13	12	7,500	12	463,000	8	86,500	8	47,500	12	12	415	3,867	8
1	....	1	1	600	1	40,000	1	700	1	7,000	1	1	14	130	9
1	....	1	1	500	1	10,000	1	1,000	....	....	1	1	25	160	10
10	....	10	10	5,150	10	592,000	6	29,000	3	37,000	10	12	421	4,541	11
8	....	13	8	2,745	8	181,500	5	13,750	4	31,500	8	11	186	1,724	12
1	....	2	1	350	1	7,000	1	1,000	1	2,000	....	....	....	....	13
1	....	1	1	400	1	15,000	....	....	1	5,000	....	....	....	....	14
7	6	7	7	1,800	8	77,400	3	655	1	2,900	9	9	74	450	15
12	....	13	12	8,594	12	583,000	10	172,886	8	98,500	11	13	100	3,618	16
3	....	3	3	960	3	67,000	3	16,000	1	2,000	2	2	7	220	17
67	4	82	67	35,815	68	2,901,700	22	274,550	36	268,200	67	74	1,296	14,022	1
53	....	68	53	25,317	54	1,849,700	13	45,050	28	172,700	52	57	1,152	9,622	2
6	....	10	6	3,050	6	192,500	....	....	3	17,000	6	6	154	1,303	3
....	....	....	....	....	....	....	....	....	....	....	....	....	....	....	4

[1] Heads of families only.

TABLE 7.—ORGANIZATIONS, COMMUNICANTS OR MEMBERS, PLACES OF WORSHIP, VALUE OF CHURCH PROPERTY, ... MORE IN 1900, BY SELECTED

	DENOMINATION.	Total number of organizations.	COMMUNICANTS OR MEMBERS.				
			Number of organizations reporting.	Total number reported.	Sex.		
					Number of organizations reporting.	Male.	Female.
	Troy, N. Y.—Continued.						
	Protestant bodies—Continued.						
	Disciples or Christians:						
5	Disciples of Christ	2	2	617	1	152	347
6	German Evangelical Synod of North America	1	1	300	1	100	200
	Lutheran bodies:						
7	General Synod of the Evangelical Lutheran Church in the United States of America	2	2	336	2	143	193
8	General Council of the Evangelical Lutheran Church in North America	1	1	500	1	219	281
9	Other Lutheran bodies	2	2	370	2	176	194
	Methodist bodies:						
10	Methodist Episcopal Church	11	11	3,416	11	1,238	2,178
11	African Methodist Episcopal Zion Church	1	1	100	1	40	60
	Presbyterian bodies:						
12	Presbyterian Church in the United States of America	14	14	3,824	14	1,205	2,619
13	United Presbyterian Church of North America	1	1	131	1	50	81
14	Protestant Episcopal Church	7	7	2,969	4	636	1,129
15	Other Protestant bodies	6	6	585	6	192	393
16	Roman Catholic Church	13	13	30,989	13	14,377	16,612
17	Jewish congregations	4	4	[1] 252	......	......	......
18	Armenian Church	1	1	331	1	252	79
19	All other bodies	2	2	135	1	20	15
1	Utica, N. Y	55	52	45,846	48	22,271	23,136
	Protestant bodies	41	41	13,455	40	4,744	8,499
	Baptist bodies:						
3	Baptists—Northern Convention	5	5	1,802	5	541	1,261
4	Congregationalists	2	2	836	2	302	534
5	Independent churches	1	1	590	1	230	360
	Lutheran bodies:						
6	General Synod of the Evangelical Lutheran Church in the United States of America	1	1	115	1	42	73
7	General Council of the Evangelical Lutheran Church in North America	3	3	1,274	3	497	777
8	Evangelical Lutheran Synodical Conference of America	1	1	280	1	120	160
	Methodist bodies:						
9	Methodist Episcopal Church	6	6	1,513	6	460	1,053
10	Other Methodist bodies	2	2	71	2	37	34
	Moravian bodies:						
11	Moravian Church (Unitas Fratrum)	1	1	280	1	95	185
	Presbyterian bodies:						
12	Presbyterian Church in the United States of America	5	5	2,979	5	1,078	1,901
13	Welsh Calvinistic Methodist Church	1	1	491	1	175	316
14	Protestant Episcopal Church	7	7	2,600	6	981	1,407
15	Other Protestant bodies	6	6	624	6	186	438
16	Roman Catholic Church	8	8	32,164	8	17,527	14,637
17	Jewish congregations	5	2	[1] 127	......	......	......
	Eastern Orthodox Churches:						
18	Greek Orthodox Church	1	1	100	......	......	......
1	Washington, D. C	289	288	136,759	259	41,634	72,723
	Protestant bodies	257	257	91,474	239	27,824	55,745
	Adventist bodies:						
3	Seventh-day Adventist Denomination	3	3	382	3	161	221
	Baptist bodies:						
4	Baptists—Northern Convention	20	20	10,777	18	3,635	7,009
5	Baptists—National Convention (Colored)	60	60	26,203	58	6,529	16,949
6	Primitive Baptists	2	2	44	2	16	28
7	Church of Christ, Scientist	1	1	347	1	91	256
8	Congregationalists	6	6	2,984	6	1,137	1,847
	Disciples or Christians:						
9	Disciples of Christ	5	5	2,170	5	959	1,211
10	German Evangelical Synod of North America	1	1	350	1	125	225
	Lutheran bodies:						
11	General Synod of the Evangelical Lutheran Church in the United States of America	9	9	2,129	8	711	1,218
12	General Council of the Evangelical Lutheran Church in North America	1	1	75	1	32	43
13	Evangelical Lutheran Synodical Conference of America	2	2	432	2	177	255
14	Evangelical Lutheran Joint Synod of Ohio and Other States	2	2	468	2	194	274
	Methodist bodies:						
15	Methodist Episcopal Church	37	37	11,019	33	3,664	6,550
16	African Methodist Episcopal Church	7	7	1,928	7	724	1,204
17	African Methodist Episcopal Zion Church	6	6	2,615	6	988	1,627
18	Methodist Protestant Church	5	5	1,415	4	479	659
19	Methodist Episcopal Church, South	7	7	1,922	6	627	1,070
20	Colored Methodist Episcopal Church	5	5	1,110	5	348	762
21	Other Methodist bodies	3	3	68	3	29	39
	Presbyterian bodies:						
22	Presbyterian Church in the United States of America	17	17	8,182	16	2,339	4,681
23	Presbyterian Church in the United States	2	2	454	2	147	307
24	Protestant Episcopal Church	38	38	13,692	33	3,747	7,877
	Reformed bodies:						
25	Reformed Church in the United States	2	2	580	1	109	161
26	Unitarians	1	1	700	1	300	400
27	Other Protestant bodies	15	15	1,428	15	556	872
28	Roman Catholic Church	21	21	43,778	13	13,245	16,734
29	Jewish congregations	4	3	[1] 698	......	......	......
	Eastern Orthodox Churches:						
30	Greek Orthodox Church	1	1	450	1	400	50
31	All other bodies	6	6	359	6	165	194

[1] Heads of families onl

DEBT ON CHURCH PROPERTY, PARSONAGES, AND SUNDAY SCHOOLS, FOR EACH CITY OF 25,000 INHABITANTS OR DENOMINATIONS: 1906—Continued.

PLACES OF WORSHIP. Number of organizations reporting— Church edifices.	PLACES OF WORSHIP. Number of organizations reporting— Halls, etc.	PLACES OF WORSHIP. Number of church edifices reported.	PLACES OF WORSHIP. Seating capacity of church edifices. Number of organizations reporting.	PLACES OF WORSHIP. Seating capacity of church edifices. Seating capacity reported.	VALUE OF CHURCH PROPERTY. Number of organizations reporting.	VALUE OF CHURCH PROPERTY. Value reported.	DEBT ON CHURCH PROPERTY. Number of organizations reporting.	DEBT ON CHURCH PROPERTY. Amount of debt reported.	PARSONAGES. Number of organizations reporting.	PARSONAGES. Value of parsonages reported.	SUNDAY SCHOOLS CONDUCTED BY CHURCH ORGANIZATIONS. Number of organizations reporting.	SUNDAY SCHOOLS CONDUCTED BY CHURCH ORGANIZATIONS. Number of Sunday schools reported.	SUNDAY SCHOOLS CONDUCTED BY CHURCH ORGANIZATIONS. Number of officers and teachers.	SUNDAY SCHOOLS CONDUCTED BY CHURCH ORGANIZATIONS. Number of scholars.	
2		2	2	730	2	$29,000	1	$900			2	3	67	417	5
1		1	1	350	1	15,000					1	1	14	150	6
2		2	2	550	2	20,500	2	3,600	1	$3,000	2	2	31	295	7
1		1	1	315	1	20,000					1	2	19	170	8
2		2	2	325	2	7,000	2	1,400	1	2,000	2	2	19	149	9
11		11	11	5,635	11	351,500			10	51,500	11	12	327	2,799	10
1		1	1	550	1	25,000	1	5,000			1	1	10	271	11
13		17	13	7,778	14	547,500	6	31,650	6	30,500	13	13	320	2,396	12
1		1	1	300	1	30,000			1	5,000	1	1	12	90	13
7		14	7	4,000	7	490,700			5	59,700	6	7	108	1,049	14
6		6	6	1,734	6	121,000	1	2,500	1	4,000	6	7	71	534	15
12	1	12	12	9,798	12	1,012,000	8	221,500	8	95,500	13	15	138	4,205	16
2		2	2	700	2	40,000	1	8,000			2	2	6	195	17
	1														18
	2														19
47		55	47	27,327	49	2,001,050	23	147,880	24	173,000	49	54	1,216	11,465	1
38	3	46	38	19,971	40	1,311,050	17	81,280	16	83,500	41	45	1,029	8,141	2
5		5	5	3,030	5	174,000	4	29,900			5	5	141	1,247	3
2		3	2	1,675	2	70,000	1	17,000	1	4,000	2	2	64	552	4
1		1	1	500	1	25,000	1	3,500	1	7,000	1	1	30	250	5
1		1	1	300	1	10,000	1	2,600			1	1	6	51	6
3		3	3	1,300	3	66,000	2	4,500	1	4,000	3	4	86	699	7
1		1	1	350	1	20,000	1	7,000	1	4,000	1	1	8	85	8
6		6	6	2,900	6	120,000	3	9,430	3	13,500	6	6	280	1,214	9
2		2	2	666	2	20,000			1	3,000	2	2	11	79	10
1		2	1	650	1	18,000					1	2	23	150	11
5		6	5	3,650	5	315,000	1	3,500	2	11,500	5	6	167	2,025	12
1		1	1	550	1	20,000	1	2,000	1	4,500	1	2	25	250	13
7		10	7	3,425	7	347,000	1	1,050	4	30,000	7	7	123	1,141	14
3	3	5	3	975	5	106,050	1	800	1	2,000	6	6	65	398	15
8		8	8	7,056	8	663,000	5	64,600	8	89,500	8	9	187	3,324	16
1		1	1	300	1	7,000	1	2,000							17
	1														18
235	43	264	232	142,311	243	10,025,122	143	1,570,609	74	612,741	263	297	5,338	56,771	1
218	38	245	215	127,291	226	8,552,072	132	940,690	61	416,860	246	274	4,797	50,801	2
2	1	2	2	700	2	20,000	1	2,400			3	3	42	304	3
18	2	21	17	12,045	18	888,500	7	35,600	2	7,500	20	25	737	8,314	4
43	17	44	43	27,337	43	962,900	33	180,386	2	1,300	57	58	482	5,599	5
	2														6
1		1	1	600	1	32,000	1	12,000			1	1	14	90	7
5		6	5	4,050	6	329,000	3	53,500		4,000	6	8	168	2,311	8
5		6	5	2,606	5	141,000	4	25,013			5	5	123	1,495	9
1		1	1	650	1	53,000	1	1,000	1	5,500	1	1	20	160	10
9		9	9	3,910	9	476,700	6	59,300	3	36,500	9	9	220	1,794	11
1		1	1	350	1	22,000	1	10,000			1	1	10	98	12
2		3	2	600	2	40,000	2	1,300	1	5,000	2	3	20	154	13
2		2	2	575	2	43,000	2	14,700			2	2	24	227	14
36	1	36	34	17,439	36	1,178,705	24	84,098	20	138,260	37	41	934	9,569	15
7		7	7	4,150	7	127,987	6	29,350	4	8,800	7	7	98	1,116	16
6		6	6	3,230	6	207,000	5	38,900	2	9,000	6	7	102	1,037	17
5		5	5	3,843	5	169,500	3	24,500	2	10,000	5	5	126	1,466	18
7		8	7	3,100	7	141,000	3	18,075	1	3,500	7	7	130	1,378	19
5		5	5	4,400	5	139,000	3	20,000	1	1,000	5	5	49	505	20
	3				1	80					1	1	4	40	21
17		25	17	12,560	17	1,198,500	7	101,450	6	57,000	17	23	606	6,809	22
2		2	2	560	2	40,000	1	6,000			2	2	30	185	23
33	5	43	33	18,267	37	1,864,850	17	208,318	13	117,500	38	46	677	6,606	24
2		2	2	1,200	2	90,000			2	12,000	2	2	38	421	25
1		1	1	700	1	100,000					1	1	20	150	26
8	7	9	8	4,425	10	287,350	2	14,800			11	11	123	973	27
13		15	13	11,670	13	1,259,550	8	514,919	13	195,881	13	19	526	5,620	28
3		3	3	3,100	3	210,000	3	115,000			3	3	12	325	29
1		1	1	250	1	3,500									30
	5										1	1	3	25	31

TABLE 7.—ORGANIZATIONS, COMMUNICANTS OR MEMBERS, PLACES OF WORSHIP, VALUE OF CHURCH PROPERTY, MORE IN 1900, BY SELECTED

	DENOMINATION.	Total number of organizations.	COMMUNICANTS OR MEMBERS.				
			Number of organizations reporting.	Total number reported.	Sex.		
					Number of organizations reporting.	Male.	Female.
1	Waterbury, Conn.	36	36	35,260	34	17,083	18,082
2	Protestant bodies	24	24	7,581	24	3,050	4,531
	Adventist bodies:						
3	Advent Christian Church	1	1	203	1	78	125
	Baptist bodies:						
4	Baptists—Northern and National (Colored) Conventions	4	4	1,326	4	691	635
5	Congregationalists	5	5	1,982	5	726	1,256
	Lutheran bodies:						
6	General Council of the Evangelical Lutheran Church in North America	2	2	516	2	250	266
7	Evangelical Lutheran Synodical Conference of America	1	1	50	1	25	25
	Methodist bodies:						
8	Methodist Episcopal Church	3	3	1,470	3	532	938
9	African Methodist Episcopal Zion Church	1	1	235	1	101	134
10	Protestant Episcopal Church	2	2	1,691	2	611	1,080
11	Other Protestant bodies	5	5	108	5	36	72
12	Roman Catholic Church	9	9	27,454	9	13,963	13.491
13	Jewish congregations	2	2	[1] 125	....	....	....
	Eastern Orthodox Churches:						
14	Russian Orthodox Church	1	1	100	1	70	30
1	Wheeling, W. Va.	43	43	22,017	37	8,826	11,025
	Protestant bodies	33	33	11,356	28	3,469	5,851
	Baptist bodies:						
	Baptists—Northern and National (Colored) Conventions	2	2	378	1	107	217
	Disciples or Christians:						
4	Disciples of Christ	-	-	760	2	294	466
	German Evangelical Protestant bodies:						
5	German Evangelical Protestant Ministers' Association	1	1	399	1	154	245
6	Independent churches	1	1	1,000	1	450	550
	Lutheran bodies:						
7	General Synod of the Evangelical Lutheran Church in the United States of America	2	2	757	2	205	552
8	General Council of the Evangelical Lutheran Church in North America	1	1	800	1	375	425
9	Evangelical Lutheran Joint Synod of Ohio and Other States	1	1	490	1	175	315
	Methodist bodies:						
10	Methodist Episcopal Church	10	10	3,438	8	1,675	1,800
11	African Methodist Episcopal Church	1	1	76	1	21	55
	Presbyterian bodies:						
12	Presbyterian Church in the United States of America	4	4	1,502	3	221	512
13	United Presbyterian Church of North America	2	2	496	2	171	325
14	Protestant Episcopal Church	3	3	995	2	105	240
	Reformed bodies:						
15	Reformed Church in the United States	1	1	240	1	100	140
16	Other Protestant bodies	2	2	25	2	16	9
17	Roman Catholic Church	7	7	10,206	7	5,222	4,984
18	Jewish congregations	1	1	[1] 130	....	....	....
19	All other bodies	2	2	325	2	135	190
1	Wilkes-Barre, Pa.	65	65	35,780	60	16,524	18,851
2	Protestant bodies	46	46	13,387	46	5,110	8,277
	Baptist bodies:						
3	Baptists—Northern and National (Colored) Conventions	5	5	781	5	284	497
4	Congregationalists	3	3	589	3	232	357
	Lutheran bodies:						
5	General Council of the Evangelical Lutheran Church in North America	5	5	1,582	5	651	931
6	Other Lutheran bodies	5	5	903	5	472	431
	Methodist bodies:						
7	Methodist Episcopal Church	7	7	3,275	7	1,191	2,084
8	Other Methodist bodies	4	4	347	4	125	222
	Presbyterian bodies:						
9	Presbyterian Church in the United States of America	4	4	2,281	4	777	1,504
10	Welsh Calvinistic Methodist Church	2	2	816	2	377	439
11	Protestant Episcopal Church	3	3	1.569	3	541	1,028
	Reformed bodies:						
12	Reformed Church in the United States	2	2	559	2	209	350
13	Other Protestant bodies	6	6	685	6	251	434
14	Roman Catholic Church	12	12	20,238	12	10,284	9,954
15	Jewish congregations	4	4	[1] 245	....	....	....
	Eastern Orthodox Churches:						
16	Russian Orthodox Church	1	1	1,250	1	850	400
17	Greek Orthodox Church	1	1	160	....	....	....
18	Polish National Church of America	1	1	500	1	280	220
1	Williamsport, Pa.	52	51	17,189	48	6,490	9,825
2	Protestant bodies	47	47	13,331	44	4,722	7,735
	Baptist bodies:						
3	Baptists—Northern and National (Colored) Conventions	7	7	1,717	7	693	1,024
	Evangelical bodies:						
4	Evangelical Association	1	1	117	1	40	77
5	United Evangelical Church	3	3	847	2	230	410
6	German Evangelical Synod of North America	1	1	500	1	200	300

[1] Heads of families only.

DEBT ON CHURCH PROPERTY, PARSONAGES, AND SUNDAY SCHOOLS, FOR EACH CITY OF 25,000 INHABITANTS OR DENOMINATIONS: 1906—Continued.

PLACES OF WORSHIP.					VALUE OF CHURCH PROPERTY.		DEBT ON CHURCH PROPERTY.		PARSONAGES.		SUNDAY SCHOOLS CONDUCTED BY CHURCH ORGANIZATIONS.				
Number of organizations reporting—		Number of church edifices reported.	Seating capacity of church edifices.		Number of organizations reporting.	Value reported.	Number of organizations reporting.	Amount of debt reported.	Number of organizations reporting.	Value of parsonages reported.	Number of organizations reporting.	Number of Sunday schools reported.	Number of officers and teachers.	Number of scholars.	
Church edifices.	Halls, etc.		Number of organizations reporting.	Seating capacity reported.											
31	4	32	31	19,892	32	$1,938,054	19	$373,675	17	$208,000	31	33	653	9,373	1
19	4	19	19	9,960	20	895,054	11	58,675	9	85,000	22	22	526	5,039	2
1	....	1	1	400	1	11,000	1	2,450	1	4,000	1	1	21	141	3
4	....	4	4	1,240	4	132,000	2	9,000	....	....	4	4	92	1,299	4
4	....	4	4	2,900	4	286,000	2	6,350	2	31,000	5	5	151	1,270	5
2	....	2	2	900	2	29,804	2	12,775	1	5,000		2	30	292	6
....	1	....	....	....	....	....	....	....	....	....	1	1	5	20	7
3	....	3	3	2,050	3	106,750	2	5,100	3	17,500	3	3	128	1,080	8
1	....	1	1	500	1	30,000	1	8,000	1	2,500	1	1	12	109	9
2	....	2	2	1,420	2	280,000	....	....	1	25,000	2	2	78	783	10
2	3	2	2	550	3	20,500	1	15,000	....	....	3	3	9	45	11
9	....	10	9	8,232	9	1,006,000	7	306,000	8	123,000	9	11	127	4,334	12
2	....	2	2	1,100	2	25,000	....	....	....	....	....	....	....	....	13
1	....	1	1	600	1	12,000	1	9,000	....	....	....	....	....	....	14
37	5	41	37	22,615	38	1,513,275	19	101,225	22	212,000	39	46	848	9,881	1
30	3	34	30	18,405	31	1,028,275	13	52,900	18	119,000	30	35	784	7,803	2
2	....			1,800	2	25,200	1	1,700	....	....	2	4	69	471	3
2	....	-	-	1,100	2	76,000	2	5,100	....	....	2	2	63	617	4
1	....	1	1	600	1	10,000	1	1,400	1	3,000	1	1	22	190	5
1	....	1	1	1,000	1	80,000	1	4,000	1	2,500	1	1	40	350	6
2	....	2	2	1,450	2	76,300	2	11,000	....	....	2	2	58	730	7
1	....	1	1	1,000	1	32,000	....	....	1	12,000	1	1	25	200	8
1	....	1	1	800	1	70,000	....	....	1	7,500	1	1	20	200	9
10	....	10	10	5,225	10	218,000	3	2,800	8	62,500	10	11	263	2,810	10
1	....	1	1	350	1	17,500	1	2,600	1	2,000	1	1	7	34	11
3	1		3	2,200	3	212,000	....	....	1	5,500	3	5	123	1,321	12
2	....	4	2	730	2	80,000	....	....	....	....	2	2	38	325	13
3	....	[illegible]	3	1,700	3	116,000	1	20,000	3	22,000	3	3	33	395	14
1	....	1	1	450	1	15,000	1	4,300	1	2,000	1	1	23	160	15
....	2	....	....	....	1	275	....	....	....	....	....	....	....	....	16
5	1	5	5	3,410	5	437,000	4	41,795	4	93,000	6	8	43	1,888	17
1	....	1	1	500	1	40,000	1	4,000	....	....	1	1	6	80	18
1	1	1	1	300	1	8,000	1	2,530	....	....	2	2	15	110	19
58	5	64	58	36,925	60	1,950,800	27	133,372	32	238,000	54	65	1,428	17,623	1
41	4	46	41	24,630	43	1,304,800	18	48,908	19	150,500	42	48	1,200	13,617	2
4	1	4	4	1,800	5	87,300	2	3,100	....	....	5		79	554	3
3	....	3	3	1,450	3	37,000	....	....	1	4,000	3	5	65	588	4
5	....	6	5	2,175	5	89,000	4	6,800	3	15,000	5		103	939	5
5	....	5	5	1,550	5	50,000	5	25,667	1	5,500	3	4	31	314	6
6	1	6	6	5,750	6	268,000	....	....	5	36,000	6	6	294	3,928	7
4	....	4	4	1,850	4	32,500	3	4,041	1	2,000	4	4	67	660	8
4	....	6	4	4,495	4	367,600	1	4,000	3	49,500	4	5	227	3,009	9
2	....	2	2	1,500	2	50,000	1	4,500	1	4,500	2	2	78	855	10
3	....	5	3	2,600	3	260,000	1	500	3	26,500	3	5	109	1,316	11
2	....	2	2	610	2	28,000	....	....	....	....	2	2	51	431	12
3	2	3	3	850	4	35,400	1	300	1	7,500	5	7	96	1,023	13
12	....	12	12	8,735	12	558,000	6	69,964	11	80,000	9	14	217	3,668	14
3	....	3	3	1,660	3	53,000	1	3,000	....	....	2	2	10	288	15
1	....	1	1	1,500	1	25,000	1	9,000	1	4,500	....	....	....	....	16
....	1	....	....	....	....	....	....	....	....	....	....	....	....	....	17
1	....	2	1	400	1	10,000	1	2,500	1	3,000	1	1	1	50	18
46	5	46	46	21,725	47	1,115,900	15	71,505	26	115,500	50	50	1,098	10,592	1
43	4	43	43	19,725	43	935,900	13	51,905	24	101,500	46	46	1,071	9,904	2
7	....	7	7	3,350	7	153,200	3	13,900	1	1,000	7	7	139	1,308	3
1	....	1	1	500	1	12,000	1	2,000	1	3,000	1	1	16	150	
3	....	3	3	1,900	3	31,200	....	....	3	11,000	3	3	91	970	4
1	....	1	1	500	1	12,000	....	....	1	1,200	1	1	25	225	6

TABLE 7.—ORGANIZATIONS, COMMUNICANTS OR MEMBERS, PLACES OF WORSHIP, VALUE OF CHURCH PROPERTY, MORE IN 1900, BY SELECTED

	DENOMINATION.	Total number of organizations.	COMMUNICANTS OR MEMBERS.				
			Number of organizations reporting.	Total number reported.	Sex.		
					Number of organizations reporting.	Male.	Female.
	Williamsport, Pa.—Continued.						
	Protestant bodies—Continued.						
	Lutheran bodies:						
7	General Synod of the Evangelical Lutheran Church in the United States of America.	5	5	1,680	5	638	1,042
8	General Council of the Evangelical Lutheran Church in North America	2	2	857	2	323	534
	Methodist bodies:						
9	Methodist Episcopal Church	8	8	3,112	8	1,061	2,051
10	African Methodist bodies	2	2	245	2	87	158
	Presbyterian bodies:						
11	Presbyterian Church in the United States of America	5	5	1,838	4	469	919
12	Protestant Episcopal Church	5	5	1,361	4	589	555
	Reformed bodies:						
13	Reformed Church in the United States	1	1	295	1	111	184
14	Other Protestant bodies	7	7	762	7	281	481
15	Roman Catholic Church	3	3	3,776	3	1,734	2,042
16	Jewish congregations	1	......	......	......	......	......
17	Spiritualists	1	1	82	1	34	48
1	Wilmington, Del.	93	93	38,095	83	15,621	19,560
2	Protestant bodies	80	80	17,329	72	5,279	9,343
	Baptist bodies:						
3	Baptists—Northern Convention	10	10	2,362	8	502	1,129
4	Primitive Baptists	1	1	10	1	5	5
	Friends:						
5	Society of Friends (Orthodox)	1	1	109	1	48	61
6	Religious Society of Friends (Hicksite)	2	2	352	2	163	189
	Lutheran bodies:						
7	General Synod of the Evangelical Lutheran Church in the United States of America.	1	1	38	1	16	22
8	General Council of the Evangelical Lutheran Church in North America	2	2	665	2	351	314
	Methodist bodies:						
9	Methodist Episcopal Church	21	21	6,210	21	2,258	3,952
10	African Methodist Episcopal Church	4	4	694	3	38	73
11	African Union Methodist Protestant Church	6	6	843	6	302	541
12	Other Methodist bodies	6	6	514	5	160	273
	Presbyterian bodies:						
13	Presbyterian Church in the United States of America	9	9	2,798	8	859	1,739
14	United Presbyterian Church of North America	1	1	114	1	40	74
15	Protestant Episcopal Church	8	8	1,945	5	274	559
16	Other Protestant bodies	8	8	675	8	263	412
17	Roman Catholic Church	10	10	20,522	10	10,326	10,196
18	Jewish congregations	2	2	[1] 207	......	......	......
19	Spiritualists	1	1	37	1	16	21
1	Woonsocket, R. I.	23	22	24,469	18	11,060	13,160
2	Protestant bodies	11	11	1,914	10	583	1,282
	Baptist bodies:						
3	Baptists—Northern Convention	1	1	384	1	128	256
4	Congregationalists	1	1	234	1	77	157
	Methodist bodies:						
5	Methodist Episcopal Church	1	1	213	1	66	147
6	Protestant Episcopal Church	2	2	494	2	145	349
7	Universalists	1	1	333	1	86	247
8	Other Protestant bodies	5	5	256	4	81	126
9	Roman Catholic Church	7	7	22,305	7	10,432	11,873
10	Jewish congregations	3	2	[1] 120	......	......	......
11	All other bodies	2	2	130	1	45	5
1	Worcester, Mass.	105	101	69,588	90	31,617	35,725
2	Protestant bodies	79	77	19,927	73	6,979	12,127
	Baptist bodies:						
3	Baptists—Northern and National (Colored) Conventions	12	12	3,368	12	1,222	2,146
4	Free Baptists	1	1	123	1	47	76
5	Congregationalists	16	16	6,699	16	2,290	4,409
	Disciples or Christians:						
6	Disciples of Christ	2	2	647	1	170	342
	Lutheran bodies:						
7	General Council of the Evangelical Lutheran Church in North America	3	3	1,243	3	549	694
8	Other Lutheran bodies	4	4	403	4	200	203
	Methodist bodies:						
9	Methodist Episcopal Church	11	11	3,115	10	1,157	1,894
10	Other Methodist bodies	2	2	316	2	118	198
11	Protestant Episcopal Church	4	4	1,807	4	640	1,167
12	Unitarians	3	2	384	2	144	240
13	Universalists	2	2	622	......	......	......
14	Other Protestant bodies	19	18	1,200	18	442	758
15	Roman Catholic Church	13	13	46,560	13	23,501	23,059
16	Jewish congregations	8	6	[1] 625	......	......	......
17	Armenian Church	1	1	1,200	1	850	350
	Eastern Orthodox Churches:						
18	Syrian Orthodox Church	1	1	400	1	250	150
19	Greek Orthodox Church	1	1	800	......	......	......
20	Spiritualists	2	2	76	2	37	39

[1] Heads of families only.

DEBT ON CHURCH PROPERTY, PARSONAGES, AND SUNDAY SCHOOLS, FOR EACH CITY OF 25,000 INHABITANTS OR DENOMINATIONS: 1906—Continued.

PLACES OF WORSHIP.					VALUE OF CHURCH PROPERTY.		DEBT ON CHURCH PROPERTY.		PARSONAGES.		SUNDAY SCHOOLS CONDUCTED BY CHURCH ORGANIZATIONS.				
Number of organizations reporting—		Number of church edifices reported.	Seating capacity of church edifices.												
Church edifices.	Halls, etc.		Number of organizations reporting.	Seating capacity reported.	Number of organizations reporting.	Value reported.	Number of organizations reporting.	Amount of debt reported.	Number of organizations reporting.	Value of parsonages reported.	Number of organizations reporting.	Number of Sunday schools reported.	Number of officers and teachers.	Number of scholars.	
5	....	5	5	2,000	5	$70,500	1	$2,000	2	$9,000	5	5	149	1,223	7
2	....	2	2	875	2	40,000	1	3,500	1	2,800	2	2	41	412	8
8	....	8	8	4,350	8	166,500	3	9,830	8	37,000	8	8	249	2,597	9
2	....	2	2	800	2	36,000	2	3,175	....	....	2	2	22	205	10
5	....	5	5	2,450	5	201,500	....	....	3	18,000	5	5	148	1,287	11
5	....	5	5	1,750	5	154,000	1	1,000	3	15,000	5	5	83	678	12
1	....	1	1	350	1	25,000	....	....	1	3,500	1	1	22	225	13
3	4	3	3	900	3	34,000	1	16,500	....	....	6	6	86	624	14
2	1	2	2	1,600	3	168,000	2	19,600	2	14,000	3	3	24	673	15
1	....	1	1	400	1	12,000	....	....	....	....	....	....	....	....	16
....	....	....	....	....	....	....	....	....	....	....	1	1	3	15	17
86	6	92	83	40,754	88	1,904,123	46	208,987	32	170,000	84	91	1,761	20,595	1
76	3	82	74	33,530	78	1,471,123	39	85,737	23	113,500	75	80	1,600	16,788	2
10	....	11	9	4,300	10	188,800	3	5,650	1	2,000	9	9	195	1,874	3
1	....	1	1	350	1	10,000	1	1,000	....	....	....	....	....	....	4
1	....	1	1	250	1	16,000	....	....	....	....	....	....	....	....	5
2	....	2	2	700	2	18,000	....	....	....	....	2	2	20	93	6
1	....	1	1	150	1	6,000	....	....	....	....	1	1	12	135	7
2	....	2	2	1,050	2	42,000	1	3,000	....	....	2	2	44	575	8
21	....	22	21	10,600	21	616,450	16	44,000	11	49,000	21	23	690	7,133	9
4	....	4	4	1,850	4	32,900	3	5,257	1	2,500	4	4	52	588	10
6	....	8	6	3,200	6	26,000	5	2,613	2	4,000	6	6	62	980	11
6	....	6	6	2,550	6	35,200	6	11,800	....	....	6	6	66	531	12
8	....	8	8	3,900	8	190,000	1	6,900	2	13,500	9	11	269	3,166	13
1	....	1	1	300	1	16,000	1	3,500	....	....	1	1	13	135	14
8	....	10	8	3,405	8	203,775	1	2,000	5	34,500	8	9	126	1,279	15
5	3	5	4	925	7	68,998	1	17	1	8,000	6	6	51	299	16
9	1	9	8	6,900	9	423,000	6	121,250	9	56,500	8	10	156	3,742	17
	1	1	1	324	1	10,000	1	2,000	....	....	1	1	5	65	18
....	1	....	....	....	....	....	....	....	....	....	....	....	....	....	19
17	4	18	1	10,275	18	665,800	7	78,700	10	83,000	19	25	386	5,540	1
9	2	9	9	2,975	10	201,300	1	2,500	4	20,500	11	13	192	1,371	2
1	....	1	1	600	1	30,000	....	....	....	....	1	2	32	237	3
1	....	1	1	325	1	45,000	....	....	1	5,000	1	1	31	236	4
1	....	1	1	250	1	26,000	....	....	1	3,000	1	1	24	228	5
2	....	2	2	650	2	35,000	1	2,500	1	10,000	2	2	28	230	6
1	....	1	1	400	1	50,000	....	....	....	....	1	1	35	265	7
3	2	3	3	750	4	15,300	....	....	1	2,500	5	6	42	175	8
7	....	7	7	6,800	7	457,500	5	72,200	6	62,500	7	11	193	4,139	9
1	....	2	1	500	1	7,000	1	4,000	....	....	1	1	1	30	10
....	2	....	....	....	....	....	....	....	....	....	....	....	....	....	11
79	21	91	78	50,440	89	3,610,713	47	501,794	30	296,600	90	109	2,232	22,038	1
60	16	66	59	34,569	70	2,629,951	36	216,244	17	141,300	75	87	1,863	15,413	2
11	1	15	11	6,615	12	448,500	9	42,000	....	....	12	20	357	2,681	3
1	....	1	1	250	1	9,000	1	3,900	....	....	1	1	17	97	4
15	1	17	15	10,640	16	1,149,000	9	87,350	5	55,000	16	17	644	5,411	5
2	....	2	2	1,000	2	43,000	1	5,000	....	....	2	2	41	502	6
3	....	3	3	1,650	3	50,410	3	25,094	1	6,000	3	4	79	640	7
2	1	2	2	750	3	20,000	2	7,450	....	....	3	3	20	131	8
10	....	10	10	5,850	10	277,000	2	11,900	6	31,600	11	12	325	2,921	9
1	1	1	1	700	1	25,700	1	2,500	....	....	2	2	35	238	10
4	....	4	4	1,973	4	294,711	....	....	2	22,500	4	5	121	937	11
3	....	3	3	1,666	3	141,300	....	....	2	22,700	3	3	37	265	12
2	....	2	2	1,500	2	95,500	1	10,000	....	....	2	2	55	580	13
6	12	6	5	1,975	13	75,830	7	21,050	1	3,500	16	16	132	1,010	14
13	....	17	13	12,471	13	889,512	10	278,050	11	152,500	13	20	364	6,415	15
5	1	7	5	2,900	3	74,000	1	7,500	1	300	1	1	3	120	16
1	....	1	1	500	1	17,000	....	....	1	2,500	1	1	2	90	17
....	1	....	....	....	1	200	....	....	....	....	....	....	....	....	18
....	1	....	....	....	....	....	....	....	....	....	....	....	....	....	19
....	2	....	....	....	1	50	....	....	....	....	....	....	....	....	20

TABLE 7.—ORGANIZATIONS, COMMUNICANTS OR MEMBERS, PLACES OF WORSHIP, VALUE OF CHURCH PROPERTY, MORE IN 1900, BY SELECTED

	DENOMINATION.	Total number of organizations.	COMMUNICANTS OR MEMBERS.				
			Number of organizations reporting.	Total number reported.	Sex.		
					Number of organizations reporting.	Male.	Female.
1	Yonkers, N. Y.	53	52	48,211	47	20,508	25,133
	Protestant bodies	36	36	9,815	33	2,925	4,470
	Baptist bodies:						
3	Baptists—Northern and National (Colored) Conventions	5	5	1,276	5	491	785
	Lutheran bodies:						
4	Evangelical Lutheran Synodical Conference of America	1	1	275	1	120	155
5	Other Lutheran bodies	2	2	191	2	121	70
	Methodist bodies:						
6	Methodist Episcopal Church	7	7	1,545	7	695	850
7	African Methodist Episcopal Zion Church	1	1	350	1	125	225
	Presbyterian bodies:						
8	Presbyterian Church in the United States of America	3	3	1,860	3	677	1,183
9	Protestant Episcopal Church	8	8	3,203	5	290	493
	Reformed bodies:						
10	Reformed Church in America	3	3	856	3	301	555
11	Other Protestant bodies	6	6	259	6	105	154
12	Roman Catholic Church	11	11	38,016	11	17,433	20,583
13	Jewish congregations	2	1	[1] 100			
14	All other bodies	4	4	280	3	150	80
1	York, Pa.	65	64	17,828	58	7,246	9,693
2	Protestant bodies	58	58	15,215	55	6,056	8,411
	Evangelical bodies:						
3	Evangelical Association	1	1	80	1	60	20
4	United Evangelical Church	6	6	1,056	6	414	642
	Lutheran bodies:						
5	General Synod of the Evangelical Lutheran Church in the United States of America	11	11	4,729	11	2,160	2,569
6	Evangelical Lutheran Synodical Conference of America	1	1	595	1	273	322
	Methodist bodies:						
7	Methodist Episcopal Church	5	5	1,606	5	648	958
8	African Methodist bodies	2	2	270	2	75	195
	Presbyterian bodies:						
9	Presbyterian Church in the United States of America	4	4	1,106	4	396	710
10	United Presbyterian Church of North America	1	1	85	1	34	51
11	Protestant Episcopal Church	4	4	751	2	25	38
	Reformed bodies:						
12	Reformed Church in the United States	9	9	2,598	8	1,061	1,487
	United Brethren bodies:						
13	Church of the United Brethren in Christ	5	5	1,379	5	545	834
14	Other Protestant bodies	9	9	960	9	375	585
15	Roman Catholic Church	3	3	2,472	3	1,190	1,282
16	Jewish congregations	3	2	[1] 61			
	Eastern Orthodox Churches:						
17	Greek Orthodox Church	1	1	80			
1	Youngstown, Ohio	60	60	17,740	54	7,306	9,793
	Protestant bodies	54	54	14,442	52	5,765	8,306
	Baptist bodies:						
3	Baptists—Northern and National (Colored) Conventions	8	8	1,448	6	392	685
4	Congregationalists	2	2	630	2	272	358
	Disciples or Christians:						
5	Disciples of Christ	3	3	1,850	3	775	1,075
	Lutheran bodies:						
6	General Council of the Evangelical Lutheran Church in North America	2	2	590	2	259	331
7	Evangelical Lutheran Joint Synod of Ohio and Other States	3	3	1,231	3	576	655
8	Other Lutheran bodies	3	3	514	3	255	259
	Methodist bodies:						
9	Methodist Episcopal Church	6	6	2,759	6	1,054	1,705
10	Other Methodist bodies	5	5	381	5	116	265
	Presbyterian bodies:						
11	Presbyterian Church in the United States of America	6	6	1,730	6	711	1,019
12	United Presbyterian Church of North America	2	2	875	2	340	535
13	Other Presbyterian bodies	2	2	160	2	89	71
14	Protestant Episcopal Church	1	1	925	1	348	577
	Reformed bodies:						
15	Reformed Church in the United States	2	2	790	2	337	453
16	Other Protestant bodies	9	9	559	9	241	318
17	Roman Catholic Church [2]	1	1	2,992	1	1,526	1,466
18	Jewish congregations	3	3	[1] 190			
19	All other bodies	2	2	116	1	15	21

[1] Heads of families only.

DEBT ON CHURCH PROPERTY, PARSONAGES, AND SUNDAY SCHOOLS, FOR EACH CITY OF 25,000 INHABITANTS OR DENOMINATIONS: 1906—Continued.

PLACES OF WORSHIP.					VALUE OF CHURCH PROPERTY.		DEBT ON CHURCH PROPERTY.		PARSONAGES.		SUNDAY SCHOOLS CONDUCTED BY CHURCH ORGANIZATIONS.				
Number of organizations reporting—		Number of church edifices reported.	Seating capacity of church edifices.		Number of organizations reporting.	Value reported.	Number of organizations reporting.	Amount of debt reported.	Number of organizations reporting.	Value of parsonages reported.	Number of organizations reporting.	Number of Sunday schools reported.	Number of officers and teachers.	Number of scholars.	
Church edifices.	Halls, etc.		Number of organizations reporting.	Seating capacity reported.											
43	8	46	43	21,282	46	$2,515,250	25	$391,450	21	$303,500	45	55	921	13,263	1
30	5	33	30	14,040	32	1,241,200	12	101,500	11	167,000	33	37	745	6,144	2
5	....	6	5	2,660	5	146,500	....	....	1	25,000	4	6	149	1,159	3
1	....	1	1	250	1	16,000	1	1,600	1	5,000	1	1	16	160	4
2	....	2	2	575	2	9,000	2	2,500	....	....	1	1	6	35	5
6	1	6	6	2,135	7	147,075	1	5,500	1	9,000	7	7	101	844	6
1	....	1	1	500	1	15,000	....	....	1	5,000	1	1	22	195	7
3	....	4	3	2,760	3	276,000	1	4,900	1	20,000	3	4	175	1,390	8
8	....	9	8	3,185	8	444,000	3	12,000	4	53,000	8	9	182	1,702	9
3	....	3	3	1,725	3	170,500	3	73,000	2	50,000	3	3	67	505	10
1	4	1	1	250	2	17,125	1	2,000	....	....	5	5	27	154	11
11	....	11	11	5,842	11	1,215,000	11	258,950	9	133,500	11	17	172	6,994	12
1	....	1	1	800	1	42,000	1	20,000	....	....	1	1	4	125	13
1	3	1	1	600	2	17,050	1	11,000	1	3,000	....	....	....	....	14
61	3	69	60	36,570	61	1,563,700	31	105,235	34	179,000	61	65	1,696	19,958	1
56	2	64	55	33,770	56	1,412,200	27	79,935	32	163,000	56	60	1,640	19,338	2
1	....	1	1	400	1	12,000	1	3,000	1	4,000	1	1	15	80	3
6	....	6	6	3,475	6	65,000	5	19,681	1	3,000	6	6	178	2,256	4
11	....	13	11	16,100	11	450,600	4	7,900	8	45,300	11	13	446	6,009	5
1	....	1	1	750	1	30,000	1	1,400	1	5,000	1	2	24	310	6
5	....	5	5	2,850	5	122,500	3	3,775	5	24,500	5	5	149	1,675	7
2	....	2	2	800	2	10,600	1	1,379	1	2,000	2	2	33	238	8
4	....	7	4	2,400	4	204,000	1	5,000	2	20,000	4	4	108	1,303	9
1	....	1	1	200	1	13,000	....	....	....	....	1	1	15	100	10
4	....	4	4	1,115	4	50,500	3	8,700	1	15,000	4	4	37	285	11
9	....	12	8	5,550	9	324,000	5	25,200	4	17,500	9	9	278	3,366	12
5	....	5	5	3,000	5	60,500	2	3,600	3	10,500	5	5	189	2,525	13
7	2	7	7	3,130	7	69,500	1	300	5	16,200	7	8	168	1,191	14
3	....	3	3	2,000	3	119,500	2	9,300	2	16,000	3	3	45	550	15
2	....	2	2	800	2	32,000	2	16,000	....	....	2	2	11	70	16
....	1	....	....	....	....	....	....	....	....	....	....	....	....	....	17
45	12	48	45	22,465	49	1,431,150	17	89,575	18	80,200	52	56	854	9,574	1
44	10	46	44	20,465	48	1,156,150	16	59,575	17	60,200	50	53	858	8,817	2
6	2	6	6	2,375	7	111,350	1	625	....	....	8	8	118	837	3
2	....	2	2	1,000	[illegible]	42,000	1	2,000	....	....	2	2	38	320	4
3	....	3	3	2,200	3	180,000	3	16,200	....	....	3	3	62	1,050	5
2	....	2	2	700	2	41,000	1	7,000	1	3,000	2	2	35	322	6
3	....	3	3	1,125	3	39,000	1	1,200	2	5,500	2	2	21	275	7
2	1	2	2	750	2	18,570	1	3,000	1	2,500	2	2	17	144	8
5	1	5	5	3,100	5	176,500	1	1,800	5	31,000	6	6	150	2,564	9
5	....	5	5	1,500	5	52,300	1	2,200	4	6,400	4	5	53	425	10
6	....	7	6	3,325	6	261,000	2	10,000	1	800	6	6	106	1,062	11
2	....	2	2	1,150	2	50,000	....	....	....	....	2	2	61	497	12
2	....	2	2	650	2	18,000	....	....	....	....	2	3	30	125	13
1	....	2	1	1,000	1	100,000	....	....	....	....	1	2	32	380	14
2	....	2	2	800	2	41,000	2	12,000	1	5,000	2	2	39	320	15
3	6	3	3	790	6	25,430	2	3,550	2	6,000	8	8	76	496	16
1	....	2	1	2,000	1	275,000	1	30,000	1	20,000	1	2	14	740	17
....	....	....	....	....	....	....	....	....	....	....	....	....	....	....	18
....	2	....	....	....	....	....	....	....	....	....	1	1	2	17	19

[1] Exclusive of statistics not reported separately by cities for part of Cleveland diocese.

TABLE 8.—COMPARISON OF ORGANIZATIONS, COMMUNICANTS OR MEMBERS, MINISTERS, CHURCH EDIFICES, BY DENOMINATIONS (IN DETAIL), FOR CON-

[The 1890 figures are exclusive of Alaska: Organizations, 26; communicants or members,

	DENOMINATION.	TOTAL NUMBER OF ORGANIZATIONS.		NUMBER OF COMMUNICANTS OR MEMBERS REPORTED.	
		1906	1890	1906	1890
	All denominations	212,230	165,151	32,936,445	20,597,954
2	Adventist bodies	2,551	1,757	92,735	60,491
3	Evangelical Adventists	18	30	481	1,147
4	Advent Christian Church	550	580	26,799	25,816
5	Seventh-day Adventist Denomination	1,889	995	62,211	28,991
6	Church of God (Adventist)	10	29	354	647
7	Churches of God (Adventist), Unattached Congregations	10		257	
8	Life and Advent Union	12	28	509	1,018
9	Churches of God in Christ Jesus	62	95	2,124	2,872
10	Armenian Church	73	6	19,889	335
11	Bahais	24	....	1,280	....
12	Baptist bodies	54,880	42,909	5,662,234	3,712,468
13	Baptists	47,910	36,673	5,323,183	3,429,080
14	Northern Baptist Convention	8,272	7,902	1,062,105	800,025
15	Southern Baptist Convention	21,104	16,238	,009,471	1,280,066
16	National Baptist Convention (Colored)	18,534	12,533	,261,607	1,348,989
17	General Six Principle Baptists	16	18	685	937
18	Seventh-day Baptists	77	106	8,381	9,143
19	Free Baptists	1,346	1,586	81,359	87,898
20	Freewill Baptists	608	167	40,280	11,864
21	General Baptists	518	399	30,097	21,362
22	Separate Baptists	76	24	5,180	1,599
23	United Baptists	196	204	13,698	13,209
24	Duck River and Kindred Associations of Baptists (Baptist Church of Christ)	93	152	6,416	8,254
25	Primitive Baptists	2,922	3,107	102,311	116,271
26	Colored Primitive Baptists in America[1]	797		35,076	
27	Two-Seed-in-the-Spirit Predestinarian Baptists	55	473	781	12,851
28	Freewill Baptists (Bullockites)	15	....	298	....
29	United American Freewill Baptists (Colored)	251	....	14,489	....
30	Brethren (Plymouth)	403	314	10,566	6,661
31	Brethren (Plymouth)—I	134	109	2,933	2,289
32	Brethren (Plymouth)—II	128	88	4,752	2,419
33	Brethren (Plymouth)—III	81	86	1,724	1,235
34	Brethren (Plymouth)—IV	60	31	1,157	718
35	Brethren (River)	111	111	4,569	3,427
36	Brethren in Christ	74	78	3,397	2,688
37	Yorker, or Old Order, Brethren	9	8	423	214
38	United Zion's Children	28	25	749	525
39	Buddhists	74	47	3,165	....
40	Chinese Temples	62	47	....	....
41	Japanese Temples	12	....	3,165	....
42	Catholic Apostolic Churches	24	10	4,927	1,394
43	Catholic Apostolic Church	11	10	2,907	1,394
44	New Apostolic Church	13		2,020	
45	Christadelphians	70	63	1,412	1,277
46	Christian Catholic Church in Zion	17	....	5,865	....
47	Christian Israelite Church	5	....	78	....
48	Christian Missionary Association	....	13	....	754
49	Christian Union	217	294	13,905	18,214
50	Christians (Christian Connection)[4]	1,379	1,424	110,117	103,722
51	Church of Christ, Scientist	638	221	85,717	8,724
52	Church of God and Saints of Christ (Colored)	48	....	1,823	....
53	Church Triumphant (Schweinfurth)	....	12	....	384
54	Churches of God in North America, General Eldership of the	518	479	24,356	22,511
55	Churches of the Living God (Colored)	68	....	4,276	....
56	Church of the Living God (Christian Workers for Friendship)	44	....	2,676	....
57	Church of the Living God (Apostolic Church)	15	....	752	....
58	Church of Christ in God	9	....	848	....
59	Churches of the New Jerusalem	133	154	7,247	7,096
60	General Convention of the New Jerusalem in the United States of America	119	154	6,612	7,096
61	General Church of the New Jerusalem	14		635	
62	Communistic societies	22	32	2,272	4,049
63	United Society of Believers (Shakers)	15	15	516	1,728
64	Amana Society	7	7	1,756	1,600
65	Harmony Society	....	1	....	250
66	Society of Separatists	....	1	....	200
67	New Icaria Society	....	1	....	21
68	Society of Altruists	....	1	....	25
69	Adonai Shomo	....	1	....	20
70	Church Triumphant (Koreshan Ecclesia)	....	5	....	205
71	Congregationalists	5,713	4,868	700,480	512,771
72	Disciples or Christians	10,942	7,246	1,142,359	641,051
73	Disciples of Christ	8,293	7,246	982,701	641,051
74	Churches of Christ	2,649		159,658	

[1] Includes figures for Alaska, not returned separately.

[4] No regular ministry.

SEATING CAPACITY OF CHURCH EDIFICES, NUMBER OF HALLS, ETC., AND VALUE OF CHURCH PROPERTY, TINENTAL UNITED STATES: 1906 AND 1890.

14,852; church edifices, 34; seating capacity, 4,800; halls, etc., 2; church property, $203,650.]

TOTAL NUMBER OF MINISTERS.		NUMBER OF CHURCH EDIFICES REPORTED.		SEATING CAPACITY OF CHURCH EDIFICES REPORTED.		NUMBER OF HALLS, ETC., REPORTED.		VALUE OF CHURCH PROPERTY REPORTED.		
1906	1890	1906	1890	1906	1890	1906	1890	1906	1890	
164,830	[1] 111,036	192,795	142,487	58,536,830	43,560,063	14,791	23,332	$1,257,575,867	$679,426,459	1
1,152	1,364	1,473	774	287,964	190,748	666	957	2,425,209	1,236,345	2
8	34	16	23	4,050	5,855	2	5	27,050	61,400	3
528	883	428	294	104,339	80,286	90	281	854,323	465,605	4
488	284	981	418	169,740	94,627	539	563	1,454,087	645,075	5
20	19	3	1	1,200	200	6	28	4,000	1,400	6
12		2		350		8		2,300		7
40	50	6	8	1,150	2,250	5	19	29,790	16,790	8
56	94	37	30	7,135	7,530	16	61	53,650	46,075	9
12	7	3	....	1,300	....	60	....	38,000	....	10
(3)	....	....	....	....	....	23	....	....	....	11
43,790	25,646	50,092	37,671	15,702,712	11,568,019	3,250	5,539	139,842,656	82,328,123	12
37,793	21,110	45,035	32,555	14,239,735	9,970,835	2,759	4,469	133,781,179	76,759,690	13
7,360	6,685	8,244	7,066	2,584,801	2,180,458	254	1,165	74,620,025	49,524,504	14
13,316	8,957	18,878	13,502	6,044,633	4,349,407	1,997	2,641	34,723,882	18,196,637	15
17,117	5,468	17,913	11,987	5,610,301	3,440,970	508	663	24,437,272	9,038,549	16
8	14	14	14	2,870	3,600	1	4	19,450	19,500	17
90	115	71	78	19,400	21,467	7	18	292,250	265,260	18
1,160	1,493	1,111	1,225	275,601	349,309	61	349	2,974,130	3,115,642	19
600	118	556	125	158,540	41,400	45	43	296,585	57,005	20
525	332	380	209	117,095	71,850	119	180	252,019	201,140	21
100	19	60	19	19,070	5,650	4	5	66,980	9,200	22
260	25	77	179	16,745	60,220	22	23	36,715	90,150	23
99	80	86	125	27,508	40,885	2	17	44,321	56,755	24
1,500	2,040	2,003	2,735	679,190	868,073	176	356	1,674,810	1,591,551	25
1,480		501		94,223		44		296,539		26
35	300	38	397	11,350	134,730	....	75	21,500	172,230	27
4	....	8	....	1,560	....	2	....	6,900	....	28
136	....	152	....	39,825	....	8	....	79,278	....	29
(3)	....	4	....	600	....	398	313	18,200	1,465	30
....	....	....	....	....	....	134	108	....	....	31
....	....	3	....	600	....	124	88	17,500	1,265	32
....	....	1	....	....	....	80	86	700	200	33
....	....	....	....	....	....	60	31	....	....	34
216	155	93	70	33,060	22,105	19	36	165,850	81,350	35
170	128	73	45	25,860	19,005	2	28	143,000	73,050	36
24	7	....	....	....	....	9	8	....	....	37
22	20	20	25	7,200	3,100	8	....	22,850	8,300	38
15	....	69	47	2,110	....	5	1	88,000	62,000	39
1	....	62	47	....	....	....	1	30,000	62,000	40
14	....	7	....	2,110	....	5	....	58,000	....	41
33	95	9	3	1,970	750	15	7	161,500	66,050	42
14	95	7	3	1,270	750	4	7	153,000	66,050	43
19		2		700		11		8,500		44
(3)	....	4	4	850	950	31	59	3,245	2,700	45
35	....	....	....	....	....	17	....	....	....	46
(3)	....	1	....	120	....	4	....	30,150	....	47
....	10	....	11	....	3,300	....	1	....	3,900	48
295	183	188	184	61,566	68,000	16	105	299,250	234,450	49
1,011	1,435	1,253	1,098	383,893	347,697	85	226	2,740,322	1,775,202	50
1,276	26	253	7	81,823	1,500	322	213	8,806,441	40,666	51
75	....	1	....	400	....	47	....	6,000	....	52
....	....	....	....	....	....	....	12	....	15,000	53
482	522	417	338	124,213	115,530	54	129	1,050,706	643,185	54
101	....	45	....	10,635	....	23	....	58,575	....	55
51	....	27	....	5,985	....	17	....	23,175	....	56
30	....	12	....	3,100	....	3	....	25,700	....	57
20	....	6	....	1,550	....	3	....	9,700	....	58
130	119	94	88	19,498	20,810	31	70	1,791,041	1,386,455	59
108	119	89	88	18,978	20,810	22	70	1,760,691	1,386,455	60
22		5		520		9		30,350		61
....	....	24	40	4,300	9,450	12	5	31,190	106,800	62
(3)	....	3	16	800	5,650	12	....	17,100	36,800	
(3)	....	21	22	3,500	2,800	....	....	14,090	15,000	
....	....	....	1	....	500	....	....	....	10,000	
....	....	....	1	....	500	....	....	....	3,000	
....	....	....	....	....	....	....	....	....	....	
....	....	....	....	....	....	....	....	....	....	
....	....	....	....	....	....	....	....	....	6,000	[illegible]
....	....	....	....	....	....	....	5	....	36,000	[illegible]
5,802	5,058	5,792	4,736	1,794,997	1,553,080	164	456	63,240,305	43,335,437	71
8,741	3,773	9,040	5,324	2,776,044	1,609,452	907	1,141	29,995,316	12,206,038	72
6,641	3,773	7,066	5,324	2,176,597	1,609,452	214	1,141	27,439,944	12,206,038	73
2,100		1,974		599,447		693		2,555,372		74

[3] Returned as a part of the Primitive Baptists in 1890, the Colored Primitive Baptist body not having been, so far as known, in existence at that time.
[4] Christian Church (South), reported separately in 1890, included in 1906 with Christians (Christian Connection).

TABLE 8.—COMPARISON OF ORGANIZATIONS, COMMUNICANTS OR MEMBERS, MINISTERS, CHURCH EDIFICES, BY DENOMINATIONS (IN DETAIL), FOR CONTI-

[The 1890 figures are exclusive of Alaska: Organizations, 26; communicants or members,

	DENOMINATION.	TOTAL NUMBER OF ORGANIZATIONS.		NUMBER OF COMMUNICANTS OR MEMBERS REPORTED.	
		1906	1890	1906	1890
75	Dunkers or German Baptist Brethren	1,097	989	97,144	73,795
76	German Baptist Brethren Church (Conservative)	822	720	76,547	61,101
77	Old Order German Baptist Brethren	68	135	3,388	4,411
78	The Brethren Church (Progressive Dunkers)	202	128	17,042	8,089
79	German Seventh-day Baptists	5	6	167	194
80	Eastern Orthodox Churches	411	2	129,606	600
81	Russian Orthodox Church	59	1	19,111	500
82	Servian Orthodox Church	10		15,742	
83	Syrian Orthodox Church	8		4,002	
84	Greek Orthodox Church	334	1	90,751	100
85	Evangelical bodies	2,738	2,310	174,780	133,313
86	Evangelical Association	1,760	2,310	104,898	133,313
87	United Evangelical Church	978		69,882	
88	Evangelistic associations	182		10,842	
89	Apostolic Faith Movement	6		538	
90	Peniel Missions	11		703	
91	Metropolitan Church Association	6		466	
92	Hephzibah Faith Missionary Association	10		293	
93	Missionary Church Association	32		1,256	
94	Pentecost Bands of the World	16		487	
95	Heavenly Recruit Church	27		938	
96	Apostolic Christian Church	42		4,558	
97	Christian Congregation	9		395	
98	Gospel Mission	8		196	
99	Church of Daniel's Band	4		92	
100	Lumber River Mission	5		265	
101	Pentecostal Union Church	3		230	
102	Voluntary Missionary Society in America (Colored)	3		425	
103	Free Christian Zion Church of Christ (Colored)	15		1,835	
104	Friends	1,147	1,056	113,772	107,208
105	Society of Friends (Orthodox)	873	794	91,161	80,655
106	Religious Society of Friends (Hicksite)	218	201	18,560	21,992
107	Orthodox Conservative Friends (Wilburite)	48	52	3,880	4,329
108	Friends (Primitive)	8	9	171	232
109	German Evangelical Protestant bodies	66	52	34,704	36,156
110	German Evangelical Protestant Ministers' Association	44	52	23,518	36,156
111	German Evangelical Protestant Ministers' Conference	22		11,186	
112	German Evangelical Synod of North America	1,205	870	293,137	187,432
113	Independent churches	1,079	155	73,673	13,360
114	International Apostolic Holiness Union	74		2,774	
115	Jewish congregations	1,769	533	[3] 101,457	[3] 130,496
116	Latter-day Saints	1,184	856	256,647	166,125
117	Church of Jesus Christ of Latter-day Saints	683	425	215,796	144,352
118	Reorganized Church of Jesus Christ of Latter-day Saints	501	431	40,851	21,773
119	Lutheran bodies	12,703	8,595	2,112,494	1,231,072
120	General Synod of the Evangelical Lutheran Church in the United States of America	1,734	1,424	270,221	164,640
121	United Synod of the Evangelical Lutheran Church in the South	449	414	47,747	37,457
122	General Council of the Evangelical Lutheran Church in North America	2,146	[1] 1,560	462,177	[1] 276,483
123	Evangelical Lutheran Synodical Conference of America	3,301	1,934	648,529	357,153
124	United Norwegian Lutheran Church in America	1,177	1,122	185,027	119,972
125	Evangelical Lutheran Joint Synod of Ohio and Other States	772	421	123,408	69,505
126	Lutheran Synod of Buffalo	33	27	5,270	4,242
127	Hauge's Norwegian Evangelical Lutheran Synod	272	175	33,268	14,730
128	Evangelical Lutheran Church in America, Eielsen's Synod	26		1,013	
129	German Evangelical Lutheran Synod of Texas	25		2,440	
130	Evangelical Lutheran Synod of Iowa and Other States	828	[1] 484	110,254	[1] 48,363
131	Synod for the Norwegian Evangelical Lutheran Church in America	927	489	107,712	55,452
132	Evangelical Lutheran Synod of Michigan and Other States	55	66	9,697	11,482
133	Danish Evangelical Lutheran Church in America	92	131	12,541	10,181
134	Icelandic Evangelical Lutheran Synod in North America	14	13	2,101	1,991
135	Immanuel Synod of the Evangelical Lutheran Church of North America	11	21	3,275	5,580
136	Finnish Evangelical Lutheran Church of America, or Suomi Synod	105	11	12,907	1,385
137	Norwegian Lutheran Free Church	320		26,928	
138	United Danish Evangelical Lutheran Church in America	198	[1] 50	16,340	[1] 3,493
139	Slovak Evangelical Lutheran Synod of America	59		12,141	
140	Finnish Evangelical Lutheran National Church	66		10,111	
141	Apostolic Lutheran Church (Finnish)	68		8,170	
142	Church of the Lutheran Brethren of America (Norwegian)	16		482	
143	Evangelical Lutheran Jehovah Conference	9		735	
144	German Augsburg Synod		23		7,010
145	Independent congregations		231		41,953
146	Mennonite bodies	604	550	54,798	41,541
147	Mennonite Church	220	246	18,674	17,078
148	Bruederhoef Mennonite Church	8	5	275	352
149	Amish Mennonite Church	57	97	7,640	10,101
150	Old Amish Mennonite Church	46	22	5,043	2,038
151	Reformed Mennonite Church	34	34	2,079	1,655

[1] Includes figures for Alaska, not returned separately.
[2] Not reported.
[3] In 1906, heads of families only. In 1890, members as well as heads of families included.

SEATING CAPACITY OF CHURCH EDIFICES, NUMBER OF HALLS, ETC., AND VALUE OF CHURCH PROPERTY, NENTAL UNITED STATES: 1906 AND 1890—Continued.

14,852; church edifices, 34; seating capacity, 4,800; halls, etc., 2; church property, $203,650.]

TOTAL NUMBER OF MINISTERS.		NUMBER OF CHURCH EDIFICES REPORTED.		SEATING CAPACITY OF CHURCH EDIFICES REPORTED.		NUMBER OF HALLS, ETC., REPORTED.		VALUE OF CHURCH PROPERTY REPORTED.		
1906	1890	1906	1890	1906	1890	1906	1890	1906	1890	
2,255	2,088	1,442	1,016	508,374	414,036	59		$2,802,532	$1,362,681	75
1,784	1,622	1,186	854	432,854	353,586	47	280	2,198,957	1,121,541	76
195	237	66	63	19,250	25,750	...	189	89,800	80,770	77
269	224	184	96	54,220	32,740	11	37	472,975	145,770	78
7	5	6	3	2,050	1,960	1	1	40,800	14,550	79
108	[1]14	85	2	38,995	325	326	...	964,791	45,000	80
55	[1]13	46	1	20,345	250	13	...	484,371	40,000	81
9	...	8	...	2,800	...	2	...	62,460	...	82
9	...	2	...	700	...	6	...	32,160	...	83
35	1	29	1	15,150	75	305	...	385,800	5,000	84
1,496	1,235	2,537	1,899	659,391	479,335	152	425	8,999,979	4,785,680	85
942	1,235	1,617	1,899	390,199	479,335	100	425	5,819,620	4,785,680	86
553		920		269,192		52		3,180,359		87
356	...	124	...	34,590	...	52	...	532,185	...	88
(3)	...	1	...	200	...	5	...	450	...	89
30	...	1	...	500	...	10	...	40,250	...	90
29	...	4	...	2,025	...	2	...	118,300	...	91
36	...	9	...	1,450	...	1	...	11,300	...	92
35	...	19	...	4,735	...	12	...	33,135	...	93
50	...	16	...	3,780	...	1	...	69,550	...	94
55	...	8	...	2,800	...	15	...	8,950	...	95
19	...	44	...	11,475	...	1	...	141,550	...	96
26	...	5	...	1,550	...	1	...	7,200	...	97
10	...	4	...	750	...	3	...	3,100	...	98
15	...	2	...	500	...	1	...	2,400	...	99
5	...	5	...	2,600	...	...	...	3,000	...	100
35	...	3	...	900	...	...	...	90,600	...	101
11	...	3	...	1,325	...	...	...	2,400	...	102
20	...	14	...	5,201	...	1	...	5,975	...	103
1,479	1,277	1,097	995	304,204	302,218	39	99	3,857,451	4,541,334	104
1,325	1,113	832	725	224,898	215,431	32	90	2,719,551	2,795,784	105
97	115	214	213	66,290	72,568	2	4	1,037,650	1,661,850	106
47	38	47	52	12,216	13,169	1	1	93,500	67,000	107
10	11	4	5	800	1,050	4	4	6,750	16,700	108
59	44	71	52	37,409	35,175	...	1	2,556,550	1,187,450	109
43	44	49	52	25,179	35,175	...	1	939,950	1,187,450	110
16		22		12,230		...		1,616,600		111
972	680	1,258	725	380,465	245,781	42	83	9,376,402	4,614,490	112
(3)	[1]54	812	112	213,096	39,345	229	54	3,934,267	1,486,000	113
178	...	44	...	15,115	...	31	...	80,150	...	114
1,084	200	821	301	364,701	189,234	230	231	23,198,925	9,754,275	115
1,774	2,043	933	388	280,747	122,892	214	432	3,168,548	1,051,791	116
824	543	624	266	214,409	92,102	93	178	2,645,363	825,506	117
950	1,500	309	122	66,338	30,790	121	254	523,185	226,285	118
7,841	4,591	11,194	6,701	3,344,654	2,205,685	1,197	1,314	74,826,389	35,060,354	119
1,311	966	1,720	1,322	582,008	471,819	41	72	16,875,429	8,919,170	120
226	201	442	379	153,520	138,453	13	29	1,509,760	1,114,065	121
1,393	[5]1,153	2,106	[4]1,248	734,068	[4]517,233	75	[4]205	22,394,618	[4]10,379,455	122
2,385	1,282	2,868	1,531	826,993	443,185	351	67	18,916,407	7,804,313	123
453	109	1,018	669	284,711	185,242	102	393	3,668,588	1,544,455	124
547	297	712	443	199,797	149,338	53	10	3,606,285	1,639,087	125
27	20	34	25	8,759	5,793	...	2	130,000	84,410	126
122	58	226	100	57,426	30,500	22	75	682,135	214,395	127
6	...	6	...	1,200	...	20	...	15,900	...	128
12	...	18	...	2,834	...	5	...	30,050	...	129
483	(5)	705	[4]306	162,847	[4]71,592	109	[4]170	2,327,098	[4]739,831	130
359	194	649	275	168,889	78,988	138	182	2,469,713	806,825	131
37	37	53	53	13,795	14,613	4	12	184,700	164,770	132
58	108	70	75	14,250	14,760	20	42	248,700	129,700	133
10	1	14	4	3,355	1,300	...	9	32,350	7,200	134
17	21	11	19	5,300	5,300	...	...	89,300	94,200	135
24	8	50	8	11,643	1,915	60	...	151,345	12,898	136
140	...	219	...	54,605	...	68	...	660,310	...	137
99	[6]40	140	[6]33	27,294	[6]5,700	57	[6]15	418,450	[6]44,775	138
22	...	31	...	9,775	...	30	...	219,300	...	139
16	...	43	...	10,095	...	23	...	95,150	...	140
78	...	37	...	7,725	...	3	...	62,856	...	141
7	...	10	...	2,315	...	3	...	16,400	...	142
9	...	12	...	1,450	...	...	...	21,550	...	143
...	49	...	23	...	7,560	...	1	...	111,060	144
...	47	...	188	...	62,344	...	30	...	1,249,745	145
1,006	905	509	406	171,381	129,340	87	103	1,237,134	643,800	146
346		207	1	77,451	70,605	13	29	500,112	317,045	147
9		8		650	600	...	...	9,100	4,500	148
131		52	98	17,487	15,430	5	33	122,275	76,450	149
141	336	4	84	1,025	200	41	20	6,700	1,500	150
34	288	29	29	7,465	7,465	5	5	52,650	32,650	151

[4] See denominational text, pages 495 and 519.
[5] Ministers for the General Council and for the Synod of Iowa, etc., not returned separately.
[6] Figures are for the Danish Church Association.

TABLE 8.—COMPARISON OF ORGANIZATIONS, COMMUNICANTS OR MEMBERS, MINISTERS, CHURCH EDIFICES, BY DENOMINATIONS (IN DETAIL), FOR CONTI-

[The 1890 figures are exclusive of Alaska: Organizations, 26; communicants or members,

	DENOMINATION.	TOTAL NUMBER OF ORGANIZATIONS.		NUMBER OF COMMUNICANTS OR MEMBERS REPORTED.	
		1906	1890	1906	1890
	Mennonite bodies—Continued.				
152	General Conference of Mennonites of North America [1]	90	47	11,661	5,879
153	Church of God in Christ (Mennonite)	18	18	562	471
154	Old (Wisler) Mennonite Church	9	15	655	610
155	Defenceless Mennonites	14	9	967	856
156	Mennonite Brethren in Christ	68	45	2,801	1,113
	Bundes Conferens der Mennoniten Brueder-Gemeinde:				
157	Krimmer Brueder-Gemeinde	6	12	708	1,388
158	Schellenberger Brueder-Gemeinde	13		1,825	
159	Central Illinois Conference of Mennonites	13	....	1,363	....
160	Nebraska and Minnesota Conference of Mennonites	8	....	545	....
161	Methodist bodies	64,701	51,489	5,749,838	4,589,284
162	Methodist Episcopal Church	29,943	25,861	2,986,154	2,240,354
163	Union American Methodist Episcopal Church (Colored)	77	42	4,347	2,279
164	African Methodist Episcopal Church	6,647	2,481	494,777	452,725
165	African Union Methodist Protestant Church	69	40	5,592	3,415
166	African Methodist Episcopal Zion Church	2,204	1,704	184,542	349,788
167	Methodist Protestant Church	2,843	2,529	178,544	141,989
168	Wesleyan Methodist Connection of America	594	565	20,043	16,492
169	Methodist Episcopal Church, South	17,831	15,017	1,638,480	1,209,976
170	Congregational Methodist Church	325	214	14,729	8,765
171	Congregational Methodist (Colored)	....	9	....	319
172	New Congregational Methodist Church	35	24	1,782	1,059
173	Colored Methodist Episcopal Church	2,381	1,759	172,996	129,383
174	Reformed Zion Union Apostolic Church (Colored)	45	32	3,059	2,346
175	Primitive Methodist Church in the United States of America	96	84	7,558	4,764
176	Free Methodist Church of North America	1,553	1,102	32,838	22,110
177	Reformed Methodist Union Episcopal Church (Colored)	58	....	4,397	....
178	Independent Methodists	....	15	....	2,569
179	Evangelist Missionary Church	....	11	....	951
180	Moravian bodies	132	92	17,926	11,745
181	Moravian Church (Unitas Fratrum)	117	92	17,155	11,745
182	Evangelical Union of Bohemian and Moravian Brethren in North America	15	....	771	....
183	Nonsectarian Churches of Bible Faith	204	....	6,396	....
184	Old Catholic Church	....	4	....	665
185	Pentecostal Church of the Nazarene	100	....	6,657	....
186	Polish National Church of America	24	....	15,473	....
187	Presbyterian bodies	15,506	13,471	1,830,555	1,277,851
188	Presbyterian Church in the United States of America	7,935	6,712	1,179,566	787,743
189	Cumberland Presbyterian Church	[2]2,850	2,791	[2]195,770	164,940
190	Colored Cumberland Presbyterian Church	196	224	18,066	12,956
191	Welsh Calvinistic Methodist Church	147	187	13,280	12,722
192	United Presbyterian Church of North America	968	866	130,342	94,402
193	Presbyterian Church in the United States	3,104	2,391	266,345	179,721
194	Associate Synod of North America (Associate Presbyterian Church)	22	31	786	1,053
195	Associate Reformed Synod of the South	141	116	13,201	8,501
196	Synod of the Reformed Presbyterian Church of North America	114	115	9,122	10,574
197	Reformed Presbyterian Church in North America, General Synod	27	33	3,620	4,602
198	Reformed Presbyterian Church (Covenanted)	1	4	17	37
199	Reformed Presbyterian Church in the United States and Canada	1	1	440	600
200	Protestant Episcopal Church	6,845	5,018	886,942	532,048
201	Reformed bodies	2,585	2,181	449,514	309,458
202	Reformed Church in America	659	572	124,938	92,970
203	Reformed Church in the United States	1,736	1,510	292,654	204,018
204	Christian Reformed Church	174	99	26,669	12,470
205	Hungarian Reformed Church in America	16	....	5,253	....
206	Reformed Catholic Church	5	8	1,250	1,000
207	Reformed Episcopal Church	81	83	9,682	8,455
208	Roman Catholic Church [4]	12,482	10,239	12,079,142	6,241,708
209	Salvationists	714	329	23,344	8,742
210	Salvation Army	694	329	22,908	8,742
211	American Salvation Army	20		436	
212	Schwenkfelders	8	4	725	306
213	Social Brethren	17	20	1,262	913
214	Society for Ethical Culture	5	4	2,040	1,064
215	Spiritualists	455	334	35,056	45,030
216	Swedish Evangelical bodies	408	....	27,712	....
217	Swedish Evangelical Mission Covenant of America	281	....	20,760	....
218	Swedish Evangelical Free Mission	127	....	6,952	....
219	Temple Society in the United States (Friends of the Temple)	5	4	376	340
220	Theosophical societies	85	40	2,336	695
221	Theosophical Society in America	14	40	166	695
222	Theosophical Society, New York	1		90	
223	Theosophical Society, American Section	69		2,080	
224	Universal Brotherhood and Theosophical Society [4]	1		....	
225	Unitarians	461	421	70,542	67,749
226	United Brethren bodies	4,304	4,526	296,050	225,281
227	Church of the United Brethren in Christ	3,732	3,731	274,649	202,474
228	Church of the United Brethren in Christ (Old Constitution)	572	795	21,401	22,807
229	Universalists	846	956	64,158	49,194
230	Vedanta Society	4	....	340	....
231	Volunteers of America	71	....	2,194	....

[1] Apostolic Mennonite Church, reported separately in 1890, included in 1906 with the General Conference of Mennonites of North America.

SEATING CAPACITY OF CHURCH EDIFICES, NUMBER OF HALLS, ETC., AND VALUE OF CHURCH PROPERTY, NENTAL UNITED STATES: 1906 AND 1890—Continued.

14,852; church edifices, 34; seating capacity, 4,800; halls, etc., 2; church property, $203,650.]

TOTAL NUMBER OF MINISTERS.		NUMBER OF CHURCH EDIFICES REPORTED.		SEATING CAPACITY OF CHURCH EDIFICES REPORTED.		NUMBER OF HALLS, ETC., REPORTED.		VALUE OF CHURCH PROPERTY REPORTED.		
1906	1890	1906	1890	1906	1890	1906	1890	1906	1890	
143	97	89	44	33,800	14,105	5	2	$303,400	$120,550	152
17	18	2	3	350	400	5	4	1,600	1,600	153
18	17	10	12	2,440	4,120	...	1	17,950	8,015	154
26	18	13	8	3,095	2,070	1	...	16,800	10,540	155
70	31	58	34	16,248	10,625	9	8	140,747	39,600	156
17	37	6	11	3,175	3,720	...	1	17,900	11,350	157
19		13		3,550		...		13,000		158
18	...	12	...	3,075	...	1	...	25,900	...	159
17	...	6	...	1,570	...	2	...	9,000	...	160
39,737	30,000	59,990	46,138	17,053,392	12,863,178	3,193	6,067	229,450,996	132,140,179	161
17,479	15,423	28,345	22,844	7,983,742	6,302,708	1,211	2,873	163,357,805	96,723,408	162
64	32	60	35	16,046	11,500	16	7	170,150	187,600	163
6,200	3,321	6,538	4,124	1,832,600	1,160,838	268	31	11,303,489	6,468,280	164
187	40	71	27	21,955	7,161	1	13	183,697	54,440	165
3,082	1,565	2,131	1,587	690,951	565,577	78	114	4,833,207	2,714,128	166
1,852	1,441	2,457	1,924	721,464	571,266	230	575	6,053,048	3,683,337	167
553	600	489	342	123,571	96,254	64	213	637,117	393,250	168
5,811	4,801	15,933	12,688	4,484,290	3,359,466	970	1,634	37,278,424	18,775,362	169
324	150	262	150	82,355	46,400	33	60	194,275	41,680	170
...	5	...	5	...	585	...	4	...	525	171
59	20	34	17	11,000	5,150	1	6	27,650	3,750	172
2,671	1,800	2,327	1,653	758,328	541,464	78	64	3,017,849	1,713,366	173
33	30	43	27	15,700	10,100	1	1	37,875	15,000	174
80	60	101	78	30,390	20,930	3	11	630,700	291,993	175
1,270	657	1,140	620	262,265	165,004	239	439	1,688,745	805,085	176
72	...	59	...	18,735	...	...	...	36,965	...	177
...	8	...	14	...	7,725	...	3	...	266,975	178
...	47	...	3	...	1,050	...	9	...	2,000	179
128	[2] 114	137	112	44,625	31,515	11	4	936,650	676,250	180
125	[2] 114	129	112	41,525	31,515	4	4	922,900	676,250	181
3	...	8	...	3,100	...	7	...	13,750	...	182
50	...	41	...	5,700	...	156	...	25,910	...	183
...	1	...	3	...	700	...	2	...	13,320	184
170	...	69	...	19,770	...	26	...	393,990	...	185
24	...	27	...	12,130	...	1	...	494,700	...	186
12,456	[2] 10,448	15,311	12,465	4,892,819	4,037,550	406	1,352	150,189,446	94,861,347	187
7,603	[3] 5,934	8,185	6,660	2,692,561	2,223,944	208	555	114,882,781	74,447,450	188
[3] 1,514	1,861	[3] 2,474	2,024	[3] 767,348	669,507	[3] 108	536	[3] 5,803,960	3,515,510	189
375	393	195	183	71,165	52,139	1	34	203,778	195,826	190
87	100	156	189	40,282	44,445	2	14	761,350	625,875	191
994	731	984	832	322,950	264,298	19	50	10,760,208	5,408,084	192
1,606	1,129	3,012	2,288	898,087	690,843	60	143	15,488,489	8,812,152	193
12	12	19	23	4,575	4,849	1	8	28,825	29,200	194
111	133	142	116	50,075	37,050	3	5	436,550	211,850	195
128	124	116	115	34,110	37,095	3	3	1,258,105	1,071,400	196
26	29	27	33	11,016	12,380	...	1	365,400	469,000	197
...	1	...	1	...	200	1	3	...	...	198
...	1	1	1	650	800	...	...	200,000	75,000	199
5,368	[3] 4,146	6,922	5,018	1,675,750	1,336,752	257	312	125,040,498	81,219,117	200
2,039	1,506	2,706	2,080	990,654	825,931	62	73	30,648,247	18,744,242	201
710	558	773	670	283,447	257,922	15	8	15,553,250	10,340,159	202
1,180	880	1,740	1,304	640,745	534,254	30	61	14,067,897	7,975,583	203
131	68	181	106	62,334	33,755	13	4	903,600	428,500	204
18	...	12	...	4,128	...	4	...	123,500	...	205
10	8	1	...	200	...	4	8	60,000	...	206
84	78	87	84	25,053	23,925	5	2	1,460,787	1,615,101	207
15,177	[3] 9,106	11,881	8,784	4,494,377	3,370,482	518	1,469	292,638,787	118,123,346	208
3,089	...	161	27	53,273	12,055	541	300	3,184,854	38,150	209
3,030	...	159	27	52,223	12,055	523	300	3,175,154	38,150	210
59		2		1,080		18		9,700		211
5	3	8	6	2,950	1,925	...	...	38,700	12,200	212
15	17	15	11	9,200	8,700	2	6	13,800	8,700	213
(4)	...	...	...	...	...	5	5	...	...	214
185	...	100	30	55,125	20,450	322	307	958,048	573,650	215
495	...	389	...	111,480	...	18	...	1,638,675	...	216
347	...	268	...	82,368	...	9	...	1,225,220	...	217
148	...	121	...	29,112	...	9	...	413,455	...	218
3	4	3	5	830	1,150	...	...	11,000	15,300	219
(4)	...	...	1	...	200	79	38	300	600	220
...	...	...	1	...	200	9	38	...	600	221
...		...		...		1		...		222
...		...		...		69		300		223
...		...		...		...		...		224
541	515	463	424	159,917	165,090	23	55	14,263,277	10,335,100	225
2,435	2,798	3,900	3,415	1,060,560	991,138	255	989	9,073,791	4,937,583	226
1,935	2,267	3,410	2,837	937,055	816,458	191	780	8,401,539	4,292,643	227
500	531	490	578	123,505	174,680	64	209	672,252	644,940	228
724	708	776	832	220,222	244,615	33	61	10,575,656	8,054,333	229
(4)	...	2	...	600	...	2	...	52,000	...	230
302	...	10	...	1,825	...	64	...	83,521	...	231

4 Greek Catholic Church (Uniat), reported separately in 1890, included in 1906 with the Roman Catholic Church.

TABLE 9.—COMPARISON OF THE TOTAL POPULATION, AND ORGANIZATIONS, COMMUNICANTS OR MEMBERS, CHURCH PROPERTY, FOR ALL DENOMINATIONS,

	STATE OR TERRITORY.	TOTAL POPULATION.		TOTAL NUMBER OF ORGANIZATIONS.	
		1906[1]	1890	1906	1890
1	Continental United States	84,246,252	[2]62,947,714	212,230	165,151
2	North Atlantic division	23,388,682	17,406,969	33,592	27,887
3	Maine	714,494	661,086	1,559	1,605
4	New Hampshire	432,624	376,530	856	783
5	Vermont	350,373	332,422	909	904
6	Massachusetts	3,043,346	2,238,947	3,088	2,547
7	Rhode Island	490,387	345,506	521	402
8	Connecticut	1,005,716	746,258	1,384	1,149
9	New York	8,226,990	6,003,174	9,639	8,237
10	New Jersey	2,196,237	1,444,933	2,802	2,085
11	Pennsylvania	6,928,515	5,258,113	12,834	10,175
12	South Atlantic division	11,413,343	8,857,922	41,655	30,423
13	Delaware	194,479	168,493	468	382
14	Maryland	1,275,434	1,042,390	2,773	2,328
15	District of Columbia	307,716	230,392	289	217
16	Virginia	1,973,104	1,655,980	6,639	4,998
17	West Virginia	1,076,406	762,794	4,042	2,989
18	North Carolina	2,059,326	1,617,949	8,592	6,824
19	South Carolina	1,453,818	1,151,149	5,385	3,815
20	Georgia	2,443,719	1,837,353	10,097	6,899
21	Florida	629,341	391,422	3,370	1,971
22	North Central division	28,628,813	22,410,417	69,023	59,847
23	Ohio	4,448,677	3,672,329	9,890	9,345
24	Indiana	2,710,898	2,192,404	6,863	6,480
25	Illinois	5,418,670	3,826,352	9,374	8,296
26	Michigan	2,584,533	2,093,890	5,635	4,798
27	Wisconsin	2,260,930	1,693,330	4,902	3,722
28	Minnesota	2,025,615	1,310,283	4,759	3,429
29	Iowa	2,205,690	1,912,297	6,290	5,539
30	Missouri	3,363,153	2,679,185	9,206	8,064
31	North Dakota	463,784	190,983	1,993	868
32	South Dakota	465,908	348,600	1,801	1,589
33	Nebraska	1,068,484	1,062,656	3,313	2,797
34	Kansas	1,612,471	1,428,108	4,994	4,920
35	South Central division	16,130,741	11,170,137	57,778	40,744
36	Kentucky	2,320,298	1,858,635	6,553	5,555
37	Tennessee	2,172,476	1,767,518	8,021	6,350
38	Alabama	2,017,877	1,513,401	8,894	6,383
39	Mississippi	1,708,272	1,289,600	7,396	5,186
40	Louisiana	1,539,449	1,118,588	3,855	2,701
41	Arkansas	1,421,574	1,128,211	6,208	4,874
42	Oklahoma[2]	[1]1,414,177	258,657	4,497	929
43	Texas	3,536,618	2,235,527	12,354	8,766
44	Western division	4,684,673	3,102,269	10,182	6,250
45	Montana	303,575	142,924	546	
46	Idaho	205,704	88,548	676	
47	Wyoming	103,673	62,555	228	
48	Colorado	615,570	413,249	1,268	
49	New Mexico	216,328	160,282	626	
50	Arizona	143,745	88,243	237	
51	Utah	316,331	210,779	542	
52	Nevada	42,335	47,355	88	
53	Washington	614,625	357,232	1,771	273
54	Oregon	474,738	317,704	1,304	[illegible]
55	California	1,648,049	1,213,398	2,897	1,996

[1] Estimated.

[2] Includes the population of Indian Territory and Indian reservations.

CHURCH EDIFICES, SEATING CAPACITY OF CHURCH EDIFICES, NUMBER OF HALLS, ETC., AND VALUE OF BY STATES AND TERRITORIES: 1906 AND 1890.

NUMBER OF COMMUNICANTS OR MEMBERS REPORTED.		NUMBER OF CHURCH EDIFICES REPORTED.		SEATING CAPACITY OF CHURCH EDIFICES REPORTED.		NUMBER OF HALLS, ETC., REPORTED.		VALUE OF CHURCH PROPERTY REPORTED.		
1906	1890	1906	1890	1906	1890	1906	1890	1906	1890	
32,936,445	20,597,954	192,795	142,487	58,536,830	43,560,063	14,791	23,332	$1,257,575,867	$679,426,489	1
10,306,946	6,176,015	32,991	26,707	11,788,803	9,872,148	2,137	2,578	626,897,510	342,227,377	2
212,988	159,846	1,511	1,342	412,838	408,452	104	256	9,955,363	6,192,400	3
190,298	102,941	851	774	254,017	250,035	61	80	7,864,991	4,457,225	4
147,223	106,315	891	802	235,661	237,000	46	110	5,939,492	4,643,800	5
1,562,621	942,751	2,983	2,458	1,313,564	1,102,772	288	313	84,729,445	46,835,014	6
264,712	148,008	493	386	195,688	166,384	50	48	9,533,543	7,583,110	7
502,560	309,341	1,414	1,175	522,941	443,979	87	92	29,196,128	16,985,036	8
3,591,974	2,171,822	9,193	7,942	3,191,267	2,868,490	623	742	255,166,284	140,123,008	9
857,548	508,351	2,875	2,204	1,015,903	803,017	174	157	50,907,123	29,490,414	10
2,977,022	1.726,640	12,780	9,624	4,646,929	3,592,019	704	780	173,605,141	85,917,370	11
4,517,061	3,295,916	39,627	29,309	12,250,279	8,914,505	1,628	2,109	114,460,588	62,009,981	12
71,251	48,679	478	401	130,267	111,172	13	26	3,250,106	2,708,825	13
473,257	379,418	2,814	2,369	810,701	718,459	81	96	23,765,172	15,445,946	14
136,759	94,203	264	206	142,311	114,420	43	36	10,025,122	6,313,625	15
793,546	569,235	6,480	4,894	1,974,332	1,490,675	242	330	19,699,014	10,473,943	16
301,565	189,917	3,428	2,160	949,812	587,338	463	751	9,733,585	3,701,483	17
824,385	685,194	8,188	6,512	2,715,567	2,192,835	229	276	14,053,506	7,077,440	18
665,933	508,485	5,290	3,967	1,774,437	1,199,908	90	101	10,209,043	5,636,236	19
1,029,037	679,051	9,624	7,008	3,063,866	2,108,566	275	248	17,929,183	8,228,060	20
221,318	141,734	3,061	1,793	688,986	391,132	183	245	5,796,859	2,424,423	21
10,669,212	6,738,989	62,256	48,264	17,844,755	13,998,428	4,806	10,640	356,256,559	198,823,535	22
1,742,873	1,215,409	9,519	8,857	3,102,819	2,815,713	379	582	74,670,765	42,138,862	23
938,405	693,860	6,580	5,944	2,132,181	1,890,300	250	543	31,081,500	18,671,131	24
2,077,197	1,202,588	8,626	7,352	2,685,352	2,260,619	423	967	66,222,514	39,715,245	25
982,479	569,504	4,882	3,761	1,353,180	1,097,069	523	1,080	27,144,250	18,682,971	26
1,000,903	556,355	4,562	3,286	1,206,385	845,208	327	482	27,277,837	14,521,341	27
834,442	532,590	4,280	2,619	1,104,317	691,631	356	719	26,053,159	12,940,152	28
788,667	556,817	5,921	4,539	1,617,467	1,203,185	368	970	30,464,860	16,056,786	29
1,199,239	735,839	8,146	6,121	2,391,498	1,859,589	646	1,455	38,059,233	19,663,737	30
159,053	59,496	1,325	335	262,251	69,590	355	451	4,576,157	780,775	31
161,961	85,490	1,461	774	285,197	149,728	240	742	4,538,013	1,761,277	32
345,803	194,466	2,847	1,822	649,132	409,462	337	818	12,114,817	6,443,689	33
458,190	336,575	4,107	2,854	1,054,976	706,334	602	1,891	14,053,454	7,447,569	34
5,726,570	3,555,324	49,594	33,993	14,478,100	9,663,965	4,957	6,105	100,383,963	50,381,948	35
858,324	606,397	5,894	4,768	1,775,123	1,504,736	285	621	18,044,389	12,112,320	36
697,570	551,673	7,400	5,792	2,323,285	1,811,942	489	533	14,469,012	9,885,943	37
824,209	559,171	8,183	6,013	2,423,175	1,702,527	379	389	13,314,993	6,768,477	38
657,381	430,557	6,997	5,001	2,041,665	1,330,542	222	254	9,482,229	4,390,173	39
778,901	399,991	3,630	2,520	1,046,850	617,245	127	186	10,456,146	5,032,194	40
426,179	296,208	5,192	3,791	1,446,892	1,041,040	685	928	6,733,375	3,266,663	41
257,100	34,176	2,709	470	598,650	88,188	1,051	378	4,933,843	243,841	42
1,226,906	677,151	9,589	5,638	2,822,460	1,567,745	1,719	2,816	22,949,976	8,682,837	43
1,696,666	831,710	8,327	4,214	2,174,893	1,111,017	1,263	1,900	59,577,247	25,963,648	44
98,984	32,478	407	164	100,665	33,942	82	112	2,809,779	885,950	45
74,578	24,036	495	143	121,775	29,527	107	97	1,726,734	281,310	46
23,945	11,705	160	43	35,250	8,385	37	76	778,142	368,625	47
205,666	86,837	956	463	255,469	120,862	190	192	7,723,200	4,743,317	48
137,009	105,749	522	381	129,745	107,925	56	92	956,605	531,925	49
45,057	26,972	181	70	40,954	19,230	37	52	798,975	270,816	50
172,814	128,115	516	280	169,369	89,695	58	157	3,612,422	1,493,791	51
14,944	5,877	67	41	15,015	9,890	10	23	492,350	208,225	52
191,976	58,798	1,416	532	341,812	126,109	217	357	8,062,986	2,408,625	53
120,239	70,524	1,086	592	270,329	142,843	138	317	4,620,793	2,829,150	54
611,464	280,619	2,521	1,505	694,510	422,609	331	425	28,065,261	11,961,914	55

[3] Oklahoma and Indian Territory combined.

[4] Special census, 1907.

TABLE 10.—COMPARISON OF COMMUNICANTS OR MEMBERS, BY SELECTED

	STATE OR TERRITORY.	ALL DENOMINATIONS.		ADVENTIST BODIES. Total.		Advent Christian Church.		Seventh-day Adventist Denomination.		Other Adventists.[1]		ARMENIAN CHURCH.	
		1906	1890	1906	1890	1906	1890	1906	1890	1906	1890	1906	1890
1	Continental United States	32,936,445	20,597,954	92,735	60,491	26,799	25,816	62,211	28,991	3,725	5,684	19,889	335
2	North Atlantic division	10,306,946	6,176,015	19,825	17,936	11,234	11,810	7,539	3,931	1,052	2,195	15,570	335
3	Maine	212,988	159,846	2,159	2,964	1,610	2,317	527	459	22	188	318	
4	New Hampshire	190,298	102,941	1,723	2,090	1,608	1,978	115	112			465	
5	Vermont	147,223	106,315	1,613	1,768	1,082	1,079	458	526	73	163		
6	Massachusetts	1,562,621	942,751	4,061	3,428	3,053	2,611	926	490	82	327	6,960	195
7	Rhode Island	264,712	148,008	940	1,458	761	950	179	108		400	2,103	70
8	Connecticut	502,560	309,341	2,042	1,692	1,645	1,358	269	91	128	243	579	
9	New York	3,591,974	2,171,822	4,022	2,412	1,145	1,048	2,614	1,176	263	188	3,295	70
10	New Jersey	857,548	508,351	599	172			451	85	148	87	550	
11	Pennsylvania	2,977,022	1,726,640	2,666	1,962	330	469	2,000	884	336	599	1,300	
12	South Atlantic division	4,517,051	3,295,916	9,618	5,039	6,598	4,139	2,939	678	81	222	187	
13	Delaware	71,251	48,679	155	117			155	26		91		
14	Maryland	473,257	379,418	401	70			401	23		47		
15	District of Columbia	136,759	94,203	382	96			382	96			75	
16	Virginia	793,546	569,235	1,164	323	507	165	576	114	81	44	112	
17	West Virginia	301,565	189,917	1,820	847	1,476	681	344	136		30		
18	North Carolina	824,385	685,194	1,652	1,632	1,388	1,549	264	83				
19	South Carolina	665,933	508,485	710	811	509	811	201					
20	Georgia	1,029,037	679,051	1,122	954	917	873	205	81				
21	Florida	221,318	141,734	2,212	189	1,801	60	411	119		10		
22	North Central division	10,689,212	6,738,989	37,994	29,040	5,439	7,094	30,229	18,983	2,326	2,963	1,998	
23	Ohio	1,742,873	1,215,409	3,291	2,461	782	953	2,334	1,189	175	319		
24	Indiana	938,405	693,860	3,394	2,289	669	455	2,029	1,193	696	641		
25	Illinois	2,077,197	1,202,588	3,258	2,431	1,054	1,019	1,906	871	298	541	1,446	
26	Michigan	982,479	569,504	7,974	5,794	451	591	7,042	4,716	481	418	168	
27	Wisconsin	1,000,903	556,355	3,866	2,541	651	613	3,194	1,892	21	36	154	
28	Minnesota	834,442	532,590	2,452	3,023	349	710	2,103	2,313				
29	Iowa	788,667	556,817	3,910	3,610	608	1,272	3,097	2,197	205	141		
30	Missouri	1,199,239	735,839	2,378	1,453	323	230	1,805	815	250	408	230	
31	North Dakota	159,053	59,496	868	95			868	95				
32	South Dakota	161,961	85,490	1,042	1,076		163	1,042	884		29		
33	Nebraska	345,803	194,466	2,872	1,132	305	98	2,415	829	152	205		
34	Kansas	458,190	336,575	2,689	3,205	247	990	2,394	1,990	48	225		
35	South Central division	5,726,570	3,555,324	8,734	3,246	2,020	1,946	6,566	1,222	148	78		
36	Kentucky	858,324	606,397	343	80			343	80				
37	Tennessee	697,570	551,673	1,452	396	351	185	1,101	211				
38	Alabama	824,209	559,171	728	688	413	688	315					
39	Mississippi	657,381	430,557	569	39	189	30	380			9		
40	Louisiana	778,901	399,991	536	177	34	51	502	116		10		
41	Arkansas	426,179	296,208	664	1,093	120	671	544	363		59		
42	Oklahoma[2]	257,100	34,176	2,617		502		1,967		148			
43	Texas	1,226,906	677,151	1,825	773	411	321	1,414	452				
44	Western division	1,696,666	831,710	16,564	5,230	1,508	827	14,938	4,177	118	226	2,134	
45	Montana	98,984	32,478	565	49			565	49				
46	Idaho	74,578	24,036	518	148	88		430	148				
47	Wyoming	23,945	11,705	76				76					
48	Colorado	205,666	86,837	2,344	414	33		2,311	414				
49	New Mexico	137,009	105,749	218				218					
50	Arizona	45,057	26,972	214	12			214	12				
51	Utah	172,814	128,115	216	37		8	216	29				
52	Nevada	14,944	5,877	76	56			76	56				
53	Washington	191,976	58,798	3,058	788	410	129	2,592	560	56	99		
54	Oregon	120,229	70,524	2,208	904	302	132	1,844	683	62	89		
55	California	611,464	280,619	7,071	2,822	675	558	6,396	2,226		38	2,134	

[1] Includes Evangelical Adventists; Church of God (Adventist); Churches of God (Adventist), Unattached Congregations; Life and Advent Union; and Churches of

DENOMINATIONS, BY STATES AND TERRITORIES: 1906 AND 1890.

BAPTIST BODIES.																
Total.		Baptists.								Seventh-day Baptists.		Free Baptists.		Freewill Baptists.		
		Total.		Northern Convention.		Southern Convention.		National Convention (Colored).								
1906	1890	1906	1890	1906	1890	1906	1890	1906	1890	1906	1890	1906	1890	1906	1890	
5,662,234	3,712,468	5,323,183	3,429,080	1,052,105	800,025	2,009,471	1,280,066	2,261,607	1,348,989	8,381	9,143	81,359	87,898	40,280	11,864	1
571,346	435,043	528,610	382,040	488,458	382,040			40,152		4,967	5,617	35,607	44,236			2
32,854	35,038	20,813	18,492	20,813	18,492							11,698	16,294			3
15,974	16,772	9,741	8,768	9,721	8,768			20				6,210	8,004			4
9,951	11,258	8,450	8,933	8,450	8,933							1,501	2,325			5
80,894	62,966	78,166	59,830	72,891	59,830			5,274				2,720	3,122			6
19,878	17,293	14,928	12,055	14,304	12,055			624		1,080	1,271	3,252	3,252			7
27,872	22,600	27,535	22,372	25,317	22,372			2,218		38	103	299	125			8
176,981	142,736	165,710	129,711	163,947	129,711			1,763		2,926	3,274	7,910	8,636			9
65,248	39,760	64,238	38,757	54,354	38,757			9,884		735	745	50				10
141,694	86,620	139,030	83,122	118,661	83,122			20,369		188	224	1,967	2,478			11
1,984,710	1,297,371	1,877,578	1,236,720	62,359	38,977	737,458	491,811	1,077,761	705,932	698	791	3,956	2,277	31,348	11,864	12
2,921	2,006	2,694	1,823	2,694	1,823											13
30,928	16,238	29,435	15,767	252		11,232	8,017	17,951	7,750			1,242	98			14
37,024	19,372	36,980	19,338	10,777	3,000		3,621	26,203	12,717							15
415,987	303,134	404,268	292,564			136,062	92,693	268,206	199,871			425	478	64		16
67,044	42,854	60,365	39,396	48,636	34,154	1,672	1,009	10,057	4,233	681	767	1,513	1,668	193		17
401,043	310,920	355,987	288,093			202,798	153,648	153,189	134,445	17	10		11	22,518	10,224	18
341,456	203,959	338,201	201,788			118,360	76,216	219,841	125,572					2,649	1,640	19
596,319	357,241	566,631	338,376			232,088	137,860	333,943	200,516			776		4,500		20
91,988	41,647	83,017	39,575			34,646	18,747	48,371	20,828		14		22	1,424		21
771,329	568,662	690,904	492,012	432,366	351,141	176,225	122,258	82,313	18,613	2,315	2,511	31,320	33,114	1,425		22
92,112	68,033	82,035	57,685	64,635	57,685			17,400		130	131	5,553	6,982	1,425		23
92,705	70,380	73,729	54,080	60,203	54,080			13,526				1,931	1,926			24
152,870	109,640	134,965	95,237	118,884	95,237			16,081		290	350	7,755	6,096			25
50,136	39,580	45,120	34,145	44,373	34,145			747		18		4,977	5,435			26
21,716	16,913	19,474	14,152	19,414	14,152			60		955	1,078	1,287	1,683			27
24,309	16,441	22,786	14,698	22,786	14,698					207	246	1,316	1,497			28
44,096	33,962	41,745	30,901	39,393	30,901			2,352		131	169	1,563	2,029			29
218,353	159,371	198,459	140,598	115		176,208	121,985	22,136	18,613		13	5,525	4,752			30
4,596	2,298	4,596	2,298	4,596	2,298											31
6,198	4,052	6,097	3,856	6,097	3,856						28	96	168			32
17,939	13,481	16,895	11,917	16,895	11,917					321	267	491	1,185			33
46,299	34,511	45,003	32,445	34,975	32,172	17	273	10,011		263	229	826	1,361			34
2,262,933	1,382,992	2,154,780	1,290,441			1,096,727	665,997	1,059,053	624,444	338	196	10,358	8,092	7,507		35
311,583	229,524	287,791	203,913			211,552	153,668	76,239	50,245		6	2,165	1,641			36
277,170	185,189	253,141	158,815			159,838	106,632	93,303	52,183			1,840	2,864	3,093		37
452,559	258,405	422,270	240,622			162,445	98,185	259,825	142,437	24	11	1,200	847	2,213		38
371,518	224,612	364,339	218,962			123,357	82,315	240,982	136,647		33	2,804	1,339	35		39
185,554	98,552	183,130	95,744			49,620	27,736	133,510	68,008	60	36	1,382	1,000			40
193,244	128,724	184,995	122,150			91,631	58,364	93,364	63,786	254	60	337	40	371		41
69,585	9,463	66,930	9,363			49,978	9,363	16,952					100	1,288		42
401,720	248,523	392,184	240,872			247,306	129,734	144,878	111,138		50	630	261	507		43
71,916	28,400	71,311	27,867	68,922	27,867	61		2,328		63	28	118	179			44
2,029	683	2,029	683	2,029	683											45
2,374	745	2,331	656	2,331	656						28					46
838	262	838	262	838	262											47
13,011	4,944	12,917	4,944	12,917	4,944					63						48
2,403	355	2,403	355	2,331	355	61		11								49
1,034	197	1,034	197	1,034	197											50
987	327	987	327	987	327											51
316	63	316	63	316	63											52
12,807	3,941	12,614	3,870	12,440	3,870			174								53
11,316	5,500	11,159	5,306	11,099	5,306			60								54
24,801	11,383	24,683	11,204	22,600	11,204			2,083				118	179			55

[1] Oklahoma and Indian Territory combined.

TABLE 10.—COMPARISON OF COMMUNICANTS OR MEMBERS, BY SELECTED

	STATE OR TERRITORY.	BAPTIST BODIES—continued.											
		General Baptists.		Separate Baptists.		United Baptists.		Duck River and Kindred Associations.		Primitive Baptists.[1]		Other Baptists.[2]	
		1906	1890	1906	1890	1906	1890	1906	1890	1906	1890	1906	1890
1	Continental United States	30,097	21,362	5,180	1,599	13,698	13,209	6,416	8,254	137,387	116,271	16,253	13,788
2	North Atlantic division									1,179	1,738	983	1,412
3	Maine									68	137	275	115
4	New Hampshire											23	
5	Vermont												
6	Massachusetts									9	10		4
7	Rhode Island											618	715
8	Connecticut												
9	New York									435	1,019		96
10	New Jersey									225	258		
11	Pennsylvania									442	314	67	482
12	South Atlantic division					2,226			659	54,665	43,560	14,239	1,500
13	Delaware									227	183		
14	Maryland									251	373		
15	District of Columbia									44	34		
16	Virginia									11,230	9,950		142
17	West Virginia					2,226				2,066	217		806
18	North Carolina								659	12,422	11,740	10,099	183
19	South Carolina									606	531		
20	Georgia									20,688	18,535	3,724	330
21	Florida									7,131	1,997	416	39
22	North Central division	19,443	14,682	3,277	1,599	2,659	2,738		185	19,931	20,551	55	1,270
23	Ohio					1,381				1,588	3,202		33
24	Indiana	6,671	5,351	2,201	1,599					8,132	7,078	41	346
25	Illinois	3,621	2,605	1,076						5,163	5,301		51
26	Michigan									21			
27	Wisconsin												
28	Minnesota												
29	Iowa									657	853		10
30	Missouri	9,048	6,654			1,267	2,738		185	4,040	3,763	14	668
31	North Dakota												
32	South Dakota									5			
33	Nebraska	103	72			11				118	40		
34	Kansas									207	314		162
35	South Central division	10,654	6,680	1,903		8,813	10,471	6,416	7,410	61,188	50,422	976	9,280
36	Kentucky	6,881	4,455	1,765		7,167	6,443			5,670	10,665	144	2,401
37	Tennessee	1,108	1,008	138			3,180	4,099	5,065	13,472	12,987	279	1,270
38	Alabama						702	1,947	782	24,601	14,903	304	538
39	Mississippi							370	368	3,970	3,070		840
40	Louisiana									982	1,602		170
41	Arkansas	2,035	1,217			1,646	146		887	3,431	2,994	175	1,230
42	Oklahoma[4]	630								687		50	
43	Texas								308	8,375	4,201	24	2,831
44	Western division									424			336
45	Montana												
46	Idaho									43			61
47	Wyoming												
48	Colorado									31			
49	New Mexico												
50	Arizona												
51	Utah												
52	Nevada												
53	Washington									193			71
54	Oregon									157			194
55	California												

[1] Includes Primitive Baptists and Colored Primitive Baptists in America.
[2] Includes General Six Principle Baptists; Two-Seed-in-the-Spirit Predestinarian Baptists; Freewill Baptists (Bullockites); and United American Freewill Baptists (Colored).
[3] Christian Church [illegible] in 1890 included in 1906 with Christians Christian Connection .

DENOMINATIONS, BY STATES AND TERRITORIES: 1906 AND 1890—Continued.

BRETHREN (PLYMOUTH)—I, II, III, IV.		CHRISTIAN UNION.		CHRISTIANS (CHRISTIAN CONNECTION).[3]		CHURCH OF CHRIST, SCIENTIST.		CHURCHES OF GOD IN NORTH AMERICA, GENERAL ELDERSHIP OF THE.		CHURCHES OF THE NEW JERUSALEM.[4]		CONGREGATIONALISTS.		DISCIPLES OR CHRISTIANS.[5]		
1906	1890	1906	1890	1906	1890	1906	1890	1906	1890	1906	1890	1906	1890	1906	1890	
10,566	6,661	13,905	18,214	110,117	103,722	85,717	8,724	24,356	22,511	7,247	7,095	700,480	512,771	1,142,359	641,051	1
4,704	2,486	....	416	17,682	21,335	53,023	2,261	11,157	9,430	3,638	3,830	337,502	290,352	39,771	18,132	2
....	5	....	....	2,210	3,451	384	60	....	75	135	289	21,093	21,523	397	293	3
15	19	....	102	1,303	1,522	431	54	....	....	60	42	19,070	19,712	4	....	4
....	6	....	264	266	335	144	40	....	....	....	....	22,109	20,465	316	262	5
621	552	....	....	2,114	2,722	43,547	499	....	20	1,535	1,684	119,196	101,890	1,527	777	6
195	66	....	50	769	972	234	75	....	....	133	130	9,858	7,192	79	35	7
49	16	....	....	103	105	521	75	....	....	46	28	65,554	59,154	866	337	8
1,572	923	....	....	5,492	7,520	5,671	1,268	....	....	578	560	57,351	45,686	9,168	4,316	9
988	439	....	....	1,406	1,489	540	35	....	....	133	323	8,460	4,912	227	105	10
1,264	460	....	....	4,019	3,219	1,551	155	11,157	9,344	1,018	774	14,811	9,818	27,187	12,007	11
502	392	....	65	25,591	19,307	1,594	91	1,985	1,697	538	467	15,685	8,469	77,820	43,775	12
42	44	....	....	....	....	74	*	....	....	59	50	....	....	75	95	13
129	103	....	15	51	....	223	....	1,204	816	237	244	812	336	3,343	1,774	14
38	8	....	....	....	....	347	15	....	....	132	98	2,984	1,399	2,170	700	15
128	63	....	....	8,266	5,770	175	....	....	....	59	2	238	156	26,248	14,100	16
....	....	....	....	708	704	74	....	781	881	....	....	228	136	13,323	5,907	17
36	3	....	....	15,909	12,736	110	....	....	....	....	....	2,699	1,002	13,637	12,437	18
....	8	....	....	....	....	23	....	....	....	....	....	456	376	2,021	2,880	19
33	55	....	....	657	97	397	40	....	....	38	48	5,581	3,880	13,749	4,676	20
96	106	....	50	....	....	171	33	....	....	13	30	2,687	1,184	3,254	1,306	21
4,128	3,150	12,982	15,922	62,330	59,948	22,489	5,028	9,783	9,987	2,318	2,197	278,687	185,359	616,578	365,442	22
323	276	8,184	8,002	24,706	25,952	2,582	564	2,980	3,352	642	657	43,555	32,281	88,787	54,425	23
135	128	1,488	1,599	21,397	19,832	1,931	134	1,999	2,575	131	104	5,406	3,081	118,447	78,942	24
967	830	123	206	8,654	5,745	5,675	1,271	1,555	1,495	712	641	54,875	35,830	105,068	60,867	25
556	466	....	436	1,018	1,834	1,580	125	320	373	161	163	32,553	24,582	10,629	5,788	26
153	74	....	....	470	579	1,704	474	....	....	11	43	26,163	15,841	1,715	1,317	27
531	387	....	....	....	....	2,387	264	21	....	67	80	22,264	13,624	3,560	1,917	28
434	377	655	1,258	3,568	2,555	1,485		918	683	75	138	37,061	23,733	57,425	30,968	29
502	229	2,433	3,926	1,177	1,627	2,644		1,053	221	375	309	11,046	7,617	166,137	97,773	30
38	35	....	....	137	....	139		....	....	....	....	5,290	1,616	147	20	31
3	....	....	....	....	....	237		....	....	....	....	8,599	5,164	1,478	490	32
178	136	....	....	169	148	994		329	332	....	....	16,629	10,045	19,613	7,715	33
308	212	99	495	1,034	1,676	1,131	640 [illegible]	613	956	144	62	15,247	11,945	43,572	25,200	34
183	149	733	1,240	4,393	3,132	1,992	131	1,339	1,388	285	168	16,062	6,640	349,944	192,390	35
18	5	139	443	2,310	2,146	137	....	....	....	14	61	996	449	136,110	77,647	36
75	8	53	376	....	....	337	3	....	....	73	64	2,426	1,429	56,315	41,125	37
....	....	....	....	1,890	687	94	....	....	....	10	....	5,395	1,683	17,970	9,201	38
....	....	....	....	....	....	92	....	....	....	....		595	210	9,864	5,729	39
....	22	....	....	....	....	63	....	....	....	24	....	1,773	1,057	2,548	202	40
....	3	....	101	157	181	82	....	737	577	54	3	344	669	21,275	14,385	41
....	....	541	130	....	....	391	16	602	811	....	....	2,677	297	32,306	2,242	42
90	111	....	190	36	118	796	112	....	....	110	40	1,856	846	73,556	41,859	43
1,049	484	190	571	121	....	6,619	1,213	92	....	468	433	52,544	21,951	58,246	21,312	44
....	....	....	....	18	....	213	....	....	....	....	....	954	345	2,008	785	45
19	....	....	....	....	....	119	....	....	....	....		1,487	105	3,252	350	46
....	....	....	....	....	....	....	....	....	....	....	....	833	339	292	48	47
99	70	190	571	....	....	1,489	147	....	....	46	41	8,951	3,217	8,635	2,400	48
6	....	....	....	....	....	....	....	....	....	....	....	270	175	1,092	65	49
....	....	....	....	....	....	78	....	....	....	....	....	405	162	536	78	50
....	....	....	....	....	....	452	100	....	....	....	....	1,174	460	250	270	51
....	....	....	....	....	....	....	....	....	....	....	....	180	50	100	....	
185	51	....	....	103	....	924	90	50	....	78	....	10,026	3,154	10,628	5,816	
127	22	....	....	....	....	591	62	42	....	50	45	4,575	2,037	10,420	4,067	
613	341	....	....	....	....	2,753	814	....	....	294	347	23,690	11,907	21,033	7,433	52 53

[4] Includes General Convention of the New Jerusalem in the United States of America and General Church of the New Jerusalem.
[5] Includes Disciples of Christ and Churches of Christ.
[6] Oklahoma and Indian Territory combined.

TABLE 10.—COMPARISON OF COMMUNICANTS OR MEMBERS, BY SELECTED

	STATE OR TERRITORY.	DUNKERS OR GERMAN BAPTIST BRETHREN.								EASTERN ORTHODOX CHURCHES			
		Total.		German Baptist Brethren Church (Conservative).		The Brethren Church (Progressive Dunkers).		Other Dunkers, etc.[1]		Total.		Russian Orthodox Church.	
		1906	1890	1906	1890	1906	1890	1906	1890	1906	1890	1906	1890
1	Continental United States	97,144	73,795	76,547	61,101	17,042	8,089	3,555	4,605	129,606	600	19,111	500
2	North Atlantic division	23,419	16,898	19,032	14,385	3,985	2,008	402	505	68,408		12,991	
3	Maine									780			
4	New Hampshire									5,210			
5	Vermont									150		150	
6	Massachusetts									14,145		470	
7	Rhode Island									1,105			
8	Connecticut									3,127		1,552	
9	New York	100		100						19,302		1,767	
10	New Jersey	143	191	43	191	100				2,466		606	
11	Pennsylvania	23,176	16,707	18,889	14,194	3,885	2,008	402	505	22,123		8,446	
12	South Atlantic division	20,681	14,000	17,095	12,366	3,008	924	578	710	4,831			
13	Delaware												
14	Maryland	4,450	2,974	3,667	2,446	616	200	167	328	400			
15	District of Columbia	256		110		146				450			
16	Virginia	11,524	7,244	9,078	6,659	2,166	397	280	188	756			
17	West Virginia	3,651	3,216	3,457	2,710	80	327	114	179				
18	North Carolina	761	525	744	510			17	15	95			
19	South Carolina	39		39						360			
20	Georgia									1,270			
21	Florida		41		41					1,500			
22	North Central division	47,280	40,584	35,177	32,191	9,634	5,048	2,469	3,345	32,007		3,415	
23	Ohio	12,872	11,798	9,076	8,490	2,592	1,542	1,204	1,766	4,004		852	
24	Indiana	14,539	12,350	9,949	10,224	3,800	1,479	790	647	1,155			
25	Illinois	4,666	4,119	3,848	3,701	716	193	102	225	17,536		1,226	
26	Michigan	1,213	844	914	560	201	240	98	44	500			
27	Wisconsin	339	199	253	170	68		18	29	1,156		196	
28	Minnesota	365	104	365	104					1,614		964	
29	Iowa	3,378	3,470	2,504	2,769	852	601	22	100	325			
30	Missouri	1,984	2,090	1,881	1,845	44	90	59	155	2,455			
31	North Dakota	1,354		1,311				43		177		177	
32	South Dakota	155	102	75	102	80				230			
33	Nebraska	1,594	1,441	1,096	998	471	396	27	47	2,105			
34	Kansas	4,821	4,067	3,905	3,228	810	507	106	332	750			
35	South Central division	2,498	1,529	2,443	1,522	36		19	[illegible]	2,690	100	695	
36	Kentucky	14	13	14	10				3	80			
37	Tennessee	1,104	1,249	1,104	1,249					410			
38	Alabama	52		52						1,505			
39	Mississippi												
40	Louisiana	98	17	98	17						100		
41	Arkansas	199	82	172	78	27							
42	Oklahoma[4]	880	73	861	73			19		195		195	
43	Texas	151	95	142	95	9				500		500	
44	Western division	3,266	784	2,800	637	379	109	87	38	21,670	500	2,010	500
45	Montana	16		16						1,500			
46	Idaho	476	40	476	40					1,200			
47	Wyoming		21						21	900			
48	Colorado	357	127	339	110		17	18		2,905		725	
49	New Mexico												
50	Arizona	36		36									
51	Utah									4,500			
52	Nevada									670			
53	Washington	453	26	453	26					574		574	
54	Oregon	410	280	410	250		20		10	311		61	
55	California	1,518	290	1,070	211	379	72	69	7	9,110	500	650	500

[1] Includes Old Order German Baptist Brethren and German Seventh-day Baptists.
[2] Includes Servian Orthodox Church and Syrian Orthodox Church.
[3] Includes Evangelical Association and United Evangelical Church.

DENOMINATIONS, BY STATES AND TERRITORIES: 1906 AND 1890—Continued.

EASTERN ORTHODOX CHURCHES—cont'd.				EVANGELICAL BODIES.[3]		FRIENDS.								GERMAN EVANGELICAL PROTESTANT BODIES.[5]		
Greek Orthodox Church.		Other Eastern Orthodox Churches.[3]				Total.		Society of Friends (Orthodox).		Religious Society of Friends (Hicksite).		Other Friends.[4]				
1906	1890	1906	1890	1906	1890	1906	1890	1906	1890	1906	1890	1906	1890	1906	1890	
90,751	100	19,744		174,780	133,813	113,772	107,208	91,161	80,655	18,560	21,992	4,051	4,561	34,704	36,156	1
45,035		10,382		66,215	49,270	26,029	28,360	12,322	12,387	13,393	15,611	314	362	7,417	12,287	2
780				64		1,713	1,430	1,713	1,430							3
5,210						357	413	357	413							4
				56		177	251	177	251							5
12,475		,200		590		1,798	1,602	1,734	1,560			64	42			6
1,105				138		648	698	575	617			73	81			7
1,575				76												8
15,100		2,435		5,755	6,222	5,555	7,078	3,296	3,644	2,165	3,331	94	103			9
1,860				762	669	3,324	3,261	1,043	982	2,281	2,279					10
6,930		6,747		58,774	42,379	12,457	13,627	3,427	3,490	8,947	10,001	83	136	7,417	12,287	11
4,831				2,603	2,377	10,977	8,792	8,044	6,077	2,606	2,715	327		1,369	1,915	12
						621	744	109	122	512	622					13
400				2,309	1,743	2,079	2,072	508	525	1,571	1,547			970		14
450						156	59	61	19	95	40					15
756						1,369	893	941	387	428	506					16
				294	565		50		50					399	1,915	17
95						6,752	4,904	6,425	4,904			327				18
360																
1,270																
1,500					69		70		70							21
23,530		5,062		98,984	78,948	69,141	66,142	63,299	58,277	2,561	3,666	3,281	4,199	22,470	16,154	22
1,810		1,342		19,225	14,673	14,364	13,747	12,394	10,884	750	1,187	1,220	1,676	15,596	11,793	23
1,155				8,872	6,738	30,621	27,780	29,255	25,915	1,013	1,376	353	489	2,633	1,886	24
13,310		3,000		15,107	10,934	2,343	2,455	1,902	2,015	441	440			2,630	735	25
500				7,700	6,677	1,351	1,458	1,348	1,433	3	25			21		26
960				13,450	12,558	111	154	111	154							27
650				7,942	6,181	274	305	274	305							28
325				10,446	9,761	10,068	10,125	8,762	8,146	239	440	1,067	1,539	80		29
2,455				1,081	1,102	603	615	603	615					1,510	,700	30
				1,784	784											31
230				1,797	1,628	103	266	103	266							32
1,985		120		6,192	3,458	1,358	980	1,243	782	115	198				40	33
150		600		5,388	4,459	7,925	8,257	7,304	7,762			621	495			34
1,995	100			1,466	509	2,455	2,101	2,455	2,101					2,813	5,800	35
80				270	213									2,813	1,250	36
410						117	1,001	117	1,001							37
1,505						37		37								38
																39
	100						66		66						3,500	40
							338		338							41
				585		2,187	576	2,187	576							42
				611	296	114	120	114	120						1,050	43
15,360		4,300		5,512	2,209	5,170	1,813	5,041	1,813			129		635		44
		1,500														45
1,200						273		273								46
900																47
2,180				345	87	94	38	94	38							48
																49
																50
4,500																51
670																52
				987	451	451		451								53
250				3,262	1,199	1,688	766	1,688	766							54
5,660		2,800		918	472	2,664	1,009	2,535	1,009			129		635		55

[4] Includes Orthodox Conservative Friends (Wilburite) and Friends (Primitive).
[5] Includes German Evangelical Protestant Ministers' Association and German Evangelical Protestant Ministers' Conference.
[6] Oklahoma and Indian Territory combined.

TABLE 10.—COMPARISON OF COMMUNICANTS OR MEMBERS, BY SELECTED

	STATE OR TERRITORY.	GERMAN EVANGELICAL SYNOD OF NORTH AMERICA.		INDEPENDENT CHURCHES.		JEWISH CONGREGATIONS.[1]		LATTER-DAY SAINTS. Total		Church of Jesus Christ of Latter-day Saints.		Reorganized Church of Jesus Christ of Latter-day Saints.	
		1906	1890	1906	1890	1906	1890	1906	1890	1906	1890	1906	1890
1	Continental United States	293,137	187,432	73,673	13,360	101,457	130,496	256,647	166,125	215,796	144,352	40,851	21,773
2	North Atlantic division	35,359	24,592	22,851	8,023	63,021	63,188	2,911	1,736	669	100	2,242	1,636
3	Maine	...	...	346	170	205	...	507	442	...	...	507	442
4	New Hampshire	...	...	10	150	80	...	...	...	...	...	...	...
5	Vermont	...	...	280	166	166	44	...	...	...	...	...	...
6	Massachusetts	...	...	2,013	684	4,388	2,501	679	457	109	...	570	457
7	Rhode Island	...	...	364	768	1,025	910	306	233	...	...	306	233
8	Connecticut	...	...	639	353	1,733	1,621	44	8	...	...	44	8
9	New York	26,183	17,409	10,029	4,232	35,342	45,807	388	158	215	56	173	102
10	New Jersey	2,305	1,890	1,584	552	4,603	4,276	...	21	...	...	...	21
11	Pennsylvania	6,871	5,293	7,586	948	15,479	8,029	987	417	345	44	642	373
12	South Atlantic division	9,582	5,219	7,963	911	5,959	9,507	6,686	1,395	5,678	762	1,008	633
13	Delaware	...	...	66	...	207	...	...	...	...	...	...	...
14	Maryland	8,384	4,405	1,738	500	2,153	3,575	115	75	58	58	57	17
15	District of Columbia	350	...	150	386	698	976	...	...	...	...	...	...
16	Virginia	564	700	932	...	915	1,187	1,021	171	988	137	33	34
17	West Virginia	95	114	1,225	...	220	350	1,385	406	785	81	600	325
18	North Carolina	...	...	2,096	...	234	386	976	108	976	108	...	...
19	South Carolina	...	...	485	...	312	800	1,101	203	1,101	203	...	...
20	Georgia	189	...	738	25	897	2,086	386	175	386	175	...	...
21	Florida	...	...	553	...	323	147	1,702	257	1,384	...	318	257
22	North Central division	220,090	149,145	27,050	3,559	20,227	35,590	31,947	15,816	2,471	80	29,476	15,736
23	Ohio	35,138	31,617	2,390	298	5,678	8,889	1,507	678	196	...	1,311	678
24	Indiana	21,624	15,274	3,020	918	1,383	3,617	1,090	380	411	14	679	366
25	Illinois	59,973	37,138	9,431	1,640	5,286	10,171	2,960	1,909	518	...	2,442	1,909
26	Michigan	20,436	10,926	2,035	170	1,530	3,693	4,335	1,540	108	...	4,227	1,540
27	Wisconsin	19,861	11,410	1,387	...	1,199	1,231	1,184	341	323	32	861	309
28	Minnesota	9,183	5,567	1,300	31	1,725	1,424	522	224	143	...	379	224
29	Iowa	11,681	6,902	2,706	75	412	537	8,328	5,303	189	...	8,139	5,303
30	Missouri	32,715	25,676	2,725	156	2,392	4,450	8,042	3,189	162	...	7,880	3,189
31	North Dakota	1,655	440	273	...	12	30	242	...	...	...	242	...
32	South Dakota	325	...	334	...	...	...	85	88	...	...	85	88
33	Nebraska	3,882	2,142	764	...	435	1,062	1,568	1,058	65	...	1,503	1,058
34	Kansas	3,617	2,053	685	271	175	486	2,084	1,106	356	34	1,728	1,072
35	South Central division	25,877	8,026	11,143	150	7,992	13,365	9,547	1,779	6,019	622	3,528	1,157
36	Kentucky	12,189	4,912	815	...	1,147	955	1,407	249	1,150	199	257	50
37	Tennessee	...	...	2,381	...	919	1,760	1,013	198	841	134	172	64
38	Alabama	710	...	1,116	150	1,141	3,168	2,124	592	1,052	166	1,072	426
39	Mississippi	...	...	2,274	...	746	1,370	1,214	197	1,018	123	196	74
40	Louisiana	4,353	1,250	592	...	1,618	3,374	455	...	455	...	...	...
41	Arkansas	250	...	1,629	...	673	744	538	60	248	...	290	60
42	Oklahoma[2]	630	...	949	...	72	...	1,296	46	382	...	914	46
43	Texas	7,745	1,864	1,387	...	1,676	1,994	1,500	437	873	...	627	437
44	Western division	2,229	450	4,646	717	4,258	8,846	205,556	145,399	200,959	142,788	4,597	2,611
45	Montana	...	...	...	...	152	140	510	122	242	...	268	122
46	Idaho	...	...	66	...	...	...	32,425	14,972	32,159	14,816	266	156
47	Wyoming	125	...	10	...	...	...	5,211	1,336	5,203	1,322	8	14
48	Colorado	833	135	346	...	853	1,062	2,755	1,762	2,194	1,640	561	122
49	New Mexico	...	...	30	...	120	50	738	456	684	453	54	3
50	Arizona	...	...	25	...	20	...	6,175	6,500	6,175	6,500	...	...
51	Utah	50	...	...	...	183	100	151,525	118,201	151,032	117,640	493	561
52	Nevada	...	...	...	...	...	...	1,105	525	1,105	417	...	108
53	Washington	...	...	1,097	...	488	150	461	34	56	...	405	34
54	Oregon	...	...	323	...	414	1,165	1,817	95	1,496	...	321	95
55	California	1,221	315	2,749	717	2,028	6,179	2,834	1,396	613	...	2,221	1,396

[1] In 1906, heads of families only. In 1890, members as well as heads of families included.
[2] See denominational text, pages 355 and 379.

DENOMINATIONS, BY STATES AND TERRITORIES: 1906 AND 1890—Continued.

LUTHERAN BODIES.

Total.		General Synod.		United Synod in the South.		General Council.[3]		Synodical Conference.		United Norwegian Church.		Joint Synod of Ohio and Other States.		Synod of Buffalo.		
1906	1890	1906	1890	1906	1890	1906	1890	1906	1890	1906	1890	1906	1890	1906	1890	
2,112,494	1,231,072	270,221	164,640	47,747	37,457	462,177	276,483	648,529	357,153	185,027	119,972	123,408	69,505	5,270	4,242	1
522,606	333,736	151,034	97,257	...	...	287,223	178,211	53,886	33,022	1,386	434	8,343	5,750	2,699	2,268	2
1,045	904	...	...	...	...	220	179	...	...	340	225	...	...	...	...	3
1,070	520	...	...	...	...	550	395	260	...	260	125	...	...	...	...	4
408	174	...	...	...	...	408	174	...	...	...	...	...	...	...	...	5
13,063	4,137	...	103	...	...	6,645	1,743	3,966	1,717	...	...	...	...	...	...	6
2,873	590	...	...	...	...	2,516	420	357	...	...	...	...	...	...	...	7
19,713	5,702	231	190	...	...	13,951	3,767	4,156	1,405	...	...	...	...	...	...	8
124,644	89,046	20,543	15,611	...	...	65,450	39,430	32,178	22,642	695	84	290	198	2,699	2,268	9
24,147	12,878	4,997	2,415	...	...	15,323	7,940	2,240	699	25	...	...	...	...	...	10
335,643	219,725	125,263	78,938	...	...	182,160	124,163	10,729	6,559	66	...	8,053	5,552	...	...	11
91,951	67,721	30,188	19,884	45,279	34,850	2,061	1,563	7,907	4,312	32	42	6,363	3,216	...	...	12
731	296	38	...	...	...	665	296	...	...	...	...	28	...	...	...	13
32,246	24,648	24,824	17,288	...	...	56	...	4,062	3,208	...	42	3,254	1,545	...	...	14
3,104	2,997	2,129	1,038	...	...	75	600	432	375	...	...	468	150	...	...	15
15,010	12,220	645	450	13,293	11,196	...	...	860	399	32	...	180	175	...	...	16
6,506	4,176	2,552	1,108	962	1,518	1,176	650	215	121	...	...	1,540	779	...	...	17
17,740	12,326	...	...	14,881	11,759	...	...	1,966	...	...	...	898	567	...	...	18
12,652	8,757	..	...	12,652	8,757	...	...	...	...	...	...	...	...	...	...	19
3,233	1,932	..	...	3,233	1,477	...	...	...	...	...	...	...	...	...	...	20
729	369	..	...	268	143	89	17	372	209	...	...	...	...	...	...	21
1,405,788	793,897	81,569	43,780	18	...	162,047	87,014	555,115	308,802	180,122	118,276	102,652	57,793	2,571	1,948	22
132,439	89,560	30,317	18,437	18	...	18,237	10,804	24,129	15,440	...	...	45,937	31,261	...	...	23
55,768	41,832	7,753	6,090	...	...	5,445	3,887	34,028	24,666	...	...	8,310	5,095	...	...	24
202,566	116,807	14,768	7,438	...	...	36,366	19,446	113,527	69,033	7,374	3,298	5,651	2,695	194	136	25
105,803	62,897	1,944	679	...	...	9,693	4,194	50,031	27,472	2,760	3,011	9,702	6,217	700	342	26
284,286	160,919	1,534	861	...	...	8,695	2,999	153,690	83,942	49,535	28,717	15,471	7,356	1,309	1,158	27
267,322	145,907	...	26	...	...	49,830	25,125	61,092	30,398	59,204	49,541	9,656	3,180	368	312	28
117,668	63,725	5,207	2,043	...	...	13,771	7,733	25,528	13,252	23,287	14,891	2,643	650	...	...	29
46,868	27,099	2,104	1,576	...	...	846	364	41,185	22,121	...	14	195	30	...	...	30
59,923	18,269	...	...	...	...	1,604	651	5,854	1,136	22,138	10,283	2,269	70	...	...	31
45,018	23,314	552	64	...	...	2,475	2,330	8,285	3,097	15,004	7,922	838	327	...	...	32
59,485	27,297	12,807	3,731	...	...	7,308	4,228	25,730	12,339	338	285	1,259	440	...	...	33
28,642	16,262	4,583	2,835	...	...	7,782	5,253	12,036	5,906	482	314	721	472	...	...	34
49,586	25,587	4,295	2,551	2,450	2,607	1,578	7,153	21,358	8,490	...	...	2,156	2,230	...	...	35
4,940	2,394	3,190	1,627	...	...	100	13	1,511	468	...	...	139	...	...	...	36
3,225	2,975	727	749	1,678	1,999	...	...	725	227	...	...	45	...	...	...	37
1,111	791	...	175	50	75	130	...	895	534	...	...	36	...	...	...	38
970	533	...	...	722	533	...	...	198	...	...	...	...	...	...	...	39
5,793	2,962	..	...	...	...	...	...	5,253	2,452	...	...	540	500	...	...	40
2,080	1,386	...	...	...	...	...	...	1,886	1,311	...	...	...	...	...	...	41
4,030	...	378	...	...	...	...	...	2,907	...	...	...	59	...	...	...	42
27,437	14,556	...	...	...	...	1,348	7,140	7,983	3,498	...	...	1,337	1,730	...	...	43
42,563	10,131	3,135	1,168	...	...	9,268	2,542	10,263	2,527	3,487	1,220	3,894	516	...	26	44
3,059	394	...	...	...	...	473	...	690	130	575	87	...	...	...	...	45
1,968	401	...	...	...	...	821	139	206	27	424	110	292	80	...	...	46
908	721	66	141	...	...	57	580	172	...	...	...	...	...	...	...	47
5,063	1,208	820	220	...	...	1,235	469	1,051	394	...	...	425	...	...	...	48
100	64	59	64	...	...	...	...	...	...	...	...	41	...	...	...	49
...	...	...	...	...	...	...	...	...	...	...	...	...	...	...	...	50
453	84	...	...	...	...	390	...	39	...	...	...	...	...	...	...	51
148	...	...	...	...	...	...	...	148	...	...	...	...	...	...	...	52
13,464	1,912	...	...	...	...	2,506	446	1,030	...	1,980	819	2,545	386	...	...	53
6,039	1,080	...	...	...	...	2,211	305	1,080	274	403	204	591	50	...	...	54
11,371	4,267	2,190	743	...	...	1,575	603	5,247	1,702	105	...	...	...	...	26	55

[3] Oklahoma and Indian Territory combined.

TABLE 10.—COMPARISON OF COMMUNICANTS OR MEMBERS, BY SELECTED

	STATE OR TERRITORY.	LUTHERAN BODIES—continued.													
		Hauge's Norwegian Synod.		Synod of Iowa and Other States.[1]		Synod for the Norwegian Church in America.		Synod of Michigan and Other States.		Danish Church in America.		Suomi Synod.		United Danish Church in America.[2]	
		1906	1890	1906	1890	1906	1890	1906	1890	1906	1890	1906	1890	1906	1890
1	Continental United States	33,268	14,730	110,254	48,363	107,712	55,452	9,697	11,482	12,541	10,181	12,907	1,385	16,340	3,493
2	North Atlantic division					1,793	1,339			1,761	1,494	2,106		499	
3	Maine									300	200			185	
4	New Hampshire														
5	Vermont														
6	Massachusetts					200	375			140	119	1,065		117	
7	Rhode Island														
8	Connecticut									550	200				
9	New York					1,047	784			500	410	245		77	
10	New Jersey					546	180			271	565			15	
11	Pennsylvania											806		105	
12	South Atlantic division														
13	Delaware														
14	Maryland														
15	District of Columbia														
16	Virginia														
17	West Virginia														
18	North Carolina														
19	South Carolina														
20	Georgia														
21	Florida														
22	North Central division	33,090	14,525	94,949	48,027	97,340	53,178	9,697	11,482	10,580	8,514	10,250	1,385	14,921	3,289
23	Ohio			8,020	5,111	100	184	1,896				1,572			
24	Indiana		29			125	182		441			30			
25	Illinois	2,547	863	14,005	7,414	2,692	1,688			2,580	1,314	563		470	50
26	Michigan	225	62	6,817	4,516	820	758	7,801	11,041	1,071	588	6,121	1,265	688	
27	Wisconsin	3,047	2,165	15,220	7,073	23,927	15,087			1,146	2,076	186		3,897	395
28	Minnesota	12,857	6,534	8,460	2,781	38,903	21,832			1,081	1,032	1,548		2,376	1,524
29	Iowa	5,523	1,593	23,082	12,276	11,027	7,069			2,836	2,211			4,121	413
30	Missouri			2,137	1,493		50							83	
31	North Dakota	4,721	576	3,717	931	11,980	2,784			64				692	
32	South Dakota	3,539	2,239	4,103	2,440	6,489	3,030			417	285	230	120	444	153
33	Nebraska	532	438	6,859	2,976	1,212	544			1,325	888			2,120	754
34	Kansas	99	26	2,529	1,016	65	30			60	120			30	
35	South Central division			13,493	286	1,421	350			200		50		145	
36	Kentucky				286										
37	Tennessee					50									
38	Alabama														
39	Mississippi											50			
40	Louisiana														
41	Arkansas			194											
42	Oklahoma[3]			541										145	
43	Texas			12,758		1,371	350			200					
44	Western division	178	205	1,812	50	7,158	585				173	501		775	204
45	Montana					1,290	165					31			
46	Idaho	64				161	45								
47	Wyoming											113			
48	Colorado			670	50	82	75							170	
49	New Mexico														
50	Arizona														
51	Utah					12					48			12	
52	Nevada														
53	Washington	60	205	892		3,195	16					119			40
54	Oregon			250		722	95					238		165	20
55	California	54				1,696	189				125			428	144

[1] See denominational text, pages 355 and 379.
[2] Figures for 1890 are for the Danish Church Association.
[3] Includes Evangelical Lutheran Church in America, Eielsen's Synod; German Evangelical Lutheran Synod of Texas; Icelandic Evangelical Lutheran Synod in North America; Immanuel Synod of the Evangelical Lutheran Church of North America; Norwegian Lutheran Free Church; Slovak Evangelical Lutheran Synod of America; Finnish Evangelical Lutheran National Church; Apostolic Lutheran Church (Finnish); Church of the Lutheran Brethren of America (Norwegian); and Evangelical

DENOMINATIONS, BY STATES AND TERRITORIES: 1906 AND 1890—Continued.

LUTHERAN BODIES—continued.		MENNONITE BODIES.												METHODIST BODIES.		
Other Lutherans.[3]		Total.		Mennonite Church.		Amish Mennonite Church.		Old Amish Mennonite Church.		General Conference of Mennonites of North America.[4]		Other Mennonites.[5]		Total.		
1906	1890	1906	1890	1906	1890	1906	1890	1906	1890	1906	1890	1906	1890	1906	1890	
67,396	56,534	54,798	41,541	18,674	17,078	7,640	10,101	5,043	2,038	11,661	5,879	11,780	6,445	5,749,838	4,589,284	1
11,876	13,961	16,868	15,800	10,493	10,077	569	2,533	1,742	144	1,711	1,472	2,353	1,574	958,008	774,544	2
....	300	....	....	....	....	....	....	....	....	....	....	....	....	20,112	23,041	3
....	....	....	....	....	....	....	....	....	....	....	....	....	....	12,529	12,354	4
....	....	....	....	....	....	....	....	....	....	....	....	....	....	17,671	17,527	5
940	80	....	....	....	....	....	....	....	....	....	....	....	....	65,498	61,138	6
....	170	....	....	....	....	....	....	....	....	....	....	....	....	7,892	7,353	7
825	200	....	....	....	....	....	....	....	....	....	....	....	....	34,663	30,815	8
920	7,619	341	470	....	....	....	299	168	....	36	46	137	125	313,689	265,551	9
730	1,079	....	....	....	....	....	....	....	....	....	....	....	....	122,511	96,377	10
8,461	4,513	16,527	15,330	10,493	10,077	569	2,234	1,574	144	1,675	1,426	2,216	1,449	363,443	260,388	11
121	3,854	2,305	1,293	1,987	1,082	56	125	165	....	....	....	97	86	1,464,023	1,279,623	12
....	....	....	....	....	....	....	....	....	....	....	....	....	....	32,402	25,786	13
50	2,565	953	525	689	336	24	125	165	....	....	....	75	64	137,156	123,618	14
....	834	....	....	....	....	....	....	....	....	....	....	....	....	20,077	16,369	15
....	....	1,021	666	967	666	32	....	....	....	....	....	22	....	200,771	154,693	16
71	....	331	102	331	80	....	....	....	....	....	....	....	22	115,825	85,102	17
....	....	....	....	....	....	....	....	....	....	....	....	....	....	277,282	276,336	18
....	....	....	....	....	....	....	....	....	....	....	....	....	....	249,169	251,477	19
....	455	....	....	....	....	....	....	....	....	....	....	....	....	349,079	275,784	20
....	....	....	....	....	....	....	....	....	....	....	....	....	....	82,262	70,458	21
50,867	35,884	33,298	23,967	5,689	5,776	6,750	7,213	3,099	1,821	8,573	4,407	9,187	4,750	1,676,275	1,260,402	22
2,213	8,332	9,778	5,988	2,365	1,736	2,877	1,965	1,245	694	1,526	348	1,765	1,245	355,444	272,737	23
77	1,442	4,808	3,732	1,138	700	1,078	929	627	853	920	405	1,045	845	233,443	179,613	24
1,829	3,432	3,755	3,014	772	273	993	2,305	267	105	146	169	1,577	162	263,344	189,358	
7,430	2,752	1,560	356	313	155	178	....	194	....	....	....	875	201	128,675	101,951	
6,629	9,140	....	....	....	....	....	....	....	....	....	....	....	....	57,473	43,696	
21,947	3,622	659	967	24	725	....	....	....	....	262	70	373	172	47,637	32,199	
643	1,604	1,669	1,454	25	28	666	908	211	....	767	509	....	14	164,329	122,607	
318	1,451	1,032	748	317	199	392	316	88	24	130	133	105	76	214,004	162,514	[illegible]
6,884	1,838	129	41	34	41	95	....	....	....	....	....	....	....	10,223	4,889	1
2,642	1,307	996	1,383	75	655	....	....	....	....	562	226	358	502	16,143	12,116	3
....	674	1,468	1,664	89	751	370	504	....	....	679	....	330	409	64,352	42,941	[illegible]
255	290	7,445	4,620	537	513	101	291	467	145	3,581	2,547	2,759	1,124	121,208	95,781	34
2,440	1,920	1,534	158	187	28	80	95	....	....	1,145	....	122	35	1,479,745	1,193,379	35
....	....	....	....	....	....	....	....	....	....	....	....	....	....	156,007	141,521	36
....	....	44	58	44	28	....	30	....	....	....	....	....	....	241,396	223,116	37
....	7	....	....	....	....	....	....	....	....	....	....	....	....	254,373	242,624	38
....	....	....	....	....	....	....	....	....	....	....	....	....	....	212,105	164,589	39
....	....	....	....	....	....	....	....	....	....	....	....	....	....	79,464	65,693	40
....	75	45	100	....	....	45	65	....	....	....	....	....	35	142,569	123,316	41
....	....	1,410	....	122	....	35	....	....	....	1,145	....	108	....	76,336	13,630	42
2,440	1,838	35	....	21	....	....	....	....	....	....	....	14	....	317,495	218,890	43
2,092	915	793	323	318	115	185	135	37	73	232	....	21	....	171,787	81,336	44
....	12	26	....	....	....	....	....	21	....	5	....	....	....	7,022	2,425	45
....	....	56	....	56	....	....	....	....	....	....	....	....	....	5,884	1,162	46
500	....	....	....	....	....	....	....	....	....	....	....	....	....	1,657	912	47
....	....	169	75	169	....	....	75	....	....	....	....	....	....	27,867	10,850	48
....	....	....	....	....	....	....	....	....	....	....	....	....	....	6,560	2,360	49
....	....	3	....	....	....	....	....	....	....	3	....	....	....	2,667	656	50
....	36	....	....	....	....	....	....	....	....	....	....	....	....	1,567	1,055	51
....	....	....	....	....	....	....	....	....	....	....	....	....	....	618	418	52
1,137	....	59	....	....	....	....	....	....	....	38	....	21	....	31,700	12,697	53
379	132	380	248	93	115	185	60	16	73	86	....	....	....	21,717	11,927	54
76	735	100	....	....	....	....	....	....	....	100	....	....	....	64,528	36,874	55

[4] Apostolic Mennonite Church, reported separately in 1890, included in 1906 with the General Conference of Mennonites of North America.

[5] Includes Bruederhoef Mennonite Church; Reformed Mennonite Church; Church of God in Christ (Mennonite); Old (Wisler) Mennonite Church; Defenceless Mennonites; Mennonite Brethren in Christ; Krimmer Brueder-Gemeinde; Schellenberger Brueder-Gemeinde; Central Illinois Conference of Mennonites; and Nebraska and Minnesota Conference of Mennonites.

[6] Oklahoma and Indian Territory combined.

TABLE 10.—COMPARISON OF COMMUNICANTS OR MEMBERS, BY SELECTED

	STATE OR TERRITORY.	METHODIST BODIES—continued.											
		Methodist Episcopal Church.		African Methodist Episcopal Church.		African Union Methodist Protes-ta^nt Church.		African Methodist Episcopal Zion Church.		Methodist Protestant Church.		Wesleyan Methodist Connection of America.	
		1906	1890	1906	1890	1906	1890	1906	1890	1906	1890	1906	1890
1	Continental United States	2,986,154	2,240,354	494,777	452,725	5,592	3,415	184,542	349,788	178,544	141,989	20,043	16,492
2	North Atlantic division	868,462	694,903	25,144	22,683	2,709	1,287	17,323	20,448	21,616	18,453	4,482	5,440
3	Maine	20,087	22,990				45	25					
4	New Hampshire	12,529	12,354										
5	Vermont	17,471	17,268									146	259
6	Massachusetts	61,626	58,477	1,364	1,342			1,215	724				8
7	Rhode Island	6,536	6,064	542	595		49	262	401				
8	Connecticut	32,878	29,411	335	158			1,229	1,012	161	154		
9	New York	291,919	242,492	4,294	3,124	115	60	6,149	6,668	3,890	4,759	3,097	3,913
10	New Jersey	106,505	82,955	5,971	5,851	1,575	281	2,180	2,954	5,248	3,459		65
11	Pennsylvania	318,911	222,886	12,638	11,613	1,019	852	6,263	8,689	12,317	10,081	1,239	1,195
12	South Atlantic division	322,482	268,572	250,341	229,010	2,883	2,128	101,532	200,954	66,984	52,227	4,018	386
13	Delaware	24,269	20,412	2,553	2,603	1,264	368	167	158	3,463	1,551		
14	Maryland	95,207	82,069	9,613	12,359	1,059	1,546	923	1,211	16,373	13,283		
15	District of Columbia	11,019	9,630	1,928	1,479	45		2,615	2,495	1,415	831		
16	Virginia	18,578	16,764	9,889	12,314	515	214	5,474	11,765	4,480	4,154		
17	West Virginia	61,641	48,925	1,002	216			86		16,004	10,652	238	245
18	North Carolina	20,805	16,433	16,797	16,156			66,356	111,949	18,271	14,351	886	141
19	South Carolina	54,097	43,200	79,220	88,172			19,058	45,880	1,840	2,665	1,603	
20	Georgia	28,579	25,400	93,626	73,248			3,630	12,705	4,970	4,390	1,096	
21	Florida	8,287	5,739	35,713	22,463			3,223	14,791	168	350	195	
22	North Central division	1,411,874	1,038,245	46,486	39,772			4,454	4,808	54,247	47,707	10,964	10,067
23	Ohio	317,584	240,650	9,812	10,025			386	194	23,494	18,931	2,443	1,657
24	Indiana	210,593	162,989	5,769	4,435			1,281	1,339	10,408	7,033	3,459	2,199
25	Illinois	235,092	165,191	9,833	6,383			870	434	5,512	5,502	308	643
26	Michigan	114,326	86,958	1,737	1,836			60	702	5,077	4,512	2,354	2,942
27	Wisconsin	54,817	41,360	164	118			86	102		12	288	427
28	Minnesota	46,351	30,837	755	489						137	80	207
29	Iowa	156,576	111,426	1,617	1,820					2,994	5,645	712	840
30	Missouri	80,334	58,285	11,318	9,589			1,765	2,037	4,712	3,359		50
31	North Dakota	10,033	4,804										
32	South Dakota	15,485	11,371	38								176	458
33	Nebraska	62,586	41,086	509	399						686	67	78
34	Kansas	108,097	83,288	4,934	4,678			6		2,050	1,890	1,077	566
35	South Central division	239,347	176,368	169,365	159,378			60,291	120,676	35,697	23,272	579	462
36	Kentucky	30,158	29,172	10,047	13,972			5,773	7,217	2,341	1,822		
37	Tennessee	46,180	42,873	23,377	23,718			6,651	12,434	2,716	2,880	422	462
38	Alabama	20,450	18,517	39,617	30,781			36,705	79,231	5,403	4,432		
39	Mississippi	50,695	31,142	28,797	25,439			5,602	8,519	4,517	3,147		
40	Louisiana	19,763	15,073	9,462	13,631			2,539	2,747	3,513	1,231		
41	Arkansas	12,569	10,076	26,903	27,956			2,404	3,601	6,658	3,946		
42	Oklahoma[1]	23,309	2,062	6,243	489			160		2,054	278	157	
43	Texas	36,223	27,453	24,919	23,392			457	6,927	8,495	5,536		
44	Western division	143,989	62,266	3,441	1,882			942	2,902		330		137
45	Montana	5,819	1,901	135	32								
46	Idaho	5,313	941										
47	Wyoming	1,612	773	45	139								
48	Colorado	24,830	8,560	1,139	788								
49	New Mexico	3,513	1,750	83	62								
50	Arizona	1,734	320	82									
51	Utah	1,537	1,048	30	7								
52	Nevada	618	418										
53	Washington	29,347	11,592	334	66						315		35
54	Oregon	18,681	9,436	60	16			40	275		15		61
55	California	50,985	25,527	1,533	772			902	2,627				41

[1] Includes Union American Methodist Episcopal Church (Colored); New Congregational Methodist Church; Reformed Zion Union Apostolic Church (Colored); and Reformed Methodist Union Episcopal Church (Colored).

DENOMINATIONS, BY STATES AND TERRITORIES: 1906 AND 1890—Continued.

METHODIST BODIES—continued.												MORAVIAN BODIES.				
Methodist Episcopal Church, South.		Congregational Methodist Church.		Colored Methodist Episcopal Church.		Primitive Methodist Church in the U. S. A.		Free Methodist Church of N. A.		Other Methodists.[1]		Total.		Moravian Church (Unitas Fratrum).		
1906	1890	1906	1890	1906	1890	1906	1890	1906	1890	1906	1890	1906	1890	1906	1890	
1,638,480	1,209,976	14,729	8,705	172,996	129,383	7,558	4,764	32,838	22,110	13,585	9,523	17,926	11,745	17,155	11,745	1
806	635	566	...	466	513	5,901	3,532	7,950	5,082	2,583	1,568	7,124	5,534	7,124	5,534	2
...	...	...	...	...	...	...	...	...	...	...	...	...	...	...	...	
...	...	...	...	...	...	...	...	...	...	...	...	...	...	...	...	4
...	...	...	...	...	...	...	...	54	...	...	...	...	...	...	...	5
...	...	...	...	...	...	1,264	575	29	12	...	...				...	6
...	...	...	...	...	...	532	194	...	...	20	50	...	...	...	...	7
...	...	...	...	...	...	...	...	...	...	60	80	...	...	...	...	8
...	...	...	...	...	...	298	496	3,609	3,751	318	288	1,427	852	1,427	852	9
...	...	403	...	...	266	...	...	91	161	538	385	375	374	375	374	10
806	635	163	...	466	247	3,807	2,267	4,167	1,158	1,647	765	5,322	4,308	5,322	4,308	11
655,261	484,952	2,812	1,834	46,354	33,076	...	...	476	66	10,880	6,418	3,784	1,929	3.784	1,929	12
...	...	...	...	...	187	...	...	...	...	686	507	...	...	...	...	13
12,642	10,604	...	...	240	44	...	...	163	31	936	2,471	122	150	122	150	14
1,922	953	...	...	1,110	939	...	...	23	7	...	35	...	...	...	...	15
157,354	105,892	...	...	1,514	1,351	...	...	38	28	2,929	2,211	184	45	184	45	16
36,632	25,064	...	...	72	...	...	...	150	...	...	...	...	...	...	...	17
151,808	114,385	...	...	2,209	2,786	...	...	...	...	150	135	3,478	1,734	3,478	1,734	18
84,266	68,092	...	...	4,850	3,468	...	...	...	...	4,235	...	...	...	...	...	19
178,307	134,600	2,656	1,655	34,501	22,840	...	...	102	...	1,612	946	...	...	...	...	20
32,330	25,362	156	179	1,858	1,461	...	...	...	...	332	113	...	...	...	...	21
123,149	98,802	1,118	1,546	3,751	1,722	1,657	1,232	18,575	15,550	...	951	6,146	4,223	6,146	4,223	22
...	...	...	...	211	...	138	69	1,376	897	...	314	1,154	822	1,154	822	
818	945	...	...	40	...	...	...	1,075	673	...	...	368	346	368	346	
7,196	7,109	...	96	603	56	331	309	3,597	3,395	...	180	266	.336	266	336	
...	...	...	...	...	...	...	...	5,121	4,592	...	409	197	168	197	168	
...	...	...	...		...	1,158	765	960	864	...	48	2,713	1,477	2,713	1,477	
...	...	...	...	...	...	...	...	451	529	...	...	830	696	830	696	
562	730	...	...	...	...	30	29	1,838	2,117	...	...	59	101	59	101	
112,058	86,466	1,118	1,450	1,980	953	...	...	719	325	...	...	78	59	78	59	
...	...	...	...	...	...	...	...	190	85	...	...	481	199	481	199	
...	...	...	...	...	...	...	...	444	287	...	...	...	...	...	...	
181	206	...	...	...	...	...	...	1,099	486	...	...	...	...	...	...	[illegible]
2,332	3,346	...	...	917	713	...	...	1,795	1,300	...	...	...	19	...	19	[illegible]
839,452	612,809	10,233	5,385	122,217	94,072	...	...	2,442	371	122	586	771	40	...	40	35
99,355	82,430	...	...	8,137	6,908	...	...	196	...	...	...	...	...	...	...	36
140,306	121,398	977	196	20,634	18,968	...	...	131	...	...	187	...	...	...	...	37
126,702	87,912	3.355	2,596	23,112	18,940	...	...	29	...	...	213	...	...	...	...	38
94,845	74,785	1,640	1,341	25,814	20 107	...	...	73	29	122	80	...	...	...	...	39
31,639	24,874	711	...	11,728	8.075	...	...	109	62	...	...	...	...	...	...	40
81,699	71,565	684	223	11,506	5.888	...	...	146	61	...	...	...	...	...	...	41
40,473	10,498	107	...	2,858	291	...	...	975	12	...	...	31	40	...	40	42
225,431	139,347	2.759	1,029	18,428	14,895	...	...	783	207	...	104	740	...	...	...	43
19,812	12,778	...	...	208	...	...	...	3,395	1,041	...	...	101	19	101	19	44
1,068	492	...	...	...	...	...	...	...	...	...	...	...	...	...	...	45
503	221	...	...	...	...	...	...	68	...	...	...	...	...	...	...	46
...	...	...	...	...	...	...	...	...	...	...	...	...	...	...	...	47
1,465	1,299	...	...	...	...	...	...	433	203	...	...	...	...	...	...	48
2,882	548	...	...	82	...	...	...	...	...	...	...	...	...	...	...	49
682	336	...	...	126	...	...	...	43	...	...	...	...	...	...	...	50
...	...	...	...	...	...	...	...	...	...	...	...	...	...	...	...	51
...	...	...	...	...	...	...	...	...	...	...	...	...	...	...	...	52
718	449	...	...	...	...	...	...	1,301	240	...	...	...	...	...	...	53
2,272	1,936	...	...	...	...	...	...	664	188	...	...	...	...	...	...	54
10,222	7,497	...	...	...	...	...	...	886	[illegible]	...	...	101	19	101	19	55

[1] Oklahoma and Indian Territory combined.

TABLE 10.—COMPARISON OF COMMUNICANTS OR MEMBERS, BY SELECTED

	STATE OR TERRITORY.	MORAVIAN BODIES—continued. Evangelical Union of Bohemian and Moravian Brethren in North America.		PRESBYTERIAN BODIES. Total.		Presbyterian Church in the United States of America.		Cumberland Presbyterian Church.[1]		Colored Cumberland Presbyterian Church.		Welsh Calvinistic Methodist Church.	
		1906	1890	1906	1890	1906	1890	1906	1890	1906	1890	1906	1890
1	Continental United States	771		1,830,555	1,277,851	1,179,566	787,743	195,770	164,940	18,066	12,956	13,280	12,722
2	North Atlantic division			617,944	454,520	523,742	381,477	8,991	6,210			5,639	4,681
3	Maine			364	224	364	205						
4	New Hampshire			842	956	842	956						
5	Vermont			1,636	1,267	432	230					652	431
6	Massachusetts			8,559	5,105	5,678	3,570						
7	Rhode Island			1,741	828	1,071	608						
8	Connecticut			2,425	1,864	2,252	1,680						
9	New York			199,923	168,564	186,278	154,083					1,837	1,789
10	New Jersey			79,912	59,464	78,490	58,759	79					
11	Pennsylvania			322,542	216,248	248,335	161,386	8,912	6,210			3,150	2,461
12	South Atlantic division			213,488	142,263	62,596	41,074	835	718				
13	Delaware			5,200	4,622	5,086	4,622						
14	Maryland			17,895	12,483	15,927	10,593						
15	District of Columbia			8,636	5,128	8,182	4,882						
16	Virginia			39,628	27,746	2,615	945						
17	West Virginia			19,668	10,952	8,514	4,275		32				
18	North Carolina			55,837	36,102	10,696	6,516	110					
19	South Carolina			35,533	26,118	8,026	6,829						
20	Georgia			24,040	14,538	2,243	1,370	599	598				
21	Florida			7,051	4,574	1,307	1,042	126	88				
22	North Central division			609,739	427,629	473,220	313,415	58,113	49,564	1,408	856	7,510	7,885
23	Ohio			138,768	103,607	114,772	82,444	2,458	2,602			2,223	2,463
24	Indiana			58,633	43,351	49,041	35,464	6,376	4,826			9	
25	Illinois			115,602	77,213	86,251	54,744	17,208	14,177	913	195	502	425
26	Michigan			37,900	25,931	36,710	25,088						
27	Wisconsin			21,243	14,154	18,077	11,019					2,579	2,641
28	Minnesota			27,569	15,055	26,412	13,732					1,063	1,166
29	Iowa			60,081	40,528	48,326	29,994	1,190	1,167			539	348
30	Missouri			71,599	53,510	25,991	17,272	28,637	23,990	410	471	73	154
31	North Dakota			6,727	3,044	6,727	3,036						
32	South Dakota			6,990	4,778	6,764	4,413					190	306
33	Nebraska			23,862	15,065	20,684	12,159	307	416			242	267
34	Kansas			40,765	31,393	33,465	24,050	1,937	2,386	85	190	90	115
35	South Central division	771		287,949	213,113	30,418	17,097	123,060	105,354	16,658	12,100		
36	Kentucky			47,822	40,880	8,543	6,917	16,916	15,458	2,042	1,421		
37	Tennessee			79,337	66,573	6 786	4,399	42,464	39,477	6,640	5,202		
38	Alabama			30,722	21,502	303	152	8,588	7,390	5,805	3,104		
39	Mississippi			22,471	18,250	192		5,991	6,353		278		
40	Louisiana			8,350	5,864		70	1,152	808				
41	Arkansas			21,156	18,022	809	494	11,990	12,282		255		
42	Oklahoma[2]	31		16,001	4,211	9,667	2,253	4,351	1,229	80	100		
43	Texas	740		62,090	37,811	4,118	2,812	31,598	22,297	2,091	1,740		
44	Western division			101,435	40,326	89,590	34,680	4,781	3,094			131	156
45	Montana			4,096	1,232	4,096	1,232						
46	Idaho			3,770	815	3,698	815						
47	Wyoming			984	364	984	364						
48	Colorado			18,957	6,968	16,055	5,902	718	231			131	156
49	New Mexico			2,935	1,275	2,864	1,275						
50	Arizona			2,884	188	2,884	188						
51	Utah			1,902	688	1,902	688						
52	Nevada			520	275	520	275						
53	Washington			16,758	4,343	14,437	3,770	615	470				
54	Oregon			10,947	5,244	9,701	3,935	540	897				
55	California			37,682	18,934	32,449	16,236	2,908	1,496				

[1] See denominational text, page 510.
[2] Includes Associate Synod of North America (Associate Presb terian Church): Reformed Presbyterian Church in North America General 8 od: Reformed Presb

DENOMINATIONS, BY STATES AND TERRITORIES: 1906 AND 1890—Continued.

PRESBYTERIAN BODIES—continued.										PROTESTANT EPISCOPAL CHURCH.		REFORMED BODIES.				
United Presbyterian Church of North America.		Presbyterian Church in the United States.		Associate Reformed Synod of the South.		Synod of the Reformed Presbyterian Church of North America.		Other Presbyterians.[1]				Total.		Reformed Church in America.		
1906	1890	1906	1890	1906	1890	1906	1890	1906	1890	1906	1890	1906	1890	1906	1890	
130,342	94,402	206,345	179,721	13,201	8,501	9,122	10,574	4,863	6,292	886,942	532,048	449,514	309,458	124,938	92,970	1
71,711	51,366					4,595	6,241	3,266	4,545	467,067	285,543	290,131	207,095	97,619	78,041	2
							19			5,520	3,291					
										4,892	2,911					4
283	219					99	222	170	165	5,278	4,335					5
2,540	1,135					341	400			51,636	26,855	393	62			6
670	220									15,443	9,458					7
173	184									37,466	26,652	1,262	150			8
10,115	9,719					,446	2,328	247	645	193,890	127,218	69,828	55,973	63,350	52,228	9
1,343	685								20	53,921	30,103	37,298	26,210	32,290	24,067	10
56,587	39,204					2,709	3,272	2,849	3,715	99,021	54,720	181,350	124,700	1,979	1,756	11
1,564	701	139,207	93,988	9,286	5,697		85			126,982	81,078	22,273	16,627	159		12
114										3,796	2,719		69			13
340	171	1,628	1,654				65			34,965	23,988	13,461	10,741	19		14
		454	246							13,692	7,476	580	301			15
		36,569	26,515	444	286					28,487	20,371	2,488	1,819			16
1,026	530	10,047	5,995	81	100		20			5,230	2,906	886	794			17
84		41,322	27,477	3,625	2,109					13,890	8,186	4,718	2,903			18
		23,395	16,561	4,112	2,728					8,557	5,742	140		140		19
		20,258	12,096	940	474					9,790	5,515					20
		5,534	3,444	84						8,575	4,225					21
49,291	39,616	14,713	10,442	75	92	3,841	4,030	1,568	1,729	183,107	107,850	132,643	83,582	26,360	14,929	22
18,336	14,710					629	951	350	487	32,399	17,454	51,328	36,255	214	156	23
2,802	2,542		79			305	246	100	194	7,653	5,185	9,216	6,761	268	172	24
9,555	6,529					512	536	661	607	36,364	19,099	9,946	5,385	4,962	2,820	25
1,017	646					173	197			26,439	18,034	28,345	15,404	11,260	6,609	26
546	432					41	62			16,527	10,457	11,459	7,765	2,312	1,349	27
	12					94	145			18,763	11,142	2,255	968	852	145	28
8,890	7,769					899	984	237	266	8,990	6,481	11,517	5,741	4,835	2,605	29
1,589	1,068	14,713	10,363	75	92	111	100			13,328	8,828	1,284	586			30
	8									2,227	892	1,059	287	165	89	31
36	59									7,065	2,649	2,711	1,883	847	594	32
2,459	2,172					170	51			6,903	4,036	2,108	1,408	482	344	33
4,061	3,669					907	758	220	225	6,459	3,593	1,415	1,139	213	46	34
1,871	465	112,354	75,291	3,340	2,712	249	76	9	18	60,285	37,222	3,142	1,586	705		35
		20,143	16,915	178	169					8,091	7,161	2,101	1,350			36
544	465	21,390	15,954	1,504	1,058			9	18	7,874	5,671	234	236			37
249		15,368	10,560	320	220	89	76			8,961	6,085					38
70		15,641	11,055	577	564					5,704	3,560					39
		7,198	4,926							9,070	5,162					40
146		7,357	4,478	854	513					4,315	2,381	60				41
362		1,323	629	58		160				2,024	105	747		705		42
		23,934	10,774	349	188					14,246	7,097					43
6,405	2,254	71				437	142	20		49,501	20,355	1,325	568	95		44
										3,290	1,104	135				45
72										1,846	364					46
										1,741	467					47
1,798	537					255	142			6,832	3,814	111	35			48
		71								869	373	70				49
										1,059	179					50
										977	751					51
										1,210	535					52
1,616	103					90				6,780	1,698	379	167	95		53
706	412									3,580	1,849	512	298			54
2,213	,202					92		20		21,317	9,221	118	68			55

[1] Oklahoma and Indian Territory combined.

TABLE 10.—COMPARISON OF COMMUNICANTS OR MEMBERS, BY SELECTED

	STATE OR TERRITORY.	REFORMED BODIES—continued.						REFORMED EPISCOPAL CHURCH.		ROMAN CATHOLIC CHURCH.[1]		SALVATIONISTS.[2]	
		Reformed Church in the United States.		Christian Reformed Church.		Hungarian Reformed Church in America.							
		1906	1890	1906	1890	1906	1890	1906	1890	1906	1890	1906	1890
1	Continental United States	292,654	204,018	26,669	12,470	5,253	....	9,682	8,455	12,079,142	6,241,708	23,344	8,742
2	North Atlantic division	185,329	127,418	2,830	1,636	4,353	....	4,666	4,020	5,833,658	2,939,986	8,916	2,734
•	Maine	....	....	....	....	....	....	....	....	113,419	57,548	384	265
4	New Hampshire	....	....	....	....	....	....	....	....	119,863	39,920	144	26
5	Vermont	....	....	....	....	....	....	....	....	82,272	42,810	138	....
6	Massachusetts	253	62	140	....	....	....	....	311	1,080,706	614,627	1,597	656
7	Rhode Island	....	....	....	....	....	....	....	....	195,951	96,755	160	31
8	Connecticut	1,012	150	....	....	250	....	....	....	299,513	152,945	476	203
9	New York	5,700	3,432	298	313	480	....	890	743	2,285,768	1,153,130	3,123	625
10	New Jersey	1,094	830	2,392	1,323	1,522	....	212	326	441,432	223,274	640	156
11	Pennsylvania	177,270	122,944	....	....	2,101	....	3,564	2.640	1,214,734	556,977	2,254	772
12	South Atlantic division	21,914	16,627	....	....	200	....	2,730	2,196	354,736	254,883	814	519
13	Delaware	....	69	....	....	....	....	100	139	24,228	11,776	65	153
14	Maryland	13,442	10,741	....	....	....	....	332	285	166,941	141,410	94	213
15	District of Columbia	580	301	....	....	....	....	....	....	43,778	37,593	18	23
16	Virginia	2,288	1,819	....	....	200	....	46	49	26,700	12,356	136	54
17	West Virginia	886	794	....	....	....	....	....	....	40,011	15,653	179	17
18	North Carolina	4,718	2,903	....	....	....	....	....	....	3,981	2,640	172	59
19	South Carolina	....	....	....	....	....	....	2,252	1,723	10,317	5,360	61	....
20	Georgia	....	....	....	....	....	....	....	....	19,273	11,228	61	....
21	Florida	....	....	....	....	....	....	....	....	17,507	16,867	28	....
22	North Central division	82,254	57,819	23,329	10,834	700	....	2,286	2,239	3,946,752	2,172,330	9,196	4,666
23	Ohio	50,732	35,846	382	253	....	....	557	257	557,650	336,114	2,066	655
24	Indiana	8,289	6,269	659	320	....	....	....	....	174,849	119,100	353	104
25	Illinois	2,652	1,783	2,332	782	....	....	1,663	1,755	932,084	475,324	1,928	922
26	Michigan	1,666	1,013	14,719	7,782	700	....	66	102	492,135	222,261	1,371	1,089
27	Wisconsin	8,386	5,966	761	450	....	....	....	....	505,264	249,164	390	322
28	Minnesota	788	730	615	93	....	....	....	....	378,288	271,769	581	460
29	Iowa	3,692	2,513	2,990	623	....	....	....	....	207,607	164,522	472	397
30	Missouri	1,284	586	....	....	....	....	....	125	382,642	162,864	980	340
31	North Dakota	817	161	77	37	....	....	....	....	61,261	26,427	237	....
32	South Dakota	1,365	1,000	499	289	....	....	....	....	61,014	25,720	109	41
33	Nebraska	1,616	968	60	96	....	....	....	....	100,763	51,503	154	19
34	Kansas	967	984	235	109	....	....	....	....	93,195	67,562	555	307
35	South Central division	2,437	1,586	....	....	....	....	....	....	1,109,096	452,841	1,072	35
36	Kentucky	2,101	1,350	....	....	....	....	....	....	165,908	92,504	123	....
37	Tennessee	234	236	....	....	....	....	....	....	17,252	17,950	133	....
38	Alabama	....	....	....	....	....	....	....	....	42,285	13,230	79	....
39	Mississippi	....	....	....	....	....	....	....	....	28,576	11,348	15	....
40	Louisiana	....	....	....	....	....	....	....	....	477,774	211,763	72	....
41	Arkansas	60	....	....	....	....	....	....	....	32,397	3,845	159	....
42	Oklahoma[3]	42	....	....	....	....	....	....	....	36,548	2,510	130	....
43	Texas	....	....	....	....	....	....	....	....	306,356	99,691	361	35
44	Western division	720	568	510	....	....	....	....	....	834,900	421,668	3,346	788
45	Montana	....	....	135		....	....	....	....	72,350	25,149	172	30
46	Idaho	....	....	....	....	....	....	....	....	18,057	4,809	186	....
47	Wyoming	....	....	....	....	....	....	....	....	10,264	7,185		....
48	Colorado	90	35	21	....	....	....	....	....	99,820	47,111		214
49	New Mexico	....	....	70	....	....	....	....	....	121,558	100,576		....
50	Arizona	....	....	....	....	....	....	....	....	29,810	19,000		....
51	Utah	....	....	....	....	....	....	....	....	8,356	5,958		4
52	Nevada	....	....	....	....	....	....	....	....	9,970	3,955		....
53	Washington	....	167	284	....	....	....	....	....	74,961	20,848		156
54	Oregon	512	298	....	....	....	....	....	....	35,317	30,231		44
55	California	118	68	....	....	....	....	....	....	354,408	156,846	22 1,[illegible]	340

[1] Greek Catholic Church (Uniat), reported separately in 1890, included in 1906 with the Roman Catholic Church.
[2] Includes Salvation Army and American Salvation Army.

DENOMINATIONS, BY STATES AND TERRITORIES: 1906 AND 1890—Continued.

SPIRITUALISTS.		UNITARIANS.		UNITED BRETHREN BODIES.						UNIVERSALISTS.		ALL OTHER DENOMINATIONS.		
				Total.		Church of the United Brethren in Christ.		Church of the United Brethren in Christ (Old Constitution).						
1906	1890	1906	1890	1906	1890	1906	1890	1906	1890	1906	1890	1906	1890	
35,056	45,030	70,542	67,749	296,050	225,281	274,649	202,474	21,401	22,807	64,158	49,194	111,879	16,268	1
13,445	26,369	51,579	49,029	57,081	34,904	54,881	34,904	2,200	...	39,317	28,906	28,688	7,374	2
1,343	2,562	2,762	2,421	...	...	...	...	...	...	4,686	3,750	188	100	3
283	672	3,629	3,252	...	...	...	...	...	...	1,993	1,204	351	250	4
740	1,966	710	968	...	...	...	...	...	...	3,030	2,409	112	...	5
3,885	7,345	35,440	34,610	...	...	...	...	...	...	12,983	7,142	4,793	786	6
70	450	1,406	1,595	...	...	...	...	...	...	1,175	998	226	...	7
976	2,354	446	179	...	...	...	...	...	...	1,478	2,129	891	299	8
4,489	6,351	4,656	4,470	1,507	953	1,484	953	23	...	10,761	8,526	10,254	2,953	9
209	100	934	363	...	...	...	...	...	...	910	541	1,709	90	10
1,450	4,569	1,596	1,171	55,574	33,951	53,397	33,951	2,177	...	2,301	2,209	10,164	2,896	11
882	1,471	2,083	1,488	34,377	22,284	34,046	22,284	331	...	1,750	1,518	5,972	234	12
37	...	250	60	...	...	...	...	...	...	...	...	222	...	13
92	665	500	603	6,541	4,736	6,445	4,736	96	...	250	382	1,783	81	14
143	475	700	600	260	...	260	...	...	...	154	128	405	9	15
37	12	76	...	7,021	5,306	6,786	5,306	235	...	20	18	463	137	16
145	65	...	...	19,993	12,242	19,993	12,242	...	...	94	56	1,450	7	17
...	...	122	...	...	...	...	...	...	...	373	255	792	...	18
...	20	160	150	...	...	...	...	...	...	121	101	8	...	19
6	169	170	75	521	...	521	...	...	...	656	533	832	...	20
422	65	105	...	41	...	41	...	...	...	82	45	17	...	21
15,216	12,005	10,156	10,807	191,777	162,198	174,501	141,318	17,276	20,880	20,236	15,793	56,785	6,728	22
2,633	2,174	1,228	907	71,338	53,500	65,191	47,678	6,147	5,822	5,003	4,961	3,152	913	23
1,608	715	253	320	52,700	42,697	48,059	35,824	4,641	6,873	2,506	1,950	4,278	147	24
4,547	1,314	2,339	1,932	19,701	16,622	18,705	15,429	996	1,193	5,165	3,424	22,792	2,026	25
1,667	2,565	1,452	1,904	7,383	10,803	3,446	5,201	3,937	5,602	1,866	1,549	3,404	101	26
784	354	919	1,394	2,180	1,750	2,036	1,687	144	63	1,342	544	1,684	689	27
715	500	1,160	1,349	1,282	803	1,282	803	...	...	1,220	1,093	7,645	110	28
505	2,613	1,482	1,238	11,236	10,673	11,082	10,401	154	272	1,388	829	4,598	1,791	29
874	853	482	1,135	3,616	4,361	3,321	4,361	295	...	786	711	1,831	228	30
...	...	72	55	...	...	...	...	...	...	...	...	2	...	31
...	...	21	105	257	602	175	493	82	109	13	...	1,049	...	32
387	290	403	190	6,086	6,031	6,045	5,673	41	358	10	161	3,201	41	33
1,496	627	345	278	15,998	14,356	15,159	13,768	839	588	937	571	3,149	682	34
1,692	1,575	973	270	7,233	1,708	7,078	1,708	155	...	1,794	1,469	8,619	1,506	35
419	300	440	100	993	567	993	567	...	...	520	434	575	1,239	36
29	1,075	95	60	2,875	1,141	2,875	1,141	...	...	77	20	1,154	...	37
...	...	...	...	30	...	30	...	...	...	533	365	784	...	38
...	...	...	...	...	...	...	...	...	...	285	120	383	...	39
85	120	250	110	361	...	361	...	...	...	...	...	68	10	40
...	25	...	...	...	...	...	...	...	...	85	16	3,467	157	41
202	26	70	...	2,974	...	2,819	...	155	...	24	...	1,060	...	42
957	29	118	...	...	...	...	...	...	...	270	514	1,128	100	43
3,821	3,610	5,751	6,155	5,582	4,187	4,143	2,260	1,439	1,927	1,061	1,506	11,815	426	44
237	20	437	...	...	...	...	...	...	...	...	...	180	...	45
100	...	54	...	310	100	113	100	197	...	...	25	138	...	46
56	50	...	...	...	...	...	...	...	...	...	...	28	...	47
406	275	723	644	720	585	720	585	...	...	229	15	1,072	28	48
...	...	...	...	...	...	...	...	...	...	...	...	10	...	49
...	...	...	...	...	...	...	...	...	...	...	...	69	...	
57	80	113	...	...	...	...	...	...	...	...	...	32	...	
...	...	...	...	...	...	...	...	...	...	...	...	6	...	
823	565	553	802	1,079	1,100	582	494	497	606	167	...	2,044	9	
334	751	667	890	2,129	1,696	1,533	493	596	1,203	60	84	690	40	
1,808	1,869	3,204	3,819	1,344	706	1,195	588	149	118	605	1,382	7,540	349	[illegible]

[1] Oklahoma and Indian Territory combined.

TABLE 11.—COLORED[1] ORGANIZATIONS, SHOWING COMMUNICANTS OR MEMBERS, PLACES OF WORSHIP, VALUE OF (IN DETAIL), FOR CONTI-

[The statistics in this table refer to 16 denominations comprising wholly colored organizations and

	DENOMINATION.	Total number of organizations.	Number of colored organizations.	COMMUNICANTS OR MEMBERS.				
				Number of organizations reporting.	Total number reported.	Sex.		
						Number of organizations reporting.	Male.	Female.
1	Total	142,776	36,770	36,563	3,685,097	34,648	1,324,123	2,203,537
2	Adventist bodies	2,439	31	31	634	29	185	420
3	Advent Christian Church	550	2	2	72	2	33	39
4	Seventh-day Adventist Denomination	1,889	29	29	562	27	152	381
5	Baptist bodies	32,122	19,891	19,833	2,354,789	18,771	846,077	1,419,941
6	Baptists—Northern Convention	8,272	108	108	32,639	98	10,694	19,108
7	Baptists—National Convention (Colored)	18,534	18,534	18,492	2,261,607	18,034	822,162	1,379,387
8	Free Baptists	1,346	197	195	10,876	175	3,397	5,554
9	Primitive Baptists	2,922	4	4	102	4	45	57
10	Colored Primitive Baptists in America	797	797	787	35,076	325	6,341	11,438
11	United American Freewill Baptists (Colored)	251	251	247	14,489	135	3,438	4,397
12	Christians (Christian Connection)	1,379	92	91	7,545	91	3,380	4,165
13	Church of God and Saints of Christ (Colored)	48	48	48	1,823	48	550	1,273
14	Churches of God in North America, General Eldership of the	518	15	14	329	14	143	186
15	Churches of the Living God (Colored)	68	68	67	4,276	67	1,686	2,590
16	Church of the Living God (Christian Workers for Friendship)	44	44	44	2,676	44	984	1,692
17	Church of the Living God (Apostolic Church)	15	15	14	752	14	291	461
18	Church of Christ in God	9	9	9	848	9	411	437
19	Congregationalists	5,713	156	156	11,960	155	4,613	7,339
20	Disciples or Christians	10,942	170	170	11,233	168	4,414	6,765
21	Disciples of Christ	8,293	129	129	9,705	127	3,849	5,802
22	Churches of Christ	2,649	41	41	1,528	41	565	963
23	Evangelistic associations	3	3	3	425	3	150	275
24	Voluntary Missionary Society in America (Colored)	3	3	3	425	3	150	275
25	Free Christian Zion Church of Christ (Colored)	15	15	14	1,835	14	740	1,095
26	Independent churches	1,079	12	12	490	12	196	294
27	Lutheran bodies	5,447	7	7	239	7	70	169
28	General Council of the Evangelical Lutheran Church in North America	2,146	1	1	15	1	2	13
29	Evangelical Lutheran Synodical Conference of America	3,301	6	6	224	6	68	156
30	Methodist bodies	44,861	15,317	15,181	1,182,131	14,447	420,767	703,320
31	Methodist Episcopal Church	29,943	3,750	3,682	308,551	3,183	102,740	169,081
32	Union American Methodist Episcopal Church (Colored)	77	77	77	4,347	77	1,785	2,[illegible]
33	African Methodist Episcopal Church	6,647	6,647	6,608	494,777	6,486	177,837	304,[illegible]
34	African Union Methodist Protestant Church	69	69	69	5,592	67	1,972	[illegible]
35	African Methodist Episcopal Zion Church	2,204	2,204	2,197	184,542	2,156	67,096	11[illegible]
36	Methodist Protestant Church	2,843	64	62	2,612	59	982	[illegible]
37	Wesleyan Methodist Connection of America	594	22	19	1,258	17	454	[illegible]
38	Colored Methodist Episcopal Church	2,381	2,381	2,365	172,996	2,309	64,988	104,[illegible]
39	Reformed Zion Union Apostolic Church (Colored)	45	45	45	3,059	36	1,139	1,562
40	Reformed Methodist Union Episcopal Church (Colored)	58	58	57	4,397	57	1,774	2,[illegible]
41	Moravian bodies	117	2	2	351	1	113	186
42	Moravian Church (Unitas Fratrum)	117	2	2	351	1	113	186
43	Presbyterian bodies	14,226	659	655	47,116	587	17,780	25,273
44	Presbyterian Church in the United States of America	7,935	417	417	27,799	356	8,935	14,963
45	Cumberland Presbyterian Church	2,850	1	1	50	......	......	......
46	Colored Cumberland Presbyterian Church	196	196	196	18,066	196	8,405	9,661
47	Presbyterian Church in the United States	3,104	44	40	1,183	34	433	638
48	Associate Reformed Synod of the South	141	1	1	18	1	7	11
49	Protestant Episcopal Church	6,845	198	193	19,098	151	5,446	10,041
50	Reformed bodies	659	2		59	2	24	35
51	Reformed Church in America	659	2		59	2	24	35
52	Reformed Episcopal Church	81	38	2	2,252	38	833	1,419
53	Roman Catholic Church	12,482	36	36	38,235	33	16,838	18,592
54	United Brethren bodies	3,732	10	10	277	10	118	159
55	Church of the United Brethren in Christ	3,732	10	10	277	10	118	159

[1] Negroes or persons of negro descent.

CHURCH PROPERTY, DEBT ON CHURCH PROPERTY, PARSONAGES, AND SUNDAY SCHOOLS, BY DENOMINATIONS
NENTAL UNITED STATES: 1906.

26 denominations comprising in part colored organizations, as shown by the first two columns.]

PLACES OF WORSHIP.					VALUE OF CHURCH PROPERTY.		DEBT ON CHURCH PROPERTY.		PARSONAGES.		SUNDAY SCHOOLS CONDUCTED BY CHURCH ORGANIZATIONS.				
Number of organizations reporting—		Number of church edifices reported.	Seating capacity of church edifices.		Number of organizations reporting.	Value reported.	Number of organizations reporting.	Amount of debt reported.	Number of organizations reporting.	Value of parsonages reported.	Number of organizations reporting.	Number of Sunday schools reported.	Number of officers and teachers.	Number of scholars.	
Church edifices.	Halls, etc.		Number of organizations reporting.	Seating capacity reported.											
34,506	1,261	35,160	33,091	10,481,738	34,660	$56,636,159	9,003	$5,005,905	4,779	$3,727,884	33,538	34,681	210,148	1,740,099	1
14	9	14	12	1,948	11	10,274	4	731	...	...	27	28	135	566	2
2	...	2	2	700	2	3,800	...	...	...	...	2	2	8	27	3
12	9	12	10	1,248	9	6,474	4	731	...	...	25	26	127	539	4
18,754	571	18,849	18,034	5,831,259	18,823	26,562,845	3,254	2,140,863	766	677,411	18,014	18,459	103,612	952,755	5
99	6	106	94	41,860	97	1,561,326	55	356,993	17	35,500	102	106	1,382	12,827	6
17,832	508	17,913	17,316	5,610,301	17,890	24,437,272	3,100	1,757,190	709	617,241	17,478	17,910	100,069	924,665	7
173	5	173	165	43,850	173	186,130	43	16,227	13	13,100	168	177	868	5,732	8
4	...	4	4	1,200	4	2,300	...	...	...	...	...	...	...	...	9
497	44	501	318	94,223	508	296,539	34	6,968	21	10,095	166	166	911	6,224	10
149	8	152	137	39,825	151	79,278	22	3,485	6	1,475	100	100	382	3,307	11
89	1	91	87	26,969	90	69,505	16	2,460	3	600	87	88	447	4,001	12
1	47	1	1	400	1	6,000	...	...	...	...	1	1	6	150	13
5	8	5	5	905	7	5,500	1	400	...	...	7	11	37	270	14
45	23	45	43	10,635	46	58,575	10	3,410	2	1,500	61	62	210	1,760	15
27	17	27	27	5,985	28	23,175	7	1,710	...	...	43	43	122	886	16
12	3	12	11	3,100	12	25,700	2	1,600	2	1,500	13	13	67	585	17
6	3	6	5	1,550	6	9,700	1	100	...	...	5	6	21	289	18
133	14	137	130	39,500	137	459,497	32	32,106	36	46,125	150	174	1,066	10,339	19
137	24	140	133	34,320	141	185,215	36	18,029	4	1,950	134	141	712	4,916	20
112	8	115	108	28,095	116	170,265	29	16,898	4	1,950	111	117	639	4,319	21
25	16	25	25	6,225	25	14,950	7	1,131	...	...	23	24	73	597	22
3	...	3	3	1,325	2	2,400	1	1,000	...	...	3	3	21	390	23
3	...	3	3	1,325	2	2,400	1	1,000	...	...	3	3	21	390	24
14	1	14	14	5,201	13	5,975	7	1,150	2	450	7	7	63	340	25
12	...	12	5	845	12	2,750	1	260	...	...	12	13	40	435	26
7	...	7	7	1,200	7	15,000	1	140	2	1,800	6	6	18	279	27
1	...	1	1	300	1	5,000		140	...	...	1	1	3	25	28
6	...	6	6	900	6	10,000	...	...	2	1,800	5	5	15	254	29
14,472	523	14,968	13,813	4,269,852	14,542	25,771,262	5,506	2,561,418	3,785	2,641,643	14,140	14,753	98,266	712,006	30
3,556	75	3,672	3,094	901,812	3,585	6,104,379	1,372	611,166	1,206	777,715	3,522	3,745	26,044	204,810	31
60	16	60	59	16,046	59	170,150	39	40,796	4	6,400	76	78	481	3,372	32
6,292	268	6,538	6,178	1,832,600	6,299	11,303,489	2,574	1,191,921	1,783	1,255,246	6,056	6,285	41,941	292,689	33
68	1	71	67	21,955	68	183,697	41	20,917	7	7,500	66	66	441	5,266	34
2,079	78	2,131	2,048	690,951	2,104	4,833,207	724	474,269	348	350,690	2,060	2,092	16,245	107,692	35
52	4	53	44	10,125	50	62,651	23	1,073	5	1,820	48	53	223	1,650	36
14	2	14	13	3,600	14	21,000	6	1,086	3	2,450	16	16	100	769	37
2,252	78	2,327	2,214	758,328	2,264	3,017,849	692	215,111	421	237,547	2,207	2,328	12,375	92,457	38
41	1	43	38	15,700	41	37,875	7	825	...	...	35	36	212	1,508	39
58	...	59	58	18,735	58	36,965	27	4,254	8	2,275	54	54	204	1,792	40
1	1	1	1	300	1	8,000	...	...	...	...	2	2	18	217	41
1	1	1	1	300	1	8,000	...	...	...	...	2	2	18	217	42
593	18	618	581	193,441	592	990,215	85	53,869	92	78,705	635	669	3,880	33,132	43
363	17	383	360	113,701	365	752,387	59	39,208	75	66,430	405	433	2,791	24,904	44
1	...	1	1	200	1	1,000	...	...	...	...	1	1	8	75	45
195	1	195	191	71,165	192	203,778	18	10,407	8	5,825	192	192	933	6,952	46
33	...	38	28	8,075	33	32,850	8	4,254	9	6,450	36	42	146	1,166	47
1	...	1	1	300	1	200	...	...	...	...	1	1	2	35	48
150	11	171	148	42,700	159	1,773,279	28	113,246	58	164,950	180	188	1,189	13,779	49
...	2	...	...	...	...	...	...	...	...	...	1	1	9	52	50
...	2	...	...	...	...	...	...	...	...	...	1	1	9	52	51
36	2	42	36	6,948	38	28,287	13	1,143	7	3,350	33	34	159	1,326	52
34	2	36	32	12,640	32	678,480	8	75,650	22	109,400	30	33	220	3,151	53
6	4	6	6	1,350	6	3,100	1	30	...	...	8	8	50	236	54
6	4	6	6	1,350	6	3,100	1	30	...	...	8	8	50	236	55

TABLE 12.—COLORED[1] ORGANIZATIONS, SHOWING COMMUNICANTS OR MEMBERS, PLACES OF WORSHIP, VALUE TERRITO-

[The statistics in this table refer to colored organizations in 43 denominations comprising

	STATE OR TERRITORY.	Number of colored organizations.	COMMUNICANTS OR MEMBERS.				
			Number of organizations reporting.	Total number reported.	Sex.		
					Number of organizations reporting.	Male.	Female.
1	Continental United States	36,770	36,563	3,685,097	34,648	1,224,123	2,203,537
	North Atlantic division	1,026	1,021	134,711	980	44,348	80,219
3	Maine	1	1	25	1	10	15
4	New Hampshire	1	1	20	1	8	12
5	Vermont	......	......	......	......	......	......
6	Massachusetts	64	64	9,402	60	2,905	5,347
7	Rhode Island	20	20	2,114	17	569	1,098
8	Connecticut	49	48	4,492	47	1,537	2,802
9	New York	203	202	30,482	187	9,782	17,854
10	New Jersey	259	257	28,015	255	8,924	18,430
11	Pennsylvania	429	428	60,161	412	20,613	34,661
12	South Atlantic division	15,250	15,163	1,741,491	14,297	636,338	1,032,207
13	Delaware	125	125	10,583	117	3,867	5,277
14	Maryland	624	620	71,797	541	23,265	36,299
15	District of Columbia	102	102	46,249	97	14,153	28,909
16	Virginia	1,983	1,974	307,374	1,817	116,271	175,333
17	West Virginia	271	268	14,949	251	6,377	7,839
18	North Carolina	2,813	2,797	283,707	2,580	105,067	165,644
19	South Carolina	2,860	2,853	394,149	2,769	142,868	240,626
20	Georgia	4,834	4,790	507,005	4,565	185,114	308,620
21	Florida	1,638	1,634	105,678	1,560	39,356	63,660
22	North Central division	2,023	2,012	166,356	1,927	55,570	101,140
23	Ohio	371	367	33,667	328	11,276	19,134
24	Indiana	202	200	23,133	197	8,100	14,548
25	Illinois	359	358	32,058	349	11,079	20,339
26	Michigan	43	43	3,235	43	1,188	2,047
27	Wisconsin	11	11	310	11	110	200
28	Minnesota	10	10	1,453	9	393	760
29	Iowa	72	72	4,108	72	1,481	2,627
30	Missouri	655	651	50,074	625	15,514	30,197
31	North Dakota	......	......	......	......	......	......
32	South Dakota	2	2	38	2	15	23
33	Nebraska	12	12	1,007	9	308	567
34	Kansas	286	286	17,273	282	6,106	10,698
35	South Central division	18,341	18,237	1,634,055	17,326	585,477	985,522
36	Kentucky	1,007	1,005	116,918	966	44,639	69,263
37	Tennessee	1,879	1,855	172,867	1,726	59,645	106,318
38	Alabama	3,734	3,715	397,178	3,485	146,186	234,680
39	Mississippi	3,877	3,863	358,708	3,657	121,925	220,909
40	Louisiana	2,085	2,067	185,918	1,950	62,965	111,937
41	Arkansas	2,094	2,081	146,319	2,042	56,895	86,742
42	Oklahoma[2]	618	616	29,115	595	11,397	16,918
43	Texas	3,047	3,035	227,032	2,905	81,805	138,755
44	Western division	130	130	8,484	118	2,300	4,449
45	Montana	6	6	135	6	35	100
46	Idaho	......	......	......	......	......	......
47	Wyoming	1	1	45	1	12	33
48	Colorado	25	25	2,507	22	776	1,535
49	New Mexico	7	7	221	7	68	153
50	Arizona	5	5	208	5	66	142
51	Utah	1	1	30	1	7	23
52	Nevada	......	......	......	......	......	......
53	Washington	18	18	614	18	229	385
54	Oregon	4	4	160	4	45	115
55	California	63	63	4,564	54	1,152	1,963

OF CHURCH PROPERTY, DEBT ON CHURCH PROPERTY, PARSONAGES, AND SUNDAY SCHOOLS, BY STATES AND RIES: 1906.

In whole or in part colored organizations. See Table 11 for denominations in detail.]

PLACES OF WORSHIP.					VALUE OF CHURCH PROPERTY.		DEBT ON CHURCH PROPERTY.		PARSONAGES.		SUNDAY SCHOOLS CONDUCTED BY CHURCH ORGANIZATIONS.				
Number of organizations reporting—		Number of church edifices reported.	Seating capacity of church edifices.		Number of organizations reporting.	Value reported.	Number of organizations reporting.	Amount of debt reported.	Number of organizations reporting.	Value of parsonages reported.	Number of organizations reporting.	Number of Sunday schools reported.	Number of officers and teachers.	Number of scholars.	
Church edifices.	Halls, etc.		Number of organizations reporting.	Seating capacity reported.											
34,506	1,261	35,160	33,091	10,481,738	34,660	$56,636,159	9,003	$5,005,905	4,779	$3,727,884	33,538	34,681	210,148	1,740,099	1
889	119	911	877	298,737	901	8,363,962	558	1,585,575	233	573,490	959	971	9,076	77,542	2
1	....	1	1	200	1	3,000	1	1,600	....	....	1	1	8	30	3
....	....	....	....	....	....	....	....	....	....	....	1	1	3	24	4
....	....	....	....	....	....	....	....	....	....	....	....	....	....	....	5
50	11	51	50	20,060	52	646,425	35	159,508	8	22,050	58	58	613	5,069	6
18	2	19	18	7,700	18	184,346	15	37,350	3	10,500	17	17	202	1,557	7
40	8	40	40	11,804	42	379,855	23	44,264	15	35,900	45	45	455	2,764	8
169	27	173	163	59,542	169	2,366,796	93	513,412	52	162,250	186	189	1,745	15,045	9
234	20	240	233	72,443	239	1,289,335	145	231,632	57	94,050	247	252	2,308	17,287	10
377	51	387	372	126,988	380	3,494,206	246	597,809	98	248,700	404	408	3,742	35,766	11
14,397	416	14,671	13,827	4,639,781	14,448	21,779,621	3,584	1,692,985	1,771	1,364,885	13,904	14,430	92,395	808,219	12
122	3	124	119	29,894	122	319,832	74	40,836	32	35,750	116	118	900	7,651	13
595	14	612	552	154,672	592	1,979,408	277	314,861	188	189,350	585	605	4,976	42,193	14
82	20	84	80	51,342	83	2,061,942	60	328,454	18	70,360	98	103	1,165	13,570	15
1,875	62	1,916	1,808	621,808	1,874	3,562,930	440	308,680	172	165,435	1,802	1,926	12,616	113,727	16
200	58	200	187	50,765	209	496,946	76	42,282	39	48,050	247	257	1,533	11,246	17
2,565	52	2,593	2,510	860,675	2,610	3,238,735	511	127,879	232	162,988	2,519	2,601	19,142	148,248	18
2,801	32	2,853	2,724	995,462	2,808	3,366,223	666	145,878	353	227,963	2,779	2,896	19,808	188,497	19
4,606	113	4,717	4,406	1,522,656	4,608	5,125,207	1,182	264,966	464	290,513	4,304	4,425	23,891	218,359	20
1,549	62	1,572	1,441	352,507	1,542	1,638,398	298	119,159	273	174,476	1,454	1,499	8,364	64,728	21
1,850	120	1,881	1,804	497,665	1,872	5,824,226	764	681,494	562	499,105	1,863	1,891	12,913	82,380	22
333	20	336	318	94,000	336	1,473,251	132	125,636	90	106,286	343	347	2,721	18,470	23
190	10	192	186	56,515	191	596,625	105	73,680	70	70,650	192	197	1,415	9,562	24
327	25	332	322	89,815	333	1,040,148	148	165,422	78	81,520	337	344	2,364	16,155	25
42	....	44	41	12,470	43	167,950	19	17,009	24	27,060	42	42	363	1,910	26
9	2	9	9	1,960	10	26,850	4	851	....	....	10	10	50	244	27
9	....	9	9	2,755	9	74,300	5	5,362	3	7,700	8	8	78	497	28
61	10	63	59	14,955	61	167,125	30	25,711	25	18,700	65	65	410	2,323	29
600	38	617	584	153,914	605	1,690,119	202	229,805	173	123,890	588	597	3,650	22,912	30
....	....	....	....	....	....	....	....	....	....	....	....	....	....	....	31
1	....	1	1	150	2	3,900	1	1,700	1	1,800	2	2	9	32	32
11	1	11	10	3,175	11	73,500	5	2,130	6	7,100	11	11	101	589	33
267	14	267	265	67,956	271	510,458	113	34,188	92	54,399	265	208	1,752	9,686	34
17,258	599	17,582	16,474	5,015,313	17,322	19,863,508	4,036	963,785	2,155	1,226,294	16,694	17,268	94,971	767,048	35
956	36	967	939	268,085	964	1,845,538	263	102,328	199	122,573	920	939	5,841	43,863	36
1,735	69	1,808	1,644	530,457	1,743	2,631,502	364	136,630	199	109,270	1,677	1,729	9,513	76,021	37
3,476	107	3,542	3,313	1,114,305	3,474	3,920,253	790	168,554	360	224,196	3,349	3,469	19,105	164,436	38
3,744	74	3,800	3,588	1,093,415	3,741	3,524,880	857	139,001	339	213,641	3,594	3,711	19,590	168,184	39
2,017	40	2,035	1,856	573,281	2,032	2,796,242	559	158,708	345	224,112	1,927	2,001	10,194	92,266	40
1,974	61	2,017	1,925	551,131	1,992	1,628,303	417	77,810	251	106,405	1,908	1,984	11,552	80,152	41
534	56	553	517	116,991	543	410,089	140	31,957	58	24,437	557	590	2,964	19,326	42
2,822	156	2,860	2,692	767,698	2,833	3,106,101	646	148,797	404	201,660	2,762	2,845	16,212	122,800	43
112	7	115	109	30,242	117	804,842	61	82,056	58	64,150	118	121	793	4,910	44
6	....	6	6	1,175	6	11,650	4	432	4	3,600	5	5	30	134	45
....	....	....	....	....	....	....	....	....	....	....	....	....	....	....	46
1	....	1	1	150	1	10,000	....	....	1	1,000	1	1	12	40	47
23	1	23	21	6,160	24	241,455	17	26,494	19	28,750	23	24	176	1,220	48
7	....	7	7	912	7	10,050	3	440	3	1,800	7	8	33	135	49
2	1	2	2	420	2	7,500	1	130	....	....	5	5	24	121	50
1	....	1	1	300	1	4,000	1	216	....	....	1	1	10	30	51
....	....	....	....	....	....	....	....	....	....	....	....	....	....	....	52
13	....	14	13	3,250	13	57,900	8	6,125	4	2,400	15	15	87	514	53
3	1	3	3	900	3	44,000	3	3,950	2	3,000	3	3	15	85	54
56	4	58	55	16,975	60	418,287	24	44,269	25	23,600	58	59	406	2,631	55

TABLE 13.—COLORED[1] ORGANIZATIONS, SHOWING COMMUNICANTS OR MEMBERS, PLACES OF WORSHIP, VALUE TIONS (IN DETAIL), FOR EACH

[The statistics in this table refer to denominations comprising in whole

ALABAMA.

	DENOMINATION.	Total number of organizations.	Number of colored organizations.	COMMUNICANTS OR MEMBERS. Number of organizations reporting.	Total number reported.	Sex. Number of organizations reporting.	Male.	Female.
1	Total	5,052	3,734	3,715	397,178	3,485	146,186	234,680
	Adventist bodies:							
2	Seventh-day Adventist Denomination	15	2	2	41	2	16	25
	Baptist bodies:							
3	Baptists—National Convention (Colored)	1,977	1,977	1,974	259,825	1,935	98,280	156,302
4	Free Baptists	21	13	13	330	13	121	209
5	Primitive Baptists	306	4	4	102	4	45	57
6	Colored Primitive Baptists in America	187	187	186	14,829	63	2,714	4,547
7	United American Freewill Baptists (Colored)	6	6	6	272	3	47	142
8	Christians (Christian Connection)	25	1	1	110	1	59	51
	Churches of the Living God (Colored):							
9	Church of the Living God (Christian Workers for Friendship)	1	1	1	25	1	10	15
10	Church of Christ in God	1	1	1	12	1	8	4
11	Congregationalists	114	21	21	1,580	21	651	929
	Disciples or Christians:							
12	Disciples of Christ	154	11	11	843	11	345	498
13	Churches of Christ	157	6	6	379	6	155	224
	Evangelistic associations:							
14	Voluntary Missionary Society in America (Colored)	3	3	3	425	3	150	275
	Methodist bodies:							
15	Methodist Episcopal Church	377	190	183	12,137	155	4,033	6,473
16	African Methodist Episcopal Church	557	557	555	39,617	527	14,324	23,852
17	African Methodist Episcopal Zion Church	389	389	385	36,705	382	13,076	23,410
18	Colored Methodist Episcopal Church	292	292	290	23,112	287	9,146	13,913
	Presbyterian bodies:							
19	Presbyterian Church in the United States of America	7	6	6	168	4	47	93
20	Colored Cumberland Presbyterian Church	55	55	55	5,805	55	2,586	3,219
21	Presbyterian Church in the United States	208	8	8	232	8	105	127
22	Protestant Episcopal Church	102	3	3	262	2	105	131
23	Roman Catholic Church	98	1	1	367	1	183	184

ARIZONA.

	DENOMINATION.	Total number of organizations.	Number of colored organizations.	Number of organizations reporting.	Total number reported.	Number of organizations reporting.	Male.	Female.
1	Total	5	5	5	208	5	66	142
	Methodist bodies:							
2	African Methodist Episcopal Church	2	2	2	82	2	24	58
3	Colored Methodist Episcopal Church	3	3	3	126	3	42	84

ARKANSAS.

	DENOMINATION.	Total number of organizations.	Number of colored organizations.	Number of organizations reporting.	Total number reported.	Number of organizations reporting.	Male.	Female.
1	Total	2,713	2,094	2,081	146,319	2,042	56,895	86,742
	Adventist bodies:							
2	Seventh-day Adventist Denomination	22	3	3	36	1	3	4
	Baptist bodies:							
3	Baptists—National Convention (Colored)	1,115	1,115	1,113	93,364	1,099	37,289	55,159
4	Free Baptists	8	5	5	290	4	72	100
5	Colored Primitive Baptists in America	20	20	19	810	10	83	142
6	Churches of God in North America, General Eldership of the	23	7	7	169	7	87	82
	Churches of the Living God (Colored):							
7	Church of the Living God (Christian Workers for Friendship)	11	11	11	765	11	287	478
8	Church of the Living God (Apostolic Church)	8	8	8	338	8	118	220
9	Church of Christ in God	1	1	1	15	1	8	7
10	Congregationalists	4	1	1	112	1	33	79
	Disciples or Christians:							
11	Disciples of Christ	156	8	8	377	8	187	190
12	Churches of Christ	190	1	1	36	1	3	33
13	Free Christian Zion Church of Christ (Colored)	14	14	13	1,635	13	665	970
14	Independent churches	38	2	2	180	2	70	110
	Methodist bodies:							
15	Methodist Episcopal Church	252	119	118	6,636	113	2,166	3,906
16	African Methodist Episcopal Church	485	485	482	26,903	481	10,247	16,636
17	African Methodist Episcopal Zion Church	65	65	65	2,404	65	932	1,472
18	Colored Methodist Episcopal Church	211	211	206	11,506	202	4,382	6,894
	Presbyterian bodies:							
19	Presbyterian Church in the United States of America	23	14	14	467	11	146	201
20	Protestant Episcopal Church	67	4	4	270	4	117	159

[1] Negroes or persons of negro descent.

OF CHURCH PROPERTY, DEBT ON CHURCH PROPERTY, PARSONAGES, AND SUNDAY SCHOOLS, BY DENOMINA-
STATE AND TERRITORY: 1906.

or in part colored organizations, as shown by the first two columns.]

ALABAMA.

PLACES OF WORSHIP.					VALUE OF CHURCH PROPERTY.		DEBT ON CHURCH PROPERTY.		PARSONAGES.		SUNDAY SCHOOLS CONDUCTED BY CHURCH ORGANIZATIONS.				
Number of organizations reporting—		Number of church edifices reported.	Seating capacity of church edifices.		Number of organizations reporting.	Value reported.	Number of organizations reporting.	Amount of debt reported.	Number of organizations reporting.	Value of parsonages reported.	Number of organizations reporting.	Number of Sunday schools reported.	Number of officers and teachers.	Number of scholars.	
Church edifices.	Halls, etc.		Number of organizations reporting.	Seating capacity reported.											
3,476	107	3,542	3,313	1,114,306	3,474	$3,920,253	790	$168,554	360	$224,196	3,349	3,469	19,105	164,436	1
1	1	1	1	150	1	1,150	1	400	...	...	2	2	13	62	2
1,924	39	1,940	1,863	640,715	1,923	1,889,648	324	67,369	53	45,355	1,882	1,938	10,066	99,776	3
13	...	13	8	1,005	13	4,750	3	300	...	...	12	12	39	273	4
4	...	4	4	1,200	4	2,300	...	...	...	...	...	...	...	...	5
86	1	87	64	21,855	86	51,950	8	548	1	450	51	51	221	1,722	6
4	2	4	1	75	6	1,100	2	6	...	...	3	3	14	127	7
1	...	1	1	150	1	500	...	...	...	...	1	1	8	75	8
...	1	...	...	...	...	...	...	...	...	...	1	1	3	15	9
1	...	1	1	100	1	500	...	...	...	...	...	...	...	...	10
19	1	19	18	5,015	21	68,420	3	1,220	7	6,850	21	25	170	1,454	11
10	...	11	10	2,605	10	11,850	1	6	...	...	11	12	58	413	12
4	2	4	4	1,175	4	3,250	3	636	...	...	5	5	28	174	13
3	...	3	3	1,325	2	2,400	1	1,000	...	...	3	3	21	390	14
171	3	182	148	43,669	172	192,580	61	7,062	52	19,905	174	187	1,186	8,444	15
505	42	517	474	153,650	501	599,907	179	46,375	120	61,403	480	502	3,012	21,616	16
375	7	387	364	121,785	377	701,841	112	22,046	57	48,103	355	358	2,456	17,202	17
284	8	296	280	93,306	284	292,676	87	20,691	60	29,906	275	294	1,440	9,996	18
4	...	4	4	1,500	4	5,900	1	800	...	...	6	7	26	190	19
55	...	55	53	21,125	53	42,331	3	85	5	1,625	55	55	291	1,997	20
8	...	8	8	2,600	7	8,700	1	20	2	2,000	8	9	45	318	21
3	...	4	3	1,050	3	30,500	...	...	2	6,100	3	3	17	180	22
1	...	1	1	250	1	8,000	...	...	1	2,500	1	1	1	12	23

ARIZONA.

2	1	2	2	420	2	$7,500	1	$130	...	...	5	5	24	121	
1	1	1	1	120	1	5,000	1	130	...	...	2	2	9	36	2
1	...	1	1	300	1	2,500	...	...	...	...	3	3	15	85	3

ARKANSAS.

1,974	61	2,017	1,925	551,131	1,992	$1,628,303	417	$77,810	251	$106,405	1,908	1,984	11,552	80,152	1
...	1	...	...	...	...	...	...	...	...	...	3	3	8	29	2
1,086	16	1,087	1,049	303,571	1,090	837,664	167	29,156	52	31,735	1,049	1,066	5,863	47,216	3
4	...	4	4	850	5	2,450	1	25	...	...	4	6	6	85	4
13	3	13	7	1,175	13	3,360	1	115	...	...	...	...	...	...	5
2	4	2	2	305	2	1,950	...	...	...	...	3	4	11	85	6
9	2	9	9	1,610	9	9,400	1	50	...	...	11	11	33	244	7
8	...	8	8	2,000	8	7,200	1	400	1	1,000	7	7	37	175	8
1	...	1	1	500	1	1,500	1	100	...	...	1	1	5	20	9
1	...	1	1	500	1	2,500	...	...	...	...	1	1	10	75	10
7	...	7	7	970	8	2,540	1	10	...	...	8	8	29	182	11
...	1	...	...	...	...	...	...	...	...	...	1	2	4	40	12
13	1	13	13	4,401	12	4,975	7	1,150	2	450	7	7	63	340	13
2	...	2	2	500	2	850	...	...	...	...	2	2	11	60	14
110	3	111	106	29,925	115	137,700	35	8,652	45	17,300	117	128	870	5,367	15
466	14	492	466	131,992	466	375,762	128	20,947	92	34,289	445	465	3,077	17,006	16
57	3	66	57	17,651	59	57,279	22	4,827	11	5,600	52	53	326	1,775	17
185	9	191	183	53,131	189	165,273	51	10,878	45	15,181	179	202	1,119	6,852	18
8	2	8	8	1,625	10	8,900	...	...	3	850	14	14	63	494	19
2	2	2	2	425	2	9,000	1	1,500	...	...	4	4	17	108	20

TABLE 13.—COLORED[1] ORGANIZATIONS, SHOWING COMMUNICANTS OR MEMBERS, PLACES OF WORSHIP, VALUE TIONS (IN DETAIL), FOR EACH

[The statistics in this table refer to denominations comprising in whole

CALIFORNIA.

	DENOMINATION.	Total number of organizations.	Number of colored organizations.	COMMUNICANTS OR MEMBERS. Number of organizations reporting.	Total number reported.	Sex. Number of organizations reporting.	Male.	Female.
1	Total	827	63	63	4,564	54	1,152	1,963
	Baptist bodies:							
2	Baptists—National Convention (Colored)	25	25	25	2,083	19	335	586
	Methodist bodies:							
3	Methodist Episcopal Church	505	1	1	16	1	6	10
4	African Methodist Episcopal Church	22	22	22	1,533	19	443	803
5	African Methodist Episcopal Zion Church	14	14	14	902	14	350	552
	Presbyterian bodies:							
6	Presbyterian Church in the United States of America	261	1	1	30	1	18	12

COLORADO.

	DENOMINATION.	Total number of organizations.	Number of colored organizations.	COMMUNICANTS OR MEMBERS. Number of organizations reporting.	Total number reported.	Sex. Number of organizations reporting.	Male.	Female.
1	Total	554	25	25	2,507	22	776	1,535
	Baptist bodies:							
2	Baptists—Northern Convention	87	4	4	1,040	4	386	654
	Methodist bodies:							
3	Methodist Episcopal Church	220	4	4	152	2	36	55
4	African Methodist Episcopal Church	15	15	15	1,139	14	325	679
	Presbyterian bodies:							
5	Presbyterian Church in the United States of America	128	1	1	116	1	14	102
6	Protestant Episcopal Church	104	1	1	60	1	15	45

CONNECTICUT.

	DENOMINATION.	Total number of organizations.	Number of colored organizations.	COMMUNICANTS OR MEMBERS. Number of organizations reporting.	Total number reported.	Sex. Number of organizations reporting.	Male.	Female.
1	Total	576	49	48	4,492	47	1,537	2,802
	Baptist bodies:							
2	Baptists—Northern Convention	141	6		269	6	103	166
3	Baptists—National Convention (Colored)	13	13	1	2,218	13	768	1,450
4	Church of God and Saints of Christ (Colored)	4	4	[illegible]	42	4	9	33
	Methodist bodies:							
5	Methodist Episcopal Church	206	1	1		1	15	38
6	Union American Methodist Episcopal Church (Colored)	1	1	1		1	20	40
7	African Methodist Episcopal Church	5	5	5		4	62	120
8	African Methodist Episcopal Zion Church	17	17	16	1,[illegible]53	16	457	772
9	Protestant Episcopal Church	189	2	2	286	2	103	183

DELAWARE.

	DENOMINATION.	Total number of organizations.	Number of colored organizations.	COMMUNICANTS OR MEMBERS. Number of organizations reporting.	Total number reported.	Sex. Number of organizations reporting.	Male.	Female.
1	Total	392	125	125	10,583	117	3,867	5,277
	Baptist bodies:							
2	Baptists—Northern Convention	16	3	3	707	2	59	76
3	Church of God and Saints of Christ (Colored)	2	2	2	54	2	25	29
	Methodist bodies:							
4	Methodist Episcopal Church	207	48	48	3,312	45	1,354	1,882
5	Union American Methodist Episcopal Church (Colored)	12	12	12	686	12	270	416
6	African Methodist Episcopal Church	39	39	39	2,553	38	689	1,281
7	African Union Methodist Protestant Church	13	13	13	1,264	11	412	725
8	African Methodist Episcopal Zion Church	4	4	4	167		44	42
	Presbyterian bodies:							
9	Presbyterian Church in the United States of America	37	1	1	125	3	50	75
10	Protestant Episcopal Church	39	1	1	35	1	12	23
11	Roman Catholic Church	23	2	2	1,680	2	952	728

DISTRICT OF COLUMBIA.

	DENOMINATION.	Total number of organizations.	Number of colored organizations.	COMMUNICANTS OR MEMBERS. Number of organizations reporting.	Total number reported.	Sex. Number of organizations reporting.	Male.	Female.
1	Total	202	102	102	46,249	97	14,153	28,909
	Baptist bodies:							
2	Baptists—Northern Convention	20	2	2	4,189	2	1,500	2,689
3	Baptists—National Convention (Colored)	60	60	60	26,203	58	6,529	16,949
4	Church of God and Saints of Christ (Colored)	1	1	1	70	1	20	50
5	Congregationalists	6	3	3	1,173	3	441	732
	Methodist bodies:							
6	Methodist Episcopal Church	37	10	10	3,115	8	1,055	1,940
7	African Methodist Episcopal Church	7	7	7	1,928	7	724	1,204
8	African Union Methodist Protestant Church	1	1	1	45	1	20	25
9	African Methodist Episcopal Zion Church	6	6	6	2,615	6	988	1,627
10	Colored Methodist Episcopal Church	5	5	5	1,110	5	348	762
11	Protestant Episcopal Church	38	5	5	871	4	199	330
12	Roman Catholic Church	21	2	2	4,930	2	2,329	2,601

[1] Negroes or persons of negro descent.

OF CHURCH PROPERTY, DEBT ON CHURCH PROPERTY, PARSONAGES, AND SUNDAY SCHOOLS, BY DENOMINA- STATE AND TERRITORY: 1906—Continued.

or in part colored organizations, as shown by the first two columns.]

PLACES OF WORSHIP.					VALUE OF CHURCH PROPERTY.		DEBT ON CHURCH PROPERTY.		PARSONAGES.		SUNDAY SCHOOLS CONDUCTED BY CHURCH ORGANIZATIONS.				
Number of organizations reporting—		Number of church edifices reported.	Seating capacity of church edifices.		Number of organizations reporting.	Value reported.	Number of organizations reporting.	Amount of debt reported.	Number of organizations reporting.	Value of parsonages reported.	Number of organizations reporting.	Number of Sunday schools reported.	Number of officers and teachers.	Number of scholars.	
Church edifices.	Halls, etc.		Number of organizations reporting.	Seating capacity reported.											
CALIFORNIA.															
56	4	58	55	16,975	60	$418,287	24	$44,269	25	$23,600	58	59	406	2,631	1
21	3	21	21	5,445	22	161,350	8	22,923	7	7,000	23	24	150	1,179	2
1	...	1	1	150	1	1,000	1	423	...	...	1	1	5	14	3
21	...	23	21	6,425	22	125,150	9	5,750	11	13,050	21	21	154	934	4
13	1	13	12	4,955	14	129,587	6	15,173	7	3,550	12	12	93	484	5
...	...	...	...	...	1	1,200	...	...	...	...	1	1	4	20	6
COLORADO.															
23	1	23	21	6,160	24	$241,455	17	$26,494	19	$28,750	23	24	176	1,220	1
3	...	[illegible]		1,100	3	48,000	1	7,000	2	3,700	4	5	55	442	2
4	...	4	2	500	4	22,000	4	4,922	3	4,650	4	4	19	91	3
14	1	14	14	3,435	15	159,455	11	6,572	12	17,400	14	14	92	607	4
1	...	1	1	1,000	1	10,000	1	8,000	1	1,500	1	1	10	80	5
1	...	1	1	125	1	2,000	...	...	1	1,500	...	...	...	...	6
CONNECTICUT.															
40	8	40	40	11,804	42	$379,855	23	$44,264	15	$35,900	45	45	455	2,764	1
5	1	5	5	880	6	11,250	2	1,700	2	2,300	6	6	48	209	2
13	...	13	13	4,121	13	106,500	7	14,650	2	1,300	13	13	127	1,162	3
...	4	...	...	...	...	...	...	...	...	...	...	...	...	...	4
1	...	1	1	200	1	1,000	1	425	...	...	1	1	6	35	5
1	...	1	1	300	1	7,000	...	...	...	...	1	1	11	40	6
5	...	5	5	1,175	5	14,600	3	3,939	2	4,500	5	5	39	270	7
14	3	14	14	4,728	15	204,505	9	23,107	8	23,500	17	17	208	946	8
1	...	1	1	400	1	35,000	1	443	1	4,300	2	2	16	102	9
DELAWARE.															
122	3	124	119	29,894	122	$319,832	74	$40,836	32	$35,750	116	118	900	7,651	1
3	...	3	3	1,050	3	24,300	...	...	...	...	3	3	30	447	2
...	2	...	...	...	...	...	...	...	...	...	...	...	...	...	3
48	...	48	45	9,890	48	112,650	24	15,397	18	18,200	47	47	356	2,775	4
12	...	12	12	3,041	12	25,400	9	5,421	1	1,500	12	14	109	657	5
39	...	39	39	8,955	39	89,710	26	12,600	8	7,650	35	35	260	2,034	6
13	...	15	13	4,825	13	38,347	11	4,375	4	5,400	13	13	109	1,463	7
4	...	4	4	1,083	4	11,925	4	3,043	...	...	3	3	20	100	8
1	...	1	1	300	1	5,000	...	...	...	...	1	1	10	90	9
1	...	1	1	250	1	4,500	...	...	...	...	1	1	4	15	10
1	1	1	1	500	1	8,000	...	...	1	3,000	1	1	2	70	11
DISTRICT OF COLUMBIA.															
82	20	84	80	51,342	83	$2,051,942	60	$328,454	18	$70,360	98	103	1,165	13,570	1
2	...	2	2	3,000	2	135,000	...	...	...	...	2	3	88	1,450	2
43	17	44	43	27,337	43	962,900	33	180,386	2	1,300	57	58	482	5,590	3
1	...	1	1	400	1	6,000	...	...	...	...	...	...	...	...	4
3	...	4	3	2,050	3	88,000	2	14,500	1	4,000	3	5	57	637	5
10	...	10	8	3,900	10	149,705	8	24,418	5	20,260	10	10	119	1,689	6
7	...	7	7	4,150	7	127,987	6	29,350	4	8,800	7	7	98	1,116	7
...	1	...	...	...	...	...	...	...	...	...	1	1	4	40	8
6	...	6	6	3,230	6	207,000	5	38,900	2	9,000	6	7	102	1,037	9
5	...	5	5	4,400	5	139,000	3	20,000	1	1,000	5	5	49	505	10
3	2	3	3	1,175	4	66,350	2	9,900	1	4,000	5	5	46	582	11
2	...	2	2	1,700	2	170,000	1	11,000	2	22,000	2	2	120	915	12

TABLE 13.—COLORED[1] ORGANIZATIONS,SH OWING COMMUNICANTS OR MEMBERS, PLACES OF WORSHIP, VALUE TIONS (IN DETAIL), FOR EACH

[The statistics in this table refer to denominations comprising in whole

FLORIDA.

	DENOMINATION.	Total number of organizations.	Number of colored organizations.	COMMUNICANTS OR MEMBERS. Number of organizations reporting.	Total number reported.	Sex. Number of organizations reporting.	Male.	Female.
1	Total	2,011	1,638	1,634	105,678	1,560	39,356	63,660
	Adventist bodies:							
2	Seventh-day Adventist Denomination	17	1	1	11	1	4	7
	Baptist bodies:							
3	Baptists—National Convention (Colored)	660	660	658	48,371	653	18,069	29,940
4	Colored Primitive Baptists in America	128	128	128	5,350	98	1,767	3,007
5	United American Freewill Baptists (Colored)	18	18	18	388	16	184	168
6	Independent churches	19	8	8	260	8	110	150
	Methodist bodies:							
7	Methodist Episcopal Church	153	107	107	6,384	77	1,733	3,225
8	African Methodist Episcopal Church	583	583	582	35,713	580	13,824	21,793
9	African Methodist Episcopal Zion Church	64	64	64	3,223	64	1,153	2,070
10	Methodist Protestant Church	8	2	2	23	2	11	12
11	Colored Methodist Episcopal Church	48	48	48	1,858	47	682	1,106
	Presbyterian bodies:							
12	Presbyterian Church in the United States of America	32	1	1	28	1	7	21
13	Presbyterian Church in the United States	81	1	1	37	1	21	16
14	Protestant Episcopal Church	141	16	15	1,410	11	495	819
15	Roman Catholic Church	59	1	1	2,622	1	1,296	1,326

GEORGIA.

	DENOMINATION.	Total number of organizations.	Number of colored organizations.	COMMUNICANTS OR MEMBERS. Number of organizations reporting.	Total number reported.	Sex. Number of organizations reporting.	Male.	Female.
1	Total	5,420	4,834	4,790	507,005	4,565	185,114	306,620
	Baptist bodies:							
2	Baptists—National Convention (Colored)	2,504	2,504	2,495	333,943	2,447	122,601	207,824
3	Colored Primitive Baptists in America	150	150	146	4,531	63	771	1,850
4	United American Freewill Baptists (Colored)	93	93	93	3,680	70	1,076	1,415
5	Church of God and Saints of Christ (Colored)	2	2	2	32	2	11	21
6	Congregationalists	85	24	24	2,150	24	895	1,255
	Methodist bodies:							
7	Methodist Episcopal Church	357	290	281	25,121	240	8,305	12,354
8	African Methodist Episcopal Church	1,226	1,226	1,212	93,626	1,201	35,011	57,350
9	African Methodist Episcopal Zion Church	68	68	68	3,630	66	1,298	2,232
10	Methodist Protestant Church	77	29	29	1,062	28	417	393
11	Colored Methodist Episcopal Church	402	402	397	34,501	385	12,852	21,026
12	Reformed Methodist Union Episcopal Church (Colored)	2	2	2	162	2	55	107
	Presbyterian bodies:							
13	Presbyterian Church in the United States of America	29	29	29	2,243	25	738	1,351
14	Presbyterian Church in the United States	227	1	1	20	1	9	11
15	Protestant Episcopal Church	121	12	9	1,001	9	431	570
16	Roman Catholic Church	77	2	2	1,303	2	644	659

ILLINOIS.

	DENOMINATION.	Total number of organizations.	Number of colored organizations.	COMMUNICANTS OR MEMBERS. Number of organizations reporting.	Total number reported.	Sex. Number of organizations reporting.	Male.	Female.
1	Total	5,442	359	358	32,058	349	11,079	20,339
	Adventist bodies:							
2	Seventh-day Adventist Denomination	56	1	1	30	1	6	24
	Baptist bodies:							
3	Baptists—Northern Convention	945	2	2	66	2	27	39
4	Baptists—National Convention (Colored)	158	158	158	16,081	155	5,848	10,158
5	Free Baptists	123	36	36	1,907	34	638	1,099
	Churches of the Living God (Colored):							
6	Church of the Living God (Christian Workers for Friendship)	2	2	2	55	2	22	33
	Disciples or Christians:							
7	Disciples of Christ	769	2	2	195	2	70	125
	Lutheran bodies:							
8	Evangelical Lutheran Synodical Conference of America	340	1	1	42	1	18	24
	Methodist bodies:							
9	Methodist Episcopal Church	2,028	7	7	710	6	175	510
10	African Methodist Episcopal Church	116	116	115	9,833	113	3,154	6,359
11	African Methodist Episcopal Zion Church	9	9	9	870	9	247	623
12	Colored Methodist Episcopal Church	11	11	11	603	11	233	370
	Presbyterian bodies:							
13	Presbyterian Church in the United States of America	473	1	1	200	1	50	150
14	Cumberland Presbyterian Church	193	1	1	50	...	...	...
15	Colored Cumberland Presbyterian Church	9	9	9	913	9	418	495
16	Protestant Episcopal Church	210	3	3	503	3	173	330

[1] Negroes or persons of negro descent.

OF CHURCH PROPERTY, DEBT ON CHURCH PROPERTY, PARSONAGES, AND SUNDAY SCHOOLS, BY DENOMINA-
STATE AND TERRITORY: 1906—Continued.

or in part colored organizations, as shown by the first two columns.]

FLORIDA.

PLACES OF WORSHIP.					VALUE OF CHURCH PROPERTY.		DEBT ON CHURCH PROPERTY.		PARSONAGES.		SUNDAY SCHOOLS CONDUCTED BY CHURCH ORGANIZATIONS.				
Number of organizations reporting—		Number of church edifices reported.	Seating capacity of church edifices.		Number of organizations reporting.	Value reported.	Number of organizations reporting.	Amount of debt reported.	Number of organizations reporting.	Value of parsonages reported.	Number of organizations reporting.	Number of Sunday schools reported.	Number of officers and teachers.	Number of scholars.	
Church edifices.	Halls, etc.		Number of organizations reporting.	Seating capacity reported.											
1,549	62	1,572	1,441	352,507	1,542	$1,638,398	298	$119,159	273	$174,476	1,454	1,499	8,364	64,728	1
1	....	1	1	100	1	75	1	16	....	....	1	1	2	13	2
642	13	643	610	130,510	641	592,138	83	44,505	51	34,075	614	621	3,100	26,907	3
122	5	122	98	28,060	122	92,806	6	2,275	12	7,450	79	79	353	2,445	4
16	1	17	15	3,325	16	3,970	3	758	1	350	16	16	52	310	5
8	....	8	1	70	8	1,050	....	....	....	....	8	9	21	335	6
102	....	103	74	18,775	100	143,300	37	26,657	30	20,075	98	105	620	4,699	7
537	38	557	528	139,179	529	580,305	126	31,258	146	81,865	516	543	3,566	24,498	8
61	2	61	60	18,598	63	101,840	23	6,142	16	15,100	59	60	339	2,791	9
1	....	1	1	50	1	1,500	1	20	....	....	2	2	3	21	10
42	3	42	38	9,640	43	36,075	14	6,378	10	2,061	44	46	197	1,383	11
1	....	1	1	200	1	1,000	1	725	....	....	1	1	5	25	12
1	....	1	1	150	1	200	....	....	....	....	1	1	6	20	13
14	....	14	12	3,050	15	64,140	3	425	6	12,300	14	14	96	1,174	14
1	....	1	1	800	1	20,000	....	....	1	1,200	1	1	4	107	15

GEORGIA.

4,608	113	4,717	4,406	1,522,656	4,608	$5,125,207	1,182	$264,966	464	$290,513	4,304	4,425	23,891	218,359	1
2,428	56	2,436	2,364	860,448	2,431	2,615,744	334	95,651	34	31,835	2,351	2,388	11,058	121,962	2
109	....	112	59	18,810	107	46,557	10	581	2	1,000	3	3	15	168	3
83	5	84	75	26,000	83	50,558	17	2,721	5	1,125	64	64	235	1,753	4
....	2	....	....	....	....	....	....	....	....	....	....	....	....	....	5
21	....	21	21	6,200	21	64,575	8	1,361	7	8,800	21	26	150	1,643	6
271	2	288	231	75,273	271	339,587	96	15,469	85	37,378	267	285	2,154	16,140	7
1,175	39	1,230	1,144	337,455	1,174	1,206,432	552	93,679	244	140,055	1,100	1,142	7,318	50,833	8
64	2	64	64	20,105	66	66,915	21	3,187	7	2,750	63	63	370	2,454	9
28	....	29	25	5,825	25	40,875	10	593	2	1,595	20	20	99	650	10
389	5	408	383	159,895	388	544,850	132	51,210	69	55,025	375	391	2,231	19,418	11
2	....	2	2	600	2	2,200	2	514	....	....	2	2	8	35	12
25	2	27	25	9,275	26	59,025	....	....		2,450	28	28	193	2,325	13
1	....	1	1	100	1	800	....	....	....	....	....	....	....	....	14
10	....	13	10	2,270	11	65,089	....	....	4	8,500	8	10	53	863	15
2	....	2	2	400	2	23,000	....	....	....	....	2	3	7	115	16

ILLINOIS.

327	25	332	322	89,815	333	$1,040,148	148	$165,422	78	$81,520	337	344	2,364	16,155	1
....		....	....	....	....	....	....	....	....	....	1	1	4	22	2
1	....	1	1	250	1	4,000	1	1,600	....	....	2	2	12	62	3
145	10	145	143	40,355	148	421,798	49	54,214	19	18,450	152	156	1,065	7,294	4
35	1	35	35	8,980	35	42,825	10	5,271	1	800	31	31	174	946	5
1	1	1	1	150	1	900	1	250	....	....	2	2	4	11	6
1	....	1	1	350	1	1,400	1	700	....	....		2	10	60	7
1	....	1	1	250	1	4,000	....	....	1	1,600	1	1	3	24	8
5	2	5	4	850	5	21,950	3	74	1	1,500	6	6	37	413	9
107	8	111	105	28,518	110	423,925	63	77,986	45	46,850	107	110	833	5,316	10
8	1	8	8	2,300	8	46,300	6	7,027	4	1,220	9	9	65	550	11
10	1	10	10	2,800	10	25,600	7	2,068	4	2,600	10	10	65	318	12
1	....	1	1	312	1	12,000	....	....	....	....	1	1	20	275	13
1	....	1	1	200	1	1,000	....	....	....	....	1	1	8	75	14
9	....	9	9	3,450	9	23,950	6	8,732	1	3,500	9	9	60	672	15
2	....	3	2	1,060	2	10,500	1	7,500	2	5,000	3	3	14	117	16

TABLE 13.—COLORED[1] ORGANIZATIONS, SHOWING COMMUNICANTS OR MEMBERS, PLACES OF WORSHIP, VALUE TIONS (IN DETAIL), FOR EACH STATE

[The statistics in this table refer to denominations comprising in whole

INDIANA.

	DENOMINATION.	Total number of organizations.	Number of colored organizations.	COMMUNICANTS OR MEMBERS.				
				Number of organizations reporting.	Total number reported.	Sex.		
						Number of organizations reporting.	Male.	Female.
1	Total	3,191	202	200	23,133	197	8,100	14,548
	Baptist bodies:							
2	Baptists—National Convention (Colored)	88	88	88	13,526	87	4,907	8,319
3	Free Baptists	31	7	7	417	7	154	263
	Churches of the Living God (Colored):							
4	Church of the Living God (Christian Workers for Friendship)	1	1	1	85	1	35	50
5	Church of Christ in God	1	1	1	35	1	9	26
	Disciples or Christians:							
6	Disciples of Christ	670	1	1	160	1	70	90
7	Churches of Christ	112	1	1	70	1	25	45
	Methodist bodies:							
8	Methodist Episcopal Church	1,726	25	25	1,553	24	486	997
9	African Methodist Episcopal Church	66	66	64	5,769	63	1,882	3,772
10	African Methodist Episcopal Zion Church	8	8	8	1,281	8	439	842
11	Wesleyan Methodist Connection of America	88	1	1	57	1	20	37
12	Colored Methodist Episcopal Church	1	1	1	40	1	15	25
	Presbyterian bodies:							
13	Presbyterian Church in the United States of America	328	1	1	22	1	8	14
14	Protestant Episcopal Church	71	1	1	118	1	50	68

IOWA.

1	Total	2,135	72	72	4,108	72	1,481	2,627
	Baptist bodies:							
2	Baptists—Northern Convention	390	1	1	35	1	13	22
3	Baptists—National Convention (Colored)	33	33	33	2,352	33	879	1,473
	Methodist bodies:							
4	Methodist Episcopal Church	1,586	2	2	58	2	21	37
5	African Methodist Episcopal Church	35	35	35	1,617	35	554	1,063
6	Protestant Episcopal Church	91	1	1	46	1	14	32

KANSAS.

1	Total	1,988	286	286	17,273	282	6,106	10,698
	Baptist bodies:							
2	Baptists—National Convention (Colored)	137	137	137	10,011	136	3,664	6,067
3	Church of God and Saints of Christ (Colored)	3	3	3	78	3	28	50
	Churches of the Living God (Colored):							
4	Church of the Living God (Christian Workers for Friendship)	3	3	3	135	3	51	84
	Disciples or Christians:							
5	Disciples of Christ	343	5	5	262	4	97	135
	Methodist bodies:							
6	Methodist Episcopal Church	1,299	23	23	765	23	246	519
7	African Methodist Episcopal Church	92	92	92	4,934	90	1,633	3,142
8	African Methodist Episcopal Zion Church	1	1	1	6	1	3	3
9	Colored Methodist Episcopal Church	19	19	19	917	19	304	613
	Presbyterian bodies:							
10	Colored Cumberland Presbyterian Church	1	1	1	85	1	45	40
11	Protestant Episcopal Church	90	2	2	80	2	35	45

KENTUCKY.

1	Total	2,748	1,007	1,005	116,918	966	44,630	69,263
	Adventist bodies:							
2	Seventh-day Adventist Denomination	19	2	2	45	2	10	35
	Baptist bodies:							
3	Baptists—National Convention (Colored)	531	531	529	76,239	506	29,796	44,681
4	Free Baptists	39	20	20	1,020	19	382	551
5	Colored Primitive Baptists in America	5	5	5	228	2	55	74
	Churches of the Living God (Colored):							
6	Church of the Living God (Christian Workers for Friendship)	3	3	3	94	3	39	55
7	Church of Christ in God	2	2	2	80	2	28	52
8	Congregationalists	18	2	2	210	2	96	114
	Disciples or Christians:							
9	Disciples of Christ	841	24	24	2,721	24	1,106	1,615
10	Churches of Christ	151	2	2	57	2	21	36
	Methodist bodies:							
11	Methodist Episcopal Church	425	93	93	7,197	85	2,172	4,220
12	African Methodist Episcopal Church	130	130	130	10,047	129	3,482	6,482
13	African Methodist Episcopal Zion Church	59	59	59	5,773	58	2,008	3,650
14	Colored Methodist Episcopal Church	98	98	98	8,137	97	3,121	5,001
	Presbyterian bodies:							
15	Presbyterian Church in the United States of America	83	3	3	198	2	50	98
16	Colored Cumberland Presbyterian Church	26	26	26	2,042	26	899	1,143
17	Protestant Episcopal Church	86	4	4	251	4	86	165
18	Roman Catholic Church	232	3	3	2,579	3	1,288	1,291

[1] Negroes or persons of negro descent.

OF CHURCH PROPERTY, DEBT ON CHURCH PROPERTY, PARSONAGES, AND SUNDAY SCHOOLS, BY DENOMINA-
AND TERRITORY: 1906—Continued.

or in part colored organizations, as shown by the first two columns.]

INDIANA.

PLACES OF WORSHIP. Number of organizations reporting— Church edifices.	PLACES OF WORSHIP. Number of organizations reporting— Halls, etc.	PLACES OF WORSHIP. Number of church edifices reported.	PLACES OF WORSHIP. Seating capacity of church edifices. Number of organizations reporting.	PLACES OF WORSHIP. Seating capacity of church edifices. Seating capacity reported.	VALUE OF CHURCH PROPERTY. Number of organizations reporting.	VALUE OF CHURCH PROPERTY. Value reported.	DEBT ON CHURCH PROPERTY. Number of organizations reporting.	DEBT ON CHURCH PROPERTY. Amount of debt reported.	PARSONAGES. Number of organizations reporting.	PARSONAGES. Value of parsonages reported.	SUNDAY SCHOOLS CONDUCTED BY CHURCH ORGANIZATIONS. Number of organizations reporting.	SUNDAY SCHOOLS CONDUCTED BY CHURCH ORGANIZATIONS. Number of Sunday schools reported.	SUNDAY SCHOOLS CONDUCTED BY CHURCH ORGANIZATIONS. Number of officers and teachers.	SUNDAY SCHOOLS CONDUCTED BY CHURCH ORGANIZATIONS. Number of scholars.	
190	10	192	186	56,515	191	$596,625	105	$73,680	70	$70,650	192	197	1,415	9,562	1
83	5	84	82	26,525	81	246,775	38	36,503	11	17,600	86	89	658	4,802	2
5	1	5	5	1,150	6	21,400	4	2,375	1	8,000	7	7	46	263	3
....	1	....	....	....	....	....	....	....	....	....	1	1	3	25	4
....	1	....	....	....	....	....	....	....	....	....	....	....	....	....	5
1	....	1	1	225	1	2,000	....	....	....	....	1	1	10	100	6
1	....	1	1	250	1	1,000	....	....	....	....	1	1	5	45	7
24	....	24	22	5,590	25	51,350	13	5,768	14	6,300	25	25	152	946	8
65	1	66	65	19,250	65	223,500	40	18,091	41	35,750	59	60	458	2,728	9
8	....	8	8	2,875	8	33,800	6	5,243	2	2,400	8	8	63	527	10
1	....	1	1	300	1	3,000	1	600	1	600	1	1	7	40	11
1	....	1	....	....	1	800	1	600	....	....	1	2	3	16	12
....	1	....	....	....	1	5,000	1	2,000	....	....	1	1	7	40	13
1	....	1	1	350	1	8,000	1	2,500	....	....	1	1	3	30	14

IOWA.

61	10	63	59	14,955	61	$167,125	30	$25,711	25	$18,700	65	65	410	2,323	1
1	....	1	1	200	1	2,100	1	1,300	....	....	1	1	6	30	2
27	6	27	26	5,970	27	53,975	10	6,031	6	3,900	29	29	177	1,233	3
2	....	2	2	850	2	15,000	1	9,000	2	400	2	2	9	30	4
30	4	30	29	7,335	30	92,850	17	7,180	16	12,900	32	32	213	968	5
1	....	3	1	600	1	3,200	1	2,200	1	1,500	1	1	5	62	6

KANSAS.

267	14	267	265	67,956	271	$510,458	113	$34,188	92	$54,399	265	268	1,752	9,686	1
132	4	132	130	33,371	132	267,542	48	12,930	21	16,234	132	132	887	5,111	2
....	3	....	....	....	....	....	....	....	....	....	....	....	....	....	3
1	2	1	1	125	2	1,800	[illegible]	100	....	....	[illegible]	3	7	56	4
4	....	4	4	1,100	5	8,550	2	1,100	....	....	3	4	23	173	5
23	....	23	23	4,250	23	27,150	10	2,119	16	8,600	21	21	120	620	6
85	4	85	85	22,530	87	170,841	40	12,863	44	24,665	85	87	596	3,128	7
1	....	1	1	30	1	150	....	....	....	....	1	1	2	11	8
18	1	18	18	5,970	18	27,625	11	5,076	9	3,700	18	18	107	502	9
1	....	1	1	300	1	1,500	....	....	1	400	1	1	5	35	10
2	....	2	2	280	2	5,300	....	....	1	800	1	1	5	50	11

KENTUCKY.

956	36	967	939	268,035	964	$1,845,538	263	$102,328	199	$122,573	920	939	5,841	43,863	1
1	....	1	1	150	1	2,000	1	300	....	....	2	2	8	49	2
505	18	506	499	148,041	510	961,202	92	41,654	29	22,550	495		3,235	25,215	3
19	....	19	19	4,680	19	11,950	5	2,975	....	....	17		93	537	4
1	1	1	1	500	1	2,000	....	....	....	....	....	498 18	....	....	5
....	3	....	....	....	....	....	....	....	....	....	3	3	9	45	6
1	1	1	....	....	1	200	....	....	....	....	1	1	2	40	7
2	....	2	2	470	2	10,000	1	250	....	....	2	2	17	135	8
19		19	19	4,875	21	43,875	5	2,233	2	800	21	21	117	841	9
2	....	2	2	500	2	850	1	35	....	....	2	2	4	30	10
92	1	95	87	22,544	92	181,146	28	7,611	48	28,970	84		549	3,633	11
129	1	132	129	33,475	130	265,930	68	23,441	62	37,403	116		690	4,461	12
56	3	57	56	16,005	57	111,350	17	6,993	16	8,950	54	86	408	3,229	13
96	1	99	93	27,140	96	196,725	42	16,361	38	21,025	91	188	548	4,184	14
3	....	3	3	850	3	5,900	....	....	2	1,025	2	2	16	136	15
25	1	25	25	7,855	25	29,410	3	475	....	....	24	24	120	935	16
3	1	3	3	950	4	23,000	....	....	2	1,850	4	4	22	273	17
2	1	2	....	....	....	....	....	....	....	....	2	2	3	120	18

TABLE 13.—COLORED[1] ORGANIZATIONS, SHOWING COMMUNICANTS OR MEMBERS, PLACES OF WORSHIP, VALUE TIONS (IN DETAIL), FOR EACH

[The statistics in this table refer to denominations comprising in whole

LOUISIANA.

	DENOMINATION.	Total number of organizations.	Number of colored organizations.	COMMUNICANTS OR MEMBERS. Number of organizations reporting.	Total number reported.	Sex. Number of organizations reporting.	Male.	Female.
	Total	2,448	2,085	2,067	185,918	1,950	62,985	111,937
	Baptist bodies:							
2	Baptists—National Convention (Colored)	1,411	1,411	1,410	133,510	1,385	45,821	83,749
3	Free Baptists	31	7	7	452	3	40	52
4	Colored Primitive Baptists in America	4	4	4	201	1	50	75
5	Congregationalists	28	15	15	845	15	264	581
	Methodist bodies:							
6	Methodist Episcopal Church	279	249	236	18,019	157	3,832	8,262
7	African Methodist Episcopal Church	178	178	177	9,462	174	3,263	6,145
8	African Methodist Episcopal Zion Church	44	44	44	2,539	41	656	1,242
9	Colored Methodist Episcopal Church	171	171	169	11,728	169	4,633	7,095
	Presbyterian bodies:							
10	Presbyterian Church in the United States	88	4	3	195	3	70	125
11	Roman Catholic Church	214	2	2	8,967	2	4,356	4,611

MAINE.

	DENOMINATION.	Total number of organizations.	Number of colored organizations.	Number of organizations reporting.	Total number reported.	Number of organizations reporting.	Male.	Female.
1	Total	1	1	1	25	1	10	15
	Methodist bodies:							
2	African Methodist Episcopal Zion Church	1	1	1	25	1	10	15

MARYLAND.

	DENOMINATION.	Total number of organizations.	Number of colored organizations.	Number of organizations reporting.	Total number reported.	Number of organizations reporting.	Male.	Female.
1	Total	1,758	624	620	71,797	541	23,265	36,299
	Baptist bodies:							
2	Baptists—National Convention (Colored)	65	65	65	17,951	53	4,480	8,382
3	Free Baptists	12	12	10	1,242	4	49	133
4	Church of God and Saints of Christ (Colored)	2	2	2	44	2	9	35
	Disciples or Christians:							
5	Disciples of Christ	26	1	1	69	1	30	39
	Methodist bodies:							
6	Methodist Episcopal Church	966	367	365	33,567	316	13,046	17,942
7	Union American Methodist Episcopal Church (Colored)	12	12	12	936	12	372	564
8	African Methodist Episcopal Church	107	107	107	9,613	97	2,693	4,953
9	African Union Methodist Protestant Church	26	26	26	1,059	26	376	683
10	African Methodist Episcopal Zion Church	14	14	14	923	14	362	561
11	Colored Methodist Episcopal Church	5	5	5	240	5	104	136
	Presbyterian bodies:							
12	Presbyterian Church in the United States of America	95	3	3	489	3	144	345
13	Protestant Episcopal Church	262	6	6	1,478	5	530	940
	Reformed bodies:							
14	Reformed Church in America	1	1	1	19	1	9	10
15	Roman Catholic Church	165	3	3	4,167	2	1,061	1,576

MASSACHUSETTS.

	DENOMINATION.	Total number of organizations.	Number of colored organizations.	Number of organizations reporting.	Total number reported.	Number of organizations reporting.	Male.	Female.
1	Total	1,638	64	64	9,402	60	2,905	5,347
	Baptist bodies:							
2	Baptists—Northern Convention	332	3	3	474	3	179	295
3	Baptists—National Convention (Colored)	26	26	26	5,274	26	1,854	3,420
4	Church of God and Saints of Christ (Colored)	2	2	2	202	2	76	126
5	Congregationalists	615	7	7	475	7	152	323
	Methodist bodies:							
6	Methodist Episcopal Church	413	3	3	88	3	33	55
7	African Methodist Episcopal Church	14	14	14	1,364	11	127	362
8	African Methodist Episcopal Zion Church	7	7	7	1,215	7	479	736
9	Protestant Episcopal Church	229	2	2	310	1	5	30

MICHIGAN.

	DENOMINATION.	Total number of organizations.	Number of colored organizations.	Number of organizations reporting.	Total number reported.	Number of organizations reporting.	Male.	Female.
1	Total	775	43	43	3,235	43	1,188	2,047
	Baptist bodies:							
2	Baptists—Northern Convention	420	3	3	436	3	135	301
3	Baptists—National Convention (Colored)	14	14	14	747	14	293	454
	Disciples or Christians:							
4	Disciples of Christ	116	1	1	25	1	10	15
	Methodist bodies:							
5	African Methodist Episcopal Church	22	22	22	1,737	22	651	1,086
6	African Methodist Episcopal Zion Church	2	2	2	60	2	19	41
7	Protestant Episcopal Church	201	1	1	230	1	80	150

[1] Negroes or persons of negro descent.

OF CHURCH PROPERTY, DEBT ON CHURCH PROPERTY, PARSONAGES, AND SUNDAY SCHOOLS, BY DENOMINA-
STATE AND TERRITORY: 1906—Continued.

or in part colored organizations, as shown by the first two colums.]

LOUISIANA.

PLACES OF WORSHIP.					VALUE OF CHURCH PROPERTY.		DEBT ON CHURCH PROPERTY.		PARSONAGES.		SUNDAY SCHOOLS CONDUCTED BY CHURCH ORGANIZATIONS.				
Number of organizations reporting— Church edifices.	Number of organizations reporting— Halls, etc.	Number of church edifices reported.	Seating capacity of church edifices. Number of organizations reporting.	Seating capacity of church edifices. Seating capacity reported.	Number of organizations reporting.	Value reported.	Number of organizations reporting.	Amount of debt reported.	Number of organizations reporting.	Value of parsonages reported.	Number of organizations reporting.	Number of Sunday schools reported.	Number of officers and teachers.	Number of scholars.	
2,017	40	2,035	1,856	573,281	2,032	$2,796,242	559	$158,708	345	$224,112	1,927	2,001	10,194	92,266	1
1,375	25	1,381	1,313	401,961	1,385	1,651,607	267	81,061	94	57,552	1,320	1,353	6,806	62,828	2
7	......	7	6	2,150	7	3,275	......	......	1	100	5	5	19	108	3
4	......	4	1	200	4	1,350	......	......	1	150	......	......	......	......	4
13	1	13	13	4,750	13	42,850	5	1,140	6	7,000	15	20	86	873	5
240	2	240	150	44,810	239	460,575	148	39,995	133	85,100	228	244	1,320	13,253	6
171	6	175	171	52,220	174	261,305	77	19,829	71	39,335	168	175	958	7,600	7
39	1	39	37	9,695	41	31,925	19	1,291	6	4,500	32	32	199	1,183	8
163	5	168	160	55,095	164	249,125	42	14,692	30	23,925	154	166	791	5,974	9
3	......	4	3	1,200	3	3,450	1	700	1	450	3	4	8	102	10
2	......	4	2	1,200	2	90,780	......	......	2	6,000	2	2	7	350	11

MAINE.

1	......	1	1	200	1	$3,000	1	$1,600	......	......	1	1	8	30	1
1	......	1	1	200	1	3,000	1	1,600	......	......	1	1	8	30	2

MARYLAND.

595	14	612	552	154,672	592	$1,979,408	277	$314,861	188	$189,350	585	605	4,976	42,193	1
58	4	58	50	18,735	58	313,963	30	46,642	6	8,400	59	62	550	6,207	2
4	......	4	4	900	4	8,050	4	1,380	1	400	8	8	72	413	3
......	2	......	......	......	......	......	......	......	......	......	......	......	......	......	4
1	......	1	1	150	1	2,500	......	......	......	......	1	1	6	36	5
363	3	373	329	85,397	363	873,775	158	111,547	129	118,950	356	370	3,262	24,788	6
9	3	9	9	2,700	9	14,850	3	4,800	1	500	12	12	62	709	7
104	......	106	104	28,230	102	337,850	57	69,951	39	38,000	97	98	709	7,120	8
26	......	27	25	7,150	26	45,050	6	1,876	1	300	23	23	89	649	9
14	......	15	14	4,535	13	44,100	10	19,025	1	4,000	13	13	86	871	10
4	1	4	4	825	4	2,750	2	290	......	......	5	5	29	134	11
3	......	3	3	1,500	3	39,500	1	6,600	3	5,100	3	4	32	330	12
6	......	9	6	2,800	6	228,000	3	28,300	5	8,700	6	7	60	549	13
......	1	......	......	......	......	......	......	......	......	......	......	......	......	......	14
3	......	3	3	1,750	3	69,000	3	24,450	2	5,000	2	2	19	387	15

MASSACHUSETTS.

50	11	51	50	20,060	52	$646,425	35	$159,508	8	$22,050	58	58	613	5,069	1
3	......	4	3	1,260	3	33,000	1	5,000	1	600	3	3	35	259	2
21	2	21	21	9,575	23	284,050	19	94,494	1	3,000	26	26	283	2,520	3
......	2	......	......	......	......	......	......	......	......	......	......	......	......	......	4
3	4	3	3	790	3	10,800	1	900	1	3,000	6	6	51	358	5
2	1	2	2	500	2	12,000	......	......	......	......	3	3	17	135	6
13	1	13	13	4,750	12	154,350	8	17,500	4	12,950	11	11	101	756	7
6	1	6	6	2,785	7	104,025	5	39,614	1	2,500	7	7	109	893	8
2	......	2	2	400	2	48,200	1	2,000	......	......	2	2	17	148	9

MICHIGAN.

42	......	44	41	12,470	43	$167,950	19	$17,009	24	$27,060	42	42	363	1,910	1
3	......	3	3	1,050	3	22,900	1	375	1	1,500	3	3	32	258	2
13	......	13	13	3,460	14	31,950	5	1,625	4	3,700	13	13	99	498	3
1	......	1	1	100	1	1,000	......	......	......	......	1	1	5	25	4
22	......	23	21	6,710	22	97,400	12	13,609	18	16,860	22	22	210	1,082	5
2	......	2	2	750	2	4,700	1	1,400	......	......	2	2	7	27	6
1	......	2	1	400	1	10,000	......	......	1	5,000	1	1	10	50	7

TABLE 13.—COLORED[1] ORGANIZATIONS, SHOWING COMMUNICANTS OR MEMBERS, PLACES OF WORSHIP, VALUE TIONS (IN DETAIL), FOR EACH

[The statistics in this table refer to denominations comprising in whole

MINNESOTA.

	DENOMINATION.	Total number of organizations.	Number of colored organizations.	COMMUNICANTS OR MEMBERS. Number of organizations reporting.	Total number reported.	Sex. Number of organizations reporting.	Male.	Female.
1	Total	772	10	10	1,453	9	393	760
	Baptist bodies:							
2	Baptists—Northern Convention	248	2	2	540	2	187	353
	Methodist bodies:							
3	African Methodist Episcopal Church	5	5	5	755	4	172	283
	Presbyterian bodies:							
4	Presbyterian Church in the United States of America	296	1	1	23	1	7	16
5	Protestant Episcopal Church	223	2	2	135	2	27	108

MISSISSIPPI.

	DENOMINATION.	Total number of organizations.	Number of colored organizations.	Number of organizations reporting.	Total number reported.	Number of organizations reporting.	Male.	Female.
1	Total	4,463	3,877	3,863	358,708	3,657	121,925	220,909
	Adventist bodies:							
2	Advent Christian Church	7	1	1	31	1	14	17
3	Seventh-day Adventist Denomination	21	4	4	77	4	29	48
	Baptist bodies:							
4	Baptists—National Convention (Colored)	2,236	2,236	2,232	240,982	2,155	81,291	153,035
5	Free Baptists	47	39	39	2,067	38	719	1,273
6	Colored Primitive Baptists in America	27	27	27	554	10	71	89
	Churches of the Living God (Colored):							
7	Church of the Living God (Christian Workers for Friendship)	5	5	5	253	5	104	149
8	Congregationalists	7	7	7	595	6	246	341
	Disciples or Christians:							
9	Disciples of Christ	105	8	8	482	8	197	285
10	Churches of Christ	47	1	1	41	1	11	30
	Methodist bodies:							
11	Methodist Episcopal Church	564	557	552	50,130	472	16,631	27,540
12	Union American Methodist Episcopal Church (Colored)	6	6	6	122	6	49	73
13	African Methodist Episcopal Church	460	460	460	28,797	455	9,983	18,352
14	African Methodist Episcopal Zion Church	144	144	144	5,602	144	2,131	3,471
15	Colored Methodist Episcopal Church	348	348	346	25,814	328	9,573	14,713
	Presbyterian bodies:							
16	Presbyterian Church in the United States of America	6	6	6	192	6	63	129
17	Presbyterian Church in the United States	262	22	19	408	13	116	180
18	Protestant Episcopal Church	81	2	2	900	2	325	575
19	Roman Catholic Church	90	4	4	1,661	3	372	609

MISSOURI.

	DENOMINATION.	Total number of organizations.	Number of colored organizations.	Number of organizations reporting.	Total number reported.	Number of organizations reporting.	Male.	Female.
1	Total	3,780	655	651	50,074	625	15,514	30,197
	Baptist bodies:							
2	Baptists—National Convention (Colored)	288	288	288	22,136	278	7,094	13,235
3	Free Baptists	121	32	32	1,531	32	628	903
4	Church of God and Saints of Christ (Colored)	1	1	1	34	1	11	23
	Churches of the Living God (Colored):							
5	Church of the Living God (Christian Workers for Friendship)	1	1	1	75	1	25	50
6	Church of Christ in God	2	2	2	620	2	328	292
	Disciples or Christians:							
7	Disciples of Christ	1,424	17	17	979	17	347	632
	Methodist bodies:							
8	Methodist Episcopal Church	1,009	115	111	8,254	99	1,806	4,185
9	African Methodist Episcopal Church	154	154	154	11,318	150	3,603	7,422
10	African Methodist Episcopal Zion Church	11	11	11	1,765	11	396	1,369
11	Colored Methodist Episcopal Church	24	24	24	1,980	24	696	1,284
	Presbyterian bodies:							
12	Colored Cumberland Presbyterian Church	3	3	3	410	3	170	240
13	Presbyterian Church in the United States	160	3	3	102	3	38	64
14	Protestant Episcopal Church	125	3	3	355	3	129	226
15	Roman Catholic Church	457	1	1	515	1	243	272

MONTANA.

	DENOMINATION.	Total number of organizations.	Number of colored organizations.	Number of organizations reporting.	Total number reported.	Number of organizations reporting.	Male.	Female.
1	Total	6	6	6	135	6	35	100
	Methodist bodies:							
2	African Methodist Episcopal Church	6	6	6	135	6	35	100

[1] Negroes or persons of negro descent.

OF CHURCH PROPERTY, DEBT ON CHURCH PROPERTY, PARSONAGES, AND SUNDAY SCHOOLS, BY DENOMINA-
STATE AND TERRITORY: 1906—Continued.

or in part colored organizations, as shown by the first two columns.]

MINNESOTA.

PLACES OF WORSHIP.					VALUE OF CHURCH PROPERTY.		DEBT ON CHURCH PROPERTY.		PARSONAGES.		SUNDAY SCHOOLS CONDUCTED BY CHURCH ORGANIZATIONS.				
Number of organizations reporting—		Number of church edifices reported.	Seating capacity of church edifices.		Number of organizations reporting.	Value reported.	Number of organizations reporting.	Amount of debt reported.	Number of organizations reporting.	Value of parsonages reported.	Number of organizations reporting.	Number of Sunday schools reported.	Number of officers and teachers.	Number of scholars.	
Church edifices.	Halls, etc.		Number of organizations reporting.	Seating capacity reported.											
9	......	9	9	2,755	9	$74,300	5	$5,362	3	$7,700	8		78	497	1
2	......	2	2	1,000	2	40,000	......	......	......	......	2		29	230	2
5	......	5	5	1,375	5	28,500	.	4,462	2	5,200	[illegible]	[illegible]	30	155	3
......	......	......	......	......	......	......	......	......	......	......	1	1	5	12	4
2	......	2	2	380	2	5,800	1	900	1	2,500	2	2	14	100	5

MISSISSIPPI.

3,744	74	3,800	3,588	1,093,415	3,741	$3,524,880	857	$139,001	339	$213,641	3,594	3,711	19,590	168,184	1
1	......	1	1	200	1	300	......	......	......	......	1	1	4	14	2
2	......	2	1	43	1	900	......	......	......	......	3	3	12	54	3
2,188	37	2,191	2,1	626,434	2,186	1,970,237	298	59,102	55	41,330	2,100	2,142	10,799	104,825	4
38	1	38	24	13,540	36	21,680	8	579	1	150	36	39	135	1,041	5
13	6	13	38	1,150	12	4,900	......	......	......	......	......	......	......	......	6
5	......	5	5	850	5	3,200	1	360	......	......	5	5	14	87	7
6	1	6	6	2,300	7	19,331	2	120		200	6	10	40	741	8
8	......	8	5	1,500	7	12,485	3	500		800	8	8	25	217	9
1	......	1	1	300	1	400	1	125	......	......	1	1	1	25	10
544	2	559	481	147,923	542	512,125	200	29,291	140	72,936	533	565	3,689	27,833	11
2	4	2	1	75	1	200	1	100	......	......	6	6	30	182	12
442	11	471	438	131,337	440	436,267	173	28,482	91	51,840	421	434	2,418	16,437	13
135	6	137	129	40,880	136	117,605	71	8,537	17	6,585	127	129	742	3,952	14
336	5	342	336	120,458	341	291,050	93	7,990	26	10,050	320	340	1,548	11,482	15
4	1	4	4	1,200	5	5,800	2	1,015	......	......	6	7	39	378	16
13	......	13	8	2,075	14	6,400	3	300	2	1,050	17	17	56	466	17
2	......	3	2	1,850	2	78,000	......	......	2	21,200	2	2	31	260	18
4	......	4	4	1,300	4	44,000	1	2,500	3	7,500	2	2	7	190	19

MISSOURI.

600	38	617	584	153,914	605	$1,690,119	202	$229,805	173	$123,890	588	597	3,650	22,912	1
262	18	264		70,181	263	712,450	73	95,534	21	30,850	269	269	1,592	9,709	2
28	1	28		5,255	29	26,800	4	2,927	3	1,100	26	26	133	806	3
......	1	......	258 28	......	......	......	......	......	......	......	......	......	......	......	4
......	1	......	......	......	......	......	......	......	......	......	1	1	4	30	5
2	......	2	2	550	2	6,500	......	......	......	......	2	3	9	190	6
14	3	14	14	3,600	15	25,830	4	8,885	......	......	13	13	94	511	7
111	2	122	99	23,784	112	262,134	40	41,602	56	27,200	103	109	657	3,999	8
140	11	142	140	38,060	141	462,105	62	50,291	81	53,415	132	134	903	5,467	9
10	1	10	10	3,460	10	70,400	7	21,250	2	2,250	11	11	63	700	10
24	......	25	24	6,064	24	46,550	8	4,332	8	4,525	22	22	150	1,073	11
3	......	3	3	1,060	3	21,250	1	100	......	......		3	12	125	12
2	......	2	2	700	2	7,100	2	3,184	1	350		2	11	76	13
3	......	4	3	960	3	41,000	......	......	1	4,200		3	18	156	14
1	......	1	1	270	1	8,000	1	1,700	......	......	[illegible]	1	4	70	15

MONTANA.

6	......	6	6	1,175	6	$11,650	4	$432	4	$3,600	5	5	30	134	1
6	......	6	6	1,175	6	11,650	4	432	4	3,600	5	5	30	134	2

TABLE 13.—COLORED[1] ORGANIZATIONS, SHOWING COMMUNICANTS OR MEMBERS, PLACES OF WORSHIP, VALUE TIONS (IN DETAIL), FOR EACH

[The statistics in this table refer to denominations comprising in whole

NEBRASKA.

	DENOMINATION.	Total number of organizations.	Number of colored organizations.	COMMUNICANTS OR MEMBERS. Number of organizations reporting.	Total number reported.	Sex. Number of organizations reporting.	Male.	Female.
1	Total	1,266	12	12	1,007	9	308	567
	Baptist bodies:							
2	Baptists—Northern Convention	210	2	2	305	1	100	200
	Disciples or Christians:							
3	Disciples of Christ	178	1	1	20	1	12	8
	Methodist bodies:							
4	Methodist Episcopal Church	746	2	2	58	2	21	37
5	African Methodist Episcopal Church	6	6	6	509	5	175	322
6	Protestant Episcopal Church	126	1	1	115			

NEW HAMPSHIRE.

	DENOMINATION.	Total number of organizations.	Number of colored organizations.	COMMUNICANTS OR MEMBERS. Number of organizations reporting.	Total number reported.	Sex. Number of organizations reporting.	Male.	Female.
1	Total	1	1	1	20	1	8	12
	Baptist bodies:							
2	Baptists—National Convention (Colored)	1	1	1	20	1	8	12

NEW JERSEY.

	DENOMINATION.	Total number of organizations.	Number of colored organizations.	COMMUNICANTS OR MEMBERS. Number of organizations reporting.	Total number reported.	Sex. Number of organizations reporting.	Male.	Female.
1	Total	1,787	259	257	28,015	255	8,924	18,430
	Baptist bodies:							
2	Baptists—Northern Convention	286	19	19	3,758	18	1,470	2,237
3	Baptists—National Convention (Colored)	70	70	69	9,884	69	2,899	6,985
4	Church of God and Saints of Christ (Colored)	5	5	5	253	5	62	191
5	Congregationalists	44	1	1	148	1	52	96
	Methodist bodies:							
6	Methodist Episcopal Church	634	21	21	1,918	21	703	1,215
7	Union American Methodist Episcopal Church (Colored)	15	15	15	538	15	220	318
8	African Methodist Episcopal Church	69	69	69	5,971	69	1,891	4,080
9	African Union Methodist Protestant Church	12	12	12	1,575	12	583	992
10	African Methodist Episcopal Zion Church	35	35	34	2,180	34	702	1,478
	Presbyterian bodies:							
11	Presbyterian Church in the United States of America	346	6	6	475	6	153	322
12	Protestant Episcopal Church	271	6	6	1,315	5	189	516

NEW MEXICO.

	DENOMINATION.	Total number of organizations.	Number of colored organizations.	COMMUNICANTS OR MEMBERS. Number of organizations reporting.	Total number reported.	Sex. Number of organizations reporting.	Male.	Female.
1	Total	63	7	7	221	7	68	153
	Baptist bodies:							
2	Baptists—Northern Convention	57	1	1	45	1	23	22
3	Baptists—National Convention (Colored)	1	1	1	11	1	4	7
	Methodist bodies:							
4	African Methodist Episcopal Church	2	2	2	83	2	20	63
5	Colored Methodist Episcopal Church	3	3	3	82	3	21	61

NEW YORK.

	DENOMINATION.	Total number of organizations.	Number of colored organizations.	COMMUNICANTS OR MEMBERS. Number of organizations reporting.	Total number reported.	Sex. Number of organizations reporting.	Male.	Female.
1	Total	6,648	203	202	30,482	187	9,782	17,854
	Adventist bodies:							
2	Seventh-day Adventist Denomination	99	2	2	74	2	14	60
	Baptist bodies:							
3	Baptists—Northern Convention	924	30	30	11,157	28	3,569	7,368
4	Baptists—National Convention (Colored)	13	13	13	1,763	12	615	1,114
5	Church of God and Saints of Christ (Colored)	7	7	7	102	7	30	72
6	Congregationalists	302	1	1	24	1	10	14
7	Independent churches	86	1	1	20	1	5	15
	Methodist bodies:							
8	Methodist Episcopal Church	2,199	7	7	1,303	6	527	728
9	Union American Methodist Episcopal Church (Colored)	7	7	7	318	7	137	181
10	African Methodist Episcopal Church	41	41	41	4,294	40	1,033	1,661
11	African Union Methodist Protestant Church	3	3	3	115	3	40	75
12	African Methodist Episcopal Zion Church	76	76	75	6,149	69	2,015	3,817
	Moravian bodies:							
13	Moravian Church (Unitas Fratrum)	9	1	1	299	1	113	186
	Presbyterian bodies:							
14	Presbyterian Church in the United States of America	831	5	5	960	4	277	473
15	Protestant Episcopal Church	843	8	8	1,779	5	402	900
16	Roman Catholic Church	1,208	1	1	2,125	1	935	1,190

[1] Negroes or persons of negro descent.

OF CHURCH PROPERTY, DEBT ON CHURCH PROPERTY, PARSONAGES, AND SUNDAY SCHOOLS, BY DENOMINA-
STATE AND TERRITORY: 1906—Continued.

or in part colored organizations, as shown by the first two columns.]

NEBRASKA.

PLACES OF WORSHIP.					VALUE OF CHURCH PROPERTY.		DEBT ON CHURCH PROPERTY.		PARSONAGES.		SUNDAY SCHOOLS CONDUCTED BY CHURCH ORGANIZATIONS.				
Number of organizations reporting—Church edifices.	Number of organizations reporting—Halls, etc.	Number of church edifices reported.	Seating capacity of church edifices. Number of organizations reporting.	Seating capacity of church edifices. Seating capacity reported.	Number of organizations reporting.	Value reported.	Number of organizations reporting.	Amount of debt reported.	Number of organizations reporting.	Value of parsonages reported.	Number of organizations reporting.	Number of Sunday schools reported.	Number of officers and teachers.	Number of scholars.	
11	1	11	10	3,175	11	$73,500	5	$2,130	6	$7,100	11	11	101	589	1
2	......	2	1	500	2	18,000	1	670	2	1,600	1	1	14	100	2
1	......	1	1	200	1	3,000	1	750	......	......	1	1	7	17	3
2	......	2	2	450	2	5,200	1	60	1	300	2	2	10	41	4
5	1	5	5	1,775	5	29,300	2	650	2	2,200	6	6	59	371	5
1	......	1	1	250	1	18,000	......	......	1	3,000	1	1	11	60	6

NEW HAMPSHIRE.

......	......	......	......	......	......	......	......	......	......	......	1	1	3	24	1
......	......	......	......	......	......	......	......	......	......	......	1	1	3	24	2

NEW JERSEY.

234	20	240	233	72,443	239	$1,289,335	145	$231,632	57	$94,050	247	252	2,308	17,287	1
19	......	22	19	6,970	19	137,800	13	21,850	1	800	19	21	379	1,646	2
63	5	63	63	20,415	67	325,835	49	69,525	7	10,900	68	68	511	4,181	3
......	5	......	......	......	......	......	......	......	......	......	1	1	6	150	4
1	......	1	1	200	1	10,500	1	4,000	......	......	1	1	19	145	5
21	......	22	21	6,271	21	102,700	10	17,600	6	11,300	21	22	213	1,724	6
10	5	10	10	2,100	10	13,800	7	2,850	......	......	14	14	64	276	7
68	1	68	68	20,042	68	371,300	31	62,214	34	52,450	66	66	610	4,601	8
12	......	12	12	3,750	12	28,800	12	5,270	1	800	12	12	121	1,628	9
29	......	29	28	8,775	30	136,000	19	27,023	5	9,800	33	33	252	1,903	10
6	......	7	6	1,950	6	35,600	1	400	2	6,500	6	6	60	400	11
5	......	6	5	1,970	5	127,000	2	20,900	1	1,500	6	8	73	633	12

NEW MEXICO.

7	......	7	7	912	7	$10,050	3	$440	3	$1,800	7	8	33	135	1
1	......	1	1	100	1	500	......	......	......	......	1	1	2	13	2
1	......	1	1	100	1	800	......	......	......	......	1	1	2	9	3
2	......	2	2	450	2	5,000	1	300	2	1,500	2	2	12	59	4
3	......	3	3	262	3	3,750	2	140	1	300	3	4	17	54	5

NEW YORK.

169	27	173	163	59,542	169	$2,366,796	93	$513,412	52	$162,250	186	189	1,745	15,046	1
......	2	......	......	......	......	......	......	......	......	......	2	3	19	110	2
26	4	27	25	13,500	25	775,076	18	264,010	2	6,000	29	29	332	3,935	3
11	2	11	9	3,610	10	79,875	4	25,988	......	......	11	11	90	619	4
......	7	......	......	......	......	......	......	......	......	......	......	......	......	......	5
1	......	1	1	150	1	3,000	......	......	......	......	1	1	7	38	6
1	......	1	1	125	1	500	1	260	......	......	1	1	4	28	7
5	1	5	3	1,775	6	90,950	4	3,325	3	11,400	7	8	127	944	8
6	......	6	6	1,600	6	42,500	4	16,050	......	......	7	7	46	276	9
35	5	35	35	12,061	36	355,300	26	65,231	13	23,700	38	39	350	2,879	10
3	......	3	3	1,100	3	10,000	2	1,100	1	1,000	3	3	13	116	11
71	3	74	70	21,716	71	736,095	29	91,748	29	67,350	72	72	590	4,258	12
......	1	......	......	......	......	......	......	......	......	......	1	1	10	97	13
3	1	3	3	1,480	3	78,500	1	500	......	......	5	5	66	617	14
6	1	6	6	2,025	6	138,000	3	17,200	3	37,800	8	8	85	1,058	15
1	......	1	1	400	1	57,000	1	28,000	1	15,000	1	1	6	70	16

TABLE 13.—COLORED[1] ORGANIZATIONS, SHOWING COMMUNICANTS OR MEMBERS, PLACES OF WORSHIP, VALUE
TIONS (IN DETAIL), FOR EACH

[The statistics in this table refer to denominations comprising in whole

NORTH CAROLINA.

	DENOMINATION.	Total number of organizations.	Number of colored organizations.	COMMUNICANTS OR MEMBERS.				
				Number of organizations reporting.	Total number reported.	Sex.		
						Number of organizations reporting.	Male.	Female.
1	Total	3,970	2,813	2,797	283,707	2,580	105,067	165,644
	Adventist bodies:							
2	Seventh-day Adventist Denomination	13	3	3	31	2	9	22
	Baptist bodies:							
3	Baptists—National Convention (Colored)	1,163	1,163	1,155	153,189	1,140	59,158	92,525
4	Colored Primitive Baptists in America	62	62	62	2,215	15	154	432
5	United American Freewill Baptists (Colored)	133	133	129	10,099	45	2,106	2,647
6	Christians (Christian Connection)	192	86	85	6,558	85	2,931	3,627
7	Church of God and Saints of Christ (Colored)	2	2	2	32	2	9	23
8	Congregationalists	54	53	53	2,666	53	1,030	1,636
	Disciples or Christians:							
9	Disciples of Christ	128	9	9	873	9	361	512
	Lutheran bodies:							
10	Evangelical Lutheran Synodical Conference of America	32	5	5	182	5	50	132
	Methodist bodies:							
11	Methodist Episcopal Church	358	173	173	10,953	152	3,708	6,233
12	Union American Methodist Episcopal Church (Colored)	1	1	1	20	1	9	11
13	African Methodist Episcopal Church	235	235	232	16,797	219	5,724	10,186
14	African Methodist Episcopal Zion Church	673	673	673	66,356	657	25,040	40,015
15	Colored Methodist Episcopal Church	39	39	39	2,209	39	876	1,333
16	Reformed Zion Union Apostolic Church (Colored)	6	6	6	130	6	62	68
	Moravian bodies:							
17	Moravian Church (Unitas Fratrum)	22	1	1	52	....	....	....
	Presbyterian bodies:							
18	Presbyterian Church in the United States of America	149	137	137	9,670	119	3,298	5,222
19	Presbyterian Church in the United States	424	4	4	95	4	34	61
20	Protestant Episcopal Church	258	27	27	1,526	25	484	929
21	Roman Catholic Church	31	1	1	54	1	24	30

OHIO.

	DENOMINATION.	Total number of organizations.	Number of colored organizations.	Number of organizations reporting.	Total number reported.	Number of organizations reporting.	Male.	Female.
1	Total	5,036	371	367	33,667	328	11,276	19,134
	Baptist bodies:							
2	Baptists—Northern Convention	474	1	1	73	1	30	43
3	Baptists—National Convention (Colored)	163	163	163	17,400	146	6,016	9,777
4	Free Baptists	82	4	4	65	....	....	....
	Churches of the Living God (Colored):							
5	Church of the Living God (Christian Workers for Friendship)	1	1	1	15	1	7	8
6	Congregationalists	253	2	2	264	2	84	180
	Disciples or Christians:							
7	Disciples of Christ	543	8	8	570	8	189	381
8	Churches of Christ	70	1	1	24	1	6	18
	Methodist bodies:							
9	Methodist Episcopal Church	2,409	35	35	2,912	25	820	1,309
10	African Methodist Episcopal Church	120	120	119	9,812	112	3,250	5,906
11	African Methodist Episcopal Zion Church	9	9	9	386	9	135	251
12	Wesleyan Methodist Connection of America	54	16	13	1,124	12	404	575
13	Colored Methodist Episcopal Church	4	4	4	211	4	97	114
	Presbyterian bodies:							
14	Presbyterian Church in the United States of America	656	1	1	67	1	21	46
15	Protestant Episcopal Church	192	5	5	446	5	132	314
16	Roman Catholic Church	606	1	1	298	1	85	213

OKLAHOMA.[1]

	DENOMINATION.	Total number of organizations.	Number of colored organizations.	Number of organizations reporting.	Total number reported.	Number of organizations reporting.	Male.	Female.
1	Total	1,444	618	616	29,115	595	11,397	16,918
	Baptist bodies:							
2	Baptists—National Convention (Colored)	305	305	305	16,952	298	6,769	9,762
3	Colored Primitive Baptists in America	5	5	5	100	4	35	60
4	United American Freewill Baptists (Colored)	1	1	1	50	1	25	25
5	Churches of God in North America, General Eldership of the	20	3	3	93	3	28	65
	Churches of the Living God (Colored):							
6	Church of the Living God (Christian Workers for Friendship)	4	4	4	79	4	35	44
7	Church of the Living God (Apostolic Church)	1	1	1	35	1	18	17
8	Free Christian Zion Church of Christ (Colored)	1	1	1	200	1	75	125
	Methodist bodies:							
9	Methodist Episcopal Church	479	39	38	1,580	32	587	828
10	African Methodist Episcopal Church	137	137	136	6,243	134	2,309	3,879
11	African Methodist Episcopal Zion Church	8	8	8	160	8	73	87
12	Colored Methodist Episcopal Church	86	86	86	2,858	83	1,125	1,602
	Presbyterian bodies:							
13	Presbyterian Church in the United States of America	179	24	24	456	22	173	260
14	Colored Cumberland Presbyterian Church	2	2	2	80	2	35	45
15	Protestant Episcopal Church	43	1	1	15	1	7	8
16	Roman Catholic Church	173	1	1	214	1	103	111

[1] Negroes or persons of negro descent.

OF CHURCH PROPERTY, DEBT ON CHURCH PROPERTY, PARSONAGES, AND SUNDAY SCHOOLS, BY DENOMINA- STATE AND TERRITORY: 1906—Continued.

or in part colored organizations, as shown by the first two columns.]

NORTH CAROLINA.

PLACES OF WORSHIP.					VALUE OF CHURCH PROPERTY.		DEBT ON CHURCH PROPERTY.		PARSONAGES.		SUNDAY SCHOOLS CONDUCTED BY CHURCH ORGANIZATIONS.				
Number of organizations reporting—		Number of church edifices reported.	Seating capacity of church edifices.		Number of organizations reporting.	Value reported.	Number of organizations reporting.	Amount of debt reported.	Number of organizations reporting.	Value of parsonages reported.	Number of organizations reporting.	Number of Sunday schools reported.	Number of officers and teachers.	Number of scholars.	
Church edifices.	Halls, etc.		Number of organizations reporting.	Seating capacity reported.											
2,565	52	2,593	2,510	860,675	2,610	$3,238,735	511	$127,879	232	$162,988	2,519	2,601	19,142	148,248	1
....		....	....	....	....	....	....	....	....	....	2	2	7	14	2
1,130	17	1,131	1,102	410,446	1,136	1,216,162	146	38,526	22	21,875	1,101	1,145	7,469	67,483	3
15	4	15	14	4,775	36	26,815	1	19	....	....	13	13	195	1,035	4
45	....	46	45	10,275	45	23,250	....	....	....	....	17	17	81	1,117	5
83	1	85	81	25,569	84	63,405	15	2,410	3	600	81	82	407	3,571	6
....	2	....	....	....	....	....	....	....	....	....	....	....	....	....	7
45	4	46	45	11,950	45	40,361	5	2,715	6	2,575	52	54	267	2,612	8
8	....	8	8	2,660	9	7,130	2	375	....	....	6	6	42	355	9
5	....	5	5	650	5	6,000	....	....	1	200	4	4	12	230	10
165	3	168	149	43,055	171	197,647	56	18,509	40	22,676	161	171	1,185	8,865	11
....	1	....	....	....	....	....	....	....	....	....	1	1	3	20	12
224	7	226	221	69,930	227	385,190	97	23,260	42	28,200	225	229	1,680	9,903	13
650	8	656	645	223,915	654	941,234	162	36,655	88	63,732	652	663	6,405	40,589	14
37	....	39	37	10,575	38	37,414	8	1,413	5	1,450	38	38	211	1,535	15
4	1	4	4	1,000	6	2,400	....	....	....	....	1	1	13	145	16
1	....	1	1	300	1	8,000	....	....	....	....	1	1	8	120	17
123	3	129	123	39,010	122	198,977	17	3,699	16	13,180	133	139	973	8,478	18
4	....	8	4	1,000	4	3,200	1	50	2	1,100	4	8	16	139	19
25	....	25	25	5,465	26	76,550	1	248	7	7,400	26	26	163	1,999	20
1	....	1	1	100	1	5,000	....	....	....	....	1	1	5	38	21

OHIO.

333	20	336	318	94,000	336	$1,473,251	132	$125,636	90	$106,286	343	347	2,721	18,470	1
1	....	1	1	200	1	5,000	1	2,900	....	....	1	1	7	41	2
145	8	147	141	43,316	147	596,371	44	59,164	19	20,100	153	156	1,194	8,378	3
....	....	....	....	....	....	....	....	....	....	....	....	....	....	....	4
											1	1	2	9	5
2	....	2	2	375	2	7,800	....	....	1	2,500	2	2	27	203	6
8	....	8	8	2,050	7	25,000	3	450	1	350	8	8	54	345	7
....		....	....	....	....	....	....	....	....	....	....	....	....	....	8
34	....	35	24	6,580	35	124,980	21	21,181	13	15,050	34	34	265	1,781	9
114	6	114	114	33,354	115	621,000	46	32,137	49	61,336	112	112	968	6,322	10
8	1	8	8	2,150	8	27,300	8	5,244	3	1,100	8	8	58	301	11
12	1	12	11	3,100	12	16,000	5	486	2	1,850	13	13	85	666	12
3	1	3	3	1,100	3	5,900	3	1,574	1	1,000	4	4	23	110	13
....	1	....	....	....	....	....	....	....	....	....	1	1	7	55	14
5	....	5	5	925	5	34,900	1	2,500	1	3,000	5	5	28	296	15
1	....	1	1	250	1	10,000	....	....	....	....	1	2	3	53	16

OKLAHOMA.[1]

534	56	553	517	116,991	543	$410,689	140	$31,957	58	$24,437	557	590	2,964	19,326	1
280	17	280	271	62,900	281	179,666	52	8,760	3	2,500	284	289	1,506	10,636	2
4	....	4	4	440	4	890	....	....	....	....	....	....	....	....	3
1	....	1	1	150	1	400	....	....	....	....	....	....	....	....	4
....	2	....	....	....	1	200	....	....	....	....	2	5	20	147	5
3	1	3	3	300	3	675	....	....	....	....	3	3	9	52	6
....	1	....	....	....	....	....	....	....	....	....	1	1	5	26	7
1	....	1	1	800	1	1,000	....	....	....	....	....	....	....	....	8
32	2	32	31	7,005	34	38,773	12	2,239	6	1,372	36	40	201	1,263	9
113	16	127	109	24,816	117	117,705	51	11,290	36	16,575	126	139	746	3,930	10
6	2	6	6	1 550	6	4,706	2	190	1	300	5	5	16	138	11
70	12	71	67	15 110	71	51,830	23	9,478	10	2,690	74	79	352	2,310	12
20	3	24	20	2,965	20	10,950	....	....	2	1,000	22	25	98	665	13
2	....	2	2	800	2	1,200	....	....	....	....	2	2	6	50	14
1	....	1	1	75	1	1,500	....	....	....	....	1	1	3	25	15
1	....	1	1	80	1	1,200	....	....	....	....	1	1	2	84	16

[1] Oklahoma and Indian Territory combined.

TABLE 13.—COLORED[1] ORGANIZATIONS, SHOWING COMMUNICANTS OR MEMBERS, PLACES OF WORSHIP, VALUE TIONS (IN DETAIL), FOR EACH

[The statistics in this table refer to denominations comprising in whole

OREGON.

	DENOMINATION.	Total number of organizations.	Number of colored organizations.	COMMUNICANTS OR MEMBERS.				
				Number of organizations reporting.	Total number reported.	Sex.		
						Number of organizations reporting.	Male.	Female.
1	Total	4	4	4	160	4	45	115
	Baptist bodies:							
2	Baptists—National Convention (Colored)	2	2	2	60	2	20	40
	Methodist bodies:							
3	African Methodist Episcopal Church	1	1	1	60	1	15	45
4	African Methodist Episcopal Zion Church	1	1	1	40	1	10	30

PENNSYLVANIA.

	DENOMINATION.	Total number of organizations.	Number of colored organizations.	Number of organizations reporting.	Total number reported.	Number of organizations reporting.	Male.	Female.
1	Total	7,127	429	428	60,161	412	20,613	34,661
	Adventist bodies:							
2	Seventh-day Adventist Denomination	66	1	1	23	1	10	13
	Baptist bodies:							
3	Baptists—Northern Convention	739	25	25	9,193	20	2,751	4,453
4	Baptists—National Convention (Colored)	103	103	103	20,309	100	7,312	11,651
5	Free Baptists	42	1	1	35	1	15	20
6	Colored Primitive Baptists in America	2	2	2	45	2	19	26
7	Church of God and Saints of Christ (Colored)	5	5	5	548	5	177	371
8	Churches of God in North America, General Eldership of the	178	5	4	67	4	28	39
	Lutheran bodies:							
9	General Council of the Evangelical Lutheran Church in North America	755	1	1	15	1	2	13
	Methodist bodies:							
10	Methodist Episcopal Church	2,379	15	15	3,631	15	1,371	2,260
11	Union American Methodist Episcopal Church (Colored)	22	22	22	1,647	22	703	944
12	African Methodist Episcopal Church	149	149	149	12,638	149	4,284	8,354
13	African Union Methodist Protestant Church	9	9	9	1,019	9	317	702
14	African Methodist Episcopal Zion Church	67	67	67	6,263	63	2,070	3,743
15	Colored Methodist Episcopal Church	5	5	5	466	5	204	262
	Presbyterian bodies:							
16	Presbyterian Church in the United States of America	1,075	6	6	536	4	47	117
17	Protestant Episcopal Church	489	10	10	1,841	8	311	860
	Reformed bodies:							
18	Reformed Church in America	10	1	1	40	1	15	25
19	Roman Catholic Church	1,032	2	2	1,785	2	977	808

RHODE ISLAND.

	DENOMINATION.	Total number of organizations.	Number of colored organizations.	Number of organizations reporting.	Total number reported.	Number of organizations reporting.	Male.	Female.
1	Total	159	20	20	2,114	17	569	1,098
	Baptist bodies:							
2	Baptists—Northern Convention	74	3	3	345	3	160	185
3	Baptists—National Convention (Colored)	4	4	4	624	4	212	412
4	Free Baptists	28	1	1	175	1	50	125
5	Church of God and Saints of Christ (Colored)	1	1	1	64	1	13	51
6	Congregationalists	42	1	1	82	1	32	50
	Methodist bodies:							
7	Union American Methodist Episcopal Church (Colored)	1	1	1	20	1	5	15
8	African Methodist Episcopal Church	6	6	6	542	4	79	208
9	African Methodist Episcopal Zion Church	3	3	3	262	2	18	52

SOUTH CAROLINA.

	DENOMINATION.	Total number of organizations.	Number of colored organizations.	Number of organizations reporting.	Total number reported.	Number of organizations reporting.	Male.	Female.
1	Total	3,048	2,860	2,853	394,149	2,769	142,868	240,626
	Baptist bodies:							
2	Baptists—National Convention (Colored)	1,317	1,317	1,317	219,841	1,296	76,071	138,702
3	Church of God and Saints of Christ (Colored)	1	1	1	8	1	2	6
4	Congregationalists	7	6	6	377	6	131	246
	Disciples or Christians:							
5	Disciples of Christ	41	6	6	202	5	66	113
	Methodist bodies:							
6	Methodist Episcopal Church	395	395	393	54,097	364	20,287	30,478
7	African Methodist Episcopal Church	632	632	628	79,220	626	31,160	47,965
8	African Methodist Episcopal Zion Church	193	193	193	19,058	189	7,368	11,065
9	Methodist Protestant Church	33	11	11	683	11	278	405
10	Colored Methodist Episcopal Church	72	72	72	4,850	72	1,942	2,908
11	Reformed Methodist Union Episcopal Church (Colored)	56	56	55	4,235	55	1,719	2,516
	Presbyterian bodies:							
12	Presbyterian Church in the United States of America	111	111	111	8,026	92	2,588	4,161
13	Protestant Episcopal Church	118	21	21	1,130	13	330	566
14	Reformed Episcopal Church	38	38	38	2,252	38	833	1,419
15	Roman Catholic Church	34	1	1	170	1	94	76

[1] Negroes or persons of negro descent.

OF CHURCH PROPERTY, DEBT ON CHURCH PROPERTY, PARSONAGES, AND SUNDAY SCHOOLS, BY DENOMINA-
STATE AND TERRITORY: 1906—Continued.

or in part colored organizations, as shown by the first two columns.]

OREGON.

PLACES OF WORSHIP.					VALUE OF CHURCH PROPERTY.		DEBT ON CHURCH PROPERTY.		PARSONAGES.		SUNDAY SCHOOLS CONDUCTED BY CHURCH ORGANIZATIONS.				
Number of organizations reporting— Church edifices.	Number of organizations reporting— Halls, etc.	Number of church edifices reported.	Seating capacity of church edifices. Number of organizations reporting.	Seating capacity of church edifices. Seating capacity reported.	Number of organizations reporting.	Value reported.	Number of organizations reporting.	Amount of debt reported.	Number of organizations reporting.	Value of parsonages reported.	Number of organizations reporting.	Number of Sunday schools reported.	Number of officers and teachers.	Number of scholars.	
3	1	3	3	900	3	$44,000	3	$3,950	2	$3,000	3	3	15	85	1
1	1	1	1	500	1	15,000	1	1,200	......	......	1	1	4	30	2
1	......	1	1	150	1	4,000	1	2,400	1	1,000	1	1	6	25	3
1	......	1	1	250	1	25,000	1	350	1	2,000	1	1	5	30	4

PENNSYLVANIA.

377	51	387	372	126,988	380	$3,494,205	246	$597,809	98	$248,700	404	408	3,742	35,766	1
......	1	......	......	......	......	......	......	......	......	......	1	1	10	19	2
23	1	25	20	9,350	21	288,900	13	48,288	4	13,500	21	21	275	3,469	3
82	21	85	81	30,928	83	851,200	48	171,013	8	28,700	101	101	872	8,611	4
1	......	1	1	150	1	3,100	......	......	......	......	1	1	5	40	5
2	......	2	2	700	2	7,200	1	2,500	......	......	......	......	......	......	6
......	5	......	......	......	......	......	......	......	......	......	......	......	......	......	7
3	2	3	3	600	4	3,350	1	400	......	......	2	2	6	38	8
1	......	1	1	300	1	5,000	1	140	......	......	1	1	3	25	9
11	4	12	11	5,825	13	257,800	10	93,025	4	11,200	15	15	260	4,796	10
19		19	19	5,980	19	65,400	14	11,125	2	4,400	22	22	150	1,150	11
143	6	143	143	42,765	144	985,790	103	196,194	51	101,450	143	145	1,374	10,683	12
9	......	9	9	3,330	9	48,000	7	7,016	......	......	9	9	73	915	13
61	6	62	60	18,285	61	339,630	38	36,308	21	37,650	65	66	513	3,672	14
5	......	5	5	2,125	5	29,535	3	2,300	1	6,000	5	5	28	355	15
6	......	6	6	1,550	6	49,500	2	5,400	3	8,300	6	6	67	581	16
9	1	12	9	4,000	9	504,900	4	16,100	2	11,500	9	10	88	1,160	17
......	1	......	......	......	......	......	......	......	......	......	1	1	9	52	18
2	......	2	2	1,100	2	55,000	1	8,000	2	26,000	2	2	9	200	19

RHODE ISLAND.

18	2	19	18	7,700	18	$184,346	15	$37,350	3	$10,500	17	17	202	1,557	1
	......	3	3	1,250	3	14,500	2	2,300	2	5,500	3	3	36	224	2
	......	4	4	2,100	4	41,146	3	13,500	1	5,000	4	4	46	372	3
1	......	1	1	350	1	10,000	1	150	......	......	1	1	26	200	4
......	1	......	......	......	......	......	......	......	......	......	......	......	......	......	5
1	......	2	1	350	1	5,000	1	2,300	......	......	1	1	10	40	6
1	......	1	1		1	1,000	1	450	......	......		1	6	62	7
6	......	6	6	2,250	6	59,700	5	5,650	......	......	1	4	42	320	8
2	1	2	2	1,200	2	53,000	2	13,000	......	......	3	3	36	339	9

SOUTH CAROLINA.

2,801	32	2,853	2,724	995,462	2,808	$3,366,223	666	$145,878	353	$227,963	2,779	2,896	19,808	188,497	1
1,304	8	1,310	1,272	487,016	1,309	1,404,648	202	45,816	29	20,015	1,286	1,315	8,242	89,200	2
......	1	......	......	......	......	......	......	......	......	......	......	......	......	......	3
6	......	6	6	1,950	6	11,935	1	2,000	2	6,000	6	6	35	388	4
4	......	5	3	450	5	3,875	1	50	......	......	4	5	12	81	5
387	6	406	360	128,	386	527,700	106	15,553	95	68,598	382	424	3,139	30,970	6
627	3	635	617	209,	628	780,447	222	53,428	145	85,175	621	646	5,225	44,187	7
183	9	186	182	79,	186	261,770	47	10,405	18	12,100	191	192	1,506	10,075	8
8	1	8	5	1,	8	3,800	4	95	2	125	9	11	47	396	9
71	1	74	70	22,400	72	106,251	22	7,579	16	9,525	68	72	381	2,828	10
56	......	57	56	18,[illegible]	56	34,765	25	3,740	8	2,275	52	52	196	1,757	11
106	1	111	104	,634	101	144,145	23	6,069	29	18,900	107	119	741	6,003	12
12	......	12	12	36,605	12	56,600	......	......	2	1,900	19	19	123	1,146	13
36	2	42	36	9,948	38	28,287	13	1,143	7	3,350	33	34	159	1,326	14
1	......	1	1	200	1	2,000	......	......	......	......	1	1	2	80	15

TABLE 13.—COLORED[1] ORGANIZATIONS, SHOWING COMMUNICANTS OR MEMBERS, PLACES OF WORSHIP, VALUE TIONS (IN DETAIL), FOR EACH

[The statistics in this table refer to denominations comprising in whole

SOUTH DAKOTA.

	DENOMINATION.	Total number of organizations.	Number of colored organizations.	COMMUNICANTS OR MEMBERS. Number of organizations reporting.	Total number reported.	Sex. Number of organizations reporting.	Male.	Female.
1	Total	2	2	2	38	2	15	23
	Methodist bodies:							
2	African Methodist Episcopal Church	2	2	2	38	2	15	23

TENNESSEE.

	DENOMINATION.	Total number of organizations.	Number of colored organizations.	COMMUNICANTS OR MEMBERS. Number of organizations reporting.	Total number reported.	Sex. Number of organizations reporting.	Male.	Female.
1	Total	3,691	1,879	1,855	172,867	1,726	59,645	106,318
	Adventist bodies:							
2	Advent Christian Church			1	41	1	19	22
3	Seventh-day Adventist Denomination		3	3	58	3	17	41
	Baptist bodies:	11						
4	Baptists—National Convention (Colored)	739	7	757	93,303	740	32,334	59,658
5	Free Baptists	30	59	6	432	5	176	236
6	Colored Primitive Baptists in America	96	96	93	3,268	28	315	631
	Churches of the Living God (Colored):							
7	Church of the Living God (Christian Workers for Friendship)		8	8	690	8	244	446
8	Church of the Living God (Apostolic Church)		3	2	142	2	57	85
9	Church of Christ in God		2	2	86	2	30	56
10	Congregationalists	48	7	7	1,039	7	427	612
	Disciples or Christians:							
11	Disciples of Christ	150	2	2	58	2	24	34
12	Churches of Christ	631	28	28	886	28	329	557
	Methodist bodies:							
13	Methodist Episcopal Church	799	218	208	13,450	171	3,969	7,838
14	African Methodist Episcopal Church	309	309	306	23,377	304	8,238	14,904
15	African Methodist Episcopal Zion Church	117	117	117	6,651	117	2,186	4,465
16	Colored Methodist Episcopal Church	209	209	209	20,634	200	7,715	12,207
	Presbyterian bodies:							
17	Presbyterian Church in the United States of America	92	20	20	1,130	18	390	674
18	Colored Cumberland Presbyterian Church	79	79	79	6,640	79	3,048	3,592
19	Presbyterian Church in the United States	188	1	1	94	1	40	54
20	Associate Reformed Synod of the South	14	1	1	18	1	7	11
21	Protestant Episcopal Church	103	9	9	275	9	80	195
22	Roman Catholic Church	25	1	1	595	....	....	....

TEXAS.

	DENOMINATION.	Total number of organizations.	Number of colored organizations.	COMMUNICANTS OR MEMBERS. Number of organizations reporting.	Total number reported.	Sex. Number of organizations reporting.	Male.	Female.
1	Total	5,051	3,047	3,035	227,032	2,905	81,805	138,755
	Adventist bodies:							
2	Seventh-day Adventist Denomination	29	2	2	58	2	12	46
	Baptist bodies:							
3	Baptists—National Convention (Colored)	1,763	1,763	1,761	144,878	1,711	53,775	88,770
4	Colored Primitive Baptists in America	43	43	43	1,280	15	195	323
	Churches of the Living God (Colored):							
5	Church of the Living God (Christian Workers for Friendship)		4	4	405	4	125	280
6	Church of the Living God (Apostolic Church)	4	2	2	173	2	71	102
7	Congregationalists	28	5	5	220	5	69	151
	Disciples or Christians:							
8	Disciples of Christ	503	16	16	1,082	16	411	671
9	Churches of Christ	627	1	1	35	1	15	20
	Methodist bodies:							
10	Methodist Episcopal Church	568	419	413	28	379	9,077	16,615
11	African Methodist Episcopal Church	442	442	440	24	429	8,304	16,249
12	African Methodist Episcopal Zion Church	11	11	11		11	193	264
13	Methodist Protestant Church	236	22	20	,200	18	276	447
14	Colored Methodist Episcopal Church	288	288	288	18,[illegible]	283	6,289	11,757
	Presbyterian bodies:							
15	Presbyterian Church in the United States of America		1	1	45	1	1	44
16	Colored Cumberland Presbyterian Church	58	21	21	2,091	21	1,204	887
17	Protestant Episcopal Church	125	3	3	217	3	82	135
18	Roman Catholic Church	255	4	4	3,700	4	1,706	1,994

UTAH.

	DENOMINATION.	Total number of organizations.	Number of colored organizations.	COMMUNICANTS OR MEMBERS. Number of organizations reporting.	Total number reported.	Sex. Number of organizations reporting.	Male.	Female.
1	Total	1	1	1	30	1	7	23
	Methodist bodies:							
2	African Methodist Episcopal Church	1	1	1	30	1	7	23

[1] Negroes or persons of negro descent.

OF CHURCH PROPERTY, DEBT ON CHURCH PROPERTY, PARSONAGES, AND SUNDAY SCHOOLS, BY DENOMINA-
STATE AND TERRITORY: 1906—Continued.

or in part colored organizations, as shown by the first two columns.]

SOUTH DAKOTA.

PLACES OF WORSHIP.					VALUE OF CHURCH PROPERTY.		DEBT ON CHURCH PROPERTY.		PARSONAGES.		SUNDAY SCHOOLS CONDUCTED BY CHURCH ORGANIZATIONS.				
Number of organizations reporting—		Number of church edifices reported.	Seating capacity of church edifices.		Number of organizations reporting.	Value reported.	Number of organizations reporting.	Amount of debt reported.	Number of organizations reporting.	Value of parsonages reported.	Number of organizations reporting.	Number of Sunday schools reported.	Number of officers and teachers.	Number of scholars.	
Church edifices.	Halls, etc.		Number of organizations reporting.	Seating capacity reported.											
1	....	1	1	150	2	$3,900	1	$1,700	1	$1,800	2	2	9	32	1
1	....	1	1	150	2	3,900	1	1,700	1	1,800	2	2	9	32	2

TENNESSEE.

1,735	69	1,808	1,644	530,457	1,743	$2,681,502	364	$136,630	199	$109,270	1,677	1,729	9,513	76,021	1
1	....	1	1	500	1	3,500	....	....	....	....	1	1	4	13	2
2	....	2	1	125	1	425	....	....	....	....	2	2	13	45	3
729	21	729	707	228,223	736	1,208,610	91	53,639	30	31,100	732	740	3,917	31,828	4
4	1	4	4	890	4	5,450	1	30	....	....	6	9	36	255	5
50	8	50	23	7,163	52	28,747	3	440	1	20	10	10	54	426	6
5	3	5	5	2,300	5	5,050	1	150	....	....	8	8	24	217	7
1	2	1	....	....	1	10,000	....	....	....	....	2	2	10	53	8
1	1	1	1	400	1	1,000	....	....	....	....	1	1	5	39	9
5	2	5	4	1,450	6	65,800	1	1,200	2	3,000	7	8	79	757	10
1	1	1	1	300	1	1,500	....	....	....	....	1	1	6	26	11
17	11	17	17	4,000	17	9,450	2	335	....	....	12	12	30	238	12
200	5	210	166	46,812	202	228,040	73	24,272	48	19,100	194	210	1,197	9,606	13
289	6	339	297	93,529	296	376,279	82	21,624	61	18,315	285	296	1,673	12,677	14
108	5	119	107	31,160	110	189,221	26	8,879	12	7,200	111	111	614	4,371	15
204	2	214	202	76,275	203	416,325	78	24,646	38	23,085	198	209	1,337	11,631	16
18	....	20	18	4,595	18	29,850	1	400	3	2,650	20	20	127	923	17
79	....	79	79	30,735	78	71,155	5	1,015	1	800	77	77	355	2,466	18
1	....	1	1	250	1	3,000	....	....	1	1,500	1	1	4	45	19
1	....	1	1	300	1	200	....	....	....	....	1	1	2	35	20
8	1	8	8	1,150	8	20,900	....	....	2	3,000	8	10	26	370	21
1	....	1	1	300	1	7,000	....	....	....	....	....	....	....	....	22

TEXAS.

2,822	156	2,860	2,692	767,698	2,833	$3,106,101	646	$148,797	404	$201,660	2,762	2,845	16,212	122,800	1
2	....	2	2	180	2	1,124	....	....	....	....	2	2	14	59	2
1,664	75	1,669	1,618	457,324	1,669	1,575,930	285	65,574	75	44,075	1,608	1,647	8,955	75,525	3
28	6	28	13	3,165	29	17,735	2	353	....	....	7	7	29	203	4
3	1	3	3	650	3	2,150	1	800	....	....	4	4	10	95	5
2	....	2	2	700	2	1,500	....	....	1	500	2	2	9	261	6
4	1	5	3	1,000	4	8,625	1	400	2	2,200	5	6	31	240	7
15	....	16	15	3,585	14	12,530	3	1,800	....	....	13	15	90	468	8
....	1	....	....	....	....	....	....	....	....	....	1	1	1	45	9
376	21	385	337	90,544	382	560,052	135	19,502	139	66,680	395	403	2,833	18,932	10
407	27	424	391	113,978	407	509,922	153	53,033	130	54,905	390	409	2,419	14,563	11
11	....	13	11	3,540	11	12,380	3	83	1	200	10	15	78	316	12
15	3	15	13	2,950	16	16,476	8	365	1	100	17	20	74	583	13
266	21	269	257	82,182	266	312,195	55	6,887	48	23,900	279	284	1,556	10,238	14
1	....	1	1	300	....	....	....	....	....	....	1	2	10	360	15
21	....	21	19	5,850	21	12,982	....	....	....	....	21	21	84	672	16
3	....	3	3	610	3	12,000	....	....	3	1,900	3	3	10	95	17
4	....	4	4	1,140	4	50,500	....	....	4	7,200	4	4	9	145	18

UTAH.

1	....	1	1	300	1	$4,000	1	$216	....	....	1	1	10	30	1
1	....	1	1	300	1	4,000	1	216	....	....	1	1	10	30	2

TABLE 13.—COLORED[1] ORGANIZATIONS, SHOWING COMMUNICANTS OR MEMBERS, PLACES OF WORSHIP, VALUE TIONS (IN DETAIL), FOR EACH

[The statistics in this table refer to denominations comprising in whole

VIRGINIA.

	DENOMINATION.	Total number of organizations.	Number of colored organizations.	COMMUNICANTS OR MEMBERS.				
				Number of organizations reporting.	Total number reported.	Sex.		
						Number of organizations reporting.	Male.	Female.
1	Total	3,037	1,983	1,974	307,374	1,817	116,271	175,333
	Adventist bodies:							
2	Seventh-day Adventist Denomination	25	4	4	70	4	19	51
	Baptist bodies:							
3	Baptists—National Convention (Colored)	1,374	1,374	1,368	268,206	1,312	102,392	153,459
4	Free Baptists	7	7	7	425	7	167	258
5	Colored Primitive Baptists in America	65	65	64	1,588	13	102	176
6	Christians (Christian Connection)	74	5	5	877	5	390	487
7	Church of God and Saints of Christ (Colored)	10	10	10	260	10	68	192
	Disciples or Christians:							
8	Disciples of Christ	277	9	9	787	9	328	459
9	Independent churches	17	1	1	30	1	11	19
	Methodist bodies:							
10	Methodist Episcopal Church	319	154	154	10,171	138	3,581	5,947
11	African Methodist Episcopal Church	117	117	116	9,889	115	3,845	6,034
12	African Union Methodist Protestant Church	5	5	5	515	5	224	291
13	African Methodist Episcopal Zion Church	75	75	75	5,474	75	2,163	3,311
14	Colored Methodist Episcopal Church	34	34	34	1,514	34	558	956
15	Reformed Zion Union Apostolic Church (Colored)	39	39	39	2,929	30	1,077	1,556
	Presbyterian bodies:							
16	Presbyterian Church in the United States of America	43	37	37	2,088	30	627	1,010
17	Protestant Episcopal Church	395	34	33	1,771	16	411	655
18	Roman Catholic Church	70	3	3	503	3	190	313
	United Brethren bodies:							
19	Church of the United Brethren in Christ	91	10	10	277	10	118	159

WASHINGTON.

	DENOMINATION.	Total number of organizations.	Number of colored organizations.	Number of organizations reporting.	Total number reported.	Number of organizations reporting.	Male.	Female.
1	Total	252	18	18	614	18	229	385
	Baptist bodies:							
2	Baptists—Northern Convention	154	1	1	7	1	2	5
3	Baptists—National Convention (Colored)	5	5	5	174	5	78	96
	Churches of the Living God (Colored):							
4	Church of the Living God (Apostolic Church)	1	1	1	64	1	27	37
	Methodist bodies:							
5	African Methodist Episcopal Church	10	10	10	334	10	107	227
6	Protestant Episcopal Church	82	1	1	35	1	15	20

WEST VIRGINIA.

	DENOMINATION.	Total number of organizations.	Number of colored organizations.	Number of organizations reporting.	Total number reported.	Number of organizations reporting.	Male.	Female.
1	Total	1,390	271	268	14,949	251	6,377	7,839
	Adventist bodies:							
2	Seventh-day Adventist Denomination	19	1	1	8	1	3	5
	Baptist bodies:							
3	Baptists—National Convention (Colored)	148	148	148	10,057	143	4,703	5,192
4	Free Baptists	30	7	7	518	7	186	332
5	Colored Primitive Baptists in America	3	3	3	47	1	10	6
	Methodist bodies:							
6	Methodist Episcopal Church	973	61	58	3,011	49	938	1,543
7	African Methodist Episcopal Church	35	35	35	1,002	35	407	595
8	African Methodist Episcopal Zion Church	6	6	6	86	6	40	46
9	Wesleyan Methodist Connection of America	11	5	5	77	4	30	37
10	Colored Methodist Episcopal Church	3	3	3	72	3	30	42
	Presbyterian bodies:							
11	Presbyterian Church in the United States of America	71	1	1	45	1	18	27
12	Protestant Episcopal Church	91	1	1	26	1	12	14

WISCONSIN.

	DENOMINATION.	Total number of organizations.	Number of colored organizations.	Number of organizations reporting.	Total number reported.	Number of organizations reporting.	Male.	Female.
1	Total	11	11	11	310	11	110	200
	Baptist bodies:							
2	Baptists—National Convention (Colored)	2	2	2	60	2	18	42
	Methodist bodies:							
3	African Methodist Episcopal Church	6	6	6	164	6	57	107
4	African Methodist Episcopal Zion Church	3	3	3	86	3	35	51

WYOMING.

	DENOMINATION.	Total number of organizations.	Number of colored organizations.	Number of organizations reporting.	Total number reported.	Number of organizations reporting.	Male.	Female.
1	Total	1	1	1	45	1	12	33
	Methodist bodies:							
2	African Methodist Episcopal Church	1	1	1	45	1	12	33

[1] Negroes or persons of negro descent.

OF CHURCH PROPERTY, DEBT ON CHURCH PROPERTY, PARSONAGES, AND SUNDAY SCHOOLS, BY DENOMINA-
STATE AND TERRITORY: 1906—Continued.

or in part colored organizations, is shown by the first two columns.]

VIRGINIA.

PLACES OF WORSHIP. Number of organizations reporting— Church edifices.	PLACES OF WORSHIP. Number of organizations reporting— Halls, etc.	PLACES OF WORSHIP. Number of church edifices reported.	PLACES OF WORSHIP. Seating capacity of church edifices. Number of organizations reporting.	PLACES OF WORSHIP. Seating capacity of church edifices. Seating capacity reported.	VALUE OF CHURCH PROPERTY. Number of organizations reporting.	VALUE OF CHURCH PROPERTY. Value reported.	DEBT ON CHURCH PROPERTY. Number of organizations reporting.	DEBT ON CHURCH PROPERTY. Amount of debt reported.	PARSONAGES. Number of organizations reporting.	PARSONAGES. Value of parsonages reported.	SUNDAY SCHOOLS CONDUCTED BY CHURCH ORGANIZATIONS. Number of organizations reporting.	SUNDAY SCHOOLS CONDUCTED BY CHURCH ORGANIZATIONS. Number of Sunday schools reported.	SUNDAY SCHOOLS CONDUCTED BY CHURCH ORGANIZATIONS. Number of officers and teachers.	SUNDAY SCHOOLS CONDUCTED BY CHURCH ORGANIZATIONS. Number of scholars.	
1,875	62	1,916	1,808	621,808	1,874	$3,562,930	440	$308,680	172	$165,435	1,802	1,926	12,616	113,727	1
3	1	3	3	500	2	800	1	15	....	....	3	3	14	53	2
1,343	21	1,367	1,318	474,358	1,341	2,641,090	254	204,659	40	44,310	1,308	1,402	9,372	86,686	3
7	....	7	7	2,050	7	7,300	2	215	3	1,700	7	7	47	315	4
47	10	47	24	5,130	38	10.830	1	67	4	1,025	3	3	44	225	5
5	....	5	5	1,250	5	5,600	1	50	....	....	5	5	32	355	6
....	10	....	....	....	....	....	....	....	....	....	....	....	....	....	7
9	....	9	9	2,775	9	5,200	2	39	....	....	9	10	51	469	8
1	....	1	1	150	1	350	....	....	....	....	1	1	4	12	9
149	3	152	134	36,835	151	262,640	51	29,681	54	36,215	140	155	1,071	8,179	10
114	3	117	114	37,550	117	309,025	65	52,812	45	47,660	106	113	724	6,516	11
5	....	5	5	1,800	5	13,500	3	1,280	....	....	5	5	32	455	12
71	4	72	71	22,265	72	102,280	40	15,649	12	9,250	71	73	477	2,796	13
33	1	37	33	8,245	33	32,650	4	328	1	600	33	33	163	1,407	14
37	....	39	34	14,700	35	35,475	7	825	....	....	34	35	199	1,363	15
28	2	28	27	7,230	31	40,640	6	2,400	6	4,975	37	40	205	2,352	16
14	3	18	14	4,720	18	42,450	2	630	4	5,700	29	29	121	2,163	17
3	....	3	3	900	3	50,000	....	....	3	14,000	3	4	10	145	18
6	4	6	6	1,350	6	3,100	1	30	....	....	8	8	50	236	19

WASHINGTON.

13	....	14	13	3,250	13	$57,900	8	$6,125	4	$2,400	15	15	87	514	1
1	....	1	1	200	1	1,000	....	....	....	....	1	1	2	12	2
5	....	5	5	1,300	5	19,600	3	1,475	....	....	5	5	25	125	3
1	....	1	1	400	1	7,000	1	1,200	....	....	1	1	6	70	4
6	....	7	6	1,350	6	30,300	4	3,450	4	2,400	7	7	49	287	5
....	....	....	....	....	....	....	....	....	....	....	1	1	5	20	6

WEST VIRGINIA.

200	58	200	187	50,765	209	$496,946	76	$42,282	39	$48,050	247	257	1,533	11,246	1
....	1	....	....	....	....	....	....	....	....	....	1	1	3	10	2
103	38	103	1	30,910	108	199,876	31	13,775	7	12,500	142	1	876	6,810	3
7	....	7	00	1,900	6	17,100	....	....	2	850	7	48	37	455	4
3	....	3	2	1,100	2	1,400	1	70	....	....	....	....	....	....	5
50	9	50	41	9,480	55	191,170	25	15,797	20	26,100	55	62	396	2,805	6
30	5	30	30	6,000	31	75,550	16	10,940	9	7,800	32	32	172	894	7
2	3	2	2	300	2	450	1	300	....	....	3	3	14	42	8
1	1	1	1	200	1	2,000	....	....	....	....	2	2	8	63	9
2	1	2	2	500	2	1,400	1	200	....	....	3	3	15	67	10
1	....	1	1	225	1	5,000	1	1,200	....	....	1	1	7	75	11
1	....	1	1	150	1	3,000	....	....	1	800	1	1	5	25	12

WISCONSIN.

9	2	9	9	1,960	10	$26,850	4	$851	....	....	10	10	50	244	1
1	1	1	1	100	2	950	2	146	....	....	2	2	8	45	2
6	....	6	6	1,160	6	20,000	1	675	....	....	5	5	27	99	3
2	1	2	2	700	2	5,900	1	30	....	....	3	3	15	100	4

WYOMING.

1	....	1	1	150	1	$10,000	....	....	1	$1,000	1	1	12	40	1
1	....	1	1	150	1	10,000	....	....	1	1,000	1	1	12	40	2

TABLE 14.—COMPARISON OF COLORED[1] ORGANIZATIONS, SHOWING COMMUNICANTS OR MEMBERS, CHURCH EDIFICES, SEATING CAPACITY OF CHURCH EDIFICES, NUMBER OF HALLS, ETC., AND VALUE OF CHURCH PROPERTY, BY DENOMINATIONS (IN DETAIL), FOR CONTINENTAL UNITED STATES: 1906 AND 1890.

DENOMINATION.	NUMBER OF COLORED ORGANIZATIONS.		NUMBER OF COMMUNICANTS OR MEMBERS REPORTED.		NUMBER OF CHURCH EDIFICES REPORTED.		SEATING CAPACITY OF CHURCH EDIFICES REPORTED.		NUMBER OF HALLS, ETC., REPORTED.		VALUE OF CHURCH PROPERTY REPORTED.	
	1906	1890	1906	1890	1906	1890	1906	1890	1906	1890	1906	1890
Total	36,770	23,462	3,685,097	2,673,977	35,160	23,770	10,481,738	6,800,035	1,261	1,358	$56,636,159	$26,626,448
Adventist bodies	31	...	634	...	14	...	1,948	...	9	...	10,274	...
Advent Christian Church	2	...	72	...	2	...	700	...	...	...	3,800	...
Seventh-day Adventist Denomination	29	...	562	...	12	...	1,248	...	9	...	6,474	...
Baptist bodies	19,891	13,289	2,354,789	1,403,559	18,849	12,614	5,831,259	3,634,054	571	783	26,562,845	10,279,599
Baptists	18,642	12,946	2,294,246	1,384,861	18,019	12,316	5,652,161	3,535,530	514	737	25,998,598	10,129,942
Northern Baptist Convention	108	406	32,639	35,221	106	324	41,860	92,660	6	72	1,561,326	1,087,518
Southern Baptist Convention	...	7	...	651	...	5	...	1,900	...	2	...	3,875
National Baptist Convention (Colored)	18,534	12,533	2,261,607	1,348,989	17,913	11,987	5,610,301	3,440,970	508	663	24,437,272	9,038,549
Free Baptists	197	5	10,876	271	173	3	43,850	800	5	2	186,130	13,300
Primitive Baptists	4	323	102	18,162	4	291	1,200	96,699	...	33	2,300	135,427
Colored Primitive Baptists in America[2]	797		35,076		501		94,223		44		296,539	
Two-Seed-in-the-Spirit Predestinarian Baptists	...	15	...	265	...	4	...	1,025	...	11	...	930
United American Freewill Baptists (Colored)	251	...	14,489	...	152	...	39,825	...	8	...	79,278	...
Christians (Christian Connection)	92	63	7,545	4,989	91	54	26,969	16,495	1	7	69,505	23,500
Church of God and Saints of Christ (Colored)	48	...	1,823	...	1	...	400	...	47	...	6,000	...
Churches of God in North America, General Eldership of the	15	...	329	...	5	...	906	...	8	...	5,500	...
Churches of the Living God (Colored)	68	...	4,276	...	45	...	10,635	...	23	...	58,575	...
Church of the Living God (Christian Workers for Friendship)	44	...	2,676	...	27	...	5,965	...	17	...	23,175	...
Church of the Living God (Apostolic Church)	15	...	752	...	12	...	3,100	...	3	...	25,700	...
Church of Christ in God	9	...	848	...	6	...	1,550	...	3	...	9,700	...
Congregationalists	156	85	11,960	6,908	137	69	39,500	19,360	14	11	459,497	246,125
Disciples or Christians	170	277	11,233	18,578	140	183	34,320	41,590	24	75	185,215	176,795
Disciples of Christ	129	277	9,705	18,578	115	183	28,095	41,590	8	75	170,265	176,795
Churches of Christ	41		1,528		25		6,225		16		14,950	
Evangelistic associations	3	...	425	...	3	...	1,325	...	...	...	2,400	...
Voluntary Missionary Society in America (Colored)	3	...	425	...	3	...	1,325	...	...	...	2,400	...
Free Christian Zion Church of Christ (Colored)	15	...	1,835	...	14	...	5,201	...	1	...	5,975	...
Independent churches	12	...	490	...	12	...	845	...	...	...	2,750	...
Lutheran bodies	7	10	239	305	7	8	1,200	1,600	...	2	15,000	15,150
United Synod of the Evangelical Lutheran Church in the South	...	5	...	94	...	3	...	550	...	2	...	1,750
General Council of the Evangelical Lutheran Church in North America	1	...	15	...	1	...	300	...	...	...	5,000	...
Evangelical Lutheran Synodical Conference of America	6	5	224	211	6	5	900	1,050	...	...	10,000	13,400
Methodist bodies	15,317	9,118	1,182,131	1,190,860	14,968	10,313	4,269,852	2,945,797	523	412	25,771,262	14,825,552
Methodist Episcopal Church	3,750	2,984	308,551	246,249	3,672	2,800	901,812	635,252	75	165	6,104,379	3,630,093
Union American Methodist Episcopal Church (Colored)	77	42	4,347	2,279	60	35	16,046	11,500	16	7	170,150	187,600
African Methodist Episcopal Church	6,647	2,481	494,777	452,725	6,538	4,124	1,832,600	1,160,838	268	31	11,303,489	6,468,280
African Union Methodist Protestant Church	69	40	5,592	3,415	71	27	21,955	7,161	1	13	183,697	54,440
African Methodist Episcopal Zion Church	2,204	1,704	184,542	349,788	2,131	1,587	690,951	565,577	78	114	4,833,207	2,714,128
Methodist Protestant Church	64	54	2,612	3,183	53	50	10,125	11,545	4	4	62,651	35,445
Wesleyan Methodist Connection of America	22	...	1,258	...	14	...	3,600	...	2	...	21,000	...
Congregational Methodist (Colored)	...	9	...	319	...	5	...	585	...	4	...	525
Colored Methodist Episcopal Church	2,381	1,759	172,996	129,383	2,327	1,653	758,328	541,464	78	64	3,017,849	1,713,366
Reformed Zion Union Apostolic Church (Colored)	45	32	3,059	2,346	43	27	15,700	10,100	1	1	37,875	15,000
Reformed Methodist Union Episcopal Church (Colored)	58	...	4,397	...	59	...	18,735	...	...	...	36,965	...
Independent Methodists	...	2	...	222	...	2	...	725	...	...	...	4,675
Evangelist Missionary Church	...	11	...	951	...	3	...	1,050	...	9	...	2,000
Moravian bodies	2	...	351	...	1	...	300	...	1	...	8,000	...
Moravian Church (Unitas Fratrum)	2	...	351	...	1	...	300	...	1	...	8,000	...

[1] Negroes or persons of negro descent.
[2] Returned as a part of the Primitive Baptists in 1890, the Colored Primitive Baptist body not having been, so far as known, in existence at that time.

TABLE 14.—COMPARISON OF COLORED[1] ORGANIZATIONS, SHOWING COMMUNICANTS OR MEMBERS, CHURCH EDIFICES, SEATING CAPACITY OF CHURCH EDIFICES, NUMBER OF HALLS, ETC., AND VALUE OF CHURCH PROPERTY, BY DENOMINATIONS (IN DETAIL), FOR CONTINENTAL UNITED STATES: 1906 AND 1890—Continued.

DENOMINATION.	NUMBER OF COLORED ORGANIZATIONS.		NUMBER OF COMMUNICANTS OR MEMBERS REPORTED.		NUMBER OF CHURCH EDIFICES REPORTED.		SEATING CAPACITY OF CHURCH EDIFICES REPORTED.		NUMBER OF HALLS, ETC., REPORTED.		VALUE OF CHURCH PROPERTY REPORTED.	
	1906	1890	1906	1890	1906	1890	1906	1890	1906	1890	1906	1890
Presbyterian bodies	659	503	47,116	29,561	618	413	193,441	114,909	18	62	$990,215	$611,176
Presbyterian Church in the United States of America	417	233	27,799	14,961	383	200	113,701	56,280	17	21	752,387	391,650
Cumberland Presbyterian Church	[2]1	......	[2]50	......	[2]1	......	[2]200	......	......	......	[2]1,000	......
Colored Cumberland Presbyterian Church	196	224	18,066	12,956	195	183	71,165	52,139	1	34	203,778	195,926
Presbyterian Church in the United States	44	45	1,183	1,568	38	29	8,075	6,190	......	7	32,850	22,200
Associate Reformed Synod of the South	1	......	18	......	1	......	300	......	......	......	200	......
Synod of the Reformed Presbyterian Church of North America	......	1	......	76	......	1	......	300	......	......	......	1,500
Protestant Episcopal Church	198	49	19,098	2,977	171	53	42,700	11,885	11	2	1,773,279	192,750
Reformed bodies	2	......	59	......	......	......	......	......	2	......	......	......
Reformed Church in America	2	......	59	......	......	......	......	......	2	......	......	......
Reformed Episcopal Church	38	37	2,252	1,723	42	36	6,948	5,975	2	1	28,287	18,401
Roman Catholic Church	36	31	38,235	14,517	36	27	12,640	8,370	2	3	678,480	237,400
United Brethren bodies	10	......	277	......	6	......	1,350	......	4	......	3,100	......
Church of the United Brethren in Christ	10	......	277	......	6	......	1,350	......	4	......	3,100	......

[1] Negroes or persons of negro descent.

[2] See denominational text, page 530, Part II.

TABLE 15.—COMPARISON OF ORGANIZATIONS OR CHURCHES, ACCOMMODATIONS, AND PROPERTY, BY DENOMINATIONS, FOR CONTINENTAL UNITED STATES: 1870, 1860, AND 1850.

[For explanation of this table, see page 13.]

DENOMINATION.	1870				1860			1850		
	Organizations.	Edifices.	Sittings.	Property.	Churches.	Accommodations.	Property.	Churches.	Accommodations.	Property.
All denominations	72,459	63,082	21,665,062	$354,483,581	54,009	19,128,751	$171,397,932	38,061	14,234,825	$87,328,801
Baptist Regular	14,474	12,857	3,997,116	39,229,221	11,221	3,749,551	19,799,378	9,376	3,247,069	11,020,855
Baptist (other)	1,355	1,105	363,019	2,378,977	929	294,667	1,279,736	187	60,142	153,115
Christian	3,578	2,822	865,602	6,425,137	2,068	681,016	2,518,045	875	303,780	853,386
Congregational	2,887	2,715	1,117,212	25,069,698	2,234	956,351	13,327,511	1,725	807,335	8,001,995
Episcopal (Protestant)	2,835	2,601	991,051	36,514,549	2,145	847,296	21,665,698	1,459	643,598	11,375,010
Evangelical Association	815	641	193,796	2,301,650	......	......	......	39	15,479	118,250
Friends	692	662	224,664	3,939,560	726	269,084	2,544,507	726	286,323	1,713,767
Jewish	189	152	73,265	5,155,234	77	34,412	1,135,300	36	18,371	418,600
Lutheran	3,032	2,776	977,332	14,917,747	2,128	757,637	5,385,179	1,231	539,701	2,909,711
Methodist	25,278	21,337	6,528,209	69,854,121	19,883	6,259,799	33,093,371	13,302	4,345,519	14,825,070
Miscellaneous	27	17	6,935	135,650	2	650	4,000	122	36,494	214,530
Moravian (Unitas Fratrum)	72	67	25,700	709,100	49	20,316	227,450	344	114,988	444,167
Mormon	189	171	87,838	656,750	24	13,500	891,100	16	10,880	84,780
New Jerusalem (Swedenborgian)	90	61	18,755	869,700	58	15,395	321,200	21	5,600	115,100
Presbyterian (regular)	6,262	5,683	2,198,900	47,828,732	5,061	2,088,838	24,227,359	4,826	2,079,765	14,543,789
Presbyterian (other)	1,562	1,388	499,344	5,436,524	1,345	477,111	2,613,166	32	10,189	27,550
Reformed Church in America (late Dutch Reformed)	471	468	227,228	10,359,255	440	211,068	4,453,850	335	182,686	4,116,280
Reformed Church in the United States (late German Reformed)	1,256	1,145	431,700	5,775,215	676	273,697	2,422,670	341	160,932	993,780
Roman Catholic	4,127	3,806	1,990,514	60,985,566	2,550	1,404,437	26,774,119	1,222	667,863	9,256,758
Second Advent	225	140	34,555	306,240	70	17,120	101,170	25	5,250	11,100
Shaker	18	18	8,850	86,900	12	5,200	41,000	11	5,150	39,500
Spiritualist	95	22	6,970	100,150	17	6,275	7,500	......	......	......
Unitarian	331	310	155,471	6,282,675	264	138,213	4,338,316	245	138,067	3,280,822
United Brethren in Christ	1,445	937	265,025	1,819,810	......	......	......	14	4,650	18,600
Universalist	719	602	210,884	5,692,325	664	235,219	2,856,095	530	215,115	1,778,316
Unknown (local missions)	26	27	11,925	687,800	......	......	......	22	9,425	98,950
Unknown (union)	409	552	153,202	965,295	1,366	371,899	1,370,212	999	320,454	915,020

INDEX.

Academies. *See* Colleges, academies, etc.
Adonai Shomo (Communistic), disappearance of denomination, 15, statistics for 1890, 514.
Advent Christian Church. *See* Adventist bodies.
Adventist bodies:
  organizations, number, 22; per minister, 92; by periods, 99, 103.
  communicants or members, number, 25–35; by classes of cities, 74, 83; per minister, 93.
  church edifices and halls, number and seating capacity, 32, 34, 35.
  value of church property, 37–40; by classes of cities, 76.
  debt on church property, 40; by classes of cities, 78.
  parsonages, number and value, 41.
  Sunday schools, teachers, and scholars, number, 87, 88.
  ministers, number and increase, 1890–1906, 91; salaries, by classes of cities, 94, 95.
  languages used in church services, 106, 107, 111.
  work, home, 126; foreign, 131; contributions, 134.
  general statistics, 148, 156–293, 380–382, 514.
—— colored organizations, general statistics, 137, 538, 564.
African immigrants, number admitted during year ending June 30, 1907, 32.
African Methodist Episcopal Church. *See* Methodist bodies, *also* Colored organizations.
African Methodist Episcopal Zion Church, loss in membership, 26. *See also* Methodist bodies *and* Colored organizations.
African Methodists. *See* Methodist bodies, *also* Colored organizations.
African Union Methodist Protestant Church. *See* Methodist bodies, *also* Colored organizations.
Akron, Ohio, 376, 381, 408.
Alabama, population, organizations, members, and value of and debt on church property, with per cent distribution and rank, 42, 43. *See also* States and territories.
Albany, N. Y., 374, 380, 408.
Allegheny, Pa., 374, 380, 408.
Allentown, Pa., 376, 381, 410.
Altoona, Pa., 376, 381, 410.
Altruists, Society of (Communistic), disappearance of denomination, 15; statistics for 1890, 514.
Amana Society. *See* Communistic societies.
American Bible Society, 12.
American Salvation Army, new denomination, 15, 518. *See also* Salvationists.
American Sunday School Union, statistics furnished by, 13.
American Tract Society, 12.
Amish Mennonite Church. *See* Mennonite bodies.
Apostolic Christian Church, new denomination, 16, 516. *See also* Evangelistic associations.
Apostolic Faith Movement, new denomination, 16, 516. *See also* Evangelistic associations.
Apostolic Lutheran Church (Finnish). *See* Lutheran bodies.
Apostolic Mennonite Church, consolidation with another denomination, 15, 518.
Arabic language, use of, in church services, 121.
Arizona, population, organizations, members, and value of and debt on church property, with per cent distribution and rank, 42, 43. *See also* States and territories.
Arkansas, population, organizations, members, and value of and debt on church property, with per cent distribution and rank, 42, 43. *See also* States and territories.
Armenian Church: salaries of ministers, by classes of cities, 96, 97; organizations, by periods, 99; languages used in church services, 107, 111; general statistics, 148, 380–382, 514.
Armenian immigrants, number admitted during year ending June 30, 1907, 32.
Armenian language, use of, in church services, 121.
Associate Church of North America, change in name of denomination, 14.
Associate Reformed Synod of the South. *See* Presbyterian bodies, *also* Colored organizations.
Associate Synod of North America (Associate Presbyterian Church), change in name of denomination, 14. *See also* Presbyterian bodies.
Asylums. *See* Hospitals, asylums, etc.
Atlanta, Ga., 374, 380, 410.
Atlantic City, N. J., 376, 381, 412.
Auburn, N. Y., 376, 381, 412.
Augusta, Ga., 376, 381, 412.
Austrian (German) language, use of, in church services, 121.

Bahais: new denomination, 16; organizations, by periods, 99; languages used in church services, 106; general statistics, 148, 156, 380–382, 514.
Baltimore, Md., 374, 380, 412.
Baptist bodies:
  organizations, number, 22; per minister, 92; by periods, 99, 103.
  communicants or members, number, 25–35; distribution for continental United States, diagram, 26; by states and territories, 46; per 1,000 population, 62; diagrams, 64, 66; by classes of cities, 74, 83; per minister, 93.
  church edifices and halls, number and seating capacity, 32, 34, 35.
  value of church property, 37–40; by classes of cities, 76.
  debt on church property, 40; by classes of cities, 78.
  parsonages, number and value, 41.
  Sunday schools, teachers, and scholars, number, 87, 88.
  ministers, number and increase, 1890–1906, 91; salaries, by classes of cities, 94, 95.
  languages used in church services, 106, 107, 111.
Baptist bodies—Continued.
  work, home, 126; foreign, 131; contributions, 134.
  general statistics, 148, 156–293, 380–384, 514.
—— colored organizations, general statistics, 137, 538, 564.
Baptist Church of Christ, change in name of denomination, 14.
Baptists. *See* Baptist bodies.
Baptists (other), explanation of term, 13; comparative statistics for 1850, 1860, and 1870, 565.
Baptists—National Convention (colored). *See* Baptist bodies, *also* Colored organizations.
Baptists—Northern Convention. *See* Baptist bodies, *also* Colored organizations.
Baptists, Regular. *See* Regular Baptists
Bay City, Mich., 376, 381, 414.
Bayonne, N. J., 376, 381, 414.
Belgian language, use of, in church services, 121.
Binghamton, N. Y., 376, 381, 414.
Birmingham, Ala., 376, 381, 416.
Bohemian and Moravian Brethren. *See* Moravian bodies.
Bohemian and Moravian immigrants, number admitted during year ending June 30, 1907, 32.
Bohemian language, use of, in church services, 121.
Bosnian immigrants. *See* Dalmatian, Bosnian, and Herzegovinian immigrants.
Boston, Mass., 374, 380, 416.
Brethren (Plymouth): organizations, by periods, 99, 103; languages used in church services, 106, 107, 112; work, home, 126; foreign, 131; general statistics, 148, 382–384, 514.
Brethren (Plymouth)—I. *See* Brethren (Plymouth).
Brethren (Plymouth)—II. *See* Brethren (Plymouth).
Brethren (Plymouth)—III. *See* Brethren (Plymouth).
Brethren (Plymouth)—IV. *See* Brethren (Plymouth).
Brethren (River): organizations, by periods, 99, 103; languages used in church services, 107, 112; work, home, 126; foreign, 131; general statistics, 148, 382–384, 514.
Brethren Church, The (Progressive Dunkers). *See* Dunkers or German Baptist Brethren.
Brethren in Christ. *See* Brethren (River).
Bridgeport, Conn., 374, 380, 416.
Brockton, Mass., 376, 381, 418.
Bruederhoef Mennonite Church. *See* Mennonite bodies.
Buddhists: new denominational family, 16; salaries of ministers, by classes of cities, 96, 97; organizations, by periods, 99; languages used in church services, 107, 112; work, home, 128; general statistics, 148, 382–384, 514.
Buffalo, N. Y., 374, 380, 418.
Buffalo, Lutheran Synod of. *See* Lutheran bodies.
Bulgarian, Servian, and Montenegrin immigrants, number admitted during year ending June 30, 1907, 32.

Bul'ockites. *See* Freewill Baptists (Bullockites).
Bundes Conferenz der Mennoniten Brueder-Gemeinde. *See* Mennonite bodies.
Butte, Mont., 376, 381, 420.

California, population, organizations, members, and value of and debt on church property, with per cent distribution and rank, 42, 43. *See also* States and territories.
Cambridge, Mass., 374, 380, 420.
Camden, N. J., 374, 380, 420.
Canton, Ohio, 376, 381, 420.
Catholic Apostolic Church. *See* Catholic Apostolic Churches.
Catholic Apostolic Churches: new denominational family, 16; organizations, by periods, 99; languages used in church services, 107, 112; general statistics, 148, 385-387, 514.
Catholic bodies, omission of family in 1906, 15.
Cedar Rapids, Iowa, 376, 381, 422.
Census inquiry, scope of, 9.
Central Illinois Conference of Mennonites, new denomination, 16, 518. *See also* Mennonite bodies.
Charleston, S. C., 374, 380, 422.
Chattanooga, Tenn., 376, 381, 422.
Chelsea, Mass., 376, 381, 424.
Chester, Pa., 376, 381, 424.
Chicago, Ill., 374, 380, 424.
Chinese immigrants, number admitted during year ending June 30, 1907, 32.
Chinese language, use of, in church services, 121.
Chinese Temples. *See* Buddhists.
Christadelphians: organizations, by periods, 99; languages used in church services, 106; general statistics, 148, 385–387, 514.
Christian Catholic Church in Zion: new denomination, 16; salaries of ministers, by classes of cities, 94, 95; organizations, by periods, 99; languages used in church services, 107, 112; work, home, 126; general statistics, 148, 385–387, 514.
Christian Church (South), consolidation with another denomination, 15, 514.
Christian Congregation, new denomination, 16, 516. *See also* Evangelistic associations.
Christian Israelite Church: organizations, by periods, 99; languages used in church services, 106; general statistics, 148, 385–387, 514.
Christian Missionary Association: disappearance of denomination, 15; statistics for 1890, 514.
Christian Reformed Church. *See* Reformed bodies.
Christian Union: change in name of denomination, 14; salaries of ministers, by classes of cities, 94, 95; organizations, by periods, 99, 103; languages used in church services, 106; work, home, 126; general statistics, 148, 385–387, 514.
Christians, comparative statistics for 1850, 1860, and 1870, 565.
Christians (Christian Connection):
omission of family in 1906, 15.
organizations, number, 22; per minister, 92; by periods, 99, 103.
communicants or members, number, 25–35; by classes of cities, 74, 83; per minister, 93.
church edifices and halls, number and seating capacity, 32, 34, 35.
value of church property, 37–40; by classes of cities, 76.
debt on church property, 40; by classes of cities, 78.
parsonages, number and value, 41.
Sunday schools, teachers, and scholars, number, 87, 88.
Christians (Christian Connection)—Cont'd.
ministers, number and increase, 1890–1906, 91; salaries, by classes of cities, 94, 95.
languages used in church services, 107, 112.
work, home, 126; foreign, 131.
general statistics, 148, 156, 385–387, 514.
—— colored organizations, general statistics, 137, 538, 564.
Church edifices: number, per cent distribution, and increase, 1890–1906, 32; number, by denominations, 149; by states and territories, 155; by denominations and states and territories, 157; by classes of cities, 375; by cities and selected denominations, 409; comparison, 1890 and 1906, 515; by states and territories, 521; comparative statistics for 1850, 1860, and 1870, 565.
Church of Christ in God, new denomination, 16, 514. *See also* Churches of the Living God (colored).
Church of Christ, Scientist:
organizations, number, 22; per minister, 92; by periods, 99, 103; percentage formed from 1900 to 1906, 105.
communicants or members, number, 25–35; by classes of cities, 74, 83; per minister, 93.
church edifices and halls, number and seating capacity, 32, 34, 35.
value of church property, 37–40; by classes of cities, 76.
debt on church property, 40; by classes of cities, 78.
parsonages, number and value, 41.
Sunday schools, teachers, and scholars, number, 87, 88.
ministers, number and increase, 1890–1906, 91; salaries, by classes of cities, 94, 95.
languages used in church services, 106.
general statistics, 148, 156, 385–387, 514.
Church of Daniel's Band, new denomination, 16, 516. *See also* Evangelistic associations.
Church of God (Adventist). *See* Adventist bodies.
Church of God (Adventist), Unattached Congregations, new denomination, 15, 516. *See also* Adventist bodies.
Church of God (Winebrennerian), change in name of denomination, 14.
Church of God and Saints of Christ (colored): new denomination, 16; organizations, by periods, 99; languages used in church services, 106; ministers, number, 146; general statistics, 137, 148, 385–387, 514, 538, 564.
Church of God in Christ (Mennonite). *See* Mennonite bodies.
Church of Jesus Christ of Latter-day Saints. *See* Latter-day Saints.
Church of the Living God (Apostolic Church), new denomination, 16, 514. *See also* Churches of the Living God (colored).
Church of the Living God (Christian Workers for Friendship), new denomination, 16, 514. *See also* Churches of the Living God (colored).
Church of the Lutheran Brethren of America (Norwegian), new denomination, 16, 516. *See also* Lutheran bodies.
Church of the United Brethren in Christ. *See* United Brethren bodies.
Church of the United Brethren in Christ (Old Constitution). *See* United Brethren bodies.
Church property: value, 1890 and 1906, 37; average per organization, 37; at specified censuses, 39; per capita, 39; by selected denominations, 40; average per organization, 44; by classes of cities, 76; by denominations, in detail, 149; in foreign missions, 131; by states and territories, 155; by separate states and denominations, 157; by classes of cities, 375; by specified cities and denominations, 409; comparison, 1890 and 1906, 515; by states and territories, 521; in 1850, 1860, and 1870, 565.
—— debt on, by selected denominations, 40; average per organization, 44; by classes of cities, 78; by denominations, in detail, 149; by states and territories, 155; by separate states and denominations, 157; by classes of cities, 375; by specified cities and denominations, 409.
—— colored organizations, general statistics, 137, 539, 543, 564.
Church Triumphant (Schweinfurth), disappearance of denomination, 15; statistics for 1890, 514.
Church Triumphant or Koreshan Ecclesia (Communistic), disappearance of denomination, 15; statistics for 1890, 514.
Churches of Christ, new denomination, 15, 514. *See also* Disciples or Christians.
Churches of Christ (Disciples or Christians), percentage of organizations formed from 1900 to 1906, 105. *See also* Disciples or Christians.
Churches of Christ in Christian Union, Independent, change in name of denomination, 14.
Churches of God in Christ Jesus. *See* Adventist bodies.
Churches of God in North America, General Eldership of the: change in name of denomination, 14; salaries of ministers, by classes of cities, 94, 95; organizations, by periods, 99, 103; languages used in church services, 107, 112; work, home, 126; foreign, 131; general statistics, 148, 385–387, 514, 538.
—— colored organizations, general statistics, 137, 564.
Churches of God (Adventist), Unattached Congregations. *See* Adventist bodies.
Churches of the Living God (colored): new denominational family, 16; organizations, by periods, 100; languages used in church services, 106; ministers, number, 146; general statistics, 137, 148, 156, 385–387, 514, 538, 564.
Churches of the New Jerusalem: new denominational family, 16; salaries of ministers, 94, 95; organizations, by periods, 100, 103; languages used in church services, 106, 107, 112; work, home, 126; foreign, 131; general statistics, 148, 156, 385–387, 514.
Cincinnati, Ohio, 374, 380, 426.
Cities: general statistics for continental United States, by classes of principal, 68–73; by separate denominations and classes of, 74–79; by classes of principal, 374; by selected denominations and specified, 408.
—— communicants or members, by specified denominations and classes of, 80–85; Protestant, Roman Catholic, and "all other," in principal, diagram, 86; by denominations, in detail, and classes of, 380.
Cleveland, Ohio, 374, 380, 428.
Colleges, academies, etc., number and students, by denominations, 127.
Colorado, population, organizations, members, and value of and debt on church property, with per cent distribution and rank, 42, 43. *See also* States and territories.
Colored Cumberland Presbyterian Church. *See* Presbyterian bodies, *also* Colored organizations.
Colored Methodist Episcopal Church. *See* Methodist bodies, *also* Colored organizations.
Colored ministers, total number, 146; by denominations, in detail, 515.

Colored organizations:
- comparison, 1890 and 1906, 137; per cent distribution and increase, 138; total number in 1906, 146.
- communicants or members, comparison, 1890 and 1906, 137; by states and territories, 145; per cent distribution and increase, 139; distribution, by sex, 140.
- places of worship, 141.
- seating capacity of church edifices, 141.
- value of church property, comparison, 1890 and 1906, 137; per cent distribution and increase, 142.
- debt on church property, 143.
- parsonages, number and value, 143.
- Sunday schools, teachers, and scholars, number, 144.
- ministers, number, 146.
- general statistics, by denominations, 538; by states and territories, 540; by separate denominations and states and territories, 542–563; comparison, 1890 and 1906, 564.

Colored Primitive Baptists in America, new denomination, 15, 514. *See also* Baptist bodies *and* Colored organizations.

Columbus, Ohio, 374, 380, 428.

Communicants or members: basis of enumeration, 24; number, by principal denominations, 24–35; diagrams, 83–85; by principal denominations and states and territories, 46–53; per 1,000 population, 62; diagrams, 64–67; Protestant, Roman Catholic, and "all other," diagram, 86; per minister, 93; by denominations, in detail, 148; by states and territories, 154; by separate states and denominations, 156; by separate states and counties, 294; by classes of cities, 374; by classes of cities and separate denominations, 380; by specified cities and denominations, 408; comparison, 1890 and 1906, 514; by states and territories, 521; by selected denominations and states and territories, 522.

—— colored, number, by denominations, 538; by states and territories, 540; by separate denominations and states and territories, 542–563; comparison, 1890 and 1906, 137; by separate denominations, 564.

Communistic societies: organizations, by periods, 100; languages used in church services, 106, 107, 112; general statistics, 148, 514.

Congregational Methodist Church, percentage of organizations formed from 1900 to 1906, 105. *See also* Methodist bodies.

Congregational Methodist (colored): disappearance of denomination, 15; statistics for 1890, 137, 518.

Congregationalists:
- organizations, number, 22; per minister, 92; by periods, 100, 103.
- communicants or members, number, 25–35; distribution for continental United States, diagram, 26; by states and territories, 46; by classes of cities, 74, 83; per 1,000 population, 62; diagrams, 65, 67; by classes of cities, 74, 83; per minister, 93.
- church edifices and halls, number and seating capacity, 32, 34, 35.
- value of church property, 37–40; by classes of cities, 76.
- debt on church property, 40; by classes of cities, 78.
- parsonages, number and value, 41.
- Sunday schools, teachers, and scholars, number, 87, 88.
- ministers, number and increase, 1890–1906, 91; salaries, by classes of cities, 94, 95.
- languages used in church services, 107, 113.
- work, home, 126; foreign, 131; contributions, 134.
- general statistics, 148, 156–293, 387–389, 514.

Congregationalists—Continued.
- comparative statistics for 1850, 1860, and 1870, 565.

—— colored organizations, general statistics, 137, 538, 564.

Connecticut, population, organizations, members, and value of and debt on church property, with per cent distribution and rank, 42, 43. *See also* States and territories.

Continental United States:
- organizations, number, 42, 69; by classes of cities, 70; reporting foreign languages, 122.
- communicants or members, distribution, by principal denominations, diagram, 26; number, 43; average per organization, 44; by separate denominations and states and territories, 46; ratio to total population, 58; Protestant, Roman Catholic, and "all other," 59; per 1,000 population, by principal denominations, 62; by classes of cities, 70; by sex, 71.
- value of church property, 43; average per organization, 44; by classes of cities, 72, 73.
- debt on church property, 43; average per organization, 44; by classes of cities, 72, 73.
- church edifices and halls, number and seating capacity, 69; by classes of cities, 71.
- parsonages, number and value, 69, 72, 73.
- Sunday schools, number, by classes of cities, 73; denominational and undenominational, by states and territories, 89; by geographic divisions, 90.
- ministers, average salaries, by denominations, 94.

Contributions, amount reported for home work, 126, 134; foreign, 131, 134.

Council Bluffs, Iowa, 376, 381, 430.

Covington, Ky., 376, 381, 430.

Croatian and Slovenian immigrants, number admitted during year ending June 30, 1907, 32.

Croatian language, use of, in church services, 121.

Cuban immigrants, number admitted during year ending June 30, 1907, 32.

Cumberland Presbyterian Church. *See* Presbyterian bodies.

Dallas, Tex., 376, 381, 430.

Dalmatian, Bosnian, and Herzegovinian immigrants, number admitted during year ending June 30, 1907, 32.

Danish Church Association (Lutheran), consolidation with another denomination, 15, 516.

Danish Evangelical Lutheran Church in America. *See* Lutheran bodies.

Danish language, use of, in church services, 121.

Data for report, how obtained, 11.

Davenport, Iowa, 376, 381, 430.

Dayton, Ohio, 374, 380, 432.

Debt on church property. *See* Church property, debt on.

Defenceless Mennonites. *See* Mennonite bodies.

Delaware, population, organizations, members, and value of and debt on church property, with per cent distribution and rank, 42, 43. *See also* States and territories.

Denominational families: changes in names of, 14; disappearance of, 15; number of new, 16.

Denominations: descriptive statements, how obtained, 11; classification at former census periods, 13; changes in names, 14; additions and omissions, 15, 16; list of, 16; rank of principal, 55–57; number, by classes of cities, 74; showing largest percentages of organizations established prior to 1800, 104; in 1850, 1860, and 1870, 565; work of, in domestic and foreign fields, 123–136; general statistics, in detail, 148; by separate states, 156; by separate states and counties, 294; by classes of cities, 380; comparison, 1890 and 1906, 514; by states and territories, 522.

Denver, Colo., 374, 380, 432.

Des Moines, Iowa, 374, 380, 434.

Detroit, Mich., 374, 380, 434.

Disciples of Christ. *See* Disciples or Christians.

Disciples or Christians:
- new denominational family, 16.
- organizations, number, 22; per minister, 92; by periods, 100, 103.
- communicants or members, number, 25–35; distribution for continental United States, diagram, 26; by states and territories, 46; per 1,000 population, 62; diagrams, 64, 67; by classes of cities, 74, 83; per minister, 93.
- church edifices and halls, number and seating capacity, 32, 34, 35.
- value of church property, 37–40; by classes of cities, 76.
- debt on church property, 40; by classes of cities, 78.
- parsonages, number and value, 41.
- Sunday schools, teachers, and scholars, number, 87, 88.
- ministers, number and increase, 1890–1906, 91; salaries, by classes of cities, 94, 95.
- languages used in church services, 107, 113.
- work, home, 126; foreign, 131; contributions, 134.
- general statistics, 148, 156–293, 387–389, 514.

—— colored organizations, general statistics, 137, 538, 564.

District of Columbia, population, organizations, members, and value of and debt on church property, with per cent distribution and rank, 42, 43. *See also* States and territories.

Domestic work. *See* Home work.

Dubuque, Iowa, 376, 381, 434.

Duck River and Kindred Associations of Baptists (Baptist Church of Christ), change in name of denomination, 14. *See also* Baptist bodies.

Duluth, Minn., 374, 380, 436.

Dunkers or German Baptist Brethren:
- organizations, number, 22; per minister, 92; by periods, 100, 103.
- communicants or members, number, 25–35; by classes of cities, 74, 83; per minister, 93.
- church edifices and halls, number and seating capacity, 32, 34, 35.
- value of church property, 37–40; by classes of cities, 76.
- debt on church property, 40; by classes of cities, 78.
- parsonages, number and value, 41.
- Sunday schools, teachers, and scholars, number, 87, 88.
- ministers, number and increase, 1890–1906, 91; salaries, by classes of cities, 94, 95.
- languages used in church services, 106, 107, 113.
- work, home, 126; foreign, 131.
- general statistics, 148, 156, 387–389, 516.

Dutch and Flemish immigrants, number admitted during year ending June 30, 1907, 32.

Dutch or Flemish language, use of, in church services, 121.

East Indian immigrants, number admitted during year ending June 30, 1907, 32.

East St. Louis, Ill., 376, 381, 436.

Eastern Orthodox Churches:
- new denominational family, 16.
- organizations, number, 22; per minister, 92; by periods, 100, 103; percentage formed from 1900 to 1906, 105.

Eastern Orthodox Churches—Continued.
- communicants or members, number, 25–35; by classes of cities, 74, 83; per minister, 93.
- church edifices and halls, number and seating capacity, 32, 34, 35.
- value of church property, 37–40; by classes of cities, 76.
- debt on church property, 40; by classes of cities, 78.
- parsonages, number and value, 41.
- Sunday schools, teachers, and scholars, number, 87, 88.
- ministers, number and increase, 1890–1906, 91; salaries, by classes of cities, 96, 97.
- languages used in church services, 108, 113.
- work, home, 128.
- general statistics, 150, 156–293, 387–389, 516.

Easton, Pa., 376, 381, 436.
Education: amount contributed for, by denominations, 126; value of property and endowments, 127.
Eielsen's Synod. *See* Evangelical Lutheran Church in America, Eielsen's Synod, *also* Lutheran bodies.
Elizabeth, N. J., 374, 380, 436.
Elmira, N. Y., 376, 381, 438.
English immigrants, number admitted during year ending June 30, 1907, 32.
English language, use of, in church services, 106–120.
Enumeration, plan of, 10.
Erie, Pa., 374, 380, 438.
Esthonian language, use of, in church services, 121.
Evangelical Adventists. *See* Adventist bodies.
Evangelical Association, comparative statistics for 1850, 1860, and 1870, 565. *See also* Evangelical bodies.
Evangelical bodies:
- new denominational family, 16.
- organizations, number, 22; per minister, 92; by periods, 100, 103.
- communicants or members, number, 25–35; by classes of cities, 74, 83; per minister, 93.
- church edifices and halls, number and seating capacity, 32, 34, 35.
- value of church property, 37–40; by classes of cities, 76.
- debt on church property, 40; by classes of cities, 78.
- parsonages, number and value, 41.
- Sunday schools, teachers, and scholars, number, 87, 88.
- ministers, number and increase, 1890–1906, 91; salaries, by classes of cities, 94, 95.
- languages used in church services, 108, 113.
- work, home, 126; foreign, 131; contributions, 134.
- general statistics, 150, 387–389, 516.

Evangelical Lutheran Church in America, Eielsen's Synod. *See* Lutheran bodies.
Evangelical Lutheran Jehovah Conference. *See* Lutheran bodies.
Evangelical Lutheran Joint Synod of Ohio and Other States. *See* Lutheran bodies.
Evangelical Lutheran Synod of Iowa and Other States. *See* Lutheran bodies.
Evangelical Lutheran Synod of Michigan and Other States. *See* Lutheran bodies.
Evangelical Lutheran Synodical Conference of America. *See* Lutheran bodies.
Evangelical Union of Bohemian and Moravian Brethren in North America, new denomination, 16, 518. *See also* Moravian bodies.
Evangelist Missionary Church (Methodist), disappearance of denomination, 15; statistics for 1890, 137, 518.
Evangelistic associations:
- new denominational family, 16.
- salaries of ministers, 94, 95.

Evangelistic associations—Continued.
- organizations, by periods, 100, 103.
- percentage formed from 1900 to 1906, 105.
- languages used in church services, 106, 108, 113.
- work, home, 126; foreign, 131.
- general statistics, 150, 156–293, 387–392, 516.

—— colored organizations, general statistics, 137, 538, 564.
Evansville, Ind., 374, 380, 438.

Fall River, Mass., 374, 380, 440.
Finnish Evangelical Lutheran Church (Suomi Synod), percentage of organizations formed from 1900 to 1906, 105. *See also* Lutheran bodies.
Finnish Evangelical Lutheran National Church, new denomination, 16, 516. *See also* Lutheran bodies.
Finnish immigrants, number admitted during year ending June 30, 1907, 32.
Finnish language, use of, in church services, 121.
Fitchburg, Mass., 376, 381, 440.
Flemish immigrants. *See* Dutch and Flemish immigrants.
Florida, population, organizations, members, and value of and debt on church property, with per cent distribution and rank, 42, 43. *See also* States and territories.
Foreign work: scope of, 123, 130; statistics, by denominations, 131–134; comparison with home, 135.
Fort Wayne, Ind., 376, 381, 440.
Fort Worth, Tex., 376, 381, 440.
Free Baptists, change in name of denomination, 14. *See also* Baptist bodies.
Free Christian Zion Church of Christ (colored): new denomination, 16; organizations, by periods, 100; languages used in church services, 106; ministers, number, 146; general statistics, 137, 150, 516, 538, 542–562, 564.
Free Methodist Church of North America. *See* Methodist bodies.
Freewill Baptists, change in name of denomination, 14. *See also* Baptist bodies.
Freewill Baptists (Bullockites). *See* Baptist bodies.
French immigrants, number admitted during year ending June 30, 1907, 32.
French language, use of, in church services, 121.
Friends:
- organizations, number, 22; per minister, 92; by periods, 100, 103.
- communicants or members, number, 25–35; by classes of cities, 74, 83; per minister, 93.
- church edifices and halls, number and seating capacity, 32, 34, 35.
- value of church property, 37–40; by classes of cities, 76.
- debt on church property, 40; by classes of cities, 78.
- parsonages, number and value, 41.
- Sunday schools, teachers, and scholars, number, 87, 88.
- ministers, number and increase, 1890–1906, 91; salaries, by classes of cities, 94, 95.
- languages used in church services, 106, 108, 114.
- work, home, 126; foreign, 131.
- general statistics, 150, 156–293, 390–392, 516.
- comparative statistics for 1850, 1860, and 1870, 565.

Friends (Primitive). *See* Friends.
Friends of the Temple, change in name of denomination, 14.

Gaelic language, use of, in church services, 121.
Galveston, Tex., 376, 381, 442.
General Baptists, percentage of organizations formed from 1900 to 1906, 105. *See also* Baptist bodies.
General Church of the New Jerusalem, new denomination, 15, 514. *See also* Churches of the New Jerusalem.
General Conference of Mennonites of North America. *See* Mennonite bodies.
General Convention of the New Jerusalem in the United States of America, new denomination, 15, 514. *See also* Churches of the New Jerusalem.
General Council of the Evangelical Lutheran Church in North America. *See* Lutheran bodies.
General Six Principle Baptists. *See* Baptist bodies.
General Synod of the Evangelical Lutheran Church in the United States of America. *See* Lutheran bodies.
Georgia, population, organizations, members, and value of and debt on church property, with per cent distribution and rank, 42, 43. *See also* States and territories.
German Augsburg Synod (Lutheran), consolidation with other denominations, 15; statistics for 1890, 516.
German Baptist Brethren Church (Conservative). *See* Dunkers or German Baptist Brethren.
German Evangelical Lutheran Synod of Texas, new denomination, 15, 516. *See also* Lutheran bodies.
German Evangelical Protestant bodies:
- new denominational family, 16.
- communicants or members, number, 30.
- salaries of ministers, 94, 95.
- organizations, by periods, 100.
- languages used in church services, 108, 114.
- general statistics, 150, 390–392, 408, 516.

German Evangelical Protestant Ministers' Association, new denomination, 15, 516. *See also* German Evangelical Protestant bodies.
German Evangelical Protestant Ministers' Conference, new denomination, 15, 516. *See also* German Evangelical Protestant bodies.
German Evangelical Synod of North America:
- organizations, number, 22; per minister, 92; by periods, 100, 103.
- communicants or members, number, 25–35; by states and territories, 46; by classes of cities, 74, 83; per 1,000 population, 62; diagrams, 65, 67; per minister, 93.
- church edifices and halls, number and seating capacity, 32, 34, 35.
- value of church property, 37–40; by classes of cities, 76.
- debt on church property, 40; by classes of cities, 78.
- parsonages, number and value, 41.
- Sunday schools, teachers, and scholars, number, 87, 88.
- ministers, number and increase, 1890–1906, 91; salaries, by classes of cities, 94, 95.
- languages used in church services, 108, 114.
- work, home, 126; foreign, 131; contributions, 134.
- general statistics, 150, 156–293, 390–392, 516.

German immigrants, number admitted during year ending June 30, 1907, 32.
German language, use of, in church services, 121.
German Seventh-day Baptists. *See* Dunkers or German Baptist Brethren.
Gloucester, Mass., 376, 381, 442.
Gospel Mission, new denomination, 16, 516. *See also* Evangelistic associations.
Grand Rapids, Mich., 374, 380, 442.
Greek immigrants, number admitted during year ending June 30, 1907, 32.

Greek language, use of, in church services, 121.
Greek Orthodox Church. *See* Eastern Orthodox Churches.

Halls: number, per cent distribution, and increase, 1890–1906, 32; number, by denominations, 149; by states and territories, 155; by denominations and states and territories, 157; by classes of cities, 375; by cities and selected denominations, 409; comparison, 1890 and 1906, 515; by states and territories, 521.
Harmony Society: disappearance of denomination, 15; statistics for 1890, 514.
Harrisburg, Pa., 374, 380, 444.
Hartford, Conn., 374, 380, 444.
Hauge's Norwegian Evangelical Lutheran Synod. *See* Lutheran bodies.
Haverhill, Mass., 376, 381, 444.
Heavenly Recruit Church, new denomination, 16, 516. *See also* Evangelistic associations.
Hebrew immigrants, number admitted during year ending June 30, 1907, 32.
Hebrew language, use of, in church services, 121.
Hephzibah Faith Missionary Association, new denomination, 16, 516. *See also* Evangelistic associations.
Herzegovinian immigrants. *See* Dalmatian, Bosnian, and Herzegovinian immigrants.
Hoboken, N. J., 374, 380, 444.
Holyoke, Mass., 376, 381, 446.
Home work: scope of, 123, 124; statistics, by denominations, 126–130; comparison with foreign, 135.
Hospitals, asylums, etc.: amount contributed for, by denominations, 126; number and inmates, 127.
Houston, Tex., 376, 381, 446.
Hungarian Reformed Church in America, new denomination, 16, 518. *See also* Reformed bodies.

Icelandic Evangelical Lutheran Synod in North America. *See* Lutheran bodies.
Icelandic language, use of, in church services, 121.
Idaho, population, organizations, members, and value of and debt on church property, with per cent distribution and rank, 42, 43 *See also* States and territories.
Illinois, population, organizations, members, and value of and debt on church property, with per cent distribution and rank, 42, 43. *See also* States and territories.
Immanuel Synod of the Evangelical Lutheran Church of North America. *See* Lutheran bodies.
Immigrants, number admitted during year ending June 30, 1907, by nationality, 32.
Immigration, influence of, on membership of denominations, 25, 28, 54; on proportion of sexes, 31; on debt on church property, 40; on membership of Roman Catholic Church, 61; on use of foreign languages in church services, 110.
Independent Churches:
  organizations, number, 22; per minister, 92; by periods, 100, 103; percentage formed from 1900 to 1906, 105.
  communicants or members, number, 25–35; by classes of cities, 74, 83; per minister, 93.
  church edifices and halls, number and seating capacity, 32, 34, 35.
  value of church property, 37–40; by classes of cities, 76.
  debt on church property, 40; by classes of cities, 78.
  parsonages, number and value, 41.
  Sunday schools, teachers, and scholars, number, 87, 88.
  ministers, number and increase, 1890–1906, 91; salaries, by classes of cities, 94, 95.
Independent Churches—Continued.
  languages used in church services, 108, 114.
  work, home, 126; foreign, 131; contributions, 134.
  general statistics, 150, 156–293, 392–394, 516.
—— colored organizations, general statistics, 137, 538, 564.
Independent Methodists, disappearance of denomination, 15; statistics for 1890, 518.
Indian (American) language, use of, in church services, 121.
Indiana, population, organizations, members, and value of and debt on church property, with per cent distribution and rank, 42, 43. *See also* States and territories.
Indianapolis, Ind., 374, 380, 446.
International Apostolic Holiness Union: new denomination, 16; organizations, by periods, 100; languages used in church services, 106; work, home, 126; foreign, 131; general statistics, 150, 392–394, 516.
International Sunday School Association, 12.
Iowa, population, organizations, members, and value of and debt on church property, with per cent distribution and rank, 42, 43. *See also* States and territories.
Iowa, Synod of. *See* Lutheran bodies.
Irish immigrants, number admitted during year ending June 30, 1907, 32.
Italian (north) immigrants, number admitted during year ending June 30, 1907, 32.
Italian (south) immigrants, number admitted during year ending June 30, 1907, 32.
Italian language, use of, in church services, 121.

Jackson, Mich., 376, 381, 448.
Jacksonville, Fla., 376, 381, 448.
Japanese immigrants, number admitted during year ending June 30, 1907, 32.
Japanese language, use of, in church services, 121.
Japanese Temples, new denomination, 16, 514. *See also* Buddhists.
Jehovah Conference. *See* Lutheran bodies.
Jersey City, N. J., 374, 380, 448.
Jewish congregations:
  omission of family in 1906, 15, 516.
  organizations, number, 22; per minister, 92; by periods, 100, 103.
  communicants or members, number, 25–35; by classes of cities, 74, 83; per minister, 93.
  church edifices and halls, number and seating capacity, 32, 34, 35.
  value of church property, 37–40; by classes of cities, 76.
  debt on church property, 40; by classes of cities, 78.
  parsonages, number and value, 41.
  Sunday schools, teachers, and scholars, number, 87, 88.
  ministers, number and increase, 1890–1906, 91; salaries, by classes of cities, 96, 97.
  languages used in church services, 108, 114.
  work, home, 128; contributions, 134.
  general statistics, 150, 156–293, 392–394, 516.
  comparative statistics for 1850, 1860, and 1870, 565.
Johnstown, Pa., 376, 381, 450.
Joint Synod of Ohio and Other States. *See* Lutheran bodies.
Joliet, Ill., 376, 381, 450.
Joplin, Mo., 376, 381, 450.

Kansas, population, organizations, members, and value of and debt on church property, with per cent distribution and rank, 42, 43. *See also* States and territories.
Kansas City, Kans., 374, 380, 452.
Kansas City, Mo., 374, 380, 452.
Kentucky, population, organizations, members, and value of and debt on church property, with per cent distribution and rank, 42, 43. *See also* States and territories.
Knoxville, Tenn., 376, 381, 452.
Korean immigrants, number admitted during year ending June 30, 1907, 32.
Krimmer Brueder-Gemeinde, new denomination, 15, 518. *See also* Mennonite bodies.

La Crosse, Wis., 376, 381, 454.
Lancaster, Pa., 376, 381, 454.
Languages used in church services, 105–123; denominations reporting English only, 106, 107; foreign and English, 107–109; specified, 111–120; alphabetical list, 121; by states and territories, 122.
Lappish language, use of, in church services, 121.
Latter-day Saints:
  organizations, number, 22; per minister, 92; by periods, 100, 103.
  communicants or members, number, 25–35; by states and territories, 47; by classes of cities, 74, 83; per 1,000 population, 62; diagrams, 65, 67; per minister, 93.
  church edifices and halls, number and seating capacity, 32, 34, 35.
  value of church property, 37–40; by classes of cities, 76.
  debt on church property, 40; by classes of cities, 78.
  parsonages, number and value, 41.
  Sunday schools, teachers, and scholars, number, 87, 88.
  ministers, number and increase, 1890–1906, 91.
  languages used in church services, 108, 114.
  work, home, 128; foreign, 133; contributions, 134.
  general statistics, 150, 156–293, 392–394, 516.
Lawrance, Marion, secretary, American Sunday School Association, 12.
Lawrence, Mass., 374, 380, 454.
Lettish language, use of, in church services, 121.
Lexington, Ky., 376, 381, 456.
Life and Advent Union. *See* Adventist bodies.
Lincoln, Nebr., 376, 381, 456.
Lithuanian immigrants, number admitted during year ending June 30, 1907, 32.
Lithuanian language, use of, in church services, 121.
Little Rock, Ark., 376, 381, 456.
Little Russian language, use of, in church services, 121.
Los Angeles, Cal., 374, 380, 456.
Louisiana, population, organizations, members, and value of and debt on church property, with per cent distribution and rank, 42, 43. *See also* States and territories.
Louisville, Ky., 374, 380, 458.
Lowell, Mass., 374, 380, 458.
Lumber River Mission, new denomination, 16, 516. *See also* Evangelistic associations.
Lutheran bodies:
  organizations, number, 22; per minister, 92; by periods, 100, 103.
  communicants or members, number, 25–35; distribution for continental United States, diagram, 26; by states and territories, 46; by classes of cities, 74, 83; per 1,000 population, 62; diagrams, 64, 66; per minister, 93.
  church edifices and halls, number and seating capacity, 32, 34, 35.
  value of church property, 37–40; by classes of cities, 76.
  debt on church property, 40; by classes of cities, 78.

Lutheran bodies—Continued.
  parsonages, number and value, 41.
  Sunday schools, teachers, and scholars, number, 87, 88.
  ministers, number and increase, 1890-1906, 91; salaries, by classes of cities, 94, 95.
  languages used in church services, 108, 114.
  work, home, 126; foreign, 132; contributions, 134.
  general statistics, 150, 156-293, 392-397, 516.
  comparative statistics for 1850, 1860, and 1870, 565.
—— colored organizations, general statistics, 137, 538, 564.
Lutheran Independent congregations, consolidation with other denominations, 15, 516.
Lutheran Synod of Buffalo. *See* Lutheran bodies.
Lynn, Mass., 374, 380, 460.

Magyar immigrants, number admitted during year ending June 30, 1907, 32.
Magyar language, use of, in church services, 121.
Maine, population, organizations, members, and value of and debt on church property, with per cent distribution and rank, 42, 43. *See also* States and territories.
Malden, Mass., 376, 381, 460.
Manchester, N. H., 374, 380, 460.
Maryland, population, organizations, members, and value of and debt on church property, with per cent distribution and rank, 42, 43. *See also* States and territories.
Massachusetts, population, organizations, members, and value of and debt on church property, with per cent distribution and rank, 42, 43. *See also* States and territories.
McKeesport, Pa., 376, 381, 460.
Memphis, Tenn., 374, 380, 462.
Mennonite bodies:
  organizations, number, 22; per minister, 92; by periods, 101, 103.
  communicants or members, number, 25-35; by classes of cities, 74, 83; per minister, 93.
  church edifices and halls, number and seating capacity, 32, 34, 35.
  value of church property, 37-40; by classes of cities, 76.
  debt on church property, 40; by classes of cities, 78.
  parsonages, number and value, 41.
  Sunday schools, teachers, and scholars, number, 87, 88.
  ministers, number and increase, 1890-1906, 91.
  languages used in church services, 108, 116.
  work, home, 128; foreign, 132; contributions, 134.
  general statistics, 150, 156-293, 395-397, 516.
Mennonite Brethren in Christ. *See* Mennonite bodies.
Mennonite Church. *See* Mennonite bodies.
Methodist bodies:
  organizations, number, 22; per minister, 92; by periods, 101, 103.
  communicants or members, number, 25-35; distribution for continental United States, diagram, 26; by states and territories, 46; by classes of cities, 74, 83; per 1,000 population, 62; diagrams, 64, 67; per minister, 93.
  church edifices and halls, number and seating capacity, 32, 34, 35.
  value of church property, 37-40; by classes of cities, 76.

Methodist bodies—Continued.
  debt on church property, 40; by classes of cities, 78.
  parsonages, number and value, 41.
  Sunday schools, teachers, and scholars, number, 87, 88.
  ministers, number and increase, 1890-1906, 91; salaries, by classes of cities, 96, 97.
  languages used in church services, 106, 108, 116.
  work, home, 128; foreign, 132; contributions, 134.
  general statistics, 152, 156-293, 397-399, 518.
  comparative statistics for 1850, 1860, and 1870, 565.
—— colored organizations, general statistics, 137, 538, 564.
Methodist Episcopal Church. *See* Methodist bodies.
Methodist Episcopal Church, South. *See* Methodist bodies.
Methodist Protestant Church. *See* Methodist bodies.
Metropolitan Church Association, new denomination, 16, 516. *See also* Evangelistic associations.
Mexican immigrants, number admitted during year ending June 30, 1907, 32.
Michigan, population, organizations, members, and value of and debt on church property, with per cent distribution and rank, 42, 43. *See also* States and territories.
Michigan, Synod of. *See* Lutheran bodies.
Milwaukee, Wis., 374, 380, 462.
Ministers: by principal denominations, 91; organizations per minister, 92; members per minister, 93; salaries, 93-98; comparison, 1890 and 1906, 515.
—— colored, number, 146.
Minneapolis, Minn., 374, 380, 462.
Minnesota, population, organizations, members, and value of and debt on church property, with per cent distribution and rank, 42, 43. *See also* States and territories.
Missionaries: number, home, 126; foreign, 131.
Missionary Church Association, new denomination, 16, 516. *See also* Evangelistic associations.
Missions, home and foreign, comparison, 135. *See also* Home work *and* Foreign work.
Mississippi, population, organizations, members, and value of and debt on church property, with per cent distribution and rank, 42, 43. *See also* States and territories.
Missouri, population, organizations, members, and value of and debt on church property, with per cent distribution and rank, 42, 43. *See also* States and territories.
Mobile, Ala., 376, 381, 464.
Modern Syriac (Nestorian) language, use of, in church services, 121.
Montana, population, organizations, members, and value of and debt on church property, with per cent distribution and rank, 42, 43. *See also* States and territories.
Montenegrin immigrants. *See* Bulgarian, Servian, and Montenegrin immigrants.
Montenegrin language, use of, in church services, 121.
Montgomery, Ala., 376, 381, 464.
Moravian bodies:
  new denominational family, 16.
  salaries of ministers, by classes of cities, 96, 97.
  organizations, by periods, 101, 103.
  languages used in church services, 108, 117.
  work, home, 128; foreign, 132.
  general statistics, 152, 397-399, 518.
—— colored organizations, general statistics, 137, 538, 564.

Moravian Church (Unitas Fratrum), comparative statistics for 1850, 1860, and 1870, 565. *See also* Moravian bodies.
Moravian immigrants. *See* Bohemian and Moravian immigrants.
Mormons, comparative statistics for 1850, 1860, and 1870, 565. *See also* Latter-day Saints.

Nashville, Tenn., 374, 380, 464.
National Baptist Convention (colored), change in name of denomination, 14. *See also* Baptist bodies *and* Colored organizations.
Nebraska, population, organizations, members, and value of and debt on church property, with per cent distribution and rank, 42, 43. *See also* States and territories.
Nebraska and Minnesota Conference of Mennonites. *See* Mennonite bodies.
Nestorian language. *See* Modern Syriac (Nestorian) language.
Nevada, population, organizations, members, and value of and debt on church property, with per cent distribution and rank, 42, 43. *See also* States and territories.
New Apostolic Church, new denomination, 16, 514. *See also* Catholic Apostolic Churches.
New Bedford, Mass., 374, 380, 466.
New Britain, Conn., 376, 381, 466.
New Congregational Methodist Church. *See* Methodist bodies.
New Hampshire, population, organizations, members, and value of and debt on church property, with per cent distribution and rank, 42, 43. *See also* States and territories.
New Haven, Conn., 374, 380, 466.
New Icaria Society (Communistic), disappearance of denomination, 15; statistics for 1890, 514.
New Jersey, population, organizations, members, and value of and debt on church property, with per cent distribution and rank, 42, 43. *See also* States and territories.
New Jerusalem Church (Swedenborgian), comparative statistics for 1850, 1860, and 1870, 565. *See also* Churches of the New Jerusalem.
New Mexico, population, organizations, members, and value of and debt on church property, with per cent distribution and rank, 42, 43. *See also* States and territories.
New Orleans, La., 374, 380, 468.
New York, population, organizations, members, and value of and debt on church property, with per cent distribution and rank, 42, 43. *See also* States and territories.
New York City, 374, 380, 468.
Newark, N. J., 374, 380, 470.
Newcastle, Pa., 376, 381, 470.
Newport, Ky., 376, 381, 470.
Newton, Mass., 376, 381, 472.
Nonchurch population, ratio to total population, 58-60.
Nonsectarian Churches of Bible Faith: new denomination, 16; organizations, by periods, 101, 103; languages used in church services, 108, 117; general statistics, 152, 156, 397-399, 518.
Norfolk, Va., 376, 381, 472.
North Carolina, population, organizations, members, and value of and debt on church property, with per cent distribution and rank, 42, 43. *See also* States and territories.
North Dakota, population, organizations, members, and value of and debt on church property, with per cent distribution and rank, 42, 43. *See also* States and territories.

Northern Baptist Convention, change in name of denomination, 14. *See also* Baptist bodies.
Norwegian language, use of, in church services, 121.
Norwegian Lutheran Free Church: new denomination, 16, 516; percentage of organizations formed from 1900 to 1906, 105. *See also* Lutheran bodies.
Norwegian Synod (Lutheran). *See* Lutheran bodies.

Oakland, Cal., 374, 380, 472.
Ohio, population, organizations, members, and value of and debt on church property, with per cent distribution and rank, 42, 43. *See also* States and territories.
Ohio, Joint Synod of. *See* Lutheran bodies.
Oklahoma, population, organizations, members, and value of and debt on church property, with per cent distribution and rank, 42, 43. *See also* States and territories.
Old Amish Mennonite Church. *See* Mennonite bodies.
Old Catholic Church, disappearance of denomination, 15; statistics for 1890, 518.
Old (Wisler) Mennonite Church. *See* Mennonite bodies.
Old Order German Baptist Brethren. *See* Dunkers or German Baptist Brethren.
Omaha, Nebr., 374, 380, 474.
Oregon, population, organizations, members, and value of and debt on church property, with per cent distribution and rank, 42, 43. *See also* States and territories.
Organizations: definition of term, 21; number, per cent distribution, and increase, 1890–1906, 22; average members per organization, 28; per minister, 92; by periods, 99, 103; general statistics for continental United States, by separate denominations, 148; by states and territories, 154, 520; by separate states and denominations, 156; by classes of cities, 374–379; by specified cities and denominations, 408; comparison, 1890 and 1906, 514, 520; comparative statistics for 1850, 1860, and 1870, 565.
Original Freewill Baptists, change in name of denomination, 14.
Orthodox Conservative Friends (Wilburite). *See* Friends.
Oshkosh, Wis., 376, 381, 474.

Pacific Islander immigrants, number admitted during year ending June 30, 1907, 32.
Parsonages: number and value, 41; for continental United States, by denominations, 149; by states and territories, 155; by separate states and denominations, 157; by classes of cities, 375; by specified cities and denominations, 409.
—— colored organizations, number and value, 539–543.
Passaic, N. J., 376, 381, 474.
Paterson, N. J., 374, 380, 476.
Pawtucket, R. I., 376, 382, 476.
Peniel Missions, new denomination, 16, 516. *See also* Evangelistic associations.
Pennsylvania, population, organizations, members, and value of and debt on church property, with per cent distribution and rank, 42, 43. *See also* States and territories.
Pentecost Bands of the World, new denomination, 16, 516. *See also* Evangelistic associations.
Pentecostal Church of the Nazarene: new denomination, 16; salaries of ministers, by classes of cities, 96, 97; organizations, by periods, 101; languages used in church services, 108, 117; work, home, 128; foreign, 132; general statistics, 152, 156–293, 397–399, 518.
Pentecostal Union Church, new denomination, 16, 516. *See also* Evangelistic associations.
Peoria, Ill., 374, 380, 476.
Philadelphia, Pa., 374, 380, 476.
Philanthropic institutions: value of property and endowments, 127; number, and inmates and patients, 131.
Pittsburg, Pa., 374, 380, 478.
Polish immigrants, number admitted during year ending June 30, 1907, 32.
Polish language, use of, in church services, 121.
Polish National Church of America: new denomination, 15, 518; salaries of ministers, by classes of cities, 96, 97; organizations, by periods, 101; languages used in church services, 108, 117; general statistics, 152, 156–293, 400–402, 518.
Population: ratio of church members to total, by states and territories, 58–61; members per 1,000, by states and territories and principal denominations, 62–68; number and per cent distribution, by classes of cities, 70; by states and counties, 294; by classes of cities and separate denominations, 380; comparison, 1890 and 1906, by states and territories, 520.
Portland, Me., 374, 381, 480.
Portland, Oreg., 374, 381, 480.
Portuguese immigrants, number admitted during year ending June 30, 1907, 32.
Portuguese language, use of, in church services, 121.
Presbyterian bodies:
- organizations, number, 22; per minister, 92; by periods, 101, 104.
- communicants or members, number, 25–35; distribution for continental United States, diagram, 26; by states and territories, 46; by classes of cities, 74, 83; per 1,000 population, 62; diagrams, 64, 67; per minister, 93.
- church edifices and halls, number and seating capacity, 32, 34, 35.
- value of church property, 37–40; by classes of cities, 76.
- debt on church property, 40; by classes of cities, 78.
- parsonages, number and value, 41.
- Sunday schools, teachers, and scholars, number, 87, 88.
- ministers, number and increase, 1890–1906, 91; salaries, by classes of cities, 96, 97.
- languages used in church services, 106, 109, 117.
- work, home, 128; foreign, 132; contributions, 134.
- general statistics, 152, 158–293, 400–402, 518.
- comparative statistics for 1850, 1860, and 1870, 565.

—— colored organizations, general statistics, 137, 538, 565.
Presbyterian Church in the United States, change in name of denomination, 14. *See also* Presbyterian bodies.
Presbyterian Church in the United States (Southern), change in name of denomination, 14.
Presbyterian Church in the United States of America, change in name of denomination, 14. *See also* Presbyterian bodies.
Presbyterian Church in the United States of America (Northern), change in name of denomination, 14.
Presbyterians (other): explanation of term, 13, 14; comparative statistics for 1850, 1860, and 1870, 565.
Primitive Baptists. *See* Baptist bodies.
Primitive Friends. *See* Friends.
Primitive Methodist Church in the United States of America. *See* Methodist bodies.
Protestant bodies:
- organizations, number, 22; per minister, 92; by periods, 99, 103.
- communicants or members, number, 25–35; distribution for continental United States, diagram, 26; by states and territories, 46; by classes of cities, 74, 86; ratio to total population, 58–60; per 1,000 population, 62; diagrams, 64–67; per minister, 93.
- church edifices and halls, number and seating capacity, 32, 34, 35.
- value of church property, 37–40; by classes of cities, 76.
- debt on church property, 40; by classes of cities, 78.
- parsonages, number and value, 41.
- Sunday schools, teachers, and scholars, number, 87, 88.
- ministers, number and increase, 1890–1906, 91; salaries, by classes of cities, 94–97.
- languages used in church services, 107, 111.
- work, home, 126; foreign, 131; contributions, 134.
- general statistics, 148, 150, 156, 408, 514.
- comparative statistics for 1850, 1860, and 1870, 565.

—— colored organizations, general statistics, 137, 538, 565.
Protestant Episcopal bodies, omission of family in 1906, 15.
Protestant Episcopal Church:
- organizations, number, 22; per minister, 92; by periods, 101, 104.
- communicants or members, number, 25–35; distribution for continental United States, diagram, 26; by states and territories, 47; by classes of cities, 74, 83; per 1,000 population, 62; diagrams, 65, 67; per minister, 93.
- church edifices and halls, number and seating capacity, 32, 34, 35.
- value of church property, 37–40; by classes of cities, 76.
- debt on church property, 40; by classes of cities, 78.
- parsonages, number and value, 41.
- Sunday schools, teachers, and scholars, number, 87, 88.
- ministers, number and increase, 1890–1906, 91; salaries, by classes of cities, 96, 97.
- languages used in church services, 109, 118.
- work, home, 128; foreign, 132; contributions, 134.
- general statistics, 152, 158–293, 400–402, 518.
- comparative statistics for 1850, 1860, and 1870, 565.

—— colored organizations, general statistics, 137, 538, 565.
Providence, R. I., 374, 380, 480.
Pueblo, Colo., 376, 382, 482.

Quincy, Ill., 376, 382, 482.

Racine, Wis., 376, 382, 482.
Reading, Pa., 374, 381, 484.
Reformed bodies:
- organizations, number, 22; per minister, 92; by periods, 101, 104.
- communicants or members, number, 25–35; distribution for continental United States, diagram, 26; by states and territories, 47; by classes of cities, 74, 83; per 1,000 population, 62; diagrams, 65, 66; per minister, 93.
- church edifices and halls, number and seating capacity, 32, 34, 35.
- value of church property, 37–40; by classes of cities, 76.

Reformed bodies—Continued.
debt on church property, 40; by classes of cities, 78.
parsonages, number and value, 41.
Sunday schools, teachers, and scholars, number, 87, 88.
ministers, number and increase, 1890-1906, 91; salaries, by classes of cities, 96, 97.
languages used in church services, 109, 118.
work, home, 128; foreign, 133; contributions, 134.
general statistics, 152, 400-404, 518.
—— colored organizations, general statistics, 137, 538, 565.
Reformed Catholic Church: salaries of ministers, by classes of cities, 96, 97; organizations, by periods, 101; languages used in church services, 109, 118; general statistics, 152, 156-293, 402-404, 518.
Reformed Church in America (late Dutch Reformed), comparative statistics for 1850, 1860, and 1870, 565. *See also* Reformed bodies.
Reformed Church in the United States (late German Reformed), comparative statistics for 1850, 1860, and 1870, 565. *See also* Reformed bodies.
Reformed Episcopal Church: salaries of ministers, by classes of cities, 96, 97; organizations, by periods, 101; languages used in church services, 106; work, home, 128; foreign, 133; general statistics, 137, 152, 156-293, 402-404, 518.
—— colored organizations, general statistics, 137, 538, 565.
Reformed Mennonite Church. *See* Mennonite bodies.
Reformed Methodist Union Episcopal Church (colored). *See* Methodist bodies, *also* Colored organizations.
Reformed Presbyterian Church (Covenanted). *See* Presbyterian bodies.
Reformed Presbyterian Church in North America, General Synod. *See* Presbyterian bodies.
Reformed Presbyterian Church in the United States and Canada. *See* Presbyterian bodies.
Reformed Zion Union Apostolic Church (Colored Methodist), change in name of denomination, 14. *See also* Methodist bodies *and* Colored organizations.
Regular Baptists: denominations comprising, 15; comparative statistics for 1850, 1860, and 1870, 565.
Regular Baptists (colored), change in name of denomination, 14, 15.
Regular Baptists (North), change in name of denomination, 14, 15.
Regular Baptists (South), change in name of denomination, 14, 15.
Religious Society of Friends (Hicksite). *See* Friends.
Reorganized Church of Jesus Christ of Latter-day Saints. *See* Latter-day Saints.
Rhode Island, population, organizations, members, and value of and debt on church property, with per cent distribution and rank, 42, 43. *See also* States and territories.
Richmond, Va., 374, 381, 484.
Rochester, N. Y., 374, 380, 484.
Rockford, Ill., 376, 382, 486.
Roman Catholic Church:
organizations, number, 22; per minister, 92; by periods, 101, 104.
communicants or members, number, 25-35; distribution for continental United States, diagram, 26; by states and territories, 47; ratio to population, 58-60; by classes of cities, 74, 83; per 1,000 population, 62; diagrams, 64, 66; per minister, 93.
Roman Catholic Church—Continued.
church edifices and halls, number and seating capacity, 32, 34, 35.
value of church property, 37-40; by classes of cities, 76.
debt on church property, 40; by classes of cities, 78.
parsonages, number and value, 41.
Sunday schools, teachers, and scholars, number, 87, 88.
ministers, number and increase, 1890-1906, 91; salaries, by classes of cities, 96, 97.
languages used in church services, 109, 118.
work, home, 128.
general statistics, 152, 158-293, 402-404, 518.
comparative statistics for 1850, 1860, and 1870, 565.
—— colored organizations, general statistics, 137, 538, 565.
Roumanian immigrants, number admitted during year ending June 30, 1907, 32.
Roumanian language, use of, in church services, 121.
Russian immigrants, number admitted during year ending June 30, 1907, 32.
Russian language, use of, in church services, 121.
Russian Orthodox Church. *See* Eastern Orthodox Churches.
Ruthenian (Russniak) immigrants, number admitted during year ending June 30, 1907, 32.
Ruthenian language, use of, in church services, 121.

Sacramento, Cal., 378, 382, 486
Saginaw, Mich., 378, 382, 486.
St. Joseph, Mo., 374, 380, 488.
St. Louis, Mo., 374, 380, 488.
St. Paul, Minn., 374, 380, 488.
Salem, Mass., 378, 382, 490.
Salt Lake City, Utah, 374, 381, 490.
Salvation Army, percentage of organizations formed from 1900 to 1906, 105. *See also* Salvationists.
Salvationists: new denominational family, 16; salaries of ministers, 96; organizations, by periods, 101, 104; languages used in church services, 109, 119; work, home, 128; general statistics, 152, 158, 402-404, 518.
San Antonio, Tex., 376, 381, 490.
San Francisco, Cal., 374, 380, 492.
Savannah, Ga., 376, 381, 492.
Scandinavian immigrants, number admitted during year ending June 30, 1907, 32.
Scandinavian language, use of, in church services, 121.
Schedules: sources of information, 10; means of verification, 11.
Schellenberger Brueder-Gemeinde, new denomination, 15, 518. *See also* Mennonite bodies.
Schenectady, N. Y., 378, 382, 494.
Schwenkfelders: organizations, by periods, 101; languages used in church services, 109, 119; work, home, 128; foreign, 133; general statistics, 152, 402-404, 518.
Scotch immigrants, number admitted during year ending June 30, 1907, 32.
Scranton, Pa., 374, 380, 494.
Seating capacity of church edifices: by principal denominations, 34-36; by denominations in detail, 149; by states and territories, 155; by separate states and denominations, 157; by classes of cities, 375; by specified cities and denominations, 409; comparison, 1890 and 1906, 515; by states and territories, 521.
—— colored organizations, general statistics, 539, 541, 564.
Seattle, Wash., 376, 381, 494.
Second Advent denomination, comparative statistics for 1850, 1860, and 1870, 565.
Separate Baptists. *See* Baptist bodies.
Separatists, Society of (Communistic), disappearance of denomination, 15; statistics for 1890, 514.
Servian immigrants. *See* Bulgarian, Servian, and Montenegrin immigrants.
Servian language, use of, in church services, 121.
Servian Orthodox Church, new denomination, 16, 516. *See also* Eastern Orthodox Churches.
Seventh-day Adventist Denomination, ercentage of organizations formed from 1900 to 1906, 105. *See also* Adventist bodies.
Seventh-day Baptists. *See* Baptist bodies.
Sex of members, distribution, by denominations, 28-31. *See also* Communicants or members.
Shakers, comparative statistics for 1850, 1860, and 1870, 565. *See also* Communistic societies.
Sioux City, Iowa, 378, 382, 496.
Six Principle Baptists. *See* General Six Principle Baptists, *also* Baptist bodies.
Slavic language, use of, in church services, 121.
Slovak Evangelical Lutheran Synod of America, new denomination, 16, 516. *See also* Lutheran bodies.
Slovak immigrants, number admitted during year ending June 30, 1907, 32.
Slovak language, use of, in church services, 121.
Slovenian immigrants. *See* Croatian and Slovenian immigrants.
Slovenian language, use of, in church services, 121.
Social Brethren: organizations, by periods, 101; languages used in church services, 106; general statistics, 152, 402-404, 518.
Society for Ethical Culture: organizations, by periods, 101; languages used in church services, 106; work, home, 128; general statistics, 152, 402-404, 518.
Society of Altruists. *See* Altruists, Society of.
Society of Friends (Orthodox). *See* Friends.
Society of Shakers, change in name of denomination, 14.
Somerville, Mass., 376, 381, 496.
South Bend, Ind., 378, 382, 496.
South Carolina, population, organizations, members, and value of and debt on church property, with per cent distribution and rank, 42, 43. *See also* States and territories.
South Dakota, population, organizations, members, and value of and debt on church property, with per cent distribution and rank, 42, 43. *See also* States and territories.
South Omaha, Nebr., 378, 382, 496.
Southern Baptist Convention, change in name of denomination, 14. *See also* Baptist bodies *and* Colored organizations.
Spanish immigrants, number admitted during year ending June 30, 1907, 32.
Spanish language, use of, in church services, 121.
Spanish-American immigrants, number admitted during year ending June 30, 1907, 32.
Spiritualists: organizations, by periods, 101, 104; percentage formed from 1900 to 1906, 105; languages used in church services, 109, 119; work, home, 128; general statistics, 152, 402-404, 518; comparative statistics for 1850, 1860, and 1870, 565
Spokane, Wash., 378, 382, 498.
Springfield, Ill., 378, 382, 498.
Springfield, Mass., 376, 381, 498.
Springfield, Ohio, 378, 382, 500.
States and territories:
population, estimated, 42; ratio of members to total, 58-61; by counties, 1900, 294; comparison, 1890 and 1906, 520.

States and territories—Continued.
organizations, number, 42, 154; comparison, 1890 and 1906, 520.
communicants or members, number, 43, 154; average per organization, 44; by principal denominations, 46–49; diagrams, 50–53; rank of principal denominations, 55; percentage of total population, 58–61; number per 1,000 population, 62; diagrams, 64–67; by denominations, in detail, 156; by counties and selected denominations, 294; comparison, 1890 and 1906, 521; by selected denominations, 522.
value of church property, 43, 155; average per organization, 44; by denominations, 157; comparison, 1890 and 1906, 521.
debt on church property, 43, 155; average per organization, 44; by denominations, 157.
Sunday schools, teachers, and scholars, number, 89, 155; by denominations, in detail, 157.
languages used in church services, 122.
church edifices, number and seating capacity, 155; by denominations, in detail, 157; comparison, 1890 and 1906, 521.
halls, number, 155; by denominations, in detail, 157; comparison, 1890 and 1906, 521.
parsonages, number and value, 155; by denominations, in detail, 157.
—— colored organizations, comparison, 1890 and 1906, 145; general statistics, 540, 542.
Statistical unit, meaning of term, 21.
Statistics, methods of collecting, 10.
Sunday schools: method of obtaining data, 12; number, by principal denominations, 86–88; denominational and undenominational, by states and territories, 89, 90; by denominations, in detail, 149; by states and territories, 155; by separate states and denominations, 157-293; by classes of cities, 375–379; by specified cities and denominations, 409.
—— colored organizations, general statistics, 541, 543.
Suomi Synod (Finnish). *See* Lutheran bodies.
Superior, Wis., 378, 382, 500.
Swedenborgian Church. *See* Churches of the New Jerusalem.
Swedish Evangelical bodies:
new denominational family, 16.
salaries of ministers, 96.
organizations, by periods, 102, 104.
languages used in church services, 109, 119.
work, foreign, 133.
general statistics, 152, 402–404, 518.
Swedish Evangelical Free Mission, new denomination, 16, 518. *See also* Swedish Evangelical bodies.
Swedish Evangelical Mission Covenant of America, new denomination, 16, 518. *See also* Swedish Evangelical bodies.
Swedish language, use of, in church services, 121.
Synod for the Norwegian Evangelical Lutheran Church in America. *See* Lutheran bodies.
Synod of the Reformed Presbyterian Church of North America. *See* Presbyterian bodies.
Synodical Conference. *See* Lutheran bodies.
Syracuse, N. Y., 374, 380, 500.
Syriac language, use of, in church services, 121.
Syrian immigrants, number admitted during year ending June 30, 1907, 32.
Syrian Orthodox Church, new denomination, 16, 516. *See also* Eastern Orthodox Churches.

Tacoma, Wash., 378, 382, 502.
Taunton, Mass., 378, 382, 502.
Temple Society in the United States (Friends of the Temple): change in name of denomination, 14; salaries of ministers, by classes of cities, 96, 97; organizations, by periods, 102; languages used in church services, 109, 119; general statistics, 152, 402–404, 518.
Tennessee, population, organizations, members, and value of and debt on church property, with per cent distribution and rank, 42, 43. *See also* States and territories.
Terre Haute, Ind., 378, 382, 502.
Texas, Lutheran Synod of. *See* Lutheran bodies.
Texas, population, organizations, members, and value of and debt on church property, with per cent distribution and rank, 42, 43. *See also* States and territories.
Theosophical societies: new denominational family, 16; organizations, by periods, 102; languages used in church services, 106, 109, 119; general statistics, 152, 402–407, 518.
Theosophical Society, American Section, new denomination, 15, 518. *See also* Theosophical societies.
Theosophical Society in America, new denomination, 15, 518. *See also* Theosophical societies.
Theosophical Society, New York, new denomination, 15, 518. *See also* Theosophical societies.
Toledo, Ohio, 374, 380, 502.
Topeka, Kans., 378, 382, 504
Trenton, N. J., 376, 381, 504
Troy, N. Y., 376, 381, 504.
Turkish immigrants, number admitted during year ending June 30, 1907, 32.
Two-Seed-in-the-Spirit Predestinarian Baptists. *See* Baptist bodies.

Union American Methodist Episcopal Church (colored). *See* Methodist bodies, *also* Colored organizations.
Unitarians:
organizations, number, 22; per minister, 92; by periods, 102, 104.
communicants or members, number, 25–35; by classes of cities, 74, 83; per minister, 93.
church edifices and halls, number and seating capacity, 32, 34, 35.
value of church property, 37–40; by classes of cities, 76.
debt on church property, 40; by classes of cities, 78.
parsonages, number and value, 41.
Sunday schools, teachers, and scholars, number, 87, 88.
ministers, number and increase, 1890–1906, 91; salaries, by classes of cities, 96, 97.
languages used in church services, 109, 119.
work, home, 128.
general statistics, 152, 405–407, 518.
comparative statistics for 1850, 1860, and 1870, 565.
United American Freewill Baptists (colored): new denomination, 16, 514; percentage of organizations formed from 1900 to 1906, 105. *See also* Baptist bodies *and* Colored organizations.
United Baptists. *See* Baptist bodies.
United Brethren bodies:
organizations, number, 22; per minister, 92; by periods, 102, 104.
communicants or members, number, 25–35; by states and territories, 47; by classes of cities, 74, 83; per 1,000 population, 62; diagrams, 65, 66; per minister, 93.
church edifices and halls, number and seating capacity, 32, 34, 35.
United Brethren bodies—Continued.
value of church property, 37–40; by classes of cities, 76.
debt on church property, 40; by classes of cities, 78.
parsonages, number and value, 41.
Sunday schools, teachers, and scholars, number, 87, 88.
ministers, number and increase, 1890–1906, 91; salaries, by classes of cities, 96, 97.
languages used in church services, 109, 119.
work, home, 128; foreign, 133; contributions, 134.
general statistics, 152, 158–293, 405–407, 518.
—— colored organizations, general statistics, 137, 538, 565.
United Brethren in Christ, comparative statistics for 1850, 1860, and 1870, 565. *See also* United Brethren bodies.
United Brethren in Christ (Old Constitution). *See* United Brethren bodies.
United Danish Evangelical LutheranChurch in America. *See* Lutheran bodies.
United Evangelical Church, new denomination, 15, 516. *See also* Evangelical bodies.
United Norwegian Lutheran Church in America. *See* Lutheran bodies.
United Presbyterian Church of North America. *See* Presbyterian bodies.
United Society of Believers (Shakers), change in name of denomination, 14. *See also* Communistic societies.
United Synod of the Evangelical Lutheran Church in the South. *See* Lutheran bodies.
United Zion's Children. *See* Brethren (River).
Universal Brotherhood and Theosophical Society, new denomination, 15, 518. *See also* Theosophical societies.
Universalists:
organizations, number, 22; per minister, 92; by periods, 102, 104.
communicants or members, number, 25–35; by classes of cities, 74, 83; per minister, 93.
church edifices and halls, number and seating capacity, 32, 34, 35.
value of church property, 37–40; by classes of cities, 76.
debt on church property, 40; by classes of cities, 78.
parsonages, number and value, 41.
Sunday schools, teachers, and scholars, number, 87, 88.
ministers, number and increase, 1890–1906, 91; salaries, by classes of cities, 96, 97.
languages used in church services, 106.
work, home, 128; foreign, 133.
general statistics, 152, 158–293, 405–407, 518.
comparative statistics for 1850, 1860, and 1870, 565.
Utah, population, organizations, members, and value of and debt on church property, with per cent distribution and rank, 42, 43. *See also* States and territories.
Utica, N. Y., 376, 381, 506.

Vedanta Society: new denomination, 16; organizations, by periods, 102; languages used in church services, 106; general statistics, 152, 405–407, 518.
Vermont, population, organizations, members, and value of and debt on church property, with per cent distribution and rank, 42, 43. *See also* States and territories.
Virginia, population, organizations, members, and value of and debt on church

property, with per cent distribution and rank, 42, 43. *See also* States and territories.
Voluntary Missionary Society in America (colored), new denomination, 16, 516. *See also* Evangelistic associations *and* Colored organizations.
Volunteers of America: new denomination, 16; organizations, by periods, 102; salaries of ministers, by classes of cities, 96, 97; languages used in church services, 106; general statistics, 152, 405–407, 518.

Washington, D. C., 374, 380, 506.
Washington, population, organizations, members, and value of and debt on church property, with per cent distribution and rank, 42, 43. *See also* States and territories.
Waterbury, Conn., 378, 382, 508.
Welsh Calvinistic Methodist Church. *See* Presbyterian bodies.
Welsh immigrants, number admitted during year ending June 30, 1907, 32.
Welsh language, use of, in church services, 121.
Wendish language, use of, in church services, 121.
Wesleyan Methodist Connection of America. *See* Methodist bodies.
West Indian (except Cuban) immigrants, number admitted during year ending June 30, 1907, 32.
West Virginia, population, organizations, members, and value of and debt on church property, with per cent distribution and rank, 42, 43. *See also* States and territories.
Wheeling, W. Va., 378, 382, 508.
Wilkes-Barre, Pa., 376, 381, 508.
Williamsport, Pa., 378, 382, 508.
Wilmington, Del., 376, 381, 510.
Winebrennerians. *See* Churches of God in North America, General Eldership of the.
Wisconsin, population, organizations, members, and value of and debt on church property, with per cent distribution and rank, 42, 43. *See also* States and territories.
Wisler (Old) Mennonite Church. *See* Mennonite bodies.
Woman's Christian Temperance Union, 12.
Woonsocket, R. I., 378, 382, 510.
Worcester, Mass., 374, 380, 510.
Wyoming, population, organizations, members, and value of and debt on church property, with per cent distribution and rank, 42, 43. *See also* States and territories.

Yiddish language, use of, in church services, 121.
Yonkers, N. Y., 378, 382, 512.
York, Pa., 378, 382, 512.
Yorker, or Old Order, Brethren. *See* Brethren (River).
Young Men's Christian Association, 12.
Young Women's Christian Association, 12.
Youngstown, Ohio, 378, 382, 512.

Zion Union Apostolic Church, change in name of denomination, 14.

○

CPSIA information can be obtained
at www.ICGtesting.com
Printed in the USA
LVHW02s1241281017
554132LV00036B/593/P

9 781333 208745